# SCHOOL AND SOCIETY



EDITED BY J. McKEEN CATTELL

VOLUME XL

JULY-DECEMBER, 1934

WITH WHICH HAS BEEN COMBINED THE

## EDUCATIONAL REVIEW

Edited by WILLIAM McANDREW

NEW YORK
THE SCIENCE PRESS
1934

THE SCIENCE PRESS PRINTING COMPANY
LANCASTER, PENNSYLVANIA

# CONTENTS AND INDEX

## VOLUME XL—JULY-DECEMBER, 1934

NAMES OF CONTRIBUTORS ARE PRINTED IN SMALL CAPITALS


ABEL, J. F., Educational Reforms in Persia, 425
Academic Freedom, T. W. GOSLING, 79; M. E. DEUTSCH, 356
Adams, Sir John, W. C. BAGLEY, 631
Adult Education, in New York City, 85; Inst. for Supervisors of, 379; Jewish, 578
Advanced School of Education, Plans for, 683
Age, School-leaving, 332; in Wales, 835
Air-minded Youth, L. L. RILEY, 366
Alabama, Teachers Colleges of, C. M. DANNELLY, 389
American, Council on Education, Standards, R. WALTERS, 100; Museum of Natural History, Annual Report, 196; Legion, and Communism, 273, Educational Resolutions, 838; Institute, Junior Science Workshop Courses, 579; Scholar To-day, G. S. FORD, 641; Assoc. for the Advancement of Science, Committee on the Place of Science in Education, O. W. CALDWELL, 673; and Meeting of Science Teachers, 684; Historical Association, Meeting of, 869
Apprenticeship Systems, European, 377
Appropriations for New York State Schools, 274
Athletes, Scholarships for, 6
Atlanta, Center for Graduate Work and Research, 717
Australia, English Children in, 177
Australian Council for Educational Research, 84

BABCOCK, R., Pioneering in Teacher Training, 67
BAGLEY, W. C., Sir John Adams, 631
Barth, Karl, Suspension of, 716
BAYLES, E. E., Comment on Bobbitt's Criticism, 690
BEARD, J. H., School Child's Health, 753
Beloit College, Curriculum Changes, 716
BENGTSON, C., Amer. Federation of Teachers, 15, 845
BENJAMIN, H., Mexico's Six-year Plan, 666
BERNARD, L. L., Second-hand Text-books, 305
BLATCHFORD, C. H., JR., Examination in English for Foreign Students, 249
BLAUCH, L. E., Course of Study in Dentistry, 220
BOBBITT, F., The Commission on the Social Studies, 201
Bonn Professor, Suspension of, 716
Books, Love of, L. W. SMITH, 494; Scientific, in Early West, J. F. MCDERMOTT, 812
Boston's Surplus Teachers, 223
BOUTWELL, W. D., Washington Meeting of National Education Association, 48
BOWDEN, A. O., Change—The Test of Teaching, 133
Boys, Transient, Education of, G. E. OUTLAND, 501
BRANDENBURG, G. C. (the late) and O. C. TRIMBLE, Professional Training in Education, 850
British, Assoc. of University Teachers, 117; Sound Films, 141; Labor Party, Education Policy of, 332; School Children, with Defective Eyesight, 437; London County Council, 541; Nutritional Investigation of, 715; School Child, Health of, 865
Brown, Chancellor, 635
BROWN, C. H., College Library Budgets, 224
BROWN, F., The Truant Child, 772
Brown Univ., Bachelor of Philosophy Degree, 179
Browning, Edward W., Bequests, 625
BRYAN, J. S., Inaugural Address, 571
Bulgaria, School System, J. S. ROUCEK, 495, 775
Business Education, National Council of, 440
BUTLER, N. M., The Challenge to Education, 512
Butler, President, and Fascism, 695
BYRNS, R., The Mental Ability of Twins, 671

CAHOON, G. P., and M. MACKAY, Teacher-training Program, 228
CALDWELL, O. W., Committee on the Place of Science in Education, 673
California, Conference on Educational Issues in, R. WALTERS, 129; Public School Crisis, 194; Population and Public Education, 241; Elementary Text-book Situation, 316; Univ. of, Professional Practise at, 835; Administration of Higher Education in, 866
CALLAWAY, E., For Peace and Foreign Trade, 65
Canadian Library Council, 210
Carleton College, President of, 719
Carnegie Corporation, Work of, 849
CARROLL, R. P., Experiment in Psychology, 188
Centennial Year in History of Education, W. C. EELLS, 875
CHAMBERS, M. M., Bequests of Scholarships and Loan Funds, 131
Change—The Test of Teaching, A. O. BOWDEN, 133
Chemistry, College, Predicting Success in, W. C. REUSSER, V. BRINEGAR and G. FRANK, 197
Chicago, Federal Loans for Teachers Salaries, 177; Back Salaries, 274; Public Schools, 346; School Board, "Economy Program," 779; University of, Students-at-Large, 8; Specialization in Child Development at, 119
Child, Development, the School and the, 66; in Chicago, 119; Guidance in N. Y. City Schools, 179; Labor Day, 440; Federal Amendment, 682; Need of the, in School Administration, G. R. JOHNSON, 877
Children's Rights, 562
China, Educational Research in Canton, S. W. DOWNS, 423
Church-related Colleges, Conference, C. J. T., 363
Civics, A New Deal for, C. STEWART, 97
Civilian Conservation Corps, H. L. FARR, 386; and Pa. State Coll., 485; Camps and Amer. Assoc. of Univ. Professors, 766
Coefficients, Prediction, Homogeneous Grouping as Technique for Improving, M. E. WAGNER and E. STRABEL, 887
Collectivism and Democracy, P. W. HUTSON, 354
College, Football and Endowment, A. C. MARTS, 14; Museum, Developing, J. H. FURBAY, 98; Club, Peoples, in N. Y. City, 118; Trustee, Qualities of, C. F. THWING, 137; Small, and Liberal Learning, D. R. FOX, 505; Years, 428; Amer-

ican, 529; of City of New York, Alumni Dinner, 685, Merited Severity, 698, Creating Guttersnipes, 699
Colleges, American, Association of, 870
Columbia University, Summer School Library, 8; Origin of Students, 57; Cultural Surveys, 319; Extension Division, 347; Loans to Students, 622; Advanced School of Education, 683; Library, 768
COOKE, D. H., Statistical Slide Rule, 149
COOPER, E. N., College in the Movies, 664
Cooper Union, 275, 331, 518, 625
Cornell Univ., Courses in Large-Scale Planning, 716; Theater, 868
Correctional Institutions, 89
Correspondence Courses, Conference, 213
Course, as a Unit of Teaching, G. FREDEN, 773
COWLEY, L. E., Student Residential Housing, 705, 758
COX, P. W. L., Commission on Social Studies, 554
Culture, National, J. E. MORGAN, 111
Curriculum, Changes, in Harvard Business School, 318; College, Functional Areas in, P. F. VALENTINE, 725
CURTIS, H. S., Education and Business, 327; Pennington, a Ford School, 450

DAKIN, W. S., Plan of Education, 844
DANNELLY, C. M., Teachers Colleges of Alabama, 389
DEARBORN, G. V. N., Children at the Movies, 127
Dentistry, Course of Study in, L. E. BLAUCH, 220
Depression and the Teacher, H. RENNICK, 775
DEUTSCH, M. E., Academic Freedom, 356
DIENNA, J. B., Transition School in the Pennsylvania State College, 253
Dollars and Books, 729
DOWNS, S. W., Educational Research in Canton, China, 423
Drought-Stricken States, 499

Economies in Local School Attendance Units, H. A. LITTLE, 526
Education, and Business, H. S. CURTIS, 327; Challenge to, N. M. BUTLER, 512; Week, 519; Secondary School, Three Hundredth Anniversary, 546; Plan, W. S. DAKIN, 844
EELLS, W. C., 1935 as Centennial Year in History of Education, 875
Emergency, in Education, Commission on, for 1935, J. K. NORTON, 105; College at Yonkers, 624; Conferences on, 821
Emotion and the Educative Process, Conference, D. A. PRESCOTT, 396
Endowment, College, and Football, A. C. MARTS, 14
Engineers, Conference on Reconstruction and Recovery, 211
England, Educational Research in, 361
English, Teachers of, Nat. Council, 414; in Elementary Grades, L. J. O'ROURKE, 454; Labor Party and Education, 651
Europe, Salaries of Elementary Teachers, 226
Excellence, The Search for, 426

FARR, H. L., Civilian Conservation Corps, 386
Fascism, President Butler and, 695
Federal, Aid, to Education, G. F. ZOOK, 41, to College Students, 86, for the Schools, 98, to Students, Regulations on, 178; Loans for Teachers' Salaries in Chicago, 177; Employment of Teachers, 243; Government and the Schools, 317; Implications of, R. A. KENT, 337; Aid for School Construction, 345; Support for Public Schools, J. B. SEARS, 433; W. KELTY, 494; Emergency Relief, Williams College, 765
FEINGOLD, G. E., Secondary Education, 825
FERGUSON, L. W., Our Presidents, 813
Fire Hazards, Elimination of, I. H. JONES, 93
FORBES, A. W., Educational Dictator for Industry, 219
FORD, G. S., The American Scholar To-day, 641
Foreign Students, Examination in English for, C. H. BLATCHFORD, JR., 249
FOSTER, W. T., "We Ain't Gwine Nowhere," 878
Foundation, Constructive Activities of, 883
FOX, D. R., The Small College and Liberal Learning, 505
FREDEN, G., Course as a Unit of Teaching, 773
French Educational Exhibit, 19
Freshman Week, Extending, F. G. LIVINGOOD, 420
FROMAN, L. A., High School Deficiencies, 324
Frontier, Challenge of, R. L. KELLY, 857
Funds, School, Responsibility for, P. JARVIS, 527
FURBAY, J. H., Developing the College Museum, 98; Better English for Student Teaching, 588

Game and the Candle, 884
Gardens, School, in Holland, 484
Geography Teachers, Nat. Council of, 656
George Washington Univ., Inter-American Lectures at, 320; Natural Science Courses, 380; New Woman's Dormitory, 868
German, Student Troubles at Göttingen, 84; Refugees, 120; Universities, Reduced Registration, 411; Scholars, Displaced, 780
Gifts, Large, A. C. MARTS, 862
GORTNER, R. A., Race Prejudice, 665
GOSLING, T. W., Academic Freedom, 79
Göttingen, Univ. of, Student Troubles at, 84
Goucher College, Program, 486
Government, Radio Broadcasts on Problems of, 518; Service, Training School for, 718
Grades, Regents, as a Cumulative Educational Record, M. E. WAGNER, 367
Graduate Work and Research, Center for, 717
GRAY, J., Visions and Voyages, 73
GREENE, H. W., Negro Doctorates, 388
Guidance, Educational, M. MCCONN, 537; Child, in London, 819

Hague, Academy, 5
Haiti, Teachers for Rural Schools, 577
Handicapped, Scout Activities for, in Norway, 208
Harvard, University, Gifts and Legacies, 88; Prize Fellowships, 180; Business School, Curriculum, 318; Film Service and Boston Fine Arts Theater, 438; Yenching Inst., 485; Visiting Professors, 519; Extra-Curricular Lectures, 548; Graduate School of Business, 578; Courses in Public Administration, 652; Children's Classes at Germanic Museum, 683; Library, 802; Scholastic Honors at, 867
Health, Education, Cultural Objectives of, C.-E. A. WINSLOW, 1; Service, in New York City Schools, 579; Teacher's Part in Promoting, J. E. BEARD, 753; Survey of N. Y. City Schools, 839; Public, Radio Talks on, 626; L. TYSON, 846
High, School, Traditional Curriculum Challenged, J. L. MERIAM, 169; Deficiencies, L. A. FROMAN, 324; Schools, of N. Y. City, 118; American, Tercentenary of, 720

Higher Education, Nonsense in, G. E. SNAVELY, 832
History of Education, Teaching of, M. O. McCLUSKEY, 449
Hobby, Birth of a, J. A. LOW, 811
Holland, School Gardens in, 484
Home-Study Assignments, M. A. STEINER, 20
HOPKINS, E. M., Prerequisites of Intelligence, 473
Housing, Student Residential, W. H. COWLEY, 705, 758
Humanities, Summer Seminars, 837
HUNTER, E., Reading of College Students, 70
HUTCHINS, R. H., Educational Function of New England, 233
HUTSON, P. W., Collectivism and Democracy, 354

Illinois, Teachers, Plight of, 453
India, Students from, in England, 315
Industry, Educational Dictator for, A. W. FORBES, 219
Intelligence, Prerequisites of, E. M. HOPKINS, 473; Test Scores, H. WOOLF, 150; C. W. REEDER, 399; Oral Group Test, R. S. SCHULTZ and G. S. MACVAUGH, 639
Interfraternity, National, Conference, 767
Inter-, Scholastic Correspondence, A. WILSON, 389; American, Educational Conference, 277, Federation of Education, G. L. SWIGGETT, 364
International, School for Refugees, Holland, 55; Universities Conference, 315; Education, Institute of, 588
Italian Students, Visit to College of City of New York, 586
Italy, Military Training in Schools, 802

JANES, G. M., Future of Phi Beta Kappa, 281
JARVIS, P., Responsibility for School Funds, 527
Jewish Pre-medical Students, 836
JOHNSON, B. L., The Librarian as an Associate in College Instruction, 632
JOHNSON, G. R., Child's Need in School Administration, 877
JOHNSTON, J. B., and E. G. WILLIAMSON, Follow-up Study of Scholastic Predictions, 730
JONES, I. H., Elimination of Fire Hazards, 93
Journalism, First School of, 392

KANDEL, I. L., The Control of Teachers, 351
Kansas Schools, 150
KELLY, R. L., Challenge of Frontier, 857
KELTY, W., Why Federal Aid?, 494
KENT, R. A., Implications of Federal Aid to Education, 337
KEPPEL, F. P., American Philanthropy and the Advancement of Learning, 401
KOTSCHNIG, W. M., Nationalism in European Universities, 265
KREY, A. C., Commission on Social Studies, 660

Leisure, W. B. McPHERSON, 492
Liberal Arts College, J. H. MILLER, 328
Librarian as Associate in College Instruction, B. L. JOHNSON, 632
Librarians in Conference, 498
Libraries, Planning for, 181; for Civilized Living, C. H. MILAM, 480
Library, of Columbia Univ., 8; International Research Institute, 19; Canadian, Council, 210; Rural School, Practice, 210; University of Liverpool, 209; College, Budgets, C. H. BROWN, 224; Humanistic, at Princeton, 242; Schools, 284; N. Y. Public, 529; of Harvard University, 802; Association, American, Officers, 121
LINVILLE, H. R., American Federation of Teachers, 616
LITTLE, H. A., School Attendance Units, 526
Liverpool, University of, Library, 209
LIVINGOOD, F. G., Extending Freshman Week, 420
London, Child Guidance in, 819; County Council, Educational Budget, 541
Louisiana, Improved Educational Facilities, 142; State Univ., Students' Strike, 766
LOW, J. A., The Birth of a Hobby, 811

McAFEE, L. O., Teacher Placement, 634
McANDREW, W., People, Performance and Publications, 25; Comments on Things Educational, 153, 289, 457, 593, 739; Books Reviewed, S. P. Abelow, 34; L. Adamic, 460; J. R. Aiken, 607; J. C. Almack, E. W. Staffelback, 297; W. E. Atkins, A. Wubnig, 32; R. H. Baker, 601; K. Beal, 752; A. A. Berle and others, 294; H. Best, 163; G. C. and R. G. Blakey, 470; R. P. Boas, E. Smith, 38; W. R. Boorman and J. Johnston, 608; L. F. Borden, 165; W. Bragg, 40; E. G. Braggini, 604; D. Brande, 301; J. B. Brebner, J. Erskine and E. D. Martin, 607; T. H. Briggs and Others, 301; A. P. Brigham, C. T. McFarlane, 39; J. Brigham, 596; M. B. Bruere and M. R. Beard, 605; A. Bryant, 34; L. Bryson, 603; J. W. Buckham and G. M. Stratton, 747; W. H. Burton, 296; O. W. Caldwell and G. E. Lundeen, 745; L. de la Chalotais, 162; E. Chamberlain, 608; J. Charteris, 34; H. C. Christofferson, 39; L. D. Coffman, 471; H. L. Cohen, 164; L. V. Coleman, 295; E. Collings, 750; J. Cottler, H. Brecht, 164; C. A. Coulomb, 603, 604; P. W. L. Cox, R. E. Langfitt, 298; T. B. Cross, C. H. Stover, 165; E. P. Cubberley, 469; F. D. Curtiss, O. W. Caldwell and N. H. Sherman, 600; L. T. Dennis, 167; W. H. Dooley, 464; H. R. Douglas, C. W. Boardman, 167; E. Dowling, C. A. Coulomb and A. A. Rapp, 604; E. R. Downing, 598; R. L. Duffus, 606; C. A. Ellwood, 35; E. R. Embree, M. S. Simon, W. B. Mumford, 162; H. Emerson, 303; E. M. Fair, 607; T. Fansler, 603; L. F. Fargo, 166; H. U. Faulkner, 294; F. K. Farris, E. E. Keener, 297; R. L. Finney and L. D. Zeleny, 160; I. T. E. Firkins, 299; O. W. Firkins, 608; C. R. Fish and H. E. Wilson, 466; E. M. Forster, 472; M. F. Gallagher, 464; C. R. Gaston, A. F. Chapin and M. M. Nagelberg, 608; C. Gauss, 461; R. W. Gavian, A. A. Gray and E. R. Groves, 602; H. George, 157; H. B. Gislason, 164; K. Glover and E. Dewey, 470; W. I. Gooch, 750; N. G. Goodman, 467; W. Goodsell, 462; D. C. Gordon, V. R. King, 32; M. Graves, M. M. Ott, 40; R. Graves, M. P. Payne, 302; J. T. Greenan, 465, and J. M. Gathany, 604; E. Greenlaw and Others, 608; H. F. Guggenheim, 466; A. L. Guptil, 37; W. J. Hale, 39; A. F. Harlow, 465; H. F. Harrington and R. E. Wolseley, 752; C. J. H. Hayes, P. T. Moon, J. W. Wayland, 294; B. L. Q. Henriques, 164; H. Hill, R. G. Tugwell, 30; D. Holt, 608; H. N. Holmes, 304; R. B. Hudson and J. C. Walker, 602; M. A. Hyde, 467; International Institute of Intellectual Cooperation, 601; E. Jacobson,

598; F. C. Jean, E. C. Harrah and F. L. Herman, 600; M. Jenkins, 472; J. E. Johnson, 161; J. B. Johnston, 742; O. G. Jones, 299; M. Josephson, 292; B. Kaessmann, H. R. Manakee, J. L. Wheeler, J. M. Gambrill, 295; I. L. Kandel, 470; G. N. Kefauver, V. H. Noll and C. E. Drake, 36, 471; E. A. Kirkpatrick, 748; G. Kleiser, 32; E. W. Knight, 161; H. Kohn, 603; A. C. Kray and Others, 29; La Mari, 38; J. H. Latane and D. W. Wainhouse, 463; E. A. Lathrop, 607; S. Leacock, 749; N. J. Lennes, L. R. Traver, 297; S. A. Leonard, R. C. Pooley, 166; R. L. Lyman and Others, 301; O. McConathy and Others, 38; J. H. McCulloch, 38; W. J. McGucken, 744; J. Martin, 38; F. Mason, 749; H. E. Mills and Others, 156; J. Mills, 304; H. C. Morrison, 295; L. M. Morsch, 607; National Education Association, 745; E. H. Naumburg, C. Lambert, L. S. Mitchell, 40; R. Niebuhr, 293; E. W. Nixon and F. W. Cozens, 598; W. M. Otto and M. E. Marye, 752; J. Ozans, 603; K. Page, 31; E. W. Pahlow, 33; F. C. Palm and F. E. Graham, 467; A. M. Palmer, G. Holton, 302; L. Parker, 303; J. E. Peabody, 304; C. A. Perry, 302; D. W. Peters, 462; W. B. Pitkin, 298; G. V. Price, 293; J. L. Rathbone, 597; W. C. Reavis, 37; T. S. Roberts, 600; A. S. Romer, 40; J. Rorty, 159; D. Rowden, 751; M. Russell, E. P. Wilson, 303; H. C. Schweikert, 608; E. Seeger, 33; G. E. Shankle, 166; W. B. Shaw, 300; A. H. Smith, 603; G. Soule, 159; D. Starch, 158; J. Stephens, E. L. Beck, R. H. Snow, 166; F. B. Strain, 304; P. M. Symonds, 468; A. J. A. Symons, 606; N. Thomas, 159; C. H. Tompson, 602; J. A. Thomson, 749; E. L. Thorndike and Others, 750; W. C. Trow, 163; B. R. Tucker, 37; B. Tunstall, 34; L. Tyson and J. C. Waller, 596; P. F. Voelker, 748; H. M. Walker, 601; L. H. Wallace, 163; E. A. Walter, 302; W. J. Whitford, E. B. Liek, W. S. Gray, 37; J. K. Wilcox, 160; J. F. Williams, 599; M. Williamson and M. S. Lyle, 471; D. Yoder and G. R. Davies, 465; H. A. Zesbaugh, 37

McCluskey, M. O., Teaching History of Education by the Laboratory-Unit Plan, 449

McClusky, H. Y., Methods of Correcting Outcome of an Examination, 566

McConn, M., Educational Guidance, 537

McConnell, R. E., Training Teachers for Emergency Nursery Schools, 778

McDermott, J. F., Scientific Books in the Early West, 812

McPherson, W. B., Leisure, 492

Manuel, H. T., Spanish-Speaking Child of the Southwest, 692

Marts, A. C., College Football and College Endowment, 14; No More Large Gifts?, 862

Marvin, Cloyd Heck, Tribute to, 550

Massachusetts Institute of Technology, Five-Year Course, 180

Mathematics, History of, G. A. Miller, 96; in Webster's Dictionary, 1934, G. A. Miller, 728

Meriam, J. L., Curriculum of High School, 169

Methods, Remedial, for Non-Readers, M. A. Tinker, 524; of Correcting Outcome of Examinations, H. Y. McClusky, 566

Metropolitan Museum of Art, Educational Work, 346; Lectures and Gallery Talks at, 869

Mexican, School System To-day, R. J. Parker, 558

Mexico, Education in Six-Year Plan, H. Benjamin, 666; School Strike in, 764; New Schools of, A. Risdon, 880

Michigan, University of, Entrance Requirements, 866

Milam, C. H., Libraries for Civilized Living, 480

Military Training, at Land Grant Colleges, 764; in Schools of Italy, 802

Miller, D. G., Education in Palestine, 189

Miller, G. A., History of Mathematics, 96; Mathematics in Webster's New International Dictionary, 1934, 728

Miller, J. H., Liberal Arts College, 328

Mills, H. C., and R. E. Eckert, Evaluation of Reading as a Unit, 261

Minnesota, University of, Follow-up Study of Scholastic Predictions, J. B. Johnston and E. G. Williamson, 730

Morgan, J. E., A National Culture, 111

Moser, W. E., Placement Bureaus, 429

Motion Pictures, Report of Office of Educ., 56; National Organizations Interested in, R. Walters, 451; Licensing, in New York State, 654

Moton, President, Resignation of, 581

Movies, Children at, G. V. N. Dearborn, 127; College in the, E. N. Cooper, 664

National, Advisory Council on Radio in Education, 245, 487; Interfraternity Conference, 767; Educational Association, W. D. Boutwell, 48; Department of Superintendence, 806

Nationalism in European Universities, W. M. Kotschnig, 265

Natural History, Amer. Museum, Lectures, 487

Nearpass, H. L., Educational Nomenclature, 217

Negro, Doctorates, H. W. Greene, 388; and American Education, J. A. Scott, 609

Negroes, Educational Leaders among, 820

Nelson, C. J., To-day's Educational Problems, 125

New, England, Educational Function of, R. H. Hutchins, 233; School for Social Research, 242, 276

New York, City, Adult Education in, 85; Schools, Financial Condition, 7; Summer Play Schools, 86; High Schools, 118; Peoples College Club, 118; PWA Funds for, 141; Bureau of Child Guidance in, 179; Budget, 223; Visual Education in, 243; Decrease in Number of Pupils, 317; Registration, 412; Teacher Qualifications, 484; Costs, 547; Health, Service, 579, Survey, 839; College of the City of, Courses for Teachers, 378; State, Oath in, 211; Appropriations, 274; Convocation of University of, 415; Association of Colleges and Universities, 441; Licensing Motion Pictures in, 654; Teachers Association, 719; Rural School Districts in, 805; University, Inst. for Supervisors of Adult Educ., 379; Doctorate of Education, 413; General Education Board's Grant, 655; Social Sciences in Curriculum, 804

Newark, N. J., University of, 87

Nomenclature, Educational, H. L. Nearpass, 217

North Carolina, Conference for Social Service, 142; Institute of Education, 143

Northeastern Univ. Sch. of Arts and Sciences, 57

Northwestern University, Appointments, 380

Norton, J. K., Work of the Joint Commission on the Emergency in Education for 1935, 105

Norway, Physically Handicapped in, 208

Nursery Schools, G. D. Stoddard, 148

Ohio State University, Appointments, 347; Educational Broadcasting, 373; New Council, 836
ONTHANK, K. W., Effect of Social Trends on Higher Education, 256
Oregon, Institutions, Registration in, 548
Orientation Courses, R. P. SIBLEY, 373
OUTLAND, G. E., Transient Boys, 301

Palestine, Contemporary Education in, D. G. MILLER, 189; Teacher Training in, 621
Parent Education, E. N. WHITE, 679
PARKER, R. J., Mexican School System To-day, 558
PATRY, F. L., Education and Psychiatry, 712
Peace and Foreign Trade, E. CALLAWAY, 65
Pennington School, H. S. CURTIS, 450
Pennsylvania, State College, Transition School, J. B. DIENNA, 253; Reorganization of School of Education, 275; and Civilian Conservation Corps, 485; University of, Museum, 654
Persia, Educational Reforms in, J. F. ABEL, 425
Phi Beta Kappa, Future of, G. M. JANES, 281; Triennial Council, R. WALTERS, 393; Purposes of, W. A. SHIMER, 421; Annals, R. W., 885
Philanthropy, American, and the Advancement of Learning, F. P. KEPPEL, 401
Pittsburgh, Meeting of American Vocational Association, 244; Univ. of, and Governor Pinchot, 128; School of Education, 840
Placement Bureaus, W. E. MOSER, 429
Political Controls of Education, 254
Predictions, Scholastic, in University of Minnesota, J. B. JOHNSTON and E. G. WILLIAMSON, 730
PRESCOTT, D. A., Conference on Emotion and the Educative Process, 396
Presidents, Our, L. W. FERGUSON, 813
Princeton Univ., Honorary Degrees, 9; Plans for New Humanistic Library, 242
Professional Training in Education, (the late) G. C. BRANDENBURG and O. C. TRIMBLE, 850
Psychiatry and Education, F. L. PATRY, 712
Psychological European Field Trip, 85
Psychology, Experiment in, R. P. CARROLL, 188; and Vocational Guidance, 516
Public Schools, Federal Support, J. B. SEARS, 433
Puerto Rico, Teaching of Spanish in, 344
Purdue University, Science Institute, 212

Race Prejudice, R. A. GORTNER, 665
Radio, Educational, Ohio State University, 377; Music on, 517; Broadcasts on Problems of Government, 518; in Education, R. WALTERS, 530; Education or Propaganda, 668; Tennessee Valley Authority and, 669; Univ. of the Air, 805; Resolution of Wisconsin Teachers, 838; Public Health, Talks on, 626; L. TYSON, 846; National Advisory Council on, in Education, 245, 487; Broadcasting, J. F. WRIGHT, 720
READ, C. B., Statistical Techniques, 535
Reading, Periodical, of College Students, E. HUNTER, 70; Evaluation of, as a Unit in "How to Study" Courses, H. C. MILLS and R. E. ECKERT, 261
REEDER, C. W., Intelligence Test Scores, 399
Registration in American Universities and Colleges, R. WALTERS, 785
Religion in Higher Education, National Council on, W. E. UPHAUS, 282
Religious Groups, Scholastic Ranking of, H. S. RUMMELL, 286
Remedial Methods for Non-Readers, M. A. TINKER, 524
RENNICK, H., Depression and the Teacher, 775
Research, Educational, Work of Australian Council, 84; in England, 361; in Canton, China, S. W. DOWNS, 423
Retiring Allowances in State Universities, 62
REUSSER, W. C., V. BRINEGAR and G. FRANK, Predicting Success in Chemistry, 197
RILEY, L. L., Air-minded Youth, 356
RISDON, A., New Schools of Mexico, 880
ROBISON, C. H., Special Students, 328
Rochester, University of, Ten-Year Plan, 143
Rockefeller Foundation, Report, 564
ROGERS, H. W., Science in Secondary School and College, 334
ROOSEVELT, F. D., Address at College of William and Mary, 569
Rosenwald County Library Experiment, 412
ROUCEK, J. S., Educational Structure of Yugoslavia, 250; Schools of Bulgaria, 495, 775
RUMMELL, H. S., Ranking of Religious Groups, 286
Russia, Extension System of Education in, 241

Salaries, of Elementary Teachers in Europe, 226; in Chicago, 177, 274
SARBAUGH, M. E., The Young College Student, 823
Scholarships, for Athletes, 6; and Loan Funds, M. M. CHAMBERS, 131; Examination, English, J. M. STALNAKER, 701
SCHULTZ, R. S., and G. S. MACVAUGH, A Short Oral Group Intelligence Test, 639
Science, Inst. of Purdue University, 212; in Secondary School and College, H. W. ROGERS, 334; at the Universities, H. T. TIZARD, 369; Natural, at George Washington Univ., 380; Teaching of, 437; Committee on Place in Education, O. W. CALDWELL, 673
SCOTT, J. A., Education and the Negro, 609
SEARS, J. B., Federal Support for Schools, 433
Secondary, School, Population, 699; Education, Anniversary of, 546; G. E. FEINGOLD, 825
SHIMER, W. A., Phi Beta Kappa Purposes, 421
SIBLEY, R. P., Orientation Courses, 373
SISSON, E. D., Twenty Years after, 781
SMITH, F. W., Stress in Education, 186
SMITH, L. W., For Love of Books, 494
SNAVELY, G. E., Nonsense in Higher Education, 832
SNEDDEN, D., Education and the Social Change, 311
Social, Service, Resolutions of N. C. Conference for, 142; Studies, Recommendations of the Commission on, F. BOBBITT, 201; N. J. WEISS, 446; P. W. L. COX, 554; A. C. KREY, 660; E. E. BAYLES, 690; Research, New School for, 242; Appointments, 276; Trends, Effect on Higher Education, K. W. ONTHANK, 256; Philosophy, Dept. of (at Cooper Union, 275; Change and Education, D. SNEDDEN, 311; New Order, School for, T. E. WILLIAMS, 542; Frontier, 581; Sciences in Curriculum of N. Y. University, 804
Soviet Union, Extension System of Education in, 241
Spanish, American University, 545; Speaking Child of the Southwest, H. T. MANUEL, 692
Spelling Tests, L. WELLER and M. E. BROOM, 103
STALNAKER, J. N., An Objective English Scholarship Examination, 701
STANLEY, B., Turkish Schools, 814
Statistical, Slide Rule, D. H. COOKE, 149; Techniques, C. B. READ, 535

STEINER, M. A., Home-Study Assignments, 20
STEWART, C., A New Deal for Civics, 97
STODDARD, G. D., Nursery Schools in the Emergency Program, 148
Straubenmuller, Gustave, in Honor of, 58
Stress in Education, F. W. SMITH, 186
Student-Teachers, J. H. FURBAY, 588
Students of Special Ability, Provision for, 439
Superintendence, Dept. of, 806
Survey, National, of the Education of Teachers, 195; Courses, P. W. WARD, 398
SWIGGETT, G. L., Inter-American Federation of Education, 364

TAYLOR, J. P., A Vermont Experiment, 17
Teacher, of Teachers, 530; Placement, L. O. McAFEE, 634; Training, R. BABCOCK, 67; G. P. CAHOON and M. MACKAY, 228; at Univ. of Vermont, 653; for Emergency Nursery Schools, R. E. McCONNELL, 778
Teachers, Control of, I. L. KANDEL, 351; Qualifications for, in N. Y. City Schools, 484; Amer. Federation of, H. R. LINVILLE, 616; C. BENGTSON, 15, 845; Better Speech for, N. J. WEISS, 875
Tennessee Valley Authority and Radio, 669
Test, Oral Intelligence, R. S. SCHULTZ and G. S. MACVAUGH, 639
Text-books, Second-hand, L. L. BERNARD, 305
THWING, C. F., a College Trustee, 137
TINKER, M. A., Remedial Methods for Non-Readers, 524
TIZARD, H. T., Science at the Universities, 369
Truant Child, F. BROWN, 772
Turkey, Schools in, B. STANLEY, 814
Turkish Language, Congress on Reform, 273
Tuskegee Institute, Resignation of President Moton, 581
Twenty Years After, E. D. SISSON, 781
Twins, Mental Ability of, R. BYRNS, 671
TYSON, L., Public Health on the Radio, 846

Union College, Installation of President, 441
Universities, Amer., Assoc. of, 589; Endowed, Support of, 848; Urban, Assoc. of, R. WALTERS, 636
University, Teachers, British Assoc. of, 117; Special Students, C. H. ROBISON, 327; of the Air, 805; Professors, Amer. Assoc., and Civilian Conservation Camps, 766
UPHAUS, W. E., National Council on Religion in Higher Education, 282

VALENTINE, P. F., The College Curriculum, 725
Vassar College, Revision of Curriculum, 580
Vermont, Experiment, J. P. TAYLOR, 17; Univ. of, and Teacher Training, 653
Vocational, Assoc., Amer., Pittsburgh Meeting, 244; Guidance, Psychology and, 516

W., R., Phi Beta Kappa Annals, 885
WAGNER, M. E., Regents' Grades, 367; and E. STRABEL, Homogeneous Grouping and Prediction Coefficients, 887
Wales, School-leaving Age in, 835
WALTERS, R., Report of Committee on Standards of American Council on Education, 100; Conference on Educational Issues in California, 129; Phi Beta Kappa, Council of, 393, Annals, 885; Conference of National Organizations Interested in Motion Pictures, 451; National Assembly on Radio in Education, 530; Assoc. of Urban Universities, 636; Registration in American Universities and Colleges, 1934, 785
WARD, P. W., Survey Courses, 398
"We Ain't Gwine Nowhere," W. T. FOSTER, 878
WEEKS, A. D., What One Studies, not How, 691
WEISS, N. J., Professor Bobbitt's Criticism, 446; Better Speech for Teachers, 875
WELLER, L., and M. E. BROOM, Spelling Tests, 103
Wesleyan Univ., Grants for Research, 839
What One Studies, not How, A. D. WEEKS, 691
WHITE, E. N., Parent Education, 679
William and Mary College, Address at, F. D. ROOSEVELT, 569; Inaugural Address, J. S. BRYAN, 571
Williams College, and Federal Relief, 765
WILLIAMS, T. E., School for New Social Order, 542
Williams, President Walter, and "First School of Journalism," 392; Resignation of, 416
WILSON, A., Inter-Scholastic Correspondence, 389
WINSLOW, C.-E. A., Health Education, 1
Wirt, Superintendent, Libel Suit against, 549
Wisconsin, Alumni Research Foundation Fellowship, 58; Teachers, Radio Resolution, 838; Univ. of, Honorary Degrees, 144; School for Workers in Industry, 653
WOOLF, H., Intelligence Test Scores of Kindergarten Children, 150
World's Fair, Educational Tours to, 516
WRIGHT, J. F., Educational Broadcasting, 729

Yale, Univ., School of Nursing, 120; Appointments, 381; Provision for Students of Special Ability, 439; Study of Federal Government, 623; Finances, 803; in China, 546; Anniversary, 681
Yonkers Emergency College, 624
Yugoslavia, Educational Structure of, J. S. ROUCEK, 250

ZOOK, G. F., Federal Aid to Education, 41

# SCHOOL AND SOCIETY

WITH WHICH ARE COMBINED THE EDUCATIONAL REVIEW, ESTABLISHED IN 1891, THE TEACHERS MAGAZINE, ESTABLISHED IN 1878, AND THE SCHOOL JOURNAL, ESTABLISHED IN 1874.

Volume 40 | SATURDAY, JULY 7, 1934 | Number 1019


## CULTURAL OBJECTIVES OF HEALTH EDUCATION


By Dr. C.-E. A. WINSLOW

PROFESSOR OF PUBLIC HEALTH, YALE SCHOOL OF MEDICINE


It is probable that the original stimulus leading to the development of education in any field has been chiefly technological. The uneducated man is a practical animal. What he desires is the mastery of tools which will help him to some immediate end. Only as the process of education itself evolves and opens new vistas to the imagination does the ideal of culture emerge.

The Academy of Plato and the Lyceum of Aristotle were primarily gymnasia. The greatest schools of philosophy which have ever existed were grafted upon training schools for the winning of athletic competitions.

So the development of the medieval university was an outgrowth of the need for professional training of ecclesiastics—an objective as technological as the preparation of engineers and chemists for their task to-day. Only later were the possible wider values of such education realized and crystallized in the classical system which proved so extraordinarily successful in the training of great leaders at Oxford and Cambridge during the nineteenth century.

The concept of classical culture was, however, too narrow and inflexible. The work of the last half century has been largely the breaking of this over-rigid mold to make place for the inclusion of widening domains of human knowledge. Modern languages, the natural sciences and the social sciences must find their place in the scheme of education; and the battle opened by President Eliot's inaugural address at Harvard College on October 19, 1869, has now been fully won. It is important to note that President Eliot, himself, was completely imbued with the cultural rather than the technological ideal. It is emphasized on every page of his numerous addresses. Yet the inevitable occurred. The inclusion of a vast mass of diversified knowledge in new and pedagogically undeveloped fields necessarily led to a technological emphasis. Narrow specialization and narrow utilitarianism tended to dominate the professional schools; and, as for the colleges, they lost for a time any semblance of concerted educational objective in a confusion of free electives, unrelated to any guiding principle of ordered cultural development. The secondary schools perhaps suffered less seriously than the colleges, but the same general tendencies were clearly manifest.

To-day, perhaps, the time has come to assimilate the welter of specialized technological education into a semblance of order guided by a more definite cultural objective; and certain tendencies of the time make such a process peculiarly imperative.

By a curious paradox, the astounding triumphs of technology have made technology relatively a less important factor in human life. A hundred years ago, the major problem—the sole problem for the mass of mankind—was to wring the bare essentials of daily living from a stubborn and resistant world. Almost the whole of a man's time was consumed in making a living and it was natural that the kind of education which helped him to make a living, "to get on in the world," was the essential thing. Technology has changed all that. It is quite certain that, if the problems of social adjustment could be solved, five hours' work a day at his chosen profession or craft could ensure to every individual an adequate standard of material prosperity. The problem of the future is no longer the performance by each individual of his own special job. The problems of the future are, first, the interrelationship of individuals in a soundly planned social order and, second, the utilization of those widening vistas of leisure time which open up before us in such a way as to promote the good life of the individual member of the state.

Even in the highest and most successful forms of professional education, thoughtful leaders are profoundly dissatisfied with the predominantly technological approaches of the past. Our law schools want their students to think of the law not as a series of precepts set down in books but as a means of promoting the widest ideals of human welfare. Our medical schools are seeking to broaden their vision from a study of symptoms to a conception of the individual human being in his familial and social environment.

The further down one goes in the educational scheme, the more important becomes the cultural emphasis on man as a citizen rather than the technological emphasis on man as merely a productive unit. The survival of civilization to-day depends far less on individual competence than on social coordination.

It has become increasingly evident that the economic crisis through which the world is passing to-day can not be overcome by the haphazard interplay of motives of individual selfishness. In pioneer days it was sufficient for each man to clear his own section of the forest and to cultivate his own farm; but the idea that rugged individualism by itself could solve the problems of modern industrial society is a form of mysticism which is born only of wishful thinking. We must have definite, purposeful, intelligent national and international planning if civilization is to survive. The need is so imperative that many nations are ready to sacrifice all that has been held to be most precious in the liberal traditions of the nineteenth century in order to attain immediate salvation. Germany, Italy and Russia have accepted dictatorships not because they desired dictatorship. No one wants dictatorship except dictators. Liberty has been abandoned in Germany and restricted in Italy and Russia because the need for a new social order was urgent. In this country we are trying a more difficult and a nobler experiment. We are seeking to accomplish the aims of national planning by common consent and not by compulsion, to create a new social economy within the framework of a democratic order and without loss of the essential values of the older liberalism. Our success is still problematical. Whether the obstructive forces of ignorance and selfishness can be overcome without Naziism or Fascism is still on the knees of the gods; but on the success or failure of this experiment may depend the course of civilization for a century to come.

What part have we to play as teachers in this historic period? Clearly, I think, to see to it that in our little individual areas of influence we are on the side of the angels—that we are educating citizens and not merely doctors or lawyers or farmers or stenographers or salesmen or bank presidents. And here at last we come to the particular topic we are to discuss this morning.

Few subjects lend themselves better to the wider cultural ideals of education than hygiene. At the very basis of all our teaching of health lies the idea of fitness for community service. Here particularly applies the splendid dictum of Matthew Arnold, "There is a view in which all the love of our neighbor, the impulses toward action, help, and beneficence, the desire for removing human error, clearing human confusion, and diminishing human misery, the noble aspiration to leave the world better and happier than we found it, motives eminently such as are called social—come in as part of the grounds of culture, and the main and preeminent part."

The bearing of the teaching of hygiene upon the social problems of to-day is, however, far more definite and specific than that implied in the cultivation of a general sense of social responsibility. In the field of community health we have a very definite concrete illustration of the most vital problems of present-day society. The triumphs of the public health campaign during the past half century constitute one of the most striking achievements in the history of the human race. During that period the mortality rates in our urban populations have been reduced by nearly one half. Think what it means to have abolished cholera and typhoid and typhus and diphtheria and scarlet fever as important causes of death, to have reduced infant mortality and tuberculosis to a quarter of their earlier figure, to have lifted one half of the total burden of death and disease and disablement from the shoulders of our city dwellers. Consider what this implies not only for the physical health and efficiency of our race but for the whole emotional and intellectual atmosphere in which we live.

Such are the opportunities which the technological advances of science have placed at our disposal. Yet we have by no means reaped the fullest possible benefits from those advances. Even in 1929 at the height of its prosperity the United States had developed community health machinery only about one half as adequate as that which was demonstrated to be necessary for sound social economy. A score or so of cities, a dozen rural counties, had really adequate health organizations with the budget of two dollars per capita which experience has shown is essential for modern health protection. At the other extreme, two thirds of the rural counties in the United States had no organized health service whatsoever.

During the past five years, even the modest achievements of 1929 have been ruthlessly sacrificed in many communities. The health budgets of Alabama have been reduced 85 per cent. The child health service of Indiana has been wrecked. Federal appropriations for aid to rural health work, meager at the best, have been entirely cut off and Congress, which can appropriate hundreds of millions for war vessels and for organized lobbies of veterans, can not find a dollar for the salvage of our health defenses at home.

The obstacles here, as elsewhere in the broad area of social planning, are ignorance and selfishness. We do not understand the difference between "economy," which means wise management of the household or the state, and "parsimony," which means not spending money. The vested interests of large taxpayers cry out for indiscriminate tax reduction, saving one dollar for prevention in order to pay out ten dollars for cure and laying up burdens of disease and disability to be liquidated in the future. The tubercle bacillus will in the end collect a tax far heavier than that which we are saving by unwise reduction in our appropriations for protection against its ravages.

In some cases I regret to say that misguided leaders have arrayed even the medical profession as a selfish vested interest active in destroying the public health machinery of the community because of alleged competition with the private practitioner. This has happened in Indiana and is to-day happening in Los Angeles County, California.

All in all, is this not a typical example of the basic problem of society as a whole—the problem of overcoming ignorance and selfishness in order to secure a whole-hearted and intelligent cooperation for the common good? If you can develop in the child a clear comprehension of the need for coordinated social planning in this special field, have you not made a step toward a truly cultural education and laid at least a foundation for the essential citizenship of the future?

Citizenship, however, is, after all, only a means to an end—not an end in itself. The one end is a good life for the individual citizen. There is real danger that this may be forgotten. It has apparently been forgotten in Germany.

We have been using the word "cultural" as opposed to "technological" to stand for the higher ideals of education; but the term is not perhaps the best for this purpose. A "culture" is something which is cultivated; and one can cultivate weeds as well as grain. Primitive peoples have their "cultures" which are often peculiarly dominant and unyielding. The cultural conception may mean simply the molding of the individual to a national or racial norm which in itself is barbarous and undesirable. What we desire is not only culture but a high and a noble culture, a civilized culture. To civilize is "to bring out of barbarism, enlighten, refine." That should be our true ideal.

The essence of the problem is admirably discussed in Clive Bell's "Civilization."[1] The author begins in an ironical vein by pointing out that in 1914–1918 we were all asked to offer our lives for "civilization" and that it behooves us to consider what this precious thing really is. He then analyzes the quality of certain very primitive cultures to see what civilization is not; and he shows that honesty, religious faith, respect for women, kindliness, industry, generosity, truthfulness, cleanliness, morality, chivalry, patriotism can not be considered as characteristic of civilization, since they appear in highly developed forms among many peoples whom no one could by any stretch of imagination call "civilized." Finally, he takes for contrast three periods which by universal consent could be taken as representative of the ideal of civilization—Periclean Athens, Fifteenth Century Italy and Eighteenth Century France. In these periods he finds two qualities predominant which are not found in such degree in any barbarous society. They are, first, a high sense of esthetic values for the sake of the spiritual experience involved and not for utility; and the enthronement of reason as the arbiter of human conduct, reason, free from traditional and emotional bonds which bears its fruit in illimitable tolerance, realizing "that what we believe is not necessarily true; that what we like is not necessarily good; and that all questions are open."

The production of such a civilized state of mind as this should be our educational ideal and not the perpetuation of a traditional culture with its petty taboos and inhibitions.

Has not the study of hygiene its essential place in a scheme of education aiming at such an ideal as this? John Dewey, in his recent address on "The Supreme Intellectual Obligation," has said:

> The obligations incumbent upon science can not be met until its representatives cease to be contented with having a multiplicity of courses in various sciences represented in the schools, and devote even more energy than was spent in getting a place for science in the curriculum, to seeing to

[1] Chatto and Windus. London, 1928.

> it that the sciences which are taught are themselves more concerned about creating a certain mental attitude than they are about purveying a fixed body of information or about preparing a small number of persons for the further specialized pursuit of some particular science. . . . The responsibility of science can not be fulfilled by educational methods that are chiefly concerned with the self-perpetuation of specialized science to the neglect of influencing the much larger number to adopt into the very make-up of their minds those attitudes of open-mindedness, intellectual integrity, observation and interest in testing their opinions and beliefs that are characteristic of the scientific attitude.

Surely in such an educational ideal as this hygiene should play an essential rôle. The old maxim, "Know thyself," still holds as a basis of true education. To understand the functioning of one's own living machine, to know its limitations and its powers, to feel the beauty of physical health and vigor as the Greeks felt it and to know how such health and vigor can be attained as we know it—this is a fundamental part of that attitude of mind which makes for civilized living.

Even more significant is the contribution of that area of hygiene which relates to the human mind and the human emotions. The savage conceives of even the physical world as dominated by emotional personality. The thunder is the voice of an angry god and the storm is an evidence of his wrath. Gradually such superstitions have given way to a conception of an external universe governed by the workings of orderly causal processes. In the inner realm such enlightenment has come more slowly. We still take our own emotions and those of others seriously, as if they were ultimate facts. Mental hygiene will slowly and gradually substitute a more scientific attitude. It will teach us that our own angry voices have origins more complex but no less a part of a causal chain of events than the thunder. As we learn "why people behave like human beings" we shall undermine some of our emotional complexes by a solvent scepticism. We shall regard the emotional reactions of others with a tolerant comprehension. We shall approach that sense of the basic importance of esthetic experience and that liberalism of the intellect which are the hall-marks of civilization.

Is such an ideal susceptible of realization in a political order such as our own? The great civilizations of the past have always been aristocracies, flowerings of small groups of favored individuals resting on a basis of slave labor or its equivalent. From a material standpoint this need no longer necessarily be the case. The resources of technological science make it theoretically possible for the whole human race to live in physical comfort without long hours of grinding toil for any one. The real crux of the matter is a psychological, not an engineering problem. Is the average individual susceptible of civilization? Will the vast increase of leisure time which confronts the human race really bear fruit in the evolution of a sense of beauty and a love of truth throughout the great mass of mankind? No one can tell; but the attempt to realize this ideal is the great challenge to education. If the spirit of Athens and of Florence can become a permeating influence in a modern democratic state our "culture" will become a "civilization."

# EDUCATIONAL EVENTS

## THE HAGUE ACADEMY

Dr. James Brown Scott, director of the Division of International Law of the Carnegie Endowment for International Peace, has made public particulars in regard to courses and lectures to be given at the Hague Academy this summer. The sessions will start in July and continue through August, and will be divided into two terms.

Dr. Scott states that:

The academy is one of the very few institutions of learning in the world which may properly be termed international in the fullest sense of the word. Its courses, as may be seen from the program for the coming Summer, deal with various phases of the legal relations between states, the several general and special subjects in this field being treated in an objective manner, with emphasis upon the development of peaceful relations between states. Moreover, the academy loses none of its international status by being situated within the territorial limits of a single state.

The lectures are given in French and cover not only the general phases of the historical development and fundamental principles of international law, but also special phases relating to juridical questions of current international interest. The instruction thus given is, of course, of a more advanced nature than that offered in universities, and the student who hopes to obtain the greatest benefit from such instruction should possess a sound basic knowledge of international law.

The sessions will be divided into eight subjects, as follows:

The course on the *Historical Development of International Law* will include the "Russian Policy of Gaining Access to the Mediterranean in the Twentieth Century," by André N. Mandelstamm, former director of the legal department of the Ministry of Foreign Affairs of Russia, and member of the Institut de Droit International, and "Jean Bodin—His Place Among the Founders of International Law," by André Gardot, former president of the Ordre des Avocats at the Court of Appeals of Angers and president of the Comité Jean Bodin.

The course on *Principles of Public International Law* will be presented by Professor Karl Strupp, of the University of Istanbul, former professor at the University of Frankfort and corresponding member of the American Institute of International Law, whose subject will be "General Rules of the Law of Peace." In the second term the same subject will be presented by Professor Erich Kaufmann, of the University of Bonn, honorary professor at the University of Berlin and associate member of the Institut de Droit International.

The course on *Principles of Private International Law* will be divided into its history from the Middle Ages onward, especially in Occidental Europe, by Professor E. M. Meijers, of the law faculty of the University of Leyden, and the "Conflicts of Law in the Matter of Time," by Etienne de Szaszy, professor at the University of Budapest and a judge attached to the Royal Hungarian Ministry of Justice.

*Special Subjects in Private International Law* will offer in the first term "The Conflicts of Law in the Matter of Aerial Law," by Professor Fernand de Visscher, of the University of Ghent and of the Catholic Faculty of Law in Lille, and in the second term, "The Recent Developments of the Principle of Domicile in English Law," by Norman Bentwich, professor at the University of Jerusalem.

## SCHOLARSHIPS FOR ATHLETES

THE following letter has been sent to the head of every institution on the approved list by Dr. Wilson Farrand, acting chairman of the Commission on Institutions of Higher Education of the Association of Colleges and Secondary Schools of the Middle States:

The Commission on Higher Institutions of the Middle States Association of Colleges and Secondary Schools reiterates emphatically its position that no college granting athletic scholarships will be considered by the commission worthy of a place on its approved list. In October last the president of every coeducational and men's college on the list stated over his signature that the institution over which he presided was living up, in letter and spirit, to the rule as stated. A request for a similar statement will be sent to each president in October next.

By "athletic scholarship" the commission means any money, or equivalent of money, paid to any student primarily because of athletic achievement or promise, including opportunities for earning money beyond a fair amount for the service rendered.

The commission does not mean by its statement that no athlete shall receive a scholarship, but simply that athletics shall not be considered either to qualify or disqualify a student from holding a scholarship. The commission feels that any athlete who holds a scholarship should conform to the regular standards exacted of all scholarship holders, and that the ratio of athletes holding scholarships to the non-athletes holding scholarships should conform approximately to the ratio of athletes to non-athletes in the institution.

The commission realizes that it is impossible for an institution to control the subsidizing of athletes by its alumni or others, but it feels that a college should not knowingly permit such subsidization, and should use every reasonable means to prevent it. We are not attempting to reform athletics, but we feel that the practise of subsidizing athletes is extremely detrimental to the maintenance of high standards in a college, and we ask the hearty cooperation of every institution on our list in the attempt to check what in some quarters has been a great evil.

Any questions in regard to the interpretation of the rule sent to the acting chairman will receive as prompt attention as possible.

## THE FINANCIAL CONDITION OF THE NEW YORK CITY SCHOOLS

A statement in regard to the financial condition of the schools of New York City has been made public by Dr. George J. Ryan, president of the Board of Education, and Dr. Harold G. Campbell, superintendent of schools.

Earlier this year both Mr. Ryan and Dr. Campbell issued statements predicting the closing of the schools next spring unless the Legislature consented to make up the $8,000,000 deficit. It was explained at the time that for the calendar year 1934 the budget allowance for schools was $130,759,983, but that this was based on the assumption that the state would fulfill its statutory obligation. If the Legislature refuses to make up this difference, it was said, $3,365,000 would have to be deducted from the appropriation for the fall term, while the remaining $4,535,000 would be taken from the spring term of 1935.

The statement is in part as follows:

Parents and the people generally are entitled to know the whole truth. We must face the facts, unpleasant as they may be. Right now there is not enough money to operate the schools this fall, even on the depression basis, with large classes and curtailed activities all along the line. To reopen the schools in September and keep them open until the end of the next school year, we must have the $8,000,000 that we rightfully should have under the terms of the Friedsam act, but which the Legislature has failed to appropriate. Even if appropriated, this $8,000,000 is sufficient only to take care of commitments already made.

Unless supplemented by additional appropriations, hundreds of physically handicapped children will go uneducated; adequate repairs to school buildings can not be made; sufficient supplies can not be bought, and we shall have to go on with overcrowded classes and overworked teachers. We have been cutting and giving money for relief purposes both out of our regular budget and out of teachers' salaries until the danger point has at length been reached.

It is pointed out that until the depression set in, appropriations were being made in accordance with a long-term program designed to provide "ultimately for the needs of all the children." According to this program, the board's 1934 budget would have been about $152,000,000, while for 1935 it would have had $157,000,000. However, the largest single year's budget on record was in 1932, when $145,300,000 was appropriated. The 1934 budget is about $22,000,000 under what it should have been.

Since the depression the schools have been falling behind and the board is unable to provide such fundamental necessities as money for books and for repairs to buildings. The statement continues:

The public must realize that children are staying in school to-day longer than ever before. The number attending high school has increased 100 per cent. in ten years. There are no jobs for children and they are forced to remain in school. These children must be provided for or the community itself will suffer. Delinquency and crime will increase and the money that is now being withheld from education will be spent during the next few years for the maintenance of reformatories. Meanwhile, the lives of countless children will have been wrecked.

As an alternative to this condition it is suggested that parents ask the governor and legislators to first appropriate the full statutory amount of state aid and, second, that they "provide, at least until the city's financial position is improved, such additional aid as may be necessary to make possible adequate educational facilities for all the children."

It is pointed out that:

Since the state's financial position is such that it is able to borrow money at slightly less than 2 per cent., the lowest rate in history, certainly there should be no hesitancy to appropriate sufficient money to provide adequate schools for the children of the state. The total sum necessary is less than the cost of one battleship, but it is enough to make useful American citizens of hundreds upon hundreds of New York City's children, who now receive inadequate schooling or none at all.

## STUDENTS-AT-LARGE AT THE UNIVERSITY OF CHICAGO

Extension of the New Plan of the University of Chicago to permit students not candidates for a degree to become students-at-large has been announced by President Robert Maynard Hutchins, following approval of the policy by the University Senate.

The University of Chicago becomes the first major American institution of higher education to admit any student who can demonstrate ability to profit by university opportunities to do so without having to meet requirements for a degree or otherwise becoming entangled in academic red tape. The Chicago plan will greatly extend existing facilities for adult education and its influence in this field is expected to be far reaching.

The statement of policy adopted by the senate was as follows: "Students, qualified for admission to the university, who are interested in further study but do not desire to register as candidates for a degree, shall be admitted as students-at-large in the university and be given the privilege of attending lecture courses and of using the library and such other facilities of the university as the appropriate dean and the instructor may recommend."

Under this plan, the qualifications for admission to the university have been broadened so that the old requirement of a certain number of high-school units no longer controls, particularly in cases of students who can demonstrate training or experience that gives promise of satisfactory college work. In the last three years, students who have not completed the high-school course, but whose record demonstrates ability and fitness for advanced work, have been admitted and several candidates for higher degrees have been admitted despite a lack of formal entrance requirements. The success of this experiment led to the adoption of the students-at-large plan.

According to a statement made by Dean of Faculties Emery T. Filbey, the university's latest departure from traditional academic paths follows as a logical development of the new plan. Under this arrangement, a student no longer graduates when he has passed a specified number of courses, but when he has demonstrated achievement by passing examinations, for which he may prepare by attending class or through study on his own initiative. In the recent June convocation, one student received a bachelor's degree after two years in the university, and thirteen others graduated after three years of study.

The students-at-large will have even greater freedom to follow their intellectual interests, but it is believed that any individual sufficiently interested in obtaining an education to study in this classification will make exceptional use of the opportunities. It will be possible for students desiring to do so to become candidates for degrees by taking the general examinations.

Admission of students-at-large is also in line with the criticism frequently made by President Hutchins of the American exaltation of academic degrees, rather than insistence on the value of a true education. "We shall shortly see the bachelor's degree required for elementary teachers and the master's for high-school teachers, as the doctorate is now almost universally demanded for teachers at the higher levels," President Hutchins said in his convocation address on June 12. "Thanks to such requirements and similar ones for entrance to professional schools, American students have in the last forty years become the most degree conscious in the world. They are not to blame. Colleges and universities have themselves informed them that nobody can get anywhere in teaching, research, or the so-called learned professions without an appropriate alphabetical series after his name."

## LIBRARY SERVICE AT THE SUMMER SCHOOL OF COLUMBIA UNIVERSITY

Library service under specialists from all sections of the United States will be studied in the thirty-fifth Columbia University Summer Session, in which 1,000 courses in every field of elementary, intermediate and higher education will be given from July 9 to August 17.

Studies in library work with children and in standard works of reference will be directed by Elizabeth Nesbitt, assistant professor of library science, Carnegie Institute of Technology, Pittsburgh, and by Margaret Jackson, librarian, Hoyt Library, Kingston, Pa. Professor Helen A. Bagley, of the School of Library Service, Drexel Institute, Philadelphia, will cooperate in two courses in "Principles of Dictionary Cataloguing."

Professors Lydia M. Gooding and Miriam D. Tompkins, of the School of Library Science, Emory University, will lecture on subject bibliographies and book selection.

Edith N. Snow, supervisor of recataloguing at the Public Library, Portland, Maine, will give a course in principles of classification, the aim of which is "to develop skill in translating the salient features of books into classification numbers."

The courses offered in library training fall into three groups. They include graduate courses leading to the degree of bachelor of science; undergraduate courses leading to a certificate; advanced graduate courses leading to the degree of master of science. Students are expected to enter the school from all parts of this country as well as from abroad.

Charles F. McCombs, superintendent of the main reading room in the New York Public Library, will lecture on "Bibliography and Bibliographical Methods," and Otto W. Fuhrmann, director of the Division of Graphic Arts, New York City, will present "History of Bookmaking."

Others who will give courses in the school are: Linda H. Morley, librarian, Industrial Relations Counselors, Inc., New York City; Amelia H. Munson, assistant to supervisor of school work, in charge of work with continuation schools, in the New York Public Library, and Edna E. Bayer, librarian at the Benjamin Franklin Junior-Senior High School, Rochester, N. Y.

Dr. Charles C. Williamson is dean of the Faculty of Library Service and Edna M. Sanderson is associate dean. Members of the Columbia Faculty who will teach during the summer are: Dena Babcock, instructor in library administration; Lucile F. Fargo, research associate; Lucy E. Fay, associate professor of bibliography; Bertha M. Frick, instructor in cataloguing; Clarissa L. Goold, instructor in library service; Alice I. Hazeltine, assistant professor of library work with children; Margaret Hutchins, instructor in bibliography; Ernest J. Reece, associate professor of library administration; Isabella K. Rhodes, assistant professor of cataloguing, and Mary M. Shaver, assistant professor of bibliography.

## HONORARY DEGREES CONFERRED BY PRINCETON UNIVERSITY

AMONG the recipients of honorary degrees conferred by Princeton University at its recent commencement were four men engaged in educational administration. In conferring these degrees Dean Luther P. Eisenhart said:

### MASTER OF SCIENCE

PETER CARTER SPEERS, of the Class of 1914, professor of industrial chemistry in Forman Christian College, Lahore, India. By his planning and efforts, and with financial support from the British Government and from American sources, a laboratory for industrial chemistry was erected there within a few years following his graduation from Princeton.

His scientific investigations have been directed toward the development of the resources of India for the benefit of her people. A teacher of wide influence who has planted in his students the seed of his mission for India which is bringing forth an hundredfold.

### DOCTOR OF DIVINITY

WILLIAM HARRIS, a Princeton-born boy and a graduate of the Class of 1892; organizer principal of the Prince Royal's College of Chiengmai, Siam, acknowledged to be the best school for boys in Siam and open to all without regard to race or religious belief; aided and encouraged by his Princeton classmates in the gift of the college auditorium; twice decorated by the King of Siam for his contributions to education and for his many public services.

He has accomplished much, he has planned much more, ever animated by the passion to transmit the traditions and ideals of Princeton to that far-distant land.

### DOCTOR OF LETTERS

TYLER DENNETT, president-elect of Williams College. His literary career, begun as an undergraduate, has been crowned by his ''John Hay''; a student and expositor of diplomatic history, principally of the Far East; for eight years associated with the State Department in Washington.

When our School of Public and International Affairs was instituted, he became its first professor of international relations. He returns to his *alma mater* having won the esteem of his Princeton students and colleagues as a scholar, a teacher and a man.

DOCTOR OF LAWS

JAMES BRYANT CONANT, president of Harvard University. He had barely completed his undergraduate and graduate study at Harvard when he joined the Chemical Warfare Service; elected to the National Academy of Sciences at the early age of 34; recently for the third time awarded a medal for distinguished work in organic chemistry. His main chemical investigations are noteworthy for their high quality, breadth of range, intuition and ingenious planning, involving adept use of methods from every field.

A quiet, imaginative, versatile, thorough scholar, a proved master of the art of fire, he now carries aloft the torch of learning, and is destined as the years go by to be classed with that other professor of chemistry who became the great president of Harvard.

# EDUCATIONAL NOTES AND NEWS

THE National Education Association has been holding its seventy-second annual meeting in Washington during the present week under the presidency of Miss Jessie Gray, of Philadelphia. SCHOOL AND SOCIETY will print at an early date an account of the meeting and several of the most important addresses.

JOHN STEWART BRYAN, publisher of *The Richmond News Leader,* was elected on June 30 president of the College of William and Mary to succeed the late Dr. J. A. C. Chandler.

DR. EUGENE C. BROOKS, head of the North Carolina State College of Agriculture and Engineering, at Raleigh, and Dr. J. I. Foust, head of the North Carolina State College for Women, at Greensboro, have tendered their resignations to the board of trustees of the Greater University of North Carolina, of which these two colleges are units. Dr. Brooks and Dr. Foust held the rank of vice-presidents of the consolidated university. Prior to the merger, each was president of his institution. They have been made presidents emeritus of the Raleigh and Greensboro units, respectively, with an allowance of $4,000 a year each.

DR. WENDELL S. BROOKS has been elected president of the newly organized College of Liberal Arts of the Billings Polytechnic Institute. For the past four years he has been president of Intermountain College. Dr. Brooks is secretary of the Western Union Association of Independent Colleges.

THE Rutgers University award for "outstanding service to agriculture and education" was presented to Dr. J. E. Russell, dean emeritus of Teachers College, Columbia University, during the annual field day program of the New Jersey College of Agriculture and Experiment Station on June 13. The award, a bronze medal, is given by the trustees of the university and was presented by Dr. R. C. Clothier, its president.

AN album of letters from some five hundred friends and alumni, expressing appreciation of his work and of his contributions to agriculture, was recently presented to Dr. Charles Franklin Curtiss, who retired in 1932 as dean of agriculture and director of the Experiment Station at the Iowa State College. An oil portrait of Dean Curtiss, painted by Robert Grafton, of Chicago, will be presented to the college.

DR. NICHOLAS MURRAY BUTLER, president of Columbia University, president of the Carnegie Endowment for International Peace and president of the Pilgrims of the United States, was the guest of the Pilgrims at a dinner given in his honor in London on July 3. The Earl of Derby presided and the American ambassador was present.

DR. JAMES BRYANT CONANT, president of Harvard University, sailed for Europe on June 30.

MISS MARTHA BERRY, of Georgia, head of the Berry Schools, who is visiting England, was presented among other Americans to King George and Queen Mary at Buckingham Palace on June 13 by Mrs. Robert W. Bingham, wife of the United States ambassador.

THE Hungarian Red Cross Medal of Merit was presented to Miss Augusta Markowitz, librarian of the Woodstock Branch of the New

York Public Library, on May 25, at reception held by the Hungarian-American Society at the Rockefeller Center, New York City.

THE John Newbery Medal, given annually to the author of "the most significant contribution to American literature for children," was awarded at the Montreal conference of the American Library Association to Miss Cornelia Meigs, a member of the department of English at Bryn Mawr College. The Newbery Medal was established in 1921 by Frederic G. Melcher, editor of *The Publishers' Weekly,* and is named in memory of the first publisher of children's books. It is a bronze medal designed by René Paul Chambellan. The winner is selected by a committee of fifteen children's librarians of the American Library Association.

FREDERIC W. ERB, who retired on July 1 after fifty years of service in the Columbia University Library, was honored recently at a ceremony in the library at which President Butler presented him with a book of more than two hundred letters of appreciation from university trustees, faculty and staff members. A silver coffee service was also presented to him.

AT the Chicago meeting of the American Federation of Teachers Raymond F. Lowry, of Toledo, was elected president to succeed Dr. Henry R. Linville, of New York City. Dr. Linville has been president of the Teachers Union of New York City since 1916, and was elected president of the federation in 1931.

THE degree of doctor of laws was conferred at the commencement of Bates College on June 18 on Dr. Dixon Ryan Fox, president of Union College, Schenectady, N. Y.

AN honorary degree of doctor of philosophy, granted by the University of Cologne, was conferred on June 3 upon Professor William Alpha Cooper, retiring head of the department of German at Stanford University. The degree was presented by Richard Heinemann, chancellor of the German consulate in San Francisco, at a dinner given in Professor Cooper's honor by faculty and students. A telegram was read from Dr. Hans Luther, German ambassador at Washington. Through the consulate he presented Dr. Cooper with a parchment-bound copy of a Wagner memorial edition of Nibelungenlied. Dr. Camille von Klenze, visiting professor from the University of Munich, read a letter from the president of the Deutsche Akademie in Munich. Members of the faculty gave him a pair of opera glasses, and his former students sent a bound volume of messages from all over the world. They also presented to the department an enlarged and framed portrait of Dr. Cooper.

DEAN FRANK M. ERICKSON, of Willamette University, received the honorary degree of doctor of education at commencement exercises on June 11. Dr. Erickson has been dean since 1931. Previously he was for six years dean of the College of Liberal Arts. He went to Willamette in 1920 as professor of education. Dr. Erickson will be acting president of the university until a successor is chosen to Dr. Carl Gregg Doney, whose resignation took effect with the close of this school year.

THE degree of doctor of laws was on June 11 conferred by Macalester College, St. Paul, Minn., on George Rowland Collins, associate dean of the New York University School of Commerce, Accounts and Finance.

DR. EDWIN B. FRED, professor of bacteriology at the University of Wisconsin, has been appointed dean of the Graduate School. He will succeed Professor Charles S. Slichter, who has been dean since 1920. Dean Slichter retired on July 1, having reached the age of seventy years. He has been appointed research adviser to the Graduate School and professor emeritus of mathematics.

AT the annual meeting of the Board of Trustees of Birmingham-Southern College, Dr. Wyatt W. Hale, acting dean, was elected dean of the college.

DR. JOSEPH S. CHAMBERLAIN, head of the department of chemistry at the Massachusetts State College at Amherst, has been made Goessmann professor of chemistry in recognition of twenty-five years' service to the college as professor of organic and agricultural chemistry.

DR. CLARENCE H. WHITE, professor of Greek, who is retiring this year after teaching for thirty-two years at Colby College, has been given the title of professor emeritus. He will teach one course in Greek art next year.

DR. WILHELM KÖHLER, director of the State Museum of Art at Weimar, has been appointed professor of the history of art at Harvard University.

PROFESSOR WILLIAM C. GREENE, of the department of English and history at the Massachusetts Institute of Technology, has been appointed for the coming year exchange professor at Stevens Institute of Technology at Hoboken, N. J.. Professor John B. Fife, of Stevens Institute, will spend next year at the Massachusetts Institute.

FREDERICK H. HARWOOD, who has been a member of the faculties of Syracuse University and the Eastman School of Music at Rochester, New York, has been appointed a member of the staff of the University of California Extension Division.

DR. JAMES SPARLING, New York City, has been appointed dean of men and assistant professor of psychology at Hiram College, Ohio, succeeding Dr. Clifton W. Hall.

THREE members of the faculty of the University of California will teach in the summer session of the University of Hawaii. Raymond G. Gettell, head of the department of political science in the University of California at Berkeley, will lecture in political science, taking the place of Dr. William H. George, who will lecture during the California summer session. August Vollmer, professor of criminology and police administration, formerly chief of police at Berkeley, will conduct courses in police administration in Honolulu. Miss Elizabeth B. Kepple, of the extension department of the University of California at Los Angeles and a member of the faculty of Pasadena Junior College, will teach oral English. Arthur E. Lindborg, formerly superintendent of education in American Samoa, and now a graduate student at California, also will serve on the faculty.

DR. HERMANN COOPER, associate in higher education, previously for two years principal of the Fredonia State Normal School, has been appointed assistant commissioner of the New York State Department of Teacher Education and Certification. Since the position was created last September, Dr. Cooper has been serving on a temporary appointment.

MRS. EDWARD MEAD EARLE, of New York City, has been appointed head of Miss Fine's School at Princeton. She succeeds the late Margaret May Fine, founder and former head mistress, who died last autumn.

WILLIAM BECKMAN VAN ALSTYNE, JR., director of the department of personnel of Princeton University for the last five years, will become associated next September with Merck and Company, manufacturing chemists at Rahway, N. J.

JUSTIN MILLER, dean of the Law School of Duke University, has been appointed a special assistant to the Attorney General to aid in the presentation of cases before the Supreme Court.

PROFESSOR J. L. STOCKS, professor of philosophy at the University of Manchester, will be the first labor candidate from the University of Oxford at the next general election.

TO perpetuate the memory of the late Dr. Gustave Straubenmuller, retired associate superintendent of the New York City schools, the Board of Education has voted to change the name of the Textile High School to the Straubenmuller Textile High School. Dr. Straubenmuller was responsible for the establishment of the school fifteen years ago.

A FULL-LENGTH bronze statue, executed by Colonel Augustus Lukeman, New York City, was dedicated to the late Dr. James Kennedy Patterson, for forty-one years president of the University of Kentucky, at ceremonies held on June 1. Governor A. O. Stanley was the principal speaker. The statue has been placed on the central part of the campus.

CLAUDE C. RUSSELL, superintendent of the schools of New Haven, Connecticut, and lecturer in elementary education at Yale University, died on June 29. He was sixty-one years old.

FRANK H. HILL, for fourteen years superintendent of the schools of Marblehead, Mass., died on July 29 at the age of sixty-six years.

AT the recent commencement exercises at Skidmore College, a grant of $10,000 a year for five years from the Rockefeller Foundation was announced to finance education in nursing at Skidmore College and Mary McClellan Hospital, Cambridge, N. Y.

A DIVISION of social sciences has been organized at the University of Michigan. The new plan will not set up another administrative or teaching unit within the university, but will bring together the faculties of the schools, colleges and departments which teach the sciences of man's history and present ways of living. As initially organized, the division will consist of the Law School, the School of Business Administration, and the departments of anthropology, economics, geography, history, philosophy, political science, psychology and sociology.

COLUMBIA UNIVERSITY has announced a plan to organize an Institute of Urbanism, modeled upon the Institut d'Urbanisme of the University of Paris. The institute will appoint a director and staff of instructors from among the various faculties of Columbia University. Lecture rooms, seminar rooms, drafting room, offices and a library will be provided. From four to ten fellowships will be available for advanced students. The purpose of the institute is to carry on researches relating to the immediate problems of the city, such as administrative organization, economic and social development and the physical facilities for urban life.

COLLEGE editors representing Harvard and Yale Universities and the Universities of Georgia, Illinois, Chicago, Texas, California, Wisconsin and Washington express their belief that prospects for employment by 1934 graduates are more favorable than last year. As reported by Wayne W. Parrish in *The Literary Digest,* more business firm representatives have visited the bureau of appointments at Yale University thus far this year than in the previous two years. W. Emerson Gentzler, director of appointments at Columbia University, finds a larger demand for specialized persons. In Georgia opportunities for work seem greater. Prospects in Texas, however, are less favorable. John P. Bardon, editor of *The Daily Maroon,* of the University of Chicago, reports: "Jobs are more plentiful but salaries in vocations chosen by college graduates are low and prospects for advancement seem low." In Wisconsin there is increased demand for graduates except in education. Few of the graduates of the University of California last year are unemployed. In Washington graduate unemployment is half of what it was last year.

INTERNATIONAL Educational Pictures, Cambridge, Mass., has recently been organized as a non-profit clearing house to promote international understanding and world peace by fostering interest in the manners, customs, industries, arts, religions, and other aspects of the peoples of the world. As a bureau it will offer a central information and film-booking division for non-theatrical films of international interest available in the United States. As a film clearing house International Educational Pictures will place orders for non-theatrical exhibitors with their nearest distributor having copies of films desired. The catalogue of the new clearing house, as described in *Educational Screen,* includes titles of 2,000 films—16 mm and 35 mm—of which 375 are said to be free, except for a small booking fee of 25 cents per reel. The films are classified under more than a hundred geographical areas, and under such other subject-headings as art, biography, entertainment, history, industries, literary dramatizations, nature, religion, science, sports and transportation. The catalogue, $8\frac{1}{2}'' \times 11''$ in size, contains thirty-two pages with many illustrations of scenes from countries all over the world.

ACCORDING to Professor Waldo Abbot, director of broadcasting, ninety-two Michigan schools had classes listening to the educational radio talks broadcast from the University of Michigan during the recently completed radio series for 1933–34. Forty-one of the ninety-two schools reported 12,157 listeners a week, with others unable to give definite attendance figures. These listeners were exclusive of the students "attending" the radio music classes conducted by Professor Joseph E. Maddy. Seventy-four of the schools are equipped with radios, in eighteen the pupils go elsewhere to listen to the programs. Only thirteen schools reported that they did not make use of the university broadcasts. Following in popularity the vocational, science and history series were civics, English poets, English language, zoology, astronomy and fine arts. Forty-seven schools asked to have the vocational series repeated and 41 requested a school health series next year.

# DISCUSSION

## COLLEGE FOOTBALL AND COLLEGE ENDOWMENT

A GREAT many colleges, during the 1920 decade, were induced to go in for football in a big way in the expectation that a winning team would be of great help in attracting both gifts and students to their campuses. The pretensions of football have been considerably deflated in the past few years (along with the deflation of many other hopes and plans); but there is still enough misapprehension among college presidents and trustees in regard to what football should or should not be expected to do for the general promotional program of a college to warrant a brief discussion of it.

We have heard many a college trustee say something like this: "What we need is a football team. I mean a team that can win games and make the newspaper headlines. If we could turn out a first-class football team, we'd have no trouble getting all the students we could admit and in getting the friendship of men with money. But as long as we dub along with a fourth-rate team nobody is going to pay any attention to us." I venture to say that this idea has been expressed in substantially these same words in the councils of every college represented here.

Well, let us examine the actual experiences of colleges with football as a promotional technique during the 1920 decade. Let us see just what football did or did not accomplish for them in dollars and cents in that ten-year period. I have taken the rather famous Bulletin No. 23 of the Carnegie Foundation, which is a very complete survey of college football, and have selected from it, just as fairly as could be done, 16 colleges which are mentioned as having spent much time and money in building up their football teams. I have selected 16 other colleges which are mentioned as having regarded football as an amateur sport and as not having spent much money to get players. I prefer not to name the colleges in either group, as I do not wish these comments to be interpreted as a criticism of any sort of any college. The colleges were selected impersonally, and I believe fairly, with the idea of having each group of 16 balance with the other in respect to geography, size, age and type. They were selected with a sincere desire to throw light upon a vital college problem and not for the purpose of proving any preconceived notion. If any one questions the fairness of the selections, he is privileged to make his own selections and to try the same experiment with his own choices.

The 16 colleges selected to represent the "football" group are situated in 13 states, in all sections of the nation. Their asset value in 1921 ranged from $550,000 to $7,500,000. They are average sized colleges. The "non-football" group are situated in 14 states, also in all sections of the nation. Their asset value in 1921 ranged from $750,000 to $8,400,000, also average sized colleges.

The aggregate property value of the "football" group in 1921 was $28,237,130. In 1930, this aggregate property value had increased to $61,295,639, a gain of $33,059,509; in percentage a gain of 117 per cent.

The aggregate value of the "non-football" group in 1921 was $27,195,348. In 1930 this aggregate property value had increased to $61,403,921, a gain of $34,208,573; in percentage a gain of 125 per cent. Thus far, the race is fairly even between "hares" and "tortoises." The latter are slightly in the lead, but not impressively so.

But the real test of the soundness of a college's financial promotional program lies in its ability to build up a stabilizing endowment. Building and equipment are essential and must be provided, of course, but the year-in-and-year-out problem of college financing is to strengthen endowment. The cornerstone of a sound college financing policy is to lay aside a dollar or more in endowment for every dollar added to equipment. The college which fails in that test soon joins in the lament of the college president who secretly bemoaned his good fortune of the gift of another building. "One more building given us and we'll be ruined." Let us then compare the endowment gains of the two groups.

In 1921 the aggregate endowment of the "football" group was $10,880,265. By 1930 they had increased this to $22,806,254, a gain of $11,925,989; in percentage a gain of 105 per cent.

The aggregate endowment of the "non-football" group in 1921 was $36,461,819. By 1930 they had increased this to $82,639,817, a gain of $46,177,998; in percentage a gain of 126 per cent. (All figures have been taken from the biennial educational surveys made by the United States Department of the Interior.)

Here we see the race develop between hare and tortoise as fable suggests. The hare has given the spectators the better show, but the tortoise has won through. The friends of the "non-football" group of colleges made gifts to endowment during the decade four times as great as the friends of the "football" group made to their colleges.

The internal financial condition of some of these colleges which depended upon football for financing strength is pitiful, almost tragic. One whose name has been publicized across the nation by its team was barely able to open its doors last September, chiefly because of a heavy stadium debt. The president of another announced recently in the newspapers that the debt on his stadium is in danger of destroying the college itself.

It is not easy, mathematically, to measure the effect of college football on student enrolment, for the reasons which influence young people to go to this or that college are not so easily tabulated as are property values. I have questioned student recruiting agents of several colleges about their experiences in this connection, and they tell me that the rating of their football teams is a factor only amongst the exceptional high-school athletes who hope to make the team. These lads are usually found to have attractive offers from several colleges and their decision is quite often based upon the best terms offered to them.

The rank and file of prospective freshmen, however, seem to be only mildly interested in the standing of the football teams, and their decisions as to which college to enter is based upon factors quite apart from football. One field agent of a college (which, by the way, is amongst the 16 colleges in the "football" group) told an amusing story of his experiences when he started his recruiting work. He armed himself with pictures of the stadium, the football games and of various social, fraternity and outside interests, and felt he was ready to "sell" his college to all prospective freshmen. He was astonished to find how much high-school seniors were interested, on the contrary, in entrance requirements, in college courses, in faculty and in accreditment of later university work. At the end of his first week in the field, he slipped back to the campus, laid aside his sports pictures, and started to learn the college catalogue by heart in the hope of being able to know more about it than the high-school lads whom he was about to meet.

The experience of these field agents whom I have questioned could be summed up fairly in this sentence taken from the Carnegie Foundation Bulletin No. 23—"As a matter of fact, the athletic reputation of a college or university, and especially its football, has little if anything to do with college registration." In a later bulletin, No. 26, the foundation again emphasizes this conclusion, "The notion that winning athletic teams bring the college increased attendance, contributions for endowment and academic purposes, or higher reputation among those whose good opinion is worth having, is erroneous."

What merit, then, does college football have? A very good deal. It is a superb college sport, an important factor in the educational program, a thrilling spectacle around which college loyalties and spirit amongst students and the younger alumni can be built. But, as a means of building student enrolment, its net rating would seem to be very low, and, as a means of building college endowment, its net rating would seem to be minus.

Arnaud C. Marts

New York, N. Y.

## IS THE AMERICAN FEDERATION OF TEACHERS A LABOR UNION?

On April 15, 1916, the American Federation of Teachers was organized in Chicago. It affiliated with the American Federation of Labor on May 9, 1916. Hence the American Federation of Teachers supposedly is a labor union.

However, the Brotherhood of Railway Trainmen and the Amalgamated Clothing Workers are not affiliated with the American Federation of Labor. Using the matter of affiliation these organizations of working people are not labor unions.

The American Medical Association, the American Bar Association and numerous professional groups can rightfully call themselves guilds. Numerous local, state and national organizations of teachers are most certainly guilds, as they work for group benefits and serve the public efficiently.

The Brotherhood of Railway Trainmen and the Amalgamated Clothing Workers also have made successful effort to advance the welfare of their groups and to give the public superior service. The Actors' Equity can claim the same purposes, but it is considered a labor union.

How do the three labor unions mentioned above differ from the American Medical Association, the Bar Association and the professional organizations of teachers? They have conducted successful strikes in order to further their demands.

Has the American Federation of Teachers ever conducted a strike? It boasts that in eighteen years of its existence such a thing has never happened. It has circulated statements containing promulgation of a ukase by Samuel Gompers relieving the teachers from the necessity of carrying on a strike or from taking part in any sympathetic strike. If you question any life-member of a labor union about this, he will say: "That is no labor union." I took pains to ask John P. Frey about Mr. Gompers' dispensation. I was assured that he had no right to make any such arrangement.

On November 14, 1902, the weekly bulletin of the Chicago Teachers' Federation announced affiliation of a large group with the Chicago Federation of Labor. The first matter to be settled was whether the new union would be called on to strike. Miss Jane Addams, in a speech on October 18, 1902, explained that the strike and the boycott were under control of the local union, not the Federation of Labor, and that sympathetic strikes were always voluntary. A letter from John Fitzpatrick made practically the same statement, since he said that the Chicago Federation of Labor had no power to call a strike.

In 1915 Mr. Jacob Loeb secured a change in the rules of the Chicago Board of Education which prohibited "membership by teachers in labor unions or in organizations affiliated with a trade union, or a federation or association of trade unions, as well as teachers' organizations which have officers, business agents or other representatives who are not members of the teaching force."[1] This rule was further revised and on June 27, 1916, sixty-eight principals and teachers were not reemployed.[2]

Two other organizations of Chicago teachers affiliated with the Chicago Federation of Labor were very small groups at this time and their existence was ignored. Chicago teachers have never gone on strike. The headquarters of the American Federation of Teachers are located there and numerous national conventions have been held in the city.

The unionized teachers of Chicago have been a powerful influence in its educational affairs. Following the war period salaries were liberally increased. Teachers of vocational subjects in high schools who had no college degrees attained the same salaries as those who held masters' degrees and who had done considerable graduate work.

In the Proceedings of the twelfth annual convention of the American Federation of Teachers, held at Chicago in June, 1928, we find: "We have elected Mr. Bogan superintendent of schools."[3] W. J. Bogan succeeded William McAndrew.

The practises of labor unions in regard to overtime are clear cut. The number of hours per week is definitely limited. When all the members of the union are employed and overtime is absolutely necessary, overtime costs the employer 50 per cent. additional.

What have been the policies of the Chicago teachers' unions with regard to overtime in evening and continuation schools? The scramble for jobs has been undignified, to say the least, despite the fact that qualified teachers, natives of the city, were unemployed. This overtime, used in teaching laboring people and their children, was always sold to the board of education at a discount.

In November, 1929, the Chicago Federation of Men Teachers issued a bulletin entitled "Overtime Now! What Next? A Warning." In 1913, to simplify teaching in a few high schools, the teaching day was lengthened from

1 Proceedings of the Board of Education of the City of Chicago, 1915–1916, p. 734.

2 *Ibid.*, pp. 3080–3091.

3 *Ibid.*, p. 97.

five to six hours. A wrangle ensued because several teachers, not entitled to the additional hour of teaching, manoeuvered to be placed on the six-hour day with 20 per cent. additional pay. In 1914 the teaching day in all high schools was lengthened to six hours, but the increase in salary was only 10 per cent. Teachers who suffered a pay cut joined the union and agitated for the restoration of pay, but it has never arrived.

The American Railway Brotherhoods have worked out strict rules of seniority in connection with promotions. Many teachers would be delighted if all desirable positions were to be secured only after experience and education were fully rated in making up programs and assigning rooms. The American Federation of Teachers has neglected this fine practise, which would be most desirable in maintaining teacher morale. The pension list in Chicago would be considerably shorter if experience and education were fairly rated.

If the American Federation of Teachers is to be a real labor union it must follow the practises and tactics of successful unions. Only then will it cease to be a sponger on the organizations of working people.

CAROLINE BENGTSON

# SPECIAL CORRESPONDENCE

## A VERMONT EXPERIMENT

"WOMEN and Children First: The Rule of Ships of the Sea Applied to the Ship of State" may seem a strange slogan for a state-wide campaign on budgets, finances and reports. But its significance is clear when interpretative comment reveals the thesis—that, if Town-Village-City reports are "interesting to women" and "clear to children," they will be sure to intrigue the tired business man and to catch and hold the attention of the busy workingman, in fact help capture for public affairs some of the new leisure time of a people whose traditional genius it is, both in age and in youth, to understand government and to share government.

This Vermont school experiment is an inevitable recent step in the evolution of a state-wide campaign on budgets, finances and reports which seeks greater efficiency and economy and their requisite, a public better informed about their own affairs. To secure such a result, a whole people must be mobilized, citizens and officials, men and women, old and young.

The first step was the publication of a State Chamber of Commerce Bulletin entitled "Making Town-Village-City Reports More Interesting," a graphic bulletin reproducing the bar charts and pie charts and graphs and drawings which had been used by the town of Springfield, Vermont, for a number of years to illustrate their town reports, so that the most important financial and social facts would be quickly clear and emphatic. This bulletin was distributed broadcast throughout Vermont as a challenge and suggestion to other towns. It attracted attention in many other states of the Union.

Then came the "Midget Town Report," a tiny booklet indicating in graphic form the topics and arrangement which might well be followed in every town report. The pleated folding made it possible to study the "Midget Town Report" page by page, or to unfold and to inspect all the pages all at once. The comment of the public was, "Why, this is an accordean." And the distributors replied, "Certainly it is. And we know the tune it plays: Lead Kindly Light." With this tiny booklet there was given out in January at ten regional county meetings of citizens and officials a big broadside budget sheet with an elaborate analysis of the town budget and the school budget, revenues and expenditures.

The next step in February was the distribution to the newspapers of the ten-year tax rate history of all the towns, county by county, the annual average rates for the towns of each county being visualized by bar charts and the annual rates of the individual towns being given in tables of figures. The newspapers were glad to publish these ten-year stories of the rise and fall of tax rates, since official town reports so often confine themselves to the thin and narrow story of one town and one year, with no material for comparison either in time or space.

Meanwhile the colleges of Vermont were approached with the suggestion that right around them in their own and adjoining counties lies admirable research material in the town reports and in the proceedings of town meetings. College study groups have been formed, and they have been invited to make graphic display of the results of their studies on town report and town policy developments in the "Graphic Review of Public Affairs—State and Local," an exhibit in connection with the annual meeting of the Vermont State Chamber of Commerce.

And so the mobilization of a whole people proceeded. But the schools, not yet. The movement was avowedly "that a child may understand." It was for the children, but not yet of them and by them. Then some meditative reminiscence and a happy incident led to the beginning of the school experiment.

Remembering that it was supremely by the use of color and charts and maps that the State Chamber for years had vividly presented to the Vermont public such causes as highway economics and development, the gasoline tax movement on a national scale, roadside improvement, planning and zoning, Vermont's state finances, the secretary of the chamber remarked in a committee conference with officers of the town of Leicester that some day some Vermont town would use color to illuminate and give distinction to their town report. He held up as an example a brightly and variously hand-colored pie chart which visualized the breaking down of a town tax rate into its different divisions.

Noting a very responsive interest on the part of a selectman of French descent, the secretary inquired how many copies of their report are printed by the town of Leicester. And then on account of the very modest number of reports quoted the question was asked whether it would be practicable for the pupils in the schools to color by hand the proposed pie charts in the Leicester town reports, and to make the reports a community product by the grace of the schools, a report of and by as well as for the school pupils. So in due time appeared the Leicester town reports, as a newspaper account said, "alone in their tinted glory."

It was all these elements in an evolving situation which helped form and ripen the idea that the creative way for the schools to study town business and town reports—these community text-books, these "Civic Bibles Printed like Ads"—is to have the pupils present graphically the facts, figures and fancies through the use of bar charts, pie charts, graphs, drawings and maps, thus entertainingly illustrating the community text-book, thus making good the slogan "A Civic Bible—Printed like an Ad."

Let them picture the facts and figures, root and branch, page after page, telling to the eye the whole story of what has happened and what is happening in their towns and neighboring towns and in other towns of similar population and character.

School pupils need not be expected to judge the merits and the demerits of the conditions and the proposals reflected in the reports of town or village or city. The pupils are performing their first duties as statesmen if they merely state the facts and figures so clearly, so vividly, so graphically that the eye hears and the ear sees. Every school should contribute to its community a museum or picture gallery of contemporaneous local affairs and should keep it contemporaneous.

To dramatize the Vermont Experiment the State Chamber of Commerce announces that they will award diplomas of supreme merit and diplomas of superior merit to the schools which submit the best collections of charts illustrating the facts and figures reflected in the town reports just published, every school presenting at least two bar charts, two pie charts and two graphs. The displays of charts and graphs will be exhibited in connection with the annual meeting of the State Chamber. Drawings, maps and pictures are left for later years, if the experiment proves to be a success this year.

That the experiment is a brilliant success in Waterbury and in a number of other towns which have written the State Chamber is indicated by the following letter just received from the principal of the Waterbury High School:

> Here at Waterbury we find considerable interest being manifested in the contest you have inaugurated. Particularly in the Social Civics Class forty odd students are zealously graphing various aspects of the Town Report which have captured their respective interests.
>
> We expect to have most of the report charted before long and will duly submit our best products at the appointed time. Kindly keep us informed as to the developments in this contest.
>
> D. P. Rowe,
>
> *Principal, Waterbury High School*

This treasured letter demonstrates that among the young there is no "political apathy," if they are given an opportunity to do something constructive. The phrases "zealously graphing," "have captured their respective interests" and "most of the report charted" are worth the "forty odd students" weight in gold to the thus comforted promoters of the experiment.

For years it has been a fond hope that some day there would appear an opportunity to apply along civic and commercial lines a principle which has been so long so well capitalized by the Agricultural Extension Service. Youth can be won to new ideas and to new methods and, by demonstrating these ideas and methods in the presence of their elders, can win over a reluctant and hesitating older generation.

So here in the field of methods of presentation of the facts, figures and fancies of Town-Village-City affairs is the longed-for opportunity. It may be that next year Vermont Town-Village-City Reports will contain many more bar charts, pie charts, graphs and drawings, because the youth of Vermont will have demonstrated what can be done graphically in making facts and figures clear and emphatic. Youth and age will thus work together in developing a technique in the presentation of facts and figures, with the object of promoting economy and efficiency and of enabling democracy to democ.

The Vermont experimenters are asking: "Why should not each and every school in Vermont, and for that matter each and every school in the United States, do what was done by the schools of Leicester and what is being done by the 'forty odd students' in Waterbury?"

JAMES P. TAYLOR

VERMONT STATE CHAMBER
OF COMMERCE

# QUOTATIONS

## THE INTERNATIONAL RESEARCH INSTITUTE LIBRARY

THE world's most important international library will be attached to the league's new $5,000,000 palace in Geneva when it is inaugurated in 1935.

A gift of $2,000,000 from John D. Rockefeller, Jr., has enabled the league to lay plans for a library research institute which will be the joy of world scholars.

Plans to organize the library as an autonomous International Research Institute now are under consideration. The institute library, although attached to the league, would be a separate institution with a distinct charter.

Approximately half the Rockefeller gift has been used to construct a beautiful building adjoining the new League Assembly Hall, the largest in the world. The remainder of the fund will go into an endowment fund.

The building will house all the most important international treaties, official publications and books printed on international political, social, economic and financial affairs. The league library is the only institution in the world to receive all government publications and official documents.

Its treaty series containing all international treaties registered with the league is the most important collection of its kind in the world. In addition the league has a chain of 120 depositary libraries scattered throughout the world.

The new library will have room for 1,000,000 volumes. At the present time only 13 years after its foundation, the league library possesses 180,000 books. Approximately 20,000 new volumes are added each year.

The new library building has three floors. On the ground floor and in the center of the building will be an information office containing the catalogue and lending department. Connected with it will be a museum room for exhibitions.

There will be a newspaper and periodical reading room, a general reading room and a lecture room all on the first floor. The second floor will contain special reading rooms divided by topics, such as legal, finance, economics, history, mandates, opium, public health and communications.—*The New York Sun.*

## THE FRENCH EDUCATIONAL EXHIBIT

THE MUSÉE PÉDAGOGIQUE, on which an article appeared in the *Educational Supplement* last year, continues to extend its activities. It is a center of documentation about everything which concerns schools, and some of its developments are of considerable interest.

Great advance is being made in the study and practical encouragement of the use of the gramophone in the schools. The purposes in view are the teaching of singing and the cultivation of musical taste, language teaching, reading aloud and recitation, as well as amusement on proper occasions—the last especially for boarders in secondary schools. In order to ensure the best employment of this method of education the Comité Française du Phonographe dans l'Enseignement, in cooperation with the Musée Pédagogique, has organized a service both of information and equipment. It has induced the gramaphone manufacturers to make a machine, described as the "modèle scolaire," specially adapted in dimensions and other characteristics for use in schools. The committee has also drawn up lists of records which, after research, have been selected as suitable for the various purposes. With the aid of the French Association of Teachers of Foreign Languages, for instance, a list of records giving readings in English, German and Italian have been approved. The English list includes pieces from Shakespeare, Shelley, Keats, Tennyson, Wordsworth, Stevenson, Browning, Herrick, Longfellow and Dickens.

The general aim is that schools should provide themselves with a library of records—a *discothèque*. A central library, which will also be a place of documentation, is in process of equipment at the Musée Pédagogique, under the active impulsion of M. M. C. Lebrun, the assistant director. The model school gramophone and the lists of records have been officially approved by the Ministry of National Education. Schools and other teaching organizations can obtain the records at reduced prices. Among the further aims of the Comité Français du Phonographe dans l'Enseignement is a fresh registering of French literary texts spoken in a simple and natural manner suitable for child auditors, rather than in the declamatory style of the dramatic artist. It is also hoped that well-chosen records may, in the absence of equipment needed for "talkies," serve as musical accompaniment for films.

There are other educational organizations and societies of various kinds with which the Musée actively cooperates, such as the French Pedagogical Society, the National Committee of Open Air Schools, and the French New Education Group, which are authorized to hold meetings or organize exhibitions in the Musée. In the last few weeks there has been an exhibition of Japanese school art, in which 800 drawings and 80 samples of manual work were shown. For the purpose of illustrated lectures and the discussion of films and projections a cinema-lecture theater has been admirably equipped. The library is being constantly extended, and an interesting initiative has been taken in forming a collection of authorized text-books used in French schools, with the addition, as far as possible, of books which were formerly employed but are now out of date.—*Paris correspondent of The London Times Educational Supplement.*

# EDUCATIONAL RESEARCH AND STATISTICS

## VALUE OF HOME-STUDY ASSIGNMENTS

IN most communities parents not only expect but desire all children, especially those attending high school, to do some studying at home. Secondary school teachers and principals also insist upon the necessity of requiring their pupils to do some home-work on contracts or assignments given to supplement the regular classroom activities. Many adverse and favorable arguments have been advanced in regard to the value of such outside preparation or study, but so far no report of any investigation of this problem has ever been seen by the writer. For these reasons, an attempt has been made to determine the value of home-study assignments by measuring the gains made by pupils in achievement tests.

It may be wise to call attention to one educational value of home assignments that has not been considered in this study. This particular value may be intangible, but in the judgment and opinion of the writer it is very significant and is really much greater than any improvement in achievement that may result from studying outside of school. Since modern homes have no or little opportunity of giving boys and girls any daily tasks that may aid in the development of a sense of responsibility, the school must provide such training. Before the present day of mechanical and electrical appliances, children had enough daily tasks or chores in the home to train them early in life in trustworthiness and dependability. It now seems necessary, however, for the school to make pupils assume some responsibility for a few daily tasks that may provide not only valuable drill or practise in what is taught in school but real opportunities for growth in character.

Although home-work may have considerable value, regardless of its effect upon formal learning or scholastic attainments, this study was limited to the problem of finding the effect of home-study assignments upon the standard test scores of seventh grade pupils in arithmetic and English. A class of 39 pupils just entering the seventh grade of a four-year junior high school was used in this research. The experiment extended over the first semester of 1933–34, a period of 18 weeks.

Since a similar investigation made two years ago in the same school had been limited to arithmetic and resulted in no appreciable difference between those pupils who had home work and those who had none, in this study it seemed wise to include two subjects, English and arithmetic. The seventh grade class in each case was divided into two equivalent groups on the basis of mental ability and achievement tests, but in the former study one half of the class was not required to do any home-work in arithmetic, while in this study one half was given daily assignments in English and the other group had assignments in arithmetic. By this plan every pupil in the class had the same amount of home-work. The assignments for five days were mimeographed and given to pupils each week, and the required written work was collected daily and corrected by the arithmetic and English teacher, respectively.

The two teachers cooperating in this experiment were given the following directions at the beginning of the semester:

(1) Groups A and B will be formed according to mental ability and achievement in arithmetic and English.

(2) Only Group A will be given daily assignments in arithmetic to prepare outside of class.

(3) Only Group B will be given daily assignments in English grammar to do outside of class.

(4) Assignment sheets will be prepared weekly with five daily lessons and will contain definite drill material only. None of this drill work will be used in class.

(5) All home-study assignments will be corrected by the teacher or a committee of pupils. These papers will always be marked and returned to each pupil on the following day for correction.

(6) Both groups will do the same work in class and will receive the same instruction, except for such comments as the teacher may write on the papers when they are marked.

(7) No direct credit will be given for this outside work in monthly marks. Pupils will not be told that no credit will be given for these daily exercises done outside of class. Both groups will take the same monthly and term tests.

(8) Gains of each group will be obtained by comparing scores at beginning of semester with those at the end.

Groups A and B were formed by using the Otis Self-Administering Mental Ability Test and the arithmetic and language usage tests of the Stanford Achievement Test,, revised form, and the Unit Scales of Attainment, Division III. By using these test results, it was possible to form 18 pairs of pupils of equal mental ability and with fairly equivalent standing in the subject tests. The average scores for these groups on each of the four arithmetic and the four English tests showed very slight differences. When the pupils were assigned to either group, the nature of the experiment was explained and their cooperation requested. They were then told that Group A would be given daily assignments in arithmetic only and that Group B would have English assignments to prepare each day. The pupils were also informed that those in either group could study the other subject outside of the recitation by reviewing the regular classwork or by getting some other supplementary work from the teacher not used in the assignment sheets.

Each teacher prepared his weekly assignments and checked the work done by the pupils very conscientiously during the semester. Before these weekly sheets were mimeographed, the exercises or problems assigned were carefully examined by the writer. Since this home-work was given specifically to supplement the regular classroom instruction, both the English and arithmetic assignments were similar to the exercises given in commercial workbooks and included no new material. Each teacher was not only very careful to see that neither the preparation of the assignments nor the checking of the pupils' papers should interfere with his instruction during the recitation period but also very eager to make these home-study assignments as practical and helpful as possible to his pupils. It is evident, therefore, that an ideal situation was created to determine how the preparation of assignments outside the classroom affected learning as measured by standard tests.

Since these seventh grade pupils spent one entire recitation period daily in arithmetic and language work, respectively, with no study period during the school day, all these special assignments had to be prepared at home or in their report rooms before the beginning of the forenoon and the afternoon session where no supervision from the English or the arithmetic instructor was possible. It is evident, therefore, that the results of this experiment will indicate how the independent study of seventh grade pupils affects their progress in arithmetic and English as measured by standard tests.

## Analysis of Data

For the purpose of comparing the progress made during the semester by the two groups in arithmetic, all the initial achievement tests or other forms of the same tests were given to the pupils at the end of the semester. Besides the two problem tests and the two tests on fundamental operations contained in the Stanford Achievement Test and in the Unit Scales of Attainment, respectively, a final objective test on the arithmetic taught in the first half of the seventh grade was given at the beginning and at the end of the semester. The average of the increases in the scores on each test for Group A, which had daily assignments in arithmetic, was compared with the corresponding averages for Group B and is shown in Table I. Besides these differences between the average gain on each test, the pairs of pupils were compared with each other, and the number of pairs in which the pupil of Group A or Group B made the greater gain in each test is also included in Table I.

TABLE I

Comparison of Gains in Arithmetic Scores Made by Pupils in Group A Who Had Home-study Assignments With Those Made by the Pupils of Group B that Had Only English Assignments

| | Stanford Achievement | | Unit Scales of Attainment | | |
|---|---|---|---|---|---|
| | Reasoning | Computation | Problems | Fundamentals | 7B Test |
| *Group A* | | | | | |
| Range | – 12 to 15 | – 6 to 36 | – 6 to 15 | – 6 to 19 | 4 to 46 |
| Average gain | 5.8 | 9.8 | 4.6 | 5.5 | 23.4 |
| *Group B* | | | | | |
| Range | – 24 to 11 | – 11 to 20 | – 5.5 to 15 | – 19 to 9 | 1 to 42 |
| Average gain | 0.5 | 4.7 | 3.9 | – 3.2 | 22.5 |
| Difference favoring A | 5.3 | 4.9 | 0.7 | 8.7 | 0.9 |
| Ratio of pairs A–B | 12 to 3 | 11 to 6 | 8 to 8 | 13 to 3 | 9 to 8 |

An examination of the preceding table clearly shows that the pupils who had daily home-work in arithmetic made greater gains in each of the five tests than the pupils of the other group. Since these differences are based on the averages of only 17 pairs, who participated in the entire experiment, no statistical evidence of their reliability is presented. Since the differences between the standard norms of these tests for the half-year covered by this experiment are only 4 points for the two Stanford Achievement tests and 3 for the problem test and 2 for the test on fundamental operations of the Unit Scales, the improvement of Group A is considerably greater than expected in each of the four tests, but the average changes in the scores of Group B vary from a loss of 3.2 points to a gain of 4.7. The pupils of Group B, in other words, failed to make the same consistent improvement as those of the other group. The differences between the average gains of the two groups all favor the group that had home assignments, and in three of the four tests they even exceed the normal or standard gain for the first half of the seventh grade.

It is interesting to note that the difference between the gains made by the two groups on the objective test on the work covered during the semester is negligible. Since the maximum possible score on this test is 100 points, a difference of .9 is very insignificant. The actual increases in the scores on this test of all the pupils ranged from 1 to 46 points.

An analysis of the semester failures in arithmetic shows that five pupils of Group A failed and only two of the other group that had no home-work. These results clearly show that the regular classroom instruction was the deciding factor both in the improvement of pupils as measured by the objective test in arithmetic and in their ability to pass the semester's work.

The last line of Table I shows that the number of pairs in which the pupils of Group A made the greater gain favors Group A in four of the tests with a tie in the other test. In the two Stanford Achievement tests the ratio is 23 to 9 in favor of Group A and on the two tests of the Unit Scales it is 21 to 11. In the case of two pairs the gains were equal on both of these tests. Since the averages of the differences between the initial and final scores on the objective test of the two groups were almost the same, the ratio of 9 to 8 also indicates that the home-study assignments had practically no effect upon the results of this test.

An analysis of the results of the English tests indicates that these home-study assignments did not have as great an effect upon the English test scores as the arithmetic assignments had on the arithmetic scores. Table II shows how the two groups compare in their gains on the language tests.

TABLE II

Comparison of Gains in Language Scores Made by Group B That Had Home-study Assignments in English With Those Made by the Pupils of Group A Who Had No Such Assignments

| | Stanford Achievement Lang. Usage | Unit Scales of Attainment | | | Conklin and Pressey Grammar Usage |
|---|---|---|---|---|---|
| | | Capitalization | Punctuation | Usage | |
| *Group B* | | | | | |
| Range | – 16 to 11 | – 10.5 to 8 | – 8.5 to 13 | – 5 to 21.5 | – 3 to 11 |
| Average gain | 0.8 | 0.2 | 5.0 | 9.5 | 3.4 |
| *Group A* | | | | | |
| Range | – 25 to 41 | 4.5 to 13 | – 3 to 16 | – 14 to 23 | – 4 to 8 |
| Average gain | 3.3 | 3.2 | 4.9 | 6.0 | 1.5 |
| Difference favoring B | – 2.5 | – 3.0 | 0.1 | 3.5 | 1.9 |
| Standard differences | 4 | 1 | 1.5 | 2 | 1.3 |
| Ratio of pairs B–A | 7 to 10 | 5 to 12 | 7 to 8 | 9 to 8 | 11 to 6 |

An examination of Table II shows considerable variation and inconsistency in the average gains of the two groups. In the first two tests Group A made the greater gains as shown in the third line of the table. In punctuation there is no significant difference, but in the last two tests on usage Group B averaged very much higher. When the average gains made by each group are compared with the differences between the standards or norms for the beginning and the end of the first half of the seventh grade, the period covered by this experiment, it is evident that in the language usage test neither group made normal progress, but with the exception of Group B in the capitalization test all the other gains greatly exceed the standard difference for every test. One reason why the first test in Table II does not show the same proportionate gains as the others is due to the wide range of individual gains of Group A pupils, from – 25 to 41. Since this test offers only two choices, guessing seems to have had an important effect upon these scores. Since Group B made greater gains only on the tests shown in the last two columns of Table II, the effect of the English assignments upon the progress of pupils as measured by these five tests is not conclusive.

An analysis of the content of the tests used to measure progress in English is necessary to explain the variations in the respective gains of each group. The grammar usage test, whose results are shown in the last column of Table II, is the only one that really measured the drill work provided by the home-study assignments in English. Since the other four tests measured language abilities not directly affected by these assignments, their results indicate only such pupil growth as may have resulted from the regular classroom instruction. The average gain of Group A that had no assignments on this fifth test was 1.5 and almost the same as the standard gain, 1.3, for the semester, but the other group made an average gain of 2.3 times as much as Group A. Since this is a multiple choice test containing four sentences in each part from which the pupil must select the one grammatically incorrect, the possibility of guessing is greatly reduced. On the basis of this test, it is evident that these English exercises done at home had a marked and pronounced effect upon the ability of pupils to detect grammatical errors in sentences.

Another factor that deserves consideration is the promotion record. As in the case of the failures in arithmetic, five of the seven English failures belonged to Group B that had home assignments in English. Since only two pupils failed in both subjects, it is evident that the home-study assignments in neither arithmetic nor English had any effect upon a pupil's ability to pass the semester's work in either subject. This is, no doubt, true because both teachers were instructed to give every pupil the same material in the regular recitation period. It is not true, however, that any of these assignments was unrelated to the subject-matter presented in the classroom, for a special effort was made to provide supplementary drill material in the topics taught during the semester. Although this drill work did not seem to aid the pupils in passing the semester's course in English, the median of Group B on the final English test given by the principal was about 5 per cent. greater than the median of the group that had only arithmetic assignments. It is evident, therefore, that any improvement that may have resulted from the work done in the preparation of these English assignments was not sufficient to modify the final marks of the pupils to any appreciable extent.

### CONCLUSIONS

The daily home-study assignments given to one half of the seventh grade pupils of a junior high school in arithmetic and to the other half in English suggest the following inferences or conclusions:

(1) Daily home-study assignments of a drill nature in arithmetic and English grammar tend to accelerate learning as measured by standard tests in these subjects.

(2) When classroom instruction is not directly modified by the work assigned for outside preparation, a pupil's chances of passing seventh grade arithmetic or English, if passing is based only on the oral and written work done during the recitation period, are not increased by problems or exercises done at home.

(3) Since the English tests included so many more specific abilities that were measured than the two, solving problems and fundamental operations, included in the arithmetic tests, the differences between the average gains of the two groups do not consistently favor the group that had English assignments. In the grammar test, however, the gain made by the group having English assignments is 2.3 times as much as the other group made.

(4) In this experiment the full value of home-study assignments is probably not revealed because the pupils did not have the benefit of a free classroom discussion of the work done at home but had to depend upon such comments as might be written by the teacher in marking their papers.

(5) Since the daily home-study assignments were planned to keep a pupil of average ability busy for only thirty minutes, they were not excessively burdensome on the pupils in proportion to the benefits obtained.

M. A. STEINER

INGRAM, PA.

## NEW BOOKS IN EDUCATION

MORRISON, HENRY C. *Basic Principles in Education.* Pp. v + 452. Houghton Mifflin. $2.50.

SEYMOUR, F. EUGENE and HALLIE S. POOLE. *A Unit Workbook in Plane Geometry.* Pp. 126. Macmillan. $0.40.

TINKER, HAROLD L. *Essays Yesterday and To-day.* Pp. xii + 691. Macmillan. $0.80.

# EDUCATIONAL REVIEW

**Edited by Nicholas Murray Butler, 1891–1919, Frank Pierrepont Graves, 1920–1924, and William McAndrew, 1924–**

## PEOPLE, PERFORMANCE AND PUBLICATIONS

By WILLIAM McANDREW

*Social-studies need housecleaning.*—The circulars sent to this reviewery to advertise oncoming books in the social studies grow warmer and warmer. Harcourt, Brace and Company send, with their Hill-and-Tugwell high-school economics, shouting print telling of the pains taken by newspapers to show the book as opposed to traditional standards. The text is a drastic departure, says the circular. Allyn and Bacon, displaying their Hughes series in civic training, stress the shift from knowledge to civic performance. Professor McKinley, after publishing twenty-five volumes of the monthly *Historical Outlook,* rechristens it *The Social Studies.* Minnesota Professor Krey continues to hammer against the custom of building a social-studies course by pieces from other schools. "It produces complete anesthesia of thought." Vassar Professor Ware finds the studies "producer-minded." That's the trouble with America, she shows it has been assumed that the problems of economic activity are problems of production, that people needed prodding to produce more. It is time the majority were thought of and economics taught from the consumer's side. Chicago Sociologist Rosander finds necessary a teaching staff determined to undertake important changes and to teach the necessity of civic planning in which government, science and education are fused into a new unity. We have never conceived, he says, our social studies as dynamic, preparing the generation for continual adjustments nor stimulating it to think creatively in civic directions. Political pap has been passed out to children to leave them content with conventional beliefs. School is attempting to stimulate pupils to creative work in language, art and handwork, but government, economics, sociology, as taught, is mostly for the status as is. Our social science courses are too dull. Notes, events, personalities and movements that have no bearing on the present are emphasized. Civic teaching is stressing structure, not the actual workings. Our boys learn of the old tyrants and how they oppressed the common people, but hear nothing of *our* privileged classes who buy immunity in the courts, undermine honest government, throw wage-earners out of work at will, make charity a hobby for the idle rich, peddle prosperity in the face of gravest distress and pillage the public treasury. What social studies need to teach is what to do here and now. Schools can tell the truth about rich tax evaders, lying advertisers, corporations that loot, politicians who fiddle while the people starve. Schools can make clear the duty to face problems rather than to avoid them. Unless education is based on realities it is a time-waster. Unless it stresses the duty of correcting civic defects it can not justify public support. Meantime Columbia Professor Kimmel, after his wide survey for the Cooper-Koos national study, continues to remove expensive and ornamental coverings from the near-corpse of civics. The so-called problems study he finds strictly avoiding conflict situations. Complacency is undisturbed. Local situations are avoided. The stealings of the Tweed Ring may be mentioned, but graft in the home town, never. What relations, asks Professor Kimmel, have your stated aims to the parts your students will play in politics and industry? How do you explain the disparity between the ideals you hold before youth and the dominant interests of the business world they will enter? Kimmel heard teachers in civic classrooms holding forth on only the forms of municipal government on the same day that the newspapers had shown the workings of the local government under its corrupt political organization. He found most teachers emphasizing fictions, while the pupils and the whole community knew the realities. Youth is taught out of school that money, however obtained, brings approval. Children have ceased to play Indian and taken to hold-ups and gun play. Nobody cares to pretend to be the policeman. The idea of reforming the social order by the present platitudes of the social studies is a phantom dream.

Got to have a new deal in the social studies, shouts Professor Mahoney in Boston University. You curriculum-makers must turn your attention to getting the generation to diagnosing democracy's ills. Until you stop tinkling the cymbals of patriotism and get down to the sorry mess in civic affairs, local, state and national, you are naught. Truly, social studies are for civic improvement. Rightly organized and properly taught, they must clean house from cellar to attic. So says Mahoney.

There is no lack of understanding as to what prevents. I quizzed the Fitchburg training class, I questioned the Yale summer students in education: What's holding you back? Their answers were the same: Fear and laziness. The men I have quoted here agree along with Professor Beard and Stanwood Cobb that the needful teaching is not above the understanding of children of twelve years and upwards. That is not the trouble. The fault lies in the lack of teaching-drive. The fear is exaggerated. Upholders of the assumption of vested interests are nowhere a majority: Dr. Kimmel finds that text-books too honest are withdrawn, but that live teachers' organizations which agitate against such removal prevent it. During presidential campaigns, he says, when a party intrenched in the city government is faced with defeat, sometimes the school board issues an order prohibiting political discussion in the classrooms. In some cities he found an interlocking corporation of business, politicians, police, grafters and criminals in control of the schools. There, pupils hearing politics discussed on every side and over the radio, reading political arguments in the newspapers, can not discuss them in the civics class. Teachers confess to being timid. That's something. If one knows what ails him, cure is more promising. Investigator Rosander is of the opinion that hope lies in the teachers' united action. Realizing the absurdity and hypocrisy of their position in a public-school system founded to teach government, politics, citizenship, as much in need of a professional freedom as is a physician or a lawyer, let teachers in their own and in their parent-teachers organization work upon the majority of the community which will see the irrefutable logic of the situation. Let teachers' organizations get tenure laws through the legislature; let them, united, stand for bringing their pupils into line with civic realities and needs. No school board dare dismiss an entire corps for doing what history and logic show it was instituted to do. At no period in the past hundred years were the times so ripe for putting the schools on a sound educational basis.

*Good fighting in California.*—The schoolmaster's blood is boiling in the Golden State. Twenty-eight thousand copies of "Why the Campaign against our Schools?" have been distributed. It describes the location and tactics of the enemy: The California Taxpayers Association, The State Chamber of Commerce, The United States Chamber of Commerce, The California State Department of Finance as organized by a former employee of the Taxpayers Association. It lists by name the persons in control of these organizations. From hearings, investigations and correspondence it quotes the details of the campaign to wreck the schools. The United States Chamber's form letter to the California Chamber is quoted, suggesting the chamber's measures to push: simplify curricula, increase class size, increase teaching hours, shorten year, discontinue evening classes and kindergartens, cut a year off elementary schooling, another off high school, transfer costs of instruction above high school from taxpayer to pupil, require fees from all high-school pupils.

How are these cuts kept in the attention of legislators? By a well-paid lobby. Who pays? The broadside quotes from vouchers and hearings, showing payment of $30,000 by light and power companies, $3,600, for broadcasting, $24,000 for advertising, various sums paid as utility employers' dues in Rotary, Lions, Exchange, Optimist, Kiwanis, Legion, Press and other clubs and moneys spent in church and community celebrations. Besides the curtailments advocated by the United States Chamber of Commerce the state organization for reduction of costs was sponsored for twenty-nine reductions and abolitions, including killing of school book funds, of classes for migratory laborers, compulsory education in two highest years, adult education, institutes and conventions, the Historical Associations and the Polytechnic.

Each chapter of Phi Delta Kappa has voted

to enter the war for the schools. Meetings with prominent laymen give and take criticism and suggestions on school procedure and plan defense and aggression. "The revolution is under way," shouts Lambda Chapter. The educator is no longer an isolated theorist. He is an alert citizen. The enemy has made himself known; he is banker, big business man, the profiteer for himself. He is the minority but tireless. He's fighting all the time, not only when the legislature meets. He's plenty scared. It matters little to him what the masses and the children need. He says the school men are not united, know nothing of finance, taxation or government. Now, says Lambda, let the school people organize the citizens in their districts. See them personally. Get their pledges. Keep after them. Card-catalogue them, find legitimate economies in education. Develop your leaders. Abandon jealousies. Stop relying on resolutions adopted at conventions. Instead, get pledges. The war is on. Brains, logic, persuasion, will win it. Organize your teachers, your parents, your churches, your service-clubs. Shame your slackers into action. You never had so big an opportunity to be what you have been urging your pupils to become—loyal citizens. The whole of American history is for you. The mass of the people are at heart with you. Hold 'em. This is not playing politics; it's making politics work.

*Adult education boom.*—Rumors rolling in from librarians and school people that grown-up America is getting hungrier for education are confirmed by the turn-out at this year's ninth annual meeting of the American Association for Adult Education held at Washington. Even late arrivals on the first day at the mountainous Shoreham Hotel, the headquarters, had to find rooms elsewhere. Witty Morse Cartwright, director, had all the wrinkles—panels, symposiums, luncheon forums, banquets, round-tables, free periods, debates, dialogues and question-boxes filling the four-day program like the stuffed peppers of the cook's menu. We want conflict, circularized the director, we crave debatable questions. We have selected topics that have had doubt, indecision and difference of opinion. Bring disagreement to the surface. Ex-cathedra conclusions are taboo; but the Socratic dialogue, the dog fight, are wanted and are to be carried out to such conclusions as may be reached. But no discussion is aimed to end discussion. The times demand action. So ran the call.

I warrant no educational program ever got nearer to its planners' hearts' desire than this one. The attendance was away above any previous meet of the association. Farmer James Russell opened the session. Director Marsh of the C. C. Camps told of his educational program. Emergency Campaigns, Literacy, Rural Schemes, Lecture Service, The New Deal, Recreation, Library Work, Labor Institutes, Museums, Negro Education, Alumni Congresses, Research, Radio, Religion, Guidance, Parent Training, Organization, Techniques, New Experiments, and whatever any seeker for light asked for were expounded and discussed by the country's recognized leaders.

William Green of the American Federation of Labor was drafted. Lyman Bryson was chosen for his California experience. The long list had George Zook, retiring commissioner of education, and John Studebaker, the new one. Frederick Keppel pleaded for art, Everett Martin and Seymour Barnard represented peoples institutes, Levering Tyson radiated, Daphne Martin studied children, Harry Overstreet philosophized, Joy Morgan editorialized, Arthur Bestor chautauquaed, Jacques Ozanne emitted mental ozone.

A climax event was President Dorothy Canfield Fisher's epic recital of what education has done and must do for the grown-ups. It has made over the mothers and pushed down baby mortality lower than ever before. Our grandmothers were in the stone age of knowledge of child care. The basic fact, said Mrs. Fisher, is that in every human soul is the wish to know. It is not satisfied by the knowledge of how to make a living. It must be helped by all the means in the power of the people so that the fathers and mothers making sacrifices to send their children to school will not themselves be intellectually and culturally starved.

*How timid teachers are* should be disclosed statistically by some of Measurer Thorndike's patient students. We get tired of hearing timidity cited as the educator's common denominator. When you pin down to naming names any imputer of this trait to our folks he can't recall any. Piffle! I have worked more than fifty years with teachers in Michigan, New York and Chicago. I can't remember any who were afraid of school boards, superintendents or principals. I have just seen a stack of teachers' letters to Richard Welling, New York, commenting on his red-hot "Civics as It Should be Taught." From the one-room school teacher up to Mr. Zook, the national commissioner, these letters pooh-pooh the idea that any one is afraid to teach the real facts about distorted democracy. "Let's have this in high school and college," urges William Kilpatrick. "I'm for your method of attack," shouts teacher Rosier from his West Virginia hill. Primary teacher Johanna Lindlof asks, "Why stop with civics classes? Get every public-school teacher supplied." Kings County wants every mother's club to study the booklet.

Among these hundred comments were three flickers of the myth that teachers are afraid. None of the correspondents admit that he himself dare not permit the pupils to discuss the defects of local government, but three say that other teachers daren't. One says they fear the corporations will get their scalps. Another remarks, "Let's form a union to teach civic truth and to protect any one who does it." Well, why not? Let the union select the teacher, decide on the educational dynamite and be ready for the explosion. There won't be any. Where the fear is, is in school boards. They do not, now, want to be exhibited as interfering with discovery of civic waste and political incompetency.

*Glimmers in these dark hours.*—Chicago's Bogan persuades his board to heal one of the stabs it made. Free education above high-school grade will be restored. Auditoriums can be provided for lectures every hour by competent college teachers. Some laboratories can be used for individual work by highly qualified students. Libraries can cooperate. All high-school graduates who apply can be given something to mitigate the terrifying prospect of leisure imposed on thousands of youth out of work and with no resource of physical, mental or moral profit. . . . Most of the Columbia professors commenting on President Butler's arguments against the child-labor amendment call them nonsense. Professor Strayer doesn't "see the validity of Dr. Butler's objections." Dr. Counts considers them "the sort of objections raised by reactionaries to all sorts of social legislation." Dr. Goodsell thinks they are "stupid." . . . University of Michigan Carrothers pleads for sympathy toward teachers who attend institutes and conventions. Speakers are too disregardful of the boredom suffered by listeners sitting in front of one who has failed to make as thorough preparation as a concert musician does. Plan your meetings as carefully as a vaudeville director plans his. Lay down the law for all speakers as to time limits, audibility and interest. Require their replies that they understand requirements. Educate chairmen how to interrupt speakers who are not being heard or are running beyond time quota. A chairman should be the audience's protector and friend. Have comment-cards passed to auditors as they enter which ask for appraisal and suggestions. Tabulate these and send summaries to each speaker. The meetings belong to the teachers. Work your democracy. . . . At last there comes an educational journal avowedly devoted to the civic wake-up. Kilpatrick, Counts, Dewey, Hullfish, Newlon, Overstreet, Rugg, Watson—twenty-seven adventurers in all—announce the launching from 66 West 88th Street, New York, next October of *The Social Frontier,* a journal of educational criticism and reconstruction devoted to serving the emerging consciousness among American teachers that they must participate fully in social processes reshaping the American order. The program includes reconstruction of educational aims, of curriculums, arts and procedure. The journal will carry articles by distinguished thinkers—news, editorial comments, plans for professional action, significant quotations from press, platform and microphone. It will appear monthly, will cost $2.00 a year, is a cooperative non-profit enterprise. Sponsors of the idea have supplied funds for the support until the infant can walk alone. The directorate is expanding to cover representatives in every American state and territory. . . . The Language-Research Institute of New York University, publishing *The American World,* a newspaper using a vocabulary of 900 words selected by Director Elaine Swenson, has educated so many of its adult readers beyond this word list and into an appetite desiring more than the mere news of the world that the institute is planning a five-cent periodical devoted to re-writes of standard magazine articles on civic problems, short stories and literary anthologies in a vocabulary expanded to 1,800 words.

## TEETH IN THE SOCIAL SCIENCES

IF the report of the American Historical Association's Commission on the Social Studies[1] is a compromise, as the association's Secretary Read says it is—it was drafted, cut to pieces at two meetings far enough apart to allow for rumination, rewritten, again discussed, again revised and sent to all members for criticism—one surmises that it must have had, all along, a jolly lot of dynamite. In its final form Charles Merriam, Ernest Horn, Edmund Day and Frank Ballou decline to sign it. Each was invited to submit a dissenting opinion, but no answer appeared before the report went to press. If any came thereafter Secretary Read sayeth not. But Dr. Ballou's reasons are printed in SCHOOL AND SOCIETY under date of June 2.

To one who digests current books and articles on the social situation no shock will come from such declarations as these:

Cumulative evidence supports the conclusion that the age of individualism and *laissez-faire* in economy and government is closing; a new era of collectivism is emerging.

There will be a larger measure of compulsory and voluntary cooperation of citizens in the conduct of national economy.

There will be increasing state intervention in matters previously left to individual discretion, a state intervention that in some instances may be direct and mandatory.

It is indispensable to develop in students a critical spirit toward the old and persisting order.

The interests of the masses of the people are to be considered paramount. No man, woman or child can be exploited without doing violence to the essential spirit of American democracy and liberty. Despite academic criticism and in view of assaults by selfish groups, this spirit must give direction to the further evolution of life and institutions in the United States.

Corporate organization and other devices of capital have greatly reduced the opportunities for individual freedom and equality.

The American people will be called upon to make choices in the proximate future.

These extracts are from the commission's conclusions on the nature and function of the social sciences. After this field is surveyed the report goes with probe, scalpel and bottles of tonic into the philosophy and purpose of education, selection and organization of materials of instruction, method of teaching, testing, the teacher, public relations, administration and next steps.

Justice can not be done to this book by abstract, analysis or quotation. It has been boiled down to concentrated nutriment. Like a testament, its pronouncements are short; they are numbered verse by verse.

It proclaims education as the highest form of statesmanship: a positive and creative attack on problems of society. Education's obligation is imperative. It must aim at efficient functioning of the emerging economy and work for changes in the attitude of the American people, especially the rising generation. It must completely and frankly recognize that the old order passes, a new arises. Knowledge and capacity are indispensable in the people if America is to survive. This knowledge and capacity is education's task. The ideals of democracy, cultural liberty, the moral equality and dignity of all men, the abolition of class distinctions, the extension of the opportunity for the fullest development of every one's creative abilities, his spiritual qualities, his individuality, the protection of liberty, these education can secure. It is its obligation to prepare the rising generation for these essentials.

The condition of America demands an increased emphasis on social instruction in the schools and a more realistic approach. It must be continuous from kindergarten through college and extend to the adult population. The teaching staff must assume professional responsibility for it, resisting the pressure of selfish interests. The people must be moved to engage in profound movements of social reform and reconstruction. The school must provide politi-

[1] A. C. Krey, G. S. Counts, W. G. Kimmel, T. L. Kelley, Charles A. Beard, Isaiah Bowman, Ada Comstock, Avery O. Craven, Guy Stanton Ford, Carleton J. H. Hayes, Henry Johnson, Leon C. Marshall, Jesse H. Newlon, John F. Steiner, "Conclusions and Recommendations." Charles Scribner's Sons, New York. 170 pp. $1.25.

cal and moral leadership for community, nation and mankind. Observation and discussion must be combined with actual participation in the government of the school and the civic activities of the community. The actual life of the school and of its district are among the greatest aids for this instruction. Many a college education has been filed away in a drawer of notebooks, gathering dust and forgotten.

The scholarship, courage and vision of a school rise no higher than the teachers. They must combine to increase these necessities. Teachers should unite for fair compensation, security of tenure and for protection from group pressure. It is ignorance that puts the public into the control of determined minorities. The commission places its trust in the improvement of the teacher rather than in perfection of technical administration.

Achievements already accomplished in government and economics indicate that the American people have the cooperative and moral powers to realize the vision of the founders of the nation.

The composers have resisted temptation to make a detailed syllabus, although they must know how generally the average worker prefers such a labor-saving device to the more fundamental outline of aims, motives and principles. In preferring the more modern belief that classroom teachers should themselves take a large share in making the exercises suitable for reaching the goal the commission has discouraged the scissors and paste-pot method. In opposing the fashionable reliance on mechanical tests and measurements these committeemen aim at some restoration of a needed philosophy of education.

This snug little book, beautifully printed, clear and courageous in its utterance, distinct and practicable in its proposals, is an eloquent confirmation of the principles that have been shouted at us from patriotic platforms, that have been sung and saluted all our lives. In dignity of utterance, in soundness of doctrine, it is a veritable schoolman's bible. It is so simple as to make fit reading for devotional ceremonies at the opening exercises of high schools, at college chapels and at teachers meetings and conventions. It outranks any work of a Committee of Ten, Classical Investigation or Children's Charter that has appeared, for its roots are in the two fundamental documents from which the nation sprang.

## ROOTED IN THE NEW SOCIAL ORDER

DR. WIRT, Mr. Rand and some senatorial hunters for mares' nests have pretty well advertised a new economics by Messrs. Hill and Tugwell.[2] I imagine what aroused the suspicions of the heresy sleuths is the subtitle of the book: "A Study of American Levels of Living and How to Improve Them." In the millennium curious students exploring the twentieth century will discover that it was its custom to single out whoever proposed to better man's condition and to call him names. Here are some samples of the most different of the passages in this book:

Under a picture of a luxurious building is the question: In this country club which is more frequent, talk of fashion and sport or discussion of the social problems of our times?

A yacht like the one pictured here costs $100,000 to run for only a few weeks in the season. This would buy a year's comfort for forty families.

Millions of poor live in misery below the point of physical health.

Tell about a rich man who injured the community; about one who benefited it.

The worker must be regarded by the responsible managers of industry as important as profits.

The worker should have a voice in the control of manufacture.

Suggest what might be done to improve the situation in occupations in which the character of the work prevents satisfaction to the workers.

An epic passage from Henry George's disturbing book, "Progress and Poverty," is quoted.

It is strange how willingly people accept the notion that millions must be destitute because there is too much food and clothing.

One must be complacent indeed to feel that his own good fortune is a reason for defending the present system.

Capital export must be coordinated with national welfare rather than left to the complete control of men dominated by the profit motive.

[2] Howard Hill, Rexford Guy Tugwell, "Our Economic Society and its Problems." Harcourt, Brace and Company, New York. 560 pp. $1.72.

Russia has silenced the notion that economic affairs are governed by adamant natural laws.

Those scraps reveal the flavor of the book.

The trouble with the Hill-Tugwell text is that it soft pedals "God's in his heaven, all's right with the world." It makes the mistake of laying down a distinct picture of the economic world as it is and of suggesting to young people that they ought to be getting ready to change it. That we who have national wealth and technical skill, says this book, should let such conditions exist is a stinging shame. Why are you studying this subject? it asks. Surely not to get knowledge for its own sake. It's up to you to do something intelligently, honestly, justly.

The already famous chapters 27, 28, and 29 are dangerous because they expose the coming citizen to practical and orderly ways of getting out of the mess we are in. Kinds of control are submitted for discussion, now, at a time when control is a word that throws some minds into tantrums. You can't pin any propaganda charge on these authors. Their fault is that they take young heads out of the sand heaps.

The pictures are unusually numerous and belonging.

As providing what the social studies advocates tell us schools have lacked too long, these forthright expounders have scored a bull's-eye.

## REAL NEWS FOR SCHOOL AND COLLEGE

For more than two and a half years there has been going into schools and colleges from The Civic Education Service in Washington a weekly journal[3] so different from the usual run of school periodicals as to delight the heart of the teacher who is tired of the washed-out and expurgated offerings that have proved harmless and next to useless in classes of current events. One thing has become a truism with observant teachers: it isn't necessary in current affairs to denature material for students. The use of newspapers for class use has brought an overdose of crime stories, sports and advertisements. Here is an offering by two historians, a professor of education and two economists, trained by writing for every-day folks. Their selection of topics, their short editorial essays, their cartoons and news photographs, their hook-up of present events with past history, their summaries and their dashes of humor constitute a weekly text refreshingly informative. The feature, "Something to think about" is composed by a master of the art of setting the mind to deliberative logic. There are no advertisements. As I see it, only a twisted mind could read propaganda or partisanship between the lines. The motive is frankly to enlighten public opinion on the people's interests.

As a reviewer is expected to criticize, I wish there could be in the material furnished to classes in the social sciences more reference to needs in the school's home community. We have done pretty well in this regard in our geography, science, hygiene, home-making and pictorial art. In civics classes the favorite themes are the big far-off things, like international affairs and doings in Washington, the contact with which for us ordinary people is of the slightest. The civic wastage and political dishonesty in our home town is much more a duty for us to know and cure, much more capable of our amendment, and a more promising field for the cultivation of civic courage. Frequent interpolation of the question "How is it in your town, city or country?" would stiffen the excellent discussion feature of this high-grade publication. These five editors have the courage and the teaching skill to awaken the coming generation to the fact that it isn't necessary to wait for a war with Japan before running a risk for one's beloved homeland. Only because *The American Observer* is so superior could one have the nerve to suggest how it could be better.

[3] Charles A. Beard, George S. Counts, Harold G. Moulton, David S. Muzzey, Walter E. Myer, *Editors, The American Observer*. Civic Education Service, 744 Jackson Place, Washington, D. C. 8 pp. 15 × 10 in. $2.00 a year. In clubs for class use $1.00 a year; 50c a semester.

## CLERGYMEN, WAR AND CAPITALISM

Parkes Cadman, Harry Fosdick, Edward Israel, Ashby Jones, William King, F. H. Knubel, Francis McConnell, John McDowell, D. P. McGeachy, Daniel Poling, William Scarlett and Kirby Page, ministers, asked 100,000 clergymen fifteen searching questions on live controversial subjects involving government. Replies came from 20,870. They were turned over for tabulation to a firm of certified public accountants. The results are in print.[4] It looks

[4] "20,870 Clergymen on War and Economic Injustice." Kirby Page, 3947 Forty-eighth Street,

to me as though the questions asked are topnotch themes for discussion in educational classes. "Do you favor?" "What are your reasons?" This provokes the style of thinking activity our school leaders are pushing into classrooms.

The percentages of replies are these: 88 per cent. for a cooperative commonwealth based on service as opposed to a capitalistic system activated by a profit motive; 79 per cent. favor a drastic inheritance tax, limiting the amount of wealth any one may inherit; 63 per cent. favor compulsory unemployment insurance administered by government; 54 per cent. advocate national labor unions; 67 per cent. believe the churches should go on record as refusing to sanction or support any future war; 77 per cent. wish the United States to make immediate reduction of armament proportionately greater than other nations are willing to promise; 82 per cent. are against military training in public high schools and colleges.

In addition to the ministers consulted, the students in eight theological seminaries were questioned. Their per cents. were higher than those quoted above. Thus may we see, dearly beloved, that the hope of the race is in its youth.

Eight hundred and twenty-two of the ministers failed to sign their names. One thousand one hundred and eighteen asked that their replies be kept secret, except for tabulation.

Englishmen believe that anonymity in opinion is more sought by Americans than by any other people. Is this rugged individualism?

## UNTRAMMELLED ECONOMICS

When teachers Atkins and Wubnig shall be called to receive their civic crowns for public service the citation should be: "For that you have composed a book on a difficult subject no paragraph of which any youth will have to read twice for its meaning." Their text is a high-school economics.[5] Its clearness and interest are nothing short of amazing. The authors have cut loose from the persisting principles formulated a hundred and fifty years ago by writers who knew only a populace of small shopkeepers and individual craftsmen. This book has no idea that teachers will let it become a basis for memorizing paragraphs and reciting them. The questioning kept up throughout the volume requires John and Mary to tell how matters lie in their own neighborhood. How can you further the betterment toward which the world is now struggling? This is the recurrent theme of this lively book. Each chapter's purposes are outlined at its beginning. There is no large controversial question omitted. The balance between the arguments for and against is cleverly maintained and then you are asked, "Which side are you on? Why?" Charts, pictures, reading lists and an index are of true workmanship. It is a masterpiece.

Long Island City, New York. 40 pp, paper. Six copies, $1.00; ten, $1.50; 50, $6.00; 100, $10,00.

[5] Willard E. Atkins, Arthur Wubnig, "Our Economic World." Harper and Brothers, New York. 411 pp. $1.68.

## VIBRANT WITH CURRENT PROBLEMS

In collecting material for college freshman classes in English Messrs. Gordon and King,[6] Californians, have hit three bull's-eyes at one shot. They have collected fifty-two pieces of masterly writing; they have selected these because of treatment of vital problems of to-day; they have chosen pieces of arresting interest full of provocation to classroom discussion. The themes and the style are by no means above high-school capacity to understand and profit by. Politics, economics, sociology, ethics, science, medicine, art, personality are here. I am somewhat sorry the makers call it a college book. Such a title makes many laymen shy and this work is bound to be read entire by every average citizen who gets beyond the title page. I am bold to say it should be rechristened "American Readings in Problems of To-day."

Connecticut Governor Cross is represented by his slashing "Young Men in Politics." Lillian Symes appears with her brilliant "Last Frontier." You will find here Bertrand Russell, Bernard De Voto, Robert Duffus, Raymond Fosdick, Glenn Frank, Stuart Chase, Sherwood Anderson, Louis Adamic and many other favorites. It is a vibrant book in line with the present revolution.

## LIVING WELL

Teacher-at-large Kleiser has long been turning out self-helper books on talking, ad-

[6] Dudley Chadwick Gordon, Vernon Rupert King, "College Readings on To-day and Its Problems." Oxford University Press, New York. 646 pp. $1.95.

dressing audiences and writing. His latest work[7] takes all life for its province, planning, working, eating, sleeping, seeing, relaxing, growing old and enjoying life. Dr. Kleiser doesn't hesitate to preach. It would be hard to write a guide to life and not preach. Any one who takes up such a book expects sermons. Those here are direct: "Don't let your ideals and enthusiasms fade," "men have mastered the art of living, don't throw away what they have proved"; "your income goes farther if you budget it; budget your time," "when you shut your desk shut your business into it; when you play, wholly play"—and so on, principles, experiences, authorities put into working directions, expressed in simple, encouraging discourse. I found that youngsters are curious to learn the ways of efficient living. Dr. Kleiser has a way of setting forth the large themes in attractive form. This is a first-class book for school and college libraries.

## HISTORY ALIVE

Ohio State University has a chair of the teaching of history. Its Professor Pahlow doesn's sit in it—stands up or walks around, stirring the atmosphere of the classroom to electric conviction that history isn't what has happened but what mankind has achieved. Pahlow has finished another book.[8]

It is one lively history of the world, as gripping as a detective story. My boy, shouts Pahlow, history is an account of your family. Your most important job is to share in running the world. How can you conduct your father's business if you don't learn how it became what it is to-day? How can you prescribe for the illness of your family without learning the history of the case? The hope of mankind lies in the power of your generation to do what no previous one has done. Study seriously that great world-enterprise that you will soon have to manage. A few thousand resolute spirits, a fraction of the misdirected heroism that went to waste in the world war, a campaign for a new order, will turn the destines of mankind around for a new life of the race.

The book bristles with enthusiasms. It puts new life into the doings of all the ancient races, grouped in key units according to the scheme of modern learning. It brings the long-neglected countries of the Orient into the drama, magnifies the great inventions—language, literature, government, agriculture, architecture, other arts and mechanics. It gives new questions and projects. It uses remarkable pictures, avoiding ruins. It prefers restorations with live people thronging the temples and forums. Even the illustrations are labeled with spicy humor. A profusely inscribed mummy case "reveals more about Egypt than its occupant ever knew." "Khafra made this stone likeness of himself in case his mummy wouldn't last." A brilliant full-page picture of a Babylonian king in his room of inscriptions carries the comment: "If you have trouble with your dates, here is where your troubles began."

Pahlow holds that teaching should make history hum. His does. He has an uncanny clairvoyant insight into the interests of young minds and a singular skill in turning them toward big ideas.

## CHINESE HISTORY FOR YOUNG FOLKS

Miss Seeger[9] in the Dalton School, New York City, can not understand why world histories have so commonly shirked our great eastern neighbors. She tried a year-course with twelve-year old children in which China, Japan and India were studied. They loved it. Now Miss Seeger writes a picturesque and fascinating story of the Chinese people, their manners, religions, arts, philosophies, literatures, campaigns and difficulties, from early days to the establishment of the republic. It is a sprightly book, abounding in new drawings and fully indexed.

## PEPYS ALIVE AGAIN

We all prefer to read our Pepys in small portions. The whole diary runs to 1,300,000 words. The New Turner Edition, unexpurgated, will be published by George Bell and Sons, London. This, like the sets currently available, is too expensive for most of us, and the volumes we seek in the public library are always out. But Arthur Bryant,[10] whose "King Charles II" is

[7] Grenville Kleiser, ''How to Succeed in Life.'' Funk & Wagnalls Company, New York. 330 pp. $2.00.

[8] Edwin W. Pahlow, ''Man's Achievement Up to the Age of Steam.'' Ginn and Company, Boston. 754 pp. $1.96.

[9] Elizabeth Seeger, ''The Pageant of Chinese History.'' Longmans, Green and Company, New York. 386 pp. $3.00.

guarantee of an accurate view of the period and a picturesque presentation, covers all the days of the journal. He sets the incomparable diarist in a living picture of the intrigues, revolutions and life of one of the quaintest epochs of England. You see the bird-like little Sam flitting from church to church, half a dozen of a Sunday, to sample the sermons. You share his delight at finding he can shave himself and save pennies. You admire the tailor's son arranging marriages for the nobility. You experience the horror of the plague and of the great fire.

His was a time of changing morals. The religious comforts of the Puritan parents ceased to have meaning for the children. As the youngsters grew up they thought they saw as failures the results of efforts to rule the terrestrial earth according to laws, not of men, but of angels. The righteous war of the fathers to exterminate pleasure, sin, idolatry and a formalized religion was seen to have ended not in the rule of the saints but in that of bootleggers and profiteers. Reformation had passed into ruin, freedom of conscience into religious oppression; the presbyter was as the old priest. The universal use of pious language had given money-grabbers, bribers and libertines a vocabulary of ideals. A large proportion of the nation was tired of virtue, nobility and self-denial. Sam sweetens his pages with declarations of his own honesty as compared with his fellow officers in the navy office, and grows rich from rake-offs and gifts from contractors.

The diary is in its own way as great a masterpiece as the Iliad or Don Quixote. At heart this navy comptroller was an artist. He had the artist's two essentials—sincerity and selection. Instinctively he knew what incident or mental process would give his work the spirit of life. He loved his art so intensely that no consideration of weariness or shame prevailed on him to omit anything essential.

His style never tires you. A genius like Frank Adams gets the hang of it. He makes a weekly column of his own twentieth century doings sparkle down the page of *The Herald-Tribune*. Mr. Bryant's biography is all of the Pepysian flavor. In his narrative, Pepys, the tremendous worker, the savior of the British navy, the cheerer of countless mortals three centuries away, walks, works, flirts and plays, very much alive.

[10] Arthur Bryant, "Samuel Pepys. The Man in the Making." The Macmillan Company, New York. 436 pp. $3.00.

## TRAITS OF A GREAT COMMANDER

The Scot who commanded the British in the last days of the world war and became Earl Haig is depicted by a fellow general in a short, simple biography, the twenty-fourth in Macmillan's series of "Great Lives."[11] You see a young man intensely loving his mother, uninterested in any particular study, pinched by what he considered inadequate income, pushed into a military school by an ambitious and determined sister, and finding his bent. His instructors come to admire his application. The colonel tells one of the Sandhurst collegians, "Your man, Haig, one of these days, will be commander-in-chief." You see the young man, without influence, by sheer attention to doing every commission at his best, rising to the top of the army. With incident and clear presentation of traits of personality the story is made vital from beginning to end.

## MASTERY IN ACTION

Tunstall's new life of the greatest of English admirals[12] is the story of terrible handicaps: one eye blinded, one arm gone, sea sickness, poor health, slight loyalty to marriage vows. But a supreme affection for his men, a Phillip-Sydney quality of self-sacrifice in the face of suffering, a masterly art of giving responsibility to the right men, an untiring pressure on Parliament for fairness to common sailors, a superb courage, shine through the plain recital of facts which make up this short and stirring story as Mr. Tunstall tells it.

## A LIFE OF SUPERINTENDENT MAXWELL

Fourteen years after William Henry Maxwell's imposing frame was carried to Evergreen Cemetery a biography[13] of him appears.

[11] J. Charteris, "Haig." The Macmillan Company, New York. 144 pp. 75 cents.

[12] Brian Tunstall, "Nelson." Great Lives Series. The Macmillan Company, New York. 143 pp. 75 cents.

[13] Samuel P. Abelow, "Dr. William H. Maxwell, The First Superintendent of Schools of the City of New York." Scheba Publishing Company, 1098 Park Place, Brooklyn, New York. 177 pp. $1.50.

Teacher Abelow tells you he got his material together through the aid of a few of the New York school superintendent's intense admirers, and he hopes that teachers who read it will be inspired by the example of a great educator so that they will carry on during these critical days. The book is frankly panegyric. In accounts of the hero's early life and of his educational experience before the creation of Greater New York the admirable qualities of an educational warrior are given proper prominence. This is commendable. The docile type of school man was so common in those days that it is refreshing to learn of one who rarely knuckled down. His predecessors conceived it their duty to take orders from the board. Maxwell acted first and defended afterwards if any board assembled had the temerity to criticize. Biographer Abelow, basing his narrative on the voluminous reports of the superintendent, evolves a statement of educational policy, raising the standard of teacher training, establishing higher pay and permanence of position, eliminating political pull and introducing new activities. Maxwell was a skilful organizer, an indomitable worker and a courageous fighter. Sometimes he would say, "I'm standing with my back to the wall with a battle axe in each hand," when if he had laid down his axes and stepped forward he could have gotten all he wanted and saved much time and sweat. His quarrels with the beloved Thomas Hunter of the Normal College, Board Presidents Little, Tift, Churchill and Wilcox, with Frank McMurry, Dr. Ira Wile, Dr. William H. Allen, Nathan Jonas and State Superintedent Skinner were childish and losing games for him. His high-horse manner towards those whom he called "my subordinates" was absurd in a public school system.

His persistence in decisions considered untenable by his legal advisers cost him many wasteful lawsuits and humiliating defeats. His implacable resentment against underlings who showed signs of independence lost him what might have been valuable support from honest and important people. He was a classic and royal type, speaking of "my board of examiners," "my school library," "my statistician," "my power." His current title among the rank and file was "the Czar." The clerks who came in contact with him adored him. The board of examiners gladly obeyed his nod. The board of superintendents, a creation of his, passed resolutions charging him with destroying good will and with making his imagination serve for facts.

All the same, he advanced public education more than any Brooklyn or Manhattan superintendent before him. He freed the schools from the thralldom of politics. He broke the tradition that the New York school system had no bonds with the educational interests of the country at large. He participated in national associations and brought many teachers to similar cooperation. He addressed himself more to improvement of teaching than to affairs of buildings and grounds. He extended the services of the two universities which are in New York so that the teachers of the city schools rose in professional standing. He was a great superintendent. Those whom he antagonized said so. One of the most persistent opponents against many of his proposals headed the movement ending in the erection of the memorial statue. He was proud of himself. He bluffed many a proposition through. He lost fights by overplaying. The residuum of advantages New York education owes to him is tremendous, no matter how many of us he vindictively persecuted. He was due to have a biography. Abelow should be commended for the labor he has undergone to make one.

## EDUCATION IS PASSING FROM STATIC TO DYNAMIC

At two New York meetings and at one in Washington there were such quotations from Duke University Ellwood's latest book[14] that I felt like a teacher of current events who hadn't read the papers. I got the book. I've read every word of it. It is one of the clearest, most courteous pieces of polemic writing that has passed through this reviewery in many a day. With gentle firmness Professor Ellwood squeezes the juice out of various theories of what sociology ought to be and drops the husks into the waste can.

Sociology at present, and all the social sciences, mirror a world in disagreement. Neither

[14] Charles A. Ellwood, "Methods in Sociology, A Critical Study." Duke University Press, Durham, North Carolina. 214 pp. $1.50.

conflicting schools nor thinking people assent to any common doctrine. There are those who conceive of sociology as a pure science measurable by the quantitative devices of physics. What can not be so measured is, to such arguers, not worth considering. This will not do. On the contrary, in this crisis it is the duty of social scientists to place their scholarship at the service of their communities at large. In separate chapters Dr. Ellwood considers the scientific method, objectivity, behaviorism, philosophical procedure, observation, statistics, anthropology, ethics, law, government and social work.

From the chapters on sociology and education comes the assertion that the teacher with social vision will have more power to mould the future than the legislator has. More than the legislator, he needs social wisdom to guide his work.

We are passing from static to dynamic education, from one that aims to conserve the social order to an education that will initiate and control social progress. Education's two chief problems are the aim and the curriculum. School people in conventions pass good resolutions affirming their aim to be civic progress and go back to their schools without doing anything to the curriculum which was never set up for civic progress. Education, supported by public funds, is essentially a program of applied sociology. School is too much concerned with the individual for his own sake. This does not assure a harmonious relation of the citizen to his community. It may be a great damage to social benefit. The proper aim of education is to add to general welfare. There is too narrow an aim of fitting the student to succeed in life. The school should work for the general advancement of humanity rather than for successful careers of individuals. The aim of education must be the efficient aider of society, the good citizen, who adds to the benefits of civic life.

Some school masters try to believe that to make a good farmer or a good office worker is to make a good citizen. A man may be an excellent engineer and a bad citizen. To be a good citizen one must help the institutional activities of his community.

The teacher must be a social leader. He must make himself active in the great campaign for the improvement of society, not a minor part of the movement, but its fundamental, most important part.

Education is the only reliable means of social progress. Revolution by force never effects advance. It may sweep away obstacles, but education has to do the building. Education directed toward its proper aim could make the normal person many times more socially efficient than he is now. It can give him an entirely different attitude toward civilization than he now has. In this point the education of the nineteenth century completely failed. It laid more stress on individual advantage than on service to the community. That justice, brotherhood and the service of mankind can not be acquired in school is absurd. Education can change human customs, beliefs and nature. It has done so in the past. The colleges are not doing their main duty—producing experts in the larger problems of community life. The superior society of the future must be produced by the trained scientific mind knowing social facts and forces.

## COLLAPSE OF COLD-STORAGE EDUCATION

No proof ever appeared that the period of childhood could be used for storing one's mind with any major part of the knowledge essential for a complete life. New social problems unconceived when you were in school have arisen which the ordinary man can not handle without instruction. While there is life there is the need and power to learn. This is the fundamental idea of an admirable study of continuation schools[15] which comes as one of the monographs of the Cooper-Koos national survey of secondary education. It notes the number, method and aims of continuation schools. New York State places emphasis on citizenship. Massachusetts considers civic training secondary and a by-product. California makes it the preponderant purpose. So say the official documents, but you know how far we get from our prospectuses. The sampling done by the authors of this monograph is tabulated to give you a clear idea of what is being done, who the pupils are, what work they find.

Evening high schools are described, their pupils, their programs and other matters of moment.

[15] Grayson N. Kefauver, Victor H. Knoll, C. Elwood Drake, "Part-Time Secondary Schools."

## HOW HIGH SCHOOLS GUIDE

THE work of Dr. Reavis[16] in the National High School Survey has a definiteness that makes his volume especially provocative to action by those in charge of secondary schools. He has selected ten instances of progressive planning for guiding pupils toward suitable life work. He has described the usage in each of these localities in such a manner that superintendents and principals will, in the easiest way, get improvement into the service in their own plants.

## LIFE'S SPRING-CLEANING TIME

PHYSICIAN AND PSYCHOLOGIST DR. TUCKER,[17] avoiding technical language or explaining it when used, sums the experience students of adolescent problems have thus far gained. He discusses conduct disturbances, moodiness, inferiority complexes, superior ability, fantasies, repression, fears, guilt, shame, egoism, undesirable habits, abnormal eating, overstudy, lying, stealing, bullying, rebellion, truancy, vulgarity, whining, dirtiness, laziness, show-off and sex problems. What youth needs is understanding and sympathy. The perpetual oncoming of youth needs a remaking of education to give him a fairer chance.

## CHILD ARTISTS

I RECALL a fuddyduddy quite eminent in the art-teaching world who forbade children to draw people, because such activity made disproportion of the human body too familiar. The University of Chicago puts out a study[18] that shows the protest of my old friend shoved far into the *Nirgendwo*. Miss Zesbaugh studied no less than 8,000 drawings of postmen by children of nine school grades in six cities. She tabulated the proportional length of heads, limbs, size of feet, place of attaching arms and legs and noted other details. A rating scale for drawings is derivable. Her conclusions are put into a form of decided value to teachers who encourage a fascinating phase of children's activity. At about the fourth grade schematic scrawls give way to forms beginning to resemble real humans. Kindergartners represent their people facing forward. Alas, as we grow older our human world goes sideways, and mark you, headed to the left. Republicans, take notice. Man is larger to the primary child and shrinks as times goes on. The pedagogical instinct should be curbed when it restricts the children's interests. Many a budding artist has been nipped by taking away desire.

## ART ADVENTURE

WITH a charming print of a little girl possessing a pan of bright colors and painting a picture of flowers Scott, Foresman and Company's adventuresome sally into a new kind of primary school reading begins.[19] It is a child's primer for the second half of the first year of reading. Experts in art teaching and in reading ability have compiled it in accordance with conclusions reached by many experiments. The result is a continuing picture gallery in colors with alluring text to satisfy a youngster's curiosity and love of pictures. The *Art Digest,* that weekly periodical which every patriotic school library ought to have, hails this adventure as an epoch-making event. French children's books are true works of art. For a generation American public schools, in a fog of fads-and-frills criticism, have been fighting the ugliness of pioneer civilization. This wonderful primer is a march with banners farther to the front.

## DRAWING FOR THE UNTAUGHT

ARCHITECT AND ARTIST GUPTILL[20] has taught freehand and pictorial drawing for twenty-five years in the Pratt Institute, Brooklyn. He offers a book which in a single volume gives the basic principles underlying drawing in pencil, ink, charcoal, crayon and brush. In it the author incorporates the definite suggestions, corrections and helps his long experience has shown necessary. He furnishes graded exercises, ways of self-criticism and hundreds of diagrams, sketches and beautiful examples of drawing.

---

Superintendent of Documents, Washington, D. C. 98 pp. 10 cents.

16 William C. Reavis, "Programs of Guidance." Superintendent of Documents. Washington, D. C. 144 pp. 10 cents.

17 Beverley R. Tucker, M.D., "Adolescence." The Stratford Company, Boston. 121 pp. $1.25.

18 Helen Ann Zesbaugh, "Children's Drawings of the Human Figure." University of Chicago Press. 74 pp. $1.25.

19 William J. Whitford, Edna B. Liek, William S. Gray, "Art Stories, Book One." Scott, Foresman and Company, Chicago. 144 pp. 68 cents.

20 Arthur L. Guptill, "Freehand Drawing Self-taught." Harper and Brothers, New York. 135 pp. 12 × 9 inches, $3.50.

### MUSIC IN THE COUNTRY SCHOOL

Silver, Burdett and Company come pioneering with a book[21] on music adapted to rural education. It is a practical manual for the program in one-room and two-room schools. The authors see the rights of the country child ignored. The book shows how fine music can be brought to him. It presents plans, detailed outlines and materials, procedures for teachers, references for county superintendents and others. A generous amount of new projects, refreshing variety lists of songs, tips on teaching them, choruses, musical games, appreciation, voice training, correlation with school subjects, radio, gramophone, rhythm bands, dances and so on, make it a lively book.

### ON WITH THE DANCE

Mr. Martin[22] is a critic on the staff of *The New York Times*. Signore La Meri[23] is director of the department of dancing of Regie Academia dei Fidenti, Italia. Each contributes a trim volume to the Barnes series of books for teachers.

The dance in the good old days was a religious rite. The gods were expert at it. King David danced before the Lord. The Greeks developed it into a high art of great beauty. The Romans debauched it. With them dancing and lewdness became synonymous. The church did much to rescue it, using it in religious ceremonies, pageants and miracle plays. Eighteenth century France set the pace again for dissolute dancing, other nations imitating. Then came, says director La Meri, a renaissance: the Russian artists, Ruth St. Denis, Pavlowa, Maud Allan, Mary Wigman, the Italians, the Scandinavians, the Orientals. All the time, Spain has maintained an art form untainted by other movements. These epochs are described by Author La Meri, who discusses ballets, free dances, the ethnologic, the Oriental, the Spanish, other European forms, and the American.

Mr. Martin is more concerned with the dancing of our day, its art, techniques and relation to other cultures. The old ballet was a story in pantomine with choreographic interpolations after the manner of the later musical comedy. The plot was a main consideration of the critics. In the modern form, dancing is the main issue; music and plot are secondary. The Martin book is a guide to appreciation.

In this Barnes series there are already seven books, including "Expression Gymnastics," "Eurythmics, Art and Education," "Social Dancing as Art," "The Free Dance" and "Shawn the Dancer."

### GRACE IN THE GYMNASIUM

Physical Instructor McCulloch,[24] Ypsilanti Normal College, makes available in unusually imitable performance his experience and convictions regarding a large assortment of developing and corrective gymnastics. It is remarkably effective in the use of motion pictures, 265 of them, and step-by-step description of moves. Expression, psychologic objectives, health, grace and confidence are developed lucidly. This book will perk up the instructor day by day and is admirably adopted as a text for his classes.

### ZEST, APPRECIATION, ENJOYMENT AND UNDERSTANDING

I have spent several pleasant hours studying a high school and college text-book by two lively-minded scholars.[25] The words at the head of this review are, in the order there given, the aim the authors say they have. Zest. The word recalls a lively woman who taught literature in a high school of my acquaintance, forty-five years ago. Zest, she said, was our form of the Persian "Zestan," a bit of orange peel or lemon rind put into a drink to quicken the tang of it. These authors' "Comprehension questions," "problems in appreciation" and plain talks on poetry, fiction, romance, drama, essay and biography do this service for the masterpieces. This book has lure. Ah, me, I wish I were a freshman with young folks and with the modern opposite of the drab stick who bored us in English I. Methinks had we used this text there had been zestan withal.

21 Osbourne McConathy, W. Otto Meissner, Edward Bailey Birge, Mabel E. Bray, Fannie W. Dunn, Frank A. Beach, Josephine Murray, ''Music in Rural Education.'' Silver, Burdett and Company, New York. 290 pp. $1.20.

22 John Martin, ''The Modern Dance.'' A. S. Barnes and Company, New York. 123 pp. $1.50.

23 La Meri, ''Dance as an Art Form.'' A. S. Barnes and Company, New York. 198 pp. $1.50.

24 J. H. McCulloch, ''Gymnastics, Tumbling and Pyramids.'' W. B. Saunders Company, Philadelphia. 177 pp. $2.00.

25 Ralph P. Boas, Edwin Smith, ''Enjoyment of Literature.'' Harcourt, Brace and Company, New York. 553 pp. $1.60.

## WAR, PROSPERITY AND CHEMISTRY

Chemical Research Director Hale[26] dedicates to his "little daughter, Ruth Elizabeth," an informative book tracing the epochs of chemistry from the early days, expounding the revolutionary changes the science has wrought.

We are near another awakening, the dominance of another force, the appearance of another star of human destiny. This is the development of biological chemistry. Nature's laboratory offers an amazing assortment of organic compounds beginning to reveal their marvelous design in atomic architecture. This is the chemistry of the immediate present and the future.

As to chemistry and war, Germany, far ahead in chemical skill, did not realize her tremendous advantage. She was easily two years ahead of the best equipped of her foes with the mightiest weapon yet given to man. Had she employed her science she could have won the world war in ten days. Finally, her chemists had their suggestion adopted. Chlorine gas was brought into the fray. Modern war was inaugurated. In future conflicts the supreme direction will be in the hands of chemists, physicists, biologists and engineers. The chemists to-day are actively engrossed in this service. The nations are chemically conscious.

The depression, impairing credits, has delayed experimentation.

How recovery will come through aid to metal production, cheaper fertilizers, chemically made building material and textiles, levulose sugar, utilization of weeds, increased irrigation, synthetic rubber, less costly transportation and so on is set forth by the author in a striking manner. With an interesting division of the entire history of the world into epochs of chemical advance, with a chapter on "Chemeconomy," and an enumeration of the great triumphs won and to be gained, with a discussion of the social revolutions such discoveries will again produce, Dr. Hale concludes his startling book.

## THE WHY AND HOW OF GEOMETRY

Professor Christofferson, Miami University, has noted that the high-school teacher of geometry has had very little more of training than the high-school geometry course itself gives. Why is this four-thousand-year-old subject given place in an American high school? Professor Christofferson calls the authorities to the stand.[27] Oxford required the study in the thirteenth century and has varied the demands down and up since then. Harvard, from foundation days, taught it. By 1887 she had reached the point of requiring it for entrance. It has steadily crept down until now it is in the junior high school. What reason other than tradition should give it this grip? The authorities quoted answer: spatial imagination, appreciation of great basal propositions, appreciation of deductive proof, ability to use this proof where applicable, habits of succinct and precise statement, orderly organization of ideas, logical memory. These are the objectives listed by a national committee. Geometry teachers will swallow them. To me they savor of mental discipline, transfer of learning, cultivation of faculty and other hoary slogans which need statistical tables of mental tests of children who have and have not been dosed with geometry. Professor Christofferson, however, brings the case down to earth by the caution that geometry values depend on the way it is studied or taught. He proceeds to elucidate settled and unsettled difficulties, axioms, postulates, definitions and the things teachers are doing intelligently or in a routine manner in thousands of classrooms. He analyzes modes of thinking and reasoning. He gives sample lessons. He discusses the use of curiosity, search and discovery found in pupils properly guided. He covers the whole field of high-school demonstrative geometry, making a veritable handbook for the teacher's guidance in getting for each pupil the most that the course can give. The author doesn't wander. He has well-defined goals and marches straight to them. Almost he persuadeth the ordinary reader to be an expert geometer.

## NEW GEOGRAPHIES

With maps tinted to show the physical contour and at the same time the political divisions, with a striking array of new pictures, with the text a continuous narrative, with intentional omission of much detail that teachers record as dull and uneducative, Brigham and McFarlane

[26] William J. Hale, "Chemistry Triumphant." The Williams and Wilkins Company, Baltimore. 151 pp. $1.00.

[27] Herbert Carl Christofferson, "Geometry Professionalized for Teachers." George Banta Publishing Company, Menasha, Wisconsin. 204 pp. $1.75.

launch a new geography of New York State and North America.[28]

The vocabulary and sentence structure has been checked with word lists for the fifth school year. It is a handsome book.

Their seventh grade geography is also ready. It covers 406 pages and is priced at $1.52. They entitle it, "How the World Lives and Works." How the expansion of Europe overseas has resulted, what the world relations of the United States are, come in for especial attention. The importance of weather and climate, the world's resources, the occupations of its people, the dependence of America on other nations, plenty of questions, projects, and tests *à la mode moderne,* make an effective working study of such facts of astronomy, agronomy, industry, science and economics as the young citizen should know. An index with pronunciation guidance ends the story. The pictures tell a large part of the wondrous tale.

### MAN AND HIS ANIMAL RELATIVES

FOR the newer and integrated aims of the modern college of liberal arts there is needed a shorter, simpler, more general treatment of biology. The University of Chicago offers a text composed with this need in view.[29] Enriched by photographs and diagrams, Professor Romer's text is a clear presentation of man, his similarity to other forms of life, his difference from them. From cells, from dinosaurs, to the 1934 inmates of old men's homes, this work is a close-connected story of our ancestors and of the contributions they have made to our living machine.

### AND THERE WAS LIGHT

NOT since the happy day in 1880 when Professor McLouth, of the Normal School in Ypsilanti, lent me Tyndall's "Heat as a Mode of Motion" have I read a science book with so much pleasure as I got from Sir William Bragg's treatise on light.[30]

It is a book for the general reader. It is a reproduction of lectures the author has given to popular audiences composed mostly of young people. The chemistry and physics of it are simple; the plates are especially attractive. The manner of discussing the eye, the colors of plants, of the sky and laboratory experiments is interest-absorbing. As a general school library book, as a supplement to the studies in high-school science, as a source from which interesting summaries may be made for enlivening classes in physics, it is unexcelled.

### REMARKABLE TEXT ON HOME-MAKING

EVEN a mere man, if he opens the Graves and Ott[31] text-book on home economics, intended for girls in the junior and senior high schools, is not likely to lay it down until he has absorbed the most of it. The 50 tips on table manners, the chapter on "How Do We Live?" the definite responsibilities of different members of the family, how children must help, sickness in the home, what shall you do after school, the singularly charming pictures, will hold him.

These two gentlewomen, teachers, one in Schenectady, one in Port Chester, treat their specialty with a breadth and at the same time a definiteness that marks the book for acclaim. They are missionaries for the realization of the third stated purpose of our constitution—domestic tranquillity. Their conception of a happy home, of the material and spiritual means of making it, is specific and modern. Their projects, problems, thought-provoking exercises and books of reference show that they know how to teach in 1934. Little, Brown and Company has given the book a beauty in line with the style of the authors.

### BUILDING AS A THRILL

THE John Day Company has seized the popular idea of large photographs filling a whole book. They have let it into the school.[32] The authors and compilers are in the Cooperative School for Student Teachers, New York. With thrilling photographs and crisp explanatory text they portray the building of a skyscraper from excavation to placing of the capstone. It is an alluring book to keep lying on the reading table of the school library.

28 Albert Perry Brigham, Charles T. McFarlane, "Our Home State and Continent." American Book Company, New York. 330 pp. $1.32.

29 Alfred Sherwood Romer, "Man and the Vertebrates." University of Chicago Press. 425 pp. $3.00.

30 Sir William Bragg, F.R.S., "The Universe of Light." The Macmillan Company, New York. 282 pp. $3.50.

31 Mildred Graves, Marjorie M. Ott, "Your Home and Family." Little, Brown and Company, Boston. 352 pp. $1.40.

32 Elsa H. Naumburg, Clara Lambert, Lucy Sprague Mitchell, "Skyscraper." The John Day Company, New York. 80 pp. $2.00.

# SCHOOL AND SOCIETY

WITH WHICH ARE COMBINED THE EDUCATIONAL REVIEW, ESTABLISHED IN 1891, THE TEACHERS MAGAZINE, ESTABLISHED IN 1878, AND THE SCHOOL JOURNAL, ESTABLISHED IN 1874.

Volume 40 | SATURDAY, JULY 14, 1934 | Number 1020

## FEDERAL AID TO EDUCATION[1]

By Dr. GEORGE F. ZOOK

RETIRING UNITED STATES COMMISSIONER OF EDUCATION; DIRECTOR OF THE AMERICAN COUNCIL ON EDUCATION

AFTER a separate existence of sixteeen years the functions of the Federal Board for Vocational Education were by order of the President in August, 1933, transferred to the Department of the Interior and two months later assigned by the secretary of that department to the Commissioner of Education. Thus ended an unfortunate situation which for a number of years had given rise to considerable misunderstanding and apprehension. Already it has been demonstrated that the two organizations can be merged in spirit and purpose and that through our present comprehensive organization the interests of vocational and general education can be developed both vigorously and harmoniously. The combined staff of the Office of Education now numbers approximately 150 persons with an appropriation during the present fiscal year for salaries and general expenses of $593,753. I believe that the present administration is entitled to the deep gratitude of laymen and educators alike for having taken this statesmanlike step in the development of sound policy relative to the relations of the Federal Government to education. We can now go forward united under one banner and in one organization.

[1] Address at the first general session of the National Education Association, Washington, D. C., July 2, 1934.

The year just closed has been one of the most distressing yet possibly also one of the most significant ones in the history of American education. Everywhere the schools and colleges, both public and private, have been compelled to resort to further economies which in many states were so severe as to constitute nothing short of an educational crisis. In such a period old methods and outworn organization pass out and something more suited to the new day takes their place. While it is as yet too early even to identify all these trends, we are at that point in the development of certain national educational policies where with far less effort than usual we have the opportunity to influence the course of events in education for a generation, if not for several of them.

Our present difficulties in the support of education go back to our fundamental law. The federal constitution did not of course confer upon the central government authority to deal with education. Hence this responsibility was reserved to the several states. They in turn abdicated this obligation to the local units within the states.

For years local communities also shirked the responsibility for the maintenance of schools. Then arose a great line of prophets from Horace Mann to P. P. Claxton, who went about the states of this Union preaching the inalienable right of little children to the cultural heritage of the ages and the necessity of universal public education as the basis for popular government. Spreading the gospel of education was engaged in with a zeal akin to religious evangelism, of which it was indeed often an integral part. The spread of free public schools into every corner of our land during the last 100 years not by governmental coercion but mainly through popular desire is one of the striking accomplishments of the marvelous age through which we have passed. The school units of those early days were no larger than those which could be attended conveniently by a group of children walking to school and which contained enough real estate to support the school through taxation. There never was even in the beginning any relationship between the number of children to be schooled and the ability of the community to support schools.

The economic and social changes of recent decades, while they have generally raised the level of educational opportunity, have on the other hand also increased the inequalities of such opportunities between and among children. The concentration of wealth makes a high-school education an easy possibility in some communities, in others junior college education is within easy reach, in still others various curricula leading to baccalaureate degrees may be obtained as against a limitation of school opportunities to the elementary grades in the case of a large proportion of children and young people not so fortunately situated.

One of the factors in this situation is the way in which the schools have been confined to the real estate property tax as almost their sole means of support. In the face of rapid increases in other types of wealth from which income was available the schools kept on levying local taxes on real estate while other public agencies, especially those carried on by the states, have been wise enough to use more modern and effective sources of taxation. In 1931–32, 80.5 per cent. of revenue receipts from taxation and appropriation for the schools came from county and local sources. Practically all this came from taxes on real estate. On the other hand, the gasoline tax generally used for the maintenance of roads is an eloquent example of the kind of a tax which can be levied successfully long after local property taxes have in many parts of the country all but broken down. While we can of course look forward confidently to the continued revival of business and industry in such a manner as to make it possible for the owners of property again to pay taxes in larger amounts than at present, I am confident that local taxes on property can never again be counted on as much as in the past to bear the burdens of interest and sinking fund for capital outlay and for general maintenance of the schools. If this statement is true we are indeed faced not with a theory but a condition that may well make those who have the welfare of our country through education at heart pause for extended consideration. We shall have to do something about it or the financial support of our educational program will be permanently impaired.

Inasmuch as I have just stepped out of federal service it is perhaps natural that I should share with you some of my observations relative to the problem of federal aid to education which have grown in part out of the brief but most interesting year during which it has been my privilege to serve as Commissioner of Education.

There are a number of considerations which bear upon this problem, but I call your attention to but two of them. First, the title to the wealth of the country which is produced by all of us working together in all parts of the country is concentrated in certain states and even in metropolitan areas of these states in a most interesting and surprising manner. It seems no more than simple justice, therefore, that a way should be found by means of which wealth may be taxed where it is located and the income therefrom distributed to the states to be used for the education of the children where they are located.

In 1913 the sixteenth amendment to the Federal Constitution was adopted. This amendment authorized the Federal Government to levy income taxes on individuals. It is doubtful whether any addition to our fundamental law of greater social significance has been made since the beginnings of our government. This amendment conferred upon the Federal Government power to levy and collect the most important modern form of taxation. In 1931–32 the income taxes collected by the Federal Government from corporations and individuals amounted to $1,056,757,000. Even in the next year when the depression was at its height receipts from the federal income tax were $746,791,404. To the extent that the Federal Government exercises this power, the states are in effect inhibited from using it for their own purposes. To a considerable extent the same kind of development has taken place relative to inheritance taxes and relative to certain sales taxes, notably on liquor, tobacco and gasoline, which otherwise could have been used more extensively by the states to support state and local functions.

Hence during the last two decades two important developments affecting the support of all state and local functions, including education, have been taking place simultaneously, namely, the breakdown of the property tax on the one hand, and the gradual assumption by the Federal Government of a number of sources of modern and effective taxes which, had they been left to the states, would at least have enabled the states and the local communities to pull themselves out of their financial troubles more quickly and easily. In view of these circumstances it has always seemed to me to be somewhat unbecoming on the part of members of Congress, as has happened so frequently in the session just closed, to advise somewhat testily representatives of state and local governments, including the schools, that if only they would "set their houses in order back home" it would be unnecessary to be asking for federal aid.

However, few people would now advocate that the Federal Government surrender the income tax and other modern taxes to the states. Our experience shows clearly that the Federal Government is far more effective in the collection of such taxes than the several states can possibly be. Moreover, through the services conducted by the Federal Government with the income derived from these sources all the people benefit, whereas a return of these several forms of taxation to the states would only emphasize the present injustices and inequalities between and among our citizens resulting from the concentration of the title to wealth in a small number of metropolitan areas. It is evident that this is not the solution of the financial problems facing the states and localities, including the schools.

I am convinced that if the Federal Government continues to levy these more modern forms of taxation, as it alone can do most effectively, it follows as clearly as can be that some proportion of the proceeds of these taxes should be returned to the states for the support of state and local governmental functions, including schools.

It is perhaps unnecessary for me to call your attention to the fact that while I am here taking a stand in favor of federal aid to education I believe that we educators should be broadminded enough to recognize that whatever financial problems face the schools also face all other aspects of our state and especially our local governments.

Many people have objected violently that certain forms of education, namely, extension education in agriculture and home economics, vocational education and education in agriculture and mechanic arts to the neglect of others have been selected by the Federal Government for special subsidy. Whatever validity there is to these objections holds equally well for the whole of education as against all other state and local needs. To the extent, therefore, that we succeed in securing federal aid for education only there will always be a corresponding tendency for the states and localities to reduce their appropriations for this service. We can not, therefore, and we ought not to want to escape the necessary close relationships which exist between the financial problems facing the schools and all other forms of local and state efforts. Would it not be wiser public policy, therefore, for us to join cordially in all efforts which may be made in Washington in the future to secure a comprehensive program of federal aid to the states and localities for all aspects of government, including the schools, rather than to pursue our own special needs too far? I believe that we ought to give this matter our earnest consideration. It would, among other things, avoid many of the problems of federal control of education.

Such a view may be too Utopian for the present time. In other words, the schools are in such a difficult position that we must of course seize every opportunity to plead their cause. The Federal Government can and should do two things—it can build the schoolhouses of the country and it can help to maintain the schools. I wish to discuss these two matters in order.

Until about a year ago I can not recall in the literature of federal aid to education any suggestion that the Federal Government should build or help to build schoolhouses, although aid for school-building purposes from the central government has long been the usual thing in Great Britain and France. Yet for years the Federal Government has been supplying generous sums of money to the states for the construction of roads. The National Industrial Recovery Act alone set aside $400,000,000 for this purpose out of a total of $3,300,000,000 for public works. Another act just passed by Congress authorizes the further appropriation of the appalling sum of $3,000,000,000 for the construction of roads during the next few years. Battleships get another huge sum and now another sum equal to that which may be spent on roads is being made available for the construction and repair of homes.

In all this staggering program where does the little red schoolhouse come in? In 1931–32 there were 245,941 of these one-room schools scattered from one end of the country to the other. While it is true that approximately $75,000,000 of the funds set aside in the National Industrial Recovery Act have been lent and granted to states and local communities for school and college buildings, the surface of the school-building program in this country has not even been scratched. Most of the money has gone to the larger communities where code wages and regulations can be observed. The rural areas as yet are both unwilling and unable to initiate public works enterprises, including schools, until there is some modification of the present situation which will enable them to take advantage of federal funds for construction purposes.

In the meantime the school-building situation languishes. Normal school construction, both additions and replacements, has all but ceased. CWA helped tremendously on school repairs, but it was of course only a temporary relief. The consolidation of small schools into modern, effective plants has all but stopped. Many of the communities which were progressive enough to take this step prior to the depression are sulkily paying interest and sinking fund on school buildings built at top prices. What are we going to do about those 245,941 one-room rural schools, a large proportion of which are a disgrace to the level of civilization which we claim to have attained?

Yet past these archaic structures suited to the civilization of a generation or two ago in which most of them were constructed, there have been built with the generous help of the Federal Government thousands of miles of hard-surfaced roads. Is a road more important than a school? Does it not raise the pertinent question as to whether we who are interested in schools should not learn the lesson learned by those interested in roads years ago. In other words, schools as well as roads should be constructed through the use of federal funds; a very small part of the sum now authorized for any of the three great construction purposes authorized by the last Congress for roads, homes or battleships would replace every one-room country schoolhouse which should be replaced with modern consolidated school plants. I for one believe that it would be entirely worth while to do so. Indeed, I can think of no action on the part of the Federal Government which would more certainly meet one of the greatest social needs of the times, namely, that of making the schools community centers suited to the educational and recreational needs of both children and adults.

I do not believe, however, that this very desirable end can be attained through the 70 per cent. loan and 30 per cent. grant provisions of the present Public Works Act. If schools are the foundation on which popular government is built the Federal Government should give school buildings at least the preferential treatment relative to grants of money which the roads have long enjoyed. Should this prove possible I am convinced that no other step which could be taken by Congress with respect to education would approach in significance a national school-building program.

On February 2 of this year Mr. Harry Hopkins at the recommendation of the Office of Education issued a release stating that it was his purpose to make available federal relief funds to employ teachers from February 1 to June 30, 1934, "in elementary and secondary schools, in communities up to 5,000 population—where the districts have made the maximum financial effort and are still obliged to close short of a normal length of school term." The pay of the teachers was not to "be higher than that stipulated for the same positions during the current year."

As soon as this order was issued the Office of Education lent several members of its slender staff and called on several of the leading men in school finance in state departments of education to help the FERA to determine the amounts of money to which the several states under Mr. Hopkins' order were entitled. It was a difficult problem which had to be met promptly, but I am happy to say that it was done successfully. As a result of this action $16,924,765 has been distributed to 33 states. Seven states each received $1,000,000 or more as follows: Alabama, $2,266,909; Georgia, $1,675,000; Oklahoma, $1,377,695; Mississippi, $1,321,876; Florida, Louisiana and Tennessee, $1,000,000 each. The smallest sums were received by Washington, $29,928, Idaho, $19,921, and Iowa, $9,514. Some of you will be interested to know that no state east of the Alleghanies and north of the Potomac River qualified for federal relief to their school teachers.

I am sure that you join me in an expression of deepest gratification that through the generosity of the Federal Government it was thus possible to keep open the schools of the country upon something like the normal basis reached during the depression in the several states. Somehow or other the Federal Government seems a bit closer to you and me as a result of this action. When to this sum is added approximately

$8,000,000 for the emergency educational program in adult education and in nursery schools together with approximately $7,000,000 for the part-time employment program of college students, and $2,500,000 for the educational program in the Civilian Conservation Corps camps, the grand total for the emergency educational program reaches the rather large sum of approximately $36,000,000. To this should be added the amounts of money distributed by the Office of Education to the several states and territories annually for the colleges of agriculture and mechanic arts, $2,550,000; vocational education, approximately $6,998,775; vocational rehabilitation, approximately $887,648; total, approximately $10,436,423. Even this figure does not include the money expended for extension education in agriculture and home economics, and the large but unestimated sum of federal money which was made available through CWA for school repairs and construction.

I wish, however, to call your attention to the fact that the $16,924,765 set aside by the Federal Government to keep the schools open was frankly intended not as federal aid to education but as relief to school districts in the states on the basis of normal school term and existing salaries. There was no attempt at equalization of any kind. If the normal school term of a Negro school was four months as against seven months for the whites, it was assumed that the states should be helped to maintain their own chosen situation. Or if the average salary of teachers in one state was $40 as against $60 in another state, the respective salary bases of the two states were used. The school districts of Iowa, for example, made themselves ineligible for further federal assistance by taking advantage of a state law, enabling them to reduce teachers' salaries to a minimum of $40 per month.

Early in the session of Congress just closed there arose an insistent demand that Congress make available through the Office of Education a direct appropriation of at least $100,000,000 to keep the schools open. The Committee on Education in the House held hearings for nearly a week, at which a great deal of evidence showing the probable needs of the schools during the year 1934–35 was presented. There was no opposition. The House Committee on Education finally reported out a bill for $75,000,000, based on the philosophy that the schools should receive temporary relief but carefully avoiding any commitment to the policy of permanent federal aid to education. Although strenuous and magnificent service was rendered by the emergency committee headed by Superintendent James H. Richmond, of Kentucky, the bill never came to a vote in either house. In effect the administration compromised through a statement made by the chairman of the Appropriations Committee in the House when he introduced the Omnibus Relief Bill which afterwards became a law. At that time the chairman of the House Appropriations Committee itemized the "Proposed application from July 1, 1934, to March 1, 1935 (8 months)." Among these items were included "Schools (subject to authorization by the President)—$48,000,000."

From this statement it is clear that no federal funds are earmarked for the schools this year. The amount which is used for the relief of school teachers will depend this year as it did last year on the action of the administration. Thus the principle of federal relief to teachers as against a possible permanent policy of federal aid to education has been maintained in the face of tremendous pressure on the part of a large proportion of the teaching profession.

Any one who believes that social and economic conditions have so changed as to make necessary or desirable regular federal aid to education can not of course be satisfied with work relief wages to school teachers on the basis of *status quo*. There is no element of equalization either for teachers or pupils in the whole business. As a matter of fact the inequalities of the depression as they affect the schools are far greater now than they were prior to the depression. Since the depression the wealthier states have reduced expenditures moderately, but Alabama has lost one half of the meager amount it had. The gap between the educational opportunities of the children in the poorer states and those in the wealthier states widens. One may well paraphrase the old parable to make it read "from the child that hath will be taken away little but from him that hath not will be taken away even that which he hath." Very few of you believe, I am convinced, that this situation can continue indefinitely. Some form of permanent federal aid to education must replace the present temporary expedient of federal relief to needy teachers.

Such a bill authorizing an appropriation of $300,000,000 during the year 1934–35 was introduced into the last Congress by Representative Deen of Georgia. The bill contained a carefully worked-out objective basis of distributing the appropriation to the states on the basis of average daily attendance of less than college grade in the public schools. The amount to be received by each state varied from $11 to $26.25 per child five to twenty years of age according to the density of farm population of the states. The states with the greatest density of farm population were to receive the smallest amount per child; those with the sparsest farm population the largest sums per capita.

Here is raised squarely the familiar question as to whether the federal agency, presumably the Office of Education, should have any kind of discretionary power under a regular system of federal aid to education. While this particular bill actually leaves some discretionary power with a small portion of the intended total appropriation of $300,000,000, it is plain that the primary intention was to arrive at an objective basis on which the federal money should be distributed to the several states and that this objective basis should be written into the law. The federal agency then automatically goes through the process of making the proper distribution.

I have no doubt that there is much to be said for this point of view. It seems to have worked well in several states, including New York, relative to the distribution of state funds to localities. Fundamentally, however, I believe that such a policy is a mistake. It goes on the assumption that the Congress is more capable of determining a technical matter of this kind than a central educational agency acting with the advice of educational experts and that such a method of distribution once adopted is good indefinitely. Our experience with the supplementary Morrill acts and the agricultural experiment station acts should teach us that the objective bases selected by Congress are likely to be a matter of logrolling in which each state receives the same amount of money, irrespective of need. Moreover, these laws as well as the Smith-Hughes and the Smith-Lever laws show clearly that once such a method of distribution is written into the law it is practically impossible to change it by subsequent legislation. I can not believe that it is wise practise to write details of this kind into the law which experience demonstrates can be changed if at all only with the greatest difficulty. I venture further the statement that if a careful examination is made of the total situation there has been far more criticism of the federal agencies for carrying out the letter of the laws than for exercising arbitrary powers where discretion was permitted. I believe, therefore, that we ought to consider this matter carefully and earnestly before we write any more meticulous regulations and objective bases of distribution into our federal laws dealing with education. In the long run I am convinced that we shall have much more federal control of education through regulations inserted in the law than from a Federal Office of Education which is clothed with discretionary power in the distribution of federal funds.

In the session just closed Congress adopted one measure of direct aid to education. I refer to the amendment to the Small Industries Bill, which authorized the R.F.C. to make loans up to a total of $75,000,000 to public-school districts for the purpose of paying teachers' salaries due prior to June 1, 1934. It is no wonder that the Chicago school teachers now have a more optimistic attitude toward life. I believe this measure will be of inestimable value to a large number of communities throughout the country.

From the amount of time which I have devoted to the problem of federal aid to education you would perhaps be justified in assuming that I think that federal aid is the most important problem of finances which is facing us. I do not hold this opinion. According to the fundamental law of the land, education is a responsibility of the several states. Now that the support of the schools through local taxation is breaking down, the first line of defense does not lie with the Federal Government but with the state legislatures. Some of them, as in Kentucky, have risen to their responsibility, but others, as in my own state of Ohio, have dawdled away months of their time uselessly and finally lacked both the courage and the vision to perform a plain duty in a crisis as real as those which confront men on the field of battle. The only difference is that in this instance innocent children are the real victims.

The real challenge to the development of education, therefore, lies back home in our several states. It is in the state legislatures where the greatest battles must be fought. They will be battles requiring the vision to effect a thorough reorganization of small school districts into larger, more effective and more economical units. They will be battles to compel the state legislature to find new forms of modern taxes which can be collected by the state and distributed to the communities on some equitable basis, thus relieving the local property tax. They will be battles requiring the active interest of laymen and professional educators alike. It is indeed a task for all of us. The situation is imminent, we must be up and at our work.

# THE WASHINGTON MEETING OF THE NATIONAL EDUCATION ASSOCIATION

By WILLIAM DOW BOUTWELL

THE seventy-second meeting of the National Education Association, which met from June 30 to July 6 in Washington, D. C., will long be remembered—

For the enervating and stifling heat and humidity which taxed the endurance and good nature of all those daring enough to come to Washington in midsummer.

For the unhappy hours spent in what must be the world's worst meeting hall, the Washington Auditorium, whose public address system failed completely at the two initial sessions.

For the silence of the White House, which sent no message to the teachers meeting three city blocks from its doorstep.

For the parliamentary tangles into which the representative assembly got itself and from which it was rescued by Miss Cornelia Adair, assisting Miss Jessie Gray.

For the adoption of the amendments to the by-laws eliminating some 150 *ex-officio* members of the representative assembly and thus making triumphant democracy in the National Education Association even more triumphant.

For the straight-from-the-shoulder address of the very recently resigned U. S. Commissioner of Education, George F. Zook, who decried the failure of the Federal Government to aid education.

For the cardboard fans carrying the picture and the platform of the winning candidate for president.

The seventy-second meeting of the National Education Association was one of the smallest in many years. Unofficial reports put registration at 4,500, or about half that of the Department of Superintendence, at Cleveland. The number of exhibits was also small. Some of the sectional and departmental meetings were well attended, for example, the sessions of the Association of Journalism Advisers, the Department of Special Education and others. In many meetings, however, the attendance was pitifully small. One speaker of national standing reported that he entered the hall to give his carefully prepared address only to find five auditors and no chairman.

Subjects of outstanding interest in this convention were federal aid to education, academic freedom, the application of the planning idea to education and the future of democracy in the United States.

The work of the National Committee for Federal Emergency Aid for Education was reviewed by its chairman, James H. Richmond, state superintendent of public instruction for Kentucky. He told of the activities in Washington in endeavoring to secure congressional and administration acceptance of the 6-point program for federal aid adopted by the advisory committee called together last fall by Commissioner Zook; how hearings had been held by the education committee of the house; how a bill carrying $75,000,000 for schools had been reported out; and how the rules committee blocked placing the bill on the calendar for vote. "What influence prevented the rules committee from letting this bill come to a vote," he said, "is still a mystery to me."

"One would be in error, however," declared Superintendent Richmond, "to conclude that we failed entirely in our efforts." Among the gains he cited first, personal assurance by the President in April and May that "he realized that an emergency faced the schools and that something should be done to aid them"; second, acceptance by Congress of the view that education needs emergency aid; and third, new realization of the importance of informing people of the needs of education.

Mr. Richmond made, at the conclusion of his address, what is probably the first public announcement of the government's program for aid to education during the coming year. This will include continuance of the emergency education program embracing vocational education, nursery schools, vocational rehabilitation and adult education. Training programs for teachers in workers' education and nursery schools are already under way. Six to 10 per cent. of the funds used will be available for supervision. Further use of emergency funds to help needy college students is probable. Emergency funds will also be used to keep schools open where closing short of the normal term is threatened, owing to financial distress.

Paying tribute to the National Education Association, Mr. Richmond said: "In the past, I confess that I have been somewhat indifferent to the virtues of the National Education Association. It was, in my mind, just another organization; but my experience in the past few months with the various members of its staff have not only convinced me of the excellent work that it is doing, but of the tremendous possibilities that now challenge this great organization."

A summary of what had been done under each of the 6 points of the advisory committee's aid program was presented by State Superintendent James N. Rule, of Pennsylvania.

Commissioner Zook, fresh from a year's service in the Federal Government, said, "The Federal Government can and should do two things—it can build the schoolhouses of the country and it can help to maintain the schools." In support of the reasonableness of federal aid to education, he pointed out: "The title to the wealth of the country which is produced by all of us working together in all parts of the country is concentrated in certain states and even in metropolitan areas of these states in a most interesting and surprising way. It seems no more than simple justice, therefore, that a way should be found by means of which wealth may be taxed where it is located and the income therefrom distributed to the states to be used for the education of the children where they are located." Turning to school building, he said: "While it is true that approximately $75,000,000 of P.W.A. funds have been lent or granted to states and local communities for school and college buildings, the surface of the school-building problem in this country has not been scratched. Most of the money has gone to the larger communities. What are we going to do about those 245,941 one-room rural schools, a large portion of which are a disgrace to the level of civilization which we claim to have attained? Past these archaic structures there have been built with the generous help of the Federal Government thousands of miles of hard-surfaced roads. Is a road more important than a school? A very small part of the sum now authorized for any of the three great construction purposes authorized by the last Congress for roads, homes or battleships would replace every one-room country school-house which should be replaced with modern consolidated school plants."

Many of the speakers voiced a dissatisfaction with the attempt to meet school needs through emergency organizations and emergency methods. Crystalizing this sentiment, former Commissioner Zook declared, "Some form of permanent federal aid to education must replace the present temporary expedient of federal relief to needy teachers."

One entire general session was devoted to the question of academic freedom, with Charles E. Beury, president of Temple University, speaking for higher education, Thomas W. Gosling, director of the Junior Red Cross, for superintendents, and Mrs. F. Blanche Preble, Chicago, for the classroom teachers. The discussions left the question still in the realm of the academic, although Dr. Gosling offered the following formula: "It is only the truth that counts and the welfare of the young who are to be taught. If the truth is known, it must be taught without fear or favor; if it is not known, as so often is the case in the challenging subjects of the current curriculum, then nothing remains for the teacher but to examine with his pupils all the facets of the problem including the teacher's own personal opinion, and to stimulate them to honest, penetrating and courageous investigation on their own initiative. . . . There are likely," he admitted, "to be some martyrs before the end is achieved."

Very practical was the resolution on academic freedom adopted by the convention. It provides a charter of liberty for teachers and objects to the "sudden singling out of teachers to take an oath of allegiance."

That this charter of freedom of speech might be put to an early test by an organization friendly, rather than unfriendly, was evident in two speeches delivered on the same day by officers of the American Legion. Edward A. Hayes, national commander, addressed an evening meeting; Russell Cook, national director of the Legion's Americanism Commission, a morning general session. "Educators who cling to patriotism of the founders of our republic," said Commander Hayes, "and who cast out the strange tenets of radical groups that are subversive to our system of government, form the backbone of future Americanism. Inversely, educators who implant subversive ideas in the minds of youth are doubly dangerous to the welfare of the country." In a somewhat similar vein Mr. Cook said: ". . . we believe the teaching of strange tenets in government has no place in the schoolroom. . . . In the last few years there has grown up a movement in which too many of our teachers are creating ideas in the schoolroom, for what is called a new social order. The American Legion is opposed to that movement. We say it is not the mission of the teacher to lead the child into believing that we should have a new social order, but that it is his mission to educate the child so that it can take its proper place in whatever social order exists when it comes to maturity. We believe the teacher's mission is to educate the child in fundamentals. . . ."

The advice of the Legion officials takes on added significance in view of the close working arrangement between the Legion and the National Education Association, set forth in Secretary J. W. Crabtree's report. More than 500 Legion posts have already received National Education Association citations for forming active education committees which "have cooperated with educational authorities of their own communities and state in devising ways and means for the maintenance and advancement of the school system during the present emergency in education." Of the Legion posts Mr. Crabtree says: "They do not dictate to the schools. They simply follow the lead of the schools in a cooperative way."

Since the idea of national planning fostered by the Administration appeals to the idealism of educators and fits in with their experience in organization for a social service, it is natural that educators should begin to think of planning in connection with education. Professor John K. Norton, of Teachers College, Columbia University, head of the Joint Commission on the Emergency in Education, presented a directory of research into educational problems by more than 150 organized groups. The commission is pointing toward educational planning on a broad scale. Mr. Carl H. Milam, secretary of the American Library Association, added his voice to this movement. "A complete system of public and school libraries which will make books and reading guidance easily available to every citizen of the United States is a necessary part of the public equipment for civilized living under the New Deal," he said. Mr. Milam advocated a national bureau, associated with the Office of Education, which would concern itself with libraries, adult education, recreation, the fine arts, music and other cultural interests.

President Glenn Frank spoke ably on a question that is buzzing in the brain of many an educator—the future of democracy. Both he and Newton D. Baker suggested their concern for the survival of democratic government under stresses and strains of modern economic conditions.

The breach between President Roosevelt and organized education was perceptibly widened in the course of the convention. The meeting was set for Washington in the hope that the President would address it. He left for his vacation while the meeting was in session. Mrs. Roosevelt was in the Tennessee Valley. "We determined to come to Washington," said Robert C. Moore, secretary of the Illinois State Teachers Association, "in the heat, thinking it probable that the President of the United States would like to address us.

We have sweated and we have sweltered, but not one single personal or official word has come from him. General Johnson, who was to have spoken for the President yesterday, was ill and left town. I believe a great national organization fighting for childhood in a time of crisis deserves the attention of the New Deal."

On the other side of the fence is the fact that this Administration has spent more than $200,000,000 for schools this year, a contribution to education greater than any from federal sources since the Northwest Territory section grants in 1787. And yet there is not a line of commendation for the Administration's contributions in the National Education Association resolutions.

Most important of the resolutions is a request for $500,000,000 from the Federal Government, to be distributed according to average daily attendance and lack of adequate tax resources. Thus, in spite of President Roosevelt's evident belief that the present system of education has definite shortcomings, organized education simply asks for money to perpetuate an Old Deal in education instead of offering a New Deal in educational organization and service. Obviously there is something to be said on both sides. Here is a splendid task awaiting educational statesmanship—to bring organized education and the Administration into harmonious cooperation.

The passage of the amendment excluding many *ex-officio* members from the representative assembly is not important. The *ex-officio's* vote was unimportant. But the passage does mark another milestone in the evolution of the National Education Association. As one leader said: "The organization must soon decide whether it will be the National Teachers Association or the National Education Association. Years ago when the teachers came in large numbers higher education pulled up stakes and left. Now the Department of Superintendence is considering separating itself. Perhaps there should be a national teachers association. But a national association of teachers can only speak for teachers; it can't speak for education in the United States."

The decline of the summer meeting and the parallel increase in significance of the winter meeting of the Department of Superintendence have created much concern among National Education Association leaders. It was a live question in the lobbies and halls. It came to the surface in a resolution calling for the creation of a committee of seven to recommend a plan of reorganization. Another question is: Who shall be selected to succeed Secretary Crabtree upon his retirement? There is every evidence that the National Education Association is approaching a crossroad, where decisions of greatest significance to its future must be made.

Henry Lester Smith, dean of education at Indiana University and long treasurer of the National Education Association, was elected president for the coming year. R. E. Offenhauer, superintendent, Lima, Ohio, and state director for Ohio, was elected treasurer.

The board of directors elected Agnes Samuelson, state superintendent of public instruction, of Iowa, to the executive committee. A. L. Whittenberg, secretary, Illinois State Examining Board for Teachers, was elected to the board of trustees. Joseph H. Saunders, superintendent, Newport News, Va., was reelected chairman of the board of trustees and Edgar C. Doudna, Madison, Wis., secretary.

Resolutions adopted were:

WELFARE OF CHILDHOOD AND YOUTH

1. The National Education Association endorses the rapidly growing practise of stressing in the classroom through units of subject-matter and through projects the cultural heritages of the various national, ethnic and racial groups.

2. In order that every child, no matter what his economic status, shall fully enjoy the right of a free education from nursery school through the university, the educational profession should ac-

tively work for the passage of the child labor amendment by states.

3. The moving picture is one of the most important means of education to-day. The National Education Association joins other organizations, educational, patriotic and religious, in demanding a high type of moving picture for the boys and girls of America. The Association hereby records itself as wholly in sympathy with the current movement to bring about reform in the moving picture industry and to encourage clean, moral films. Particularly does the Association condemn the showing of stories or scenes which threaten the integrity of the American home, ridicule sacred institutions, glorify lawlessness, and make juvenile delinquency a subject of jest or an incitement to imitation. The practise of block booking of pictures to exhibitors whereby worthy pictures and objectionable ones must be taken in lots is recognized as largely responsible for the unsavory character of contemporary moving picture programs and is condemned without reserve.

4. The National Education Association urges complete and scientific instruction in the schools regarding the effects of alcohol and narcotics on the human body and the social organization, and expresses its disapproval of any false advertising or propaganda on this subject.

5. The National Education Association endorses the plan of the United States Office of Education for the creation of a Continuing Commission on Youth Problems.

The Association recommends the expansion of the educational program of the Civilian Conservation Corps, with the purpose of equipping the boys for regular occupation after discharge.

### TEACHER WELFARE

1. The financial difficulties of the schools have been accompanied by increasing discrimination against and unjust discharge of teachers. The need for tenure has never been more imperative. The Division of Research of the National Education Association is strongly urged to assist the tenure committee in its investigations and it is recommended that sufficient space in the *Journal* be allotted from time to time adequately to present the cause of tenure. It is further urged that the Committee on Tenure make a report to each annual session of the Representative Assembly. The Board of Directors of the Association is instructed to provide from current funds the sum of ten thousand dollars to be used, or as much thereof as may be necessary, for the purpose of the tenure committee.

2. The National Education Association unalterably opposes further retrenchment in services and activities in the schools and the reduction of salaries. It is convinced that the time has come for vigorous effort to restore both services and salaries to normal levels.

### SOCIAL LEGISLATION

1. Recognizing that proper housing conditions are essential in leading children through education into the fruition of ethical character and good citizenship, the National Education Association endorses the social policies of slum clearance and of providing sanitary, attractive and comfortable homes within their means for the underprivileged classes.

2. The National Education Association endorses the principle of unemployment insurance for all workers, including teachers. It also endorses the payment by the state of pensions to widowed mothers who need such aid.

### SCHOOL SUPPORT AND ADMINISTRATION

1. Since the annual income of the nation's schools has been reduced more than five hundred million dollars, the National Education Association pledges itself to make every effort to have introduced in the next session of Congress and to secure passage of a bill providing a direct grant of not less than five hundred million dollars to be distributed to all public school districts, according to average daily attendance and lack of adequate tax resources, to reestablish education at the 1930 level. It is understood that this grant shall not entail any federal control of schools.

2. The National Education Association reaffirms its stand that the major part of local education costs should be borne by the state.

3. The National Education Association strongly advocates the enactment of scientific tax laws in all states, to the end that all forms of wealth shall bear their just shares of the costs of education and government. Pending the release of real estate from the disproportionate tax burden which it now bears, the National Education Association urges educators and lay friends of the schools to engage in the important task of securing equitable assessing.

4. The National Education Association unqualifiedly endorses the principle that all school affairs, including budgets and the appointment of teachers and officials, should be under the management of school authorities without interference from political or other special groups.

5. The National Education Association urges its members to be active in informing the public of the purpose and work of the schools, of the facts in regard to school costs, and of the effects of proposed changes. The following avenues of disseminating information are suggested: addressing meetings of organizations, utilizing the opportunities afforded by the press and the radio, and in-

ducing parents and other citizens to visit school classes and exhibits.

PREVENTION OF WAR

War is the greatest menace to civilization. As an important step toward the elimination of war, legislation should be passed by the United States Congress prohibiting profits on the manufacturing and sale of munitions and other war equipment. Children should be taught the truth about war and its costs in human life and ideals and in material wealth. The *Journal* of the National Education Association should carry frequent articles concerning war, its costs and its consequences.

NATIONAL EDUCATION ASSOCIATION ADMINISTRATION

1. The National Education Association has been carried on for years under a cumbersome plan of organization. It is generally believed that there are too many boards, committees, trustees and directors, whose duties overlap. A committee of seven, at least three of whom shall be classroom teachers, shall be appointed to recommend to the meeting of the Representative Assembly in 1935 a plan of reorganization under the present charter and to consider the need of changes in the charter. The Representative Assembly recommends that an adequate appropriation be made for this committee.

2. Beginning with the 1935 convention, provision shall be made for registration of members and delegates each day of the convention.

3. The National Education Association endorses the plan of having one day of special emphasis on rural education in American Education Week, beginning with 1934.

APPRECIATION

The National Education Association acknowledges the many courtesies and the hospitality of the District of Columbia. It extends special thanks to Superintendent Ballou, the educational staff of the District, the teachers and pupils, the Boy Scouts of America, the High-School Cadets, the Army, the Marine and the Navy Bands, the press, the National Broadcasting Company and the Columbia Broadcasting System, the headquarters staff of the National Education Association, and others who have cooperated in making successful the seventy-second annual convention of the National Education Association.

MYRTLE HOOPER DAHL, *Chairman*
AMY H. HINRICHS, *Secretary*

The following statement on academic freedom was submitted and adopted with the idea that it would become a permanent plank in the National Education Association platform:

Teachers are under the obligation to present all points of view on controversial issues, and therefore should have the right to express their own opinions on such issues without danger of reprisal by the school administration or by pressure groups in the community.

The teacher should also be guaranteed the constitutional rights of freedom of speech, press and assembly and the right to support actively organized movements which they consider to be in their own and the public interest. The teacher's conduct outside the school should be subject to no external controls to which other citizens are not subjected.

The sudden singling out of teachers to take an oath of allegiance is a means of intimidation of teachers which can be used to destroy the right of academic freedom.

The following amendments to the by-laws were adopted:

Amend Article I by adding Section 11. The Representative Assembly shall be composed of the President, the twelve Vice-Presidents, the Secretary and the Treasurer of the National Education Association, the United States Commissioner of Education and the Delegates elected from the various affiliated State and Local Associations, as provided by By-Law.

Amend Article II, Section 9, to read—The President, the twelve Vice-Presidents, the Secretary and the Treasurer of the National Education Association, and the United States Commissioner of Education shall be ex-officio Delegates to the Representative Assembly.

# EDUCATIONAL EVENTS

## EDUCATIONAL BUDGET OF THE LONDON COUNTY COUNCIL

THE London County Council met early in May to decide on the education estimates for 1934–35. On capital account £160,000 was voted and on maintenance £10,820,035. These estimates were formulated by the Municipal Reform Party when in power, and the present Labor majority in submitting them made it clear that they would bring up supplementary estimates as their policy developed.

According to a summary given in the London *Times,* the £11,000,000 voted is not the total cost of education in London. Sums expended by other committees bring the total to £12,651,957. Of this £7,860,017 falls on the ratepayers. The percentage of the total borne by the rates is now 62.1, against 61.7 in 1933–34. In 1930–31, the last full year in which the Board of Education paid 50 per cent. of approved net elementary education, the rates bore 51 per cent. and the Exchequer 45 per cent. For the coming year the Exchequer will only bear 33.8 per cent. compared with 34 per cent. in 1933–34.

The Finance Committee reports with reference to the capital expenditure of £160,000 that in addition provisional sums of £60,000 in respect of expenditure under the Education Acts and £20,000 under the Children and Young Persons Act, 1933, are included in the estimates, making the total provision £240,000.

Mrs. Lowe (chairman of the Education Committee), in submitting the estimates, said that the Labor majority was not responsible for them. They were the estimates of the Opposition when in power. The Labor majority would shortly bring forward proposals, particularly in regard to capital expenditure, which the Education Committee was about to discuss.

Sir John Gilbert said he understood that the present majority intended to bring up supplementary estimates as opportunities arose. When those estimates were brought forward the Municipal Reform Party would deal with them on their merits. If such proposals were considered either unnecessary or wasteful the Reform Party would oppose them. He believed that the estimates submitted were effective, dealt adequately with London's needs, and enabled the council to maintain its proud position at the head of the education authorities of the country. On elementary education, excluding special schools, it was proposed to spend £8,151,163; on special schools £875,663, and on residential schools chargeable to public assistance £615,540. On all forms of higher education no less than £3,004,591 was to be spent. He pointed out that in considering those figures it should be remembered that there had been a great drop in the child population in the schools which made the average cost per scholar much larger. In 1914–1915 the average roll was 727,052 children. For the current year 1934–35 it was estimated that the average roll would only be 546,000 children, a drop of 181,000 since the beginning of the War. Last year it was estimated that the average roll would be 570,000, so that even since last year it was estimated that there would be a drop of no fewer than 24,000 children in the roll of the schools. Gross peak expenditure was in 1921–22, when it reached £15,525,354. This year the gross expenditure would be £12,651,957. If the £700,000 10 per cent. cut on teachers' salaries was added, to make the comparison exact, expenditure could be put at 13½ millions, against 15½ millions in the peak year.

Rate expenditure for 1921–22 worked out at £7,641,182, while for the current year it was actually more at £7,860,017. Average expenditure per child was £7 18s. in 1921–22 compared with no less than £10 4s. per child in the current year. The council had 87 central schools with accommodation for 32,000 children.

Mr. Charles Robertson, vice-chairman of the Education Committee, said he was not proud of the estimates. On capital account nearly a million was spent in 1927–28. The estimates were now down to £96,000. The elementary school children of London were not getting their due share. The child population was decreasing and the child becoming more valuable. It was their bounden duty to provide adequate schools for the youth of London.

Mr. Latham, chairman of the Finance Committee, said that it had not been possible to revise the estimates, and Labor was not enthusiastic about them.

## AN INTERNATIONAL SCHOOL FOR REFUGEES IN HOLLAND

A SPECIAL correspondent of *The Christian Science Monitor* writes from London: "In the autumn of last year the Society of Friends in London formed a committee to deal with the German refugee problem, and one important aspect of this problem, the subject of education, soon occupied their attention. A number of teachers were among the refugees, and children who had left Germany with their parents. It was decided to try to provide work for a small proportion of the refugee teachers by opening a school in a country where the authorities would be sympathetically inclined and where the children would not be too far away from their own country. After eliminating Denmark and Switzerland as geographically unsuitable, it was decided to look for a suitable house in Holland. The Dutch authorities proved to be extremely helpful and so Dutch Friends approached Baron van Pallandt, who offered to rent his property, Castle Eerde, at a reduced rate. Funds were raised and an international board was formed comprising Quakers from England, Holland and Germany, an inspector of education from Amsterdam and a famous Dutch psychologist. As a result of this prompt and energetic action a new coeducational boarding school was opened at Castle Eerde, near Ommen, in April.

"Castle Eerde is a stately eighteenth century house near the German frontier. It is a particularly fine example of Baroque architecture surrounded by a moat. The Baron has made the grounds into a bird sanctuary. The classrooms are in converted stabling and open out upon the gardens and playing fields. In this quiet and beautiful place fresh hope is being awakened in the refugees who, through no fault of their own, have suffered deeply.

"The school has already demonstrated its international nature by accepting Dutch and French pupils, one stateless child and Dutch and English teachers, in addition to the refugees themselves. It is hoped that this international feature will continue to be one of the school's important aspects. More Dutch children are expected to enter as soon as certain regulations demanding the employment of a qualified Dutch teacher have been complied with. In the meantime lessons in the Dutch language are given daily, teachers and children attending the class together.

"As there are few boarding schools in Holland this venture is regarded as an interesting experiment. An innovation as uncommon in most European countries as in Holland, is the appointment of a woman as head. The eldest pupil is a boy of seventeen, but the board find their confidence well placed and feel the head is proving to be highly suitable."

## REPORT ON MOTION PICTURES OF THE OFFICE OF EDUCATION

A REPORT on motion pictures prepared by Dr. Cline M. Koon, specialist in radio and visual education of the Office of Education, with the assistance of a committee of leaders in the field called together by United States Commissioner of Education George F. Zook, has been issued. It is one of the more than forty reports on motion pictures in education presented by various nations at the meeting of the International Congress of Educational and Instructional Cinematography held in Rome.

Following are significant facts given in the report:

> It is estimated that 70,000,000 persons attend motion picture performances every week in the United States.
>
> On an average, each child in areas where motion pictures are physically available goes to the movies once a week.
>
> Three out of four of the pictures that are shown relate to sex, crime or romantic love.
>
> The child retains two thirds as much as the adult from his attendance at the movies.
>
> Motion pictures change children's attitudes and these changes have a lasting influence.
>
> Motion picture appreciation courses in high schools offer a new and promising method for building better standards of judgment of films on the part of children.
>
> The Department of Commerce reports that 190,000 non-theatrical motion picture projectors are in use, including home sets.
>
> Thirty-two states have film libraries.

At the present time, most of the non-theatrical projectors in school auditoriums and public halls are 35 millimeter silent projectors. The steady growth in the use of 16 mm films in classrooms is reflected in the reports from six cities showing an increase in showings from 101,170 in 1931–32, to 148,943 in 1932–33, an increase of more than 47 per cent.

Motion pictures increase the effectiveness of instruction. Pupils studying with one group of historical films learned 19 per cent. more than those who did not, and learned more quickly; remembered 12 per cent. better; and outside of their classroom work, voluntarily read 40 per cent. more supplementary material in American history. But it is estimated that less than 10 per cent. of all public schools are making systematic use of motion pictures in classroom instruction.

In conclusion the report states that:

> In comparison with the theatrical motion picture, the non-theatrical picture in the past usually lacked technical excellence, was used comparatively little, and with varying regularity. Many agencies have pioneered in the development of the educational

film, but the result in the United States to-day is chaotic and disorganized. The principal reasons for this condition seem to be the past policy of the Federal Government to leave to private industry and voluntary endeavor many activities that the typical European government would assume, and the educational system of the country which is not centralized in the Federal Government, but, in main, is left to each of the forty-eight states. Private industry is deadlocked over the fact that producers can not afford to make films until a sufficient number of projectors is sold to make the work profitable, and the projector concerns can not sell their apparatus because there is no comprehensive library of suitable films available for their use.

Commendable efforts are being made in many places to overcome these difficulties, according to the report, but there is a great need for a national films institute to assemble, edit, classify, publicize and catalogue non-theatrical film material, and to set up a convenient and economical distribution system, and to produce and stimulate the production and effective utilization of educational films.

## ORIGIN OF THE STUDENTS OF COLUMBIA UNIVERSITY

Enrolling students from ninety-five foreign countries, Columbia University since 1910 has developed steadily as a world center of education, as shown in a survey made by Dr. Frank D. Fackenthal, secretary of the university. During the period 346,427 men and women, of whom 9,425 were from other lands, have studied at Columbia. Every state in the Union as well as Alaska, the Hawaiian and Philippine Islands, Porto Rico, the Canal Zone and the Virgin Islands are represented.

Canada, China and Japan lead foreign countries in the number of their residents who have attended Columbia. Canada accounts for 2,213; China, 2,062, and Japan, 1,220. Cuba, Germany and Great Britain are next on the list, followed by France, Mexico, South America, Norway, Switzerland, Nova Scotia, India and Korea.

Nearly 50 per cent. of the 923 United States territory students were residents of Porto Rico. The Philippine Islands are a close second with 328, followed by the Hawaiian Islands, Alaska and the Virgin Islands.

The metropolitan area has supplied the majority of students for the past thirty-four years. Greater New York residents numbered 123,084 in the period from 1910 to 1934, with 47,656 from other parts of New York State. New Jersey sent 36,544. Pennsylvania ranks fourth with 16,349; Ohio, with 10,511, and Connecticut with 10,272, are fifth and sixth.

Massachusetts, Michigan, Virginia, North Carolina and Texas are listed next, followed by Illinois, Indiana, Georgia, Missouri, California and Maryland. Maine and Minnesota sent almost the same number of students, as did Iowa and South Carolina. Nevada ranks last, with fifty-one students.

## THE SCHOOL OF ARTS AND SCIENCES AT NORTHEASTERN UNIVERSITY

The Board of Trustees of Northeastern University proposes to establish a School of Arts and Sciences in the day division, the first class to be admitted in the fall of 1935–36. The course of study will be arranged on the cooperative plan and will normally require five years to complete. After a freshman year consisting of thirty-five consecutive weeks of study, students in the new school will alternate on the cooperative plan during the remaining four years on the same program now working successfully in the Schools of Business Administration and Engineering. The degree of bachelor of science, with specification in the field in which the student has concentrated his work, will be awarded upon the completion of not less than 144 term hours of study, one term hour comprising fifteen hours of class work with the necessary outside preparation. Candidates for the first freshman class must have completed an accredited high school program of four years.

The new School of Arts and Sciences is to be not merely another college of liberal arts, but a new project intended to fill a distinct educational need. In addition to providing a broad background of liberal subjects, it will aim also at developing in its students a vocational competence so that at graduation they may be fitted to do some specific kind of useful work.

During the upper four years students alternating between the university and industrial plants will have an opportunity of experiencing various fields of business and of learning how to adjust themselves to the industrial world. Incidentally, this makes it possible for upperclassmen to earn a substantial part of their college expenses.

## FELLOWSHIPS OF THE WISCONSIN ALUMNI RESEARCH FOUNDATION

Establishment of a limited number of special fellowships in the natural sciences, for young men of "very exceptional talent and originality," has been made possible at the University of Wisconsin for the coming year by a grant of $10,000 from the Wisconsin Alumni Research Foundation. The grant is in addition to a grant of $139,321 given to the university to aid its research program during the coming year. This represents an increase of about $17,000 over the amount appropriated by the foundation last year.

According to Professor Charles S. Slichter, retiring dean of the Graduate School, stipends for the special fellowships will vary, but will be above the average. In selecting the candidates, who should not be over twenty-five years of age, emphasis will be placed on unusual scholarship, exceptional personality and originality. In order to find suitable candidates, who will be appointed at any time during next year, a thorough search is now being made throughout the country.

Ordinarily each year the foundation has used income from the invested capital in supporting university research. But during emergency which obtained last year and still continues, the trustees of the foundation have decided that they could render no more useful public service than to add to the customary support they give the university a material sum from the anticipated income of the coming year to help to meet the critical financial condition confronting its research program.

With the aid from the foundation continued for the coming year, the university will be able to carry on its plan, started last year, of master-apprentice graduate instruction. This plan permits graduate students to work as apprentices in the laboratory with mature scholars directing major research projects.

## IN HONOR OF GUSTAVE STRAUBENMULLER

The Board of Superintendents of New York City recently passed a resolution in appreciation of services to the city schools of the late Gustave Straubenmuller.

Dr. Straubenmuller died on May 13. He retired three years ago after having spent fifty years in the educational system as teacher, assistant superintendent, district superintendent and associate superintendent. From 1916 to 1918 he was acting superintendent of schools.

In the tribute, the Board of Superintendents said:

Almost every important progressive movement that has come to fruition in our public school system within the past two decades has been influenced by the vision of this fine schoolmaster.

He played a large part in improving methods of teaching geography and foreign languages and in the development of nature study, school gardens, visual instruction, school libraries, vocational schools, including particularly the Textile High School, continuation schools, junior high schools, classes for physically and mentally handicapped children, and training schools and colleges for teachers.

He was foremost in movements to enrich culturally the lives of our children by enlisting the cooperation with the public schools of museums of art and of natural history, botanical gardens and other such institutions, so that their treasures might be made available to our pupils. He proposed the establishment of a high school for gifted students, to be known as an arts and crafts school.

The crowning glory of Dr. Straubenmuller's notable work as an educator was his service for the five years prior to his retirement as chairman of the committee on revision of the courses of study in elementary and junior high schools. This extensive project, which involved the making and the progressive improvement of courses of study, will be an enduring monument.

Dr. Straubenmuller was a deep student of educational and related problems, and through his knowledge of foreign languages was able to bring to his work and to the deliberations of this board the best thoughts of other countries, as well as our own. To the last he kept alive the inquiring and open-minded spirit of the student and the scholar. Through his willingness to try new ideas and plans he combined in his work the best of the conservative and the progressive. He was always professionally minded. In spite of obstacles, he continued to maintain high ideals of service and achievement. He believed that education should have a strong ethical purpose.

By his untiring personal endeavor, his lovable traits of character, his deep and accurate scholarship, his broad and diversified interests and his unimpeachable professional integrity, he enhanced the prestige of the board on which he served for nearly twenty-five years, and elevated to a high plane the cause of free public education.

His counsel and leadership will be sadly missed, but his memory and influence will long remain.

# EDUCATIONAL NOTES AND NEWS

DR. HENRY LESTER SMITH, professor of school administration and dean of the School of Education at Indiana University, was elected president of The National Education Association at the recent meeting in Washington, D. C.

DR. ALBERT BUSHNELL HART, professor of government, emeritus, at Harvard University, celebrated his eightieth birthday on July 1.

DR. JOHN C. HESSLER, professor of chemistry at Knox College and formerly dean and acting president of James Millikin University, has been appointed president of the university to fill the vacancy created by the resignation of Dr. J. H. White. Dr. White's resignation became effective on June 19 and Dr. Hessler assumed the office on July 1.

FREDERICK WOLFF OGILVIE, professor of political economy at the University of Edinburgh, has been appointed president and vice-chancellor of the University of Belfast.

ON the occasion of his retirement as principal of Stuyvesant High School, New York City, Dr. Ernest R. von Nardroff was recently the guest of honor at a testimonial luncheon given by former and present members of the faculty. Dr. Frederick H. Law, chairman of the English department, presented to Dr. von Nardroff a scroll decorated and engraved in gold and black by Dr. Max Rabus. Another gift was a wrist watch. Dr. von Nardroff has been principal of the school for twenty-six years.

AT the seventy-fifth anniversary of Lake Erie College the degree of doctor of laws was conferred on Dr. Robert Sessions Woodworth, professor of psychology at Columbia University, son of Lydia Ames Sessions, the first president of Lake Erie College.

AMONG honorary degrees awarded by Knox College was the doctorate of laws conferred on Miss Jane Addams. Dr. John Huston Finley, editor of *The New York Times,* member of the Knox class of 1887, once president of Knox College, delivered the commencement address.

DR. WALDEMAR WESTERGAARD, professor of history at the University of California at Los Angeles, has been appointed a corresponding honorary member of the Institut Historique et Heraldique de France.

DR. FRANKLYN B. SNYDER, who has been since 1918 professor of English at Northwestern University, has been elected a fellow of the Society of Antiquaries of Scotland, in recognition of his "Life of Robert Burns."

DR. CHARLES GROVE HAINES, of the University of California at Los Angeles, has been elected a member of the Institut International de Philosophie du Droit et de Sociologie Juridique, for meritorious work in legal philosophy and sociological or realistic jurisprudence.

PROFESSOR PAUL D. MUESCHKE, of the department of English at the University of Michigan, is the recipient of the Henry Russel Award for 1934. Professor Mueschke has been on the faculty since 1922.

MISS EFFIE ISABEL RAITT, for twenty-two years director of home economics at the University of Washington, was elected president at the twenty-seventh annual session in New York City of the American Home Economics Association in succession to Dr. Frances Zuill. Miss Mabel V. Campbell, of the University of Missouri, was elected vice-president.

DR. CHARLES H. KEENE, of the University of Buffalo, was elected president of the American Association of School Physicians at the annual business meeting held in Buffalo on June 27. Dr. John Sundwall, of the University of Michigan; Dr. James F. Rogers, of the Department of the Interior; Dr. Charles C. Wilson, of Evansville, Indiana, and Dr. Haven Emerson, of New York City, were named vice-presidents. Dr. William A. Howe, chief of the medical inspection bureau of the New York State Department of Education, was elected secretary-treasurer.

CHARLES H. COMPTON, assistant librarian of the St. Louis Public Library, was elected president of the American Library Association at the final meeting of the conference in Montreal. Other new officers of the association are Mildred H. Pope, State Library, Olympia, Wash., first vice-president; James T. Gerould, Princeton University, Princeton, N. J., second vice-president; Mathew S. Dudgeon, Public Library, Milwaukee, treasurer, and Eugene M. Stevens, Federal Reserve Bank, Chicago, trustee of endowment funds. Members elected to the executive board were Carl L. Cannon, Yale University Library, New Haven; Louise Prouty, Public Library, Cleveland, and Ida F. Wright, Public Library, Evanston, Ill.

PROFESSOR LEON J. RICHARDSON, director of university extension, was recently appointed dean of the summer session of the University of California. He succeeds the late Dr. Harold D. Bruce. Professor Richardson was dean of the summer session in 1902, 1903 and 1904, and was acting dean in 1905 and 1913.

DR. CHARLES L. ANSPACH, head of the department of education and psychology at the Michigan State Normal College, Ypsilanti, has been appointed dean. Professor H. Z. Wilber, director of extension, has been appointed director of the summer session and Dr. H. L. Turner, director of rural education, has been appointed director of the laboratory schools.

RAYMOND B. ALLEN, associate director of the New York Post-Graduate Medical School, became associate dean of the Columbia School of Medicine on July 1.

AMONG the visiting professors at the summer sessions at the University of Chicago are Joseph G. de R. Hamilton, Kenan professor of history at the University of North Carolina; James H. Hanford, specialist in English literature at Western Reserve University, who will be the Frederic Ives Carpenter visiting professor of English; William S. Cooper, professor of botany at the University of Minnesota; W. H. Greaves, professor of public speaking at Yale University; William G. Hale, dean of the University of Southern California Law School; Roscoe T. Steffen, professor of law at Yale University; Edson R. Sunderland, professor of law at the University of Michigan, and William C. Van Vleck, dean of the Law School at the George Washington University.

DR. LEOPOLD VON WIESE, director of the Research Institute in Social Science at Cologne, Germany, formerly secretary and a founder of the German Sociological Society, president of the International Institute of Sociology, founder and editor of *Kölner Vierteljahrshefte für Sozialwissenschaften,* has been appointed lecturer on sociology at Harvard University for the second half of 1934–35.

PROFESSOR M. E. HAGGERTY, dean of the School of Education of the University of Minnesota, is giving courses on higher education at Teachers College, Columbia University, during the summer session.

GEORGE R. CRESSMAN, assistant superintendent of Chester County, Pa., schools, has been elected supervising principal of Doylestown schools. He succeeds Carmon Ross, who was recently elected president of the State Teachers College at Edinboro.

LAURENCE W. LANGE, of the New York Telephone Company, has been appointed director of student personnel and admissions at the New York University College of Arts and Pure Science and College of Engineering. The council of the university recently passed a resolution of appreciation to Mr. Lange's predecessor, Theodore A. Distler, Jr., who resigned to become dean of Lafayette College at Easton, Pa.

DR. PAUL R. SPENCER, superintendent of schools at Peekskill, N. Y., has been appointed principal of the Trenton, N. J., Senior High School.

DENTON M. ALBRIGHT, of Rochester, Pa., assumed the duties of superintendent of schools in Lewistown on July 2. Mr. Albright has been superintendent of schools in Rochester for the past eight years.

DR. FORREST R. BLACK, professor of law at the University of Kentucky, has been granted leave of absence for next year. He will go to Washington to become chief attorney of the Agricultural Adjustment Administration. Dr. Black will act as assistant to Jerome Frank, general counsel, and as a member of the board of strategy will seek to formulate a constitutional theory to justify the validity of the Agricultural Adjustment Administration when it reaches the higher courts.

DR. CARROLL D. CHAMPLIN, professor of education at the Pennsylvania State College, has been granted sabbatical leave for the first semester of next year to study the methods of teacher training used in central Europe. He will also spend several weeks in Italy, Greece and the Holy Land.

DR. HEINRICH JORDAN is offering a course in

"Recent Developments in the Philosophy of the State" at the summer session of New York University. The course, which will continue for six weeks, was made possible by a grant from the Carl Schurz Memorial Foundation. Dr. Jordan was formerly in the German diplomatic and consular service and for more than three years he was vice-consul with the German Consulate General in New York. In this capacity he was charged with fostering intellectual cooperation between his homeland and the United States. Previously he had been secretary to the German Legations in Bogota and Stockholm and an attaché to the German Consulate in Lithuania.

HELEN PURCELL, chief of kindergarten and elementary instruction in the Pennsylvania State Department of Public Instruction, died on July 1.

HOLMES COWPER, head of the College of Arts and Sciences and professor of singing at Drake University, died on July 2 at the age of sixty-four years. Professor Cowper had been at Drake since 1909.

A CONFERENCE ON HIGHER EDUCATION was held at the University of Oregon on July 11, 12, 13 and 14. Among the speakers were Frederick M. Davenport, congressman from New York; Dr. F. J. Kelly, chief of the division of higher education, Washington, D. C.; Dr. James W. Angell, professor of economics at Columbia University, New York, and an international authority on finance; Dr. George W. Frasier, president of Colorado State Teachers' College, and Dr. F. L. Hovde, assistant director of the famous General College of the University of Minnesota. Four main topics were taken up: "Responsibility of Higher Education to Students"; "Responsibility of Higher Education to Commonwealth"; "Responsibility of Higher Education in Adult Education," and "Responsibility of Higher Education for Social Planning." Open forums were held each afternoon in all sections, and a general summary was presented on the last day.

THE first annual meeting of the Southern Intercollegiate Mathematics Association, which was organized at Shreveport, Louisiana, last fall at the instigation of Dr. I. Maizlish, of Centenary College, was held at Louisiana State Normal College, Natchitoches, on May 5, with Dr. Maizlish presiding. Its purpose is to stimulate an interest in mathematics in colleges and universities by holding annual competitions in algebra, trigonometry, analytic geometry and calculus. Winners of this year's preliminary contests were: Millsaps College, Jackson, Miss.; Simmons University, Abilene, Texas; the University of Arkansas and Louisiana State University. The winner of the final contest, held at Natchitoches, was the Louisiana State University. The award was a silver cup which will become the permanent possession of the school first winning it three times. The second annual meeting will be held next year in the early part of May, in Shreveport, La.

THE thirteenth summer educational exhibit at Columbia University will open on July 16 with a display of 50,000 books, in addition to visual education materials and classroom equipment. The exhibit, twice as large as last year, is expected to attract teachers, principals and school superintendents from all parts of the United States. It will be held in the main gymnasium of the university and will continue for three weeks. Ten university presses will be among the exhibitors showing the most advanced books for elementary, high-school and college use. Teaching by means of still and moving pictures, drawings and colored slides will be illustrated. The organization of special work, such as making a classroom newspaper, will be described.

THE *American Library Journal* reports that a gift for the extension of the Williston Memorial Library has been voted to Mount Holyoke College by the General Education Board. The sum, not to exceed $375,000, represents about seventy per cent. of the estimated cost of the enlargement and reconstruction of the library and is donated on condition that the college furnish the remaining money needed, and that the total cost of the reconstruction be limited to $555,000. The program provides for the retention of the entire present building and the erection of a tower 36 feet square at the end of the present stack wing, opposite the tower of Clapp Laboratory. This will contain the main entrance on the ground floor and the stair hall. Flanking the tower on each side will be a wing extending north and south forty feet beyond the line of the present building. The addition will be in collegiate Gothic style, of brown sandstone from local quarries, to harmonize with the architecture of the present library.

The John Simon Guggenheim Foundation recently announced the award of five scholarships to Latin-American scholars. The scholarships were endowed by Mr. and Mrs. Simon Guggenheim as a part of the foundation which was set up in memory of their son, John Simon Guggenheim. The winners are: Dr. Atilia M. Varras, chief of the Sanitary Inspection Service of the northern zone of Chile, who will study in the fields of preventive medicine and public health. Alfredo B. Vasquez, professor at the National University of Mexico, who will study Mayan linguistics and translation of the Maya Codex. Dr. Alfonso Dampf, chief of the entomological laboratory of the Mexican Ministry of Agriculture, who will study various phases of the effects and habits of black flies. Dr. Luis H. H. Rivero, of the University of Havana, who will pursue taxonomical and biological studies of West Indian fishes. Dr. Ramon E. Gaviola, of the University of Buenos Aires, who will pursue studies in the field of physical chemistry. The scholarships, awarded without regard to race, color or creed, carry a value of $2,000, plus travel expenses.

According to the *Lincoln State Journal*, Nebraska, Judge Munday, of Red Cloud, member of the State Normal Board, offered a resolution at the board meeting which largely takes the selection of faculty members out of the hands of the presidents of the four state normal schools. The new plan was adopted. In the past presidents have been in the habit of recommending one person for vacancies and usually the board acts only on the one recommendation. Under the new rule there is to be more latitude for applicants and more for the board in making selections. Presidents of normal schools are required under the new rule, whenever there is a vacancy in the head of a department or teaching position, to notify the state superintendent, the State University Registration Bureau and other registration bureaus. Ten days before a board meeting presidents of normal schools are to submit to the board a summary of the qualifications of all applicants and his first, second and third choice. This, however, does not bind the board to the election of any one of the three candidates recommended by the president. According to the *State Journal*, as a result of this rule the board, meeting at the capitol, elected no heads of departments or teachers for permanent positions which were submitted by presidents, but did elect some temporary faculty members.

The Cornell Cosmopolitan Club lists, in the recent report of the retiring president, Donald C. Martin, a number of activities which have promoted international good-will throughout the university and in Ithaca. For thirty years the club, with its slogan, "Above all nations is humanity," has administered to the needs of foreign students. Cornell is the home of one of the ten largest groups of foreign students in America. In a recent study of the distribution of alumni, made at Harvard, Cornell led Yale, Harvard, Princeton and Columbia in the number of alumni in foreign lands. Students attending Cornell this year number 130 and represent 36 countries and all the continents. John L. Mott, son of John R. Mott, is assistant to the dean of the university faculty and in charge of the foreign students. He is also secretary of the International Association. This year he directed a group of fourteen Turkish students sent to the United States by the Government to study the English language and American methods of education. Groups planning to visit Cornell include nearly 400 Italian students sent by Premier Mussolini and a number of students from Japan.

# DISCUSSION

## RETIRING ALLOWANCES FOR TEACHERS IN STATE UNIVERSITIES

What shall we do with our professors who get old? They may try to remain young, but that is an impossibility. It may be possible to be quite efficient, although getting old. Maybe, in some cases, there is a lack of real efficiency even in younger years. Over the country in general we have poorhouses for those who are in need and who are unable to make a living. The elderly professor may have reached the age at which he is mentally or physically unable to make a living, but he does not want to go to the poorhouse, and we do not want to send him there.

Unfortunately it is true in many cases that the professor is paid a very meager salary during his working years, and when he becomes old he is just turned out to get along as best he can. He was unable to save enough money from his small salary to care for his old age, and so he must depend on relatives or go to the poorhouse. Of course he can end it all by dying.

The giving of retiring allowances or pensions to professors who have been connected with educational institutions for a number of years, and who have reached a retiring age, is a subject which is attracting considerable attention at the present time. The United States Government, a number of years ago, arranged plans for caring for the old age of those who have given years of service in governmental positions. Most of the religious denominations take care of their ministers when they have reached a retiring age. Many large industrial organizations have systems of retiring pensions for their employees.

Some years ago the Carnegie Foundation started a movement to take care of educators of advanced age. They first tried outright pensions in certain limited classes of institutions, and they hoped the idea would grow and be used by other classes of institutions. The expense became too heavy and the plan was changed. They organized an Annuity Association, and this organization adopted the plan of having teachers contribute a small percentage of their salaries each year, which contribution was to be matched by the institution, or others, and then a retiring allowance would come to the professor when he reached the retiring age. Some institutions have taken the place of the Annuity Association and handle the plan themselves. In these cases the teachers contribute a certain amount from their salaries annually, and the institution either contributes a like amount or guarantees the retiring allowance. In at least one case an outside organization assumed the payment of the annuity on condition that the professor would contribute so much of his salary for a definite period of years or longer.

The writer has made an attempt to find the present status of retiring allowances in the forty-three state universities of the country. Letters of inquiry were sent to each institution and replies were finally obtained from all the institutions. The facts were tabulated, and copies of the tabulation were sent to all the institutions for any possible corrections. It is believed that the tabulations given below are entirely correct, but as there are so many modifications of methods and so many different plans in use it is possible that some errors may be found. Some institution may have a very exact and well-worked-out system, but it may differ from an exact system, somewhat similar to it, used in another institution. Some have no system but give allowances of some sort or other. Some have two or three plans working in the same institution. Some give part-time work with full-time pay or part-time pay; some give part-time pay with optional work or with no work involved. It is therefore difficult to prevent overlapping in the tabulation of the plans in use.

The following are summaries of the information secured. The separate items under the different heads are all put under one consecutive set of numbers for convenience in referring to them.

### SUMMARIES OF RETIRING ALLOWANCES IN STATE UNIVERSITIES

#### (a) *Methods of Giving Retiring Allowances*

(1) The following 13 state universities have the plan of the Teachers Insurance and Annuity Association of America or a similar plan for the retirement of their teachers: Arkansas, California, Colorado, Maine, Michigan, Missouri, Ohio, Pennsylvania, South Carolina, Utah, Vermont, Virginia, Wisconsin.

(2) The following 12 states have their own plans. In some cases the institutions have a modification of the Annuity Plan. In some cases they have the Annuity Plan coupled with some other plan of their own; in some they have only their own plan, hence states appear in both this list and the one given above. Where an institution has only the Carnegie Annuity Plan its name does not appear on this list: California, Florida, Illinois, Kentucky, Louisiana, Maine, Minnesota, Nevada, Ohio, Oregon, Vermont, Wisconsin.

(3) The following 11 states give a part-salary for part-time work, or a full salary for part-time work, or some sort of help to retiring teachers: Alabama, Florida, Iowa, Kansas, Missouri, Ne-

braska, New Mexico, North Carolina, Oklahoma, Wisconsin, Wyoming.

(4) Combining the above lists, the following 28 states have some sort of payments made to retiring teachers in the state universities: Alabama, Arkansas, California, Colorado, Florida, Illinois, Iowa, Kansas, Kentucky, Louisiana, Maine, Michigan, Minnesota, Missouri, Nebraska, Nevada, New Mexico, North Carolina, Ohio, Oklahoma, Oregon, Pennsylvania, South Carolina, Utah, Vermont, Virginia, Wisconsin, Wyoming.

(5) The following 15 states have no plan for retiring allowances in their state universities and do not give any help to their retiring teachers in these institutions: Arizona, Delaware, Georgia, Idaho, Indiana, Maryland, Mississippi, Montana, New Hampshire, North Dakota, South Dakota, Tennessee, Texas, Washington, West Virginia.

*(b) Amounts Given for Retiring Allowances*

(6) The Annuity Plan usually calls for a payment by the teacher of 5 per cent. of his salary annually for a number of years, and this is met by a like amount paid by the state or some other individual or organization. Some still have the original Carnegie plan not entirely completed. The states having this plan are listed under No. 1.

(7) The following 6 states have individual pensions or some of the more complicated plans: Alabama, California, Michigan, New Mexico, Ohio, Virginia.

(8) In the following 7 states each case is considered separately with no necessity of uniform action or any necessity of giving any retiring allowance: Alabama, Kansas, Nebraska, New Mexico, North Carolina, Oklahoma, Wyoming.

The following (9 to 14), have definite plans.

(9) Retiring teachers are given one fourth of their regular salary each year after retiring in Nevada.

(10) Given one third of their regular salary in Louisiana.

(11) Given one half of their regular salary each year after retiring in Florida, Iowa and Oregon.

(12) Given 20 per cent. of regular salary each year, plus 1 per cent. of the regular salary for each year of service in the institution in Kentucky.

(13) Given 25 per cent. of salary each year, plus 1 per cent. of salary for each year of service in the institution, with a total limit of 50 per cent. of the regular salary in Illinois.

(14) Professors given $2,500 a year after retiring; associate professors given $2,000 a year in Minnesota.

*(c) Retiring Ages*

(15) The following are the ages at which teachers *may* retire:

| Age | States |
|---|---|
| 50 | Wisconsin (special cases). |
| 65 | Alabama, California, Colorado, Illinois, Maine, Nevada, Ohio and Utah. |
| 68 | Minnesota and South Carolina. |
| 70 | Florida, Kentucky, Louisiana, Michigan, Missouri, Oregon and Virginia. |

(16) The following are the ages at which they *must* retire:

| Age | States |
|---|---|
| 65 | Arkansas (may be reappointed annually if in good health). |
| 68 | Illinois. |
| 70 | California, Iowa, Kentucky, Louisiana, Michigan, Minnesota, Missouri, Montana, Nevada, Ohio, Oregon, Pennsylvania and South Carolina. |
| 73 | Alabama. |

(17) In the following the time of retiring is at the option of the Board: Missouri, Montana, North Carolina, Utah, Virginia, Wisconsin.

*(d) Use of Libraries and Laboratories by Retired Teachers*

(18) Retired teachers are given the use of libraries, laboratories, etc., in 23 states: Alabama, Arkansas, California, Florida, Illinois, Iowa, Kansas, Kentucky, Louisiana, Maine, Michigan, Minnesota, Nevada, North Carolina, Ohio, Oklahoma, Oregon, Pennsylvania, South Carolina, Utah, Vermont, Virginia, Wisconsin.

(19) Retired teachers are not given use of libraries and laboratories, except by special permission, in Indiana, Missouri and West Virginia.

(20) No ruling in other states as to the use of libraries and laboratories by retired teachers.

*(e) Place of Residence after Retiring*

(21) In 15 states teachers on retiring allowances may reside anywhere: Alabama, California, Colorado, Florida, Illinois, Kentucky, Michigan, Minnesota, Nevada, Ohio, Oregon, Pennsylvania, Utah, Virginia, Wisconsin.

(22) Teachers on retiring allowances must not reside elsewhere in Kansas.

(23) No statement from other states as to residence.

*(f) Holding of Other Positions after Retiring*

(24) The following 15 states permit retired teachers to accept other positions: Alabama, California, Colorado, Florida, Illinois, Kentucky, Michigan, Minnesota, Nevada, Ohio, Oregon, Utah, Vermont, Virginia and Wisconsin.

(25) The following 2 states do not permit the

holding of other positions: Kansas and Pennsylvania.

(26) No reports from other states.

The question of providing retiring allowances is one which is being widely considered at the present time in all varieties of institutions. The system in use in Florida, for example, is just being put into effect in this year 1934. Movements to adopt retiring systems are being carried out or agitated at this time in the state universities of Delaware, Missouri, Montana and North Carolina. Teachers are not organized for such matters as labor is organized, hence they have but little to say in planning retiring systems.

The university professor must make a complete preparation for his work. His education is expensive and covers a number of years. His preparation requires an expenditure of as much time and money as does the preparation of the physician, the lawyer, the business man or the man in any other activity of life. His salary usually does not compare with that of the lawyer or the physician, for example, hence the need of retiring allowances. To keep abreast of the advancement in his line of work and at the same time to save money is almost impossible.

Another situation might be mentioned. The age of retirement from teaching has had a tendency to be lowered in these later years, as is indicated in the summaries given above. At the same time the average length of life has been considerably extended. The result of these two changes is that the years of retired life for the teacher are more in number than they have been in the past—another reason for retiring allowances.

J. N. Swan

University of Mississippi

## FOR PEACE AND FOREIGN TRADE

Among the most important social movements of our day is that toward international peace. Another problem, for the United States particularly, is the salvation and development of our foreign trade. The orderly increase of our international commerce, with security of investment and profit, will require long years of peace for its accomplishment. International peace and international trade go hand in hand. Educators, considering these problems, must ask themselves, "How can the schools help to create universal peace, how may they assist in the promotion of international trade?"

One of the ways to accomplish these things is to train a group of men and women, who, at the completion of their education, will have an extensive and intensive knowledge of other countries, who will have a forward-looking and unprejudiced spirit and an ability and skill for adapting themselves to whatever new situations may arise with regard to other nations.

Because the United States occupies such a prominent place in the affairs of the world, the business which falls to our Department of State becomes greater in volume every year. It is increasingly evident that this department will need at some time in the near future an enlarged personnel to carry on its task, which becomes more burdensome and more important each year. The enlarged personnel should come, in large part, from our colleges and universities. A certain number of our honor graduates should be prepared for such positions, which, though they do not offer great financial rewards, should give security of tenure and present an opportunity for public service.

Likewise, as business conditions continue to improve, our American companies doing business abroad will need trained men for the foreign field.

Perhaps it may be argued that the number of Americans needed in the services indicated above is not and will not be very large. Yet, the demand for minor executives and office workers, as foreign trade does increase little by little, should help to absorb some of the surplus of college graduates who now compete against each other in fields decidedly overcrowded. There are some professions which are not likely to need many more college graduates for some years, since our slowly increasing population does not permit them to expand very much. On the other hand, our government is putting forth efforts to increase our foreign trade, and it is likely that this latter will expand.

Young persons, to be trained for positions having contact with foreign governments or with foreign commercial companies, need to study many subjects, but surely among these subjects are foreign languages. The proper approach to a foreign diplomat is the friendly one, especially easy to the American who can address the stranger in the tongue of his native land. It is said that a famous Italian visiting in this country was so impressed with the fact that President Roosevelt spoke with him in Italian that he immediately telephoned long distance to Mussolini to tell him of it.

Some business firms have the practise of choosing for the foreign field, not new men, but experienced and capable ones from their own force, who are given intensive study in the necessary foreign language for a few weeks before they sail. Any one who has ever studied a foreign language realizes that the few weeks of study will not prove adequate for all the situations the employee will meet. A foreign language is no easier to learn "at a glance" than salesmanship or engineering. Therefore, the young man who is looking forward to employment with one of the many companies doing business abroad should not be deterred from beginning, in college, his preparation in foreign languages, the same as he begins there the study of economics, commercial law and international relations.

Furthermore, a planned and permanent peace between the United States and other countries requires that public sentiment in our country be forward-looking and, above all, lacking in foolish and fatal prejudices against foreign nations. Grade and high-school pupils, therefore, should be taught subjects and attitudes which make for international peace. A recent investigation in racial prejudices of high-school students indicates that such prejudices are strong in them, but that those who have taken French and Spanish are much less prejudiced against the people of those nationalities than the rest of the student body.

The opportunities offered in a class in foreign language for teaching an appreciation of an alien nation are very great, and general information may be given on various subjects. Anything that can be read or studied in English may be read or studied in the foreign language as well. Famous literary themes, information about great men and discussions on art may be presented in simplified form, even in an elementary course. Folk songs of the foreign country may be sung as they were meant to be, in the language in which they were composed. After some proficiency is secured by the student, material as mature as would be offered in English may be presented. Historical documents, for instance, may be read in their original language.

Due consideration should be given the foreign languages, experiments should be made of their usefulness in the modern curriculum. They should not be discarded simply because some theorist cries, "Traditional! Out with them!" Let us do some coldly scientific thinking on the subject. Let us arrange some experiments to determine whether the teaching of foreign languages may serve a social purpose. It may be found that they fit just as well into our new era of American life as some other subjects.

ELIZABETH CALLAWAY
CENTRAL MISSOURI STATE
TEACHERS COLLEGE

# QUOTATIONS

## FITTING THE SCHOOL TO THE CHILD

DR. HAROLD G. CAMPBELL, superintendent of the public schools of New York City, would reduce the number of failures in elementary schools by making the educational clothing a better fit for the wearer. Dr. Campbell has named a committee to study ways and means.

What he has in mind may be indicated by two statements in the letter outlining the duties of the committee. First: "If we find a child who wants to be and has within him the ability to be a good musician, we should seize upon it, and build our course of study for that child around that interest and that ability." Again: "Every child has some interest, some ability, great or little, latent or apparent. It is for us to find these interests and abilities, and to formulate our courses of study upon them. We must be the searchers of the hearts and minds of these children and make contact with their inner selves. We must create interests where we find none."

With thirty or forty pupils to a teacher in the elementary schools, it would seem a large order to undertake to make acquaintance with their inner selves, to discover and stimulate individual interests and supply them where lacking. But at least it is refreshing to find the New York superintendent proclaiming that education should not be conducted on the principle of mass production, and he is able to show that something is being accomplished, as things are, in dealing with pupils as individual human beings.

In an interview supplementing his letter, he pictured a system in which every school would provide classes for children of superior intellect, for those mechanically inclined, and for those with poor vision or hearing, each child pursuing a curriculum suited to his individual needs and abilities. He said that in the high schools progress in the establishment of such a system had been made. It may be taken as representative of the American spirit as opposed to that in countries where dictators rule the schools as they rule everything else, and the chief end of education is the glory and maintenance of the dictatorship. For this proposal in New York is in keeping with freedom of thought and speech. But there remains the question how the school teacher, already burdened with cares and duties, is to become the intimate acquaintance of the inner selves of forty or fifty boys and girls.—*The Boston Transcript.*

# SPECIAL CORRESPONDENCE

## PIONEERING IN TEACHER TRAINING

It all began years ago, so each of the three directors of the college told us during our seminars with them. After these seminars it seemed plausible enough, even inevitable, that some such teacher-training institution as the Graduate Teachers' College of Winnetka should make its appearance along the North Shore of Chicago.

People like Flora Cooke, Perry Smith and Carleton Washburne never reach the ultimate, because their goals are steadily pushed forward. At one time their horizons were probably much less distant than they are to-day. Perhaps they have almost reached those earlier horizons by now (at least we students thought so). Yet there was one problem facing them which was never ending, for their staffs continually changed and with each new teacher came a new problem. There was no place to which they could turn for teachers with assurance that the new members of the staff would have the right kind of teacher training fitted for their duties. Out of this condition must have arisen the desire to have a school for the training of their own teachers. It needed but a suggestion from one of them to pull all three into the plans for just such a school. But before the first group of students arrived in the fall of 1932 the idea of limiting the school to only prospective teachers for their own schools had been abandoned.

With these three educators all carrying out their ideas and aspirations within a few miles of each other they could not but come together in this latest and perhaps most influential project, that of fitting teachers to carry on and add to the ideals known as progressive education. They had a more than usual bond to make them unite. Back in the sixth grade Perry Smith and Carleton Washburne were students in the Francis Parker School, where Miss Cooke was a teacher. The two of them were early brought in contact with certain educational procedures and a philosophy which had been a part of the Parker School since its founding in 1900. Then in later years when both were ready to start their permanent workshops it was in the village of Winnetka that the two located, one in the public schools and the other in the North Shore Country Day School. For fifteen years they have worked together for the mutual benefit of the community and at all times each has been intensely interested in what the other was doing. Though the Francis Parker School was a few miles distant, both of these men kept in close contact with the educational primal stuff from which they had sprung and looked to Flora Cooke with as much admiration and respect as they had in those days when school-going was such an interesting experience.

On paper we were a heterogeneous group that made up the first class. Of the seven, six had traveled rather widely and all had had interesting backgrounds. One had taught in Australia for three years; one, a Hindu, worked in Tagore's school for five years and had then gone to London for two years' study in the London

Day Training College; another had had his first years of teaching in the Near East. I say we were not of the same ilk "on paper." Yet down deep within us there must have been a common motif. After all, did we not come from widely varying backgrounds and habitats to spend a year in a college which would not be in existence until we arrived? Also the fact that each one began his year's work in the elementary grades and only later proceeded to the high-school level showed that we were interested in much more than a preparation for English or science or music. One of the seven displayed a quality common to all of us, I think, when she decided to leave the college in the second quarter and return to her pottery-making, which had thus far been less a vocation than an avocation. Finally, there was a definite feeling among us all that whatever the immediate prospects were, eventually we should go to some new community and strike out for ourselves. One of the group is by this time doing as much in his own country of India. The rest will do likewise when their times arrive.

We were told in the beginning that the Graduate Teachers' College would hold to the principles of progressive schools, and that the directors and dean were interested in giving us what we wanted and not alone what they thought we should have. Naturally enough, there was no great disagreement, for the problems facing those responsible for the college were the problems each of us students wanted to tackle. Our work was to be as completely functional as possible, theory and practise meeting at every step of the way. The courses of study were to be means by which problems could be faced and solved, and thus we students were partially responsible for what our teachers gave us.

We went into the classroom for half of each day to work with carefully chosen teachers. We were partners in the work of teaching there, sometimes helping in special projects, at other times working with individuals, and again, observing or taking over the class completely. As problems of method or theory arose we threshed them out either with the teacher of the classroom or in the seminars we held later in the day. There was no set time for staying in any place—we remained as long as we thought we were getting what we wanted. Frequently we had a chance to take a unit of work and complete it under the supervision of our teacher-in-charge. Thus two of the students worked in high-school English classes where the unit ended in morning exercises. Another carried through a one-act play, and all of us aided in one way or another in the presentation of a Gilbert and Sullivan Operetta.

There being three schools in the college, and each of them having much to give us, we tentatively divided our time equally among them. However, we were free to remain in any one school as long as we liked. The writer, for instance, after spending three months in one school, went back later in the year for another five weeks in order to prepare for a special unit of work in biology. Though the general approach to the child as an individual and as a member of the group held in all three schools, the methods used were strikingly in contrast, and this fact contributed much to the vitality of our classroom experiences. Then, too, each school had its own peculiar contributions to make, for example, individualized instruction or parent-school relationship or motivated work.

The curriculum naturally centered around our individual interests. Two of us were especially interested in English, two in the social sciences, one in nursery school and the other two in the entire twelve grades from an administrative as well as teaching point of view. Yet with all these differences in special interests there were two problems common to the entire group. One was the attempt to reach some philosophy of education and the other was to understand the child. A nucleus for a course of study readily presented itself. First there would be the philosophies of education underlying each of the three schools and, secondly, there must be some course in mental hygiene. With those two courses, each of us combined a third of more individual interest. These courses were all seminars conducted by the directors, the psychiatrist for the Winnetka Public Schools, or by various teachers who were qualified to do so. Our courses changed three times during the year, as we went to the different schools, giving us approximately twelve weeks in each course. There were no text-books in any of the courses, but a well-selected bibliography was suggested by each leader of a seminar. In one of the philosophy seminars, for example, we read parts of Plato's "Republic," Rousseau's "Emile," Pinkevitch's "New Education in the Soviet Republic" and Washburne's "Remakers of Mankind." Late in the year most of the group took up some form of handwork with such satisfying results that we recommended some similar work should be made a part of the curriculum for every one in the future.

The seminars met regularly once a week, but special meetings were called when the need arose. The methods varied in the seminars according to the subject-matter. In one of the philosophy courses we had dinner together and then sat about the fire discussing problems which arose out of our reading, such as "indoctrination," "individualism," "training for a society already set up *vs.* a society in flux." This discussion was followed by a lecture hour at which parents also were listeners. In another seminar each of the students prepared a unit of work which correlated English and social science. (In this case the leader of the seminar was working on just such a course to be tried the next year in his own classes.) A seminar on the "Reorganization of Science in the Junior and Senior High School" was made up of students and the entire science staff, including the manual training and home economics instructors, plus one teacher of social science. In our discussions we were actually working out a proposed new curriculum in science for that school. The mental hygiene seminars centered around a few general principles of behavior, but most of the time we worked with case studies which we had all read, cases brought in by the students from the classrooms, or the mental attitudes of the students themselves, such as those dealing with religion or sex.

Looking back upon the work in the Graduate Teachers' College now, it is as adventurously and romantically educational as all of us thought it was last year. Then, we were almost too engrossed in the fun of "being educated to be educators" to evaluate the unique and fundamental soundness of the new college. Now, after almost a year of teaching (each of the students was placed for the following year) it is possible to gain a perspective of last year's experience and to make a comparison with the other years of college and university study. As I look back upon my undergraduate work, the short period of graduate study and the year in a European university, they all lack the dynamic reality which so characterized this new Graduate Teachers' College. There was so much to get in our all too few months together that one couldn't be bothered with uninteresting material. We students objected when the subject-matter was too elementary, and when we saw no relation between our seminar reading or discussion and the problems we were faced with; we did not trust to luck that "some day it would come in handy" but rather said we were not interested and wished to get along. Teachers or leaders of seminars respond quickly enough in the right set-up.

Specifically, the year stands out as one of freedom. The courses to be taken were as much a matter for us to choose, I suppose, as is educationally possible. The suggested reading was "suggested," and though most of it was done, there were books which received only a cursory going through. We all found time for browsing and the "unrequired reading" was an important part of the year. Except for one or two seminars, such as the "Social Science-English" and "Reorganization of Science in the High School" seminars, where we were working on units requiring preparation of written material, there were no papers to write, nor were there examinations to prepare for. Not once were we quizzed in the ordinary sense on our preparation. Yet the leaders of the seminars would have had no great difficulty in detecting slipshod work. And then when June came and we were ready to say our "au revoirs" we had no degrees given us by the directors of the college. One of them had asked us about degrees or some formal signification of the year in the Graduate Teachers' College, and I think a majority expressed their disapproval. Frankly, the year couldn't be summed up that way at all. But we did have a graduation dinner, and the same emotions I had had at my earlier college graduation came into full force that evening. We were all together, sixty faculty members and six students. (The mere ratio signifies more than this entire article.) Instead of one great speaker brought from the outside, we had our three directors from the inside, Perry Smith,

Flora Cooke and Carleton Washburne. The last named presented to each of the six his "diploma," which in reality was a certificate on which was written the student's educational background, his specific work within the college, and a brief comment as to the college's estimation of him and his work. It was a great way to close our year in Winnetka—a year of growth together, faculty and students; a year where each person, teacher or pupil had to contribute or all of us lost.

RUSSELL BABCOCK
WINNETKA PUBLIC SCHOOLS
WINNETKA, ILLINOIS

# EDUCATIONAL RESEARCH AND STATISTICS

## A STUDY OF THE PERIODICAL READING DONE BY COLLEGE STUDENTS

AN interest in the types of reading done by college students and the actual interest such students take in the present-day happenings of the world led me to devise a brief test and questionnaire which I circulated in classes at the Wisconsin State Teachers College at Milwaukee. I especially aimed at getting a fairly reliable distribution of freshmen and juniors. The data on the sophomore and senior students that I obtained came incidentally from the groups that I tested, made up mainly of freshman and junior students.

The method used was the circulation of a mimeographed blank which contained a matching test, a group of questions and a line giving the name of the four classes with the direction that the year in college was to be underlined. The matching test consisted of 35 names, mentioned prominently in the news of February 4, 1934, on one side, and 37 possible descriptions to fit these men on the other. For example, Emma Goldman was to be matched with the inscription "famed anarchist," Max Raskin with "Milwaukee city attorney" and William M. Magee with "president of Marquette University."

The questions were the following: If you could read only five magazines a month, which would you choose? What person in the world would you like most to meet? Who is the greatest man that ever lived? Who is the greatest woman that ever lived? Could you write a paper on the Roosevelt recovery program without consulting references? What is your major subject? No time limits were imposed on the test or on the questions which followed. Because the test was of the imperfect matching type the element of guessing by the process of elimination was lessened. All the tests were given at approximately the same time throughout the college.

Of the 35 possible correct answers there were two scores as high as 33, both made by juniors. One freshman made a zero score. The freshman class had the lowest rating, with an average score of 11. The sophomore class had the highest, with a rating of 17.1. The juniors and seniors slumped with scores of 16.5 and 15.8, respectively. The probable errors of the means of the freshman and junior groups are .30 and .76, respectively. Those of the other classes are a bit higher. By means of the probable error of the differences of the means it is found that the differences between the freshman and the sophomore and junior classes are significant. The difference between the freshman and senior class might very likely be due to chance. The probable error of the difference here is more than half the difference. It is usually held that the obtained difference to be statistically significant and indicative of a real difference must be four times the probable error of the difference. The evidence then would indicate that there is a considerable increase of ability to identify these personages of recent fame. The sophomores and the juniors score significantly higher. However, the seniors do not. There is an indication of a slump the last two years in college. The introduction of specialized college work in the various academic fields probably hindered the impetus to read about and study current problems.

The history and economics majors made the highest scores, with ratings of 20.1 and 16.8, respectively. The art students with 9 and the music students with 9.8 had the lowest scores. Other scores were English, 10.7; chemistry, 11.4; languages, 12; biology, 12.6; elementary education, 12.7; physics, 13.6; mathematics, 13.7; kindergarten-primary, 14.4; and exceptional division, 15.5. Because of the lack of numbers the differences in many cases are not significant, but merely indicate what my limited data indicate. The differences between art and history, between art and economics, between music and history, between music and economics, between history and mathematics, between history and languages are some of the statistically significant mean differences. These differences are likely due mainly to the particular inclinations of those students who make up these groups. Those in the economic and history departments could hardly be interested in their major fields without being interested in current trends. Those interested in artistic fields are likely to pass over the news rather rapidly and with less care. The environment in some of the courses would likewise tend to emphasize or neglect those factors being tested.

Another method used to secure an indication of the efforts students make to follow recent developments was brought out by the question—Could you write a paper on the Roosevelt recovery program without consulting notes? Of the seniors 67 per cent. said they could, while the juniors were not so sure, only 52 per cent. answering yes. The sophomores indicated that only one third of those writing could, while the freshmen indicated that only 37 per cent. of their group could write such a paper. In view of the fewer seniors and sophomores represented, their scores are less valuable. Fifteen per cent. more juniors than freshmen admit their ability to do this job. I believe it can be safely assumed that many who answered yes could not write a very acceptable paper. Those who answered no were more likely aware of their limitations in respect to this problem.

In answer to the question—If you could read only five magazines a month, which would you choose?—the following periodicals were found to constitute the big ten. They follow in order with the percentage of those reporting who chose those magazines. The first ten chosen by the seniors are also shown.

I classified the types of readings done by the years in school and for the total of all the classes. The following magazines rated among the first ten of all the four classes: *Literary Digest, Atlantic Monthly, Readers Digest* and *Harper's*. Educational magazines begin to be mentioned about the junior year. Their titles are scattered and no one received great mention. The increased mention of *Progressive Education Magazine* might be attributed to the blanks filled out by elementary practise teachers. While the *American, The Saturday Evening Post* and *Liberty* rated strongly among the first- and second-year students, they were less frequently mentioned during the third year and did not make the first ten among the seniors. Although great variations were found between the readings of members of the same class, serious types of publications were mentioned very frequently. Only five of the college big ten group contain fiction material. Much intellectual and broadening matter is contained in them. Only two of the first ten of the senior group contain fiction content.

All four classes selected Franklin D. Roosevelt as the person they would like most to meet. He received 67 per cent. of all mentions. Mussolini was named by 12 per cent.; Einstein by 7 per cent.; Hitler by 5 per cent.; and Mae West and Gandhi by 4 per cent. Others named were "an eligible bachelor," "a generous millionaire," Sinclair Lewis, George Arliss, E. R. Downing, composer of "Star Dust," Lenin,

All-college Big Ten

| | | |
|---|---|---|
| 1. | *Literary Digest* | 42 per cent. |
| 2. | *Atlantic Monthly* | 34 " " |
| 3. | *Readers Digest* | 31 " " |
| 4. | *Time* | 26 " " |
| 5. | *Harper's* | 24 " " |
| 6. | *American* | 20 " " |
| 7. | *National Geographic* | 19 " " |
| 8. | *Saturday Evening Post* | 13 " " |
| 9. | *Nation* | 12 " " |
| 10. | *Liberty* | 11 " " |

Senior Big Ten

| | | |
|---|---|---|
| 1. | *Harper's* | 38 " " |
| | *Atlantic Monthly* | 38 " " |
| 3. | *Literary Digest* | 28 " " |
| | *Time* | 28 " " |
| 5. | *Readers Digest* | 24 " " |
| 6. | *Current History* | 17 " " |
| | *Nation* | 17 " " |
| 8. | *Survey* | 14 " " |
| | *Forum* | 14 " " |
| | *Progressive Ed.* | 14 " " |

Ramon Navarro, Dillinger, Roy C. Andrews, Litvinoff, Byrd, Norman Thomas, Stalin, Bing Crosby, Clark Gable, Anne Lindbergh, Colonel Lindbergh, Willa Cather, Walter Damrosch, Eva Le Gallienne, W. A. Ganfield, Emma Goldman, G. B. Shaw, Bob LaFollette, H. G. Wells, Clarence Darrow, Helen Wills Moody, Fritz Kreisler, Amelia Earhart, Helen Keller, Dr. Alexander, of Columbia University, Paderewski, Will Rogers, Alfred Adler, J. P. Morgan, Jean Parker and Wayne King.

The greatest woman that ever lived was Jane Addams, according to 26 per cent. of the students voting, Madame Curie was chosen by 17 per cent., while Florence Nightingale was selected by 13 per cent. Others securing votes were Queen Victoria, Frances Perkins, Joan of Arc, Helen Keller, Queen Elizabeth, Catherine the Great, Cleopatra, Eve, the virgin Mary, Clara Barton, Sappho and Mrs. Coolidge.

The greatest man was Abraham Lincoln, who secured 32 per cent. of the votes. Jesus Christ was given 27 per cent., although He probably would have scored an overwhelming victory if the statement had been made that He was to be included. Many expressed surprise that Christ was to be included and they signified that they would have voted Him this honor if they had know that He was to be included. Edison was third with 9 per cent., followed closely by Washington and Napoleon. Others mentioned were Aristotle, Charlemagne, Knute Rockne, F. D. Roosevelt, Karl Marx, Copernicus, Newton, Bismarck, Hitler, Eugene V. Debs, Plato, Moses, Spinoza, "my father," Shakespeare and Pasteur.

The results of this survey would seem to indicate that our colleges are not especially successful in stimulating students to read and study current history and trends. Twenty-six per cent. of all the college students were unable to score more than eight correct answers. At least that many fairly obvious answers were included in the test, with such personages as Mayor Hoan, Adolf Hitler, Samuel Insull, Senators Johnson, of California, and Duffy, of Wisconsin, Alfalfa Bill Murray, Local Meteorologist Coleman and City Attorney Max Raskin. The highest mean made by the second-year students included less than half of the correct answers. It would seem that college students should do much better than was shown on this test. It would seem, too, that more than 44 per cent. of those replying would claim the ability to write a paper on the Roosevelt recovery program.

It is to be regretted that students majoring in subjects such as art and music rate so poorly on this test. It seems especially desirable that their education be more liberal rather than vocational. Perhaps greater integration of college courses and fields would tend to correct these inequalities.

It would appear that college students at the Milwaukee State Teachers College read a rather selective group of periodicals. Relatively few educational magazines are mentioned. It would seem that in a teachers college, especially, more emphasis would be placed on magazines pertaining to teaching and psychology. It is probable that familiarity with such publications would find more such magazines among those regularly sought and read. The results on the matching test would indicate that these magazines could not have been read very carefully. At least 16 of the 35 persons to be identified are consistently mentioned in such magazines as *Time, Nation* and the *Literary Digest*. The other 19 names are of local and state interest. Newspapers are probably read hastily and with little care.

The lists of greats is conspicuous in its lack of great educational personages. One student would like to meet Dr. Alexander, of Columbia University, and another Alfred Adler, the psychologist. The choices seem to favor statesmen and politicians. Idols of the teaching profession have not as yet become established, it would seem. John Dewey, Edward Thorndike and similar personages were not once mentioned.

ELDEN HUNTER

WISCONSIN STATE TEACHERS
COLLEGE, MILWAUKEE

## NEW BOOKS IN EDUCATION

*Guide Book for Foreign Students in the United States.* Pp. 119. Institute of International Education, New York.

MONROE, PAUL and FRIEDRICH SCHNEIDER, Editors. *International Education Review.* Pp. 437–562. J. P. Bachem, Köln.

*Sixty-seventh Annual Report of the State Board of Education Showing Condition of the Public Schools of Maryland for the Year Ending July 31, 1933.* Pp. 345. Illustrated. State of Maryland Department of Education, Baltimore.

# SCHOOL AND SOCIETY

WITH WHICH ARE COMBINED THE EDUCATIONAL REVIEW, ESTABLISHED IN 1891, THE TEACHERS MAGAZINE, ESTABLISHED IN 1878, AND THE SCHOOL JOURNAL, ESTABLISHED IN 1874.

Volume 40 SATURDAY, JULY 21, 1934 Number 1021

## VISIONS AND VOYAGES[1]

By JESSIE GRAY

PRESIDENT OF THE NATIONAL EDUCATION ASSOCIATION

I HAVE thought of this great association as a treasure chest. The amount of the treasure is not to be measured by what we can take out for ourselves, but how much we can put into the chest, as riches to spend for others. The teachers of this nation have put into it their loyalty, cooperation, zeal and industry. They have worked that children shall not be deprived of their rightful heritage. The association pays tribute to the dauntless courage of the teachers of America, and I dedicate myself to a year of service in assisting them with their problems.

Everything that has happened this year, in the cycle of happy service, has emphasized the truth of the foregoing statement. In the greater knowledge of that experience, let us review our plans, our accomplishments through organization, realizing how pitifully weak the individual is and how magnificently strong the service and the devotion of 200,000 members, guided by a marvelously trained, dedicated staff, under the leadership of an executive secretary whose courage and rectitude have won laurels and distinction.

Our unfinished work, our plans in the making, will be our vision and challenge for the next year's voyage. Our treasure chest has bulged with increased understanding, loyalty, cooperative endeavor and all that adds to the fulness of life. The teachers have woven into the fabric of the nation devotion, dedication, sacrifice and the ineradicable pattern that children must be well taught in order to dream dreams and catch the vision without which the people perish. It has been their extravagant gladness to put thirty million children in their midst, to help make each life and to keep all happy and content in the making—unmindful of the howling wolves of selfishness that would have destroyed our schools.

The National Education Association again pays tribute to the spiritual motherhood and dauntless courage of those teachers who collectively have done more than their share in carrying on despite every discouragement. They know full well that it is only "in the fertile soil of education and preparation that democratic principles can grow into cooperation, understanding and the fulfilment of our best hopes." Their professional contribution not only has held education true to its mission of interpreting life through sympathy, benevolence and interdependence, but it has expressed concretely, in every way, the ardent hope for the success of this association—our cooperative endeavor—through our collective wisdom, voice and influence.

During this year your faithful, ever-vigilant executive secretary, Mr. Crabtree,

[1] Address before the General Session, Washington Auditorium, Washington, D. C., July 3, 1934.

took up the cudgels to defend, primarily, the sacred trust of education from chiselers who would have cut our tree of life down to its roots. Can't you see him instant in season and out of season calling the land grant banks to a halt, the tax economists to an accounting, because they know neither how to raise taxes yet nor how best to apportion them so that the relative importance of governmental functions shall be held in the righteous balance of finer judgment. To those in our midst whose foolish remarks were unsound and unwise, he also uttered a challenge for the ethics of leadership to look to its wisdom and constructiveness. To those editors of newspapers and magazines whose influence was deplorably weak for education, if not actually antagonistic, the tide has turned to a greater helpfulness because of his powerful influence. Not only has he defended American education in its hour of greatest need, but he has given an inspirational leadership in the improvement of the schools so that they may be more worthy of defense.

The growth in membership, 7,865 in 1912 to well-nigh a quarter of a million in 1934, is another testimonial to the vision, devotion and dynamic influence of Mr. Crabtree. His vision saw the possibility of enlarged headquarters and a way to its fulfilment. His acumen evolved the plan to finance it from life memberships. They have leaped ahead from 73 in 1917, when he came, to 4,954 in 1934. We owe a debt to Mr. Crabtree that can never be paid except through clearer vision, consecrated devotion and a life free from greed, guile and malfeasance.

During this year, your president has visited 87 cities in 27 states. It has been her privilege to speak to 300,000 people, to address state conventions, national groups, local associations, parent-teacher associations, city and national clubs, Chambers of Commerce, Rotary, Kiwanis and Lions Clubs, Forums, as well as members of Boards of Education. She has traveled 40,000 miles by train and plane. Everywhere, teachers were busy developing visions of stewardship and making voyages to discover how to make the school more appreciative of its community and the community more appreciative of its schools. Whenever there was a call for faith and courage, there was a sure answer in holding education true to its mission.

Memberships have increased, through sacrifice in many cases. The division of membership reports $9,407 extra revenue, showing 4,704 more memberships. Seventeen state associations reported increased members, and eight states report an increase in their National Education Association memberships. We find ourselves on the upward march! This is glorious news indeed! It was due, no doubt, to the dynamic membership committee appointed early in the year. They worked valiantly to interpret the activities and advantages of our national organization. Praise be to them for their fine results!

The privilege of membership is the privilege of service and constructive suggestion. It is a matter of pride to participate in group action that states social and economic goals for a nation, cares for legislation, secures retirement for teachers, guides and develops international relations, takes care of rural and adult education, promotes library service and kindergartens. It is a matter for condemnation to accept gains from organization and not support it by membership. It seems hardly honest in the last analysis, does it? How can teachers say to their government, "I do my part," if they refrain from doing their part through organization toward the general welfare and common defense of their own group?

Our management this year, always wonderful, has been a miracle. Through strictest economies we find ourselves at the end of a very expensive year $7,500 within our income, although we were obliged to call for funds to finance the extra work of the Commission for Federal Emergency Relief, for which nothing had been budgeted. Publicity was tremendously increased and that demanded extra finance also. We express our appreciation for the spontaneous response when the National Education Association was left with the greater part of the burden of financing the Commission on the Federal Emergency Relief. Eleven state organizations sent $630, 163 local associations sent $2,574 and two departments sent $275. Added to this was $500 from the Phi Delta Kappa; $1,500 from the American Council; $37 from individuals and $378 from the unemployment fund, making a total of $5,894.

Another expression of appreciation is due the National Broadcasting Company, whose half-hour broadcast each week represents a contribution of $2,500, or $100,000 for forty weeks of free service. This program has helped to sensitize our nation, helped to keep the public informed of the schools, their services and costs, the value of education, the attack on it, and the result of those attacks. It has aroused us all to the plight of education. We also thank Past President Florence Hale for her cheery challenges in the varied and interesting programs which have reached and convinced millions of people. This service she, too, gave freely and gladly.

This year, our immediate plans were made for a greater information of lay organizations to defend education as the cornerstone of democracy. In this plan, the division of research gave the scientific facts, the division of publicity sent them forth to be used in defense of education through all affiliated lay organizations. To each American Legion Post, a special citation was sent for its work in the defense of education during this emergency.

Our journal has never functioned better in interpreting the crisis, its cause, its extent and how to end it. A series of special features included "The Interpretation of Education" (October, 1933); "Working Together" (November, 1933); "Emergency Federal Aid Imperative" (February, 1934); and "Secondary Education for the New Day" (May, 1934). (Teachers who clamor for news of what is being done should read, mark and inwardly digest, since membership can only be turned into service when informed as to fields of service and how to function therein.) The journal this year has presented a perfect course in cooperative endeavor. The new era in education will result when we, too, spread eagle wings to fly from inertia, and call: "I do my part. Why don't you do yours?"

Throughout the year, the journal makes the report of work well done, as well as the announcement of new plans for the next bit of progress. It has kept the members and the profession generally in close touch with the work of the Joint Commission on the Emergency in Education, as well as with the progress of the National Commission for Federal Emergency Aid for Education and the statements of the Committee on Social and Economic Goals. In this great effort to interpret education in a national field, teachers who have not read their journals are greatly at fault. Faculties that have not used the journal as the basis of discussion are prolonging the crisis, which can not pass away till every one cooperates through understanding and participates in the well-planned program to end it. Teachers can make their contribution in meeting citizens and revealing to them the program for the welfare of the schools. This service offers an opportunity for them to show that they are neither indifferent nor mercenary in their profession. You and your journal are invincible! Carry its message of the schools to the people. Beyond the profession itself, it maintains 3,300 contacts with press associations, religious, business, labor and lay magazines, writers, cartoonists, speakers, radio stations and others who have influence in forming public opinion.

The journal each year sponsors American Education Week in cooperation with the Office of Education and the American Legion. Last year it gave suggestions and materials to 3,000 communities. Think of that stupendous contribution! It distributed a million pieces of literature which produced untold good, not to mention an income of $6,671. Already it has planned the coming year's program for American Education Week. You, no doubt, will accept many of its suggestions. It is a part of your membership value in a vision of greater future usefulness.

Through this same division of publications, we have heard the report of the Joint Commission on the Emergency in Education. This committee, early in the summer of 1933, published its findings on the financing of education. The plan has been discussed in every section of the nation in nine regional conferences held in Kansas City, Chicago, Atlanta, Cincinnati, Detroit, Hartford, Birmingham, Washington and Cleveland. Eight hundred extra consultants were appointed from lay organizations and officers of teacher organizations and school systems. They drafted a charter of educational finance which has been studied by all lay organizations to help in the solution of the vexing problem of financing the schools. The work of this great interpretative group was helped by a study outline prepared by the field secretary of the association for lay study of the report. The commission was augmented this year by the addition of two members appointed by our President. As a result of the decision by the executive committee in Cleveland, in February, 1934, it will continue its work on educational recovery and reconstruction. The division of research also prepared monthly reports for these 800 consultants, compiled a directory of 400 committee reports relating to educational recovery and tabulated reports on rural school conditions in 2,000 counties. It supplemented the report and work of the joint commission by publishing four pertinent pamphlets: (1) "Essentials of Taxation"; (2) "Evaluating the Public Schools"; (3) "Current Status of the Kindergarten," and (4) "Federal Emergency Aid for Education Imperative."

The research division has planned, in response to the legislative commission, a state school legislative reference service. It will be financed by the association and will serve to help states plan for far-reaching improvements in school systems. No doubt it will suggest new tax bases, a larger administrative unit, a better way of selecting members of boards of education, as well as limiting their numbers. Strange, is it not, that in our nation there are on an average of two members of boards of education for each teacher?

Planning this year for a more complete interpretation of the schools to the public by us has brought forth the eighth yearbook of the Department of Classroom Teachers, called "Teacher and Public." It is full of actual experiences that have won public understanding and defense for schools. It was written by teachers from their actual experiences. The ninth chapter of the 1934 yearbook of the Department of Superintendence, called "Helping Citizens Know Their Schools," also gives additional help for the interpretation of the school. One of the outstanding contributions of the year for interpreting the schools to the people has been the publication by the National Congress of Parents and Teachers of a 200-page book called "Our Public Schools." This gives simple, concrete information about schools, so that parents may be helped to protect education against unwise economies and unjust slashes of the school budget. It was prepared by our field secretary, Charl Williams. Nineteen leading educators and experts have written chapters in simple, interesting, non-technical language, telling the story of the development, organization and maintenance of our public schools and their purpose in the new social order. This book should also be discussed in faculty meetings, so that teachers and public may "speak the same language" in defending education in coming legislative sessions.

The journal has also sponsored vitalized commencement programs to register that finer interpretation of schools in students' minds, so that they will continue their interest and support, when they, in turn, shall be taxpayers. It has been my privilege to attend six commencements this June and they bore marvelous testimony to a superfine kind of program and teaching.

Too much praise can not be given our division of publicity. Side by side with it goes the work of the research division. When you hear teachers say "What does the NEA do for me?" take out this one year's list of accomplishments and its plans for the future and let it answer the question.

Under all the activity of the National Education Association is the sure foundation of scientific data produced by the research division. It carried on this year the following studies concerning teacher welfare and school efficiency:

(1) For the committee on the economic status of the teacher, it collected, checked and tabulated 30,000 monthly reports; thus securing the first reasonably accurate status of the American teacher.

(2) For the Department of Classroom Teachers, it reviewed 42 investigations in school publicity and prepared 39 statistical charts and tables, as well as editorial assistance in "Teacher and Public."

(3) For the retirement committee, it collected information on the effects of the depression on 22 state retirement systems.

(4) For the legislative commission, it collected the data concerning the need for Federal Emergency Aid. It helped draft the six-point program; conducted six nation-wide telegraphic surveys of educational conditions and prepared 200 pages of reports to support the survey.

(5) For the Department of Elementary School Principals, it contributed several chapters to the thirteenth yearbook.

(6) For the committee on social and economic goals, it conducted a survey of social-civic education.

(7) For the Department of Superintendence, it collected data, drafted the final chapter of the twelfth yearbook and helped in the development and management of 77 topic groups at the Cleveland convention.

It also issued five research bulletins: (1) "Constructive Economy in Education"; (2) "Current Conditions in the Nation's Schools"; (3) "Five Years of State Revenue Legislation, 1929–1933"; (4) "Education for Character. (a) The Social and Psychological Background"; (5) "Education for Character. (b) Improving the School Program."

It has answered 2,000 letters and issued special circulars dealing with the NIRA; school-building construction; unpaid salaries of teachers; the schedule of high-school classes; expenditures for school books; and school legislation of 1933. For next year there are already visions for increased service which you may read in Dr. Carr's report.

The year's work would be very incomplete without mention of the heroic work of our legislative commission, with Dr. Sidney Hall as chairman. Late in the summer, to give teachers a voice to state the relative value of their services, we formulated a code to state fair minimum credentials and salaries of teachers. It was hoped that we could prevent the scaling down of salaries below codes offered by the various industries. It was offered to the administrative officers of the NRA in a special conference and rejected because no government employees were permitted to make codes. In early October, 32 national groups met under the leadership of Dr. James N. Rule, state superintendent of Pennsylvania, to discuss the crisis in education. As a result, a six-point program for legislation enactment was drafted. Dr. James H. Richmond, state superintendent of Kentucky, was made chairman of the National Committee for Federal Emergency Aid for Education, and Mr. James W. Cammack was made his first assistant. You know the program. It was perfectly reported in the journal. You know how generously you responded to financing it. The grilling work of watching and waiting and moving the bills was in large measure carried on by Mr. Cammack.

Thirty-three states received sums to keep rural schools open in communities of 5,000 population or less. Approximately $17,000,000 was spent by the state superintendent and the state emergency relief commission without any federal control. This act has been completed and has ceased. In addition, approximately $9,000,000 were released for employing teachers who did not have positions; nursery, adult education, continuation, rehabilitation and special classes for handicapped pupils and vocational courses were given.

Through PWA about $70,000,000 were spent for erection of school buildings on a 70–30 basis by local districts and Federal Government, respectively.

To pay teachers salaries incurred before June, 1934, the Sabath Amendment of the Home Industries Act has been signed for loans to school districts to pay salaries in arrears.

I have given you a vision of organization activities with which you have entrusted us this year—to increase understanding among us, to interpret education to our fellow citizens, to thwart and nullify inimical forces that would negate the finest influence of school services and deny them support. The vision is not complete without a danger signal. There are 200,000 members in the National Education Association. The indifference of the 800,000 inert members of the profession is the first menace. Inertia in four fifths of the physical body would be paralysis. Moreover, the greatest criticism comes from those whose psychology is to criticize, to call off attention from their own inactivity. Making a contribution of service cures much fault-finding. If there has been no participation in the program of understanding, planning, achievement, in all honor there should be no adverse criticism. Drones may shirk, but workers work!

There is also a tendency on the part of some educators to take the cream of the profession and abrogate to themselves the credit of the success which belongs to the profession as a whole. To skim off the successes and deny the defeats is unsportsmanlike and entirely unprofessional. Teachers who do much experimentation should guard against exploitation of their best work by those who had no part in it.

To ask any other organization to make the teachers' cause, in itself, synonymous with theirs is to deny the ability of the profession to organize for its own defense, or else to admit the weakness of professional organization to insure its own defense and secure its own aims. Every lay organization is basically and essentially interested in education and must become defenders of education. All political parties must be interested in the support of education. Every profession must also be interested in and defend education per se, not the teacher separated from her work. The profession itself is its own paramount defender. Therefore, teachers who have passed on to other organizations their memberships and affiliation, in the hope of protection, have separated themselves from their work and are no longer under the defense of education. Of those teachers we ask, "Have you given your profession 100 per cent. of your support?" "If not, why not?" We urge a united profession, with faith in ability to plan and work cooperatively for all progress and prestige of the group as a whole. We urge the ideal that our profession best defends itself through fine service, fine ethics and loyalty within the group.

Organizations, like clocks, go from the motion members give them and, as organizations, are made and moved by us; so by us they may be ruined. Wherefore our organization depends rather on us than we on our organization. Let us, therefore, strengthen ourselves in service, spirit and dedication that it may be well with all of us because of each of us.

Our vision for next year must include greater cooperation with our wonderful lay organizations, more scientific information, definite work for tax reforms and restoration of school budgets, social contacts with homes, and clubs, articles for magazines, larger administrative units. (In some places there are 4,285 teachers to one member of a Board of Education. On an average, there is one board member for two teachers in the United States, and in twelve states there are more board members than teachers! From this statement, we can see visions of interesting work in the voyage ahead.

And, teachers, we must put America first, not merely in the assertion of rights, but in the glad assumption of duties, not in splendid icy isolation, but in warm-hearted cooperation. In Flanders Fields, Allan Seegar says the soldiers had "*felt* dawn." We, too, must feel dawn—the stir of vitality that wakes us to a new endeavor, the thankfulness for work to do. "Listen to the salutation of the dawn. Look to this day, for it is life. In its brief course, lie all the verities and realities of your existence; the bliss of growth, the glory of action, the splendor of beauty. For yesterday is but a dream, and to-morrow is only a vision, but to-day well lived, makes of every yesterday a dream of happiness, and every to-morrow a vision of hope. Look well, therefore, to this day, for such is the salutation of the dawn," as you begin your voyage into a happy new year of service.

# ACADEMIC FREEDOM[1]

By Dr. THOMAS W. GOSLING

NATIONAL DIRECTOR, AMERICAN JUNIOR RED CROSS

At one time academic freedom referred primarily to teaching. It meant the right of the teacher without let or hindrance to teach whatever he pleased. It assumed that the teacher would choose to teach only within the field in which he had special qualifications. It assumed also that students were under no compulsion to attend the teacher's lectures or to pay him any fees for his labors. Thus from the beginning the freedom of the learner was involved in the freedom of the teacher.

The social situations which made this kind of academic freedom possible are no longer the conventional patterns. A free society in which instruction is offered only to those who want it and who are qualified to profit by it and in which any one may teach if he can gather an audience is scarcely to be found anywhere in America. Even where instruction is offered under the

[1] An address at the convention of the National Education Association, Washington, D. C., July 3, 1934.

auspices of private organizations or societies, the teacher is expected to conform to regulations and the students in their attendance respond to certain social compulsions. Thus academic freedom has taken on new meanings as society has become more highly organized. It is now interpreted in a manner which includes many kinds of freedom under many different circumstances. Whereas academic freedom was once understood to involve the right freely to express opinions on matters of abstract principle of a purely impersonal nature, now after gradations and increments of meaning it is thought by many to confer the additional privilege of making personal attacks for purely personal ends.

### The Price of Progress

As one takes a long look backward and views the slow, intermittent, but persistent upward struggle of mankind he is deeply impressed by the part which freedom of thinking and freedom of expression have played in the human drama. It never has been altogether safe to think outside of the patterns of convention and to speak without restraint. Socrates propounded his doctrines for the enlightenment of the young men of Athens; he was charged with making "the worse appear the better reason"; and he paid for his hardihood by being forced to drink the poison hemlock. But his death did not end all. Through his disciple Plato and a host of followers he gave to Athens a position of distinction and of leadership which for centuries has supplied positive direction to human affairs. Galileo, imprisoned for proclaiming that the earth is round, lives on, while even the names of his persecutors have scarcely a place in the memory of men; and the earth still revolves daily on its axis, and relentlessly follows its orbit around the sun. Countless men have dared to speak the truth and have been willing to pay the price. "The blood of the martyrs is the seed of the Church." The fact is that without free utterance even at a price the moral and spiritual progress of the world would be seriously impeded if not altogether restrained.

### Freedom in the Schools

On this occasion we wish to deal specifically with the freedom of the teachers in the public schools. Are there any principles which may be accepted as policies and as guides of conduct? Are there standards of action which apply to teachers and not to other members of the community? Are teachers to be encouraged to think of their rights without giving due consideration to their duties also?

There is a realm of at least tentatively exact knowledge in which no one is privileged to express opinions contrary to accepted facts. For example, no one should be permitted to teach arithmetic to elementary school children unless he is willing to teach that two and two make four; nor should any one be permitted to teach plane geometry to high-school pupils unless he accepts the doctrine of the three dimensions of space. It is possible of course that the higher mathematics will refute our present conceptions and make it necessary for us to impart new doctrines wholly opposed to those which are now conventional. In the meantime, while the scholar continues to make his researches and to discover new truths, he teaches the known facts of the present to those who on account of their immaturity have need of safe guidance in a world which does not yet know all. Thus we have no difficulty and no argument in disposing of the question of freedom in areas where little or no controversy exists.

When we come, however, to other fields over which float the clouds of uncertainty, we find a wholly different set of problems. These become especially acute in the teaching of biology and of the social sciences. It would be helpful in resolving the difficulty if both teachers and the general public would recall the memorable words which Isocrates used in his defense of the sophists: "Remember it is not my case alone which is at issue but the education of our youth—upon which the future of others must depend." Thus it is not the whim or the predilection or the prejudice of either the teacher or the general public that counts at all in this matter. It is only the truth that counts and the welfare of the young who are to be taught. If the truth is known, it must be taught without fear or favor; if it is not known, as so often is the case in the challenging subjects of the current curriculum, then nothing remains for the teacher but to examine with his pupils all facets of the problem, including the teacher's own personal opinion, and to stimulate them to honest, penetrating and courageous investigation on their own initiative. To go beyond this is to violate the intellectual and the spiritual integrity of the learner; it is to erect the barrier of predetermined judgment between the mind of the pupil and the truth which he is seeking; it is exalting the right of the individual teacher above the welfare of the social group. The rights of the learner are as sacred as the rights of the teacher.

A careful observance of this distinction between indoctrination and free discussion will make it easier for the American teacher to include in his courses of study much vital material which hitherto has been excluded from the classroom. It is highly important that our young people should be aware of a multitude of problems which have a direct bearing upon the social, economic and political welfare of the nation and that they should be prepared in the schools to deal with these problems intelligently and fearlessly after the days of formal schooling are over. In this phase of the teacher's work academic freedom means the right to discuss all questions freely, dispassionately, honestly, and to enjoy immunity from attack.

The attainment of this kind of academic freedom rests largely in the hands of the teachers themselves. There are likely to be some martyrs before the end is achieved; but if the teaching profession in the interest of the public welfare will take and hold a consistent and determined position, much individual suffering and hardship may be avoided.

### Freedom to Participate in Civic Activities

There is another kind of academic freedom which teachers now most earnestly desire. They are not content to live segregated lives, shut out from participation in the affairs of the world. Their former isolation from the stream of normal activities has brought upon them a certain condescending sympathy which at times has proved highly offensive. They are asking for the full recognition of their rights as citizens and they are asserting a claim to just appraisal of their services to society. The public should applaud this virile attitude, because it means that the youth of the land will be taught by men and women who have strength and courage. Only such are fit to teach the children of America.

This new kind of academic freedom will make available to the nation vast resources of energy, intelligence and idealism at a time when they are sorely needed. The financial depression has revealed the teachers to themselves. It has brought to them a sense of their social utility; it has found them ready and eager to make sacrifices for the children and their families; and it has made them acceptable to communities which did not fully realize their worth before. It is unthinkable that having once achieved this social status, teachers will fail to move on into other areas of service.

The whole theory of academic freedom is predicated not solely or primarily upon a just conception of individual rights, but chiefly upon a broad view of social welfare. It is highly important in all fields of human activity that the truth shall be known. The truth is not ascertained by the counting of noses or by the casting of ballots. Least of all can it be determined by the use of force or compulsion. Truth is a special gift to open minds operating in an atmosphere of honest inquiry and of untrammeled freedom. The state, which is society in an organized form, has a peculiar interest in fostering and maintaining the conditions under which truth may be revealed. The progressive discovery and application of new truths constitute the indispensable requisites of national safety and of national progress.

The particular service which our American teachers are prepared to render to-day is to keep open the avenues of discussion and of discriminating inquiry concerning the state of the nation. Unfortunate occurrences beyond our borders have shown how easy it is to conscript public opinion and to make it subservient to the requirements of centralized authority. Even in normal times in America it is difficult to have clear thinking and honest expression. All of us find ourselves hedged in by the compulsions of the various groups with which we are affiliated. Our coterie of friends, our clubs, our political and professional organizations, our business associates, all tend to impose upon us certain formulas of thinking; they almost seem to be in a conspiracy of silence and of repression from which we can free ourselves only by vigorous self-assertion—not the bombastic self-assertion of the egotist but rather the quiet and determined insistence of the individual upon his intellectual and spiritual independence. This condition, characteristic of common experience, is accentuated in periods of crisis, for these tend to marshal all forces to a common end. It is in those very times, however, that there is the greatest need of constructively critical judgments which may safely find public utterance. "Eternal vigilance is the price of liberty." It is equally true that the silence of the people is a sign that tyranny is near.

With some conspicuous exceptions, our American teachers as a body are strong supporters of the American doctrine of democracy. They are prepared under a guarantee of freedom of speech to defend this doctrine not at all as a fixed and unchanging creed, but as a definition of a living and growing organism with inherent power of adaptation to the developing genius of the American people.

## Freedom to Participate in School Administration

Within the field of school administration, academic freedom is likely to show rapid development. There is evidence of an increasing conviction that there has been too much authoritarianism in American education. The ideal school administration exhibits a maximum of cooperation and a minimum of authority. The school systems which have attained the highest distinction and which are recognized as leaders in public education have been successful in enlisting large numbers of their staffs in cooperative endeavors for the benefit of the children. The executives have been leaders who have interpreted their functions generously and unselfishly. They have not arrogated to themselves unusual dignities and powers. They have sensed a high responsibility to provide suitable and adequate teaching materials; to make the conditions of teaching as pleasant and inspiring as possible; and to discover and to develop merit everywhere. The financial situation of the past few years has made these commendable efforts unusually difficult; at the same time it has drawn teachers and administrators more closely together in sympathetic understanding and has tended to unify the profession to the great advantage of all.

The next step in the development of this new and wholesome relationship will follow when teachers are released from the fear which is the normal consequence of autocratic administration. There should be no fear in a school system except that which accompanies incompetence and dishonesty.

The machinery for the attainment of the new goals lies in the development of strong professional organizations which will conduct continuous studies of all kinds of school problems and which through intrinsic worth will make themselves indispensable helpers in the heavy tasks of administration. The teachers themselves are likely to be given as much freedom of expression as they will take. In their own interest, they will develop codes of ethics with accompanying agencies for enforcing their purposes. They will not be able to tolerate inefficiency, dishonesty or self-seeking. Their own freedom will depend upon their fitness for self-government. In the new era, the best administrator will be the person who has the highest capacity for inspiring cooperative effort and for organizing and leading willing and efficient helpers. What Charles William Eliot said of the best type of college president may be said of the best type of school administrator: "He will manifest no desire whatever for arbitrary power over masses of human beings, or for what is ordinarily called fame or glory."

### OBSTACLES TO FREEDOM

The chief obstacle in the way of attaining academic freedom is likely to be found in the inertia or the fear or the self-interest of those who have not been accustomed to accord this freedom to others. It will be found also in that strange multifarious public opinion which is curiously averse to the acceptance of new ideas. Doubtless in coming into this new freedom teachers will commit many excesses. Some, for example, will forget that if they have rights, they have also correlative duties. The right to freedom of speech involves the accompanying duty to deal justly with all men and to observe the principles of decency and honor. These are essential limitations upon academic freedom. When these limitations are not observed, teachers will subject themselves to merited criticism. It may seem at times that their charter of freedom should be revoked. But the struggle for freedom can not be stopped. It is the assertion of the universal in man; as such it may suffer reverses, but never permanent defeat.

The opponents of academic freedom may properly be reminded that in the long run less of harm will be done by the abuse of freedom than by efforts to suppress it. We are attempting in America to develop a cooperative society founded on good will, fair dealing and mutual helpfulness. Faith in the common man and faith in the ultimate triumph of truth over falsehood are fundamental to the success of our program. If we have faith, we shall tolerate error because we shall know that it can not survive. It is better for us all that error should be brought out into the light rather than that it should be permitted to hide in dark places and do its mischievous work in secret. Light, freedom and life are both the means and the end of our struggle.

### CONCLUSION

Thus academic freedom in its various forms is seen to be only one phase of that spiritual freedom to which we all aspire. It is essential not only for the happiness of the individual, but also for the strength and the well-being of the state. A denial of freedom is a denial of a universal human imperative. Any attempt at denial can end only in tragedy.

# EDUCATIONAL EVENTS

## WORK OF THE AUSTRALIAN COUNCIL FOR EDUCATIONAL RESEARCH

ACCORDING to information sent us from the Australian Council for Educational Research, the Carnegie Corporation of New York has during recent years in various ways shown an interest in Australian education and has made grants of money available for various purposes. Its largest single benefaction has been the grant made for the support of the Council for Educational Research, but it has in addition given grants for adult education, for libraries and for Australian educationists who have wished to go abroad. Dr. James E. Russell and Dr. L. D. Coffman have visited Australia in order to make observations on behalf of the Carnegie Corporation. Word has recently been received that the president of the corporation, Dr. F. P. Keppel, hopes to visit Australia in the early part of next year.

The Carnegie Corporation has recently arranged for the preparation of a number of sets of books and materials for assisting in the teaching of art in secondary schools. Each set consists of approximately 125 books and 900 photographs and color reproductions. The value of each set is about two thousand dollars. The Carnegie Corporation has notified its intention of supplying three of these sets for use in Australia, and has asked the Council for Educational Research to advise it in the matter of making the best possible use of the sets.

The corporation has also made arrangements to finance a comprehensive survey of library facilities in Australia. The investigation will include not only public and university libraries, but also libraries in all types of schools. The survey is to be carried out by Ralph Munn, who is in charge of the Carnegie Library at Pittsburgh, acting in cooperation with Mr. E. R. Pitt, who is in charge of the Public Library at Melbourne.

The council has on hand the preparation of a comprehensive report on secondary education in Australia. It is hoped in this report to do for Australia what the report on "The Education of the Adolescent" (Hadow Report) did for England. Chapters are being prepared by educationists associated both with the Education Departments and with private secondary schools. The report is being prepared under the editorship of Dr. P. R. Cole, who also edited the council's book on the Primary School Curriculum.

## STUDENT TROUBLES AT THE UNIVERSITY OF GÖTTINGEN

ACCORDING to press dispatches to *The New York Times,* an open fight by students of the University of Göttingen against Nazi rule was a fresh contribution on July 16 to the general discontent in Germany. In the revolt, the first instance of the kind under the Hitler régime, 1,000 fraternity men battled with brown-shirted Nazi students in defense of their ancient colors.

The fight broke out after the fraternity men had held a meeting at which they protested vigorously against the dissolution of the ancient university society. Fire hoses were turned on the combatants and finally order was restored after the arrest of ten leaders, who were charged with "breach of the peace and incitement to revolt."

Two fraternities were suspended until further notice by the president of the university, acting under pressure of the Nazi-conducted students' federation.

The incident was viewed as significant, since it provided the first instance of open revolt among German students, the vast majority of whom have been ardent supporters of the Nazi movement from its earliest days. It was also taken as an indication of the extent of dissatisfaction that was climaxed by the bloody June 30 "purging" of Nazi ranks.

The national executive body of the Hitler Youth organization has forbidden the public burning of school caps taken from well-to-do youths on the ground that this leads to the destruction of substantial quantities of raw materials, which in Germany's situation can not be allowed. The collection of the caps and presentation of them to rag dealers is recommended.

It should be explained that local Hitler Youth enthusiasts recently have been making bonfires of these caps as a symbol of that abolition of class distinctions which is said to be in progress. The continued wearing of caps after leaving school by youths of the moneyed classes apparently has caused ill-feeling among their fellows in the working classes.

## EUROPEAN PSYCHOLOGICAL FIELD TRIP

UNDER the auspices of the American Peoples College in Europe a field trip in the psychology of social change will be given under the direction of Dr. Goodwin Watson, professor of psychology, Teachers College, Columbia University. This trip, which commences on August 15 and lasts for five weeks, is especially designed for those who have the opportunity to travel only between the end of summer school and the beginning of college. Russia, Scandinavia, England and Scotland are the four countries in which a survey will be made of various theories and practical application of psychological methods. For a laboratory Dr. Watson will use Moscow and Leningrad under the communist régime, London with the traditional English method of democracy, and Denmark with its use of universal adult education to achieve social aims. The group, which is open to both men and women, will attend the meetings of the section of psychology of the British Association for the Advancement of Science, which meets in Aberdeen this year.

This psychological field trip is one of several short European study tours being planned this summer for those with short vacations by the American Peoples College in Europe in addition to its longer travel courses. With its headquarters in the heart of the Tyrolean Alps the college was founded five years ago under the auspices of a group of progressive American educators interested in bettering international understanding and in making European study and travel possible for young Americans of limited means.

Dr. John Dewey, of Columbia University; Dr. Harry A. Overstreet, of the College of the City of New York, and Dr. Jay B. Nash, of New York University, are members of its educational advisory board. The New York office of the college is at 545 Fifth Avenue.

## ADULT EDUCATION IN NEW YORK CITY

THE *New York Herald Tribune* reports that after an eighteen months' program of free adult education in New York City, the State Education Department, in cooperation with the New York City Board of Education and the New York State Temporary Relief Administration and various other organizations will continue with a new summer session, offering more than 376 different subjects in a series of free courses for adults, seventeen years of age or older. This summer session will continue through to the fall, when it is planned to further extend the free day adult educational programs.

On December 18, 1932, more than 3,400 students registered in the various classes in response to that first announcement. Now 700 teachers are actively employed. They give instruction to approximately 25,000 men and women, in classes conducted in various settlement centers and public-school buildings throughout the city. The students who have enrolled for instruction in one or more subjects are taught five days a week, making an aggregate weekly student attendance of 75,000. Thus, even with such figures compiled in the regular average student attendance, there is also the constant turnover and transient groups, which run into unlimited numbers. In one instance in the engineering courses, from an enrolment of 1,300 students, 177 students have found employment during a period of seven weeks. In this case the student found that his time had been profitably passed in the state classes. The program of the State Adult Education Department serves to give the unemployed person an opportunity to study any subject he desires.

A grant has been obtained from the General Education Board by New York University to include also a period of six weeks' teacher-training for those teachers already engaged in the New York adult education project. These special teaching activities will be under the direction of Dr. L. A. Wilson, assistant commissioner for vocational and extension education, New York State Education Department, assisted by Dr. Ned H. Dearborn, of New York University. An attendance of approximately five hours a week will be required of all teachers. This training is only for teachers now on duty.

For the public, however, the following free summer courses will be offered: Agriculture, art, commerce, drama, general cultural subjects, homemaking, industry, music and technical branches. These courses will cover subject-matter and classes in nearly every field of trade and commercial and cultural endeavor. The public is invited to enroll for study free of charge. No special requirements are demanded, except in the trade extension courses.

The schools which will be open for general registration throughout the month of July in Manhattan are Central Needle Trades School, Central High School of Business and Arts, East Side Continuation School, Harlem Girls' Continuation School, New York Urban League, Unit of the Dance, Music and Drama; Wall Street Y. M. C. A., West Side Continuation School and Y. M. C. A. at 179 West 137th Street. The schools in Brooklyn are Brooklyn Girls' Continuation School and Brooklyn Urban League. The Bronx Vocational High School will serve the Bronx.

## FEDERAL AID FOR COLLEGE STUDENTS

The Federal Emergency Relief Administration, according to an announcement by Aubrey Williams, acting administrator, will assist 100,000 needy young men and women to earn their way through college next year by paying them for part-time jobs. Thirteen and a half million dollars have been appropriated for the school year of 1934–35, about $1,500,000 a month for nine months.

This is an enlargement of a movement begun last year at the suggestion of several college and university authorities, some of whom brought the matter before President Roosevelt personally. In part, it represents an effort to lessen unemployment this winter.

Results of the student-aid program, under which about 75,000 students were enabled to stay in college last year, are said to have been so satisfactory that Harry L. Hopkins, federal emergency relief administrator, has authorized expansion of the work.

By increasing the percentage of enrolment that each qualifying institution may aid, 25,000 more students can be added. Last year the colleges were permitted to assist ten per cent. of their enrolment; this year they may help twelve per cent.

The 100,000 students will be divided between men and women in each institution in proportion to the number of each registered. Each student will be allowed to earn up to $20 a month, and allotments to the colleges will be based on an average of $15 a month for each student.

The FERA funds will be allotted through state emergency relief administrations to non-profit-making institutions. The students will work part time on socially desirable projects, including the kinds customarily performed by students working their way, such as clerical, library and research jobs. Regular class instruction is excluded.

An addition to the kind of work to be done will be assignments to teaching adult education and extension classes, supervision of recreational activities, and other services that will increase the usefulness of the colleges to near-by communities. Some of the students may be assigned to local emergency relief administrations to assist in specialties, such as health work, nutrition, vocational agriculture and home making.

General supervision of the student-aid program is in the hands of Dr. L. R. Alderman, of the U. S. Office of Education, director of the educational division of the Federal Emergency Relief Administration.

## SUMMER PLAY SCHOOLS IN NEW YORK CITY

Following the recommendation of Associate Superintendent William E. Grady, in charge of summer play activities, according to the *New York Sun,* the establishment of thirty additional vacation playgrounds at public schools has been approved by the New York City Board of Superintendents, bringing the total number of school play yards in operation this summer up to 454. The regular staff of playground instructors employed by the school board has been augmented by the assignment of 300 relief teachers.

The new play yards have been made possible through the establishment at vacation playground centers of summer "day camps," staffed by 425 teachers on the relief rolls, in addition to the 300 assigned to regular playgrounds. Since there would be duplication of work if playgrounds and "day camps" were in the same buildings, it has been decided to remove the vacation playground staffs and place their members in new locations. The new arrangement adds sixty-eight to the original number of play centers.

There were opened on July 9 fifteen new summer play schools, which will be conducted during July and August in settlement houses, community and church centers and in public school buildings with some teacher service supplied by the Board of Education through its Department of Extension Activities. The organizations conducting Play Schools provide the additional funds needed for food, supplies and teacher service.

Children attending the schools will be carefully examined by physicians with the cooperation of the Board of Health. Where remedial defects are found, the home visitor or social worker in the school will see that the children have proper care in a clinic, at home and in the school.

The Child Study Association, through its summer play schools committee and staff, acts in an advisory and organizing capacity and offers to directors and teachers a short series of discussion meetings on teacher-child relationships and on program-planning with demonstrations of procedures, with the use of clay, paints and wood. This training has this year for the first time been made available to teachers who have been allocated to these organizations from the Works Division of the Department of Public Works.

Children attending the play schools are of many and varying backgrounds, races and nationalities and economic status. The program which is most flexible grows out of the children's own interest and experience and is carried on in buildings and out-of-doors. When the children come in the morning they discuss with their teacher plans for the day or perhaps the week. They may want to learn more about the foods they eat or the clothing they wear and where and how this food and clothing come. The children with their teachers may visit a neighboring store or larger market, a near-by dock or railroad terminus. Such a trip may lead them on their return to school to construct a train or boat, to paint a picture of the dock, to fashion fruits out of clay, or to write a story about their trip. A well-prepared, nutritious meal is provided at noon for every child and the time is used not only for eating but for social training as well. After lunch is finished the children rest. Following the rest period there may be shower-baths or swimming and then perhaps some out-of-door games or a story-telling time. Before leaving school light refreshment is provided.

Of the fifteen play schools, three or four will be used as observation centers. Emphasis will be placed on parent and teacher guidance, on the use of the out-of-doors for an integrated program of educational and recreational activities that might be adapted to a playground, on constructive lunch procedures, and on a class in homemaking for boys and girls together.

One or two new schools are being opened this summer for more privileged groups of children. This is also a new departure and opens a new field of work for the play school.

## THE UNIVERSITY OF NEWARK, N. J.

At a meeting of the trustees at the Mercer Beasley School of Law and the Newark Institute of Arts and Sciences held on July 13, it was voted to merge the two institutions to be known in the future as the University of Newark. The trustees of both schools became the board of trustees of the new institution.

The two schools will retain their names as departments of the university and will open late in September in quarters to be selected later. The law school now has quarters in the Industrial Building, with a student body of about 250, and the institute at 17 Academy Street, with about 600 students. The resources of the two schools amount to about $175,000.

The merger has been under discussion for several years, and some months ago the name of the university was incorporated.

Franklin Conklin, Jr., who was president of the Newark Institute, was elected president of the new university. The vice-president is Arthur F. Egner, who was president of Mercer Beasley. William Morgan, who was secretary of the institute, was made secretary of the university, and Harrison P. Lindabury, treasurer of the law school, takes that post in the university.

Mercer Beasley, which was opened in 1926, gives degrees of bachelor of laws and master of laws. The institute was organized in 1910 and gave college courses which were accepted as credits toward a degree at New York University. It was announced that the new university would apply to the State Board of Education for permission to grant degrees of bachelor of arts, bachelor of science and bachelor of commercial science.

The faculty of the law school will remain as at present and its work will be under the supervision of a committee comprising members of its present executive committee. The college faculty will be announced later. The standing committee of the Newark Institute will supervise the work of the college department.

At one time it was proposed to include in the merger the New Jersey Law School, Dana College and Seth Boyden School of Business. Negotiations, however, fell through.

## GIFTS AND LEGACIES FOR HARVARD UNIVERSITY

Harvard University received in gifts and legacies during the year 1933 a total amount of $2,601,469.60. These were in addition to income paid as capital by the trustees under the will of Gordon McKay, and to sums received for pensions from the Carnegie Foundation.

The class of 1909 made a gift of $100,000 to the university. This follows the custom of a large gift from the twenty-fifth reunion class at every commencement.

The list follows, all gifts of not less than $25,000 being listed under the name of the donor:

Anonymous—Additional gift for the Society of Fellows Foundation, $453,212.19.

Anonymous—Additional gift for the ''Geophysical Research Fund of Blue Hill Observatory,'' $26,932.36.

Earl Willson Bemis—To establish the ''Elizabeth F. Bemis Fund'' in memory of his mother, the income only to be used for the general purposes of the Harvard Astronomical Observatory, $50,000; to establish the ''Elizabeth Willson Stone Fund'' in memory of his grandmother, the income only to be used for the general purposes of the Gray Herbarium, $50,000; total, $100,000.

Two Hundred and Fifty Associates of the Harvard Business School—For research, and for the current needs of the library of the school, $35,000.

Anonymous—To establish the ''Eleanor Husted Leal Fund,'' the income from which shall be used by the Cancer Commission of Harvard University for cancer research, $50,000.

Estate of Annie S. Coburn (Mrs. Lewis Larned Coburn)—On account of her bequest, ''to be held as a fund to defray the expense of maintenance of all said articles (articles bequeathed by Mrs. Coburn to the President and Fellows of Harvard College for the William Hayes Fogg Art Museum) and, if sufficient therefor, to purchase additional paintings or pottery for the said Fogg Museum,'' $18,503.70; on account of her bequest, ''to be known as the Lewis Larned Coburn Memorial Fund in memory of my husband, who graduated from the Law School of Harvard University in 1861, the income therefrom to be used to give scholarships to students in said Law School'' . . . , $38,273.19; total, $56,776.89.

The Commonwealth Fund—For research in criminology in the Law School, $8,500; additional, for fellowships in the Medical School, $16,775; additional, for graduate instruction in the Medical School, $15,562.50; total, $40,837.50.

General Education Board—Additional, for the Graduate School of Education in conducting its ''Growth Study,'' $15,000; for the School of Public Health in conducting its ''Growth Study,'' $18,000; additional, for advanced work in the humanities in the Divisions of Ancient and Modern Languages, $35,603.90; total, $68,603.90.

The Harvard Fund—Additional, many subscriptions, $75,638.31.

Harvard-Yenching Institute—For expenditures payable through Harvard University, $50,000.

Estate of James Loeb—On account of his bequest, ''to be known as and entitled The Loeb Classical Library Foundation . . . the income of said foundation shall be used to defray . . . expenses involved in carrying on and completing the Loeb Classical Library, bequeathed by Mr. Loeb to the college'' . . . . Upon completion, the annual income is to be used ''for the encouragement of special research at home and abroad in the province of archeology and of Greek and Latin literature'' . . . , $100,000.

Estate of Wallace Macfarlane—On account of his residuary bequest, ''to the President and Fellows of Harvard College . . . the same to be used for such college or university purpose or purposes as said President and Fellows shall determine,'' $100,111.14.

Estate of Miss Caroline E. Peabody—Her bequest, to establish '' 'The Andrew Preston Peabody Fund'; the income to be used for the purchase of books for the University Library'' . . . , $100,388.89.

Estate of William L. Richardson—His bequest, ''for the endowment of a Professorship of Obstetrics, the income only to be used for the salary of the professor,'' $100,000; his bequest, "to be known as the Jeffrey Richardson Fellowship in the Harvard Medical School, the net income thereof to be awarded each year by the Faculty of Medicine to some deserving student, upon his graduation from the Harvard Medical School, who desires to continue his studies either here or abroad" . . . , $40,000; on account of his residuary bequest, "the income only to be used for such purposes of the university as the President and Fellows shall from time to time determine," $376,154.35; total, $516,154.35.

The Rockefeller Foundation—For the Division of Anthropology, $15,000; "for chemical research to determine the heats of organic reactions," $8,000; toward the support of the Graduate School of City Planning, $29,855.04; for fellowships and salaries, $4,600; for research in geophysics, $10,000; for advanced work in the humanities in the Divisions of Ancient and Modern Languages, $12,500; for research in industrial hazards, $95,471.68; for the *Journal of Industrial Hygiene*, $2,000; for researches in physiology and in physical chemistry, $24,-999.96; for research in the field of international relations, $28,780.59; for research in the social sciences, $65,852.64; total, $297,059.91.

Estate of Stuart Wyeth—Additional, on account of his residuary, unrestricted bequest, $26,-749.67.

Other contributions less than $25,000, $504,004.56.

## CONFERENCE OF EDUCATIONAL WORKERS IN CORRECTIONAL INSTITUTIONS

A CONFERENCE of Educational Workers in Correctional Institutions will be held under the auspices of Governor Lehman's Commission for the Study of the Educational Problems of Penal Institutions for Youth at Teachers College, Columbia University, on August 10.

Dr. N. L. Engelhardt, professor of education at Teachers College, will preside over the opening session, at which recent trends in correctional education will be discussed. There will be a luncheon meeting at the Faculty Club presided over by Dr. J. W. Ellis, commissioner of the Department of Institutions and Agencies at Trenton, N. J., at which Sam A. Lewisohn, chairman of the commission to investigate prison administration and construction in New York State, and Lewis E. Lawes, warden of Sing Sing prison, will speak. The evening session will be presided over by Dr. William F. Russell, dean of Teachers College, when addresses will be made by Calvin Derrick, superintendent of State Home for Boys, Jamesburg, N. J., and Dr. William E. Grady, associate superintendent of schools, New York City.

Arrangements have been made for five round tables in the afternoon presided over by Dr. Edgar A. Doll, director of research, Training School, Vineland, N. J.; Dr. V. C. Branham, deputy commissioner, Department of Correction, State of New York; Dr. Jesse F. Williams, professor of physical education, Teachers College, Columbia University; Edward R. Cass, general secretary, American Prison Association, New York City, and Miss Jane Hoey, assistant director of the Welfare Council of New York City.

Those taking part in the discussions will include Dr. F. Lovell Bixby, director of education, Bureau of Federal Prisons; Dr. James L. McCartney, director of classification, Elmira Reformatory; D. D. Scarborough, director of education, Attica Prison, and the Hon. William Hodson, commissioner of public welfare, New York City.

The purpose of the conference as outlined in the program is as follows:

It is easily apparent that some part of the prevention of crime is involved with programs for the treatment of convicted offenders. Furthermore, it is believed that that element of treatment which might be included under the term "education" can be made much more effective in rehabilitating the criminal than it has been in the past, or is now. Increased effectiveness in correctional education will result only when there is a pooling of the ideas of experts in the correctional field and of experts in the educational field. This conference is a step in that direction. When we can know more definitely than at present *what* education can be most valuable in a prison or reformatory, and then *how* to apply that education most effectively we shall have reached a goal worth attaining. Doubtless it would be worth while to know whether or not there is any sound basis for the arguments advanced by some of the critics of our penal system who say that no educational program can be effective as an agency in reforming the criminal. What is needed now is a scientific approach to the whole problem of education in correctional institutions. This is a task which can be accomplished when the forward-looking penologist combines his effort with that of the expert educator.

# EDUCATIONAL NOTES AND NEWS

Dr. Herbert L. Spencer, principal of the Henry Clay Frick Training School for Teachers since 1928, has been appointed dean of the college at the University of Pittsburgh by Chancellor John G. Bowman, filling the vacancy created by the resignation of Dean Lee Paul Sieg, who has become president of the University of Washington in Seattle.

Dr. Lucy L. W. Wilson, who retires this year as principal of the South Philadelphia High School for Girls, after serving for twenty years, will join the faculty of Temple University. Dr. Wilson will give courses in progressive education and on gifted and under-privileged pupils.

A breakfast in honor of Dr. W. E. Praeger, who is retiring from the department of biology at Kalamazoo College to become professor emeritus was given on June 10 by professional associates and friends. Professor Praeger was presented with a volume of congratulatory letters; addresses were made by representatives of graduate and undergraduate students and by Professor Praeger. Through the cooperation of a group of friends of Kalamazoo College with the department of biology of the University of Michigan, a tribute was paid to Professor Praeger by the establishment of the William E. Praeger Fellowship at the Biological Station of the university, at Douglas Lake, which is to be awarded yearly to a student of the college.

At a recent meeting of the Birmingham Branch of Alliance Française, Dr. Antony Constans, head of the French department of Birmingham-Southern College, was decorated by Vice-Consul Simon Klotz, on behalf of the French Government, as Officier d'Academie.

Williams College conferred at commencement the degree of doctor of science on Dr. Winterton C. Curtis, professor of zoology at the University of Missouri.

The University of Glasgow has conferred the degree of doctor of laws on the Rev. H. J. Cody, president of the University of Toronto.

Among the honorary degrees conferred at the annual graduation ceremony at St. Andrews University on June 29, the degree of doctor of laws was conferred on Miss McCutcheon, head mistress of St. Leonards and St. Katharine's Schools, and on John M. Dawson, director of education, County of Perth. Principal Sir James Irvine, vice-chancellor, performed the capping ceremony.

Professor Frederick S. Boas, president of the Elizabethan Literary Society of London, has accepted an invitation to serve as visiting professor of English literature at Columbia University during the coming year.

Dr. A. C. Eurich, of the College of Education of the University of Minnesota, will be a visiting member of the staff in educational psychology at the summer session of Stanford University.

Professor T. Moody Campbell, of Wesleyan University, who recently declined a call to become head of the department of German at the University of North Carolina, has accepted an appointment to succeed Professor James Taft Hatfield as chairman of the department of German at Northwestern University.

Louis A. Alexander, of the University of Rochester, has been promoted to a junior professorship of education.

Dr. Edna Frances Heidbreder, associate professor of psychology at the University of Minnesota, will become professor of psychology at Wellesley College.

Dr. Waldo H. Dunn, head of the department of English at the College of Wooster, has resigned to become professor of English at Scripps College, Claremont, California. Dr. Dunn was a visiting professor of English at Scripps College in 1931–32.

Dr. J. K. Galbraith, research assistant on the Giannini Foundation of Agricultural Economics of the University of California, has been appointed instructor in economics at Harvard University.

Walter G. Whitman, associate director of research of the Standard Oil Company of Indiana, has been appointed head of the department of chemical engineering at the Massachusetts Institute of Technology. Professor Whitman succeeds the late Professor William P. Ryan, who died in June, 1933. Since that time Dr. Warren K. Lewis has directed the affairs of the department as acting head.

DR. T. SMITH TAYLOR, who for the last nine years has had charge of the Physical Laboratory of the Bakelite Corporation at Bloomfield, New Jersey, was recently appointed head of the department of physics at Washington and Jefferson College, Washington, Pa.

JOHN E. ALCOTT, for the last six years Massachusetts state supervisor of vocational art education in industry and business, and head of the department of design of the Massachusetts School of Art, has joined the staff of the advertising firm of John Donnelly and Sons.

LOUIS M. KLEIN, head of the department of languages in Harrison High School, New York, has been chosen principal of the school to succeed Holland D. Roberts, who resigned last month to accept an instructorship in English at Stanford University.

GUY N. HARTMAN has been appointed to the superintendency of the Somerset County schools, Pennsylvania. He succeeds W. H. Kretchman, who has held the position for many years and who will retire this month.

DR. ALLAN W. ROWE, professor of chemistry at Boston University, has been elected a trustee of Norwich University, Vermont.

CHARLES E. RUSH, associate librarian of the Yale University Library, has been elected a member of the Board of Trustees of Connecticut College for Women, to fill the unexpired term of the late George S. Palmer.

R. E. BLACKWELL, director of public relations at Franklin College during the past seven years, has resigned to accept an appointment as assistant to the president of the University of Louisville.

AT the recent annual meeting of the Board of Trustees of Birmingham-Southern College, Mrs. William H. Stockham was elected president of the board. During the past year Mrs. Stockham was vice-president and chairman of the executive committee.

DR. I. M. LINFORTH, chairman of the department of Greek at the University of California, has been appointed professor of Greek language and literature in the American School of Classical Studies, Athens, Greece.

LLOYD K. GARRISON, dean of the University of Wisconsin Law School, has been appointed chairman of the new National Labor Relations Board by President Roosevelt. It is reported that Dean Garrison may be able to serve only temporarily on the board, since he has leave of absence of less than three months from the university.

THE Bulgarian Government has appointed Clayton E. Whipple, of Perry, N. Y., adviser in the reorganization of the rural education system now being inaugurated by the Ministry of Economy and Education. Mr. Whipple, who is the representative of the Near East Foundation in Bulgaria, has been in charge of rural extension work in connection with the Foundation's Folk School at Pordim, near Plevna.

DR. W. A. WARDIA, dean of arts at the University of Bombay, India, lectured on "The Bearing of Religion on the Politics and Political Problems of India" before the agricultural assembly of the Iowa State College on July 20.

DR. FRED M. FLING, head of the department of European history at the University of Nebraska, died on July 6 at the age of seventy-three years. Dr. Fling was one of the founders of the *Historical Outlook*. Last January he was reelected a member of the committee of one hundred electors of the American Hall of Fame.

ACCORDING to press reports, Governor Gifford Pinchot of Pennsylvania plans to lay before the next legislature a demand for a complete investigation of academic freedom at the University of Pittsburgh. In a letter to Dr. John G. Bowman, chancellor, Governor Pinchot made plain his attitude on the dismissal of Dr. Ralph E. Turner, professor of history. The university received a state subsidy of $1,188,000 for the 1933–35 biennium. The governor cited the Dr. Turner incident as one of a series of similar actions taken by the university, "which indicate that its purposes as an institution of higher learning have been perverted to conform to the views of a small group of wealthy and powerful men."

THE eighth International Congress of Philosophy is to be held in Prague from September 2 to 7. Immediately following, from September 11 to 15, the sixth International Moral Education Congress will be held in Cracow. It is hoped by the committees in charge that delegates and visitors may be able to attend both congresses.

Appraisal and Readjustment in Education was the subject of the fifth annual educational conference which was attended by several hundred superintendents, principals and teachers at the University of Michigan on July 10 and 11. Included in the program were topics and speakers as follows: "Planning—A Democratic Concept," by Arthur B. Moehlman, professor of administration and supervision, University of Michigan; "Problems Facing Our Michigan Educational System," by Dr. Paul F. Voelker, state superintendent of public instruction, and "Major Decisions of the Washington Meeting of the National Education Association," by E. T. Cameron, Michigan Education Association. "The Significance of the Resolutions Adopted by the Washington Meeting of the National Education Association," by Dr. Paul T. Rankin, supervising director of research and adjustment, Board of Education, Detroit; "Plans of the Joint National Commission on the Emergency in Education and National Reconstruction," by Dean J. B. Edmonson, School of Education, University of Michigan; "A Program for Educational Recovery for Michigan Schools," by Dr. Eugene B. Elliott, Michigan Education Association; "A Review of the Goals of Public Education in Michigan," by Dr. S. A. Courtis, professor of education, University of Michigan, and "The Social and Economic Developments in the Tennessee Valley and their Educational Implications," by Dr. Floyd Reeves, Tennessee Valley Authority.

"Current Educational Issues in California" was the general topic of a five-day conference for state educational leaders held at the University of Southern California from July 16 to 20. Dr. Vierling Kersey, superintendent of public instruction for the State of California; Dr. Fletcher Harper Swift, professor of education, University of California; Walter R. Hepner, chief of the division of secondary education, California State Department of Education; Dr. A. A. Douglass, professor of education, Claremont Colleges; Dr. O. R. Hull, professor of education at the University of Southern California; Dr. Harry P. Smith, professor of education at Syracuse University; and A. R. Clifton, Percy R. Davis, H. S. Upjohn, and John Sexson, superintendents of Los Angeles County, Santa Monica, Long Beach, and Pasadena schools, respectively, were the leaders at the morning sessions and afternoon round table discussions. Five special topics discussed include "Reorganization of Educational Programs," "Progressive Practises in Secondary Education," "Local Units of School Administration," "The Support of Public Education" and "Public Education and the Public."

A child development service to care for the special guidance and training of children who are brought to the attention of various social agencies in Lexington and Fayette County, Kentucky, has been established at the University of Kentucky in cooperation with the Lexington Junior League. Dr. Graham B. Dimmick, assistant professor of psychology, will be in charge of the project.

George Washington University has been selected by Senator Royal S. Copeland's Education and Law Conference to take over the college, university and teacher-training aspects of the experiment in character education which is now being conducted under special Congressional appropriation in the Washington Public Schools. Acceptance by the university of this responsibility was announced recently by Dr. Charles R. Mann, chairman of the Committee on Educational Policy of the Board of Trustees of the university, to whom the matter was referred by the board with power.

Six British universities, including Oxford and Cambridge, the *Christian Science Monitor* reports, decided recently to augment their 1933 summer plans to assist the unemployed, and, as a result, the Universities' Council for Unemployment Camps has been formed. At Eastnor last year, camps for unemployed men and boys were established and the universities planned to organize at least ten similar ventures. The aim of the program, the correspondent states, has been publicized as "combating the disastrous effects of unemployment by providing camps of a definitely educative character." With this end in view, the organizing council has issued through the press an appeal for funds. The estimated cost of a camp for 100 men is £200. Each camp lasts for not less than a month. Most of the time is to be spent in recreation, but part of the time is devoted to regular work that does not "encroach upon the proper sphere of paid labor." Opportunities are provided for classes of various kinds. The camps are staffed by members of the universities. The funds are drawn from several sources. University members pay some of the expenses, and the unemployed contribute from their benefit allowance. The chief source, however, is outside contributions. The entire scheme is being fostered by the Ministry of Labor and the National Council of Social Service.

# DISCUSSION

## SOME SUGGESTIONS FOR MAKING OUR OLDER COLLEGE AND SCHOOL BUILDINGS LESS DANGEROUS IN CASE OF FIRE

WHEN we realize the seriousness of this whole problem of fire it is surprising that more careful intelligent consideration has not been given to making many of our older wooden buildings safer for our students and teachers. In some of the more recent buildings, too, there is a very real danger from the same cause on account of a lack of understanding of what really happens when a fire first starts and of how a building should be planned so that the students may get out in an orderly, natural way when the danger comes.

It has been the custom in recent years, when the older buildings have been considered unsafe, to put up a lot of iron fire-escapes outside the buildings. These, in many cases, have proved almost as hazardous, when there has been confusion and panic, as the fire itself.

In many institutions, especially where there are dormitories, it is the custom to have regular fire drills, which are a help, of course; but it is not usual in these drills for the students to be required actually to get out on the fire-escapes and make their way to the ground as they would have to do in case of real danger.

In many buildings with which we are all familiar it would be a pretty difficult process to find one's way along a smoky corridor, out through a window which may be frozen down, on to a dark fire-escape which leads perhaps to a piazza roof and from there find the stairs that lead to the ground. After all, the outside fire-escape is a makeshift method of attempting to solve this serious problem.

The real solution is to do something inside the building so that the stair halls and the corridors on the several floors will be kept clear of smoke until sufficient time is gained for the students all to be safely out; and in many old buildings this is not a difficult thing to do.

To explain what really happens when there actually is a fire and the students are warned of it either by the alarm bell or by the scream of some one who has discovered smoke: The students immediately rush from their rooms into the corridors, in which there may be smoke enough to alarm them; then they race to the nearest staircase and perhaps find that smoke is already pouring up. The natural impulse then is not to go down but to race for another stair as far away as possible, only to find perhaps even more smoke pouring up that one. Then the confusion and panic begin and priceless moments are lost in the indecision of not knowing definitely what to do.

As a matter of fact, a building never burns so rapidly that there is actual danger from the fire itself, and there is always plenty of time for everybody to get out in a quiet orderly way if it is so planned that the halls and corridors and at least one enclosed stair hall can be kept clear of smoke for a very few minutes at the start.

In planning a new building, whether it is of fireproof construction or not, this is easy to accomplish, and the building inspectors usually are intelligent enough to require it, but it is surprising to see in some comparatively new buildings how little real understanding there seems to be of the essential requirements of the problem.

In visiting a fairly new dormitory recently I realized, in going over it, that there were two staircases quite open to the corridors on the several floors, and opposite them, across the corridor, there were elevator shafts with open wrought iron doors. These shafts extended from the basement to the upper floors and into the roof space above. It was a modern fireproof building, but it would be quite possible to have the building flooded with smoke from the boiler room or the laundry or the many storerooms and trunk-rooms in the basement.

It proved quite a simple thing to build partitions with wired glass to enclose the two staircases on each floor and to put panels of wired glass behind the grilled doors of the elevators, and in this way arrange to keep the corridors and stairs clear of smoke and make it possible for the students to go down one or both staircases to the ground. They were planned really too near together but were perfectly safe, as both extended to the basement with an outside door at the rear of the building.

Any old wooden building may be made nearly as safe, as far as the lives of the students are concerned, as the most modern fireproof one if such alterations are made as to allow the students two enclosed means of egress in order that one at least shall be clear of smoke for the few minutes necessary to get every one out of the building.

The problem is a simple one if the old building has a staircase at each end, which is a very common plan. We recently made a big dormitory of this type perfectly safe at a cost of less than two hundred dollars, and thousands must have been spent in past years on iron fire-escapes all over the outside. Some of them went down on to piazza roofs which connected with an adjacent building, and some were entered at the top through small windows in closets and in some of the girls' bedrooms. Had the fire ever come it would have been almost impossible to get the girls out.

In many buildings it requires a good deal of ingenuity to work out a satisfactory arrangement, but it is always possible so to change conditions that a perfectly safe building is the result. It is true that anything that can be done along these lines will not help to prevent the building burning to the ground, but it will make the lives of the students nearly as safe as they would be in a fireproof building.

There is a type of classroom building which is very difficult to deal with, and thirty or forty years ago there were many of them built. They have one main entrance hall in the center from which one or two open staircases go to the upper floors, and these buildings are usually three and sometimes four stories high. To make things a little more dangerous the boiler room is often directly under the entrance hall, and sometimes there are open stairs going down to the basement corridor which leads to the boiler room and the service and toilet rooms. Often, too, the original old steam boiler is still hard at work trying to heat the building, having been patched up numerous times to make it pull through one more winter.

In these buildings usually the only thing to do is to build at each end an outside enclosed stair hall and open the corridors through to each one. Then it may be necessary to put in new doors, without locks, between the different classrooms so that these new stairs may be reached without having to go into the corridors which open into the smoke-filled central hall.

In planning a new non-fireproof building it would be well to make the walls of the stair halls of some fireproof material and to have metal-covered doors with wired glass; but an old wooden building may be considered perfectly safe if the stairs are really enclosed, and it is not necessary that these stairs be built of fireproof material. If there is enough fire in one of these stair halls to cause the stairs themselves to burn there will be so much smoke in the enclosure that no one will think of trying to get out of the building in that way. They will instinctively go to the other stair. And in no case should a closet be built under these stairs, or anywhere else in the stair hall, in which brooms or oily cloths or other inflammable material may be kept.

In the modern plan of boys' dormitories where there are separate staircases leading up to two apartments on each of the floors there are several arrangements possible that will allow the boys on one staircase to get through the adjacent suite into the next hall, or this may be accomplished by outside iron balconies connecting the adjacent suites.

Another type of building which really ought to come under closer inspection, by school and college authorities, than is usual, is the fraternity and sorority house. Many of them are old houses built originally for single families and they are now being occupied by perhaps twenty or thirty persons. In some cases there is only one central hall and stair, and if this were filled with smoke with perhaps actual fire on the first floor it would be serious. Sometimes in these buildings it is possible to open new doors between the rooms and so arrange things that every one can reach a low roof without going into the hall, and thus be out of danger. These buildings should be carefully looked over and when they are found to be dangerous some careful plan of safe exits should be arranged.

As to the manner of lighting the halls and corridors of these buildings at night, the different states and cities vary considerably in their requirements as to new buildings. In old ones there should be enough light to light the halls dimly all night and there ought, of course, to be no dark corners, and also there should be a red light over the door leading to each stair hall.

There is another thing which should be given careful attention in making an old building safer in case of fire. In many dormitories there are clothes chutes which extend from the laundry in the basement up through the building, and in the older buildings it was customary to sheath them up with wooden sheathing and fit them with wooden doors. Sometimes they open into linen closets and the doors in this case will usually be found open. They are a real danger, as they will carry fire and smoke quickly up to the upper floors of the building.

It is a difficult thing now to try to line them with metal, but there should be a metal-covered door in the basement and all the doors should have spring hinges to hold them shut and no devices for holding them open.

A case came to our attention recently where burning sparks were drawn up a clothes chute of this sort and came out through an open door on to the floor of a room that had been freshly oiled. In a moment the floor was ablaze over the whole room. By a fortunate chance the only person in the room was near the door and got out safely. Oil has been for years a common way of treating wooden floors, but for this reason it probably is not a good material to use. Wax is much better, except on floors that have to be scrubbed with water; it is safer on account of fire and also it is a cleaner and better material in every way.

In conclusion, I will try to make a brief clear statement of the problem and its possible solutions. In the majority of cases fires start in the basement of a building and burn very quickly through into the first floor. The smoke then spreads through the different open rooms and halls and is immediately drawn up any open staircases to the upper floors. This is the time it is usually detected and the alarm given.

Most of the danger in case of fire comes from the halls and corridors being filled with a sufficiently dense smoke to cause asphyxiation within a very short time after the start of the fire.

If the corridors and stair halls can be kept clear of smoke even for a very few minutes in the beginning it will be perfectly simple for every one to leave the building in an orderly manner without any hurry or confusion.

To accomplish this result there should be at least two separate stair halls located as far apart as possible and these should be enclosed, absolutely, from the top story down to the ground level and there should be a door at the bottom opening directly out on to the ground. There should be no locks on the doors leading to these stair halls. The doors should be planned to swing into the stair hall and they should have spring door checks which will keep them always closed, and there should be no hooks or other devices for holding them open. In a building so planned the students will come from their rooms, when the alarm is given, into the upper corridors in which there will be no smoke. They will go to one or the other staircase and a glance will show if it is clear of smoke and if it is they will go safely down and be out of danger.

For the person who is in charge of the buildings of an institution, whether it is the president or the head master or the superintendent of buildings and grounds, or some one else, it is quite natural to feel that his buildings are safe. He is familiar with them all, and if they are old ones and he sees they are equipped with outside fire-escapes he naturally takes it for granted that everything probably is as nearly safe as is possible. He may worry a little and wish they were fireproof, but he lets it go. I would like to suggest, however, that after reading this he personally make a visit to each one of his buildings, and, in the light of what I have tried to explain, go over them slowly and carefully and try to picture to himself just what each person would have to do to get safely out in case of a real fire. Unless he is quite satisfied that every student can get safely and quickly out of the building without danger, I want to impress upon him his personal responsibility for the lives of the students and urge that something be done and done immediately.

I. Howland Jones
Andrews, Jones, Biscoe
and Whitmore, Architects
Boston, Mass.

## HISTORY OF MATHEMATICS IN AMERICA

The Mathematical Association of America recently published a small volume entitled "A History of Mathematics in America before 1900" edited by D. E. Smith and J. Ginsburg. Teachers of mathematics who are interested in the development of their subject in our own country will naturally welcome the opportunities which this volume of 209 pages presents to become better acquainted with various evidences of the remarkable mathematical progress made in our country during the recent centuries. In 1890 F. Cajori published under the auspices of the Bureau of Education a somewhat similar but larger volume (400 pages) under the title, "The Teaching and History of Mathematics in the United States," in which the greater part of the developments noted are considered under the following two headings: "Influx of English Mathematics, 1776–1820," and "Influx of French Mathematics," and it is stated (page 45) that "French and German authors were almost unknown" during the former of these two periods.

In the recent volume these two divisions are fortunately not adopted, and some of its statements are in disaccord therewith. For instance, the interest of Benjamin Franklin (1706–1790) and of Thomas Jefferson (1743–1826) in the French mathematicians is emphasized and it is noted that "even before the Revolution the American Philosophical Society was more closely related to France than to England" (page 76), and that "during the War of Independence it was natural that there should be a distinct lessening of British influence upon the schools of those colonies which were to become the United States" (page 75). Such differences of view may partially explain the fact that in this later volume no reference is made to any of the statements contained in the earlier one relating to the same general subject. Its title is incidentally noted on page 161 of this later volume.

While the authors of the two books on the history of mathematics in our country express different views in regard to various special questions they agree as regards the facts that few outstanding contributions to the development of mathematics were made in America before the latter half of the nineteenth century and that before this time the mathematical instruction in our schools was much below the level of that which is now being offered. It is interesting to note a somewhat similar but more recent mathematical awakening in Asia, especially in India and in Japan, so that the European preeminence in mathematical investigations is being threatened in a friendly manner from different directions. The United States of America has taken the lead in these advances outside of Europe and some of our universities now offer unsurpassed advantages for research along certain lines.

Unfortunately the earlier of the two books on the history of mathematics in our country has no index and the index of the recent work on this subject is very incomplete even as regards the items which are noted therein. The statement that these references "are reserved for such as relate to some mathematical contribution or to some important historical event" is not very illuminating, since readers naturally have different views as regards what constitutes a contribution or an important historical event. On page 117 it is stated that the *Monthly* was made the official organ a year after the founding of the Mathematical Association of America. This is misleading, since the founding of the association and the adoption of its official organ were accomplished during the same meeting. Such inaccuracies are, however, not numerous, and some of them will probably be corrected in later editions of this volume.

G. A. Miller
University of Illinois

# SPECIAL CORRESPONDENCE

## A NEW DEAL FOR CIVICS

"Only the most short-sighted student of the world scene can maintain, in the light of the accumulated knowledge of the last four years, that the industrial and social jungle-law heretofore obtaining will suffice for the ever-increasing complexity of modern life. The increasing emphasis upon social values is inevitable. And just as inevitably must education whip itself into line."

These words of Mr. J. Ray Stine, principal of Central High School, Akron, Ohio, form the ideological basis for the recent reforms introduced by him into the 9B civics course at Central High. It is his contention that the first step toward the reform of a system is a thorough understanding of that system. To this end he has evolved a combination lecture and motion picture unit given once a week to augment the regular ninth grade civics course.

This series of nineteen lectures deals solely with local problems, for it is felt that before larger phases of national activity are approached the smallest must be mastered. There is, in addition, the fact, well known in educational psychology, that the uninformed mind derives the most good from familiar objects and experiences.

Though each lecture can not at present be accompanied by a motion picture, the gaps are being filled in as rapidly as it is feasible. Subjects discussed cover all important aspects of civic life. A selection of a few titles from the whole will show the diversity of material covered: "The Cost of Education—High School"; "The City Water System"; "Street Maintenance and Repair"; "The City Park System"; "The Public Libraries"; "Public Utilities—City Franchises"; "The City Service Clubs"; "Food and Sanitary Inspection."

A consideration of the enumerated topics will show the manifold advantages deriving from presentation by means of the motion picture, for no adequate understanding could be given by any other method save an inspection trip, and this is obviously impractical.

To buttress the impression given by the lecture, a skeleton outline, mimeographed and covering very completely the material delivered in the lecture, is given to each student. A glance at the divisions included under the study of the Akron City sewerage system will show the method very clearly; they include "History," "Volume of Sewage," "Finances," "Need for Treatment," "The Treatment Process," "Final Effluent." Each of these has a very detailed number of subdivisions.

Included with each skeleton outline are a number of thought questions which are developed in class the following day. It is herein that the social integration occurs and the national questions are brought out. Tests have proved that retention is much greater and student interest much higher than under the old text-discussion method under which the student was forced to be satisfied with verbal descriptions and rather incomprehensible generalizations.

There is only one objection which can be levelled against this technique, and that is—expense. Upon inspection, however, this objection will be found to be no objection at all. There will be difficulties, of course, and each school must settle them according to local conditions. Mr. Stine's experiences, in view of his eminent success, should prove of great suggestive value.

First, the camera and projector were his own equipment; to those who argue that this condition may not exist in other schools, it may very readily be answered that service clubs and private individuals interested in the educational welfare of the city are very generous in assisting both financially and otherwise in the production of films of this nature. Recourse may also be had to moneys collected from school dances, to class gifts, to the pooling of funds with other interested high schools, and so on.

By using the narrow gauge, home-projector type of film, costs were very materially reduced. Most of the work of photography was done during summer vacation, as the occasion offered. Mr. Stine has found that persons with whom he had to deal were always more than willing to extend every form of cooperation at their disposal. A rubber company, for instance, on several occasions gave him the use of one of their blimps, from which he obtained unusual and informative shots from the air.

To supplement action shots taken on the scene, Mr. Stine made several animated drawings to illustrate many processes which were—because of the physical nature of the machinery being photographed—impossible to photograph. This demonstrated, far better than any amount of description or charting could, the processes involved.

The possibilities, it will be seen, are infinite, and will vary with circumstances which are peculiar to each city. At present, Mr. Stine contemplates filling in the remaining subjects in the semester's program. After that there remain the industries—the rubber factories, the clay products companies, the foundries, the cereal mills, the machine shops; there are the department stores. It is a flexible system whose limits are at present not even defined.

Pending compilation of the results of a very comprehensive test which was given at the end of the semester's work in civics, definite information upon the lecture-motion picture plan can not be announced, but it is very certain that a conclusive step forward toward the awakening of the social consciousness has been taken in this, the fifth year of the depression.

CHALMERS STEWART

## THE PROJECT METHOD OF DEVELOPING THE COLLEGE MUSEUM

THE college museum is probably one of the most valuable parts of an institution. However, it is usually neglected, or relegated to some dusty attic room where nobody ever has access to the material, or else is so meager that it is not worthy of the name.

At the College of Emporia we have been working out a system of projects during the past few years which are intended to build up a strong museum of comparative anatomy. Thus far our projects have been concentrated on building up a collection of mounted skeletons. Students in the zoology classes are given their choice of making drawings of skeletal parts or of mounting one skeleton to be left as a permanent part of the museum equipment. Students in more advanced classes of biology are likewise encouraged to take projects on a larger scale in lieu of the traditional laboratory routine requirements.

We have found interest so great in this new type of project that we have been forced to look outside our own community for materials. After having mounted many specimens of rabbits, frogs, rats, cats, dogs and many other local species, we contacted a distant zoological garden and circus farm, from which source we have secured during the past two years one South American llama, two lions, one leopard, one Indian elephant and one African hippopotamus.

The mounted skeletons of all these animals have now been added to our department museum as permanent equipment. The students have spent endless hours of hard work preparing these skeletons and they have learned a great deal about osteology from articulating these bones. The last one to be completed is the hippopotamus, which is now being given the finishing touches and will be on exhibition soon.

In addition to mounting the skeletons of these animals, the students made drawings of the various systems of these large animals and wrote up reports about these findings.

In a remarkably short time we have thus added thousands of dollars worth of equipment to the biology department, and at the same time have tripled the student-interest in the work. There has been some loss of routine work in certain courses, but we feel it has been compensated for in the increased interest and effort which has been applied to the projects.

J. H. FURBAY

# QUOTATIONS

## FEDERAL AID FOR THE SCHOOLS

SURPRISE is probably the most general American reaction whenever education comes out of its cloister and proclaims a dollars-and-cents consciousness of its value. Educators as a rule are modest folk, used to working without too much appreciation of their efforts, and often against odds. But, gathered in convention at Washington last week, the National Education Association adopted a resolution urging introduction of a bill in Congress which would ask for a grant of $500,000,000 for aid to public schools.

It is time the attention of the American people and their government was called to the need of increased support for education. Never have the schools been allowed to feel a depression so keenly as they have felt that which began in 1929. True, recovery plans have not entirely overlooked the impairment which educational institutions have suffered. Aid has been given to students and to teachers whose schools were closed. But the setback which education received during the period of national economic chaos has by no means been offset.

A noteworthy commentary on the conditions under which American educators are working is found in reports from the United States' largest and second largest cities. New York's Mayor LaGuardia has expressed concern over the possibility that the schools might not open in September unless the state comes to their aid at the present special session of the legislature. New York City faces a school deficit of $8,078,000. Chicago school teachers are about to be paid out of a congressional loan, but the whole world knows of their long distress and of the fact that other city employees, apparently for political reasons, received infinitely better treatment than the patient teachers.

Is not a school teacher as much of an employee of the city as a street sweeper or a dog-pound attendant? Did the fictitious setting apart of Chicago's schools as an independent body demote the teachers? The mayor controls the schools through appointments to the school board as much as ever mayors did, and the City Council has to approve the school budget before any school taxes can be raised.

Moreover, many teachers are being overloaded with work, while the city hall as usual contains a great many unnecessary but politically useful employees. And, as usual, numbers of these are still overpaid.

If the Chicago pay situation is very complex, the issues are not. A city is responsible for its teachers. There should be no difference because many a city hall employee is efficient in bringing out the vote on election day and the school teacher is not.

Big-city conditions are simply part of a dark picture. In many rural communities schools have been closed, and in many others the school year has been drastically reduced, while teachers' wages have suffered cut after cut.

The public has yet to hear what specific purposes the $500,000,000 congressional grant to public schools would serve. Use of the funds no doubt will be outlined in the near future. One thing is certain, however. That is, more substantial federal aid is due education than has yet been given to it.—*The Christian Science Monitor.*

EVERYBODY knows that the constitution of the United States made no reference to education. There is no conveyance by the states to the federal government of power in relation to schools. If the federal government is to be justified in participating in the educational program of the states, it can be done only under a very specious appeal to the general welfare clause in the preamble.

Many advocates of federal subsidies for the schools do not believe that federal control or interference is involved. Inevitably, federal control must accompany federal support. My experience in handling federal subsidies for education, under the limited acts now in existence, taught me that you must have federal control and interference or you will have misappropriation of funds and waste. The method whereby the federal government has stimulated certain types of education in the states, through lands and moneys, under the Morrill, Smith-Hughes, Smith-Lever, and related acts, is well known. . . .

Reason and experience both indicate that federal money can not be expended wisely and efficiently except by exercising federal control and supervision, and even then there is considerable waste. Witness, for example, the huge pork barrels, such as the appropriations for rivers and harbors and other matters which are the result of log-rolling, trading and political self-interest. If we embark upon a program of turning over federal money to schools without any strings on it, it is only a question of time until the waste, extravagance and misuse of these funds will result in a reaction or a change. The alternative is federal control. . . .

It should be noted that in 1930, there were 128,840 fewer children under five years of age in the United States than there were in 1920. We have passed the peak of population increase. Social and economic pressure, resulting in birth control, have halted the population increase in a way similar to the situation which has long existed in France and some other countries. This definitely means that the burden of supporting schools will be relatively less in the future than it has been in the past. The proportion of children to adults will be less; and the amount necessary for capital costs of schools will be greatly reduced, and there will be a slight reduction in operating costs.

It is evident that there is no necessity for federal financial assistance to the schools under normal conditions as no state, even in prosperous times, has ever expended more than a trifling proportion of its resources on its schools.—*Dr. John J. Tigert in The Review of Reviews.*

# REPORTS

## REPORT OF THE COMMITTEE ON STANDARDS OF THE AMERICAN COUNCIL ON EDUCATION[1]

It is an interesting circumstance that the American Council on Education should form a new Committee on Standards at the very time the North Central Association of Colleges and Secondary Schools is issuing a new statement of policy regarding accrediting which deliberately excludes the word "standards" from its official vocabulary.

Composed as it is of representatives of a dozen national and regional associations covering professional as well as college and secondary school interests, the Committee on Standards doubtless thereby tends to conservatism; tends to seek that worthy conservative objective: "The happy mean between too much stiffness in refusing and too much easiness in admitting variations in things once advisedly established."

Actually there is no real issue involved in the avoidance of the word "standards" by the North Central Association and its fresh adoption by the American Council. For all its banning of "standards" in its terminology, the North Central's "bases of accrediting" and "total pattern maps" have teeth in them; and your Committee on Standards, despite its conservative name and allegiance, has liberal leanings and a desire for broad rather than narrow criteria.

Upon this aspect of the make-up of the committee the chairman, at the initial meeting in Washington on April 7, ventured to say:

[1] Presented at the meeting in Washington, D. C., on May 18 and 19, 1934.

Most of us here to-day are veterans at this game. We have inspected and inspected and inspected. Running true to conventional pedagogical form, we ought to be hardboiled Gradgrinds with an obsession for facts. It happens, however, that the personnel of this committee, whatever its other characteristics, has this in common, that we are predominantly liberals.

We know the advantages of formal and definite standards in a pioneer era, in the range from secondary schools to professional schools. The ''Carnegie unit'' served a useful purpose in the period when a foot-rule of this sort impressed boards of education and helped to raise the minimum educational level in many parts of the country. In the professional field the criteria which developed from Dr. Flexner's study of medical education in 1909–10 had the outcome of reducing the number of medical schools from 166 to about 70; and hardly any one who knows about the old proprietary medical school would question that there has been a tremendous benefit to the medical profession and to society by the rigorous application in this field of fixed standards.

A good deal of water has flowed under the bridge and to-day we find that the Carnegie Foundation for the Advancement of Teaching, following its Pennsylvania Study, is in the lead with proposals to drop the old Carnegie Unit; and the American Medical Association, through its Council on Medical Education and Hospitals, is preparing for a re-study of the objectives of medical education and a survey and reappraisal of all medical schools in this country.

Two factors account for these and other activities and for our own liberalism in viewing standards.

The first is the improvement in scientific measurement as applied to education. We know now that the time-clock of the Carnegie unit does not record intellectual accomplishment. Educational psychology has given us better instruments in standardized subject-matter tests, in the new-type tests, in scholastic aptitude tests, in professional aptitude tests as applied to medicine and law.

The chief element in our own thinking, I venture to say, is our scientific spirit. We have more of what John Stuart Mill called a healthy skepticism. We show this by our criticism, in the scientific spirit, of the methods and results of these new scientific devices.

The second factor accounting for our liberalism is, I believe, the fact that American higher education is advancing out of the pioneer stage into that of the university ideal. We are interested in buildings, equipment, finances; but we realize that any educational institution must be judged by what William James called its *tone*. A vague word; not scientific; yet every one of us here, when we have gone to and fro on our inspections, appreciate that the truly important thing about any school, college, university is precisely the quality of its student body and of its faculty which James so aptly termed its *tone*.

The chairman expressed his belief that the new Committee on Standards, working in the spirit indicated, has possibilities of usefulness in American education by "synthesizing the findings of various studies, the judgments of experienced workers in the varied fields of classification and accrediting; and by crystallizing findings and judgments into fundamental principles stated with simplicity and directness." The chairman quoted the statement of the purpose of the committee, as given by Dr. John Henry MacCracken: "To deal with the principles of classification and accrediting rather than with the application of these principles."

An excellent presentation of the new attitude toward accrediting advocated by the North Central Association was given by the U. S. Commissioner of Education, Dr. George F. Zook. When he was president of the University of Akron, Dr. Zook was a prime mover in the study which resulted in the North Central's present policy.

The probability "that the standards of the future will be general in character" was set forth by Dr. Zook in addressing the committee. General optimum standards will be substituted for minimum specific standards. Under this conception an institution will be at liberty to choose its own methods. In some instances the institutional machinery may be elaborate and formal; in other instances it may be possible for an institution to perform the function effectively through machinery which is less imposing and much more informal.

Dr. Zook stressed that, given this liberty as to ways and means, an institution will be expected to accept appropriate responsibility and to demonstrate that its methods, plan and organization are effective in attaining the general principles called for in the standard as they apply to the objectives which the institution has set for its goal.

As to the new program of the North Central Association, Dr. Zook said that it has two equally important functions—accrediting and stimulating. There will doubtless long continue to be a very real necessity for what we now call the accrediting of institutions. That the accrediting procedure of the old type had served its day and had been valuable Dr. Zook freely granted, but he insisted that "we must establish accrediting procedures that are more scientific and much more carefully carried out." He expressed his thought that schedules of information, no matter how much improved, can not replace the need for personal inspection. He favored visits to each institution seeking accrediting by a committee of two or three members staying at least two days.

As to stimulation Dr. Zook thought that at least an equal amount of energy should be expended in aiding institutions already included in the accredited list as in considering institutions applying for inclusion. The new standards will be ideals toward the attainment of which the institution seeking accrediting and the one which has long enjoyed that status may work with equal zeal.

Dr. Zook stated, in closing, the conclusion reached by those who put through the North Central study that "the association should have but one list of accredited higher institutions."

The following questions are now before the Committee on Standards for study and discussion:

1. What is the relationship of regional and state lists of accredited institutions to functional lists?
2. Shall the American Council adhere to regional lists for colleges of arts and science?

3. Should an institution which has a law school not accredited be included on the accredited list?
4. What should our attitude be toward the junior colleges which are increasing in such numbers?
5. Should junior colleges be included with the regular list of colleges of arts and science or be included with the list of secondary schools or be listed separately?
6. Should the council utilize functional lists so far as professional schools are concerned?
7. Should teachers colleges and engineering colleges be treated as professional schools or as colleges of arts and science?
8. Should the council list American institutions in foreign lands such as those of Constantinople, at Cairo and in China?
9. What part may the Federal Government appropriately play in the determination of educational standards?
10. What, if anything, should be done regarding the classification of institutions which fall outside the regular fields, such as theological seminaries, Emerson College of Oratory in Boston, Springfield International College, etc.?
11. Has the faculty of the institution a share of responsibility for educational policy and a relation to the governing board—this implying, on the one hand, due provision for freedom of teaching and investigation and security of tenure; and, on the other hand, protection of the interests of the institution as to needful elimination and resignation at short notice.

At the April 7 meeting of the committee a good start was made in the consideration of a half dozen of the foregoing questions. Subcommittees have been appointed for further study and later report.

The following (all of whom attended the April 7 sessions in the offices of the American Council on Education) comprise the Committee on Standards:

Dr. Katharine Rogers Adams, principal of Kingswood School, Cranbrook, Bloomfield Hills, Michigan, representing the American Association of University Women.

Alexander B. Andrews, of Raleigh, N. C., representing the Section on Legal Education, American Bar Association.

Dr. Doak S. Campbell, of the George Peabody College for Teachers, representing the American Association of Junior Colleges.

Dr. William D. Cutter, of Chicago, representing the Council on Medical Education, American Medical Association.

R. N. Dempster (*secretary*), of the Johns Hopkins University, representing the Middle States Association of Colleges and Secondary Schools.

Dr. Frederick J. Kelly, of Washington, D. C., representing the U. S. Office of Education.

Dr. O. R. Latham, president of Iowa State Teachers College, representing the American Association of Teachers Colleges.

Dr. John H. MacCracken, of Washington, D. C., representing *ex officio* the American Council on Education.

Dr. Shelton Phelps, of the George Peabody College for Teachers, representing the Southern Association of Colleges and Secondary Schools.

Dr. James A. Reeves, of Seton Hill College, representing the National Catholic Educational Association.

Dr. H. W. Tyler, of Washington, D. C., representing the American Association of University Professors.

Dr. Raymond Walters (*chairman*), president of the University of Cincinnati, representing the Association of American Colleges.

Dr. W. E. Wickenden, president of the Case School of Applied Science, representing the Society for the Promotion of Engineering Education.

Professor George A. Works, of the University of Chicago, representing the North Central Association of Colleges and Secondary Schools.

Dr. George F. Zook, of Washington, D. C., director of the American Council on Education.

For the work of the committee during the coming year, the chairman has appointed the following sub-committees to consider specific problems:

*Committee on Philosophy of Standards:* Miss Adams, Messrs. Cutter, MacCracken, Reeves, Tyler, Walters and Zook.

*Committee on Regional and State Lists and Functional Lists:* Messrs. Andrews, Dempster, Kelly, Phelps and Works.

*Committee on Professional Fields:* Messrs. Andrews, Cutter, Latham, Walters and Wickenden.

*Committee on Nomenclature:* Messrs. Campbell, MacCracken, Walters and President David A. Robertson, of Goucher College.

RAYMOND WALTERS,
*Chairman*

# EDUCATIONAL RESEARCH AND STATISTICS

## A STUDY OF THE VALIDITY OF SIX TYPES OF SPELLING TESTS

SPELLING is a tool subject, one which is learned because of its value in written discourse. The purpose of teaching spelling in schools is the inculcation of the habit of using the correct letters in their proper sequence in given words, to insure the communication of ideas which are intended to be communicated by the person writing the words. It should be kept in mind that people need to spell correctly only in written discourse.

Spelling is quite objective, and it is strongly standardized. There is only one correct way to spell a word. For this reason, spelling, like arithmetic, seems to lend itself readily to objective testing of pupil achievement. It would seem that educators should have little difficulty in devising adequate and appropriate spelling tests. Yet this is not as easy as it may seem.

A considerable amount of time is spent in schools in teaching spelling, and yet most classroom teachers content themselves with using the traditional column dictation technique in measuring the spelling achievement of their pupils. It is true that there has been some research completed on the problem, using column dictation, sentence dictation, oral recall, written recall, two response, multiple (four) response, and completion type tests.[1] In only one of the investigations, however, that by Epler, are six such types of spelling tests considered. The findings of these several studies lend themselves to the following conclusions: (1) Educators are able to construct spelling tests of different types of reasonably good validity; (2) the column dictation test is still the most valid measure of spelling achievement, with the sentence dictation spelling test almost as satisfactory; and (3) methods of measuring achievement in spelling have not yet been finally established.

It is the purpose of this discussion to report an investigation of the validity of six types of objective spelling tests. The types of measuring instruments used include those utilized by earlier workers interested in the problem: (1) A two-response, written recall spelling test[2]; (2) a two-word, multiple-response written recall spelling test, similar to the spelling test included as Part I of the Cross English Test[3]; (3) a four-word, multiple-response written recall spelling test, similar to the spelling test included as Part I of the Columbia Research Bureau English Test[3]; (4) a completion spelling test[4]; (5) a column dictation spelling test; and (6) the New Stanford Achievement Test, Dictation Exercise.[5]

Each of the five teacher-made spelling tests listed above included fifty words, chosen from the Buckingham Revision of the Ayres Spelling Scale and from the Iowa Spelling Scales. These lists of fifty words included the same number of words of a given difficulty, with the difficulty levels ranging from easily spelled words to words which were spelled correctly by only a few pupils. After the preparation of the five spelling tests, they were administered to pupils

[1] Nora Epler, "A Study of Objective, Teacher-made Spelling Tests." *Unpublished master's thesis*, University of Southern California, 1933. 62 pages. W. S. Guiler, "Validation of Methods of Testing Spelling." *Journal of Educational Research*, 20: 181–189, 1929. R. V. Hunkins, "An Experiment in Column versus Dictation Spelling." *Elementary School Journal*, 19: 689, 1919. R. L. Morton, "The Validity of Times Sentence and Column Tests in Spelling." *Journal of Educational Research*, 5: 444–447, 1922. J. S. Orleans, "The Ability to Spell." SCHOOL AND SOCIETY, 23: 407–408, 1926. D. P. Phillips, "Comparison of the Two-Response and Dictated Recall Types of Spelling Tests." *Journal of Educational Research*, 23: 17–24, 1931.

[2] This test was presented in mimeographed form to the pupils, as follows:

*Directions:* In this test, some of the words are spelled correctly, and some are spelled wrongly. Look at each word carefully; if it is right, place a check in the space beside the word, and under R; if it is wrong place a check in the space after the word, and under W.

*Example:*

| R | | W |
|---|---|---|
| | verry | x |
| x | brave | |

[3] Published by World Book Company, Yonkers-on-Hudson, New York.

[4] This test was presented in mimeographed form to the pupils, as follows:

*Directions:* In this test the first letter of a word or the first two letters of the word are given. Fill in the blanks with the letters which are not given, in order to finish spelling the word. After each blank is a definition or another word which means the same thing as the word which you are to spell.

*Example:*

(b——— (A place to sleep on; a couch.)
(h——— (a place in which to live; an abode.)

[5] Published by World Book Company, Yonkers-on-Hudson, New York.

in grades two to five in the Benjamin Franklin School of San Diego. One hundred and seventy-four pupils responded to all six tests. The pupil responses were scored, the scoring was checked for accuracy, and the scores were entered and checked on a data sheet. The statistical computations, based on the pupils' responses, were completed twice with the aid of statistical tables and calculating machines to insure accuracy.

Table I includes the measures summarizing the six score series.

TABLE I

SUMMARY MEASURES FOR SIX SERIES OF SPELLING SCORES. N = 174

| Test | From Range | To | Mean | $PE_M$ | SD | V |
|---|---|---|---|---|---|---|
| Two-response | 0 | 40 | 17.2 | 0.56 | 11.4 | 66.2 |
| Two-word | 0 | 42 | 23.4 | 0.80 | 16.2 | 69.5 |
| Four-word | 0 | 40 | 20.4 | 0.51 | 10.1 | 49.5 |
| Completion | 0 | 49 | 10.7 | 0.49 | 9.7 | 90.7 |
| Column dictation | 0 | 35 | 13.8 | 0.35 | 6.9 | 49.4 |
| Sentence dictation | 0 | 59 | 28.8 | 0.61 | 12.1 | 42.0 |

*Note:* All constants in this table are quoted only to the first decimal place, excepting the probable errors of the mean.

The data in Table I clearly show one fact: the tests are discriminating. Each test included words within the achievement of most pupils, and words difficult for all pupils. No pupils completed correctly the spelling of the group of words included in the five teacher-made, objective spelling tests. The most interesting fact presented in Table I is the marked differences in mean values among the first five tests, since the original fifty words in each list used in these tests were of equal difficulty. The relative variability of three of the tests is quite similar: the column dictation, sentence dictation and four-word, multiple-answer spelling tests. Peculiarly enough, these three types of tests were found by Epler to be the most valid of the six types of tests.[6]

The intercorrelations describing the relationships between the six paired series of test scores are given in Table II.

[6] Nora Epler, *loc. cit.*, page 35.

TABLE II

MEASURES OF RELATIONSHIP FOR SIX SERIES OF SPELLING SCORES. N = 174

| Tests | (1) | (2) | (3) | (4) | (5) | (6) |
|---|---|---|---|---|---|---|
| Two-response | | .927 | .778 | .759 | .351 | .262 |
| Two-word | .004 | | .832 | .797 | .496 | .308 |
| Four-word | .020 | .016 | | .784 | .425 | .311 |
| Completion | .022 | .018 | .018 | | .193 | .497 |
| Column dictation | .045 | .037 | .042 | .049 | | .823 |
| Sentence dictation | .047 | .047 | .047 | .037 | .017 | |

*Note:* Coefficients of correlation are given in the upper right portion of this table; probable errors of these coefficients, in the lower left-hand portion of the table.

Since all the coefficients of correlation in Table II are positive, it follows that the six tests measure the same thing or things to some extent. The first four tests validate each other remarkably well, and yet these four tests do not validate the column dictation and sentence dictation spelling tests, which were found to be the best measures of spelling in earlier studies. It appears that the last-named two tests are measuring something different than is measured by the first four tests listed in Table II. The column dictation and sentence dictation spelling tests validate each other very satisfactorily. The writers suggest that perhaps vocabulary skills and proofreading skills are demanded in the first four tests more than in the last two tests in Table II, and the presence of these variables influencing the scores on the four tests may cause the values of the coefficients of correlation given in Table II. Since Epler did not find similar results in grades 7 and 8, it may be also that grade level as well as interfering variables may account for the writers' findings.

In conclusion, the writers' findings indicate that column dictation and sentence dictation spelling tests seem still the most valid measures of spelling achievement. Intensive research in test construction and in the use of different types of objective spelling tests is needed at all grade levels of the elementary school, since methods of measuring achievement in spelling are not yet finally established.

LOUISE WELLER

BENJAMIN FRANKLIN SCHOOL

M. E. BROOM

STATE TEACHERS COLLEGE
SAN DIEGO, CALIF.

# SCHOOL AND SOCIETY

WITH WHICH ARE COMBINED THE EDUCATIONAL REVIEW, ESTABLISHED IN 1891, THE TEACHERS MAGAZINE, ESTABLISHED IN 1878, AND THE SCHOOL JOURNAL, ESTABLISHED IN 1874.

Volume 40 SATURDAY, JULY 28, 1934 Number 1022

## WORK OF THE JOINT COMMISSION ON THE EMERGENCY IN EDUCATION FOR 1935[1]

By Dr. JOHN K. NORTON

PROFESSOR OF EDUCATION, TEACHERS COLLEGE, COLUMBIA UNIVERSITY

WE are just completing three of the most disastrous years in educational history. For the first time, a depression has brought serious harm to the schools and has resulted in restriction and even denial of educational opportunity to millions of children. School terms have been cut, in some instances almost to the vanishing point. All phases of the educational program have suffered. Those which represent the response of the schools to twentieth-century conditions have suffered most. Today, thousands of American communities are attempting to train for citizenship in the twentieth century in schools which in scope and procedure belong to the nineteenth century. A quarter of a million teachers are serving under conditions which are inferior to those provided the unemployed under the relief program.

For over a year the Joint Commission on the Emergency in Education has struggled to alleviate the conditions which have just been described. We have vigorously supported a series of immediate emergency measures. Comprehensive and current figures concerning closed schools, shortened terms, unpaid teachers and wrecked school programs have been collected and widely disseminated by radio, newspapers, periodicals and other avenues of publicity. The American people now recognize the gravity of the educational crisis.

A working group of consultants from every state in the Union has been organized. They have come together in a series of regional conferences in which plans for aggressive action have been made and put into operation. An extensive survey has been made to determine the agencies and organizations which are friendly, and which are hostile, to education and to discover the means whereby their attitudes toward education are expressed. This study has suggested bases for both defensive and offensive action.

The Joint Commission has actively supported the Legislative Commission and the National Committee for Federal Emergency Aid for Education in securing financial assistance for the schools from the national government. Such aid has been secured in various forms to amounts totaling tens of millions of dollars. This money has meant financial salvation to thousands of hard-pressed school districts and to tens of thousands of unfortunate teachers. Responsible officials of the administration have been brought to the place where they recognize that there is an educational emergency and are willing to do something

[1] Address before the General Session of the National Education Association, July 2, Washington, D. C.

about it. These and other measures developed by the Joint Commission to deal with the immediate emergency will be continued and supported with vigor during the coming year. It is too early to say that the crisis has passed. We must continue to be alert to the demands of the current emergency.

There are also clear signs that educational recovery has begun. Selfish interests find less response to their demands for ill-considered retrenchment. School terms, portions of the educational program which have been eliminated, budgets and salary schedules are being restored by a rapidly mounting number of communities. The attitude of the public is better than it has been for four years.

The officers of the National Education Association and the Department of Superintendence recently instructed the Joint Commission on the Emergency in Education to broaden the scope of its work to include an appraisal of the present educational situation and the development of a long-term program designed not only to facilitate educational recovery, but also to effect improvements in educational procedures demanded by changed conditions.

The Joint Commission has started work on this additional assignment. As we have struggled with the problems of the immediate emergency, it has become increasingly clear that genuine educational recovery will involve more than a mere replacement of the 1929 situation. Many of the current difficulties of the schools have their roots in conditions which existed long before the onset of the depression. The added weight of the depression has caused certain weak supports in the educational structure to crash. We can not achieve a satisfactory recovery until these weak timbers have been replaced by stronger ones.

We have long known that the means by which education is financed in this country constituted one of the weak places in our educational structure. The property tax, overburdened and poorly administered by the local community, stood in the road of educational advance throughout the decade of the twenties. When the depression came it failed almost completely in hundreds of communities. It will not do merely to return to the 1929 plan for the financing of education. During the next decade we must fundamentally redesign and reconstruct the plan for the financing of education in this country. The Joint Commission has already sketched the blueprints for this new plan. It summoned a national conference of thirty school executives, tax experts and economists to draft the outlines of a modern program for the financing of education. The report of this conference provides a sound basis for the reformation of our system for the financing of the schools. During the coming year the Joint Commission will seek to enlist the whole profession in a united attack on this key problem.

The time has come to forget our nineteenth-century provincialisms concerning the financing of education. The twentieth century has created conditions and released forces that can no longer be dealt with solely on a local basis. This has been recognized by other areas of government. It must be recognized by education.

In every state we should resolutely set to work to develop a program for the financing of educational facilities appropriate to the needs of the twentieth century. Universal education suited to the needs of all should be provided at public expense from early childhood and until such time as proper employment is advisable and obtainable. Suitable educational facilities should be made readily available for all adults.

The Federal Government should assist the states in providing an acceptable minimum or foundation of educational support in every community. We can no longer permit the chance circumstance of the wealth that happens to be located in the individual community, or in the individual state, to determine whether a child shall be provided excellent or mediocre school facilities or no educational opportunity at all. The time has come to proclaim the principle of a national minimum or foundation program of financial support for the education of every child who lives under the American flag, whether he happens to live in Middletown, Maine, Arkansas or California.

This proposal represents no fundamentally new doctrine. For a century we have accepted the principle that the wealth which a child's father happens to possess should not be the factor which determines whether he is to go to school or to be illiterate. We have long pooled our resources on a local basis to provide that indispensable service of a democratic nation—free and universal education. It has long been accepted in theory, and is increasingly being recognized in practise, that the same principle applies to the state as a whole. We agree that the chance that a child has to obtain an education should not depend upon whether he happens to live in the northwest or southeast corner of a state. All citizens within a state should assist, according to their ability, in paying for the education of every child.

Conditions have now developed which require that this principle should also be applied in the nation as a whole. No new principle is involved. Rather we are preserving under changed conditions the equality of opportunity which both in its origin and development is perhaps the most distinctive American principle in existence.

The achievement of genuine educational recovery calls for thought and action in another direction. What is to be the rôle of education in making America a better place in which to live? The troubles of the last four years have served to sharpen understanding of the problems which lie at the root of these difficulties. How are we going to convert an economy of potential abundance into one of actual abundance? How are we going to achieve that modicum of material well-being and security which is essential to cultural and spiritual health? How are we to accomplish sufficient regulation of our common affairs that we can avoid chaos and achieve stability, and at the same time protect individual initiative and liberty in certain vital areas? These are the great unsolved questions which confront us who have the privilege of living in this potent twentieth century. There is no easy answer to them. There is no final and permanent answer to such problems except that which can be given by a more universal and vital program of education.

Nothing now stands between the American people and the realization of the noblest civilization which has yet marked man's upward struggle but lack of intelligence. There has recently been issued by a responsible economic source—the Brookings Institution of Washington, D. C.—the results of an extensive investigation into the economic capacity of America to produce. This study should offer encouragement to every right-thinking American citizen. It was conducted for the specific purpose of determining whether America, in its most prosperous years, was utilizing its full productive capacity.

This investigation sought to discover whether there is justification for the contention that we lived beyond our means in the gay twenties, both in our private and public expenditures. We have been told that the depression of the last four years is "the morning after" the gay joy-ride of the twenties, during which we spent money and wickedly burned up capital, like drunken sailors. Our profligacy in the field of public expenditure has been held up as a horrible example of economic sin. The expenditures for education have been cited as a particular instance of extravagant spending.

What light does the investigation of the Brookings Institution shed upon these contentions? The conclusion can be stated in a few words: Instead of living beyond our means in 1929, the peak year of prosperity, "our economic society lacked almost 20 per cent. of living up to its means" in that year. In 1929 our income was fifteen billion dollars less than it could have been if we had used the labor force and the capital goods already in our possession in a manner which would have involved no violation of practical operating conditions.

If we had used this wasted economic power, we could have brought up to $2,000 the incomes of the 16,400,000 families in the United States who in 1929 received less than this amount. This is the conclusion of the Institute of Economics of the Brookings Institution. I would like to add that, if this wasted economic productivity had actually been used, it would have paid the total bill for public education—kindergarten, elementary, high school, college and university—more than five times.

What can education do to develop the requisite intelligence so that possibilities may become realities? The coming decades will present the greatest opportunity which has yet challenged any generation of teachers. We must seek the support of all men of intelligence and good-will to the end that we may cooperatively develop schools appropriate to the requirements of the remarkable age in which we are living.

If I had some power to claim the thought of large numbers of citizens at this time, I would not begin by deluging them with statistics of the breakdown of the schools, nor by taking them through a short course in the financing of education. Rather, I would ask them to look at life as it is and to decide what it suggests concerning the development of education in the future. The crucial problems which confront the schools to-day grow out of the fact that there are too many persons who have not faced the implications for education of the unsolved problems which afflict our society.

The Joint Commission on the Emergency in Education recently issued a publication entitled "Evaluating the Public Schools." We urge that you give this pamphlet serious attention, and think through the philosophy which lies back of it. It calls for a closer alliance between educators and the public in general. It urges something more than educational interpretation, important though that may be. It offers definite suggestions whereby school people may sit down with public-spirited citizens to discover through honest and cooperative thinking the answer to the most crucial educational questions.

In a democracy the people must ultimately decide important questions of social and economic policy. This is particularly true with respect to the public school, because this institution touches the everyday lives of the people so closely. Since the people must decide, let us see that they decide wisely and on the basis of a full presentation of the evidence.

I warn you that there are interests in this nation who because of selfishness or limited vision want no democratic decision as to the rôle of education in our civilization. For four years they have been proclaiming a gospel of negation and despair. They urge the acceptance of a peasant standard of living and a peasant standard of educating as the easiest way out of our present difficulties. Let no teacher accept this coward's solution for the difficulties of the depression. Teachers have no higher duty than to join with all men of social purpose in opposing this defeatist doctrine.

We have heard much about the new deal during the past year. But in a sense there is nothing less new in American life than the new deal.

The founding of this nation was one of the great efforts of history to offer mankind a new deal—a new deal in which religious tolerance, political equality, and economic justice would replace the persecution, inequality and injustice that cursed our forebears of Europe through the middle ages and into the modern period. It is because millions of courageous men and women dreamed and dared that they crossed an ocean to found a land in which equality of opportunity would be the watchword.

The new deal viewed in proper, and nonpartisan, perspective is nothing more than a cleansing of those springs of social justice and equality of opportunity which gave America its original impetus, and should forever refresh its upward march.

There is a third area which will deserve especial attention in the years just ahead if complete educational recovery is to be achieved. I refer to the whole matter of the professional organization of teachers. If there ever was any question about the necessity of strong professional organizations—local, state and national—the experience of these depression years must have dispelled it. Education has suffered in these trying times. But I assure you it would have suffered far more severely if it had not been for these agencies of educational defense and advance.

Many local and state associations enrol less than 100 per cent. of eligible members. The national association enrols less than 20 per cent. of its potential membership. Here is a situation which all of us should strive to correct as rapidly as possible. We can urge 100 per cent. enrolment on the basis of the record of these organizations in a time of crisis. But I prefer not to dwell on the past accomplishments of professional associations, but rather to emphasize what it is possible for them to accomplish in the future.

Educational associations should become agencies of unified and long-term educational planning. American education is about to undergo a reconstruction and expansion more fundamental than it has experienced in any other period of its history. The orderly social and economic revolution through which the country is passing places upon the schools greater demands and new responsibilities. Unemployed youths whose services can not be absorbed by industry must be provided with proper educational opportunities. The work of the schools in preparing for social and economic citizenship must be increased in effectiveness. The preparation of teachers for the new age requires far-reaching changes. The relation of education to other governmental functions, the organization of educational opportunity for the leisure time of adults, the coordination of the schools with libraries and playgrounds—these and a score of other problems press for careful consideration and constructive action in shaping a new program of education for a new age.

This situation places a heavy responsibility upon the educators of the nation. Logically, it is they who should offer the leadership needed in order that schools appropriate to the demands of our times may be developed. Already, thousands of teachers, working through a variety of educational organizations, are coming to grips with the problems which must be met in the years which lie just ahead, if education is fully to accomplish its purposes.

An investigation just completed for the Joint Commission on the Emergency in Education reveals that no less than 400 educational committees and commissions have recently prepared reports or are now conducting investigations, which are pertinent in planning educational recovery and reconstruction. The results of this study are now available in printed form under the title: "A Directory of National Deliberative Committees in Education."

One can not study this directory without realizing that there are already within our profession untapped resources for educational progress. It is the duty of professional associations to capitalize and to coordinate the vast amount of work which is already in progress in the profession, looking toward the improvement of educational procedures and results.

We should no longer be satisfied with educational associations which look ahead one or two years. Every organization—local, state and national—should have at least a ten-year program made up of long-term as well as immediate objectives. In the development of such a program each association should draw upon the best thought of its membership of all ranks. It should seek the advice of experts both within and without the profession, in order that its platform may be as defensible as careful research and mature experience will permit. To a far greater extent than in the past, professional organizations should seek the active cooperation of larger numbers of laymen. Education as we have it to-day came from the people. Education as it should be to-morrow should come from the people.

The Joint Commission urges the creation in every state of an effective council for general educational planning which will capitalize the thought and influence of the groups just described in the development and support of a comprehensive, long-term educational program. The time has passed when we can hope to win great educational victories solely through our own efforts in promoting a series of opportunistic projects.

The Joint Commission, acting under its new instructions, will provide materials which will be valuable to state educational associations in developing long-term programs. It is the intention of the commission to seek the resources requisite to the effective discharge of this important responsibility.

I have briefly indicated a few of the major objectives of the Joint Commission for 1935. We expect to continue certain activities designed to meet the immediate difficulties of education. We also expect to carry out the recent instructions to outline the elements of a long-term program for educational recovery and reconstruction. This will involve work in at least three directions:

First, there will be a series of activities designed to facilitate the movement already underway looking toward the revision of methods for financing the schools.

Second, there is need to encourage more effective means whereby the teaching profession and public-spirited citizens in general may arrive at considered decisions as to the rôle which education should play in solving the economic and social problems which have been clarified by the events of recent years.

Third, there is need for materials out of which professional organizations may develop long-term programs for the continuous improvement of educational procedures and results.

In offering this preliminary view of plans for the coming year, the Joint Commission has no illusions as to the difficulty of the work which it has been instructed to do. It will need the advice and support of its consultants and of the whole profession even more than during the past year. We offer no philosophy of self-satisfaction with education as it is to-day or as it has been in the past. Rather, we are urging that teachers dream great dreams and see great visions as to what education may mean to every state and to the nation as a whole.

The road which lies ahead is no easy one. Every step of educational advance in the twentieth century will be contested, as it was in the nineteenth century, by the forces of ignorance, prejudice, greed and narrow vision. But these forces can be defeated. They break and run in the face of intelligence, open-mindedness, courage and social vision. Intelligent and courageous teachers and parents can supply these indispensable ingredients of educational and social advance.

The twentieth century offers the American people the greatest opportunity of the ages to achieve a civilization which is full and fine—that will fulfil the American dream of equal opportunity for all. It also offers a situation full of great dangers. We can follow a course that will lead to stagnation, deterioration and decay. America must choose the road it will take! We who work in the schools and colleges of the nation have it within our hands to influence the decision. Let us catch the vision and summon the courage to march on.

# A NATIONAL CULTURE—BY-PRODUCT OR OBJECTIVE OF NATIONAL PLANNING[1]

By JOY ELMER MORGAN
NATIONAL EDUCATION ASSOCIATION

I SHALL speak quite informally. I would like first to pay a word of tribute to the Payne Fund, which has made possible the activities of the National Committee on Education by Radio and which had made considerable contribution to the development of interest in radio, even before the National Committee came onto the scene. I doubt that there has been at any other point in the history of this republic an expenditure of a similar amount of money so significant and prophetic as that which the Payne Fund has contributed to a development which is so new that the great majority of our people have quite overlooked its significance. At a time when the nation as a whole has been almost totally blind to the effects of this new institution, when governments, state and national, have been peculiarly neglectful and unappreciative of the significance of radio as an instrument of education and culture, the Payne Fund has stood by with its eyes turned toward the future and has helped to keep alive a great purpose and a great ideal. I have faith to believe that some time, if not now, the nation will awaken to the significance of the program which the National Committee on Education by Radio has been urging and that these years of pioneer beginnings will eventually be crowned with results of the utmost importance for American life and culture.

I would like also to pay tribute to my colleagues on the National Committee on Education by Radio who without compensation, without thought of advantage to themselves, often at great sacrifice, have carried on during these difficult years when we have had not only the uncertainties of a pioneer development but in addition the difficulties which grow out of the confusion created by the collapse and chaos of our economic system. I would like also to extend a word of greeting and to pay tribute to you who have come here to-day to con-

[1] Statement by Joy Elmer Morgan, chairman, National Committee on Education by Radio, and editor, *Journal of the National Education Association*, before a National Conference on the Use of Radio as a Cultural Agency in a Democracy, called by the committee, Washington, D. C., on May 7, 1934.

sider the place which this new instrument of radio should have in our national culture.

The preceding speaker, Mr. Harold B. McCarty, director of the Wisconsin State Radio Station, has described the activities of that station on behalf of a great state. As an opportunity for human betterment I would rather have the management of a radio broadcasting station in any American state than the presidency of its university. The influence of radio on the masses of the people is immediate and intimate. When it comes into their homes with the high purpose and fine spirit and the strict confidence which a wisely managed public institution inspires, it may become a mighty power for lifting the level of enlightenment so that every human institution will be better in consequence.

Our subject this morning refers to national planning. There is a popular fallacy in certain quarters that national planning represents an effort to force people or events into some preconceived mold. The exact opposite is true. It is the spirit and purpose of planning to get at the facts, the fundamental needs and wishes, and on the basis of those fundamental needs and wishes to work out step by step the procedure needed to realize them so that all the factors which enter into the situation will be brought together in a harmonious whole. No planning is preconceived. We might as well speak of preconceived growth of a tree. Planning has its own internal laws and the planner seeks to discover those laws and to apply them, just as young Charles W. Eliot has spent years studying the development of this city and laying out plans which will look forward several generations to make sure that it will be the best and most beautiful city that human ingenuity can provide. No plan is final, and it is a part of the technique of planning that provision is made for constant and continuing adaptation and replanning as new conditions develop. Our automobiles are planned. They represent a tremendous coordination of artistic and engineering skill. They have been replanned several times within the brief history of automobiling and they are still being replanned. That process will go on and should go on until we eventually arrive at the most perfect mechanism for transportation that the human mind can conceive.

We are asked this morning to discuss the question as to whether a national culture is a by-product or an objective of national planning. The discussion of culture in any connection is difficult because it is one of those words which means different things to different people and which applies to values that are somewhat intangible. Were I to talk about such a product as the automobile, for example, that is something definite and tangible. We can think of it in terms of its separate parts. Every one knows what those parts are—that it has an engine, chassis, steering apparatus, seats, and so on. We know what those parts are expected to do and each of us can estimate in his own way their effectiveness and the effect of the whole mechanism. We can form our own answers to such questions as these: Is it dependable? Is it safe? Is it beautiful? Is it economical?

When we begin to talk about culture we can not be so sure of the meaning which others will attach to our words. To some it means manners; to others it means knowledge of certain things which every one is supposed to know. To still others it is synonymous with civilization. Certainly there must be in all culture worthy the name the elements of taste and appreciation. My idea of a definition of culture is a concept which includes the entire life of a people in so far as that life is undebatably excellent and happy. We need not ask that any one shall agree with us as to the meaning of culture, but we do have a right to ask him in the name of culture to do what he sincerely thinks in his own heart is best. If we can get the masses of the people to dedicate themselves to do what in their own hearts they think best, there will be advance and growth. If they will ask themselves the simple questions—What is true? What is right? What is good? What is beautiful?—and will seek to answer those questions in their own way, the outcome will be a national culture in the truest and finest sense.

The first axiom in that process of building a culture—and a culture is always in the process of building—is freedom of thought and freedom of speech. That freedom is by all odds the greatest achievement of modern times. Nothing in our mechanical civilization with all its great inventions compares in significance with the idea of freedom of speech and thought. It is the foundation of all scientific and technical advance which has made possible the mechanism which carries radio into our homes. Without freedom of thought and speech we could not have had these things. Without freedom of thought and speech we can not have their social and political equivalent. We can not make in social and political realms the progress which we have made in the material realm. The idea of freedom of thought is the first of three great ideals which underlie modern civilization.

The second of those ideas is the idea of progress. For untold centuries the human race went along with the thought that tomorrow would be like to-day and yesterday and that every one would do exactly as his fathers had done. But gradually there began to develop the idea that there could be progress. I do not mean progress merely in the sense of the material things of life. Much more fundamental is the progress which can be made in the lives of men, in their personal growth, in their tastes, attitudes, and in their ways of conducting themselves within the family, within the neighborhood, within the state, the nation and the larger family of nations.

Horace Mann, whose centennial as the first chief state school officer in America we shall celebrate in 1937, went about this country talking and writing on the improvability of man. It is highly significant that a great teacher, a great writer and orator had to go about preaching the improvability of man, that he had to talk to parents, speak in schoolhouses and before legislatures, and to issue circulars and periodicals to get the people to recognize that the lives of men could be improved through the process of education. The idea of progress is second only to freedom of thought. Freedom of thought made science possible. The idea of progress made the common school possible. The first great development of the common school came during the 1890s and when that generation which was in the schools in the 90s came onto the scene of action, America had a period of the most rapid advance which has ever been known in any civilization.

The third of these three great ideas which underlie modern civilization is still relatively new and little understood. It is the idea of planning. It is closely related to the other ideas. It requires freedom of thought and it requires a willingness to believe that progress is possible. In the first phase of its development, planning has dealt too largely with space. We have laid out our country crudely. We have divided it into states, into sections, into cities and towns, looking only at the immediate need. We have not given enough attention to the time factor. The result has been waste. Things have had to be done over many times because of a lack of foresight. Planning considers a problem in its totality; it looks forward for a year or two years or ten years or fifty years or even for hundreds of years, and this is particularly important in the development of a national culture.

We may build a machine in a day; we may grow a crop of grain in a season; we may even grow a forest in a generation, but a national culture is a product of longer and slower growth. It is culture that makes the difference between men and beasts, between weak and brutal people and a strong and noble humanity. It is made up of the ideas, the skills, the habits, the manners, the institutions, the social patterns and, most of all, of the feelings of the people. All the activities of a people, all their decisions and institutions, will come eventually to reflect their fundamental feelings and in turn to shape those feelings. The depreciation of a national culture is therefore far more serious than the depreciation of a national coinage. If it is important that those who manage our coinage and our money and banks shall be inspired with the spirit of trusteeship, it is doubly important that that spirit of trusteeship should govern the management of radio broadcasting, the greatest medium which exists for the spread of human culture.

Our present American radio set-up, which puts radio broadcasting in the hands of private radio monopolies deriving their revenue from advertising, is dead set against each of these three fundamental ideas which underlie modern civilization. Genuine freedom of thought is impossible when the machinery through which thought must flow on a national scale is in the hands of monopoly groups supported by competitive business enterprises which have an immediate interest in keeping the facts from the people. The very points at which facts are most needed if the people are to govern themselves wisely are the points at which freedom of speech is most certain to be denied.

For example, one of the great needs in American life to-day is a realistic regulation of the powerful corporate groups which are constantly seeking to dominate government and to exploit the people. The necessary reforms are impossible so long as radio broadcasting is financed by advertising, paid for by the drug trade which resists regulation, paid for by the public utilities which are seeking to maintain their excessive charges for service, paid for by parasitic industries which wish to continue to make money from the weaknesses and indulgences of men and women. If we do not deal with these fundamental issues our civilization will crash over our very heads, and if they are to be dealt with intelligently, the people must have the facts. Most of our people are still living in the Stone Age so far as their knowledge of politics and sociology is concerned. We have done relatively little to correct this condition during these years when our civilization has been on the very brink, ready to go so far over the cliff that it may be impossible to bring it back and to reestablish it. The very idea of freedom of speech over the radio is inconsistent with the idea of making profits.

May I pause to say parenthetically that I can conceive of no greater violation of trusteeship than the way the radio groups have exposed the child mind to commercialism. For untold centuries we have regarded the mind of the child as sacred, to be protected by the parents who love him, by the church with its dedication to the eternal verities of life, and by the teacher who is licensed by the state to teach the truth and who like the parent is motivated by desire for the child's welfare. For the first time in human history we have turned over this tender child mind to men who would make a profit from exploiting it—to men who have no real understanding of the consequences of their acts, for, if they had, they would hang their heads in shame and make their apologies to generations yet unborn. If you wonder what the effects of radio broadcasting are on the child mind simply listen to the conversation of children. Notice the words they use, the songs they sing, their attitudes and manners. You will discover that the advertising agency is taking the place of the mother, the father, the teacher, the pastor, the priest, in determining the lives of children.

One of the primary traits of a civilized person is sincerity. It is very hard to define the difference between the individual who is sincere and the one who has what I describe as the "smartalecky" attitude. Yet probably the very survival or defeat of civilization hinges there as to whether the masses of our people shall be motivated by sincerity or by this flippant "smartalecky" thinking that sounds good, that sells goods in the cheap and superficial sense, but which has no relation to the fundamental spirit and purpose which has made life in America what it is.

It is impossible to exaggerate the significance of abusing the child mind in this way. The minds of children can be so filled with triviality, vulgarity, flippancy and insincerity that it will be almost impossible for them during their entire lifetimes to overcome the effects of these attitudes which are built into the very fibers of their being during the formative years. There is no occupation they can pursue, no relationship which they can maintain with their fellows which will be unaffected by these fundamental tastes and attitudes. Their family life, their choice of vocation, their relations with their fellows, their political decisions, will be colored by this vague, indefinite, but tremendously powerful subconscious self which is being built up by what goes into their minds and which is certain eventually to come out. We may well fear the suppression of important facts because the owners of radio do not wish the public to have those facts. Perhaps we should fear even more this debasing of the child mind.

The present radio set-up in the United States is also inherently inconsistent with the idea of progress. In the end the character of an institution will be determined by the ultimate test which is applied to its operation. What is that ultimate test for commercialized radio? It is this: Will it pay in dollars and cents? Will it make a profit for the advertiser? And the bigger the profit the more he will be willing to pay for time on the air. The primary questions are not: Is it true? Is it right? Is it good? Is it beautiful? but, Will it pay? And if making it pay means the destruction of progress and the negation of culture, progress and culture will go by the board. America to-day is operating on a momentum which was acquired in the days before radio. It is operating on a momentum which the people acquired before the motion picture began teaching crime and gambling and the cheap and flippant attitude toward the verities of life. No one knows what will happen when this country comes into the hands of those who have been exposed to the propaganda of the moneychangers and of the debasing material which they have broadcast into the lives of the people.

Likewise the commercial operation of radio on the basis of advertising support is inconsistent with planning. Sales and profits are things of the moment. The salesman wants what he can make now. He is not thinking of to-morrow. He wants the best hours on the air when the largest number of people are free to listen. This hand-to-mouth policy is inconsistent with farsighted planning. The common school, on the other hand, is an example of farsighted planning. It does not expect to make a profit to-day or at the end of the month or even at the end of the year. It looks ahead for a generation and in the end yields a vastly larger service because it does look ahead and make provision for the future.

American culture which has brought this

nation farther in a brief space of time than any other nation ever traveled in a similar period has been planned in the home, in the school and in the church. Shall we now turn the management of our culture over to the moneychangers whose mismanagement of business and industry has so nearly wrecked our civilization and who are in a fair way to wreck it completely if the people do not soon again exert their rights?

The elements which make up radio broadcasting can be so planned as to make a positive contribution to American life. They can be deliberately set to arouse ambition, to develop taste, to spread information, to encourage people to study and to participate actively in the intellectual, artistic and civic life of the nation; or they can be deliberately set to make people satisfied with triviality, to leave them unawakened to industrial wrong and political stupidity, groping as blindly in the midst of confusion as though these modern instruments for the spread of enlightenment did not exist. Whether radio is to do one or the other of these two things will not be a matter of accident. They will not be by-products; they will come because some one wants them and works at the task of bringing them about.

May I suggest in closing that if we wish to make the most of radio broadcasting we devote ourselves to certain fundamental principles. The following statement of principles is like that which I suggested some two years ago before the parliamentary committee in Canada which was then studying the entire subject of radio broadcasting in the dominion.

*First and foremost, all air channels to belong to the people free from any suggestion of ownership by private parties.* This question has never been fully decided by the American people. The question has never gotten to the Supreme Court in its ultimate form. Let us hope that when it does there will be no question as to who owns the air.

*Second, listener interests and needs to determine programs.* We have a billion dollars invested in our receiving sets. With all the inflated values in the studios and equipment, the capital of commercial broadcasting is not over one hundred million dollars. On the financial side alone the listener should be supreme. Yet for all practical purposes the listener is still disfranchised in the determination of radio programs.

*Third, cultural uses of radio to precede commercial uses.* In spite of the public interest clause in the Radio Act of 1927 the consistent interpretation has been to place the commercial uses of radio above the cultural uses. It is simply impossible consistently to get the best hours—when the most people are free to listen—for the best uses of broadcasting.

*Fourth, the assignment of radio channels to be so managed as not to destroy state sovereignty.* It has been one of the astounding facts of these years that this principle has been so almost universally unrecognized that there has not been in a single American state a governor who would fight through to the last ditch for the rights of the people whom he represents and whom he is sworn to serve. State sovereignty in any real and effective sense under to-day's conditions is impossible without this right to have some control over the voice that reaches out into the homes of the people of the state with a possibility of informing or of misinforming or of keeping from them the information which they should have.

*Fifth, the child mind to be safeguarded from selfish exploitation.* No one should be allowed to advertise anything to the child mind. We should look upon the effort to go over the heads of parents, the church and the school, to the child mind with something of the horror that we would look at the poisoning of a spring or well. It is not something to be exploited in the name of private gain, I care not how good the product may be. The fundamental issue is whether we are going to expose the child mind or conserve it as the most precious heritage of the race.

*Sixth, freedom of speech to be safeguarded from interference by either commercial or political forces.* You have heard that fine description of the way they manage their political campaigns over state-owned radio stations in Wisconsin. That spirit and that method of management extended to every locality and to the nation as a whole would transform political life in America. It would substitute intelligence for demagoguery; it would give us the facts we need to deal wisely with the complex issues of our day. The local communities and the states are the training fields for national leadership. We need to conserve the political and cultural vitality of the locality.

Finally, let us always remember that a culture or a civilization exists fundamentally in people's minds and if it does not continue to exist in their minds and in their feelings, it will soon cease to exist at all. If we are to have freedom of speech it will be because people want freedom of speech and are willing to exert themselves to maintain it. To-day nine tenths of the people of the world live under governments where the hands of the clock have been turned back and where the lamps of learning have been turned low or put out so that freedom of speech does not exist. Let us insist upon maintaining in our democracy these fundamental ideas of freedom of speech, of progress and of planning.

# EDUCATIONAL EVENTS

## THE BRITISH ASSOCIATION OF UNIVERSITY TEACHERS

ACCORDING to the London *Times,* the claim of the Association of University Teachers that the range of its work is world-wide was borne out at the recent meeting at University College, at the first Oxford conference.

China, the Antipodes, India, the Middle East and the American continent were represented, as well as many of the countries of Europe, in the several commissions into which the conference resolved itself. The proceedings are summarized in the *Times* as follows:

At one of the sessions on Saturday, after members from several countries had spoken of university problems, one of the speakers, Professor H. Fischer, president of the German Association of University Professors and Teachers, was asked by Professor Norman Bentwich, professor of international relations at Jerusalem, whether his association took any action for the protection of academic freedom.

Professor Fischer replied that Germany, looking back on her long tradition of scholarship, might be trusted to protect academic freedom to-day and in the future.

On Sunday the members had to choose between overcrowding in universities, the place of vocational education, the interchange of teachers and the problems of extra-mural work, with the wise proviso that each commission sought divergencies of view rather than any definite agreement at this stage.

Professor Roman Dyboski, Cracow, Poland, told the section on overcrowding that people with university diplomas had been known to apply for positions as porters, and that routine office work was being done by graduates all over Europe. In Warsaw recently the engagement of some graduates as waiters had almost caused a riot.

There was agreement that higher entrance standards would go some way to meet the problem of overcrowding.

In the section on vocational training, over which the president, Professor Frank Smith, of Leeds, presided, the breach between specialized and cultural education evoked a keen discussion.

Mr. W. Doran, Liverpool, said that too close concentration by the student affected his perfection in the subject itself, since he had difficulty in expressing himself, and it was almost impossible to assess his achievement.

Dr. Esther Crane, of Goucher College, Baltimore, suggested that the remedy lay in beginning the specialized training earlier, but on a broader basis.

Professor H. W. Tyler, Massachusetts Institute of Technology, said the solution lay in flexibility, particularly since the demands of industry changed so rapidly nowadays.

There was strong support for residence as a method which would do much to correct the isolation of the specialist, but Miss A. M. Trout, Southampton, suggested that the methods of the older universities were being accepted without adequate scrutiny.

Nationalistic prejudices in countries as far apart as Burma and Wales, demanding the translation of scientific books into the vernacular, were among the problems discussed by the section on adult education.

## REPORT ON THE HIGH SCHOOLS OF NEW YORK CITY

DR. JOHN L. TILDSLEY, acting head of the high-school division of the Board of Education of New York City, has presented a report on the work of his division to Dr. Harold G. Campbell, superintendent of schools. In this report Dr. Tildsley advocates setting back the school age to sixteen years, rather than setting it forward as has been advocated by labor leaders. He says in part:

> This proposal of mine is based on two unpopular doctrines: one, that the boy reaches at sixteen a physical development which makes it improbable that employment under modern efficiency conditions will impair his health; the second, that there is a saturation point for many boys and girls, beyond which further schooling of the accepted type is profitable neither for them nor for society.
>
> I am very skeptical whether in the long run in a well-planned school system it is desirable or efficient to have, in the same school of second grade, pupils with very wide variations in learning capacities, interests and objectives.
>
> I believe, therefore, that with a view to better education for all and at a decreased cost the automatic passage of every pupil from the 8B grade to the high school should not be continued. Either as a result of a test or on the basis of the school record combined with the test results, the thousands who are now sent to high school foredoomed to failure should be retained in the present elementary schools until they have completed the compulsory school age or be sent to special rehabilitation schools manned by elementary teachers at elementary salaries.
>
> We are now graduating about 17,000 pupils from the high schools of this city each term. Seven thousand graduated with this working power I have described and with certain other definite qualities, habits and attitudes would be a far greater asset to the city and in the long run to the taxpayers than will the 17,000 we are now graduating.

Dr. Tildsley continues:

> I believe it is a fair estimate that for 20 per cent. of the pupils in our high schools, that is, for between 40,000 and 50,000 pupils, the courses of study, the subjects offered, as now taught, are not the best media for the fullest development of these pupils. Unfortunately most of them need to be re-educated.
>
> In the process of seeking the best solution in the high schools with our great numbers and resulting large classes and crowded conditions, we are impairing the education of the 200,000 while not succeeding in solving the problem for the 40,000.
>
> The present per capita cost of high school instruction is about $160 and of elementary school $110, a difference of $50 a year per capita. If the estimate of 40,000 pupils in the high schools who have not the learning capacity for the grade of work assigned them is approximately correct, then the proposed plan might possibly result in a better education for these pupils at a saving of $2,000,000 a year.

For the more intelligent pupils Dr. Tildsley proposes the establishment of honor schools, one or two in each of the larger boroughs.

## THE FIRST PEOPLES COLLEGE CLUB IN NEW YORK CITY

A PLAN to meet the needs of hundreds of young wage earners in our big cities who are leading isolated lives and eager for a satisfying use of their leisure time has been evolved by the American Peoples College in Europe on whose educational advisory board are some of America's most discerning educators.

A series of peoples college clubs are to be established under the auspices of the college in metropolitan centers throughout the United States in which young men and women may live within easy commuting distance of their jobs and have an opportunity to continue their education in their spare time.

The term "peoples college" comes from Denmark where the peoples colleges or folk schools are open to all adults regardless of former schooling. The American Peoples College in Europe is based on the Scandinavian idea that a desire to learn is a better entrance requirement than a collection of grades and credits, and that examinations are a relic of the past. Founded five years ago by a group of American educators interested in bettering international understanding and in making European study and travel possible for young Americans of limited means, the college's activities are guided by such men as Professors John Dewey, William H. Kilpatrick and Goodwin Watson, of Columbia University; Professor Harry A. Overstreet, of the College of the City of New York; Dr. Jay B. Nash, of New York University; Dean Alvin Johnson, of the New School for Social Research, and Dr. Nat T. Frame, of the University of West Virginia. At the present time many young Americans are in Europe taking field trips varying from one to sixteen months in length and many more will be going over before the summer is over to visit its Tyrolean center and travel under its auspices.

Denishawn House in Van Cortlandt Park, built originally by Ruth St. Denis and Ted Shawn, has been procured by the college for the first of the clubs in New York City. The beautiful Tunisian building with its large trees and a patio garden makes an ideal setting for the educational and recreational activities that will make up the weekly program. Recreation is recognized as playing an important part in an individual's development and every facility will be used for hiking, dancing, singing, outdoor sports and amateur theatricals.

In a statement made by S. A. Mathiasen, director of the American Peoples College in Europe, he says:

We know from our experience with widely varying groups in the United States that there are literally thousands of young people in every large city for whom such an educational center would meet a great need. They have discovered a real desire for education in its truest sense, but they can not afford to leave their jobs. They want to live in pleasant surroundings with an atmosphere in which life may be lived with a certain dignity and graciousness. They want interesting friends and companions among other young men and women with whom they may share ideas and good times—an accomplishment not always simple to achieve in the life of modern cities.

We believe that there are great things to be done in the United States during the years immediately before us, and that the great group of wage-earning young people should not only be alert to what the possibilities of American life are, but should be so trained that they take an active part in determining that the best possibilities are realized.

Our idea is to have an hour or so each evening and longer periods week-ends spent in consideration of various ideas with the lecture discussion method. The subjects to be considered will be as broad as life itself, dealt with, however, not as academic abstractions, but in their relationship to actual living. Resident leaders will be in charge of the program, inviting as guest speakers leaders in various fields of thought in the United States and Europe. Shorter working hours per week make it possible to carry on a stimulating educational program and still leave the individual some time for himself.

Mr. and Mrs. Mathiasen will themselves live at the Denishawn Center next winter, and applications for membership in the first of these peoples college clubs are now being taken at the New York office of the American Peoples College in Europe, 545 Fifth Avenue, although the club will not officially open until October 1.

## SPECIALIZATION IN CHILD DEVELOPMENT AT THE UNIVERSITY OF CHICAGO

THE University of Chicago has recently set up an organization to provide for specialization in child development at the level of the Ph.D. The plan furnishes a general background of instruction in the basic sciences contributing to an understanding of child development, such as psychology and biology, and of the social institutions which exert the chief influence on the child's development, such as the school and the family. It also provides the opportunity for specialization and research in any aspect of development, such as physical growth, mental growth, behavior, nutrition, education, the influence of social factors, heredity and environment, etc.

For the present the programs of instruction and research are organized and supervised by the department of education in cooperation with the University Committee on Child Development. This department accepts programs of work, planned and carried out in each case with the supervision of a special committee, which include appropriate courses in any department of the university. Departmental requirements have been modified in the case of students in child development to make possible the inclusion of this work from other departments. The committee which supervises the student's program includes a representative of the department of education, the Committee on Child Development and the department in which the student's research lies.

The University of Chicago has for some time been provided with a considerable list of courses of instruction, facilities for research and laboratory schools, including a school for problem children. It now has the machinery by which these facilities can be more effectively utilized by the student who wishes to specialize in child development than was formerly the case.

## THE SCHOOL OF NURSING AT YALE UNIVERSITY

Yale University has announced that beginning with the class that enters this fall, students in the Yale School of Nursing will be given the degree of master of nursing upon completion of the basic course in the school. The Yale school is believed to be the first school of nursing, not only in this country but in the world, to make the completion of the college course an entrance requirement.

The Yale school, which is now completing its eleventh year, was the first school of nursing to be organized independently of a hospital or medical school, with the emphasis placed on nursing education in relation to preventive medicine. The part of public health nursing in the community health and welfare activities has been particularly stressed. Graduates of the school, because of their broader preparation, are in constant demand, and despite the many thousands of unemployed nurses, it has not been possible to respond to the requests for graduates for advanced positions in teaching and administration in both the institutional and public health fields.

The university also made public the resolution of the corporation on the retirement of Professor Annie W. Goodrich, dean of the school, at the end of the present academic year, when she will be succeeded by Professor Effie J. Taylor. The vote is as follows:

Voted, That the title of dean emeritus be conferred upon Dean Goodrich and that the secretary be directed to convey to her the grateful appreciation of the president and fellows for her eleven years of distinguished service to the university as organizer and first Dean of the School of Nursing. Experienced, untiring, scholarly, she has brought the school to the forefront in its field, has been accorded many honors in recognition of her service to public health and stands out as America's foremost figure in nursing education.

Dean Goodrich has been honored twice by the French Government for her work in public health. She received the Walter Burns Saunders Medal in 1932 as the nurse "who has rendered the most praiseworthy services to the profession." She also holds the Distinguished Service Medal, and the honorary degree of doctor of science from Mount Holyoke College.

## REFUGEES FROM GERMANY

The Emergency Committee in Aid of Displaced German Scholars (2 West 45th Street, New York) reports that more than 1,300 scholars were displaced, of whom six to seven hundred have emigrated or are likely to leave Germany within the next few months. In addition, between 5,200 and 5,500 professional people have had to emigrate because they have lost their positions in Germany and find themselves without any means of livelihood. Some 7,000 students had to leave the universities and other institutions of higher learning before completing their studies. Of these, 1,500 to 1,600 have sought refuge outside Germany. Thus, the total number of people belonging to the academic and professional groups who at present have to create a new existence for themselves in foreign countries is more than 7,500.

These figures were established at a meeting of the "Experts Committee for Academic and Kindred Refugees from Germany," which met recently in London. The committee forms part of the organization set up by James G. McDonald, the high commissioner for refugees coming from Germany. The London meetings were presided over by Dr. Alfred Einstein Cohn, of the Rockefeller Institute for Medical Research and member of the Emergency Committee in Aid of Displaced German Scholars, New York, which up to now has placed more than sixty German scholars in American institutions of higher learning. Dr. Stephen Duggan, director of the American Institute of International Education, and secretary of the emergency committee, attended the meeting. The Academic Assistance Council in London was represented by Professor C. S. Gibson, professor of chemistry in the University of London. Dr. Chaim Weizmann represented the institutions of research and higher learning in Palestine. There were furthermore present representatives of most of the academic and professional committees in the various countries which have been set up in collaboration with the High Commission to help in the settlement of academic and professional refugees. The student group was represented by the International Student Service.

The outstanding result of the meeting was that it became clear, provided sufficient funds are forthcoming, that most of the displaced scholars and most of the students can be taken care of and permanent places found for them, while, given a coordination of effort, under the auspices of the High Commission for Refugees Coming from Germany, a great many of the professional people may hope to create a new existence for themselves. It is expected that by July, 1935, 140 scholars will be absorbed by universities and similar institutions of learning, while 150 will have found places in research laboratories attached to industries, hospitals, etc. It is reasonably certain that another 130 scholars can be maintained after July, 1935, on grants, thanks to the work of such organizations as the Academic Assistance Council and the Emergency Committee in Aid of Displaced German Scholars, etc. Thus, 420 of the emigrated German scholars will by July, 1935, have been enabled to continue their work. As to the remaining scholars, the committee decided to make every effort to create further research scholarships and to elaborate group research schemes.

Gareth Maufe, representing the International Student Service, reported that his organization was at present in touch with 1,594 émigré students, or more than 90 per cent. of the total number. Help has been given in three main ways: By providing scholarships for continuation of study, which has been done as economically as possible by augmenting these scholarships by free places in families or "au pair" position; by scholarships for retraining, especially for those who had formerly studied German law and who must now look to new occupations, this work in England having been made possible with the help of the Jewish Refugee Committee at Woburn House; by providing employment, although it has been impossible to do this in England, owing to the Home Office regulations. The organization needs another £8,800 to complete its work.

## OFFICERS OF THE AMERICAN LIBRARY ASSOCIATION

CHARLES H. COMPTON, assistant librarian of the St. Louis Public Library, was elected president of the American Library Association for 1934–35, according to the announcement made at the last general session of the Montreal conference. According to the *Bulletin* of the association "Mr. Compton's most conspicuous services to the association have perhaps been given as chairman of the first committee on American Library Association Activities and as chairman of the Committee on Salaries and Employment. His keen interest in such other fields as publicity, publications and state-wide library service, however, give him an exceptionally broad background for his presidential administration."

Other new officers of the association are:

*First Vice-president,* Mildred H. Pope, State Library, Olympia, Washington.

*Second Vice-president,* James Thayer Gerould, Princeton University Library.

*Treasurer,* Matthew S. Dudgeon, Public Library, Milwaukee, Wisconsin.

*Trustee of Endowment Funds,* Eugene M. Stevens, Federal Reserve Bank, Chicago.

*Members of the Executive Board:* Carl L. Cannon, Yale University Library, New Haven, Connecticut; Louise Prouty, Public Library, Cleveland,

Ohio; and (to fill the vacancy caused by the election of Miss Countryman) Ida F. Wright, Public Library, Evanston, Illinois.

*New Council Members:* Louis J. Bailey, State Library, Indianapolis, Indiana; Mrs. Mary Duncan Carter, McGill University Library School; Rudolph H. Gjelsness, University of Arizona Library; M. Louise Hunt, Public Library, Racine, Wisconsin, and Althea H. Warren, Public Library, Los Angeles.

# EDUCATIONAL NOTES AND NEWS

A SPECIAL committee has been named from among the trustees of the Johns Hopkins University to make recommendations for a successor to Dr. Joseph S. Ames, retiring president. The committee includes Newton D. Baker, chairman; B. Howell Griswold, Jr., Carlyle Barton, Dr. Thomas R. Brown and Walter S. Gifford.

DR. CHARLES CHRISTOPHER MIEROW, for nine years president of Colorado College, has been appointed professor of biography at Carleton College to succeed Dr. Theodore O. Wedel, who recently resigned to accept appointment as secretary of college work for the Episcopal Church. Dr. Mierow spent last year in Rome, where he served as visiting professor at the American School of Classical Studies.

DR. CHARLES E. PRALL, dean of the College of Education of the University of Arkansas, has been appointed dean of the School of Education of the University of Pittsburgh. He will fill the vacancy created by the death of Dr. Grover H. Alderman in November, 1930. Since Dr. Alderman's death the post has been held by Dr. L. P. Sieg, who was acting dean up until July 1, when he left to become president of the University of Washington at Seattle. Dr. Prall will take office on September 1. He has a background in public school and university administration. He was for fifteen years superintendent of schools in Iowa cities. Dr. Prall, who is forty-three years of age, received his master's degree from the University of Chicago in 1926 and his doctorate from Iowa in 1928.

AT the recent commencement at Beloit College the class of 1923 at the alumni dinner presented a portrait of Dr. Melvin A. Brannon, who was president of Beloit College from 1917 to 1923 and was until a year ago chancellor of the University of Montana. Dr. Brannon responded to the address of presentation and later delivered the commencement address. The portrait was painted by Paul Trebilcock, of Chicago.

DR. R. B. VON KLEINSMID, president of the University of Southern California, was recently decorated while in Tokio, Japan, with the Third Order of the Rising Sun. The medal was given in recognition of his work in improving friendly relationships between the United States and Japan and for effective assistance in aiding American-born Japanese. Dr. von KleinSmid is chancellor of the Los Angeles University of International Relations, which is affiliated with the University of Southern California.

ROBERT MCNAIR DAVIS, who has been dean of the School of Law at the University of Kansas the past five years, has resigned administrative work to devote his full time to teaching. Dr. W. L. Burdick, who has been a member of the Kansas faculty for thirty-six years, and who was acting dean following the death of James Woods Green, will again become acting dean. Added to the law faculty will be E. R. Latty, of New York City, as associate professor, and M. A. Kallis, of Chicago, as acting associate professor.

DR. FRANK A. HARTMAN, professor of physiology at the University of Buffalo, has been appointed professor of physiology at the Ohio State University.

PROFESSOR GREGORY BREIT, of New York University, has been appointed professor of theoretical physics at the University of Wisconsin.

DR. GEORGE M. JANES, professor of economics and head of the department at Kenyon College since 1925, has retired with the title of emeritus professor of economics.

INSTRUCTORS in education recently appointed at Yale University include: Earl P. Andreen, Hazel B. Baxter, William T. Bryan, Charlotte

M. Burnham, Allegra J. Ingleright, Paul H. Sheats and Edwin R. Van Kleeck.

IN response to the demand from the Rio Grande Valley for extension center work, the University of Texas will transfer Dr. James Knight, adjunct professor of educational psychology, from Houston and its surrounding area to the valley for next year. This is the first time a permanent center has been conducted in the valley, although extension courses have been offered on a limited scale in previous years.

MRS. SARAH PORTER ELLIS has succeeded Miss Neale S. Knowles as head of home economics extension work at the Iowa State College.

PROFESSOR S. W. HUNTON, who for fifty-one years has been head of the department of mathematics at Mount Allison University, Sackville, New Brunswick, retired at the close of the academic year.

THE appointment of Professor Frederick Ogilvie, professor of political economy at the University of Edinburgh, as vice-chancellor of Queen's University, Belfast, has been announced. The post has been vacant since Christmas, when Sir Richard Livingstone assumed office as president of Corpus Christi College, Oxford.

C. J. FORDYCE, fellow and classical tutor of Jesus College, Oxford, has been appointed to the chair of humanity in the University of Glasgow, in succession to Professor William Rennie, who has become professor of Greek.

W. M. WILLIAMS, lecturer in education at Armstrong College, University of Durham, has been appointed professor of education at the University College of Wales at Swansea.

ARTHUR B. PERRY, head of the department of English, has been appointed principal of the Boys' School, Milton Academy, Massachusetts, to succeed Frank E. Lane, who has resigned. Mr. Perry has been a member of the staff of the academy since 1921. He will continue his work in the English department.

THE Leon Fellowship for research in education for 1934–35, of the value of £400 for one year, has been awarded by the University of London to William Frederic Floyd, who holds the Teacher's Diploma of East London College, King's College, and of the Institute of Education.

WILLIAM PENN LOOMIS has been appointed to the staff of the Pennsylvania Department of Public Instruction. He is chief of industrial and continuation education, succeeding Paul L. Cressman, who resigned recently to become an assistant superintendent of public instruction in Michigan.

DR. NICHOLAS MURRAY BUTLER, president of Columbia University and of the Carnegie Endowment for International Peace, returned to New York City on July 16 after a short stay in Europe.

DR. EDGAR J. FISHER, dean of Robert College, Constantinople, has returned to America for the summer and will again teach at the Summer School of Syracuse University.

PROFESSOR PETER MANNICHE, principal of the International Peoples College at Elsinore, Denmark, recently gave an address under the direction of the National Council of Education at Aurora, Ontario. Dr. Manniche is on his way to Denmark after lecturing in India, China and Japan. His lectures are concerned with the folk high schools of Denmark, not controlled by the state. These are endeavoring to prove that culture should not be only for the rich.

DR. FREDERICK P. KEPPEL, president of the Carnegie Corporation, and Dr. A. Z. Reed, of the Bureau of Educational Inquiry of the Carnegie Foundation for the Advancement of Teaching, were the principal speakers at the dinner of the American Society for Engineering Education, given on the occasion of the recent annual meeting at Ithaca.

DEAN FREDERICK E. BOLTON, of the University of Washington, delivered the commencement address at Seattle Pacific College, on "The Place of the Church College in the New Deal."

GEOFFREY WINTHROP YOUNG writes as follows to the London *Times* on the death of Dr. Fritz Beck: "Dr. Beck, director of the German and Foreign Academic Exchange Bureau, whose death during the week-end massacre in Munich is now announced, will be gratefully remembered by hundreds of English and other foreign students and visitors to Munich. A philosopher and an organizer, he was largely responsible for creating the international residential hostels in connection with the university, as also for the cooperative feeding and mutual help organizations which ameliorated the lot of the poor German student after the war. A man of wide and lively sympathies, international view-point and outspoken courage, his 'disappearance' was assumed by himself and his friends to be only a matter of time. But he never allowed the threat to interfere with the vigorous prosecution of his philanthropic activities."

A WIRELESS dispatch to *The New York Times* gives the information that Dr. Oscar Staebel, leader of the Reich students' organization, and Ernst Zaeringer, leader of the German Studenthood, have retired. In their place Bernhard Rust, the Minister of Education, has appointed Andreas Feikert, a political science student, who will combine the leadership of both offices. Dr. Staebel has been a particularly ardent advocate of the introduction of Nazi culture into the universities and the abolition of the "old Heidelberg" spirit and the "reactionary" dueling corps. There were riots at the University of Bonn and the University of Göttingen as a result. Corps regalia were banned and Borussia and other select corps were proscribed. The retirement of Dr. Staebel and Herr Zaeringer was also preceded by prolonged friction between the Reich students' organization and the Studenthood which at some universities produced a complete deadlock. The system is said to have been working so badly that the authorities contemplate extensive changes, especially for bringing student activities more tightly under the direction and control of the Ministry of Education.

A THREE-DAY conference on "Individual Development and Guidance" will be held by Teachers College, Columbia University, from July 31 to August 2. Dr. Frederick P. Keppel, president of the Carnegie Corporation, will be chairman of the opening session at 8 P. M. in the auditorium of the Horace Mann School. The principal speakers at this session will be Dean William F. Russell, of Teachers College; Professor John M. Brewer, of the Graduate School of Education of Harvard University, and Dean Max McConn, of Lehigh University.

THE University of Pittsburgh conducted a summer conference on elementary education as a part of its twenty-eighth summer session. Guest speakers for two assemblies were Dr. James N. Rule, superintendent of public instruction for Pennsylvania, and Miss Bess Goodykoontz, assistant commissioner in the Office of Education at Washington and a former member of the university faculty in education. Dr. Rule's subject was, "The Future and the Elementary School Teacher." Miss Goodykoontz discussed "New Ideas in Elementary Education." Demonstration teaching and sectional conferences in geography, reading, arithmetic and the social studies were held. Participating in the conference were Dr. G. A. Yoakam, of the University of Pittsburgh; Miss Mabel Snedaker, visiting lecturer from the University of Iowa; staff members and demonstrators from the University Summer Demonstration School, and administrative officials of the Pittsburgh public schools.

THE Executive Committee of the International Federation of Sociological Societies and Institutes has decided to hold the twelfth Congress of the International Institute of Sociology at the Universal Exposition to be held at Brussels, Belgium, in 1935. The date proposed for the congress is about August 25, 1935. The Belgian government and other governments interested in the exposition will be patrons of the congress. The subject for general discussion will be "The Elementary Forms of the Social Life," but other sociological subjects will be given a place on the program. The authors of papers and other communications are requested to make known the titles of their papers not later than December 31. These should be sent to the secretary-general of the International Institute of Sociology, Professor G. L. Duprat, of the University of Geneva. All inquiries concerning the congress should be addressed to Professor Duprat.

THE organizing committee of the Second Pan-American Conference on Education, which will meet in Santiago, Chile, has announced that Columbia University, the University of Nôtre Dame and the University of Minnesota will send representatives. With the exception of Brazil, Haiti and the Dominican Republic, which have not as yet responded to the invitation, delegates are expected to be present from all nations.

Special arrangements will be at the service of the delegates to facilitate discussion of different points of view in regard to public education.

NEW YORK UNIVERSITY has reported that registration in several summer divisions of the university has increased for the first time since early in the depression. The number of students will not be known until the close of registration for the final six weeks' term of the Washington Square College on August 6, but a slight increase over last year is indicated. Divisions which reported enrolments greater than last year included the intersession term of the School of Education, which increased from 180 in 1933 to 203 this year; the School of Commerce, where the twelve weeks' evening term increased from 480 to 557 and the six weeks' day term increased from 231 to 243; the special study group of Washington Square College, which increased from 75 to 126, and the School of Retailing, which increased from 27 to 40. Enrolment in the summer session of the School of Education has already exceeded by 12 per cent. the expectations based on the experience of the regular 1933–34 session just closed. To date 1,947 students have enrolled, as compared with the complete figure for 1933 of 2,227.

AT the University of Michigan the regents recently passed a resolution to the effect that the present Bureau of Reference and Research in Government be changed from its status as a subdepartment of the Department of Political Science to a Bureau of Reference and Research in Government affiliated with the Department of Political Science; that there shall be an Advisory Committee for the Bureau composed of the deans and/or chairmen of the Law School, the School of Education, the Departments of Political Science, Economics and Sociology, or their authorized representatives; that there shall be a director of the bureau who, by and with the advice of the Advisory Committee, shall prepare the budget, formulate the program of research and service, and select the personnel, and said director is hereby authorized to sign vouchers against the budget; that monies now in the budget of the department of political science for the year 1934–1935 allocated to the subdepartment, be transferred to the budget of the Bureau of Reference and Research in Government; that the present relationship between the former Bureau of Reference and Research in Government and the League of Michigan Municipalities as approved by the Regents at their meeting on June 27, 1916, be continued with this newly constituted bureau; that in order that the research projects of the bureau shall be intimately correlated with research in allied fields, the director and advisory committee of the bureau shall present all proposals for research to the advisory committee of the Division of the Social Sciences for its comment.

THE London Playing Fields Society reported at its recent meeting considerable progress in providing the working men and boys of London greater opportunities for playing games. The society, which for 44 years has striven to encourage the people of London to play games, now permits the playing of cricket and tennis on most of its fields on Sunday. Football, however, has been prohibited because of the resulting excessive wear to the grounds. Children of the elementary schools are allowed the free use of the society's playing fields, wherever possible, providing the children are properly supervised.

# DISCUSSION

## SOME OF TO-DAY'S EDUCATIONAL PROBLEMS

EVERY age has had its philosophers, Greece and Rome, even the dark ages, have added their numbers. One of the major themes of these philosophers has been the training of youth. However, with your permission we shall leave these earlier writers and turn to the twentieth century by stopping at the seventeenth to consult Comenius, who lived three centuries before his day. He discusses universal free education for rural and urban, rich and poor, dull and stupid. He says "not all the children of the rich and powerful only, but all alike, boys and girls, both noble and ignoble, rich and poor, in the cities and towns, villages and hamlets should be sent to school." He declared that men are born to be men, and since we do not know what the Divine Providence has destined man to be he should be educated. Speaking of the dull and stupid, he continues, "They need the more assistance to throw off their brutish dullness and stupidity as far as is possible. . . . Do we fear their folly? The more we occupy their thoughts, so much the less will the folly that arises from emptiness of mind find place." He did not believe that only those with a high intelligence quotient should be admitted to the "garden of letters," but that "every one should receive a universal education and that at school."

Philosophers of the eighteenth century continued to discuss and enlarge on the Comenius pattern. Condorcet during the French Revolution sensed the changes that were to come in the new economic order of the nineteenth century and asked for a system of free education that would prepare children and adults to evalue the social changes of their own day. He hoped also that education would insure industrial workers against the dangers from the effect of monotony of their daily labor.

The philosophers of the eighteenth century and Condorcet, in particular, influenced our own revolutionary leaders so that we find Jefferson, author of the Declaration of Independence and third president of the new republic, advocating free public elementary schools, which by 1833 were assured.

Massachusetts had been a colonial leader for free schools since her beginning and in the early years of the new republic, under the able guidance of Horace Mann, she continued her lead. She was joined by other states, especially those states carved out of our western lands, which set a precedence for government aid to schools through the ordinance of 1887 and in the later grants of public lands.

From 1833 to 1933 the nation has slowly worked toward the perfection of a policy securing free schools for all classes. We have, however, been short-visioned in not teaching our children and our adults to evaluate the social changes that have been slowly taking place in our industrial and social order of this epoch.

Until the last two or three decades populations were not so seriously affected by these changes because of free lands and, too, the masses have not been so aware of our relatively slow change from an agricultural to an urban society. The present crisis has, therefore, come to them as a distinct shock. We find ourselves to-day in a new era with more than 50 per cent. of the population in cities, badly governed, with free lands gone, and with no adequate protection for the ideals built at such cost through the centuries.

Late government reports indicate more than 2,200,000 children of school age deprived of educational opportunities; the abandonment in some localities of free public high schools; the drastic cutting of the length of school terms; the reduction of teachers' salaries so that one in every three teachers is receiving less than $750 per year when she gets it. School districts now owe teachers more than $40,000,000; it is estimated 25,000 teachers are unemployed; the school terms in one out of four cities have been so shortened that they are now shorter in these cities than they were 100 years ago.

If this array of facts is not sufficiently convincing, more can easily be added. Unless action is taken promptly, we stand to lose our inheritance of the past, particularly the achievements of our own country along the lines of elementary, secondary and higher education.

In some of our higher schools of learning there has been fostered a notion that the "garden of letters," to use the terms of Comenius, is only for the especially gifted. We have been almost if not quite possessed by the idea. If time permitted, it would be of interest to examine the educational and psychological philosophy that has contributed to this short-sighted theory in a democracy.

One of our national figures in a recent publication writes:

> We are making the same mistake in education we made in agriculture a generation ago. Then the great problem was to make two blades of grass grow where one grew before, but we never thought about marketing the two blades. We are educating and turning out into an unsafe world 30,000,000 young people. We are trying to find out ways of educating everybody. The question now is what are we going to do with our product, boys and girls, when we get them educated.

I should like to raise the questions: What are we going to do with them if we do not educate them and why is it that we can not make a safe world to receive them, or, at least, a safer world?

Only yesterday we fought a terrible war to

make the world safe for democracy. Had we put the money, the energy, the sacrifice (omitting the horrors) into making a literate and happy electorate we would not find ourselves in the present unhappy confusion. The ballot in the hands of an ignorant voter has been our undoing. That ignorance has been the shortsighted policy of those dominating our economic structure as well as that of the unlettered.

The challenge of the new epoch is here. Is it too late to bring to it that which is best and enduring of the old, or shall we dream of the good old days, which can never return, and drift into a new dark age?

It is my faith that enough leadership is still ours that we may salvage that which is best (our Christian integrity, our schools, our youth) and with government aid move out and possess the land.

Schools need at once federal and state aid with the greatest possible control in the hands of those who understand local needs. This might, perhaps, come through the English federal pattern, but whatever the plan, it is the present significant challenge which must be met if western civilization is to be maintained.

CANDIS J. NELSON
SEATTLE PACIFIC COLLEGE

## CHILDREN AT THE MOVIES

As a physician, etc., I have long considered that many "sound-movies" are extremely unsound, hygienically speaking, but far too moving to the emotional aspect of the minds of many folk, especially children. Yesterday, a Saturday, purely by chance I had a simple experience strongly corroborative of this growing suspicion.

Allured by its announcement of an excellent film of dramatic humor by good actors, I attended one of our larger up-town movie theaters, arriving at a little past one o'clock. Already there were present, at a charge of a dime each, well over a thousand boys and girls, most of them in age from two years to sixteen, far more boys than girls, and, scattered about, a few adults. There was none too much fresh air and no green fields or trees or birds or flowers for this holiday!

Besides the humorous drama-reels (to which, I found, some of the more intelligent children did pay attention), the usual "news"-excitement, and the "sex-appeal-" and tragedy-movie advertisements (which seem to be taking more and more time in these theaters), the program consisted of two long, noisy, rapid animal-films, mostly in the "jungle." This was a strange and unnatural African jungle in Asia where Bengal tigers and many huge and quarrelsome lions and gentle elephants and horrid savages roamed maniacally and roared and fought and climbed beetling rocks and leaped and fought again and struggled and died or ran away, and so on pretty fairly continuously for two hours or so. It was mostly a phantasmagoric nightmare of rushing noisy horror, much, much worse than "realistic"—tragic, exciting, disturbing, inflaming, inciting in every breathless beholder vivid impressions of battle, bloodshed and death. And was it generally enjoyed! I'll say that of a certainty it was. But one may be certain that some of these children did not enjoy it, really, as much as the majority did.

But a thousand little boys and girls in general looked on and listened spellbound and gaped and trembled and cheered at times, and took it all in to their very brains and spinal cords and autonomic nervous systems as one more two-hour orgy of "recreation" and fun on a fine Saturday holiday. Many would get up and roam about the theater for one purpose or impulse or another, and so added not a bit to the general semineurotic chaos.

This sort of thing of course is going on daily all over America, often with the added incitement of sexual turbulence and suggestion, in this case by chance inconspicuous and perhaps relatively innocuous anyway. And yet the third film (of humorous drama) was dominated throughout by the success of a heroic gang of kidnappers and of "high-class" thugs.

Who or what laboratory has the psychobiologic apparatus or child-welfare outfit adequate to measure or even to estimate the personality-damage done, say to a thousand boys and two hundred little girls by holiday afternoons of which this is only one ordinary sample? The ever-habituating nervous systems of these excited youngsters feel the costs and store them up with the interest on them, as the years go by—for a day of strain and stress.

Probably this feeble protest would not have

been thought of for publication even by a psychiatrist, had his afternoon's unintended observation not resulted in a forceful demonstration to himself—namely, of a feeling of much nerve-fatigue both emotional and intellectual. This was an experience quite foreign to most moving pictures even in these, their worst, days of noise and vulgar license. What then of the impressionable minds and the plastic nervous systems of children, some of whom were not as yet always certain in their walk to say nothing of their feeling and of their thoughts?

When will some one really make a real beginning of really doing something about it? Surely to-day's amusement and recreation will to-morrow be generally admitted to have been yesterday's crime against childhood and thus against normal human development. Before long it must be generally admitted by selectmen and their congeners in the cities, as now all but universally by psychiatrists, that in such orgies of bloodthirsty excitement more than elsewhere nowadays are sown the vital seeds of nightmare, sleeplessness, fears, neuroticism, hysteria and of cruel dispositions and trains of thought—potential malefaction, banditry and even homicide—savagery toward both our "poor relations," the brutes (which some of us greatly admire and even love), and toward mankind itself. The nervous systems of children are more plastic and impressionable and retentive and basically constructive than most parents and teachers as yet have realized—or so I believe.

GEORGE VAN NESS DEARBORN

U. S. VETERANS' HOSPITAL
NEW YORK, N. Y.
JUNE 10

# QUOTATIONS

## GOVERNOR PINCHOT AND THE UNIVERSITY OF PITTSBURGH

GOVERNOR PINCHOT'S joining with the assailants of the University of Pittsburgh on account of the dismissal of a popular professor of history, Dr. Ralph E. Turner, is loosening the tongues of a number of friends of the institution. This week representatives of twenty-one churches in the Wilkinsburg district, at a community service and with only two of the assemblage dissenting, united in a statement commending the university's policy applying to teachers.

Because Dr. Turner, former chairman of the Pennsylvania Security League, was active in working for social legislation and in combating sweatshops, several labor organizations and civic groups took the position that he was being penalized on account of his political liberalism. It was recalled that four instructors were dismissed some years ago in connection with alleged radical activities. Some of the younger alumni talked of petitioning for the resignation of Chancellor John G. Bowman. Steps were taken for an investigation of the Turner dismissal by the American Association of University Professors.

Although Dr. Turner himself has said little, he has given the impression that he was removed because of dissatisfaction among the "business men trustees" of the institution.

One of the first reactions to this was an intimation from David L. Lawrence, State Democratic Chairman, that in event of the election of a Democratic Legislature state funds for the university, amounting in the last biennium to $1,188,000, might be shut off.

Eventually the university's side of the case was given to the public by Chancellor Bowman in a letter to Representative Henry Ellenbogen. The letter, after referring to the charge that it was the policy of Pitt "to discharge every professor who may have liberal tendencies or who may be active in movements to promote social justice," declared: "It is therefore clear that the University of Pittsburgh should be responsive to public opinion and that its policy should be formulated to promote the common good."

The chancellor indicated that the sole reason for the removal of Dr. Turner was the complaint that the instructor had become flippant and sneering toward religion. It was declared to be one of the basic policies of the university to conduct its teaching in a manner that would not destroy the reverence of Catholics, Jews and Protestants for their respective faiths. The chancellor continued: "It is this policy which, in our judgment, Dr. Turner did not adequately fulfill. His failure is not concerned at all with the New Deal. It is concerned with an attitude toward faith and toward spiritual growth." Part of a letter written by a minister, in which it was charged in particular that Dr. Turner had ridiculed students who had been faithful in attending Sunday school, was included.

Although Dr. Turner denies that he has an attitude of irreverence toward religion, it is stated that the chancellor has "stacks" of letters and complaints from ministers, students and parents on the subject.

Meanwhile Governor Pinchot, who is *ex officio* a trustee of the university, wrote Chancellor Bowman a letter in which it was stated that Dr. Turner's dismissal was "one of a series of similar actions taken by the university under your direction which indicate that its purposes as an institution of higher learning have been perverted to conform to the views of a small group of wealthy and powerful men." There was this reference to the Mellons, who have contributed millions to the upbuilding of the university and are represented on the board of trustees: "If the Mellons want a school to teach their ideas, then let them support it. The Commonwealth can not." The governor's letter concluded with the statement that if the facts are as he understands them he will have no choice but to recommend to the next regular session of the Legislature a thorough investigation of the Turner case and the history of academic freedom at the University of Pittsburgh.

A number of the alumni interrogated declare that the Pinchot "lecture" to the university on academic freedom is wholly gratuitous; that the fact that Dr. Turner was employed for nine years in spite of his political liberalism at least suggests that there was no objection to him on that ground. It is stated that there remain in the faculty many who are as liberal as he. Still there is the question of why the instructor was fired just after having signed a new contract.

Supporters of the chancellor say that inasmuch as the dismissed professor received a year's salary, the contract may have been only a part of the plan to make the discharge as easy as possible.—*The New York Times.*

# SOCIETIES AND MEETINGS

## CONFERENCE ON CURRENT EDUCATIONAL ISSUES IN CALIFORNIA

SUGGESTIONS having national pertinence developed at a conference for educational leaders, held July 16–20, at the University of Southern California when the topic "Current Educational Issues in California" was considered by some two hundred superintendents and principals of the southern counties of the state.

The financial issue is dominant in California, inasmuch as the state surplus of about $40,000,000 which existed when the late Governor Rolph took office has become a deficit of $29,430,000. This situation has followed action by the 1933 Legislature and the electors of the state which "changed the state tax structure by returning the utility corporations to the local tax rolls and substituting a general sales tax." As stated by Chief Deputy Superintendent Willard S. Ford, of the Los Angeles City Schools, speaking at the conference, the same authorities "changed the basis of the support of education by transferring the county support of education to the state."

Superintendent Ford declared that the present method of distributing state aid "fails to eliminate inequalities of educational opportunity and of financial support." He discussed the major financial problems, including the principle of equalization of educational support and the provision of a minimum educational program. As to taxation he compared the amounts provided by the state to the counties and the sums formerly raised by the counties, and told how the elimination of the county school tax has affected the total tax rate for counties.

Dealing with his topic on a nation-wide basis, Professor Fletcher Harper Swift, of the University of California, analyzed "Sources of School Revenue and Taxation." In answer to the question "What is the relative importance of federal, state and local funds?" Professor Swift gave figures for 1930 showing that local funds furnished 72.7 per cent. of total public school receipts; state funds 16.7 per cent.; county funds 10.6 per cent.; federal aid and miscellaneous sources 4.1 per cent.; permanent funds and school lands 1.3 per cent.

Regarding appropriations from state sources for the benefit of public schools, Professor Swift presented statistics revealing that seven states provide no such appropriations at all; that in fourteen states such appropriations are relatively negligible; that in twelve states they are an important but not chief source; that in nine states state appropriations are the "sole source except income from permanent funds"; that in four states they are the "chief but not sole source"; that in three states—New York, Ohio and South Carolina—state appropriations are the sole source. Tables were presented showing types of taxes and the number of states levying them for school purposes.

Professor Swift gave a summary of the plan for a model income tax prepared by the National Tax Association. This plan is based upon "the principle that every person having taxable ability should pay a direct tax (proportioned to his ability) to the government under which he is domiciled." It is maintained that for carrying out this principle the personal income tax is better than any other tax. Some of the recommendations given are as follows:

The tax should be levied upon entire net incomes of persons only; it should not be collected from business concerns, either incorporated or unincorporated.

The personal income tax should be levied on a citizen's entire income from all sources; exemptions now granted in many states on state and local bonds, real estate mortgages, etc., should be discontinued as rapidly as the circumstances permit. . . .

Personal net income should be defined substantially as a good accountant would determine it. The tax systems of Wisconsin, Massachusetts and New York offer satisfactory models for such definition.

Small incomes should be exempted. Exemptions for a single person should not exceed $600; for a husband and wife, $1,200; and further exemption of $200 for each dependent, not to exceed three.

The rate of tax shall be the same for all kinds of income.

Rates should be progressive—minimum, one per cent., maximum should not exceed 6 per cent.

Administration should be in hands of state, not local officials.

The state personal income tax is a source of school support, "all or part earmarked for schools," in twelve states as follows: Arkansas (since 1929), Delaware (1917), Massachusetts (1917), Minnesota (1933), Montana (1933), New Mexico (1933), Oklahoma (1913), South Carolina (1922), South Dakota (1933), Utah (1931), Vermont (1931), Washington (1932), held invalid. In eleven states the proceeds of a personal income tax are credited to the state general fund which is a source of school aid: Alabama (1933), Arizona (1933), Georgia (1929), Mississippi (1914), Missouri (1917), New York (1919), North Carolina (1921), North Dakota (1919), Tennessee (1929) from intangibles, Virginia (1919), Wisconsin (1911). In six states there is a personal income tax, but "none or a negligible part reaches schools": Idaho (1931), Indiana (1933), Kansas (1933), New Hampshire (1924) from intangibles, Ohio (1931) from intangibles, Oregon (1929).

Professor Harry P. Smith, of Syracuse University, addressed the conference on "What the Public Needs to Know about Public Education To-day." People should be made aware that, with the increasing complexity of social life, the school becomes "a specialized institution of modern society for the performance of specific functions." Professor Smith discussed the function of the layman, the function of the professionally trained staff in the school, the complex curriculum of an industrial society and the financial support of the schools, the last including "the significance of increasing state support and the demand for federal aid."

Dr. Vierling Kersey, superintendent of public instruction, State of California, presented "Plans that Will Help the Public Become Informed." Dr. Kersey began by saying that "the public to-day is propaganda conscious, advertising shy, high-pressure resistant," but that nevertheless "the public is ready and anxious to be fact-minded about public education." Among "the most powerful in-school influences in shaping community attitudes," the speaker listed physical education—sports and contests which he estimated "result in about 30 per cent. favorable opinion"; extra-curricular activities such as club events ("about 70 per cent. favorable"); music—glee club, band, orchestra ("about 90 per cent. favorable"); school organizations—school paper, assembly ("about 40 per cent. favorable"); what children report at home concerning actual instructional experiences ("about 80 per cent. favorable where there is any. Very little result, however"); "from what the administrators and instructors radiate through their life in the community—service organizations, community organizations, churches, clubs, lodges. (The sum total of these influences is about 65 per cent. favorable.)"

Declaring that "the press is probably giving the public what the public wants to read about public education," Superintendent Kersey expressed his thought that the chief basis of different educational news must be by changed desire on the part of readers.

A great educational opportunity is offered by the movie, "which is just now being forced to be conscious of its need to be socially conscious."

Superintendent Kersey set forth "ideals that would help our public with its attitudes toward public education." These included "only constructive criticism of the profession by the profession. Critics outside our profession have usually found a predecessor within the profession." . . . "Always be sure that in educational programs first things are first: character, citizenship, culture."

Among practical plans for informing the public about public education, Superintendent Kersey listed a community advisory council; school-parent and school-citizen organizations; teacher contacts and connections; labor, church, lodge, club; parent forums; radio programs; press releases. "Keep everlastingly at it. A public relations program is never completed."

Other subjects and speakers at the conference were "Reorganization of Educational Programs," Dr. Walter R. Hepner, California State Department of Education, and Dr. Emil Lange, Long Beach City Schools, with Deputy Superintendent Arthur Gould, of the Los Angeles City Schools, as chairman of the discussion group; "Progressive Practises in Secondary Education," Professor A. A. Douglass, of the Claremont Colleges, and Dr. W. B. Featherstone, of the Los Angeles City Schools, with Principal R. C. Ingalls of the Garfield High School, Los Angeles, as chairman of the discussion group; "Local Units of School Administration," Superintendent A. R. Clifton, of the Los Angeles County Schools, and Professor O. R. Hull, of the University of Southern California, with Superintendent P. R. Davis, of the Santa Monica City Schools, as chairman of the group discussion.

RAYMOND WALTERS
UNIVERSITY OF CINCINNATI
LOS ANGELES, JULY 20, 1934

# REPORTS

## BEQUESTS OF SCHOLARSHIPS AND LOAN FUNDS

"FROM very early times," says the Supreme Judicial Court of Massachusetts, "the founding of scholarships in universities has been favored by the law, and such scholarships are none the less public charities that they are open to the rich as well as the poor." It then proceeded to uphold the validity of a bequest to Harvard College of a permanent fund, the income of which was directed to be used "to pay the fees of tuition and instruction, the costs of text-books, room rent, and reasonable board of such descendants of (four named persons) as may be students at Harvard College." The court remarked that payment of tuition fees and the cost of text-books, room rent and reasonable board of university students is a strictly educational object, and that a direction requiring that preference be given to relatives of the donor or to any other class of persons he favors, is a lawful exercise of his rights and powers.[1]

The foregoing decision was quoted with approval in a West Virginia case, where a bequest for founding scholarships at Lafayette College at Easton, Pennsylvania, for young men of poor parents residing in Marshall and Ohio Counties, West Virginia, and Belmont County, Ohio, was qualified by a provision in the will giving preference to sons and descendants of certain relatives of the testator. It was held that preference to descendants of the donor does not render a bequest of a scholarship fund non-charitable.[2]

[1] *Dexter* v. *Harvard College*, 176 Mass. 192, 57 N. E. 371 (1900).

However, if a bequest is strictly limited to use by the testator's descendants, and there is no provision for its use for general educational purposes in those years when his descendants fail to use it or when no such descendants may be in existence, it does not create a charitable trust. This is the holding of the Kentucky Court of Appeals in a case wherein a decedent gave to DePauw University in perpetuity all his estate remaining after his wife's death for the purpose of the education of the descendants of two named persons. Said the court: "This devise was in no sense for a general public use, nor was it given with motives free from the stain of everything that is personal, private, or selfish. It is confined solely to the education of the descendants of two individuals only. If it had been given for the general purposes of education, or if it had been given into the hands of trustees for the education of poor children, or the children of the state, county, or a designated community, it would have been valid and upheld as a devise for a charitable use." Despite this holding, the court permitted DePauw University to retain the property, on the ground that a favorable decision of the circuit court in 1891, from which an appeal had been granted but not taken, made the point *res adjudicata* and not subject to subsequent judicial investigation.[3]

Frequently wills bequeathing scholarship funds are contested on the ground that they contain insufficient directions regarding the administration of the fund, thus leaving too great a discretion in the hands of the designated trustees. Wherever the general intent of the donor is plain, the courts are inclined to uphold the trust and, if necessary, to advise the trustees regarding their duties. Thus in Connecticut a will was upheld which made a contingent residuary bequest to trustees directed to apply the interest thereof "to support through a course at the Sheffield Scientific School . . . the candidate passing the best examination preparatory to said course of study. Said candidate must be born or living in Danbury, Connecticut, to be eligible, and examinations shall be held for new competitors as often as the scholarship is vacated." The court held that the word "support" was not intended to be limited to bare necessities of any kind, but to include a comfortable living for the student beneficiary. However, the donor could not be thought to have wished to provide a student with money greatly in excess of his needs; and consequently the trustees were advised that if the income of the fund should in the course of time come to exceed greatly the amount required for the comfortable maintenance of one beneficiary, it would be their duty to apply the excess toward the support of another eligible student, since it was the manifest desire of the donor to have the income used for the support of worthy and eligible young men pursuing studies in the Sheffield Scientific School.[4]

Another example of judicial intervention to interpret and effectuate the donor's intent is afforded by a recent Louisiana case, where the income of the residue of an estate was bequeathed in equal parts to Tulane University and Loyola University, for scholarships of $1,000 to run for four years and then be granted to new beneficiaries and so on indefinitely. The income was sufficient to provide fourteen such scholarships at each university. The will was not explicit as to how the beneficiaries were to be selected, but named two trustees to have custody of the fund and stipulated that on the death of either or both of these trustees, their successors should be appointed by "the gentlemen of the faculties." When the two trustees refused to pay over the income of the fund unless they were given a voice in the awarding of the scholarships, it was held that the will evidenced no intent to give them such a power, but rather displayed faith in the university faculties. Accordingly, the trustees were required to pay over the income, and the selection of the beneficiaries was left to the discretion of the universities.[5]

Thomas E. Mitchell, of Georgia, left a legacy of $125,000 value to Vanderbilt University, the net income thereof to be used "according to the best judgment of the Trustees . . . to assist poor, worthy and deserving students, who may

[2] *Gallaher* v. *Gallaher,* 106 W. Va. 588, 146 S. E. 623 (1929).

[3] *Johnson* v. *DePauw University,* 116 Ky. 671, 76 S. W. 851 (1903).

[4] *Hoyt* v. *Bliss,* 93 Conn. 344, 105 Atl. 699 (1919).

[5] *Succession of Breaux,* 175 La. 269, 143 So. 246 (1932).

be *bona fide* residents of Georgia." A subsequent clause of the same will expressed the testator's desire that the university lend the funds to the selected students, taking interest-bearing notes, "since, in my opinion, such a method of assisting students by loans is better adapted to the formation of character than to make absolute gifts to such students." A legacy of equal amount and on the same terms was also bequeathed to the University of Georgia. Vanderbilt University sought permission to deviate from the express terms of its trust by extending the benefits of the fund to students from other states, showing that tuition and living expenses at the University of Georgia were much lower than at Vanderbilt, so that poor students in Georgia would naturally attend the former; and that after diligent efforts, including the mailing of circulars to its graduates and to high schools located in Georgia, offering to lend the funds at 5 per cent. interest, after three years it had been able to lend only about $2,000 to four students, leaving a balance of accumulated income of more than $24,000. The court held that the terms of the will did not conclusively require the assistance to be given in the form of interest-bearing loans, but merely expressed the donor's preference thereof, leaving to the trustees full discretion as to whether they would offer loans or absolute gifts. Hence there was nothing in the terms of the trust making its literal performance impossible, and the deviation prayed for could not be allowed.[6]

Bequests establishing student loan funds will not be invalidated by reason of the fact that they require the loans to bear interest, nor because they make the loans available to students without discrimination between those who are poor and those who are wealthy. When William D. Morgan bequeathed the residue of his estate to the Eastern Illinois State Teachers College for the establishment of a fund to be loaned at a reasonable rate of interest to indigent students, and administered by a committee consisting of the president, the business manager and the professor of mathematics, his heirs contested the will on the ground that the requirement of interest would take the bequest out of the class of charitable trusts and thus create an invalid perpetuity. The court denied this contention, pointing out that the interest would be applied solely to the charitable purpose of the fund. It also held that no specification of the residence of beneficiaries was required and that any student at the college would be eligible, regardless of residence.[7]

A bequest to a trustee, who was directed to invest the fund for ten years and then turn it over to Northwestern University to form two funds for loans to medical students and law students, respectively, limited to "worthy students about to enter the senior year in the respective courses," to enable them to pay their tuition, was also upheld by the Illinois Supreme Court. The will provided that the loans were to be for four years at 4 per cent. interest and that members of the Masonic Order were to receive preference. It was contested on the ground that worthy students might be wealthy, and that loans to wealthy students would not constitute a charitable purpose. The court destroyed this objection by construing the word "enable" strictly, holding that one could not be "enabled" to do what he was already able to do; but commentators on this case have been quick to point out that a valid charitable trust need not necessarily be exclusively for the benefit of the indigent, especially when it is for an educational purpose.[8]

M. M. CHAMBERS
OHIO STATE UNIVERSITY

[6] *Vanderbilt University* v. *Mitchell,* 162 Tenn. 217, 26 S. W. (2d) 83 (1931).

[7] *Morgan* v. *National Trust Bank of Charleston,* 331 Ill. 182, 162 N. E. 188 (1928).

[8] *Summers et al.* v. *Chicago Title and Trust Company,* 335 Ill. 564, 167 N. E. 777 (1929).

# EDUCATIONAL RESEARCH AND STATISTICS

## CHANGE—THE TEST OF TEACHING

PROBABLY every one will agree that teaching involves change in the mind and action of the one taught. Most of us who teach, however, often know little of the character and amount of this change in the mind of our pupils. Doubtless also many of us will admit that the amount of change produced in our students is a fairly accurate measurer of the effectiveness of our teaching. Likely every one will also admit that there are at least two kinds of change in the individual when he learns a group of related facts. One is found in the memory, which retains what one learns. This is noted by the increase in the already meager or large store of facts which the memory may possess and the "mental" background which is in constant process of reconstruction. The other type of change is in the attitude not only toward what he learns but also toward the larger conception of himself and the world about him. This is often referred to generally as the "universe of discourse," the attitudes toward life, the "mind-set," biases, prejudices and emotional tone. But it is precisely in this area of prejudices and emotional tone, the modification of the attitudes and the alteration of the schemes of values that is most functional in the control of conduct. Moreover, it is in this area that we have the least accurate measuring stick.

And in the matter of producing change in attitudes and the control of conduct lies the chief interest of the state when it taxes itself for the purpose of supporting schools and encouraging the education of the young. The chief purpose of the state in maintaining schools at public expense is found, first of all, in the development of good citizens, intelligent, self-supporting men and women who have higher standards of living and conduct. The state does not care so much about the amount and kind of facts one possesses as it does about the attitudes entertained regarding them.

The teaching profession has developed fairly accurate methods of testing, measuring the amount of facts one acquires in and out of school. Fairly accurately the deposits in memory can be determined and the efficiency one has developed in using the materials learned. The profession has known in the past little about the amount and kind of change in the attitudes of students and in the shifting of the scheme of values.

Recently, however, there have been some advances in constructing and refining certain measuring units in the field of social and emotional attitudes, schemes of values and the like. Among these are the Allport-Vernon test—"A Study of Values." By using this test, the present writer endeavored to determine the amount of change in the schemes of values produced in his classes in social psychology for the two terms in the academic years of 1931–1932 and 1932–1933.

In the fall and winter quarters of 1931–1932 a class of 25 students and in the corresponding quarters of 1932–1933 a class of 31 students, both classes in the fourth year of college in social psychology, are the subjects from whom data for this paper were obtained. The material of the course was gauged to suit the background and ages of these students. The range in ages extended from 19 to 46, and most of the members of the class had had some experience in teaching.

At the first meeting of the class in each year all members were given the Allport-Vernon "Values" test. When the class assembled, no purposes of the work in the course were announced, no comments were made about the course in any form nor were any reasons for giving the above test stated. Neither was there any reference to the test throughout the entire quarter. The material presented to the two classes and the methods of instruction as nearly uniform as possible were as follows: Kimball Young's book—"Social Psychology"—was used as a basic text. His source book on the same subject was also assigned as required reading, together with certain other collateral readings from anthropological literature dealing largely with certain phases of primitive life.

Class periods an hour in length were conducted in the form of lectures, discussions, reports, themes on topics in the field of interest selected by the student, round table discussions, quizzes and personal conferences. The writer prepared the lectures and conducted the discussions in harmony with the general outline of the text but amplified many of the points briefly treated by the author of the text. The writer made no attempt to bend the discussions and to plan the lectures to support nor to conform to any particular standard of esthetics, religion, politics, economic theories or to indoctrinate the class with any particular view of school of thought further than the point of view of the author of the text. It is admitted, however, that any teacher either consciously or unconsciously possesses and propagates some more or less definite attitudes in his discussions. It would be impossible not to have some point of reference. But no conscious effort was made to indoctrinate the class with his personal biases. Trained in the social science field and particularly in anthropology and sociology he naturally possesses the modern view-point in these subjects.

About the middle of the course the Allport A-S Reaction Test was given in order to determine the types of personality which students in the class possessed. But no comments nor explanations as to purposes were made. The term personality here is used in the broad sense represented by Allport in his recent writings on the subject.

At the end of the course the same attitudes test, mentioned above, was given and no comments nor explanations were made further than to state that the results of these tests in no way would influence the passing or failing the course or the grades earned in the class.

In this experimental study the writer wished to answer the following questions: (1) Exactly how much change is produced by the process of instruction and the materials of teaching in the class in the schemes of values which these students hold? (2) What effect does the type of personality, *i.e.,* whether ascendant or submissive, have upon the readiness with which changes are produced and what is the amount of such changes that may be made in the individual student? (3) How much does the factor of age play in changing attitudes? (4) Is there any difference between the sexes and the amount and kind of change made? (5) Is there a tendency to reduce the average quantitative measure of attitudes of the class to the norm of social values as determined by the Allport test?

All the change which is indicated by the results of this experiment certainly may not be wholly ascribed to the work of this class; for these students must have had, during the period of instruction involved here, other influences operating in producing a certain amount of the alteration in attitudes here recorded. But it is certain that the material presented had most to do with producing a change since the plan was calculated to bring up for discussion points in other subjects related to the five fields represented in the social values included in the test and to call attention to these in daily contact in and out of school. In all probability many of these concepts would have been passed over in the ordinary run of the student's classroom life had they not been brought up for consideration.

If the material were treated here in much more detail than our space admits many other facts than those we give here could be brought to light. If we should consider each of the five fields in detail in which social values are considered and if we could treat each item statistically, we could doubtless secure more detailed information about the significance of the changes. But since we are limited we will confine our report to the larger aspects of the problem, as indicated by the questions to be considered.

And since our space for making this report is so limited it is unnecessary to give any description of either the "Values" test or the ascendant-submissive reaction study of Allport and Vernon. We give the report of only six from the list of 56 students' reactions—two, with the least change in attitude, two with average change and two with the greatest amount of change in their values and attitudes.

Data yielded by this experiment, of which that in Table I is only a sample, warrant the following answers to the questions asked on this page.

(1) The average change produced in the individual student in each of the six categories considered, barring one or two extreme cases, ranges around 20 per cent. and the extremes from 15 per cent. to 50 per cent.

(2) There is no particular type of personality which resists change in attitude. The ascendant type changes as frequently and as much as the submissive. There is no correlation between the type of personality and the amount of change in attitude that may be produced.

(3) Age has little to do with the readiness with which change may be made. The older members of the class show as much change in their schemes of values as do the younger students. Apparently the matter of age and experience which these students brought to the class affected little their susceptibility to the influence of the teacher, though the prestige of

TABLE I

CATEGORIES IN THE TEST

| Student | Theoretical | | Economic | | Esthetic | | Social | | Political | | Religious | | Total |
|---|---|---|---|---|---|---|---|---|---|---|---|---|---|
| | B. | A. | B. | A. | B. | A. | B. | A. | B. | A. | B. | A. | |
| M.D. f21 s | 39 | 28 | 20 | 26 | 43 | 30 | 32 | 26 | 25 | 30 | 21 | 40 | 58 |
| R.S. m23 a | 20 | 31 | 33 | 30 | 36 | 17 | 23 | 38 | 30 | 31 | 38 | 33 | 54 |
| L.M. m26 a | 50 | 43 | 25 | 29 | 23 | 21 | 34 | 36 | 25 | 34 | 23 | 17 | 30 |
| J.M. m46 a | 38 | 34 | 45 | 37 | 28 | 25 | 30 | 35 | 25 | 30 | 14 | 19 | 30 |
| L.N. f42 a | 28 | 26 | 25 | 24 | 28 | 31 | 41 | 41 | 23 | 23 | 35 | 35 | 6 |
| V.M. f23 s | 39 | 37 | 29 | 26 | 31 | 32 | 37 | 37 | 22 | 24 | 22 | 24 | 10 |
| Total change for 2 classes | | 223 | | 218 | | 255 | | 234 | | 211 | | 260 | 1401 |
| Aver. change per student per category | | 4. | | 3.9 | | 4.6 | | 4.2 | | 3.8 | | 4.6 | |

In the above table the words at top of columns are the categories in the test. The column on the left contains the information regarding each student. The capital initials represent the individual student. The small letters and number under the initial mean "f" for female, "m" for male, "s" for submissive personality in the A–S reaction test and "a" for Ascendant on the test. For example, M.D. student is a woman 21 years of age and submissive.

The columns under the categories Capital B. means the score earned on the "Values" test before studying the subject and A. represents the score after the end of the course. The amount of change in attitude is the difference between the score under B. and A. The horizontal column at bottom of the table contains under each category the total amount of change in the two classes combined and the last horizontal column gives the average change per student per category for the combined number of students in both classes. The vertical column to the right indicates the total change in the six students in the table and 1,401 is the total amount of change for the two classes. The six students given in the table are typical of the two classes.

the teacher is no doubt a large factor in effecting these changes. That is, one teacher may be able, with the same material and students, to produce, on account of his ability and prestige, greater change than another teacher. Likely the chief factor which did operate in this experiment or other similar investigations is the degree of intelligence.

(4) Neither is there any correlation between the sexes and the amount and kind of change which may be brought about.

(5) There is no evidence that teaching students in the manner in which this class was taught would tend to reduce or elevate the general level of social values of the students to the average or norm established by the makers of this test.

Finally, the material used in instruction, the methods employed and the personality and prestige of the teacher are likely to be the most important factors in producing change in attitudes and controlling conduct.

A. O. BOWDEN

NEW MEXICO STATE TEACHERS COLLEGE

## NEW BOOKS IN EDUCATION

DAWSON, HOWARD A. *Satisfactory Local School Units.* Pp. x + 181. George Peabody College for Teachers, Nashville.

DE ROSA, MARY. *Artful Bachelors.* Pp. 199. Arthur H. Stockwell, London. 6s.

FELDMAN, W. T. *The Philosophy of John Dewey.* Pp. vii + 126. Johns Hopkins Press. $1.75.

GAVIAN, RUTH W. and others. *Our Changing Social Order.* Pp. xv + 577. Illustrated. Heath. $1.80.

KEFAUVER, GRAYSON N. and others. *The Horizontal Organization of Secondary Education.* Pp. viii + 273. U. S. Government Printing Office. $0.20.

# SCHOOL AND SOCIETY

WITH WHICH ARE COMBINED THE EDUCATIONAL REVIEW, ESTABLISHED IN 1891, THE TEACHERS MAGAZINE, ESTABLISHED IN 1878, AND THE SCHOOL JOURNAL, ESTABLISHED IN 1874.

Volume 40 SATURDAY, AUGUST 4, 1934 Number 1023

## SOME QUALITIES OF A GOOD COLLEGE TRUSTEE

By Dr. CHARLES F. THWING

PRESIDENT EMERITUS OF WESTERN RESERVE UNIVERSITY

WHAT is the type of man or woman who is worthy to be a member of a chief board for conducting a college or university? The answer is manifold. In particular, there are several constructive elements which should belong to the members of a board of college trustees.

The first of these elements I shall call intellectual comprehensiveness. Intellectual comprehensiveness—an awkward term indeed—stands not only for intellectual breadth but also for intellectual height and depth. It embodies the cubical relations of the mind. In his "Annual Reports," President Eliot characterizes certain of his associates who embody this signal quality. For instance, of Martin Brimmer, he says:

> . . . he was distinguished for patience, courtesy, sound judgment, and gentle decision. He made the finest use of wealth and leisure, devoting both to the promotion of art, charities, good government, and education. Public-spirited, magnanimous, upright, and serene, he was a true type of the republican gentleman.[1]

Of Senator George Frisbie Hoar, who died in 1904, Eliot writes:

> He was three times chosen an Overseer by the alumni, and was always glad to give his counsel to the University, so far as the engrossing duties of his public functions permitted; but the chief way in which he served the University was by illustrating on the most conspicuous stage the republican ideal of a public life inspired by worthy sentiments and affections, simple, disinterested, and earnest, and guided by well-read lessons from history and biography, and a deep-rooted religious faith. All his life he stood for the old-fashioned New England virtues of the modest home, the county court-house, the town meeting, and the village church.[2]

The quotations might be continued concerning members of other distinguished families and concerning individuals. Of Harvard College alone a sufficient number of citations have been made to illustrate the truth that men of comprehensiveness of judgment represent the type giving the best service as trustee or other officer of a university.

A second characteristic of a worthy member of the governing board is what I shall call interpretative mindedness. Members—trustees or regents—should seek to understand the judgment, and the grounds for judgment, of their fellow members. They should be gifted with the spirit of intellectual altruism. They should seek out the principles embodied in a mass and maze of complex and antagonistic details. They should be able to transfer the lessons of the past into the present, and they should be able to forecast the future. Their spirit should be kindly, not only because of its human and humane values, but also because such a spirit adds to the facility of interpretation and gives assurance of the truth-

[1] "Annual Reports," Harvard College, 1895–96, p. 5.

[2] *Ibid.*, 1903–04, pp. 5–6.

fulness of interpretations. Hardness of heart dulls the intellectual acuteness and slows up intellectual facility.

United with this quality should also be found the element of conciliatoriness. Every board consists of individuals, and individuals represent individualisms. But every board is to be guided by certain general principles, to move along certain recognized methods and to be inspired by certain definite motives. The trustee is to find out at what points seemingly opposing principles may unite, at what points differing methods may coincide, and to seek to unite all diverse forces into efficiency. The wise despot of a board of trustees, if he ever do exist, is wise enough not to be a despot. Democratic is the wisest, and, comprehensively, the best board. The board that is most democratic in method is most likely to be aristocratic in its constitution, and sound in its conclusions. Such a mood of conciliation is vastly promoted by what Bagehot, in speaking of the first prerequisite of an elective government, calls "mutual confidence."[3] The members of a board of trustees, whether they be seven or seventy, must have confidence in each other. This confidence is to be intellectual, in respect for each other's judgment, and, moreover, is to have regard for each other's preferences, purposes, and even prejudices. Such mutual esteem is simply a mark of gentlemen who are engaged in doing a great public duty, in carrying forward a great public trust under similar conditions and by similar methods. Yet differences are sure to arise. They awaken discussions. But discussions will seldom become dissensions or divisions in case members have confidence in each other. Whenever members are in peril of division, the board, like those who are concerned with an elective government, are to seek to possess a calm mind. In calmness, the best minds are judicial and judicious, and in such a mood such minds can surely find a way out of entangling and opposing premises unto sound conclusions.

As President Gilman, writing of trustees, says:

> They must not only be men of honor, wise and unselfish, but they must be able to get on with one another. The board must include so many persons that a diversity of views may be represented; it must be so limited that the personal attention of every member is secured. Probably the world recognizes chiefly the largeness of Johns Hopkins' bounty, its largeness in amount, in scope, and in freedom from minor restrictions; but he might have failed in the choice of men to administer his trust. On the contrary, he made a capital selection, from among laymen, resident in Baltimore, in middle life, independent, and acquainted with affairs.[4]

In a word, trustees in their relation to each other should incarnate the virtue and the grace of conciliatoriness.

A further quality of the best trustee I shall call emotional steadiness. Emotional steadiness stands for calmness and poise of the heart under sudden or repeated blows. It means stability. It represents a constant and firm control of the feelings. Even small bodies of trustees are in danger of being stampeded unto unwise conclusions. New facts, too, important, structural or even trivial, may result in the substitution of unsound for sound judgment. Emotional steadiness may save a board not only from doing wrong things, but also from doing right things in a wrong way. An instance celebrated in academic annals is the dismissal of President Tappan of the University of Michigan in the year 1863. Even if Tappan, as was charged, was arbitrary in his administration, even if his personal relations to the students[5] were

[3] Bagehot. "Works," Vol. IV, p. 258.

[4] D. C. Gilman, "The Launching of a University," p. 29.

[5] Samuel F. Cook, "Reminiscences of an Old-Timer," pp. 6, 15: "From all sides I heard the charge, in tones which indicated that it was regarded as a serious matter, that the students of the

not of a cordial character, the arbitrariness of the dismissal was inexcusable, and proved to be indeed lamentable.

It may be added that a successor of Tappan, Angell, said to me forty years after Tappan's dismissal that Tappan was the ablest of all the presidents of the University of Michigan. Immediately after his dismissal Tappan went abroad and never came back. It should also be said that near the close of his life, the regents formally asked Tappan to return, but he did not accept the invitation.

A dismissal based largely upon partisan political grounds, grounds which had special significance in the midst of an excited national campaign, that of President Andrews from Brown University, is also most significant.

Emotional calmness and poise would have avoided these most regrettable disasters at the University of Michigan and at Brown University.

Moreover, the element of progressiveness has special value in the constitution of a college trustee. For academic boards are prone to conservatism. They are more inclined rather to accept the accumulations of the past laboriously gathered than to run the risk of a partial or complete loss of a yet richer good. They are loath to try for the better under the peril of losing all the good. They are also loath to struggle for the best under the peril of losing the better. Age and experience create such a mood, and such a mood commands respect. But it is ever to be remembered that the future of a college is longer than its past. The worth of the service in the centuries yet to be is richer than its worth already won in the centuries completed.

To secure members of this progressive type, it is well to elect men when they are young. The typical trustee board is too old. Seldom should an old man be chosen. If a board is subject to constant renewal by an automatic process after a service of three or five years, men of any age may fittingly be elected; but if the place is regarded as permanent, only those who have not passed beyond mature middle life are to be selected.

Yet another fundamental quality of a trustee should be what I shall call institutional mindedness. The trustee is to bear in mind that he is both a legislator and a judge. To him, therefore, are committed the two primary and related elements, the theoretical government and the fundamental administration of a university. These two elements precede in logical order the executive. He is, therefore, to have vision without visionariness, firmness in conclusion without stubbornness, conservatism in the use of funds without niggardliness, carefulness without fussiness, generosity without profuseness, a sense of duty for the passing year without neglect of the rights of the next decade and of the following centuries. He is ever to weigh the superficial, which may be splendid and vocal, in comparison with the profound, which is often silent and sober. He is to know and to feel that the depths are silent

---

University had free access to the home of the Chancellor, and that the seniors, especially, were expected to be frequent callers; and that no one left the house without being invited to help himself to some of the ample supply and variety of liquors ready to hand on the spacious sideboard, while the Doctor indicated the choicest vintages, descanted on their age and excellence, and joined with his guests in sampling them.'' . . .

''Why anyone connected with the University should have taken the pains to drape Dr. Tappan, either the man or the University Chancellor, with a coat of whitewash, to obscure the real man by means of an historical blotch, will long remain an enigma.

''For as the years glide by, the fact will be more and more apparent that Doctor Tappan *kicked himself out of bed with both feet;* by his persistent abuse of the Legislature for having and fostering an Agricultural College, so as to cut himself off from any chance of approach in behalf of the University, and his contemptuous defiance of the liquor prohibition sentiment of the State.''

and the shallows may be noisy. To each is he to give just heed. Institutional mindedness is as remote from personal mindedness as the sunshine of noon is unlike the flickering of the candle at twilight.

In this element of institutional mindedness it is to be pointed out that the trustee is to recognize that he is not to be immediately and directly concerned with the education which the college offers, and especially with the instruction as a chief method and means of education. He is not a so-called educator. Any attempt on his part to dictate the content or the form or the emphases in instruction is liable to result in disaster. The instruction which a faculty offers is to be fundamentally and permanently remote from the legislative and formal administration of a board of trustees. The disregard of this separation is a not uncommon tendency and weakness of a board.

If there be a type of trustee, as in some institutions there is, who may be called a "dummy," there is also at the other extreme the executive trustee who seeks to do duties which do not belong to him. Such matters of administration as the details of the course of study, the number of hours which an individual professor should teach, the discipline of students, represent administrative duties which do not concern his office. He is to deal with tendencies and movements in a course of study, with the amount of work which the whole professorate should do and with the general good order of the college; but he is not to deal with specific and individual details of any one of these principles or methods. Such details belong primarily to the executive, who, if he be at all fitted for his place, has both the right and the obligation to perform.

Among the more important of what may be called the exterior duties of a trustee is the proper investment of endowment funds. These funds are held in trust. The qualities which go to constitute a good trustee of a private estate are the qualities demanded in an academic trustee. These qualities are sound judgment respecting funds, real or personal, prudence, caution, vigilance, a sense of proportion and always, of course, integrity. All interests personal to himself are to be absolutely prohibited. The record of the investment of the funds of the American college, for almost three hundred years, is a record of wisdom, honesty and of productiveness. Whatever losses have occurred, and they have been few and small, have arisen, as in the case of most bank failures, in the desire, first, either to get a high rate of interest, or, second, to promote some private or personal undertaking. But the college has been remarkably free from such adventures and adventurers. The ideal college of the future will be even still more free from such evil influences.

The most marked instance of a lack of sound judgment in the investment of funds is found in the early history of the Johns Hopkins University. In the legacy which Mr. Hopkins made to the university were included fifteen thousand shares of the stock of the Baltimore and Ohio Railroad. Mr. Hopkins' confidence in the prosperity of that railroad was absolute. He enjoined the trustees, moreover, to watch over and to protect the interests of that road. At the time of his making his legacy, the annual dividends were ten per cent. The chairman of the finance committee of the road was made president of the board of trustees of the university. Mr. John W. Garrett, the president of the road itself, acted as chairman of the finance committee of the university board. This double combination was most unfortunate. The subsequent failure of the railroad to pay dividends threatened the bankruptcy of the university.[6]

[6] D. C. Gilman, "The Launching of a University," pp. 29–30.

The confidence, however, which the community has in the integrity—both intellectual and moral—of a board of trustees has usually been well merited. Such confidence is a most precious asset. Without it, no college can worthily exist. With it, there is no worthy academic opportunity which is denied unto it. The ideal college is the splendid outcome of a long, heroic struggle. The trustees of such a college represent the best elements of the community.

# EDUCATIONAL EVENTS

## EDUCATIONAL SOUND FILMS IN GREAT BRITAIN

UNDER the auspices of the British Film Institute, 4, Great Russell Street, London, W.C.1, a private demonstration of educational sound films was presented at the Academy Cinema, London, on June 21, before teachers and educationists. *Nature* discussed the demonstration as follows:

As Mr. H. Ramsbotham, M.P., parliamentary secretary to the Board of Education, pointed out in his introductory address, such films must not be accepted without reservation, for they should always be looked upon as being supplementary to the teacher himself. The production of the films shown was a piece of pioneer work and experimental in character, and the venture augurs well for the future of the cinematograph in education, especially if the producers receive the constructive criticism from teachers for which they ask. There is little doubt that, provided it is not abused, the sound film will prove an important asset to the teacher of the future. The seven films presented on this occasion clearly showed not only the expert film producers we have at our command, but also where the film will be a useful aid and where it will prove an unwelcome intruder.

The films of the life-history of the thistle, the growth and irritability of roots, and the physiology of breathing were examples of good educational films—useful tools in the hands of a responsible teacher. They showed the value of the cinematograph film in photomicrography and in demonstrating those types of motion too slow to be watched normally. The film of wheatlands in East Anglia, too, was a good lesson in economic geography and rural science, and demonstrated the possibilities of the film in transporting a class to the actual scene of action, which otherwise has to be done, rather inefficiently, by laborious verbal teaching and much reading. Such films indicate the lines along which it is to be hoped the cinematograph in education will develop. On the other hand, certain films shown depicted the dangers inherent in the cinematograph as a teaching factor. That on kitchencraft, for example, merely illustrated the processes involved in making a pork pie. Most domestic science teachers would prefer their pupils to learn such a lesson by doing it themselves. But this is only the experimental stage, and though there is much to learn, a great deal of good work has already been done. To add to their value, the films are produced under authoritative direction. The films shown were made by Gaumont-British Instructional, who are to be congratulated on the excellent production, beautiful photography and useful running commentary. The whole performance will be presented later in provincial towns.

## PWA FUNDS FOR NEW YORK CITY SCHOOLS

ASSURANCES that New York city's application for a PWA loan of $13,127,670 to build ten new elementary schools and four new high schools will be approved "as rapidly as is consistent with sound practice," have been received by President George J. Ryan, of the Board of Education of New York City, from Mr. Harold L. Ickes. The elementary schools will cost $5,026,120, and the high schools $8,101,550.

Mr. Ickes's assurances were given in response to a request of President Ryan and Colonel Walter Jeffreys Carlin, acting chairman of the school board's committee on buildings and sites, for speedy approval of the application, which consists of only part of the aggregate total of $45,000,000 sought in federal loans for new school construction in the city.

The fourteen schools awaiting final approval, together with their approximate costs are:

HIGH SCHOOLS

Franklin K. Lane, Jamaica Avenue and Eldert Lane, Queens, $3,486,000.

Andrew Jackson, 115th Avenue and 204th Street, South Bellaire, Queens, $2,527,800.

Tottenville, Summit Avenue, Tottenville, Staten Island, $976,900.

Oakwood, Maplewood Avenue and Amber Street, Oakwood, Staten Island, $1,110,850.

ELEMENTARY SCHOOLS

*Manhattan*

P. S. 43, 129th Street and Amsterdam Avenue, $1,101,000.

*The Bronx*

P. S. 80, addition, East Van Cortland Avenue and Mosholu Parkway, $246,000.

P. S. 107, Seward and Croes Avenues, $713,000.

*Brooklyn*

P. S. 201, addition, Twelfth Avenue and Eighty-first Street, $257,000.

P. S. 225, addition, Humboldt and Ripple Streets, $335,500.

P. S. 247, Twenty-first Avenue and Seventieth Street, $510,000.

*Queens*

P. S. 2, Twenty-first Avenue and Seventy-sixth Street, North Woodside, $301,700.

P. S. 48, 108th Avenue and 155th Street, Jamaica, $384,100.

P. S. 146, Queens, 159th Avenue and Ninety-eighth Street, Howard Beach, $548,000.

P. S. 149, Queens, Ninety-third Street and Hayes Avenue, Jackson Heights, $629,820.

A $2,000,000 federal loan already granted is now being used to buy furniture for about fifteen new schools, which were completed months ago, but which have been delayed in opening because of lack of funds to provide equipment. The schools will open in the fall.

## IMPROVED EDUCATIONAL FACILITIES IN LOUISIANA

ACTING on the recommendations of the Louisiana Tax Reform Commission and State Superintendent of Public Instruction, T. H. Harris, the current session of the Louisiana Legislature has passed constitutional amendments which point to improved educational facilities for the state.

The amendments provide:

1. That a minimum educational program for the state with average annual salaries of $1,000 for white teachers and proportionate allowances for other items included in the set-up be inaugurated.

2. That the support of the schools be adjusted in such a manner that the state will supply approximately two thirds of this minimum cost and the parishes (counties) will supply the other one third. In the past the order has been reversed. The state has supplied about one third of the cost and the parishes have supplied the other two thirds.

3. That a parish wishing to maintain a higher standard of schools than is included in the minimum program may do so by voting special taxes not to exceed five mills on the assessed value of property in the parish.

4. That the State School Fund be divided into two parts and distributed as follows: Three fourths of the money will be apportioned to the parishes on the basis of the number of educables in the several parishes. The other one fourth will be used by the State Board of Education as an Equalization Fund to aid the poorer parishes in maintaining the minimum program without the necessity of voting any of the special taxes permitted in parishes that wish to maintain a program better than the required minimum.

In order to make this program effective, it is necessary that the State School Fund be increased to $10,000,000. The Legislature has provided new sources of revenue to care for the increase in the State School Fund, exemption from taxation of homesteads up to $2,000 in value, and state assumption of parish road bonds. The first receipts from the new taxes will be divided between the school fund and the homestead exemption fund as follows: The State School Fund will receive thirty-five per cent. of money, and the homestead exemption fund will receive sixty-five per cent. When the State School Fund reaches $10,000,000 the schools will cease to share the new money.

The new plan of distribution depends on the action of the people at the polls in the November election when the constitutional amendments will be placed before the voters for approval. Regardless of whether or not the constitutional amendments pass, the schools will gain materially in the amount of money available for their support.

## RESOLUTIONS OF THE NORTH CAROLINA CONFERENCE FOR SOCIAL SERVICE

THE following resolutions were passed at the recent meeting of the Committee on Education of the North Carolina Conference for Social Service:

1. We heartily endorse the eight months' school term established by the last legislature as being the basis for future development of an adequate school opportunity for all children of the state.

2. We request the General Assembly to continue the maintenance of the state-supported eight-months' term out of revenue derived from sources other than *ad valorem* taxes.

3. We request the General Assembly to liberalize the laws to enable local units to provide necessary supplements to the state-provided minimum; such supplements to be limited in such ways that the state-supported school system will not be endangered.

4. We request and strongly urge our General Assembly to so increase the appropriations for schools that every school employee will have at least a living wage.

5. We recommend a character development program, all pervasive, but as definite and purposeful as possible, throughout the entire curricular and extra-curricular activities of the school.

6. We recommend provision for an adequate survey of the vocational education needs of the state with definite steps to be taken in meeting the situation as found in the rural and urban communities.

7. We recommend a survey of the library needs of the state and the provision of adequate funds for library leadership and materials.

8. We commend the leadership of the State Superintendent of Public Instruction, A. T. Allen, for calling upon the citizenship of the state to take a part in the reconsideration and reconstruction of the curriculum.

9. We believe North Carolina has been able to provide better schools at less cost than the average in other states because we have maintained the county as the unit of school administration; we, therefore, strongly urge our General Assembly to continue this policy of the county as the unit of school administration, with professionally trained and adequately paid people in the office of county superintendent, so long as the counties continue to administer any other function of local government.

## THE TEN-YEAR PLAN OF THE UNIVERSITY OF ROCHESTER

THE report of the committee on the ten-year plan for the future development of the college at the University of Rochester has been submitted by the dean to the faculty for consideration. The movement was originally initiated by President Rhees in 1932. A summary of the conclusions of the committee follows:

(1) The maintenance of a teaching personnel which, within our general scheme of development, is the best that can be obtained. In securing additions to our teaching force, we feel that the trustees should not be limited by the salaries being paid at present in the department to which the addition is to be made. On the other hand, it should be borne in mind that the present faculty has not been assembled by chance. Those members of it, whose work is regarded as distinctive, should receive salaries commensurate with their worth to the institution.

(2) Equivalence of educational opportunity in the College for Men and the College for Women, applying, with due regard to the different interests of men and women, to teaching personnel and breadth of offering. Provision should be made for some professors and other members of the faculty to spend full time in each college. At present it may be desirable that some members of the faculty spend alternate years on each of the campuses. Equivalent opportunities for men and women will probably mean that in the College for Women there should be additional activities especially adapted to the needs of its students. Such an activity already exists, for example, in the course in nursing.

(3) Provision for adequate scholarships and other student aid for undergraduates and for satisfactory library and teaching equipment for undergraduate instruction.

(4) Provision for the needs of graduate work in respect to

- (a) Necessary additions to the teaching personnel.
- (b) Scholarships and fellowships.
- (c) Library and teaching equipment.

(5) Provision for suitable arrangement for leave of absence.

(6) Provision for suitable arrangement for attendance at meetings of learned societies.

(7) Provision for visiting professors.

## THE NORTH CAROLINA INSTITUTE OF EDUCATION

"EDUCATION in the Program of Reconstruction" was the general subject of the program of the five-day Institute of Education, sponsored jointly by the State Department of Public Instruction, North Carolina Education Association and North Carolina Congress of Parents and Teachers held from June 25 to 29.

The sessions were divided among three centers, Raleigh, Chapel Hill and Greensboro. The program was divided accordingly into three different topics, industrial, vocational and adult education, secondary and higher education, and elementary education, respectively.

A number of national and state officials took part in the program, including Governor Ehringhaus, J. C. Wright, assistant U. S. commissioner of vocational education; A. T. Allen, state superintendent, and Dr. Sidney B. Hall, Virginia superintendent of public instruction.

Authorities in different fields of education came from colleges in many sections of the North, South and Mid-West. They included Professors Edward H. Reisner, John K. Norton, John J. Coss, Jesse H. Newlon and Lois Mossman, from Columbia; Professor Edwin H. Reeder, of Vermont; Dean Malcolm MacLean, from Minnesota; Professor George B. Zehmer, from Virginia; Deans W. K. Green, of Duke, and T. E. Browne, of State, and President Graham, Dean Bradshaw and Professors M. R. Trabue, N. W. Walker and R. M. Grumman, of the university.

Other speakers included William T. Pork, president of the Citizens' Library Movement; Jonathan Daniels, editor of the Raleigh *News and Observer,* and School Superintendents Guy B. Phillips, of Greensboro, and T. Wingate Andrews, of High Point.

## HONORARY DEGREES AT THE UNIVERSITY OF WISCONSIN

AMONG the degrees conferred at the recent commencement of the University of Wisconsin by President Glenn Frank were the degree of doctor of laws on Dr. Karl Taylor Compton, president of the Massachusetts Institute of Technology, and on Dr. Albert Russell Mann, provost of Cornell University.

The citations follow:

KARL TAYLOR COMPTON

You have brought to the field of physical investigation a productive eminence, marked by breadth of knowledge, ingenuity in experimentation, and lucidity of exposition; your research in pure science reflects a rare union of precision and originality of mind, and your research in applied science reveals the imaginative power of inventive genius; your brave innocence of belief that a man can concurrently serve at the altar of productive scholarship and carry the distracting obligations of the administrator has, in your case, been justified; you have declined to pursue your researches on the side-lines of the social turmoil or sound-proof your laboratory from the cries of the street, but have manifested a living sense of the social implications of all science, erasing in your own person the frontier between the physical sciences and the social sciences in unique awareness that physics is quite as social as sociology; despite the draft that public service is making upon your energies, you compel us to speak of your research in the present tense; at the behest of the President of the United States, your disciplined judgment has been brought to bear, freely and fruitfully, upon the crucial problem of the relation of science to government.

ALBERT RUSSELL MANN

You have brought an adequate science and an active social sense to the enrichment of the content and methods of agricultural education alike in the United States and in Europe; you have contributed and are contributing a stimulating leadership to the development of soundly progressive policy in the Association of Land Grant Colleges and Universities; your captaincy of the New York State College of Agriculture gave breadth and depth and reach to its service in the life of that commonwealth; you have displayed extraordinary genius in driving fundamental research and practical application abreast without soiling the purity of research or slowing down the process of practical utilization; as Provost of Cornell University, you are sharing in the guidance of a great university through the mazes of social and economic change.

# EDUCATIONAL NOTES AND NEWS

EIGHT universities have bestowed honorary degrees on Dr. Conant since he took office as president of Harvard University. The first was given last December and the remaining during the recent commencement season. The awards are as follows: LL.D., University of Chicago, December 19, 1933; Sc.D., Columbia, June 5, 1934; Sc.D., Stevens Institute of Technology, June 9; H.D., Boston University, June 11; LL.D., New York University, June 13; Sc.D., Tufts, June 18; LL.D., Princeton, June 19; LL.D., Yale, June 20.

IN presenting Dr. George Frederick Zook for the degree of doctor of laws at the University of Michigan, Professor John G. Winter, head of the department of Latin, made the following citation to President Ruthven: "George Frederick Zook, United States Commissioner of Education, recently appointed director of the American Council on Education. Widely known by his colleagues for his effective participation in the work of various educational organizations, especially the North Central Association of Schools and Colleges, unwearied in his efforts to develop better standards of the appraisal of colleges, he seeks to clarify the aims and methods of instruction and to express their relation to state and society. In his administration of an important division of the federal government he has demonstrated his capacity to plan and to achieve."

At the Greater University of North Carolina the appointments have been announced of Dr. W. C. Jackson as dean of the Woman's College, Greensboro; of Colonel W. J. Harrelson, as dean at North Carolina State College, Raleigh; and of R. B. House, as dean of the university at Chapel Hill.

Dr. A. O. Bowden, president of the New Mexico State Teachers College, has been appointed director of the California Branch of the School of American Research of the Archeological Institute of America, which has its headquarters at the University of Southern California. Dr. Edgar L. Hewett, president of the institute, will continue to direct the field work.

Dr. Eugene Bewkes, head of the department of philosophy and formerly dean of students at Colgate University, has been made director of the School of Philosophy and Religion, and Dr. Rodney L. Mott, formerly dean of students in the department of social science at the University of Chicago, has been appointed director of the School of Social Sciences.

Recent promotions at the University of Michigan include Leonard L. Watkins, from associate professor to professor of economics; Stanley Patterson, from assistant professor to associate professor in economics, and Lowell J. Carr, from assistant professor to associate professor in sociology.

Dr. Arthur W. Melton and Leonard W. Doob have been appointed instructors in psychology at Yale University, and Dr. Frances L. Ilg has been appointed instructor in the Clinic of Child Development.

W. R. Niblett has been appointed lecturer in education at Armstrong College, Durham.

At the Ohio State University, Professor Joseph S. Myers, director of the School of Journalism, Professor Wallace S. Elden, of the department of classical languages, and Professor George R. Twiss, of the department of education, have been appointed professors emeritus.

Dr. William M. Leiserson, professor of economics at Antioch College, has been appointed by President Roosevelt to membership in the National Railway Mediation Board.

Dr. Edwin E. Witte, lecturer on industrial relations at the University of Wisconsin and director of the Wisconsin Legislative Reference Library, has been appointed chairman of a technical sub-committee of the Committee on Economic Security, to study unemployment, old-age insurance and a social program.

Professor Otto Schmitz, known in Germany as the intellectual leader of the Christian Students' movement, has been expelled from his professorship in the University of Münster by order of the Reich Ministry of the Interior. The Ministry gave no explanation, but it is said that Professor Schmitz aroused the displeasure of the authorities by opposing the destruction of the Christian Students' organization for the benefit of the Storm Troops and other strictly Nazi bodies.

Professor Neil C. Arvin, head of the department of French at the University of Rochester, has been decorated by the French Government and has been designated an officer of the academy.

Dr. Orlo H. Maughan, extension assistant in farm management at Cornell University, has taken up his work in Washington as a statistical assistant for the Farm Credit Administration.

Dr. Allen E. Sedgwick, professor of geology at the University of Southern California, has been elected president of the Board of Education of the Los Angeles city schools.

G. C. Mann has been appointed chief of the Division of Adult and Continuation Education for the State of California. He succeeds L. B. Travers, who recently resigned.

Dr. Charles C. Wilson, of Evansville, Ind., has been elected by the Board of Education director of health and physical education in the Hartford, Conn., public schools.

AT the Ithaca meeting of the Society for the Promotion of Engineering Education, Professor C. C. Williams, of the State University of Iowa, was elected its president for the coming year. Professor Williams succeeds Professor W. E. Wickenden, president of the Case School of Applied Science. Other officers elected were Professor H. P. Hammond, of the Brooklyn Polytechnic Institute, and Dean G. C. Shaad, of the University of Kansas, as vice presidents. Professor F. L. Bishop, of the University of Pittsburgh, was reelected secretary, a position he has held for the last twenty years, and W. O. Wiley, of John Wiley and Sons, New York, was elected treasurer.

A SUPPLEMENT to the June issue of *La Pediatria* is dedicated to Professor Rocco Jemma, who occupies the chair of children's diseases at Naples, on the occasion of the culmination of his thirty years' professorial activity. It contains a biographical note, a bibliography of his 137 contributions to literature, congratulations from pediatrists of all countries, abstracts from his "Festschrift," and an account of a ceremony held in his honor.

DR. ARVID WALLGREN, professor of pediatrics and chief of the Children's Hospital at Gothenburg, Sweden, delivered the Theodore B. Sachs resident lectures in tuberculosis of the University of Illinois College of Medicine, on June 6 and 7. These lectures have been established at the college for a five-year period by the Chicago Tuberculosis Institute.

HENRY ROSEMAN LANG, from 1896 to 1922 professor of Romance Languages and literature at Yale University and since 1922 professor emeritus, died on July 25 in his eightieth year.

EMILY F. WHEELER, formerly dean of women at Northwestern University, died on July 27, at the age of eighty-four years.

MISS ELIZABETH A. GREENER, for the last twenty years principal of the school of nursing and superintendent of nurses at Mount Sinai Hospital, died on July 27 at the age of fifty-nine years. For the last two years she was president of the New York State League of Nursing Education and she had been president of the New York State Nurses Association and the Michigan State Nurses Association.

PROFESSOR JAN WADIJ, director of the Ukrainian College, was killed by an assassin at Lwow, Poland, on July 25. Professor Wadij, who taught the Ukrainian language, was the author of a recent manifesto signed by leading Ukrainians condemning the terrorist activities of the Ukrainian Nationalist organization.

TWENTY-SEVEN guidance demonstrations were arranged as part of a conference on individual development and guidance held at Teachers College, Columbia University, from July 31 to August 2. The demonstrations included individual Stanford-Binet intelligence examinations with gifted children, auditory aids in speech improvement, measuring musical talents as a contribution to guidance and the audiometer in a group test of hearing.

TEACHERS of vocational agriculture from two hundred Ohio communities assembled on July 23 for the annual midsummer conference at the Ohio State University to discuss their work in relation to the economic and social adjustments affecting agriculture. The first three days were devoted to a conference in which phases of the New Deal program for agriculture were discussed. The remainder of the week was spent in informal conferences. The program was arranged by Dr. J. I. Falconer, of the department of rural economics, and Dr. L. E. Jackson, of the department of agricultural education, in cooperation with Dr. Ray Fife, of the state department of education. Dr. Fife supervises the work of teachers of vocational agriculture. In addition to speakers from the state department and from the university, several others addressed the group. Among them were Dr. Kenneth Dameron, deputy NRA administrator of wholesale and retail codes, Washington, D. C.; Dillon S. Myer, chief of the AAA compliance section, Washington, D. C.; Ernest Rice, general agent for the Farm Credit Administration, Louisville, Ky.; L. R. Schoenmann, regional director for the Land Policy Section; J. S. Cutler, regional director for the Soil Erosion Service; Dr. C. G. McBride, executive secretary of the Ohio Milk Marketing Commission; J. W. Wuichet, acting state agent for the corn-hog adjustment program; John

Slipher, assistant state agent in charge of tobacco and wheat adjustment; C. S. Vickers, field manager for the Ohio Poultry Improvement Association.

Fellowships for study abroad have been announced by the Institute of International Education. A total number of thirty fellows will attend universities in Austria, Czechoslovakia, Hungary, Italy and Switzerland during the coming academic year. These fellowships provide the recipients in practically all cases with board, room and tuition charges. About the same number of students from these five countries will study in the United States. During the past six years the institute has brought two hundred and seventy-seven students from Austria, Czechoslovakia, Hungary, Italy and Switzerland to the United States and has sent one hundred and eighty-five American students abroad for study in these countries. The value of these "exchange fellowships" during that period was $250,835.

Gifts to Cornell University received during the academic year 1933–34 ending July 1 amounted to $1,012,338.73, according to the report of the controller. The Cornellian Council, the fund-raising organization of the alumni, is credited with $188,533.06, of which $68,250 was unrestricted as to its use by the president and the board of trustees. Over 5,000 Cornell alumni made voluntary contributions. The Medical College in New York City received gifts amounting to $68,758.82 during the year. Of the $755,096.85 which came directly to the university the largest donation was $500,000 from the estate of Henry H. Westinghouse, '74. This sum is now a part of the permanent endowment of the university and the income will be used for the College of Engineering. The gifts specify a wide variety of purposes, including scholarships, loan funds, research projects, equipment, books, plant equipment and improvement, current expenses, prizes and additions to endowment. A number of gifts were unrestricted as to use and enabled the university to offset a declining income caused by a slight shrinkage in enrolment as well as a reduction in income from investments.

Committees of New York City teachers, under the direction of Lawrence A. Wilkins, director of modern foreign language study in the city's senior high schools, are developing new types of courses with civic understanding and sympathy in view. The new courses will seek to stimulate the pupil's search into the everyday life, geography, history, industries, governments, culture, traditions and ideals of the countries where the language is spoken. A committee in each of the languages, French, Spanish, Italian and German, is preparing a suggestive outline for each term. The course in Spanish, for example, includes a review of the early discoveries and the contributions of Spain to the new world —of the economic results of the introduction of sheep, cattle, horses, sugar-cane and barley; the political and religious contributions in countries colonized by Spain, a study of Spanish missions in California and Texas. Adequate study of these subjects would involve an acquaintance with painting, pottery, weaving, feather-work, and work in gold and silver, as well as music, especially programs of Spanish-American music broadcast by the Pan American Union in Washington.

A dispatch to the *Christian Science Monitor* reports that a minimum wage of $800 a year for public-school teachers will be recommended to the Ontario Department of Education, according to a resolution passed recently by delegates representing Ontario's seven normal schools. It was pointed out in the resolution that some teachers are receiving only $250 a year. That teachers holding permanent certificates be granted a high-school assistant's certificate when academically qualified, on completion of a second-year course at normal school, was a further recommendation. A third resolution asked that permanent certificates granted after completion of the second-year course at normal school be designated as permanent superior first-class, permanent superior second-year certificate, or permanent superior kindergarten-primary certificate.

According to an Associated Press dispatch, twenty-six schools and camps for women during the summer months have been established in twenty-four states and the District of Columbia by the Federal Emergency Relief Administration. Others will be established later. No work will be done on public out-of-door projects.

Students will be chosen by the state relief administrations from unemployed women. Members of the staffs of the camps and schools, except the directors, also will be chosen from the unemployed. The subjects to be taught include vocational training and guidance, household management, English, social science, health education and similar subjects.

# DISCUSSION

## NURSERY SCHOOLS IN THE EMERGENCY PROGRAM[1]

WHILE nursery schools of any kind appear somewhat strange and radical to many people, the truth is that such schools were originally established in this country over a hundred years ago by Mr. Wilderspin. Having seen them prosper on a small scale in New England and New York, he predicted that they would soon spread to the entire country so that every child could be taken care of in a neighborhood school. But he underestimated the tremendous size of this country, and he could not foresee that many other developments in education were to be considered paramount, chiefly with respect to rural education, secondary education and higher education. So slow has been the extension downward of public education that we have included the kindergarten only during the past thirty years, and in spite of intensive efforts for five-year-olds we still have facilities for only one child out of four.

During the present emergency, when the morale in families became particularly low, it was apparent that something might well be done to improve conditions for very young children, and at the same time to furnish a measure of economic security to that small but important sector of our population engaged in the practise of teaching. Emergency nursery schools, then, were set up for four major purposes: (1) To restore unemployed teachers and allied workers to socially useful services; (2) to develop the physical and mental well-being of preschool children in needy, underprivileged families; (3) to assist parents in meeting the nutritional, physical and social needs of their children; (4) to set up an environment and daily program appropriate for preschool children as a demonstration for schools, homes and welfare agencies.

About 2,500 new units were established in 36 states, giving full-day care and guidance to approximately 50,000 children and employing perhaps 10,000 people altogether. Of course a program on this small scale has merely scratched the surface of the tremendous problem of improving the health, development and education of these young children. But it has served its main purpose in demonstrating that a good life really can be provided for children of this age under educational auspices and that parents do welcome the assistance which the nursery school gives. They welcome it not only because of the direct benefits to their children, which even the non-scientific person can see and understand, but because of the better insight which they are able to get by contact with good nursery school practise. That state commissioners of education are aware of the advantages to be gained from this new extension of education is indicated by the fact that 31 commissioners out of 36 requested a renewal of the program for the coming year, and in 22 of these states they have asked for summer programs.

The experience of other countries endorses the nursery school idea. As Mrs. Roosevelt has said, England has taken to this movement with great enthusiasm: we find public endorsement of it from king and archbishop. In their reconstruction programs, particularly with respect to slum removal, the English are finding the nursery school invaluable. Russia too believes in them whole-heartedly, and with extraordinary energy has proceeded to set up public schooling for children at all ages. Already they have over three million children in nursery school and kindergarten programs. So great has been the impact of European experience upon the nursery school movement that we find the Child Welfare Committee of the League of Nations making the following recommendations:

> We are struck by the serious character of the psychological effects produced by the depression upon children and of the strained and discouraged

[1] Given at the White House, Washington, D. C., May 21, 1934.

family atmosphere which is inevitable in homes suffering from unemployment.

The committee emphasizes the necessity for removing children from the pernicious atmosphere of their own homes during the greater part of the day and sending them to nursery schools, recreation centers or reading rooms so that they may enjoy the quietness and freedom from care and irritation that are essential conditions to their proper development.

Some school superintendents dwell upon the paramount position of "normal schooling," the implication being that we should not attempt new things in education until everything is right and good at other levels. Needless to say, every one wants the normal school term established and maintained with the highest possible standards so that at no age will children be allowed to suffer through inadequate or incorrect school procedures. However, such a stand need not deter one from trying experiments at other levels. Children below the age of five or six have their health, character and personality to develop also, and such development is always found to have a high place in the aims of education. As a matter of fact we are not at all sure that these high aims can be realized unless we start with a positive program of assistance and guidance for children well below the conventional school age. Moreover, it is possible that if schools do not want to undertake this early sponsorship for the children's health and education, some other organizations may step into the breach. It seems clear, then, that we should extend education to such ages and areas as will enable us all to realize better the essential aim of any educational process. However stated, this aim will always have as its chief emphasis the welfare of children.

It is foolish to say that we can not afford to do these things for children, since few states have taken adequate steps toward renovating their taxation and budgetary arrangements. Almost every state spends enough on passenger cars alone to pay its educational bills many times over, and such incidentals as cosmetics or tobacco taken separately will pay the costs of a state's complete educational program. We should not talk glibly about not having the wealth to do what we think ought to be done as long as such conditions are the rule. Rather we should look forward courageously to a reexamination of the sources of our wealth and to its socially adequate distribution.

George D. Stoddard

University of Iowa

## A STATISTICAL SLIDE RULE

At last the statistician, particularly in the fields of education and psychology, may be on a parity with the engineer when it comes to facilitating computation. A study[1] which has been under way for two years has resulted in the production of a genuine calculating slide rule adapted to the statistical calculations of education and psychology. This statistical slide rule, models of which have been produced by the Keuffel and Esser Company, is comparable to the engineer's log log duplex in versatility and number of scales. Ten of the seventeen scales are standard slide-rule scales, (A, B, C, D, CF, DF, CI, CIF, K, L), which take care of the usual processes of multiplication, division, powers, roots, reciprocals and logarithms. The remaining seven scales make the statistical slide rule virtually "self-contained" for ordinary statistical computations. They enable the user to read either $1-r^2$ or $\sqrt{1-r^2}$ for a given setting of r, to read areas under the normal curve for given abscissae—or *vice versa,* and to calculate intelligence or other quotients based on two ages given in years and months. The gauge point (.)6745 is marked on the C and D scales, including their variants.

An abstract of the study, with cuts of both faces of the statistical slide rule, appears in the July, 1934, issue of the *Peabody Journal of Education.* This abstract gives a description of the scales and summarizes the research which was made in attempting a tentative evaluation of the rule. It is predicted that the statistical slide rule will provide a valuable *vade mecum* for the individual student or research worker, including, of course, the educational psychologist.

Dennis H. Cooke

1 E. R. Enlow, ''A Statistical Slide Rule,'' Contributions to Education, No. 130, George Peabody College for Teachers, Nashville, Tennessee, 1934. Unpublished doctoral dissertation. Abstract in the *Peabody Journal of Education,* July, 1934.

# QUOTATIONS

## THE KANSAS SCHOOLS

KANSAS has an antiquated system of support for its schools. For more than seventy years Kansas has depended upon local taxes on real estate and personal property for the support of its schools. That was all very well back in the days when all the property of the citizens of Kansas was their land, horses, cattle and other visible goods. It is all wrong now.

Kansas is the forty-eighth state in the rank of states which seek to support their schools at least partially by a state tax. As time has gone on the burden has grown increasingly upon the holder of a homestead, whether urban or rural. The prosperous have escaped their share of the load. The load has fallen on the shoulders of the man who owns a home and is paying monthly into a building and loan association or mortgage company to hold this home; or on the farmer who is jumping sideways to be able to make a living for his family and pay the interest on the mortgage on his farm.

It is high time that we gave up these ox cart tactics. We must devise some sort of a system to provide adequate support of schools, at least partially from some other source than a tax on real and personal property. Only recently a well-known citizen of Kansas died, leaving an estate of about three milllion dollars. He had been paying taxes on real property less than that on the average farm or home. Still more recently another citizen died in Topeka, leaving an estate of a million dollars, with practically no taxes on real estate.

It would take more than a philosopher to determine just how this problem should be solved, but it can be solved and it will be solved. Somehow the thing should be worked out so that through either an increased inheritance tax, a selective sales tax, a luxury tax, segregation of the income tax, or some other form of tax, the burden of support of the public schools should fall more equally on the shoulders of the Kansas citizens who should pay this tax, and less on farms and real estate in towns.

The proposal of the Kansas State Teachers Association that new sources of revenue should be found for the support of the public schools is sound. The very fact that the teachers themselves are now proposing such a thing shows that they have their feet on the ground and that they know more about this thing than we have thought they knew.—*Emporia Gazette.*

# EDUCATIONAL RESEARCH AND STATISTICS

## THE RELATION OF INTELLIGENCE TEST SCORES OF KINDERGARTEN CHILDREN TO THEIR READING TEST SCORES IN THE FIRST GRADE

THIS study originated in the problem of separating the beginner in first-grade reading who learns at a slow rate from the one whose reading progress will be normal or rapid. The testing program was carried out in the kindergartens and first grades of the public school system of Gary, Indiana, for three consecutive semesters. The following problems occurred in connection with the effort to group the children according to ability.

(1) Are intelligence test scores of value in the selection of kindergarten children for different types of reading instruction in first grade?

(2) After establishing homogeneous grouping how does the reading achievement of children in first grade compare with their intelligence test ratings made at the close of kindergarten training?

(3) How much are test scores affected by the fact that a foreign language is spoken in the home?

At the end of their last semester in kindergarten the pupils were given the Detroit First Grade Intelligence Test. Their scores, together with the teachers' estimates of ability to succeed in first grade, were used for classification into two groups. One group, called 1C, was given special help in reading and remained in the first grade three semesters. The other group was placed in 1B and followed the usual first grade reading program. The same teacher handled both classes and was free to make transfers from one group to the other, depending on the pupil's progress.

Each child who had been given the intelligence test in kindergarten was given the Detroit Word Recognition Test at the end of one semester of reading, either as a member of a 1C or a 1B class. One exception occurred, in the 2B group, which had the test only after two semesters of instruction. It was possible to give the reading test to two groups after their second semester in the first grade. These classes are numbered (I) after one semester of reading, and (II) after two semesters of reading. They include the same children except for failures and transfers. One thousand and six children were tested both on the intelligence and the reading test. For convenience the groups are designated by the following plan:

| Group | Present grade | Terms completed | Number |
|---|---|---|---|
| 2B | 2B | 1B and 1A | 231 |
| 1A(II) | 1A | 1B and 1A | 351 |
| 1A(I) | 1A | 1B | 379 |
| 1B | 1B | 1B | 253 |
| 1B(II) | 1B | 1C and 1B | 62 |
| 1B(I) | 1B | 1C | 76 |
| 1C | 1C | 1C | 67 |

The data concerning these groups at the end of a year in kindergarten follow in Table I. In Table II the results of the achievement test are given with the correlation coefficients comparing the intelligence test with the reading test.

TABLE I

Chronological Age of Kindergarten Classes with Their Mental Age on the Detroit First Grade Intelligence Test

| Group | Number | Chronological age | | | Mental age | | |
|---|---|---|---|---|---|---|---|
| | | $Q_1$ | $Q_2$ | $Q_3$ | $Q_1$ | $Q_2$ | $Q_3$ |
| 2B ........ | 231 | 5-8 | 5-11 | 6-3 | 5-4 | 5-11 | 6-5 |
| 1A(II) | 351 | 5-8 | 5-11 | 6-3 | 5-2 | 5-7 | 6-3 |
| 1A(I)... | 379 | 5-9 | 6-1 | 6-5 | 5-2 | 5-7 | 6-3 |
| 1B ........ | 253 | 5-8 | 6-0 | 6-4 | 5-6 | 5-11 | 6-5 |
| 1B(II) | 62 | 5-8 | 6-0 | 6-4 | 4-10 | 5-0 | 5-3 |
| 1B(I)... | 76 | 5-9 | 6-0 | 6-4 | 5-9 | 5-0 | 5-2 |
| 1C ........ | 67 | 5-9 | 6-1 | 6-4 | 4-11 | 5-0 | 5-3 |
| Total ... | 1,006 | 5-9 | 6-0 | 6-4 | 5-2 | 5-7 | 6-3 |

According to Table I the quartile points for the chronological and mental ages of these groups are markedly different. With four exceptions the mental ages are lower. This was to be expected for the groups taking 1C work, since those classes were selected on the basis of low scores in the intelligence test. For the groups as a whole the data of Table I indicate that they are below average in ability. However, the reading achievement of these same pupils was higher than the norms given for the Detroit Word Recognition Test according to the data of Table II.

TABLE II

Detroit Word Recognition Test Scores Compared with Norms and Correlations between the Reading Test and the Intelligence Test

| Group | Number | Scores | | | Norm | Correlation |
|---|---|---|---|---|---|---|
| | | $Q_1$ | $Q_2$ | $Q_3$ | | |
| 2B ........ | 231 | 19.8 | 24.5 | 31.0 | 20 | .21 ± .04 |
| 1A(II) ... | 351 | 22.3 | 28.4 | 33.2 | 20 | .26 ± .03 |
| 1A(I) ... | 379 | 9.1 | 13.4 | 18.5 | 12 | .22 ± .03 |
| 1B ........ | 253 | 13.1 | 18.0 | 23.1 | 12 | .30 ± .04 |
| 1B(II) ... | 62 | 10.7 | 13.7 | 17.1 | 12 | .30 ± .08 |
| 1B(I) ... | 76 | 1.9 | 3.6 | 6.2 | 4 | .24 ± .07 |
| 1C* ........ | 67 | 3.7 | 6.3 | 9.4 | 4 | .24 ± .08 |
| All 1A...... | 583 | 20.4 | 26.5 | 32.2 | 20 | |
| All 1B...... | 694 | 10.5 | 15.2 | 20.5 | 12 | |
| All 1C...... | 143 | 2.4 | 4.8 | 7.9 | 4 | |

* The 1C norm is an estimated one.

From this table we note the superiority in score of the classes 2B and 1A(II) after two semesters of reading. The other group having two semesters of work, the 1B(II), was originally a 1C class, which accounts for the low median score. The 1B group which made a median markedly above the norm was the same group which showed superiority in the mental test, according to Table I.

The correlations given in Table II indicate that the intelligence test scores obtained from the Detroit First Grade Intelligence Test are not good prognostic measures of reading success in first grade, although such scores can be utilized in establishing classes for different types of reading instruction. The effectiveness of the plan can not be judged by its results since it was begun to achieve those results. The data show that the teaching was effective either because of, or in spite of, segregating the duller children. The median score of all the groups was above the norms in all but one instance.

The correlation between intelligence and reading test scores was greater after the second semester of instruction. This may be due to the wider range in achievement after two terms of work. More training apparently scatters the class in reading ability and tends to cause an increase in the correlation between reading achievement and capacity as measured by an intelligence test.

The first grade reading problem in the Gary schools was further complicated by the large number of children from homes where a foreign language was spoken. In this connection a study was made of two groups selected from the classes reported above. These children were from the same classrooms so far as possible. Ninety-four were from homes in which a foreign language was spoken and one hundred from English-speaking homes. We shall refer to them hereafter as the "Foreign" and the "English" groups. The following table gives items which were compared.

TABLE III

COMPARISON OF TEST RESULTS FOR CHILDREN WITH DIFFERENCES IN LANGUAGE BACKGROUND

| | Foreign | English |
|---|---|---|
| Mean, Intelligence Test | 19.1 ± .67 | 26.6 ± .77 |
| Mean, Reading Test | 4.8 ± .13 | 5.5 ± .10 |
| S.D. Intelligence Test | 9.7 ± .94 | 11.5 ± .07 |
| S.D. Reading Test | 1.9 ± .09 | 1.5 ± .07 |
| Correlation between tests | .37 ± .06 | .54 ± .05 |

Although the English group made higher scores on both tests, the Foreign group scored almost as high on the reading test. It is probable that the English group made intelligence test scores more closely approximating their true ability than the Foreign group. This is further indicated by the wider scatter in the standard deviation for the English group in the intelligence test scores. The difference of seven points in the means of the two groups on the intelligence test represents a six months' difference in mental age. That the difference is so insignificant after a semester of first grade certainly raises the question as to whether the Foreign group was actually more dull. Studies by Serota, Pintner, Giardini and Root indicate that foreign language groups often show an apparent inferior intellectuality which is not consistent with later accomplishment. The data of this study confirm these previous investigations.

From this study of the value of a group intelligence test in the selection of pupils for different types of reading instruction in first grade it was concluded that:

(1) The classsification of pupils according to intelligence test scores gave homogeneous groups, since there was little overlapping of high and low reading scores between two adjacent class groups. However, after one semester of training, differences in ability which appeared to be of significance for reading instruction were materially lessened within each group. Children who were expected to make slow progress in school were able to exceed the reading test norms, either because of, or in spite of, homogeneous grouping.

(2) Intelligence tests administered in kindergarten are not good prognostic measures of reading success in first-grade classes, although there is a small correlation between their rating and the reading test score obtained after one or two semesters of training.

(3) In selecting homogeneous groups at the first-grade level the importance of the home language must be emphasized. Intelligence test ratings obtained in kindergarten correspond more closely to reading test scores in first grade for children from English-speaking homes than for those from foreign language homes. In communities with a large foreign population the home language should be considered a factor in determining test results in the primary grades.

HENRIETTE WOOLF

## NEW BOOKS IN EDUCATION

BURTON, WILLIAM H. *Introduction to Education.* Pp. 833. Appleton-Century. $3.00.

LENNES, N. J. and L. R. TRAVER. *The Lennes Essentials of Arithmetic. Grades Three, Four, Five, Six, Seven and Eight.* Pp. 160 each. Laidlaw.

SHUMAN, JOHN T. *Spelling for Trade and Technical Students.* Pp. 133. Christopher. $1.25.

# EDUCATIONAL REVIEW

**Edited by Nicholas Murray Butler, 1891–1919, Frank Pierrepont Graves, 1920–1924, and William McAndrew, 1924–**

## COMMENTS ON THINGS EDUCATIONAL

By WILLIAM McANDREW

### DYNAMITE IN SUMMER COURSES

Among the patriots who deserve a wreath this year is modest Milton Loomis, director of the summer session of New York University. Did you see his bulletin? There has long been a suspicion that this lively Alma Mater has been threatening old Status Quo with the divorce court. Loomis seems to be helping her to it. First on the bill comes a course, "Education for Social Reconstruction," with fascism, socialism, changing morals, labor troubles, discussed by apostles a college professor might have been afraid to mention ten years ago. Amongst them are constructive instructors programmed for "preparing the teacher for the new day," "youth and the changing world" and so on. There is an entire course on Young America and the New Order. Crime, The New Economics, Education Wreckers, School Management in the Depression, The New Industrial Education, Community Service, Leisure Problems, Teacher Organization, Politics and School, Patriotism and Student Activities are some of the offerings in addition to a goodly number of old academic standbys. I notice Mary Fox, Royal Copeland, Matthew Woll, Harry Laidler and Norman Thomas on the teaching staff, along with a strong battery of conservative professors.

### STANDPATTERS AND FREETHINKERS IN THE N. E. A.

William Boutwell's account of the Washington convention of the National Education Association, as printed in School and Society last month, is, I'll say, having been bewildered by the multiplicity of different sorts of things happening at the same time, a triumph of reporting that should be called to the attention of the Pultizer prize commission. Boutwell is head editor of the U. S. Office of Education and very properly abstemious of criticism directed against any educational organization. He knows, but says nothing, of the whispering campaign against one of the men prominently advocated for the position of president of the association. The charge against him was that he is tainted by the doctrines of John Dewey, Russell, Counts, Watson, Kilpatrick, Bagley, Snedden and Columbia University. People that I love were prejudiced by dread of this influence, but I, as many do, like much that disagrees with me. Good land, why pick Columbia as the black sheep, while New York University, her neighbor, is fully as tarred with Deweyism? Would that some researcher might find the center of educational resistance to a new order so that we of the old guard might hold a convention there. Where can educational calm be found? California says, "It is not in me." Colorado can not claim it, nor Texas, Utah, Illinois, North Carolina, Michigan, Wisconsin, Alabama nor Minnesota, as judged by warm anti-traditional articles in their state educational journals. Teachers have so long been twitted with being in a rut that you would think the allegation that any one is kicking over the traces would bring admiration for him.

Robert Le Diable Moore of Illinois threw a good bomb into one session attacking teachers' "meek attitude and their milk-and-water resolutions." Illinois, he said, is the junk yard of school wreckers, wealthy robber barons making children pay for bankers' blunders.

After reading Eunice Barnard's *New York Times* report of American Legion Cooke's attack on teachers for telling children we need a new social order, I went to Milo Whittaker's meeting and heard this DeKalb, Illinois, professor applauded for telling us we do need a new social order and the rising generation must so be taught. He has been canvassing hundreds of high-school pupils and finds an amazing number of them recording their belief that God's in his heaven, all's right with the world, our society is O. K.

Hard on Legionnaire Cooke's exhortation, the association's committee on social-economic goals leaps out of the Cooke house and calls for "a new era of civic interests and social interpretations." Legion Commander Hayes was hot for oaths of allegiance, while a plank offered for inclusion in the association platform condemns, says *The Times,* oaths of allegiance because they are means of intimidating teachers.

Contemporaneous with these revolts the rabbinical assembly of America resolved that the failures of political democracy are due to its corruption and abuse by private economic interests. "We pledge ourselves to the elimination of those economic influences which pervert democracy and threaten liberty. We shall support a planned economy, a control of industry and a broader distribution of wealth." "Our present scheme of living is a denial of brotherhood." The rabbis called upon education to establish a new social order.

In the lobby of the headquarters hotel I heard one old-time member of the National Education body remark, "The combination of Legion and N. E. A. principles is likely to make a very explosive mixture."

## TELL SOME RICH WIDOW

THE cheeriest of all educational banquets occurs in Pittsburgh every June when those who have won awards of the Frick Educational Commission are handed their boons. Riding to the roof garden of the William Penn Hotel in an elevator full of teachers in gala dress you would scarcely believe these vivacious folks belong to the end of a ten-months school term. When you see the entire company in the big banquet hall, buzzing with talk, merry with laughter, gay with bright colors and flowers, you will well wish old-time Americans who used to word-paint teachers in drab hues might see these handsome Pittsburghers.

The H. C. Frick awards, I was told, were suggested to the donor by Pittsburgh's front-rank citizen, Dr. Brashear, wheelwright, instrument maker, astronomer, scientist and member of the board of education. "Don't give a building," he urged. "Don't offer competitive prizes to children, paying them for attending to their studies. Put the money into something that will benefit all the children, prize-winners and dumb bells. Help the teachers who want to grow." The management of the fund was put into the hands of a commission, Dr. Brashear and associates. They canvassed teachers for suggestions. Yearly help to professional study is the chief benefaction resulting. At the banquet, George Gerwig, long-time secretary of the board of education, author of service books for high schoolers, now an officer of the commission and a member of the board of education, introduces a speaker to tell the beneficiaries and their friends how lucky Pittsburgh is educationally. Musicians from the schools radiate harmony. Marshall McCoy tells the company how the checks are to be passed out. At various stations in the hall are banners, "Harvard," "California," "Sorbonne," "London," "Rome," "Pittsburgh," "Oxford"—this year, 74 universities and several travel tours. "Ready," sings the musical McCoy, "Go." Five hundred thirty-nine awardees are, without fuss or confusion, soon at their stations and holding the checks of the commission in their happy hands.

Who has selected the places where these teachers are to do their summer study? There's another fine thing about the awards. The teacher chooses his own brain-garden. Already the large majority of teachers in Pittsburgh have taken advantage of this broadening influence. The former participants have a Phoebe Brashear Club further to spread the benefits of the knowledge gained. The whole scheme of the commission, publications, lectures, scholarships for teachers, is so direct a public service, so intelligently managed, that if known it will appeal to every school officer and board member in the country as a model. I have long thought that the rich and kind-hearted widows sprinkled through the United States have been neglected by the school superintendents. I have been told by experts that there are people who want to give money where it would do the most good and don't know what to do with it. Tell 'em about the Pittsburgh plan and suggest they endow one for your town.

## TENURE-INSURANCE REVIVAL

A REFORM that costs the school board and the people no money ought to be pushed at this time. School trustees, thinking of the grievous blows educational workers have been dealt, are more likely to respond to appeals for something involving no cost than might at other times be the case. Now is the time to extend to backward school systems a plan of tenure that will protect teachers and superintendents from dismissal when their work is of high grade and their character first class. Surveys and standard tests have reached a point that enables determination whether teaching and administration is over the average. Enough sound psychology is at hand to demonstrate the fallacy that fear of losing one's place is an efficient motive to keep us up to good work. The fortunate public servants in school systems where tenure laws function may well assist their brothers and sisters in the backwaters where old master-servant traditions obtain. There are plenty of such miasmatic places. Edgar Knight's revision of his "Education in the United States" brings school history up to date. His disclosures of the fragile threads that hold good teachers in service are astounding.

In one southern state, this promise from teachers is exacted: I will take a vital interest in all phases of Sunday School work, donating my time, service and money without stint for the uplift and benefit of the community. I will abstain from all dancing, immodest dressing and any other conduct unbecoming a teacher and a lady. I promise not to go out with young men except in so far as it may be necessary to stimulate Sunday School work. I promise not to fall in love, to become engaged or secretly married.

Knight, of course, admits that this is an extreme case, but Arthur Moehlman finds that the general ease with which local jealousies, political schemes and personal prejudice can prevent the reengagement of a competent teacher, principal or superintendent is nothing less than scandalous.

The school superintendency is behind teaching positions in security. But everybody who knows administration can show how much more the efficiency of school service depends on the head than upon the rank and file. Good armies with poor generals lose, said Commander Pershing, poor armies with good generals win. The persisting Marcy idea that a superintendency is a reward, a gift; the failure to see that a good man working out long-time policies can not be supplanted without shameful loss to boys and girls, are errors that can be mitigated by a united effort of educators. Professor Moehlman urges teachers' associations to select raw treatments of classroom workers and to bombard the perpetrators with publicity. The Department of Superintendence, when fraternal protection is proposed, applauds unanimously; but when leadership in a positive campaign gets organized, pedal frigidity ensues in the committee as in the Detroit meeting; or death takes the chairman, as it did John Chewning after the Minneapolis convention.

A curious deterrent appears occasionally in the form of fear, by superintendents enjoying intimate friendship with their business-men boards, that fraternal action in the case of any brother martyr flavors of labor-unionism. Meantime every school sociology that comes to this office for review has reached the conclusion that the union has been labor's main protection. As one required to read an abundance of educational literature every month, I note an almost universal conviction that public education is making itself over more rapidly than ever before. It is hard to avoid the belief that University of Chicago Professor Judd is sound in his contention that, unless the school system exerts itself to save its generals from persistent sniping, any rebuilding it does will continue to be abandoned here and there half done. A stiffer program of protection is due from the state and national associations. A wider extension of tenure laws in the interest of the people who pay for the schools is imperative.

## CONVENTION TALK AND MISFORTUNE

INTELLIGENT looking schoolmasters have been known to say that they get more out of conversation in the lobbies than they do from listening to addresses from convention platforms. This is, of course, unthinking nonsense, as if the boiled-down and self-tested thoughts of a selected speaker were worth less than the gossip of the moment. Lobby talk, when it concerns convention doings, is docility or unsubstantiated disagreement. But for refreshing sociability and collection of odds and ends of news give me one of the easy chairs in the rotunda of the headquarters hotel. The annual jolt, there, to patriotism is meeting superintendents who have failed of reappointment. At the Washington meeting I met seven whom I have good reason to believe have maintained school systems on a high grade. They have hard work to keep from telling in detail how they happen to be adrift. To most listeners this is like an invalid's recount of ailments. The American lack of reason in terminating a school superintendent's service really is a disease spotting districts in every part of the country. One of the unfortunates, it seemed to me, in asking his friends if they knew of vacancies, had the right idea of expressing his condition: "I'm out—politics." Nothing more. Such is the history of the American school superintendency that everybody understands those three words.

# MONTHLY SURVEY OF EDUCATIONAL BOOKS

*She of the Social Sciences.* Vassar President Henry Noble MacCracken notes the surprising growth of social studies.[1] No disciplines have evolved more swiftly. For at least a century to come the social sciences will depend on the inevitable record of science and the emotional nature of man, utilizing each and applying them to human wants. Dr. MacCracken reviews especially the forty-four years teaching of Professor Herbert Mills, now emeritus, bringing into Vassar the solidest sort of teaching in the civic field commonly accepted as a male preserve. At Vassar, Professor Mills was the recognized leader of the doctrine that the proper study of mankind is the man of to-day as well as the man of yesterday. Mills at once created, says Dr. MacCracken, not only his pupils' respect for hard work but a passion for justice in every social field.

There are two papers by Professor Mills in the volume. He accepts the full responsibility of college to develop leaders with preparation for bettering the social order. He was so stimulating, testifies Sociologist Margaret Banning, that nothing in the world seemed worth doing except attacking some of the social ills. More candidates for positions as social workers came from Vassar than from any other college or university. During this depression, says Mrs. Banning, other women seem finding out for the first time things that our Vassar graduates have known for years. "The depression is not so incomprehensible to us as to other women. Monetary history, banking, speculation, railroad control, labor problems, live topics that have eaten their way into almost every household were themes of intense discussion in the Mills seminars with plenty of heat. Indoctrination was shunned. The Socialist's side, the Bolshevist's, the Communist's, the labor leader's, got full recognition. The courses seem to Eunice Avery, as she looks back upon their presentation in 1908, to have been planned with an uncanny sense of what would be needed to-day.

[1] Herbert Elmer Mills and fourteen contributors, "College Women and the Social Sciences." The John Day Company, New York. 250 pp. $2.50.

*Chosen Freely.* These studies were always elective. Three quarters of the Vassar graduates have had them. A total of 6,209 women studied economics between 1890 and 1930. Since 1929 the classes in social science electives are filling up. Applications for September, 1934, show an increase of 50 per cent.

Fourteen Vassar graduates have articles in the volume. These women are professors, welfare commissioners, visiting teachers, some are in public health service, in vocational guidance, in politics, in research, in business and in various fields of civic work. Their papers in the book cover education, public health, philanthropy, politics, labor problems and an analysis of the occupations of Vassar alumnae. Mrs. Fitts, who gives her occupation as "minister's wife and homemaker," writes a satisfying "Praise of Domesticity."

There is good punch in "Politics and the College Woman." The educated woman in general has had a negligible influence on the political situation. Women stay out because there is so little in common between their conception of usefulness and party politics as it exists in the United States. In their attitude they contribute largely to the moral defeatism of the country's present political philosophy. Educated women are a large part of a critical audience. When you come to controlling an electorate, even a local one, college women are nearly always helpless. They are over-indifferent to office-holding, partly because of their fastidiousness. They find it too humiliating to play to the crowd. When the Vassar questionnaires come back from the graduates, continues Mrs. Banning, they show the sound purposes of living; the respondents are educators, mothers, wives, actresses—but politics is, except in one case, not mentioned among interests and activities. They read recent books and articles on current problems and solutions. They quote Keynes and Laski. Their criticisms are pungent. But they talk as though active participation in remedying the situation is far from their plans.

Any observer of social trends must ponder whether Mrs. Banning's lament is more applicable to college women than to college men. The Yalensian canvass, concluding that "politics is too dirty to touch," is significant enough, isn't it? The proceedings of educational conventions, from their beginnings to 1930, indicate that we had no thought of politics as part of our business. We are in a nation-wide flood of educational repentance, as School-historian Edgar Knight shows, point by point. The 1787 conception of a public education to be set up was with intent for training for cooperative government; that is, school for society—that is, preparation for politics. Stupendous chances for money-making lured us to dancing around the golden calf. The flood of books on social science that comes to this review shop shows many a Moses lifting up his voice. The stone tablets are due; that is, curriculums leading to the original American proposal.

*Retarded Reform.* You might arouse interest by asking your most advanced history class to select a period described by each of the following extracts and to give reasons for each answer.

"At present, tendencies threaten to kindle passions that have heretofore flamed in destructive fury."

"Problems confronting us are grave. Their gravity comes from indisposition to recognize them frankly and to grapple boldly with them."

"A civilization has concentrated wealth in the hands of a fortunate few at a time when resources are so great that the poorest could have all the comforts and conveniences enjoyed by the rich. Amid poverty and want the manufacturers cry, 'Give us a market'; 'Give us but work,' cry idle men."

These are from a book printed in 1883, fifty-one years ago, and now reprinted by a foundation.[2]

In that year a beginning Latin book was printed, based on the inductive method, which was attacked by a goodly number of eminent scholars as using a wasteful and mind-damaging method. There is no record in the annals of the publishers of it that any school board forbade a principal to use it in his classes. The book before me, "Social Problems," by Henry George, was stricken from a principal's high-school library list by a school board known to me, and the schoolmaster warned to stop lending his copy to high-school seniors. Needlework was taught school girls in England for the frankly expressed purpose of keeping them from thinking on disturbing ideas.

Tom Johnson, Cleveland's reform mayor, used to say that this is the book on political economy, so free of technical terms, so readable and vivid, that it converted him from his unpatriotic ways. John Dewey, the schoolmaster's most revered apostle, has recently said that every word of "Social Problems" applies to our present condition in a more intense degree than when it was written. President Butler considers George prophetic in appeal and insight. Roy Foulke has been reviving in Dun and Bradstreet's analytical reports, Frederick Bird has been reproducing in *The Review,* the diagnoses made by Henry George fifty years ago and showing their application to present conditions. The world has come to rank George, says Dr. Dewey, among the world's less than twenty great social philosophers from Plato down.

Political dangers, social pressures, concentration of power, the rights of man, over-production, unemployed labor, effects of machinery, wage-slavery, taxation, the farmer, are some of the chapters of the book. The directness and simplicity of it are appealing.

Robert Schalkenbach devoted his fortune to

[2] Henry George, "Social Problems." The Robert Schalkenbach Foundation, 11 Park Place, New York. 256 pp. $1.00.

endowing the foundation which is devoted to distributing the literature of this civic apostle. At a dollar each, the foundation publishes "Progress and Poverty," "Protection and Free Trade," "The Land Question," and "The Life of Henry George." John Dewey's address, "Steps to Economic Recovery," is issued at five cents.

*Psychology for Recovery.*[3] What country has recovered most from the bottom of the depression: United States, Great Britain, Germany, Sweden? Why?

Why does business turn down when it's up, and turn up when it's down?

Which cost the United States more—the world war or the depression?

Has the number of stockholders in America's great corporations declined or increased since 1929? Why?

How many bank failures were there since 1928? Why?

Dr. Daniel Starch, whom you remember as college professor of psychology in Iowa, Wellesley, Wisconsin and Harvard, also as author of texts on educational psychology and measurements, went into business psychology twenty years ago, became a director in boards of gas, electric and utilities investment companies and heads a firm of consultants in commercial research.

His new book, "Faith, Fear and Fortunes," a startling exposition of what ails the world, answers the questions at the head of this review and turns topsy-turvy a number of beliefs that the man on the sidewalk treasures. It is a psychologist's answer to the question, Why do we have booms and depressions? Must we have them again?

Economics is a science of behavior. We are all in business. Business is more concerned with human feelings than it is with mathematics. Values are mental. All business is done in the human mind. Values are emotional and contagious. All Americans want the same thing at the same time. Booms and panics depend on mob psychology. Dr. Starch describes and interprets tulipomania, the South-Sea bubble, the Mississippi scheme, the Florida boom. Diocletian, 1,700 years ago, tried the NRA and failed. Only two parts of the New Deal, according to the author's chapter on the psychology of it, have had a beneficial effect—the psychological effect of calming unreasonable fear, the gold embargo. The only way to get better times is to keep people at work, to find new things to do. Almost any business can with thought find new ways to keep its people busy. Every concern should have a brain-trust of one or more persons engaged in long-range thinking, creating new ideas, new projects. There are millions of Americans able to buy new things. The year 1933 was the best year ever enjoyed by the electric refrigeration industry and the second best for makers of washing machines. The ordinary manipulations of men and governments are but ripples. Know the titanic tides of human desires, emotions and rivalries. Know psychology.

Whether you have a head for economics, or, like me, are confused by its abstractions, you won't put this book down until you finish it, for its verve, its survey of old and new, its vivid analyses of conditions give it high readability.

*This Overturn.* Evils of an old order are attacked. Its religious or philosophical sanctions are undermined. Satire exposes its absurdity and uncovers its corruption. Intellectual activity destroys an old loyalty to a régime and the régime's faith in itself. New dogmas are put forward that come to seem more reliable than the old. A crisis comes. The old ruling classes because of their weaknesses are unable to carry on. New rulers take possession, often without violence. That is what revolution is. We are in one or entering. Mr. Soule's[4] book opens with an interpretation of four revolutions, English, American, French and Russian, bringing out some common characteristics, economical, political and war-like. He considers what revolution is not, and what part the mob plays in one.

Then come considerations of the changes under the surface of American life, machine influence, occupational upsets, business changes, debts, foreign trade and evils of the present crisis. You see the Hoover resistance and the

[3] Daniel Starch, "Faith, Fear and Fortunes." Richard R. Smith, 420 Lexington Avenue, New York. 226 pp. $2.00.

[4] George Soule, "The Coming American Revolution." The Macmillan Company, New York. 314 pp. $2.50.

planning, fermentation, the new deal dealt, the new deal played. All this is interesting enough of itself. Critic Soule's comments make it more than warm.

The constructive estimates on what is likely to come are what will touch you most. Capital entered its planned intercorporate unions and in many cases resisted requirements that it should bargain with collective labor. Organized business fights plans to regulate the selling of securities or the trade in food and drugs. This is, of course, to preserve the profit system against consumers' interest. Continuance of the present claims of business will make want in the midst of plenty more real than in this depression.

The aims originally expounded by President Roosevelt will be more strongly urged by the majority of the people—more equal distribution of incomes, higher standards of living, more security for every one. This must be planned.

Then, point by point, the author measures the present aspects of the American mind and the social situation, comparing it with the conditions of the previous revolutions. In some respects the American overturn is well on its way, in others it is behind former records. These appraisals are of the most stimulating conjectures I have seen in print.

*At These Crossroads.* Get rid of the notion that we are recovering something, warns Norman Thomas[5] in his new conribution to the Macmillan series on public affairs. We don't want to recover old usages. They failed us. Capitalism has broken down because its own methods killed it. Its doom is not due to enemies without so much as to its own follies and vices.

After a recount of specific large swindlings Mr. Thomas asks what is worth saving. There is the belief in democracy bolstered pretty well on occasion by the powers that were. The Fascist despises it. The Communist promises that his scheme will make it true. The Supreme Court whittled our constitutional rights almost completely away during the great war. Toward the Negroes we have practised more brutality than Hitler against the Jews. The Daughters of one holy revolution try to enforce birth control against other attempts at betterment. Liberty of speech, press and assembly has lost ground.

Fascism and Communism are surveyed, analyzed and compared with Socialism and Bolshevism. The Roosevelt revolution is described as a turn from laissez-faire to state capitalism. The excellence and deficiencies of the New Deal are discussed. In considering the social forces in America the author finds the labor union the strongest manifestation of the strength of the workers as producers and consumers. The New Deal has not put new principles into the Democratic party in the states. Antagonistic attitudes of radical groups toward one another can be reconciled on many points of agreement.

We won't go backward. No Coolidge epoch can be recovered. Some are hoping for an extension of the New Deal into a capitalist collectivism without ruthless intolerance. Three other roads are possible: catastrophe, as in world war, Fascism or some form of Socialism. The situation under each outcome is outlined and the superiority of the cooperative commonwealth expounded. No miracle can make the next generation just as well off as the last, bad as it was. We shall be much worse off or much better. The kind of brains that made our marvelous inventions must bring forth abundance and must end the long night of exploitation, poverty and war.

*Perpetual Propaganda.* A reformed advertising man, James Rorty,[6] resists believing that America has a class civilization. But when he tells you of the studies newspaper and magazine publishers make of their readers, estimating their numbers in a classification as "rich," "poor" or "middle class," when you consider how most people place you in some grade or other, you may be willing to admit that the now famous Commission on Social Studies has a basis for proposing that America change itself to a classless society.

This Rorty book is built on the methods, morals and menace of advertising. But its

[5] Norman Thomas, "The Choice Before Us. Mankind at the Crossroads." The Macmillan Company, New York. 249 pp. $2.50.

[6] James Rorty, "Our Master's Voice." The John Day Company, New York. 394 pp. $3.00.

author is a sociologist, economist, philosopher and Declaration-of-Independence American. His ability to pull the wool away from your eyes is uncanny. He is a tart satirist but an intimate observer filled with wonder at our persistence in the capacity that P. T. Barnum played upon in the realm of suckerdom. Here are startling facts about our favorite newspapers and magazines, the radio, the boughten testimonials, Behaviorist Watson, the movies, the steps to discount the Payne Fund's studies of the effect of motion pictures on children, *The Saturday Evening Post,* Beecher, Elbert Hubbard, Ivy Lee, Bruce Barton, the Tugwell Drug Bill, the patent medicine game and an abundance of things very much in the public mind.

The part the schools play in advertising tooth paste and brushes, how teaching for consumers' interest is blocked, the long way the teacher has to go before he gets free from the domination of big business, the use of schools in favor of the National Electric Light Association, and other educational references are cited to show that "business can control the schools and universities when it wishes."

What few newspapers can afford to print, what a live American feels he ought to know, is here a-plenty and not without pepper. It is a hard book to lay down. It puts the detective story into the shade.

*New Deal Publications.* We oldsters are having trouble in learning the A.B.C.'s of our government. PCC in one place means Planning and Coordinating Committee; in another, Production Credit Corporations. A book just issued by the American Library Association[7] has in its index 86 alphabetical denominations of New Deal Commissions, boards and councils. If you need to know the authority behind the EIBW or who compose the ECPC, Mr. Wilcox's compilation will tell you. He has furnished what he calls a fairly complete check list of the publications of all the emergency administrations for the year ending April 15, 1934, and information on how you may get what you want. All the material in his list is in the John Crerar Library, Chicago, and available for inter-library loan.

*Education for Social Order.* The collaboration of Professor and Mrs. Zeleny, of the Minnesota State Teachers College at St. Cloud, with University Sociologist Finney, of Minneapolis, has produced a notably practical treatise on education's social responsibilities.[8] Scarcely was the type set when Finney, in his fifty-eighth year, clergyman, economist, philosophy and education professor at Wesleyan and Minnesota Universities, clear and constructive author of forward-looking books, passed on. His philosophical approach to school problems, Dr. Zeleny's concern with management and scientific technology of teaching, Mrs. Zeleny's studies of rural and city life, give their book a notable balance and usefulness.

You have typical communities pictured, the teacher's embarrassment by the traditions of the district, the teacher-pupil conflict, the nature of culture, change and the curriculum, the lags of education, the social morale of the school.

The much exploited extra-curriculars betray a sociological blindness. They are carried to extremes. Their importance as an educational benefit is overestimated. The school paper goes home. Father and mother are bewildered by the new notion that education is dances, parties, play-acting, yells and turning somersaults. To what end? The children can not tell. The teachers haven't disclosed. Perhaps they don't know. All the live schools have these things; so must we. I sat beside a pretty high-school miss at a class dinner at Erie. She made a ringing speech for more class spirit. "What would you do with it if you had it?" I whispered to her. "Search me," she whispered back. Absurdities of "the child-centered school" are here discussed and awkward attempts at moral education. Self-government schemes seldom go far enough. The most important contribution the school can make for full citizenship is to inform the learner adequately as to what politics is and what it needs. Only very

7 Jerome K. Wilcox, "Guide to the Official Publications of the New Deal Administration." American Library Association, Chicago. 113 pp. $1.00.

8 Ross L. Finney, Leslie D. Zeleny, "An Introduction to Educational Sociology." D. C. Heath & Company, Boston. 341 pp. $2.40.

recently have educational leaders come to realize how much more than teaching the anatomy of the structure of government is needed. Prospective citizens must have constructive opinions on all kinds of civic problems, for the solutions depend on the votes of the people. Since votes are likely to be influenced by propaganda, education should teach how to be fortified against it. Training for citizenship requires a wide enlightenment in the field of politics, economics, sociology and history.

Copious questions and bibliography, a glossary and a good index fit the book for use in departments of education, teachers colleges, training classes and teachers' reading circles.

*Shall the Nation Help the Schools?* The question of federal aid to education is not new, but it is freshened by the disclosures of war time as to the amount of illiteracy in America greater than that of several European nations. The depression has turned many observers to the need of help wanted from all the states to aid the more unfortunate commonwealths. The H. W. Wilson Company has compiled an informative handbook[9] of twenty-five articles and numerous shorter extracts by Edward Reisner, John Norton, William Carr, Glenn Frank, William Russell, Ray Wilbur and others, bristling with argument for and against.

These Wilson people certainly know how to save your time. This book begins with a brief for debate upon a resolution "that substantial grants should be made by the federal government for public elementary and secondary education." The affirmative and negative arguments are given in bare outline. There follow fourteen pages of bibliography. Then come 175 shots from the great guns and firings from the rank and file—speeches, magazine articles, editorials, letters to the press and extracts from books. Among the negatives appear former Secretary Wilbur warning against anestheticizing local effort, Professor Lischka, of the National Catholic Welfare Conference, arguing that the Constitution does not guarantee education, and Wyoming-professor Reusser suggesting a revision of the state taxes. From the U. S. Chamber of Commerce comes a cry for state sovereignty—"the Constitution is for that." "To take funds from the wealthier states is spoliation." From *The Saturday Evening Post* is reprinted Albert Atwood's sneer at fancy hemstitching and turnip-raising on which he intimates the schools are spending money. The Catholic Education Association's report is here, and President Coolidge's opposition to the expansion of subsidies. There are arguments from *The Catholic Educational Review*. Compiler Johnsen found, against federal aid, matter that fills in the book 46 pages; for aid there are 51 pages. In these latter is Columbia Law-professor Joseph Chamberlain's exposition of Constitutional general-welfare power and federal-aid's legitimacy as established by the courts. Dean Russell's classical study of the alleged Constitutional obstacles leads the affirmative side.

*Vitalized History of Education.* William H. Payne, professor of education at the University of Michigan, used to give us, in 1884, portions of Gabriel Compayre's "History of Education." As I now recall it, we were all refreshed by them. When, later, I undertook to furnish a class of intending teachers with material on the history of American education, the poor dears were dreadfully bored. No, it wasn't my fault. Examine our early books on this subject and note what dry and dull strings of facts and dates they are.

In this magazine I once poured enthusiasm on Edgar Knight's account of American education's beginnings and progress. Without any pride of consistency I do the same for his later work on the same theme.[10] This author has sensed the epic quality of the great movement in which America, putting into practise the vision of philosopher-statesmen, has led the world. Our earlier national histories of education left the reader with the notion that there was a school belt starting from Massachusetts, running across New York, and confining itself to the territory north of the Ohio River. Professor Knight takes away none of New En-

[9] Julia E. Johnsen, "Federal Aid to Education." H. W. Wilson Company, 950 University Avenue, New York. 213 pp. 90 cents.

[10] Edgar W. Knight, "Education in the United States." Ginn and Company, Boston. 627 pp. $2.60.

gland's glory, but he rounds out the picture with the work of Marion for South Carolina, Murphey's pioneering in her neighbor to the north, Ruffner's and Wise's in Virginia, Perry's in Alabama, and others in various commonwealths north and south. The educational pioneers are woven into the story with singular effectiveness, giving it a personal flavor of high interest. The striking passages of Thaddeus Stevens's triumphant argument in the Pennsylvania legislature are given at length, as are enough of Horace Mann, Henry Barnard and others of our educational ancestry to give us the flavor of our professional forbears.

The educational revolution of 1787, when for a public school system the statesmen of the day abandoned the selfish individual aims of a schooling for distinction, for scholarship, for the saving of souls, for ornament, for getting into a superior caste, is expounded in a new fullness. The reason a school system lagged behind these proposals and later grew strong with but little regard to the promises of civic betterments that brought it forth is fully presented.

In the villages I have called home even the country doctors have prided themselves on acquaintance with the great personages who have built their profession. Knight has produced a work which makes our educational builders as interesting and as worth knowing as any Galen, Paracelsus or Lister. In 1890 you could find many schoolmasters who had heard of John Locke, Comenius, Froebel, Rousseau, Herbert Spencer and Alexander Bain and who would hesitatingly name Horace Mann as perhaps comparable to the less important of these notables. As one acquaints himself with the educational philosophy of Jefferson, Noah Webster, Stanley Hall and Henry Morrison; as one reads citations from Charles Hubbard Judd and John Dewey in the educational journals of Europe, South America and Asia; as one sees our own leaders reviewed here he gets a conviction that for real educational philosophy, science and practical workings his country is not sitting below the salt.

Recommended that you read without delay the remarkable chapter 18, "The Lean Years."

*La Chalotais the Modern.* It was a year after Rousseau's "Emile" appeared that Louis Rene de la Chalotais, 60 years old, for his last 9 years attorney-general to the Parliament of Bretagne, issued his plan for national education.[11] He was concerned as a legislator with practical problems, but the philosophy implicit in his plan is important. Many of his then unheard-of innovations have become educational commonplaces in modern practise.

The human race, he held, is able to be improved. It needs improvement. National education to that end is a paramount duty. Public education is not directed toward the greatest public usefulness. It aims to perfect itself in its useless formalism. None of its pupils ever completes it properly. Out of a thousand, scarcely one preserves or uses his books for the rest of his life. On going out into the world a youth is interested in forgetting as soon as possible all that his pretended educators have taught him.

La Chalotais's effort as a practical statesman to put to work the aspirations of his time was hailed by Diderot and Grimm as epoch-making. He demands the wresting of education from the church. It must be a state function. Its teachers must be citizens—not those who give preference to heaven instead of to their native land. The purpose of education must be to enkindle the spirit of citizenship—in this case, to train Frenchmen.

His plan outlines in detail what should be taught and how. All the studies are detailed, the current practises criticized, better ways suggested.

For universal education, he is weak. The common people must know their place. Education is to make the good citizen of the better class.

*Advancing Neighbors.* From the University of Chicago Press comes a superb piece of beautiful book-craft, an account of education in the Dutch islands of the East Indies.[12] The authors tell a picturesque story of the people of Sumatra, Java and other races, their religions and daily life. Contrary to the myth of a lazy,

[11] Louis de la Chalotais, "Essay on National Education." Longmans, Green and Company, New York. 176 pp. $2.50.

[12] Edwin R. Embree, Margaret Sargent Simon, W. Bryant Mumford, "Island India Goes to School." University of Chicago Press. 120 pp. $2.00.

luxurious existence in the Tropics, the islanders are hard and diligent workers. They carry burdens no white man could bear. A baby totes his bundle as soon as he can walk. Native law and justice are swift. Manners and customs of castes are carefully ordered. When a wave of communism reached Java the leaders of the people staved it off. One village council decreed, with unconscious humor: No citizen may join a Communist party; if he does so he shall lose his communal rights in this village.

The government and industry—rubber, spices, etc.—of the island are described.

You learn what education was before European control. The Dutch set up schools to train administrators. Failure. The native aristocrats considered their sons good enough as they were. After various trials, Holland has built up a system with farm instruction, trade schools, continuation classes, centers for training teachers, institutes for popular literature, officials' instruction and colleges of medicine, law and engineering. The Dutch have built up in Island India one of the most effective series of schools that exists in any colonial empire. This account goes thoroughly into an appraisal of the aims and methods of the service.

The survey was made by the Institute of Pacific Relations, the cost paid by the Julius Rosenwald Fund. The illustrations are full-page cuts exquisitely rendered. The volume is issued to aid international understanding.

*Where Youth is Organized.* "Away with the punishment of children; cruel treatment drives them into crime. Use good example, firm discipline that they understand." These and similar exhortations appear on the school posters of the Russian Soviet. Many are reproduced in William Trow's[13] account of the "Young Pioneer" movement in Russia. It has killed the Boy Scouts. They were too military, too capitalistic, too remote from the industrial and political duties of the citizen. Professor Trow, who teaches educational psychology in the University of Michigan, has collected five interesting essays by Russian educators, setting forth the activities employed in character education and the aims which direct it. There is so much here of what our advocates of character training are trying to do that it would be foolish to let your anti-Bolshevik notions keep you from it. The writers are refreshingly certain and aggressive.

*Doctors Behind a Cook Book.* The principal may please the domestic science department by presenting a beautiful kitchen encyclopedia,[14] sponsored by physicians. Twelve thousand proved recipes, food values, marketing, forty pages of balanced menus suitable for various occasions, meals for weight-reducing, time tables, garnishings, table setting, carving, economies, sick-room service, child-feeding, cooking equipment, abundant pictures, many in color, and a stout binding are some of the excellencies recommending this work of Mrs. Lily Haxworth Wallace, national president of the American Associated Clubs of Domestic Science, chairman of the Home-Making Department of the New York City Federation of Women's Clubs, and director of domestic science for *The Woman's World.*

*Progress for the Blind.* A hundred years have now passed since America set up schools for the education of the blind. As a memorial volume[15] Harry Best revises and expands his previous works and offers an encyclopedic treatise on blindness and its prevention, the number and condition of blind persons in the United States, provisions for children, for adults, homes and work for them, pensions, indemnities, organizations and so forth.

Efforts to reach and help those who sit in darkness are increasingly determined. It may mean that a new day is dawning for them in which their estate will be higher than it has been hitherto in this world. In the fulness of faith, efforts will be brought to bear until the affliction will be lifted and blindness shall be

[13] William Clark Trow, "Character Education in Soviet Russia." The Ann Arbor Press, Ann Arbor, Michigan. 199 pp. $1.25.

[14] Lily Haxworth Wallace, "Woman's World Cook Book." American Medical Association, Chicago. 468 pp. $2.50, including a year's subscription to *Hygeia,* the Association's monthly health magazine.

[15] Harry Best, "Blindness and the Blind in the United States." The Macmillan Company, New York. 724 pp. $6.50.

no more. So does the author prophesy in the light of advances going forward.

*Sixty Vocations.* A well-arranged and attractively narrated book on vocations in 1934[16] comes from Little, Brown and Company. Its pictures are full-page photographs beautifully done and showing good-looking people at good-looking work. Messrs. Cottler and Brecht put the facts of wages, preparation, nature of work and so on for each of sixty vocations into narrative form with conversations between applicant and employed. The jobs are grouped for the mechanically minded, the artistic, those who work with people, the sellers, the advertisers and the nature lovers.

*He Knows Boys' Clubs.* Organizer of many clubs of boys, Mr. Henriques[17] puts his experience into an enthusiastic compendium, telling the aims, activities, financial desirabilities and management successes of this social service. Self-government by the boys is a basic principle with this worker. He makes much of the training of youth for its responsibilities of leadership toward a better society. He is a broad-minded psychologist of boy character and a foe to monotony.

*A Gentle Killing of Formalism.* Minnesota University Professor Gislason[18] could well be given a prize by audiences for the human treatise he has written on speech-making.

He notes the usual chasm between the listeners and the orations of school boys. We are all sympathetic with these youngsters, but what they say makes no real impression on us. We are interested only in their words and manner. We know they are speaking a piece.

I was principal of a school once that got pretty well out of this defect. Miss Eleanor Nightingale was the doctor. Her cure was to discourage the writing of speeches and of compositions that were to be spoken. Instead, Miss Nightingale had the speaker write heads: "1. To show the audience that Washington means much to-day," "2. To elicit the audience's admiration of his self teaching," "3. To arouse admiration for his generosity," and so on. Every outline was based on audience effect. Even when the previous grammar-school elocutionary aspiration cropped up, the Lady Nightingale would interrupt with a gentle "Wait a minute; better talk with them than at them."

Now, after these many years, I find Dr. Gislason's comforting assurance that this is a long-proved propriety. Only a very talented speaker can deliver a memorized address without loss of effect. Wendell Phillips, Webster, Gladstone and other masters whom the author names avoided writing their speeches. They composed out of doors, walking or cutting down trees.

Dr. Gislason treats of the damage done a speaker by the wrong placing of an audience. Henry Ward Beecher would confess to an audience, "I can't talk with these bare seats in front chilling me. May I wait until the ushers induce some hospitably minded friends in the rear of the hall to fill these benches?" It is odd to note how teachers, who insist that their listeners be seated to the teacher's best advantage, subject visiting speakers at conventions to the cold rebuff of empty seats down front. Some intelligent souls in McKeesport, Bloomsburg, Lockport and Hartford have remedied this defect. Southern teachers fill the front seats.

Dr. Gislason's treatise is so reasonable, so engaging, so appreciative of modern conditions as to take its place among the best books. It does not discourage by technical requirements. It sparkles with anecdotes emphasizing principles. Its illustrative extracts are of superior merit. Its repudiation of formalism, its foundation upon common experience make it an alluring book to read. Its clear and convincing presentations, its questions, exercises and recommended readings, mark it as a successful text in high school and college.

*Schools and One-Act Plays.* Dr. Cohen, head of the English Department of New York City's mammoth Washington Irving High School, reminds that the reputed first English comedy was written for performance by school boys[19]

[16] Joseph Cottler, Harold Brecht, "Careers Ahead." Little, Brown and Company, Boston. 312 pp. $2.50.

[17] Basil L. Q. Henriques, "Club Leadership." Oxford University Press. 114 5th Avenue, New York. 250 pp. $1.50.

[18] Haldor B. Gislason, "The Art of Effective Speaking." D. C. Heath and Company, Boston. 183 pp. $2.48.

[19] Helen Louise Cohen, "One Act Plays by Mod-

and that no form of literature holds so many attractions for students as does drama. I recall Dr. Cohen's classes theatrical. Her rehearsals were vitalized experiences in manners, voice, posture, timeliness, taste and management. What struck me as a refreshing contrast to other experiences was that, with fewer rehearsals than I was accustomed to, this quietly merry director sat with the audience, unworried, as the real performance was given. She relied on the student managers she had trained at rehearsal. Her present book is Dr. Cohen's seventh. It contains, in full, twenty-one single-act plays by O'Neill, Dawson, MacKaye, Synge, Dunsany, Milne, Stark Young, Maeterlinck, Galsworthy, Tarkington, Chekhov, Thornton Wilder, Lady Gregory, and others with critiques, study suggestions, vocabulary tests, and illuminating comments on workmanship, theaters of to-day, little playhouses, repertory companies, stage design, play-making, school dramatics and so on.

Courses in writing short plays do produce successful writers; but the opening of a vast field of culture for thousands who never become playwrights is the main justification. There are, here, accounts of the procedures in English and American schools.

Sixty thousand high-school pupils out of 120,000 in 390 American high schools studied are actively participating in school dramatics. Over seven hundred amateur societies in Great Britain are performing one-act plays. South Dakota is well up in the front line of a similar movement in the United States. The book contains costume illustrations designed and drawn by Dr. Cohen's students.

*Literature through the Ages.* To afford the student characteristic examples of the major streams of European literature in convenient form, to illustrate the literary and philosophic background of the English-speaking peoples, Professors Cross and Stover[20] meet the return of the course in general literature as noted in many colleges. The editors desire to aid in the broader view of culture thus attainable by the present generation. They present translations of Greek, Roman, Hebrew, Celtic, Norse, German, Spanish, Italian, Welsh, Dutch, Russian, Scandinavian and Oriental masterpieces which have influenced modern culture. The compilers group the works of antiquity according to poetry, philosophy, satire, etc. They follow the same plan with works of the middle ages and of subsequent epochs. Brief biographies of authors, critical estimates of their works, explanatory notes handy on the immediate page and an index by types of literature help the book to serve its purpose.

*The School Library by a Live Educator.* Lively-minded Lucile Fargo, admired by teachers, beloved by boys and girls, author of attractive stories of school and life, has written another library book.[21] It seems to me I could not undertake to be principal of a school without having several copies to pass out to teachers so as to talk with them about portions of it every now and then. Whether she is discussing the exasperating problem of missing books, the way to keep pupil self-government from running riot, teaching the use of a library, the qualities of a school librarian, home reading, helping the teachers of different subjects or any of the hundreds of problems learned by her experience or gathered from the long lists of books and papers she has studied, the author's temperament keeps dullness away from every page. She has made a fascinating book, distinguished for completeness, admirable for arrangement, facile because of analyses at the head of each chapter, lucid with pictures and drawings, handily utile because of an index made with a canny knowledge of what her readers will want and ought to be able to find economically.

*A Story of St. Francis of Assisi.* Lucille Borden[22] tells a colorful story of the son of a merchant of Assisi. He has a noble friend in Rome who dresses him in princely garb and sends him to the reception given to the daughter of the Doge of Venice. This spirited girl ad-

ern Authors.'' Harcourt, Brace and Company, New York. 579 pp. $1.40.

20 Tom Peete Cross, Clark H. Stover, ''Readings in the Literature of Europe.'' D. C. Heath and Company, Boston. 1194 pp. $4.00.

21 Lucile F. Fargo, ''The Library in the School.'' American Library Association, Chicago. 479 pp. $3.00.

22 Lucille Papen Borden, ''Sing to the Sun.'' The Macmillan Company, New York. 380 pp. $2.00.

mires him. He runs off in dread of the consequences of being found out. Home again in Assisi he comes under the spell of the teachings of the gentle and happy Francesco. Hither, too, comes the imperious lady. She also, melts in the radiant humanity of the strange gospel and sings to the Lord and the beauty of his world, to Brother Sun, who, fair and radiant, splendid and free, makes with his brightness the light by which we see. It is a tale of noble souls, of great love, happiness, beauty, sweet Lady Poverty, song, cheerful labor, smiling fields, sunny skies, olive groves and happy endings.

*Essays that Charm.* Variety, novelty, humor, adventure, thrills, civic obligation, are some of the qualities of a new school book on essays begun by the late Professor Leonard, of the University of Wisconsin, and completed by his colleague, Professor Pooley.[23] The younger author has helped the teaching by a discussion at the close of each of the thirty selections. A who's who opens each essay. Unemployment, the inquiring mind, a better war, how to behave when sick, Professor Leonard's own "Greatest Show on Earth," are some of the themes. There is a rich humanity in this book conveyed with singular charm.

*Poets of Romance.* Extended selections from poetical works, prose extracts showing what poets have said about poetry, personal letters, facsimile reproductions of manuscript and critical biographies make a distinguished volume prepared for college classes and for high school libraries.[24] It is a notable piece of work at an amazing price, done by an experienced critic and two university professors. It has an index of authors, titles and first lines.

*A Heath-University of Chicago Joint Project.* The Heaths, forty years ago agents and directors of the University of Chicago Press, have entered a joint publishing agreement with the university for issuing nine series of foreign language texts originated by the Chicago faculty as a pioneer experiment in teaching method. The basic principle of these 85 books is reading with enjoyment from the beginning. Additional titles are in preparation.

*Lore of the Commonwealths.* Do you know what state is named by a word meaning "this is the place"? What one, from "white with snow"? What commonwealth is "the blue-hen state"? What "the gem of the mountains"? "The Bonanza"? You're likely to guess wrong on "the Switzerland of America." What state has for its motto, "let the welfare of the people be the highest law"? What state has on its seal one eagle protecting another? What state flag is quartered? Of what states is the apple blossom the official flower? Who adopted the columbine? The black-eyed Susan? The yellowhammer is the legally selected bird of what commonwealth? The chickadee? The answering information is in Dr. Shankle's[25] picturesque compendium. He spent three years searching official documents, verifying traditions, collecting answers from questionnaires and engaging in personal correspondence. He sent to each state librarian proof sheets of his book for correction and additions. He has compiled an encyclopedia of state lore, history, nicknames and odds and ends which he has put into orderly classification. He has reproduced here all the state flags and seals. He has traced the names of mottoes to their original sources, Latin, Greek, Spanish and Indian. He has included a bibliography of state histories and an architectural description of state capitols. Here is a boon for puzzled librarians and bothered teachers confronted with embarrassing questions of the curious. Intended as a book of reference it has one of the wonderful indexes that have given Halsey Wilson international fame. Its facts are so intimate, its style so engaging that you will find yourself reading it by the hour for pure pleasure and concluding it is indispensable for a school or college library. Perhaps you are wrong in your surmise as to how Rhode Island got its name and will be surprised at the explanation that it is a corruption of the

23 Sterling A. Leonard, Robert C. Pooley, "Introducing Essays." Scott, Foresman, and Company, Chicago. 295 pp. $1.00.

24 James Stephens, Edwin L. Beck, Royal H. Snow, "English Romantic Poets." The American Book Company, New York. 817 pp. $3.00.

25 George Earle Shankle, "State Names, Flags, Seals, Songs, Birds, Flowers and Other Symbols." H. W. Wilson Company, New York. 512 pp. $3.50.

Dutch "Roodt Eylandt," the red island. Maybe you will abandon your "arid zone" idea in favor of an Arizona meaning "the maiden's land," which is prettier than another possible derivation "the place of chastisement." Dr. Shankle gives you for each locality all the derivations that are common, all the nicknames, all the songs, birds and flowers proposed for recognition and tells you the authority for each explanation. The Wilson Company also issues in a 16-page booklet at 25 cents, special rates for quantities, all this material for each of Massachusetts, Minnesota, Virginia and Washington. The company has copies for other states in preparation.

*Making a High-School Principal.* Dr. Cubberley's introduction to the new Houghton Mifflin work on high-school supervision[26] frankly puts into words what many a school superintendent has noted with amazement and regret, that the high-school principal is concerned less with securing good teaching than the elementary schoolmasters are. In fifteen years, says Dr. Cubberley, the elementary school principal has been made over. The change is passing up into the high-school principalship. This Douglass-Boardman book gives the movement a strong shove. Its opening chapter is a thorough and persuasive argument for the betterment of high-school teaching. Subject specialists are dangerous and effective at the same time. Some one must keep the idea of the whole forest in the minds of these tree experts. The best preliminary training for high-school teachers anywhere leaves a tremendous amount of necessities unlearned. Few humans grow as well as they might unless outside forces work on them. Who is to call up and direct the impulses? An utterly unfounded obsession that high-school teachers are superior to those considered as lower down does ossify many good people. Who is to keep them aware that they are part of the public school scheme and obligated to the same purpose of developing the all-around useful citizen? All the surveys come through with exposures of alarmingly poor high-school teaching. Whose business is it to see that their defects are cured? None of the objections to high-school supervision are permitted by these two authors to score. Encouraging, positive, detailed, their diagnosis is a good spanking of what is still the average high-school principal, though it is done with the velvet glove.

Having told the patient the unpleasant truths and interpolated good professional encouragement, the two doctors treat the whole case completely. Here is an efficient, a workable and an imperative scheme of high-school organization, regimen for department heads, planning, inspection and appraisal of teaching, conferences, follow up, types of supervisory services, lists of books the principal should have certain teachers read. There is a general bibliography and a full index.

The authors, convinced that teachers are human beings, sound the praises of cooperative work for high-grade teaching but cling to the thesis that high schools are not logically an organization for the unbothered happiness of teachers. A democratic supervision which is all camaraderie, popularity and sentimental acquiescence in teachers' whims is little better than graft of the taxpayers' money. This book is no apology.

*Home Made.* Here is a charming rendition of every-day duties of great moment. I imagine Dr. Dennis[27] realizes that the diurnal affairs around the house are charged with powers of unhappiness and delight. With a refreshing sense of the opportunities at hand in every home, be it ever so humble, she goes into having fun indoors, sharing with grandmother, fatigue, worry and the devil-to-pay, letting your affection be visible, foster parents, death in the family, parents as persons, jealousy, humor versus ridicule, why people quarrel, teasing, the father's part, the children's share, learning to overcome anger and fear, sex education, hospitality, courtship and marriage. If there is any feature of home life you have in mind the chances are this wise home doctor covers it here. Nothing is syrupy, everything is sane and practical.

Tolerance, understanding and generosity solve

[26] Harl R. Douglass, Charles W. Boardman, "Supervision in Secondary Schools." Houghton Mifflin Company, Boston. 564 pp. $2.75.

[27] Lemo T. Dennis, "Living Together in the Family." American Home Economics Association, Mills Building, Washington, D. C. 187 pp. $1.10.

the secret of a happy home. Like most valuable things they cost effort. But oh, boy, how it pays! Tell your mother she looks swank in that dress. Remember birthdays. Don't be an affection hog. See whether you can't arrange that one evening a week is family play-time for all to have fun together. Don't forget dad in your letters home. It costs nothing to add "and father" to "dear mother." It is good to stretch the truth in the right direction. A husband, in this book, always tells his wife after they come from a party that she was the prettiest girl there. "Of course I know," she says, "that it isn't true. But after years of married life if he still says so it means more to me than if I really were." More than that, Doctor, if he says so often enough it will be true to him. So will she.

This is a book primarily for boys and girls of high-school age. It has a great deal in it that was gleaned from frank talk with them. If you know a rich widow who wants to do something pretty in memory of her dear departed, suggest that she supply all the high-school libraries with copies. Every town has conceited cubs and catty girls that should be put through a course in it. It is a good tonic antidote for a parent-teacher's club that has had an overdose of John B. Watson stuff. Its questions at the end of each chapter are prime.

*Improving the Preparation of Teachers.* Gist of attack and defense in the gentlemanly warfare waged by some professors in liberal arts colleges against the promoters of professional training for teachers is contained in Yearbook 22 of the National Society of College Teachers of Eductaion.[28]

Fowler Brooks has collected the essence of discussions at the 1934 convention of the association. They are concerned with professional training, fitting for teaching, the new social order, the teaching of government, cooperation, importance of the history of education, intellectual growth, research, visual aids, current criticism, social factors and needs of the future.

Editor Brooks has retained the freshness and stimulus of the debates of live topics so that his report is full of nutrition for the school man in service. Professor Peik finds that teachers colleges now supply 9 per cent. more educational practitioners than are prepared by universities and other colleges. In a tenth of these newer institutions graduate work is now offered. The larger teachers colleges plan to prepare for all types of educational positions. Their faculties have, over the liberal arts college courses, the advantage of experience in public-school teaching. Teachers colleges have more student-teaching while studying and more supervision. Their instructors are more educationally and less scholastically minded.

It is strange that this last fact, often called a defect by liberal arts professors, is put forward as a planned-for superiority by the teachers college directors.

Of liberal arts institutions and teachers colleges combined, 66 per cent. are the former. But they produce only 40 per cent. of the nation's teachers.

Professor Crecraft raps the timid administrators who are afraid of stimulating discussions on politics in the classroom, not trusting the preparation of their teachers. The public-school system was established to furnish the political intelligence needful to maintain and improve popular government. If, he says, the nation is to succeed in operating representative democracy, education must teach politics better. This is not yet adequately recognized in the preparation offered public school teachers and superintendents.

Dr. Reisner points out the futility of mere descriptive and analytical study of government. It is too dead. We will never have right civic attitudes until controversial political problems are a large part of the subject of school activities. The machinery of government is interesting; but the way it works is the main political concern of the properly educated citizen.

Kenneth Williams and Ernest Horn enter the ring for the championship of liberal arts colleges or teachers colleges on the question of whether too much professionalism is fostered by the teacher training institution. Ernest closes, waving this olive branch: "The prospective teacher is to be pitied if enrolled in an institution in which the college of liberal arts and the college of education spend time firing blasts and counterblasts of criticism at each other."

[28] Twenty-one contributors, "Studies in Education. XXII. Abstracts of Papers." University of Chicago Press. 60 pp. 60 cents.

# SCHOOL AND SOCIETY

WITH WHICH ARE COMBINED THE EDUCATIONAL REVIEW, ESTABLISHED IN 1891, THE TEACHERS MAGAZINE, ESTABLISHED IN 1878, AND THE SCHOOL JOURNAL, ESTABLISHED IN 1874.

Volume 40 | SATURDAY, AUGUST 11, 1934 | Number 1024

## THE TRADITIONAL CURRICULUM OF THE HIGH SCHOOL IS CHALLENGED BY THE ACTIVITY CURRICULUM OF THE ELEMENTARY SCHOOL[1]

By Professor JUNIUS L. MERIAM

UNIVERSITY OF CALIFORNIA AT LOS ANGELES

I HAVE taken the liberty to change the form of the title of this paper, from that assigned me, to its present form in order that I may emphasize the one curriculum as pitted against the other curriculum. The high school and the elementary school as distinct organizations are of less concern just now. Then, too, this title, in the form of a declarative sentence, is indeed a declaration of opposition between two forces—and forces they are.

This title reminds me of numerous observations when a small boy on a farm. It was regarded for the welfare of the poultry division that occasionally a rooster from a neighbor's flock be introduced to our flock. There was usually a sharp conflict between the home rooster and the newcomer. The adult farmer is author of the saying: "A cock fights best on his own dung hill." However, sometimes the new rooster carries off the honors. Sometimes, too, there is an honorable draw between them.

Now I feel quite at home in both of these curriculum camps. But I wish to do more than merely look on at this "cock-fight." I prefer to play the rôle of umpire in this conflict. But do not expect a conflict between bantam roosters, but rather a Plymouth Rock of traditional fame, challenged by a Rhode Island Red with a considerable amount of red activity.

The word challenge is a strong term. The party on the challenging side believes that it sees in the party challenged certain deficiencies or certain characteristics not in harmony with the party of the first part. They are irritating. The aggressor is usually of the self-proclaimed progressive type. He wishes to mend matters. He is sufficiently self-centered to believe that he can contribute to the improvement of the other party.

I plan the conduct of this challenge in three parts; "rounds," if you please.

(1) I shall endeavor to point out in the traditional curriculum of the high school certain policies, certain practises that are definitely deficiencies in the judgment of one who dares to be frankly critical and honestly helpful.

(2) I shall try to place the activity curriculum strictly in the open. This new movement has unquestionably marked virtues, so marked as to warrant it playing

[1] Read before the Department of Secondary School Principals of the National Education Association, Cleveland, on February 27, 1934.

the rôle of David going out to meet Goliath. But let me be sufficiently judicious to remark that unless some of its gross inadequacies are overcome serious misfortune will take place.

(3) I wish to show how the traditional curriculum of the high school can meet this challenge with such professional spirit and timely courage that real victory is accorded both of our contestants.

To attempt to evaluate the traditional curriculum of the high school within the first third of this paper is a dangerous undertaking; yet more dangerous to try to expose those phases which warrant a challenge by the activity curriculum of the elementary school. I feel sure I shall express views with which many—even most—of you will not agree. I have no apologies to make. Sincere professional disagreements are tonic in educational endeavor. I shall say some things very baldly because of my strong convictions and by reason of not having time to "beat about the bush."

The North Central Association of Colleges and Secondary Schools took the initiative, in 1928, asking that an extensive study be made "that we may know where we stand in secondary education." The Office of Education at Washington was invited to conduct this survey. Commissioner Cooper was director and associated with him was a staff of experts in secondary education. The results of this study are published in 28 monographs, issued by the Office of Education.

This series of monographs can not give us the whole of the picture of secondary education, but is probably the most reliable account we have of current secondary school practise and theory. I shall base my evaluations on representative portions of this survey supplemented by my own observation and experience in secondary schools.

*Monograph No. 5. "The Reorganization of Secondary Education"*: Here we come very abruptly upon one of the occasions for the challenge by the "Activity Curriculum." And I make bold to say that I suspect few of you secondary school men are aware of how this "reorganization of secondary education" contributes to instigating this challenge. Believe it or not: Extensive reorganization has been effected and is now continuing with little significant regard for the real curriculum work of the school. Reorganization for the purpose of organization—an administrative affair. I have examined this volume of 423 pages, in search of sufficient occasion for reorganization. The first paragraph in this unwarranted long monograph tells the story. "The chief purpose of this study has been to determine what existing forms of American secondary-school organization are of greatest promise. . . . in particular, to discover the effects of the junior high school movement upon practice in school organization. . . ." Koos, in his book, "The Junior High School," indicates various forces responsible for this reorganization movement.

(1) Time is wasted. Pupils do not progress as rapidly as do European pupils. Therefore, reorganize.

(2) Pupil mortality is great in the upper grades. Therefore reorganize to induce pupils to continue in school—as though continuance in school is a virtue irrespective of the nature of school occupation.

(3) School authorities desire their schools to be known as "progressive," even if the change made is a mere superficial regrouping of grades.

I invite you school principals to be frank and honest—courageously so. I invite you to agree with me that the subject-matter courses of seventh, eighth and ninth grades have been given little significant change by reason of the much-boasted reorganization of secondary education. Likewise, grades ten, eleven and twelve. You will recall this when you face the challenge of the "Activity Curriculum."

It is well to look into reports upon the more prominent of these school subjects.

*Monograph No. 20. "Instruction in English":* Here we find many statistical tables and charts presenting a variety of time allotments. Aims of teaching composition—fifteen of these nicely charted, followed by eighteen more labeled "Specific Aims of Written Composition," also nicely charted; then twenty aims of oral composition nicely charted. Fifty-three aims for composition! Chapters follow treating in similar fashion the other two traditional divisions of this traditional English, *viz.*, grammar and literature. In the conclusion of this English survey we find three significant statements:

(1) There is . . . in composition a preoccupation with matters of form and surprisingly little concern with having something to say.

(2) The stress upon grammar technicalities . . . seems curiously unwarranted. . . .

(3) In the division of literature . . . intensive study of a few set classics persists in a large number of courses.

Are you principals sufficiently intimate with your students to realize that such composition, grammar, classics, are positively obsolete in the current life of red-blooded, buoyant American youth?

On this score a challenge by the activity curriculum is forthcoming. And closely related to English are all the foreign languages. Let me surprise you by putting in this same group the conventional high-school music, art—yes, and physical education.

*Monograph No. 23. "Instruction in Mathematics":* The reorganization of secondary education, referred to above, has left almost undisturbed the arithmetic of grades seven and eight—formerly of the elementary school, now of the junior high. True, some schools report the addition of so-called "general mathematics," but under this caption one readily recognizes chapters from the traditional arithmetic, *e.g.*, fundamental operations, percentage, areas, graphs, arithmetic of business, etc., etc. Algebra in grade nine of the junior high school retains the earmarks and nearly all the other marks of the algebra in the high school before reorganized. This survey reveals in the senior high-school mathematics "more emphasis on disciplinary and cultural values than on practical outcomes. . . ."

It is playing with fire to even question the prominence accorded this time-honored and almost sacred division—Mathematics. Are you principals willing to secure honest statements from your students as to their likes and dislikes in mathematics from grade seven on; and are you willing to be strictly consistent in your advocacy of functional mathematics and your administration of mathematics courses? Again, I am anticipating the challenge which the activity curriculum is soon to make.

*Monograph No. 21. "Instruction in the Social Studies":* The survey shows that in the great majority of schools the arrangement of courses in this group is largely as existed before the "reorganization of secondary education." The prevailing plan is:

| | | |
|---|---|---|
| United States history | grades | 7, 8 |
| Geography | " | 7 |
| Community civics | " | 8, 9 |
| World history | " | 10 |
| Modern European history | " | 11 |
| American history | " | 11, 12 |
| American government | " | 12 |

You and I went through this same program.

The survey concludes to this effect: Some schools claim great activity in curriculum revision. Other schools have not engaged in such activities. But in both groups the actual content of instruction in geography, history, civics is essentially as formerly. And these three distinct subjects of earlier years are now combined in a most peculiar arithmetical sum, "the social studies," but each retains its own identity.

Again, I ask you principals if you are in the classroom enough to sympathize with pupils who are obliged to work upon geography quite foreign to lives they are living; on history so much in the past as to have little vital contact with present life; on forms of government rather than on the governing of life. Here is another warrant for a challenge by the activity curriculum.

I have gone far enough in presenting representative situations in your high schools. Have I been unfair in thus boldly questioning the accepted values of English—grammar, composition, literature; in raising serious doubts as to the conventional worth of arithmetic, algebra, geometry; in daring to even intimate that geography, history, civics are not real social studies at all? But I am earnestly endeavoring to prepare you for a challenge that will surprise—even shock—those of you who are not conversant with the activity curriculum of the elementary school.

I have known secondary school principals well enough in the past quarter of a century to hear some of your own thoughts just now. To this effect: Whatever be the truth of what has been here exposed, we are not responsible. Social custom, you say, selects teachers prepared to teach these subjects in the conventional way and social custom supplies text-books loaded with content to be taught. And further, college entrance requirements dictate the courses and the units with which the high-school graduate must be equipped.

Here is a fifth warrant for the challenge soon to come. And you may expect its first appearance at this point. But before this challenge is made, it is imperative that the activity curriculum of the elementary school be somewhat examined.

Now we are in trouble. English grammar, algebra, American history, these we know. But what is this activity curriculum? Evidence indicates that nobody knows, though many think they do. It is interesting to note that within the past two weeks three studies of these activities have been made public: (1) The National Society for the Study of Education presents its thirty-third Yearbook on "The Activity Movement." (2) The Informal Teaching Committee of the New York Principals' Association presents an "Analysis of Trends in an Informal Unit [Activity] Teaching Program." This is published in the January issue of *Teachers College Record*. (3) "A Critical Survey of 1,000 Activities" was presented this morning before the American Education Research Association by the writer of this paper.

I wish to give you first an epitome of the findings and the conclusions of these three studies. You, as secondary school principals, probably think that three such studies would clarify the issue and give expression to a notion of the activity curriculum satisfactory to leading educationists as well as to the intelligent public. But not so. The keen and able critic, Bagley, characterizes the activity program as "fundamentally fallacious" in certain respects; as "totally blind to two fundamental facts"; as "perilous" in other respects.[2] Such criticism is cutting and severe. My own studies of this activity curriculum, in theory and in practise, have led me to agree so far with these criticisms of Bagley and others that I am unable to see in the activity curriculum, as it now is, a challenge worthy of any retort by the traditional curriculum of the high school. I hope, however, to show certain underlying principles in this activity movement so in tune with modern life—of the best type—that you principals will be pleased with the challenge.

In attempting to give you a very limited word-picture of these three quite extended studies, it is obviously impossible to adequately present many phases regarded as

2 See Thirty-third Yearbook, National Society for the Study of Education, Part II, p. 77.

important. I think I can contribute perspective by calling to mind the "project-method" of teaching, so popular a decade or so ago. Simply this. Teachers recognized that pupils had difficulties in learning the old school subjects—even indispositions towards such learnings. They recognized that these same pupils acted readily and joyfully in their own affairs—projects they were called. Only a little pedagogical ingenuity was needed to put these two—normal life projects and formal class subjects—together and, presto, we had the effective project method of teaching the three R's. This procedure was extensive in the elementary schools. It was used only a little in high schools.

The activity curriculum is an extension of this project-method. I shall briefly present four aspects of this movement, as it now appears in practise.

(1) The Activity Curriculum emphasizes child life. Of the normal boy it is said: "He cries, he laughs; he sees, he hears, he feels, he tastes; he runs, he walks, he rests; he eats, he sleeps, he wakes; he whistles and sings; he listens to stories and tells big whoppers, too; he quarrels and even fights at times; he asks questions and gives expression to an apparently independent self; he plays, he works—and sometimes shirks. All this and much more is characteristic of the boy," and of his sister.[3] Normal child life is full of movement, rich with joy and gladness and safely allowed large freedom. In harmony with this child life, the activity school provides generously for physical movement—physical exercise and play, excursions and construction work. The school encourages joy and gladness by basing the program upon interests rather than upon discipline. The child is granted large freedom to choose what he is to do and freedom to change as he sees fit.

(2) The Activity Curriculum emphasizes social contacts. The "socialized recitation" has been a stepping stone to this new movement. The school has become a social unit. A large measure of informal democracy reigns. Self-government is allowed. And more—increased contacts are made with the out-of-school community, social and industrial. Cooperation is claimed. Group spirit prevails in the school; parents make more positive contributions to the school in response to the extended interests of the pupils. All this is due to the so-called "social studies," as one of the prominent divisions of the new school curriculum.

(3) The Activity Curriculum emphasizes a principle called "integration." This is a new term in our educational nomenclature. But the term is obviously used with two distinct meanings. By some, the reference is to a unit in the life of a child. To use Kilpatrick's language: ". . . a unitary sample of actual child living." By others —a larger number indeed—integration is essentially a further development of the earlier term "correlation." Under this notion an activity unit of study carries out the principle of integration when it provides for a correlation of the variety of school subjects. Thus the term is used in relating school subjects around an activity as center.

(4) The Activity Curriculum emphasizes the method aspect of learning. More than a quarter of a century ago, the psychologist James emphasized the idea that impression depends upon expression. Later, learning by doing was emphasized. And now we have—Activity is a learning process. Here is the most conspicuous feature in this activity curriculum. The traditional subjects, with their skills and knowledges, are intimately and almost continually related to the activity. A statement from the last Yearbook expresses the prevailing situation. ". . . the children's effort is utilized in enriching the required subject-matter and in furthering its learning.

3 In *Childhood Education,* April, 1925.

What the learner does in this way is regarded as a means of getting the subject-matter learned."[4] Here we have essentially the project-method.

In each of these four aspects, a serious weakness is present.

(1) The activity curriculum as it now prevails coddles and pampers children by catering to their interests. The extreme freedom granted pupils in this new movement becomes a license based on coddling rather than on child welfare. I fear it reflects against the teacher's ability and preparation to guide, rather than does credit to child judgment and self-control.

This serious weakness is not a challenge to the traditional curriculum of the high school.

(2) The much-vaunted cooperation in social experience jeopardizes hard, serious, individual work and continued effort. The discipline of accomplishing tasks, laid out by adequately prepared teachers, is lacking. Too much superficial work is done under the guise of social cooperation.

This second serious weakness is not a challenge.

(3) "Integration" has no significance when used to indicate a unit in the normal life of children, and to effect a correlation of school subjects about a life activity is to make relationships without value and heap indignities upon the beautiful activities of childhood.

The Activity Curriculum now in practise is not a creditable challenge at this point.

(4) Activities used to motivate uninviting subjects-to-be-studied as a method of stimulating the learning process is positively belittling to our teaching procedures and greatly lowers the valuation of the life activities of children.

Let us not countenance a challenge here.

This Activity Curriculum of the elementary school is seriously jeopardized by the four weaknesses presented above. But candid judgment must thus evaluate this curriculum as described in educational literature and as seen in schoolroom procedure. This is the natural consequence of the efforts of teachers whose enthusiasm for progress is not governed by adequate study of principles involved. You who are responsible for the direction of secondary education are invited to look beneath these weaknesses. The Activity Curriculum in principle is far more than it has yet appeared to be. I invite your attention to three commendable aspects and to the challenge they make.

(1) The Activity Curriculum of the elementary school is sufficient unto itself and the immediate lives of the pupils; it is not a stepping stone to high-school work. To the high credit of our secondary schools, pupils in the lower schools have never been called upon to pursue certain grammar or arithmetic or geography as prerequisites for admission to high school. The activity curriculum pays no disrespect to the high school by utterly disregarding preparation for high-school work.

Here is the first challenge: that the high school assign itself the task of serving youth (12 to 18 years of age) without regard to college entrance requirements. Secondary schools have long been so enslaved to college entrance that the majority of youth are sacrificed for the relatively few. The challenge is direct—that you in secondary schools provide that education which equips youth for participation in home and industry and society. All high schools should be trade schools, in the sense that secondary education serve the large majority instead of the small minority. This is not a new message. But most of our high schools serve the higher institutions rather than youth in the everyday walks of life: they are under the domination of the college entrance rather than public service.

[4] Thirty-third Yearbook, Part II, of the National Society for the Study of Education, page 71.

The Progressive Education Association has announced a unique adventure. Twenty-seven high schools selected on the basis of progressive tendencies have an arrangement with a goodly number of colleges and universities whereby their graduates will be admitted to freshman standing without complying with the usual requirements. This leaves the high school free to serve local interests. The results of this experiment will be watched with great interest. In the meantime, are our high schools willing to serve their own students rather than higher schools? There is evidence that college students would probably be of higher order than at present. But that is not our concern just now.

(2) The Activity Curriculum of the elementary school takes its subject-matter directly from real life and thus avoids the abstractions which constitute practically all the subjects of the traditional curriculum. The challenge now is of large dimensions. It calls for a discontinuance of English literature, grammar, composition; of arithmetic, algebra, geometry; of geography, history, civics. Freed from college entrance requirements and social custom, this new procedure in dealing with real activities would be strictly normal. But this challenge must be made more specific.

For some years there has been a distinct tendency to stress in English courses the preparation for wholesome leisure. But let us take a long stride forward. Increasing leisure time is upon us. Better preparation is imperative. In the high school connected with the University of Missouri twenty years ago, we provided a leisure reading room. In this room we placed all the wholesome reading books we could command. A teacher was present, not to teach and make assignments, but to be a leading companion with students who were allowed at least one hour each day in this room. The room was equipped for comfort; rocking chairs, sofas, a variety of chairs and tables, flowers and plants—even canary birds. But we must now provide much further. Music rooms are needed, providing opportunity for choral work and instrumental, and for appreciation. Art and museum rooms are needed, richly supplied with pictures that please and inspire. The moving picture merits a large place in schools, to supplant the unwholesome commercial supply or as a means of helping to improve the choice by moving picture fans. Dramatic work in our high schools is too largely superficial and demoralizing. It is largely for petty show. It merits much more time, attention, guidance, leading to a much higher type of wholesome self-entertainment. A great variety of game rooms are needed, suitably equipped. The social dance, too, a large factor in the recreational life of youth, needs the guidance of our schools. Many complaints are made against the social life of high-school youth. The schools are largely responsible. Composition, algebra, foreign language, history, etc., etc., an uninteresting daily grind with tedious home assignments, all drive the youth to seek relief in social life, not always wholesome.

Two hours each day of such leisure activities under helpful guidance would be appropriate, not as a teaching-learning situation, but as a part of normal life that rightfully belongs to youth.

This is the challenge for one third of the school day.

The Activity Curriculum calls for another two-hour period each day in a variety of work activities, *e.g.,* wood shop and metal, print shop and office, cooking and sewing, laundry and hairdressing, etc., etc., etc. Everybody busy two hours each day in wholesome occupation. What an influence upon habits of industry!

The Activity Curriculum calls for a third two-hour period devoted to acquiring an understanding of the very complex environment in which we live—nature all about us and human nature all around us. Here is an education far more fundamental than the so-called fundamentals in our schools.[5] But the studies must relate to concrete issues, not to generalizations composing our traditional school subjects. (Professor Bruner, in the January, 1934, issue of the *Teachers College Record,* lays emphasis upon this type of fundamental education.)

Thus the large, inclusive, three-in-one challenge invites the high school to provide a daily program of three two-hour periods, one for leisure activities, one for work activities, one for informational activities. This encompasses the range of the life of youth and does not direct all to college.

You principals are now wondering about the disciplines of English grammar, the algebraic equation, the sequence of history. A third challenge of the Activity Curriculum invites you to recognize such disciplines, so far as they have values, as strictly incidental to the larger values in the activities of real life. As pointed out above, too frequently the activity curriculum, as the project-method before it, serves as a teaching situation, a motivation for learning. Various researches in the elementary school field indicate that the formal skills are yet better acquired when the acquiring is strictly incidental to the activity in which they function. Thus, secondary schools may be justified in placing grammar, algebra, history and all allied subjects on the reference shelf, to be used only as the development of an activity calls for their use.

The Activity Curriculum of the elementary school is a school organization of child life and its environment for the purpose of enriching child life. This Activity Curriculum is a bold break from tradition, but for the sincere purpose of greater service to children, for their improvement.

The Activity Curriculum of the elementary schools looks upon the traditional curriculum of the high school with sympathy. It realizes the great pressure from above, *i.e.,* requirements stipulated by higher institutions. It realizes also the great pressure in the undercurrent of social custom, expressed in the traditional curriculum. But far more does it realize the yet greater pressure of modern life—service to youth.

The traditional curriculum of the high school is challenged by the activity curriculum of the elementary school to do three things: (1) Render service to youth, irrespective of college entrance; (2) help boys and girls to participate in the vital issues of current life, in leisure and in work, irrespective of the traditional school subjects; (3) help adolescent youth to evaluate school *arts* as incidental to life *acts.*

Supplement

A general organization for scheduling an "Activity Curriculum" is proposed.

| | Leisure | Work | Information |
|---|---|---|---|
| Sec. 1. | 8:30–10:30 | 10:30–12:30 | 1:00– 3:00 |
| 2. | 10:30–12:30 | 1:00– 3:00 | 8:30–10:30 |
| 3. | 1:00–3:00 | 8:30–10:30 | 10:30–12:30 |

| | | |
|---|---|---|
| *Reading:* | *Shops:* | *Raw Products:* |
| Fiction | Carpenter | Farming |
| Travel | Cabinet | Mining |
| Science | Metal | Fishing |
| Poetry | Paint | Etc. |
| Etc. | Etc. | |
| *Music:* | *Household arts:* | *Manufacturing:* |
| Choral | Cooking | Textiles |
| Instrumental | Sewing | Rubber |
| Orchestra | Art-Crafts | Metal |
| Appreciation | Etc. | Foods |
| Etc. | | Etc. |
| *Picture:* | *Office:* | *Commerce:* |
| Painting | Stenography | Trade |
| Moving | Correspondence | Transportation |
| Etc. | Bookkeeping | Etc. |
| | Etc. | |

[5] Compare "Fundamentals in the Elementary School Curriculum," N. E. A. *Proceedings,* 1909: 169–175.

| | | |
|---|---|---|
| *Dramatics:* | *Industry:* Printing Garage Weaving Gardening Etc. | *Government:* Courts Police Etc. |
| *Games:* Cards Social Athletic Etc. | *Etc.:* | *Recreation (study of):* Travel Sports Etc. |
| *Dance:* Social Folk Etc. | | *Etc.:* |
| *Etc.:* | | |

Such a schedule calls for:

(1) The school divided into three sections (large school or small).

(2) The platoon system—the whole plant occupied all the time.

(3) Long sessions—not too long. Only one exchange of classes, at 10:30, in addition to the half-hour for lunch.

(4) No assignments or home work—but interest leads to much work done by guided choice.

# EDUCATIONAL EVENTS

## ENGLISH CHILDREN IN AUSTRALIA

*The Christian Science Monitor* states that out of 1,000 children transferred during a period of 18 years from poor surroundings in England to a sunny, healthy farm school in Western Australia only six have had to be returned. The Fairbridge Farm School at Pinjarra with this record claims to have shown that this is a successful form of emigration, satisfactory both to the emigrants and to the country of their adoption.

Out of this thousand there are 300 still at the school and 700 are at work in Australia—none being unemployed. So well known are the Fairbridge boys and girls that during the last two years there were about 1,000 applications for the 100 due to leave the school.

A movement has been set on foot by the Child Emigration Society in London to extend the farm school idea to the other Dominions as the founder, Kingsley Fairbridge, originally intended. It was planned to fill the empty spaces of the Empire with British stock, and to give the poorer children from the crowded cities a new life which would turn them into good Australians, good Canadians, good South Africans, as the case might be. It is hoped to raise £100,000 to establish three more farm schools.

At a meeting held in London recently the Prince of Wales appealed for funds and headed the list himself with a donation of £1,000.

Under the Fairbridge method the children, boys and girls, are taken overseas when about eleven to twelve years old. They are housed on the 5,000-acre Pinjarra estate in cottages which become their homes. They receive the state education until they are fourteen and for the last eighteen months are trained as well on the farm. When they go out to employment, an after-care and savings system helps them until they can stand alone. Among old students unemployment, even in these latter difficult years, has been unknown. Over 600 individual savings accounts under the trusteeship of the farm officials has grown by the end of 1932 to a sum of over £7,835.

At present the cost of maintaining the Pinjarra School is shared by the Commonwealth and Western Australia Governments and that of Great Britain. Both countries regard it as good business for each, and not a mere matter of sentiment. England is relieved of a certain number of poor children and the Dominion gets the same number of first-class citizens.

## FEDERAL LOANS FOR TEACHERS SALARIES IN CHICAGO

The *Monitor* bureau reports that with a $25,447,240 federal loan assured the school board of Chicago is looking forward to the immediate prospect of paying its public school teachers for seven months of uncompensated service. An Illinois Supreme Court decision on August 1 on the constitutionality of the loan cleared the way.

This decision is said to be bringing to an end Chicago's "educational dark age," a period of more than three years when teachers worked with few and uncertain pay days. Pay checks amounting to $21,591,000 are ready to go out. The loan means also a significant departure in government finance, according to students of local government, for according to the American Municipal Association this will be the first time a branch of local government in the country has received credit from the Federal Government for operating expense.

The *Monitor* writes:

> To most Chicago teachers, the approaching pay day means coming out from under a burden of debt and worry which has made their task of teaching a most difficult one for more than three years. To students of municipal government, it means a step in the direction of easing the interest burden of local government.
>
> To the municipal government experts, this forecasts the possibility of federal loans to cities, which would enable them to borrow at lower interest rates than are now possible. Since many governmental units, like the Chicago Board of Education, finance themselves by issuing anticipation warrants on taxes due but not collected, and must pay high rates of interest on such loans, federal credit would do much to relieve the burden of interest in such localities, it was said.
>
> Of course, further legislation would be necessary for such borrowing, as the recent act of Congress applied only to school districts which are able to give as security land not used for school purposes.
>
> Chicago is peculiarly well situated to offer security. Even when it had not a cent in its cash box to pay a single teacher, it has held property worth millions in the downtown district, leased to owners of skyscrapers.
>
> One entire block in the heart of the "Loop", bounded by Madison, Monroe, State and Dearborn Streets, is school property. Frontage of such Loop landmarks as the First National Bank and the Boston Store is also owned in part by the board as is the site of the municipal airport. Yet, until the Supreme Court handed down its decision, there appeared no way for the board to realize cash from borrowing on these valuable holdings.

## REGULATIONS GOVERNING FEDERAL AID TO STUDENTS

The University of Texas reports that under the provisions of the Federal Emergency Relief Administration it is enabled to provide for its students 651 jobs, of which 428 are for men and 223 for women students, on the basis of the percentage of men and women students in the total enrolment. Of these jobs at least 50 per cent. go to freshmen, or to students who were not students in January.

The principal regulations governing the allotment of jobs include the following:

> Funds allotted shall be used to pay students for doing socially desirable work, including the sort customarily done in the institution by students who are working their way through college, such as clerical, library, and research work. Regular class instruction shall be excluded, but students may be assigned to extension, adult education, recreation and other activities that increase the usefulness of the college to the community. Each institution shall pass on the acceptability of its own work projects. All jobs must be under the direct charge of the institution.
>
> Inasmuch as the principal objective of using relief funds for student aid is to increase the number of young men and women going to college, funds allotted shall not be used to replace college funds heretofore available for student aid. Ordinary maintenance work about the college, waiting on table in dining halls and other routine activities that would have to be carried on anyway shall be financed from the usual sources, not from FERA funds. Violation of the spirit of this provision shall be considered a cause for withdrawing a college's entire allotment of student aid funds and assigning it to other institutions.
>
> The students shall be selected for the jobs on the following considerations:
>
> Need—the student's financial status shall be such as to make impossible his attendance at college without this aid; character and ability to do college work—the students shall be of good character and judged by the usual methods of determining ability employed by the particular college, shall possess such ability as to give assurance that they will do high grade work in college; status as to present attendance—at least 50% of the funds allotted to the institution shall be paid to students who were not regularly enrolled in any college or university during January, 1934; equitable division between sexes—jobs shall be allocated between boys and girls in proportion to the enrollment of each in the particular school.
>
> The hourly rate of pay shall be such as is commonly paid by the institution for the type of service rendered but not less than 30 cents an hour.
>
> No student shall work more than 30 hours in any week or 8 hours in any day.

Each institution benefitting from the terms of this relief program is permitted to give part-time employment to 12 per cent. of its enrolment of full-time students as of October 15, 1933.

## THE BUREAU OF CHILD GUIDANCE IN THE NEW YORK CITY SCHOOLS

DR. LEON W. GOLDRICH, director of the Bureau of Child Guidance in the New York City schools, recommended the establishment of a child guidance unit in each of the five boroughs and the enlargement of the present staff of the bureau in his annual report to Dr. Harold G. Campbell, superintendent of schools.

At the present time, according to a summary of the report appearing in *The New York Times*, the only unit of the bureau is in Manhattan, and the work of the other boroughs is done through that office. There is an increasing demand by teachers, supervisors and social agencies for more intensive service of the bureau. Its work has received encouraging indorsement from leaders in crime prevention and juvenile delinquency. Dr. Goldrich believes that the bureau should be extended so that its services may be available to all the schools in the city and to all departments in the city's educational system.

Out of one group of 586 children who were examined and for whom treatment was given or recommended more than 60 per cent. made definite improvement and approximately one third were entirely freed from the difficulties for which they were referred to the bureau.

The report goes into the economic and social plans of the New Deal with the work of the public-school system and points out that if the gains already made are to become permanent, the schools of the country must educate all the children and adults in such a way that the new social life will be thoroughly understood. During the last school year the bureau stressed the fact that mental hygiene, like physical and personal hygiene, has positive and constructive educational values for all children.

The bureau during the last school year continued its cooperative relationship with the Crime Prevention Bureau, the Welfare Council, the Juvenile Protective Association of Brooklyn, the City Committee on Mental Hygiene, the local colleges and hospitals and the New York Principals' Association.

It is reported that during March and April, twenty-two Civil Works Administration workers were assigned to the bureau, and that in the first ten months of the school year, 1,884 children were examined by the personnel of the bureau and the C. W. A. workers. Of this number, 919 were given psychological examinations or group tests, or were tutored in arithmetic or reading by C. W. A. workers under the direction of the regular staff. Nine hundred and twenty-four children were studied and recommendations made or treatment given. Of this number 673 were referred to the bureau for the first time and 251 were carried over for treatment from the previous year. The intelligence quotient tests showed a particularly high amount of retardation in reading and arithmetic.

Complete physical tests were given to 192 children by the bureau, of which thirty-three were found to be without any physical defects; 41 per cent. of the others had one defect; 40 per cent. had two and 19 per cent. had three or more. It is stated that malnutrition was particularly noteworthy and that 26 per cent. of those examined showed either mild or severe malnutrition.

## THE BACHELOR OF PHILOSOPHY DEGREE AT BROWN UNIVERSITY

BROWN UNIVERSITY, the first institution in the United States to award the degree of bachelor of philosophy, will discontinue the degree for students entering in September or thereafter. For students completing liberal arts courses, the degree of bachelor of arts only will be awarded.

Under the new plan, the A.B. degree will be awarded either for the satisfactory completion of present A.B. admission and graduation requirements, which include the study of Latin or Greek, or for the satisfactory completion of present Ph.B. admission and graduation requirements, which do not include Latin or Greek. Students will be expected to choose one of the two programs and to keep within the present limits of the program chosen.

Although all liberal arts students in the class of 1938 and thereafter will be awarded the A.B. degree only, should any member of the present undergraduate classes now engaged in a Ph.B. program prefer the Ph.B. degree, his preference will be respected.

The degree of Ph.B. was introduced at Brown University by President Francis Wayland in 1850 as one item in his celebrated and drastic proposal of a new educational program. It was adopted in order to open the college to students who had not had the regular classical training of the preparatory schools. At first the degree was regarded as inferior to the A.B. degree because students were admitted without the usual classical training and also because the requirements for the degree in college were not so large. For entrance, slightly more mathematics was required for the Ph.B. degree than for the A.B., but no Latin or Greek.

In 1873, however, the requirements for a Ph.B., before entrance and in college, were stiffened. In 1903 the number of units required for entrance was raised to the number required of A.B. candidates. Successively in 1918 and 1919 the standards for the degree were raised, and for many years the two liberal degrees, A.B. and Ph.B., have stood on equal footing in respect to the number and difficulty of requirements. The chief difference between them has been the requirement of ancient languages for the A.B. and more mathematics for the Ph.B.

## THE NEW PRIZE FELLOWSHIPS AT HARVARD UNIVERSITY

TEN boys from the Middle West, with exceptional school records, have been awarded the first of the new prize fellowships at Harvard College for entering freshmen of unusual ability and promise. The fellowships are an experiment, for they are awarded regardless of financial need, but at the same time carry maximum stipends of $1,000 in the freshman year and $1,200 each year thereafter, depending on the financial resources of the recipients.

This affords unusual opportunity for talented boys of limited means who would otherwise find it difficult to obtain a college education. The selection was based on considerations of character, originality and initiative, as well as school records, and the results of the scholastic aptitude tests and any other college board examinations that may have been taken. Detailed information about the candidates was obtained from the schools and from members of the community from which they came. Applications were restricted to boys living in and attending school in Ohio, Illinois, Wisconsin, Michigan, Indiana and Minnesota. Among the 250 candidates for the fellowships, one hundred and five were the highest ranking scholars in their graduating classes.

In commenting on the establishment of these fellowships President James Bryant Conant said:

> We hope ultimately to establish Prize Fellowships of this kind in other sections of the country. The fellowships are regarded as prizes to be competed for by outstanding students, whatever their financial circumstances, so the stipend varies from a minimum of two hundred dollars to a maximum of one thousand dollars for the freshman year.
>
> In determining the fellowship winners the committee places emphasis on originality, ambition and initiative. There is a great deal of evidence showing that we can select young men of real ability before they enter college.
>
> At present it is difficult for a student to work his way through college. We should note that many potential leaders are lost because of the fortuitous circumstance that they are not able, for financial reasons, to complete their higher education.
>
> We hope to have eventually at Harvard such scholarship funds that ten per cent. of each entering class may be taken care of by awards sufficient to carry the very promising men through college.
>
> The universities in this country should be the apex of a pyramid based on our highly developed school system. A path to the top should be open to all of exceptional talent.

## FIVE-YEAR COURSE IN TECHNOLOGICAL TRAINING AT THE MASSACHUSETTS INSTITUTE OF TECHNOLOGY

A NEW departure in technological training to meet a growing demand for engineers with a thorough understanding of the social and economic implications of their profession was announced recently by President Karl T. Compton in a statement that the Massachusetts Institute of Technology will offer a new five-year course which will include advanced studies in the social sciences and economics.

The new course, which in no way affects the regular four-year courses in science and engineering, has just been approved by the faculty and the corporation. It will be offered next autumn in nearly all the professional fields of the institute's curriculum.

Dr. Compton announced that:

This new course will include essentially the same professional studies as at present in any one of the departments of engineering or science, but will also include an increasing program of more advanced studies in the fields of economics and the social sciences running through the last three years of the five-year course. In the fifth year a considerable amount of time will be devoted to a thesis on some subject which combines the professional and economic aspects of the problem which is chosen. On satisfactory completion of the fifth year there will be awarded the degree of bachelor of science in the professional field, such as civil or electrical or mechanical engineering, or chemistry or physics or biology, and also the degree of master of science in economics and engineering.

It was General Francis A. Walker, as former president of the Massachusetts Institute of Technology, who first had a clear vision of the coming economic importance of the engineer's work and reduced this vision to practise by the introduction of economic studies into the regular program of professional training at this institution. Later, under the influence of Professor Davis R. Dewey, an offshoot of this work in economics developed into the present important and flourishing department of business and engineering administration.

It is our conviction that the five-year course now being established represents another important step in the training of men in applied science, with a realization of the social implications of their work. It will constitute an introduction to the ideas and techniques through which the social and economic effects of engineering are woven into the complex pattern of our present civilization.

Three considerations point to the importance and timeliness of this new development in technological education. The first of these is the certainty that applied science will play an ever-increasing rôle in determining our economic and social life. The second is the increasing necessity for organized cooperation, with economic and social controls, whether along the lines of the "new deal" or on some different basis, but which, in any case, creates an urgent demand for men with an engineering training and a broad conception of relative social values and economic processes. The third of these considerations is the desirability of developing a cooperative approach to economic problems by the engineer and the economist, in somewhat the same way as has proved so fruitful in the cooperation of the engineer with the physicist, the mathematician, the chemist and the biologist.

In the past it has been predominantly true that social and economic life have been in many respects transformed by the work of the scientist and engineer. The analysis of these changes and the attempt to direct them has, however, been made by an almost entirely separate group of men classically trained in principles of economics or perhaps trained only through business or political experience.

Out of these conditions I believe that there will grow a new field for the engineer. Of course, there will always be a need for engineers who are highly trained in scientific specialties, and who confine their activities to creative work in these fields. Such engineers pursue highly individualistic careers. I believe that there will also be an increasing demand for men of engineering training and broad social interests in the field of public service. In any case, it is certainly true that the world needs men of first class professional training, combined with an understanding of economic processes and a broad conception of social values. This new five-year course is designed to aid in the development of men to supply this need.

## PLANNING FOR LIBRARIES

National planning for libraries was the chief subject discussed at the fifty-sixth annual conference of the American Library Association recently held in Montreal. The council specifically indorsed:

Federal aid for libraries and assumption by the national government of responsibility for leadership in the library movement.

The enactment of a law in every state providing for the certification of librarians.

State aid for school libraries.

Close coordination of university and other large libraries to increase the accessibility of research materials to all scholars and advanced students.

Federation and coordination of public libraries in large systems, each system to serve a metropolitan area, a large county or several counties.

Several months ago the Executive Board appointed a Planning Committee consisting of Harry M. Lydenberg, Ralph Munn, Louis R. Wilson and Carl H. Milam. They and President Countryman solicited and received helpful suggestions from many sources, outside as well as inside the library profession, and in the light of these suggestions made recommendations to the council looking toward national planning. The Planning Committee's statement to the council is printed in full in the August issue of the *Bulletin of the American Library Association.*

Because of the alarming shortage of books in public libraries throughout the country the council adopted the following resolution on the recommendation of the Board on the Library and Adult Education and the Library Extension Board:

A serious shortage of books exists in public libraries everywhere, due to increased demand and decreased income during the last four years. Former book stocks are worn out, new books cannot be purchased; thus the library has lost in part ability to keep its readers in touch with current developments and is not now rendering its full contribution to national recovery.

Trustees of every library are asked by the Council of the American Library Association to call this acute situation to the attention of appropriating bodies and urge more adequate funds for books. Such an increase in book funds should not be made at the expense of personnel equally necessary for effective service.

Further use of white collar workers on work relief projects in and for libraries was advocated by the council on the recommendation of the Library Extension Board and the Board on the Library and Adult Education in the following resolution:

It is the opinion of the Council of the American Library Association in session at Montreal, June 25, 1934, that many work relief projects of a highly desirable and useful type can be set up in libraries to utilize effectively the services of educated and trained persons from many professions, including librarians now unemployed and without adequate means of subsistence. Libraries generally have demonstrated that they can conduct and supervise work relief projects with effectiveness.

These workers can be utilized in libraries in such capacities as:

1. Surveyors of library facilities and needs. (a) State-wide, under the direction of state library planning committees and in cooperation with state planning boards; (b) In metropolitan areas, counties, and other regions under similar direction.
2. District or neighborhood representatives of the library, who will establish contacts with individuals and groups, with and through schools and other community institutions, and who will introduce and extend library service into sections not adequately served under present conditions.
3. Assistants within the library to prepare booklists and indexes, collect and arrange pamphlets, government documents and other materials, particularly in technical and special fields, and in many similar ways add to existing library facilities.
4. Advisers and leaders of study and discussion groups with the general objective of increasing the educational value of the library's services.
5. Statistical workers to study financial, loan and other records in order to assemble information needed in planning more economical and efficient service.

In view of the opportunities libraries offer for the profitable employment of many skilled professional workers, the Council urges that the services of greater numbers of the more able professional workers be made available, even if they are not completely destitute.

The Executive Board voted to call a midwinter meeting of the American Library Association Council in Chicago, from December 27 to 29. The next annual meeting of the association will be in Denver in 1935.

# EDUCATIONAL NOTES AND NEWS

DR. BRUCE R. BAXTER, dean of the School of Religion at the University of Southern California, has been elected president of Willamette University, Salem, Ore. He will succeed Dr. Carl Gregg Doney, who has been president of the university since 1915.

DR. DIXON RYAN FOX, professor of history at Columbia University and president of the New York State Historical Association, will be installed as the twelfth president of Union College on October 12. Dr. Nicholas Murray Butler, president of Columbia University, will be the principal speaker.

DR. WILLIAM E. MASTERSON, dean of the University of Idaho College of Law, has been appointed dean of the University of Missouri School of Law. He succeeds James L. Parks, who died on March 6.

THE title of emeritus professor of history in the University of London was conferred on Professor F. J. C. Hearnshaw on his retirement from the university chair of medieval history at King's College.

DR. HARRY KURZ, head of the department of Romance languages at Knox College, has resigned to accept a similar position at the University of Nebraska.

DR. HEINRICH JORDAN, formerly in the German diplomatic service, has been appointed assistant professor of philosophy at Carleton College. During the present summer session he has been a member of the faculty of New York University.

DR. EDWARD B. SHAW has been promoted to be associate clinical professor of pediatrics at the University of California Medical School, San Francisco.

MARY E. HALLER, associate professor of mathematics in the University of Washington, has been appointed head of the department of mathematics of Gooding College.

SAMUEL ENGLE BURR has succeeded Henry E. Snaveley as superintendent of schools at New Castle, Del. Mr. Snaveley is retiring from the position after having held it for a period of sixteen years. Since 1930 Mr. Burr has served as superintendent of schools at Glendale, Ohio, a suburb of Cincinnati. Before going to Glendale he was director of educational and psychological research in the public schools of Lynn, Mass. William Slade, Jr., of Shaker Heights, Ohio, has been elected to succeed Mr. Burr as superintendent of the Glendale public schools. Mr. Slade has served as the principal of the Moreland School in Shaker Heights for a number of years.

THE resignation of N. P. Neilson as chief of the California State Division of Health and Physical Education has been announced.

DR. PAUL W. GATES, associate professor of history at Bucknell University, has been granted a leave of absence in order to make a study of the land policy for the Agricultural Adjustment Administration. The survey is to be completed in time for the next session of Congress.

MRS. FRANCES FOSTER has been appointed editor of *Progressive Education*, the official journal of the Progressive Education Association.

DR. FREDERICK B. ROBINSON, president of the College of the City of New York, returned from a trip to Europe on August 6.

DR. HENRY FAIRFIELD OSBORN, honorary president of the American Museum of Natural History, sailed for Europe on August 1.

DR. EDWIN W. KEMMERER, professor of economics at Princeton University, has returned to New York after spending six weeks at Angora preparing a report for the Turkish government on the country's financial situation. The report is the last of seven comprising a study of Turkey's economic situation.

DR. NICHOLAS MURRAY BUTLER, president of Columbia University, on August 7 addressed the thirty-fifth annual convocation of the summer session of the university. His subject was "This World Needs Another Alexander Hamilton."

SUPERINTENDENT JOSEPH C. BROWN, of Pelham, N. Y., addressed the students of the summer school of Yale University on July 31. He spoke on "Some Significant Trends in Elementary Education."

THE list of speakers during the autumn term at Rutgers University in the Kirkpatrick Chapel will include: Presidents Clarence A. Barbour, of Brown University; William Mather Lewis, of Lafayette College, and H. W. A. Hanson, of Gettysburg College, and two former presidents of Rutgers University, Dr. John M. Thomas and Dr. William H. S. Demarest, now president of the New Brunswick Theological Seminary. Professor William Lyon Phelps, of Yale University, and Governor A. Harry Moore, of New Jersey, will also speak.

PROFESSOR RICHARD THAYER HOLBROOK, head of the department of French of the University of California, died on July 31 at the age of sixty-four years.

DR. WILLIAM BENJAMIN SMITH, professor emeritus of Tulane University, died on August 6, at the age of eighty-three years. Dr. Smith began his work as a teacher in 1871. In 1881 he became professor of mathematics at Central College, Missouri. In 1885 he was appointed professor of physics at the University of Missouri, becoming professor of mathematics in 1888. He was called to Tulane University in 1893, where he taught mathematics until

1906, when he was transferred to the chair of philosophy. In 1915, on his sixty-fifth birthday, he was made professor emeritus.

DR. HAROLD GOLDER, dean of the Graduate School of the American University, died on August 3 at the age of thirty-eight years.

HERBERT N. MORSE, since 1928 assistant state commissioner of education of New Jersey, died on August 4, at the age of sixty-two years. He had been associated with the State Department of Public Instruction for thirty-five years.

THE REV. WILLIAM ERNEST BLOMFIELD, late principal of Rawdon College, Leeds, died on July 23, at the age of seventy-one years.

PROFESSOR F. W. BURSTALL, formerly vice-principal of the University of Birmingham, England, died on July 17, at the age of sixty-eight years. Professor Burstall, who became vice-principal of the university in 1925, retired in 1930. He was made emeritus professor and a life governor of the university.

HARVARD UNIVERSITY and Phillips Exeter Academy benefit under the will of Mrs. Mary A. Sawyer, of Cambridge. The will gives $15,000 to the academy to found three scholarships and $4,000 for the library. Harvard University receives $5,000 to establish the George Carleton Sawyer Scholarship in memory of her husband.

A MOVEMENT to obtain improved library facilities for North Carolina was initiated at a recent meeting at Chapel Hill attended by more than one hundred representatives from all sections of the state. It was found that much had been accomplished through the efforts of the Citizens' Movement, organized in 1928, in 1925, only 21 per cent. of the people having had public library service, while to-day there are 41 per cent. in this class. The state ratio of 11 people per library book in circulation has been reduced to five. The delegates unanimously indorsed the work of the State Library Commission at Raleigh, of which Marjorie Beale is the director, and passed a resolution to be presented to the next Legislature, asking for increased funds for the work. Through this state agency rural school children, teachers, clubwomen and others interested in intellectual advancement are reached. William T. Polk, of Warrenton, was elected chairman of the Citizens' Movement.

A SELECTED group of not more than twenty-five students who have still to complete a half or a whole year of the regular four-year high-school course will be admitted as members of the freshman class at the University of Louisville on September 13 in an experiment being conducted by the College of Liberal Arts. Selection will be on the basis of the applicant's record in the high school, the scores made in certain standard psychological and subject-matter tests and recommendation by the high-school principal. In the case of an individual who has already shown pronounced interest and ability in a certain field, special privileges and opportunities may be given to enable him to devote more than the usual amount of time to this field. Each of the applicants admitted in this special group will be given greater freedom in the matter of class attendance than is permitted other freshmen. Through tutorial relation the student will receive close individual attention from some faculty member in an effort to give every possible opportunity for the development of initiative and self-reliance.

IN a memorandum to the Senate of Glasgow University, the Students' Representative Council has requested two changes in the faculty of arts. The first of these has to do with the establishment of a faculty of education and the second with the raising of the age of admission to the university. The students point out, in support of the first recommendation, that teachers have for a long period advocated the establishment of specialized work for preparing students planning to enter the teaching profession. They propose that a separate faculty be established, that courses be organized with the needs of teachers definitely provided for, and that a distinctive degree be granted for the completion of the curriculum.

AT the meeting of the London Education Committee on July 7 the general purposes sub-committee submitted a comprehensive statement of educational developments to be undertaken in the financial year 1934–1935, and succeeding years. Altogether the committee proposed expenditure on capital account of £851,519, of which £511,400 was new money, *i.e.,* after taking into account £340,119 in the estimates of 1934–35. This would be spent as follows: 1934–35, £90,500; 1935–36, £323,780; 1936–37, £320,-

112; 1937–38, £95,127, and £22,000 in succeeding years. On maintenance account the committee proposed to spend £100,475, £124,920 in 1935–36, £118,650 in 1936–37, and £117,600 in 1937–38. The plan includes the provision of eight new public and elementary schools and sites; extra playing space; rebuilding or modernization of ten elementary schools and plans for modernizing ten further schools; rebuilding or remodeling of five secondary schools; "refresher" courses for teachers; partial rebuilding and expansion of two technical institutions; improvement of dental services, and a number of other improvements. Mr. Robertson, in submitting the plan, said that the educational machine had been slowed down of recent years. The new majority were putting right the failings of the late majority. A recommendation that Armistice Day shall in future be known as "Armistice Day and Peace Day" with a view to propagating the idea of peace in the council's schools was carried.

THE English Labor party has announced that it proposes to remove the poverty bar from English education, with complete educational equality and final abolition of the system under which the quality of education offered to children depends on the income or social position of their parents. Under the new program, all secondary schools would be free, obtaining from public funds the money now obtained from fees. England and Wales, to which the Labor project would apply, have almost no free secondary schools, although many "free-placers" from the lower schools get scholarships in county secondary schools. These correspond roughly to American high schools. With the new plan the age for leaving school would be increased from fourteen to fifteen years, and eventually to sixteen, and wage-earning employment out of school hours would be barred by law to those under the age. Antiquated or unsuitable school buildings would be replaced or remodeled, classes would be reduced in size, only trained and certified teachers would be employed, and open-air recovery schools for ailing children would be established.

THE University of London has received from the Carnegie Corporation of New York an offer to provide $22,500 annually for three years to aid the Institute of Education in developing its relations with students from the Dominions and Colonies. The sum is intended to provide fellowships for short periods to picked students from the Dominions and to enable the institute to invite a senior university teacher from one of the Dominions to hold for a limited period the post of adviser to oversea students. The Senate, with the concurrence of the Court, has accepted the offer and has conveyed to the corporation the thanks of the university for the generous gift.

PROBATE of the will of Alice Stephen Baroness Northcote shows that she left the bulk of her fortune of $1,825,000 to assist migration to Australia of British children. The will directs formation of the "Northcote Children's Emigration Fund," in memory of her husband, to assist poor children, especially orphans, to emigrate from Britain to Australia and to establish and equip themselves there.

*The Christian Science Monitor* reports that under arrangements with the London County Council and the local education authorities in England and Scotland, the South Australian Education Department, through the League of Empire, has a plan of interchange of teachers. The arrangement usually is for one year and applies to certificate primary assistant teachers only, of not less than five years' service, who have passed through the Teachers' College. Applicants pay their own expenses and the passage money between the two countries both ways. Teachers are not employed during the whole period in one school but must accept various appointments as the occasion requires. The plan is said to work well and there are usually a fair number of applicants for the positions, which are limited to those between the ages of 25 and 45 years. There are now several South Australian teachers "doing the round" of schools in England and a corresponding number teaching in South Australia.

INTERNATIONAL COLLEGE, an American institution at Izmir, Turkey, closed its doors temporarily at the end of this academic year, according to an announcement recently made by William W. Patton, chairman of the board of trustees. The college is one of the six institutions affiliated in the Near East College Association. It is explained that the trustees are studying plans for the future and that the closing was necessitated since the enrolment had dropped, partly due to local economic conditions, and also to the improved educational facilities provided by the Turkish Government.

# DISCUSSION

## AFTER THE PRESENT STRESS IN EDUCATION, WHAT?

SOME time ago I had occasion to "cast up accounts" of our public schools. Here is the story that pressed upon the minds and hearts of friends of the public schools, as no story has done in the whole history of education in this country.

(1) Current treatment had left a social stigma upon teachers and had placed upon them a grievous financial handicap. In the minds of those who hold the purse strings of public treasuries education seemed to have lost prestige and dignity and to be of less concern than material interests.

Here are some significant facts that appeared: A large increase in public school enrolment, with further additions probable as the new labor laws show their real force; an enormous decrease in school funds; increase of the teacher's load to meet increase of enrolment and decrease of funds; cuts in teachers' salaries ranging from 10 to 40 per cent., and still further loss through payment by "warrant," which carries a material discount in cashing; one quarter of all teachers in the country paid less than the minimum "blanket code" for industrial workers. All this in the face of increased cost of living.

Why go further into the harrowing details? These terse statements tell the story. The logical result of it all is lowered spirit and vitality from lack of means and from worry, overtaxed strength because of severer demands upon it, inevitable loss of efficiency.

The whole structure of society rests predominantly upon the teachers. As are the teachers, such in impressive degree the manners and morals, private and public virtues, intelligence and culture, and in general the social and even the justifiable financial status of the country. They are in an important sense at the controls of physical, mental, spiritual and industrial progress. The teachers deserved to be returned to a position of self-respect and financial competence, so that they might have means to advance their qualifications for teaching, through ever-present opportunities for observation and study, without worry as to the wherewithal to assure their daily bread. Their treatment was not conducive to the peace of mind necessary for the most effective work.

Real teachers could not object to sacrifice at such times—sacrifice in time and money, but they should not sacrifice to the point of loss of efficiency. Sacrifice should be equable throughout municipality, state or nation, not eased in some cases and massed in others.

(2) The schools themselves. Here is the vital issue: Many schools were closed; a vast number of schools reduced their term-length more or less drastically; more than two million children of school age were not in school; school programs were slashed at the expense not only of spiritual and intellectual values, but of general physical well-being. To which should be added that activities of the CWSA as then directed still further aggravated the situation.

The facts were patent and well advertised. There is no need of further specification. The public school is the Palladium of the Republic or ought to be. It could hardly lay claim to it at that time.

What has been said as to the teacher's relation to society applies equally to the school. The teacher is the school. When the teacher loses prestige the school loses also. When the school suffers the whole of American life suffers.

It is not a matter of eloquent words of homage to our public schools, not a matter of popular platitudes as to education, which mean little because they have no vital grip upon those who use them. If it had not been for the sincere and uneffusive words and work of a goodly number of teachers and administrators schools would have suffered severely even before the present unpleasantness. Do we really grasp the meaning and implications of education? I am reminded of a slurring remark reported to me as coming from one of the managers of the Century of Progress Exposition when consulted as to an exhibit of education—"What does it (education) amount to? What is education anyway?" Education at the exposition was conspicuous for its inconspicuousness.

If any enterprise needed a square deal, whether by the route of code or otherwise, the school and its teachers had a superior claim, in order to remove a dangerous condition into which public education was falling—how dangerous will not fully appear till we see its effects in reduced morale and efficiency, reduced intelligence, thought power, loyalty and devotion, and, on another side even more fundamental, reduced physique and mental and physical soundness.

Economy? Yes, always. But economy in the elimination of waste evident in the flush times of the twenties, and, in emergencies, economy in things that can be spared temporarily, not economy that is a new and more vital waste that will eventually shame us in a less efficient product of our schools and in weaker management of municipal and federal affairs by the generation now suffering in its schooling. This false economy had crippled the schools to a degree that was intolerable.

Friends of education demonstrated to the Federal Government that a real emergency, comparable to other emergencies, existed in the public schools, with the result that the government came to the rescue and appropriated many millions which partly made up for default in local and state appropriations. To-day these funds are finding their way into the schools, so that unemployed teachers are taking up their work again, schools are reopening and children are returning to their studies. But teachers' salaries are not yet being restored toward normal; neither is the average curriculum regaining its losses. Restoration evidently will be a long and painful process. Federal aid is relieving but is not curing the situation. The damage already done is beyond repair. We may partially atone for it by speedily restoring schools and teachers to the level absolutely necessary for safety.

After symbols and codes, what?

Statutes, symbols, formulas, codes never settle anything. Only education, and only the right type of education at that, is potent.

It is in order to study the schools calmly and see what adjustments ought to be made to bring education into its own. One who has been conversant with the inner development of public education must frankly, even shamefacedly, confess that responsibility for the present plight lies in appreciable degree on public education itself. It is occasion for deep repentance and resolve. As present stress lays bare educational conditions and achievements, as well as lack of achievements, the ineffectiveness of the school's functioning in certain vital matters comes clearly to view. A fair analysis of our public education discloses conditions that call insistently for curative treatment. Let us face the situation with honest and timely confession.

(1) Any one who has been conversant with the economics of the public schools knows that there has been waste and even in some cases, extravagance. This has inevitably worked against the best constructive work in training hand, intellect and character. Waste and extravagance are widely scattered infestations of public and private life. They have trespassed on the territory of beneficiently intentioned organizations labeled with mystic letter symbols. It would not be logical to suppose that the schools would escape, even if there had not been ocular demonstration that they had suffered from the same distemper. One is tempted to be fatalistic enough to think that there can be no progress without a percentage of waste (though the public schools had too much)—but extravagance, never. We must repair and improve school economics. We can do it and can bring in a régime that is truly progressive.

(2) The Federal Government gives strictly emergency relief. Its recent appropriation is a temporary matter. To live permanently from the government chest invites disease. As soon as possible we must revert to traditional principles which are absolutely essential for any healthy public service. Local initiative and responsibility are the foundation walls for any sound construction in education.

The legitimate functions of the Federal Government are: (1) To come to the rescue in emergencies; such emergencies ought to be rare; common sense and financial wisdom will reduce them to a minimum. (2) To equalize educational opportunity when a state finds itself unable to do so; this emergency also ought to be rare. (3) To act as a "clearing house" for results of explorations in education and as a repository of educational facts. (4) To inform and to encourage as to higher results in education and educational administration, to point the way, and to inspire, even constrain, communities to follow it, but not to carry them. If it remains true to these functions, and if local responsibility and initiative play their part virilely, a sound and progressive educational system is assured. Otherwise a definite bid is made for decadence in education—for an educational proletariat.

(3) No unit of government, from school district to state, has any right to mortgage its assets to the very limit. The finances of each must be regulated in such a way that there will be a reserve for emergency—reserve in money or means or both—so that the right of way ahead will be clear. In this connection school funds should be rigidly segregated and safeguarded. Let us not get in the way of feeding on crumbs from the Federal table.

(4) Most important and timely. Our school system has advanced by its own momentum in large measure. It has been just growing without any thorough-going thought and prevision. Neither idealistic nor pragmatic philosophy has been justly applied to it. Evidence is multiplying that the complacent feeling as to education that has prevailed is giving way to at least a suspicion that the system has not worked and, as at present organized and administered, will not work, satisfactorily. It is a most opportune time to study, summarize, take account of stock, explore the ground, ascertain our assets and liabilities, our prospects, and what educational common sense ought to suggest as reasonable objectives. It is not a time to grasp nervously at specious remedies, which are liable to be no more than palliatives, perhaps not even that; nor is it a time to persuade ourselves that nothing short of an absolute revolution will answer our problems. The trouble is not difficult to find; remedies are simple and not far to seek. True enough, far-reaching changes must be made, but the matter is largely one of emphasis, method and teaching efficiency.

Particularly in our analysis must we survey the boundaries of popular education, which has never adequately been done. Let us set up intelligently the bound marks, temporary ones at least, for in an infinite enterprise like education nothing can be regarded as fixed. In times like these thought is stimulated; it goes deeper and truer than in times of ease and self-complacency. If we set this thought to working in earnest, without extravagance or radical stimulants, it should land us on solid foundations away from the shifting sands where educational oratory, eloquent writing and superficial theory and action have left us.

FRANK WEBSTER SMITH

## A PROPOSED EXPERIMENT IN PSYCHOLOGY

THERE has been an attempt on the part of some psychologists to divide people into two personality classes—introverts and extroverts. The introvert is self-conscious, shy, hesitant, evasive, etc. The extrovert is bold, impulsive, direct, etc. A third classification might be mentioned: the ambivert. The ambivert is an individual who has some of the traits of both the introvert and the extrovert, perhaps with either introversion or extroversion dominating.

Classification is important, but more important is the question as to how people become introverts or extroverts. Without going into a long wordy argument as to whether these traits are due to heredity or environment I should like to suggest an experiment relative to the matter. It seems that one might well be conducted in some of our larger school centers.

For example, in a school that has a large number of pupils in the fourth, fifth or sixth grade, without interfering with administrative affairs, a group of introverts might be assembled in one room and a group of extroverts might be assigned to another room, say about thirty in each group. These could be classified with the help of psychologists, psychiatrists, social workers and with the use of some of the personality tests now available.

In almost every group as we find them to-day there are certain individuals who do most of the talking. There are others who do very little, if any. If we should have a group of the outspoken, leader type together for one semester or a year, it would seem that some of them would become quiet, acquiescent, introvertive. On the other hand, if the quiet, inactive ones were together for a year, perhaps some of them would become active, aggressive, of the leadership or extrovertive type.

If some of the superintendents who have the proper organization and the right kind of assistance would conduct some experiments of this kind, they might easily make a very valuable contribution to education.

Robert P. Carroll
School of Education
Pennsylvania State College

# SPECIAL CORRESPONDENCE

## CONTEMPORARY EDUCATION IN PALESTINE

It is the irony of fate that one of the oldest surviving races which taught the world some of its most fundamental and enduring lessons and produced the greatest pedagogical genius of all history, the Master Teacher, should see its native land languishing in comparative ignorance and illiteracy until the close of the recent war. From the time when the troops of Titus plunged Jerusalem ankle deep in blood until General Allenby marched peaceably through the city gates in 1917, the little land of Palestine, once the hub of the world, was torn mercilessly between rival powers. While writhing under the heel of foreign dominance by a power whose culture belonged to an obsolete and forgotten world,[1] Palestine had no opportunity to keep pace with the rapid developments which heralded the modern age. To the well-known axiom that education usually reflects the cultural status of a nation, Palestine was no exception. It remained for the introducers of western culture at the close of the world war to rescue education from its medieval backwardness and inefficiency in this land, once "flowing with milk and honey," but then little more than a barren, undeveloped desert.

The immediate background of contemporary education in Palestine was the climax of a Moslem rule of over seven hundred years. During this period, practically nothing was done to keep pace with the world's progress in any line, and education was well-nigh forgotten.[2] At the time of the British occupation in 1918, the educational system was essentially that established by the Turkish law of 1869.[3] What secondary and higher elementary schools there were in existence were controlled by Imperial officers and were comparatively efficient. The lower elementary schools, however, were in the control of local committees, most of which operated schools which were poorly organized and woefully inefficient. This situation was slightly bettered in 1913, when the control of the Imperial officers over these local schools was somewhat strengthened. Nevertheless, the compulsory use of a foreign language, Turkish, even in the elementary classes, along with the inefficient administration and instruction in the school system, made it anything but desirable. Theoretically, the Ottoman educational system was compulsory and gratuitous, but this had only a partial practical significance, and the education of girls was almost totally omitted.[4]

The first important step towards reconstruction was taken in the formation of an Educational Committee by the Zionist Organization in 1914. It was not until after the British occupation in 1918, however, that a total rehabilitation of the educational system was achieved. The quasi-military government which conducted Palestinian affairs between the occupation and the set-up of the civil administration under the British Mandate in 1920 appropriated money for educational purposes, reopened a number of schools, provided teacher training facilities for Arab teachers, and instituted Arabic as the medium of instruction in government schools. Since 1920, the government has officially recognized the Zionist educational system as of equal standing with the Arab. Hence, a dual system of public education is operating in Palestine at present on a linguistic and racial basis, the Arab public system and the Hebrew public system.[5]

The government department of education directly controls the Arab system and maintains it out of public funds, while it indirectly controls the Hebrew system by periodic inspection

[1] The Moslems.

[2] *Cf.* Reports of the Experts, submitted to the Joint Palestine Survey Commission, October 1, 1928, p. 18 *f.*

[3] *Cf.* Bowman, "Education in Palestine," "The Year Book of Education," 1932.

[4] *Ibid.*

[5] *Cf.* Palestine Government, Department of Education, Annual Report, 1929–30.

to see that these schools are kept up to the government standards. The Jewish Agency, a world Jewry organization, directly controlled the Hebrew system until August, 1932, when its administration was transferred to the Keneset Yisrael, "the Congregation of Israel" or "the organized Jewish Community of Palestine."[6]

Elementary education is free in the Arab schools, the funds for their operation being provided by the government, while a small tuition fee is charged for higher education. In the elementary town schools, however, a small fee of 100 mils is collected from well-to-do pupils in order to assist in paying for the library, sports, gardens, etc. The Hebrew system has not yet been established on a free tuition basis even in the elementary schools, for it is largely dependent on gifts and funds raised by various Jewish organizations throughout the world, the government providing only about 10 per cent. of the necessary finances. Hence, in most Hebrew elementary schools a minimum tuition fee of less than 5 dollars a year, or about 10 cents a week, is charged.[7]

Education in neither system is made compulsory by the government, but the Hebrew authorities have voluntarily instituted compulsory education for the Jewish children. This has worked quite effectively in the first grades of the elementary school, but due to the extreme poverty of the people, many of the children are unable to complete their elementary education. Approximately 70 per cent. of the Jewish children of elementary school age are now in school.[8] The remaining 30 per cent., however, are not all left entirely without schooling. Many of them have entered school, but have been forced to leave before completing the first eight grades. In 1931 it was estimated that about one third of the Jewish children are eliminated from school at the end of the third year, at the age of nine or ten; another third likewise drop out in the sixth or seventh year, and scarcely a third are able to remain throughout the eight-year course.[9] The success of their attempt at compulsory schooling is clearly seen, however, when the figures reveal that, though the Jews form only about 20 per cent. of the population of Palestine, they contribute 42 per cent. of the children in the schools.[10] This indicates that universal elementary education among the Arab population is still far from being achieved. This is not so much the result of a lack of desire for education, but is the consequence of insufficient facilities for providing education for all.

The education of girls presents another marked contrast in the two systems. The Hebrew schools give equal attention to the education of boys and girls. In 1932, 53 per cent. of the enrolment in these schools was made up of girls. At this same time, the female enrolment in the Arab system was only 19 per cent. of the total. The Hebrew system also is coeducational, while the Arab system maintains separate schools for boys and girls. The Arabs seem still to be in the throes of their Moslem background in their attitude towards the education of women, but they are slowly emerging from this to a new view-point. It will perhaps not be long before women will have an equal opportunity with men in the Arab public schools of Palestine.

The elementary schools both of the Arab and Hebrew systems are the most important part of the educational structure of Palestine at present. It has often been the practise in the East to neglect the elementary education of the masses and to concentrate attention on higher education for a selected group. This has now been abandoned in an attempt to spread literacy universally throughout Palestine.[11] There were 303 elementary schools in the Arab system in 1932, with a total enrolment of 24,696 pupils, while only 12 schools offered secondary work, with a total enrolment of 317 pupils.[12] In the Hebrew system, at the same time, there were 109 elementary schools, with an enrolment of

[6] *Cf.* "Facts and Figures concerning the Jewish Public School System of Palestine," recorded by the Waad Leumi (The National Council, or Executive Committee of the Keneset Yisrael), p. 4.

[7] *Ibid.*, p. 15.

[8] *Ibid.*, p. 14.

[9] *Ibid.*

[10] *Cf.* "Fifteen Years of Jewish Achievement in Palestine," a report published by the Zionist Organization of America.

[11] *Ibid.*

[12] *Cf.* Report by His Majesty's Government in the United Kingdom of Great Britain and Northern Ireland to the Council of the League of Nations on the Administration of Palestine and Trans-Jordan for the year 1932.

15,576 pupils, as compared with 5 secondary schools, in which 1,529 pupils were in attendance.[13]

In the Arab system, four years of elementary education are provided in the rural schools. The first year is called "preparatory," and the others are grades 1 to 3. In some instances higher grades are added. Since there are no kindergartens for boys in the government schools, the preparatory class may be thought of as taking the place of them. In the town schools 7 years of schooling are usually provided, the first being preparatory, and the remainder ranging from the first to the sixth grade. The course of study given in the town schools is broad, practical and comparatively up-to-date. The subjects taught are Arabic language, penmanship, arithmetic, geography, history, nature study, hygiene, science, drawing, manual work, geometry, English, English penmanship, religion and physical training.[14] The studies in the village and rural schools are practically the same, save that special attention is given to agricultural instruction, both theoretical and practical. In the town girls' schools needlework, embroidery and practical hygiene are introduced during the first four years, while infant welfare finds a place in the sixth year of the course.

The Hebrew system provides elementary education for practically all Jewish children, schools being found even in the smallest villages. The regular elementary course is of 8 years' duration, the first year being preparatory and the remaining years ranging from grades 1 to 7. Not more than a third of the pupils, however, are able to remain in school long enough to complete the full course. The studies offered are much the same as those given in the Arab system, but Hebrew is substituted for the Arabic language, the Bible and the Hebrew religion are taught, and singing is introduced. In the rural schools less emphasis is given to English, and gardening is substituted for manual work.[15]

There are three types of Hebrew school, the Mizrachi, the General, and the Labor schools.

[13] *Ibid.*
[14] *Cf.* Palestine Government, Department of Education, Annual Report, 1929–30.
[15] *Ibid.*

The first represents the orthodox religious group of the Zionist movement. In these schools the traditional religious curriculum is at the center, with a minimum of modern secular training finding its place in the periphery. The General schools introduce the study of the Bible and the Rabbinical writings as the basis of Hebrew literature, history and culture, and respect the ancient religious traditions and ceremonies, yet the inculcation of these is left more to the home, and a liberal secular course of study is more characteristic of these schools. The Labor schools are found in the rural sections, and reflect their environment in the type of work offered. The instruction in these schools is centered around practical activities, attempting to correlate the training given with the life of the rural population they serve. These schools are not anti-religious, and they insist, as do the others, on a good knowledge of the Bible as the basis of Hebrew culture.[16]

Secondary education in Palestine presents another difference between the Arab and Hebrew systems. The Arab secondary school is continuous beyond the elementary level, following the educational ladder system. A four-year course is designed for these secondary schools, which leads directly to the college or university. A small tuition fee is charged from well-to-do pupils, and day-school facilities for secondary education are provided only for boys. A boarding school, known as the Women's Elementary Training College, was opened in 1919, to which girls are admitted for training with a view to teaching in the elementary schools. There are 11 government secondary schools in Palestine. Nine of these offer the first two years of the secondary course, one in Jaffa offers the first three years, and one, the Government Arab College in Jerusalem (formerly the Men's Training College), is equipped to give the full four-year course. The secondary curriculum is very similar to that found in the United States, geometry, trigonometry, physics, chemistry, botany and zoology being introduced in addition to the type of work offered in the elementary schools. In both the Men's and Women's College, special training in pedagogy is given for those who desire to become elementary teachers.[17]

[16] *Cf.* "Facts and Figures," p. 12.

The Hebrew secondary school overlaps the elementary school, organized somewhat on the pre-war German plan. The secondary course is of 8 years' duration, the first 3 years being considered elementary, corresponding to the fourth, fifth and sixth grades in the Arab elementary system, and to the fifth, sixth and seventh grades in the Hebrew elementary system. The completion of this course qualifies one for entrance to a college or university. The course of study given in the first 4 years is parallel to that given in the elementary schools. The last 4 years introduce into the curricuulm philosophy, physics, chemistry, biology, drawing and painting, and another language besides Hebrew and English. Along with the secondary schools might be mentioned 4 teacher training colleges, which give a five-year course following the elementary school, the first 3 years of which correspond to the secondary schools, while the last 2 years are characterized by professional training in preparation for teaching.[18]

In higher education, the Hebrew system surpasses the government Arab system. The government maintains some students at the American University at Beirut, at the Helwan Training College near Cairo, and at various British institutions of higher learning, but has no university of its own. The Hebrew system is capped by the Hebrew University, located on Mount Scopus, at Jerusalem. This is a new university, officially opened in 1925, for the purpose of becoming the intellectual center of Hebrew culture throughout the world. Its avowed intent is to conserve the ancient culture of the race, and to conduct research in scientific fields for the benefit of the world. The university is in a strategic location to study archeology, to do research in medicine based on the study of parasites and conditions found in Palestine which are practically unknown to the rest of the world, to delve into Oriental languages and cultures, and to promote internationalism. This little country is on the threshold of both occident and orient, and its present scholars have both the traditional background of an oriental language and culture from the days of Abraham to the present, plus the advantage of active participation in modern western life previous to their return to Palestine. Just recently, a gift was made for the establishment of a chair of international peace.[19] Originally, the university was largely engaged in research, giving no degrees. At present, however, regular academic work is being offered, leading to a degree. Thirteen master of arts degrees were the first degrees given in January, 1932.[20] No social, racial or religious distinctions are made, but matriculation is open to all students who are intellectually qualified.[21] Instruction is given largely in Hebrew, but lectures are often delivered in several other languages. The new Wolffsohn Memorial library was dedicated in April, 1930. This library contains some rare specimens of antiquity, besides such modern treasures as the original manuscript of Einstein's theory of relativity, presented by the scientist himself.[22] This library is the largest in the Near East, and is second only to the library of the League of Nations in the international character of its collections. Since the Nazi revolution, many Hebrew students have been fleeing to Palestine to complete their studies, and the university is constantly growing. It is gaining world recognition, and if financial difficulties do not handicap too seriously, it will doubtless soon be rated as a first-class modern university of the highest rank.

The kindergarten has been an extremely significant part of the educational progress of Palestine, particularly in the matter of health education and the prevention of disease. Eye diseases, head and skin troubles and other maladies have been remedied, and undernourished children have been cared for. Meals are served to needy children, and they are protected from harm, both physical and moral, by being taken from the streets into the kindergarten. The Hebrew system has been particularly active in kindergarten work, maintaining 139 such schools in 1932.[23] One particular advantage which the Hebrew children gain from atten-

[17] *Cf.* Palestine Government, Department of Education, Annual Report, 1929–30.

[18] *Ibid.*

[19] *Cf.* Hyman, "The Hebrew University, Jerusalem," *National Student Federation of America News Service,* Vol. I, No. 7.

[20] *Cf.* Report by His Majesty's Government.

[21] *Cf.* "The Hebrew University is Expanding Its Work," *New York Times,* Sunday, March 31, 1929.

[22] *Ibid.*

[23] *Cf.* Report by His Majesty's Government.

dance at the kindergarten is a knowledge of the Hebrew language, which assists them in their further education. Jewish immigrants have come from all over the world, and there are more than fifty languages and dialects spoken.[24] Hence, an introduction to Hebrew at the kindergarten level is a distinct aid in preparing the pupils for later instruction with Hebrew as the medium.

Several progressive steps in Palestinian education have been made in various directions. Practical agricultural education is particularly stressed in order to teach the people how to till the ground to provide for themselves a better living. Over 200 village schools have land for gardens, the care of which is insured by a supervisor of school gardens with two assistants. In these gardens the pupils receive an elementary agricultural training. On Arbor Day, 1932, over 12,000 trees were planted in the government schools.[25] Manual training and technical education are finding a large place in the educational system, an exhibition of arts and crafts being held at Jerusalem during the winter of 1932. Kitchens are maintained in many schools where undernourished children are fed, and where over 4,000 children are receiving instruction in cooking and dietetics.[26] There are 4 institutions where instruction is given to the blind. At two of these handwork alone is given, while the other two have introduced academic instruction on the elementary level. Two girls from these institutes have completed the teacher training course at the Women Teacher's College, and one boy is studying at the Hebrew University. There are three institutions where deaf and dumb children are trained, and one for the care of mentally defective children. There are also psychiatrists both at Jerusalem and Tel-Aviv who attend cases of mental deficiency sent them by the school authorities.[27] Physical training and athletics are finding a prominent place in the schools, with frequent interscholastic meets and a general athletic meet held annually at Jerusalem.[28] School hikes and summer camps are frequent, besides the increasing activity of the Boy Scouts and the Girl Guides. In addition to this, all schools receive medical inspection by the department of health, or by qualified physicians who report to this department.[29] In these many respects, education in Palestine is becoming more and more progressive.

In addition to the two main school systems which have been discussed, there are three types of school which are organized separately. These are the Moslem schools, the Christian schools and the Jewish schools which are not under the jurisdiction of the Hebrew public system.[30] They are private institutions, and are not significant in a discussion of public education.

What is the immediate problem of public education in Palestine? It is the problem of finance. The Arab public system is failing to remove much illiteracy among the Arab population of Palestine, because it has insufficient funds to establish the proper number of schools and to give free education to all. In 1932, 5,271 pupils who applied for admittance were turned away because of inadequate facilities to care for them.[31] The immediate problem of the government is to establish the school system on a financial basis which shall make it possible for every child to receive free education. Then compulsory education can be instituted, and the problem of illiteracy solved. The Hebrew system faces a similar problem. They have been partially successful in establishing compulsory education and providing a minimum of elementary training for most of the Jewish children. Yet, many of these must drop out of school very early, and a few receive no education at all. In the fall of 1931, the Jewish Agency was so nearly bankrupt for educational funds that the schools were not opened. Finally, the teachers agreed to contribute one month's salary to the educational budget, and the schools were reopened in February, 1932.[32] The Zionist Organization of America is making a plea for financial support for educational purposes at the present time. The immediate problem, then, facing educational authorities of Palestine, both

24 *Cf.* Reports of the Experts submitted to the Joint Palestine Survey Commission, p. 19.

25 *Cf.* Report by His Majesty's Government.

26 *Ibid.*

27 *Ibid.*

28 *Ibid.*

29 *Cf.* Palestine Government, Department of Education, Annual Report, 1929–30.

30 *Cf.* Report by His Majesty's Government.

31 *Ibid.*

32 *Ibid.* *Cf.* also "Facts and Figures," p. 7.

Hebrew and Arab, is to secure enough funds to increase the educational facilities to an extent which will make possible free compulsory education.

Other problems connected with Palestine's educational set-up at the present time are the private schools which are not under government control and the dual system of educational administration. Eventually, the private schools must be brought under the control of a central authority in order to keep their standards high. They may remain private schools, but should be required to conform to certain qualifications established by the department of education. If the differences of religion and language and culture between the Arabs and the Hebrews were not so marked, a unified system of education should take the place of the present dual system. But in view of these differences, it is England's problem to discover whether it would be wise to attempt to unify the system or to continue it as it now is.

DONALD G. MILLER

NEW YORK, N. Y.

# QUOTATIONS

## THE PUBLIC SCHOOL CRISIS IN CALIFORNIA

ALREADY there are signs of renewed attacks upon the public school system of California. The State Legislature convenes in January, and there is trustworthy authority for the statement that legislation is being prepared to repeal the teacher tenure law, to abandon kindergarten and adult education and to remove the fixed charges in the State Constitution that guarantee the right of free public schools to every child.

The threatened attack upon teacher tenure is an unblushing attempt upon the part of certain politicians to make the appointment and removal of school teachers a political racket.

In this they are said to be aided and abetted by politically interested organizations which would profit by providing jobs, and, of course, to have more jobs to provide more teachers must be dismissed.

The agencies would work hand in glove with the politicians.

The politicians would do the dismissing for political reasons, and the agencies would furnish the replacements for a commission.

Fortunately that fraudulent scheme is so obviously fraudulent the electors are certain to defeat it by voting for an amendment to the State Constitution prohibiting the application of the spoils system to the positions of school teachers.

The other propositions are not so obvious in their intent to undermine our system of free education for all the children of all our people.

They are put forward by pinchpenny politicians who want to save on education, not for the avowed purpose of balancing the state budget, but to have more money to squander on their friends and supporters.

By cutting out the kindergarten they plan to sacrifice children, who have no votes, and find a few extra jobs for friends who have, and who in return will vote and work for them.

They would abolish adult education for a similar reason. No adult interested in his or her further education would be likely to vote for the type of politician willing to cripple our public schools.

The proposal to remove the fixed charges in the State Constitution that guarantee the right of free schools to every child is false economy in its worst form, and is a menacing attack upon the very foundations of our American democracy.

Our debt of a free education for our children is as sacred as any debt the state can owe, and it must be paid in full.

To repudiate the debt of a free education would be a crime against the principles of an enlightened democracy, and a further offense against our financial stability, since in better education lies our surest hope of being able to pay all other debts.

No state was ever saved from insolvency by condemning its citizens to ignorance.

No state was ever put into bankruptcy by buying school books.

It is none too soon to prepare against the attacks upon education which are certain to be made at the next session of the Legislature.

In the last session more than 300 bills were

introduced, if not for the purpose of wrecking our public school system, at least for purposes which could have had no other effect.

As many if not more are now in course of preparation and it is the duty of parents to prepare to oppose all that are pernicious.

The way of preparedness for parents is to study the various school propositions and let the legislators know that whatever other economies may be effected there must be none threatening the security, efficiency and freedom of public school education.—*Los Angeles Examiner*.

# REPORTS

## THE NATIONAL SURVEY OF THE EDUCATION OF TEACHERS

Professor E. S. Evenden, of Columbia University, has made public the report of the national survey of the education of teachers conducted for the past three years under the direction of the U. S. Office of Education. Professor Evenden as associate director was in active charge of the study, authorized by Congress in 1930.

There is an oversupply of teachers in such numbers as to be professionally demoralizing alike to employed and unemployed teachers. The plight of the thousands of teachers who are now unemployed and who would not be considered for reemployment because of incompetence or because their educational and professional preparation are definitely below present standards, is a matter to arouse our sympathy and to challenge the various group, state and national relief organizations and the agencies for vocational rehabilitation.

So far as the schools are concerned, however, the elimination of that group is a matter for congratulation instead of condolence, since it makes possible a desirable advance in standards.

In the first place, each state, county or city school system responsible for the placement of teachers should make, if it has not already done so, an analysis of all the unemployed teachers for whom it can be considered in any way responsible. Such an analysis should determine the number of unemployed teachers whose educational and professional preparation is entirely satisfactory according to present standards for each type of teaching position.

If only such teachers and those who bring their preparation up to that standard are considered, a large part of the oversupply is automatically removed. Plans should then be developed for employing the unemployed adequately prepared teachers at a rate not to exceed 20 per cent. of the new teachers needed by that school system each year.

This rate of absorption would permit the institutions preparing teachers to run at 80 per cent. capacity, which would enable them to keep their programs intact and would not call for radical expansions or reorganizations if, after four or five years, they were called upon to increase their load by 25 per cent.

During the time that the surplus is being gradually absorbed some of the unemployed teachers will have found other fields of work or will have added to their professional preparation in order to keep it up-to-date. This plan does not provide for the immediate relief of the capable unemployed teachers who may not be employed for a period of one or more years.

They, however, are better off with the prospect of employment than at present and undoubtedly numbers of them beyond the number employed could be used for substitute work and for evening and vacation schools which would represent part-time employment at least.

In the second place the present large annual additions to the surplus of teachers must be stopped immediately if any satisfactory adjustment to this perplexing problem is to be made. This can not be done without having available the records which will make it possible to predict the number of new teachers for each type of position needed and without having the cooperation of the state certification authorities and of all the institutions in which teachers are prepared.

State action to check over-production involves five major steps:

First, the establishment of the standards of educational and professional preparation which the state will consider satisfactory for each of the different kinds of teaching positions.

Second, the preparation of a list of approved institutions within the state in which the programs and facilities for the preparation of teachers for each type of position meet the adopted standards.

Third, the preparation of estimates of the number of teachers for each different type of position that will be needed each year for a period extending at least ten years into the future.

Fourth, the allocation of the maximum number of each type of teacher that will be certificated from each of the approved institutions and the number that will be accepted from other states and all other sources.

Fifth, the enforcement of restricted certification which would permit teachers to teach only in those positions or those subjects for which they are prepared.

This program must include all higher educational institutions within a state—both public and private—which have been approved as institutions qualified to prepare teachers or other educational workers.

The quotas allocated to individual institutions should be raised or lowered in terms of any changes in the total demand and, whenever it is possible to do so with reasonable accuracy, the quotas should be changed in terms of the relative merits of the graduates of the institutions on the approved list.

So far as the problem of raising the level of educational preparation of American teachers is concerned there is evidence that significant progress has been made but that there is still much more to be done. Since conditions are now more propitious for raising standards than ever before, it is recommended that all states take advantage of the opportunity to raise the level of preparation required for all new teachers as well as for those in service.

No new teachers should be employed nor any former teachers reemployed who do not meet the present generally accepted standards of two years beyond high school for elementary teachers and four years of college work for teachers in the secondary schools.

Furthermore, every state which has not already done so should set a date as near as educational and economic conditions in the state will warrant when all teachers admitted to the schools will have a minimum of four years of educational preparation above high school.

This goal of equality of initial preparation for all teachers—rural, elementary, junior and senior high school, refers only to equivalence in the amount and quality of the educational preparation but does not and should not imply identity of content.

## THE SIXTY-FIFTH ANNUAL REPORT OF THE AMERICAN MUSEUM OF NATURAL HISTORY

One of the fundamental ideas of the founders of the museum was that it should be an institution for education. This ideal is continually before us, and the museum for years has been exerting a great influence in the educational field. Its activities in this field may be grouped under two main headings, namely: "Technical Education" and "General Education."

Under the first is our school service, college and university contacts, teacher training courses and adult education program. Under the second heading is our public guide service, special exhibitions, conventions and other public meetings and contributions to leisure time problems and to outdoor education.

In spite of reduced funds and although the board of education for financial reasons was obliged to withdraw the corps of teachers which had been previously assigned to the museum to supplement our own teaching staff, we have been able to continue our educational program in practically all its branches.

What is meant by the museum's "school service"? It means that small nature collections and other visual instruction aids are loaned free to any public school in Greater New York. It means that lantern slides and motion picture films of the museum are available for supplementing classroom instruction. It means that lectures and talks in the exhibition halls, special instruction for the sight conservation classes and expert guidance through the halls are being given to school children and their teachers. It means that five auto-trucks are daily delivering loan material to the schools and thereby are placing at the disposal of teachers aids which they can not get in any other way. This is a service that is used by more than 93 per cent. of the schools of the city and made more than 31,000,000 contacts with school children in 1933. The following statistical table indicates the extent of this service and its importance:

| | 1930 | 1931 | 1932 | 1933 |
|---|---|---|---|---|
| Attendance at lectures, classes and guiding | 247,629 | 226,552 | 220,482 | 191,556 |
| Children's Science Fair | 39,250 | 30,657 | 37,275 | 44,745 |
| Visitors to Bear Mountain nature trails | 200,000 | 283,000 | 300,000 | 350,000 |
| Contacts made by lending lantern slides | 15,588,403 | 17,392,790 | 17,019,882 | 17,014,690 |
| Contacts made by lending motion picture films | 3,764,505 | 7,423,708 | 10,458,181 | 9,012,628 |
| Contacts made by lending circulating collections | 3,210,741 | 2,590,753 | 3,816,863 | 4,775,176 |
| | 23,050,528 | 27,947,460 | 31,852,683 | 31,388,795 |

But our educational program goes a great deal farther than this. An important—if not the most important—contribution of the museum to technical education is the teacher training courses, which give practical instruction in how to recognize objects in nature and how to use visual aids. During the year five of these training courses have been given by our staff, and the over-registration is a clear indication that they are of real value to teachers.

The department has continued its contacts with colleges and universities of the city and vicinity. Several courses have been given at the museum for which college credit is given. These institutions are finding it most helpful to make more intensive use of our collections in their own courses.

In the field of general education the museum has made its contribution by serving as host to visiting educational and scientific bodies. These included the fiftieth anniversary meeting of the American Ornithologists' Union, which included the finest exhibition of bird paintings ever brought together; the Children's Science Fair in cooperation with the American Institute, also the Congress of the Junior Science Clubs; the Flower Show of the New York Horticultural Society; a series of symphony concerts, given in our auditorium by the New York Civic Orchestra, under the auspices of the State Department of Education; a conference of unemployed teachers, conducted by the New York State Department of Education, and many others. Members of the educational staff of the museum are serving on the Adult Education Council, on the President's NRA Committee on the Use of Leisure Time.

In outdoor education, the museum has continued to operate the Trailside Museum and the Nature Trails at Bear Mountain in cooperation with the Commission of the Interstate Park. This work is immediately in charge of Mr. William H. Carr, and the museum's share is financed through contributions from Mr. Felix M. Warburg. Mr. Carr reports that the attendance for the summer of 1933 was more than 350,000.

The department sponsors one club activity for school children, the Junior Astronomy Club. Its 150 active members attend lectures and discussions, make observations and write and publish the *Junior Astronomy News,* which goes to 150 associate members of the club, in twenty-six states and in London and Paris.

# EDUCATIONAL RESEARCH AND STATISTICS

## PREDICTING SUCCESS IN FIRST-YEAR COLLEGE CHEMISTRY

RECENT attempts to predict success in college chemistry by means of Chemistry Aptitude, Chemistry Training or Intelligence Tests has not yielded very reliable results. There are those who hold that aptitude in a given field is far too complex a function to permit measurement by any single test. Others hold that while aptitude may be a complex function, its most essential elements may be measured by comparatively simple tests. Experimental results of the prediction of success in college chemistry are few in number and not entirely in agreement.

Bray[1] studied the relation of the Iowa Chemistry Aptitude Test given at the beginning of the first quarter session and the Iowa Chemistry Training Test given near the end of the quarter session. He concludes from this study that the Iowa Chemistry Aptitude Test is a fairly ac-

[1] W. J. Bray, "Aptitude and Its Relation to Achievement in General Chemistry," *Science Education,* 16: 439–442, December, 1932.

curate instrument for predicting the success of the superior students.

Cook[2] compared intelligence ratings and results of the Iowa Chemistry Aptitude Test with achievement in high-school chemistry. Three measures of achievement were used: (1) Powers General Chemistry Test, (2) gain as measured by the Powers Test, and (3) total scores on teachers' objective tests given throughout the semester. He found that scores on the Chemistry Aptitude Test are of somewhat less value than IQ's calculated on the Terman Group Test of Mental Ability and that predictions made on the basis of either the Iowa Aptitude Test or the Terman IQ's are not reliable for purposes of predicting success in high-school chemistry.

Cornog and Stoddard[3, 4] have shown that the predictive power of the Iowa Chemistry Aptitude Test is greater than the general intelligence examination or the high-school record of the student. Their results show that the correlations between Chemistry Training and marks or Chemistry Aptitude and marks range from .73 to .26, with an average correlation between Chemistry Training and marks of .57 and an average correlation of Chemistry Aptitude and marks of .44.

Smith and Trimble[5] believe that it is possible to predict the performance of the best and poorest students through the use of the Iowa Chemistry Aptitude and Iowa Chemistry Training Tests. They report a correlation between Chemistry Training and final marks of .79 and a correlation between Chemistry Aptitude and marks of .42.

In the foregoing studies there seems to be about as much relationship between intelligence test scores and marks in chemistry as between Chemistry Aptitude or Chemistry Training test scores and marks in chemistry. In none of the studies has a criterion been built up by a combination of Intelligence and Chemistry Aptitude or Intelligence and Chemistry Training. It may be possible that the chemistry tests and intelligence tests measure sufficiently different functions in the learning of chemistry to make a combination criterion of value for purposes of prediction.

### The Problem

The problem of this study is to compare predictions of success in first-year college chemistry, made from Intelligence Test scores, from Chemistry Aptitude Test scores, from Chemistry Training Test scores and from combinations of the chemistry tests and intelligence. More specifically, the problem is to determine which test or combination of tests is the best criterion for prediction.

### The Data

The data for this study are the results of three tests: The Ohio Psychological Examination, Chemistry Aptitude Tests of the Iowa Placement Examinations, Chemistry Training Tests of the Iowa Placement Examinations and marks earned in chemistry during the first year in college. The Ohio Psychological Examination was given to all students included in the study, either during the latter part of their senior year in high school or at the opening of their freshman year in college.

Chemistry Aptitude Test, Series CA1, Revised Form B was given by the Chemistry Department of the University of Wyoming to 46 freshmen during the first week of school in the fall of 1931. Chemistry Aptitude Test, Series CA1, Revised Form A was given to 34 freshmen in the fall of 1933. Chemistry Training Test, Series CT1, Revised Form B was given to 40 freshmen in the fall of 1931. Chemistry Training, Series CT1, Revised Form A was given to 47 freshmen in the fall of 1932. Chemistry Training, New Series, Form X was given to 22 freshmen and Form Y of the same series to 11 freshmen in the fall of 1933. The Chemistry Aptitude Tests were given to freshmen who had had no high-school chemistry, whereas the Chemistry Training Test was given to those who previously had had high-school chemistry.

[2] Gerhard A. Cook, "Use of the Iowa Chemistry Aptitude Test in Foretelling Success in High School Chemistry," *Science Education*, 16: 51–54, October, 1931.

[3] Jacob Cornog and George D. Stoddard, "The Chemistry Training of High School and College Students," *Journal of Chemical Education*, 6: 85–92, January, 1929.

[4] Jacob Cornog and George D. Stoddard, "Predicting Performance in Chemistry," *Journal of Chemical Education*, 2: 701–708, August, 1925.

[5] Otto M. Smith and H. M. Trimble, "Prediction of the Future Performance of Students from Their Past Record," *Journal of Chemical Education*, 6: 93–97, January, 1929.

The three term marks in chemistry given throughout the year were recorded for each student.

### TREATMENT OF THE DATA

Form 17 of the Ohio Psychological Examination was used for all students included in the study.

Scores on Forms A and B of the Chemistry Aptitude Test were considered comparable and the scores of the 80 freshmen were treated as one group. Scores on the Chemistry Training Tests, Forms A and B and Forms X and Y, were not considered comparable because of the differences in means and standard deviations of the groups on which the norms were computed. The scores on all the training tests were, therefore, changed to z-scores to form a comparable series. Chemistry marks, as recorded in the office of the registrar, were assigned the following values:

| Marks | 1 | II | III | IV | Inc. Con. | Fd. |
|---|---|---|---|---|---|---|
| Values | 1 | 2 | 3 | 4 | 5 | 6 |

These values were then averaged for the three term marks assigned to each student. In a few cases the average mark was computed for two terms.

The three zero-order coefficients of correlation and probable errors were computed for the two groups. Table I shows these correlations.

TABLE I

ZERO ORDER CORRELATIONS

| Variables correlated | Product-moment correlation | Probable error | Number of cases |
|---|---|---|---|
| Chemistry Aptitude and marks | .570 | ± .053 | 75 |
| Chemistry Training and marks | .575 | ± .052 | 116 |
| Intelligence and marks (Aptitude group) | .400 | ± .065 | 75 |
| Intelligence and marks (Training group) | .425 | ± .052 | 113 |
| Chemistry Aptitude and Intelligence | .540 | ± .055 | 75 |
| Chemistry Training and Intelligence | .450 | ± .050 | 116 |

It will be noted from the table that scores on the Chemistry Aptitude Test and scores on the Chemistry Training Test correlate with average marks in chemistry, .570 ± .053 and .575 ± .052, respectively, whereas the Intelligence Test scores correlate with average chemistry marks in the two groups, .400 ± .065 and .425 ± .052, respectively. The difference between the correlation of Chemistry Aptitude and marks and Intelligence and marks is .17 ± .057, and the difference between the correlation of Chemistry Training and marks and Intelligence and marks is .15 ± .050. The differences are both approximately three times as great as their probable errors. While the differences between these correlations can not be said to be completely significant, there are 98 chances in 100 of a true difference. From the differences in the above correlations it would appear that both the Chemistry Training Test and the Chemistry Aptitude Test are better criteria for the prediction of success in first-year college chemistry than is the Ohio Psychological Examination.

The problem of the study is to determine further whether or not the Intelligence Test results added to the Chemistry Test results would be a better criterion for prediction than the results of either the aptitude or training tests taken alone. This problem can be answered by computing the multiple correlation between Chemistry Aptitude and Intelligence with marks and between Chemistry Training and Intelligence with marks. If the Intelligence Test measures factors other than those measured by either Chemistry Training or Chemistry Aptitude Tests, one would expect the multiple correlations to be greater than the zero order correlations. If, on the other hand, most of the factors measured by the intelligence tests are also measured by Chemistry Training and Aptitude Tests, one would not expect any increase in the multiple correlations over the zero order correlations. Table II shows the multiple correlations to be almost identical with the zero order correlations.

It is evident that nothing of value has been added to the criterion by the addition of the Intelligence Test to either the Chemistry Training Test or the Chemistry Aptitude Test.

TABLE II

MULTIPLE CORRELATIONS

| Variables correlated | Multiple correlation | Number of cases |
|---|---|---|
| Combination of Chemistry Aptitude and Intelligence with average marks | .570 | 75 |
| Combination of Chemistry Training and Intelligence with average marks | .570 | 113 |

Another measure of the predictive value of a criterion is the size of the probable error of a predicted score which is measured by the probable error of estimate. The criterion which yields the smallest probable error of estimate is the best for prediction. Table III shows the probable errors of estimate of predicted chemistry marks from six criteria.

TABLE III

PROBABLE ERRORS OF ESTIMATE

| Criteria | Probable error of estimate |
|---|---|
| $PE_{(est)}$ of marks predicted from Chemistry Aptitude | .76 Point |
| $PE_{(est)}$ of marks predicted from Intelligence (Aptitude group) | .85 Point |
| $PE_{(est)}$ of marks predicted from combination of Intelligence and Chemistry Aptitude | .76 Point |
| $PE_{(est)}$ of marks predicted from Chemistry Training | .59 Point |
| $PE_{(est)}$ of marks predicted from Intelligence (Training group) | .66 Point |
| $PE_{(est)}$ of marks predicted from combination of Intelligence and Chemistry Training | .59 Point |

All errors of predicted marks are larger for the group which took the Aptitude Test than for the group which took the Training Test because of the smaller number of cases in the aptitude group. None of the predictions are very accurate. A chemistry mark predicted from the Aptitude Test has a relatively large error; *e.g.*, there is a fifty-fifty chance that a predicted mark of 3 would vary from 2.24 to 3.76 and a fifty-fifty chance that it would vary beyond these limits. Or again, there is a fifty-fifty chance that an average chemistry mark of 3, predicted from the Training Test, would vary from 2.41 to 3.59, and a fifty-fifty chance that it would vary beyond these limits. The errors of prediction are not reduced when combinations of Training and Intelligence or Aptitude and Intelligence are taken as the criterion.

CONCLUSIONS

(1) Both Chemistry Training and Chemistry Aptitude, as measured by the tests used in this study, correlate more highly with average marks in chemistry than do the Intelligence Test scores.

(2) A more accurate prediction of success in first-year college chemistry can be made from either the Iowa Chemistry Aptitude Test or the Iowa Chemistry Training Test alone than from the Ohio Psychological Examination alone.

(3) A prediction of success in first-year college chemistry based upon a combination of the Intelligence Test scores and Chemistry Training Test scores is no more accurate than a prediction based upon Chemistry Training Test scores alone.

(4) A prediction of success in first-year college chemistry based upon a combination of the Chemistry Aptitude Test scores and the Intelligence Test scores is no more accurate than a prediction based upon the Chemistry Aptitude Test scores alone.

(5) Neither the Chemistry Aptitude Test nor the Chemistry Training Test yields a sufficiently high correlation with chemistry marks to make it a very valuable basis for prediction of success in first-year college chemistry.

W. C. REUSSER
VAUGHN BRINEGAR
GUY FRANK
UNIVERSITY OF WYOMING

## NEW BOOKS IN EDUCATION

LUMLEY, F. H. *Broadcasting Foreign-Language Lessons.* Pp. viii + 90. Bureau of Educational Research, Ohio State University.

THOMAS, EDITH and T. R. BAROUS, Editors. *Alumni Reading List.* Second series. Pp. xi + 209. University of Michigan Press.

TYLER, TRACY F., Editor. *Radio as a Cultural Agency.* Pp. viii + 150. National Committee on Education by Radio, Washington.

# SCHOOL AND SOCIETY

WITH WHICH ARE COMBINED THE EDUCATIONAL REVIEW, ESTABLISHED IN 1891, THE TEACHERS MAGAZINE, ESTABLISHED IN 1878, AND THE SCHOOL JOURNAL, ESTABLISHED IN 1874.

Volume 40 SATURDAY, AUGUST 18, 1934 Number 1025

## QUESTIONABLE RECOMMENDATIONS OF THE COMMISSION ON THE SOCIAL STUDIES

By Professor FRANKLIN BOBBITT

UNIVERSITY OF CHICAGO

A RATHER startling social document has recently made its appearance. It seems to be important chiefly as evidence of the degree of strength and soundness of one of the factors upon which the future of our nation depends.

For a century or two, our economic, political and other social affairs have been growing increasingly complex and have been requiring corresponding enlargement of the social intelligence of the population. During the last generation particularly, the growth of large-scale corporationism and of technology has been bewilderingly rapid and has produced a social complexity that calls to-day for greatly enhanced enlightenment. If this is not achieved, the nation sooner or later, it seems, will be overwhelmed.

From the beginnings of our national history, we have assumed that the way to meet increased responsibilities was to raise the general level of intelligence. As a consequence, the public schools, which had a simple task in the simple world of a century ago, now bear a heavy responsibility in the complex world of to-day. And we have had faith both in the power of a generally distributed intelligence and in the potential ability of our people to attain the necessary levels of discernment.

Leadership in the enlightenment necessary for a wise management of economic and political affairs is entrusted to the specialized economists, political scientists, sociologists, historians and geographers. They are the custodians of the accumulated wisdom of mankind relative to the management of social affairs. Society supports them for that work. It is for them then, as their function, to extend this wisdom by research, to keep it organized and to place it at the disposal of all our citizens for their guidance. The custodians of the social science are the *ex-officio* leaders of the nation in that thought that should guide our people along the wholesome and fruitful lines of progress and which should help them to see the errors and dangers that are to be avoided.

During the past two or three decades, particularly, the population has been seriously mismanaging its economic-political affairs and running into difficulties, which have come to a head during the past five years. Clearly, our people have not attained the degree of enlightenment that is now necessary for guiding its social affairs with wisdom and competency. The custodians of social understanding either have been lacking in their supply of it or there has been inefficiency in distributing it to the population.

Recognizing this deficiency, the American Historical Association, in cooperation with other national social science groups, arranged five years ago for an official "Commission on the Social Studies." The duty of this body was double: (1) To note the route along which the nation should be guided in its progress forward, as shown by their social science; and (2) to explain in sufficiently detailed and understandable fashion the educational program necessary for so educating the population that it can follow the route which is indicated by the social science. Because of the gravity of their responsibility and the difficulty of the problems, the commission was given five years for the work and a generous grant by the Carnegie Corporation, which enabled it to work under highly favorable conditions. This was justified by the fact that no body of men in this broad land, at this critical time, has been charged with so fundamental and so heavy a responsibility. Those who guide the nation's thought guide the nation.

The five years are at an end. In a small document[1] of 23,000 words—the equivalent of about seventy-five ordinary book pages—they present their conclusions. As representatives of the nation's authorized custodians of the social science, it is to be viewed as the authoritative pronouncement of that specialized group. It purports to be the highest wisdom that the nation has to present relative to the route forward and to the acquisition of competence to travel it.

If the commission has succeeded in its work, the thought of this document should be memorized by every citizen in the land: it would show them the way forward to which they are to hold, and the qualities and powers they must maintain within themselves in order to keep the course. Especially should it guide those who are educating the oncoming generation.

If the commission has failed in its task, it shows that the specialized custodians of the thought needed for social guidance are unequal to the demands upon them, and that the nation lacks guidance. Beyond understanding there is nothing reliable to which it can turn. It can guess and grope in the fog; it can operate on the basis of wishes, emotions and benevolent paternalism; it can plunge now this way and now that in blind trial and error and rationalize it by calling it "experimentation"; but amidst the complexities and perils of to-day those methods promise to be about as successful as a blind man's driving in swift motorcar traffic. Any guidance except that of intelligence will lead but to disaster. Even the amount of intelligence that we have may not succeed; but it is the only thing that holds out any measure of promise. If it fails, the nation which thought it was moving toward the promised land moves toward the abysses.

It is then our national duty to scrutinize with all care the route which the expert interpreters of social wisdom have pointed out to us in this document as the one the nation ought to follow. While the followership can not lead, it is for them to check the guidance accorded by their leaders.

*A*

Let us then note the way forward as this is charted by those who represent the nation's most expert pilots. The commission

[1] American Historical Association, Report of the Commission on the Social Studies: "Conclusions and Recommendations of the Commission." New York: Charles Scribner's Sons, 1934. Pp. 168.

Abstract of the report appeared in SCHOOL AND SOCIETY, XXXIX (May 26, 1934), 680–82.

The report was signed without reservations by: Charles A. Beard, Ada Comstock, George S. Counts, Avery O. Craven, Guy Stanton Ford, Carlton J. H. Hayes, Henry Johnson, A. C. Krey, Leon C. Marshall, Jesse H. Newlon, and Jessie Steiner; and with reservations by Isaiah Bowman. Four members of the commission refused to sign the report. These were: Frank A. Ballou, Edmund E. Day, Ernest Horn, and Charles E. Merriam. Superintendent Ballou presented his reasons in SCHOOL AND SOCIETY, Volume XXXIX, page 701.

writes: "Cumulative evidence supports the conclusion that, in the United States as in other countries, the age of individualism and *laissez-faire* in economy and government is closing and that a new age of collectivism is emerging."

The commission does not make concrete what this collectivism in the United States is to be by naming those other countries that we are to accompany. If they do not mean the outstanding exponents and exemplars of collectivism, namely, Italy, Germany and Russia, they ought to have made the matter clear by naming the countries that they had in mind. We must therefore assume that they meant those best-known ones; and that the United States, in the judgment of the representatives of those who best know, moves toward the repressive anti-democratic fascism of Italy and Germany, or toward the communism of Russia. If the commission means otherwise, it should explain what it means.

In further interpretation of the matter, the commission says:

> As to the specific form which this "collectivism," this integration and interdependence, is taking and will take in the future, the evidence at hand is by no means clear or unequivocal. It may involve the limiting or supplanting of private property by public property or it may entail the preservation of private property, extended and distributed among the masses.

The commission seems to have been divided in mind whether this collectivism toward which we move, rightly in their judgment, is to take the form of communism by the "limiting or supplanting of private property by public property" or some type of fascism in which there is to be the "preservation of private property, extended and distributed among the masses." The clear antipathy of the commission to private property, except as it is distributed among the masses, is significant. It is also significant that they frequently refer to the free-born citizens of America as "the masses." Within that phrase is the implication of serious civic degeneracy. Then in this disability of the population, they find their justification for advocating a generous state paternalism to care for those who have lost their powers to care for themselves.

Having told us obscurely, in the first paragraph quoted, the kind of collectivism meant, in this second paragraph they name the protective euphemism that they intend to use in their report in their references to fascism and communism, namely, "integration and interdependence." This obscure phrase is clear enough for the initiate to understand and innocuous enough not to alarm the uninitiated. Not once in its report does the commission use either term "fascism" or "communism." If it looked upon these as threats to the nation, it seems that it would have named them at least once in warning against them. But instead, it always refers to them by the use of favorable euphemisms which will not awaken the wide-spread popular antagonism toward any form of collectivism. Favorite terms of reference are: "closely integrated society," "economy marked by integration and interdependence," "an economy managed in the interests of the masses," "the emerging economy," "the new order," "collectivism" and "the steadily integrating social order." They seem to expect those who speak their special language of proletarianism to understand, and the others to be too dull to be offended. It is obvious that the commission has little respect for the intelligence of the American population. As a matter of fact, their whole report grounds itself back upon their low valuation of the potential intelligence, independence of spirit and competence of "the masses," and the consequent need of a régime of state paternalism to care for a population no longer competent for individual self-management. They further say:

Almost certainly [the oncoming age] will involve a larger measure of compulsory as well as voluntary cooperation of citizens in the conduct of the complex national economy, a corresponding enlargement of the functions of government, and an increasing state intervention in fundamental branches of economy previously left to individual discretion and initiative—a state intervention that in some instances may be direct and mandatory and in others indirect and facilitative. In any event, the commission is convinced by its interpretation of available empirical data that the actually integrating economy of the present day is the forerunner of a consciously integrated society in which individual economic actions and individual property rights will be altered and abridged.

The deliberately obscured phrases of this pronouncement by a representative commission from among those who are assuming both theoretical and practical economic-political leadership in our country should be carefully examined and the meaning brought out into the light. Their terms are doubtless to be interpreted in the way in which the things referred to are working out in those "other countries" which are traveling the road which the commission thinks we are to travel. When they say, then, that there is to be "compulsory as well as voluntary cooperation of citizens in the conduct of" fascism or communism, we can visualize in the concrete what their obscure phrases mean by viewing the large amount of compulsory and the small amount of voluntary cooperation in Italy, Germany and Russia. If that is not what the commission means, they will grant that the matter is important enough for them at least to explain in a few clear-cut and unambiguous terms exactly what they do mean.

Democracy in our land has had a long and honorable history. Its measure of success has been such as warrants a full and sympathetic consideration by the commission, rather than the curt dismissal without any attempt at explanation that it receives. The refusal of this authoritative body even to grant democracy a hearing seems to violate principles of scientific accuracy, balance and tolerance which they laud so definitely and justly in their report. Failure on their part to live up to their own standards may be regarded by the population, to whom they are *ex-officio* leaders of thought, as failure of trust.

As one analyzes the report of the commission, there can be no uncertainty relative to their satisfaction in viewing the collectivistic trend. They make no attempt to discover whether this trend is an evil to be counteracted and prevented by education or a good that is to be accepted and promoted by education. They seem simply to accept it without questioning it. They are so certain that it is a thing of promise, which is to be embraced and furthered, that the alternative of preserving democracy seems not even to have occurred to them.

The commission seems to write, however, with an uneasy conscience. Voices from our democratic past, with its high hopes and enthusiasms, still echo in their memories. And in their report, some of the familiar phrases work through to the surface and float like wreckage of things gone:

The commission deems possible and desirable the retention and fulfillment of the historical principles and ideals of American democracy. . . . (p. 23.)

. . . a supreme purpose of education in the United States . . . is . . . to shape the form of that society in accordance with American ideals of popular democracy and personal liberty and dignity. . . . (p. 39.)

The great purpose of the American public school . . . is to prepare the younger generation for life in a highly complex society that is committed to the ideal of democracy. . . . (p. 46.)

These brave, and shall we also say, pathetic, words in an expiring age yet come easy to those who confess they have lost the faith, since as historians the phrases are deeply engraved in their now rejected mental autonomisms. They show that they do not mean them, however, by never following them up in their proposals and by their denunciation with fervor, and often with bitterness, of the things involved, and which they conceive to be inevitably involved, in democracy. They trounce with all the humorless zeal of a proletarian such horrors as "individualism," "property rights," "individual enterprise," "acquisitive egoism," "predatory groups," "special privilege," "privileged minority," "gross inequalities in income and wealth," "harnessing of science to individualism in business enterprise" and the "subjection of public welfare to the egoism of private interests."

It is difficult to explain, in a way favorable to the commission, their frequent lip-service to democracy, when the whole tenor of their report is denial both of its legitimacy and of its desirability. One can not believe that they are uninformed relative to the differing natures of collectivism and of democracy and of their total irreconcilability. It is equally difficult to believe that they use the slogans of democracy as a mere protective smoke-screen for a communistic offensive. It would be too transparent. The only plausible explanation that the present writer can find for their contradictions is that their paeans to democracy spring from their automatisms as tributes to a dying age of revered memory.

*B*

The second of the two major functions of the commission was to formulate, in general outline at least, a plan of education for the nation that would make the population proficient in the management of its economic, political and other social affairs in the difficult period that lies ahead of us. Since, in the judgment of the commission, this is to be some form of collectivism, of which all kinds are really much alike in spite of their terminology and their pretenses, the educational problem is then how to educate the people in general for a willing and child-like submissiveness to the wise and benevolent few who are to think and plan their affairs for them.

Their problem is a new one for American education. Our public schools were designed to meet the needs of a nation of individuals, each of whom was to be a full-statured, independent and self-reliant freeman in his own right. Each was to be actuated by a sense of his individual responsibility and vigorous in the self-directed discharge of it. Persons were still to be persons, not "masses," and they expected to do their own thinking and planning and to be rewarded when they thought straight and planned sanely; and equally they expected to be punished with failure, if they were superficial and childish in their thinking and careless in their planning. Hence education was expected to mature their powers of thought and judgment and to set them on their feet as self-reliant grown-up men and women.

But now, we are told, that type of human living and of education is to be superseded. Men are to be nurslings of the state. The integrators and directors of the interdependent coordination, to borrow the commission's impressive phraseology, are to think and to plan for the masses. If this function were left to the people, they would get things badly mixed. In the emerging economy, human beings are no longer to have the adventure of making their own mistakes. Things are to be planned and managed by those who do not make mistakes.

It is obvious that the first step in making the people submissive is to indoctrinate them fully with the spirit and philosophy of state paternalism. They must see themselves clearly as the happy children of the all-wise and beneficent state. They began life in the happy condition of irresponsible children. Now that they can not get into their vocations before the age of twenty or twenty-five, they must continue to be paternalistically cared for until the age when their characters are pretty well finished and shaped for life. They come to adulthood accustomed to paternalism and liking it, since they have never known anything else. They are well prepared to continue it for the rest of their lives. They retain enough manhood not to want to continue to be burdens upon their own fathers and mothers; but as the great All-Father, the State, beckons benevolently to them, they gladly accept its vast and all-protective paternalism. They would nestle in its bosom, children that never grew up.

Clearly the social conditions have paved the way to a national acceptance of the philosophy of state paternalism, in which submissiveness and obedience are essential factors. Indoctrination has only to build upon foundations already securely laid. The business of education is to make the population conscious of the ideals, standards, purposes and values of the easy, juvenile, collectivistic way. It will protect them from all ideas of a contrary character that would only confuse their standardized and sweetly harmonious thinking. This philosophy is then to be emotionalized and quickened as a religion, since there is nothing that will prevent contrary thought quite so effectively as an atmosphere of contrary emotion.

> From this point of view [the commission writes] a supreme purpose of education in the United States, in addition to the development of rich and many-sided personalities, is the preparation of the rising generation to enter the society now coming into being through thought, ideal, and knowledge, rather than through coercion, regimentation, and ignorance, and to shape the form of that society in accordance with American ideals of popular democracy and personal liberty and dignity.

The commission, of course, knows that collectivism requires the submission of all to the plans of the few; but they see that self-submission is both more effective and more pleasant than enforced submission. Self-regimentation along the lines of the indoctrination is better for all concerned than official regimentation. Coercion is made unnecessary, if one can be brought to travel the road because he likes it and has been made competent in reading the road-signs.

The central thought of that paragraph, which the commission seems deliberately to have obscured by its irrelevant opening and closing phrases, is this: We must educationally aim at indoctrination so as to avoid the necessity of coercion.

From the commission's point of view, this is essential. Every nation that is now collectivizing its population is forced to use a full measure of coercion; and this is because education has not yet sufficiently shaped the population for self-regimentation. The commission realizes that the traditions of freedom in our country will make even "the masses" impatient of the restraints inherent in fascism or communism. Hence they must be carefully prepared in ideals and thought "to enter the society now coming into being." This ought not, however, in America to be difficult. Conditions have already shaped the current generation for an all-comprehensive paternalism. The people already have favorable attitudes. And the high level of native intelligence has been awakened by our schools. We have only to develop a properly colored and unconfused kind of "thought, ideal and knowledge" in order to succeed, in a way that European nations have not succeeded, in evading coercion and regimentation. This is accomplished as we achieve a full self-regimentation, actuated by enlightened self-interest. The function of the school is to attach the needed enlightenment to the self-interest.

If this is not the thought of the commission, it is for them to explain what their thought is. Since they have chosen to chart the future for the nation and for education in obscure phrases of hidden meaning, we are forced to interpret them in terms of the commission's central doctrines. Those of us who are engaged in the education of the rising generation greatly need to draw upon the best understanding that the country has to offer. We know that the expert custodians of the social science—assuming that they are genuinely expert—are the only ones to whom we can legitimately turn. We try here to decipher the meanings of those who seem either not to have been expert or not to have played fair with us. If our interpretations are mistaken, the members of the commission have yet time to explain their meaning in clear and honest terms.

*C*

This document is to be viewed as a symptom. The nation is sufficiently science-minded to realize that the rough-and-ready knowledge of common sense is no longer adequate for grappling with our baffling economic and political ailments. The nation is like a very sick man. Only the best doctors are qualified to diagnose, to prescribe and to direct the treatment. Hence the nation, in its representatives, the government, turns to its custodians of social science as the expert physicians. The rightness of the method of turning to the best available science for guidance can not today be questioned.

The science of the experts may yet be insufficient for properly guiding the treatment. But there is, and in the nature of the case, can be no proper substitute. We go forward to success on the basis of the wisdom of the experts; or we fail. Those are the only alternatives before the country.

The country is then compelled to ask: How competent, in their organization and interpretation of the social science, are its specialized custodians? As the nation drifts in all sorts of directions, do they see, and are they able to point out, the one right direction? Or are they themselves so unanchored in their understanding as to be swept from their moorings and lose all sense of proper direction?

This document is a good index of their preparedness to hold firmly and consistently to a course in the midst of storm. This body had a clear and definite commission. It was asked to provide guidance to the nation in its most fundamental function of educating 130,000,000 citizens for social competency. It was given highly favorable conditions for its labors. The work was under way before the storm broke. They had then four years of viewing the raging cross-currents as motive and opportunity for bringing their science to bear in a diagnostic way and for showing the nation and the educational profession the course to which we must hold if we are to ride out the storm unharmed, and continually to meet those of the future. How well did they meet this responsibility?

Their report shows that they moved in the same direction as the major currents of the storm. Either they did it because they were intellectually unanchored and blind like the rest, or because in the clearness of their vision of the realities they saw that the currents, by miraculous and fortunate chance, were carrying us in right directions. Now which of these is the proper explanation?

The answer is to be ascertained in the character of their report. If it shows them in an emotionalized state of exhilaration, and oblivious to all besides the thrills of the new country they are being carried into—if they are enthusiastic evangels of the new movement and oblivious to even the presence of alternatives—then we can be assured that they are not the voices of the social science.

On the other hand, if the report soberly shows the alternative possibilities, gives each a proper hearing, carefully weighs the factors and cautiously points out the clear reasons why one course is to be approved and all contrary ones to be disapproved, if it does these things in the convincing and yet unemotional manner of the clear-seeing, science-directed physician or engineer, then the internal evidence of the report is that, as pilots to the nation, they can be trusted. Beyond all others, they are the ones who merit our confidence.

The tone of the commission as it presents its basic—shall we call it thought or emotion?—is that of the revolutionary hysteria that grips all the collectivizing nations. They laud scientific methods; but it seems to be rationalizing after-thought. They show no evidence, in spite of their claims, of having used it in arriving at their conclusions.

The report of the commission is an ominous symptom of unpreparedness on the part of the custodians of the social science to lead the thought required for guiding aright the onward progress of the nation.

The American Historical Association and allied groups which sponsored the commission now bear responsibility for properly dealing with this astounding document. If it meets their approval, it is their duty to popularize its ideas and recommendations, to work them into the national consciousness, and thereby make them effective for the guidance of progress. If, on the other hand, they do not approve, then it is their clear duty promptly and unequivocally to repudiate the report as not representing the thought of the specialists in social understanding. If they approve and remain silent, they will be derelict in social duty. If they employ silence as their method of repudiation, then as the *ex-officio* leaders of social thought for the country, they will be remiss in their leadership.

# EDUCATIONAL EVENTS

## SCOUT ACTIVITIES FOR THE PHYSICALLY HANDICAPPED IN NORWAY

A SPECIAL dispatch to *The Christian Science Monitor* from Oslo, Norway, discusses the progress of the boy and girl scout movement among the physically handicapped.

In Oslo scouting among boys at the school for the deaf was started in 1930 by the chemist Erling Willoch, who himself had been a scout since 1915. The head master at the school for the deaf gives some of the school hours to scout training, which is proving its value in widening the outlook of the deaf, stimulating their initiative, and making them more contented. To start with, Mr. Willoch found that he had to give all the instruction himself, but now he takes the boys fortnightly, and a deaf patrol leader gives weekly instruction. Six to eight deaf scouts now join the ordinary scouts who patrol the ski tracks in Nordmarka and Ostmarka on winter Sundays, when as many as 60,000 ski runners are out. Patrolling the most crowded tracks, smoothing them and guiding the stream of skiers has proved effective in preventing mishaps. This patrolling has resulted in the reduction of accidents from about 100 in Nordmarka in 1929–30 to about 20 in 1933–34.

The troop of deaf girl guides in Oslo, started by Miss Kristine Johansen, Strömmen, are said to strive earnestly to keep their scout promise and law. There is also a troop of deaf girl guides at Holmestrand. This guide patrol grew out of a series of concerts given here under the auspices of a group of grown-up girl guides at the head of whom is Miss Fjeld, herself a guide for sixteen years. Miss Fjeld realized they might start a girl-guide patrol, and a year ago the first patrol of fifteen was started among these disabled girls, and on the anniversary this year four more girls were initiated. Their program resembles as closely as possible that of the ordinary guides. The theory of scouting they take fully, and the girls who have hitherto been only conscious of their physical inferiority, now enjoy the opportunity for equality which is involved in the scout's promise and duties.

According to the *Monitor,* the matron of the cripples' working home is highly pleased with the influence of scouting on the girls. She finds they are keener, more enthusiastic, happier and more grateful for what is being done for them. It is also encouraging to see how many practical things they are capable of doing. This year they are going to have a camp.

The girls stop two years at this home, then go back to their respective homes. Contact is being kept up by correspondence, and if there is a girl guide troop in the vicinity intercommunication is established.

In Trondheim, besides a two-year-old troop of deaf girl guides there is a troop of blind guides. With these one important point is to get them out in the open like other children. This in itself makes a vast difference to them, opening the world of nature. They learn quickly and remember well.

At Stavern, Miss Marie Treschow has started a troop among the bedridden children. She has an assistant who teaches the children practical things, like making little presents. Otherwise the main part of the training is done by correspondence. Monthly the children receive a letter which is sent from bed to bed, and each one of the children copies out in a little book the things they are to learn from it. These books are made as interesting and entertaining as possible with illustrations, riddles and instruction. From time to time the leaders come out to visit the children. To these children, the sense of sharing other children's activities, and feeling that they have got something of value to do, is found to be of inestimable consequence. In Bergen, a similar troop is being started, and in Finmark it is already under way.

At the school for mentally undeveloped children at Röstad, Levanger, north of Trondheim, a troop has been started and, although this is perhaps the most difficult of all these scouting enterprises, it is found interesting and encouraging, for the children are aroused to activity and initiative.

## THE LIBRARY OF THE UNIVERSITY OF LIVERPOOL

WE learn from the London *Times* that Harold L. Cohen, of Liverpool, England, whose family have been associated with the city for four generations, has made a gift of £100,000 to the University of Liverpool for the erection of a new library.

Mr. Cohen's decision is conveyed in the following letter, which he has sent to Lord Derby, chancellor of the university:

I believe that the number of students in the University of Liverpool has now seriously outgrown its library facilities. I realize that library accommodation must be of vital importance to many of the young men and women in this university who do not live in hostels and who may not have readily available places for quiet reading and study.

My wife and I and our children are natives of Liverpool and my family have lived in the city for four generations. We have received so many kindnesses from our fellow-citizens that it occurs to me that I might find an opportunity for expressing my gratitude for all these benefits if I were to try to secure for the young men and women of the university a chance of obtaining for themselves and future generations of students the benefits that come from a good university library.

May I, therefore, offer to you as chancellor the sum of £100,000, which I understand is the amount required to pay for a library worthy of the university to which you have for over 25 years devoted so much of your time and thought.

Lord Derby has expressed to Mr. Cohen the profound gratitude of the university.

The main university library is at present housed in the Tate Library, the gift to the university of Sir Henry Tate in 1892. With the great increase in the library and the number of readers, the present accommodation is now altogether inadequate. The university council for some years have felt some anxiety for the library situation and have recognized that the only satisfactory solution is the erection of a new building. This has now been made possible by Mr. Cohen's offer. Mr. Cohen has already shown his interest in university library matters by a gift to the endowment fund of the library and by bearing the cost of the furnishing and equipment of the library in the new building of the Students' Union. Mr. Cohen's father, the late Alderman Louis Cohen, Lord Mayor of Liverpool in 1899–1900, founded and endowed a chair of dental surgery at the university in 1920.

It is intended to erect the new library on the site of the old School of Architecture in Ashton Street. Operations will begin in January.

## THE CANADIAN LIBRARY COUNCIL

THE formation of a Canadian Library Council to meet problems essentially Canadian in character but affiliated in some way with the American Library Association was considered at the Montreal conference, according to the *Bulletin* of the association. This action was taken at a business meeting of several hundred Canadian librarians following the Canadian reception at the Redpath Library, McGill University, on the evening of June 26, and was the outgrowth of suggestions presented the previous day at the open meeting of the Library Extension Board for Canadian librarians. Mary J. L. Black, Public Library, Fort William, Ontario, Canadian member of the Library Extension Board, presided at both meetings.

As soon as the resolution setting up the council was adopted, an organization committee was named and a nominating committee of three elected.

Officers chosen at a later meeting were: *President,* John Ridington, University of British Columbia Library, Vancouver; *First Vice-president,* Fred Landon, University of Western Ontario Library, London; *Second Vice-president,* Aegidius Fauteux, Municipal Library, Montreal; *Treasurer,* Henry Munro, superintendent of education, Halifax, Nova Scotia; *Secretary,* Edgar S. Robinson, Vancouver Public Library.

An executive committee consists of Estelle Vaughan, Gerhard R. Lomer, W. J. Sykes, Angus Mowat, and E. L. Hill, with George H. Locke and Miss Black, *ex-officio* members.

At the open meeting for Canadian librarians, John Ridington spoke of the need for a central Canadian library agency and traced the history of concerted interest on the part of Canadian librarians in their problems from its beginning in a Canadian meeting at the Seattle conference in 1926.

The Toronto conference in 1927 was the occasion for another Canadian library gathering, which Mr. Ridington termed "the most enthusiastic meeting he had ever attended." It was there that the suggestion was first made and approved that some organization should be established which would form the bond of contact between those engaged in library work throughout the entire Dominion. A Canadian library association was formed, but the practical difficulties of working without a secretariat and the lack of funds to establish such an office proved insuperable.

Another Canadian project of the Toronto conference, however, was carried through with great success. This was the survey of library conditions and needs in Canada which was accomplished through a grant from the Carnegie Corporation of New York. The published report, "Libraries in Canada," has given great impetus to library improvement and extension in many of the provinces.

## RURAL SCHOOL LIBRARY PRACTICE

A STUDY of rural school library practices and services has been made by Edith A. Lathrop, of the Office of Education, in cooperation with the Carnegie Corporation of New York, the American Library Association and an expert advisory committee.

The survey, made in 42 states, included visits to 364 rural schools of all types and 55 county libraries in 24 states. Library service was studied also in 23 city school systems and in the library practise schools of Teachers College, Columbia University, and of the University of Chicago.

The investigation showed a great need in rural schools for books especially suitable for children in the lower elementary grades. Restricted use of books and periodicals as sources of information in development of school projects is also reported. Recreational reading, an integral part of programs in many larger schools, was found to receive little attenion in small rural schools. It was discovered also that comparatively few persons in charge of rural school libraries have received training in library work.

But the rural school library picture is brightened here and there by numerous successful practices, local or state-wide. State supervisors of library schools direct library demonstrations and experiments in some instances. Teacher-training institutions offer courses in library technique for rural high-school teachers, and occasionally, where there is no county library service, offices of county superintendents of schools circulate books.

Some rural communities encourage reading in elementary classes by offering such books as

Arabian Nights, Pinnochio and other favorites instead of the old-fashioned reading texts. Individual differences of readers are recognized. Not all children read the same books or the same number of books. Puppet shows and other forms of dramatization replace dull book reviews, and lantern slides are often used. Children even build and furnish libraries as well as doll houses.

Alabama is experimenting with methods for improving administration of rural school libraries. Southern California rural-school supervisors are studying school library problems. North Carolina has carried on four types of demonstrations, one of which provides for an itinerant librarian. In Minnesota, county teachers' institutes have been used as mediums for library instruction. Groups of rural teachers in New York meet with the state school library supervisor for the purpose of learning how to organize their libraries.

Further evidence of the endeavor to provide better library service for at least some of the 40,000,000 persons in the United States without public library facilities, is the number of state and local school-library surveys. Such surveys have been made in California, Florida, Illinois, Indiana, Iowa, Kentucky, Massachusetts, Michigan, Missouri, Nebraska, New York, North Dakota, Ohio, Oregon, Pennsylvania, South Carolina, Virginia and Washington. Most of these surveys show forward-looking practices, but a quite general failure to make the library a dynamic factor in the rural school. Problems to be solved in making the library an integral part of the rural school include methods of financing and administration.

## THE TEACHER'S OATH IN NEW YORK STATE

GOVERNOR LEHMAN of New York signed the Ives bill on August 10 requiring an oath of allegiance to the State and Federal Constitutions from teachers in both public and private schools.

The Governor had vetoed a similar bill at the regular session, but in a memorandum he said that the new bill had been amended to meet some of the objections he had voiced.

The text of the new law reads:

After October 1, 1934, it shall be unlawful for any citizen of the United States to serve as teacher, instructor or professor in any school or institution in the public school system of the State or in any school, college, university or other educational institution in this State, whose real property or any part of it is exempt from taxation under section 4 of the tax law unless and until he or she shall have taken and subscribed the following oath or affirmation: "I do solemnly swear (or affirm) that I will support the Constitution of the United States of America and the Constitution of the State of New York, and that I will faithfully discharge, according to the best of my ability, the duties of the position of .................... (title of position and name or designation of school, college, university or institution to be here inserted), to which I am now assigned."

The oath required by this section shall be administered only by the officer or person, or in the case of a board or body by a member of the board or body, having authority to employ such person as a teacher, instructor or professor in such school, college, university or institution, and each is hereby authorized to administer it.

The officer, person or member administering such oath shall make a record or notation of the fact in the books or records of the school, college, university or institution, and forthwith transmit the oath as taken and subscribed to the Commissioner of Education, who shall file it in his office, where it shall be subject to public inspection.

It shall be unlawful for an officer, person or board having control of the employment, dismissal or suspension of teachers, instructors or professors in such a school, college, university or institution to permit a person to serve in any such capacity therein in violation of the provisions of this section.

This section shall not be construed to require a person to take such oath more than once during the time he or she is employed in the same school, college, university or institution, though there be a change in the title or duties of the position.

The provisions of section 30 of the civil service law shall not apply to a person who is required to take the oath prescribed by this section.

This act shall take effect immediately.

## CONFERENCE OF ENGINEERS ON RECONSTRUCTION AND RECOVERY

MEMBERS of the American Society of Mechanical Engineers and the American Institute of Chemical Engineers and professors and alumni of various colleges of engineering met at Johnsonburg, N. J., on Saturday, August 11, at the engineering camp of the Stevens Institute of Technology, to begin a nine-day conference on current economic and industrial problems. At the opening session on Saturday evening, the president of the Bell Telephone Company of New Jersey spoke on "Collectivism and Individualism in Industrial Management."

In the course of the following week, twenty-five conference sessions were planned on the theme "An Economic Appraisal of the New Deal" and under this head controversial economic and industrial questions will be considered from the point of view of the engineer, through addresses, forum sessions and seminars. At the final session, on Sunday evening, August 19, the speaker will be General Hugh S. Johnson, National Recovery Administrator, or, if necessary, his personal representative.

Ordinarily two sessions of the conference have been held each morning and one each evening. Members of the conference had the afternoons free for recreation and sports.

The schedule of evening sessions of the Conference was as follows:

August 11—Chester I. Barnard, president of the Bell Telephone Co., of New Jersey, on "Collectivism and Individualism in Industrial Management."

August 12—Malcolm C. Rorty, president of the American Management Association, on "Democratic Premises and the New Deal."

August 13—William J. Cunningham, professor of transportation in the Harvard University School of Business Administration, on "An Analysis of the Railroad Situation."

August 14—James D. Mooney, president of the General Motors Export Corporation, on "Paper Money and Gold in International Trade."

August 15—Charles B. Ames, chairman of the Board of the Texas Co., on "Oil Production and Control under NRA."

August 16—W. M. Persons, consulting economist, on "Government Experimentation in Business from 1776 to 1933."

August 17—Q. Forrest Walker, economist, R. H. Macy and Co., on "Distribution Problems under NRA."

August 18—Walter Rautenstrauch, professor of industrial engineering in Columbia University and others, in a panel discussion of "Can the Procedures of NRA Accomplish Its Objectives?"

August 19—General Hugh S. Johnson on NRA.

Of the morning meetings, two will deal with "Costs and Prices under NRA." Dr. W. D. Ennis, professor of economics of engineering at the Stevens Institute of Technology and director of the conference, presided at these two sessions. "Labor under the New Deal" was discussed in two sessions at which the speakers were Emanuel Stein, professor of economics at New York University, and Professor C. R. Daugherty, of the University of Pittsburgh.

Other speakers announced for morning sessions include Lyman Bryson, of the Des Moines Forum, on "The Revolt of the Small Business Man"; Louis M. Faulkner, deputy chamberlain of the City of New York, on "Rehabilitation of City Finances"; K. W. Jappe on "Tariff Bargaining"; Leon B. Lent, executive officer of the Code Authority of the Scientific Apparatus Industry, on "Economics of Industry Planning"; Benjamin S. Kirsch, counsellor at law, on "Legalities of NRA"; Henry R. Hayes, formerly president of the Investment Bankers Association, on "Some Aspects of Utility Investments"; Professor Paul H. Nystrom, of Columbia University, vice-chairman of the Retail Code Authority, on "Effects of the New Deal on Selling and Advertising"; James A. Farrell, formerly president of the United States Steel Corporation, on "Trade in a Changing World," and Professor John D. Black, of Harvard University, on "Agricultural Planning under AAA."

## THE SCIENCE INSTITUTE OF THE SUMMER SESSION OF PURDUE UNIVERSITY

THE Science Institute was organized as a part of the Summer Session of Purdue University for the purpose of bringing to students, faculty members and other persons outside the university who are interested, the latest developments in the various fields of science.

During the current Summer Session four series of lectures, field trips and informal discussions were offered in the fields of astronomy, botany, psychiatry and neurology.

From June 18 to June 23, Dr. W. B. McDougall, naturalist of Yellowstone National Park, gave a series of lectures embracing such subjects as symbiosis, plant interrelations, plant communities and the vegetation of the Rocky Mountains. These lectures were well attended mainly by graduate students, high-school teachers and faculty members.

In the second week of the institute Dr. J. R. Oliver, of the Johns Hopkins University Medical School, gave eleven lectures on "The Nature and Treatment of Mental Diseases." Among other groups in regular attendance at Dr. Oliver's lectures was a group of forty ministers from various parts of Indiana. The average attendance at these lectures was above two hundred.

Dr. Clifford Crump, designer of the Perkins Observatory and a well-known authority in the field of astronomy, gave daily lectures during the week of July 2 to July 7 on some of the recent discoveries in astronomy. Dr. Crump's lectures were well attended and created much interest in the subject.

From July 9 to July 14 Dr. C. J. Herrick, neurologist and head of the department of anatomy of the University of Chicago Medical School, presented the more recent discoveries concerning the anatomy and functions of the cerebral cortex. Professor Herrick's lectures were of special interest to advanced students in psychology and physiology.

The Science Institute is said to be doing more to stimulate interest among our graduate students in scientific work than any other organization of the Summer Session. While attendance at the lectures is entirely voluntary and in no case is credit in any regular course involved, the increasing number of regular attendants at the lectures is a fair indication of their value to the university community. The lectures are all open to students, faculty members, and others who are interested. No registration is required and thus far no attempt has been made to keep an accurate record of attendance. One of the most gratifying aspects of the Science Institute is the increasing tendency of various groups to remain after the lectures for informal discussion of some scientific question. These informal sessions frequently last for over an hour and are of material assistance to students in clarifying hazy or inaccurate concepts.

## CONFERENCE ON SUPERVISED CORRESPONDENCE COURSES

A CONFERENCE on supervised correspondence study was held at Teachers College, Columbia University, during the week of August 6. Dr. Frank W. Cyr, professor of education, Teachers College, acted as chairman of the conference. The general consensus of opinion was that supervised correspondence study in the high schools offers a possible solution of the problem of how boys finishing the high-school course can be provided for until employment opportunities increase.

"We are up against the problem in this country of keeping the boy occupied in school until he can find a job even though he has completed the regular course," according to L. P. Arduser, director of the High School Service Department of the International Correspondence Schools. "We can't keep the boy out of work and out of school at the same time. Supervised correspondence study in the high schools, because of its low comparative costs, makes it possible for the high school to widen its curriculum and provide for a larger student body without making unbearable the burden of taxation."

Professor F. W. Dunn, professor of rural education, Teachers College, stated that there are many rural high schools whose student body is not large enough to justify the wide variety of courses required to fit the curriculum to the individual and that supervised correspondence study provides a practical means of achieving this aim of present-day education. S. C. Mitchell, superintendent of schools, Benton Harbor, Michigan, pointed out that no high school, no matter how large, can undertake to offer as a part of its regular curriculum a course which only one or two students may need, but that the system of supervised correspondence study makes available all the hundreds of courses offered by correspondence schools and university extension courses. He stated that the Benton Harbor High School has an enrolment of over 700 students and that last year 132 were enrolled for correspondence study.

Supervised correspondence study consists of an arrangement between the local high school and a university extension division or correspondence school, whereby the high school is able to offer one or a group of its students any one of the great number of courses offered by these two types of educational institutions. Adopted by some 150 high schools, it has enabled the schools to fit the curriculum to the natural aptitudes and inclinations of the individual students, while avoiding the great increase in costs which such enrichment of the curriculum would ordinarily entail. A member of the school faculty is appointed to supervise and assist in the correspondence study. A regular period during the school day is allotted for this work.

The three-day conference was held in connection with the course in supervised correspondence study procedure now being given in the Teachers College Summer School, under the direction of Dr. Cyr, assisted by Superintendent Mitchell, of Benton Harbor. Among those attending the conference were: Professors K. O. Broady and A. A. Reed, University of Nebraska; Professor J. O. Keller, Pennsylvania State College; Director James A. Moyer, Massachusetts State Department of Education; Dr. Wayne W. Soper, New York State Education Department; Ralph Newing and L. P. Arduser, International Correspondence Schools; James McKinney, the American School, and Professors H. D. Kitson, F. W. Dunn and P. R. Mort, Teachers College.

# EDUCATIONAL NOTES AND NEWS

R. E. Priestley has been appointed vice-chancellor of Melbourne University, Australia. This is a newly created administrative post. Mr. Priestley is a fellow of Clare College, University of Cambridge, and secretary of the General Board of the Faculties and the Board of Research Studies.

Dr. H. G. Hotz, for the past fifteen years professor of education in the University of Arkansas, has been appointed acting dean of the College of Education, to succeed Dean C. E. Prall, who was recently appointed dean of the College of Education at the University of Pittsburgh.

Dr. Edward Henry Lauer has taken over his new work as dean of the College of Liberal Arts of the University of Washington.

Major Edwin Howard Armstrong, known for his work in radio communication, has been appointed professor of electrical engineering at Columbia University, to succeed the late John H. Morecroft.

Dr. Joseph M. Murray, a research associate of the Roscoe B. Jackson Memorial Laboratory, has been elected head of the department of zoology at the University of Maine. Dr. Murray will retain his position as a member of the laboratory staff and will take up his work at Orono in September of this year.

Roy F. Thompson, of New Haven, Conn., has been appointed associate professor of forestry at the Iowa State College to succeed Professor D. B. Demeritt, who resigned recently to become head of the department of forestry at the University of Maine. Since 1913 Mr. Thompson has served as assistant forest economist for the forest taxation inquiry of the U. S. Forest Service.

Dr. Albert Eugene Casey, associate in pathology at the Rockefeller Institute for Medical Research, has been appointed associate professor of pathology at the University of Virginia.

Dr. Albert J. Rooks has completed forty years of service with Calvin College, Grand Rapids, Michigan. Professor Rooks joined the college when the literary department was a theological school. He became its principal when it was reorganized in 1900, and became dean of the College of Literature in 1919. He now is professor of Latin.

Mary R. Chamberlin, who served as assistant superintendent in the New Rochelle, N. Y., schools since her appointment in 1899, has retired on a pension. A resolution expressing appreciation for her efficient service was adopted by the Board of Education at a recent meeting.

Dr. Earle E. Eubank, head of the department of sociology of the University of Cincinnati, recently conducted a two-day Social Welfare Institute in the City of Akron. The institute was under the direction of Dr. H. O. DeGraff, head of the department of sociology of the University of Akron. Social welfare institutes are conducted annually and constitute a part of the civic policy and program in which the university is actively engaged.

Dr. Marvin A. Brooker, associate economist at the Florida Experiment Station, has been appointed chief statistician of the U. S. Farm Credit Administration, with headquarters at Columbia, S. C.

To celebrate the tenth anniversary of Professor A. Broderick Cohen as director of the summer session of Hunter College, the teaching staff gave a tea on August 9. During Professor Cohen's administration as director, the summer session has grown both in the introduction of new fields of study and in the student body, the enrolment having increased from 1,758 in 1925 to 2,766 this summer, a gain of 57 per cent.

DR. CHALFANT ROBINSON, curator of medieval history and professor of paleography at Princeton University, has been elected a member of the Institut Historique et Heraldique de France.

ARMON JAY LAWRENCE, assistant professor of economics at the University of Kentucky, has been made editor of *Modern Business Education,* a quarterly publication sponsored by the Southern Commercial Teachers' Association. The appointment was made by Professor B. Frank Kyker, of the University of North Carolina, president of the association.

ALIDA C. BOWLER, of the U. S. Children's Bureau, has been appointed superintendent of the Carson Indian School and Reservation of Nevada. It is understood that Miss Bowler will have opportunity to reorganize the educational system of the reservation.

DR. WILLIAM L. SLATE, director of the Connecticut Agricultural Experiment Station at Storrs, has been appointed to the chairmanship of the State Planning Commission.

DR. WILLIAM EUGENE MOSHER, director of the School of Citizenship and Public Affairs at Syracuse University, has been appointed chief of the investigation of the Federal Power Commission into electric rates.

DR. HARRY MORGAN AYRES, professor of Old English at Columbia University, has announced that he will seek the Democratic nomination for senator from Connecticut.

DR. KARL NICKERSON LLEWELLYN, Betts professor of jurisprudence at Columbia University, will be an independent candidate for a place on the New York State Democratic Committee in the primary elections to be held in September.

DR. JOSEPH MOORE JAMESON, since 1913 vice-president of Girard College and for the last fifteen years head of the department of physics at Pratt Institute, died on August 6 at the age of sixty-four years.

DR. CHARLES W. E. MILLER, professor emeritus of Greek at the Johns Hopkins University, died on August 8 at the age of seventy-one years. Professor Miller was formerly editor of *The American Journal of Philology.*

DR. WILFRED HAROLD MONRO, professor emeritus at Brown University, for forty years professor of history at that institution, died on August 9 at the age of eighty-five years.

ALTON GILBERT HOLT, president and superintendent of instruction of the American Conservatory of Music, died on August 7 at the age of sixty-one years.

EUGENE C. GIBNEY, director of extension activities of the New York City Board of Education since 1919, died suddenly on August 13. He was 52 years old.

DR. WILLIAM HENRY BALLARD, for fifty-seven years connected with the Hamilton, Ontario, Board of Education, died in his eighty-eighth year on August 8.

DAME JESSIE PHIPPS, chairman of the Education Committee of the London County Council, died on August 8 at the age of seventy-nine years. Dame Phipps was born in the United States.

ARRANGEMENTS for the dedication of a plaque at the University of Wisconsin to the memory of Dr. S. M. Babcock have been made for October 22, Dr. Babcock's birthday. The memorial committee consists of E. G. Hastings, agricultural bacteriology, *chairman;* E. B. Hart, agricultural chemistry; and Noble Clark, assistant director of the Wisconsin Experiment Station. The plaque, which is the work of Lorado Taft, is a gift of the friends and admirers of Dr. Babcock through a committee of which the late Professor E. H. Farrington was the active head.

DR. WILLIAM P. DEARING, president of Oakland City College, Oakland City, Ind., was the commencement speaker at the University of Kentucky summer session commencement exercises held on Friday afternoon, August 17. Dr. Dearing's subject was "The Heritage of the American Youth." At the summer session commencement exercises students who have completed work toward their degrees in the first or second summer term will receive graduation certificates.

THE National Schoolmart, an exposition sponsored by Teachers College, Columbia University, and by the School of Education of New York University, opened on August 15 in New York City and will continue through August 24. The exposition will include displays of construction materials, architectural products and services, auditing systems, school furniture, typewriters and other business machines and various other aids to modern education. Work done in educational fields will also be illustrated. The exposition will be held in connection with the twenty-third annual convention of the National Association of Public Business Officials. This will be held at the Port Authority Building from August 21 to 24, inclusive. Speakers at the opening ceremonies on August 15 included: Dr. George J. Ryan, president of the Board of Education; Dr. Harold G. Campbell, superintendent of schools; Dr. Hamilton Holt, president of Rollins College, and Dr. Edison Ellsworth Oberholtzer, superintendent of schools at Houston, Texas.

WITH the discontinuance this year of the Barnard Summer School for Women in Industry the American Museum of Natural History has opened a day school. Political science, sociology, trade unionism and other subjects are being taught by a staff of nearly fifty instructors under the direction of Professor C. Drummond Jones, of New York University. The classes begin at nine o'clock in the morning and continue through the evening. This group is one of thirty or forty similar groups planned. Headquarters are in Washington, and Miss Hilda Smith, formerly of the Vineyard Shore School for workers at Kingston, N. Y., has been placed in charge by the Federal Government. Camps for women are included. While only women are to be admitted to the camps, the school at the museum includes both men and women in about equal numbers. Each will receive a federal subsidy or "scholarship."

THE Rockefeller Foundation has appropriated $1,000,000 to McGill University as an endowment for the department of neurology. The foundation had previously contributed $232,000 toward the erection and equipment of the neurological building. The $1,000,000 takes the place of the $50,000 a year contributed annually to carry on work in neurology under the direction of Professor Wilder Penfield.

BY the will of Professor Henry R. Lang, emeritus professor of Romance languages at Yale University, the university receives $30,000, of which $10,000 is to found a traveling fellowship in English, in memory of his late wife, Alice Derby Lang; $10,000 is left to found prizes in classical literature and $10,000 for patients in the infirmary. Smith College receives $10,000 for students who show special proficiency in Greek.

THE University of Pennsylvania has announced that its officers, faculty members and employees who received only 90 per cent. of their basic salaries and wages during the year ended June 30 are being paid an additional 3¼ per cent. A balanced budget has been preserved for 1933–34 by limiting operating expenses to $5,246,000, a reduction of approximately $602,000.

FORTY-SEVEN members of the class of 1935 at Princeton University have qualified for the "no-course" plan of study adopted last May for high-ranking seniors. Instead of taking four courses a term, as upper classmen have done since the inauguration of the four-course plan in 1925, the students will take a three-course schedule for the first term of their senior year, which begins next month, and will take no courses at all during the second term. Instead, they will have weekly conferences with departmental supervisors. To qualify for this plan an undergraduate must attain a first group average in his major field of study and maintain a second group general average throughout his junior year. Less than one tenth of the class of 1935 has met these requirements.

THREE new departments will be added for the 1934–35 session of the Louisiana State University College of Arts and Sciences. They are the Departments of Fine Arts, Religious Education and Philosophy. Philosophy will be taught by Dr. Frederick W. Meier, who has offered courses in this field at the university this summer. The religious courses, which are open to all students, are optional, but students wishing to take a course not offered by the denomination which they indicated as their preference in registering must secure the written permission of their parents or guardians. The work in this department is being financed by the respective religious organizations and it is expected that other denominations will offer courses. The instruction will be of university grade and will be offered by instructors of approved academic rank. University credit will be given on the successful completion of the courses.

THREE buildings on the Ohio state fair grounds will be used this fall as a cooperative dormitory center for 100 men students at the Ohio State University. Two buildings, used each year for junior fair exhibits, will provide sleeping and study quarters for the students, who will be selected for their scholarship and financial need. A third structure, the clubhouse, will serve as kitchen and dining-room. Selection of the three buildings was made by Earl H. Hanefeld, director of agriculture, and other university officials, after Governor George White had authorized their use by students who could not otherwise attend the university. Most of the residents will be freshmen, but a small group will be chosen from the upper classes to help new students with their studies and to supervise dormitory activities. The two buildings selected for sleeping quarters contain 100 exhibit booths, partitioned on three sides. Each booth will provide bed and locker space for one boy.

DR. HAROLD H. AXWORTHY, director of the Bureau of Community Service at New York University, reports that approximately 1,500 students were expected to receive benefits of the Federal Emergency Relief Administration at the university during the coming academic year. The students will be employed on a part-time basis in the various divisions of the university. They will receive from $10 to $20 per month for nine months. It is the desire of the Relief Administration to aid as many new students as possible, in addition to former students who were forced to drop their school work during the past two years because of financial reasons. The two groups will comprise half of the FERA group and present students the other half. Dr. Axworthy will supervise the selection of the students and will interview applicants from Washington Square College. He will be assisted in the selection of the students by the following members of the faculty: Dr. Ralph E. Pickett, school of education; Professor John H. Prime, school of commerce, accounts and finance; Professor R. D. Niles, school of law; Professor Louis Menk, college of fine arts; Professor William R. Bryans, college of engineering, and Laurence W. Lange, university college of arts and pure science.

# DISCUSSION

## EDUCATIONAL NOMENCLATURE

NOT long ago I had occasion to do some extensive reading covering nearly all phases of education and psychology. Without presuming to infer that I read all or even liberal parts of every book or magazine article that has been written on these subjects during recent years, I did absorb enough to make me realize how confusing much of our educational literature must be to the young student in teacher-training institutions or to the young teacher who is making an honest effort to obtain a more professional background by reading widely among the books, magazines and reports with which we are so richly endowed. What is needed is a standard list of names, symbols, abbreviations, formulas, and the like, so that even an ordinary, beginning teacher may have some chance to understand what writers on educational subjects are trying to convey to them.

For the purposes of this article, let us take only one phase of the subject, that of educational measurements and the closely allied field of educational statistics. Is it necessary to have so many ways of expressing the same thing, as in the case of "average," "mean," "arithmetic mean," "arithmetical mean," "arithmetic average" and "arithmetical average"? Clearly, we have too many equivalents in our educational terminology.

In addition to the richness of the English tongue as a cause of this duplication of terms, the rapid development of new ideas in education during the past quarter of a century has also contributed to the confusion. Some writer hits upon an idea and calls it "average deviation." Another educator may work out the same thing entirely independently and call it "average variation," because "deviation" and "variation" are synonymous. But "average" also has its synonym in "mean," so the next writer comes along with "mean deviation," and only time is necessary for the other possibility to appear as "mean variation." Now, the second, third and fourth forms are just as good as the first one, but they are no better, so why not fix upon the original form and let it go at that? After all, it is merely a matter of individual opinion and by no means as vital as is the simplification of our educational terminology. And, remember, the fellow who started the above-mentioned mixup in terms was responsible not only for the confusion of the terms themselves, but also for that of all their abbreviations. Thus the poor reader must keep in mind that A.D., M.D., A.V. and M.V. all mean the same thing. "He who puts in motion a wrongful act is guilty of the consequences thereof," as our legal brethren would say.

Considerable confusion often arises when two things are considered identical when they are merely equivalent. For things to be identical they must be alike in every particular, while they may be equivalent in certain respects if they are equal. Thus a pound of butter is equivalent in weight to a pound of feathers, but the two are by no means identical. The fact that certain statistical terms are of equivalent value has caused them to be confused and used interchangeably as though they were identical. This accounts, in part, for the variety of terms meaning the same thing which one finds in educational statistics and measurements. Thus, "accomplishment quotient," "achievement quotient," "attainment quotient," "subject ratio," "accomplishment ratio" and "achievement ratio" are used interchangeably by various authors, because, though derived in more than one manner, their values are equivalent.

The prize example of useless duplication and reduplication which I found in my reading was in the various ways of expressing the idea of the "normal curve." Not satisfied with this rather simple expression, the writers on measurements and statistics have proceeded to give us their various notions of what this commonly used idea should be called. As a result we have, if I have not missed any of them, the following: "normal frequency curve," "normal surface of frequency," "normal probability curve," "normal curve of probability," "Gaussian curve," "normal curve of distribution," "normal distribution curve," "curve of error," "probability surface," "biologic curve," "symmetric curve," "symmetrical curve" and "binomial graph."

The need of standardizing educational terms is very evident to one who makes even a cursory study of modern educational literature. That we have allowed these sources of confusion to creep into our nomenclature is hardly in keeping with our profession. The world looks to us for leadership in the matter of accuracy and clearness of expression. We can not rightly face our classes and insist that our pupils or students observe all the rules of correct diction, while our educational leaders continue to invent new ways of expressing ideas already labeled by others. Why can not the authorities in the various fields get together and agree on some one of the several suggestions that have been made for various ideas? Why all this useless duplication, triplication and even more than quadruplication?

If the reader still thinks I am unduly concerned about this matter, and that no standardization is necessary, I would suggest that he glance through the following list of a few of the other equivalent terms in the field of measurements and statistics that I ran across in my reading:

Non-verbal test and non-language test; old style test, old type test, subjective test, and traditional test; practise test and instructional test; prognosis test, prognostic test, aptitude test, vocational guidance test, and vocational test; rearrangement test and continuity test; recall test, single answer test, single response test, and direct-recall test; shorthand test and stenography test; achievement test, accomplishment test, attainment test, and subject-matter test; survey tests, general survey tests, general tests, and general achievement tests; coefficient of variability and coefficient of variation; frequency surface and surface of frequency; correlation table and scatter diagram; frequency table and distribution table; raw-score-G table and G-score table; test and examination; ''Aussage'' test and testimony test; best answer test, best-answer test, best answer exercise, and best-answer exercise; Binet tests, Binet-Simon tests, and Binet-Simon scale; difficulty test, power test, and scaled test; discussion test and essay type test; ethical test and moral test; general intelligence test, mental alertness test, intelligence test, mental test, psychological test, classification test, and point scale; relative ability and brightness; ability grouping and homogeneous grouping; accidental error and variable error; achievement age (A.A.) and subject age (S.A.); chronological age and time age; pedagogical age and educational age; age-grade-distribution table and age-grade table; A.Q., abbreviation for achievement quotient, accomplishment quotient, and arithmetic quotient; A.R., abbreviation for accomplishment ratio or achievement ratio, which in turn are the same as the accomplishment quotient or the achievement quotient; array and array of measures; Avg. Dev. and A.D., abbreviations for average deviation; bar diagram and bar graph; basic age and physiological age; range and absolute range; rate and speed; coefficient of reliability and coefficient of self-correlation; percentile scale and percentile table; age score, age-score, age equivalent, and age-equivalent; derived score and transmuted score; G score, G-score, grade score, and grade status; quotient score and ratio score; measures of central tendency and average measures; C.I., abbreviation of coefficient of intelligence or classification index; product-moment correlation, short method of correlation, the Galton-Pearson product-moment method of correlation, and the Pearson product-moment method of correlation; rank correlation, the Spearman rank method of correlation, and the Spearman rank-differences method of correlation; credit point, credit hour, and credit unit; percentile curve and ogive (also sometimes used interchangeably with cumulative frequency curve); quartile deviation, quartile-deviation, semi-interquartile range, median deviation, median-deviation, and probable error; standard deviation, root-mean-square deviation, the mean-square deviation, the error of mean square, the mean error, and the mean-square error (the abbreviation is usually $\sigma$ (sigma), though *S.D.* is also widely used); intelligence quotient and mental ratio; interval, step, class interval, class-interval, group interval, group-interval, step interval, and step-interval; assumed mean and guessed mean; median, mid-score, and mid-measure; mental tests and intelligence tests; age norm, achievement norm, and attainment norm; percentile and percentile point; sector diagram, pie graph, circle graph, and circle areas graph; equivalent form, duplicate form, and duplicate test; constant error, systematic error, and recurring error; variable error, accidental error, and chance error; examinee, the subject, and the testee; histogram and column diagram (related to the frequency polygon, frequency curve, smoothed frequency curve, smoothed frequency polygon, frequency surface, and curve diagram).

Homer L. Nearpass

Santa Barbara, Calif.

## AN EDUCATIONAL DICTATOR FOR INDUSTRY

Much complaint has been made because no provision was made by the industrial codes for apprenticeship, or for any method by which ambitious boys could secure a more extensive educational preparation in the industries than merely being broken in on a job. Most codes provided for a short learning period, long enough to learn a single operation, but that was all. Apprentice courses that had long prepared boys for skilled work were forced to close.

On June 27 President Roosevelt suddenly changed the situation by a single executive order. It was issued without giving those interested in the subject a chance to find out what it would contain or to offer constructive criticisms. The order, in effect, states that any employer may engage apprentices regardless of the codes on obtaining a certificate from an agency designated by the Secretary of Labor. It further authorizes the Secretary of Labor to prescribe such further rules as may be deemed necessary.

No one knows just what the Secretary of Labor will do with these powers. But there are no restrictions as to what the Secretary may do along the line of detailed requirements. By the simple act of withholding the certificate unless the requirements are met, the Secretary of Labor may regulate apprenticeship in the minutest detail.

The first few years of employment form one educational period that is one of the most important and one of the most neglected. It is in these years that habits are formed that lead to advancement or in the downward direction to blind alley jobs or unemployment. In the past this educational period has been left to the judgment or to the neglect of the individual employer. Under NRA the boys in this period were generally excluded from proper training and forced into jobs where they could be exploited or into unemployment. Now the opportunities are to be reopened under the name of apprenticeship. And it will be done under the control of an educational dictator.

To guide the education of boys under so many and varied kinds of employers is a task that should require the best educational talent that is available. For this educational expert, the President selects the Secretary of Labor. Regardless of the qualifications of the present Secretary of Labor, are educators satisfied to have what is probably the most powerful educational positions in the country to-day filled by a person primarily in the labor field?

A. W. FORBES

WORCESTER, MASS.

# SPECIAL CORRESPONDENCE

## A COURSE OF STUDY IN DENTISTRY

THE American Association of Dental Schools is bringing to completion a three-year curriculum study which is likely to prove an important landmark in dental education. The major outcomes of this project are a suggested undergraduate course of study in dentistry and a statement of general principles and plans on which dental educators can cooperate in mutual understanding.

The need for a thorough study of the dental curriculum had become apparent to a number of leading dental educators several years ago. The field of dentistry and its responsibilities had in the last generation undergone a remarkable expansion. Dentistry in the past consisted principally of restorative services, and dental education was aimed primarily at developing in the students proficiency in providing dental restorations for patients. Owing to important clinical investigations and research studies made during the past quarter of a century the emphasis in dentistry has been undergoing a marked change. It has been learned that certain common disorders of the teeth may produce serious, sometimes fatal, ailments in other parts of the body and that superficially perfect dental service, judged by standards of mechanics and esthetics, may hide or induce local pathologic processes which have far-reaching consequences for the health of the individual. The result of these discoveries has been an increasing tendency to regard dentistry as a health service, which imposes important new obligations on the dental profession. Leaders in dental education had come to realize the importance of adjusting the education of the oncoming dentists to these new conceptions in order that the dental profession might in the future render to the public a service that is in keeping with its responsibility for the health of the people.

At the same time a considerable amount of confusion had arisen in dental education because of the variety of curriculum plans which had been evolved. One group of dental schools had three-year curriculums based on two years of preprofessional education in college, another group had four-year curriculums based on one year of education in college, and a third group had four-year curriculums based on two years of study in college. This situation hampered the discussion of the problems of dental education and it stood in the way of progress.

The general plan of the curriculum was the subject of much discussion by the American Association of Dental Schools, beginning as early as 1924. This discussion was greatly stimulated by the "Report on Dental Education in the United States and Canada" made to the Carnegie Foundation for the Advancement of Teaching in 1926 by Dr. William J. Gies. The report stated that, although the practise of dentistry can not be made an accredited specialty of medicine, it should be developed into "the equivalent of an oral specialty of the practise of medicine" and it added:

> In this view of an enlarged dentistry, its practitioners would be trained to give the service not only of dental surgeons and dental engineers as at present, but of oral sanitarians and oral physicians as well. Instead of examining only the teeth and mouth of a patient, as is now usually the case in a restricted view of their responsibility, they would also suitably enquire into and keep careful records of the state of the patient's health, particularly as it affects or is modified by conditions of the teeth and mouth. Dentists would plan

their procedures to meet not only the local indications but also the possible requirements of extra-oral relationships; would also recognize and note the significance of outstanding symptoms of systemic disease, and warn or advise the patient accordingly, or explain his need for a physician's attention; and could effectively discuss, with a physician, the oral conditions in their relation to a patient's general welfare. Prevention of diseases at all ages would become an inherent and predominant motive.

The educational implication of the enlarged view of dentistry was evident. Dr. Gies suggested that attention should be directed to the content of the dental curriculum and he emphasized the need for improving dental teaching and dental research, in order that the dental profession might take its rightful place in the promotion of human welfare.

Finally, after considering these matters for several years, the association made a request of the Carnegie Corporation for a grant to assist in conducting a curriculum survey. The corporation responded in 1930 with an appropriation of $20,000 to support a study designed (1) to discover the services which dentistry should render to meet oral health needs, and (2) upon this foundation, to organize a course of study that would serve as a basis for adequately preparing men and women to render the services required of dentistry. An additional grant of $10,000 was later made by the Carnegie Corporation for the support of the survey.

The association appointed a committee of five deans of dental schools to have general charge of the survey. As finally constituted the committee consists of the following deans: Wallace Seccombe, University of Toronto, *chairman;* John T. O'Rourke, University of Louisville, *secretary;* Arthur D. Black, Northwestern University; H. Edmund Friesell, University of Pittsburgh; Harry M. Semans, Ohio State University. This committee selected as its educational advisers two well-recognized educationists, Floyd W. Reeves, of the University of Chicago, and W. W. Charters, of Ohio State University. Also, it appointed the writer as executive secretary to devote his entire time to the survey.

The survey has been an extensive project. The types of oral diseases, disorders and deficiencies were ascertained; studies were made of the services required of dentistry in its new relationships, and the objectives of undergraduate dental education were formulated. Subcommittees, consisting of a total of forty dental teachers, then outlined the content of the various courses to be taught to dental students, and more than a hundred dental teachers assisted in reviewing the proposed courses. Finally, the courses were arranged in a suggested curriculum, which included the following subjects: Orientation in dentistry; personal hygiene; materials used in dentistry; physics; organic chemistry; physiological chemistry; anatomy; histology and embryology; oral anatomy; physiology; nutrition; bacteriology; materia medica; pharmacodynamics; pathology; oral hygiene and oral prophylaxis; application of preventive principles in dentistry; radiography; diagnosis and treatment planning; orthodontics; operative dentistry; oral medicine; anesthesia; oral surgery; dental prosthesis; principles and practise of medicine; technical composition; history of dentistry; social and economic relations of dentistry, and practise management.

Some of the subject-matter in the curriculum is new, much is old. The requirements of dental health service and the demands of an adequate program of dental education made it necessary to pioneer in the suggestions for teaching material. At the same time much subject-matter now generally taught was found to serve the purposes very well. All the material incorporated in the curriculum was placed there because it was regarded as necessary to attain the stated objectives of undergraduate instruction in dentistry.

A determined effort has been made to correlate the subject-matter of the courses. The instruction in the clinical subjects was outlined first and the instruction in the preclinical subjects was then definitely planned to give the proper background for clinical study. The outline for each subject was prepared with the entire curriculum in mind.

The American Association of Dental Schools at its annual meeting in Chicago, held from March 19 to 21, devoted the major portion of its program to a consideration of the report of the survey. The principal features of the study were outlined at general sessions and the reports on the various subjects of the dental curriculum were fully presented by the subcommittees at group conferences. The dental teachers studied the reports and made suggestions for the final report. The report of the survey was well received and enthusiastically discussed by the dental teachers.

The Curriculum Survey Committee presented to the association a series of recommendations relating to policies and plans for dental education. These recommendations, all of which were adopted, were as follows:

1. That the objectives of undergraduate dental education be the education of students in order that they may—
   (a) Be competent in the maintenance of oral health and the treatment of oral diseases, disorders, and deficiencies, with understanding and appreciation of the relationships between oral and systemic conditions in health and disease.
   (b) Cooperate effectively with persons engaged in allied fields of service.
   (c) Have interest in, and desire for, continuing professional study after graduation.
   (d) Practise dentistry with due regard for its social, economic, and ethical relationships.
   (e) Cooperate effectively in community life.
2. That two years of education in the liberal arts and sciences be required for admission to the dental school.
3. That a minimum of six semester hours in general chemistry and six semester hours in biological science be required in the preprofessional curriculum, and that courses in English, Sociology, Economics, and Psychology be recommended.
4. That the undergraduate dental curriculum be a four-year course.
5. That the curriculum to be submitted by the Curriculum Survey Committee be adopted as a guide to the member schools of the Association.
6. That provision be made in the students' schedule for extra-class study in accordance with the hours included in the recommended curriculum.
7. That the member schools of the Association be urged to develop adequate library facilities and to promote their effective use.
8. That dental education be further developed as an autonomous field of professional education.
9. That provision be made for a medium of publication to stimulate interest in the study and discussion of the important problems of dental education and to disseminate information on these problems.
10. That the faculties of the member schools of the Association be urged to appoint standing committees to study the recommendations of the Curriculum Survey Committee and to investigate current problems in dental education.

The action of the association in adopting the recommendations of the Curriculum Survey Committee does not make the recommendations mandatory on the dental schools. It merely makes the recommendations a statement of approved principles and plans for the guidance of the dental schools and persons and organizations concerned with the problems of dental education. It is, of course, apparent that the recommendations will probably have an important effect in the development of future policies and plans regarding education in dentistry.

The enthusiastic reception of the report by the dental teachers is a clear indication of their great interest in the problems of dental education. Also, it is a sign that much progress is being made in training men and women for the practise of dentistry. Dental education is putting its house in order and it is doing this in a most creditable manner.

The final report of the Curriculum Survey is now being prepared. It will be published by the American Association of Dental Schools some time during the coming summer.

The curriculum survey had scarcely gotten under way when the committee had forcibly impressed upon it the need for improving the quality of the teaching in the dental schools. Other important related problems also called for attention. These problems were so large that adequate study of them would have required resources far more extensive than those at the disposal of the committee. It was therefore decided to concentrate on the undergraduate curriculum as the first step in the further improvement of dental education and its adjustment to the new demands made on dentistry. The association, recognizing the need for additional investigations in dental education, continued the committee and charged it with making further studies and obtaining the necessary funds therefor, the studies to deal with methods of teaching in dentistry, with graduate instruction and the education of dental teachers, research workers and specialists and with student personnel. The committee is now making plans to discharge the added responsibilities laid upon it.

L. E. Blauch,
*Executive Secretary, Curriculum Survey Committee, American Association of Dental Schools*
Northwestern University

# QUOTATIONS

## BOSTON'S SURPLUS TEACHERS

Boston's Teachers' College is facing a problem common to all normal schools and, in fact, other educational institutions, yet perhaps more acute in this case than in some others. This is the question what to do for the graduates it is continually turning out. Less than a decade ago, the college was hard put to supply teachers enough to meet the demand, owing to the increase of population, particularly in the North and West Ends. Then three factors entered, which, operating together, have so diminished the demand that it is said that at the present time no less than twelve hundred graduates of the college—we do not vouch for the accuracy of this figure—are without teaching positions.

First, the restrictive immigration laws cut down the influx from abroad, thus materially limiting the foreign population in these areas. Then came the rapid growth of the parochial schools, which are private institutions, under no obligation to secure their teachers from the graduate list of the Teachers' College. Thirdly, a fact in itself of social interest, the size of the American family has so diminished as to affect noticeably what otherwise would be the normal growth of population in the city.

Various expedients have been adopted by the School Committee to cope with the human accumulation which is being ground out annually by the Teachers' College. The course has been lengthened from three to four and even five years, and although the graduates are given a degree, they are not now entitled to employment until they have had a year of experience in substitute teaching, at the end of which they are required to pass a stiff examination before receiving a certificate that they are qualified to teach. Even with these brakes applied, the number of graduates continues to mount in greater proportion than they can be supplied with places in the public schools.

As the situation now stands, the Teachers' College is slowly but surely attaining something of the status of a college of liberal arts, which the city can not afford as an educational luxury on the side. A school for training in the liberal arts could be maintained appropriately enough by one of the existing colleges, but as an institution supported by the city of Boston, and without the facilities for placing its graduates, it is something of an extravagance, from the strictly economic point of view. The idea of abolishing the college can not be entertained, unless a substitute is provided, for it is an indispensable agency for the proper training of the teachers for the Boston schools, even if its whole output can not be used. The college certainly provides a baffling problem for the School Committee, who have been giving it much thought. If a solution can be found, one more municipal worry will be out of the way.—*The Boston Evening Transcript.*

## THE SCHOOL BUDGET

The proposed school budget shows a reduction in the item that is at the foundation of the whole public school structure—the day elementary school, including the junior high school. The decrease is not large, but would be relatively larger if the junior high school item were separately shown in cost as it is in numbers. According to the estimate there will be an actual reduction of 10,000 in the number of elementary day school pupils next March compared with last. This signifies in part the changes that are taking place in the age-groups of our population. The decrease would be still greater if the children were not remaining longer even in the elementary school.

Yet growth in numbers goes on apace and shows itself markedly beyond the elementary school. While the estimated decrease in the day elementary school instructional budget is somewhat more than $60,000, the increase for the day high schools, the continuation schools, the evening high and elementary and trade schools exceeds $1,300,000. These increases are based on estimated increased attendance, with a relatively greater cost per pupil than in the lower ranges. The sum of it is that the estimated increase of $1,415,362.39 is due to larger attendance in the post-elementary classes and this in turn is due to the fact that many pupils are remaining in school because of lack of employment, even when the compulsory school age has been passed. Doubtless some of these should have other than the regular high-school training, but it is nevertheless best, for adults as well as themselves, that they remain in school.

The salary schedules being what they are, the attendance being what is estimated, the pupil-load (which has been increased) remaining what it is, the making of the education budget is only a matter of arithmetic. In what is known as the "special school fund," which provides for the cost of all items other than salaries of members of the supervising and teaching staffs, the increase is greater than on the instructional side, carrying the sum of the increases to $3,184,959.62, and the total expenditure for all purposes to $139,795,372.10. In this special fund the outstanding increases are for repairs, ordinary and special, replacements, alterations, supplies and equipment, which have been in large part put off from year to year. These two items alone call for an increased expenditure of more than $1,600,000,000. The personnel item is somewhat less than last year.

This tentative budget is presented as being the lowest with which, as Superintendent Campbell said, "we could possibly reach and operate the schools at all," but it is also "as high as is within reason." The public has an opportunity to help determine its final content. —*The New York Times*.

# REPORTS

## COLLEGE LIBRARY BUDGETS AND THE INCREASED COST OF BOOK PURCHASES[1]

MUCH attention has been given to the crisis in education, but little has been written of the progressive deterioration of college and university libraries under their greatly curtailed book budgets and the ultimate effect of present administrative policies upon the research and instructional work of our colleges. University administrators have too often picked the library budget as the first item to be cut when curtailment becomes necessary. In some cases the book appropriations have been entirely wiped out.

During the June meeting of the American Library Association at Montreal, the Committee on German Periodicals reported that in spite of reductions in prices in terms of foreign currencies, the cost of importations had greatly increased, owing to the reduced purchasing value of the American dollar. As a result subscriptions to scientific periodicals, almost a necessity for research workers, have been cancelled and valuable sets have been broken. Even if subscriptions are resumed in future years there will be very considerable gaps. An essential requirement for research is that the results of research in all countries be available to the investigator. If the present curtailment in library book budgets is continued for any length of time, there will undoubtedly be danger of duplication in research, for the investigator will not have available the results of similar studies at European institutions.

The association has been successful in obtaining very considerable reductions in the prices (in foreign currencies) of many expensive scientific periodicals. The publisher (Springer) of the great majority of German scientific periodicals has reduced the prices (in marks) of his publications for the first four months of 1934 over 45 per cent., as compared with the prices of the same periodicals during a similar period in 1933. Nevertheless, the importations of foreign books and periodicals are costing American libraries at least 50 per cent.

[1] Based on Report of A. L. A. Sub-Committee on German Periodicals presented at Montreal meeting, June, 1934.

more than they did two years ago. One large library on the Pacific coast reports that notwithstanding many cancellations the costs showed a very decided increase this year. Another library states that even with reductions and cancellations of high-priced periodicals the cost of all its importations for the first four months of 1934 was exactly 50 per cent. more than during the first four months of 1933. These increased costs are occurring at the very time when the college and university library budgets are being heavily reduced. The result is that much-needed and much-used material will not be available to research workers in the future unless there is a radical change in policy. There has already been a deterioration in the quality of service to investigators rendered by many formerly outstanding libraries.

The effect of curtailment in the purchases of library books and periodicals has been strongly stated during the last few months by several administrative experts—not librarians. Librarians themselves have been strangely silent in the present-day crisis confronting their libraries. In SCHOOL AND SOCIETY[2] John C. Christensen, controller of the University of Michigan, states:

> The curtailment in the purchase of books during the past few years will seriously hamper the work of our colleges and universities if continued over a long period. The needs of the library, as well as the teaching and research units, must be considered carefully in any study of the economical operation of our institutions.

From the School of Education, University of Chicago, John Dale Russell, a man who has had much experience in the study of university and college budgets, makes the following statement, in an article entitled "Practical Methods for Reducing the Cost of Instruction."[3]

> An item of instructional expenditure that has been eagerly pounced upon as offering the opportunity for curtailment in the present emergency is the library budget. It is extremely unfortunate that the necessity of reducing these appropriations has been felt just at the time when instructional methods are being developed which are likely to increase the use of the library. Certainly the discontinuance of book purchases and the undermanning of the library staff can not continue for longer than one or two years without making a noticeable reduction in the quality of the instruction. . . .

In an editorial in the *Journal of Higher Education*,[4] Dr. W. W. Charters, of Ohio State University, writes:

> . . . the library facilities of the colleges and universities, as a class, are scandalously inadequate for the education of students, which is the only reason for the existence of college librarians and college professors. The book, the teacher, and the student are the triangle of education. Every one amiably agrees that books are more important than buildings, but it is immeasurably easier to secure a $500,000 building than to raise the budget for library facilities by $25,000 a year. . . . The first responsibility of the administrative officers is to secure an efficient faculty, and the second is to provide an adequate supply of books and teaching equipment.

The president of another large university stated orally that the lack of adequate library facilities was the reason for the omission of some departments in his university from the report issued by the American Council on Education and listing departments of various universities, which were considered qualified to give the doctorate.[5] While some administrators, probably greatly to their chagrin, have been forced to recognize the effect of past curtailments, yet there are many more who seem to take the position of the president of a local Iowa school board. To a request for the purchase of a few books for the high-school library, he replied, "Didn't we buy six books last year?" The head of another school board, even more materially minded, refused to honor a requisition for library books, "because those we have bought the last few years are all worn out and it's no use buying library books to wear out."

If the question of funds for the library were left to the decision of the faculty who use the library rather than to the deans and administrative officers whose use is not so intimate, the library might fare better. Among the nine

[2] 39: 731, June 9, 1934.

[3] *Journal of Higher Education*, 5: 24, January, 1934.

[4] 5: 225–26, April, 1934.

[5] American Council on Education. Report of Committee on Graduate Instruction, April, 1934.

recommendations adopted by the faculty of the University of Wisconsin in 1933 relative to retrenchment and reorganization necessary to balance the budget, the following was included:

4. On the Library: that the library receive no cut which would cripple its effectiveness in all scholarly activities.[6]

There have been many articles published on possible methods of reducing college budgets. In so far as these articles mention the library they deplore the present tendency to slash the book budgets. Yet there are indications that many universities and colleges have selected the library as the chief place where curtailment can be made. Eventually, as has been pointed out, these cuts, if continued for any length of time, will have a serious effect on American scholarship. The cuts are especially unfortunate at a time when the cost of importations has increased so tremendously, owing to the decreased purchasing value of the dollar. There is a distinct need for a clearer understanding by university administrators of the results which will inevitably follow the present restriction of library purchases—which, in fact, are only a very small per cent. of the total college expenditures, in many cases less than 2 per cent. and in some cases less than one.

CHARLES H. BROWN,
*Chairman, A. L. A. Sub-Committee on German Periodicals*
IOWA STATE COLLEGE LIBRARY

## SALARIES OF ELEMENTARY TEACHERS IN EUROPE

A REPORT of the Board of Education, London, printed in *The Educational Supplement* of the London *Times,* on the salaries of elementary school teachers in England, Wales, France, Germany and Italy, follows.

Table I gives the position in England and Wales. In 1930 these scales were paid in full. As from October 1, 1931, they were subjected to a deduction of 10 per cent., and from July 1 of this year the deduction will be reduced to 5 per cent. From the net salary thus received the teacher pays 5 per cent. by way of superannuation contribution.

[6] SCHOOL AND SOCIETY, 37: 770, June 17, 1933.

TABLE I

| Scales | Men Min. | Men Annual increment | Men Max. | Women Min. | Women Annual increment | Women Max. |
|---|---|---|---|---|---|---|
| | £ | £ | £ | £ | £ | £ |
| 1 | 168 | 12 | 312 | 150 | 9 | 246 |
| 2 | 168 | 12 | 330 | 150 | 9 | 258 |
| 3 | 180 | 12 | 366 | 162 | 9 | 288 |
| 4 | 192 | 12 | 408 | 180 | 9 | 324 |

### FRANCE

As regards the position in France, the information given by the Board of Education is as follows:

Teachers in France are civil servants. The salaries of elementary school teachers (men and women), under Article 185 of the law of July 13, 1925, range from 10,500 francs to 19,000 francs.

Head teachers receive supplements of from 800 to 3,500 francs (according to the size of the school).

Teachers in the city of Paris receive a communal supplement of 500 francs, rising by increments of 500 francs to 2,000 francs for every five years of service in Paris.

The salaries of teachers in higher elementary schools range from 16,000 to 36,000 francs (Department of the Seine, 26,000 to 46,000 francs); the supplement for head teachers is 3,000 to 6,000 francs (Department of the Seine, 7,000 to 10,000 francs).

In addition to the salaries and supplements already mentioned, French teachers receive allowances for children and allowances for residence, as well as other supplements for special qualifications in teaching.

A law of December 31, 1933, made the following reductions in the salaries of civil servants:

| | | | |
|---|---|---|---|
| 2 per cent. on salaries of | 12,001 to | 15,000 francs |
| 3 " " " " " | 15,001 " | 20,000 " |
| 4 " " " " " | 20,001 " | 25,000 " |
| 5 " " " " " | 25,001 " | 30,000 " |
| 6 " " " " " | 30,001 " | 50,000 " |
| 7 " " " " " | 50,001 " | 100,000 " |

A further law introduced in April of this year by the present French Government cancelled these provisions and introduced a new scale for reductions in salaries as follows:

| | | | | |
|---|---|---|---|---|
| 5 per cent. | on salaries from | 0 | to | 20,000 francs |
| 6 " | " " " | 20,001 | " | 30,000 " |
| 7 " | " " " | 30,001 | " | 50,000 " |
| 8 " | " " " | 50,001 | " | 80,000 " |
| 9 " | " " " | 80,001 | " | 100,000 " |
| 10 " | " " " | over 100,000 francs | | |

GERMANY

The following information is supplied concerning Germany:

According to the Elementary School Teachers' Salary Law (Volksschullehrer-Besoldungsgesetz) of May 1, 1928, the basic salary scale for permanently appointed teachers in public elementary schools in Prussia is as follows:

2,800 marks per annum
3,050 " " "
3,300 " " "
3,550 " " "
3,800 " " "

and then by increments of 200 marks to a maximum of 5,000 marks a year. Women teachers receive 10 per cent. less than the scale, except when the teaching periods are the same for men and women.

The law also provides for eight different kinds of pensionable allowances (Stellenzulagen) varying from 300 to 700 marks a year, which are paid to head teachers of schools of different sizes and to teachers for special work.

In addition to these pensionable allowances, the elementary school teachers receive (1) a housing allowance (*Wohnungsgeldzuschuss*) based partly upon their grade in the Civil Service and partly upon the locality in which they officially reside; (2) children's allowances.

A reduction of 5 per cent. in salaries of unmarried teachers and of 2½ per cent. in the case of married teachers was imposed by the Prussian Government in June, 1932.

In addition to this the German Government has passed three successive economy measures reducing the salaries of teachers and Government employees:

(1) December, 1930—a cut of 6 per cent.

(2) June, 1931—a further cut from 4 to 8 per cent.

(3) December, 1931—A further cut of 9 per cent.

The basic salary scales for teachers in higher elementary schools (Mittelschulen) are as follows:

3,300 marks a year
3,550 " " "
3,800 " " "
4,050 " " "
4,300 " " "

and then by increments of 200 marks a year to a maximum of 5,500 marks a year.

The law also provides for three different kinds of pensionable allowances varying from 300 to 900 marks a year according to the size of the school for head teachers and second teachers in large schools. The higher elementary school teacher also receives housing and family allowances.

The salaries of higher elementary school teachers are subject to the same reductions (already mentioned) as the salaries of elementary school teachers.

ITALY

In Italy, according to the Board of Education, the following is the position:

Elementary school teachers in Italy are paid according to the appropriate Civil Service salary scales. Their basic salaries range from 5,900 to 10,000 lire, with active service supplements beginning after two years' service of 1,300 to 1,800 lire.

Family allowances and allowances for each minor child up to a maximum of three are also given.

A royal decree of November 20, 1930, reduced salaries, active service supplements and family allowances by 12 per cent.

A further reduction was made by a royal decree issued on April 14, 1934, which was to come into force on April 16. According to this decree there was to be a reduction of:

6 per cent. when the total amount of salary and active service supplement was between 500 and 1,000 lire a month.

8 per cent. when it was between 1,000 and 1,500 lire a month.

10 per cent. when it was between 1,500 and 2,000 lire a month.

12 per cent. when it was over 2,000 lire a month.

It would have been interesting at the same time to obtain similar information concerning the United States of America, but the Board of Education say that the scales of salary paid to elementary school teachers in the United States vary from state to state and it is not possible to furnish a reliable statement of existing practise on the incomplete information available.

# EDUCATIONAL RESEARCH AND STATISTICS

## DOES A TEACHER-TRAINING PROGRAM ADEQUATELY PREPARE TEACHERS?[1]

How satisfactorily does a teacher-training program equip teachers for problems which they meet in their first teaching situations? A follow-up study looking toward an answer to this question was instituted in the year 1928–1929 by the directors of teacher training in the University of California. Dr. George A. Rice, director of practise teaching in the university and principal of University High School in Oakland, California, sent a questionnaire to those graduates of the university who were engaged in their first year of teaching under full certification. In 1929–1930 the questionnaire was sent again to first-year teachers. An analysis of these two follow-up returns has been presented previously.[2]

In the spring of 1932 a reorganized questionnaire was sent to the teachers who had completed their teacher-training course in 1930–1931. The questionnaire contained three questions which encouraged the beginning teachers to express freely their opinions concerning valuable features of their training or to suggest means for increasing the value of the training program. Two further questions asked definitely for opinions concerning the value of college courses. The questionnaire contained four check lists by means of which the teachers indicated the desirability or undesirability of changing certain supervised teaching activities and certain professional courses in the university. A fifth and a sixth check list asked for the extra-curricular activities and the community responsibilities which engaged the time of the teacher in his first teaching position.

Two hundred and sixteen questionnaires were returned. Sixty-six came from former student teachers who had not obtained positions. Opinions expressed on these sixty-six papers are incorporated in the following discussion.

The first question on the questionnaire was:

> As you look back upon your preparation for teaching, in what ways, in your opinion, might it have been improved? What experiences should you have had which you did not have? In what respects did you find yourself well prepared or poorly prepared when you taught in your first position?

The former student teachers suggested sixty-eight ways of improving preparation for teaching. These sixty-eight suggestions were made in a total of four hundred and twenty-four statements. About 30 per cent. of the statements were recommendations for more varied experiences with pupils, subject-matter and methods. They called for the teaching of more subjects, minors as well as majors; for more experience with pupils at different age levels; for wider acquaintance with the content of high-school courses; for more substitution teaching in Oakland schools, other than University High School; for experience with more kinds of classes, students and situations; for several consecutive periods of teaching in one day. Not only should the training be more varied, according to these teachers, but the period of training should be more extended. A longer term of actual practise teaching, with less time for theory, more visiting, more observation and demonstration, a longer daily period of practise teaching were some of the suggestions for lengthening the training. The third group of suggestions in point of frequency was for more experience with extra-curricular activities, with home rooms, with study halls and with special assemblies and special programs. Broader experiences in class management and discipline stood fourth in the list of suggestions. Two view-points were expressed. Some of the teachers wished more instruction in management and discipline, other recommended that practise teachers be given the

[1] A follow-up study of the teacher-training program at the University of California.

[2] G. P. Cahoon, "What Training Do Beginning Teachers Need?" *University High School Journal*, 10: 2, 131–159, August, 1930.

opportunity to settle their own problems. Closely connected with the second of these viewpoints is the fifth group of suggestions which call for increased responsibility to be placed on student teachers.

When replying to the first question of the questionnaire many of the former student teachers indicated, in addition to means for improvement, those features of their preparation which they had found valuable. The statement occurring most often was the general one that the training course was useful or excellent. But 110 of the 140 statements named some valuable phase of training. Experience in classroom management was the most frequently mentioned item. The specific features of management in which the student teachers had received aid were: Providing for individual differences; class discipline; supervising classroom projects, and meeting unusual classroom situations with ease. Other features of the training program which these teachers recognized as valuable were: Experience in lesson planning; variety of experiences offered, including substitution, short-unit courses, section meetings, observation and study-hall experiences; contacts with supervising teachers; adequate academic training. It is interesting to note the similarity between the list of benefits which the beginning teachers derived from their preparation and the list of suggestions which they made for improvement in preparation.

The second question of the questionnaire read:

> Will you suggest the ways, if there are any, in which you might have profited during your first year of teaching by assistance from the supervisory staff of University High School?

Four types of aids were mentioned in a total of only 59 statements. Aids in organization and methods would have been welcomed most frequently during the first year "on the job." Specifically, the teachers needed help in organizing and teaching a subject for which there had been little preparation, in organizing work to make the best use of time in a day's program, in selection of materials and activities for pupils of different age and ability levels. Lists of references, texts, work-books and similar aids were mentioned with next greatest frequency. Some of the teachers would have welcomed the opportunity to write to the supervising teachers at University High School as problems presented themselves. Others would have appreciated in-service assistance in extra-curricular and professional problems and activities.

The third question of the follow-up form was:

> Do you consider that you would have profited by a reorganization of subject matter in your academic courses? If so, along what lines?

More than half of the 77 answers emphasized the need of relating the subject-matter of college courses more definitely to high-school courses and to the needs and interests of children. Standing next in frequency to suggestions for practicability were suggestions that cultural courses replace some of the intensive, concentrated preparation. Almost as many suggestions, however, stressed the need for more intensive preparation, particularly in specialized fields.

The fourth question of the questionnaire was:

> What changes, if any, would you suggest in the professional courses?

More than twice as many suggestions were made for reorganizing professional courses as had been made for reorganizing academic courses. The greatest stress was placed on the plea for desirability of relating professional courses more definitely to high-school courses: give more practical suggestions for teaching high-school subjects; give definite applications to high-school situations in educational psychology and in secondary education courses; place more emphasis on pupils and on materials and subjects related to pupil interests and needs; allow observation of class-room practise in high school before practise teaching begins. Second to the need for coordination between professional and high-school courses, the beginning teachers felt the need for reorganization within the professional courses and curricula. Some suggested shorter courses and elimination of overlapping. A few recommended such improved methods as smaller classes, less detail, and more discussion groups.

The fifth question on the follow-up form read:

Of what specific deficiencies in your preparation have you become aware, such, for example, as lack of conversational practise in teaching a modern language, lack of knowledge of formal grammar, lack of knowledge of the content of high school courses in your teaching field?

The 176 reactions to this question overlapped to a considerable extent the suggestions for reorganization of academic and professional courses. Lack of knowledge of what and how much to teach for a given course was listed more often than any other deficiency. But the teachers recognized almost as frequently the lack of subject-matter background in their teaching fields. They also realized their lack of experience in such particular skills and methods as conversational practise in modern language, and knowledge of good texts and work-books. A few teachers mentioned deficiencies in training for counseling, vocational guidance and extra-curricular activities.

The first check list of the questionnaire was a list of supervised teaching activities: classroom teaching, conferences with supervising teacher, general meetings, methods sections, conferences with department supervisor, substitution in Oakland schools, observation, discussion groups. The teachers indicated whether they would advise giving more time or less time to each of these activities or whether they would advise no change in present practise. On the whole, the beginning teachers seemed satisfied with the present time allotment for the activities on this list. For only general meetings was there a fair proportion of suggestions for "less." There was a tendency to vote for more classroom teaching, more substitution and observation and a larger number of discussion groups.

The second check list was preceded by the question:

Will you indicate the emphasis which from your experience you believe should be placed on the following matters in supervised teaching?

The items in the list were: Directed study, class management, lesson planning, construction of tests, special teaching techniques, practise in study halls, practise in working with extra-classroom activities, school health programs, use of reference materials, cafeteria management, teaching pupils at different levels, administrative experience, home-room practise. In general, the beginning teachers indicated that the supervised teaching activities should be emphasized no less than at present. In fact, there was a tendency to advise increased emphasis, especially on class management, experience in extra-curricular activities and home-rooms and the teaching of pupils at different levels.

The third check list named certain techniques of supervision: Close supervision in the classroom, demonstration teaching by supervising teachers, conferences before class with the supervising teacher, conferences after class with the supervising teacher, help in class management from the supervising teacher, adaptation of class work to needs of individual students. Close supervision by the supervising teacher in the classroom was the only item which the beginning teachers thought should receive less emphasis than it receives at present. Increased emphasis was recommended for demonstration teaching by supervising teachers and for adaptation of class work to the needs of individual students.

The fourth check list was composed of the titles of five courses in the department of education at the university. The teachers indicated by check whether they thought the time given to each course should be more than, less than or the same as it is at present. On the whole there was satisfaction with present offerings, with a slight tendency to ask for "more." Seven subjects not on the list were added by the teachers.

The fifth check list asked for the extra-curricular activities of these beginning teachers. Most of the teachers had extra-classroom duties. Sixteen duties were listed. Each of five responsibilities—home room, class adviser, club sponsor, faculty committee work, assistance in the athletic program—demanded time from a third or more of the teachers. Many of the teachers had more than one extra-curricular duty. No doubt these facts explain why so many of the teachers advised more contact with these activities during the practise teaching experience.

The sixth check list was headed, "Community Responsibilities Assumed by Teachers." Fourteen responsibilities were checked. Each of three community responsibilities—church, fraternal organizations, professional educational organizations—was being carried by between a fifth and a third of these beginning teachers.

Each teacher who returned a questionnaire indicated the type of school in which he was teaching, the subjects in which he had been trained to teach and the subjects which he was teaching. About two thirds of the group were teaching in junior or senior high schools. The others were distributed among elementary school, junior college, combined high school and junior college, college, university, business college, night school, private tutoring.

A comparison between the subjects taught by teachers in training and the subjects taught by the same teachers in service showed that over two thirds of the beginning teachers were teaching predominantly those subjects in which they had received training. Only a tenth of the teachers were teaching predominantly subjects in which they had not been trained.

### SUMMARY AND CONCLUSIONS

This summary is based only on the analysis of responses to the questionnaire of 1932. It does not take account of the numerous modifications which have been effected in the teacher-training program at the University of California since the questionnaire was sent out.

In general, the beginning teachers of this study expressed satisfaction with their training. Most of them seemed to feel that their experiences in directed teaching and in their academic and professional courses had enabled them to meet, in the main, the demands of their first teaching positions.

However, many of these former student teachers were meeting situations which had not been anticipated in their training, in spite of the fact that most of them had had directed teaching experiences with two classes in two distinct situations. Because they had been plunged into unanticipated experiences they advised a longer training period, with greater variety of activities. Many principals assign to beginning teachers a variety of subjects and in addition expect them to take charge of a home room, manage a study hall, be adviser for a club, assist in the athletic program or plan assemblies. Hence these former student teachers wished that their training had given them more varied classroom experience with pupils at different age and ability levels, with their minor as well as their major subjects, with related subjects in their general fields (as with biology if a physics or chemistry major), and with subject-matter and method content of high-school courses in their subject fields. Similarly, they wished that they had experienced wider contacts in club work, home-room activities, study-hall supervision, assembly planning, playground work, counseling and arranging of health programs.

Many of the teachers expressed the desire for a practise teaching period longer than the present semester of twenty weeks. Several recommended more than one period of teaching per day, particularly teaching two or three consecutive periods of different subjects for at least a few days. Variety and quantity are of course interrelated. To provide appreciably more variety in contacts and experiences would necessitate a longer teaching period.[3]

The problem of class management and discipline seems to be a persistent one. This problem might be partly solved by extending the teaching period and by providing greater variety in classroom and extra-classroom experiences. A wider contact with different types of activities and groups would give wider experience in management and in the handling of discipline problems. Many student teachers seemed to feel that they were not given sufficient responsibility for the management of a class, and that student teachers in general had not the "prestige" necessary to encourage good classroom discipline.

Besides suggestions for extending the training program there were suggestions for changing certain training procedures. The majority of these suggestions for reorganization of the teacher-training program had to do with the

[3] A second semester of directed teaching, known as Education 323, has been provided at the University of California for those who have completed the regular directed teaching course (Education 320). During this second semester students may obtain the longer teaching period and the greater variety of experience suggested above. Between sixty and seventy student teachers have availed themselves of this opportunity in each of the past two semesters.

unification of the program and with the relating of theory to practise. Academic and professional courses should be more practical: they should show how to apply theory to practise by being more closely adapted to the needs of high-school pupils; they should contain information concerning the content of various high-school courses and the activities associated with these courses—such information as might be obtained from well-written course-of-study outlines; they should give more attention to a wise grouping of teaching subjects and to training in a field rather than in one or two subjects. The elimination of overlapping of content in professional courses would allow time for this better organized training. A number of the teachers proposed that all, or nearly all, educational work be placed in the fifth, or graduate, year and be more closely correlated with the directed teaching experiences.

Some of the needs mentioned above might be met through special problems courses in the large subject-matter fields (science, mathematics, English, social studies, etc.). These courses could present content, teaching methods, special devices, techniques and supplementary aids for the high-school courses within each field. Perhaps they might outline courses in related fields. They could provide a better articulation between the academic courses at the college level and the related high-school courses. They could give training in the various practical contents and skills not taught in college courses but essential to the high-school work. They could provide training in the use of numerous special materials which now is received, if at all, only during the actual directed teaching.

There are some conspicuous omissions among the responses on these questionnaires. Over 200 of the 216 teachers seem to have passed through their period of training indifferent to the information, ideas and attitudes that look toward professional growth. A total of twelve suggestions mentioned such items as professional magazines, state requirements and laws, teachers' insurance, professional obligations and expenses, the high-school organization as a unit, a teacher's relations to the principal and other employees of the school organization, and relations to Parent Teacher Associations. Only two acknowledgments were made of helpful suggestions received along these lines during the training period. Professional organizations received no mention at all. Teachers in general receive constant criticism for lack of professional outlook, ignorance of professional literature, neglect of professional organizations. Possibly the training period is the time when teachers should become conscious that these problems demand consideration. It is interesting, perhaps significant, that only one teacher mentioned, as an important outcome of her preparation, pleasurable anticipation of teaching as a profession.

There is a hopeful sign of progress in the proportion of teachers who are instructing in subjects for which they were trained. The number of teachers so employed was distinctly greater than the number that reported proper placement in answer to the previous questionnaire.[4]

The large number of statements made by these teachers is significant. The 216 papers contained over a thousand statements which presented more than 200 different suggestions. This abundance of statements indicates that the beginning teachers are alert and thoughtful concerning their own teaching problems. It is a not unreasonable supposition that this attitude is partly a result of their training. Probably the teacher-training program neither will nor should incorporate all the suggestions which these teachers made. No doubt reorganizations will be made, but any teacher-training program must leave problems to be solved by the teachers themselves. In fact, a few of the teachers of this study stated that a training program has done its duty when it has shown the teachers how to go about solving their problems and has pointed the way to the important fields of information. A university teacher-training program faces the continuing problem of selecting those experiences which shall provide teachers with a sufficiently rich cultural background, with essential facts and techniques, with an awareness of important educational problems and with an eagerness for continual improvement.

G. P. CAHOON
MINNETTE MACKAY
UNIVERSITY OF CALIFORNIA

[4] *Ibid.*, p. 152.

SCHOOL AND SOCIETY

WITH WHICH ARE COMBINED THE EDUCATIONAL REVIEW, ESTABLISHED IN 1891, THE TEACHERS MAGAZINE, ESTABLISHED IN 1878, AND THE SCHOOL JOURNAL, ESTABLISHED IN 1874.

Volume 40 SATURDAY, AUGUST 25, 1934 Number 1026

# THE EDUCATIONAL FUNCTION OF NEW ENGLAND[1]

By Dr. ROBERT MAYNARD HUTCHINS
PRESIDENT OF THE UNIVERSITY OF CHICAGO

I AM here to-night to utter a Macedonian cry. If occasionally it sounds hysterical, I beg you to remember that it is of the nature of such a cry to be so. If on occasion it sounds uncomplimentary, I hope you will understand that this is merely the result of limitations of time. I can not remind you at the end of every paragraph that my purpose is to give you the highest compliment in my power and that my incidental brutality is intended simply to reveal in clearer light the opportunity that is before you. For I propose to show that the educational function of New England is to lead. My chief criticism of you is that you are so modest that you do not realize it. I wish to urge New England to-night to resume its rightful and natural place at the head of American education. I do not greatly care whether you do this from anger or ambition. I shall try to arouse both in you, in the hope that one or the other will result in the action which the country needs.

And first of all I wish to enumerate the general and pervasive contributions which New England has made. The preparatory schools, colleges and universities of this region have done three things for all of us. In the first place, they have set high standards of scholarship for students and teachers. They have required them to meet the standards erected and have declined to temporize or soften under pressure. I do not say that these standards have in all cases been the wisest; I do say that New England has adhered to them. Its resistance to mediocrity in the staff and in the student body has strengthened the resistance of all other educational institutions.

In the second place, New England has maintained freedom of thought, speech and teaching. Academic people who have not lived outside New England may not realize that the battle for academic freedom is a battle not yet won. Such freedom has become a commonplace in this part of the world. In less happy climes business men, parents and men in the street often feel called on to request the expulsion of a professor if he disagrees with them, and sometimes succeed in securing it. The example of the New England universities, and notably Harvard, has made it more respectable than it once was to demand that the teacher be permitted to say what he thinks, inside and outside the classroom. To be sure, we must take care that he is competent in his field; but that is to be determined not by the general public, but by his colleagues.

In the third place, New England has

[1] The Stearns Lecture before Phillips Academy, 1934.

elevated education throughout the country by constantly raising teachers' salaries. Such improvement as we have witnessed in the profession has been largely the result of this phenomenon. The level of academic compensation on the Atlantic seaboard is much higher than anywhere else. It would be lower everywhere else if it were not as high as it is here. No important university in the East has reduced salaries during this depression. Elsewhere every university but one has reduced them. If it had not been for New England that one would have done so; and the rest would have done it more.

These three contributions of New England are of the greatest importance. Unfortunately, however, I must also recite New England's sins against American education. They are sins of commission and omission. The requirements New England has established for entrance to, progress through and graduation from a school, college or university have had a dreadful effect throughout the country. New England invented the horrid machinery composed of course grades, course credits, course examinations, required attendance and required residence through which we determine by addition, subtraction, multiplication, division and a logarithm table the intellectual progress of the young. Of course this machinery has nothing to do with education and constitutes in fact one of the prime obstacles in its path. With the exception of Harvard, New England retains it in all its menacing vigor and thus makes it difficult to modify it elsewhere.

New England, too, and here Harvard has been the chief offender, has extended this vicious principle into new educational territory by requiring the bachelor's degree for entrance to professional schools. Such a school acquires mystical prestige by being called graduate. A law school, for example, is a good school if its students have spent four years in college. It is a poor one if they have lingered only three. It is really not respectable if they have devoted only two to the pursuit of the liberal arts. Of course there is not the slightest basis in fact or theory for this view. In fact, students who have not spent four years in college are likely to do better in law school than those who have. In theory there is no reason why a student who has completed his general education and wishes to specialize should not do so in professional subjects instead of non-professional ones. Yet New England has given impetus to the adding machine system by deciding that you can tell whether a student will succeed in a professional school by adding up the years he has devoted to football and fraternities.

The influence of the College Board Examinations has on the whole been pernicious. They have not been adopted outside New England; they have been modified here. Nevertheless, they have served to spread abroad the erroneous and dangerous doctrine that the purpose of the secondary school is to prepare for college. This notion has prevented the high school from developing its own program in terms of the needs of its own students. Its course of study has been formulated to meet collegiate requirements whose chief distinction is their rigidity, antiquity and remoteness from the real world. Of course this notion could not prevail indefinitely. The high school is not preparatory to college. The great mass of its pupils never go there. The high school has had at length to work out its own curriculum; but one of the reasons why it is not a very good one is that the high school is still confused as to what it is about. Nor have the College Boards been without painful repercussions on New England. The separation of the high-school course of study from the College Board curriculum is now great enough to make it most inconvenient for a high-school boy to take the examinations. As a result he does not go to a New England college or university.

Outside New England we are coming to the view that we do not know very much about selecting students at entrance. One middle western university, after trying various arithmetical computations in this connection, with no result except to admit some students who should have been excluded and exclude others who should have been admitted, finally announced a formula which I offer as the best that can be constructed at this stage. The announcement was as follows: "Any student will be admitted who commends himself to the Board of Admissions by reason of his personal qualities and scholastic aptitude." Under this formula age, years in secondary school, credits, grades and previous condition of servitude are not controlling. The student will be enrolled if on the whole he deserves a trial in college. The university knows that such a trial is the only real test. Its formula has this important consequence—it leaves the secondary schools free to frame the best course of study they can. It imposes neither the methods nor the subject-matter of their program. As one who has prepared students for the College Boards I can testify to the limitations they set to education. The teacher must prepare the pupil for the examinations first of all. In the school I taught in I did not dare try to educate my charges. It would have confused their minds.

We are witnessing in the West the collapse of all formal requirements. Our problem now is not to keep students out of educational institutions but to find or create those they can profitably go to. The most footless question that university presidents have been debating in recent years is, Who should go to college? Where else is there to go? To-day adults can not get jobs. Boys and girls of college age can hope to find them only by accident. Because of the technological improvements of recent years industry will require in the future proportionately fewer workers than ever before. The great problem of the high school now is not to hold its pupils, but to get rid of them. Their graduates can not get work and demand that classes be provided for them by an overburdened staff in overcrowded buildings. The public junior colleges and the state universities in urban centers have been swamped by the tide that has swept over them since the depression began. If these students are forbidden to enter educational institutions, what will become of them? All of them can not be absorbed into the army, navy or Civilian Conservation Corps. We should not encourage them to try to get into jail. The answer is that we must expand the educational system of the country to accommodate our young people up to their eighteenth or even their twentieth year. If existing schools and colleges are not adapted to the needs of all these students (and they certainly are not) we must establish new ones for them. If existing methods of selection and instruction can not be employed we shall have to invent others.

New England's contribution to methods of selection I have already described. Her contribution to methods of instruction is individualized teaching. This, where it takes the form of the small class, has had a destructive effect on education elsewhere. All the evidence is that a small class merely as such is no better than a large one. New England's insistence on the small class has given even the high school in the West the impression that only in such classes can education be conducted. The diminished resources of public education have thus been lavished on a kind of teaching it could have done very well without. The tutorial system is a contribution of New England which the rest of the country can not accept if it means that every student will have individual instruction in every subject all the time. The rest of the country can hope to supply able students with individual instruction in fields in which they are particularly interested and qualified. It should not attempt, for financial and educational reasons, to give it to every student every hour of every day. It is far too costly; it can not be demonstrated that it is worth the cost. The problem of the rest of the country is not to increase the amount of individualized teaching; it is to reduce it. We must find some way to cut down the number of miscellaneous small classes and discover some more economical and effective method of teaching the large number of students with whom we perforce must deal.

Nor can the rest of the country adopt the so-called house plan or college plan now being introduced at Harvard and Yale. If this plan is a housing plan it can of course be imitated; it already exists in other places. If, however, the proposal is to conduct education in small residential units in which faculty and students can live and study together, if in short the plan is the plan of Oxford and Cambridge, then it can have no followers in the West. The cost of the scheme is a fatal objection now. But assuming the money were available, we could not attempt it in the western universities, where co-education is the rule and where 50 per cent. or more of the students must live at home if they are to attend the university at all. I do not deny the merits of the British plan; I do assert that it can not be instituted in the West.

Even though the plan will not be instituted in the West its effects there are not likely to be salutary. It will be taken as another evidence that New England believes that the purpose of the higher learning is principally social and moral. This lesson New England has taught us too well already. It has already convinced us that athletics, architecture, personality, character and gentlemanliness are the essence of the intellectual life. The example of eastern colleges is always offered to refute a western president who wants to make his university an educational institution. Education and scholarship can be carried on in ramshackle buildings, with students who live at their homes and professors who live at theirs. Education and scholarship can flourish even if professors and students associate with one another only for intellectual as distinguished from social and athletic purposes. Of course I should not expect a university to refuse gifts of beautiful and useful buildings. I should not expect students and teachers to decline to speak to one another except on subjects on which they will later take or give examinations. Nor should I expect a university to ignore the moral virtues. I should insist, however, that the intellectual virtues are the proper preoccupation of a university; that the moral virtues may best be developed by concentration on the intellectual ones; and that learning how to be clubby is not the highest learning that may be achieved in a university. The emphasis in the house plan on the non-intellectual aspects of university activity is not an emphasis the country needs.

The house plan will have one other effect upon the West. It will separate it still farther from New England. The junior college is rapidly becoming the characteristic educational institution of the country outside New England. The depression has stimulated its growth. Three new ones were established in Chicago three weeks ago. The junior college takes its students through to the end of the sophomore year. I believe that it will become more and more the usual thing for the student to attend a junior college in his home town. If he goes to a university he will enter it as a junior. The house plan is built on the idea of a solid social and educational bloc enclosing the student from the sophomore or even the freshman year to graduation. This means that it will be almost impossible for the junior college graduate to attend a university where the house plan is in vogue; and New England will be cut off once again from the American educational system.

Recent events suggest that New England is withdrawing farther and farther into itself. General examinations and reading periods, which the rest of the country can adopt, hardly atone for the loss of New England's leadership in attacking the great problems of organization and subject-matter which now confront the institutions of the South and West. I can illustrate the seriousness of those problems by a brief reference to the junior college. There are 450 of these colleges in the country. They are two-year units, admitting their students as freshmen and graduating them as sophomores. Since 50 per cent. of their population leaves them every year they have the greatest difficulty in developing a coherent program. Their course of study is either two years more of high school or a pale imitation of the first two years at the state university, usually the weakest part of the curriculum of that institution. Many of their students are there because there is no other place for them to go. What shall be done about it? Should the junior college take over the last two years of the high school? Should the high school take over the junior college? What sort of students should the junior college admit? What sort of curriculum should be formulated for them? What is to be done with the students who we decide should not be admitted? These questions are pressing for answer. At all levels of education we face similar problems. But not since Mr. Eliot presented us with the elective system, which was not an unmixed blessing, has New England given us an important idea which we may use in meeting such problems. To-day we are in a desperate plight. Public education in some western and southern states has now collapsed. In many others it is on the verge of collapse. The state universities have received terrible blows from legislatures who have seen their states laid waste by the depression. The endowed colleges and universities are many of them barely able to maintain themselves. And yet we must now reconstruct our whole program to meet the new conditions which the economic situation has thrust upon us. We must reorganize the educational system and redefine the purposes of its units. We must create new units to accommodate students whom industry can no longer absorb, but whom we have never regarded as our responsibility before. We need ideas, courage, imagination now as at no earlier period. Where shall we hope to find them if not in New England? There are situated the strongest institutions in the country. They can enlighten us if they will. For forty years they have turned their backs to us and devoted themselves to their own affairs. The great developments of those years have occurred at levels which New England has ignored; they have occurred in the public schools; the elementary schools, the high schools, the junior colleges. We have been without the leadership which only New England can give us. We can do without it no longer.

Compelled by circumstances, the country outside New England is proceeding nevertheless to frame a new educational system. New England can help in its construction if it will. The educational system that is developing is this. The primary school will complete its work in six years. After it will come a new kind of preparatory school, which we may as well call the high school. This pupil will enter at twelve and leave at about 16. At about sixteen he will enter upon one of two courses of study, the one cultural and the other technical. Each of them will be designed as though the student were to terminate his education in them. Actually most students will regard the completion of one of these courses of study as the completion of formal education. These curricula will take the student from his sixteenth to his twentieth year. At the latter age he should go to work unless he is interested and qualified in some scholarly or professional field.

The cultural course of study will be given in an institution called the college, even though it begins and ends two years earlier than our present colleges. If convenient, the college may also administer the technical course of study. If it is not, it may be given by technical institutes specially created to take charge of it. In any event the end of these two courses of study would be intended as the end of education for the great majority of the young people of the country. The colleges and technical institutes that I predict will be numerous. They will be local. Attendance on them will be as customary as attendance at high school is to-day. The ordinary youth will thus complete his education at home. And he will complete it in an institution adapted to his individual needs and capacities. If he wishes he will do so at public expense. The expense to the public will be more than justified.

Many of the present four-year colleges of liberal arts outside New England will become technical institutes or colleges of the new variety that I have described. They will admit their students at about sixteen and graduate them about twenty. They can not afford and should not attempt the expensive and difficult work of which the present junior and senior year in New England colleges are composed. They should abandon those years. The strongest of the present colleges may, however, develop in another direction. They may devote themselves to what may be called non-professional specialization in arts, literature and science. They would admit their students at the beginning of the junior year to a three-year curriculum leading to the M.A. degree. This degree will, I believe, supplant the B.A. at this point. The B.A. at present means little. The curriculum which leads to it is a strange mixture of general education, specialized study and vocational training. The one common denominator of the B.A. degree in the colleges and universities of America is that it takes four years to get it. Eventually, I think, the bachelor's degree will be granted at the end of the present sophomore year, on graduation from the new colleges that I foresee. Then it may mean something. It may mean that its holder has a general education.

University work outside New England will begin with the beginning of the junior year. Although universities may operate some of the new colleges and technical institutes that will arise, they will not do so under the delusion that collegiate work is university work. They will operate them to assist the new colleges and technical institutes in formulating their programs. Universities which do not wish to conduct such experimental work should abandon their freshman and sophomore years. As long as they continue them they serve to confuse the students, the faculty and the general public about the aims and activities of the university. The university will consist of the professional schools, which the student will enter if he chooses at the opening of the junior year, and customary divisions of arts, literature and science. University students will be carefully selected. As we have seen, the selective principle can not operate below this point because by definition the institutions below the university are designed to accommodate all or almost all the population that is of an age to attend them. No one will be permitted to enter the university who can not demonstrate his interest and ability in some field of knowledge. The hordes who are now allowed to proceed to the B.A. or even the Ph.D. merely because they are the offspring of voters will be excluded. The university will devote itself to scholarly and professional work and the cultivation of the minds of those who have minds to cultivate.

Now you will observe that this program from the elementary schools through the university means a thoroughgoing reorganization of the educational system. It provides for a tremendous expansion and diversification of educational opportunity. Hence it meets the most pressing social need of America to-day. At the same time by disentangling the purposes of the high school, the college and the university it clarifies the responsibilities of each educational unit. With depleted resources and increased burdens the West and South are struggling toward some such plan. New England can help us in our struggles if it will.

With deference I venture to suggest what New England might do for us. Nothing would advance the higher learning in America so much as an announcement from the strong colleges and universities of New England that they had abandoned their freshman and sophomore work. If they then went on to develop a three-year course of study to the master's degree they would do still more for us. They would show us not only the organization we should adopt, but also the subject-matter we should treat of. New England need not take this step from philanthropic motives alone. New England faces the choice between resuming the leadership of American education and becoming an excrescence on it. If it becomes an excrescence on it, it will lose all contact with students from outside New England. If the strong colleges and universities in this part of the world will begin their work with the junior year, they may expect to enlist in increasing numbers the graduates of junior colleges and of the new colleges which I have described. If Yale and Harvard are going British I suggest that they go the whole way and eliminate work which in England is regarded as of public-school grade. The first-year man at Oxford and Cambridge is the equivalent of a junior here. I suggest that we make our juniors first-year men.

With deference I recommend that the great preparatory schools of New England become colleges. This would mean that they would cease to be preparatory schools. They would take their students through to the end of what we now call the sophomore year. They would correspond to the gymnasium, the lycée and the English public school. Their qualified graduates might go on to the university if they cared to do so. If they did not, they could feel that they had had an education.

The location and environment of the New England preparatory schools are better for collegiate work than those of the New England universities. The preparatory schools can do the teaching that is now done in the freshman and sophomore years of universities better than the universities can do it. The object of a preparatory school faculty is to teach. The faculty knows how to do it and wants to do it. A university faculty is selected to advance knowledge. It does not want to teach and does not know how to do it. As a result freshman and sophomore teaching is relegated to youthful instructors whose one ambition is to get out of it as soon as possible into the more respectable, remunerative and rarefied atmosphere of scholarly research. To turn the New England preparatory schools into colleges of the sort I have described would relieve the universities of a burden they do not want, give the schools an opportunity they are equipped to grasp, introduce some education into the two most wasteful years of the university course and set an example for the country.

The object of these new colleges should be to give a sound general education to the students in them. One of the virtues of the organization that I foresee is that it would compel us to find out what a sound general education is. I can not truthfully say that New England has done much for us lately in helping us to find out what the curriculum should contain. The principal differences between New England and the rest of the country have been on the issue of Greek and Latin. As formulated, the issue was not worth fighting over. The classical position degenerated into a defense not of reading and understanding the great books of the ancient world, but of studying their language in infinite detail and as an end in itself in such a way as to create in the student a profound distaste for the ancient world and all its works.

I put it to you that if we are going to convince our fellow-citizens that education is an affair of the intellect we must have a course of study that will corroborate instead of refuting our pretensions. New England has a great intellectual tradition. If it will now revitalize that tradition it may discover in the process what a general education ought to be. It may even discover a new classicism more worth fighting about than the old. With deference I suggest to the New England preparatory schools (after they become colleges) a course of study based upon ideas. In general, ideas are to be found in books. Many of these books are written in ancient languages. It is not indispensable, though it is highly desirable, to study them in the languages in which they were written. The course of study, therefore, would consist largely of books, great books and not parts of these books, but all of them. The rest of the curriculum would be devoted to learning how to deal with ideas—how to recognize them, analyze them, develop them and apply them. This used to be done through what was called the *trivium:* grammar, rhetoric and logic. A course of study composed of the classics and the *trivium* would make the college an intellectual enterprise and college education an intellectual experience. The graduate would have had no vocational training. He would have trained his mind. I suggest that he would be better equipped to meet practical situations than one whose training had been given him through the medium of little imitation practical situations in the classroom.

I suggest also that the graduate of such a college would be better equipped to go into the university than one who had passed through a preparatory school of the variety that exists to-day. But New England must show us, too, how to make the university an intellectual affair. In this behalf the New England universities might attempt also a return to classical models. They might recall that once the three "departments" of a university, and the only ones, were medicine, theology and law. To-day we should certainly add the natural sciences at the base of medicine and the social sciences which are the foundations of the law. These three fields were not studied professionally; the object of studying them was to understand them. To study the law to learn how to practise it and to study it to understand it are two quite different things. Nor in those days were these three fields studied in isolation from one another. Each one penetrated and was penetrated by the rest. The propositions and facts were the same; the ultimate references were different. So wherever he was working the student never lost sight of the unity of the universe and the unity of thought. Not crammed with little useless facts, busy applying in more specialized fields the knowledge he had of the classics and the *trivium,* he might come at last to comprehend man and nature and the relations between the two.

With colleges and universities aiming to attain these ends, we might have an educational system in America that would give us the trained intelligence we need, that would furnish direction to our people, and that would produce at last an enlightened nation. To lead us to the achievement of these ideals is the educational function of New England.

# EDUCATIONAL EVENTS

## THE EXTENSION SYSTEM OF EDUCATION IN THE SOVIET UNION

A DISPATCH to *The Christian Science Monitor* states that "Free-Day-Universities," which compare with the extension departments of American universities, have developed widely during the past few months within the Soviet Union. They are evidence of the new desire which is being encouraged by the authorities, for something more than the narrowly specialized education which accompanied the Five-Year Plan for industrialization.

Last September a group of professors at the Leningrad Chemical-Technological Institute organized a series of lectures on art and literature, to be given on "free days," the general holidays which come once in every six days. These lectures proved so popular that the director decided to continue them as a permanent part of the work of the institute, and to include lectures on history and the sciences.

The plan was taken up by other technical institutes in Leningrad and elsewhere, and today practically every higher school in the Soviet Union arranges free-day lectures on cultural, as distinguished from technical, subjects. The most popular lectures attract audiences of several thousand men and women.

In many schools these extension lectures gradually have shaped themselves into courses and those who attend them are enrolled as students. In Moscow, 50,000 persons have been thus enrolled, and the number in other cities is in proportion. While some factory and office workers attend these lectures, the greatest interest is shown by students at technical schools, whose narrowly specialized training has given them little opportunity to study literature, history or even the wider aspects of sciences.

During this summer lectures are being given in the various municipal parks of the Soviet Union. Teachers from the nearest institutes have volunteered to give courses, and the Commissariat of Education has retained several of the most popular lecturers to travel from city to city. In this spontaneous fashion is growing up a sort of Soviet "Chautauqua" movement.

Up to the present time, Soviet educators have devoted most of their time and money toward the drive against illiteracy, and for the technical equipment of specialists in the expanding factories. Now the official figures show that illiteracy has largely disappeared, and a sufficient number of training schools for technicians has been established. Time can be spared for the clamorous demand for more general knowledge.

## POPULATION TRENDS IN RELATION TO PUBLIC EDUCATION IN CALIFORNIA

NUMEROUS articles that have appeared recently in discussion of current trends of population in California and in the United States as a whole have been summarized in a report of the California State Department of Education. A number of carefully directed and scientifically conducted research studies also have been reported making some effort to predict probable future trends of population as well as providing exhaustive analyses of past and present trends. The gist of these discussions and reports are summarized as indicating:

1. That birth rates have decreased almost continuously in the United States as a whole and in California since 1921.
2. That the excess of births over deaths has decreased almost continuously for an even greater period, and that the decrease has been much greater in California than in the United States as a whole during the past ten years.
3. That increases in population due to immigration have decreased materially in recent years, both in California and in the United States as a whole.
4. That increases in population in California due to migration from other states has decreased remarkably since 1930.
5. That the percentage of the total population

found in those age-groups which contribute to public-school enrolment (5 to 19 years of age) has decreased since 1930 both in the United States as a whole and in California.

6. That the actual total population of children of elementary school age (5 to 14 years of age) has decreased in California since 1930.
7. That decreases in total population in California have occurred in the earlier age-groups (0–4 and 5–9 years) beginning in 1930.

## PLANS FOR THE NEW HUMANISTIC LIBRARY AT PRINCETON UNIVERSITY

THE appointment of a committee by the Princeton board of trustees to supervise the raising of funds for the university's new humanistic library has been announced by President Harold Willis Dodds and preliminary architectural plans for the projected structure were placed on display in the main reading room of the present library building.

Designed to satisfy all the customary requirements of a library, and, in addition, to supply an intellectual center for the work of the social science and humanistic departments, the plan of the building is revolutionary in that every upper classman and graduate student in these departments will have an individual desk and locker immediately adjacent to the books covering his field of study.

Charles Z. Klauder, of Philadelphia, assisted by Ides Van Der Gracht, of New York, has designed the building, which will occupy the northeast corner of the campus, bounded by Nassau Street on the north, Washington Road on the east and the university chapel on the south. It will replace the Pyne Library, erected in 1897, which has been greatly overcrowded for some years.

The committee for raising funds is headed by Walter E. Hope, of New York City, assistant secretary of the Treasury under President Hoover. Other members are Charles W. McAlpin, Frederick P. King, Whitney Darrow, George M. Moffett, Raymond B. Fosdick, Charles Scribner, Jr., Jarvis Cromwell and William E. Stevenson, all of New York City; Professors Edwin W. Kemmerer and C. Rufus Morey, of Princeton; Henry B. Thompson, of Greenville, Del.; Wilson S. Arbuthnot, of Pittsburgh; Harry H. Langenberg, of St. Louis; John Stuart, of Chicago, and Fitz Eugene Dixon, of Elkins Park, Pa.

## THE NEW SCHOOL FOR SOCIAL RESEARCH

THE New School for Social Research, Inc., has received permission in an order of Supreme Court Justice Hofstadter to transfer all its property at 66 West Twelfth Street without consideration to a new corporation of the same name chartered recently by the Board of Regents of the State of New York with power of conferring degrees in its Graduate School. The former corporation was a membership organization without such power, while the new one is formed under the Education Laws.

The petition of the membership corporation, signed by Alvin S. Johnson, president and director of the school, included a letter written to the new corporation stating that the plans for the school to confer degrees had been realized through the action of the State Board of Regents, and said the transfer of property would be made "to enable you to amplify and conduct, without interruption, and in accordance with the policies heretofore pursued by the undersigned, any business and affairs of the New School and its graduate faculty." The transfer did not become effective until Justice Hofstadter approved it.

The property includes the land and building at 66 West Twelfth Street and all the contents. The petition said that assets of the old corporation consist of $15,000 cash, $60,000 in notes receivable, $13,400 as the value of the reference library, and $51,900 for furniture and furnishings. The liabilities, which are assumed by the new corporation, consist of a first mortgage of $250,000, a second mortgage of $100,000 and a serial mortgage bond issue, on which interest is payable out of the net income of $371,500. The present value of the land and building is stated to be $916,484.

The petition said that the interest of the school would be promoted by the transfer because "upon the reorganization in 1933 of German university life by the National Socialist revolution scores of professors of international reputation were dismissed or given indefinite furloughs." It added that "your petitioner, as an American institution, believing in academic liberty, invited a number of the most outstanding of the scholars to form themselves into a graduate faculty of political and social science at the New School, thus serving a dual purpose of offering them a livelihood with academic fredom and making available for graduate students in this country German university methods having a definite character and value of their own."

In conclusion the petition reads: "After the graduate faculty was established it became increasingly apparent that many serious graduate students would have liked to matriculate and follow the courses offered by the faculty had the New School been organized with requisite authority to permit it to grant graduate degrees in the social sciences. This authority now having been obtained through the action of the Regents of the State of New York the interests of your petitioner will be promoted."

## VISUAL EDUCATION IN THE NEW YORK CITY SCHOOLS

MISS RITA HOCHHEIMER, assistant director of visual education, in her annual report to Dr. Harold G. Campbell, superintendent of the New York City schools, states that about forty-five per cent. of the schools, with a pupil population of 1,000,000 children, are now convertible into motion picture theaters for visual education purposes.

The Board of Education's drive for general motion-picture reform is linked with the spread of the "learning-by-seeing" movement through the use of moving pictures and stereopticon slides in the schools. Associate Superintendent John S. Roberts, who supervises all visual instruction work, is now engaged, at Dr. Campbell's request, on a survey to determine how the schools can help to effect the production and distribution of better films.

In addition to the 300 schools equipped with motion picture projectors, 635 schools, or 90 per cent. of the total number, are equipped with one or more lantern slide machines. The supply system of the bureau of visual instruction includes four film libraries serving eight school districts, with two new libraries soon to be established.

Weekly picture service was maintained last year to thirty-three schools in Manhattan, thirteen in the Bronx, thirty-five in Brooklyn and ten in Queens. The bureau has 175 separate films designed for use in connection with courses in geography, nature study, health education and biology.

Miss Hochheimer states that the pictures have not only added to the children's factual knowledge but have destroyed barriers of distance, changed attitudes and enlarged vocabularies.

To correlate the pictorial material more closely with curricular subjects, a city-wide program of teacher training in visual instruction has been begun. The program involves demonstration lessons and discussions for principals and teachers in all school districts.

Listed in the report as significant steps in the visual instruction movement are the development by the health education committee of the Principals Association of lantern slides suitable for health education in the first grade; the study by a subcommittee of visual aids for use in vocational guidance; the preparation, in cooperation with Savel Zimand, administrative director of the Bellevue-Yorkville Health Demonstration, of an intensive program of visual health instruction for the schools of that district, and the request by the advisory board on industrial education for help in plans for safety education in industrial high schools.

## EMPLOYMENT OF TEACHERS BY THE FEDERAL EMERGENCY RELIEF ADMINISTRATION

EMPLOYMENT of 40,000 unemployed teachers in a nation-wide campaign against illiteracy has been announced by Aubrey Williams, acting administrator, as the goal of the emergency program which is being financed by the Federal Emergency Relief Administration.

The campaign, in which state relief directors have been enlisted, is expected to reach 2,000,000 persons whose requirements are not now included in state educational programs. The major part of the program concerns itself with the education of adult workers now unemployed.

As formulated by the Education Division of the FERA, under the leadership of Dr. L. R. Alderman, the new "five-point program" includes literacy classes, vocational training, vocational rehabilitation, general adult education and nursery schools.

Literacy classes are to be organized in every community where the need exists and a sufficient number of adults unable to read and write can be interested in the program.

Vocational training, for the adult unemployed, will include trade, industrial and commercial education, home economics, agriculture and counsel for better vocational adjustment.

The adult education phase of the program will include workers' educational classes, a venture in an unexplored field which was undertaken by the Education Division last winter; parent education, avocational training, hobbies and handicraft training and general academic, informal and cultural education. The workers' educational classes will be in reality discussion groups under the direction of specially trained teachers.

Beginning with the August allotments to each state for relief purposes, provision has been made for the emergency educational program. In addition, each state received an allotment of teachers who could be employed in this work.

All the relief funds must be used for educational purposes and not connected with local school budgets.

## THE PITTSBURGH MEETING OF THE AMERICAN VOCATIONAL ASSOCIATION

THE ninth annual convention of the American Vocational Association will be held in Pittsburgh, from December 5 to 8.

Preliminary preparations for the December convention have been going on for the past several months. A local steering committee has been organized with Dr. Ben G. Graham, superintendent of the Pittsburgh public schools, as honorary chairman. The other members are Frank M. Leavitt, associate superintendent, Pittsburgh public schools, chairman; Fred W. Boland, director of trade training, Pittsburgh public schools, vice-chairman; and Dr. G. D. Whitney, director of vocational teacher training, University of Pittsburgh, secretary.

Among the materials being prepared for the convention is an illustrated booklet describing the activities of the public schools of Pittsburgh and vicinity and the types of industries in the Pittsburgh area. This booklet will be distributed to all delegates and guests. Other pamphlets illustrative of vocational education in its several aspects are being organized.

The Hotel William Penn has been chosen for convention headquarters. Practically all meetings will be held there. This hotel is conveniently situated within easy commuting distance of the University of Pittsburgh and the Carnegie Institute of Technology, the two institutions in Pittsburgh engaged in the preparation of vocational and industrial arts teachers. The Clifford B. Connelly Trade School, one of the largest public trade schools in the country, is only a short distance away.

Local coordinators have been appointed by the steering committee to work with the vice-presidents of the American Vocational Association. These are: *Agriculture,* A. K. Getman and Ray Seamans; *Commercial,* Jacob Spies and D. D. Lessenberry; *Home economics,* Elisabeth Amery and Emma M. Watts; *Industrial arts,* R. W. Selvidge and Glen U. Cleeton; *Industrial and Part-time,* Thomas H. Quigley and Aida C. Bishop, Joseph W. Fleming; *Rehabilitation,* Oscar M. Sullivan and M. M. Walter; *Vocational guidance,* Edwin A. Lee and Harry A. Snyder. The vice-presidents of the sections will be responsible for arranging the programs, while the local coordinators will assist in effecting arrangements in Pittsburgh and in conducting the meetings.

Teachers, supervisors and superintendents, as well as college and university professors and administrators in the Pittsburgh district, have been selected as committee chairmen. The following are responsible to the local steering committee for the specific items with which they have been charged:

*Service clubs,* Dr. S. E. Weber; *Hostess organization and coordination,* Ella Ruth Boyce; *Tours,* Dr. Herbert L. Spencer; *Local arrangements,* Dr. A. M. Goldberger; *Reception,* Irene E. McDermott; *Industrial contacts,* John D. Beatty; *Hotels,* R. M. Sherrard; *Membership,* Dr. A. S. Hurrell; *Service,* Dr. John A. Hollinger; *Registration,* Dr. Samuel Fausold; *Exhibits,* James R. Glenn; *Information,* Joseph M. Speer; *Entertainment,* Dr. Coit R. Hoechst; *Printing,* John Hawthorne; *Music,* Dr. Will Earhart; *Banquet,* Elmer G. Miller; *Publicity,* Theodore A. Siedle.

The officers of the American Vocational Association are: *President,* Ray Fife, state supervisor of agricultural education, Ohio; *Vice-presidents,* A. K. Getman, state supervisor of agricultural education, New York; Elisabeth Amery, state supervisor of home economics education,

Maryland; R. W. Selvidge, professor of industrial education, University of Missouri; Jacob Spies, supervisor of commercial education, Cheboygan, Wisconsin; Edwin A. Lee, superintendent of schools, San Francisco; Oscar M. Sullivan, state director of re-education, Minnesota, and Thomas H. Quigley, professor of industrial education, Georgia School of Technology; *Treasurer,* Charles W. Sylvester, director of vocational education, Baltimore; *Executive secretary,* L. H. Dennis, Washington, D. C., and *Director,* Dr. George P. Hambrecht, state director for vocational education, Wisconsin.

### THE NATIONAL ADVISORY COUNCIL ON RADIO IN EDUCATION

October 8 and 9 are announced as the dates for the forthcoming annual assembly of the National Advisory Council on Radio in Education which will be held in Chicago. Five sessions will be at the Drake Hotel and one in the Hall of Science at the Century of Progress Exposition.

"The Importance of Radio Broadcasting in a Changing Social Order" is to be the general subject of the conference. Among the speakers will be Secretary of the Interior, Harold L. Ickes; Dr. John H. Finley, associate editor of *The New York Times;* Walter Damrosch; Professor John Erskine; President Robert M. Hutchins, University of Chicago; President Walter Dill Scott, Northwestern University; Dr. Frederick P. Keppel, president of the Carnegie Corporation of New York; President Robert G. Sproul, University of California; President Lotus D. Coffman, University of Minnesota; David Sarnoff, president of the Radio Corporation of America; Dr. Harry Woodburn Chase, chancellor of New York University, and others.

Carl H. Milam, secretary of the American Library Association, is chairman of the committee on program which includes Levering Tyson, director of the council, President Hutchins and President Scott. Private *versus* government control of radio will be one of the topics of discussion.

## EDUCATIONAL NOTES AND NEWS

Professor Eugene Allen Gilmore, since 1930 dean of the College of Law at the University of Iowa, and for eight years previously secretary of public instruction and governor-general of the Philippine Islands, has been elected to the presidency of the university.

Professor Pendleton Howard has been elected dean of the College of Law at the University of Idaho to take the place of Dean W. E. Masterson, who was recently elected dean of the School of Law at the University of Missouri. During the past year Dr. Howard was a visiting professor in the Law School of Northwestern University. He has been professor of law at the University of Idaho since 1929.

Dr. Vern O. Knudsen, chairman of the department of physics at the University of California at Los Angeles, has been appointed dean of the Graduate School.

Dr. E. T. Grether, associate professor of economics at the University of California, has been made acting dean of the College of Commerce. He takes the place of Dean Henry F. Grady, who has accepted a position with the Federal Administration in Washington.

Dr. A. C. McIntosh has been appointed Kenan professor of law emeritus after twenty-four years of service as a member of the faculty of the University of North Carolina. His work will be taken over by Dr. James H. Chadbourne, while Professor Mulder, the new member of the staff, will assume the courses formerly taught by Dr. Chadbourne.

Dr. Harlan C. Koch, head of the department of secondary education of the University of Nebraska, has been appointed to the position of assistant director of the Bureau of Cooperation with Educational Institutions at the University of Michigan, to succeed Dr. Wray H. Congdon, who has resigned to become director of admissions at Lehigh University.

W. H. Orion, director of physical education of the Santa Barbara Public Schools and director of municipal recreation in Santa Barbara City, has been appointed chief of the Division of Health and Physical Education by the California State Department of Education to take the place made vacant by the resignation of N. P. Neilson. Mr. Orion began his work with the State Department of Education on August 15.

DR. JACOB GOODALE LIPMAN, professor of soils and dean of agriculture at Rutgers University and director of the New Jersey Agricultural Experiment Station, has been awarded the Chandler Medal of Columbia University for 1934. Dr. Lipman is a native of Latvia, and began his study of the science of soils on a New Jersey farm. The medal will be formally conferred at Columbia in November.

NEW appointments at Colgate University include Thomas Roberts, who has been made professor of music, and the following instructors: John F. Fichten, 3d, fine arts and head of survey in that department; Raymond O. Rockwood, William M. Shankwiler, Howard Dwight Williams and August Oran Spain, history; Andrew Louis, German; Herman Arno Brautigam, Biblical literature; Charles Frank Phillips, Carl Tristan Arlt, Lawrence William Towle and Leonard Palmers Adams, economics; Raymond J. Myers, zoology; Eugene Bahn, public speaking, and J. Leslie Hart, physical education.

ROBERT B. LYONS, director of the high-school band and orchestra at Streator, Illinois, has been elected assistant professor of music and director of the band of the University of Idaho.

JAN RUHTENBERG, Swedish architect, has been appointed a member of the faculty of the School of Architecture of Columbia University. Mr. Ruhtenberg, one of the leaders of the modern movement in German architecture, will teach design.

THREE of the faculty of Birmingham-Southern College who were away last year on sabbatical leave are returning to their regular duties this fall. J. Horace Coulliette, professor of physics, spent his sabbatical year at Columbia University; Douglas L. Hunt, associate professor of English, engaged in advanced study and taught one class in freshman English at Vanderbilt University, and Robert S. Whitehouse, associate professor of modern languages, spent the year studying at Johns Hopkins University.

DR. PITMAN B. POTTER, professor of political science at the University of Wisconsin, is summer director of the Students' International Union at Geneva. This organization annually assembles two dozen or more students from colleges in the United States and Europe at its round table conference during July and August.

J. R. MACKAY, of Saskatoon, Canada, was elected president of the Canadian Teachers' Federation at the concluding session of the annual convention on August 13. Miss Jessie Norris, of Montreal, was elected first vice-president and C. N. Crutchfield, Shawinigan Falls, Que., again was chosen secretary-treasurer. Executive members are: Miss Jacqueline Macdonald, of Charlottetown, P.E.I.; H. V. Corkum, Mahone Bay, N.S.; E. J. Alexander, Saint John, N.B.; Miss Dorothy Seiveright, Macdonald College, Quebec; Miss Etta Lane, Toronto; Miss M. A. Strangways, Prince Albert, Sask.; E. J. Thorlakson, Calgary.

WE learn from the *Western Journal of Education,* San Francisco, that Vierling Kersey, California State Superintendent of Public Instruction (incumbent); G. Vernon Bennett, formerly city superintendent of Pomona and more recently connected with the University of Southern California, and John Harold Swan, of the Junior College, Sacramento, are candidates for election to the office of California State Superintendent of Public Instruction.

DR. ROBERT GORDON SPROUL, president of the University of California, has accepted the invitation of Newton D. Baker, *chairman,* to become a member of the "Committee for the 1934 mobilization for human needs."

DR. CLIFFORD L. JAMES, professor of international trade and finance at the Ohio State University, has been granted a leave of absence to serve as an economist on the Federal Trade Commission.

DR. JACOB VINER, chief administration economist, adviser and assistant to Secretary of the Treasury Henry Morgenthau, Jr., will relinquish his official post before the end of the year, according to a United Press dispatch. After his retirement Dr. Viner is expected to resume teaching at the University of Chicago and the Graduate Institute of International Studies at the University of Geneva.

DR. WILLIAM P. DEARING, president of Oakland City College, Indiana, addressed the summer session graduating class at the University of Kentucky on August 17. Approximately one hundred and sixty-five students received degrees at the annual summer school commencement exercises.

JAMES RICKARBY CAMPBELL, founder of the Kingsley School at Essex Fells, N. J., died on August 16, at the age of seventy-four years. After teaching in several schools and colleges, Mr. Campbell founded the Kingsley School in 1900. Having rounded out nearly half a century in educational work, he retired as headmaster emeritus in 1926.

DR. WILLIAM T. VLYMEN, retired principal of the Eastern District High School of New York City, died on August 13, at the age of seventy-four years. Dr. Vlymen had been connected with the city school system for a period of forty-eight years.

DR. HENRY M. MAXSON, superintendent of public schools in Plainfield, N. J., for thirty-five years, died on August 20, at the age of eighty-one years.

THE twentieth National Recreation Congress will be held in Washington, D. C., from October 1 to 5. There will be no papers. The *Journal* of the American Medical Association reports that the congress will divide itself into discussion groups beginning Tuesday morning and continuing through the day and each morning thereafter. Wednesday, Thursday and Friday mornings at 11 o'clock the entire congress will come together to hear reports from these discussion groups. Wednesday, Thursday and Friday afternoons will be left free for special meetings. General meetings will be held each evening, with addresses by prominent speakers. Headquarters will be at the Wardman Park Hotel.

THE fourth biennial conference of the National Council of Parent Education for workers in family and parent education will be devoted to a consideration of "Social Philosophy for Education in Parenthood and Family Life." It will be held in Washington, D. C., on November 1, 2 and 3, at the Wardman Park Hotel, and will be preceded by a meeting of the council. While this conference is arranged and conducted by council member organization representatives and by professionals affiliated with the council, all members of the professions whose work includes any form of family and parent education are invited to attend.

THE opening date for the Pan-American Conference on Education has been fixed for September 9. The local organizing committees are making final preparations for the meetings, which will be held at the University of Chile. A special exhibition of scholastic material is planned. It is stated that delegates will try to reach an understanding looking toward a certain uniformity in studies.

THE International Congress of Librarians will be held in Spain in the first ten days of June, 1935, according to Dr. William Warner Bishop, chairman of the International Library Committee. Probably some of the meetings will be at Madrid, and some at Barcelona or elsewhere.

THE first of fifteen regional institutes for adult education supervisors under the auspices of the Federal Relief Administration was held at the George Peabody College for Teachers from July 22 to August 1. The institute was attended by supervisors from Alabama, Kentucky, Mississippi and Tennessee. It was under the direction of Dr. Doak S. Campbell, of the Division of Surveys and Field Studies. Those appearing on the program were Dr. L. R. Alderman, director of the Emergency Education Program; Dr. Walter D. Cocking, Commissioner of Education in Tennessee; President Bruce Payne, of Peabody College; State Superintendent W. F. Bond, of Mississippi; Dr. Chas. W. Knudsen, of Peabody College; Miss Marguerite Burnett, State Department of Education, Delaware; Miss Wil Lou Gray, State Department of Education, Columbia, South Carolina, and Lieutenant Colonel Walter L. Simpson, state relief director of education for the state of Tennessee. Detailed plans for carrying on the work of adult education in the four states were worked out.

A CONFERENCE for workers on college curriculum problems was held at the George Peabody College from July 30 to August 2. The conference was sponsored by the Curriculum Laboratory under the direction of Dr. Doak S. Campbell and Dr. Hollis L. Caswell, of the Division of Surveys and Field Studies. The purposes were to observe in the Curriculum Laboratory the work of various groups on state and city curriculum problems and to work out plans for further participation of higher institutions in curriculum programs. Sixty-four official representatives from fourteen states attended the conference. In addition there were approximately a hundred visitors attending the sessions.

Work is progressing rapidly on the library and the chemistry building at the University of Arkansas, Fayetteville, as well as on a building for the Medical School at Little Rock, the ground-breaking ceremonies being held on July 30. The cost of each of the three buildings approximates half a million dollars. Their erection at this time is made possible by a grant from the Federal Public Works Administration. It is expected that they will be completed in the late spring or early summer and ready for occupancy at the beginning of the school year in September, 1935.

Dr. John S. Roberts, associate superintendent in charge of junior high schools of New York City, in his annual report urges early consideration of a ten-year plan to place all seventh, eighth and ninth grade students in Junior High Schools, eliminating two years from the secondary schools and one year from the high schools. "There is a ten-year plan or building program which would eventually result in placing all seventh, eighth and ninth year pupils in the city in the Junior High School which would result in the cutting out of the ninth year from all senior high schools and the conversion of 8B schools into 6B schools in all parts of the city, with perhaps the exception of a few in outlying districts." Dr. Roberts recommended "that this tentative plan be given consideration by the Board of Superintendents at an early date."

Fifty British school boys sailed from London on August 6 to explore and survey a hitherto unmapped area of Newfoundland. This is the third expedition organized by the Public Schools Exploring Society. Surgeon-Commander Murray Levick is in charge of the expedition.

An Associated Press dispatch from Bonn, Germany, states that Nazi measures to cut down college attendance have been strikingly successful. There are only 4,953 students enrolled for the summer semester at the University of Bonn, as compared with 6,022 in 1933. Freshman enrolment has been reduced by more than 50 per cent. Only 321 students were admitted, compared with 771 in 1933.

Improvement in the education of the underprivileged in Mexico, especially in the rural districts, is the purpose of an extensive school building program. There are now 18,000 rural schools in the Republic, but between now and 1939 it is planned to spend more than one fifth of the entire budget of the Department of Education on the construction of such schools. The secretary of education, Eduardo Vasconcelos, in an interview with a United Press correspondent, stated that in the next three years more than 11,000 rural schools will be built, bringing the total number to almost 31,000.

Dr. T. L. Yuan, director of the Chinese National Library of Peiping, at a recent luncheon of the Duke University library staff, completed arrangements for the establishment of an exchange system between this institution and the Peiping library. In addition to financial grants, the library has as a nucleus a collection of Chinese incunabula consisting of approximately 500,000 volumes dating from the ninth century. This library corresponds to the Library of Congress in the United States, and is now in process of expansion.

Chile's Republican militia has organized a cadet school for sons of militiamen. These children, the United Press reports, range from six to seventeen years in age and will take the same oath as that sworn by the militia. The first cadet school, named Caupolican after the famous Indian warrior who successfully defended Auracania against the Spanish conquistadores in the colonial days, is one of a series of similar institutions to be established throughout the republic. The cadets will be taught strict military discipline and will be instructed in the lore of past patriots. The body will be non-political, as is the militia itself.

A recent Associated Press dispatch from Madrid related that the Spanish state, true to the prophecy of church authorities, has found it "materially impossible to fulfill its plan to substitute lay for religious education within the time it prescribed. As a result, the education of all except a comparatively small number of Spain's youth still remains in the hands of the church. The state felt confident, at the time the law of religious congregations was passed last summer, that sufficient facilities would be provided by October 1 to substitute lay for religious advanced education and that the change from religious to lay elementary education would be possible by the first of this year. Catholic Church statisticians challenged this ability after checking up available and potential facilities of the state. After several temporary postponements the government has announced that it has found it impossible to make the change at the present time and that the substitutions will be indefinitely postponed. The government based its failure to effect the substitution within the time designated "on the failure of previous governments to make any preparations for the change." Many churchmen now predict that a complete substitution of lay for religious education in Spain may never be effected.

WORK has been started on the $500,000 main building of the Lester School and Henry Lester Institute of Technical Education in Shanghai. The institution, the first of its sort to be erected in China, has been made possible by the will of the late Henry Lester. It has been designed to afford technical education for students of all nations, but will offer special inducements to Chinese students.

*The Christian Science Monitor* reports that the salaries of the Yugoslav National Representatives are to be reduced by 20 per cent. and with the money saved 500 additional school teachers are to be engaged. Most of the other state officials also are to suffer substantial salary cuts.

# DISCUSSION

## EXAMINATION IN ENGLISH FOR FOREIGN STUDENTS

A FOREIGN student wishing to attend an American college finds it necessary to satisfy both the American immigration authorities and the admissions officer of the college which he selects. Although the Immigration Act of 1924 is based on the quota principle, it provides for certain non-quota immigrants of which one group is defined as follows:

> An immigrant who is a bona fide student at least 15 years of age, and who seeks to enter the United States solely for the purpose of study, at an accredited school, college, academy, seminary, or university, particularly designated by him and approved by the Secretary of Labor. . . . (*Section 4e, in part.*)

Consular officers of the United States are authorized to issue a non-quota or student visa on satisfactory proof that the applicant is entitled to be approved as a non-quota immigrant. The applicant must designate the "accredited school, college, academy, seminary, or university" and he must present to his local American consul proof that this institution accepts his credentials.

With the passage of the Immigration Act large numbers of foreign students seeking to take advantage of American educational opportunities requested our colleges to issue the necessary certificates of admission. The registrars of these colleges at once saw the need for substantiating the credentials presented by these applicants and in 1928 requested the College Entrance Examination Board to hold at centers abroad a special examination designed to assist them in judging the ability of foreign students to undertake with reasonable hope of success college courses conducted in the English language. After giving careful consideration to this request, the board decided to act favorably upon it, believing that the cost of the examination would eventually be borne by the examinees. To make possible the administration of this examination until such time as it should be self-supporting, however, the board sought outside assistance. In view of the importance of having the examination conducted efficiently and in a manner to command the respect of those who should come in contact with it, the Carnegie Endowment for International Peace granted to the board an allotment of five thousand dollars. In accepting this grant, the College Entrance Examination Board said:

> The Board has a sense of satisfaction in feeling that the act of the Carnegie Endowment for International Peace is the recognition of a great beneficent foundation of the value and promise of

the service now offered by the College Entrance Examination Board to the cause of international education.

If the foreign student is asked by his college to take "The Examination to Test Competence in the Use of the English Language," he applies to the College Entrance Examination Board and pays the ten-dollar fee. Thereupon the board makes arrangements with a suitable person for the conduct of the examination the following April at a convenient place for the candidate. On the first day he presents himself to the supervisor for the three written parts of the examination and on the following day his use of spoken English is tested by means of ten or fifteen minutes of conversation with the supervisor. The papers written at the examination are graded by the College Entrance Examination Board and together with the supervisor's report upon the oral test are transmitted to the college that the student wishes to enter. The college thus has an opportunity to judge for itself whether or not the applicant has sufficient mastery of English. If it believes that he would be unsuccessful in college because of an inadequate knowledge of English, it can so advise him in order that he may be saved a long, expensive and fruitless journey.

The Examination to Test Competence in the Use of the English Language has been held every April for the past five years at places in Europe, Asia and South America. On account of the exceptional conditions resulting from the world-wide depression, however, fewer candidates have presented themselves than was expected, a total of 236 candidates having been examined. It is interesting to note that each year a group of candidates for the educational scholarships offered by the Commission for Relief in Belgium has presented itself in Brussels and that in 1931 a group of eighty graduates of Soviet engineering schools took the tests at Moscow. Recent letters indicate that foreign governments expecting to send students to the United States will require them to demonstrate their fitness by means of this examination.

The colleges that have made use of this examination report that it has proved of great practical value and that it has served to set before foreign students the necessary standard of preparation in English. The late Professor Adam Leroy Jones, of Columbia University, who served on all the more important committees dealing with this examination, said: "Experience at Columbia shows the great value of this examination and indicates that it has very important possibilities." It is the hope of those who are most interested in this undertaking that in the absence of satisfactory evidence of proficiency in the English language colleges will make use of this examination.

C. H. Blatchford, Jr.

# SPECIAL CORRESPONDENCE

## THE DEVELOPMENT OF THE EDUCATIONAL STRUCTURE OF YUGOSLAVIA

The schools of Yugoslavia are of two classes: (1) The schools under the Ministry of Education concerned with scientific training, and (2) the schools under other authorities concerned with agriculture, craft, trade and industry and military training.

In this article we shall be concerned with the schools of the first group. Until very recently these schools were organized on the basis of the laws in vigor in various districts before the union. It is only the present régime which has unified scholastic legislation in Yugoslavia; and the establishment of one unified scholastic organization has thus adjusted education to the cultural requirements of the future of the nation.

Education is classified in three grades: (1) Primary education embraces kindergarten schools, and primary schools with the higher national schools, domestic and popular schools; (2) middle education comprises the gymnasiums, teachers' training schools and theological schools; (3) higher education comprises the high schools and universities. Art educations are provided in the schools of acting, music, painting and sculpture and architecture.

The state program devotes the greatest attention to the renewal and foundation of schools, especially in districts which were victims of the war or where previously there were no schools. Old and worn-out buildings are replaced by new ones in accordance with modern hygienic and pedagogic principles, and in backward districts new schools are being built with expedition.

Since the Liberation the following schools have been built and opened: 2,735 lower schools, 69 middle schools, 9 art schools and 16 high schools and faculties.

Under the heading of primary education are included all institutions which bear the general name of "national" schools, as also the "popular" schools.

The building and upkeep of national schools is borne by the municipality, while the state department appoints and pays the teaching staff. In order to hasten the erection of schools, the banovinas (provinces) and the state grant assistance to needy municipalities, while the law of national schools of 1929 makes provision for a special fund for granting to municipalities loans at a low rate of interest.

A preparatory stage to primary education is the kindergarten school. The establishment of

TABLE 1

| Years | Schools | Teachers | Pupils |
|---|---|---|---|
| 1918–19 | 115 | 939 | 17,594 |
| 1929–30 | 194 | 1,730 | 20,159 |

these is compulsory for larger towns and industrial centers, and optional in other places. Kindergarten schools accept children from the conclusion of the fourth year of age.

The primary school is the provision for elementary education, and on completion of four years is extended in the higher national schools. The 1929 reform established national education on a modern basis. Uniformity of organization was introduced, not only in management but also in type. Compulsory school attendance, which hitherto had varied as to duration (between four and eight years) was extended to eight years over the whole country. Children are enrolled in primary schools in their seventh year. Those children who, on completion of primary school, pass on to popular, middle or professional schools are exempted from attendance at the higher national school. This reform permits the adaptation of education to the local conditions and needs. The principle of continuous activity of the pupil is established as

TABLE 2

| Years | Schools | Teachers | Pupils |
|---|---|---|---|
| 1918–19 | 120 | 2,053 | 42,672 |
| 1929–30 | 171 | 4,128 | 74,800 |

the method of instruction, and this involves the obligation on the teacher to have regard for the individuality of the pupil and his family and social conditions. Coeducation of boys and girls is established, but where circumstances permit they are separated in separate schools or departments. Education is general, compulsory and gratuitous, and is given in the country's language. For children of national minorities, wherever there is a group of such, the Yugoslav national schools comprise also departments where education is given in their national language. These are opened wherever there are 25 pupils of one nationality. In places where there are several departments of the same national minority, these form a separate school which has its separate director. Primary schools may give only the regular syllabus of instruction, while higher national schools may give the regular or shortened course (according to local conditions). The law devotes great attention to the safeguarding of the health of the pupils. Provision is made for the systematic establishment of school baths and clinics, the permanent and compulsory examination of pupils and teachers, and the removal of infectious, especially tuberculous children from the schools. On social grounds school kitchens and children's hostels are established.

Special schools make provision for children of insufficient and defective development. These may be state, banovina (province) or private establishments. They are equipped as boarding establishments.

Domestic schools are provided for girls after completion of primary school instruction. The erection and upkeep of these schools is borne by the state or the banovina budgets. They are

TABLE 3

| Years | Schools | Teachers | Pupils |
|---|---|---|---|
| 1918–19 | 24 | 287 | 2,300 |
| 1929–30 | 39 | 634 | 7,538 |

first opened in culturally-backward districts and are equipped as boarding establishments.

Temporary adult schools and courses for the purpose of national education are organized in connection with the national school local needs, such as hygienic, cooperative economic, for housewifery, illiterates, etc. They are established through private initiative, and the instructors' salaries are borne by the banovina and the state. Instruction is on practical lines.

The popular schools form a class between the primary school and the middle school. They are established in towns with the object of providing general education to fit their pupils for

TABLE 4

| Years | Schools | Teachers | Pupils |
|---|---|---|---|
| 1918–19 | 11 | 118 | 865 |
| 1929–30 | 14 | 146 | 1,445 |

crafts, trades and industrial callings. The education is gratuitous and in the language of the state. For children of national minorities separate departments are formed, as in the primary schools, where instruction is given in their maternal language.

The development of popular schools since the Union is illustrated in Table 1.

The second group is provided by the middle (secondary) schools.

Not until the Law of Middle Schools of 1929, was the education of Yugoslav gymnasiums placed on a uniform and modern basis. They comprise three types: modern gymnasiums, technical schools and classical gymnasiums. Incomplete gymnasiums have four classes; full gymnasiums have eight. The greatest number of modern gymnasiums is established as the general type of middle school, with faculty to open departments of the other two types. Instruction is gratuitous.

Gymnasiums may be state or local authority gymnasiums, and the already existing private ones are recognized by law on condition that they comply with the law's provisions. National minorities which desire to provide middle school instruction in their national tongue have the option of special gymnasiums.

Every school is obliged to have a library for teachers and one for pupils. In places where there exists no public library the teachers' library may be transformed to serve as a public library.

The forming of societies among the pupils for intellectual, moral, esthetic and physical exercise is permitted.

Safeguarding of the health of the pupils is provided for through school baths and clinics, and by one permanent doctor to each school. On sociological grounds the establishment of boarding institutions is countenanced.

The instruction is directed to achieve a cultural-moral influence in the spirit of the Yugoslav idea. And the teachers are obliged to accommodate their teaching to the individualities of the pupils, with regard to their circumstances. The class teacher and the class committee composed of the teachers of respective

TABLE 5

FACULTIES

| University | Theology | | Law | | Philosophy | | Technical | | Medicine | | Veterinary | | Agriculture | | Total | |
|---|---|---|---|---|---|---|---|---|---|---|---|---|---|---|---|---|
| | Teachers | Students | Teachers | Students | Teachers | Students | Teachers | Students | Teachers | Students | Teachers | Students | Teachers | Students | Teachers | Students |
| Belgrade | 22 | 266 | 29 | 2,947 | 97 | 1,192 | 63 | 1,780 | 62 | 672 | — | — | 24 | 341 | 297 | 7,198 |
| Zagreb | 21 | 104 | 20 | 1,160 | 67 | 1,258 | 88 | 555 | 128 | 421 | 25 | 269 | 45 | 64 | 394 | 3,831 |
| Ljubljana | 16 | 105 | 19 | 354 | 37 | 337 | 44 | 469 | 14 | 78 | — | — | — | — | 131 | 1,341 |
| Skoplje | — | — | — | — | 20 | 146 | — | — | — | — | — | — | — | — | 20 | 146 |
| Subotica | — | — | 15 | 352 | — | — | — | — | — | — | — | — | — | — | 15 | 352 |
| Total | 59 | 475 | 83 | 4,813 | 221 | 2,933 | 195 | 2,804 | 205 | 1,171 | 25 | 269 | 69 | 405 | 857 | 12,870 |

classes are responsible for the organizations and instructions of the pupils in each class, while the council of teachers is responsible for the instructions as a whole and the educations in the school. Pupils on completion of four classes present themselves for the lower school certificate, and on completion of eight classes for the higher school certificate (certificate of maturity).

The development of gymnasiums since the Union is illustrated in Table 2.

The teachers' training schools have as their object the professional educations of teachers of national schools and the training of them for their functions of national education and culture. They are state institutions and equipped as boarding establishments. Only the already existing private and day training schools are recognized in so far as they conform to the provisions of the Law of Teachers' Training Schools of 1929, when the diversities under which the training schools had developed in Yugoslavia were removed.

Attached to the teachers' training schools is a national school serving as a practising school, together with a garden and land for practical agricultural instruction.

Admission to teachers' training schools is open to pupils holding the lower school certificate on passing the special entrance examination. The course of instructions lasts over five years and is uniform for all pupils of the school. For the purpose of training teachers for minority schools, the schools accept members of national minorities, and courses of instruction in the language desired are organized.

The development of the teachers' schools since the Union is illustrated in Table 3.

The object of the theological schools is to educate youths for the professions of priest and religious instructor. They are maintained by the state or by state grants. All are equipped as boarding establishments. The course of instruction and direction is prescribed by the state in agreement with the respective churches, and for Roman Catholic schools by the Church alone. In the Orthodox schools admittance is open to pupils holding the lower school certificate, while to Roman Catholic schools only on completion of the full gymnasium course. The instruction is of six years' duration in the former and of four in the latter. The religious education of Moslems is provided in the Great Medresa of Skoplje and the Sherifate school of justice at Sarajevo; that of Israelites at the Theological Middle College of Sarajevo. All three rank as full middle schools.

The development of theological training since the Union is shown in Table 4.

Higher education in Yugoslavia is provided in two higher pedagogical schools, one high school of industry and commerce and three universities.

Table 5 illustrates the numbers of staff and students at the end of the school year 1929–30.

Joseph S. Roucek
Pennsylvania State College

## THE TRANSITION SCHOOL IN THE PENNSYLVANIA STATE COLLEGE

In the Pennsylvania State College the various lines of study are organized into corresponding schools. It often happens that students who seem to have ability for liberal arts work fail in the more technical schools and express the desire to transfer to liberal arts. To test the ability and will of these students whose records in the original schools leave doubt as to their capacity, the Transition School was established in 1925 under the direct supervision of Arthur Ray Warnock, dean of men, with the cooperation of Dr. Charles W. Stoddard, dean of the School of the Liberal Arts.

The records of the students who passed through the Transition School to the Liberal Arts School are self-explanatory. From a group of 69 who made the transition in the period from 1930 to 1934, only 20 have failed to maintain the average necessary for graduation, but these 20, in all but a few cases, sustained an average necessary for college attendance. The remainder of this group made either fair or good records, and in the cases of 5 the records were excellent, representing 7 per cent. of the total. This compares with the entire Liberal Arts School, in which 20 per cent. of the total enrolled students made excellent marks.

It must be understood that students placed in the Transition School are on virtual probation, for their ultimate transfer to liberal arts depends directly upon their records in the probation section. And in this connection the Transition School serves a dual purpose. It affords a medium for students to find themselves, and also serves to quicken the slackers who have so fallen in their work as to approach complete failure. Misfits are a problem in any college, and a method so conclusively helpful as this in placing them is worthy of serious consideration. That 71 per cent. of the students forced into the Transition School by failure in other schools were able to maintain a satisfactory standard of work in liberal arts, and in most cases to gain a degree, is conclusive evidence that the school has proved its worth.

Paralleling the work of the Transition School, The Liberal Arts School established a probation section for its delinquent freshmen, who make such poor records in their first semester as to make necessary some sort of private instruction. This section was placed in charge of Dr. Willard Waller, eminent sociologist at the college, who attempts to teach these students the best way to take notes, to read, to concentrate and to write examinations. He also tries to discover personal inhibitions in the students which would naturally result in poor work. Since the section was established in 1931, 41 per cent. of the number admitted have remained in school, a surprisingly large total, considering the type of students who entered the section.

Thus it seems worth the while, judging from the records of the Transition School and the Liberal Arts Probation Section, to make a determined effort to resurrect the seemingly poorer students and to so handle them as to enable each to make a success of his college career.

JACK B. DIENNA
PENNSYLVANIA STATE COLLEGE

# QUOTATIONS

## POLITICAL CONTROLS OF EDUCATION

AT Harvard's two hundred and ninety-eighth commencement, where Dr. Dodds received the degree of doctor of laws, both he and his host, President Conant, made speeches placing strong emphasis on the maintenance of academic freedom. Both lauded the splendid war-time record of President Lowell and, in effect, pledged their respective institutions to maintain similar freedom in the future.

These pledges could not have been offered at a more opportune time, for in the following weeks there have been threats against academic freedom as vicious as any we have seen since 1919. The "red raids," inspired or prosecuted by vigilante committees and aimed at labor agitators, have been followed by serious demands for similar raids on university faculties. No faculty member, if the raiders have their way at the University of California, for instance, can hold his job as long as he has "dangerous ideas" (*i.e.* ideas different from the raiders'). It is even suggested, according to news reports, that the California library is to be searched for subversive documents. Presumably this would be followed by a book-burning spree in the best Goebbels style.

It seems hard to believe that this program of suppression can really be carried out in the Pacific Coast universities, but the tendency is there at least. At a time when the international situation is tense and labor disputes are in progress at many points in the country, it is a great satisfaction to see Harvard and Princeton recommit themselves so specifically to a policy of academic freedom. A dictatorship—fascist or proletarian—is the only alternative over a long period.—*The Princeton Alumni Weekly.*

IN *The New Republic* of April 18, 1934, appeared a review of "Just Plain Larnin'," a novel by James M. Shields, published by Coward-McCann, New York. Mr. Shields, principal of a school in Winston-Salem, North Carolina, for the past thirteen years, told in his book of the tyranny exercised by conservative boards of trustees over schoolmen who try to tell the truth about "disagreeable matters" such as economics. The reviewer, William McAndrew, former superintendent of schools for Chicago, corroborated Mr. Shields' view and praised his book warmly. Now Mr. Shields has an object lesson of his own to put into his next book. He has just been removed from his post for no assigned reason, and at a time of year when it is particularly difficult for an educator to obtain new employment. He believes he was dismissed for his political and economic views, and for expressing them as he did in a book that attracted nationwide favorable attention. The city school board, after at first trying to pass over the matter in silence, has done the expected thing and denied that Mr. Shields' book had anything to do with his dismissal. It says that he was removed because the board understood that he was "trying to obtain a position in the North." We doubt whether there is one intelligent person in Winston-Salem who believes this explanation. Long before his dismissal, citizens of that community had been predicting that his frankness in discussing local situations under thin fictional disguise would cost him his position. The school board has acted as might have been expected, not only in Winston-Salem but in almost any other community anywhere in the country. There is precious little free speech for teachers at present, and there won't be until several things have happened, first of which is that educators as a class shall wake up and fight for their rights as citizens and human beings.—*The New Republic.*

SOME six weeks ago we called attention to the strange case of John W. Finch, dean of the University of Idaho School of Mines. His appointment as director of the Bureau of Mines had been agreed to by the President. Professor Finch came to Washington prepared to take the office, but when his commission was sent for, Mr. Roosevelt's signature was found lacking. Instead there was a notation: "Held up temporarily because of political objections by P. M. G." Now, however, the President has signed the commission notwithstanding the objections, and Dr. Finch has been sworn in. His bureau is under Secretary Ickes, and there appears to be no doubt that it was the head of the Interior Department who took the matter up afresh with the President and induced him to overrule the objections of the P. M. G. The atrocious crime of the new director of the Bureau of Mines was that he had voted for Hoover in 1932. But Secretary Ickes rightly and vigorously insisted that in filling a highly technical position, competence and experience should be the test, not partisanship. At any rate, the President completed the appointment, apparently upon that principle.—*The New York Times.*

SOME 30,000 German teachers assembled at the week-end at Frankfurt for the Reich meeting of the National Socialist Teachers' Association formed last year from a large number of separate organizations and now comprising about 300,000 teachers of all grades. Among a number of addresses on various points of Nazi policy the chief was a speech by Dr. Rust, the German Minister of Education. He thought the occasion opportune for replying to questions asked abroad whither Germany was marching, and for explaining the events of June 30.

In the past, he said, France and Great Britain had experienced hours of heavy battles and grave decisions, but they had never been confronted with the problem of their very existence, either at Waterloo or at Sedan. That was why they misunderstood Herr Hitler's action in judging and executing his former associates, and had talked of the revival of the brutal Middle Ages in Germany. "Gentlemen in France and Great Britain," the Minister exclaimed, "at the end of the Middle Ages you had united realms, whereas Germany had emerged from that era disunited and bleeding." Now she was engaged in the hard fight for national unity and greatness. It was the duty of the present generation to solve this problem now or never.

Referring to the question on the lips of many old Nazi fighters about the establishment of a real Nazi economy, Dr. Rust said that it would come when all Germans had become National Socialists and servants of the National Socialist State. National Socialism would exist in the German schools when it had been created by a new class of German teachers. They were to be trained in the National Socialist Teachers' League in order to create the new type of human being demanded in Germany. If they wished to gain control over German youth they must live and march with the people's army of the future like the highly esteemed military officer. In addition to scientific and professional education, the teacher's chief task was the development of character, last and not least, through physical training. Dr. Rust concluded by assuring German teachers of the same protection for their honor as that given to the family and the workman.

Other speeches pointed out the need of impressing on German youth Germany's right to possess colonies.—*Correspondent, Educational Supplement of the London Times.*

# SOCIETIES AND MEETINGS

## CONFERENCE ON EFFECT OF SOCIAL TRENDS ON HIGHER EDUCATION

"What are the responsibilities which changing social conditions are placing upon higher education?" was the theme of the conference on higher education recently (July 11, 12, 13, 14) held at the University of Oregon. "Are new social, economic and political trends bringing new tasks to education and if so in what ways, and by what steps may the schools, particularly the higher institutions, meet these changing demands upon them?"

The conference was attended by more than six hundred, chiefly teachers and administrators in higher education, together with secondary school teachers and representatives of business, the professions and governmental and public service agencies. For three days members discussed in general sessions and forum meetings problems confronted by higher education as a result of recent changes in society and in ideas of social goals, and listened to reports of experiments and innovations in various institutions designed to meet more adequately responsibilities placed upon them by these social changes. Although individuals often failed to agree both with respect to the precise nature of the changes which are taking place and of educational procedures, the net impression gained is that educators in the main are awake to the needs for readjustments in their programs and are aware of the significant connection of education with business, finance, politics and government, and not least with the movement for more systematic and orderly social planning.

The majority of delegates in attendance were from the Pacific Northwest states, but the conference drew significant representation from a much wider area. Principal addresses were delivered by Dr. F. J. Kelly, specialist in higher education, U. S. Office of Education; Dr. Frederick M. Davenport, former congressman from New York and university teacher; Dr. James W. Angell, professor of economics, Columbia University; Dr. F. L. Hovde, assistant director of the General College, University of Minnesota; Dr. George W. Frasier, president of Colorado State Teachers College.

In addition to the general sessions at which the addresses were discussed by selected panels and from the floor, forum sessions were held daily centering around responsibility of higher education to (1) students, (2) commonwealth, (3) adult education, (4) social planning. Chairmen of the forums who shaped their programs, guided discussion and reported "findings" were, respectively: (1) Dr. Elam J. Anderson, president of Linfield College; (2) Dr. Samuel C. May, director of the Bureau of Public Administration, University of California; (3) Mr. Alfred Powers, dean of General Extension, Oregon State System of Higher Education; (4) Mr. Marshall N. Dana, chairman of the Pacific Northwest Regional Planning Division, Portland.

At the closing banquet of the conference Dr. Kelly summarized and "philosophized upon" the outstanding findings of the conference. He opened with the emphatic statement that "not only has higher education, as represented by large and small colleges and universities, kept pace with rapidly changing conditions, but it is quietly but firmly taking the lead in social trends, and further, it expects to act as a guide to keep democracy from falling into chaos." In his summary he observed that: *First:* Colleges and universities have already under way projects to solve the problem of millions of people, now finding themselves with much free time due to industrial changes, of what to do with their new and often unexpected leisure. Adult education represented by extension classes, correspondence classes and even regular campus classes have been formed especially for these people at many institutions.

*Second:* Institutions have recognized that students must be trained not only to "make a living" but must also be trained for "living rather than for working alone." To answer this call, institutions have adopted as objectives the training for avocation as well as for vocation, instilling in students a desire for social service, and inculcating in them an appreciation of the arts.

*Third:* The educational period is being extended in part as an inevitable consequence of the decreasing social need for youth to become "producers" at an early age, in part to meet the need for an extended educational preparation for complex modern life. Higher institutions must accordingly shape their programs to provide suitably for great numbers of students for the majority of whom a general education is more appropriate than the more specialized studies designed for scholars and the higher level professions. To prepare for more useful and enjoyable lives should be the aim for the majority, having in mind the nature of the society in which they live and their probable adult activities. The General College of Minnesota and the lower division program of Linfield College in Oregon were cited as examples of this type of education offered, not as a substitute for advanced and professional studies for those who are qualified and interested, but as a type of education more adequate to the actual needs of the majority of the large and increasing proportion of young people who, unless they are to be left footless in their communities between the time of finishing high school and that when society is ready to give them employment, must be provided for in the educational program.

*Fourth:* The colleges and universities must be expected to furnish real "experts," whose activities may greatly change the entire procedure of democratic government. In place of settling matters of state by calling for "opinions" of heterogeneous groups, the experts will be called to present facts for a basis of action.

At the first meeting Dr. Norman F. Coleman, president of Reed College, Portland, asked the frank question, "Are schools and colleges still bound by the old tradition that success in life is achieved by personal gain and by fulfilling personal ambition to 'get ahead' materially?"

Dr. Coleman spoke on "Present Social Trends." These he divided into three general classifications: first, a definite trend toward more leisure time for all people; second, an obvious trend away from dependence on personal gain; third, progress in cooperative activity, manifested by increase in the numbers of forums, discussion groups, clubs, and even the increase in governmental activities, such as the AAA and CWA.

Education has a great opportunity to provide means of worthwhile employment of the great amount of leisure time that is now and will in the future be available to the people, Dr. Coleman said. "The high school or college graduate of to-day can not expect to start out and get ahead by the 'personal gain' method," he declared. "The fall of many executives in big business has diminished the prestige for this phase of life. This is already reflected in the attitude of the youth of to-day. Personal profit is much less than formerly the main spring of life and career.

"The great mass of people on the relief rolls, the necessity for helping the less fortunate, is bringing about the definite feeling that material wealth is something that must be distributed rather than hoarded, if people are to be happy and enjoy life. Cooperative activities that make for better conditions will continue to develop."

Dr. Angell discussed financial aspects of the "new deal," particularly banks and monetary adjustments, granted the necessity for radical revision but pointed dangers in some of the policies of the administration.

The talk provoked a warm discussion, in which Dr. James H. Gilbert, dean of the College of Social Science and professor of economics, T. M. Hicks, Jr., manager of McMorran and Washburn, Eugene, and Dr. E. B. Mittelman, professor of business administration and economics at the University of Oregon, participated.

Institutions of higher education, by and large, have not lagged behind changing orders and new economic conditions, but have adapted themselves to them, declared Dr. W. J. Kerr, chancellor of the Oregon System of Higher Education, who addressed the conference luncheon on July 12.

The state-supported institutions arose because of a demand on the part of the public for a leadership that could cope with the current conditions of whatever time the particular institutions were founded, he pointed out. This charged the institutions with the duty of keeping abreast with current conditions.

During the past few years, since the advent of the present economic condition, institutions of higher education like other activities have suffered decreases in income. In the main they have met this difficulty, not only by taking salary and expense cuts, but by cooperating with each other, eliminating rivalries and proceeding on the basis of the greatest good to the state.

As an example of the cooperative spirit and organization in higher education, Dr. Kerr cited Oregon, where one board of higher education has recently replaced four other boards. Under this system economies have been possible and efficiency has been maintained.

The outstanding need in the government today is more and better politically trained leaders in Congress and elsewhere, recruited especially from young men and women to whom the country has given a higher education training at a great cost, it was declared by Dr. Davenport. Dr. Davenport, who was the main speaker at the evening session on July 12, was for many years congressman from New York and has devoted years of study to politics and government. His topic was "Importance of the Educated Politician in the New Order."

Dr. Davenport soundly scored individuals and agencies who denounced politicians, without at the same time upholding those individuals who are earnestly training to do a good job in public office. This attitude, he pointed out, has driven many worthy men and women out of the field of public service and made way for persons of lesser ability who often have special and selfish interests.

"The American people, their humorists, their editors and critics ought to teach the young men and women of the present generation that, next to enlisting in war in a great emergency, there is nothing more difficult nor important than enlisting in and fighting in public service," the speaker declared.

Dr. Davenport also condemned the tendency to point the finger of scorn at such a body as the national congress. "There is nothing which has had more certain effect in enfeebling that body, burdened as it is with complexity of problems and gravity of decision," he said. "If the sentiment of the people at home is hostile to their public servants, consciously or unconsciously the public servants can not do their best. If the American people would expect more from Congress they would receive more."

The absolute necessity for the politician in government was pointed out by Dr. Davenport, who held that this class of persons was even more important than the "experts," many of whom are now prominent in government. "The true politician is the man who persuades people to behave like rational human beings," he stated. "He has a peculiar sensitivity particularly to the emotional processes of the popular mind. He knows how to mellow and modify the pressure groups, such as financiers, labor leaders, veterans and the farmer. His is the task of moulding disparate and often hostile interests into something like mutual understanding.

"The 'expert' should be on 'tap' but not on top. He will learn that it is one thing to spawn the idea, and another to keep it alive. The politician must deal constantly with social variables, and the expert, if he is to be of any use, must learn that too. When the 'expert' becomes political minded, however, he becomes very valuable." As an example, Dr. Davenport declared that the plain politician could never interpret and discuss the gold and credit price level problem without the expert nearby.

The plans and workings of the General College, University of Minnesota, one of the new and daring experiments in higher education, were set forth by Dr. F. L. Hovde, assistant director of that college, on Friday morning, and provoked one of the liveliest discussions of the conference. Some of the ideas and ideals of general education advocated by the educator were described as "high-spirited youthfullism," "veneer form of education," "insufficient training for the highly complex society which demands experts to cope with its intricate problems, rather than mediocre minds which 'dabble' in a host of fields."

Compliments and questions, some critical, were showered upon the speaker from the audience and from the discussion panel consisting of Dr. W. A. Bratton, dean of Whitman College, Mr. Otto Hartwig, labor representative on the Oregon State Industrial Accident Commission, Salem, and Dr. C. Gilbert Wrenn, of Stanford University.

"Education to-day is faced with the problem of training young and adult people for living as well as working," declared Dr. Hovde, as the chief reason for setting up a college that departs radically from the traditional academic objectives of training of leaders, researchers, scholars and professional men.

A new light was thrown on higher education as the able young educator described the "general college" plan now under way. The college focuses upon the needs of the student of to-day. It recognizes that often students have kinds of intelligence that examinations are not yet sensitive enough to measure.

Courses in the General College are of an entirely new type. Visual aids, such as motion pictures, are freely employed. Students see the inside workings of government, business, politics, newspapers and social agencies. Some of them join the writing laboratory, others spend much of their time in the art studio, others devote their time to science. "But we make up for lack of personal teaching in these classes by individual guidance through a student personnel program. Incidentally we save enough by handling large groups in class not only to pay for the personnel program but actually to make the per student cost of the general college program remarkably low."

Lecture classes are often large, since a research study has shown that this method is effective for many types of courses, Dr. Hovde said. Examinations are not given by courses, nor necessarily by those who teach them, but cut across course lines so that by the "comprehensive" method of testing an idea of what the student has actually learned can be obtained.

The entire resources of the university, such as the testing bureau, health service, speech clinic, psychiatrist and social worker, are utilized for the students in the general college. Other courses in the university are also thrown open to these students, so that it is actually possible to "tailor-make" a curriculum for the individual, Dr. Hovde pointed out.

Continuation of the learning process of college days into and throughout life after college should be held up as an objective or social aim in education, it was declared by Dr. Frasier, in the main address delivered on Friday evening.

The chief task of the American college to-day, according to Dr. Frasier, is to rethink its purpose in terms of a changing society, and to graduate men and women better equipped to take their part in the competitive world.

"The result of a real society-centered college education is to teach a student to love and appreciate good music and keep on through life with this enjoyment; aid him to learn to appreciate the beautiful and artistic in pictures, house decorations, clothing, and in all surroundings, even after college days; to lead him to develop an interest in games that add happiness and healthfulness to life and to play them throughout life. If, in addition to these, he learns about his body, its functions and care, and keeps on practising good health habits, if he learns to be a good citizen of a college community and keeps on being a good citizen in a larger community, if his interest in the social sciences in college develops and interest in the world lasts, if the good English he learns to speak is carried into everyday life, if a love of the best in books and magazines developed in college leads him to read the best during his lifetime, if he has developed a social consciousness that makes him interested in his fellowmen, and if he loves justice and hates injustice, the student has achieved the real social aim in education."

If such an aim is to be achieved in American education, according to Dr. Frasier, several readjustments must be made. Colleges and universities must admit any one who can profit by a university education. Expert teachers must be provided, an intelligent administration instituted, a vital personnel department introduced, and extensive, all-inclusive libraries be provided.

Dr. Frasier's address gave rise to a host of questions, challenges and complaints from the audience. Discussion leaders were: Dr. John L. Kerchen, director of the Worker's Education Bureau of America; Dr. C. D. Clark, head of the department of sociology at the University of Kansas; Mr. R. E. McCormick, superintendent of schools, Bend, Oregon; and Dr. Samuel H. Jameson, professor of sociology at the University of Oregon.

Dr. Kerchen urged that education be readjusted to fit the workers, who make up three fourths of the population of America. Dr.

Clark questioned the advisability of setting up definite objectives in modern education. "Objectives," he said, "have to be merged according to the changing social plan and conditions, and can not be lined up according to a rigid standard."

Demands made upon higher education to-day, with changing social orders and economic conditions, are bringing about changes that a few years ago would have been regarded as revolutionary by academic minded educators, it was declared on Saturday by Dr. Kelly in his comprehensive analysis of "Trends in Higher Education."

"Higher education to-day is rapidly adopting the objectives of personal development, rather than remembered facts," Dr. Kelly declared. "It is becoming 'student-centered' rather than 'subject-centered,' and the emphasis is upon learning rather than teaching."

Due to the demand for adult education by those who did not have the opportunity of the usual preparatory school training, and the thousands of young men and women not employed who did not complete their training in lower schools, many institutions are "letting down the bars" for admission. Dr. Kelly cited examples of colleges and universities where no specific courses are required for admission, and others which have established special colleges or departments for these students.

"A new aim of education, the education of youth for the state, for service to society, is permeating America," declared Dr. Kelly in his Saturday morning general session address. He pointed out the necessity for student personnel work to guide in individual development.

"Courses are being instituted that have abiding interest for the student, that deal with realities understood by students. Examinations are being divorced from faculty supervision, and are not being based on the course alone, but on knowledge gained independently by the student. These also test his ability to apply that knowledge to varying situations."

"The real test of liberal education is whether the student continues to learn worthwhile things after he graduates," Dr. Kelly said. "As long as the student looks to the teacher as the responsible party in his educational enterprise, he is not preparing for independent use of his powers. Learning, not teaching is the heart of the college. Only when colleges create an atmosphere of student zeal for learning, not credit earning, will they be preparing for democratic living."

"If democracy is to persist," emphasized Dr. Kelly, "the general level of understanding of all the people must be broadened in the field of social, economic and political problems. Colleges must not limit their service to a select few. Young people must be broadened in the field of social, economic and political problems in order to be given a basis of social intelligence. To that end courses adapted to the needs of the many are being introduced. Our complex society requires a longer period of education than formerly, and the colleges are fitting into that need.

Bluntly and emphatically, "three axioms" in education, universally believed by American people, were branded as absolutely false by Dr. Frasier, at the luncheon meeting on Saturday. These "axioms" are: that too many teachers are being educated in America, that students for teachers' colleges should be selected on a "quota" basis, and that institutions to train teachers should be located in or near large cities.

"Decidedly there are not too many teachers in this country when hundreds of thousands of children have been without schooling this year, when even in our large cities as many as 50 pupils are herded into one room, to be taught by one teacher, when we have been unable to provide adequate staffs for adult education in hundreds of places," Dr. Frasier declared.

"The cry should not be for less teachers, which if kept up will destroy not only quantity but quality, but for a reawakening on the part of the people to the realization that better school facilities are needed, that every child should have the opportunity of a real education."

It is impossible to select intelligently for a quota, Dr. Frasier stated, in commenting on the second "axiom." If the selection is purely on an academic or scholastic basis, many socially minded students, with valuable abilities, will be excluded, he pointed out. Often the brilliant student lacks many of the abilities needed for a teacher.

Teachers' colleges should be located where

the best possible surroundings can be obtained, rather than in cities, the speaker declared. Health, opportunities of recreation, satisfactory building sites and room for expansion are items to be considered.

Taking as a topic, "What should the teacher get in college if he is going to do the best possible job?" Dr. Frasier outlined five things he considers essential: (1) Have a health consciousness; the teacher must be an example of health for his pupils. (2) Be a good citizen, and be conscious of social, economic and governmental problems. (3) Be cultured, have an appreciation of the good and the beautiful, know science, history, geography, literature, art and music. (4) Have a wide and extensive knowledge of the subjects he teaches. (5) Be master of the techniques needed in teaching, such as the use of child psychology and lesson presentation.

On the final day each of the four forums presented, through their chairmen, conclusions which they recommended to the entire body. These reports, together with principal papers, will shortly be issued as proceedings of the conference.

KARL W. ONTHANK
UNIVERSITY OF OREGON

# EDUCATIONAL RESEARCH AND STATISTICS

## AN EVALUATION OF READING AS A UNIT IN A "HOW TO STUDY" COURSE

DURING the past two years considerable experimentation has been carried on in the high schools from which the University of Buffalo draws a large proportion of its student body to determine whether instruction in study techniques, through a course in "how to study," might raise the level of performance in high school and also facilitate the student's progress in later college work.[1] These study courses were taught by members of the university staff and carried a half-unit of Regents' credit, so that students accorded them the same amount of time and attention as was given to their regular subjects. Those who elected the course were predominantly high-school juniors, many of whom were looking forward to college work. Comparisons on general measures of ability and achievement showed that they might be regarded as a random sampling of Buffalo high-school upper-classmen.

### I

The present report is devoted to an analysis of one section of this course, the instruction and drills on reading speed and comprehension. About six weeks were spent on this particular unit, and it was probably given more emphasis throughout the course than any other topic. Before taking up this section of the work, the students had been given a month's work in elementary psychology in which they became acquainted with the laws underlying the learning process and had participated in experiments demonstrating some of these principles. It was hoped that they would approach the problem of reading with the intention of applying this knowledge to the improvement of their reading techniques.

The content of this unit included lectures and discussions on the mechanics of reading, analysis of methods of deriving more meaning from the printed page, extensive vocabulary work and the use of a large number of reading selections as practise exercises for increasing speed and comprehension. These reading drills were usually short articles (1,000 to 1,500 words), although a few long *New York Times* feature articles (3,000 to 4,000 words) were also included to afford practise in more sustained reading situations. The same method was used in conducting all the drills. In each case the student received a folder containing the reading selection and a series of detailed questions, usually of the multiple-choice type, on the article to be read. The students were instructed to read the article as rapidly as was consistent with accurate comprehension, without referring to the questions until the reading had been completed. The drills were carefully timed with a stop-watch, and the time placed on the black-

[1] These "how to study" courses represent one approach to the problem of the articulation of high school and college which is being investigated at the University of Buffalo under a grant from the General Education Board.

board at ten-second intervals. As soon as a student finished the article, he placed it in the folder, noted the time on his sheet and began work on the questions. Thus each drill yielded two measures—a statement of rate in terms of words per second and a comprehension score.

based on the reading drill results. These data, given in Table I, show very definitely that speed alone has been increased by the instruction given these groups. The extent of increase appears to be a function of the group, for School C, which shows much less gain than the other

TABLE I

THE AVERAGE SPEED AND COMPREHENSION ON THE VARIOUS READING DRILLS USED WITH THE "HOW TO STUDY" GROUPS

| Reading drills | School A | | | School B | | | School C | | |
|---|---|---|---|---|---|---|---|---|---|
| | N | Speed* | Comp. Per cent. | N | Speed | Comp. Per cent. | N | Speed | Comp. Per cent. |
| 1st ........ | 14 | 3.31 | 77.1 | 33 | 4.86 | 76.7 | 15 | 3.66 | 76.0 |
| 2nd ........ | 13 | 5.21 | 68.4 | 31 | 4.85 | 77.7 | 20 | 3.79 | 70.5 |
| 3rd ........ | 14 | 7.14 | 75.7 | 31 | 5.70 | 86.5 | 21 | 4.78 | 70.0 |
| 4th ........ | 13 | 8.08 | 81.5 | 28 | 6.09† | 72.5† | 21 | 5.24 | 89.1 |
| 5th ........ | 14 | 11.05 | 79.3 | 31 | 5.94 | 91.6 | 20 | 6.69 | 68.0 |
| 6th ........ | 15 | 9.58 | 64.0 | 30 | 9.66 | 80.7 | 19 | 5.28 | 64.2 |
| 7th ........ | 15 | 9.98† | 53.8† | 29 | 10.21† | 49.1† | 20 | 5.83† | 35.5† |
| 8th ........ | 14 | 10.31† | 63.4† | 29 | 10.39 | 75.9 | 19 | 6.38† | 54.2† |
| 9th ........ | 15 | 9.85 | 61.3 | 27 | 11.34 | 77.0 | 19 | 6.44 | 64.2 |

* Speed as measured by the number of words read per second.

† These drills were twice as long as the others, and comprehension was measured on a different basis (free response questions).

The results reported here are derived from classes in three of the high schools which cooperated in this study. While in each school a control group, composed of students carefully paired on a number of criteria, was used to measure the outcomes of the course as a whole, administrative difficulties made it impossible to select pairs for each unit of the course. To afford some check on the values of the reading section, however, two third-year English classes were selected in each school and given a number of the tests that the study students took. Since these English students showed about the same level of achievement for the preceding year as the study students,[2] they afford some indication of how much improvement might be expected in these functions without special training, and have therefore been designated in this report as the control group.

II

The first analyses of the effects of a "how to study" course on reading achievement were

schools, has a relatively larger number of foreign-born students and ranks lower on the various tests of intelligence and achievement given these students. Although a great deal of emphasis was placed on accurate comprehension of materials, the study groups in two of the schools show a drop, while the third group just holds its own. It is interesting to note that the Pearsonian $r$ between speed and comprehension, which was slightly positive on the first drill ($r = .20 \pm .08$), becomes negative on the last one ($r = -.17 \pm .08$). Contrary to the belief that the necessity for greater concentration required by the increased speed would also improve comprehension, almost an opposite trend becomes established through the reading drills.

To determine whether this lack of increase in comprehension might be merely a function of the highly timed drills on short selections, an analysis was made of the performance of the study and control groups on the Nelson-Denny test which was given at the beginning and at the end of the training series. The significant point in these results, which are summarized in Table II, is that the study groups do not show even

[2] The average grade for the preceding semester for the study group was 80.34 ($\sigma = 6.76$), while that of the control group was 81.26 ($\sigma = 6.02$).

TABLE II

A COMPARISON OF THE PERFORMANCE OF THE STUDY AND CONTROL GROUPS ON THE NELSON-DENNY READING TEST

| Group | Pre-test* (Form A) | | | End-test* (Form B) | | | Gains in Form B over Form A | | |
|---|---|---|---|---|---|---|---|---|---|
| | Voc. | Par. | Total | Voc. | Par. | Total | Voc. | Par. | Total |
| *Study* | | | | | | | | | |
| School A | 35.6 | 41.9 | 77.4 | 38.4 | 38.7 | 77.1 | + 2.8 | − 3.2 | − 0.3 |
| School B | 32.6 | 41.6 | 74.2 | 34.4 | 41.9 | 76.3 | + 1.8 | + 0.3 | + 2.1 |
| School C | 29.9 | 31.6 | 61.4 | 30.3 | 34.1 | 64.4 | + 0.4 | + 2.5 | + 3.0 |
| *Control* | | | | | | | | | |
| School A | 27.0 | 34.1 | 61.1 | 29.4 | 35.2 | 64.7 | + 2.4 | + 1.1 | + 3.6 |
| School B | 29.2 | 37.6 | 66.8 | 31.1 | 37.3 | 68.4 | + 1.9 | − 0.3 | + 1.6 |
| School C | 24.8 | 34.9 | 59.7 | 30.3 | 36.0 | 66.0 | + 5.5 | + 1.1 | + 6.3 |

* The pre-test was given to schools A and C in November, 1932, and to School B in February, 1933. The end-test was given in all schools in May, 1933.

as much gain as the control groups, in spite of the fact that they had had considerable practise in reading situations.

The first part of the Nelson-Denny test gives a measure of the student's vocabulary. Although the study students had spent a number of periods during this unit analyzing words and mastering, through appropriate drills, the more basic Latin and Greek roots, prefixes and suffixes, they showed no gain over the untrained groups. Even if reading ability becomes fixed at a certain level, it would seem that vocabulary would continue to increase, since acquaintance with words is almost a purely additive process. Yet the consistency of the results from these three schools suggests that intensive drill of this type does not result in higher scores on a vocabulary test.

The second section of the Nelson-Denny test, which consists of a number of paragraphs from typical college texts with a series of multiple-choice questions on each, was completed by many students within the twenty-minute time allotment, so that the study group, of whom this is especially characteristic, could not effectively register their increased speed of reading. What stands out most strikingly, of course, is that these students did not utilize whatever advantage they may have had in speed to check over their answers carefully enough to excel in comprehension.[3]

III

The lack of improvement in each group during this period constitutes an interesting problem. A study of the norms of the Nelson-Denny test showed that when students of the same educational level were considered (high-school juniors) there was an increase of 8 points to the senior year norms, and that when students of the same reading ability were considered (college freshmen)[4] there was a gap of 20 points between their mean score and that of college sophomores. Yet the present groups, both experimental and control, increased on the average only 2 points over a period of at least four months, just about the amount the authors claim for practise effect (1.4 points), apparently indicating that no improvement occurs in the last two years of high school.[5] The reliability of the test was checked by correlating the results of Forms A and B for the various groups studied, and the resulting coefficients checked rather closely with the one reported in the test manual ($r = .914 \pm .013$). Interestingly enough, the relationship was slightly higher for the study group than for the control group. Students, therefore, tended to keep the same relative ranking in respect to reading ability,

[3] An interesting problem is raised as to whether this was due to the fact that they were trained (in the drills) not to look back. If so, the use of such drills may be criticized on the grounds that they build up habits which do not function in normal reading situations.

[4] The norms of this test are consistently too low for the high-school population of Buffalo.

[5] This point was substantiated through correspondence with the authors of the test, who attribute the increase from one year to the next almost entirely to the more rigorous selection of students with each advance in educational level.

whether or not they were subjected to special training.

To measure the long-time effects of instruction in reading techniques, a study was made of the reading ability of the study and control students after a lapse of several months. In October, 1933, all students who had taken the Nelson-Denny test the preceding year were tested for speed and comprehension on a long *New York Times* article (4,200 words). It was felt that such a selection would correspond to a normal reading situation more closely than a series of unrelated paragraphs, and that it should afford, therefore, a measure of the reading ability a pupil usually calls into play.

TABLE III

A Comparison of the Performance of the Study and Control Groups on a New York Times Selection Given Five Months Later

| Measure | Study | Control | Diff. / S.E. Diff. |
|---|---|---|---|
| *School A* | | | |
| Number | 11 | 56 | |
| Speed | 6.75 | 4.14 | 4.28 |
| Comprehension | 53.7 | 64.4 | 1.89 |
| *School B* | | | |
| Number | 25 | 77 | |
| Speed | 6.87 | 5.45 | 2.10 |
| Comprehension | 59.0 | 56.5 | .78 |
| *School C* | | | |
| Number | 15 | 33 | |
| Speed | 4.97 | 3.95 | 3.55 |
| Comprehension | 53.4 | 62.6 | 2.11 |

As is evident from Table III, the same trend appears, for only in respect to speed of reading do the trained students show an advantage over the untrained groups. In two of the three differences on reading rate, the ratios are entirely significant, so that it may fairly be concluded that a study course will operate to increase speed in reading. It is interesting to note, however, that the rate of reading, as far as the study groups are concerned, has dropped very materially from the level reached the preceding May. There seems little question but that part of the increase in speed of reading characteristic of those students who had received training in this phase of study is to be traced to the stimulation of the teacher and that it does not carry over into other reading situations.

The results tend to reverse in favor of the control students on comprehension, for although the differences are not reliable, the two larger ones favor the untrained groups. In Schools B and C the students who served as controls for the course as a whole were also present at this testing, and the similarity of their achievement on both speed and comprehension to those who were selected as controls for this particular unit shows that the trend holds rather consistently for any untrained students in the senior high school. Correlations between speed and comprehension on this test also showed the same trend toward a slightly negative relationship that was evidenced on the last reading drill.

In summary it might be pointed out that: (1) High school juniors, with and without training, apparently do not increase in reading ability, as measured by a standardized test, over a period of at least four months. (2) Study courses through the unit on reading increase speed of reading in the test situation. The gain is more noticeable at the end of the training series but does persist to some extent to a similar reading situation several months later. (3) Special training in reading techniques does not increase comprehension, at least as measured in this study. Not only is there no gain in comprehension for students in the "how to study" courses on the specific drills used, but they show no superiority to untrained students on the end-test, and even rank slightly lower than the control groups on a measure of comprehension obtained after a lapse of several months.

Henry C. Mills
Ruth E. Eckert
University of Buffalo

## NEW BOOKS IN EDUCATION

Foran, Thomas G. *The Psychology and Teaching of Spelling.* Pp. xi + 234. Catholic Education Press. $2.40.

Jernegan, Marcus W. and others. *Growth of the American People.* Pp. xvi + 804 + lvii. Illustrated. Longmans, Green. $1.96.

Jones, Edward S., Editor. *University of Buffalo Studies.* Vol. IX: *Studies in Articulation of High School and College.* Pp. xiii + 319. University of Buffalo.

# SCHOOL AND SOCIETY

WITH WHICH ARE COMBINED THE EDUCATIONAL REVIEW, ESTABLISHED IN 1891, THE TEACHERS MAGAZINE, ESTABLISHED IN 1878, AND THE SCHOOL JOURNAL, ESTABLISHED IN 1874.

Volume 40 | SATURDAY, SEPTEMBER 1, 1934 | Number 1027

## NATIONALISM IN EUROPEAN UNIVERSITIES

By WALTER M. KOTSCHNIG

GENERAL SECRETARY OF THE INTERNATIONAL STUDENT SERVICE, GENEVA

THERE are few periods in history which equal in content of revolutionary change the days in which we are living. Old forms of thought and life are being abandoned over night, as new forces break forth and assert themselves. These have wrought changes in every field of human endeavor—in politics and economics, in individual relationships and in social concepts, in the field of education as in that of religion. Nationalism has been the most powerful amongst these forces. The economic nationalism of this country, the nationalist-imperialist policy of Japan, the Fascist revolution in Italy and the success of National-Socialism in Germany testify to its strength.

The universities have not been spared. On the contrary, in Germany and Italy at least, they have undergone changes which go beyond anything which may have happened in other fields. There are good reasons for these changes. On the one hand, the new nationalist leaders, Mussolini as well as Hitler, have concentrated their efforts on the universities as institutions designed *par excellence* to formulate the new nationalist ideas and to bring forth a new leadership able and determined to put these ideas into practise. On the other hand the universities were the more vulnerable, the more ready to accept the new gospel, because for a long time past they had been suffering from a lack of purpose, from the absence of any clear idea of learning and leadership. As a result they had lost the loyalty of their students, who were hungering for leadership and who, not finding it in the universities, had turned to prophets in the streets, whose apocalyptic visions or entrancing descriptions of the promised land seemed to give them purpose and direction.

Thus it is not surprising that Italian students, of whom more than 90 per cent. are organized in the *Gruppi Universitari Fascisti,* were amongst the first to acclaim the Italian university reform which imposed upon every university professor an oath of allegiance, making it incumbent upon him to refrain from the diffusion of any "anti-national" and "subversive" ideas opposed to the Fascist régime. Similarly, German students led the campaign against so-called "foreign" elements in the German universities, which culminated in the law of April 25, 1933, directed against Jewish professors and students and those who were not in sympathy with the National-Socialist revolution. We know the results of that law—between eight hundred and a thousand professors, lecturers and assistants removed from their positions; six to eight thousand students unable to continue and finish their studies. We also know the repercussions abroad—the protests of those who have looked upon the German universities as amongst the finest achievements of the human mind, the endeavors to help those who are the victims of nationalist persecution and the wholesale condemnation of the Hitler régime. And we also remember the petitions signed by eminent scientists against the Italian law, imposing the oath of allegiance upon Italian university professors.

All these protests have been of no avail. The nationalist régimes continue to flourish; youth marches on on the road of Nationalism. The Fascist hymn of *Giovinezza,* eternal youth, the *Horst-Wessel-Lied* in Germany continue to hold the students in thrall, to inspire them as no formula or syllogism of the old university was able to do in the past. So powerful is the appeal of the new Nationalism which the universities are to serve, that even professors reared in the ideas of the humanistic university pay little heed to their loss of "academic freedom," but on the contrary attempt to justify the restrictions put upon them. Such results can not be explained by simple political changes, such as the accession to power of just another political party which may be dislodged again to-morrow. What has arisen is a new philosophy, a new *Weltanschauung* which can only be understood and interpreted in terms of fundamental principles. As far as the universities are concerned a new conception of learning and "truth" is gaining ground which can only be rejected or modified in the light of other conceptions of learning and truth.

The difficulties of such an undertaking are obvious, for while it is fairly simple to analyze the conception of the present-day universities in those countries where Nationalism has not led to a complete revolution in values, it is exceedingly difficult to arrive at a clear idea of the nationalist conception of the university. It is buried in a jungle of phrases and slogans. To go one step further, it is next to impossible to evolve an idea of the university which by its inner consistency and cogency would be adequate to the present-day world and yet be free of nationalist errors. However, the attempt has to be made unless we are resigned to see our own universities engulfed by nationalistic philosophy.

In a recent publication[1] I have defined the character of a university as determined by the idea of knowledge which it professes to advance, by the type of man it purports to produce, and by the economic, social and political condition of the community in which it finds itself. If it is admitted that these are, indeed, the constituent elements of the university, it becomes obvious at once that our universities have degenerated in more than one respect and that they are far from holding the high place which was theirs in the past.

To begin with, we hold no common idea of learning; there is no unity of knowledge. Individually known facts are without fundamental meanings as long as they are not related to a higher principle, an idea with which they can be coordinated and by which—within limits—they can be explained. The history of the universities is ideally the history of man's search after that idea.

There have been periods in this history when men believed that the all-embracing principle had been found. Never has the power and the influence of the universities been so great as during these periods. There is, to clarify our meaning by way of a few examples, the period of scholasticism with its conception of the *unitas intellectus* of Thomas Aquinas, in which faith and knowledge became one. It made the universities centers both of religion and of intellectual achievement. Its way to truth was through faith; its attitude one of devotion; its essence religion. The university found its deepest oneness in the oneness of God.

[1] "The University in a Changing World" (London, 1932).

The period of enlightenment established the goddess of reason as arbiter of truth and falsehood. It conceived the world as essentially built on reason. In reason it found both the unity of the world and the way to understand it. Elements from this period entered into the thought of German idealistic philosophy, which found the true essence of all things in the idea which man forms of them. Thus subject and object became one. "Pure thought is the annihilation of the contrast, the reunion of the originally united," says Steffen in his *Grundzüge der philosophischen Naturwissenschaft*. The university finds the way to truth through the intellect, philosophy is its essence. Through it man takes part in "primal knowledge" (*Urwissen*) in which all partial knowledge converges.

Auguste Comte and his Positivism opened a new period. Philosophy had to cede supreme place to the natural sciences and their methods. The new possession which all the universities in all their faculties have in common is the scientific method. Again there is no real difference between man and matter. Man is matter, and as such can be explored by the same methods as are used in the natural sciences. All standards of value become taboo. At last things are to be seen as they are: "science without presuppositions" is born.

There followed, as was only to be expected, an unparalleled development in the natural sciences, which laid the foundations for the technical progress of modern society. At the same time the universities became more and more barren in their understanding of man. Far from grasping the genius of Shakespeare, philology delighted in counting the number of words he had used. Economics attempted the impossible task of interpreting economic behavior in terms of quantities. The study of the secretion of glands was firmly believed to yield a complete understanding of psychological facts. To the thinker of true insight, however, life remained a greater mystery than ever.

"Utility" became a poor substitute for "value," for such was the ignorance of man, such the lack of knowledge of the essence of man, that all efforts to tear from nature its secrets, all the great inventions and discoveries, helping man to control matter, only put the new problem of how to use these discoveries. No answer was given, no answer could be given in so far as the nature of man did not yield its secrets to quantitative methods or to a process of deduction based on a knowledge of matter. Starvation in an age of plenty, ever new conflicts between individuals and communities, the most terrible war of all ages, and revolution after revolution were the results.

As the chaotic, the unknown is always inferior to the ordered and clearly perceived, man became the slave of the machine, of the "progress" which he himself had created. The failure of the universities obviously does not lie in the fact that they did not take the lead in the ordering of human relations, individual, social and international—this can not be their task and never has been—but that they failed to engender knowledge which, in the hands of physicians, teachers, politicians, might have offered a key to the complex nature of present-day society.

Incidentally, in their desire to be useful, the universities adopted all kinds of courses, from the noble art of ice-cream making to hotel-keeping, which turned them into the kind of bedlam which has been so forcibly denounced by Abraham Flexner. What a contrast with the universities of Paris and Bologna in the Middle Ages or the University of Berlin at the beginning of the nineteenth century!

To each idea of knowledge corresponds a conception of the kind of man the university purports to produce. In other words, it is not only the task of the university to advance knowledge, but to aid in the education of its students. Scholasticism, with its idea of learning, aimed at bringing forth the "scholar-saint," the period of enlightenment had its concept of the "rational man," the idealistic philosophy of the early 19th century knew the "scholar and ethical personality," while positivism proclaimed its idea of leadership in the terms, "knowledge is power."

In the measure to which it became obvious that this knowledge obtainable by positivist methods, and therefore also the power which they conveyed, was exceedingly limited, all attempt at the creation of an "élite" became frustrated. Mr. Babbitt established himself as controller of the destinies of the university, which henceforth was to furnish the world with good doctors, lawyers and business managers, for Mr. Babbitt needed them for his comfort. It was to produce docile citizens, for Mr. Babbitt disliked to be reminded of the shortcomings of this best of all worlds. And as Mr. Babbitt was prepared to pay for services rendered, university men and women sold their ability, their skill and knowledge to the forces of self-interest which dominate the world to-day, and block the way to a fuller and freer life.

When in a combination of three constituent elements two grow increasingly weak, it is evident that the third gains disproportionate importance. This is exactly what has happened. The third constituent element of the university, which we found in the economic, social and political structure of its land and epoch, has become all powerful. Conditions differing from country to country, the unity of the idea of learning, as well as the common conception of an "élite" to be created within the universities, has been shattered. At all times the universities have exhibited differences corresponding to the differences in national character and environment. These were not in the past, however, sufficient to destroy the common foundation. To-day universities have next to nothing in common. They do not exist any more as institutions of learning, but as exponents of socio-economic systems, whether communism or nationalism or liberal democracy. For as it is impossible to spread "subversive" liberal ideas through German or Italian universities so, I understand, it is not conducive to promotion for an American professor to teach and live with communist ideas, though he may hold them to be the truth. It has been said that a free country is one in which no particular person can be blamed for the existing tyranny! The saying can be applied to universities. Even Mr. Babbitt is at times of a retiring disposition.

Thus nationalism can not claim to be original in its efforts to purify the universities under its sway from teachers, teachings and taught who are opposed to the prevailing nationalist philosophy. Even its ruthlessness in intolerance can be easily matched by the ruthlessness with which Soviet Russia banned all bourgeois influences from the universities. What is, however, remarkable is the endeavor to recreate the university in the spirit and philosophy of nationalism, to find a new "absolute" idea of learning and to arrive at a new idea of the "élite" which is to be born in the universities. It is in order to understand these efforts that we have had to deal at some length with what has gone before, the process of disintegration which characterized the last four or five decades in the history of higher learning. Being in opposition to that last period, the new nationalist school of thought excels in criticism of and attack upon the past, while it is still in many ways nebulous and indefinite in its constructive program. However, we can foreshadow future developments by analyzing the line of attack of the protagonists of a nationalist conception of the university.

The main attack is directed against the positivist conception of "science without presupposition." In this respect such divergent schools of thought as nationalists, communists and Catholics meet on common ground. It is pointed out that science without presuppositions is unthinkable. Three arguments recur in contemporary nationalist literature. First, it is emphasized that choice confronts the seeker even before he begins his work. Not only the object which he is going to investigate depends on this choice, but also the viewpoint from which he will approach the object. This choice depends on certain presuppositions, on the scale of values held by the scientist. He is at the mercy of what a recent German writer has called "the unescapable 'perspectivity' of all forms of intellectual conception of the world." Secondly, it is said that research without the affirmation of final values must of necessity lack in that passion for truth which alone yields results. Thirdly, these values determine, consciously or unconsciously on the part of the scientist, the selection of the relevant findings within the sum total of the actually perceived manifestations.

That there is a good deal of justification in this reasoning, particularly as far as the first and third arguments are concerned, needs no elaboration. The second point, put somewhat differently, simply testifies to an awakening of the desire to arrive at an inner cohesion of all knowledge, the all-embracing principle of earlier ages.

The second attack made by the nationalists is directed against the onesidedness of all knowledge in the past. It is held that it was concerned only with the realm below or above living reality. Positivism, dealing only with matter, led to a mechanistic conception of the world, utterly unfitted to explain life, to interpret living organisms such as the state or the nation, their growth and decay. It was dealing with things below the human level and its knowledge was at best partial. The Neo-humanists on the other hand, it is claimed, conceived the world in terms of abstract ideas and concepts, equally unfitted to do justice to the living historic reality. They conceived "the thing in itself," "man in himself," *i.e.*, irrespective of time and space, of historical and national conditionings. The "totality" of the living entity escaped them, for it is inseparably bound up with historic reality. There is a living soul in man and his world which can not be reached either by positivist methods or by the rationalist, deductive processes which characterize the Neo-humanist.

In the light of these two objections it is possible to penetrate the verbosity of modern nationalist writers and to obtain a glimpse of what they are after. They postulate a new realism which would give a clearer insight into the world as it is, an understanding of the processes of life which manifest themselves in the individual as well as in the communities of which he is a part. Instead of seeking eternal laws which exist irrespective of time or space, they want to understand the finite, that which exists. Instead of seeking "the man in himself," they are seeking the "German man" or the "Italian man." To understand him completely, they have to see him in relation to the finite manifestations of human existence which are to be found within the nation, the entity which determines and characterizes the existence of the individual. There is no man who lives like Robinson Crusoe on his island. Every one of his acts is conditioned by his being a German, an Italian or a Frenchman.

It is the nation then and its outward form, the state, which become the pivot of all learning. All partial knowledge finds its meaning only when it is related to the nation and the state. According to the nationalist conception, it is the supreme function of the university to bring the essential traits of the specific nation, in their all-powerful influence upon the individual, from the unconscious into the conscious, and to conceive and interpret all partial findings of scientific endeavor in terms of the supreme values embodied in the nation. Science and every form of learning must be subordinated to this aim. A recent German exposition of the nationalist conception of a university quotes Nietzsche: "All culture begins with the opposite of what we praise as academic freedom, with obedience and subordination, with discipline and service." Italy is satisfied with positing the National Fascist State as the supreme value to which everything else is subsidiary, and in which all knowledge finds a new unity of meaning and purpose. Every one can partake in the search for Fascist truth, though he may not be of Italian origin, if he only affirms the values inherent in the concrete Fascist state. Jews and foreigners have held and are holding positions of high esteem in the Fascist universities, and no one would think of interfering with their work. Fascism may refute *abstract* ideas such as "man in himself," yet the Fascist universities are based on an idea, the concrete conception of the Fascist state, and whoever accepts that conception, whoever sees its cogency, may serve it.

Germany has gone one step further. Not only is all knowledge to be related to the one point of reference, the National State, but only those of German descent, of German blood, can think in terms of the German nation. In one word, learning and knowledge in the German sense is open only to Germans. Thus man and matter, subject and object, become one again as in the days of Steffen; but a whole world divides Steffen from the protagonists of National Socialist science. He found a unity in "pure thought," man recreating the thing in idea, while to-day biological facts, *the thing,* determine the thought of man. A new materialistic determinism has arisen, more formidable than the economic determinism of Karl Marx. Marx admitted some modicum of individual freedom in certain fields, *e.g.,* "religion is a private matter." In National Socialism there is no escape from the domination of the blood, not what you are but who your ancestors were is essential. This domination of the blood is not confined to the humane sciences, sociology or psychology. Even in the natural sciences, methods and findings are determined by particular national "view-points" which are not freely chosen but depend upon the national characteristics of the scientist. Once this thesis is admitted, all Jews and other foreign elements must of necessity be removed from the universities and the life of the state. These people of foreign racial stock can not adequately use even the language of their adopted country as a means of expression. Shortly after the German revolution, posters prepared by the German Student Union appeared in the German universities, demanding that no Jew should be allowed to speak or write in German. "If a Jew writes in German, he lies," ran the text. And it found its climax in a demand that any books written by Jews should be marked "translation from the Hebrew!" The number of exiled professors and of students unable to continue their studies in Germany is a natural sequence to this new idea of learning.

While Fascism spared Italy this "organic" conception of the universities, there are other elements which the Italian and German universities of 1934 have in common. There is first of all the intolerance with regard to "subversive ideas," the infringement upon or annihilation of what has been known hitherto as academic freedom.

From what has gone before, it is hardly

necessary to insist that the restrictions of academic freedom practised in Italy and Germany are not simply to be regarded as the whims of dictators. They are but the logical consequence of the new place assigned to the university within the state or, more fundamentally speaking, of the new conception of learning. To attack these restrictions is "to strike at the heart of the nation," as a contemporary Italian professor puts it; to deny them is to deny the universities themselves.

The above quotation illustrates the extraordinary fact we have already mentioned, that even university professors reared in the traditions of the humanist university have attempted to justify the restrictions put upon them. And there is no doubt that the overwhelming majority of the students have joyfully submitted to the demands of state and nation, that the student organizations not built upon nationalist ideas have dwindled away, and that most of the students are now organized in the Nationalist formations, the *Gruppi Universitari Fascisti* and the *National-Sozialistische Studentenbund.* There is a new sense of liberation and of exhilaration to be noticed in the universities, particularly of Italy, which is the very opposite of what one might have expected, yet further reflection easily leads to an explanation of what to the liberal world appears so paradoxical. Italy and Germany believe they have found the "all-embracing principle" to which everything relates, which gives purpose to all human endeavor. Having found it, all their uncertainty has been put to rest; they have emerged from an all-pervading, agonizing anarchy, to find direction and what appears to them meaningful coordination in the idea of the nation-state. Far from resenting any loss of freedom, they feel that now at last true liberty has come to them; and they rejoice in it. I quote from an article on the Fascist university, written by a leading Italian scholar: "Life which lacks liberty is without meaning, without liberty there is no life, no humanity, no ethical reality, but with liberty comes the ordering of the whole of life—political, juridical, economic and cultural—because if it is true liberty it is at the same time duty and right, direction and limit, creation and the ordering of that same creation."

There remains but one fundamental aspect of the new national universities to be discussed—their endeavor to create a new "élite." Let it be stated from the outset that they have restored the educational function of the universities to the important place which it ought to hold, and which it does not hold in our own universities owing to the absence of any clear idea of the type of person to be brought forth. Whether we can agree with the idea of the new "élite" now prevalent in countries like Italy or Germany is another question. In the universities of these countries "education" has in a sense become the primary function of the university. The same Italian author whom we have quoted above puts it very clearly: "Having made the country for the Italians, it was necessary to make Italians for the country." And the National-Socialist head of a German university writes of his duty to his students, "Building up a national character and will is the task of the university."

The ideal of the man to be produced is inherent in the nationalist idea of knowledge. To be educated means to identify oneself with the essence of what constitutes the German or the Italian nation. The task is facilitated by seeing in Hitler or Mussolini the personification of the true German or Italian type. Thus German university youth emulates Hitler, as Italy's youth shapes itself after the image of Mussolini. In a more abstract sense the new nationalist universities purport to produce the type of man who, fully conscious of the intrinsic national characteristics of his people and inspired by its greatness, lives for the fulfilment of its destiny. As power—not only that which comes of a nation's cultural achievement, but also sheer physical might—is held to be essential to real greatness, the will to power has to be developed. Military training and science as well as physical education become integral parts of the curriculum. *Libro e Moschetto*—books and rifles, is the slogan of Fascist university youth. German university youth is not only organized in storm troops, but obliged by the universities to take part in military training. It is not surprising that with this "heroic" conception of the scholar, women should have been relegated to an inferior position, and that it is the aim to restrict their numbers in the German universities to 10 per cent. of the total enrolment. This is part of the iron logic of National Socialism.

Certainly there is nationalism in one form or another in most of the other European countries, and it has left its imprint upon the universities. There are none, however, in which the victory of nationalism has been so complete as in Germany and Italy. They are the only countries which have evolved the totalitarian conception of the university in a nationalist sense.

Does our analysis of that conception allow us to draw any conclusions which are not simply condemnatory? The answer, we believe, is "yes."

To begin with, it brings home the extent of weakness in purpose and aim of our universities. The ease, not to say the alacrity, with which the German universities, formerly model institutions of higher learning, surrendered to the impact of nationalism, ought to serve as a warning to other countries. What happened to Germany yesterday may happen to-morrow to them.

It is not as if the nationalist conception of the university had nothing to offer. From a formal point of view, indeed, it offers everything: a new idea of knowledge which professes to correlate the hitherto unrelated and an educational ideal which has proved to be most powerful. Though one may reject this idea and ideal as fundamentally unsound, it has to be admitted that they have stirred great numbers of professors and students in Italy, where the system has had time to produce results, to valuable efforts in research, for every scientific achievement carries with it the supreme reward of being taken as a new proof of the greatness of the Italian nation. Nor can there be much doubt that the emphasis on the totality of life, on the historical and ontological conditioning of man in Germany, will lend a new impetus to the study of the social sciences, so sorely neglected in the past. And it may well be that, though these problems are approached with presuppositions which are exceedingly one-sided or definitely wrong, more light will be shed upon them than has been obtained by applying to them the methods of the natural sciences or the abstract formulas of a rational mind.

The western world is not prepared to accept the presuppositions of the Nationalists, their political or biological determinism. Yet we feel profoundly the need for a dynamic unity of conception such as they have found, which will give cohesion to our efforts and release to our energies. Where shall we look for it? Some are returning to Scholasticism. Are we with them, to find the oneness of man, the oneness of knowledge in the oneness of God again? Or are there, in view of the growing agnosticism, the breaking up of the world of believers into innumerable groups and denominations, any other ideas or concepts which carry conviction, which will answer the anxious questioning of man's restless mind? These are the questions which our tragic and harassed generation puts to the university. The future of the university will depend upon the answer it can give.

# EDUCATIONAL EVENTS

## CONGRESS ON THE REFORM OF THE TURKISH LANGUAGE

A STAFF correspondent of *The New York Times* gives a summary of the proceedings of the second Congress for the Reform of the Turkish Language, which began on August 19 in the Dolma Bagtche Palace, when the report of the permanent commission created by the first Congress two years ago was examined. The object of the proposed reform is to give the Turkish people an essentially national language free from all extraneous influences. It is expected that Mustapha Kemal Pasha, who is primarily responsible for the movement, will attend all sessions, as he did at the last congress.

The dispatch states that for many centuries Arabic and Persian have been the predominating influence in the language used by Osmanli Turks, Arabic because the Koran is written in that language, and the teaching of it has been obligatory, and Persian because of the richness and beauty of Persian literature.

These two languages, it is stated, had the same relation to Turkish as Greek and Latin have to the languages of Christian nations. The upper classes even used them to the exclusion of the original Turkish, which they regarded as vulgar. Moreover, until the end of the nineteenth century, Turkish official documents were so full of Arabic and Persian words as to be quite unintelligible to any person not possessing a perfect knowledge of both languages.

The permanent commission appointed by that congress has collected some hundred thousand purely Turkish words. The sources that have been explored include the Turkish provinces, other Turkish-speaking countries such as the Caucasus, Central Asia, etc., and old Turkish books. The congress, it is expected, will not only adopt these words officially but will also revise the grammar and invent new words from root words now in use.

Turkish public opinion, although admitting the desirability of some reform, is divided on the extent and rapidity with which reforms should be adopted. A radical view is that every foreign word should be expunged from the language forthwith, but more moderate opinion favors the retention of certain Arabic and Persian expressions so generally used as to have become part of the Turkish language. This element insists that whatever reforms are made should be carried out gradually by persuasion and example rather than by force, otherwise the change following so soon the adoption of Latin characters in writing and printing may lead to chaos.

## THE AMERICAN LEGION AND THE ALLEGED TEACHING OF COMMUNISM

CRITICISM of alleged communistic tendencies in American schools, colleges and universities was expressed by Edward A. Hayes, national commander of the American Legion, in an address at the sixteenth annual convention of the California department of the legion held in San Francisco on August 13, 14 and 15. Because of the recent general strike in San Francisco, said to have been incited by communists, the issue was dramatically present throughout the convention.

"Intellectual people sneered at the American Legion and other organizations for a number of years when we were calling attention to things going on right under their very noses. They are not sneering now," said Commander Hayes. He declared that "the activities we are combatting have been going on since before the war," and he continued his exhortation to the legionnaires as follows:

> There is no place in this country for people who don't have the proper sense of the rights of others. If you are going to safeguard and transmit to posterity the government you are pledged to uphold then you have the right to see that those who wish to teach overthrow of the government do not get a chance to teach it.
>
> This must be done legally, properly and in a disciplined manner. As your national commander I am asking you to go back to your communities without the attitude of mind that you are trying to crucify anyone. I ask you to check the teachers in your schools and if you find any teaching pupils to forget Washington or Lincoln or others who have taught us patriotic ideals, put your finger on those individuals. Be sure you get the facts and then let the people of your community know the truth.

That theories which are radical or pacifistic are being taught at certain institutions of higher education was charged by Commander Hayes, and he included ministers and other church leaders. "It is not an insurrection of the ignorant that we need fear. It is the laziness of the intellectual."

As a part of its program, the American Legion is asking all state departments to help in having 25,000 legion speakers appear before grade and high schools, colleges and civic and luncheon clubs on Constitution Day, September 17, and during the week following.

The general purpose behind Constitution Day is given as aiming "to stimulate a study and appreciation of the United States of America and the rights, benefits and privileges guaranteed thereby, and to reawaken the faith and confidence of all our citizenry in our constitution and to bring about a rededication to the principles set forth in that document, thus helping to defeat the inroads of radical groups who seek to tear down the constitution and our form of government."—R. W.

## APPROPRIATIONS FOR NEW YORK STATE SCHOOLS

GOVERNOR HERBERT H. LEHMAN, of New York, signed on August 25 the appropriation bill amounting to $13,346,000 for the schools of the state. To raise the necessary funds he signed at the same time the one per cent. supplementary income tax law.

*The New York Times* states that the tax is in effect a reenactment of the 1933 special emergency levy denoted as a "gross" tax which was repealed last spring after being applied, with modifications, for one year only. Before the payments became due on April 15 it was amended to allow the customary exemptions of $1,000 for single persons and $2,500 for heads of families and an additional $400 for each dependent on it. It differs from the normal income tax, to which it is additional, in that the percentage is not scaled according to size of income. It is to be computed without consideration of capital gains or losses.

The tax becomes payable next April on the basis of 1934 incomes. It is expected to raise $14,000,000 which would cover the $13,346,000 added appropriation for education.

Governor Lehman had recommended that if the appropriation were made there should be a corresponding tax measure. The Republicans in the Assembly, however, forced through the Porter bill making the appropriation but omitting any tax. In the Democratic Senate the bill was passed with the tax appended. Thus amended, it was returned to the Republican Assembly, where it was adopted under protest. The Governor signed the bill without comment.

The Republicans in both houses took the position that as the appropriation was necessary to bring state aid for education up to the full $116,000,000 called for under the basic formula of the Friedsam act, it was the Governor's duty under the executive budget system to initiate the tax.

Increments under the Friedsam act had been suspended since the last year of President Roosevelt's administration as Governor in 1932. Governor Lehman, following that precedent, had omitted the $13,346,000 increment from this year's budget. The Republicans attempted to provide for it at the regular session, but were blocked by the Democrats. A bill suspending the Friedsam act increments to conform to the reduced appropriation was passed by the Democratic Senate but defeated in the Republican Assembly.

## PAYMENT OF BACK SALARIES AT CHICAGO

CHICAGO has received from the Reconstruction Finance Corporation a loan of $22,300,000 for the payment of back salaries to teachers and other employees of the Board of Education, which in many cases have been in arrears for over six months.

More than $35,000,000 in non-educational property of the school board has been pledged as security for the loan. The first interest payment on the bonds, amounting to $2,935,000, falls due in December, 1935, and the first principal payment of $250,000 is due the following year. The City of Chicago has given assurance to the Reconstruction Finance Corporation that in future all city salaries will be paid when due.

This is the first time since April, 1931, that school workers have been paid in full, with definite assurance that the board will meet its future obligations regularly. From that date the Board of Education has been continually behind from one to eight months. The trouble began in 1927 and distress for the teachers was precipitated by the reassessment order of the State Tax

Commission in May, 1928, which slowed tax collections.

Until April, 1931, the former School Board managed to meet payrolls nearly on time, and then its financial position collapsed entirely. The board's arrearage continually mounted and the school problem became of national concern.

In March, 1933, Mayor E. J. Kelly took office, succeeding the late Mayor A. J. Cermak. He first led a drive for the Kearner-Skarda Act, which hastened tax collections. He reorganized the Board of Education, which elected James B. McCahey president, and under his leadership instituted an economy program which stabilized finances.

Payments made range from $892 for certain teachers in the elementary schools to $3,391 for principals of the largest high schools. Thirty-two high-school principals received from $2,558 to $3,391; four thousand high-school teachers, from $1,071 to $2,261; elementary school principals, of which there are 175, $1,785 to $2,856; ten thousand elementary teachers from $892 to $1,487. The average payment to each elementary instructor was $1,050.

## THE ESTABLISHMENT OF A DEPARTMENT OF SOCIAL PHILOSOPHY AT COOPER UNION

THE establishment of a department of social philosophy at Cooper Union, N. Y., displacing the People's Institute, which for thirty-six years has functioned as a public forum and as a pioneer center of American adult education, has been announced by R. Fulton Cutting, president of the Board of Trustees.

Dr. Everett Dean Martin, who since 1922 has been director of the institute, has been appointed head of the new department, which has received a grant of $45,000 from the Carnegie Corporation to aid in carrying on its work for the next three years. The free public lectures and the other educational work will be continued under the direction of Dr. Martin. The institute, which has depended entirely upon voluntary contributions, will finance the work.

Approximately 2,000,000 people have attended the free lectures held four nights a week. Classes have been held in an auditorium near the Union, as well as in branches of the New York Library, and in several settlement houses, and have given instruction to about 1,500 students annually in philosophy, literature, biology, psychology, anthropology and natural science.

The founding of a department of social philosophy carries out the wishes of Peter Cooper, founder of the union, who indicated in his deed of trust that instruction in social and political science was one of the principal objects of his benefaction. The institute was founded in 1897 as an experiment in realizing his purposes.

Under the administration of Charles Sprague Smith, as well as of Dr. Frederick C. Howe and Edward F. Sanderson, who succeeded him, the People's Institute carried on welfare activities in addition to its regular educational work. These activities were aided by John Collier, the present Commissioner of Indian Affairs, who grew up in the service of the institute and was on its staff for many years.

Among the community organizations which the institute helped to found were The Marine League, The People's Symphony Concerts, The National Board of Review of Motion Pictures, The Community Center Movement, The Training School for Community Workers, The Educational Dramatic League, Play Streets, An Immigrant Information Station, National Child Health Committee, The People's Chorus, and the Ukrainian Needlecraft Guild. During the past twelve years the institute activities have been confined to adult education.

Distinguished leaders in education, finance, sociology and other fields constitute the advisory council of the institute. They include Frank L. Babbott, Earl Barnes, Alfred J. Boulton, R. R. Bowker, John Graham Brooks, Nicholas Murray Butler, John Dewey, John L. Elliott, John H. Finley, Glenn Frank, Franklin H. Giddings, Mrs. J. Borden Harriman, Mrs. L. Emmett Holt, Charles H. Ingersoll.

## REORGANIZATION OF THE PENNSYLVANIA STATE COLLEGE SCHOOL OF EDUCATION

ANNOUNCEMENT has been made of the reorganization of the School of Education of the Pennsylvania State College as a professional school on the upper division-graduate basis. Provision for the work of the first two college years has been made through cooperation with the School of the Liberal Arts by the organization of a common two-year curriculum in that school which is expected to meet the need for cultural and basic courses, thus leaving the professional courses and activities for the upper and graduate divisions. Candidates having completed the lower division work with a satisfactory record will be admitted to the School of Education on the basis of comprehensive and other examinations, character and personal interview.

A five-year integrated professional curriculum will be provided, permitting prospective educational leaders to drop out of the school for professional experience after receiving each of the first two degrees (bachelor and master) and requiring them to integrate this professional experience with their further study until the highest degree is attained. A fundamental principle of the reorganization which has been in effect at the institution for several years is the essential unity of theory and practice in professional training. Courses taken during periods of residence at the college carry over and are applied in actual school work during intervals between periods of study, which intervals, in turn, provide opportunity for research and experiment in actual school situations and contribute practical school experience for the interpretation and enrichment of further study for the next degree. The plan of reorganization provides that the professional degrees, master of education and doctor of education, shall be administered by the school of education, while the academic degrees of equivalent ranks, with majors in education, shall continue in charge of the Graduate School of the College.

The organization of the school for the performance of its various functions consists of the following standing committees of the faculty: Committee on Pre-professional Guidance, furnishing advisory service in the lower division of the college; Executive Committee, chiefly administrative in function; Committee on Admission, Examinations and Personnel; Committee on Professional Standards and Advanced Study. The work of the committees is coordinated through the dean who is *ex officio* a member of all of them.

The objectives sought in the reorganization are listed as:

1. To delay until a later point in the College course the selection of candidates for training in order to eliminate those manifestly unfit and to secure a higher quality of intellect and character.
2. To control the number of teachers trained by the College and keep it in a reasonable relation with the needs of the State for new teachers.
3. To work in closer coordination with the Department of Public Instruction and with the State Teachers Colleges.
4. To provide a better guidance service for prospective teachers.
5. To maintain the recognized standards and qualifications of the best teacher-training institutions.
6. To limit enrolment in the professional courses to students in the upper division of the School of Education or to those who present equivalent qualifications.
7. To avoid duplication and waste.
8. To strengthen and integrate the professional curriculum.
9. To take the first necessary steps toward putting the school on a graduate basis.
10. To reduce the several undergraduate and graduate curricula to a single integrated curriculum which may be taken in segments with professional experience between periods of study.
11. To place the administration of the strictly professional degrees (M.Ed. and Ed.D.) under the Education Faculty.
12. Likewise, to hand over the non-professional work to other faculties under which it is regularly offered in the form of service courses, and thus secure the maximum preparatory and cultural values.
13. To transmute the inordinate emphasis now placed upon academic credit into a deliberate exaltation of superior ability and a significant accomplishment.

## APPOINTMENTS AT THE NEW SCHOOL FOR SOCIAL RESEARCH

THE Graduate Faculty of Political and Social Science, the "University in Exile," at the New School for Social Research, which was recently granted the power of conferring degrees, will add six more German professors to the staff for the next academic year, which begins on October 1.

The degrees, master of social science and doctor of social science, will be conferred on the successful students by the Board of Regents of the State of New York, acting on the advice of the graduate faculty. In the last academic year, 200 students took courses. Owing to their new degree-conferring power, the graduate faculty expects a higher number of students for the coming year.

The new members of the faculty are the following:

Hans Staudinger, economist and formerly secretary of state for Prussia, will act as professor of economic and business administration. Dr. Staudinger, who also was a former ministerial director to the Prussian Ministry of Trade and Industry, has initiated wide reforms in industrial and business education in Prussia.

Albert Salomon, formerly professor of sociology at the Pedagogical Institute in Cologne and editor of *Die Gesellschaft*, will act as professor of sociology.

Erich Hula, a specialist in public law and political science and a former lecturer on international law at the University of Cologne, will act as professor of public law and political science.

Dr. Alfred Kähler will lecture on economics and labor legislation. He was formerly teacher and then director of the Volkshochschule Harrisleefeld in Schleswig-Holstein, one of the best-known German institutions for the adult education of workers.

Fritz Lehmann will lecture on banking and business economics. He formerly conducted seminars on banking at the University of Cologne.

Carl Mayer, a specialist in economics and sociology, was formerly a member of the faculty at the Institute for Social and Political Science at Heidelberg. More recently he was a lecturer at the Akademie der Arbeit at the University of Frankfurt.

With the new additions, the teaching staff of the "University in Exile" includes eighteen professors, seventeen Germans and one Italian.

## THE INTER-AMERICAN EDUCATIONAL CONFERENCE

THE United States and the majority of the Latin-American countries will be officially represented at the Second Inter-American Conference on Education to be held at Santiago, Chile, from September 9 to 16. While the conference was planned by the Inter-American Federation of Education, it is being held under the auspices of the Chilean Government whose ministry of foreign affairs transmitted the invitations to other American governments.

The purposes of the conference are to bring together representative educators of the American continents; encourage a close union of the peoples of America by means of public education; advance cultural and educational relations between colleges and universities of every kind in the countries of America, and make easier exchange of ideas, experiences and practices in educational technique and scientific research.

The working program of the conference is not yet ready for publication but it will be arranged from the topics proposed by the participating countries, each of which is entitled to submit three subjects for discussion. It must include "character education" and "vocational education," two items assigned to it by the first conference held at Atlanta, Georgia, in 1929.

The official delegation from the United States include:

Dr. William F. Notz, dean of the Georgetown School of Foreign Service, Washington, D. C., a school which trains persons of more than average talent not only for foreign service positions in the United States Government but also for foreign trade conducted by private bodies. Dean Notz himself offers courses in public finance, banking and exchange, and economics and, because both of his training and of his position, will bring to the conference an unusual fund of knowledge and a keen interest.

Miss Faith Hunter Dodge, a journalist and instructor in Spanish in the schools of Chicago, has traveled widely in Latin America, speaks and writes Spanish fluently and has a main interest in carrying to and bringing from the conference those things that are useful in rousing classroom children to know and appreciate the lives of children in their neighbor countries.

Dr. Harold Benjamin is assistant dean of the school of education of the University of Minnesota. He took passage on the steamer Santa Elisa on August 11 and will reach Santiago some days before the discussions open. Trained mainly in institutions of the Western United States, Dr. Benjamin knows of Latin America and its cultures. His special fields are secondary education and psychology in both of which he can find much of value at a meeting such as the coming conference.

Dr. J. C. Wright, chairman of the delegation and Assistant Commissioner for Vocational Education of the United States Office of Education, left

New York on Saturday for the conference. Dr. Wright's interest is, of course, mainly in the many types of technical and vocational education offered both in the United States and abroad. After the closing of the conference he will take advantage of his trip to South America to visit Argentina, Uruguay and Brazil, and study several phases of education in those countries.

# EDUCATIONAL NOTES AND NEWS

Porter H. Adams, formerly president of the National Aeronautic Association and a member of the Vermont legislature, was elected on August 25 to the presidency of Norwich University, Vt. He is a direct descendant of John Adams and John Quincy Adams.

E. Kenneth Smiley has resigned his position as dean of the Junior Division at the University of North Dakota to be assistant to the dean of admissions at Lehigh University.

Dr. Richard E. McArdle, chief of the section of silviculture of the Pacific Northwest Forest Experiment Station, Portland, Ore., has been elected dean of the School of Forestry of the University of Idaho, to take the place of Dean Francis Garner Miller, who died last March after a period of service of seventeen years.

Professor Edward S. Noyes, associate professor of English at Yale University, has been appointed associate dean of freshmen. He will take over the duties of registrar of the freshman class, chairman of the committee of counselors and adviser on study programs for entering freshmen.

Ashbel G. Gulliver, associate professor of law, has been appointed assistant dean of the School of Law at Yale University. Myres S. McDougal, of the faculty of the University of Illinois College of Law, has been appointed visiting associate professor of law.

Five new members have been named to the faculty of Bard College, residential unit of Columbia University at Annandale, N. Y. They are George H. Genzmer, librarian and lecturer in English; Cyril Harris, assistant professor and fellow in English; C. Ray Carpenter, lecturer in psychology; Francis M. Summers, instructor in biology, and John T. Baker, visiting lecturer in philosophy.

Dr. Willard L. Thorp, formerly a professor at Amherst College, has been appointed director of the Consumers' Division of the National Emergency Council.

Professor Clair E. Turner, of the department of biology and public health of the Massachusetts Institute of Technology, was recently appointed special consultant by the United States Office of Indian Affairs. He attended the Navajo Educational Conference held at Fort Wingate, New Mexico, from August 27 to September 1, making an address on "Health Education."

Dr. Barbara Nachtrieb Armstrong, associate professor of law at the University of California, has been granted leave of absence to accept a membership on the National Committee on Economic Security.

John Coatman, professor of economic relations at the University of London, has been appointed news editor of the British Broadcasting Company.

The honorary doctorate of natural science has been conferred by the University of Frankfort-on-Main on Professor Henry Fairfield Osborn, honorary life president of the American Museum of Natural History.

Dr. Bruno Gebhard, a director of the German Museum of Hygiene, Munich, was the guest of honor on August 24 at a luncheon attended by public health officials at the Metropolitan Life Insurance Building, New York City. Dr. Gebhard is on his way to attend a meeting of the American Public Health Association at Pasadena, Calif., in September.

Dr. Thomas S. Baker, president of the Carnegie Institute of Technology, has returned after two months spent in Europe.

Dr. Roscoe Pound, dean of the Harvard Law School, has returned to the United States, after spending the summer abroad.

The Rev. George F. Smythe, who died on August 25, was formerly professor of Latin at

Kenyon College and up to the time of his death dean of Bexley Seminar of that institution. He was eighty-one years of age.

WALTER SCOTT PERRY, for forty-one years the director of the School of Fine Arts at Pratt Institute, Brooklyn, died on August 23 at the age of seventy-nine years.

DR. IRA A. MACKAY, dean of the faculty of arts and sciences of McGill University and formerly professor of law and philosophy at the University of Saskatchewan, died on August 20 at the age of fifty-nine years.

EDWIN L. MILLER, assistant superintendent of the Detroit public schools, died on August 21 at the age of sixty-six years. He was founder and president of the North Central Association of Colleges and Secondary Schools.

EMILE BOURGEOIS, professor of history at the Sorbonne, died on August 25 at the age of seventy-seven years. In 1923 Professor Bourgeois was one of six French professors who gave a series of lectures on French civilization at the summer session of Columbia University.

THE University of California has received from the Carnegie Corporation the sum of $17,000 toward the support of a study of bureaucracy to be conducted by Dr. Robert A. Brady, associate professor of economics.

GIFTS of more than $158,000 to the Chautauqua Institution have been announced by President Arthur E. Bestor. This support will assure the continuance of Chautauqua, which has conducted its program and summer schools under a receivership since December, 1933.

A FIRE broke out at Gordon Hall at the University of Mississippi on August 25. The west and center wings of the large boys' dormitory were destroyed. The hall was unoccupied during summer while undergoing repairs and it is thought probable that the fire was started by an electric wire. The damages were estimated at $50,000.

A UNITED PRESS dispatch from Austria reports that many grade and high schools in the states of Styria and Carinthia may postpone the opening of fall sessions because the buildings are in use as concentration camps. It is said that there are not enough jails to accommodate those held in detention, most of them as the result of the July revolt.

THE Division of Publications of the National Education Association will found a journal in accordance with the recommendations of the National Association of Journalism Advisers. It is the purpose of this project to help make school publications more effective mediums for school interpretation and to help editors and advisers keep in touch with events, movements and plans related to school life. This project will include the founding and development of the National Association of Student Editors, whose official organ will be known as "vitalized school journalism." This organization is to be a medium for the dissemination of education ideals among the students of the nation and a clearinghouse of information and ideas relating to school life and journalism. It will keep editors and advisers in touch with current movements and events which should be interpreted to students and parents and encourage the study and publication of local school history. With the help and direction of the Division of Publications, it will carry out various activities in creative school journalism and research for the benefit of members.

A CWA survey of living costs at the State University of Wisconsin shows that students spend as little as $350 a year. The amount spent for the past year, reported by the students who lived the most economically, averaged $348.78 for the 252 days of the university term. This figure, according to the survey, represents the average minimum expense for a whole year of study, and was accomplished by students living together in small groups, and either cooking their own meals or dining regularly in the cost dining rooms of the state university. The average cost of attending the state university for a year ranged from the low average minimum to a high average of $447.70, the figures showed. The figures were obtained by interviewing more than 700 students of varying economic circumstances and living in all types of student houses. It is the first time that actual expenses have been listed by the students themselves and the results are lower than previous official estimates of the average cost of a year at the university.

ON a scale said to have never before been attempted, the residents of the mountain and river-bottom population of Arkansas will have an opportunity to obtain the rudiments of education. Preliminary plans for an adult education program that will benefit a large number of the 96,918 illiterates have been announced by E. B. Matthews, director of vocational education for Arkansas. This winter 700 or 800 teachers, educated members of mountain communities and river settlements, will go to the remote mountain regions. Classes will be conducted in churches, homes and schoolhouses. Since the original program was initiated last winter as a phase of emergency relief work, it is estimated that the enrolment in adult classes was about 7,000.

A MIGRANT nursery school has been undertaken under the auspices of New York State and the Federal Government at Brant, N. Y. Each year families from Buffalo spend the summer harvesting berries, vegetables and other produce on farms along the south shore of Lake Erie. Heretofore the mothers have had to take their small children into the fields or leave them for care at the homes where the workers reside. The plan was started by New York State this summer to care for these children. Food is provided by federal funds. Katherine A. Walsh and Dorothy L. Hotaling, of the New York State Department of Education, are directors.

REPORTS compiled by Dr. Edgar L. Morphet, research director of the State Department of Education of Alabama, show sharp drops in school enrolment and in the amount of money spent annually for education. Public schools made payments amounting to $21,495,577 in the peak year 1930–31, but in 1932–33 spent only $14,114,640. Because of the receipt of federal aid during the 1933–34 scholastic year, however, expenditures will be normal when figures are compiled after the fiscal year ends on October 1. The white public school enrolment dropped from 436,739 students in 1928–29 to 422,100 in 1932–33. The average white school term in 1930–31 was 153 days and in 1932–33 was 132 days.

DR. M. D. COLLINS, State Superintendent of Schools of Georgia, has announced a program, contingent on the appropriation of funds by the state legislature, allowing students to study whatever subjects they may prefer. This program, which calls for a greatly altered curriculum, will be followed from the elementary grades through the high schools and on into the colleges. It is designed to fit students for earning a living, regardless of the point in their formal education at which they leave school.

A CORRESPONDENT from India to the London *Times* reports that, after many years of preparation the executive of the Indian Public School Society reported to its members that the necessary funds and building plans were ready for the foundation early next year of the country's first school to be modeled on all that is best in the English public-school tradition combined with Indian culture and environment. The plan has the full sympathy of the Government of India, some members of which sit on the society's committee, and through their mediation the school will be able at a small cost to occupy the former buildings and grounds of the Imperial Forest College and Research Institute on the Chand Bagh estate at Dehra Dun. There will be accommodated between 100 and 150 boys whom it is hoped to enroll at the beginning. The society has about £150,000 for the extensions required for the ultimate objective of 420 boys paying an annual fee of 1,000 to 1,200 rupees [£75 to £90] each. A selection committee in England will be asked to appoint a head master, and it is contemplated that six or seven house masters and a number of assistant masters will be public-school men.

THE enrolment of foreign students in Italian universities has increased from 487 in 1913–1914 to 2,287 in 1932–1933. Of the latter 1,851 were enrolled in universities proper, and 436 in other institutions of higher education. Foreign students represent 4.5 per cent. of the total number attending Italian universities. The majority of these students study medicine and surgery, Bologna University having the largest number, followed by Rome.

THE annual report of the Children's Fund of the state of Michigan, reported by the *Journal* of the American Medical Association, shows that during the year ended April 30, 1934, a total of $452,395.11 was expended by the Children's Fund of Michigan to carry on its work in emergency relief, child health, child guidance, research and dependency. Because of the depression some programs were eliminated and others were curtailed. The greatest expenditures continued to be in the field of child health. During this fifth year of the fund's existence, about 280,000 children received some form of service. The feeding of malnourished children in the Detroit area was carried on as a supplemental program to that of the social service committee of the Detroit school system. Eight dental clinics were maintained in school buildings, with an extraction clinic at Grace Hospital for serious cases and a tenth clinic at the Boys Club of Detroit. Thirty-six counties and two urban areas were served by the all-year dental program, and twenty additional counties received the benefit of the ten weeks summer program, which was given over entirely to corrective processes as heretofore. Eleven counties in the state were served by two traveling ophthalmologists, who examined children's eyes and prescribed glasses when necessary. The fund purchases glasses when parents are not able to afford them. At the beginning of the year all grants for research not done directly in the fund's laboratory were discontinued with the exception of the study of childhood tuberculosis carried on through the St. Vincent de Paul Society by Dr. John A. Johnston, of Henry Ford Hospital. The fund did not reduce its appropriation to the Michigan Children's Aid Society, which is used in helping dependent children in the less prosperous sections of northern Michigan, where the population is scattered. The children taken care of under this grant are supported wholly by the fund during the whole year. Green Pastures, summer camp for Negro children at Little Pleasant Lake, Jackson County, was also operated to its full capacity by the Urban League for Negroes. Grants included one to a special committee of the Wayne County Medical Society that helps indigent persons receive medical treatment from practicing physicians.

# DISCUSSION

## THE FUTURE OF PHI BETA KAPPA

THE eighteenth triennial council of Phi Beta Kappa is to meet at Cincinnati in September, and several proposals as to the future policy of the society have been made. One is that measures be taken to increase the endowment of the foundation by approximately $1,500,000, in addition to the present total of $267,587. Such a plan in times like these is a grandiose scheme. Many college presidents are telling their alumni that the day of large endowments has gone by and that the colleges must depend on the yearly gifts of many. But aside from this practical consideration, the question arises as to why Phi Beta Kappa should become another educational bureaucracy as it inevitably would with the resources afforded for publicity and propaganda by such a large endowment. Are there not at present enough bureaus attempting to lay down the law in educational matters? Should individual colleges be further standardized according to the ideas of a small body of men? The council meets but once in three years in a democratic capacity.

One proposed use of this large endowment is to give fellowships to worthy scholars, but how these are to be bestowed has not been stated. Another proposal is that the initiation fees and keys of new members be presented to them without charge. Now as to fellowships, the society, unlike a university, is not very well equipped for making wise choices. As for the free keys, things given away are not usually valued very highly. A third proposed use of the endowment is for a subsidy for *The American Scholar,* a quarterly recently established by the society. According to statistics published only about 7 per cent. of the membership are subscribers. What great need does the publication fill? Most of the articles are of a popular and journalistic character written by professional writers whose names are familiar to readers of current magazines and newspapers. What peculiar and original service, then, does the magazine give that it should be sponsored by Phi Beta Kappa?

The fact is that giving power to a few persons would lead to bureaucracy and standardization. One minor example is the uniform initiation ritual sent out from headquarters. One chapter used it and then went back to its own ritual adopted fifty years ago. Why not? The society goes back to the stirring days of

1776 and has always been democratic; it has always been an undergraduate society; honorary members of mature age have been elected from time to time, but these have constituted a very small minority. The proposals enumerated would change the society entirely. Why should Phi Beta Kappa sell its birthright for a mess of pottage?

GEORGE MILTON JANES

KENYON COLLEGE

# SPECIAL CORRESPONDENCE

## THE NATIONAL COUNCIL ON RELIGION IN HIGHER EDUCATION

TWELVE years ago, under the leadership of Professor Charles Foster Kent, there came into existence an association of persons interested in the religious life of the students in our colleges and universities. This organization, now known as the National Council on Religion in Higher Education, is sponsored by a board on which such nationally known figures as Dean Herbert E. Hawkes, Dr. Harry Emerson Fosdick and Mr. Cleveland E. Dodge serve. From the beginning the basic concern of the council has been to improve the status of religion as a subject in the college curriculum and to develop such attitudes as would make religion a reconstructive and stabilizing force in meeting the stupendous tasks of modern life. A major function has been to locate gifted young men and women looking toward leadership, among undergraduates, in religion and kindred fields, to subsidize their graduate training in the best educational centers at home and abroad, and to place them, when prepared, in situations where they can render the maximum service. To date 145 fellows have been appointed. Now nearly 100 are at work in nearly 100 institutions.

The chief interest during the first years was to provide better equipped teachers of religion. But a natural development, if the whole of campus life was to be affected, was to appoint fellows who were concerned with the spiritual values discoverable in all the activities of man. As the council has grown, it has therefore come to function through six closely coordinated groups: (I) History and Literature of Religion, (II) Philosophy, (III) The Process of Education, (IV) Ethics and Social Philosophy, (V) Psychology and (VI) Child Psychology and the Home. These groups regard themselves as distinct and purposeful units in an integrated whole. In addition to conducting separate seminars at the annual meetings of the council, some now hold special winter conferences to discuss the research projects of individual members. Thus, in February, the Psychology Group met at Columbia University—having for its theme "The Contributions of Psychology to the Determination of Educational Goals." Four sessions were built around the following papers: "The Approach to Purposive Psychology," "The Situation Approach," "The Mental Hygiene Approach" and "The Understanding (Spranger) Approach." At about the same time the Process of Education Group held a conference at Drew University on "Experiments in the Reorganization of Content and Method in Higher Education in the Interest of Spiritual Values." Changes taking place at Ursinus College, Drew University and Bucknell University were examined and appraised. This conference was unique in the way students took active part.

The single annual event in the life of the national council that helps the fellows maintain a sense of corporate unity and purpose is a conference, spoken of as the Week of Work. There, as implied above, the six separate groups devote a series of morning seminars to their respective professional interests. The evening sessions, bringing all together, contribute the chief integrating factor of the Week of Work. Here the basic purpose of the council and its relation to the current affairs of society are kept to the fore. At the 1933 week, held at Colgate-Rochester Divinity School from September 5 to 11, Professor Eduard C. Lindeman, of the New York School of Social Work, led these sessions on the theme, "The Philosophy and Techniques of Social Change." An expert in drawing out, directing and synthesizing the thinking of the conference, as well as in furnishing fresh data, he helped us examine the present assets and liabilities in American life; to analyze the claims of communism, socialism, liberalism, fascism and education as instruments of social change;

to point out the economic, political and intellectual factors in the present crisis in Western culture; and to discover a constructive outlet for the intellectual in the present crisis.

One can readily understand the difficulty with which a group of 150 intellectuals with such extremely divergent religious, social and economic philosophies is held intact. The tension has become greater under the stress of each succeeding year. A small minority, far to the left, has felt that the council has been sailing under false colors, and that instead of calling ourselves a "Council on Religion" we had better be known as a society for social education. At the Week of Work last year a special committee was asked to study the attitudes of the fellows present and try to reach an intelligent consensus. Reporting for the committee, Dr. Millar Burrows, of Yale Divinity School, said:

> As educators we share a common purpose to develop in students religious insights and a concern for the achievement of spiritual values. We are endeavoring to help students to face honestly and constructively the problems of religious reconstruction in the modern world. In realizing these religious objectives many find that they can work within the historic tradition, others that their study leads them to radical departure from traditional positions. The Fellowship includes members of the Jewish, Roman Catholic, and Protestant faiths. In our relationship as Fellows, we maintain the principle of individual freedom of thought, and we find stimulus and challenge in our contrasting points of view, and an impulse toward new search for an adequate understanding of religion.
>
> We are concerned with the production of a culture which will make possible vital spiritual growth. To achieve this end members of the group tend to move in varying degrees toward such reforms as socialization of the means of production; redistribution of wealth; social equality in race relations; repudiation of war as an instrument of national policy. Agreeing in a desire to arouse an earnest concern in our students for these matters we differ as to whether our educational responsibility involves: (1) an endeavor to influence students in the direction of these specific reforms; or (2) an attempt to cultivate in students a critical attitude and a sense of social responsibility, leaving them free to work out their own program.

This report, with the discussion that grew out of it, was a step in the direction of clarifying our purpose; but the council still felt the need of a special committee on purpose to take a year to make an unhurried survey of the total membership, and reach a more satisfactory basis upon which to proceed. This committee has recently put into the hands of the board members and the fellows a preliminary document that will form the basis of study at the 1934 Week of Work. This document, not now ready for publication, sets forth a revised statement of purpose, suggests the desired characteristics and equipment of the individual fellows, and outlines a challenging program in relation to the reconstruction of religion and the transformation of society and education. In closing its report the committee on purpose ventured the faith that the quest of religion is the most unifying factor, and that we should, through finding unity in diversity, seek the transformation of modern life so that the highest spiritual growth is made possible for all.

The coming Week of Work, to be held again at Colgate-Rochester Divinity School from September 4 to 10, promises to be one of the most significant and crucial in the short life of the national council. It will be significant because of the dynamic form in which the program is conceived. The desire of the separate groups to relate their subject-matter to the momentous problems involved in change is evident from the themes which are, in order: I, "The History of Religion and Its Interpreters"; II, "The Place of Philosophy in American Culture"; III, "Experiments in Effecting Desirable Changes in the Colleges"; IV, "Adjusting Social Science Teaching to the Demands of the Changing Social Order"; V, "The Contribution of Psychology to the Determination of Educational Goals," and VI, "The Relation of the Family to a Changing Society." The general sessions will consider "The Future of the Liberal Arts College and Its Ideal in American Society." President William Mather Lewis, of Lafayette College, and Professor Sidney Hook, of the Department of Philosophy of New York University, are among those presenting papers. The Week of Work will be crucial in that we shall find out whether there is a purpose and a future program sufficiently unifying and inclusive to hold us together.

WILLARD E. UPHAUS

# REPORTS

## ACCREDITED LIBRARY SCHOOLS

THE Board of Education for Librarianship, by virtue of its charter, is authorized to accredit and classify library schools. In accordance with the minimum requirements for library schools adopted by the council of the American Library Association, a library school must give in a single academic year at least one coordinated professional curriculum credited as a full year of study.

The American Library Association conducts no course in library science nor is it responsible for the instruction offered by any institution.

Each of the accredited library schools, with the exception of those indicated in (1) below as training school librarians only, offers a general basal course in library science. Some of them, particularly those which offer advanced curricula, also give opportunity for specialization in certain fields of library science, as noted in (3).

The prospective student is urged to examine carefully the catalogues of the library schools to determine the curriculum best suited to his own needs and to consider the location of the school in relation to the fields of library service which may have a particular appeal for him. He is advised also to consult the director of the library school in regard to details of the curriculum, specialization, transfer of credits, opportunities for positions and similar information.

Summer courses in library science, with the exception of cumulative courses given as the equivalent of, or credited toward the completion of, the full professional curriculum, can not be considered the equivalent of a library school curriculum. Such cumulative sessions are noted under (9). No library school credits correspondence courses toward completion of a professional curriculum.

The accredited library schools are listed below geographically, then alphabetically according to the form of name in common usage as indicated by capital letters. The date of establishment and the classification under the minimum requirements for library schools follow the name. Accredited curricula only, given in the regular term or summer session, are listed. Information supplied by the schools is given in the following order:

(1) Curricula in the regular year, with degree or certificate awarded.
(2) Minimum entrance requirements.
(3) Specialization in types of library service.
(4) Fees, including tuition, registration, matriculation, etc. (Minimum and maximum figures refer respectively to residents and non-residents of the state.)
(5) Estimated cost of trips and field work.
(6) Estimated cost of text-books and supplies.
(7) Estimated cost of board and room per year.
(8) Scholarships or loan funds.
(9) Summer courses credited toward completion of professional curricula.

### EASTERN STATES

*Simmons College School of Library Science,* Boston, Mass. (1902) Type II and Type III. (1) (a) General (b) Library work with children. B.S. (2) (a) and (b) Three academic years, including knowledge of typewriting, German and French; or college graduation, including French and German (3) See (1) (b) above; also elective courses in school library work (4) $255 (5) $12–55 (6) $40 (7) $350–525 (8) Scholarships and loan funds available to undergraduates only.

*New Jersey College for Women Library School,* New Brunswick, N. J. (1927) Type III. (1) General. B.A. or B.S. (2) Three college years (4) $175–275 (5) $50 (6) $40 (7) $450–525 (8) Scholarships and loan funds.

*New York State College for Teachers Department of Librarianship,* Albany, N. Y. (1926) Type III. (1) and (3) School library work. B.S. in L.S. (2) Two college years (4) $200; $10 for residents of N. Y. State preparing for state positions (5) $70 (6) $30 (7) $320–525 (8) Scholarship and loan funds (9) Same as (1), admitting only those in, or under appointment to, high school library positions in N. Y. State.

*Pratt Institute School of Library Science,* Brooklyn, N. Y. (1890) Type III. (1) General. Certificate (2) High school graduation, two modern languages, plus library experience and examination, or college graduation (4) $200 (5) $50–65 (6) $30–35 (7) $400–500 (8) Scholarships and loan fund.

*Columbia University School of Library Service,* (1887) Type I. (1) (a) First year, General. B.S. (b) Second year, Advanced study. M.S. (2) (a) College graduation (b) College graduation, one year of accredited library school study and one year of library experience (3) Specialization in various fields of library service (4) $340 (5) $25 (6) $40 (7) $540–630 (8) Scholarships and loan fund (9) Same as (a) in minimum of four summer sessions; also courses credited toward (b).

*Syracuse University School of Library Science* (1908) Type III (Tentative). (1) and (3) General, with specialization in library work with adults and with young people. B.S. (2) College graduation (4) $352 (5) $15–50 (6) $15–20 (7) $350–535 (8) Scholarships and loan funds (9) Same as (1) in 4–6 summer sessions.

*Drexel Institute School of Library Science*, Philadelphia, Pa. (1892) Type II. (1) General. B.S. in L.S. (2) College graduation (4) $255 (5) $50 (6) $40 (7) $430–490 (8) Scholarship, covering tuition fees; loan fund.

*Carnegie Institute of Technology, Carnegie Library School*, Pittsburgh, Pa. (1901) Type III (Tentative). (1) and (3) (a) General (b) Work with children (c) Senior high school library work. B.S. in L.S. (2) College graduation (4) $310 (5) and (6) $40 (7) $325–400 (8) Scholarship and loan fund.

MIDDLE WESTERN STATES

*University of Chicago Graduate Library School* (1928) Type I. (1) and (3) Advanced study and research in various fields of library science. M.A. and Ph.D. (2) Bachelor's degree from an accredited college, a year of library school training and a year of library experience (4) $100 per quarter (7) $147–380 per quarter (8) Four fellowships of $1,000 each and a few research assistantships and half-tuition scholarships; loan fund (9) Same as (1).

*University of Illinois Library School* (1893) Type I. (1) (a) First year, General. B.S. in L.S. (b) Second year, Advanced study. M.A. or M.S. (2) (a) College graduation, *preferably with A.B. degree* (b) College graduation, one year of library science *with at least a B average*, library experience, and fitness for advanced professional study (3) Specialization in various fields of library service (4) $90–145 (5) First year, $30 (6) First year, $20; Second year, $15 (7) $400 (8) One $300 scholarship and small loan fund for second year students only (9) First semester only of (a) in two consecutive summer sessions; also courses credited toward (b).

*Kansas State Teachers College of Emporia* (1928) Type III. (1) and (3) School library work. B.S. in Education plus library certificate (2) Three college years (4) $54–84; (6) $25–30 (7) $125–225 (8) Loan funds.

*University of Michigan Department of Library Science* (1926) Type I. (1) (a) First year, General. B.A. in L.S. (b) Second year, Advanced study. M.A. in L.S. (2) (a) A bachelor's degree from an approved college and a reading knowledge of French and German (b) Same as (a), plus one year accredited library school study (3) Specialization in various fields of library service (4) $113–153 (5) $5–15 (6) $35 (7) $450 (8) Loan fund (9) First semester only of (a) in two summer sessions; also courses credited toward (b).

*College of St. Catherine Library School*, St. Paul, Minn. (1929) Type III (Tentative). (1) and (3) General, with emphasis on college, school and children's library work. B.S. in L.S. (2) College graduation (4) $215 (5) $15 (6) $40 (7) $450–700 (8) Scholarships.

*Western Reserve University School of Library Science* (1904) Type II. (1) and (3) (a) General (b) Library service for children (c) High school library service. B.S. in L.S. (d) Second year advanced training in library service for children. M.S. (2) (a)–(c) College graduation (d) College graduation and one year of library science (4) $325 (6) $25 (7) $350–450 (8) Scholarships and loan fund (9) (a)–(c) only, in five consecutive summer sessions.

*University of Oklahoma School of Library Science* (1929) Type III. (1) General. B.A. in L.S. (2) Three college years (4) $13–63 (5) and (6) $50 (7) $300 (8) Loan fund (9) First semester's work only, in two consecutive summer sessions.

*University of Wisconsin Library School* (1906) Type III. (1) General. Diploma. Under certain conditions, curriculum is also accredited by the College of Letters and Science toward a bachelor's degree (2) Junior standing and examination (4) $69–119 (5) $15 (6) $40 (7) $270–375 (8) Loan fund.

SOUTHERN STATES

*Emory University Library School* (formerly Library School, Carnegie Library of Atlanta, Georgia) (1905) Type II. (1) General. B.A. in L.S. (2) College graduation (4) $160 (6) $40 (7) $400 (8) Loan funds.

*Louisiana State University of Library Science* (1931) Type II. (1) and (3) (a) General, with elective courses in library work with children, county libraries and college and university libraries (b) School library work. B.S. in L.S. (2) College graduation (4) $90 (5) $55 (6) $25 (7) $245–420 (8) $2,000 scholarship and fellowship fund; loan fund (9) Same as (1) (a) and (b).

*University of North Carolina School of Library Science* (1931) Type II and Type III (Tentative). (1) and (3) General, with elective programs in public, school and college library work.

A.B. and L.S. or a certificate (2) College graduation, or senior standing in Univ. of N. C. (4) $163–263 (5) $35 (6) $16 (7) $283–328 (8) Scholarships and loan fund (9) Selected courses.

*George Peabody College for Teachers Library School*, Nashville, Tenn. (1928) Type III (Tentative). (1) and (3) School library work. B.S. in L.S. (2) College graduation, 36 quarter hours in one liberal arts field, 18 quarter hours in modern language, 16 quarter hours in education and psychology (4) $225 (5) and (6) $30 (7) $210 minimum (8) Scholarships and loan fund (9) Same as (1).

*Hampton Institute Library School* (Negro), Virginia (1925) Type III (Tentative). (1) General. B.S. (2) Four college years (4) $175 (5) $20 (6) $30 (7) $180 (8) Scholarships.

WESTERN STATES

*University of California School of Librarianship* (1919) Type I. (1) (a) First year, General. Certificate (b) Second year, Advanced study. M.A. (2) (a) College graduation (b) College graduation and one year library science with at least a B average, and library experience (3) Specialization in various fields of library service (4) $50–200 (5) and (6) $50 (7) $350 (8) Loan fund.

*University of Denver School of Librarianship* (1931) Type II (Tentative). (1) General. A.B. or B.S. to four year students, B.S. in L.S. to college graduates (2) Three college years (4) $244–262 (6) $17 (7) $225–450 (8) Loan funds.

*University of Washington Department of Librarianship* (1911) Type III (Tentative). (1) and (3) (a) General. B.A. in Librarianship (b) Second year advanced course in library work with children. Certificate (2) (a) Graduate standing with B average; 20 college credits each in French and German; (b) graduation from an accredited library school (4) $68–188 (5) $50 (6) $10 (7) $400 (8) Loan fund.

CANADA

*McGill University Library School*, Montreal, (1927) Type II. (1) General. B.L.S. (2) College graduation (4) $150 (5) $75 (6) $35 (7) $480–500 (8) Scholarship.

HALF-YEAR CURRICULUM IN SCHOOL LIBRARY WORK[1]

*The University of Tennessee Department of Library Science*, Knoxville, Tenn. (1928) was accredited under the former Minimum Standards for a Curriculum in School Library Work (Bulletin of the A. L. A., Vol. 20, pp. 444–52), as a 16 semester hour curriculum in school library work with credit toward B.A. or B.S. (2) Two college years (4) $61–142 (5) and (6) $25 (7) $500 (8) Scholarships and loan funds (9) Same as (1).

[1] Standards for less than a full year of professional instruction are under revision.

# EDUCATIONAL RESEARCH AND STATISTICS

## SCHOLASTIC RANKING OF RELIGIOUS GROUPS

A RECENT study by Fry[1] shows that certain religious denominations in the United States contribute disproportionately to the number of individuals who attain eminence. There are, for example, thirty-two times as many Unitarians and six times as many Episcopalians represented in the 1930–31 edition of "Who's Who in America" as the numerical strength of these groups would lead one to expect. Similarly, certain other denominations fall behind their expectancy of representation in "Who's Who." Table I shows the relationship between representation and total membership for each denomination having one hundred or more representatives in "Who's Who."

[1] C. Luther Fry, "The Religious Affiliations of American Leaders," *The Scientific Monthly*, p. 241, March, 1933.

TABLE I

DENOMINATIONAL REPRESENTATION IN "WHO'S WHO" IN PROPORTION TO GENERAL CHURCH MEMBERSHIP

| | |
|---|---|
| Unitarian | 32.50 |
| Reformed | 6.52 |
| Universalist | 6.43 |
| Episcopalian | 6.07 |
| Congregationalist | 4.96 |
| Quaker | 4.40 |
| Presbyterian | 3.11 |
| Christian Scientist | 1.27 |
| Methodist | .89 |
| Baptist | .70 |
| Disciples of Christ | .61 |
| Lutheran | .32 |
| Roman Catholic | .13 |

The present study was undertaken to investigate the possibility that the members of the eight denominations most strongly represented in the student body of the University of Missouri, considered as groups, might exhibit varying capacities for scholastic achievement. The degree of "scholastic achievement" of each denominational group will be indicated by the average scholastic index of the group, based on grades received by individual members. Certain other relevant characteristics of the groups will be shown for purposes of comparison.

The names of the individual students studied were obtained by random sampling of the records in the office of the registrar. Only two qualifications for inclusion in the samples were imposed—(1) the individuals must have been recent high-school graduates and (2) they must have entered the university direct from high school. Information concerning religious affiliation or preference was obtained from the personal information forms filled in by each student at matriculation.[2] In order that all individuals studied might have had sufficient time to complete a regular four-year course, with normal progress, no student entering after the first semester of the year 1929–30 was included. All samples were obtained from matriculants of the period 1925–29.

The scholastic index of each student was determined by the following conventional formula, adapted to the grading system in use in this institution: Scholastic Index =

$$\frac{4E + 3S + 2M + I}{E + S + M + I + F} 100,$$

where E, S, M, I and F designate the number of semester hours of excellent, superior, medium, inferior and failure grades, respectively. The index of each denominational group was obtained by applying the formula to the totals for the individual members comprising the group. Each group was tested for stability by adding successive groups of ten individuals and determining the cumulative scholastic index after each such addition. After relative stability, indicated by successive fluctuations of less than a whole point, was obtained, the group was considered ready for analysis.

Table II shows the mean scholastic index, probable error of the mean and the coefficient of variability for each group.[3]

TABLE II

Ranking on Basis of Scholarship

| Group | Mean SI | PEm | CV |
|---|---|---|---|
| Jewish | 198.24 | 4.07 | 36.23 |
| Methodist | 192.30 | 3.96 | 36.24 |
| Episcopalian | 186.43 | 3.85 | 35.26 |
| Entire group | 182.36 | 1.36 | 38.10 |
| Christian Scientist | 182.14 | 4.40 | 35.46 |
| Disciples of Christ | 180.31 | 4.07 | 40.09 |
| No preference | 179.75 | 4.09 | 40.09 |
| Presbyterian | 174.32 | 3.95 | 38.68 |
| Roman Catholic | 173.62 | 3.98 | 37.75 |
| Baptist | 172.64 | 3.81 | 38.78 |

The probable error in each case indicates the range within which the true mean might reasonably be expected to lie if the total population sampled were included in the study.

The coefficients of variability indicate the relative homogeneity of the various groups in terms of the dispersion of the individual averages around the central point of balance. It will be noted that the Episcopalians are the most homogeneous group, and the Disciples and those indicating no denominational preference the most heterogeneous.

In this connection, it should be remarked that the distributions of the individual indices comprising the groups of Baptists, Episcopalians and Methodists show positive skewness, the first two to a marked degree, indicating that the mean scholastic index is drawn upward from the point of greatest concentration of individual indices by the presence of a comparatively large number of high-ranking individuals. The other groups show negative skewness, indicating the marked influence of low-ranking individuals on the group average.

A comparison of the ranking order based on average scholarship indices with that determined by Fry, based on representation in "Who's Who," discloses a number of discrepancies. Table III, which includes the seven denominations common to both lists, shows these differences.

[2] These statements of affiliation or preference are probably entirely ingenuous, reflecting merely the influence of family training. The study might well be designated as a study of the scholastic achievements of sons and daughters of members of certain sects.

[3] For purposes of comparison, a sample of those students who claimed no church membership or preference was included.

TABLE III

COMPARATIVE RANKING ORDER

| On basis of representation in "Who's Who" (selected) | On basis of average scholarship |
|---|---|
| (1) Episcopalian | (1) Methodist |
| (2) Presbyterian | (2) Episcopalian |
| (3) Christian Scientist | (3) Christian Scientist |
| (4) Methodist | (4) Disciples of Christ |
| (5) Baptist | (5) Presbyterian |
| (6) Disciples of Christ | (6) Roman Catholic |
| (7) Roman Catholic | (7) Baptist |

The Christian Scientists are the only group occupying the same position in both scales. The Methodists are in fourth position in Fry's scale, and in first position in average scholarship. The Presbyterians, second in Fry's scale, are only fifth in scholarship. The Disciples are two places higher in scholarship than in representation in "Who's Who." The other denominations show shifts of less significance.

The greatest discrepancy occurs in the case of the Jews. Table I leaves the Jews entirely out of account, while Table II shows them leading all denominations in scholarship. Fry was unable to include them in his study for two reasons: (1) few adherents of the Jewish religion are found in "Who's Who" and (2) it is impossible to obtain accurately comparative data

TABLE IV

LOW RANKING STUDENTS AND GRADUATES

| Group | Number in group | Dropped for deficiency: Number | Dropped for deficiency: Per cent. | Bachelor's degrees: Number | Bachelor's degrees: Per cent. |
|---|---|---|---|---|---|
| Jewish | 142 | 27 | 19.01 | 42 | 29.58 |
| Methodist | 141 | 33 | 23.40 | 66 | 46.80 |
| Episcopalian | 133 | 33 | 24.81 | 30 | 22.56 |
| Christian Scientist | 98 | 28 | 28.57 | 22 | 22.45 |
| Disciples of Christ | 143 | 35 | 24.48 | 46 | 32.17 |
| No preference | 141 | 44 | 31.21 | 44 | 31.21 |
| Presbyterian | 133 | 31 | 23.31 | 47 | 35.34 |
| Roman Catholic | 123 | 39 | 31.71 | 42 | 34.15 |
| Baptist | 140 | 36 | 25.72 | 47 | 33.57 |
| Total | 1,194 | 306 | 25.63 | 386 | 32.33 |

on the total number of individuals embracing the Jewish faith.

Table IV presents further evidence concerning the scholastic characteristics of the groups. The Jewish group shows the smallest percentage of fatalities by way of the elimination rules,[4] with the Presbyterians next in order. The Catholics suffer the greatest depletion of ranks from this cause.

In tenacity, as indicated by the percentage who continue in the university and are graduated, the Methodists are easily in the lead. The Christian Scientists and Episcopalians show the smallest proportion of students who obtain degrees.

CONCLUSIONS

On the basis of scholastic achievement, the groups studied fall in a definite order, with the Jews, Methodists and Episcopalians above the average of the entire group, and the Christian Scientists, Disciples, those who claim no church membership, Presbyterians, Catholics and Baptists below the average. The difference between any two adjacent denominational groups is slight, but the difference between those at the extremes of the scale, the Jews and the Baptists, amounts to twenty-five points, or one fourth of a grade interval, and may be regarded as significant.

Slight agreement between the two ranking scales was found. As noted above, only the Christian Scientists occupy a position in the scholastic scale corresponding to their position in the scale based on representation in "Who's Who." The Jews, Methodists, Disciples and Catholics are found higher in the scholastic scale than in the other, while the Episcopalians, Presbyterians and Baptists are lower.

H. S. RUMMELL

UNIVERSITY OF MISSOURI

[4] In the University of Missouri, as in most colleges and universities, students who fall below a certain standard of scholarship are dropped from the rolls.

## NEW BOOKS IN EDUCATION

LATANÉ, JOHN H. *A History of American Foreign Policy.* Revised and enlarged by David W. Wainhouse. Doubleday, Doran. $4.00.

NIMKOFF, M. F. *The Family.* Pp. x + 526. Houghton Mifflin. $3.00.

PERKINS, JEANETTE E. *Others Call It God.* Pp. xx + 141. Harper. $1.50.

# EDUCATIONAL REVIEW

**Edited by Nicholas Murray Butler, 1891–1919, Frank Pierrepont Graves, 1920–1924, and William McAndrew, 1924–**

# COMMENTS ON THINGS EDUCATIONAL

**By WILLIAM McANDREW**

## BLAME FOR TOO MANY TEACHERS

THE New York City Board of Education examiners report that the outlook for prospective teachers is very dark. Students are advised to seek other employment. Applicants now on the eligible list, says the report, have waited so long and are presumably so rusty that new examination should be required before they are appointed. A sad note in the report is the observation that these certified intending teachers are bitter against the school authorities. Resort to influence and "pull," with no result, has only intensified resentment. Their attitude toward education, toward society, toward life itself is unquestionably antagonistic, says the report. They are embittered toward those in authority. They have become indifferent to what the public is used to expect of teachers in the way of decent and restrained behavior in public. Many have embraced a radical social and political philosophy.

This report of the examiners refers to what the newspapers have reported of unemployed teachers from time to time crowding the hall at meetings of the board of education and giving vent to anger in ways not approved in books of etiquette. You have only to imagine yourself in their situation to understand the difficulty of keeping to good manners. A certificate-holder feels like a person who legitimately holds a steamer ticket but who sees the vessel setting off at each new term crowded full. The proposition to cancel certificates and to require new examinations will naturally be fought by the ticket holders. They have an association of unassigned teachers and have, before now, defeated similar proposals. When William Maxwell was superintendent he proposed that there should be a continuing list of eligible teachers added to by each subsequent examination. Applicants, whether new or old, were to be listed in order of standing. This was to insure the schools the presumably best-prepared whenever appointments were made. If your chances were imperiled by your low rating you could enter each new examination with intent to get a higher mark. The legislature saw the applicants' side of the case and passed a law forbidding the merging of eligible lists. All on schedule one must be taken care of before any on list two are considered. In the appointment of teachers and superintendents, or in their discharge for incompetence, American boards of education have been notoriously more accommodating to individuals than careful of the efficiency of educational service. Persons, not performance, has been the rule in all the school systems I have known.

The distress of the New York unemployed teachers is, of course—and more's the pity—typical of unappointed applicants in all the states. It is made no less unbearable for them by the fact that they have been given their tuition free and were never, as West-Pointers are, given assurance of positions if they fulfilled requirements. When I was in normal school, fifty-four years ago, every one of us knew that getting places would be a gamble and that there were more graduates than vacancies. But the flight of girls into matrimony and boys into business made vacancies, even in Michigan, frequent, while any one who would go west of the Mississippi was sure of a place.

Ten years ago there were enough warnings to warrant the reduction of training-school output. Naturally the teachers colleges resisted the reduction of enrolment and of their faculties. Overproduction of teachers, lawyers, engineers, physicians, apparently of trained people for anything except straitened living, is evident, whatever field is surveyed. The 500 observers quoted by Walter Pitkin[1] agree that acting, journalism, librarianship, the ministry, professional music, law, medicine, dentistry, nursing, illustrating, painting, design, architecture, decorating, aviation, bond-selling, insurance, stenography and other occupations which he names, have more than enough unemployed

[1] "New Careers for Youth." Simon and Schuster, New York. 1934.

efficient workers to fill all vacancies that will occur for several years to come. That is no solace to a person who wants to teach and can't. What can you say to these people? Shall you say that the education that has been given them is full of valuable knowledge and skills that are applicable in every field? Shall you say that no one of their teachers ever assured them they would have employment? Shall you advise them to consider teaching only one of the many diminished opportunities left and that they should join the procession of daily trampers from office to office, from shop to shop, asking for jobs? What else can you say? Pitkin's advice is to examine the employments which he lists as the most promising, to apply for them, and to accept the hard fact that America as a whole must accept a lower standard of living than it is accustomed to. We who are teaching or who have taught have been accepting it for ourselves for three or four years already.

## FEAR OF RADICAL THINKING

THERE are not a few sober thinkers who are saying too many people have become oversaturated with education. Many years ago I remember Mrs. Julia Ward Howe saying that her husband, Samuel Howe, who had fought on the side of the Ypsilanti brothers to free Greece from Turkish rule, found the Greeks so highly educated that they all felt they had to be generals. Higher education had made them unwilling to perform the humbler work their country needed most. But I fail to see how there can be an overproduction of education. Yet it is plain enough that the offering which Mr. Flexner and Mr. Nock and the professors of my college days deemed the only proper education has failed to succor us in this hour. Not a thing taught me in high school or college is of any help in this time of trouble. Neither knowledge or trained brain is mine to show how this rich country with invention and natural wealth enough to do it shall afford comfort and happiness to every inhabitant who is willing to work. If your education has given you the means of showing the solution why are you so infernally secretive about it?

The appalling fact is that the opportunity of getting food, clothing, warmth and shelter is approaching the danger point for millions of honest and industrious people. Everybody knows that the fundamental purpose of preparing food is to eat it; of making cloth is to wear it; of procuring fuel is to burn it; of building a house is to get into it. Everybody knows that all these processes have been bedevilled by the purpose of making money out of them. As far as you and I as individuals are concerned our education has been at fault in not teaching us how to grow food, weave cloth, mine coal and build a house. This nonsense is implicit in the back-to-the-land fantasy and doesn't help the unemployed teachers at all. The sort of teaching you are likely to see is that a state, a nation, founded on a promotion of general welfare can and should as a government by all the people provide that the fundamental operation of providing food, clothing, warmth and shelter shall be divorced from profit and be conducted solely for the general welfare, as are light-houses, highways, parks and schools. This is a radical philosophy.

The New York examiners report that many unemployed have embraced radical social and political philosophies. When associations of ministers are pledging themselves "to support a planned economy, a control of industry and a broader distribution of wealth," is that not embracing radical social and political philosophies? And who is it that would blame unemployed teachers from doing the same? Are those who are most sympathetic with the unemployed, are those who are working to keep them, afraid of radical social and political philosophies? Not yet? So far, the dread of radical philosophies has rested chiefly in managers of educational institutions supported largely by contributions of the gentlemen who are responsible for exclusion of general welfare from operations of government. So far the influence of public-school boards as studied by Claude Arnett[2] in the replies is in a majority of cases opposed to any teaching that proposes a planned economy, a control of industry and a broader distribution of wealth. But teachers, in their National Education Association, are proposing to teach that "we need a new social order and a new social interpretation."

[2] "Social Beliefs and Attitudes of American School-Board Members." Emporia, Kansas, Gazette Press. 1932.

## AN OGBURN HOROSCOPE

WE came away from the University of Chicago's Conference of Administrative Officers of Public and Private Schools with the feeling that reliable lights had been set in the murk of the path ahead.

Professor Ogburn, whose own brand of humor throws bright flashes on the most solid of social statistics, said the present atmosphere has so inspired him that in his university courses he tries to avoid all past and present tenses in the use of his verbs.

Naturally Dr. Ogburn's estimate of the financial future in education made us all prick up our ears. His appraisal of income trends, based on a less rapid increase of population and on increasing invention is that wealth and income will be greater during the next twenty-five years. Whether this will mean more money for schools who can say? There will be fewer pupils in the elementary grades, more in the third than in the second, more in the second than in the first. The expansion of high schools, taking in as high as 90 per cent. of those of secondary school age, the consequent growth of college enrolment, are going to require a large amount of money so that adjustment of individual teachers' salaries upwards is doubtful. Competition for the tax-payer's dollar will be more keen. There is not much doubt that our people will demand social insurance. This will take fourteen or fifteen per cent. of our total wage-earning bill, if European figures are a guide. Most of this will be paid by taxpayers. This will leave less for schools.

This speaker wondered how the tremendous multiplication of knowledge of facts and principles is going to be covered by education. Will it be by specialization or by increasing the years spent in school?

Another change is seen in the fact that marriage is increasing and people are wedding earlier. This calls for more educational provision for adults.

Adult education suffers, now, from the competition recreation offers. Increased leisure brought by shorter hours of labor may surfeit the population with amusements and boredom and turn folks to the greater satisfaction of education.

## THE EDWARDS FORECAST

MY young friend, Newton Edwards, is, like Professor Ogburn, southern born. His part in this Chicago conference was to estimate future implications of present trends. He, too, considered the effect of changing proportions of adult and infant population. In 1850 there were 1,120 adults for each 1,000 children; in 1930 there were 2,013 adults. If at the present time we had that 1850 ratio we would not have merely 33,000,000 children to educate; we would have 63,000,000. This reduction of the proportion of children is going on. The tax on each adult if education costs per child remain constant will decrease. Productive labor is being taken from the shoulders of youth. We have the paradox that the decline in child population increases high-school and college enrolment. Those who are clamoring for a reduction of education in the higher grades should be urging the begetting of more children.

Professor Edwards's charts on child distribution were conclusive in support of state and federal aid to schools. The number of children born in the large cities lacks 20 per cent. of being sufficient to maintain a stationary population. In the town the deficit is 7 per cent. In the non-farming villages there is a surplus birth of 30 per cent.; on the farms the surplus is 50 per cent. No other nation has a mobility of population equal to ours. Born and raised in one community more of our people live elsewhere than is the case with any other country. As the whole argument for tax-supported education rests on the safety and welfare of the community, unless state and federal government more equitably distribute school moneys the danger of poor communities dumping their ill-educated population on other localities will become a serious menace. Moreover, this mobility requires a type of education preparing a youth for meeting different conditions than those of the place in which he spends his school days.

Professor Edwards's statistical demonstration that the education of the future must be much more definitely adjustable was impressive. Life is demanding a higher degree of intelligent skill. The day when muscle and common sense insured success has passed. Twenty-five per cent. of our workers are on jobs that did not exist ten years ago. This calls for vocational training emphasizing ability to tackle new problems instead of the present narrow, technical type of training.

Society is going collectivist. The burden of

training for social welfare and service will profoundly change the type of rollicking good-time selfishness common in high schools. It demands honest-to-goodness attention to the public weal.

### THE SCHOLASTIC WALL

Paul Voelker, Michigan's new state superintendent of schools, tells the Detroit Rotarians we are doing wrong by trying to smear scholarship and science on all the high-school boys and girls. Neither God nor the founders of the republic intended this. The high schools are bound by college entrance requirements. Less than two per cent. reach the college goal. Of these, one per cent. achieve high scholarship. Our teachers call a boy "dumb-bell" when he fails in mathematics or language. Charles Lindbergh was kicked out of Wisconsin University because he couldn't learn biology. But after he spanned an ocean and came back the hero of the hour the president of Wisconsin called him back and handed him a college degree. Our schools measure only scholastic intelligence. But what the country lacks is financial, economic, political, social, artistic intelligence. Between such and youth we have built the scholastic wall.

And, oh, Paul, in scores of towns in that beautiful state of yours are schools out of which have been ripped music, art and studies aimed at schooling economic, political and artistic intelligence. It has been done because your college-intoxicated school folks are spending their depleted funds to keep in repair the scholastic wall built from the blue prints of college requirements. *Si quaeris amoenam stupiditam circumspice.*

## MONTHLY SURVEY OF EDUCATIONAL BOOKS

*History This Generation Should Know.* "Robber Barons" is a startling title for biographies of "successful" Americans. You expect exaggerated stories of evil-doers and heated reproaches from a mind frenzied by a sense of injustice. Mr. Josephson goes quite a different road. His talent is for biography. He has done lives of Rousseau and Zola. He is strong in presenting a phase or movement or obsession of an epoch while making a story of people. The present volume[3] is an account of exploitation of American resources, material and human, from 1861 to 1901, forty years of fooling most of the people most of the time and of making the intended equality, life, liberty, happiness, perfect union, domestic tranquility, common defense, justice and general welfare a vanishing dream. The chief actors in this tragedy, Vanderbilt, Cooke, Gould, Fisk, Huntington, Stanford, Carnegie, Frick, Rockefeller, Hill, Harriman and Morgan, play here their picturesque parts again until the economic revolution is consummated and the stage holds a unified industrial society in the grip of a masterful hierarchy. A tribe of financial giants grew up, fought one another and learned the more remunerative value of union. They captured the industrial pass through which the commerce of the country flows. Entrenched there they have been as able to take toll of business as were the barons who planted their castles on the routes of trade.

Fascinating, wonderful, compelling admiration, were these American freebooters. While the productive labor in factories and farms, the movement of ships and railways present the picture of beautiful order, discipline and rhythm, following the regularity of days and seasons, the great exploiter puts them through a mad dance and comes out loaded with plunder. He must plan with clairvoyant foresight. He must move without faltering step, strike without mercy. He must show infinite resourcefulness, efficiency, sagacity. School teachers and preachers dilate upon his qualities. He is made a hero. The type of the successful baron of industry rose to a zenith of glory. He sunned himself in the admiration of public opinion. The press extolled him. He is presented as the high product of the land of opportunity. He is democracy's nobility, the self-made man.

The railroad presidents, the copper barons, the steel-masters and big merchants come into the rule of the nation, lay leaders of churches, trustees of universities, owners of newspapers, figures of fashionable society. They flood the elections with greenbacks and are boosted into

[3] Mathew Josephson, "The Robber Barons." Harcourt, Brace and Company, New York. 474 pp. $3.00.

the Senate. Professors in endowed universities see that Mr. Rockefeller and Mr. Pullman "are superior in creative genius to Shakespeare, Dante or Homer." Instructors who protest against the concentration of wealth find themselves out of employment.

If done in blank verse the story would be an epic of iron men crushing out the sap of liberty from the republic, changing the national hero from a Washington to an Insull, a Van Sweringen or a Henry Ford.

This man, Josephson, could write a gripping high-school text for these days—"How we got into this fix." For his paragraphs and chapters hang together. His theme stays on the ground of fact. His sense of civic values is in the cherished tradition of the statesmen who visioned the patriot dream. He is easy to recite from. Your pupils would not have to be prodded to study the lesson.

*Religion and These Times.* Dr. Niebuhr's[4] much-discussed review of this present stimulates and provokes. It sees no hope of economic salvation under the private ownership of productive processes.

The industrial oligarchy which controls society may contain those who are privately the kindest and most considerate of men, in which case they will do what they can to soften the inevitable injustice of their rule by personal generosities. The philanthropies of our overlords very frequently spring from an honest desire to alleviate human suffering. But the generosities of even the most sensitive do not extend to the point of yielding the sources of their power in the interest of a larger justice. If one should go this length his actions are resented by other members of his class.

There is something pathetic, says Dr. Niebuhr, about the simple confidence of our social scientists and preachers of economic righteousness in the redemptive power of their advice. They ascribe to disinterested ignorance what should be attributed to interested intelligence.

With illustrations from recent events the author contemplates the life and death of civilizations, the prophecy of doom, the brief glory of the business man, the social struggle here, fascism, individualism, Christianity, communism and barbarism in the spirit of vengeance.

[4] Reinhold Niebuhr, "Reflections on the End of an Era." Charles Scribner's Sons, New York. 307 pp. $2.00.

Attempts to perpetuate a dying system beyond its day such as we are now witnessing will increase manufacturing costs and lower living standards. They will be as inimical to a free exchange of ideas as to the free exchange of goods. Modern fascist Germany, striving to revive a dead system, controls all organs of propaganda and maintains hysteria.

It is the Niebuhr method to set readers to contemplation of large issues, to doubt that the author's own views will elicit general concurrence, but to reason matters through to a conclusion. In this case his verdict is that the liberal culture of the present time is unable to give guidance and direction to a confused generation which faces the break-up of a social system and the task of building a new one. To try to combine political radicalism with a historical interpretation of religion is bizarre and capricious. The place of religion in furnishing spiritual guidance in these times is the theme of the book as a whole.

*Cheer in American History.* Dr. Price,[5] social-science professor in Teachers College, Kansas City, has composed a moving history of American confidence as exhibited by national leaders and public behavior. He treats of optimism as a cultural product, a moving force, a legitimate aim of education, a collective wisdom transcending individual folly or foresight. Belief in America has changed the attitude of adverse critics. Its exponents survive in memory and fame. The pessimists fade out. The original democratic ideals recur in waves of popular feeling. Campaigns for abolition of poverty can not be stopped. Science works toward removal of obstacles. Art continues the pursuit of happiness.

American education is both a form and a fertilizer of optimism. We send ten sons and daughters to college for every one so provided for by Europeans. In 1930 our expenditure for education was half of the world's total. Horace Mann's contention that education is the supremest welfare of mankind has been accepted as a belief by the American masses. They hold that every boy and girl should have the education justified by the abilities of each.

The idea of democratic education is young. It is still more of an idea than a fact. The

[5] Guy V. Price, "Optimistic America." Western Baptist Publishing Company, Kansas City, Missouri. 297 pp. $2.25.

fuller it develops the capacities of the citizen, the more ably will it secure general welfare. The passing of the frontier has made educational opportunity a right more highly prized. The optimism that is embedded in the schools, rooted in effort toward a better society, is basic. Americans look on education as the sovereign civic remedy. It is for this reason that we are in a wide movement for extending schooling to greater numbers of adults. This is one of the most significant departures. Its greatest possibility is the interpretation of social trends by master-teachers.

The human spirit is taking fresh stock of its heritage. The measure of success is the nobility of human aims and the heroism of persistence, strong in will to strive, to seek, to find and not to yield.

Dr. Price is free from the gush of the "inspirational" address. His conviction of the value of optimism as a force that gets worthwhile things done is accompanied by a determination to present and resolve such despairs, sneers and cantankerous wailings as he can find. He interprets a kaleidoscope of speeches, editorials, broadcasts and writings of courage and doubt. He calls on the philosophers, the historians, the politicians, the educators, the scientists, the financiers, employers, labor leaders, ministers and croakers for the views they have printed. He connects these into an engaging narrative. He offers an exposition and defense of a great faith, a magazine of ammunition for the embattled schoolmaster.

*American Heroic Age.* Smith College History-professor Faulkner[6] makes of the sixteen years from 1898 through 1914 a stirring story of those who while America was making her fortune strove to keep her from losing her soul. You are favoring the study of biography as a means of building character. Here are the lives and deeds of men showing the stuff you want developed in the rising generation. Professor Faulkner tells this history in a style that will stir young and old. He is direct, exact and of unremittent holding power. His accounts of the deeds of U'Ren, La Follette, the first Roosevelt, Wilson, Hughes, Folk, Phelan, Tom and Hiram Johnson, Mark Fagan, Altgeld, Dewey, Brand Whitlock, Golden Rule Jones, Heney, Carrie Chapman Catt, Anna Howard Shaw, Elizabeth Cady Stanton and Ida Tarbell cover efforts that these present times need knowing more of. The flavor is of a sort of heroism as valuable in this crisis as the daring of the Adamses, Reveres, Ethan Allens and Marions.

Professor Faulkner covers the fields of big business, labor strivings, transportation tyranny, women's revolt, children's rights, religious changes, science struggles, health campaigns, economics and the new democracy. The service of the so-called muckrakers, the influence of the stage, of literature, of the arts and of education are given rightful prominence. The stoppage of the forward sweep in 1914 brings out vividly a new sense of the tragedy of the great war and the renewed strength it gave to the forces of evil that were breaking under an attack worthy of a heroic age.

*Brain-Trust Observations.* Nine timely essays by those whom the publishers call members of the brain trust and others[7] are those presented as lectures at Swarthmore College. They cover how codes are made, agriculture relief, labor programs, economic planning, business, monetary policy, international aspects and banking reform.

*The Social-Science Flavor.* Professors Hayes and Moon, of Columbia, with Professor Wayland, of Virginia State Teachers College, offer a history of the world in two books.[8] The first runs from the beginnings of civilization through the religious upheaval in Europe. The second begins with European expansion, treats of revolutionary foundations of present civilization, deals with Latin-American overturn, the growth and setbacks of democracy, and peers into the future. The Orient is given attention. The emphasis is upon the cultural, social and political doings of mankind. Each unit is summarized by review questions and

6 Harold Underwood Faulkner, "The Quest for Social Justice." The Macmillan Company, New York. 390 pp. $4.00.

7 A. A. Berle, Jr., John Dickinson, A. Heath Onthank, Leo Pasvolsky, Alexander Sachs, Herbert J. Tily, Willard L. Thorp, Rexford G. Tugwell, Leo Wolman, Clair Wilcox, Herbert F. Fraser and Patrick Murphy Nalin. "America's Recovery Program." Oxford University Press, New York. 253 pp. $2.00.

8 Carleton J. H. Hayes, Parker Thomas Moon, John W. Wayland, "World History." Book I, 911 pp. Book II, 912 pp. $1.60 each. The Macmillan Company, New York.

study helps. Pictures and maps abound. It is late historical research put into the form which long teaching experience has found able to hold interest and to make history real.

*Model for a State History.* I can see days of delight for the school children and teachers of Maryland when Ginn and Company's history of that old state[9] gets into their hands. Two Baltimore librarians with access to priceless archives and pictures, two teachers of history equipped with experience in late knowledge of unit technology, easy-word lists and lesson lore, combine to make a text that seems to me as near perfection as could be hoped for in this human world.

They carry a continuous and adventuresome tale from 1633, for three hundred years, to now. The story is gripping; the facts, interesting; the maps and pictures, profuse and delicious.

*Cherishing Old Houses.* The American Association of Museums has issued a beautiful volume[10] by its director describing and illustrating with handsome plates some of the famous American residences that are preserved and open to the public. An important feature of the volume is its counsel for the extension of the movement, suggestions for administration, finances, restorations, furnishings, collections, attracting visitors and interpretation. There are forty-eight pages of a list of historic mansions and dwellings arranged by states. There is a bibliography and index. Our historic sense, says Author Coleman, is awakening. Old houses are being treasured everywhere. The automobile is gratifying our desire to visit historic spots. Americans are taking afternoon tea in the old open houses or on the lawn. We are getting more quietly sociable.

*Morrisonic Meditations.* It is a red-letter day when a Henry Morrison book appears. Here comes another of the cogitations of this educational democrat.[11] The schoolmasters, teachers and students, he says, are keen to be told how to educate. What they most need is educational thinking, a valid understanding of what education itself is. They desire the instruments of navigation. They lack knowledge of destination. Like a ball and chain the "systems" of teaching clog our progress. The Jesuits in the seventeenth century developed a scheme of pedagogical procedure, with pupil performance, memoriter work, erudition, cupidity and emulation. Our schoolmastery is flavored with these conceptions. Every time we hear a recitation, record a grade, publish a class standing, award a prize or confer a degree, we are doing what the old Jesuit teachers would do if they were set down in this year of grace, if it is such. Every time we devise a standardized text, and most times when we put on a pedagogical experiment, we are trying how better to carry into effect the Jesuit system. They were supremely good schoolmasters, whatever we may think of their theory of education.

There is an epic quality to Dr. Morrison's progress here through history, biology, sociology and psychology. His discourse has singular dignity and beauty. It is everywhere clear and easy to read. The amount of material drawn from experiments and from writings of the moderns is extensive but always digested. What our human material is—physically, mentally and emotionally—spreads over these pages in a brilliant panorama, always with the educational implications discussed and illuminated.

For ages, notes the author, pretty much all intellectual attack on the problem of education was purely speculative and in general addressed to the issue, what education ought to be, rather than to what education is. Speculative theory easily degenerates into sheer mysticism. A ball is hung over a baby's crib "to awaken in the infant's dawning mind the idea of completeness." A creative education for children "struggling to be free" wants to re-create civilization without reference to fifty-thousand years of social experience. A choice bit of mysticism keeps bubbling up in the slogan "education is not preparation for life; it is life." It sounds good. We could say similarly of eating; it is not a means of sustaining life;

[9] Beta Kaessmann, Harold Randall Manakee, Joseph L. Wheeler, J. Montgomery Gambrill, "My Maryland." Ginn and Company, Boston. 424 pp. $1.32.

[10] Laurence Vail Coleman, "Historic House Museums." American Association of Museums, Washington. 187 pp. $2.50.

[11] Henry C. Morrison, "Basic Principles in Education." Houghton Mifflin Company, Boston. 452 pp. $2.50.

it is life. Growth is not an approach to maturity; it is maturity. The democratic platform is democracy. The promise to pay, is pay. Nevertheless, the education of childhood and youth is of necessity nothing but the preparation for right living in adult life.

My mental picture of dear old Jean Jacques Rousseau after his treatment by the Morrison soap and water is that of a seventeenth century horse doctor prescribing for a sick automobile.

Many a discussion of mental discipline and transfer of learning have I had to read in these ten years of reviewing educational books. If I were not afraid of being charged with using an outmoded Jesuit practise I would bestow a medal upon Sir Henry for the best discussion of these bugaboos in the fewest words.

Pretty well toward the end of the book I find this striking hint of the schoolmaster's real task:

Remoulding the world to meet the heart's desire would probably produce a world you wouldn't like. But the force of circumstances, which is and always has been the law, is inevitably and always forcing the individual into conformity with the general trend of all evolution; sometimes with misery to himself and disaster to society, sometimes—always in the long run—with happiness to himself and hence to society. It is as ridiculous to suppose that we can invent education or society as it would be to suppose that we could invent a new body or a body of natural law. Through understanding the educational process and obeying the law there is every reason to suppose that we can devise instructional procedures which will mitigate and in the end eliminate the misery which is otherwise inseparable from adjustment by variation and survival.

*Burton's Coup de Maitre.* It is strange that the doctor's and the lawyer's professional books are so much thicker than ours. Professor Burton's[12] conviction that a teacher is not equipped until he has studied sociology, psychology, biology, anthropology, economics, politics and the history of civilization is easily defended. The timidity of writers on education as shown by the shortness of their books is not fanciful. They know how transitory the place of teaching is in the conception of those who enter the ranks. Our author declines to baby his students. He says the profession requires hard study. The oversupply of candidates shows this to be the time to select those with the capacity and desire to make a real profession of teaching. If any one, he says, finds these lessons too hard, that is a pretty good sign that such a one is not needed as a teacher.

I'll say Professor Burton is over-critical of his own book. He has the knack of making hard parts interesting. His style is conversational. He assumes no expert knowledge in the reader. The presentation is uniformly that of a teacher who leaves no underbrush cluttering the trail.

The book announces its purpose as developing a scientific and philosophic attitude toward education, recognizing the problems and helping in their solution and depicting the education now current in the United States.

There is a gap between the advanced scholars of education and the teachers in the classrooms. The implications of the science and of the philosophy of education are not realized in teaching practise. Dr. Burton does not attempt to reconcile the various doctrines as some of your friendly expounders endeavor. At many places in the book he repeats this creed:

Education is a social science based on a philosophy.

It is the fundamental institution by which society and civilization guard and perpetuate themselves.

The individual is entitled to consideration according to his contribution to society. He attains happiness by supporting a community spirit aiming at the happiness of all.

This requires both discipline and freedom.

On this the author has built a commanding work, broad, critical, encouraging and constructive. It represents the intense labor of years. It entitles him to acclaim.

The organization of it is education, society and the individual; aims; values; education as a science; its methods; its philosophy; nine chapters on the origin, development and present nature of education in the United States; the curriculum; the pupil population; the laws of pupil growth; administration; guidance; vocational training; classroom practise; teaching as a profession; duties; working condi-

[12] William H. Burton, "Introduction to Education." D. Appleton-Century Company, New York. 833 pp. $3.00.

tions; funds; rewards; legal status; personal requirements.

There is in the chapter on aims a valuable list of changes in American society. Education is obligated to modify its practises because of them. Some of those emphasized by Dr. Burton are the relations of labor and employers, the threat to the standard of living, the complexity of finance not understood by financiers; the attempt at social planning, the overdose of nationalism, the entrance of government into business, the increase of political crookedness, greater control of government by self-seeking groups, decrease of understanding of government and participation in it by the average citizen, growing disrespect for law.

These changes, insists Dr. Burton, demand education for citizenship. Formal civics has proven worthless but persists. Alteration of the study is opposed by interests who do not wish the citizen to become too well informed about the inner workings of business and government.

The curriculum is covered in a masterly chapter. The American college originated as a training ground for preachers. The subjects thought necessary, Greek and Latin, have maintained a hold in spite of protests. Surrounded by a glamorous memory, supported by the prestige of great men who studied the old curriculum, the only one available, this core of the college curriculum has persisted, regardless of the fact that its purpose has disappeared. Latin is a vocational subject leading to the occupation of priest or Latin teacher.

There is an interesting account of algebra's entrance as a historical accident.

School boards forbid controversial subjects in the classroom. If this is to prevent propaganda it is right. If it excludes analytic, informative, judgment-forming discussion it is wrong. The school is society's instrument for bettering civilization. It is essential that the deficiencies of civilization be discussed.

These are problems which high-school pupils should consider from every side—capitalism; socialism; rugged individualism; cooperation; our forms of government, municipal, state, national; the acts of our political representatives, local and others.

From these samples you may see that here is no timid yesterday-book. The teaching aids in it, projects, readings and reports are ample and requiring your mind to come to judgment.

*Stopping Recitation Waste.* From the Laidlaws come three notably ingenious books of self-teaching in spelling, English and arithmetic.[13] The lesson is on one side of the page, next to it is the practise space with printed directions as to what the pupil is to do. At the end of each mastery unit is a score sheet for the pupil to set down his record. The teachers who prepared these manuals have transferred themselves, lesson by lesson, to a place at the pupil's side as he advances at his own gait independently of his faster or slower neighbor. Pupils mark their own or one another's papers. If difference of opinion arises the teacher decides. At the top of each page appears "The perfect score is 25. My score is ——." The pupil corrects his errors from the answers read by the teacher or furnished to the worker on the sheets issued to the school separate from the book. In the speller are provisions for use of the pupil's own misspelled words, for pronunciation, for drawing, for vocabulary development and other desirables. The English book involves oral and written composition descriptions and stories from pictures. It covers the commonly accepted essentials of the study. The arithmetic is designed to meet the demands of the more exacting courses of study retained in the stiffer schools, the courses that require elementary geometry, measurement of volumes and extraction of roots. You select or omit pages according to your radical or liberal theories. The material is based on an analysis of thirty different courses of study now used in the United States. Practise in fundamentals is distributed according to research on the difficulties of learners. Problem-solving receives more than usual attention. The pupil is not to be allowed to leave an exercise if his result is incorrect until he has found and corrected the error.

Each work is a complete text for the grade, requiring no other book. Any one who has noted the large aggregate waste of separate

[13] John C. Almack, E. H. Staffelback, "The Stanford Speller." 82 pp. 24 cents. N. J. Lennes, L. R. Traver, "Essentials of Arithmetic." 162 pp. 44 cents. Florence K. Ferris, Edward E. Keener, "Everyday English." 162 pp. 44 cents. Laidlaw Brothers, Chicago.

pupils' time resulting from recitation on the traditional plan will be impressed by the provision made here for keeping everybody at work.

*The High-School Principal To-day.* There is a notable freshness in the new book on high-school management put out by the American Book Company.[14] Both authors are specialists in secondary education on the faculty of New York University. The new conception of responsibility for all children of high-school age is accepted ungrudgingly as an opportunity for big public service. Get your out-of-school young folks into your orchestras, dramatic societies and other activities that will help them and the community at large. Belie the slam that high school is a private club. The whole town owns it. Break the tradition that alumni do not include former students who failed to graduate. The returning youths whom the depression is sending to you are worth receiving with more than a spirit of resignation. Treat them as homecomers. Make it worth their while to stay.

These authors find college domination and academic tradition among the worst retarders of the public service obligated on high schools by the source of their financial support from the taxed community whose main interests are not college preparation. These traditions, stereotyped into "high standards of scholarship," "departmental teaching" and "mental discipline," are hanging on too long in a society that has been unredeemed by them.

These two investigators believe that the high-school czar has retired voluntarily or perforce. His successor extends a welcome to the students to recognize the school as a community plant to be perfected by cooperating experiment and improvement. The folderol and make-believe self-government scheme, playing at passing laws and holding court, is passing out. Pupil assemblies and committees are deliberating and recommending business of the school, in which they have direct interest. Of course, a principal can settle everything. If he does he is missing a big chance to prepare his youngsters for cooperative government in town, county, state and nation. He is obstructing potential civic leaders of whom too few, God knows, are functioning with educated civic virtues in the out-of-school world. This is a great book, 689 pages. From its discriminating history of American high schools through its multiplicity of administrative duties, supervision of instruction, nature and needs of pupils, guidance, curriculum and personal traits of a worthwhile principal, it is specific, experienced, reasoned, documented, indexed and unafraid.

A refreshing frankness in admitting the backwardness of a large contingent of the high-school army is accompanied by timely warning of what will happen to them if they continue their haughtiness.

*Truth for Guidance.* Walter Pitkin[15] gathers the observations made by half a thousand business men, employers and a staff of thirty research assistants and makes a detailed summary of to-day's opportunities. He has made a survey that will be of priceless value to high-school principals, vocational advisers and school superintendents.

The boys and girls now in school may have to join the lost tribes already roaming in search of work, unless a different attitude of mind is taken by the oncoming generation. The standard of living expected—and not unreasonably—by their predecessors can not be attained. It would be a tragedy of disappointment and broken spirit if their parents and teachers let them go forth with the dreams of the pioneer days. Yesterday two big mistakes were made—the boys' hope for big money jobs, the girls' expectation of marriage into social prestige. Every sane observer knows that these fairy-tale rewards for hard work are not now attainable. The very rich and the very poor will continue to become middle-class in outlook and income. This, insists Walter, will make life better than it is and was. Everybody will be the gainer by living at the lower pressure that is coming. Shorter hours of work, easier tasks, earlier retirement in middle age, greater diversity in jobs and life will give the generation little wealth and more comfort and human friendliness.

Cheery philosopher Pitkin goes with his

[14] Philip W. L. Cox, R. Emerson Langfitt, "High-School Administration and Supervision." The American Book Company, New York. 689 pp. $3.00.

[15] Walter B. Pitkin, "New Careers for Youth." Simon and Schuster, New York. 236 pp. $1.50.

usual bluntness into the upsetting facts which threaten youth's sweet dream. There's no more room at the top. Every tempting employment is out of sight behind a swarm of applicants. There is a new struggle for existence. The dramatic leaps into fortune must be forgotten and a long up-hill pull expected. Present-day high-schoolers, as shown by canvasses, the author quotes, are of the opinion that there is a demand for engineers, architects, doctors and accountants. The appalling fact is that there is almost no chance in these fields. What was instilled into me in my school days and in turn spread by me, a generation later—that hard work and honest loyalty is sure to bring promotion to high place—has had so many disproofs even in the days of its universal preaching that I wonder the researchers have been so long showing the fallacy of it. Twenty-five years ago, I heard Washington Gladden, coiner of the phrase "tainted money," tell graduating high-school boys and girls that the "success" reward stressed in week-day and Sunday-school teaching is fallacious and wicked. Virtue, as was said of old, is its own only reward. Be good and you will be good; that is what must satisfy you. It is not true to say that you will be happy. The general can not say, "Fight and you will be happy." He says, "We must fight." The real man says, "I can do without happiness." Pitkin exhorts to this good doctrine of the old sages of the porch.

Educated in Ypsilanti schools, pretty good for their kind, graduated by Michigan University, he is no soft critic of the isolation of teaching from the real truth of community conditions. He counts fifty honor men from five universities who regret that ever they went even to high school. They are lost in bewilderment, unable to hold their own in a world which refuses to be what was expected. The more scholarly they are, the more bitter.

What the nature of employment is, the chances in each, are detailed. There are enough teachers available to fill for the next ten years all the vacancies that occur. The overcrowded fields are discussed; so are the promising occupations. The counsel on how to act in the different world that confronts us is reasoned carefully and with sympathy for the puzzled youth born to these trying times.

*Exercises in Pupil Self-Government.* In the public schools and in the University of Toledo Professor Jones has been experimenting for several years in leading young persons to get the feel of the orderly procedure on which the proper outcome of deliberative bodies in government depends. I have seen his high-school and college classes practising the intricacies of parliamentary law with a remarkable surety and unusual skill. Two manuals[16] by him are based on the belief that the public schools are obligated in a democracy to equip the citizen with ability to get expression of the public will from the public rather than from newspaper editors and party politicians. These books are lessons and practise in parliamentary procedure. They dramatize the meetings, give the actual working of chairman and group members in the various situations, explain why the rules are as they are, supply immediate access to authority by an ingenious arrangement of indexed sheets covering various contingencies and emphasize the duty of being prepared to conduct civic meetings in the community.

The questions that come up in school clubs, assemblies, pupil-participation schemes and so on furnish bases for the various lively exercises.

*Life and Letters of a Professor.* Memoirs and letters of Oscar Firkins, professor of comparative literature, University of Minnesota, portray the character of a critic, essayist, playwright, poet and teacher, a man of unique personality.[17]

Handicapped by shyness, suffering from imperfect eyesight, oppressed by failure in commercial and educational ventures, this boy of the middle west is discovered by the revered Maria Sanford, head of the rhetoric department of the University of Minnesota, who found his correction of student papers she had given him so well done that she pushed him into an instructorship. With a deficiency of self-assertion and push he rose by sheer merit to be the university's prize exhibit of scholarship and culture, a teacher whom ambitious students importuned for permission to enter his class. When William Archer, the English dramatic

16 O. Garfield Jones, "Junior Manual for Group Leadership." 91 pp. 80 cents; "Senior Manual." 124 pp. $1.00. D. Appleton-Century Company, New York.

17 Ina Ten Eyck Firkins, "Memoirs and Letters of Oscar Firkins." University of Minnesota Press, Minneapolis. 315 pp. $2.50.

critic, came to New York he said the one American he cared most to meet was Oscar Firkins. The Minnesota professor became dramatic critic of the *New York Weekly Review*. He followed Higginson as literary reviewer for *The Nation*.

In this volume Richard Burton furnishes an estimate and appreciation, attempting an understanding of this "gifted, strange and mysterious personality." Unable to use his eyes, Professor Firkins studied languages and foreign literature by the aid of his devoted wife, who read to him works in Greek, Latin, French, Spanish, Italian, Norwegian and Anglo-Saxon "while she did not understand a word in any of them."

Firkins's mother, wonderful woman, learned to read at five years of age. She was not allowed to have "Uncle Tom's Cabin," appearing serially in the family newspaper. The sheets were used to paper the walls of the kitchen. But little girl Ten Eyck read the story, although it was pasted upside down.

Netta Wilson furnishes an engrossing appraisal of Firkins as a teacher. He had a genius for imparting a vivid account of a whole book. He knew how to master extension and detail. He was an artist of epigram and aphorism, so spontaneous with them that any discourse of his without them would have been detected as a pose.

His class-discipline was strict and dignified with an atmosphere of mutual respect. There was no lateness, no slipping out early, no easy absence, no looking out of the window. Questions dropped on you without warning. On the first day everybody got a secret number. Oral corrections of themes were made by number. The other fellows could not enjoy hearing you wigged for they wouldn't know who number 14 was. Praise for work was given out by name.

Records of grades were secret, like professors' salaries. Hardly any one failed, strict as the requirements were, for everybody worked, including father. Rarely did he ask his classes to buy a book. When he used "Palgrave's Golden Treasury" he suggested a fifty-cent edition.

There are 219 pages of letters in the volume. They are on intimate personal matters, on European travel, on current happenings and policies, on the destiny of the Republic.

He writes the dean a letter explaining a negative vote on a girl's thesis. She had been attracted by "the new freedom" into a discussion of sex. "She is innocent," wrote the Professor. "But innocence launched on a sexual theme, when she is armed with courage but unfurnished with common sense, goes great lengths in the direction of the silly and the nauseous. She tells more than once that a sexual act is blameless when impulsive. She rather fondles the women who yield to physical desires. She is no more immoral than a parrot who swears. I do not think that naiveté which makes innocence the mouthpiece of license is entitled to a master's degree from an institution which stands for self-discipline rather than for unchecked impulse and which prefers a modicum of good sense even in its graduate students."

In a letter to a newspaper editor, Professor Firkins repudiates the assumption that the alleged unanimity of the faculty in calling for war-preparedness is significant. "In the first place, Dr. Burton is not with the majority. In the second place, agreement on such matter loses force in the exact measure of its completeness. Had only three fourths or, better still, only two thirds of the respondents concurred, the fraction would have been weightier than the total. A perfect consent points to docility or imitation. When all the wheat-stems in a field bend south that doesn't mean that each stem is choosing south. It means the wind is from the north."

There are 26 pages of short, pithy observations from Firkins's notebooks, on poetry, drama and literary masters. There are 22 pages of titles of books, plays and articles by this prodigious worker.

*Mother of State Universities*. The talent of condensing the archives of 116 years into 157 pages without making men and events into dried units in a herbarium is possessed by Wilfred Shaw,[18] so long a director of alumni relations with the University of Michigan that facts and figures come from him at the slightest provocation. He does give them a lively human interest. His history of the university, easily read at a sitting, is a moving story of educational pioneering, remarkable men, regrettable warfare and happy outcomes. Handsome drawings and

[18] Wilfred B. Shaw, "A Short History of the University of Michigan." George Wahr, Ann Arbor. 157 pp. $1.25.

impressive portraits embellish the book. Its analytic appraisal of the men who made the university the model of every state institution of higher education west of the Atlantic states is a high order of biography. Every one who knows anything of Michigan places Shaw himself among the master builders.

*Writing to See.* In a unique book for those who wish to become writers Mrs. Brande[19] has some remarkably effective exercises on using the eyes and the ears, how to make a familiar scene radiate new charms. The story-writer's reservoir is his unconscious mind. If you are not one who habitually puts impressions into your inner self you can learn to enrich your possessions. How to look and listen is detailed here with much skill. The book is expressly for those who want to write. As compared with the multitudes in high school the number having the longing for authorship is, as every prodding teacher of composition knows, so small that it would be as absurd to assume that the students are to be developed into writers as to hold that sculptors, painters or office holders are to be made out of all school children. Mrs. Brande's chapter on seeing to write seems to me to carry an unescapable implication, of which, considering her purpose, she properly says nothing. This is that writing in the manner she prescribes exercises for is a prolific means of sharpening observation. Thereby comes a fuller and richer life. This is one of the great aims of education, isn't it? I am bold to say that an English teacher who will apply in class work the remarkably sensible doings the maker of this book proposes for the aspiring literary artist will be generously repaid. Here are set forth the advantages of encouraging in yourself a duplex personality, of harnessing the unconscious, of working on schedule, of reading, of originality, of self-criticism, of rest and recreation and of many odd performances you never thought of. As a reader for publishers, a magazine editor and adviser to writers, Mrs. Brande gained an experience which is set out here in a decidedly taking style. Wonderful to say, it is a book on writing that writers endorse. Among the reviews that led me to send for it William Benet's calls it the best book he ever came across. Harry Hansen says he never read more valuable advice. The *Sun* review called it surely one of the most sensible manuals ever written.

*Literature Study as an Adventure.* Nine teachers have a hand in the beautiful anthology of poetry and prose which the Houghton Mifflin Company offer for the senior high school.[20] It is one of four literature books for the junior and senior organizations. It fulfils college-entrance requirements as to old English selections, includes the whole of "Henry Esmond," specimens from the principal literary masters of England and a wealth of questions, class activities, composition helps, tests, college entrance questions, library adventures and supplementary reading lists.

Comprehension is the first objective. The notes are at the bottom of the pages. To cultivate imagination there are questions of unusual import abounding. For encouraging a taste for reading on higher levels many suggestions have been interpolated. There are 72 pages devoted to a history of English literature. The authors indicate what selections need to be read for college entrance, what should be read intensively. There are hints at preventing the college requirements from stifling the growing love of literature and an abundance of jolly good stuff as antidote. All through the volume is the doctrine that reading should be an adventure.

The high schools are swamped with new pupils that are there because they must be. This book will make the stay of such more worth while.

*English as Actually Taught.* A detailed account of objectives, methods and results in English teaching in the University High School, Chicago, appears as monograph 4[21] of the publications of the laboratory schools of the University of Chicago. It is an exposition of corrective reading, elementary and advanced training in usage, English of community life, types of world literature, epochs, creative writing, plays and production, short story, novel, essay,

19 Dorothea Brande, ''Becoming a Writer.'' Harcourt, Brace and Company, New York. 148 pp. $2.00.

20 Thomas H. Briggs, Max J. Herzberg, Emma Miller Bolenius, Katherine L. Carey, George J. Crane, George W. Norwell, Bert Roller, Mellie John, DeWitt T. Starnes, ''English Literature.'' Houghton Mifflin Company, Boston. 770 pp. $2.12.

21 R. L. Lyman, Harold A. Anderson, Gladys Campbell, Edith E. Shepherd, Russell Thomas, Arthur E. Traxler, ''English Instruction in the University High School.'' University of Chicago Press. 178 pp. $1.50.

poetry, individualization of instruction, student publications, clubs, voluntary reading and kindred topics.

The study is especially valuable not only for full accounts of the methods found to be most effective but for the honest appraisal of promising ones that failed to meet expectations. Notable is the discussion of the lack of adequate tests of appreciation of good literature.

*Dickens in the Classroom.* The novels of Dickens averaged more than four hundred thousand words each. He could string description, conversation and sentimentality along page after page and charm readers with writing not at all vital to the story. The Victorian readers never felt this as a weakness in story-writing. Present-day Americans find some of Dickens's pages dull. Messrs. Graves and Paine[22] condense for school use David Copperfield so that two hundred thousand words give the story that Dickens told in five hundred thousand. The masterpiece is selected on account of the variety and fame of its characters, its pictures of social conditions and its humor. Mr. Paine, who directs the teaching of English in the schools of Elizabeth, New Jersey, selected the novel as a result of experiment with high-school classes and getting their votes that Copperfield was the most satisfying book of the course. He begins with a fourteen-page life of the author, gives hints on how to read him, and stresses his value as a delineator of social history. Footnotes explain words and allusions. For each chapter there are study questions in the manner of an experienced teacher more concerned with developing your opinion, enjoyment and taste than with grinding your industry and memory.

*Bright Idea in English.* Mr. Walter of the University of Michigan guessed two years ago that readers would like a yearly record of what America is saying. His thirty-six essays gathered during that year and printed in one volume proved him right. Here he comes again[23] with a collection that for variety, timeliness, importance and workmanship is proof that the editor knows who's who and what's what. Mr. Roosevelt, Mr. Lippmann, Dean Gauss, Mr. Gavit, Mr. Rorty, Sherwood Anderson are here. Politics, sociology, education, science, sport, music, biography, literature and art are represented. Each author is pleasantly introduced by the manager of the show.

*Leisure and the Little Theater.* The cheerfully persuasive recreation promoter, Mr. Perry,[24] of the Russell Sage Foundation, adds another volume to the bright library he is writing on what we can profitably do with our growing leisure. He finds 1,020 groups of Americans promoting little theater projects, wherefore he bids you rejoice. What plays do these people want? What do they get? How do they run their tournaments? What are college dramatic societies doing? The high-school clubs? How are the play-writing contests progressing? What are the most helpful books on stagecraft, costuming, makeup, acting, stage-managing, playwriting, property, pantomime, school and church dramatics? All these things Sir Arthur tells you in one small volume embodying a monumental job of canvassing the whole country for the facts.

*Art in College.* Somewhere in the attic is a parchment for which I paid $10 in 1886. It says I am a bachelor of arts. It doesn't say what arts. The courses we took to get that reward had nothing in them which in common speech, then or now, are considered to be in the art realm. However, the Association of American Colleges sends me a bright book[25] which shows that the mistake was mine in being born too soon. Ten years ago, say the authors, no other subject of importance was so generally neglected by colleges. In 1925 President Frederick Keppel of the Carnegie Corporation found collegiate art giving reason for encouragement and hope but none for satisfaction whatsoever.

There are 633 institutions in the United States covered by this report. Of these, 208 offer no art. This is 32 per cent. of the entire number. Of the men's colleges, 59 per cent. have no art. Of the women's higher schools, 86 per cent. offer art. What the 60 art courses are, how many of each are given, details of

22 Robert Graves, Merrill P. Payne, "David Copperfield." Harcourt, Brace and Company, New York. 490 pp. $1.00.

23 Erich A. Walter, "Nineteen-Thirty-Four Essay Annal." Scott, Foresman and Company, Chicago. 374 pp. 90 cents.

24 Clarence Arthur Perry, "Work of the Little Theatres." Russell Sage Foundation, New York. 228 pp. $1.50.

25 Archie M. Palmer, Grace Holton, "College Instruction in Art." Association of American Colleges, 111 Fifth Avenue, New York. 62 pp. $1.00.

their presentation, the outlook for the future, and the association's art program are treated extensively.

*Art in Daily Life.* Two college women[26] have prepared a sumptuously illustrated book on objectives and methods in art for every one. Their purpose is improvements in personal appearance and in home surroundings. Their list of abilities aimed at are singularly clear and well organized. There is a fine chapter on creating an interest. By treating the lessons as problems and by bringing into art teaching the new and approved procedures that are revolutionizing school subjects they are performing a pioneering work in a subject that has long been a beggar at the schoolhouse door. Balance, proportion, repetition, rhythm, line, emphasis, color, clothing, home-furnishing, stage-setting, costuming and kindred topics are discussed and made the basis of remarkably educative exercise.

The authors appeal to the teacher to know what she is after in the case of each learner and to so present the problems that they become a challenge to the pupils' best thinking and manipulative efforts. The problem is not an end but an educative force. So make it.

*Art as Personal Interpretation.* Miss Parker writes alluringly of the enrichment of life by art.[27] Your instincts and sensibilities are good guides. The books on esthetics contradict one another. Construct your own theory. Try some form of expressing yourself artistically. Art releases energy, forces and tranquilizes it. Children draw pictures with great satisfaction, though you can not see the sense nor beauty in their productions. The book is an answer to the cry of spiritual starvation and reveals the satisfactions derivable from art in its various forms.

*A New Summary of Alcohol.* Laws requiring that the effect of alcohol on the human body shall be taught are still part of the statutes of many states. Whether they are obeyed or not, a concise, modern, popular exposition of facts is a boon to every one in charge of the growth and information of the generation. A former health commissioner of New York, now professor of public health in Columbia University,[28] Dr. Emerson concludes his informative and easily comprehended little book with the observation, "If the school children are taught facts about alcohol as these are known from scientific and experimental services of the medical and social sciences they will be in a position to determine a rational personal and political attitude toward beverage alcohol. They can thus avoid the extremes of partisanship, the pitfalls of exploitation of voters and the misinterpretation of knowledge by commercial interests and the press. These have made a pitiful exhibition of our people during the last twenty years."

The author restricts himself to physiology. The morals of the problem he leaves to others. Those of us, he says, who grew up in the nineteenth century under misinformation, extravagance of expression, biased and fanatical teaching of the effects of alcohol need the balanced and reliable statements which modern medical science offers.

In the press, among politicians, among economists, clergy and men of business, contradiction of fact is the rule. What alcohol does to the body isn't now to be settled by opinion or speculative authority. Laboratory records are available to put conclusions on a strictly quantitative basis. These data have brought to a unanimity of opinion physiologists, dietitians, immunologists, clinicians, psychologists and psychiatrists.

There are thirty-seven essentials in foods. Alcohol is not listed among them. It is excluded from the diet of persons requiring skill, accuracy, rapidity or muscular response. It is not advised by physicians for the diet of healthy persons of any age. It is a drug and, if unsuitably used, a poison. It creates a temporary sense of well-being. The physician prescribes it to release the body from dangerous inhibitions, not for the stimulation of other functions. In whatever amount taken it is not a digestant, a gastric tonic or a stimulant to digestion. It is dangerous in cases such as obeying traffic signals, operating machinery or transportation dependent on other than well-trained animal power. Students of automobile accidents are seriously recommending suspension of licenses of persons known to have driven a car within four hours after taking an alcoholic drink. Forty-six per cent. of adult persons dying from accidents are alcoholic at the time of injury.

26 Mable Russell, Elsie Pearl Wilson, "Art Training through Home Problems." The Manual Arts Press, Peoria, Illinois. 214 pp. $2.85.

27 Lockie Parker, "Art and People." The John Day Company, New York. 126 pp. $1.75.

28 Haven Emerson, M.D., "Alcohol, Its Effects on Man." D. Appleton-Century Company, New York. 114 pp. $1.00.

It is injurious in the case of snakebite. In no amount is it necessary for life. Even moderate drinkers die earlier on the average. A cocktail before meals is deleterious in its immediate and after effects. It costs a staggering amount of public money in the care of persons who from its use are put in hospitals, jails, asylums and poorhouses. These facts Dr. Emerson establishes from records and averages.

What is left? Strong drink makes one feel other than what he is—either cheerier or more depressed, braver or more cowardly, sillier or more dignified. It gets a dull after-dinner speaker applauded by a muddled audience that can't think. It appears to be the great fooler. Such is the curious working of the American mind that resentment against the exaggerations of reformers drive a large multitude of the population into refusal to face the implications of demonstrable fact.

*Self-Teaching in Biology.* James Peabody taught biology in the Morris High School, New York, in such a manner that the state high-school commissioner caused the subject, using the Peabody syllabus, to be a required course in the schools of the commonwealth. Truthful James has translated his teaching methods into a manual by which the high-school students mostly teach themselves.[29] It fits into Mr. Peabody's school text-book. It is constructed on the problem method. It requires independent observation and thought. It expects pupils to progress at different rates. It has detachable leaves enabling the teacher to take out those needed at the time. It requires the application of drawing. It involves some valuable exercises in self-analysis.

*Romance in Real Chemistry.* Oberlin Chemistry Professor Holmes' chronicles of laboratory discoveries[30] has the swing of an adventuresome saga. It is composed for laymen and handles the subjects they listen to with eagerness when some one who knows and is not handicapped by technical terms can be questioned. Chemist Holmes has the Tyndall-Huxley talent for preserving the fascination of the true story. The very titling of the chapters is alluring; the lightest substance known, the elixir of life, brimstone or cornerstone, chaining the sun, the house of the future. These are archives of the chemists' battles to outwit the forces of nature and improve them. This appears to be the age of chemistry more than it is the machine era. Wrong distribution of profits, overproduction, menace of leisure threaten us, warns Dr. Holmes, but the cause is not the advance of science and invention. A ten-year moratorium of scientific research would be absurd. In his detailed account of chemical warfare the author declines to become excited over any alleged menace by chemistry. This is an excellent school library book in aid of the science teacher.

*Curious Facts in Electric Service.* From the title of Mr. Mills's book[31] you would hardly expect the engaging stories that fill it. But if you knew the author as previous writer of "Letters of a Radio Engineer to His Son," "Within the Atom" and "The Realities of Modern Science," you would expect here something choice. You'll have it. He talks of the vivisection of speech in the electrical laboratories and of the discoveries aiding mechanical reproduction of sound. He describes electrical brains, extension of the senses, television and a great many of the problems and triumphs of the electrical engineer.

*Notable Sex Book.* Mrs. Strain,[27] in her treatment of how to meet the normal sex interests of children and how to guide these instincts from infancy through adolescence, has done a fine piece of work for parents, teachers and social workers. She is clear, sympathetic, dignified and far-seeing. She proposes a normal, constructive, natural approach to the knowledge children are keen to possess and which they will get in undesirable and injurious form unless those obligated to give them proper training undertake the duty. Mrs. Strain shows how the obstacles to proper teaching may be removed. She knows mental hygiene. She expounds a method of escape from emotional conflicts and sexual maladjustments in later life. She gathers a hundred common questions and answers them frankly. She treats of the love impulse, learning social standards, playground problems, vulgarities, explaining birth and babies, sex delinquencies, and so on. It is a sound, sane, scholarly book based on science, medicine and a wide experience in teaching.

29 James Edward Peabody, "Work Test Book in Biology and Human Welfare." The Macmillan Company, New York. 158 pp. 40 cents.

30 Harry N. Holmes, "Out of the Test Tube." Ray Long and Richard R. Smith, New York. 373 pp. $3.00.

31 John Mills, "Signals and Speech in Electrical Communication." Harcourt, Brace and Company, New York. 281 pp. $2.00.

32 Frances B. Strain, "New Patterns in Sex Teaching." D. Appleton-Century Company, New York. 250 pp. $2.00.

# SCHOOL AND SOCIETY

**WITH WHICH ARE COMBINED THE EDUCATIONAL REVIEW, ESTABLISHED IN 1891, THE TEACHERS MAGAZINE, ESTABLISHED IN 1878, AND THE SCHOOL JOURNAL, ESTABLISHED IN 1874.**

Volume 40 | Saturday, September 8, 1934 | Number 1028

## THE SECOND-HAND TEXT-BOOK BUSINESS

By Professor L. L. BERNARD

WASHINGTON UNIVERSITY

In the summer of 1933 a special committee of the American Association of University Professors, of which I was chairman, made a study of the second-hand text-book jobbing business as it affects a number of educational and scholarship matters. This study has been continued since the report of 1933, and further supplementary studies are now in process. A great deal of interest in the results of the investigation has been manifested by professors, authors, publishers and book dealers. It seems desirable, therefore, to publish a brief summary of the findings to date. Other findings will be published by the investigators as interest and results seem to justify such action.

Within the last few years the business of selling second-hand college text-books from large central stores through mail order channels has grown to large proportions. This is not a new business, but its present magnitude is new. Nearly forty years ago a New York firm, Hinds and Noble, issued a fairly voluminous catalog of second-hand text-books and apparently did a profitable business. There are now at least five of these large mail-order jobbing businesses, three of which are located in the Middle West and two in the East. Some of these firms advertise more than half a million volumes in stock. Their sales have grown to such proportions that they have made serious inroads upon the publishers' sales of new books and have in some cases cut the royalties of authors to a minimum. The depression since 1929, with consequent hard times, is thought to have aided the second-hand text-book sales at the expense of sales of new books by the publishers. Both publishers and authors are restive under this condition, and in many cases even teachers have made serious complaint because of the increased use of second-hand text-books. The following summary will present the chief findings of our investigation as the professors see the matter. Future articles will give the view-points of the publishers, the book dealers and the students.

1. Forty-five per cent. of those professors answering the question regarding the effects of the second-hand text-book jobbing business upon student work reported that they had observed no appreciable effect of the business upon student efficiency. One sociologist reported a "lack of uniformity and quality of information received from the texts." Another said, "Class preparation frequently suffers by reason of the delay experienced by students who seek to obtain second-hand copies from jobbers, often to find their search fruitless and the time wasted." A teacher of French responds: "In language study, serious demoralization. Translations written between the lines often corrupt the student's habits of work. Expecting to sell the text, the

student does not put into it the notes he needs.'' A social science teacher complains that students owning second-hand text-books frequently depend on marginal notes and do not read the text consistently. Another language teacher reports that he and other instructors in his department change their text-books yearly in order to preclude the use of interlined second-hand copies by their students, but that the handling of second-hand texts purchased from the jobbers by the local book store has rendered this means of protecting the student ineffective.

2. Only 20 per cent. of the correspondents had observed no effect of the second-hand text-book jobbing business upon student preservation of text-books. Fifty per cent. of the replies stated that it increases the tendency of the students to dispose of their books once their class work is finished. A political science teacher comments favorably upon this fact as follows: ''(a) The student who would in any case make use of his textbook for future reference probably even now does not sell it. For the others, the pin-money received from the sale of the book, no doubt, contributes more to the happiness of mankind than would a forgotten book in an attic or a basement. (b) To the student who buys the second-hand copy, the saving in money may be of significance. (c) It is to be remembered also that a very large number of text-books, by their very nature, are pretty close to useless to the student who has completed the course. The text-book is a means or a tool to an end. You will readily recall a number of *required* courses in which the textbook is neither of use nor of interest to the student who has completed the course and whose chosen field is far removed from that of the required course.'' A language teacher takes the opposite view, saying, ''Under temptation of ready money, students sell grammars needed for future college courses, not to mention of essential value as part of the library of a cultivated person.'' A dean of engineering states that he knows of ''several cases where books have been sold which will be needed for reference in later courses.'' Another teacher regards the effect as detrimental and expresses the belief that final comprehensive examinations at the end of the four-year course would stimulate the student somewhat to retain his text-books. Several correspondents speak of the practise of jobbers having representatives at their colleges at the close of each session buying up as many books as they can obtain, sometimes offering as little as ten cents a copy, a price which is frequently accepted by the student at that time of year.

3. Only one person expressed a ''doubt whether the appearance (entrance into business) of the jobbers has had any noticeable effect'' upon publishers' sales. Others estimated the effect from a ''moderate decrease'' to ''disastrous.'' This is of course a matter about which the publishers can speak most intelligently, and the reader is directed to communications on this point from the publishers included in a later article.

4. One teacher reported ''no information'' as to the effect of the second-hand text-book jobbing business upon authors' royalties. One expressed doubt on this point. All others agreed that there is an unfavorable effect, one correspondent—not the one mentioned above—characterizing it as ''disastrous'' and another estimating it at a 50 to 75 per cent. reduction in royalties. Another complained that the effect was such that in most cases the author's compensation no longer justified him in undertaking the expense of preparing the text-book.

5. Fifty-five per cent. of those answering this question were of the opinion that the ablest men are not discouraged from preparing text-books by the activities of

the second-hand text-book jobbing business. One man believes that it will have a favorable effect. He says: "It seems not to have been a barrier thus far. The present system may even have the advantage of discouraging the mediocre from entering very largely into the textbook field, since only the very best books (written by the best men) can be made profitable." Another correspondent takes a less optimistic view, stating that "a good man has frequently preferred to give lectures, go into administrative work, etc., rather than write the text book which he could have done better than anyone else." Another correspondent says, "My impression is that publishers have lately encouraged the more popularized writings of the second-rate men."

6. In reply to the question as to the influence of the second-hand text-book jobbing business upon the financial security of the publishers, one correspondent said "none," one said "slight," another advised, "Let the publishers take care of themselves." A fourth replied at length as follows: "My impression is that there need be no worries on this score. Some publishers, in order to get a book in a particular field in which good books are already available accept very mediocre or even poor manuscripts and as a consequence suffer heavy losses. These they hope to counterbalance by larger profits from some of their better books. The extensive use of second hand copies keeps these additional profits lower. But considering the whole situation, the publishers can be safely trusted to hold their own." Several correspondents mentioned recent failures and mergers of publishers and another "the pooling of advertising by four large publishing houses" as evidence of adverse effects. A majority of those answering considered the effects as adverse.

7. Three teachers replying ventured no opinion on the question as to the effect upon the collateral publication of books of research. Two were inclined to consider the effect negligible. A large majority considered it seriously discouraging. One of the writers made a variety of observations on this matter which are presented as follows: "If publishers made more profits on textbooks and authors received larger royalties, then publishers could afford to publish books of research at a very small profit or even at a loss and authors could afford to accept contracts with little or no royalty. (a) Textbook writers and research book writers are not necessarily the same persons. (b) Nothing in the whole history of publishers supplies any basis for assuming that publishers would be inclined to strike such a balance between textbooks and books of research. (c) Why should the students be the ones to pay for the publishing of these research volumes? In my opinion, what is much needed right now is to find a way of reducing the price of textbooks for students."

8. Opinion seems to be about equally divided between those who hold that the second-hand text-book jobbing business has stimulated revisions as a means to the outwitting of second-hand dealers and those who hold that publishers are afraid to bring out new editions in the face of the extensive use of second-hand editions, some of them long out of date. Apparently these two groups of correspondents have in mind two different classes of text-books, the former referring to those having sufficient popularity or being used in such large classes as to justify revisions in spite of or because of second-hand competition and the latter referring to a class of text-books with such a small normal demand as to render revision in the face of second-hand competition a highly doubtful policy. A few correspondents were inclined to believe that there was no appreciable effect upon revisions because of the competition of second-hand books.

9. Again, opinion was about equally di-

vided as to the effect of the second-hand business upon the prices of new books, with a small minority opining that there was no effect. One of the strong partisans for the second-hand jobbers remarked: "Here appears the vicious circle. The second hand book trade gained momentum because publishers insisted upon unreasonably high prices. The sale of used copies has cut into the sale of new copies and forced the publishers to raise the prices still higher." Another teacher says, "Large sales of second-hand books must have the effect of increasing the price of new offerings, since the publisher will want immediate returns to reimburse the cost of printing and advertising." One editor of a text-book series says that the competition of the second-hand jobbers "raises the price outrageously."

10. There seemed to be no definite information among teachers as to the effect of the second-hand market upon the price of second-hand text-books. Fifty-five per cent. of the replies expressed no opinion. Fifteen per cent. ventured the opinion that there was no effect. Twenty-five per cent. held that the prices were increased, and 8 per cent. that they were lowered. The statements of store managers on this point were also conflicting.

11. All but two persons replying found themselves unable to express an opinion or to give facts regarding the effect of the second-hand text-book jobbing business upon the decentralization of educational publishing. One of these said there is no effect and the other doubted if any connection could be established. The publishers, however, appear to hold the opinion that it helps to promote local publication and the mimeographing of texts.

12. The most commonly expressed opinion was to the effect that publication of new books is reduced by the competition, but three of the correspondents were convinced that there is a counter movement to stimulate publication of new books to circumvent the second-hand book jobbing trade. One correspondent said that the search for new texts, sometimes hastily prepared, was replacing the urge to bring out new editions as a more effective method of meeting competition.

13. The teachers voted at a ratio of five to two that the second-hand text-book jobbing business should be discouraged. Those opposed to the business stated such reasons as the following: "In the interest of student learning."

"I believe that jobbing of used books that have reference value, such as technical books, should be discouraged, for the reason that persons interested in these books for study purposes will need them so long as they continue to pursue the subject." "It would be better not to encourage this. Interferes with the choice of books. I have wanted to make a change in a text but a supply of new copies in the bookstore has stood in the way. They have not sold because of 2d-hand books." "In our language studies we do not like to use marked texts, and condemn and avoid them as much as possible." "It may become . . . a nation wide corruption." One dean of Liberal Arts reports that he had been compelled this year to deal with "an epidemic of textbook stealing" from students' rooms, the motive of the thieves being to sell the books for cash to the representative of the jobbers on the ground at the end of the school year.

14. Those opposed to discouraging the second-hand jobbing business offered such reasons as the following: "If second hand trade conserves human energy and facilitates communication why should we oppose it even if capitalistic enterprise suffers?" "Helps students to economize during the depression." "Good, if the students are given the benefit of the reduction in prices." "Puts text books in every student's hands."

15. Teacher proposals for the discouragement of the second-hand text-book jobbing business ran as follows: "The school might require the purchase of new books by a class order. However, this is obviously unenforceable. The publishers must handle the problem." "Publishers might undertake the jobbing of second hand texts themselves." "There are two ways by which the present development of the second-hand trade can be minimized: (1) by having teachers impress upon students the desirability of keeping books for reference purposes, in cases where the books have permanent value; (2) by an agreement among book stores operated under school or university auspices to refrain from organized participation in the trade. In the case of ———— University, representatives of second-hand concerns are given accommodations during their periodical visits, and the University Book Store itself buys and sells used books. Such practice certainly tends to stimulate traffic of this sort. In correspondence with the McGraw-Hill Book Co. about a year ago, I suggested the possibility of an agreement among publishers to deal in second-hand books in much the same way that automobile manufacturers have been forced to deal with the used-car problem. The two situations have much in common." "It seems to me that much could be done by reducing the prices of books. I can see no particular virtue in the high-priced bindings of texts since they are more or less ephemeral. If they were put up in paper covers they would serve the purpose and then would not be such attractive wares for the jobber and they would not sell at second-hand very well. Books for libraries should be made as at present and then a certain percentage might be offered for sale to students who are interested in keeping the books. The high-grade bindings of the present make the books last and we cannot blame the students for turning them into ready cash. In this way the price ought to be reduced sufficiently to do away with much of the desire to buy or sell the second-hand volumes. I have decided to use a book no more than two years, no matter if it is entirely satisfactory in order to avoid the second-hand problem. But even there I may be defeated for some administrations will not permit a change of texts until the bookstore shelves are cleared of the one in use. A more liberal return privilege by publishers would help this situation." "The best method is to get the local dealers to refuse to purchase second hand books and for teachers to encourage students to keep them." "(1) By using new texts, (2) by changing textbooks often and urging bookstore to buy only new texts."

16. Fifty-five per cent. of the professorial correspondents favored the publishers entering into the second-hand book business, if it should prove to be practicable, and all but one of these favored the payment of a 5 per cent. royalty to the authors on resales. He was of the opinion that such a procedure would prove to be too complicated to be workable. One correspondent argued: "(a) Certainly the object of low priced textbooks for students would not be achieved by this method. (b) Would such a plan cause publishers to delay unreasonably new editions? Would there be a temptation to profiteer both for the publisher and the author?" Another correspondent expressed himself as absolutely opposed to publishers entering the second-hand jobbing business, but he gave no reason for his stand. The other correspondents expressed no opinion.

17. About one third of the correspondents favored in theory the establishment of their own book stores by the publishers as a coercive measure to bring the local book stores around to a more favorable plan of cooperation with them. A fair majority of the answers expressed the belief that such a measure would not prove to be profitable to the publishers.

18. A text-book rental system controlled

by the publishers appeared to the teachers to be even less practicable than did the plan for publishers' stores.

19. Neither was there much expectation that practicable arrangements between publishers and local bookstores could be made, since the book stores' profits on second-hand books are so much greater than on new books. One teacher reports that on going into the local book store just before classes started in the fall he found nothing but second-hand books on the shelves for one of his large courses. He asked the attendant, "Where on earth did you get all of those second hand books?" "We collected them all the way from Missouri to California," she replied proudly. The text in question was his own, and he could not share the attendant's elation, because he would get no royalties on the 150 second-hand copies. Another correspondent states, "Complaint is made here that the agents (of the publishers) are more concerned about finding new manuscripts than in discussing sales progress with the book store." A number of correspondents suggested that the publishers should take back unsold copies, and another points out that this practise might prove ruinous to the publishers unless the local book stores would agree not to sell second-hand books in competition with the new books.

20. Suggestions for securing student cooperation were somewhat various. One answered, "Nothing but information." Several suggested that students might be urged to keep their books for future reference and to build up libraries. Others thought that nothing could be done. One suggested an appeal to the spirit of fair play and especially a student discount. Another proposed that "faculty members should insist that students buy new and up-to-date texts." A few correspondents expressed great hopes from student-faculty cooperative stores that would boycott the second-hand book jobbers. Another still was quite cynical about the interest of students in the larger questions of the promotion and rewarding of publishers and authors for their services and declared that they are concerned chiefly with getting text-books at the lowest prices possible. Another said that the frequent revision of text-books has convinced the student that it is useless and even stupid for him to preserve his text-books for future reference, since they will soon be out of date. Still another wrote at length in a somewhat similar vein: "With the rigid rules relative to the return of unsold books which means loss to the stores they are inclined to look out for number one. Often they under-order and then students find 2d-hand books. If the seriousness of the situation were presented from the various angles they would probably co-operate. They have a case also. College papers publish articles on the 'text-book racket.' They accuse professors of revising too often merely to get their royalties." "A fair presentation would be given consideration by them. College papers can do much to present the situation."

22. Three general comments by teachers seem to be worth quoting under the heading of further suggestions, since they represent three points of view that are rather frequently expressed. The first may be regarded as a "safe policy" comment: "Frankly I do not see any practical program for dealing with this situation. Moreover it is important to be properly considerate of the student's view point and need. Even in good times it is possible to press students too hard in the matter of buying books. On the other hand, I regard it as very desirable to cultivate the habit of owning certain books and building up a personal library. I believe the best thing professors can do is to point out the advantages of this and encourage personal own-

ership of important books but avoid anything that smacks of pressure. In relation both to students and to dealers, I think that authors and teachers can easily stir up antagonisms which will injure their interests far more than they will help. It may be, however, that someone can devise a practical plan which will be of advantage to all of us." The second represents the "competitive" view-point: "The publishing houses must in the last analysis determine the extent of the menace to their business. If the menace is serious, they have no option but to get in the game on their own account." The third implies that the trouble is fundamental to the present economic order: "The problem is part of the general chaos and absurdity of a profit economy and is probably insoluble as long as this economy is retained."

# EDUCATION AND SOCIAL CHANGE

By Professor DAVID SNEDDEN

TEACHERS COLLEGE, COLUMBIA UNIVERSITY

(1) THE query "Should education *follow* or *lead* social change?" is often heard among educators these days, and occasionally even from faculty members of Teachers College.

When thus broadly stated this query is probably no less futile than such other naïvely stated problems as: "Which comes first, the chicken or the egg?"; or "Which is mightier, the pen or the sword?"; or "Which is more important, heredity or environment?" Nevertheless, there are certain issues implied by the query which deserve close consideration by constructive thinkers who are seeking to extend the functional efficiencies of school and college educations.

(2) The term "social change" will be taken here to include any and all inventions, religious innovations, political reconstructions, novel philosophical theories, popular movements, natural cataclysms, and the like, which presently or ultimately affect profoundly the conditions and behaviors of large numbers of human beings. Hence, the appearance of great innovating or organizing leaders—Pericles, St. Paul, Constantine, Mohammed, Saladin, Ghenghis Khan, Rousseau, Darwin, Marx; or of signal discoveries—iron, the compass, printing, gunpowder, bacteria, steam power, electric power, photography; or of "movements" of or among peoples—Teutonic migrations, Crusades, destruction of feudalism, American colonization, rise of business corporations, French Revolution; or even more glacial-like trends—industrialization, falling birth rates, spread of democracy, decay of orthodox creeds, emancipation of women, growth of public education—will all be taken as at least symptoms and evidences, if not as "causative" agencies, of important "social changes."

It is important, too, to give separate consideration in our thinking to the visible primary and to the inferred secondary effects of particular changes. The "spreads" of Christianity, Moslemism and Protestantism very visibly involved profound *religious* (social) changes. But, less visibly, they seem to have also involved political, economic, racial, familistic, cultural and other profound, even if less tangible, secondary or derivative social changes.

And it is widely believed by social scientists, though the evidence is often still very obscure, that striking *economic* changes—capture of trade routes by Greeks, Romans, Venetians, Portuguese and English in succession; inventions of McCormick reapers and railways; development of the limited-liability business corporation; evolution of scientific agriculture and the like—often have profound secondary political and even religious and cultural effects.

(3) Of most importance for the problems to be considered in this paper is the fact that in large proportions of the social changes which become important in history at least three phases, functional conditions or stages may very commonly be distinguished: (a) First, there is an innovating discovery, personality, event or other seemingly unique inciting cause. (b) Second, there is a limited social area of persons or conditions which seem nearly "ripe" as soil for the acceptance, promotion or "growth" of the social change. (c) Third, there is the world at large, including often vested interests opposed to the change, throughout which the innovations spread slowly or rapidly, according to a variety of conditions which can usually be understood only in close relationship to particular case situations.

The realistic student of social changes can well search for these phases or stages in historic and contemporary events: Karl Marx, mining and factory proletariat, political socialism or communism; Luther, German burghers, world-diffused Protestantism; Darwin, intellectuals, present-day intellectual liberalism; Pasteur, a small contingent of applauders, all modern biological science; Sarajevo, Slavic and German jealousies, the World War; Baden-Powell and South Africa, middle class parents, the Boy Scout Movement; Booth, slums, Salvation Army.

Various interesting evolutions can be analyzed, and even forecasts made, by curious minds as they survey actual present-day or prospective "social changes" incited by: The inventions of the Wright brothers; the preachings of Margaret Sanger; the teachings of John Dewey; the leadership of Mussolini; the inventions of radio; the U. S. annexation of the (Panama) Canal Zone; the defeat of Hughes in California in 1916; the development of the "holding" corporation; the inceptions of Mormonism and Christian Science; the invention of the gas-engine; the beginnings of rubber cultivation in the Orient; the leadership of Ghandi; and hundreds of others.

(4) Now in considering "education" (as the widely dispersed functionings of schools and colleges immediately directed by teachers and professors) and social change it is obvious that few if any tangible interconnections can be traced as between purposed school educations in the past and the inciting events or personalities involved in the "first stages" referred to above.

In other words, "social changes" are commonly "started" by inventors, profound thinkers, highly "wilful" personalities; by catastrophic events; and occasionally by "accidents"—as in some of Creasy's "Fifteen Decisive Battles."

Of course a particular educator or the innovations of particular educators may at times figure among these "matches to magazines." But the social sciences give us no justification to look to armies of educators in the past or under any conceivable conditions in the future for such innovations any more than to armies of priests, merchants, artists, mechanics, peasants, engineers or military leaders.

Even where conditions favor the selective grouping of highly talented persons—as in medieval monasteries, modern universities, gigantic business corporations, metropolitan newspapers, etc., striking innovations seem seldom to originate from among these. (How seldom, for example, do university faculties, even in our day, produce great innovating writers, inventors, explorers, quasi-fanatical theorists, Messiahs or political leaders?)

Hence any notion that school teachers in large numbers—to say nothing of the ''educations'' they are employed, authorized or permitted to give—could collectively originate any significant social changes seems sociologically preposterous.

(5) But let us now jump to the third of the phases or stages of social change referred to above. That is, after innovations or changes have been launched by particular persons or discoveries or events; and after these innovations have been easily, perhaps gladly, accepted by limited contingents representing, as it were, fully prepared soil; the stage of wide diffusion of the beneficial features of such changes, often against opposed vested interests, and frequently in the face of lethargic indifference.

In this third area, obviously, schools and teachers in schools have great opportunities and responsibilities. More than that: large proportions of the alleged or actual aims of schools and educators down through the ages have been directed towards realization of just such ends. Once this approach is appreciated, each reader of these lines can adduce numerous striking examples. For example:

(a) A handful of innovating American ''rebels'' in 1776 led a political revolt in order to obtain political liberty and rights of self-government. They found at least a strong minority of the ''colonials'' ready to follow, to fight, to accept the new doctrines and practises. After winning the revolution, willing beneficiaries thereof used various school educations to extend and hold their gains through a hundred years to come.

(b) First one and then a few ''cranks'' discover and promote smallpox vaccination; then a long contest must be waged by the ''progressives'' against vested medical interests, as well as religious and other prejudices. Eventually a ''majority'' accept. Then schools teach the virtues of vaccination, and authorities even forcibly vaccinate the children of a still resistant minority of opponents.

(c) Among North American Indians the first innovators to use white men's steel hatchets and knives (to replace stone cutting tools) needed to exercise almost no educative procedures to procure numberless imitators—the superiorities of these new tools being so obvious.

But similar innovators, adopting the white men's religious faiths, were not similarly imitated. Rather, they were viewed with dislike and suspicion. Even when missionaries and monastic orders came to help with vigorous school educations the new and supposedly superior creeds and rituals were (except in rare cases) reluctantly accepted and easily discarded. Why?

(d) Lenin, Kemal Pasha, Mussolini, Hitler, have all been prominent political innovators: They found enough aids—often young men with firearms, ready to give support, to become fighting proselyters in turn. Result—the core of a social change. Next: harnessing and redirection of schools to prepare nation-wide, one-party support for the innovations.

(6) In all these cases do schools *lead* or *follow* social changes? Public schools certainly do *not lead* in the innovating and militant minority or second stages of such changes. How could they? Such minority groups may, indeed, organize *as means* to their ends private schools, as well as a host of other highly pragmatic educative agencies—clubs, propagandist journals, leaflet advertising, ''war'' songs, etc.

On the other hand, *do* or *can* schools *lead* in furthering, in popularizing these social changes, once they have achieved the support of ''majorities''? They certainly can do so, and even for ages past they have even often done so—it being remembered that Hitlers, Constantines, Torquemadas, burgher classes and other oligarchs, if aided by some armed retainers or zealots, are in effect "majorities" as respects real authority and power. "One with God (or the devil, sometimes) is a majority."

(7) Let us now examine the second of the three stages of "social change" referred to above.

It is probably always in some degree true that the appearance of a great mind, a great discovery or a great event of other kinds would produce no significant effects unless surrounding conditions within at least substantial proportions of a population were favorable or "ripe." The discovery of America about 1000 A. D. aroused no interest—and probably would not have done so even if the discovery had then been made by a Mediterranean navigator. A Darwin in the sixteenth century, a Karl Marx in the seventeenth, a Marconi in the eighteenth, a St. Paul in 200 B. C., would doubtless all have sown their seeds on stony ground.

Now it could well be a commendable ambition on the part of a class of educators of vision to prepare the soil for the coming of the seeds which a discoverer, a daring leader, an opportunity, might bring.

In some degree this could be done by purposive educations of *demand* or *consciousness of need* coupled with conscious promotion of beliefs that means to practical satisfactions of such need may yet be discovered. At present, whether educated thereto by their schools and colleges or otherwise, substantial proportions of American adults are keenly conscious of needs for, and of probable eventual discoveries of means for meeting such needs, in such areas as: prevention and cure of cancer, infantile paralysis, etc.; certain kinds of town planning; less expensive and more efficient residence building; more reliable commercial banking; and other areas.

Perhaps very few adult Americans are at all interested or clearly conscious of needs in such areas as: Great poetry; improvements of liberal college educations; improved breeds of poultry; reconstructions of statute-making procedures in state legislatures; or defence against Japanese imperialism. Hence, even if one or more great poets, innovating college presidents, poultry breeders, legislators or war alarmists should appear in our midst it may be doubted whether they would be looked upon as other than "cranks," mild fanatics or nuisances.

And, of course, there are many areas in which large numbers of well-read persons are intensely conscious of "needs" but have no confidence that any means can be found, short of a divinely sent Messiah, of relieving such needs. They know that great numbers of us acutely need stable prices, productive work for all, extermination of mosquitoes in the tropics, more efficient court procedures, diminished fecundity of inferior stocks, elevation of consumer tastes for moving pictures and fiction, and less eagerness for profits on part of able-minded, daring speculative enterprisers. But they think that only incurably romantic visionaries believe that any remedies for such social "shortages" will be available in our times—and even if "great men" should appear to give the needed inventions or leadership. Hence such doubters can not be prepared as "soil" for reforms or reconstructions, even when they represent no vested interests which might be at stake. But perhaps ardent "reformers," believers in cures for such shortages, can cultivate receptive groups somewhere off the main highways of current skepticism or lethargy. Have not nearly all mankind's important social changes been "cultivated" at first by small groups of so-called visionaries almost in secret?

# EDUCATIONAL EVENTS

## STUDENTS FROM INDIA IN ENGLAND

THE number of Indian students in the universities and university colleges of Great Britain and Ireland, according to the *Educational Supplement of the London Times,* underwent some diminution in the year ended September 30 last. In his report to the High Commissioner for India on the work of the Education Department for 1932–33, Dr. Thomas Quayle, the secretary, states that while the decrease is mainly due to the financial stringency prevailing in India, as elsewhere, there is reason to believe that Indian parents and guardians are beginning to realize that the excellent facilities now available in India in all branches of education render it increasingly unnecessary for their sons or wards to proceed abroad for further study or training.

Even so, of the 2,700 young men and women from the Empire oversea in our universities and university colleges, three fifths come from India. Including men reading at the Inns of Court, there are some 1,700 or 1,800 young Indians studying in the British Isles, as compared with about 2,000 two or three years ago.

The High Commissioner for India, Sir Bhupendra Nath Mitra, who has given close personal attention to the whole subject since his appointment three years ago, informs the Government of India in his covering letter that he views with equanimity the decrease in the total number of Indian students, since it appears that any loss in quantity has been more than made good by improved quality. In the academic year an Indian achieved the honor of being elected a Fellow of Trinity College, Cambridge, and no fewer than 80 post-graduate degrees were won. In addition, the remarkable number of 27 Indians obtained the high professional qualifications of F.R.C.S., England, or M.R.C.P., London. At Cambridge an Indian obtained a Cricket Blue, and both there and at Oxford an Indian was elected president of the union.

There is, however, another side to the picture. The High Commissioner again urges Indian parents and guardians to assure themselves well in advance of sending their children and wards to Europe: first, that the requisite training is, in fact, not available in India; and, second, that the would-be students are in every way fitted, by physique, temperament, training and the assurance of adequate financial resources, profitably to prosecute further studies in the West. This axiom is still insufficiently appreciated in India. The result is that numbers of young Indians come to this country who, through no fault of their own, not only are unable to derive any benefit from their sojourn, but, indeed, suffer in health, pocket and peace of mind.

The High Commissioner writes that while it is a fallacy to suppose that there is any tendency to bar Indians because they are Indians, it is equally fallacious to imagine that an Indian ought to be admitted merely because he is an Indian. It is relatively easy for well-qualified Indian applicants to obtain admission, provided that they apply in good time. The poorly-qualified applicant is much harder to place, and when placed, too often proves a disappointment to himself, his college and the High Commissioner.

In respect to professional and practical training, Sir B. N. Mitra is satisfied that there is no ground for imagining that discrimination is practised against Indians who are both qualified to receive training and are prepared to submit to the ordinary customs of each profession or each branch of profession in respect of premium, wages and the like.

## THE INTERNATIONAL UNIVERSITIES CONFERENCE AT OXFORD

THE Association of University Teachers took the initiative in convening an International Conference of university representatives which took place at University College, Oxford, from June 29 to July 2. According to *Nature,* the conference was called for the discussion of general problems of university organization and development in the light of the experience of different countries and it was, so far as is known, the first definite effort to establish some measure of international association between universities for the specific purpose of considering university affairs.

Forty universities abroad and in the Dominions appointed delegates to attend the conference, as well as certain university associations, while British universities were represented by the council members of the Association of University Teachers and by delegates from Oxford, Scotland and the British Federation of University Women. There were present among the foreign representatives the presidents of both the French and the German University Federations and the vice-president of the American Association of University Professors.

The proceedings began with a dinner in University College on June 29, at which the foreign delegates and those of Oxford, Sir Michael Sadler and Mr. George Smith, with the Warden of All Souls College, were the guests of the council of the Association of University Teachers.

The first day of the conference was devoted to a series of accounts of the origin, constitution and aims of the university associations which already exist, given by representatives of each association. These included associations in England, Scotland, France, Germany, the United States, Hungary, Switzerland and Mysore; but the Swedish and Italian associations unfortunately could not be represented.

On the second day the conference divided into four commissions, dealing, respectively, with: (1) overcrowding in universities; (2) vocational training in universities; (3) coordination of the machinery of interchange of teachers; (4) adult education in the universities. Reports from these sections were presented by the sectional leaders to the conference for discussion on the last morning.

These committees were not actually instituted by the present conference, which felt that the ground should be explored further with fuller material in hand before action is taken. In order to prepare for this, the conference resolved that an International Conference Committee should be instituted and that the university associations in each country, or single national universities where such exist, or *ad hoc* committees in other countries, be invited to nominate an officer to act as a member of this committee, the duty of which will be to maintain international contacts and prepare material for future conferences. Professor R. C. McLean, of University College, Cardiff, was appointed by the conference to act as secretary of this committee.

The conference then agreed to accept provisional invitations from France for 1935 and from Germany for 1936 as the scenes of the next two conferences.

## THE ELEMENTARY TEXT-BOOK SITUATION IN CALIFORNIA

A STUDY of the text-book situation in the elementary schools of the various states of the country has been completed by the California State Superintendent of Public Instruction. The study covers the two-year period 1932–33, 1933–34. It involves only states supplying free text-books to elementary children. The purpose of the study was to make a comparison of conditions in California with general conditions elsewhere throughout the country so far as the supply of text-books for children is concerned.

According to the report, the general situation reveals a few very significant facts: As teachers have larger and larger classes, due to reduced numbers of teachers because of restricted budgets, the text-book plays a more and more important part in the educational program. With less time per individual child the only way to avoid serious losses in instruction is to have adequate supplies of books.

The text-book budget for the present school year has suffered a severe cut. In California local budgets of school districts have been cut approximately 50 per cent. while the state budget for state printed text-books was cut approximately 30 per cent., a cut which has caused replanning of the program of supplying books to the children of the elementary schools of California. While in many states two and three children have been required to use the same text-book at the same time, in California no child has been denied his copy of the books the state supplies. The total list of desirable texts for California elementary schools is not, however, as complete as it should be. The cooperation of the State Printing Plant in Sacramento has helped to reduce costs of the state of printing of text-books. A report of the situation for California elementary schools shows that:

> During the two years 1932–33 and 1933–34 the total cost for printing and distributing free state text-books was approximately $925,800. The 800,000 children in the elementary schools of the state received during this two-year period approximately 2,500,000 books or three new books each during the two years. The average cost per

pupil per year was less than sixty cents. These cost figures indicate a lower cost per child per number of books supplied than has ever been possible under private non-free text-book purchasing by individual children.

In many districts in the State of California books, aside from those supplied by the state, have not been available because of lack of funds.

During the last four years in round numbers 4,300,000 books have been printed and supplied to the elementary schools of California.

At present California has an excellent program of text-books and it is among the best in the country.

State printing now supplies a book of excellent quality and of superior wearing character.

The state printing plant is one of the largest printers of text-books in the United States and the largest one in the West.

## THE FEDERAL GOVERNMENT AND THE SCHOOLS

ACCORDING to an Associated Press dispatch from Washington, scattered reports indicate that again this year hundreds of schools may not open next month; hundreds more probably will not have funds to see them through two semesters; thousands of teachers will be jobless, and more thousands of children will not have a chance to obtain instruction.

There are no plans to keep open with government funds the doors of financially embarrassed schools. But there are some to extend additional aid to college students and to use more unemployed teachers this year for adult education and nursery schools.

The Relief Administration has authorized employment of 100,000 college students on part time at an average of $20 a month. Last year the figure was 75,000. This means 12 per cent. of the enrolment of an institution will be eligible for the relief work during the coming terms, against 10 per cent. last year.

Forty thousand teachers will be used in nursery schools and in adult instruction. While relief funds last year paid the salaries of 40,000 teachers, 10,000 to 14,000 of them served in rural schools which otherwise would have been shut down.

Harry L. Hopkins, relief administrator, is reported to have refused the use of further relief money this year to keep rural schools operating. To permit country schools, chiefly in the South, to wind up their terms last year $17,000,000 was set aside. But Mr. Hopkins believes that Congress should provide cash specifically for such use. This it failed to do at the last session.

The drought has accentuated the critical condition in education. A committee of relief and the educational authorities have been studying the problem, and recommendations on college activities have been placed before Mr. Hopkins. Their nature has not been disclosed. The problems of elementary and high schools are being considered in a separate report not yet ready.

While officials state that the condition this year is more hopeful than it was a year ago, the best available evidence indicates that the serious decline in teachers' salaries at least has been checked and that in some instances restorations are being made. In some municipalities, moreover, financial conditions have improved and will be reflected in more funds for schools.

The U. S. Office of Education says prospects are that the drop in college enrolment apparently will be halted this year. Two years ago it fell off $3\frac{1}{2}$ per cent. and last year about $6\frac{1}{2}$ per cent.

No general increase in enrolment is expected. This may come next year, as college attendance usually lags somewhat behind recovery in industry.

## DECREASE IN THE NUMBER OF CHILDREN IN THE NEW YORK CITY SCHOOLS

RECORDS of the Board of Education of New York City, as reported by *The New York Sun*, show that since 1930 there has been a steady reduction in the number of new children enrolled in the primary grades. This has been going on long enough to counterbalance the stay-in-school tendencies in the upper grades, so that the total elementary-junior high-school registration has begun to decline. In the senior high schools, however, the enrolment still continues to rise.

In 1930, the records show, 106,000 children were enrolled in the first-year classes of the elementary schools, an increase of 2,000 over the preceding year. Since then there has been a progressive decrease as follows:

| | | | |
|---|---|---|---|
| 1931 | 103,961 | 1933 | 97,673 |
| 1932 | 100,022 | 1934 | 95,665 |

These figures are for March of each year and since the March figures are usually below those for September there may be a slight increase above 95,000 in the first-year enrolment later this month. This gain will be temporary, however, and it is expected that by next March the registration in this grade may approach the 90,000 mark.

The cumulative effect of these registration cuts is being reflected in the teachers' unemployment situation. In addition to the 5,000 unemployed teachers on the eligible lists there are hundreds of regular teachers in excess.

The official budget estimates of the Board of Education are based on an expected registration of 754,500 children in the elementary schools this autumn, a drop of 10,000 from the corresponding period of last year.

In the other divisions, however, there will be marked increases. The junior high schools expect an increase of 4,000, bringing the total number of pupils to 118,000. The senior high schools, continuing their record-breaking growth, will probably gain 12,000 students, bringing the total number to 252,000. The largest comparative increase, it is expected, will be shown in the industrial classes in continuation schools, where 105,000 will be registered as against 88,000 last March.

## CHANGES IN THE CURRICULUM AT THE HARVARD BUSINESS SCHOOL

THE Harvard Graduate School of Business Administration recently announced for next year a group of new courses which will deal particularly with current economic and political changes and their implications. The impact of government on business and of business on government will be discussed in a course in "Industry and Government," given by Professor Philip Cabot. Professor Sumner H. Slichter will offer a new course in "Industrial Relations," and Elton Mayo, professor of industrial research, and Lloyd Warner, assistant professor of social anthropology, will offer a seminar in the "Human Problems of Administration."

Professor Cabot's course will give students a realistic picture of some of the governmental problems which business men must face and solve if they are to retain control of their business. In addition, Professor Cabot writes of his course:

> Great changes will certainly come and may come swiftly. We have always been a disorderly people, but the chaos which now prevails is a new phenomenon for the nation, and we must ask and answer, "What caused it?" When considered at first glance, it might appear that the causes are the world war and the world-wide depression which followed it. But these causes are not adequate to explain the political and economic phenomena which confront us; we must look deeper. The root-causes are, I think, changes in the race composing the nation and in the environment in which we live. The best form of government for any people at any time is the child of race and environment.

Professor Slichter's course will consider the revolutionary changes taking place in industrial relations and the development of the art of collective bargaining, which is a paramount labor problem of the present. Emphasis will be laid on the interpretation of past and current experience in different types of collective bargaining. Since the most highly developed forms of collective bargaining appear with trade unions, special study will be made of the experience in bargaining with trade unions, both those affiliated with the American Federation of Labor and independent organizations; but company unions and employee representation plans also will be studied.

The official statement further reads as follows:

> With all the changes now taking place the difficulties faced by all types of administrators multiply constantly. The course given by Professor Mayo and Professor Warner will examine these difficulties in the light of various researches which contribute to our knowledge of human problems involved in industrial and business organization. Most of these human problems are rarely considered in political and economic studies. The reading and discussion in the course will follow recent developments in physiological and psychopathological studies, certain inquiries of the French Sociological School and studies of primitive people undertaken by "functional" anthropologists. Although no detailed study is to be made in this course of Pareto's Sociology, some attention, nevertheless, will be given to the practical importance of certain of Pareto's theories for the administrator. If administrators are to deal wisely either with politics, business or labor relations these problems of human nature and getting along together become constantly more important.

## CULTURAL SURVEYS AT COLUMBIA UNIVERSITY

CULTURAL surveys of the leading countries of Europe, in which nearly 150 teachers and investigators will participate, will be instituted by Columbia University at the beginning of the academic year.

Representatives of many of the faculties will unite in interpreting the cultures of Germany, France, Italy and Spain at evening meetings under the auspices of the division of university extension. The courses are said to involve a change in the "old linguistic conception" of modern language departments.

Fifty-five lectures will be devoted to the culture of Germany, sponsored by the Department of Germanic Languages, of which Professor Robert Herndon Fife is executive officer. They will be given in cooperation with the departments of anthropology, chemistry, fine arts and archeology, geography, history, mechanical engineering, music, philosophy, Romance languages and sociology; the Schools of Business, Architecture, Law and Medicine; Teachers College and Union Theological Seminary, and with scholars from other institutions.

The opening lecture, dealing with the geographical background of the German people, will be delivered by Dr. J. Russell Smith, professor of economic geography. The racial origin of the German people will be discussed on October 2 by Professor Franz Boas, of the department of anthropology.

Among the other lecturers and their topics are: "The Industrialization of Germany," Professor Walter Rautenstrauch; "Social Insurance in Germany," Professor Samuel McCune Lindsay; "The German Contribution to Bacteriology," Professor Charles N. B. Camac; "The German School System," Professor Thomas Alexander; "Women in Modern Germany," Professor Hugh W. Puckett; "Architecture in Modern Germany," Professor Emerson H. Swift; "Contemporary German Sculpture and Painting," Stanley Hart.

Five lectures will be delivered by visiting professors. Professor Henry-Russell Hitchcock, Jr., of Wesleyan University, will speak on "Garden Architecture in Germany"; Professor Alfred Remy, of Fordham University, on "German Lied"; Professor Elmer E. S. Johnson, of the Hartford Theological Seminary, on "Caspar von Schwenkfeld and the Religious Sects"; Dr. Paul Tillich, of Union Theological Seminary, on "Contemporary German Philosophy" and "Religious Trends in Modern Germany."

Fifty-six lectures on the culture of France have been arranged by the Department of Romance Languages. Prehistoric and Celtic France will be the subject of the first lecture by Dr. N. C. Nelson. Other speakers will explore the history of French civilization, concluding with a survey of contemporary movements. The list of speakers and their topics includes: "Public Education in Modern France," Professor I. L. Kandel; "The Literary Movements in Contemporary France," Professor A. G. H. Spiers; "Political and Social Life in Contemporary France," Professor C. J. H. Hayes; "France and Her Present Problems." Dr. Robert Valeur.

Sixty lectures comprise the program on the culture of Spain. "Jewish Civilization in Spain" will be discussed by Salo Baron, professor of Jewish history, literature and institutions on the Miller Foundation. "Architecture from Plateresque to Baroque" will be the theme of Dean Joseph Hudnut, of the School of Architecture. The monarchical tradition of Spain will be explained by Dr. Carleton S. Smith in a lecture on "The Catholic Kings and the Hapsburgs." Lectures on contemporary Spain will take up the novel and drama, poetry, art and music. Professor Mercedes J. Benardette, of Hunter College, will speak on "Le Cid and the Castilian Epic"; Dr. N. C. Nelson, of the American Museum of Natural History, will lecture on the prehistoric period of Spain. Edward Rochie Hardy, Jr., of the General Theological Seminary, will have as his topic "Christian Hispano-Roman Literature."

The department of Hispanic Languages, headed by Professor Federico de Onis, is carrying out studies in the traditional culture of Mexico and Spain with the collaboration of the departments of philosophy and anthropology. Financed by the Council for Research in the Humanities, this work will continue for several years. The Hispanic Bibliography now contains more than 400,000 bibliographical items, covering all aspects of the civilization of Spain, Portugal, Spanish America and Brazil, including not only literature and language, but history, art, economics, religion and science. Development of an "Archive of Hispanic Folklore," which will contain classified material for the study of traditional culture, is under way at the Casa de las Espanas.

In carrying on collective research, the Casa is working in close cooperation with the Center for Historical Studies of Madrid. The instruments for scholarly study and research which it is accumulating are said to be in a great measure unique.

## INTER-AMERICAN LECTURES AT THE GEORGE WASHINGTON UNIVERSITY

INTER-AMERICAN lectures this summer at the third annual seminar of the George Washington University, unlike previous sessions, were devoted to intensive and comprehensive review of the three key nations in South America, namely, Argentina, Brazil and Chile. Each lecture course, covering a period of one week or more, is planned to help to lay the foundation for an eight-month series of studies to be regulated by the Inter-American Center of the university.

Dr. Cloyd H. Marvin, president of the university, in announcing this summer's course pointed out that it was the forerunner of an attempt to bring about closer academic and cultural relationships with students, scholars and educational institutions in the other Americas, and with students of the United States who wish to obtain a broader understanding of, and a keener insight into, the history, thought and culture of the Central and South American republics and those of the Caribbean area.

It is the understanding that the Inter-American Center, in addition to offering regularly constituted courses and special lectures, will encourage directed research and scholarly publications in the broad field of Pan-American problems. It will endeavor to facilitate the interchange of university students and professors, and will try to promote closer cooperation in historical, scientific, philosophical, artistic, literary and bibliographical matters.

Washington, as the center in the United States for Latin-American information, offers to the George Washington University opportunities provided to no other university devoting a large part of its curricula to the problems in the middle and southern regions of the Western Hemisphere. Latin-American embassies and legations of the Department of State, Congress and the White House afford unlimited facilities for the dissemination of news.

Dr. A. Curtis Wilgus, head of the Inter-American Center, has announced that during the coming fall, winter and spring months a council of specialists will advise the center on courses, projects, lectures, the establishment of fellowships and scholarships, arranging and supervising radiocasts and the granting of degrees to individuals possessing exceptional qualifications.

# EDUCATIONAL NOTES AND NEWS

DR. GEORGE W. ROSENLOF, director of secondary education and teacher training in the Nebraska State Department of Public Instruction, has been appointed professor of secondary education in the University of Nebraska, succeeding Dr. Harlan C. Koch, who goes to the University of Michigan.

CHARLES DAVID ABBOTT, formerly of the department of English of the University of Colorado, has been appointed director of the university libraries at the University of Buffalo. The Lockwood Memorial Library building, the gift of Thomas B. Lockwood, of Buffalo, will be opened late this fall.

DR. ARTHUR H. COMPTON, professor of physics at the University of Chicago, sailed for Europe on August 3 to fill the George Eastman visiting professorship at the University of Oxford.

DR. WESLEY C. MITCHELL, professor of economics at Columbia University, has been appointed Hitchcock professor at the University of California and will give a series of nine public lectures on economic planning by the government during September. The lectures will be given under the auspices of the Hitchcock Foundation.

DR. CARL R. MOORE, professor of zoology at the University of Chicago, has been made chairman of the department of zoology, succeeding Dr. C. M. Child, who will become professor emeritus on October 1.

Two professors at Yale University have been appointed to endowed chairs. Dr. Harry M. Hubbell has been designated Talcott professor of Greek, and Dr. Austin M. Harmon has been named to the Lampson professorship of Greek.

HENRY GRATTAN DOYLE, formerly dean of the Junior College of the George Washington University, has been appointed dean of Columbian College. He has been a member of the George Washington University faculty since 1916.

SYRACUSE UNIVERSITY, which gives a two-year graduate course to student deans, has been successful in obtaining a number of appointments for its graduates. These include: Margaret Anderson, dean of women at Otterbein College, Westerville, Ohio; Gladys Beach, dean of women, Blackburn Junior College, Carlinville, Ill.; Ruth Cope, superintendent of Balentine Hall, University of Maine, Orono, Me.; Inez Duncan, social director and assistant dean of women, Judson College, Marion, Ala.; Mary Heffernen, director of the department of physical education, Cortland Normal School, New York; Sarah Lutes, assistant dormitory manager, Syracuse University; Helene Turner, assistant dean of women, University of Arizona; Lois Flint, dean of women at Illinois Wesleyan University, Bloomington, Ill.

RECENT appointments to the Louisiana State University include: Robert Penn Warren, formerly of Vanderbilt University, assistant professor of English; A. D. Folweiler, assistant professor of forestry; Jesse Hair, instructor in physical education; H. L. McCracken, professor of economics; S. A. Caldwell, instructor in economics; Charlotte Davis, instructor in public school music, Northeast Center; Alex B. Daspit, instructor in government, substituting for R. Taylor Cole, on leave of absence; Henry Janin, instructor in French, substituting for Professor H. A. Major, on leave of absence.

M. GEORGES DENGLER, French architect, arrived in this country on September 4 to join the faculty of the department of architecture of the University of Pennsylvania. M. Dengler, who will serve as professor of design, received the Grand Prize of Rome in 1931.

DR. CYRIL E. SMITH, formerly assistant professor of history at the Louisiana State University, has accepted a similar position at Marquette University. The appointment of Dr. Smith fills a vacancy that was created when the Rev. Francis S. Betten, S.J., retired last year as head of the department of history to devote his time to writing.

DR. WALTER M. FUCHS, formerly professor at the Technische Hochschule, Aachen, Germany, was recently appointed research professor at Rutgers University.

DR. HARRY HELSON, professor of psychology at Bryn Mawr College, will be exchange professor at the University of Southern California during the next academic year.

DR. CLAUDE A. BUSS, formerly with the United States foreign service in China, has been appointed to the faculty of the Los Angeles University of International Relations of the University of Southern California.

L. B. ROGERSON, since 1921 auditor of the University of North Carolina, has been appointed assistant comptroller at the Chapel Hill division of the consolidated university.

*The Experiment Station Record* states that at the Washington College and Experiment Station, Rex E. Willard, head of the department of farm management and agricultural economics, has leave of absence for one year to become regional director of the Pacific Northwest Planning Division of the Agricultural Adjustment Administration. His territory will include Washington, Oregon and Idaho, with headquarters at Washington College.

ELDON B. ENGLE, assistant professor of soils at the University of Nebraska, has been given a year's leave of absence to accept a position with the Soil Erosion Service, U. S. Department of the Interior. Harold Hedges, research associate in rural economics, has also been granted a year's leave of absence, beginning on July 1, for the purpose of acting as secretary of the Bank for Cooperatives at Omaha.

As part of the Greek Government's drive to remove Communist teachers from the schools, Achilles Dimitriades, an instructor in French, has been condemned by a Federal Constabulary Court to spend a year on the island of Arapi.

DR. JAMES BRYANT CONANT, president of Harvard University, has returned to this country from abroad after spending a vacation in the north of Wales.

Dr. Harold B. Allen, since 1926 director of education for the Near East Foundation in Greece, Albania, Syria, Bulgaria and Palestine, has returned for a visit to this country. Previous to accepting his present post, Dr. Allen was president of the New York Association of Agricultural Teachers and Principals.

Dr. Wilder Penfield, clinical professor of neurological surgery, McGill University Faculty of Medicine, received a ceremonial chalice at the twenty-first reunion of the class of 1913 of Princeton University. The chalice has been dedicated by the class to commemorate outstanding accomplishments of its members and will be retained by Dr. Penfield until another award is made.

Dr. Charles Elkanah Hodgin, dean emeritus of the University of New Mexico, died on July 28, at the age of seventy-six years. Dr. Hodgin was professor of education at the university from 1897 to 1913, when he became dean of the School of Education.

Judson Perry Welsh, formerly assistant dean of Pennsylvania State College and president of the Bloomsburg Normal School, Pa., died on August 30, at the age of seventy-eight years.

Dr. Harry T. Collings, professor of commerce at the University of Pennsylvania, died on August 29, at the age of fifty-four years.

Katharine Lehan McElroy, supervisor of schools in Cambridge, Mass., died on August 27. She had been connected with the Cambridge schools for forty-five years.

Warren M. Van Name, principal of Dewey Junior High School, Brooklyn, N. Y., died on August 28 at the age of sixty-four years. He became principal of Public School 136 in 1914, and after he reorganized it in 1919 as Dewey Junior High School, he became principal of the latter institution.

A large educational exposition, which was formally opened by Mrs. Franklin D. Roosevelt at the Education Building of New York University, on September 6, will continue until September 14. It is the work of students in the free adult classes organized in December, 1932, under the State Education Board in conjunction with the New York City Board of Education and the Temporary Emergency Relief Administration. Officials of the State Education Department in announcing the exposition said that the adult education program had proved so successful that it was proposed to incorporate it as a part of the country's educational system. The Federal Government has authorized a grant to send experts to New York to study the exposition so that they may be qualified to supervise the work to be started throughout the United States. There are 700 instructors in the adult classes and an average daily attendance of more than 25,000 students.

By the will of the late John W. Hamilton, retired Methodist Episcopal bishop, the sum of $1,000,000 will ultimately revert to five religious and educational institutions. After the death of near relatives the income from the estate is to be allowed to accumulate until the following successive gifts can be made: the American University, $250,000, for founding the Franklin Hamilton School of Divinity in memory of Bishop Hamilton's brother; the Methodist Historical Society of Boston, $150,000, for founding a Franklin Hamilton Methodist Historical Building; Mount Union College, Ohio, $200,000, for establishing a Jay Benson Hamilton School of All Sciences; the University of Southern California, $200,000, for founding a Helene Hamilton School for Bible Study, and the College of the Pacific at Stockton, $200,000, for establishing a Gordon Battelle Hamilton School of Law.

The bulk of the $200,000 estate of the late Captain Ralph M. Yardley, Chicago architect, who died recently, will go towards the establishment of a perpetual scholarship fund for high-school graduates of Mansfield, Ohio, under terms of his will. Interest from the fund will pay annually college tuition and general expenses for one boy and one girl, who would otherwise be unable to afford higher education.

Dr. Walter Hullihen, president of the University of Delaware, has announced that no student group has been sent to Germany this summer under the university foreign study plan. The reason given was the uncertain conditions in Germany and central Europe. Although the project is sponsored by the University of Delaware, the groups are composed of students from other colleges.

FOR the fourth year the Massachusetts State College has found it necessary to limit by trustee resolution the size of the entering classes. There will be admitted approximately 75 women and 225 men. The limitation of enrolment has been made necessary by the fact that facilities are not available to give adequate instruction to, nor to house a greater number of students. The enrolment at the college has practically doubled during the past five years. During the past few years an increasing demand for the admittance of women students to the college has been felt. The pressure for admittance of men has remained more nearly constant during the same period.

THE Wisconsin School of the Air, a radio program prepared by the University of Wisconsin for classroom use, is beginning its fourth year of broadcasting on October 1. H. B. McCarthy is the program director. These courses are approved by the State Department of Public Instruction and the State Teachers Association for reception in schools. Ten broadcasts, two each school day, will be available to teachers. Among the subjects included are creative art, Wisconsin history, nature, character inspiration and music, stories for children.

THE program of visual education used in Pennsylvania schools has won international recognition, according to a bulletin given out by the State Department of Public Instruction. Dr. Charles F. Hoban, director of the State Museum of Harrisburg, who returned recently from attending the International Congress of Educational and Instructional Cinematography held in Italy, stated that the program has been adopted by forty-three nations, including Austria, France and Germany, and that Italy is preparing to adopt it. Pennsylvania was the first state to inaugurate a systematic program of visual aids for school children. It also provides special instruction for all school teachers prepared in the state teachers colleges. In the schools photographs, lantern slides and motion pictures are used wherever possible to give the students a clearer idea of what they are studying. In addition, such subjects as local history, civics, geology and botany are studied with the aid of field trips.

THE New York Employing Printers Association will offer eleven courses in its school this fall. Registration will begin on September 24 and the courses will start about October 15. The courses were self-supporting last year when 191 students enrolled and 148 were graduated. Einar Schatvet, chairman of the educational committee, stated that it was hoped that many employers would be in a position this year to pay a part of the tuition charges. The courses will be in advertising typography, applied design and layout, cost finding, advanced accounting, elements of printing, selling, estimating, advanced estimating, mechanics of printing, proofreading, public speaking and speech development.

A UNITED PRESS dispatch states that the medical school of the university at Rosario, Argentina, was closed by government decree on August 29, at which time students abandoned the buildings they had previously seized in an uprising against alleged harsh disciplinary measures. The government had postponed election of a rector when the students voted to strike. An investigation is being made to determine damage to university buildings in order to sue the student leaders.

A CORRESPONDENT of the London *Times* reports that the ever-increasing importance attached to military training in the new German educational system is illustrated by the recent introduction into the Munich higher grade schools (which belong to the state) of a compulsory course of musketry drill and rifle practise. All boys of the four senior classes—*i.e.*, 16, 17, 18 and 19 years of age—must devote two hours every fortnight to this addition to the curriculum. They are assembled—about fifty together at a time—in a large state institute, where firearms are served out. Half the boys are supplied with Regular Army rifles, the rest with small calibre rifles, but they take turn and turn about with each type of weapon. The instruction, which is given by officers (either active or retired) in mufti, consists of taking an Army rifle to pieces, learning the names and functions of the various parts, and reassembling them; and also of regular musketry drill. The course has only been in existence a few weeks, but shooting practise is to be introduced shortly. The military instructors also deliver lectures to the boys on their duty to their country. The correspondent reports that much care is taken to keep these proceedings secret. When the instruction is over the rifles must be handed in again. The boys are said to be strictly forbidden to take a rifle out of the building, or to show themselves armed at a door or window.

AT a meeting of the Indian Public School Society held recently a plan for the establishment of a public school along English lines was approved, and a Board of Management was appointed, consisting of Sir Joseph Bhore, Sir Frank Noyce, Sir George Anderson, Education Commissioner with the Government of India, Sir Firoz Khan Noon, Minister for Education in the Punjab; Sir Phiroze Sethna, and Mr. Amarnath, Mr. Atal and M. S. A. Hydari, of the Indian Civil Service. Mr. Hydari will also be honorary secretary. The board will make the final selection of the headmaster, and other masters he may wish to bring from England, after consultation with Lord Halifax and a selection committee to be set up in England. The board will also be responsible for the preliminary arrangements for opening the school. Afterwards its functions will be taken over by a Government Board of Governors with the viceroy as chairman. The objective of the Indian Public School Society is a school of 420 boys paying an annual fee of £75 to £90 each. The sum of £150,000 has been collected to erect the school, which will be run on English lines adapted to Indian needs and environment.

# DISCUSSION

## WHAT TO DO ABOUT HIGH SCHOOL DEFICIENCIES

OFFICIAL figures from most universities indicate that the depression has had an adverse effect upon registration. This does not necessarily mean, however, that adult education has not taken on new life during the last four years. Some have even gone so far as to say that there has been a bull market in the field of adult education.[1] It is not the purpose of this article, however, to discuss the present total demand for education on the part of adults, but rather the increased demand by a fairly restricted group.

One of the most unpleasant tasks which I face in interviewing prospective students is the necessity of informing them that if their high-school work has not been completed, they will be required to make up any deficiency before the university can grant them a degree. One may say that this is too trite even to mention, because it is expected that all persons graduate from high school before embarking on a university course. Such certainly is expected of the younger student of high-school age, or thereabouts; but can we hold the same requirements for middle-aged or nearly middle-aged students who for various reasons did not complete their high-school course? In many cases these persons may have had the opportunity to complete their high-school work, but because they did not realize its value at the time, and could not be convinced by others, they dropped out at some time during the course, or in some cases never even entered high school. Perhaps in the majority of these cases, the opportunity did not exist for them to continue until graduation.

Some may say that the answer to all this lies in the providing of high-school evening classes. In most cases I think this is the solution. In the case of the younger person who still has time to complete his high-school course before starting his university training, and even in the case of some of the older people, it might be wiser to take up high-school work rather than university work. There are many middle-aged persons who feel the need for further education and who decide to do university evening session work along with their regular occupation. Having been out of touch with school work for

[1] See *Journal of Adult Education*, January, 1934, "A Bull Market in Education." Benjamin Fine, pages 52–55.

a number of years, and in some cases lacking innate ability, they find it much more difficult than they had anticipated. In addition they find that despite their initial enthusiasm, pursuing education in the evening together with working during the day entails a sacrifice which they are unwilling to make. This is one of the reasons for the large percentage of beginning students who fail to complete their evening session courses. For this group it seems quite clear that the high-school evening session provides sufficient opportunities. It certainly makes it less costly for them to discover that it is impractical for them to undertake university training. But there are some who are willing and, because of innate ability and breadth of experience, are capable of successfully carrying on university work, although they have not completed their high-school prerequisites. Not only are they capable of handling this work, but to send them back to the high-school evening session would deaden their desire to continue their formal education. For these persons high-school evening session work would be so easy they would not feel that it was worth while. There is likewise the question of time. It is assumed that one spends a large portion of his time during high school in the classroom. But in the university the class recitation is supposed to be preceded by an even longer period of preparation. The amount of class time, therefore, in the working off of high-school deficiencies is relatively greater than that of university work. Persons are less reluctant to give up their time if all the preparation, which involves more time than the actual class work, may be done at home.

At the present time many of our day universities will not admit persons who do not have a high-school diploma. Most universities interested primarily in providing educational opportunities for adults, however, allow such persons to take the work which they desire, but will not grant them a degree. The following situation might easily arise. Two persons have taken exactly the same work at, say, some evening session division of a university. Let us suppose that Mr. "A" is a young student who has completed his high-school work before entering the institution, but Mr. "B," who is perhaps twenty years Mr. "A's" senior, has a high-school deficiency. If Mr. "A's" work has been of the required quality, and if he has taken the requisite amount of work, he is granted the degree; but Mr. "B" is denied this final recognition, even though his record might be far superior to that of Mr. "A's." The university might be much more pleased to have Mr. "B" rather than Mr. "A" considered as one of its products. All of us who have taught adult classes will agree, I think, that the seriousness with which the more mature person undertakes his work aids him materially in the retention of the most valuable portion of the work which he has completed.

Some institutions have said that allowances can always be made for special cases, and each case should be treated on the basis of its merits, but the difficulty of all this is that Mr. "B" of our example would never have taken all the work which I have assumed that he did, unless he were working toward some goal. In some states the requirements are such that the educational institution has little choice in the matter. True it has, at least formally, the right of conferring all degrees, but it constantly must guard against such procedure as may be frowned upon by the state departments of education. This is especially true in dealing with pre-professional requirements.

The suggestion has been made that this dilemma is more apparent than real, since the adult's educational philosophy should be so built up that the degree is meaningless, that the knowledge obtained is the important thing. The newer educational approach, which is very clearly brought out by the growing use of comprehensive examinations, is striving toward measurement of attainment rather than specific knowledge of individual and unrelated facts. This process makes education even more valuable, and perhaps easier, for the adult. Even if it is true that knowledge is the important consideration, and especially does it sound altruistic, mass methods are being used in the handling of individuals in many cases to the same extent as in the handling of goods in our present large-scale productive processes. The individual, therefore, wishes some convenient and easily recognized standard which follows from his achievement. One of the first questions which is put to the applicants for many positions is "Are you a college graduate?" During the last few years employers have been able to automatically eliminate all applicants who do not possess a university degree, and still have a very wide choice because of the large number of unemployed college graduates. It is very embarrassing to explain that all the work necessary for a degree has been completed, but because of a high-school deficiency, the degree can not be granted; furthermore in many cases the opportunity to explain is not given. Even if given the opportunity, most persons would feel somewhat hesitant before outlining this anomalous situation.

If the type of person for whom I am making this plea is so very capable, why not ask him to take examinations in his high-school subjects in order to complete his prerequisites? There are several difficulties to be encountered in this procedure. First, it is very difficult to get access to the examinations. I mean by that, before a person may take high-school examinations in order to establish credit, he is usually asked to show evidence that he has covered the material in such a way that he is likely to pass the examination. This evidence is naturally very difficult to show unless he has taken formalized course work. This is no criticism of the high schools. They can not be expected to allow just any one to come into their examinations. Second, high-school examinations at least in a number of subjects tend to be very detailed. Such detailed knowledge is not supposed to be the foundation for his university work. A student might excel in a college literature course, and yet not be able to pass fourth-year high-school English without covering the particular literature assignments for that course. Is this specific knowledge which is obtained in these high-school courses absolutely necessary to the adult before he can make a creditable showing in similar but more advanced university courses?

Many of our educational institutions are willing to grant degrees beyond the rank of a bachelor's degree upon the basis of achievement. I have in mind the honorary degree. Should an institution in the granting of its honorary degrees eliminate all candidates who do not possess high-school diplomas? It does not seem reasonable that they should, and certainly a number of persons have received honorary degrees, although they have not completed their high-school training. Putting the situation at its worst then, we are willing to confer advanced honorary degrees on these outstanding individuals purely on the basis of attainment, but can not, or at least in most cases do not, grant them bachelor's degrees.

Could not something be done for these exceptional mature individuals who have not completed their high-school work, but who have successfully demonstrated their ability to carry on university work? Perhaps each institution should handle this matter according to its own best judgment. But then the question arises as to whether a particular institution is not lowering the somewhat uniform standards which are observed by all. Competition among the universities is becoming very keen. This is, no doubt, most unfortunate, but nevertheless this condition exists and we are forced to face it. If one institution alone sets up the facilities for this class of students, it may be attacked immediately by other institutions on the basis of lower standards. This matter is always brought into the open when such a student wishes to transfer from one institution to another.

The problem seems to the writer to be so large that it can not be settled without a great deal of careful thought and study. I have no completed plan to offer. But would it not be reasonable to say to the mature student, deficient in his high-school work, who has clearly demonstrated his ability in handling university work, that he will be allowed to graduate in a normal way? Perhaps it would be reasonable to require even more in the way of scholarship from these special cases than from the student who presents the usual prerequisites at the time of his entrance into the university. Most universities require that the student do average work for the four years before he is allowed to graduate. It would not be asking too much, I think, to require superior work from these special students, in terms of the usual grade, say a "B" average.

Some have felt that there is no such thing as a "self-made man." But if there is, he is forced to attain his position under a decided handicap. In spite of these disadvantages, however, there have been numerous examples in this country of "well-educated" men who have had very little formalized school work. My suggestions merely have to do with making it easier for these individuals. Selecting the deserving cases from the undeserving ones would be a difficult task, but not insurmountable, and it would certainly give some encouragement to those students who are most serious in their educational pursuits, and who are probably obtaining the most from their efforts.

LEWIS A. FROMAN,
*Acting dean of the Evening Session*
UNIVERSITY OF BUFFALO

## EDUCATION AND BUSINESS

FEW would claim that we have made the same progress in education in the last fifty years that we have in electricity or mechanics or in many other fields. We have shortened the time of learning, but not on the scale that we have shortened the time of digging ditches or making clothes. There are about 800,000 teachers in this country, reaching some 30,000,000 children. If we are to suppose General Motors or United States Steel extended to some such proportions, there would be a highly paid executive at the head, who would be making the plans and determining the form of organization. While education is recognized as a matter of great national concern, the organization and planning is left to the states, counties, cities and separate school districts.

Suppose General Motors has a training school for those who are making its radios, and it finds that it already has 100,000 trained people for 75,000 positions. We can scarcely imagine it spending much money in advertising to get new students. It would either shut down its school or raise the standard for its employees.

We should know how many new teachers we need each year and not train many more than that. It is expensive for the country to give and for the student to receive three or four years of training for a position that does not exist. Business would assign to each normal school and teachers college a quota of students to be accepted each year. It would know where vacancies were going to occur, and have the teachers ready.

Our doctrines of states rights and local autonomy interfere with any idea of general organization or planning. But there seems to be no reason why we should not keep track of vacancies and people available.

If there were a great industry in this country with 800,000 employees, we should expect them to have a research staff of several thousands of scientists, working continuously on its problems. This is the way the great progress in electricity and mechanics has been made. I was talking recently with a young man who was a member of the research staff of the Hudson Motor Company. He said he was one of twelve men who were working continuously designing the body of the Hudson car. He said his special work was designing the door. At the Dow chemical works, I was told that they had a group of 270 research chemists, who were giving their lives to the devising of new products and new methods of separation and combination for the chemicals in the ground waters of eastern Michigan.

This country is more concerned or should be in the study of its economic, social, criminal and educational problems than it is in its problems of physics or engineering, but we have the great Bureau of Standards working on these physical problems, because business needs this information. We have no group of scientists at all comparable who are working on our social and educational problems.

Our present depression is costing us some forty billions of dollars a year. It is admitted that at least half of this calamity is due to psychological causes, and that its psychological after effects will be far reaching. Most of the progress we have made has been due to a new hope and faith. If we believe that psychology deserves a place among the sciences, we should have a thousand psychologists working on this side of the problem.

HENRY S. CURTIS
ANN ARBOR, MICH.

## SPECIAL UNIVERSITY STUDENTS

THESE comments are suggested by the notice regarding students-at-large at the University of Chicago, in the issue of SCHOOL AND SOCIETY for July 7, containing this statement: "The University of Chicago becomes the first major American institution of higher education to admit any student who can demonstrate ability to profit by university opportunities to do so without having to meet requirements for a degree."

The University of California has not only extended this privilege for many years but has extended it to residents of the state without charging tuition. If "qualified for admission but not desiring to register for a degree," the students have been classed as regular but with special programs. Mature applicants not qualified for admission as regular students but "who by reason of special attainments may be prepared to undertake certain courses in the university" (University of California Circular of Information) have been admitted for many years to special status in order to take a limited group of related subjects.

Most applicants for special status, however, have not qualified for either kind of status but have tried to use special status as a back door to a standard institution not charging tuition.

While the statement quoted at the outset may be true of the major private institutions, an examination of catalogues indicates that these privileges are almost without exception extended by the state universities belonging to the Association of American Universities.

C. H. ROBISON
UNIVERSITY OF CALIFORNIA
AT LOS ANGELES

# SPECIAL CORRESPONDENCE

## THE LIBERAL ARTS COLLEGE FUNCTIONING THROUGH STUDENT ACTIVITIES

THE bipolar nature of college administration can no longer be denied. Whether the president does the whole job or whether, as is the case at Bucknell, he has someone who is responsible for the administration of the so-called extra-curricular activities makes little difference. The liberal arts college functions through the curriculum and it functions through the manifold activities in which students engage when, theoretically, they are not studying. It is possible, I suppose, to eliminate extra-curricular activities from the campus, but so long as they are permitted to exist they must be supervised and administered as carefully as the offerings of the curriculum. This was the conclusion of the Rollins conference of 1931, which met under the chairmanship of John Dewey to discuss the true college for the modern age. We quote briefly from their report:

> It is recognized that so-called extra-curricular activities are really a part of the educational offerings of the college and should be subjected to the same critical analysis, selection and guidance desirable in other phases of the curriculum.

Which is more important in molding attitudes and in shaping lives may even be a matter for debate. Our subject, therefore, has sufficient justification through reference to the most recent philosophy of the liberal arts college. That this philosophy of education is not a new discovery may be a substantiated claim of many, but that it is now receiving more than ordinary attention can scarcely be denied.

In 1930 the writer, then dean of freshmen, in his report to President Hunt and the Board of Trustees of Bucknell University recommended the establishment of a personnel office which would be made responsible for coordinating all the forces in the university in order to effect adequate supervision of student affairs and to turn these activities to desirable ends. Until such a proposal was made a part of President Rainey's program it received inadequate recognition. In the meantime the Survey Committee on "Personnel" and the Committee on "Student Activities and Organizations" which were appointed by President Rainey and functioned for the entire year 1931–32 revealed intolerable conditions with respect to student life on the campus. Data concerning individual students were found to be scattered all over the campus, fraternity presidents constituted the only student government body, unsatisfactory relationships between students and faculty were conspicuous, every conceivable form of graft existed in student organizations, neither a centralized nor a decentralized system of supervision was in evidence, campus politics was rampant, and for the most part an unwholesome situation prevailed. A spirit of urgency dominated those who took the problem seriously.

Deans Haggerty and Judd, survey experts and widely known educators, called in by the president to consider the ten survey committee reports, including the two mentioned above, recommended that a dean of students be appointed by the president and that he be made responsible for general supervision and coordination of all matters relating to student life. Based upon this recommendation the president and the board of trustees established an administrative division, responsible directly to the president and responsible for the supervision and coordination of all matters pertaining to student life except admissions, classroom instruction and student discipline. The dean of students was the name given to the new office.

### UNDERLYING PRINCIPLES OF THE OFFICE

The following underlying principles were immediately drawn up by the new administrator and were to be kept in mind to govern the construction of the personnel administrative organization at Bucknell:

A. A college personnel organization must be an entirely separate department, not connected directly with the regular administrative or disciplinary offices.

B. It should be responsible directly to the president and through him to the board of trustees.

C. There should be a coordination and concentration of all the resources of the university for the purpose of promoting the best interests of individuals in all their aspects.

D. Every independent and interrelated part of the program should be constructed with the unified final structure in mind.

E. There should be an elevation of the faculty advisory idea rather than a substitution of a system which places all responsibility for guidance and supervision upon a single individual or upon a small group of individuals.

F. There should be a closer correlation between theory and practise, between what we are teaching in our classrooms and what the students practise in their organizations and activities. This is particularly true with respect to government, business, morals, religion, dramatics, citizenship, and music and art.

G. There should be a closer correlation between scholarship standing and participation in extra-curricular activities.

H. There should be faculty-student supervision and government of student affairs in order to achieve:

   a. Adequate supervision and at the same time to teach students to look for and guard the highest values to be derived from their own activities.

   b. Unity of student and faculty aims in the educational process.

I. There should be the highest possible degree of student responsibility in the management of student organizations and activities, but student standards should be made to conform to the highest teachings and ideals of the institution as a whole.

J. Graft should be eliminated. No student should be allowed to make profit at the expense of other students and all business activities should be open and above suspicion.

K. Campus politics should be controlled, rather than driven under cover, and turned to desirable ends. Desirable ends are achieved "when an individual's policy determines his membership in a particular clique or party." Undesirable ends are achieved "when clique membership determines in advance what the policy of all the members of such a clique shall be. Freedom of thought and action in this case are denied to the individual."

L. The philosophy of the calendar should give relative prominence to athletics, dramatics, religion, social life and other student interests.

M. Organizations and activities which do not contribute to the educational process should be eliminated and careful scrutiny should be given to all new organizations that seek recognition on the campus.

N. The university should be placed at the center of student loyalty and all group loyalty should be subordinated.

O. So far as possible all extra-curricular activities should be made intra-curricular activities.

P. Every staff member in the university should be a personnel man or woman, in sympathetic if not in active contact with the personnel office.

### ADMINISTRATIVE ORGANIZATION

The need for an organization to coordinate the services which the university is prepared to render outside of the teaching function, and to supervise all student activities and organizations, has been met through the creation of a personnel council, a student-faculty congress, a committee on personnel research, a committee on student measurements, a publication board, an artist course committee, a budget committee, and the inauguration of certain practises in the personnel office itself.

*Personnel Council:* There are six significant aspects or divisions of the personnel council, as follows:

a. In every respect the president of the university is head of the personnel council. The council is a coordinating agency. It is responsible for the total atmosphere and conditions on the campus. It should be sensitive to the offerings of the college as a whole.

b. Just as the president must have group chairmen to administer the academic group functions, so he must have someone responsible for the personnel division. This person should be closely in touch and in sympathy with the president's program at all times. He should have freedom of action, to be sure, but only within the limits of the president's plan for the college program as a whole.

c. The first group on the personnel council consists of certain "experts," individuals, responsible, not for student organizations and activities, but for certain services which the university is able to render to students. This group includes:
   (1) The psychologist.
   (2) The vocational counselor.
   (3) The chairman of the committee on measurements.
   (4) The chairman of the committee on personnel research.
   (5) The chairmen of the five academic groups.
   (6) The college physician.
   (7) The chairman of freshman week.
   (8) The dean of women.

d. The second significant group on the personnel council is the central committee. It consists of twelve faculty advisers who supervise the twelve major activities and interests of students. In addition to advisers on dramatics, citizenship, social relations, publications, athletics, honorary and professional societies, musical activities, literary activities, religious activities and forensic activities, there are advisers on government and on business relations. The central committee serves as an advisory council for the dean of students and for the individual advisers who compose it. It is also an active part of the student-faculty congress. The twelve advisers are appointed by the dean of students.

e. The third major group on the personnel council is the student council. This council is composed of students representing eighteen student interests as follows: Forensics, honorary and professional societies, religion, intersorority council, interfraternity council, non-fraternity group, men's dormitory council, women's house government, athletics, literary activities, music, dramatics, publications, citizenship, freshman class, sophomore class, junior class and senior class. These student representatives are elected by their respective interest groups.

f. The remaining members of the personnel council are the dean of the university, the registrar and the comptroller. They are *ex-officio* members.

### THE STUDENT-FACULTY CONGRESS

The twelve faculty advisers, comprising the central committee of the personnel council, sit with the student council, consisting of eighteen representatives from interest groups on the campus, and together they legislate on all matters except those having to do with academic affairs and student discipline. The twelve faculty members do not represent the faculty in the strict sense of the word; they are on the congress because they are definitely interested in the student activities they represent.

Instead of numerical representation, or group representation, the congress is constructed along the lines of student interests. It will be seen that the congress operates as a concrete illustration of democratic government. The dean of students serves as the executive branch. He has veto power over the actions of congress. Recently the congress has adopted the rules committee system whereby any proposed legislation presented to the congress, instead of being voted through hurriedly, is read and passed on to an appropriate committee. This committee at the next meeting of congress reports the proposal and it is acted upon by congress. At all the meetings of the congress the adviser on government, who is professor of political science, sits by the president of congress, who is a student, and difficult questions of government are referred to him, thus giving him an opportunity to teach the principles of good government.

Two statements have been used to define the general powers of congress. First, "The student-faculty congress has jurisdiction with reference to matters which pertain to members of two or more interest groups." Secondly, matters are limited only by the words "academic" and "disciplinary." A third statement should be added. Each of the interest groups which is recognized is vested with authority to exercise jurisdiction over non-academic and non-disciplinary problems which pertain exclusively to its respective field of interest. In carrying out this authority, these groups are under the direct supervision of the twelve advisers. These men have authority to see to it that the various interests and activities on the campus are in keeping with the best policies of the university. So long as an interest-activity does not clash with another interest-activity or with the general welfare of the student body, the congress has no right to interfere. The moment an interest-activity does interfere, the congress should step in for the good of the whole.

This, then, is the general field of congressional activity and responsibility: First, to demonstrate constantly a system of self-government; secondly, to have jurisdiction over all non-academic and non-disciplinary matters pertaining to the members of two or more interest groups; and thirdly, to see to it that the activities of individuals or groups shall contribute to the welfare of the university as a whole.

Space does not permit a detailed discussion of such committees as the publication board, the research committee, the committee on measurements or of the activities of the adviser on social relations or on business management. Suffice it to say that these groups and individuals function as a part of a coordinated whole.

We can not claim for Bucknell a completely satisfactory situation. We do claim one of the broadest experiments on student-faculty cooperation we know anything about. We are combining student enthusiasm and the poise and mature judgment of faculty members in an honest attempt to create an atmosphere of honesty and sincerity where students can learn to live and work and play. Realizing that the typical American college campus is a complicated maze of organizations, activities and influences, we are beginning to think intelligently in terms of making the so-called extra-curricular activities contribute their share to the educational process.

J. Hillis Miller

Bucknell University

# QUOTATIONS

## EVOLUTION IN COOPER UNION

A feeling of great personal loss will be felt by thousands who year after year attended lectures of the People's Institute, the creation of Charles Sprague Smith, who for so many years guided it. Now the institute is gone, ending thirty-six winters and springs of cultural opportunity for New Yorkers. In the large hall of Cooper Union and in classes at several branches of the Public Library men and women, young and old, of diverse occupations and interests, came of an evening to hear Dr. Everett Dean Martin or one of his colleagues discuss social problems, esthetics, scientific research, literature, art and philosophy. Scores of those who came for the first time returned to become students in courses prepared for mature minds.

Mixed with any lament for the passing of the institute as a distinct entity must be intense relief that Dr. Martin is to be able to carry forward his work under Cooper Union itself as head of a new Department of Social Philosophy. This may mean that in a new form the People's Institute will live and grow and serve former students and generations of new students. The announcement of R. Fulton Cutting, president of Cooper Union's board of trustees, and the comments of Henry deForest Baldwin, of the People's Institute, give some assurance that the old institute's spirit may thrive in its new body.

Mr. Baldwin recalls that when the institute was established in 1897 it was "an experiment in realizing Peter Cooper's purposes." It was one of the early agencies for free education of adults in this city. With no school building of its own, its influence touched many lives and social movements. For more than a generation the institute "wrestled with the problem as to how most effectively to put the ideas of Peter Cooper into operation."

The purpose was not the imparting of information for use in the occupations of its students. Rather it strove "to guide students in adjusting themselves to their life conditions, to give them higher satisfactions." If this sounds abstract or remote from public interests, those who drank at the fountain know how real was the gratification.

A fine old institution in its own right, Cooper Union should gain in prestige by addition of a Department of Social Philosophy. The functions of the new department may be perpetuated, it is hoped, far beyond the three years of life assured to it by the Carnegie grant. The English essayist Hazlitt once wrote that "the past is as real and substantial a part of our being as the future can possibly be." The future of Cooper Union is sure to be influenced by the distinguished past of the People's Institute; the two having been long associated, the passing of one becomes the nourishment of the other.—*The New York Sun.*

### THE EDUCATION POLICY OF THE BRITISH LABOR PARTY

A LABORITE view of what public education should provide has been set down by the executive committee of the British Labor party in a report for submission to its conference in October. Compulsory education up to the age of 16 is demanded, along with the establishment of a well-staffed and well-equipped system of free secondary education, to be provided for all children "as a matter of right." The program is put forward with sharp criticism of the policy of the present government in Great Britain.

The report cites the increasing number of boys and girls employed between the ages of 14 and 17 as an argument for making school attendance compulsory until the child is 16. In support of universal free secondary education —with the abolition of fees at schools receiving grants—the report argues that a child's individual personality can best develop in an atmosphere of comradeship and equality.

An environment which offers abundant opportunity for constructive work and open-air activity is also declared necessary, and to this end the demolition of antiquated and unsuitable school buildings is urged. In elementary schools an immediate reduction of classes to forty children and eventually to not more than thirty is demanded. Special training and certification are recommended for all teachers, and better equipment, more books and facilities for practical work and play are asked for schools. Wage-earning employment for children outside of school hours is opposed in the report, which calls for more open-air and nursery schools to aid defective and ailing children.

It is proposed to give local education authorities full power to provide free meals as part of the schools' normal activities, and to impose on them the obligation of insuring that every school child will have a proper diet. The Laborites also favor the restoration of salary cuts to teachers, the reestablishment of the system whereby the government pays not less than 50 per cent. of the educational expenditures of local authorities and the building of new schools.—*The New York Tribune.*

# REPORTS

### THE SCHOOL-LEAVING AGE

WE learn from the London *Times Educational Supplement* that H. Ramsbotham, Parliamentary Secretary to the Board of Education, London, has furnished R. D. Denman, M.P., with the following statement showing those countries in which whole or part-time school attendance up to or beyond the age of 15 is compulsory:

#### I. BRITISH DOMINIONS AND COLONIES

*Australia:* 14 is the upper age limit for compulsory school attendance at the elementary schools in all parts of Australia, but in South Australia, Victoria and Western Australia apprentices in certain trades are required to attend continuation classes (where such cases have been established) for about three years.

*New Zealand:* A law of 1920 raised the age to 15, but this has not yet been put into force, and 14 is the present leaving age.

*Canada:* Alberta: 15 is the school-leaving age. British Columbia: 15 is the school-leaving age. Manitoba: 14 is the normal school-leaving age, but children who are not regularly employed may be required to attend school till they are 16. New Brunswick: in towns education is compulsory up to 16, but children over 12 can be exempted if they have passed the seventh standard and are obliged to start earning. Nova Scotia: 16 is the school-leaving age in towns, but children over 12 can obtain exemption, if they have reached the required standard, or if they are over 13, for employment. Ontario: adolescents of 14 to 16 who have not attained university matriculation standard must attend school for the full time, unless they have obtained exemption on the plea of circumstances compelling them to go to work, in which case they must attend part-time courses where such courses are provided. Saskatchewan: children must attend school until 15 unless they have obtained the high-school entrance standard.

*Union of South Africa:* Attendance is compulsory up to 16 in the Cape Province, Transvaal, and the Orange Free State. In Natal it is compulsory till 15.

*Southern Rhodesia:* An Act of 1930 made school attendance compulsory for children of European descent up to the age of 15.

*South-West Africa:* By an Ordinance of 1926, attendance was made compulsory for children of European descent up to the age of 15.

## II. European Countries

*Estonia:* The actual upper age limit of compulsory school attendance is 14, but a law which has not yet been put into force has been passed extending it to 16.

*Germany:* According to the German Constitution, compulsory school attendance should cover a period of at least eight years in the elementary school, followed by attendance at a continuation school until the completion of the eighteenth year. The actual age at which attendance becomes compulsory is determined by the different state legislatures, but in most parts of Germany attendance at the elementary school is compulsory from 6 to 14, and part-time attendance at a continuation school up to the age of 18. The Minister of Public Instruction in Prussia issued a decree on April 1, 1934, instituting a "year in the country" for children leaving the elementary school. The children who are obliged to spend this year in the country are released from the obligation to attend a continuation school during that period.

*Hungary:* The upper age limit of compulsory attendance is 15. From 6 to 12 in the elementary school, followed by three years in a continuation school.

*Luxembourg:* Attendance at the elementary school is compulsory till 13, and all children are then obliged to attend part-time continuation courses for two years.

*Norway:* The upper age limit of compulsory school attendance is 15, but a child who has obtained the leaving certificate and passed through the seven classes may leave at 14.

*Rumania:* The law provides for compulsory part-time attendance at continuation schools or classes from 14 to 18, but in practise this compulsion has not been enforced.

*Russia (Union of Soviet Socialist Republics):* According to the Soviet plan attendance is compulsory up to 15, but in large parts of the Union attendance beyond the age of 12 has probably not been enforced.

*Switzerland:* In the following Swiss Cantons attendance at the elementary school is compulsory up to or beyond the age of 15: Aargau, Bern, Fribourg, Geneva (rural districts), Grisons, St. Gall, Solothurn, Thurgau, Valais, Vaud. In addition to these cantons some form of part-time school attendance beyond the age of 15 is compulsory in the following: Appenzell (a. Rh.), Appenzell (i. Rh.), Baselland, Baselstadt, Glarus, Nidwalden (for boys), Obwalden (for boys), Schwyz (for boys between 16 and 18), Uri, Zug (for boys between 17 and 19), Zurich (girls between 16 and 18 must attend domestic continuation schools; industrial and commercial apprentices are also required to attend continuation schools).

*Sweden:* Attendance at the elementary school is compulsory from 7 to 14. Children who do not pass on to another school must attend continuation classes for from two to three years, until a required standard has been reached, or until the age of 18.

*Yugoslavia:* Compulsory instruction covers a period of eight years, from 7 to 14 or from 7 to 15.

## III. United States of America

The upper age limit for compulsory school attendance is 15 years or over in all the American States, with the exception of Georgia, Louisiana, North Carolina, South Carolina and Texas. As a general rule, however, regular attendance is required up to the age of 14, and from 14 to 16 (or later) only for those young people who have not completed the eight standards of the elementary school or have not obtained exemption for employment. In many of the states attendance at continuation schools (where such schools exist) is compulsory beyond the age of 15 for young people who have obtained exemption from full-time attendance before the close of the normal period.

# EDUCATIONAL RESEARCH AND STATISTICS

## SCIENCE IN SECONDARY SCHOOL AND COLLEGE

THIS article is concerned with some relationships existing between grades achieved by college students in the various elementary science courses in college. These relationships were computed separately for the group that had had in secondary school the particular science considered; and for the group that had not previously taken it. The average of the correlations between grades in the three sciences and intelligence is .47, and the average of the correlations between course grade in the sciences and general academic standing is .75. These correlations are also less variable (.67 to .81). To a very slight extent these correlations between course grade and general standing are too high, since the grade in the specific science is included in the general academic standing. However, this grade in a

TABLE 1

SCIENCE TAKEN BOTH IN HIGH SCHOOL AND IN COLLEGE

| Class | Correlations of intelligence and grade in course: Chemistry First science taken in college | Physics Second science taken in college | Biology | Correlations of academic standing for 4 years and grade in course: Chemistry First science taken in college | Physics Second science taken in college | Biology |
|---|---|---|---|---|---|---|
| 1930 | .28 | .53 | .40 | .79 | .67 | .62 |
| 1931 | .58 | .33 | .57 | .77 | .80 | .81 |
| 1932 | .52 | .63 | * | .79 | .81 | * |
| 1933 | .42 | .46 | .31 | .67 | .72 | .51 |
| Average | .45 | .49 | .43 | .75 | .75 | .67 |
| p.e.'s | .03 to .07 | | | p.e.'s .02 to .05 | | |
| SCIENCE TAKEN ONLY IN COLLEGE | | | | | | |
| All classes | .36 | .45 | | .59 | .71 | |
| p.e.'s | .07 and .06 | | | p.e.'s .05 and .04 | | |

* Too few cases for a correlation (less than 40).

Table 1 indicates a moderate relationship between intelligence, as measured by the Thorndike test, and college grades in biology, chemistry and physics. The range of the correlations is considerable (.28 to .63). The average r. (.47) seems to be a little higher than most correlations reported between course standing and intelligence for college students.

Table 1 shows a considerably larger relationship existing between course grade and general academic standing for 4 years than is the relationship between intelligence and course grade. specific science is but 1/20 of the general standing, since 5 courses are taken each year for 4 years and hence the spuriousness of the correlations here can be only slight. In this connection it might be of interest to report the average intercorrelation of term-by-term standing of men for these four classes, which is .66 (average of 112 correlations).

Table 2 gives the number of cases and the average intelligence test score of students who have taken a specific science both in secondary school and in college, and of those who have taken the science only in college. There is no observable difference in intelligence between those students who elect either biology or chemistry or physics in secondary school and those who do not. No measures of the reliabilities of these averages were obtained, since there were no observable differences of any significance in any of the comparisons.

TABLE 2

TAKING AND NOT TAKING SPECIFIC SCIENCES IN SECONDARY SCHOOL AND INTELLIGENCE

| | Took in Secondary School Cases | Took in Secondary School Avg. int. | Did not take in Secondary School Cases | Did not take in Secondary School Avg. int. |
|---|---|---|---|---|
| Biology | 145 | 65 | 169 | 66 |
| Chemistry | 344 | 69 | 99 | 68 |
| Physics | 342 | 70 | 112 | 69 |

Table 3 presents the general academic standing, for 4 years, of the men who studied a given science in both secondary school and in college, as compared to those who studied the science only in college. There are no observed differences except in physics, where, on the average, men who have had physics in secondary school achieve a general academic standing 4 per cent. above the men who have not had physics in secondary school. This difference may be due to the superior intelligence of the former group.

TABLE 3

AVERAGES, SIGMAS AND SIGMA DIFFERENCES

| | Biology Cases | Biology Avg. | σ | Chemistry Cases | Chemistry Avg. | Physics Cases | Physics Avg. |
|---|---|---|---|---|---|---|---|
| *Academic Standing:* | | | | | | | |
| In high school and college | 152 | 3.27 | | 359 | 3.36 | 357 | 3.40 |
| In college | 177 | 3.28 | | 103 | 3.34 | 119 | 3.29 |
| *Grade in Course:* | | | | | | | |
| In high school and college | 152 | 3.03 | .09 | 359 | 2.74 | 357 | 3.43 |
| In college | 177 | 2.76 | .08 | 103 | 1.97 | 119 | 2.88 |
| σ Difference | | | .13 | | | | |
| Chances in 100 | | | 98 | | | | |

Men who take but one science in college have a general academic rating which is less than 3 per cent. poorer than men who have more than one science in college (3.27–3.35).

Table 3 also gives the specific science course grades of men who have had that science in secondary school and of those men who did not have that science in secondary school. The last two lines of this table give the sigma difference of the grades in biology and the probability that this difference is due to something other than chance. The sigma differences for chemistry and physics were not obtained since, by comparing each of these distributions with the distribution of biology, it was apparent that the chances in 100 that the difference was due to something other than chance were 100. The course grades of students who had a specific science in secondary school are consistently higher than the course grades of students who take that science for the first time when in college. This relation is slight for biology and very definite for chemistry and physics. The grading system used is: A–5, B–4, C–3, D–2, E–1, F–0. D is passing, but for graduation a student must have a general average not less than 2.5. Students who take chemistry in college, without having had it in secondary school, achieve, on the average, a grade of 2.04. In other words, their chances of passing the course are 50–50 and their chances of obtaining a grade acceptable for graduation are 1 in 4 (from distribution curve).

The average grade of men in their first science taken in college is 2.67, as compared with their grade of 3.22 in the second science taken in college (from a distribution not included herewith); an increase of 21 per cent. The grading by these three departments varies considerably. The department which grades lowest is chemistry. Since this subject is required of most freshmen, it is usually the first science taken. To counteract the resulting difference in populations of the three science groups, we treated them separately, finding the average grade for each group. The average of these three average grades is a truer measure. We now find that the figures are 2.68 and 2.87, respectively, and the difference in grades in the first and second science groups drops 7 per cent. The higher grades made by the second science group may or may not be due to transfer. In these 4 classes, which were the subject of this study, the average increase in academic standing from term to term is, on the average, 10 per cent. This in itself may be due to transfer. However, we know that there are many potential elements here, such as choosing easy courses, choosing courses in which high grades are given, and all the devious means by which a student may accomplish a grade which is in excess of his real ability and production in a course.

TABLE 4

| | Cases | Average academic standing | Average grade | Cases | Average Intelligence |
|---|---|---|---|---|---|
| Biology | 329 | 3.28 | 2.88 | 314 | 66 |
| Chemistry | 462 | 3.36 | 2.56 | 443 | 69 |
| Physics | 476 | 3.37 | 3.30 | 454 | 70 |

Table 4 demonstrates the marked variation, by departments, that exists in grading and shows that this variation is not warranted by differences in native ability nor in general academic standing.

### CONCLUSIONS

*From Table 1:*

(1) Grades in science courses are, to a moderate extent, a function of intelligence. It might be expected that this relationship would be more pronounced.

(2) Grades in chemistry and physics are more closely related to general academic standing than to intelligence. This relationship might be more marked.

(3) When students take chemistry before taking physics, there is a higher correlation between physics and intelligence, and a higher correlation between physics and academic standing than between chemistry and intelligence and chemistry and academic standing. These facts may be due to intellectual maturity, transfer of training (general or specific), better grading by the instructor or other factors.

*From Table 2:*

(4) No tendency is observed for bright or dull students, who subsequently come to Lafayette, either to take or not to take biology or chemistry or physics in high school.

*From Table 3:*

(5) To a slight extent, students who have had physics in high school tend to achieve a superior general standing in college.

(6) There is no relationship between general scholarship in college and the selection of biology or chemistry or physics in high school. There is a slight tendency for those who have had physics in high school to achieve a superior scholastic record in college.

(7) Students who have had a specific science in both high school and college achieve a higher grade in that science in college than do students who take that science for the first time in college. This relationship is slight in biology and very definite in chemistry and physics.

(8) Students who take chemistry for the first time in college have, on the average, only a 50–50 chance of obtaining a passing grade and one chance in four of obtaining a grade acceptable for graduation.

*From Tables 2 and 3:*

(9) There is considerable discrepancy between grades in the three sciences—biology, chemistry, physics. This discrepancy may not be accounted for by differences in intelligence nor in general academic accomplishment.

HERBERT W. ROGERS

LAFAYETTE COLLEGE
MAY 21, 1934

## NEW BOOKS IN EDUCATION

BOGEN, EMIL and LEHMANN W. S. HISEY. *What About Alcohol?* Pp. 112. Scientific Education Association, Los Angeles.

BOND, HORACE M. *The Education of the Negro in the American Social Order.* Pp. xx + 501. Prentice-Hall. $2.75.

KOOS, LEONARD V. and staff. *Summary.* Bulletin, 1932, No. 17, National Survey of Education. Pp. ix + 232. U. S. Government Printing Office. $0.25.

LENNES, N. J. *A First Course in Algebra.* Pp. xii + 456. Macmillan. $1.36.

LICHTENSTEIN, ARTHUR. *Can Attitudes Be Taught?* Pp. ix + 88. Johns Hopkins Press. $1.25.

# SCHOOL AND SOCIETY

WITH WHICH ARE COMBINED THE EDUCATIONAL REVIEW, ESTABLISHED IN 1891, THE TEACHERS MAGAZINE, ESTABLISHED IN 1878, AND THE SCHOOL JOURNAL, ESTABLISHED IN 1874.

Volume 40 | SATURDAY, SEPTEMBER 15, 1934 | Number 1029

## THE IMPLICATIONS OF FEDERAL AID TO EDUCATION*

By Dr. R. A. KENT

PRESIDENT OF THE UNIVERSITY OF LOUISVILLE

THE subject on which I have been asked to speak at this time is "The Implications of Federal Aid to Education." My approach to the discussion of this will be objective as far as I am able to make it so. While there has been a great deal of controversy of opinion over federal aid to education, there is at the same time a great deal of material that is factual.

Perhaps the best immediate approach is to take a brief survey of what the Federal Government is doing and has already done in the way of support to education.[1] It may be surprising to some of us to know that the beginning of federal aid to education dates back to the Revolutionary War period. On October 10, 1780, Congress passed a resolution that the Western Territory, which had been claimed by several colonies and was later ceded to the United States, should be disposed of for the common benefit of all the states, and that the manner and conditions of the sale of these lands should be expressly regulated by Congress.

This was followed by the Ordinance of 1785, which contained the clause reserving from sale "lot No. 16 of every township for the maintenance of public schools within the said township." The importance and implications of this stipulation could not possibly have been realized at the time of its passage. It established a precedent whose influence was so far reaching as to reach down to the present time, and marked the beginning of a permanent policy of using public lands for public education. It was unquestionably the corner-stone of federal aid to public education in the United States.

The Ordinance of 1787 for the government of the Northwest Territory contained the declaration that "Religion, morality, and knowledge being necessary to good government and the happiness of mankind, schools and the means of education shall forever be encouraged." The Ordinance of July 13, 1787, made no grants of land for education, but laid the foundation for a general development of free public education throughout the United States.

This ordinance was immediately followed by that of July 23, 1787, for the sale of public lands in Ohio, under which Section 16 in each township was to be reserved for the maintenance of public schools, and "not more than two complete townships to be given perpetually for the purpose of a university." Congress granted lands for schools to Ohio when it became a state in 1802 and for a university in 1803.

Similar grants of land for educational

* An address delivered at an Educational Conference at Northwestern University, July 17, 1934.

[1] I am indebted to Dr. F. J. Kelly, of the U. S. Office of Education, for the facts in this summary.

purposes were made by Congress from time to time to the territories and states in the Northwest Territory. Beginning with 1803 a corresponding grant was made in Tennessee, which marked the beginning of a similar Congressional policy to the new states in the South and West.

About 1820 was begun the practise of granting to each state on its admission to the Union two townships of saline lands, and from 3 to 5 per cent. of the net proceeds of the sale of all public lands within the borders of the state. These grants of land and money were in many cases used in part or in whole for education. By the "Internal Improvement Act" of 1841, 500,000 acres of public lands were given to each state admitted after 1800, and these grants were devoted to education after 1845.

In 1850 the "Swamp Land Grant Act" was passed. Under this, fifteen states received over 6,000,000 acres. In twelve of these states a part or all of the proceeds from the sale of these lands was given to education.

On July 2, 1862, the first Morrill Act was passed. This provided for colleges of agriculture and mechanical arts and donated public lands to the several states and territories which maintained these institutions. The amount of public land so appropriated was equivalent to "30,000 acres for each senator and representative in Congress to which the states are respectively entitled with the apportionment under the census of 1860." The proceeds from the sale of these lands constituted a permanent fund or endowment. The income from these lands for the fiscal year ending June 30, 1933, amounted to $967,107. Sixteen of the land-grant colleges received $534,191 from other land-grant funds for the same year.

In 1887 the Hatch Act was passed. This provided for the establishment of agricultural experiment stations in connection with the colleges established in the several states under the provision of the Morrill Act of 1862. In 1906 the Hatch Act was amended by the Adams Act to provide for an increased annual appropriation. For the fiscal year ending June 30, 1933, the colleges received $1,456,347 from the Hatch-Adams funds.

In 1890 the second Morrill Act was passed, and was amended in 1907 by the Nelson Act. The annual appropriations from the Morrill-Nelson funds now amount to $50,000 for each state and territory, for the benefit of the land-grant institutions. The total annual appropriation under this act is now $2,550,000.

In 1914 the Smith-Lever Act was passed. This provides for cooperative extension work in the agricultural colleges which receive benefits under the Morrill Act of 1862. For the year ending June 30, 1933, the amount distributed under the Smith-Lever Act was $6,200,833, with $930,574 additional cooperative extension funds.

In 1917 Congress passed the Smith-Hughes Act. This provides for cooperation between the Federal Government and the several states in the promotion of vocational education in agriculture, in the trades and in industries, and for the preparation of teachers of subjects in the same classifications. In 1929 this act was supplemented by the George Reed Act to provide for further development of vocational education. During the year ending June 30, 1933, the government appropriated under this act $2,600,000. Under the George Ellzeg Act an additional federal appropriation was made, amounting to $3,100,000. The amount spent from these funds by the states and territories for the year ending June 30, 1933, was $8,739,865.

In 1924 the Clarke-McNary Act was passed. This was primarily to provide for the protection of forest lands, and although subsidizing education was not mentioned in the act, the land-grant colleges received some financial benefits. For the year ending June 30, 1933, the amount which they thus received was $59,751.

In 1925 there was enacted the Purnell Act. This was for the more complete endowment of the agricultural experiment stations. Only the land-grant institutions which were primarily or exclusively for white students participated in the benefits of this particular legislation, and the total amount which they received under this act during the year ending June 30, 1933, was $2,653,860.

In 1928 Congress passed the Capper-Ketchum Act. This provided for further development of agriculture and experimentation work at the agricultural colleges of the several states. The total amount spent under this act for the year ending June 30, 1933, was $1,479,632.

For the year already indicated the Federal Government spent upon its military training program in 124 colleges and universities and in 100 high schools and academies $6,698,219.

For the year ending June 30, 1933, the last fiscal year of the Federal Government for which we have complete returns, the United States distributed for the support of education under the several acts and for the purposes above enumerated a total of $28,697,323. This figure does not include monies spent to maintain the United States Military Academy at West Point, the United States Naval Academy at Annapolis, the United States Coast Guard Academy at New London, Connecticut, appropriations made to Howard University, the Gallaudet College for the Deaf, special schools for Indian children, special schools for Eskimo children or the United States Office of Education.

The facts which have just been recited warrant certain deductions:

*First,* the grants which Congress made to the several states for the support of public education began with the Ordinance of 1787.

*Second,* it must be recognized that the original grants of the Ordinance of 1787 such as the first one made to the state of Ohio, was a Federal grant, a subsidy for both the elementary schools and for the university. This was not a grant by the state or territory of Ohio, it was an enactment by Congress which compelled the government of Ohio to reserve certain lands for the support of special types of educational institutions.

*Third,* that this was no chance act of Congress is proven conclusively by its subsequent acts in making corresponding requirements, beginning in 1803, to the states carved out of the territory in the South and West.

*Fourth,* since Federal aid to education was begun at a time contemporary with the adoption of the Constitution of the United States, it is obvious that such aid was accepted in the earliest years of this Constitution as consistent with it.

*Fifth,* beginning with the Morrill Act in 1862, which was an appropriation again of public lands, Congress has maintained, and from time to time materially increased, specific appropriations for definite types of educational institutions and programs.

*Sixth,* the general policy of Federal Aid to Education in America is a policy which by reason of its inception in the very earliest period of the independence of this country, and by its uninterrupted and materially increasing volume from time to time, has become as permanent as any policy which the Federal government pursues, that is not explicitly enumerated under the Constitutional provisions specifying the powers given to the Congress. This is the first fundamental implication of Federal Aid to Education.

Let us now consider what the effect of federal aid upon education has been. Since about 1885 there seems to have been two main developments in this matter.[2] One is the remarkable increase in the amount of aid and the range of uses to which it has been put. The other is the equally notable increase of federal control over the money appropriated. It is natural that the two should go together.

Take, for example, the aid for agricultural education. The Morrill Act of 1862 required only that the state which accepted the grant should maintain at least

[2] See "Introduction to American Government," Ogg and Ray, page 624.

one agricultural college and make an annual report to Congress upon it, showing the institution's progress and the condition of the fund received from the Federal Government. Many of the states sold their lands at shamefully low prices. As a result Congress in 1889 prohibited states which entered the Union after that date from selling any of the lands allotted to them under the Morrill Act at less than $10 an acre. The second Morrill Act, that of 1890, required that the Secretary of the Interior satisfy himself that the subsidized institution in each state was satisfactorily fulfilling the purposes of the act, before he paid the allotment to the institution. Thus federal supervision was introduced.

The Nelson Act of 1907, which increased the subsidy, at the same time entrusted the administration of the whole system of aid to the then Bureau of Education.

At the beginning of the present century occurred a step of still greater importance. The Smith-Lever Act of 1914, for the support of extension work on the part of agricultural colleges, seems to be the first Congressional legislation which required a state to appropriate a sum of money to assist in carrying out the purposes of the act, before it might receive federal aid. Here appears for the first time the so-called 50-50 rule, or matching the federal dollar. It has been incorporated in practically all federal school aid since that time.

As far as agricultural extension is concerned, the federal act allotting funds for this purpose requires that each agricultural college maintain a distinct division for the administration of extension work in agriculture and home economics, that there be a director of this division who must be acceptable to the Federal Department of Agriculture, that all the plans for the division be submitted to this department, and finally that all money for agriculture extension work, whether derived from national, state or local sources, be administered through this single division of extension.

The Smith-Hughes Act reaches down into the states and dictates the conditions under which they may share in this allotment, requiring every participating state to have a board of vocational education.

It may not be amiss to mention here, by way of illustrative comparison, federal aid to highways. Next to public schools, highways form the principal item of public expense. Beginning with 1912, the Federal Government made appropriation to be used on rural roads over which mail was carried. This has been steadily increased until at the present time we have a rather fixed subsidizing of road construction. There is another 50-50 plan.

The type of road must be approved by the federal engineers, and a suitable allotment for materials must be regularly provided by the state itself. Inspection and approval of roads seeking Federal subsidy are made by the Bureau of Public Roads of the Department of Agriculture. An authority upon this subject states that the effect of this system has been to stimulate state expenditure for road building and to increase enormously the supply of good roads available throughout the country. It has also improved the road construction and materials.[3]

A very recent development in the national recovery program gives some most interesting information from an entirely new angle, that of the Rural Rehabilitation Program. Among the activities of this program is that of "Providing the services of trained specialists in agriculture and home economics to aid in formulating plans for subsistence farming and home making operations and in supervising the execution of such plans." "The successful consummation of the Rural Rehabilitation Program requires definite official co-

[3] See Young, "New American Government and its Work," page 630.

operation between Federal, State and County Emergency Relief Administrations, the Agricultural Adjustment Administration and the Extension Service of the United States Department of Agriculture and Agricultural Colleges."

"County Extension Agents are joint employees of the United States Department of Agriculture, the Colleges of Agriculture, and of the counties in which they are located. They are responsible for disseminating useful and practical information relative to the art and science of agriculture and home economics. They know the farm people, rural leaders, resources and conditions of their counties. They are informed relative to the program and policies of the Agricultural Adjustment Administration. They maintain offices in which literature on agriculture and home economics is available for distribution, and through which services of specialists of the Land-Grant Colleges and United States Department of Agriculture may be obtained. It is imperative that the experience and resources of the Extension Service be utilized in this program."

State and county extension workers are to "assist in outlining plans, in giving subject matter information to groups of rehabilitation people, and in giving expert advice and assistance in setting up and operating community work centers and other work projects. . . . Extension workers should also be available for advising on the location and operation of work centers and for giving public addresses and otherwise assisting in informing the public relative to the Rural Rehabilitation Program."

In the personnel set-up in each state for the administration of this program the state relief administration is recommended to organize a State Rural Rehabilitation Department, and to employ a state director of rural rehabilitation and a home economics assistant. But note that this director and assistant shall "be acceptable to the State Director of Extension." For each county having 50 or more relief cases there is to be a county rural rehabilitation supervisor, "dependent for advice on the county agricultural agent." These county or district supervisors are to "be recommended by the State Extension Service and appointed by the State Relief Administration." They also shall "enjoy the facilities of the County Extension office with respect to the use of bulletins, literature, etc."

Exactly parallel provisions are made with regard to personnel for home economics.

I have gone into considerable detail with respect to this Rural Rehabilitation Program because it contains implications of far-reaching import to considerations of federal aid to education. In the first place, it is clearly stated that "County Extension Agents are joint employees of the United States Department, of the Colleges of Agriculture, and of the counties in which they are located." Now on what basis of fact does this statement rest?

The answer is simple. There are two parts to it. The Smith-Lever Act requires:

(1) that each college benefitting under it shall maintain a distinct division for the administration of extension work in Agriculture and in Home Economics;
(2) that there shall be a director of this division;
(3) that this director shall be acceptable to the Federal Department of Agriculture; and
(4) that all plans for the division be submitted to the Federal Department.

The county agricultural extension agent is paid by funds from (a) the Federal Government, (b) the State Government, and (c) the county. He must be acceptable to the director of the State Extension Department.

The two parts to the answer then are, that the agent's pay and his appointment are contingent directly or indirectly upon

Washington. Here then we have a local official who is dependent upon the action of Congress for part of his wage, and must be acceptable to a state official, who in turn must be acceptable to a federal official. This, it would seem, is the factual basis for the statement that the county extension agent is a joint employee, with the Federal Government one of the employers.

His status as to pay and appointment are, I hope, thus made clear. This is one implication of importance to any one interested in federal aid to education.

The next implication is the power which the Federal Government is assuming to use because of the facts first stated. It is highly significant that in this case a joint employee is by one employee directed, without alternative, to discharge certain duties, without the consent of the other two employees having been obtained, or without their even having been consulted, as far as is indicated. Nor is there any lack of clarity as to obligation of the joint employee in this case. The wording of the statement from Washington is, "It is *imperative* [italics mine] that the experiences and resources of the Extension Service be utilized in this program." Read that sentence again and ponder it.

Now who drew up that and all other provisions of the Rural Rehabilitation Program? They were approved, at any rate, by Colonel Lawrence Westbrook, director of Rural Rehabilitation, Federal Emergency Relief Administration; Dr. H. R. Talley, chief, Planning Division, Agricultural Adjustment Administration; and Dr. C. W. Warburton, director of extension, U. S. Department of Agriculture.

Let there be no mistake. I am not making and shall not make the slightest reference other than this to the merits of the Rural Rehabilitation Program as such. That has nothing whatever to do with the point at issue. The point is that this case is a most outstanding illustration of the assumption by the Federal Government of the right to direct the activities of a service and personnel which it supports financially only in part, with no apparent limit on that direction, short of complete control.

If the Federal Government, because it helps to support an educational activity, can reach its authority down and arbitrarily direct the personnel of that activity, then the Federal Government is in reality using state and local (in this case county) funds to subsidize its program, for the county agent is paid by state and county as well as federal money. Moreover, it does this without asking or obtaining consent of these subdivisions of government, and the whole situation represents a reversal of the original purpose of the federal aid act, which was for the Federal Government to subsidize the state and the county.

Some one will say this recent procedure has been taken as the result of an emergency. This is true. But I submit to you that the appeals of the several groups that have been made within the past two or three years for federal aid to education have been made on the basis that an emergency exists. If you accept appropriations on grounds of emergency, you can not divorce funds so appropriated from any legitimate conditions of administering these funds, contingent upon that same emergency. And in addition, retraction of federal authority, if exercised, will be more difficult than obtaining the appropriation has been up to date.

Please bear in mind that not a single penny emergency appropriation has been voted by Congress directly to education. What education has received of federal funds for emergency purposes has been allotted from CWA, PWA and FERA funds. In the administration of these allotments the Federal Government through its appropriate agencies has had a determining voice, and justifiably so.

What authority the government would

assume were it to make appropriations directly to education can be estimated only on the basis of what it has done up to date. The record shows a markedly growing tendency on the government's part to take over more and more authority in connection with the actual distribution as well as the administration of all the program whose support is only partly provided by federal funds. The history of federal aid to education from its inception up to the present time seems to bear out this statement. It is supplemented by the history of federal aid to public highways. And the two histories bear some most striking similarities.

This is a second major implication in the consideration of federal aid to education.

A third implication is inextricably tied up with political patronage. The intimate history of government during the past fifteen months or so has revealed, in most striking manner, the limits to which men's selfishness and ambition will take them. The case of the governor found guilty under federal indictment is common public information. But what about the governor who, with the front of a Hitler or a Mussolini, makes levies directly on faculties of the state educational institutions for money to support his campaign for the Presidency? What about the governor who promises all that the FERA asks, in order to get its allotment, and then after receiving it does not carry out a single promise because the funds can not be administered to bear upon political patronage? What about United States Senators—good Democrats, too—who are reported on unimpeachable authority to be bitter against cabinet members who are interested in finding men who can do jobs well, rather than mere party men? How about a part of the educational emergency program itself which necessitated a special administrative order, issued and signed by President Roosevelt himself, before it could be pried loose from patronage-hungry senators, who already knew that politics were not to be taken into consideration in the project? What about the intimate story of some appointments pressed for the TVA?

Not one of the above references but what has back of it a real, red-hot story. My friends, any one who thinks that sums of money which might be appropriated by Congress directly to education, in quantity anywhere nearly approaching the amounts asked for by any one of several major organizations, would escape the onslaught of political patronage—that person is thinking in a world that does not exist.

This is a third fact that is implicit in federal aid to education. Some doubtless will be inclined to question, even seriously, this assertion. They will point out that this menace has not been present, certainly in any serious degree, among the aid that Congress has already granted to education. On the other hand, remember that grants to higher education, that is, to *one* institution, in each state is one thing. Grants in aid that might benefit *all public schools* in a state are an entirely different consideration, and become of immediate interest to the office-holder who is interested in the votes of the state as a whole. This will be of more interest even than aid for highways, because the latter at any given time can not be as widely diffused over the state as aid to public schools.

There are some other implications which I have purposely left until last because they are more familiar to you, and which I need not do more than mention. If we assume that aid would be given on some ratio such as the present 50-50 basis, there is some very good ground for believing that the general results would be comparable with those coming from aid to roads. State expenditures might be stimulated. Furthermore, the *quality* of educational privileges offered in some states would undoubtedly be tremendously improved over what it is now.

Now it is in those states where such improvement is most needed that it has the least possibility of occurring, for such states do not usually have money available to make the improvement. I suppose that there is no more widely accepted implication of federal aid to education than that such aid would in some way be used as an equalization fund for needy states. Indeed, this fact, which constitutes the core of the argument for federal subsidy, is the core of the argument against it, at least in the judgment of many. Why should Massachusetts pay money to help support the schools of Mississippi or Montana?

There is tied up in the controversy at this point an issue which seems to be of major importance. The Supreme Court of Tennessee has stated:

> . . . that the legislature, under the constitutional provision, may as well establish a uniform system of schools and a uniform administration of them, as it may establish a uniform system of criminal laws and of courts to execute them. . . . The prevention of crime, and preservation of good order and peace, is the highest exercise of the police power of the State, whether done by punishing offenders or educating the children. . . . The object of the public school system is to prevent crime by educating the people. . . .

The Supreme Court of Kentucky has said the following:

> Power to levy taxes is an essential attribute of sovereignty. That is so because the necessity of conducting government requires that money be raised for the purpose by some sort of taxation. So is the power to educate the youth of the state, to fit them so that the state may prosper; else the taxes raised could scarcely meet demands made upon a government in these times.

The Congress of the United States in the Ordinance of 1787 declared that "Religion, morality, and knowledge being necessary to good government and the happiness of mankind, schools and the means of education shall forever be encouraged."

The Congress since 1787 has steadfastly, consistently and without interruption been developing federal aid to public education on all levels, showing a realistic commitment to the Ordinance of 1787 in no uncertain terms.

In the light of these facts, I therefore assert that the Congress not only has the right, but also that by precedent, by settled legislative policy and by the very social principles underlying our government is under definite obligation to assist in seeing that "the means of education shall forever be encouraged."

The major part of what I have said will by some be interpreted as argument against federal aid. It has been my purpose as far as possible to point out objective facts rather than to engage in a controversy. Some of these facts point one way, and some the other. The case in favor of federal aid to public schools is nowhere put more cogently as far as I know than in an address by Dr. Zook, until recently U. S. Commissioner of Education, published recently in SCHOOL AND SOCIETY.[4] With the main points of his contention I heartily agree. That agreement in no way decreases the force of any of the implications which are here pointed out.

# EDUCATIONAL EVENTS

## THE TEACHING OF SPANISH IN PUERTO RICO

THE attempt, begun soon after the transfer of Puerto Rico from Spain to the United States, to make the national language the medium of instruction in the public schools is reported to have failed, and pupils will now be taught the three R's in their native tongue.

[4] George F. Zook, "Federal Aid to Education," SCHOOL AND SOCIETY, July 14, 1934.

José Padin, commissioner of education, has directed that English be retained as a special subject, and American text-books will be used until Spanish texts can be prepared. English will be taught throughout the elementary schools from the first grade. The order does not apply to high schools. Approximately 85 per cent. of the pupils leave school before the fourth grade.

Dr. Padin and his supporters believe the change is based on sound pedagogical principles, which will result in liberalizing the educational process and, eventually, in a more thorough knowledge of English. He maintains that children have been hampered by being forced to do their class work in a foreign tongue, which many seldom hear outside the schoolroom.

The Commissioner of Education contends that by making English a special subject in the elementary schools, and having it taught intensively by carefully selected teachers, more satisfactory results will be obtained. In upper grades English will receive more attention than other subjects.

Although the order was unexpected the language problem has been studied and discussed for years. Seven years ago a committee from Columbia University surveyed the insular school system and urged the complete elimination of English from the lower grades.

Dr. J. J. Osuna, dean of the College of Education of Puerto Rico, began his service twelve years ago by advocating English, but is said to have become convinced that the educational welfare of the children requires the change to Spanish. Both Dr. Osuna and Dr. Padin are American university men who use English as readily as Spanish.

## FEDERAL AID FOR SCHOOL CONSTRUCTION

More than half the public school construction now going on in the United States is being financed by the Public Works Administration. According to a statement made by Administrator Harold L. Ickes more than $210,000,000 have been added to the capital outlay for school-building construction as a direct result of the PWA program for the expenditure of $3,700,000,000. According to Mr. Ickes, had it not been for federal assistance through public works there would have been only a negligible amount of school construction this year.

Some idea of the extent of PWA's contribution to increasing the nation's educational facilities may be gained from the following:

> Through the middle of August PWA had allotted $133,866,269 for 1,071 educational buildings in every section of the country.
>
> A major portion of this money—$98,358,325—is being spent on elementary and secondary schools.
>
> Of the total amount allocated $122,910,358 is for 936 non-federal projects and $10,955,911 for 135 federal projects. As many of the non-federal allotments are for grants only (30 per cent. of the cost of labor and material involved), it is estimated that construction resulting from the PWA program will be approximately $210,000,000.

Mr. Ickes pointed out that the significance of the PWA contribution to the country's capital investment in schools is all the more striking in view of the fact that school construction was at a virtual standstill until the public works program began to function.

From a peak of $433,000,000 spent on public elementary and secondary school construction in 1925 there was a steady decline until 1932 when only $210,996,262 was expended. The expenditures for 1933–34 would be far under this figure had it not been for PWA assistance.

Every section of the country has benefitted from the allotments which range in size from a grant of $600 for a one-story frame building in Edom, Texas, to a loan and grant of $8,285,000 to Los Angeles for repairs, replacements and reconstruction of 130 school plants. The construction now under way includes new schools, additions, gymnasiums and auditoriums, swimming pools, libraries, dormitories and shops. There has been the widest possible geographical distribution of funds. Three grade schools are under construction in Honolulu. At the same time new facilities are being provided in San Juan, Puerto Rico.

A number of universities and colleges have shared in the PWA program. Among them are Purdue University, William and Mary College at Williamsburg, Virginia, the University of Minnesota, the University of Utah, Virginia Polytechnic Institute, Arkansas State University, the University of Toledo, the Oklahoma Agricultural and Mechanical College and the Agricultural and Mechanical College of Texas.

## THE PUBLIC SCHOOLS OF CHICAGO

A SPECIAL correspondent to *The New York Times* reports that three quarters of a million children have returned to the Chicago schools; 250,000 have enrolled in the parochial and suburban schools, the others entering the city's public schools. Opening of the schools was delayed by the shortened term—an economy measure.

It is stated that after retreating, both educationally and financially, for four years, the schools are advancing in some directions. The most important fact is that the school teachers have been paid in full for the first time in three years and are assured that hereafter they will receive their salary checks on time. A $25,000,000 loan by the Federal Government, secured by valuable Loop property owned by the school board, made this possible.

William J. Bogan, superintendent of public schools, said:

> We look forward to the new year with hope and enthusiasm. Our teachers have suffered immeasurably during these years when their salaries were as much as seven months overdue, and some have lost their insurance, homes and investments, but they are overjoyed at the opportunity of teaching again with a sense of security as to a living income. We expect this improved morale to be reflected in efficiency of teaching and administration, the benefit accruing directly to the pupils.

Other educational advances include the construction of five new high-school buildings, aided by a federal loan. Three of these have been completed, two more will be ready in February —they will seat 15,799 students. These include the new Lane Technical High School, on a twenty-acre campus, housing in one building more than 7,000 pupils, and the Steinmetz High School with room for 3,000 pupils.

Another important advance in the face of the depression and a decreased school budget will be the opening next week of three junior colleges, for which 4,500 have already enrolled. They take the place of the Crane Junior College, abandoned a year ago.

Superintendent Bogan expects a rapid extension of the junior college system. Government action in providing financial aid for needy students is a factor. About 400 of the new junior high-school pupils will each be entitled to the $15 a month grant, for which they will do miscellaneous work in the school system.

Although a substantial increase in high school and junior college attendance is anticipated, a decrease in total school enrolment is expected by the school board, for two reasons. One is the 117,000 decrease in Chicago's population since the 1930 government census. A Washington bureau recently issued estimates of increase in population of various cities, but the decline here is about 30,000 a year, compared to the usual 60,000 a year growth.

Another reason is the lower birth rate, which has registered a decrease in enrolment in the lower grades for several years, ranging from 1,200 to 2,000 a year. This trend is expected to reach the high schools in two or three years.

The schools are still suffering the severe handicaps inaugurated last year in the name of economy. Again the city's educational system will be compelled to dispense with junior high schools and other modern practises, principals will be burdened with trying to administer two schools each, and high schools will get along without deans. Teachers once more will carry the load of six classes a day instead of five—the acknowledged maximum of efficiency.

## EDUCATIONAL WORK OF THE METROPOLITAN MUSEUM OF ART

CHANGES in the educational work of the Metropolitan Museum of Art aimed at making its instruction facilities more easily available to the public have been announced by William M. Ivins, Jr., acting director of the museum.

Free lectures and gallery talks have been provided for on Saturday and Sunday afternoons and individual or group appointments on other days have been arranged at a small fee. From now on, the series of free gallery talks and lectures would run through the week, except for Monday and Friday, the regular pay days at the museum.

One series of seven lectures, covering the seven most popular sections of the museum, will be given on Tuesdays, Wednesdays and Thursdays, rotated so that one may hear the series in succession or get all the lectures by attending them on one day a week for seven weeks.

Another of the series, held on Saturdays, will cover the entire museum in a series of talks running chronologically through the season. Individual appointments, of which there were

4,067 for groups and individuals during 1933, will be continued. Public school teachers with their classes will continue to be admitted free on any day, including pay days, and museum instructors will continue to talk to the classes on any subject the teacher desires.

Another change announced by Mr. Ivins is in connection with the free courses for public school teachers, for which in the past they have been certified for credit toward professional advancement.

This year, through the courtesy of the College of the City of New York, these courses will now count as courses of that institution. The courses will still be free, but if a teacher desires credit, it will be necessary to register at City College and pass its requirements regarding examinations.

A folder listing the lectures will be published three times a year.

## THE EXTENSION DIVISION OF COLUMBIA UNIVERSITY

IN the extension division of Columbia University more than fifty new courses have been added. Most of them are concerned with the complexities of government and business resulting from new political developments. It is said that never before in the history of the extension division has there been so great interest in contemporary problems. The new curriculum has been built around the leading issues in public affairs, including social reconstruction, the relationship of government and business, foreign trade and the stock markets.

Professor Schuyler C. Wallace will present a series of lectures entitled "The Process of Government—The New Deal." In this course consideration will be given to the Agricultural Adjustment Act, to the recovery and transportation acts and to the financial policies of the administration. Farm and drought relief and labor policies will be discussed.

A study of business processes and social reconstruction, illustrated by events in the United States since the establishment of the NRA, will be made, under the direction of Dr. L. R. Robinson, by W. H. Reeves and Professor Milton Handler. Dr. Handler will lecture on government regulation of business competition. He will take up the regulation of advertising, trademarks, the common law and statutory regulation of competitive practises, etc. Professor J. W. Angell will explain the effects of currency depreciation on international trade in a course which will survey world trade currents to-day, the foreign trade of the United States, foreign exchanges and tariffs. Another addition to the curriculum will be a discussion of methods and problems of financing foreign trade. Banking and legal problems arising in connection with credit instruments will be analyzed by Mr. Reeves. Organization and administration of security syndicates will be the subject of a course to be given by Russel Murray, Jr.

An investigation of the food-production industries, particularly the cost characteristics of each type of industry and the volume of output and earnings, will be made under Dr. E. H. Hempel. Geographic, technical and financial factors in the location of plants will be noted. An industrial engineering survey of the food industries, disclosing their economic characteristics and factors influencing their stability as manufacturing enterprises, will be the basis of a considerable part of the course. Under the direction of Erich A. Otto, a survey of social and economic conditions surrounding the individual enterprise will be made, with emphasis on the increasing tendency toward coordinating industry with national economy.

The financial problems confronting the City of New York will be presented by Professor Joseph McGoldrick, comptroller of the city. He will review the city's recent financial history, the transit question and the plans proposed for the city's future development. Examination will be made of the work of the Board of Estimate, the Board of Aldermen and the Municipal Assembly. Professor McGoldrick will also discuss the changes suggested for the city charter.

Professor Roswell F. Magill, of the School of Law, will lecture on the tax system, with particular attention to constitutional limitations upon state and federal taxation and to the legal problems involved in excise, inheritance, income and property taxation.

## APPOINTMENTS AT THE OHIO STATE UNIVERSITY

NEW heads for four Ohio State University departments and the student health service are included in a list of personnel changes announced by President George W. Rightmire. These, including appointments, resignations and promotions, have been approved by the board of trustees. All new appointments are made to fill vacancies in the regular staff.

Dr. Carl L. Spohr, member of medical faculties at Ohio Medical University and Ohio State University since 1898, has been made acting chairman of the department of pathology, succeeding the late Dr. Ernest Scott.

Dr. Guy-Harold Smith has been named chairman of the department of geography, succeeding Dr. Charles C. Huntington, who recently resigned that position. Dr. Smith has been a member of the Ohio State geography faculty since 1927.

The trustees have accepted the resignation of Dr. Raymond J. Seymour, member of the teaching staff since 1904, as chairman of the department of physiology, and has approved the appointment of Dr. Frank A. Hartman, professor of physiology at the University of Buffalo, as the new department chairman. Both Dr. Huntington and Dr. Seymour will continue as members of the faculty, their resignations applying only to administrative duties involved in department chairmanships.

Dr. John W. Wilce will be the new director of the University Health Service, which replaces the Student Medical Service. Dr. Wilce, a former football coach, has been professor of physical education and associate physician in the health service. Under the new arrangement made for this service, staff members will be given ranking in the department of medicine, as follows: Dr. Wilce, professor of medicine; Dr. M. F. Osborn, associate professor; Dr. J. A. Beer, Dr. Shirley Armstrong, Dr. Charlotte Winnemore, assistant professors; Dr. J. M. Foley, instructor. A new University Health Council will serve in an advisory capacity.

University trustees have approved a plan by which administration of the department of English for the coming year will be in the hands of a committee whose members are Professors M. O. Percival, H. R. Walley and J. F. Fullington.

Dr. M. B. Ogle, chairman of the department of classical languages and member of the faculty since 1925, resigned to accept a professorship at the University of Minnesota. Other resignations which have been accepted include those of G. Arnold Logan, instructor in accounting; Vesta Shimel, assistant professor of education; Myril Shaw, assistant research engineer at the Engineering Experiment Station, and Wilmer M. Stevenson, instructor in pathology.

New appointments include: Thomas T. Frost, instructor in pathology; Paul J. Graber, instructor in accounting; Gaile A. Carbaugh, instructor in education; Anne Vance, part-time instructor in the University School; William A. Van Til, instructor in the University School; Phillip T. Knies, instructor at the dispensary, and Frank A. Riebel, instructor in physical education.

Among the promotions recently approved are those of Dr. Horace B. Davidson from resident pathologist to assistant professor in pathology, and Edgar Littlefield, from assistant to instructor in fine arts; Allen McManigal, engineering drawing, from assistant professor to associate professor, and Leo G. Staley, physical education, from instructor to assistant professor.

# EDUCATIONAL NOTES AND NEWS

ROBERT P. BARNER, principal of the Rochester, Pa., Senior High School, has been elected superintendent of the schools of Rochester, Pa. Mr. Barner entered the Rochester school system in 1922 and has served as teacher, assistant principal, principal of the junior high school and of the senior high school.

DR. FRANK L. EVERSULL has assumed his work as president of Huron College, S. D. Dr. Eversull was formerly principal of the Senior High School of East St. Louis, Ill.

MILTON F. STAUFFER, dean of the School of Commerce at Temple University, has been appointed assistant to President Charles E. Beury. Harry A. Cochran, associate dean of the school of commerce, has been promoted to succeed Mr. Stauffer as dean.

CLAUDE W. OWEN has been promoted to be dean of Bluefield College, W. Va.

DR. FRANK P. GRAVES, president of the University of the State of New York and State

Commissioner of Education, was in charge of the ceremonies at the dedication of the new amphitheater of the New York State Fair on September 4. The building has been named the Wing Coliseum in honor of Professor Henry Hiram Wing, for many years head of the department of animal husbandry of the New York State College of Agriculture at Cornell University, as an expression of appreciation and in recognition of his distinguished contribution to the dairy industry and to the science of animal husbandry not only of New York State but throughout the world. Owen D. Young, regent of the university, delivered the dedication address and the address of acceptance was made by Professor Wing.

DELISLE BURNS, Stevenson lecturer in citizenship at the University of Glasgow, will open the fall term at the New School for Social Research, New York City, with a series of three lectures on "Present Day Politics in Great Britain," beginning on Thursday, September 27, at 8:20 P. M. Mr. Burns is coming to this country under the auspices of the Institute of International Education. Since 1919 he has been an active member of the Labor Party in England, and has held various executive offices in the party organization. He has been lecturer in logic and philosophy in the University of London and lecturer in social philosophy at the London School of Economics.

DR. ALBERT T. POFFENBERGER, professor of psychology and executive head of the department of psychology at Columbia University, was elected president at the New York meeting of the American Psychological Association. Dr. J. E. Anderson, of the University of Minnesota, and Dr. E. S. Robinson, of Yale University, were elected directors.

DR. CLARENCE M. DANNELLY, a former president of Kentucky Wesleyan College, and recently the chief supervisor for the Tennessee Valley Authority research program in the colleges of Alabama, has been appointed to a professorship of education in the extension division of the University of Alabama.

Two recently appointed deans at the University of Missouri will take up their work at the beginning of the coming academic year. These are Dr. William E. Masterson, formerly dean of the School of Law at the University of Idaho, who will succeed the late James L. Parks as dean of the School of Law, and Dr. Carl Agee, who will succeed Dean G. D. Edwards as head of the Missouri Bible College. Dr. Agee has been associate dean of the Bible College and professor of the New Testament at the university for the last four years.

AT Syracuse University, Professor L. C. Dillenback, for the past four years professor of design at the Columbia University School of Architecture, has been appointed professor of architectural design, and Erwin O. Christensen, for four years educational director of the American Federation of Arts, Carnegie lecturer on the history of architecture and art.

TEN new appointments have been made at Connecticut College. These include Robert Fulton Logan, painter and etcher, a member of the department of fine arts, and Mrs. Chase Going Woodhouse, director of the Institute of Women's Professional Relations at the Woman's College of the University of North Carlina, who will combine research in this field with teaching as a part-time professor of social science. Other appointments are: Dr. Ida Craven Merriam, in the department of economics; Dr. Hamilton Smyser, Dr. Rosamond Tuve and Dr. Pauline Aiken, in the department of English; Dr. Federico Sanchez, in the department of Romance languages; Dr. Paul R. Burkholder and Dr. Harriet B. Creighton, in the department of botany, and Vivian Roberts, in the department of home economics.

RECENT appointments at the New Jersey College for Women include: Dr. Mary M. Thomson, instructor in psychiatry at Columbia College of Physicians and Surgeons, college psychiatrist; Eleanor J. Flynn, formerly of the University of Chicago and the Pennsylvania College for Women, assistant professor of sociology; Margaret B. Martin, formerly assistant director of Hampton Institute Library School, acting director of the library school; Oscar Lassner, formerly professor of music at the Leipzig Conservatory, lecturer in music; Lucinda Moles, University of Barcelona, instructor in Spanish; Susan d'Orssaud Ravacon, instructor in French.

CAMERON RALSTON, of Beaver Falls, has been

appointed director of religious activities of Washington and Jefferson College.

COLONEL JOSEPH FAIRBANKS has been elected president of the board of trustees of St. Johnsbury Academy, Vermont. He succeeds the late President Perley F. Hazen. Dr. Frank E. Farmer, of St. Johnsbury, has been elected vice-president.

L. T. BLACK, assistant superintendent of Butler County schools, Pa., won the annual award of the Nathan C. Schaeffer Memorial scholarship of $600. Mr. Black, who has been teaching for the past thirty-one years, plans to use the scholarship by enrolling in Teachers College of Columbia University for graduate studies in teacher training and supervision in the department of higher education.

A. E. BACON has been appointed superintendent of schools at Wilkes-Barre, Pa. He succeeds Harry H. Zeiser, who died in May after his reelection for a fifth term. For the past four years Mr. Bacon has been prncipal of the new Elmer L. Meyers High School.

CHARLES E. METZGER, formerly head of the commercial department, Bernardsville, N. J., High School, head of Lower School, Bordentown Military Institute, and principal of the Pennington, N. J., High School, has been appointed director of the Temple University High School, to succeed Millard E. Gladfelter, now registrar of the university.

DR. J. M. TINLEY, associate agricultural economist on the Giannini Foundation of Agricultural Economics at the University of California, has returned to Berkeley from Washington, D. C., where he has been a member of the staff of the Agricultural Adjustment Administration for the past seven months.

DR. JESSIE M. PANGBURN, of the Spearfish State Normal School, has been elected president of the South Dakota State Branch of the American Association of University Women.

FRANCIS X. SWIETLIK, dean of the Law School at Marquette University and grand censor of the Polish National Alliance, has been elected president of the Warsaw convention of Polish Residents Abroad.

FOR the fourth consecutive year, Dr. Henry L. Banzhaf, dean of the Dental School at Marquette University, has been chosen president of the Dental Educatonal Council of America. Dr. Banzhaf is a past president of the American Dental Association.

WILLIAM D. OVERMAN, of the department of history of Waynesburg College, has been appointed curator of history and archivist of the Ohio State Archeological and Historical Society, Columbus.

WILLIAM G. KIMMEL, executive secretary of the investigation of social studies in schools of the American Historical Association and managing editor of *The Social Studies,* has agreed to act as editorial adviser in social studies for the Houghton Mifflin Company.

DR. GEORGE C. BRANDENBURG, head of the department of education at Purdue University and director of its summer school, died on September 3. He was fifty-five years old. Dr. Brandenburg is known for his work on child development and personality. In 1906 he became principal of the high school at Humboldt, Iowa, and from 1910 to 1913 he was superintendent of schools at Brighton, Colo. From an instructorship in educational psychology at Purdue in 1914, Dr. Brandenburg was promoted successively to an assistant professorship in 1917, to an associate professorship in 1918 and to a professorship in 1920.

THE second Pan-American Conference on Education was officially opened at Santiago, Chile, on September 9, in the Congress Building, with President Arturo Alessandri, members of the cabinet and diplomatic corps and other government officials participating in the program. With the exception of Paraguay, every country in the Americas was represented by delegates. President Alessandri expressed confidence that the conference would prove successful. He said that the proper education of the younger generations in the Americas would gradually create an anti-war feeling, bringing the countries into closer relations, developing understanding and cooperation. Minister of Education Osvaldo Vial in officially opening the session pointed out the importance of the conference and expressed the willingness of Chile to support all constructive plans.

THE Pennsylvania Association of Deans of Women will hold its annual meeting at Harrisburg at the Penn-Harris Hotel on November 2 and 3. Nationally known speakers will address the meeting. The officers this year are: *President,* Mrs. Lillian K. Wyman, Philadelphia; *Vice-president,* Lillian E. Johnson, Slippery Rock; *Secretary,* Mary Cyril Aaron, Greensburg; *Treasurer,* Gertrude Bricker, Philadelphia.

RECOMMENDATIONS that a scientific study be made of the state financial condition along with its educational and social obligations are contained in the 1934–35 platform adopted by the North Carolina Congress of Parents and Teachers meeting at Chapel Hill. The congress is the board of managers of the Parent-Teacher Institute which meets annually at the University of North Carolina for group conferences and study. The 1934–35 platform demands "an efficient eight-month school term, changes in the school curriculum, a 25 per cent. increase in teachers salaries and wise economy in government."

WITH the appointment of Miss Nellie X. Hawkinson as professor of nursing education, a program of nursing education has been initiated at the University of Chicago. The *Journal* of the American Medical Association states that the committee of nursing education, appointed by President Hutchins last winter after a tentative plan for the organization of the courses had been approved, will be responsible for the formulation and adoption of the sequence of studies leading to degrees. Sequences for teachers of nursing, supervisors and administrative officers in schools of nursing are being planned as the first step. The degree will be given through the Division of Biological Sciences, although the courses included will be offered in education, home economics, psychology and other departments as well as in the science departments.

STARTING with the autumn quarter, the Ohio State University's school of nursing will abandon the three-year curriculum and will offer only a five-year course. During the coming year all nurses will be housed in regular university dormitories under the administration of the Women's Self Government Association. They will be eligible for all university organizations open to women. According to Miss Ruth Alice Perkins, director of nursing education, a cooperative plan has been instituted for graduate nurses who have completed three-year courses and who wish to continue their education. In return for thirty-six hours a week of general service in the hospital, graduate nurses will receive board, room, laundry of uniforms, incidental fees at the university, and a small cash allowance each month. Part-time graduates will work six hours a day for six days a week, with a full day off each week. Graduate nurses from hospitals meeting the entrance requirements will receive credit for the courses they have completed and enter the five-year course with junior standing. On this basis, approximately two and a half years are required to complete the work for a bachelor of science degree in education.

# DISCUSSION

## THE CONTROL OF TEACHERS

THE enactment of the Ives Law, requiring all teachers in public and private educational institutions which are exempted from taxation to take an oath of loyalty, provides an occasion for some interesting comparisons. This law arose presumably out of the fear that teachers may conduct radical propaganda in the schools. A similar fear was expressed in the English House of Commons in 1927, and it is pertinent to quote both the questions to and the answer of the President of the Board of Education on the subject.

In the House of Commons, on February 17th, Sir Basil Peto (Barnstaple) asked the President of the Board of Education:

(1) Whether his attention has been called to the activities of the Teachers' Labour League in promoting the spread of Socialism among children attending the elementary schools; and what steps he proposes to take to prevent party politics being taught to school children?

(2) Whether he intends to introduce legislation for the purpose of preventing the propagation of disloyal and seditious doctrines among school children, such as described in his speech at Liverpool on 6th January?

Major Sir Granville Wheler (Faversham) asked the President: Whether his attention has been drawn to the Teachers' Labour League; and if so, whether he will take steps to secure that no teacher shall in school hours or on school premises teach or influence the scholars in favour of the policy of any political party?

*Lord Eustace Percy:* I am aware of the activities of the Teachers' Labour League, but it would be easy to exaggerate the importance of this particular body. Its membership is insignificant and includes a number of teachers who are not now teaching in any school under public control. I believe the House can confidently rely upon the strong opinion of the teaching profession as a whole to counteract such propaganda. The standards of the teaching profession itself are the only sure protection against evils of this kind, but I am, of course, prepared to deal effectively with any teacher who can be shown to have abused his position in this way. I do not think new legislation on the subject is required.

*Mr. Trevelyan:* How many cases have there been of teachers teaching politics in the schools?

*Lord Eustace Percy:* I do not think that arises out of the question.

*Mr. Trevelyan:* One of the questions refers to "promoting the spread of Socialism among children," and asks what steps the Noble Lord proposes to take to prevent party politics being taught to school children. I ask how many cases have come to the Noble Lord's notice of any teachers teaching any kind of politics in the schools?

*Lord Eustace Percy:* The question on the Paper is whether the Teachers' Labour League exists in order to encourage such teaching being given in schools and to enable such teaching to be given. In view of the declared objects of the Teachers' Labour League and in view of the declarations at the last conference of the Labour Party in regard to the use of the schools for that purpose, I think the question is fully justified.

*Mr. J. Hudson* (Huddersfield): Can the Noble Lord say if the general opinion and good sense of the teachers of the country can be depended on to deal with this matter? [*Hon. Members:* "He has said so!"] . . .

*Lord Eustace Percy:* In reply to the Hon. Member from Huddersfield, I confidently rely on the teaching profession, as I said to-day, and as I said in the speech to which the Hon. Member has referred, but I think public attention should be called to the activities of those who are trying to put pressure on the teaching profession.

On another occasion in the same year a deputation of the Royal Society of St. George presented a resolution of the society requesting the President of the Board of Education to require the direct and systematic teaching of patriotism and flag exercises in the schools "as the most practical and effective antidote to disloyal and revolutionary propaganda." The President replied in part as follows:

When it came to the question of a mandate from the Board, it had always been one of the principles of educational administration in this country that as little as possible should be laid down by the central Department; that the Department, in matters of teaching, curriculum, pedagogics, and so on, should act by advice—by instruction in the sense of suggestion—by the issue of teachers' handbooks rather than by direct regulation. If a general mandate were confined to a question of ceremonial it would do more harm than good. . . .

It ought to be clearly laid down by the Board of Education, by local authorities, by the teaching profession, and by everybody who had anything to do with education, that patriotism was the very foundation of the whole of our teaching in the schools. The method by which that patriotism was taught must be mainly in the hands of the teaching profession. The problem was mainly a teaching and not an administrative one. The Royal Society of St. George might suggest to the bodies representing the teaching profession that they should form a joint committee to investigate the matter in order to reach joint conclusions. It was on the agreed conclusions of the people who actually had to do the teaching that progress in this matter must depend. They could rely on the Board to do everything that the central administration could do to assist this work.

Earlier in the same year the President of the Board of Education, in meeting charges of misuse of the schools for party ends, discussed the teaching of citizenship, patriotism and political propaganda and referred at the same time to the danger of using abstract ideas with pupils who are not ready for them.

A teacher's reasoning or arguments will soon fade from his pupil's mind; but a child in whose mind half comprehended words have taken the place of tangible things grows up only too easily a man greedy of phrases and impatient of facts.

This truth applies with even greater force to a far more important subject—the teaching of Citizenship. Let me here repeat what I said publicly a year ago with reference to those passages in the old Code which laid down that the "moral instruction" given in the schools should inculcate, among other things, "love of one's country"—"That requirement is loyally carried out by the teachers in our schools, not because it is in the regulations, but because they believe in it. The public may feel confident that the teaching profession realises to the full its responsibility in this matter and would sternly condemn any teacher who failed in this duty." . . .

Especially, perhaps, in this country do we need to bring children up to patriotism through the performance of practical duties, because that is, after all, the way in which we, as a people, have attained national unity. Just because our practical sense of national union is so strong, we have been content with a constitutional language of peculiar vagueness, a language in which any child may easily lose its way. There is, in fact, no subject in regard to which the teacher should be given more freedom than this subject of patriotism and citizenship. There is certainly none in regard to which he should have a more anxious sense of responsibility, for here he must, in an especial degree, rely on his own judgment. If governments, whether local or central, begin to prescribe to the teacher a certain method of teaching, or even attempt to influence him, in such matters, we run the risk of all those evils that we have seen in various forms, both in the Prussia of the past and in the Russia of to-day.[1]

The essence of these quotations is the emphasis placed upon the teachers as members of a profession and on the recognition of professional obligations. Only on this basis can a genuine profession of teaching at all levels be established, unless, of course, teaching is to become an instrument of a totalitarian state. What happens to the teaching profession in a totalitarian state is nowhere better illustrated than in Nazi Germany. Under the Republic the German elementary school teachers had finally succeeded in securing that professional status for which they had struggled since 1848. Under the new régime all teachers as part of the civil service have been required to subordinate their own views to National Socialism and to familiarize themselves with its ideology. The most important books on National Socialism must be provided in official libraries, and heads of departments may even examine their subordinates on them (Decree of July 11, 1933). By a law of April 7, 1933, committees of politically reliable persons were appointed to examine into the records of all members of the educational service. This law was followed by dismissal of teachers reported to be opposed to the new régime. Teachers' councils, whose creation after 1918 introduced a wholesome check on bureaucratic control, were virtually set aside by an order issued by the Minister of the Interior in August, 1933. The new attitude was clearly expressed by the Minister of Education for Saxony.

In the light of recent information I take this opportunity to state that the Ministry of Education can have confidence only in those teachers' associations of which not only the executive officers, but also every individual member is willing to give assurance in writing that he has adopted without reserve the principles of a consciously national and Christian education. The national Revolution is not satisfied with the mere outward semblance of a change. Those capable of no greater change than that can not expect to be called upon as co-workers. The new German school demands a whole German teacher who finds in the principles of Christian philosophy the motive and power for unselfish devotion to its cause. It will know how to find such men and with their help to build the new German school.[2]

This principle has now been extended to all institutions for teacher preparation and to the selection of those who are to become professors in the universities. Admission to the teacher preparation institutions as well as to the universities depends finally not on scholarship but on participation in the activities of Nazi youth organizations and the recommendation of the local leaders (*Gauleiter*) of the National Socialist Party. In the same way no one may become a *Dozent,* the first rung on the professorial ladder, who has not, in addition to meeting the traditional requirements of scholarship, also been closely affiliated with Nazi organizations, completed the necessary periods of labor service (*Arbeitsdienst*) and spent at least three months

[1] The complete passages from which these quotations are taken may be found in an article by the author on "The Making of Citizens in England," in "Essays in Comparative Education," pp. 35 *ff.* (New York, 1930).

[2] W. Hartnacke, "Neubau des deutschen Schulwesens," (Leipzig, 1933).

in one of the new *Dozentenakademien* for political indoctrination. Scholarship and research have been subordinated in the same way to Nazi policy, since, in the words of the leading educational propagandist of the Nazi régime, Ernst Krieck, "absolute freedom of teaching is absolute nonsense." While research must be free, freedom can not be allowed to researchers.

Here lies the real danger of laws like the Ives Law just enacted. Combined with the tendencies described by Dr. Jesse K. Flanders in his "Legislative Control of the Elementary Curriculum" (New York, 1925), control of the teaching of history and social sciences, and the Tennessee Law on the teaching of evolution, such laws militate against the development of a genuine profession of teaching, as self-determining and as respected as the professions of law or medicine, engineering or architecture. To talk, on the one hand, of the development of free citizens capable of discrimination and judgment, and, on the other hand, to keep those responsible for this development in leading strings is nonsense. The totalitarian state is at least honest—those who are to produce obedient, acquiescent, uncritical followers must themselves be uncritical, acquiescent and obedient. If only those patriots who suspect teachers in particular of subversive activities and who base their patriotism on loyalty to the Constitution and the wisdom of the Founders of the Republic would remember Washington's statement that "in proportion as the structure of government gives force to public opinion it is essential that public opinion be enlightened" (the real contrast between a democracy and a totalitarian state), they might refrain from controlling those who are appointed to diffuse this enlightenment. This does not mean that teachers can be absolutely free, but it does mean that the limitations of their freedom should be those that come from thorough professional preparation and from membership in a profession; it means, as the President of the English Board of Education implied in the quotations cited earlier, that, if a free society can not rely on the good sense of the teachers, external restrictions are likely to do more harm than good.

I. L. KANDEL

TEACHERS COLLEGE
COLUMBIA UNIVERSITY

## COLLECTIVISM AND DEMOCRACY

I HAVE read with amazement the vehement criticism which Professor Bobbitt[1] has leveled at the final report of the Commission on the Social Studies of the American Historical Association. Having studied the report myself, I am at a loss to understand how he could have read into it the threat to democracy which he charges it to be.

The commission having written that "the age of individualism and *laissez-faire* in economy and government is closing and that a new age of collectivism is emerging," Professor Bobbitt endeavors to pin the red tag on them. They must mean fascism or communism, says he, but they are too tricky, too underhanded, to use those terms openly. He charges them with using "deliberately obscured phrases," "hidden meanings," language "clear enough for the initiate to understand and innocuous enough not to alarm the uninitiated," "favorable euphemisms" to conceal direful plotting.

The commission's suggestion that such "collectivism" may "involve the limiting or supplanting of private property by public property or it may entail the preservation of private property, extended and distributed among the masses," means to Professor Bobbitt the inauguration of "a régime of state paternalism to care for a population no longer competent for individual self-management." In the commission's prophecy that "Almost certainly [the oncoming age] will involve a larger measure of compulsory as well as voluntary cooperation of citizens in the conduct of the complex national economy, he can see only "the large amount of compulsory and the small amount of voluntary cooperation in Italy, Germany and Russia."

The critic then comments on the tributes to democracy which he admits are contained in the report. "It is difficult to explain," he says, "in a way favorable to the commission, their frequent lip-service to democracy, when the whole tenor of their report is denial both of its legitimacy and of its desirability. One can not believe that they are uninformed relative to the differing natures of collectivism and of democracy and of their total irreconcilability."

In this last sentence we have the kernel of Professor Bobbitt's criticism. It gives us the

[1] SCHOOL AND SOCIETY, XL (August 18, 1934), 201–8.

fundamental assumption which is at the root of his disagreement with the commission. Are collectivism and democracy totally irreconcilable? Are individualism and democracy synonymous terms? To these questions Professor Bobbitt's answer is in the affirmative; the commission's answer is in the negative.

As I read the report, the commission is no whit less zealous in its stand for democracy than is its critic. The commission advocates collectivism to *preserve* democracy. They define democracy and their paragraphs are shot through and through with the spirit of allegiance to it. They face the facts of the accelerated evolution of material civilization; they recognize that the family economy of frontier days has given way to the minute specialization of each man's labor and a correlatively intricate interdependence of mankind. Who is to control this national and world economy upon the successful functioning of which the individual must depend for the very elements of existence? The commission assumes that adherence to democratic principles calls for *social* control, and they argue for the development of such social intelligence in the common man that he may participate in cooperative action.

The democracy expounded by Professor Bobbitt is that of Thomas Paine. Government is a necessary evil; let us have as little of it as possible. Individualism, unfettered and free, is the essence of democracy. Self-reliance, self-dependence, and individual responsibility were the virtues which our public schools were designed to inculcate, he says, and the alternative offered by the commission as he sees it is that "Men are to be nurslings of the state."

The argument interestingly parallels the views expressed by the opponents of ratification of the Constitution in 1788. They, too, felt that they were faced with a dangerous collectivism. In the "new plan" of government they envisioned an instrument which would destroy the liberty they so lately had gained.

The philosophy persists. Only five years ago the mass of the American people were singing the praises of Rugged Individualism. Yet the most casual student, it would seem, must be conscious of the steadily expanding collectivism which has characterized our history. The very tax-supported public school to which Professor Bobbitt attributes the original purpose of strengthening individualism was at its inception regarded by its enemies as destructive of individualism.

To-day the newspaper mirrors an accelerating collectivism. Mayor La Guardia opens fourteen new play sites and promises sixty-one more before the end of 1935. The people of the city of New York have found that as individuals they can not provide for their recreatory needs, but collectively they can do something to counteract the abnormalities of urban existence. In the Tennessee and Columbia River valleys, the people of the United States are engaged in creating vast resources of electric power. A few weeks ago President Roosevelt initiated a project which will eventually stretch a thousand miles of forest across our treeless prairies. Conservation of soil and of moisture are the reasons given for this extension of collective activity and of the public ownership of property.

Does Professor Bobbitt shudder at the trend which these straws signify? Does he feel that such measures are an annulment of democracy?

What is democracy? The commission offered a long, wordy definition (p. 12). But this product of their deliberations was only a verbose paraphrase of Lincoln's homely words—government of the people, by the people, and for the people. In our nation of subsistence farmers a century ago but *little* government was necessary; in our intricate, highly organized society of to-day, *much* government is necessary. Necessary for what? Necessary for the realization of those principles of equality and liberty which we designate as the fundamental attributes of a state of democracy. So long as the supreme power resides in the people and is exercised by representation, *much* government does not mean a denial of democracy.

(This statement is not to be interpreted as a general endorsement of the commission's report. It is confined strictly to the portion that elucidates the point of view with which Professor Bobbitt disagrees. There are other portions which I am inclined to question seriously and to call for supporting facts, but this paper is not intended to be a general appraisal.)

Percival W. Hutson
University of Pittsburgh

## ACADEMIC FREEDOM

OUR attention has been called to an excerpt from the *Princeton Alumni Weekly,* published in SCHOOL AND SOCIETY for August 25, 1934 (page 254) dealing with "Political Controls of Education," and mentioning the name of the University of California.

For that reason it seems appropriate to send you herewith a copy of the statement made to the Academic Senate of the University of California on August 27, 1934 by Robert Gordon Sproul, president of the university. Your readers would, I think, be interested in this statement, which reads:

Day by day in these troubled times the position of university administrative officers grows more difficult as they face questions involving academic freedom or the right of free speech. Both radicals and reactionaries would use the university as an agency of propaganda and each group attacks bitterly those who strive to preserve its integrity as an institution for the discovery and dissemination of knowledge. It seems to me desirable, therefore, to announce to this Senate and to the public the principles which guide the president in these matters and which may be said to be, in a certain sense, the policy of the university:

The function of a university is to seek and to transmit knowledge and to train students in the processes whereby truth is to be made known. To convert, or to make converts, is alien and hostile to this dispassionate duty. Where it becomes necessary, in performing this function of a university, to consider political, social or sectarian movements, they are dissected and examined—not taught, and the conclusion left, with no tipping of the scales, to the logic of the facts.

The university is founded upon faith in intelligence and knowledge and it must defend their free operation. It must rely upon truth to combat error. Its obligation is to see that the conditions under which questions are examined are those which give play to intellect rather than to passion. Essentially the freedom of a university is the freedom of competent persons in the classroom. In order to protect this freedom, the university assumes the right to prevent exploitation of its prestige by unqualified persons or by those who would use it as a platform for propaganda. It therefore takes great care in the appointment of its teachers; it must take corresponding care with respect to others who wish to speak in its name.

The university respects personal belief as the private concern of the individual. It equally respects the constitutional rights of the citizen. It insists only that its members, as individuals and as citizens, shall likewise always respect—and not exploit, their university connection.

The University of California is the creature of the state and its loyalty to the state will never waver. It will not aid nor will it condone actions contrary to the laws of the state. Its high function—and its high privilege, the university will steadily continue to fulfill, serving the people by providing facilities for investigation and teaching free from domination by parties, sects or selfish interests. The university expects the state, in return, and to its own great gain, to protect this indispensable freedom, a freedom like the freedom of the press, that is the heritage and the right of a free people.

MONROE E. DEUTSCH,
*Vice-president and provost of the University of California*

BERKELEY
SEPTEMBER 5, 1934

# SPECIAL CORRESPONDENCE

## AIR-MINDED YOUTH TO-DAY AND TO-MORROW

ALONG the air-ways of America there is Port Kenyon in Ohio. It is far enough away from any great urban center to develop its own interests and constituency and far afield from the immediate rewards of an industrial community, but near enough in spirit to understand and interpret the significance of the life of to-day and to-morrow to the youth of this post-war period. For this field opens an untried door into the world of to-morrow for the students of Kenyon College and comes to them as the gift of one of their own colleagues, Wilbur L. Cummings, of the class of 1902. The project of planning and pursuing the dream of the donor becomes a project in cooperative thinking and doing for this college of liberal arts. It comes into being with an almost Aladdin-like summons out of one man's interest in flying, from a sportsman's venture to the matured reflection of the discerning man of the world as to its cultural contribution—an unusual experience for this man but one most likely to occur, as he sees clearly enough, within the everyday experience of the next generation. As Mr. Cummings says: "When I was in college Henry Ford and his horseless carriage industry awakened little interest of a serious sort at all. My children are privileged to live through the period of expansion to see it as the greatest industry in their world. Now as they enter into maturity aviation is so far advanced as to turn their attention in a much more compelling way. It needs no prophet to forecast the beginnings of a tremendous development within the next twenty-five years and that not merely of technical skill and progress but of far wider changes in the social life of to-morrow. It may be a hobby or a sport and it is in no way to be despised for that. In its participation, however, it affords a training as flexible and adaptable to a new age as any possible interest can afford."

Accordingly, this venture is launched as a college enterprise. There is the flying field, less than half a mile from the Kenyon campus, approximately 1,600 and 1,900 feet in length, on which is built a fully equipped hangar with two Fleet and Fledgling Biplanes, two-place, dual control, for student instruction, each with 100 and 185 H. P. Kinney motors. In the Mather Science Hall on the campus is the aeronautics laboratory, which provides several types of airplane motors, engine parts and skeleton construction models. The course of instruction announced follows that prescribed by The United States Department of Commerce for Licensed Transport Pilot Ground Schools. This schedule affords an introduction for those who choose flying as a vocation but in no wise offers a course of study as a technical accomplishment. The study as outlined is largely theoretical and presents the necessary basic information for a thorough understanding of the art of flying—air commerce regulations, history and construction of airplanes, meteorology, principles of aerial navigation, aircraft instruments and parachutes. Basic courses in physics and mathematics in the first and second years prepare the student in his second year for the course as outlined. Flying is not included in the course but is permitted as a private venture in the two later years of college life. While the machine work affords practical experience, it becomes a necessary cooperative enterprise and no student escapes the responsibility of maintaining the mechanical efficiency of the whole plant. The course centers, therefore, the active interest of the student. It may be a hobby for most, no doubt, and it may demand time and energy which once the playing field claimed. It therefore requires more physical hours than its college credits grant. Of the 120 credit hours required for graduation, to this course is allotted 3 credit hours, which signifies a full year's participation.

In a very real sense this enterprise partakes of the character of a youth movement. It centers its responsibility in its beginnings upon the shoulders of Donald McCabe Gretzer, whose career as student, pilot and teacher brings to this new enterprise the unusual gifts of leadership of the younger generation. In laboratory and on the field this youthful instructor and his youthful colleagues are busily engaged in an absorbing occupation with something of the Montessori touch about it all. Mr. Gretzer holds membership in the American section of the International League of Aviators. On the recent occasion of the dedication of the field he was privileged to present to Mr. Cummings a diploma of honorary membership in that organization—a distinction given in America as a recognition of this college enterprise and the second award only to non-professionals, the first being given to President Coolidge.

In this day of transition this enterprise stands out as a venture unique in its possibilities and promises. It captures the imagination and provides speculation of future trends which to-day are but dimly outlined. It well may be a poet's dream, but poets, as Shelley said, are the great legislators of the world. One remembers that vignette of William Blake of Homo Sapiens standing in his infinitesimal insignificance with eager looks and outstretched arms before a great ladder reaching into the infinite. Underneath is the caption: "I want! I want!" It is a parable of that moment of tension or of balance when, somewhere between the two worlds in transition we picture to-day as passing and becoming, man gathers up his tested experience and, reviewing it wholly for the moment, stakes his all on the future in one great plunge. There is no man of to-day, however obscure, but feels the pulse of this world at his breakfast table every morning. He sees himself as Samuel Butler saw him: "We are children of the plough, the spade and the ship; we are children of the extended liberty and knowledge which the printing press has diffused. By the institutions and state of science under which a man is born it is determined whether he shall have the limits of an Australian savage or those of a nineteenth century Englishman"—and, we may add, of a twentieth century man of affairs.

That man's evolution from the post-war-born youth of to-day is being determined as never before by the significant direction which applied science presses upon every phase of his life. For two thousand years this power has been largely dormant and man's mechanical progress limited to his immediate touch. His world is the heritage of a fine quality of life, disinterested and kindly in many ways. Concern with what we call the machine, however, has been looked upon with indifference if not disdain. There was a time when, for a brief moment in the ancient world, Archimedes and Hero of Alexander, by invention and emphasis, sought to turn their world to the wonders of mechanical adaptability. But that progressive moment was thwarted by the indifference of the intellectual class to such pursuits, and war and political disorder added a further blockade. So the great gulf of the future was fixed between the cultural and the practical in educational ideal and effort.

No more than three generations behind him now the youth of to-day sees the industrial revolution enter upon the scene through the door of Watt's steam-engine and within a generation almost the social order is stirring with change. Within his own generation this youth stands at the door of a change as momentous and one for which he is better prepared to cope than his fathers. Now is given a social and cultural promise in the power of mechanical tools and weapons placed in the hands of the common man. Though we raise the warning cry against the machine as possible master, the fact remains within the forefront of the common consciousness that by this machine increased power is granted—a power that quietly works and observes man's will more than ever his busy limbs could do. So youth stands to-day gathering up the lost threads of the ancient world to live at home in a world where the interpretation of nature is being largely determined by the projection of himself through the machine. In this new democratic setting there is a promise of a greater world unity. If the ancient ideal gave us a culture of quiet rest and contemplation with its vision of a universe of truth, beauty and love, the world of youth's making to-day works "without haste" in keeping with its ancient heritage, but, adventurous and courageous, defying the static of tradition, it works "without rest," in keeping with the experimental progress of man's spirit upon new adventures in cooperative thinking and doing.

The post-war youth who now enters upon his college career chooses his electives instinctively under the preference and the guidance of this changing social scene. He knows enough to value the time and energy released from toil and rest. He wants and knows that he wants the proper preparation of mind to use it. He must understand this industrial scene not necessarily, be it said, because of his own future as a possible administrator of affairs. He is not unmindful of that ambition, but he measures with much more detachment than a former generation the old emphasis upon industrial success and utilitarian education. He knows how the exaggeration of the practical tends to stifle and reject the theoretical, and when the emergency comes and the machine breaks down he is more disposed to value the background of the theoretical. Air-minded youth to-day seeks to understand the principles of the machine as a far superior equipment for his task than merely knowing how to run the machine.

Within the life of the older generation have come the telephone, motor car, radio, movie, airplane—all serving to accelerate activity and observation. For their children man's ancient dream of flying is now a given reality, but it comes to them enriched by the experience gained through social knowledge and applied science and so promises comprehension of life in larger sort than ever before. To the youth of to-day this new avenue of interest is as fascinating and as varied as any game could ever be. It feeds the natural urge to the understanding and doing of mechanical skills. It finds complement in man's cultural life and social skills as well, so that even the competitive drive of sports may yet yield place to this cooperative doing that serves his learning. In many ways vocational avenues are enlarged and a freedom of choice that develops a man's capabilities to the utmost is promised. The new leisure and the new machine may encourage a far greater measure than ever before of cultural and scientific understanding. Time was, when the only observation hobby granted was a walk in the country where, as a turn away from sport, science taught its rudiments in geology or botany, or beauty found its answer in esthetic contemplation. If the imagination found no release here, one was as restlessly unoccupied as when waiting impatiently at a railway station for a belated train. That condition hardly exists for this post-war college youth to-day. He need not sit and wait while things labeled science are brought him on a platter. Science is so much a part of the ordering of his life that he responds to its demands with eager insistence.

Here it would seem that, by a happy coincidence, a study in aeronautics holds possibilities of active relationship between youth and his natural and social surroundings. He ought to find himself at home in his world through familiar occupations and appliances and be prepared to participate in this doing for testing and trying knowledge of all kinds. Such training holds cultural value of a high sort as one turns to the many avenues of esthetic interest it gives. It was the problem of riding upon the air that brought stream-lined cars into the region of fact and value. The beauty of moving clouds is by no means lost in pursuing the study of meteorology. The beauty of a changing landscape quickens an interest in nature's unconscious rhythms in form and design as well as calling for observation of the keenest demand. No better grounding in applied science than the avenue of aerodynamics wherein the motion of the wind on a floating object yields utilitarian as well as esthetic contemplation. While in no sense is this a complete vocational course, its utilitarian advantages enter into fields far removed from the technical. It opens up for civil engineering new problems in design and promotion. It gives to medicine avenues of investigation of altitudes upon the human body. To the lawyer it forecasts many complications of interests and enters into governmental theory and practise with larger and larger fields of interest. Architecture will find ways of building landing fields on the tops of skyscrapers. Bankers will provide capital for greater air lines and transatlantic ventures.

The most marked social change in the immediate future will be the opportunity of greater leisure, to which the flying machine will contribute the greatest part. The old bread and circus program that looked upon man as a creature to be governed and kept quietly in his place is challenged by this machine. In the facility and speed of transportation and intercourse, that man disappears. Applied science works its will not only in response to utility demands, but because of man's eager desire to know the why of things. Here his primary interest is not in the running of the machine but in the working out of its principles. This turn of emphasis means eventually an entire reversal of judgment on the vocational aspects of education, for, as Ernest McCullough observes of such efforts to-day, "half the engineering schools in the country could be eliminated or turned into low-grade trade schools with immense benefit to the country."

Something of that benefit accrues to the liberal arts colleges for their consistent devotion to cultural values first. Our great urban universities were keenly sensitive and better equipped to sense a changing demand. In the midst of the change many a college stood as ill-content as the old homestead in its urban expansion. Soon adding this to that as necessity demanded the old home became a great factory of learning and assumed the guise of a glorified showboat. Likewise many a little college on its rural hill began to feel its isolation. Though it bravely upheld its cultural traditions the busy urban world passed it by. That was the time when this practical insistence upon running the machine as an end in itself gave home economics and industrial technique the only avenue of academic expansion and salvation. That was the time when industry was glad to be relieved of its responsibility for apprenticeship discipline. Fortunately, however, before this tide had reached its flood, the big, busy neighbor beyond found that though something was gained much was lost. And the loss was in those human cultural elements which the old homestead in its ancient glory once fostered. But since return by that road was now closed a new order of smaller preceptorial units within the greater group arose to restore as far as possible the old scene and confess that the present trend was too complicated for satisfactory handling. So it happens that the old ideal of Mark Hopkins's log in its forest setting proves its worth again, and, modified by the experience gained from industrial processes and results, enters upon its new phase.

That is the situation as Kenyon College sees it. It is glad of the happy circumstance that makes possible this endeavor within its own group. It sees the concern of to-day with the technique of an industrial order and seeks to coordinate that interest with its established tradition. But just as its elective courses met their demand by never being used so literally as to bring confusion, so in this instance two conditions are met—the education of facts, principles and knowledge to meet the complexities of contemporary life, and the presentation of material so as to awaken the student's deepest interest and finest choices. It is a way of meeting the trend of the day towards technical interest so specialized as to reward with scant attention the intellectual artistic and cultural interests. It seeks to use that trend and preserve its higher appreciations. By the turn of events to-day the problem of leisure presents that opportunity. The material for man's teaching is right at hand, for man is, primarily, a creature to be taught, as L. P. Jacks says. If the youth is to be quite at home in his world his larger participation in practical affairs will be supplemented by a broad intellectual and cultural foundation. The educational emphasis becomes a matter of the artist's choice—that selective discrimination of subject-matter in natural and applied science as it appears in the everyday affairs of our industrial civilization. We acknowledge, with John Dewey, that "any subject is cultural in the degree in which it is apprehended in its widest possible range of meanings."

It is the old cultural problem of leisure as the end of education that presents itself under this new guise to-day. We have leisure. Work for the masses, however, is so much of a routine and deadening nature as to make neither hard nor difficult demands upon mind and body. In the changed social scene much newly released energy is at stake and unless through industrial processes some way of understanding is provided, what preparation can best cope with such a situation?

Call flying a sport and a hobby. It is all that and more. Its real educational value is that it introduces the man to the aviation industry at a time of its beginnings and provides him with a keen appreciation of the varied factors involved in aircraft production and use. Enough knowledge and experience is gained to give a man an ideal preparation for whatever vocation attracts him. The aeronautical industry will soon go forward under the impetus of private owners and users of flying machines. It will have in such a group a new order of captains of industry, awake not only to mechanical skill but to a social responsibility of a more cooperative cast.

It is a matter of some significance at the present moment that along with their interest in distinctive forms of applied science, the air-minded youth of to-day, who will be these captains of to-morrow, are giving increasing choice to interpretative social studies, economics, sociology and government. It is an alliance in interest which the present youth group contributes to the making of the man of the future. It is an alliance of interest between these cultural and empirical choices which this venture at Kenyon is now privileged to provide. The college rests its future upon it. Air transportation as the method of communication wherever feasible is officially approved. In the furtherance of its work the college sends out under its own power and from its own air-way its president and pilot-professor as representatives of this alliance. "It is not the purpose of this course," adds Dr. William Foster Peirce, the president of Kenyon College, "to develop commercial pilots, but only to fill a need for knowledge of aeronautics which many young men believe to be a part of a liberal education. That interest is satisfied and as a by-product a cultural and healthful form of mental and physical recreation is provided, the moral value of which is far-reaching. Moreover, the rather rigid discipline which aviation imposes creates a source of values in the mastery of self of inestimable worth."

LESTER LEAKE RILEY

KENYON COLLEGE

# QUOTATIONS

## EDUCATIONAL RESEARCH IN ENGLAND

RECURRENT cycles of lean years have prevented local education authorities from making full use of their powers to aid research, conferred upon them by Section 74 of the Consolidated Education Act of 1921. Now that the economic outlook appears to be brighter and the President of the Board of Trade is able to speak hopefully of expanding trade and commerce, it should be possible for some encouragement to be given both by the Board of Education and by local authorities to the investigation by teachers and students of problems connected with schools and scholars. An impulse to such encouragement is likely to be forthcoming in the discussions at the British Association early next month, when the education section will explore some of the findings of educational research, such as the results of intelligence testing and the relative merits of teaching methods. Laboratory work, the taking of notes and response to ocular demonstration are to be considered. The discussions are likely to gain actuality from the fact that there is already in existence a Scottish Council for Research in Education, and the experience of this organization will be of value to those who are endeavoring to form a similar body in England.

There is undoubtedly advantage to be gained from a closer association of individuals and societies engaged in education inquiries. For overlapping is avoided and work that is necessary can be indicated and undertaken in directions where it is most needed. In this country, where, as the Board of Education reminded us in a pamphlet last year, "the freedom of teachers from official control in questions relating to curricula, syllabuses and methods of teaching" is one of the main respects in which our educational system differs from that of foreign countries, valuable information regarding experiment in technique, in closer understanding of difficult types of children, not only in elementary, but in other schools should be forthcoming. Opportunity is afforded to teachers from time to time to study conditions abroad, but there is need for study here, of the change over from the infant to the primary school stage, from the primary to the senior school, and particularly for a fuller inquiry into the reactions of young children to junior county scholarship examinations. The valuable reports of the consultative committees have pointed the way to further exploration of methods of teaching, and an additional stimulus is afforded by the excellent memoranda on curricula published during recent months by the London County Council. From recorded results of teaching, it should be possible to learn, without any cut-and-dried formulae, what should be the standard of attainment of the normal child and what should be done to help the child who blossoms late to go on to some form of higher education. On this point some remarks contained in the recent Report of the London School Medical Officer are of value. He reminds us that "children develop physiologically and mentally at varying rates. . . . The slow developing children are none the worse for this. They continue to develop much longer than the others and eventually may attain the same or even a higher development of mind and character." And he goes on to say: "When scholarships are awarded on examinations taken at a given age, the precocious children are given an unfair advantage at the expense of the more slowly developing children who may be superior in the end." These are wise words and provide evidence of the need for much greater understanding of the difficulties of the normal child, difficulties which are too often passed over in dwelling on the cases of the subnormal, the abnormal and the defective. There is here, undoubtedly, a field for investigation. But it is not an educational inquiry alone which is required. Health, nutrition and environment are all related to the problem. There is rightly much talk of individual understanding of both younger and older wrongdoers, but a great deal of preventive work could be accomplished if much more care were exercised in the early years of schooling, with or without consultation of the child guidance clinic. Very often an excellent beginning is made in the infant school, for it is here that, influenced by the great educational minds of the past and by our no less great contemporary, Madame Montessori, the clearer understanding of child psychology has made the greatest headway. It was said not long ago, with good reason, that the greatest educational advance in this country during the present century has been made in the infant school. It should be recalled with emphasis that this advance has been due in great measure to the teachers themselves, who have been eager for experiment and have often provided material from their own resources.

The question arises, therefore, whether failure to achieve a similar advance in the primary school is due to the external examination at the age of eleven, for the junior county scholarship examination is in reality an external examination, and whether it hinders the free adoption of methods which can be adapted to children of varying types. There is some reason to believe, as Sir Frederick Menzies suggests, that "the educational and physical needs of the children are, unfortunately, not infrequently in conflict," and that "often it is the educational need that must suffer." With wise organization and skilful understanding there seems no reason why either education or health should lose. Enlightened local education authorities have provided a very considerable number of open-air schools in recent years. There are at present some 147 schools with accommodation for over 14,700 children. Hitherto they have been used mainly for subnormal, tuberculous, or very delicate children; but so far very little has been done in investigating the results of open-air schooling on the normal child, normal so far as intelligence goes, but who may be late in developing. Nor do we know much of the influence of open-air teaching on the nervous child or on the child with a "difficult" temperament. Many excellent private schools are aware of the changes worked in a child's character and mentality by an open-air life and by practical work in a garden or in touch with animals. Well-to-do parents are able to choose the school which they feel will fit the child. It is otherwise with the majority of people, and unless they live in the area of an authority which is able to meet the needs of special groups, the child must take his chance. But even though an actual open-air school may not be available, careful investigation in the school itself may enable the thoughtful and careful teacher to select the children for whom larger quantities of sunlight and fresh air are required, with closer individual attention, and more constant medical supervision. In London some of these desiderata are forthcoming in playground classes, but if they are to be successful they must be run, as Sir Frederick tells us, "magnificently."

Where open-air classes are well run, the medical reports seem to prove an advance in health and greater steadiness in nerve and temperament. Less is known about the results in regard to education and intelligence. There is here a field for further research. Nor do the greater authorities appear to have used, so far, the opportunities available in the scattered homes, in cottage homes, and in the boarding schools which they have inherited from the late Poor Law guardians, to study individual children or to ensure that those foster parents who are in charge of the boys and girls—sometimes from infancy to adolescence—are given teaching on health matters and some measure of psychological knowledge. A few experiments which have been made on these lines have been found to be valuable. But in these homes, among children coming from different environments, there are opportunities for the study of aptitudes and of character and for investigating the results of good food, rest and physical training as well as of occupations and amusements which must react favorably on the administration. For the most fruitful result of educational research is the barrier which it presents to mass instruction and mass treatment, and the more work that is accomplished on these lines the greater will be the achievement in happy and healthful childhood.—*The London Times Educational Supplement.*

# SOCIETIES AND MEETINGS

## THIRD ANNUAL CONFERENCE OF THE CHURCH-RELATED COLLEGES OF THE SOUTH

THE third annual conference of the church-related colleges of the South was held at the George Vanderbilt Hotel, in Asheville, N. C., on Wednesday, August 15. Approximately one hundred educators registered for the meeting, and the greatest interest was manifested in the topics discussed during the one-day session. Dr. Robert L. Kelly, secretary of the Association of American Colleges, not only brought the greetings of the association, but made a most valuable contribution in discussing the history of the efforts made last year to secure aid from the federal government for the non-tax-supported institutions of learning. Dr. John E. Bradford, a member of the executive committee of the new National Commission on Church-related Colleges, brought the greetings of this group, and discussed briefly the objective, aims and functions of the church-related colleges.

The chairman, Dr. Charles J. Turck, of Centre College of Kentucky, explained at the outset that the program had been arranged with the thought that the public mind of America, regardless of the church affiliations or church indifference of the many millions that compose it, must be brought to understand the public service that is rendered by the church-related colleges. "We can assume that we representatives of church-related colleges accept the fact that higher education under church auspices has definite spiritual values, but many thousands of our fellow-citizens do not share our church loyalty or our enthusiasm. Are there any principles which will convince the average American, regardless of his religious faith, that the church-related colleges are public institutions, serving the whole public in effective ways, and deserving the interest and support of that public?"

The program was an endeavor to give an affirmative answer to this question. The first topic, "*Resolved,* that the privately endowed colleges are institutions of public service, and consequently no discrimination should be drawn between privately endowed colleges and state-maintained institutions in the matter of federal or state relief measures in the field of education," was discussed by Dr. Harvey W. Cox, Emory University, Georgia, and Dr. Spright Dowell, Mercer University, Georgia. The paper prepared by Dr. Francis P. Gaines, Washington and Lee University, Virginia, was read by Dr. J. W. Gaines, Bethel College for Women, Kentucky. The second topic, "*Resolved,* that the best interests of our democracy require many small colleges of liberal arts, widely scattered throughout the nation and adequately equipped to serve the public," was discussed by Dr. Henry N. Snyder, Wofford College, South Carolina, and Dr. Stewart W. McClelland, Lincoln Memorial University, Tennessee.

The third topic read, "*Resolved,* that the church-related colleges represent a great saving to taxpayers and should be encouraged to serve more effectively the areas where they are." The speakers were Dr. R. C. Grier, Erskine College, South Carolina, and Dr. Dice R. Anderson, Wesleyan College, Georgia. The final topic was, "*Resolved,* that all colleges should charge fair tuition rates and employ fair and equitable methods of soliciting students. (Query, would a code of ethics in the field of higher education be helpful?)". Dr. Weldon Thomas Myers, professor of English in Converse College, South Carolina, represented the president of that institution, Dr. Edward M. Gwathmey, who was detained by illness in his family. The other speakers were Dr. Lawrence T. Lowrey, Blue Mountain College, Mississippi, and Dr. Charles J. Turck, Centre College of Kentucky.

The officers for the fourth annual conference, to be held in August, 1935, were selected as follows:

*President,* Dr. Charles J. Turck, Centre College of Kentucky; *Vice-President,* Dr. Spright Dowell, Mercer University, Georgia; *Secretary-Treasurer,* Dr. W. M. Alexander, Department of Colleges, Board of Christian Education, Methodist Episcopal Church South, Nashville, Tennessee; *the Executive Committee:* The three officers and Dr. D. M. Key, Millsaps College, Jackson, Mississippi, and Dr. P. P. Burns, Howard College, Alabama.

The report of the findings committee, which was read by Dr. W. P. Few, Duke University, North Carolina, and which was afterwards adopted by the unanimous vote of the conference, was as follows:

It is the sense of this conference that non-profit-making colleges and universities, whether tax-supported or non-tax-supported, are all alike public institutions and render public service, and should, therefore, be treated alike in all federal relief measures in the field of education. With such a principle assured by the national government, each institution would have to decide for itself whether it wishes to qualify for federal aid.

We believe that the interests of American life will be best served by many institutions of the liberal arts college type, scattered widely over the country—institutions that emphasize sound scholarship, the development of personality and the training of Christian character.

These institutions are now providing higher education for more than half of the college students of this country, and they thus effect vast savings to the taxpayers. They should be recognized as public institutions, and in all possible ways they should be encouraged to serve, and be made strong for serving, the areas where they are located.

We believe that a serious situation is developing in connection with the competition for students by institutions of higher learning and that on the part of tax-supported institutions. It is expected by the students that their college education must be financed in whole or in part by the college. We accept the principle that in all ordinary circumstances the tuition of the student, in an institution of higher learning, should be paid by him or by his parents or in some other way by endowed scholarships or gifts or loans by interested friends. In all actual cases of need, scholarships or loans should be awarded to worthy students to the extent of the need and the ability of the college to finance the necessary scholarship funds.

We note with regret that in some of our colleges, supported by tuitions and endowment, there is a tendency to exceed this limit, and that on the part of tax-supported institutions there is a tendency to charge no tuition or to fix tuition rates so low that all students are enjoying the equivalent of large scholarships. This constitutes an unfair burden on taxpayers and an unwise pauperizing of the students themselves, and sets up a ruinous sort of competition with non-tax-supported institutions.

We call upon all institutions of higher learning to fix and maintain reasonable tuition rates that are fair to the students, to the faculty, to the donors of endowments, or to the tax-paying public that sustains the institution. We pledge our cooperation to the committee of the Association of American Colleges, now studying this whole problem, and urge a prompt and thorough report on the present situation and on methods of cooperation that may help to remove the unfair practises prevailing to-day.

W. P. Few, *Chairman*

After the adoption of plans to secure adequate publicity for the principles which the conference espoused in these findings, and a renewed expression of loyalty to the ideals of the church-related colleges, the conference adjourned.

C. J. T.

# REPORTS

## THE INTER-AMERICAN FEDERATION OF EDUCATION

The Inter-American Federation of Education is born of the hope of the teachers of the Americas that there may be some agency, channel and conference through which they may work, in cooperation without alien design and pressure, for the progressive betterment of their peoples through education and for their own improvement by the exchange of information and method.

The germ of a federation of this character may be found in the sessions devoted to education in the commendable series of conferences originating and held in Latin America prior to the first Pan American Scientific Congress, which through Chile's courtesy and initiative included the United States of America in its membership.

The section on education of the second Pan American Scientific Congress held in Washington during the winter of 1915 to 1916 may truly be called the first Pan American Conference on Education. Over two hundred papers, dealing with every kind and grade of educational endeavor, were contributed by outstanding educators from the Pan American Republics. These papers were later printed by the Government Printing Office in Washington as part of the *Proceedings* of the congress. The assistant secretary general of this congress, now serving as chairman of the organization committee of the Inter-American Federation of Education, conceived at this congress the idea of a federation of teachers who could lay a basis for dependable accord of their peoples by an intelligent and appropriate program of popular education, with emphasis upon those subjects in the early school life of their peoples that would increase their civic understanding and earning power.

With this purpose in mind, as a delegate to the third Pan American Scientific Congress, meeting in Lima, Peru, during the winter of 1924 to 1925, I submitted a resolution before the section on education, later approved by the congress, which recognized that the complementary economic interests and common development of the Pan American Republics can best be achieved by a program of common preparation of their peoples in the social and vocational subjects. This resolution came from my profound conviction that there must be far wider continental spread of social information about human relations and reactions if our politically motivated and government-controlled Pan American conferences are ever to achieve the objectives which these conferences would promote. Social vision through education in social and vocational subjects are basic and vital in any program of Pan American accord.

In 1928 the National Education Association of the United States authorized me to present in person a plan for the federation of the teachers of the Americas before the ministries of education, leading educational associations and educators in the Latin American countries. The plan called for an early preliminary organization conference in which the constituent countries would participate through national cooperating committees in each country to be appointed by a leading national education association, if possible, or by the ministry of education. It was, and is, the hope of the federation that there be the largest measure of private teacher initiative in its organization, administration and deliberations.

On accepting the principle of federation these associations and ministries of education were asked to name committees, one for each country, with chairman and secretary, with whom the organizing secretary of the proposed federation, designated by the National Education Association of the United States, might later communicate on behalf of the sponsoring association, namely, the National Education Association, for the purpose of determining time, place and agenda for the first or preliminary organization conference of the proposed Inter-American Federation of Education.

Encouraged by the interest and support received by the organizing secretary in the Latin American countries, the president of the National Education Association of the United States issued on January 24, 1929, invitations to all ministries of education for the appointment of delegates to an informal Inter-American Educational Conference to be held in Atlanta, Georgia, from July 1 to 3 at the time of the 67th annual meeting of the association. Supplementary invitations were sent by the organizing secretary to all associations and persons with whom he had established contacts. Dr. Uel W. Lamkin, president of the National Education Association, stated in his letter of invitation that the conference was called in order to further the plans of the federation to which the National Education Association stood in an initiatory relation, and expressed the hope that members of the National Cooperating Committee of the proposed federation might serve as delegates to represent their respective countries.

On March 1, 1929, the organizing secretary invited the following well-known Latin American educators to form with him a small committee on program and promotion of the Atlanta conference: Ernesto Nelson, Argentina; Mario de Brito, Brazil; Ramiro Guerra, Cuba; Moises Saenz, Mexico, and Jose D. Crespo, Panama.

By June 20, 1929, the following countries had appointed national cooperating committees: Argentina, Brazil, Costa Rica, Cuba, Dominican Republic, Guatemala, Haiti, Honduras, Mexico, Panama, Peru, United States, Uruguay and Venezuela. These committees were named by ministries of education, except in the following countries: Argentina, by the Asociacion Nacional del Profesorado; Brazil, by the Asociacao Brasileiro de Educacao; Honduras, by the Sociedad Magisterio Nacional;

Panama, by the Asociacion de Maestros de la Republica; the United States, by the National Education Association; and Uruguay, by the Asociacion de Profesores de Ensenanza Preparatoria y Secundaria.

Cooperation in the work of the federation as proposed at the Atlanta conference has since been received from all the remaining countries except Colombia. It is gratifying to note at this point that Colombia has accepted the invitation to be represented at the second conference of the federation and has named so distinguished an educator, diplomat and scholar as the representative of that country. Since the adjournment of the Atlanta Conference, cooperating committees have been named by Bolivia, Chile, Ecuador and Paraguay. It is expected that El Salvador and Nicaragua will soon name their committees. Delegates from ten countries took part in the preliminary organization conference of the proposed federation, July 1 to 3, 1929, in Atlanta. The program of the conference centered around two major themes: Character education and vocational education, including preparation for farm, home, office, factory, store and home industry.

The Atlanta Conference by resolution:

(1) Declared the formation of the Inter-American Federation of Education and approved the plans and purposes of this federation as proposed by the organizing secretary, Dr. Glen Levin Swiggett;

(2) Named Dr. Swiggett chairman of the organizing committee of the federation to include, in addition to the chairman, representing the United States, representatives, one each for Guatemala, Venezuela and the Dominican Republic, with representatives from additional countries on nomination of the chairman;

(3) Recommended the appointment of an advisory or honorary council, one from each country, to cooperate with the organization committee;

(4) Recommended that the discussion of character and vocational education be emphasized at subsequent conferences of the federation; and

(5) Accepted invitation extended by the Cuban delegation to hold a second conference in Havana in 1931. (Invitations to hold a second conference had also been received from Mexico and Uruguay.)

Brazil, Mexico and Uruguay have accepted since the Atlanta conference invitation to be represented on the organization committee of the federation. The ministries of education of all participating countries constitute the advisory council of the federation. They are expected to cooperate with the organization committee of the federation and to advise and support the National Cooperating Committees of their respective countries.

Due to political and economic conditions in Cuba and other countries invited by the chairman on behalf of the organization committee to hold the second conference of the federation, it has been impossible to hold until now the second conference, the first inter-American conference on education ever held in a Latin American country, which will take place in Santiago, Chile, from September 9 to 16, 1934.

In conclusion, I beg to remind the readers of SCHOOL AND SOCIETY of an earlier article by me on this subject in that journal and to quote from this article the following paragraphs which well express the vision, purpose and difficulties of the Inter-American Federation of Education:

The growth of the Inter-American Federation of Education will be slow if it remains true to its present purposes. It believes that dependable Inter-American accord can only come from a cordial continental popular desire for Inter-American understanding. The latter is impossible until through education there can be established in these twenty-one democracies permanent bases for friendly social action. Fifty years of fairly fruitless efforts for Pan American accord should convince us of the futility of methods to establish effective Inter-American agreements, many of which are social, by governmental agencies, acting separately or cooperatively through governmental conferences. Successful cooperation among these republics demands that there first be prepared ground for common action; otherwise, resolutions proceeding from conferences will continue meaningless and without ratification.

Inter-American accord must wait upon the building of a real public opinion; and the latter upon the education of our peoples by programs and methods that are continental in aim and purpose. Expanding and deepening opportunities for education will lessen illiteracy, improve the franchise and strengthen the sense of need among all Inter-American nations for friendly cooperation; in the understanding that mutual advantages are individual advantages. Continental political agreements, even based on economic interdependence, can not be assured of any great measure of permanence unless they rest upon a social urge or need coming from a well-informed public opinion.

Another reason for the slow growth of the Inter-American Federation idea or project lies in the fact that few Latin-American countries have one outstanding, nationally representative, educational association. Many of these countries will have several similar associations. In time these associations may merge into a great organization that will represent and speak for the teachers, one for each country, as may truly be said of the National Education Association of the United States. The Inter-American Federation was conceived in the hope that some time it may become a federation of these education associations.

GLEN LEVIN SWIGGETT,
*Chairman of the Organization Committee*

# EDUCATIONAL RESEARCH AND STATISTICS

## REGENTS GRADES AS A CUMULATIVE EDUCATIONAL RECORD[1]

WITH the present emphasis on the cumulative record card as an indispensable instrument in the educational phase of guidance, the present investigation regarding the value of the New York State Regents Examinations in this capacity is perhaps timely. That the Regents examinations provide secondary school cumulative record cards, standard throughout New York State, is evident. The validity of these examinations as a predictive device, within at least the one university studied, has been established.[2]

Relationships were established between high-school performance as measured by both the total "academic" Regents average and the various individual Regents subjects and college success as measured by the total freshman-sophomore college average and by department averages and individual college courses. The students for whom these data were analyzed were 661 freshmen, who entered the college of arts and science of this university for the years 1925–29. In addition, partial analyses were made for the entrants of 1930 and 1931, about 500 additional cases.

For the purposes of contrast, the following tests and examinations were related to the various college criteria: (1) The American Council on Education Examination[3] standard[4] scores for total and sub-tests; (2) the Iowa Content Examination for High School Seniors and College Freshmen[5] total and sub-test standard scores; (3) the Cooperative English and French Tests;[6] (4) the American Council Economics Test;[7] (5) the Columbia Research Chemistry Test;[8] and (6) the Nelson-Denny Reading Test.[9]

The average of all Regents marks, excluding such "non-academic" subjects as music, shop-work, commercial courses and the like, gave the highest single relationship—of those investigated—with the freshman-sophomore college average. Relationships between it and individual college course or class grades were also at the top, or very nearly so. It was, in fact, the best single all-round predictive device which we studied. For most fields of college learning, it surpassed, in size of relationship, individual high-school subject grades within the particular field, as well as content and "college aptitude" scores.

Average high-school success is probably the best measure of a student's attack upon things academic. Such an average probably irons out

[1] This study was made possible through a grant from the General Education Board. The statistical computations were made by Eunice Strabel, to whom the author is indebted for conscientious and accurate performance.

[2] Mazie Earle Wagner, "The Prediction of College Performance," "Articulation of High School and College," *The University of Buffalo Studies*, 9: 1934, Part II, 125–173 and 184–209.

[3] Prepared by L. L. and Thelma Gwinn Thurstone; published by the American Council on Education, 744 Jackson Place, Washington, D. C.

[4] C. L. Hull, "The Computation of Pearson's *r* from Ranked Data," *Journal of Applied Psychology*, 6: 385–390. 1922.

[5] Devised by G. M. Ruch, G. D. Stoddard and others. Published by the Bureau of Educational Research and Service, University of Iowa, Iowa City, Iowa.

[6] Published by the Educational Records Bureau, New York, N. Y.

[7] Constructed by H. Taylor, T. N. Barrows and Ben D. Wood; published by the World Book Company, Yonkers-on-Hudson, N. Y.

[8] Constructed by E. R. Jette, S. R. Powers and Ben D. Wood. Published by the World Book Company.

[9] Prepared by M. J. Nelson and E. C. Denny. Printed by Houghton Mifflin Company.

the effects of special likes and dislikes for subject-matter and teachers, special high and low tides of motivation, as well as emotional and physical ill- and well-being. This process of minimizing the maxima and minima of performance—the net effect of averaging—leaves the best picture of a student's general performance and the best measure of his future general and specific academic success.

It comes somewhat as a surprise that those special abilities involved in the study of a particular field should be swamped by this measure of general attack upon things academic, this average of academic motivation and aptitude. But such is the case. When predicting college language, for instance, the Regents average may be used with better success than any high-school language previously attempted. The same holds true for other fields of learning.

Another surprise was the high predictive value of such language Regents grades as were at hand. In the absence of a Regents average, any language Regents grade or language school average is the next best measure of future college success. This is true for subject prediction as well. For instance, high-school French or German average predicts average college performance practically as well as the Regents average; and again Regents Latin III (Cicero) grades are more closely related to average college physical science or mathematics performance than any other measure examined.

Next in order of predictive value to the Regents average and language grades, in the forecasting of specific field or class performance, is high-school success in the same field of learning. Regents English IV, for instance, is exceedingly valuable in foretelling college English success.

A study of the relative guidance value of such tests as were available showed: (1) That the Iowa High School Content Examination is inferior to the Regents average. It is usually less related to specific subjects than this same average, never markedly better. (2) For the prediction of general college success, the American Council Psychological Examination is definitely inferior, at least at this college, to the Regents average, the Regents marks in English, history and science, and to the Iowa High School Content. In specific field and class performance, it is inferior, in all but a very few cases, to the Regents average, Regents language marks, Regents grades in the particular field being studied and to the Iowa High School Content.

(3) For specific class performance, at this college, the following are as good as the best single Regents predictive measure: The Cooperative English Test for the English; the American Council Economics Test for economics; the Columbia Research Chemistry Test for chemistry, and the Nelson-Denny Reading Test in the social sciences. Except for the Economics Test, none are reliably better than the best Regents measure.

The question will arise: Can generalizations from these results be made to cover other than New York State situations? The following investigations would indicate that wherever high-school grades are well standardized, *e.g.,* in large cities, grades from the secondary school may be used to advantage to predict success or failure in college: (1) Carson[10] at the University of Pittsburgh found a particularly high relationship (r. 72) between a high-school and freshman college average for Pittsburgh high-school graduates attending his university. (2) Scates,[11] at the University of Chicago, found a definitely higher relationship for students coming from Chicago high schools than for those from all high schools. (3) The present writer,[12] at the University of Buffalo, also found definitely higher relationships for students coming from Buffalo schools than for those from non-Buffalo secondary schools.

In conclusion, the best placement tests are suggested for specific course prediction in non-New York State regions, the school average for the prediction of general college success for students from large cities (the Regents average for all students from New York State schools), and batteries of placement tests for general college success prediction for students from small high schools of variable student achievement.

MAZIE EARLE WAGNER

UNIVERSITY OF BUFFALO

10 F. H. Carson, "A Study of Some Factors Influencing the Academic Success of Freshmen Students during Their First Semester at the University of Pittsburgh," M.A. Thesis, 1928.

11 D. E. Scates, "Selective Admission and Selective Retention of College Students at the University of Chicago," Ph.D. Thesis, School of Education, University of Chicago, 1926.

12 M. E. Wagner, *Op. cit.*

# SCHOOL AND SOCIETY

WITH WHICH ARE COMBINED THE EDUCATIONAL REVIEW, ESTABLISHED IN 1891, THE TEACHERS MAGAZINE, ESTABLISHED IN 1878, AND THE SCHOOL JOURNAL, ESTABLISHED IN 1874.

Volume 40 SATURDAY, SEPTEMBER 22, 1934 Number 1030

## SCIENCE AT THE UNIVERSITIES[1]

By H. T. TIZARD, F.R.S.

SECRETARY OF THE BRITISH DEPARTMENT OF SCIENTIFIC AND INDUSTRIAL RESEARCH

AT the Imperial College I have colleagues who have had over twenty-five years experience of successions of boys from secondary schools. They say, without hesitation, that the standard of general education has increased steadily throughout that period. I am newer to the work; and when I reflect that so many of the present generation of secondary schoolboys who find their way to universities come from the poorest homes, I think the standard of general education is to be praised rather than decried. I think also that the man who has ideas of his own, and a capacity for doing something really well, is more useful and more interesting, even though he may be unable to express himself adequately in his own language, than one who is merely capable of describing other people's work and ideas in elegant English. When all these allowances are made, however, there is undoubtedly room for improvement. There are many scientific men who write beautiful English; and yet I suppose there is no gap in his equipment that the average scientific man deplores more in after-life than his difficulty in writing and speaking his own language well. I say this feelingly, as to me writing is a forced labor, and I am never satisfied with the result; but with practise one can acquire a certain proficiency, and with the example of T. H. Huxley as an inspiration no one need altogether despair. My complaint of many young students of science to-day is not so much that they do not write clearly and concisely as that they do not seem to want to, which indicates insufficient practise and instruction at school to acquire a taste. Again, I should agree with the committee that "a competent knowledge of one modern language (French or German, the latter in particular) is, quite apart from its cultural value, an essential element in the equipment of the adequately trained scientist." Much of the best scientific literature is written in German, and if a scientist can not read German scientific papers, he is severely handicapped. At the Imperial College we found it necessary many years ago to institute special classes in German. It should not be necessary.

The schoolmaster is, however, in a quandary. There is a limited number of hours in the day, and if he taught all the subjects that he is advised to teach to all the boys—for every one naturally thinks that his own special subject should form part of a liberal education—he would only succeed in producing a race of smatterers. He has to choose a happy mean between teaching more and more about less and less, or less and less about more and more; and he not unjustly complains that during the

[1] From the address of the president of the Section of Educational Science, British Association for the Advancement of Science, Aberdeen, September, 1934.

last year of a clever boy's life at school he is hampered in his choice by the regulations and practise of universities. Schoolmasters at grant-aided secondary schools are in a special difficulty, for most of their pupils are not able to proceed to a university unless they win entrance scholarships. If university authorities complain that students are lacking in general education, it is for them to do their best, by altering the conditions of entry, or the standard of scholarships, to help schoolmasters to remedy the defects. I propose, therefore, to discuss briefly what changes are desirable. I shall base my remarks on the regulations of London University, and my own college in particular, but I think the regulations of other universities are sufficiently similar to make the discussion of general interest.

The first university examination is the matriculation examination. A matriculation examination, I take it, was originally intended to be an examination the successful passing of which entitled a candidate to be admitted to the privileges of a university. The London University matriculation examination has long ceased to be anything of the sort—at any rate, so far as students of science are concerned. It would seem more appropriate to regard it as an examination which entitles successful candidates to be admitted to the privilege of becoming bank clerks. Certainly few university schools of science will admit a student at the normal age of eighteen on the strength of his having passed the matriculation examination; some further proof of his proficiency is required. At the Imperial College we have a special entrance examination which mainly consists of papers in mathematics and science, but includes papers in English and a choice of foreign languages; but I can not say that a candidate is refused admittance if he fails to do well in the English and language papers, but does well in the other subjects.

The next university examination is the intermediate examination. The original object of such an examination was to test the progress of a student in his special subject of study at a university, after he had given evidence of a sufficient general education at the normal age of entry. In fact, if we agree that a university is a place where students learn to teach themselves, under the guidance of distinguished teachers, instead of learning under the strict discipline of school, the main object of an intermediate examination should be to test a student's capacity to teach himself, and therefore to satisfy the authorities that he is fit to proceed with a course of study leading to a degree. Nowadays, as the matriculation examination or its equivalent is passed by most intending students at the age of fifteen or sixteen, their remaining years at school are devoted to the special subjects of the intermediate which many of them pass before they enter the university. They are encouraged to do so by university authorities. It saves us trouble, and gives the student time to acquire a larger stock of specialized knowledge in his undergraduate career. The next obvious step will be to take the degree examinations at schools, leaving the universities free to concentrate on postgraduate work!

While these changes have been taking place in school curricula, the standard of science entrance scholarships at universities has steadily risen; and as most science scholarships go to boys who intend to study physics or chemistry at the university, the schools are encouraged—some would even say forced—against their will, to concentrate their advanced teaching on physics and chemistry. It is true that only a small proportion of the boys at any particular school intend to compete for scholarships, but it is impossible to segregate such boys altogether, and the standard of scholarship examinations, therefore, sets the pace for the higher school forms.

The object of a scholarship examination is to discover the boys of greatest promise, not the boys who have been most successfully crammed. I think that schoolmasters are inclined to attach too much importance to the character of the papers set and to give too little credit to the examiners for intelligence. It is not always the boys who get the highest marks who win the scholarships, and it is not so very difficult for an intelligent examiner to distinguish between an active and a congested brain. At the same time, I do agree with the criticism that the papers set are usually too difficult. There is too great an element of luck about a hard paper; and first-rate ability in a candidate is shown more by the way he answers a question than by his knowledge of detail. I remember giving practical effect to these opinions when I examined in the Final Honor School of Chemistry at Oxford fourteen years ago. One of the two papers I set in physical chemistry was so apparently easy that I feel sure that a more cheerful group of candidates never sat in the examination schools. I am confident, too, that there never was an occasion when an examiner found it easier to distinguish between the relative merits of different candidates. The first-class man answered the questions briefly, accurately and to the point; the second-class man wrote pages of irrelevant matter, to impress the examiner; and the third-class man made elementary mistakes.

It is not so easy as it may seem, however, to change the standard of scholarship examinations, and thereby to encourage a broader education. About a year ago we decided to review our policy at the Imperial College. Students come to the college with science scholarships from many sources; but the chief sources are the board of education, who award royal scholarships tenable only at the college as well as state scholarships tenable at any university in England and Wales; the London County Council; and the college itself. For the past five years our scholarship examinations have been held in January at the suggestion of a group of head masters of public schools, who advised that by doing so we should attract better candidates. We have not found this borne out by results; we have not had enough good candidates in any year since the change to justify us in awarding the full number of scholarships; and many of the better candidates have subsequently competed for and gained royal scholarships or state scholarships which are higher in value. Our general experience leads us to believe that very few, if any, students of first-rate ability, who have specialized in science at school, are prevented from going to a university for lack of financial assistance. On the other hand, we believe that no scholarships are deliberately made available to assist able students who have not specialized in science at school to study science at a university. We have therefore decided to make the experiment of changing the character of our January scholarship examination. We propose to set papers in general science and mathematics of quite a low standard, together with papers of a higher standard in history, foreign languages and English. The details are not yet settled, but head masters and head mistresses were notified of the change this year, and their criticism and cooperation were invited. The scheme has had a mixed reception. We have received many encouraging, but many critical letters. Much of the criticism can be summed up by the phrase, actually used—"It would not suit my Sixth, and I should not alter my Sixth to suit it." Now schoolmasters can not have it both ways; they can not say, on the one hand, that they are forced to specialize unduly at schools by the standard set by examiners for science scholarships, and, on the other hand, that they do not propose to make any change if university authorities listen to their criticisms. We intend to go on with the experiment, without any great hopes of the result; some one must make a start, and the most unpromising experiments have often given surprisingly good results. At the same time, I fully realize that what one particular college does can not solve the difficulties of the schools. If it is really the general view that the school education of a student of science is too narrow, then the best practical step is to reform the university matriculation examination, and make it appropriate to the normal age of entry. If one of the larger universities did this, the effect would be considerable. If it is not considered worth while, then criticism of the general education of the science student loses most of its point.

I have put before you some problems of the present; I want now, before I conclude, to touch briefly on a problem of the future.

All university education in science and technology is designed primarily to produce teachers or professional scientists or technicians. Most engineering students intend to become practising engineers; most chemists who do not enter the teaching profession become research chemists or chemical engineers; most students of biology become doctors or professional biologists. A few graduates in science break adrift, and turn with success to other occupations: to the law, for example, to general administration, or even to literature! Of His Majesty's present ministers, one took a degree in biology at a Scottish university, and another a degree in chemistry at an English university. But these are rare exceptions; most science graduates are specialists skilled in a particular branch of science, and ignorant of other branches. A hundred years ago it was not difficult for a scientific man to follow in detail the work of others; now it is as much as a specialist can do to keep abreast of the progress of knowledge in the particular field in which he is interested. No one studies science at a university as a general education, as men study classics, philosophy and history; indeed no one can, for no university supplies the opportunity. "Modern Greats" at Oxford includes the study of history, economics, philosophy and "the structure of modern society," but not of science!

During the present century there has been a struggle to secure a wider recognition of the value of scientific study and research, not only for the advancement of knowledge, but for the progress of civilization. Now that this recognition is widespread; now that we all see plainly the great influence of scientific discovery on social developments; now that specialized departments of science are flourishing at universities; surely an effort should be made to provide for men who have no desire to become specialists, but who wish to study the broad principles and applications of science, for their own education, and as the best preparation for after-life in many spheres of human activity. The place of the specialist in industry and in the machinery of government is assured. Large establishments have grown up, mushroom-like, to meet the demand for industrial research. Biological research is also gaining recognition, but more slowly, for public opinion has not yet been educated to the point of realizing that, in the long run, it would be fatal to attach more value to industrial research than to applied biology. With all this increase of scientific activity, there has arisen an urgent need for skilled administrators and men in public life who have a real knowledge of the principles and methods of science; not the kind of knowledge that is derived from conversation, listening to broadcast talks and reading popular books, however good these may be, but that which is gained by serious study. We can not complain that there are few such men among the present generation; it is a great thing that there has been a change of attitude of mind. But unless something is done, there will be no greater number in the next generation.

Is the time ripe for action on the part of the universities? I think it is. The great accession of knowledge in all branches of science may often seem bewildering; but its effect has been to make the main principles clearer, and easier to teach, for a connecting thread runs through them. The foundations of science have been laid; they will be strengthened in the future, but it is unlikely that they will be rebuilt. The structure that is built on them grows ever more coherent; it can be studied as a whole, without examining in great detail any of its parts. The subjects of the university school I have in mind will include the study of the foundations and philosophical background of science; of its history; of the history of social development; of the applications of science to industry, agriculture and medicine; of problems of population and health—and the like. The student will learn that law and order in the universe is not a faith but a reality; and that science is "nothing but trained and organized common sense." He will learn too, I hope, to acquire the spirit of that unprejudiced search for truth which is the basis of all fruitful scientific inquiry.

These are but vague suggestions; the practical thing to do is to make a start; and the best way to make a start is to select the right man to direct such a school—and there are men available—to put him in the right environment, and to give him the opportunity to work out his own ideas. That good would result I have not the slightest doubt.

# ORIENTATION COURSES

By Professor R. P. SIBLEY
CORNELL UNIVERSITY

THE historian of college education in our time may well be puzzled by the dearth of comment on one of its most striking features, the introduction and development of so-called orientation courses. The fact that these courses have made surprisingly little stir in the academic world, and no stir at all in the world outside, he may perhaps associate, whether as cause or consequence, to the other fact that their development has been very rapid. Even a dozen years ago orientation courses were not common and the name carried no definite meaning. In some places it meant a modest attempt to instruct freshmen in the history and traditions of alma mater; to inform them about their relations with administrative officers; to warn them about academic rules and penalties; to introduce them to the college library; to advise them about activities *extra-curriculum,* about the local churches, and in a discreetly general way about fraternities; to exhort them to take care of their health—in short, the miscellaneous program now oftener relegated to a freshman week. In other places the orientation program consisted of talks by representatives of the various departments of instruction who, appearing in series, explained the organization and sequence of their courses and tried to make clear why an intelligent freshman might wish to specialize in each of these inviting fields. Elsewhere the orientation course, labeled, perhaps, "Foundations" or "Fundamentals," was really less of an innovation than the foregoing; to constitute it portions of the Christian Evidences of a generation ago were combined with general advice on morals, health and habits of study, and whatever else a Y. M. C. A. secretary would refer to as the problems of college life.

Now useful and edifying as orientation courses of these kinds may be, obviously they have little bearing on the other courses of the curriculum. They may orient the freshman for a campus career; they are not much concerned with orienting him in the intellectual life. But the more daring experimenters felt that right here is the truly important work to be done. Freshmen lose interest not because the subjects we oblige them to study are trite and jejune, but because the courses of instruction we offer are unconnected with one another and unrelated to situations in real life. College teachers are specialists. Cultivating each his own province in the world of ideas, they act as though each province were rimmed round with walls, its borders patrolled by jealous guards and beset by inhospitable tax collectors. From them their pupils inevitably get the notion of a world of knowledge necessarily cut up into insulated parts. Teachers and taught need to be reminded, time and again, that the only divisions in the rational world are divisions which were imposed by the human mind and merely as convenient devices, different ways of viewing and comprehending a genuinely corporate whole. Furthermore, being specialists, college teachers are usually pedants; they tend to overrate technical knowledge, especially in their own several fields. Freshmen wanting a general education must be protected, then, from the college teacher whose interest lies in a specialty which he cultivates with narrow exclusiveness and professes with unbalanced zeal.

Thus one supposes it was with the intention of liberalizing by enlarging, and especially of unifying by correlating the subject-matter of freshman education that more and more college faculties have projected more and more ambitious programs of orientation until now in some institutions quite half the time of the first college year is monopolized by them and it is seriously proposed that at least as much of the succeeding years shall be. Nearly all are essentially "survey" courses, and often so called. They attempt to explain, according to modern science, how the physical universe came to be what according to modern science it is; they review the cultural history, especially the social history, of man; they propound what seem to the collective wisdom of those in charge to be the most significant political, social and economic problems of civilization to-day; they hint plainly at solutions. In making and dispensing these novel courses men of many departments usually join wits; experts in anthropology, astronomy, biology, economics, government, history, psychology and sociology are invited to put their *imprimatur* upon the joint offering, though the actual administration of it may usually be entrusted to a few men, rarely to a single man. Even text-books have been prepared covering the content of such courses; and if in general the matter in them is still regarded as experimental and plastic, most likely orientation will yet go the way of other pioneering courses and crystalize into a formulary on which multitudes of text-books play unimportant variations.

But how are these new orientation courses working out? Well; all or nearly all critics agree that they are a grand good thing for the instructors who give them. About their value to freshmen, the putative beneficiaries, there still survive doubts. For reasons which every college teacher will understand, adverse criticism has issued mainly from institutions that have not experimented, from critics who have no first-hand familiarity with the results. From time to time results of student polls are published, indicating comparative popularity for orientation. Occasionally one hears an enthusiastic expression quoted from some faculty man to the effect that with the orientation background he is getting students better prepared for later specialization. But a thorough, detailed and avowedly dispassionate report upon the actual performance of any orientation course is yet to be written, so far as the present writer has been able to discover. Unable himself to offer a record of experience, he hopes it will not prove too unprofitable if he tries to set down some theoretic advantages and weaknesses of the orientation idea as he understands it.

In the first place, some of us regard it as a promising symptom that college teachers of science have been willing to sponsor a survey course at all. Systematic studies in the history of the sciences never have had a vogue in this country; few teachers of a science have shown any interest in the historical approach to their subject. Can they really be coming to the conclusion that a passable comprehension of the purport of current scientific theories is possible for an otherwise liberally educated man, even though he has no laboratory acquaintance with the sciences in question? Are they, too, beginning to suspect that though acquaintance with the laboratory technique of at least one science may be uniquely valuable, it is nevertheless wasteful of time and money to insist on a laboratory accompaniment to every beginners' course? A similar cause for congratulation might be welcomed in the contributions to the orientation course made by history, economics and sociology; for in these fields also it has become rather fashionable to send even freshmen to the "sources," to set them "research problems," to disparage such second-hand knowledge as can be obtained from text-books, encyclopedias, surveys and summaries. Here again one may fully recognize the value that inheres in learning and practising a technique of investigation in some study while one very much doubts that in preparing college underclassmen for citizenship in the world of ideas the attitude and training of an original investigator, working on an individual "case" or "project," make a proper substitute for a wide ranging interest, perspective and sense of proportion.

It is no very profound education, to be sure, which even a conscientious learner will gain from these survey courses. What they do give can not be better described than by piecing together some remarks of Newman's from another connection. Of the contributions made to our education by our own senses but still more by other people and by books, he writes as follows:

> These informations constitute the furniture of the mind, and make the difference between its civilized condition and a state of nature. They are its education, as far as general knowledge can so be called; and, though education is discipline as well as learning, still, unless the mind implicitly welcomes the truths, real or ostensible, which these informations supply, it will gain neither formation nor a stimulus for its activity and progress. . . . These various teachings, shallow though they be, are of a breadth which secures us against those *lacunae* of knowledge which are apt to befall the professed student, and keep us to the mark in literature, in the arts, in history, and in public matters. They give us in great measure our morality, our politics, our social code, our art of life. They supply the elements of public opinion, the watchwords of patriotism, the standards of thought and action; they are our mutual understandings, our channels of sympathy, our means of co-operation, and the bond of our civil union. They become our moral language; we learn them as we learn our mother tongue; they distinguish us from foreigners; they are, in each of us, not indeed personal, but national characteristics. . . . Even the most practised and earnest minds must needs be superficial in the greater part of their attainments. They know just enough on all subjects, in literature, history, politics, philosophy, and art, to be able to converse sensibly on them, and to understand those who are really deep in one or other of them. This is what is called, with a special appositeness, a gentleman's knowledge, as contrasted with that of a professional man, and is neither worthless nor despicable, if used for its proper ends; but it is never more than the furniture of the mind, as I have called it; it is never thoroughly assimilated with it. Yet of course there is nothing to hinder those who have even the largest stock of such notions from devoting themselves to one or other of the subjects to which those notions belong, and mastering it with a real apprehension; and then their general knowledge of all subjects may be made variously useful in the direction of that particular study or pursuit which they have selected.

These uses of the opinions and professed facts which a survey course is intended to impart seem to me important for a college freshman who very possibly has slid through high school without adding appreciably to his mental furniture. And then there is another value more explicitly noted in Newman's observation that opinions and professed facts furnish us not only with "a broad foundation of thought for ourselves" but with "a medium of intercourse between ourselves and others." Before the system of free electives enriched (and bedeviled) the college curriculum, in the days when they were studying the same subjects together in the same classroom, fellow-students did share and traffic in a common fund of thought, did occasionally compare mental notes and swap ideas as well as smokes and wearing apparel. It is small wonder if they are not so apt to, to-day. It is small wonder if boys around the fraternity dinner-table, "specializing" in anything from business administration to zoology, should find the highest common conversational denominator in "dates" and sports. Surely a good word can be said for orientation courses if by supplying a common subject-matter, novel and usually interesting to young folks just out of high school, they help boys and girls to educate one another.

Theoretically, however, the faults of orientation are, to say the least, quite as obvious as the virtues. If survey courses in the gross engender distaste for detail and impatience with the drudgery of scholarship, if they tend to encourage unscrupulousness in grasping at conclusions and put a premium on glib generalizing, then these weaknesses may be expected particularly to mark the orientation course; particularly, because in the orientation course conclusions are made to matter so much—are indeed about all that matters. A generation eager for short cuts, interested in product but not in process, will find its idea of education realized in the orientation course. In the published preface to one well-known orientation course we read that its purpose is "to assist the individual in the very important problem of forming well-defined conceptions of the Cosmos and of his relation to it." "Very important," certainly. The formation of an adolescent's *Weltanschauung* is always important to him. But in this highly important business of forming a personal philosophy, will orientation only assist? Will it not, more likely, present the philosophy ready-made? That seems to be the fear of such critics as Mr. O. G. Jones,[1] who protests that modern orientation is as authoritarian in animus and method as ever medieval scholasticism. To our young people the authority will appeal not the less effectively because it is not a religious but a secular agency which disclaims any interest whatever in any "cause" except the triumph of truth.

The possible content of an orientation course is so multifarious, the possible points of view are so many, that a rigid selection and control must be exercised if the presentation is to be coherent. These needs are provided for. This sight-seeing tour called orientation is carefully conducted. The conductors are usually a body of earnest gentlemen imbued with a mighty missionary zeal. Beyond most college teachers, certainly, they are bent on doing good to their young charges. They aim at nothing less than the intellectual salvation of Juventus. Before joining the party in the capacity of guides, it is complained, they have put off the disinterestedness of science, have assumed the rôle of propagandists, purveyors of a saving faith rather than interpreters of scientific hypotheses. Their concerted creed (continue the critics), being better grounded than the propaganda of a single layman like Mr. Wells or the other authors of individual "Outlines," carries much more weight, especially with those young folks who have been flatteringly chosen to receive it because of their "superior intelligence." Yet the possession of superior intelligence does not guarantee that its possessors have arrived at the same stage of mental and emotional development. If, as oftener happens, the orientation course is made compulsory for all freshmen, no effort at all is made to ascertain whether *Juventus individuus* is ready for his Pisgah prospect.

It may be said that this fear of indoctrination could as well be directed against all effective teaching. Every teacher worth his salt lays before his pupils the conclusions he has reached and the evidence for those conclusions; he can not help hoping, and ought not if he could, that they will find the evidence convincing and come to believe as he does. The material of the orientation course, the information and speculation of which it is composed, doubtless accurate, certainly interesting, have been in enlarged form the substance of a dozen separate courses in the several sciences; why should they suddenly become suspect as "propaganda" when they are brought together in an orientation course? Obviously, because something new emerges in combining them. Despite his absorption in his own *metier* the teacher of any other course rarely cherishes notions of its transcendent worth for all men. A professor of Greek, of mathematics, of biology, of economics, not often claims saving power for a knowledge of the aorist, of least squares, of the Mendelian law, of the theory of diminishing returns. All other subjects, all other instructors, are competing with one another for a share in the student's interest; the "orienters" alone have proposed to instructors not only that they should cooperate but that they should combine "to assist the individual in the very important problem of forming well-defined conceptions of the Cosmos and of his relation to it." This really does seem a bit novel in secular education.

It is doubtless true that in their actual working not many orientation courses do much to justify the fears expressed above; but that is equivalent to admitting that any scheme of rep-

[1] SCHOOL AND SOCIETY, March 8, 1930.

resentative and wholesale orientation will not really orient the individual. Most of us feel with Dickens that there is a "lingering personal retail interest within us that asks to be satisfied." To *orient* has commonly been used reflexively; one orients oneself, not somebody else. A man's orientation—does it not amount to his philosophy of life? As such maybe one man or several men can not impart it to others by the machinery of lectures, assigned readings and recitations. Possibly the only orientation very profitable to a man is that which he has worked out in personal experience and grown into. When he has to stand off and look at it, perhaps he had better think of it as the goal rather than the spring-board of his intellectual striving. Orientation courses may still have value, however, even though they do not orient. Some of them are likely to be retained for long, in reduced dimensions and under a less pretentious name and purpose, for those students who desire a comprehensive view both of the interrelations of the sciences and of modern scientific ideas about our physical environment and social institutions. Indeed they may be supplemented by similar courses designed for students with similar desires in the field of the humane arts.

# EDUCATIONAL EVENTS

## EUROPEAN APPRENTICESHIP SYSTEMS

THE recent appointment by the Secretary of Labor, acting under an executive order of the President, of a Federal Committee on Apprentice Training under NRA Codes, and the responsibility placed upon the public schools for cooperating with industry in providing this type of training where needed, lends interest to reports on apprenticeship training policies followed in England, France and Germany. These reports have recently been received by the State Department from consuls in the three European countries.

Consul Raymond H. Geist, German consul, writes: "The foundation of German industry is its stock of highly trained mechanics and skilled laborers. Even in these years of depression everything possible has been done to sustain the apprenticeship system in Germany. The training of apprentices is considered not only an economic necessity but also a social duty toward the youth of the nation."

While trade schools, sponsored chiefly by guilds, are the principal source of training for artisans, large industries—iron, machine, chemical, instruments, optical goods and textile industries—maintain plant-owned schools approved by the state. Employers are required to provide time for workers to receive instruction supplementary to their occupations, in trade and continuation schools. So alive is the German Government to the need for careful training of apprentices that it has passed a law providing that employers can engage only the number of apprentices that the authorities feel they can adequately train. Thoroughness of training is insisted upon.

In England, a report from Robert B. Macatee, consul in London, shows apprenticeship training for retail salesmen formerly undertaken by the industries is rapidly dying out, As a result government schools have been established to provide such training in a number of the principal cities.

The Institute of Certified Grocers, a grocery trade association, is promoting practical and technical classes in schools throughout the country. The Draper's Chamber of Trade, the textile trade association, sponsors a summer school at Oxford or Cambridge, for textile employees and also cooperates in organizing workers' classes in the all-year-round schools and in textile plants. A similar policy has been followed by the National Federation of Meat Traders' Associations.

In France, where, up to the time of the war, workers received their occupational training through apprenticeship programs carried on by employers, public schools are now being used for this purpose, according to a report from George Tait, consul in Paris. A special apprenticeship tax upon employers defrays in large part the cost of these apprenticeship schools.

The detailed reports of the American Consuls

in London, Paris and Berlin on apprenticeship in England, France and Germany are contained in a vocational education bulletin recently issued by the Federal Office of Education.

## EDUCATIONAL BROADCASTING FROM THE OHIO STATE UNIVERSITY

AN innovation in educational broadcasting will be offered during the autumn quarter when the department of education of the Ohio State University conducts an evening radio course for teachers.

Entitled "The School and its Relation to the Community," the class will be conducted each Wednesday and Friday at 9 P. M. from the campus station, WOSU. The first session each week will be devoted to a talk on some phase of the subject by a faculty member, while in the Friday night broadcast a group of educators, business and professional men or parents will meet with the original speaker for a discussion of the subject. Participants in these round-table sessions, which will be broadcast, will come from various Ohio cities.

As a further step in its plan, the department of education hopes to have organized listener and discussion groups of teachers and parents throughout the effective radius of 70 miles of the station for further consideration of subjects covered in the course.

Wherever possible, it is announced, the department will send representatives to participate in these local meetings. The course carries no credits and no expense for those enrolled.

The lectures that so far have been scheduled are:

October 3, "Why Must the School Become a More Active and More Intimate Community Force Than It Has Been in the Past?" Vice-president J. L. Morrill.

October 10, "How Can the School and the Home Cooperate Effectively?" Professor John L. Clifton.

October 17, "How Can the School and Political Institutions of the Community Cooperate Effectively?" Professor E. E. Lewis.

October 24, "How Can the School and the Industries of the Community Cooperate Effectively?" Professor William E. Warner.

October 31, "How Can the School and Other Cultural Agencies, Such as Libraries and Museums, Cooperate Effectively?" Dr. Harlow Lindley.

November 7, "How Can the School and Other Character-forming Agencies of the Community Cooperate Effectively?" Professor H. Gordon Hullfish.

November 14, "How Can the School Serve Community Needs through a Program of Guidance?" Professor W. H. Stone.

November 21, "How Can the School Conduct Its Public Relations so as to Best Serve the Community?" Professor Ward G. Reeder.

November 28 and December 5, "How Can the School Fulfil Its Community Responsibilities during a Financial Depression?" Professor H. H. Davis.

December 12, "How Can the School Serve the Adult Community so as Not to Interfere with but to Improve Its Service to the Rising Generation?" Professor O. G. Brim.

December 19, "Summary and Prospects for the Next Quarter," Professor R. H. Eckelberry.

## COURSES FOR TEACHERS IN THE COLLEGE OF THE CITY OF NEW YORK

THE School of Education of the College of the City of New York has announced a special program of afternoon courses for teachers enabling them to prepare for higher degrees or to take professional courses for "alertness" credit.

Most of the courses count toward the degrees of B.S. and M.S. in education. Those who meet the full admission requirements with the required grades may take work leading to the degree of B.S. in education without cost; others are required to pay moderate fees.

The courses in education are:

Seminar in educational research.
Seminar in modern language teaching.
History of education, with special reference to the city of New York.
Contemporary movements in education.
Contemporary psychology.
Educational psychology.
Experimental educational psychology.
Psychology of high-school subjects.
Psychology and education of exceptional children.
Psychology of adolescence.
Problems of child behavior.
Statistics as applied to education.
Educational measurements.
Intelligence tests.
Clinic in intelligence testing.
Philosophy of education.
Educational sociology.
Teaching in the primary grades.

Observation and criticism of teaching in elementary schools.
Technique of progressive teaching.
Teaching of arithmetic.
Safety education.
Museum methods and practise.
Kindergarten practise.
Kindergarten extension.
Manual and oral expression in the kindergarten.
Teaching ungraded children.
English and citizenship for foreign-born.
Mechanics of visual instruction.
Nature study.
Observation and practise teaching in secondary schools.
Problems in secondary school teaching.
Teaching literature, economics, history, mathematics in high school.
Teaching of German: theory.
Romance languages: theory.
Methods and materials for teaching Spanish: theory.
Teaching of science.
Teaching biology.
Methods of teaching Gregg shorthand.
Teaching Pitman stenography.
Special problems in commercial teaching.
Teaching office technique: calculating machines, office practise.
Health education: applied physiology and health.
Folk dancing and athletics for girls.
Methods of teaching dancing: (classical, characteristic and national dances; clog, tap and athletic dancing; rhythmic gymnastics and dancing).
History of physical education.
Physical education and practise for high-school teachers.
Social hygiene and sex education.
Kinesiology and anatomy in relation to education.
Physiology in relation to health education.
Vocational information.
Vocational guidance, placement and follow-up.
Problems in vocational education.
Teaching of modern millinery construction.
Methods of teaching home economics.
Method and content in handwork: manual arts; projects for the kindergarten; teaching of pottery; developing creative power; artistic photography.
Theory and practise of art weaving.
Method and content in art weaving.
Review course in English in preparation for teaching in high school.
Review course in French in preparation for teaching in high school.
Survey course for supervisors in modern languages.
Review course in teaching general science.
Survey course for first assistants in science: organic chemistry, biochemistry; modern advances in physics.

In addition, the School of Education offers a complete schedule of courses in art, biology, chemistry, English, the social sciences, literature, mathematics, languages, public speaking, speech correction and secretarial subjects.

## THE INSTITUTE FOR SUPERVISORS OF ADULT EDUCATION AT NEW YORK UNIVERSITY

More than a hundred supervisors, district superintendents, superintendents and principals in charge of the Federal emergency education programs in New York and Connecticut attended the Institute for Supervisors of Adult Education from September 14 to 21, held at New York University.

The program was arranged by Dr. Ned H. Dearborn, acting director of the new Division of General Education, in cooperation with Dr. Lewis A. Wilson, assistant commissioner of education in the New York State Education Department, and Dr. N. S. Light, director of the Bureau of Field Service in the Connecticut State Department of Education.

The conference discussed needed developments in adult education, opportunities in general education for adults and Americanization through adult education. The program was arranged according to general subjects that included consideration of the major functions and duties of supervisors of adult education, planned to serve the purposes of the Emergency Education Program, encouraged and supported by the Federal Emergency Relief Administration and developed with the assistance of the U. S. Office of Education.

Topics discussed included the significance of adult education, analyses of existing programs in adult education, determining and stimulating local programs, counselling and educational advisement, selection of leaders, constructive supervision, interests of adults in fine and applied arts and physical and social recreation for adults.

Dr. Harold G. Campbell, superintendent of schools of New York City, was toastmaster at a dinner on September 15, at which the speakers were Frederick I. Daniels, executive director, Emergency Relief Administration, New York, who discussed problems of the New York State Relief Administration, and Miss Helen Hart, state supervisor of relief, who spoke on the contributions of adult education to relief work.

Speakers on the regular program included Edward Corsi, director, Emergency Home Relief Bureau, New York City; Dr. Harry Overstreet, professor of philosophy and psychology, College of the City of New York; W. H. Pillsbury, superintendent of schools, Schenectady, New York; Dr. Franklin J. Keller, director, National Occupational Conference, New York City; John W. Herring, executive director, American Committee on Economic Policies, New York City; Miss Caroline Whipple, supervisor of adult education, New York State; Dr. L. R. Alderman, director, educational division, Emergency Relief Administration, Washington, D. C.; Professor David Snedden, Teachers College, Columbia University, and Dr. Dearborn.

## NATURAL SCIENCE COURSES AT THE GEORGE WASHINGTON UNIVERSITY

A NATURAL science course, based upon newly defined objectives and teaching methods, will be introduced this autumn into the Junior College curriculum of the George Washington University.

The traditional introductory course in the field of natural science focuses the student's attention in the laboratory upon the minutia of plant and animal life, with the aim of imparting detailed factual material. The student through the new "Survey in Biology" will be familiarized with plants and animals in their natural environment and in their relationship to man, the objective being inculcation of a love of nature and a knowledge and appreciation of his surroundings. Instead of equipping the student with a series of facts in a highly specialized field, the Survey in Biology will aim to provide him with a background of understanding and powers of observation. The course is designed to take the student away from the atmosphere of laboratory and microscope, and into the open where he will relate his study to every-day life.

In the Survey in Biology there will be few laboratory periods. Through frequent observation trips extensive use will be made of the National Museum, the Zoological Park, the Bureau of Fisheries, the local food markets, the countryside about Washington and other places where materials can be studied to best advantage. As a substitute for the expensive and elaborate equipment of the laboratory, there will be used simple implements which may be retained and used after college years are past, as, for example, the hand lens rather than the microscope.

It is hoped to give students the broad view of the field of natural science which should be a part of the well-rounded cultural course, and, for the student who wishes to specialize, to lead naturally to advanced work in botany, zoology, geology or bacteriology.

The Survey in Biology will be under the direction of Dr. Paul William Bowman, who has been made head of the newly established department of biology.

A similar adjustment in courses and teaching has been made in the physical sciences. A course entitled Introduction to Physical Science will consist of a general survey of physics in the first semester and of chemistry in the second.

## NEW APPOINTMENTS AT NORTHWESTERN UNIVERSITY

THE appointment of seventeen new members to the faculty of Northwestern University has been announced by President Walter Dill Scott. Seven schools of the university are represented. The College of Liberal Arts heads the list with six new members, while the professional schools of dentistry and law have added two each to their faculties.

Professor T. Moody Campbell, formerly of Wesleyan University, has been appointed chairman of the department of German, replacing Professor James Taft Hatfield, who retired from teaching last spring after forty-four years of continuous service.

Dr. Walter F. Dodd, Chicago attorney and authority on constitutional law, has been appointed lecturer in political science. He was formerly on the faculty of the University of Illinois, the University of Chicago and Yale University.

The School of Law has added two assistant professors in Carl B. Spaeth and Gerald L. Wallace. The former graduated from Dartmouth College in 1929. He received a Rhodes

Scholar appointment and studied at Oxford for four years. On his return to the United States he did graduate work at Yale University and taught at Temple University last year. Professor Wallace is a graduate of the University of Illinois and did graduate work at Yale University. For the past two years he has been attorney for the New York Housing Commission.

Dr. Eugene Skinner, of Western Reserve University, and Dr. James H. Pearce, of Baylor University, have been added to the faculty of the School of Dentistry. Dr. Skinner will become an associate professor of applied physics and Dr. Pearce, who graduated from Northwestern in 1928, will join the staff of the prosthetic department.

Other appointments are:

*School of Commerce,* J. L. Miller, University of Washington, instructor in marketing; LaGrand Cannon, power sales engineer, Commonwealth Edison Company, lecturer in public utilities.

*School of Speech,* Harold Ehrensberger, formerly editor of *Little Theater Magazine*, instructor in modern drama; Theodore Fuchs, formerly executive director of the Drama League of New York and lighting director for the Theater Guild, instructor in stage lighting.

*School of Education,* William Gellerman, formerly superintendent of schools, Kent, Wash., instructor in education.

*School of Music,* Albert Noelte, Chicago composer, visiting professor of vocal composition.

*College of Liberal Arts,* Dr. Leonard Beach, instructor in English; Ralph Scott, instructor in English; Dr. Orlando Park, assistant professor in zoology; Carson Webster, instructor in art.

*School of Journalism,* J. L. Frazier, lecturer in typography.

## APPOINTMENTS AT YALE UNIVERSITY

A NUMBER of visiting professors will join the faculty of Yale University at the opening of the college year. Dr. Hajo Holborn, who since 1931 has occupied the Carnegie chair of modern history and international relations at the Berlin School of Politics, has been appointed visiting professor of history. Dr. Holborn is known for his work in two fields—the Weimar Constitution, on which the Republic of Germany was founded, and the Reformation. At Yale he will give in the Graduate School a seminar on modern German constitutional history, and a lecture course on the Renaissance. Dr. Carl J. F. Skottsberg, professor of botany at the University of Upsala, Sweden, has been appointed Bishop Museum visiting professor of botany. The Bishop Museum of Honolulu, which is affiliated with Yale, nominates annually a visiting professor who gives instruction and directs research in the problems of the Pacific area. Professor Skottsberg is director of the Botanical Garden at Gothenburg. Dr. Albrecht Götze, of the University of Marburg, will come to this country as visiting professor of Assyriology and Babylonian literature. His chief work has been in the Hittite language, a field in which Dr. Edgar H. Sturtevant, professor of linguistics at Yale, is also a specialist. Dr. Götze, who is professor of Semitics at the University of Marburg, received his doctorate at the University of Heidelberg, and, after teaching there in 1930, joined the faculty at Marburg. Dr. Millar Burrows, head of the department of Biblical literature at Brown University, will join the faculty as Winkley professor of Biblical literature in the Divinity School. From 1930–32 Dr. Burrows was engaged in teaching and research in Palestine, being director of the American School of Oriental Research at Jerusalem in the second of these years. He is president of the Board of Trustees of this school, in which a number of American universities and theological seminaries are cooperating. Dr. Burrows's work at Yale will be in studies of the religion of the Old Testament and the religion of the New Testament, and of the early environment of Christianity in Palestinian and Hellenistic Judaism.

At the beginning of the second term, Dr. Samuel F. Bemis will join the Yale faculty as Farnam professor of diplomatic history. Professor Bemis, who has been professor of history at George Washington University since 1924, won the Pulitzer history prize in 1926. In addition to his work in the Graduate School, he will give several undergraduate courses, one consisting of a discussion of relations between the United States and the different Latin-American countries. His appointment is part of the program of the university to give its students training in the field of international relations which will prepare them for careers in the service of the government.

# EDUCATIONAL NOTES AND NEWS

DR. WALTER WILLIAMS has resigned as president of the University of Missouri, effective on December 31. He will continue as dean of the School of Journalism, which he founded in 1908, at a time when there was no school of journalism in the United States. Dr. Frederick A. Middlebush, dean of the School of Business and Public Administration, has been appointed acting president.

DR. MORTON GOTTSCHALL has been appointed dean of the School of Liberal Arts and Science at the College of the City of New York by the Board of Higher Education. Dr. Gottschall has been acting dean for the past year and a half, following the resignation of Professor Daniel W. Redmond.

ERNEST A. HARDING, superintendent of the schools of Bergen County, N. J., has been appointed by the State Board of Education to be assistant commissioner in charge of elementary education. He will be succeeded in Bergen County by George R. Zimmerman, of Englewood.

THE Board of Education of New York City has announced the appointment as principal of the Stuyvesant High School of Sinclair J. Wilson; as principal of the new Benjamin Franklin High School of Leonard M. Covello, and as principal of Evander Childs High School of Dr. Hymen Alpern. Mr. Wilson, who is acting director of high-school organization, succeeds Dr. Ernest R. von Nardroff, who retired in June. The school to which Mr. Covello has been appointed specializes in arts, crafts and music. Dr. Alpern succeeds the late Henry I. Norr.

DOUGLAS GOLD, superintendent of Browning, Montana, schools for the past fifteen years, has been elected to succeed Jesse G. Ragsdale as superintendent of the Butte, Montana, schools. K. W. Bergan, who has been superintendent of the Cascade school system for nine years, will go to Browning to succeed Mr. Gold.

MAJOR L. L. LAMMERT, head master of the Wenonah Military Academy for the past nine years, has resigned to accept a teaching position at Woodbury High School of New Jersey.

RECENT promotions at the College of the City of New York include to the full rank of professor, Dr. Carroll N. Brown, Greek; Dr. Edward E. Whitford, mathematics, and Dr. Canute Hansen, hygiene. Three assistant professors have become associate professors. They are Dr. Bertram T. Butler, geology; Dr. Owen A. Haley, government, and Dr. Bennington P. Gill, mathematics. Instructors who have been made assistant professors are as follows: Dr. Harold H. Abelson, education; Dr. Ralph Gordon, English; Dr. Robert Jahrling, education; Dr. Oscar I. Janowsky, history; Michael J. Keleher, English; Dr. Leo Lehrman, chemistry; Dr. Leonard P. Sayles, biology, and Dr. Herbert P. Wirth, mathematics. Lecturers to become assistant professors are Howard G. Bohlin, drafting, and George A. Wilson, music.

BERNARD M. PEEBLES has been appointed head of the department of Latin of the Graduate School of Fordham University.

DR. ADOLPH W. ALECK, formerly instructor in psychology at New York University, has been appointed professor of psychology at the Wagner Memorial Lutheran College.

GEORGES CONNES, professor of English literature at the University of Dijon (France), has been appointed by the University of Buffalo visiting professor in the Department of Romance Languages for the first semester of the coming year. To this chair a different French scholar is appointed each year.

DR. OSCAR E. HUBBARD, for two years with the Institute of Human Relations at Yale University, has become psychiatrist at the Fairfield State Hospital, Newtown, Conn.

MAURICE JAMES, of the department of biology at the University of Colorado, has been appointed curator of the museum at the State Agricultural College, Fort Collins, Colo.

K. H. McFALL, superintendent of the Randolph, Ohio, schools, has been appointed director of admissions at Mt. Union College.

DR. CHARLES F. ROOS has resigned as chief of the research section of the research and planning division of the NRA to accept a professorship of economics at Colorado College.

AN Associated Press dispatch reports that Lloyd K. Garrison, chairman of the National Labor Relations Board, has decided to return to his work as dean of the University of Wisconsin Law School.

DR. JAMES C. BONBRIGHT, professor of finance in the School of Business at Columbia University, has been named vice-chairman of the Power Authority of New York State.

FATHER SYLVESTER BRIELMAIER, professor of moral theology and canon law at Capuchin College, Wausau, Wis., has been appointed international librarian at Rome.

PROFESSOR RALPH MUNN, director of the Carnegie Library, Pittsburgh, who, in collaboration with E. R. Pitt, of the Public Library, Melbourne, has been making a survey of library facilities in Australia, has returned to the United States. His report will be published by the Australian Council for Educational Research.

SIR WALTER HAMILTON MOBERLY, vice-chancellor of the University of Manchester, has been appointed chairman of the University Grants Committee, in succession to the late Sir Walter Buchanan Riddell. He will assume the duties of the post on January 1.

SIR GEORGE NEWMAN, chief medical officer of the British Ministry of Health and of the British Board of Education, has been recommended as a member of the General Medical Council for five years from October 9.

DR. WILLIAM WHITEHEAD WATTS, professor emeritus of geology in the Imperial College of Science and Technology, South Kensington, has been elected president of the British Association for the Advancement of Science.

IN recognition of his bibliography of French literature covering the years 1800 to 1930, Professor Hugo P. Thieme, head of the department of Romance languages at the University of Michigan, has been honored by the French Academy, which has awarded him the Prix de l'Academie.

DR. THOMAS REED, professor of political science at the University of Michigan, has been granted a leave of absence to make a survey of municipal and county government units for several eastern municipalities.

DR. VIRGINIA C. GILDERSLEEVE, dean of Barnard College, arrived from Europe on September 14, to resume her work as dean of the college. While abroad Dean Gildersleeve attended the meeting of the International Federation of University Women in Budapest.

HERBERT H. BATES, for thirty-seven years principal of the Cambridge, Mass., Training School for Teachers until his retirement thirteen years ago, died on September 6.

THE REV. ELLIOTT SPEER, principal of Mount Hermon School, was shot by an unknown person on September 14. He was thirty-five years of age.

DR. ROGER WILLIAMS SWETLAND, for thirty-six years head master of Peddie School, a boys' college preparatory school at Hightstown, N. J., died on September 15, at the age of seventy-three years.

DR. CHARLES R. FAY, formerly professor of history and economics at Erasmus Hall High School, New York City, died on September 13. Dr. Fay, who was sixty-seven years old, retired last year after thirty-three years of service.

PROFESSOR P. A. WADIA, for the past seven years dean of the faculty of arts of the University of Bombay, India, and chairman of its board of economics, political science and philosophy, delivered a public lecture at the University of California on September 6. His subject was "Modern India and Its Problems."

THE twenty-first annual meeting of the Association of Urban Universities will be held at the Brown Hotel, Louisville, Ky., on November 1 and 2. Members will be the guests of the University of Louisville, whose president, Dr. R. A. Kent, is also president of the association.

THE eighteenth annual convention of the American Federation of Teachers was the largest in its history. About a hundred and fifty delegates were in attendance representing over seventy locals in twenty states and the District of Columbia. The report of the secretary-treasurer showed that eighty-two new locals had been formed since the last convention and that the membership had doubled in one year. It was stated that this is due in large part to the fact that "teachers have begun to realize the necessity of organization as the next step in the fight against the retrenchment of the legitimate costs of education."

THE next annual meeting of the Australian Council for Educational Research will be held at Melbourne, from September 28 to October 1. It is being held a little later than usual in order that the chief executive officer, Dr. K. S. Cunningham, who is attending the International Conference on Education in South Africa as the Australian representative, may be able to attend.

A LECTURE and study-group program has been arranged for the 1934–35 season by the Child Study Association of America. The Consultation Service will open its seventh season with an extension of its program to offer individual consultation to adolescents and young people, as well as to the parents of young children, and to serve as a rounded family consultation service for practical guidance in all matters pertaining to the well-being of the family as a whole. A course in leadership training has been organized, which will offer to qualified students training in parent education leadership, and to accredited leaders in the field, continuous experience in group techniques. An evening course in religious education will be given by authorities on the philosophy of religion.

THE Rand School of Social Science, New York City, is offering this year five afternoon courses for teachers which will include alertness credit. Each course will consist of fifteen two-hour sessions, and all will start in the week of September 24. The following courses will be given: "Historic Highlights in Music," by Adele T. Katz; "Introduction to Sociology," by Alter E. Fischhof; "The Life of the Mind," by Joseph Jastrow; "Appreciation of Modern Literature," by David P. Berenberg; "Social and Political Philosophy," by Abraham Edel.

SCHOLARSHIPS have been awarded to twenty-nine students entering Columbia College. Ten of the awards are Pulitzer free scholarships for the most promising graduates of New York City's public high schools, while nineteen are special honor scholarships given to boys from widely distributed areas. Candidates for the Pulitzer scholarships are chosen from the standpoint of scholarship and financial need. According to the terms laid down by Joseph Pulitzer in founding these scholarships, each winner who enters Columbia College will receive free tuition and an annual cash allowance of $250 during his four years in college. Holders of the scholarships may choose to attend any college of the first rank in the United States, but those who enter colleges other than Columbia receive only the cash allowance.

A FIVE-DAY Training Conference on Emergency Education Problems for Unemployed Teachers, sponsored by the Federal Government and directed by the Kentucky State Department of Education, was held at the University of Kentucky during the week of September 3. Approximately 150 teachers attended the conference, which is part of the federal relief plan for "white collar" workers.

THE new oath of loyalty to the Constitution, required of school teachers of New York State by recent legislative action, will be administered by October 1. Associate Superintendent Stephen F. Bayne, in charge of personnel, has sent a request to the State Department in Albany for 50,000 copies of the oath. Dr. George J. Ryan, president of the Board of Education, is reported to have said that although the teachers had already taken an oath of loyalty they will be required to subscribe again. Previously the teachers signed forms on which the oath was printed when they placed their signatures on the payroll for the first time. The method of administering the new oath has not been determined. The duty may become that of a school official, a notary or a commissioner of deeds.

THE Institute of International Education has announced that forty-six American students have been granted fellowships for study in Germany next year. These fellowships, with the exception of six which cover tuition only, provide the recipient with room, board and tuition. In addition to the forty-six students in Germany there will be forty-three German students studying in this country on scholarships administered by the institute. Professor Stephen P. Duggan, director of the institute, in commenting on the American German student exchange, said that the number of American students applying for fellowships in Germany was smaller this year, giving some evidence of decreased interest on the part of American students in attending German universities. However, he pointed out that the fact that there has been no decrease in the number of fellowships for German students placed at our disposal by American colleges and universities would seem to indicate that our institutions have not lost interest in maintaining educational relations with Germany and in having German students as their guests.

UNDER the American scholarship plans of the English-Speaking Union twelve British public school boys will spend one school-year in various American private schools. Through these scholarships, which were initiated seven years ago by the Rev. F. H. Sill, head master of Kent School, Kent, Conn., a number of well-known American schools offer to selected British public school boys a school-year in America free of all cost, with the exception of the necessary incidental, medical and traveling expenses.

THE Dominion Bureau of Statistics at Ottawa, in a bulletin entitled "The Cost of Education," shows that the expenditure on Canadian schools and institutions of higher learning, public and private, amounted in 1932 to about $165,000,000, of which $20,000,000 was spent on universities and colleges, about $35,000,000 on high schools and $110,000,000 on elementary schools. The bureau estimates the expenditure on schools at about 3.5 per cent. of the earnings of the Canadian people.

A UNITED PRESS dispatch reports that the Morris Schools of Argentina face bankruptcy after a quarter-century of effort to place them on a firm foundation, by an Englishman, the late William C. Morris. Teachers' salaries are two years in arrears. Pupils do their exercises on the backs of used envelopes. Interclass notes are written on blank margins of newspapers. The blackboard ration for each class is one chalk daily. The schools, which have educated more than 150,000 children, will wind up in six months unless 700,000 pesos are found to clear the debt accumulated in the last three years. William Morris, a wandering preacher, without religious affiliations, is said to have sauntered into the Boca lower dock district of Buenos Aires in the late '90s, with a Bible and little else. Mr. Morris opened his first class with four pupils from the gutter. He begged from business houses for his Boca children whom he managed to feed, clothe and teach. Toughs held him up twice but ended by contributing to his enterprise. In ten years he had five schools, and to-day there are fifty-five, with 15,000 students enrolled, still fed, clothed and taught. Before the death of William Morris four years ago, his schools already were poor. Government subsidies dropped off and to-day these subsidies are 250,000 pesos behind. The government may take over the schools to prevent the turning loose in the streets of the 15,000 children.

THE general health of the Indian children living on New York State reservations compares favorably with that of the average rural white children of the same age, according to a report made by the Medical Inspection Bureau of the State Education Department, which has completed medical examinations of the school children on six of the eight Indian reservations. The report states, however, that malnutrition is more prevalent among Indian children than among rural white children and explains that this is due to lack of proper food, poorly prepared food and crowded homes with the consequent inadequate accommodations for rest and sleep for the growing children. The Onondaga, St. Regis and Tuscarora reservations have consolidated schools, each of which has the services of a public health nurse through whose efforts an average of more than 50 per cent. of the defects found in medical examinations were treated. There is a trend toward consolidation of the Indian schools with the public schools of the vicinity. An example of this is the closing of the one-room schools on the Tonawanda reservation and the transportation of the Indian children to the schools of the village of Akron.

DR. SOLOMON LOWENSTEIN, chairman of the German Jewish Children's Aid, Inc., New York, N. Y., has announced that arrangements have been made to bring 250 German Jewish children to the United States and that the first group of twenty would sail from Germany soon. Dr. Lowenstein said the children would be between 6 and 15 years old, but that most of them would range in age from 11 to 14. They are to be placed in private homes, in various parts of the United States under the supervision of professional social workers. They are not being brought here for legal adoption, as both the parents are living in many cases. The children will be educated in this country and receive training in vocations that will aid them later in earning a living. Miss Cecelia Rezovsky, who is executive director of the German Jewish Children's Aid, will send information concerning the children to those interested.

MORE than 700,000 jobless boys and girls were sent to special schools in England on September 4, in accordance with a new governmental measure. *The Christian Science Monitor* reports that the decision was reached to lower the age for the payment of unemployment insurance subscriptions, which has hitherto stood at 16—to meet the school-leaving age of 14. The Ministry of Labor is to bear 75 per cent. of the cost of the scheme. The Ministry of Education is in general charge of the curriculum, and local education authorities are attending to details. The schools to which the 700,000 children are being sent are not the ordinary type of school, since they are being attended by young unemployed people over 14 years of age. They aim, in the first instance, to keep students mentally and physically fit during the period of unemployment so that they may be able to accept any offer of work. So far as possible, classes are conducted on the premises of the 160 Juvenile Unemployment Centers which already exist. New buildings are being erected only when essential. The centers are districts where 50 or more unemployed juveniles are living. Attendance is compulsory and free of charge. Classes are held, so far as possible, in the daytime and it is intended that no one teacher shall have more than twenty-five students.

# DISCUSSION

## THE CIVILIAN CONSERVATION CORPS

THE Civilian Conservation Corps is the first practicable step toward building a sound future society. In the camps we are trying out those social principles which heretofore have existed only in men's minds or upon paper. The camps are not burdened with generations of precedent nor are they hindered by internal inertia. The CCC was created to fill a present need, to solve a problem become acute. Our chief need today is to train young men to get along as happily and comfortably as possible in the new civilization so recently thrust upon us. Whereas professors of education and elderly school teachers publicly advocate new social training and cling to the old régime in practise, we of the camps live and teach a new life. Graduate study, service in the public schools, together with experience as educational adviser in four camps, has convinced the writer of the great field of social possibilities within the CCC.

From this pioneering in society we hope to find a corrective for our faults of the past two decades. For normal earnings we hope to reestablish that respect which crashed in the burly scramble for margin profits. In nature, sports and hobbies we expect to revive that normal human interest which has been submerged by snappy roadsters and expensive parties. The task is hard. An official of an eastern reemployment committee states that the greatest handicap to a young man's progress to-day is the memory of the over-stuffed payrolls of the late twenties. Few people can be content with a normal income, so general and persistent is the effect of the false prosperity of 1928.

The President established the camps in an effort to remove potential delinquents from the streets. As long as the markets of backward nations swallowed the flood of our manufactured goods, as long as the West remained opened to malcontents and ne'er-do-wells, so long was the old order able to provide a living for all. On the eve of the normal adjustment period came the war. Now for three years we have been at rock bottom seeking a way out. Like a captain whose boat has been loaded carelessly we must adjust the cargo to secure a sailing balance. The hordes of young people ranging throughout our land by the way of brake rods and trucks led the President to create the camps. In a like manner, the amazing percentage of young people confined in our prisons must have influenced him to say the word that lifted 300,000 young men from the back alley and street corner into the freshness of the forest. With the elimination of youth from industry it has become an obligation to provide young people with a period of orderly camp life where they may think out a philosophy of their own, free from worry and temptation.

Along with this social gain has come economic relief. In recent enrolments financial need has been a prime factor in selecting the new men. CCC boys can not afford to take their opportunity lightly. To the boy whose monthly allotment brightens the home he has recently left, the year's job and his camp home is a stimulus to do good work. The fortunate boy may look upon formal education as a lark, but your CCC boy uses his opportunity as the foundation stone in a determined effort to continue to earn an honest living. The enormous amount of forest work completed and the endless variety of skills acquired by the men are proof that they have earned their right to the camp life by showing good works.

Reason is the standard of the camps. No false expectations or demands are set up. Believing that the enrolled men are average Americans the goal of the camps is within the reach of all; men are not encouraged to gaze at the peaks alone. Is it socially necessary that all men be great? Why make men uncomfortable to attempt something no one cares for? Have we not already despised the common things too much? To secure happiness a man must let his bucket down where it is now. As a consequence of normal standards the boys are not continually hounded to try something without use or interest, and that irritable tension so obvious in formal education is avoided.

Just as the camps exercise reason in setting standards, so common sense governs the selection of subject-matter. The boys are not given jobs that are hopelessly elaborate nor are they required to observe foolish discipline. On the other hand, they are encouraged to study and understand the things which recur in daily life. In the camps the boys do not remain on jobs for which they are not competent. If a boy can check tools accurately, all is well and good, but if he enters many poor reports he is given a simpler assignment. Courtesy, promptness, neatness in appearance and thoroughness are the watchwords of all. Whereas in formal education parental whims and pride are allowed to override the sensible deductions of educational experts, in the camps a boy is judged by what he can do. Our situation in the woods without the accepted conveniences of life is balanced by a freedom to practise those social principles which are denied formal education because of custom and inertia.

To pass to another phase of the work, the camps are more interested in the needs of large groups than in the desires of the few. Instruction, work programs and recreation are based on serving the many rather than the few. Volley ball, touch football, soccer, baseball and swimming take the place of tennis, golf and rowing. In a word, the camps are building a stable society by preparing men to understand and appreciate those things which are normally the lot of us all. Although Harvard University places the highest value on the educational theory of individual differences the camps are glad to champion the opinion of other schools which are adopting the belief that group training is more worthwhile than that of the individual. The sentimentally democratic worship of individualism would ruin camp morale.

The proper index of the value of the camps is the faith of the people. From Vermont to Oregon one hears only good reports of the CCC. Not a single politician has dared cry, "graft," "regimentation" or "impracticable." Parents are grateful that the boys are given a job and they appreciate the monthly check. And the wealthy are relieved to know that annually one third of a million young people are being taught respect for law and order and to appreciate the value of property. Daily contacts with local residents and interviews with prominent people have brought the conclusion that the CCC is establishing confidence in the future.

A greater index of the value of the camps is the rush for enrolment openings. In the Chicago area in July there were six applicants for each position available. No, the camps are not terrible places to which a man goes only as the lesser of many evils. Boys already in camp are on the alert to help friends and relatives get their turn. Perhaps some people are lukewarm to the NRA, the AAA and other items of the New Deal, but the Civilian Conservation Corps has the support of the whole nation. If those congressmen who recently prolonged the opportunities of 300,000 boys until next April could have known how fervently other thousands await their chance in the CCC, they would have made an appropriation, not for nine months but for nine years.

If the camps are discontinued delinquency will become a national menace over night. The NRA has quite sensibly favored the employment of adults in industry, and it stands to reason that young people have been practically eliminated from the working class. At last youth has the time for self-development. Yet what profiteth it a man if he be given time without guidance or environment? If inmates of penal institutions become depraved without employment, how much greater is the danger to youth, vibrant and eager to mould the entire world? Shall we set up a statue of a loafing bum and pull down that dedicated to the virtue of labor?

Our Civilian Conservation Corps is like the Medieval Church. Out of ancient barbarism and insecurity the church fashioned modern civilization. The camps are not stop-gaps to be discarded, come again the good old days. The camps must foster a philosophy and send out groups of boys who will spread a desire for a simple life among the people. As the church exemplified what it preached, so the CCC has built an idea from which all may graft a healthy branch.

HENRY L. FARR

180TH CO., CONN.

## THE PRESENT STATUS OF NEGRO DOCTORATES

ADDITIONAL data collected by the writer on Negro holders of the Ph.D. and equivalent degrees show that remarkable progress is being made with respect to this educational effort. The last report on this subject (see SCHOOL AND SOCIETY, September 16, 1933) indicated that at least 85 colored men and women had received the degree from 33 American and European universities since 1876. During the scholastic year 1932–33, 15 of those doctorates were conferred.

A careful check-up on the present status, which has been confirmed by official transcripts and statements by the several institutions, indicates that 16 Ph.D.'s have been awarded to Negroes during 1933–34. This means, then, that in 58 years 107 Negroes have received this award. The degrees have been conferred by 38 American and European universities. The University of Chicago (16), Columbia University (10), the University of Pennsylvania (9), Harvard University (8), Yale University (6), and Boston University (5) have contributed one half of the total number. It is significant that 61 or about 57 per cent. of all these doctorates were produced during the past four years and at the time of the nation's most acute economic disturbance. Eighty-seven have been granted since 1920. The fields of practical arts, such as home economics, agriculture, mechanical arts, business administration, health and physical education record no Negro doctorates, in so far as the data of the study establishing this report show.

Of eight fields in which these degrees were granted the leading ones are social and political science (24), physical sciences (18) and biological sciences (17). When physical and biological sciences are combined under the heading, "Natural Sciences," science then can be said to lead all other fields of knowledge in this respect.

It is noteworthy that all these doctorates have been won in over 90 per cent. of the cases from the very best American graduate schools. This statement has support when an examination of recent studies of institutions "distinguished" for graduate work in certain fields is made. Such studies would reveal something of the high quality of the doctoral degrees of this report.

It is worthy of note also that 83 of the 107 Negro holders of this degree received their basic college education from 45 Negro and 40 white colleges. The leading schools in this respect are Howard (15), Fisk (8), Lincoln, Pennsylvania (5), and Virginia Union (5). These facts seem important when it is noted that only since 1921 has a Negro college fully equipped itself from the point of approved academic standards to send its graduates to accredited graduate schools.

Almost all Negro doctorates are employed. Four have deceased. Over 95 per cent. of them are connected with the 47 regionally accredited institutions for Negroes. The greatest single number may be found at Howard University and the city of Washington, D. C. A few are in government service and research work. One has attained the rank of associate professor at the University of Chicago while two are "associates" at two other leading "white" institutions.

Although it is notably true without question

that the Negro's stride in winning doctoral degrees has been most rapid and remarkable, there is much yet to be done in this respect if the Ph.D. is to be accepted continuously as the passport to fame in American higher education, and when it is remembered also that there are only now 15 colleges for Negroes which have met in full the standards of regional accreditment, including in most cases the requirement of the Ph.D. for the headship of major departments.

HARRY W. GREENE

WEST VIRGINIA STATE COLLEGE

### INTER-SCHOLASTIC CORRESPONDENCE

MAY we call the attention of the reader to the work that the World League of International Education Associations has done and is doing in high schools to bring our students in contact with students of other countries, so as to give them a clearer understanding of those countries.

That closer contact is secured through interscholastic correspondence. In a large number of countries, an official center for such correspondence exists. In 1929 a meeting was held in Paris, of the then existing centers, which the director of the World League attended and presided. At that meeting steps were taken to improve the systems of distribution of such correspondence.

It is not necessary to emphasize the importance and benefit to the students of such contacts. The friendship thus made and the information thus acquired are strengthened by the work done in the school, by students interested in world affairs. Discussions, lectures, assembly programs constitute the activities of such groups. The World League, with headquarters in San Francisco, has at present a membership of 350 such groups in the United States and abroad. Several of those groups join together and hold, once or twice a year, regional junior international institutes. At those institutes the representatives of different high schools take part in debates, model assemblies, symposiums on world affairs, open-forum discussions, etc.

The World League has for the last three years sponsored a world-wide radio program on May 18, International Good Will Day, in which several countries took part.

Our latest project for 1935 and the following years is the building up in the high schools of International Museums which would consist of exchange of students' work—art, handicraft, etc. Maybe later—books, music, national costumes; anything that might be of interest to the students and that could form part of a museum will be added. We have already the cooperation of several countries.

Our organization has been endorsed by a large number of educators all over the world, and has been asked in the past to participate in almost every international educational convention. It has also been approved of by the State Board of Education of California.

For further information application should be mailed to World League of International Education Associations, 521 Phelan Building, San Francisco, California.

ALICE WILSON,
*Director*

# SPECIAL CORRESPONDENCE

### FACULTY IMPROVEMENT AND LIBRARY USE IN THE TEACHERS COLLEGES OF ALABAMA

THE state teachers colleges in Alabama limit their program of services to the preparation of teachers for elementary schools. If all is not well with the elementary schools, obviously all can not be well with those institutions responsible for training their prospective teachers. The two systems are intimately linked together. This close relationship is evidently the intention of those who direct the educational destinies of the state, since the control of the teachers colleges is vested in the State Board of Education.

At least two factors, which at present affect adversely the elementary schools in Alabama, have unfortunate influence on the teachers colleges, namely, salaries and certification. Salaries in the white elementary schools reached their peak in 1929–30, when the average amounted to $754. This sum has suffered the amazing reduction of 57 per cent. during the subsequent years! In the scholastic year of 1932–33 the average paid these teachers was only $325. Provisions for certification of school teachers in Alabama permit high-school graduates, through successful examination, to receive lower grade certificates. Anticipating penurious salaries and confronting the possibility of entering into competition with those who have no professional training, high-school graduates with the best promise of successful teaching experience hesitate to enroll in teachers colleges and prepare for service in elementary schools. Hence, the enrolments in the teachers colleges have decreased and other difficulties of natural consequence have been encountered, such as disturbing financial problems, heavier teaching loads and the need of instructional equipment.

The entire public school situation in Alabama was carefully analyzed the middle of last January. That analysis was based on reports from 63 of the 67 counties in the state and disclosed a tragic situation. Prior to January 1, 200 schools, employing 588 teachers and enrolling 20,000 children, had actually closed for the remainder of the school year 1933–34. Schools to the number of 1,390, or 48 per cent. of all schools in the counties reporting, were expected to close by the first of February. Put in other words, all schools in 19 counties were expected to close by February 1, all schools in 24 additional counties and 80 per cent. of all schools in the remaining counties were expected to close by February 15.

But not only during the current school year have public schools been in distress in Alabama. In 1932–33 the white rural elementary schools were open for only 115 days on an average for the state at large. In 27 counties, the term was less than 100 days. In 33 counties the term was the shortest since 1919; in 44 counties it was the shortest term during the past decade. One county had a school term of only 49 days. For all the counties, the term was from one to 85 days shorter than at any time during the past ten years. Phrased financially, the condition was such that the total amount spent for instruction in white rural elementary schools in 1932–33 was nearly $2,000,000 less than the amount spent in 1920!

Federal aid, as an emergency measure, came to the assistance of the public school program in Alabama at a timely moment. This aid has prevented the collapse of the schools for the present year as predicted by the January analysis. Many hundreds of schools have been kept open in rural communities, and thousands of teachers and children have worthwhile employment until summer vacation calls them from the schoolroom.

The problem of preventing a future collapse of public education must now challenge the statesmen, educational and political, of Alabama and the nation. Seen in its acute stages in Alabama, this is a national problem. The welfare of the entire nation depends on educated citizens in all the states of the Union.

A study of these teachers colleges now being made reveals at least two bright features in the midst of distress, namely, remarkable progress in the improvement of faculty personnel and unusual use of library facilities by students. These are factors of vital importance in instructional efficiency and are of wide interest to educators.

### Faculty Improvement

Perhaps the most thorough study of education in Alabama that has ever been made was a survey conducted in 1919 by specialists from the former Bureau of Education, Department of the Interior, Washington, now called the U. S. Office of Education. In that study reference was made to the faculties of the state teachers colleges as possessing "a relatively low standard of academic and professional training but a relatively long experience in teaching. Less than half the members of the faculties have completed college or university courses leading to academic or professional degrees." The colleges at that time were normal schools, maintaining what might be called junior college status.

In 1926 a study of the colleges revealed the information that a third of the faculty were without baccalaureate degrees. Considerable improvement was noted in 1932, with but 7 per cent. lacking such degrees. During the present scholastic year, only a single member of these faculties is without a bachelor's degree, and that faculty member is a graduate of a normal school, with many years of teaching experience and further professional training.

In 1926 only 19 per cent. of the teachers college faculties in Alabama held the master's degree; by 1932 the number holding it had increased to 50 per cent.; and during the present scholastic year, 64.8 per cent. of the faculties hold that degree.

Whereas in 1926 a bare 2 per cent. of these faculty folk held the doctor's degree, in 1932 9 per cent. held it. During the present scholastic year of 1933–34 this number has increased to 16.9 per cent. of the faculty group. One institution (Florence) has more than a fourth of its entire faculty of all ranks holding this highest earned degree.

In connection with this improved academic and professional standing of these faculties it is interesting to note their lengthy college-teaching experience. Individually the range is from the beginner with but a year of experience to the veteran with 43 years of experience. Institutionally, the range is from an average of 8.1 years of college teaching to 13 years, with an average experience for the combined faculties of 10.3 years.

### FINANCES

The startling fact of this remarkably rapid faculty improvement in these institutions is that it has been accompanied, unfortunately, by radically reduced income and greatly reduced cost of instruction.

For the school year 1932–33, two of the institutions (Florence and Livingston) received approximately 50 per cent. of what they received during the school year of 1922–23, ten years before! One of the other institutions (Jacksonville) received $23,000 less in 1933 than it did in 1923; and the fourth college (Troy) in 1933 had a smaller income by more than $47,000 than it had ten years previously. Receipts of the four colleges in 1929 amounted to $1,118,228; in 1933 they amounted to $319,669, which is 28.6 per cent. of their 1929 income. State support in 1933 was only 23.4 per cent. of what it was in 1929.

The cost of instruction and the total educational expenditures in these colleges, both in aggregate amounts and on a per student basis, greatly exceed the appropriations for support received at present from the state. In one college (Jacksonville) the state appropriation totaled $28,277 for 1932–33, whereas the instruction cost was $44,133, with the total educational expenditures amounting to $70,756. On a per student basis, the state appropriated $46.88, whereas the instruction cost was $73.19 and the educational expenditure was $117.34. Conditions are somewhat similar in the other institutions.

Combined disbursements in the colleges were in 1933 practically a third of what they were in 1929. The instruction cost in 1933 likewise was just about a third of what it had been four years before.

In only one college (Jacksonville) did the instructional cost of 1933 exceed that of 1923, and yet in that institution the instructional cost of 1933 was only 50 per cent. of what it was in 1929. Two colleges (Livingston and Troy) spent for instruction in 1933 less than half of what they spent in 1923; and each of them spent in 1933 approximately 20 per cent. of the amount spent for instruction in 1929. The fourth institution (Florence) spent $9,000 less for instruction in 1933 than it did in 1923, and only about 40 per cent. of what it did in 1929.

The only conclusion to be reached from this presentation of figures, along with the improvement of faculty personnel in these colleges, seems to be that teachers are having to carry or "tote," as is often said in the South, too much of the educational burden. Adequate compensation, including a sufficient amount for living necessities, further cultural and professional advantages and savings for the rainy day and old age must be provided these faculties if continued progress along the present desirable pathway is to be expected.

### LIBRARIES

Compared with many larger colleges, the number of volumes in the libraries of the state teachers colleges in Alabama is exceedingly small. They meet, however, the minimum standards for accreditment both in the American Association of Teachers Colleges and in the Southern Association of Colleges and Secondary Schools. The former association requires 15,000 volumes and the latter 12,000 volumes as minimum numbers. The smallest of the libraries reports 15,846 volumes, the largest reports 20,515, with an average of 17,306. The colleges are, therefore, at least meeting the accredited standards for their type of institution. In this there is nothing more than passing commendation, coupled with the knowledge that institutions do not prosper best in barely meeting minimum standards.

The remarkable feature connected with the

libraries of these colleges is the use which students are reported to be making of the available books. In the *New York Times* of February 25, 1934, President Constance Warren, of Sarah Lawrence College, reported the students in that institution as using an unusually large number of books, namely 49.2 volumes per student for the year. All will agree that this manifests a fine intellectual interest on the part of those students; it is most impressive as to student initiative and seriousness of purpose. President Warren states: "According to available statistics the highest average withdrawal from any other college library was 27 volumes per student."

With this information as a background it is interesting to know that the monthly withdrawal of books from the libraries of the state teachers colleges in Alabama for a period of from a week to a fortnight ranges from a per student average of 2.5 volumes in one institution to an average of 4 volumes in another. The session of nine months makes the yearly withdrawal range from 22.5 to 36 per student. Teachers colleges may not have been included in the gathering of the above statistics quoted by President Warren. The statistics reported by her at least furnish a comparative basis whereby claim may be made that these particular institutions in Alabama rank high amongst the colleges of America in the use that is made of their library books.

Large use is also made of reserve books in the instructional programs of these institutions. Librarians report that the monthly per student use of reserve books is seven in one institution and 10.7 in another. Simple multiplication by nine gives the yearly average. These teachers colleges seem to be well in line with the current trend in the collegiate world, which seeks to make the library a real center of scholastic activity on the campus.

The libraries in these teachers colleges greatly need enlargement, need additional professional members of the library staff, need to be housed in separate buildings and have other obvious needs. The faculties of the institutions also need enlargement, increased salaries, smaller class groups in many instances, more time for research and contributions to professional literature, and have other needs which it is not necessary to enumerate in this connection. But it is encouraging to see evidences of progress in matters of supreme importance in the work of teachers colleges even in the midst of tragic difficulties, both within the institutions themselves and in the elementary schools of the state which they serve.

CLARENCE M. DANNELLY
ALABAMA EDUCATION ASSOCIATION

# QUOTATIONS

## PRESIDENT WALTER WILLIAMS AND "THE FIRST SCHOOL OF JOURNALISM"

WALTER WILLIAMS, president of the University of Missouri, never had a Ph.D. degree. Nor had he a bachelor's degree. He did not have even a high school diploma. His school was the newspaper office and his teachers were practitioners in an occupation which he has seen develop into a profession. In that development he may say, both as founder of the first school of journalism and as an earth-encircling observer of affairs, that he was and is a part of all that he has met. Coming up from an early journalistic experience in a small town, he knew what would be most helpful to young men and women in preparation for the most demanding of callings.

While recognizing technique to be essential, he was also aware, as he has said, that technique alone does not make a master. Something beyond it is required in "doing the professional deed." In his own case he endowed technique with a spirit characteristic of a research student. Far from the shores of communication with other lands, in a valley of self-sufficiency, it is the more remarkable that he should have been so deeply interested in international relations. It is but an academic version of the familiar characterization of a Missourian, as was once said of Professor Shapley, a native of Missouri, to affirm that he was born into a scientific attitude of mind. He has to be shown. He demands to know the why and wherefore of things. Thus the newspaper man became the head not only of the School of Journalism but of the State University.

It has been said of the true journalist that he must know the truth, or as much of it as he can acquire; be eager to tell it and then know how to tell it. It is this last qualification that makes him the greatest of educators. Dr. Williams is obliged by illness to relinquish the duties of the presidency, but it will be good news to journalists throughout the world—for it is said that the graduates of his school are to be found in the ranks of nearly every important newspaper staff—that he still is to remain head of the first school of journalism.—*The New York Times.*

Where was the first school of journalism inaugurated in the United States? This question is of historical importance because of the contradictory statements that frequently appear.

In your editorial "Journalist-Educator" you pay tribute to the distinguished Walter Williams, retiring president of the University of Missouri, and credit him as "founder of the first school of journalism." The editorial closes with the statement: "It will be good news to journalists throughout the world . . . that he still is to remain head of the first school of journalism."

I agree with everything you say about the genius, distinguished record and magnificent achievement of President Williams. Would it not be a further tribute to him to straighten out the record regarding this long-mooted question of "the first school of journalism"?

Where does General Robert E. Lee stand in conferring this honor? The official records at Washington and Lee University, in Lexington, Va., establish this fact:

"General Lee's marvelous progressiveness, his practical vision of our future civilization, reached its culmination in his organizing in 1869 the first collegiate instruction ever given in the principles and practice of journalism."

The record continues: "Recent history confirms and illustrates his far-seeing wisdom. The twentieth century editor is rapidly becoming the leader and molder of American civilization, surpassing in area and effectiveness the preacher, the teacher, the legislator, the business magnate. Every American citizen, old or young, rich or poor, millionaire or day laborer, finds his ideals and convictions, his hopes and fears and innermost convictions, molded and directed by the newspapers and magazines he reads every day."

General Lee "refused all other offers after Appomattox, to dedicate the ripest years of his glorious life" to this service when he became president of Washington and Lee University. The record states further:

"It was here in that hour of sectional hatreds and division that this divinely inspired educator [General Robert E. Lee] in 1869 founded the first American school of journalism."

Perhaps I can be of some service to you in establishing the facts in this important historical question. While conducting exhaustive investigations as historian-general for the semi-centennial memorial of the Civil War, published in ten volumes under title, "The Photographic History of the Civil War," by the Review of Reviews Company, our large research board agreed that the honor of founding this first school of journalism belongs to General Lee.

This in no way detracts from the distinguished service rendered by Walter Williams and the University of Missouri. General Lee's "school of journalism" was discontinued at Washington and Lee University shortly after his death. It has recently been reestablished as a memorial to him.

While General Lee was the founder of the first school of journalism in America (and this probably means in the world), Walter Williams organized and directs the "oldest school of journalism in continuous operation in America." The honors, therefore, are sufficient to give both historical position in the annals of world journalism.—*Francis Trevelyan Miller, President, Historical Foundations, in The New York Times.*

# SOCIETIES AND MEETINGS

## THE TRIENNIAL COUNCIL OF THE UNITED CHAPTERS OF PHI BETA KAPPA

With the largest attendance on record—246 delegates representing 113 chapters and 12 associations—the eighteenth triennial council of the United Chapters of Phi Beta Kappa met at Cincinnati on September 10, 11 and 12 and forwarded a new program having among its chief objectives "to serve the state as a champion of the humane studies for cultural ends" and "the setting up of criteria which will represent to the student the ideal attitude toward liberal scholarship."

The first business session on the morning of September 10 and the banquet on the evening of September 11 were held in the Hotel Gibson. The open session and reception to delegates, senators and officers on the evening of September 10, the two business sessions on September 11 and the business session on the morning of September 12 were held at the University of Cincinnati. On the afternoon of September 10 the visitors enjoyed a tour of Cincinnati and visits to Miami University and Western College at Oxford, Ohio.

How Phi Beta Kappa may be of service in promoting cultural ends was indicated by Dr. Clark Sutherland Northup, of Cornell University, in his report as president of the United Chapters at the morning session of September 10. Dr. Northup listed ways as follows:

> Providing cheap and attractive editions and translations of the great classics, ancient and modern, studies of classical times and cultures, celebrations of great anniversaries, . . . popular biographies of the great cultural figures and leaders in education and the arts of peace, plays and pageants illustrating the history of culture, prizes for excellence in cultural studies. . . .

Dr. Northup's reference in his presidential report to *The American Scholar* as an expression of the literary and cultural interests of Phi Beta Kappa was amplified in the statement of the editorial board of this new quarterly magazine, presented by Dr. Will D. Howe at the closing session.

*The American Scholar* was established in January, 1932, as "a journal of intellectual life, scholarly but not technical," with articles selected to give "a cultural synthesis of the various fields of research, practical affairs, and abstract thought." Mr. Howe praised the work of the editor, Dr. William Allison Shimer, and told of the faithful cooperation of members of the editorial board. The quarterly has had a splendid success, as revealed by quotation and comment in newspapers and college and alumni magazines, by readers' letters and by paid subscriptions. With improving economic conditions the prospects are favorable, Mr. Howe said, for the quarterly to pay its way completely.

### Criteria of Scholarship

The changed attitude which Phi Beta Kappa is taking toward the measurement of scholarship was shown in the report of the secretary, Dr. William Allison Shimer, presented at the morning session of September 10, and in the addresses of President Frank Aydelotte, of Swarthmore College, and President David M. Robertson, of Goucher College, at the evening meeting of September 10. That chapters are using criteria of scholarship other than "the accumulation of course grades or marks" was declared by Dr. Shimer. He listed these other criteria as "broad honors work, comprehensive examinations, the accumulative record, and subjective estimates by tutors and teachers." He cited particularly the present practise of the Harvard Chapter in "postponing more elections to the end of the year when the results of honors work and comprehensive examinations can be considered."

In presenting the topic, "Selecting Students for Phi Beta Kappa," President Aydelotte referred to complications when chapters insist upon particular subjects such as Latin and Greek.

> There is in many chapters what I consider a foolish prejudice against the study of the natural sciences, even when these subjects constitute—as they very well may—a part of a liberal education. I approve strongly of confirming Phi Beta Kappa to liberal as opposed to technical and vocational courses, but I think the society must accept in each generation the definition of a liberal education which is believed in at that particular time.

President Aydelotte maintained that the really valuable basis for selecting students for Phi Beta Kappa is not to average their grades in all subjects but to find their competence in the subject or group of subjects to which they have devoted themselves. The real test of ability, Dr. Aydelotte thought, lies not so much in what the student does or does not know as in how well he knows what he knows best. With the older methods of selection upon averages of grades there has been a creditable correspondence between election to Phi Beta Kappa and worthy success in later years. The correspondence would be greatly improved, Dr. Aydelotte believed, if the test of selection for the student were the same as it is in his mature performance, *viz.*, his ability in the field in which he is concentrating.

In his discussion of "Selecting Colleges for Phi Beta Kappa," President David A. Robertson, of Goucher College, set forth the principles which were followed by the new committee of qualifications, of which he is chairman. Dr. Robertson emphasized that "Phi Beta Kappa is not and has no desire to be an accrediting agency." He told of the action taken by the 1931 council setting up a new procedure for granting charters by which a committee of impartial experts obtains data and arranges personal inspections of institutions desiring chapters. The committee considers all the material relating to the institutions and makes recommendations to the senate of Phi Beta Kappa, which in turn recommends to the council.

Dr. Robertson referred to the proposed constitutional amendment providing for election to Phi Beta Kappa of a small number of students in "colleges in which there are not yet chapters of our society." The proposed provision for a national council chapter was opposed in a resolution passed by the council at a business session, and it and other plans for amendments were referred to a new committee on the constitution.

"Principles of Phi Beta Kappa Organization" were considered by Dean Roscoe Pound, of the Harvard Law School, in the third address of the evening of September 10.

Various aspects of the aims and methods of Phi Beta Kappa activities as related to the nation were presented at the banquet on the evening of September 11 by "a battery of Ohio speakers": Charles P. Taft, II, of Cincinnati; President Edmund D. Soper, of Ohio Wesleyan University; Judge Florence Allen, of Cleveland, and Murray Seasongood, formerly mayor of Cincinnati.

Greetings to the council were given at the several sessions by the Honorable Russell Wilson, mayor of Cincinnati, by Dr. Raymond Walters, president of the University of Cincinnati, and by Lester A. Jaffe, president of the Cincinnati chapter of Phi Beta Kappa.

## ITEMS OF BUSINESS

President Northup, in his president's report, referred to the death during the last triennium of four senators of Phi Beta Kappa: President John Grier Hibben, of Princeton; Dr. Henry Suzzallo, of the Carnegie Foundation for the Advancement of Teaching; Professor Adam Leroy Jones, of Columbia University, and President Julian A. C. Chandler of the College of William and Mary.

Upon recommendation of the committee on qualifications, chapter charters were voted by the council to the Connecticut College for Women, Florida State College for Women and the University of Utah. The council approved senate action authorizing the chapters of the University of Pennsylvania and the University of North Carolina to have sections for their respective colleges for women.

In his report as secretary, Dr. Shimer told of a bequest from the estate of Miss Isabelle Stone, Wellesley, 1905, with a possible maximum value of $26,000, which is to establish a fellowship in honor of the donor's mother. The Mary Isabelle Sibley Fellowship is to be awarded to women between 25 and 35 years of age alternately in the fields of (1) Greek archeology, history, language or literature, and (2) French language or literature.

The report of Treasurer David Layton showed that the total balance in the endowment income accounts is $12,771, a decrease of $7,231 during the triennium, "a result, no doubt, of the depression." The total endowments of the United Chapters of Phi Beta Kappa as of July 31, 1934, are $267,735.

Dr. Oscar M. Voorhees gave his report as historian of Phi Beta Kappa, and he was instructed by the council to proceed with the history of Phi Beta Kappa's first century, with the aid of a committee of five professional historians.

Although the council approved the broad program presented by the senate, it did not accept the proposed amendments to the constitution. These proposals would have established alumni chapters, a council chapter providing for election by the senate of a limited number of student members in colleges not having charters at present, and would have eliminated district organizations of Phi Beta Kappa. The council authorized an *ad interim* committee to work over amendments for the constitution to be made up of ten members, including three senators and seven official representatives of district organizations. Instructions to this committee were to have a report ready for submission to each chapter of the United Chapters a year in advance of the next triennial council meeting.

Among the resolutions passed by the council was one calling upon the secretary to obtain from various alumni groups of Phi Beta Kappa information as to their activities, so that a program can be prepared giving "suggestions for enlarged usefulness."

Dr. Charles Francis Thwing, president emeritus of Western Reserve University, presided at the evening session of September 10.

Officers were elected as follows: *President,* Dr. C. S. Northup; *vice-president,* Dr. Robert A. Millikan; *secretary,* Dr. W. A. Shimer; *treasurer,* Dr. W. Randolph Burgess; *historian,* Dr. O. M. Voorhees.

The following were elected *senators:* Dr. George Henry Chase, John Kirkland Clark, Dr. James Bryant Conant, Dr. W. H. Crawford, Dr. H. A. Farr, Dr. John H. Finley, Dr. Christian Gauss, Dr. Frank P. Graves, Dr. T. H. Jack, Dr. Walter Lippmann, Dr. C. S. Northup, Dr. Ellen F. Pendleton, Dr. David A. Robertson, Dr. Owen D. Young.

Dr. Albert Shaw was elected a senator for life.

RAYMOND WALTERS
UNIVERSITY OF CINCINNATI

## CONFERENCE ON EMOTION AND THE EDUCATIVE PROCESS

THE committee on emotion and the educative process of the American Council on Education held a conference at the Malvern Hotel, Bar Harbor, Maine, from August 23 to August 26. A group of about twenty experts in the various branches of knowledge that bear upon education assayed out present understanding of emotional processes and their effects, and discussed needed research and experimentation. The fruits of the discussions will be incorporated in the committee reports, to be published next summer, after they have been studied by the committee and subjected to wider criticism. The conference was sponsored by the Josiah Macy, Jr., Foundation, of which Dr. Ludwig Kast is the director. It is this foundation which made the grant under which the committee is undertaking its two-year study of emotions as they influence the educative process.

The conference was opened during the morning of August 23, under the chairmanship of Professor Daniel A. Prescott, of Rutgers University. After an address of welcome by Dr. Kast, the first paper, "The Physiological Bases of Emotion," was presented by Dr. Walter B. Cannon, of the Harvard Medical School. At succeeding meetings the following papers were heard: "Emotion and Sex," by Dr. Lawrence K. Frank, of the General Education Board; "The Emotional Orientation of Children," by Dr. George D. Stoddard, director of the Child Welfare Research Station at the University of Iowa; "Emotion and the Intellectual Processes of Learning, Reasoning and Imagining," by Dr. F. L. Wells, chief of the psychological laboratory at the Boston Psychopathic Hospital; "Personality Maladjustments in Children," by Dr. David M. Levy, psychiatrist of New York City; "The Emotional Climate of Schools as Influenced by the Interplay of Personalities," by Dr. Mark May, secretary of the Institute of Human Relations at Yale University; "The Emotional Climate of Schools as Influenced by School Practises," by Dr. Laura Zirbes, of the Ohio State University; "Emotion and Esthetic Experience and Expression," by Dr. Thomas Munro, curator of education at the Cleveland Museum.

Other persons attending the conference and participating in the discussion were President James R. Angell, of Yale University; Dr. Madison Bentley, head of the department of psychology at Cornell University; Miss Marian Carswell, principal, Hubbard Woods School of Winnetka, Illinois; Dr. Frederick H. Lund, of Temple University; Dr. John H. MacCracken, associate director of the American Council on Education; Dr. C. R. Mann, director, American Council on Education; Dr. James S. Plant, director, Essex County Juvenile Clinic, Newark, New Jersey; Professor Herbert N. Shenton, head of the department of sociology, Syracuse University; Dr. Vivian T. Thayer, director, Ethical Culture Schools, New York City; and Dr. M. Ernest Townsend, president of the New Jersey State Normal School, Newark, New

Jersey. Professor Edward Sapir, of Yale University, a member of the committee, was unable to attend.

Numerous interesting concepts were advanced at the conference. It was pointed out that the expression of emotion, as such, is standard and untrainable, emanating as it does from the lower brain centers. Nevertheless, the cortex does participate in the evaluation of emotion-provoking situations and, through it, control over emotional reactions can be secured. Hence educators must concern themselves with cortical learning that prevents the arousal of emotion or reorients it, if they would secure that self-discipline which is essential in civilized communities. Perhaps another way of putting it would omit the use of the term emotion entirely: A major goal of education should be the achievement of an optimum balance between desire and realization. This would prevent both excessive frustration and anarchistic freedom.

The function of experience as the major factor in the patterning of our desires was repeatedly pointed out. This is particularly patent in connection with learning how to express and satisfy sexual needs in culturally approved ways and in understanding the manner in which family relationships, such as parental overprotection, parental rejection or sibling rivalry, determine the emotional needs of school children. Because of the patterning influence of folk-ways, too, the fear of wild animals, of snakes and of lightning remains characteristic of children in a period when they should be afraid of automobiles, of disease germs and of war. The growing individual in society, then, resembles a growing micro-organism in a culture. By varying the cultural media the patterns through which the individual seeks to achieve his desires may be modified.

A school may be described as a constellation of human relations very influential in building up the cultural and emotional desire patterns in children. Possibly we should give up describing the school in terms of the extremities of grades, subjects and marks and restate it in terms of lines of force operating between individuals. Much of the irritation and fatigue that teachers suffer might be changed to interest and a feeling of professional value if they saw themselves as playing truly dynamic rôles in the lives of individual children. A teacher seeking to discover in terms of emotional need why a child behaves as he does would face a class with a vastly different attitude from one who felt it her first duty to bring every child in class up to the standard test norm in arithmetic. Particularly is this important in esthetics where "biologically adequately aroused emotions" become attached to symbolic or intermediate forms that render the emotional experiences both more subtle and more complex. Through esthetics teachers have the means of assisting children to experience and to express emotion, and to reorient this desire for experiences that are rich in feeling. By this they may mold a unified personality uncloven by conflicts within.

The discussions of needed research and experimentation uncovered numerous areas needing immediate study. Long-term, continuous, coordinated researches into the emotional development of children were mentioned as especially desirable. At the same time there seems to be some danger of pushing experimental techniques too rapidly in a field where the clinical method may still yield rich returns. For example, we are greatly in need of studies to show the sources of the "value patterns" of young people. Here no single individual or branch of knowledge is sufficiently broad to conduct the research nor is the rigid control of conditions essential to scientific experimentation likely to yield definitive findings. Rather a combination of describing, of testing, of probing clinically and of observing behavior may be needed with the sociologist, the physiologist, the psychologist, the psychiatrist, the parents and the teachers all participating as consciously contributing members of a coordinated research.

The general tenor of the conference discussions did not give hope of the easy discovery of basic principles that might be stated authoritatively to school people for guiding them in their dealings with children. On the other hand, no note of pessimism was struck. Instead, a unanimous feeling of the importance of adding to our knowledge of the genesis and orientation of desire and of the effects of frustration and anxiety was expressed, and the opinion repeatedly advanced that the rigid controls of science should not be permitted to stifle the careful observation and description of experiments undertaken on the basis of philosophical considerations.

At the Bar Harbor meeting the committee added Dr. George D. Stoddard, of the University of Iowa, as a permanent member of the committee, and completed plans for prosecuting its study more diligently during the coming year.

Daniel A. Prescott,
*Chairman*

# EDUCATIONAL RESEARCH AND STATISTICS

## ATTITUDES OF AVERAGE AND SUPERIOR STUDENTS TOWARD SURVEY COURSES

In two previous years studies have been made of student opinion of two freshman survey courses given at Syracuse University. The first year's study aimed to ascertain the attitudes of students toward the survey courses primarily under the heads "interest," "profit (increase in enlightenment or understanding)" and "success in presentation." An anonymous list of questions was used at the last meeting of one of the courses, and the results indicated that the students liked the survey courses.[1] Particularly high rating was given both courses in answer to the question asking for a ranking of all their courses in terms of "profit." The following year the second study, accompanied by a shift in one of the courses from two general lectures with one section meeting to three section meetings with no lectures, ascertained that the students liked the section method of presentation better than the use of general lectures. The course changing to the section method of presentation moved up statistically relative to both the other survey course and the general curriculum on the question concerning "success in presentation," although the "profit" index, curiously enough, was relatively constant.[2]

This year the same wording of questions and methods of measurement were employed with the addition of two other questions. The students were asked to give a list of the grades they received in their various courses during the first semester. These were then averaged in tabulation and the A–B and C–D groups segregated with a view to ascertaining any differences between the attitudes of superior and average students. Another new question was introduced, asking students whether they were aware of the general field (not specific departments) in which their future major specialization would lie. Answers to all the questions were interesting.

(1) No significant divergencies in attitude appeared between the A–B and C–D groups; in both survey courses these groups, in their percentages of combined first and second rankings given to the courses, closely approximated the percentages derived from the unsegregated total groups. Such minor statistical divergencies as appeared suggested differences between the two survey courses (one course, *e.g.*, is required of all, while the other is an alternative to mathematics) rather than generic differences between the survey course and other types of course. The mass effect of the figures was to indicate that the two survey courses are equally well adapted to the needs of both A–B and C–D groups.

(2) There were 362 answers to the other new question, as to general fields of interest for future specialization. Of these 20.7 per cent. answered, "I do not know." Natural science (including mathematics and psychology) was favored by 26 per cent.; languages and literature (including English and Bible) by 25.1 per cent. The social sciences (including history and philosophy) were indicated as the choice of 28.2 per cent. Does this indicate that some guidance by professors in charge of major work could be attempted profitably as early as the sophomore year?

(3) Corroboration of the results of the previous studies was a feature of this year's study; the statistical results were remarkably consistent in the favorable rating given to the survey courses. Political Science 1 (responsible citizenship), for example, was scored in the three successive years in the following manner: 1932 (139 answers), first and second rankings combined on the "interest" question (chance = ± 40 per cent.) 52.6 per cent; 1933 (287 answers) 51.5 per cent.; 1934 (371 answers) 50.5 per cent. On the "profit" question this survey

[1] See School and Society, 36: 914, 15, July 2, 1932.

[2] See School and Society, 38: 969, 121, July 22, 1933.

course in the three successive years scored 62.8 per cent., 66.3 per cent. and 67.1 per cent. "Success in presentation" was scored 44.6 per cent., 57.9 per cent. and 53 per cent. This course is required of all students in liberal arts.

(4) The most striking feature of the study was a shift in the figures of the other survey course, Philosophy 1, indicating a factor which was not at all the object of the study. The scores of this course for the three successive years are as follows: On the "interest" question, first and second rankings combined (chance $= \pm 40$ per cent.), 1932 (215 answers) 47.7 per cent., 1933 (151 answers) 57 per cent. and 1934 (214 answers) 77 per cent.; on the "profit" question 62 per cent., 67.7 per cent. and 78.5 per cent. In "success in presentation" Philosophy 1 was scored 34.9 per cent., 68.2 per cent. and 79.1 per cent. in the three successive years. This course is required, alternative to mathematics; it is the course which changed to the section method, abandoning general lectures, between the first and second studies. This year there returned to the course a colleague who has been with the course since its inception in 1922, but who had been on a leave of absence covering the period of the two previous studies; indeed, the lecture method used in the course in 1932 had been in part a means of providing for this leave of absence without excessive increase of teaching load. The changes incident to the return of this experienced teacher to the course seem definitely reflected in the advance all along the line of the scores of this course. These statistics are a dramatic indication of the importance of maturity and professional experience on the part of university teaching personnel, even at the freshman level. This probably holds in a peculiar way of survey courses.

The three studies taken together suggest the importance of such repeated self-criticism by college and university departments. Recurrent or radical statistical divergencies mean something, although what they mean may not always be clear. When supplemented where possible by measurements of senior and alumni opinion, such studies may furnish faculty members valuable points of reference for course or curricular revision. We know so little in an exact way of what we do for our students at this level that even the most meager scientific measurements may prove useful aids to the further practise of the art of education.

PAUL W. WARD

SYRACUSE UNIVERSITY

## SHOULD INCREASES IN GRADES FOLLOW INCREASES IN INTELLIGENCE TEST SCORES?

IN the issue of SCHOOL AND SOCIETY for June 16, 1934, Dean W. H. Thompson, of the Municipal University of Omaha, gives the results of a survey made among American universities and colleges showing that significant increases have occurred in the scores on intelligence tests taken by entering freshmen.

To show the increase in intelligence test scores for the last four years, the following table gives the quartiles for the entering freshmen in the College of Commerce and Administration of the Ohio State University.

TABLE I

INTELLIGENCE TEST SCORES FOR FRESHMEN, 1930–1934

| | 1930 | 1931 | 1932 | 1933 |
|---|---|---|---|---|
| Q 3 ........ | 72 | 82 | 88 | 90 |
| M ........ | 47 | 60 | 69 | 73 |
| Q 1 ........ | 23 | 32 | 44 | 52 |

It is very evident that each entering class has scored higher than its predecessor, and that the 1933 group is the best class, judged by intelligence test scores, that the college has had in the four years passed. Furthermore, these scores are comparable, because the same test has been used over the four years, and the percentiles have been determined from the norm set up in 1930.

Passing by any explanation for the increase in test scores, the following question is raised: Has scholastic accomplishment improved to the same degree? In other words, are freshman grades getting better, too? It would be interesting for the same 188 institutions who reported to Dean Thompson to report on their experience with freshman scholarship.

An answer from the College of Commerce and Administration of the Ohio State University is ready now. Table II gives the quartile points on the first quarter grades for the same students reported in Table I. At Ohio State grade points are computed as follows: A–4; B–3;

C–2; D–1; E–0. Total grade points divided by hours carried equals the point ratio.

TABLE II

Point Ratio Quartiles for First Quarter Freshmen, 1930–1934

| | 1930 | 1931 | 1932 | 1933 |
|---|---|---|---|---|
| Q 3 | 2.52 | 2.66 | 2.73 | 2.62 |
| M | 2.06 | 2.05 | 2.11 | 2.12 |
| Q 1 | 1.52 | 1.52 | 1.69 | 1.66 |

It is very evident that any gain in scholarship has been slight. The same fact is brought out when the record for the entire freshman year is studied. The following table gives the results for all freshman students in these same classes who finished the first year. The ratios are cumulated for the three quarters covered.

TABLE III

Point Ratio Quartiles for Entire First Year for Freshman Classes of 1930–1934

| | 1930 | 1931 | 1932 | 1933 |
|---|---|---|---|---|
| Q 3 | 2.60 | 2.67 | 2.68 | 2.72 |
| M | 2.12 | 2.13 | 2.15 | 2.20 |
| Q 1 | 1.75 | 1.77 | 1.75 | 1.90 |

What is the explanation for the fact that while intelligence test scores are rising, grades are remaining practically stationary? A few typical answers will be cited:

(1) *Educational standards have been increased.* Some instructors state that as fast as the level of intelligence increases in their classes, the requirements are stepped up likewise. These instructors believe there should be no changes in the distribution of grades. Education is competitive and the least efficient in every group should be dropped out.

(2) *Fixed grade patterns.* Instructors have well-defined patterns for the distribution of grades and tend to follow their pattern, irrespective of the intellectual level of their classes. Some of these patterns are fixed in terms of percentages, while others are the results of mental attitudes.

(3) *Grading on class average.* Results of written work, tests and other requirements are averaged for a class, and each member of that class is graded in terms of his personal accomplishment. Letter grades will tend to fall into fixed percentages. Since good classes will show the same distribution as poor classes, no changes in grade distribution will occur with increased intelligence.

(4) *Student attitudes.* High-scoring students on the intelligence test are satisfied with a mediocre scholastic record. A minimum effort on their part will bring an average grade in practically any course. They find more interests in non-academic activities than in the classroom. It is a very common saying among students that one should not try to make a score on the intelligence test. Too high a score is apt to be embarrassing in relation with the instructors. There is plenty of evidence to prove that students are not working up to the level of their ability and intelligence.

(5) *Inefficient teaching of brilliant students.* Instructors become adjusted to teaching to a certain level of intelligence. When the level changes, they do not change. No efforts are made to adjust the instruction to a higher level and to appeal to the ability of the superior student. It is no wonder some keen minds have been restless, with the performance of their instructors.

Undoubtedly, other explanations are available. Whatever they may be, the fact remains that scholastic achievement has not kept pace with the gain in intelligence. If the thesis is logical that there should be a definite relationship between the two factors, then a distinct challenge is thrust at instructors and administrators to ascertain the cause for the present discrepancy and to seek a remedy for it.

C. W. Reeder

The Ohio State University

## NEW BOOKS IN EDUCATION

Bagley, William C. *Education and Emergent Man.* Pp. xiv + 238. Nelson.

Jones, John Price. *The Technique to Win in Fund Raising.* Pp. 230. *Inter-River Press.*

Leary, Daniel B. *Educational Psychology.* Pp. xiv + 363. Nelson.

Sharman, Jackson R. and others. *Current Problems in Camp Leadership.* Pp. 120. Ann Arbor Press. $1.25.

Wilson, Lester M. and I. L. Kandel. *Introduction to the Study of American Education.* Pp. vii + 328. Nelson.

# SCHOOL AND SOCIETY

WITH WHICH ARE COMBINED THE EDUCATIONAL REVIEW, ESTABLISHED IN 1891, THE TEACHERS MAGAZINE, ESTABLISHED IN 1878, AND THE SCHOOL JOURNAL, ESTABLISHED IN 1874.

Volume 40 | SATURDAY, SEPTEMBER 29, 1934 | Number 1031


## AMERICAN PHILANTHROPY AND THE ADVANCEMENT OF LEARNING[1]


By Dr. FREDERICK PAUL KEPPEL

PRESIDENT OF THE CARNEGIE CORPORATION


I DON'T suppose that any one in this audience has ever heard of the *Penang Gazette,* an English newspaper published in the Straits Settlements, and yet a recent leading article in that journal has furnished me with the text for my observations on this occasion. The article in question was entitled "Scientific Philanthropy," and it devoted two full columns to a surprisingly accurate and comprehensive record of the activities of American foundations, with the conclusion that they furnish one of the most significant contributions to our culture in the United States. Since these matters apparently proved of interest to the business men and planters of Penang, it occurred to me that they might also be of interest to the young scholars of Providence.

Perhaps, before I am through, you will wish that I had never seen the paper from Penang. The subject is one to try the patience even of that most patient of human gatherings, an academic audience. I have tried to make it as non-committal as possible by using that mellow and gracious phrase, the advancement of learning. But what is learning? The very term tempts one to analysis and classification which will satisfy no one, not even the classifier. Does learning include both scholarship and research? Does it lose caste by being applied or becoming vocational? When and how does science lose its purity? It would be much easier for us all if there existed an accepted body of doctrine about such matters, but there does not. We shall have to admit that there are many questions upon which honest men may differ.

After all, however, the phrasing doesn't really matter. If a man has what I am enough of an Irishman to call a passion for dispassionate inquiry, if he has reached or even approached the frontiers of existing knowledge in the field of his interest, if he has at hand, or can make for himself, the tools he needs, then whatever he actually accomplishes contributes, it seems to me, to the advancement of learning.

As to the relation of philanthropy to this advancement of learning, I hope we can proceed upon two or three very simple assumptions. First, that such advancement is a desirable national objective; second, that research and scholarly inquiry, though just about the least mercenary of occupations, do rest upon an economic basis; third, that donors are sincere, reasonably intelligent, and are doing their best to do good and not harm with their money, and that foundation trustees and executives possess these same qualities and moreover face their responsibilities in no spirit of

[1] Address before the Graduate School of Brown University, Commencement, 1934.

arrogance or cock-sureness, recognizing that money confers no rights of direction or control, that it is always secondary in importance to the idea and the worker. They know that they are fumbling and feeling their way. Here, as elsewhere, age and experience are likely to lead to humbleness of heart. If, for example, I had been asked to make this address ten years ago, when I was just beginning my foundation service, I should have known much better what to tell you than I do to-day.

Most of what I shall have to say will deal with the type of philanthropy which has taken the form of the foundation, not because I think it of predominant importance, but rather because the cobbler should stick to his last. One can not, however, sort out foundation gifts and their results from the broad stream of philanthropy. They constitute but one part of the whole.

When John Harvard made his modest gift to the Massachusetts Bay Colony, when the Connecticut clergy brought together their books at Saybrook, when Trinity Church in New York opened its vestry room to Samuel Johnson and his handful of students, when the College of Rhode Island set a new standard of liberality in its charter, all these and similar steps laid the foundations of American scholarship. In the years which followed, every endowment of a chair in a college or a bed in a hospital, each gift of a science laboratory or of a library, took its place in the structure that has been erected on these foundations. In recent years have come superb gifts and bequests for the general purposes of some particular institution, as, for example, those of Mr. Rockefeller to the University of Chicago, and those of Senator and Mrs. Stanford. The names of Sterling, Eno, Duke, Eastman, Baker, Cook, Whitney, Harkness, among many others—each recalls some princely donation. The degree to which American universities have become custodians of trust funds is not generally recognized. Within fifteen years the funds of this character held by four institutions alone, Chicago, Columbia, Harvard and Yale, have risen from less than twenty to more than eighty million dollars. Even at the lowest period of the depression, Dr. Richard Penrose left some $10,000,000, the income of which will be used almost exclusively for research. And remember that all these gifts are over and above the establishment of the independent foundations, with which we associate the names of Buhl, Carnegie, Couzens, Falk, Guggenheim, Macy, Milbank, Rockefeller, Rosenwald, Sage and others.

Though they can hardly be classed as philanthropic, we must mention, as part of the picture, the contributions of industry and commerce for research, on the one hand, and, on the other, the allocations from public funds—those of the Federal Government for the scientific bureaus and for such organizations as the Library of Congress, of the states for their universities, and of cities and towns for their local institutions. It has been estimated that in 1927 some $217,000,000 was spent for scientific research in the United States, and that of this total, more than 90 per cent. came from industrial and commercial bodies. I should not like to have to guarantee either figure, but that American business has contributed a very large sum to research, there can be no question. Much of it is necessarily routine and utilitarian in character, but this is by no means always the case. The work of Langmuir of the General Electric Company, for example, is recognized the world over, and I happen to know of three contributions by officers of the American Telephone and Telegraph Company, one in endocrinology, one in the physics of light and the chemistry of pigments, and one in personnel analysis, none of them having anything to do with the telephone, and all made "on company time." At the peak, the aggregate contributions for research and education from public funds must have reached an even higher figure than those from business, and the recent drastic cuts are for the most part, I am confident, temporary in character. To complete the record and not necessarily to imply that it represents a desirable trend, one must mention another source of support for scientific inquiry, namely, the earnings of previous discoveries. A number of non-profit-making research corporations have recently been established within universities which control patents and apply the earnings to new investigation.

The aggregate amount contributed from all these sources during the first and second decades of our century may never be equalled, perhaps never approached, during the lifetime of any one in this room, and even if we take the sharply reduced figures of the past year or so, these represent a degree of available financial support for the advancement of learning undreamed of during the previous history of mankind.

I think we can recognize two controlling motives which have prompted American men and women to give money during their own lives, or to leave it after death. One is the age-old and world-wide desire to relieve human suffering and distress, and the other, more special to our own land, is based on an almost mystical belief in education and what it can accomplish. Underlying both in the great majority of cases has been the same religious motive which has dotted our country-side with churches and sent our missionaries to distant lands. It is interesting to observe, however, that the man who created the phrase, the stewardship of wealth, and who practised so generously what he preached, was not himself a communicant of any church. After all, a gift, great or small, is a very personal thing. Something has touched the giver's heart, perhaps the suffering of some one dear to him. I am told that the philanthropic funds spent for the study of cancer alone in the United States amount to more than $400,000 annually.

Until very recently, few if any of the donors and few of those to whom they first entrusted their funds, had any conscious thought of research or creative scholarship. Some one, perhaps some one of you in this room, could make an important contribution to our cultural history by tracing the inevitable, but very gradual, intrusion of this idea—the slow shift of the center of interest and activity from the palliative to the constructive. It would be possible, for example, to show how the activities of those concerned with what we used to call "charity" led them into general sociological inquiry, and later into such fields as mental hygiene. Similarly, the health activities led, first, to support of the recognized medical sciences of anatomy, physiology and pathology, then to newer and at first not wholly acceptable branches such as bacteriology, embryology, biochemistry, genetics, and these in turn back to fundamental study in the basic fields of general biology, physics and chemistry.

In the case of gifts originally prompted by an interest in education, in contrast to the desire to relieve suffering, the path would, I think, follow somewhat different lines. A professor here and there must have tired of repeating to his students what he himself had learned in his own youth. Some doubtless went forward just from mental curiosity and the creative urge; others were stimulated by the needs of a developing civilization, as, for example, in geology or agriculture. As to the processes of education itself, men began to realize that the content of courses and the programs of study, in school, college and university alike, could not be settled once and for all, but were dynamic things. In the teaching of law, medicine, engineering and the like, the master-prentice conception, the didactic lecture, gradually gave way before a more professional attitude. Moreover, education came to be studied for its own sake, and one after another various citadels of the realm of assertion were attacked.

It is high time for me to turn to the one element in the whole complicated picture where I can make any pretension whatever to competence, but let me again remind you that the foundation is only one element in the picture. This plan to project the giver's shadow on into the future is at least as old as Ptolemy the First and the library of Alexandria. It flourished in the medieval church. It built up the city companies of London. And it had the compliment of being transplanted to our shores by Benjamin Franklin.

In the aggregate present American foundations account for a substantial share of the country's wealth. The last published report records 129 of them, with a total capitalization of some $800,000,000—more than half of this total being concentrated in seven trusts which have already distributed more than $280,000,000 from income and, in some cases, from principal. The peak was reached in 1928 when $92,000,000 of additional funds were received. Since then new funds have come in, but the total has probably decreased, both through distribution of capital and through depreciation of securities.

One has only to run over the highly interesting analyses prepared by Dr. Evans Clark of the Twentieth Century Fund to see how hopeless would be the task of trying to find the proportion of the funds granted by these trusts which go directly to the advancement of learning, but, on the other hand, it is very clear that a substantial proportion of such funds must be so credited. Dr. Clark's own estimate is that about $10,000,000 of the $54,000,000 distributed in 1931 were for the encouragement of research, and this figure does not include the sums voted to medicine and public health, where the research element is clearly important and significant.

Let me mention, in passing, one or two matters of detail. It is a curious fact that two of the most fruitful sources of help to American scholarship came from men who themselves had never been in the United States. For long years, the only substantial source for grants to scientific inquiry was the Smithsonian Institution, and, more recently, a striking number of Rhodes scholars returning to the United States from Oxford have taken up scholarly careers. For some reason, the proportion of Americans doing so is higher than in the case of the scholars appointed from the British Dominions and Colonies.

The community trusts, which give the donor of limited means the chance to share in the joys and responsibilities of foundation activities, have not, thus far, contributed much toward scholarly inquiry, but in the future their contribution may be substantial.

If I am not mistaken, the first foundation to be specifically dedicated to research was the Carnegie Institution of Washington, chartered in 1902. Shortly afterward came the Rockefeller Institute for Medical Research. Other examples, outside the universities themselves, of institutions endowed for research are the Woods Hole Laboratory, the Hispanic Museum, the Huntington Library, the Brookings Institution. For a decade, the largest single gift by a foundation directly in the interest of research was that of the Carnegie Corporation to the National Research Council in 1919. It is now evident, however, that the Rockefeller group will have to go well beyond this figure to carry out its purpose of providing the world with a 200″ reflecting telescope, to be installed in southern California.

Now learning does not advance itself. Some man or some woman, and it is impressive in these latter days to see how often it is some woman, some individual, at any rate, does the advancing. (I wish the English language furnished us with an inclusive pronoun for occasions like the present, but it doesn't.) Andrew Carnegie used to say, "Find the efficient man, and give him what he needs." He discovered this rule in his business and carried it into his philanthropy. How is the foundation to find the efficient man, and how does it know what he needs? There are always many more projects to be fostered, many more individuals to be helped than there are resources at hand to provide for them. The larger foundations consider fully a thousand proposals a year, many, if not most of them, involving at least ostensibly the advancement of learning. The task of selection would be hard enough within a single field; it is doubly hard as between competing fields, as is necessarily the case for foundations of broad, as contrasted with specialized, charters.

Contrary to the general impression, the foundations do not merely sit in judgment upon applications presented to them with due obeisance. It is really more often a question of the foundation catching the man with a constructive idea than it is the other way round. Generally speaking, the man with the idea must be caught in one of two nets, either in the institution which employs him—college or university—and to-day we must add institute or museum or library—or in the learned society of which he is a member. The two patterns are, so to speak, superimposed one upon the other.

At first, foundations negotiated directly. To-day there are advisory and supervisory groups of various kinds. For example, the first $2,000,000 given away by the Carnegie Corporation was given wholly on the basis of direct negotiation between the corporation and the institution concerned. Seventeen years later, 68 per cent. of the annual program was based upon consultation with some representative advisory body. In a single recent year, the records showed that our corporation had been in consultation with no fewer than 68 national scholarly organizations of one kind or another.

These include, for example, the great professional bodies, the American Medical Association, the Bar Association, the American Library Association, the national engineering societies. There are also the bodies of scholars interested in some particular subject or group of subjects: the American Historical Association, the Modern Language Association, and the like. There are also broader groupings of scholars, such as the American Association for the Advancement of Science, the National Academy of Sciences, and the like. There are also state and local academies, historical and other associations, some of which have earned the right to a place in the picture. More recently have come representative councils, such as the National Research Council, already mentioned, which deals with the natural sciences, the Social Science Research Council, and the American Council of Learned Societies, the last named dealing primarily with scholarship in the humanities. Many of the larger universities have now research councils of their own, to coordinate the work within their own walls. It is an elaborate and complicated pattern, perhaps too elaborate and too complicated, but at any rate these councils and other advisory bodies which provide a check and balance, do much to protect the foundations from the danger of arbitrary decisions, and to permit the trustees to concentrate their responsibility upon what is really their primary business, namely, to exercise an intelligent layman's judgment as to which of many competing fields of activity should be continued, which have reached the area of diminishing returns, which new fields should be entered.

The process of selection for a foundation is hard enough in any event. It is further complicated by the fact that there are fashions in research just as there are fashions in hats and gowns. To-day we have the endocrines, the cosmic rays, middle-American archeology, heavy hydrogen, the outer galaxies, pioneer belts. There are also fashionable techniques, the bombardment of the atom, the partial correlation, the private life of the long-suffering banana fly, the photo-electric eye, linguistic atlases. For a while we were all excited about the possibility of deliberately planned cooperative research. We are not so sure to-day. It was, by the way, the degree of foundation support going to enterprises of this kind a few years ago which evoked the cry from my predecessor on this platform, Professor Zinsser of Harvard:

> Research councils and foundations organize cooperative researches, thinking that the shy truth can be snared by the noisy advance of a well-drilled company of technicians, forgetting that discovery was ever a solitary task, in which cooperation must be spontaneous, asked as the need arises by one lonely seeker from another.

The greater part of foundation funds devoted directly to the advancement of learning are voted in terms of problems to be solved, large or small. These are attempts to answer some question or group of related questions formulated by an individual who has already won his spurs, or, more rarely, by a team of such individuals. Such, for example, would be the researches in the velocity of light by the late Dr. Michelson, or the program of the three coworkers at the University of Toronto who discovered insulin—with the aid of a foundation grant, by the way, of only $8,000—or the much larger and more elaborately organized group which prepared for President Hoover the "Report on Recent Social Changes."

There is, however, a second field of activity, hardly less important. In this case, the objective is not so much the answering of some particular question as the preparation of an individual, some carefully selected man or woman, to ask and answer questions of his own later on. This second field includes the great body of fellowship grants, travel allowances, refresher grants, as the English call them, for workers mid-stream in their careers, exchanges of professors and laboratory workers and the like. For fifteen years the Rockefeller Foundation has been contributing on an average nearly $1,000,000 annually to provide opportunities of these kinds for selected men and women, not all of them Americans, to be sure. While the Rockefeller gifts in this field have been outstanding, the Rhodes scholarships, the Commonwealth and Guggenheim fellowships, the allowances granted by the various Carnegie groups, as, for example, to workers in international law, all deserve more than the passing mention which it is possible to give in this place.

There is a third type of foundation activity which has a place in the picture, which may be called the oblique attack. The Laura Spelman Rockefeller Memorial, for example, spent large sums, millions of dollars in fact, in our Southern states, not so much to help selected individuals or to further any specific researches in its chosen field of the social sciences, as to create conditions in certain strategically located institutions under which research might thereafter flourish.

The scholar sometimes assumes that the whole problem for the foundation is to decide which piece of inquiry to support, his own or that of some else. He doesn't realize that before the foundation can reach that question at all, it must decide how much of its available resources shall be devoted directly to the advancement of learning, and how much to other purposes falling within the provisions of its charter and perhaps, as I have intimated earlier, lying closer to the ideas of the donor. In a word, there are plenty of other things to be done with the money. We have, for example, the pressure coming from groups organized to advance all sorts of worthy social purposes, to meet their administrative expenses in whole or in part. We have the appealing opportunities to help the under-privileged, the Negro, for instance. We have the opportunities to wage such campaigns as that of the General Education Board for better school conditions in the South, or to finance a restatement of our common law. Then we have the whole range of contributions to educational institutions for their general purposes. This is a less insistent demand than it was say in 1920 and 1921, when the General Education Board and the Carnegie Corporation jointly contributed nearly $10,000,000 for endowment among a number of colleges, conditional upon certain funds being raised from other sources.

A program which touches contributions to new knowledge indirectly rather than directly, and which is more typical of present-day policies, is that which the Carnegie Corporation has recently completed whereby the sum of $1,393,300 was distributed to undergraduate college libraries in the United States and Canada for the purchase of books of their own choosing. There is always the exciting possibility that a gift of this kind may have its share in stimulating the Newton or Kant or Darwin of to-morrow.

Within the past four years, all foundations have turned aside from their normal programs, and quite rightly, to meet emergency conditions, and even when there is no general depression to contend with, unforeseen opportunities are constantly cropping up to do some particular job which, though it lies outside the program, seems at the moment eminently worth doing.

Let me say a special word about the enterprises involving the regrouping of existing knowledge. Some recent general surveys have proved to be of great usefulness. There are also the experimental applications of ideas based on new knowledge, the so-called demonstrations. In all sorts of fields, in public health, in child guidance, in what we call progressive education, the demonstration is an essential factor.

Then we have the whole question of the diffusion of knowledge, as contrasted with its advancement. Broadly speaking, the state recognizes its responsibility for financing this diffusion of knowledge *in the classroom,* but when we step out of the classroom into that vaguely defined territory which is called adult education, we find this responsibility only rarely recognized, and the foundation finds many an opportunity to cooperate with the library, the museum, the editor and publisher, and to-day the radio chain as well. And may I point out that this is an exceedingly difficult field, since in each case consideration must be given not only to an understanding of the facts, but to the art of presenting these facts to an audience without technical preparation. If there be any question as to the need of more effective diffusion of existing knowledge, let us consider the New Deal. Practically every one of the facts upon which an intelligent layman might base an opinion is known and is a matter of record somewhere, but they have never been diffused, and meanwhile the layman is deafened and confused by the voice of assertion, *pro* and *con,* from Congress, from the press, from the platform, from the man on the street.

And after all knowledge is not everything. We are just beginning to remember, after a long period of forgetfulness, the place which the arts may play in any balanced human life. The arts appeal directly to our emotions, and these emotions are perhaps more truly ourselves than are our conscious mental processes. As to the degree to which money can really advance the cause of the arts, we are still groping, but even groping costs money, a surprisingly large amount of it.

Having shown how many and how appealing these opportunities are, let us turn back from them to research and scholarship. Since the turn of the century, there has been then this stream of financial support for the scholar from the general funds and endowment of colleges and universities, libraries, museums and hospitals, from public funds, from individuals and corporations, from the income and principal of independent foundations. In one way or another, enormous and quite unprecedented sums have been devoted to the stimulation of research and scholarly inquiry. Has it been worth while? Certainly the tools of scholarship and research are available as never before, and while the scholar and research worker are not so honorably recognized as elsewhere, nevertheless their position in this regard has improved, and their economic position has become distinctly stronger, both in comparison with other callings in the United States and with that of scholars in other lands.

On the other hand, our new learning should by this time have emancipated us from old superstitions and old bigotries. It has done so only in part, and it hasn't prevented the growth and spread of new slogans and other substitutes for thinking and knowing.

That the addition to the world's store of knowledge has been enormous goes without saying. Whether the same may be said of the quality of the work is more open to question. We have our scholars and investigators of high distinction, but in proportion to population they probably can be matched, man for man, in countries which do not provide one tenth of the purchasable aids to learning. It would be interesting to speculate as to the reasons for this. It may be, for example, that in a civilization so newly emerged from the pioneering era, our level of what the French call *la culture générale* is inevitably relatively low, and that this low base line is necessarily a deterrent factor. We may have had also to reckon with the competition of other callings for our more gifted young people, measured not only in financial reward, but in the more intangible factors of public esteem and social distinction. There are those who would add that lavish financial support has made the scholar's path too easy for those who follow it. This certainly has been true in individual instances, but whether they are numerous enough in the aggregate to create a factor of importance, I should personally question.

It must, alas, be admitted that there is a good deal of bunk connected with this whole question of research and scholarship. The foundations must accept their share of the blame. Without the least intention of doing so, they have over-stimulated certain fields, they have spoiled certain individuals, for your man of scholarship is a human, often a very human being. They have, I fear, been the chief offenders in forcing the techniques of research which developed in the natural sciences, where experimentation is relatively simple, where verification is usually possible, where controls are available, into the social sciences and the humanities, where conditions are very different.

But I submit that the foundations are not the only sinners. It is a very fine thing for a college or university to want its faculty to be a productive, a creative body. It is a very poor way of reaching this objective to put a premium upon *any* research, *any* publication, and far too many promotions have been made, too many salaries have been raised, too many men have been relieved from academic chores, for research and publication which a very little outside inquiry on the part of the institution in question would have demonstrated to be perfunctory, unimaginative and unimportant.

On the basis of present evidence, one could make a pretty fair case either for or against the defendant, but after all, isn't it too soon to try to pass judgment? The recipients of the newer type of fellowship, the man and woman who have served their apprenticeships in the elaborate recent inquiries, are few of them beyond their thirties. This whole group of younger people can hardly be said to be "in production" as yet. Twenty, or even ten, years hence, the whole world may be familiar with a number of names now quite unknown, and the same may prove true of certain discoveries already made, the significance of which is not now realized.

I am too prudent a man to hazard a guess as to the future financial support of scholarly inquiry in America, but if any of you should wish to do your own guessing—and from the nature of your present activities this may well be possible—here are some of the factors to be taken into consideration. Certain of them are relatively stable: the income from the existing university and other institutional endowments, public funds within fairly well-defined limits, current contributions from individuals and commercial organizations within even narrower limits, which I shall discuss in a moment. Other factors are less stable. As I have pointed out, the total capitalization of foundations has probably decreased, and there is a chance that it will decrease still further. Whereas in the past most trustees outside the Carnegie group have merely been permitted to distribute principal, in a number of recent trusts they have been instructed to do so, in the case of the Rosenwald Fund within a specified term of years. New foundations will inevitably be created, but their capitalization and the degree to which they may contribute to the advancement of learning are obviously unpredictable.

A rough subdivision of the different fields of inquiry may help you to make a more accurate, or, shall I say, a less inaccurate guess as to the prospects in the particular subject in which you may be interested. Dr. Waldo Leland states, with the authority of an honored alumnus of Brown, that "The natural and physical sciences deal with man's environment, the most remote as well as the most immediate; the social sciences with man in his associations with other men; while the humanities concern themselves with the manifestations of his spiritual existence." These three together pretty well cover the field. It is a convenient classification if you don't press it too far and if you are careful to remember that certain disciplines lie across the boundaries, as, for example, psychology, history and anthropology.

We can not discuss the possibilities of new sources of philanthropic support for scholarship without giving some consideration to what is going on in the minds of the people at large, to what Professor Whitehead would call our intellectual climate. I think it is fair to say that the average American looks upon the natural sciences, the humanities and the social studies, in three different ways. He trusts science, he doesn't understand it and doesn't pretend to, but he trusts it. His imagination is stirred by what science has already done, on the one hand to relieve suffering, to promote comfort and convenience, to lighten toil, and, on the other hand, to create dividends, to make new money. If he is naturally generous and in a position to give, he will do so for one or both of these reasons.

As to the humanities, he doesn't really think much about them. His chief source of inspiration, the daily paper, which is giving increasing space to science, neglects the humanities, unless there happens to be a story, as there was in the case of the opening of the Egyptian tombs. Which reminds me to say that archeology, particularly when it involves exploration and excavation, furnishes the one outstanding exception to my generalization. Buried treasure has its fascination for young and old alike. Otherwise the average man gives the humanities lip service, but regards all that kind of thing as clearly outside his particular business.

The popular reaction to the social sciences is the hardest to describe. We are all greatly concerned with what may be called the end products of economics, of social and political behavior, of education. How could it be otherwise? But when it comes to probing beneath the surface down to the underlying problems of the distribution of wealth, of social or anti-social conduct, of good or bad government, of good or bad education, then we hesitate. I am not sure how many of us have a definite suspicion that such activities may threaten the existing order, or whether it is not rather a vague sense of lurking danger in any meddling with other folk ways, but certainly the average man is far from comfortable in the presence of any deep-lying social problems, and in no mood to contribute toward their solution by supporting the very steps he extols when they are applied to problems in natural science.

While I insist that you must do your own guessing, let me give you some general impressions held by those who, from the nature of their responsibilities, have had to give attention to these matters. Scientific inquiry may count upon continuing to receive individual corporate and public contributions, plus a fair share from the income of existing endowments of universities and foundations. Thus far philanthropic gifts to scholarly inquiry in the humanities has been indirect rather than direct, the building up of great book collections and the expansion of academic departments, and the same may be said of the allocation of public funds. *Ad hoc* foundation grants have been relatively few in comparison with those in other fields. Some, indeed, have been outstanding, as, for example, those of the Rockefeller group to the Oriental Institute of the University of Chicago. Foundation activity in the humanities is likely to increase, but not with great rapidity. It is doubtful whether many important individual gifts will come from the present generation, though perhaps we can look for better things from the generation now in school and college.

Now as to the social sciences. These, like the humanities, have profited by the increase in the general wealth of the universities, both tax-supported and endowed, and scholars in both types of institution have the preparation and the courage to undertake fundamental researches in the social sciences. As to the financing of projects requiring specific appropriations, allotments have been made from the general research funds of the universities themselves, and some important individual gifts have been received, though from a small group of donors. The chief contributors, however, have been the larger foundations, and they are likely to remain the chief contributors, though not on the lavish scale of recent years. This will mean, I think, long-range studies rather than hasty attempts to meet current difficulties. As Mr. Hoover once said, research under forced draft is not likely to get you anywhere.

This statement is made in face of the fact that whenever foundations get into trouble, as they do from time to time (witness the report of the Industrial Relations Committee to Congress in 1915), it is practically always because of something they have done, either directly in the social field, or in the applications of social theories to education.

Fortunately, the trustees of these foundations, or, it would be more accurate to say, most of the trustees, recognize that social order can never be imperiled by the truth, and have the courage to stand up under criticism for acting on this belief. They have not been frightened off by the obvious presence of a lunatic fringe. They take comfort in the fact that studies in controversial fields which they support are usually attacked with equal ardor from the left and from the right. Their interest and support have not dried up as a result of inevitable mistakes and failures.

Basic research in education deserves a special word. I know many crimes have been committed in its name, many claims have been based upon it (though very seldom by the worker himself), which can not be substantiated, but after all allowances are made, I should personally place the genuine accomplishments high in the list of our national achievements since the turn of the century, and look forward to even richer opportunities in the future.

Upon a somewhat similar academic occasion four years ago, I stated that fundamental research in all the fields we have been discussing would probably offer the most important opportunities for foundation activity. I still think so, and I believe this to be true also for individual donors who make their gifts after deliberate thought and not upon impulse. I confess, however, that my reasons for the belief have shifted considerably during the four years. To-day I have less confidence in the measurability of results, less in what money can do, less in the power of organization, but, on the other hand, I take much greater comfort in the thought that any number of failures can be retrieved, and more than retrieved, by some one success, a real success.

Let me close by expressing my sincere hope that some of you, through the success of your own scholarly work, may do your share in justifying the contributions of American philanthropy to the advancement of learning.

# EDUCATIONAL EVENTS

## REDUCED REGISTRATION OF STUDENTS AT GERMAN UNIVERSITIES

A WIRELESS dispatch to *The New York Times* states that only 4,000 male and 700 female students who have successfully passed the test of the labor service army will be admitted to the German universities and technical high schools this fall, according to an announcement made by the German Student League.

The average number of new students in recent years has been 12,000, and in some of the more prosperous post-war years it approached 20,000. The maximum number for any one year, as fixed by the Ministry of Education, is 15,000 of whom 5 per cent. may be females.

Under the new regulations governing higher education in Germany every prospective university student must first pass through the labor service army, and on his admission to a university automatically becomes a member of the German Student League, of which Andreas Feickert is the dictatorial leader.

The *Times* correspondent says:

The reduction in the number of new students is in line with the policies of the National Socialist State, which places more emphasis on practical work and seeks to reduce the "intellectual proletariat." How rigid the sifting-out process has become is evident from the following figures:

The German preparatory schools released in the Spring of this year 39,579 graduates. Under the maximum ruling of the Education Ministry the number obtaining the right to university training was reduced to 15,000. Of the latter, 8,000 male and 1,000 female students entered the labor service army as the final preparation.

That even of these less than half were finally admitted was explained by officials of the German Student League as resulting from the fact that some gave up their plans to study, some preferred to stay in the labor service to become officers and the rest were unable to pass tests designed to determine their general fitness to become intellectual leaders in the Third Reich. In these tests devotion to National Socialist principles is decisive.

The class entering the universities this Fall will be the first to undergo the new and revolutionary schooling methods worked out by the National Socialist authorities. According to an order issued by Herr Feickert, the new students will live in so-called comradeship homes, will wear a uniform instead of the gay-colored student cap and ribbons and will be subject to discipline by the Student League. The comradeship homes will be the club-houses of the student corporations, which are the equivalent of the American fraternities, and the homes of previous student leagues now merged into the National Socialist League.

The purpose of all this, according to Student League officials, is to revamp German student life in accordance with the principles of the Third Reich. The drinking and dueling student of the Student Prince type is to disappear; drinking bouts are to be eschewed in favor of sports. Dueling with the saber, at least in the first student year, is to be replaced with fencing with the foil and compulsory dueling is likely to be abolished entirely. In later years the students are to be employed during their free time in the practical work of the Third Reich.

## REGISTRATION IN THE NEW YORK CITY SCHOOLS

The registration of pupils in the public schools of New York City for the new academic year has increased by 10,818 over the figure of a year ago, according to a report by Eugene A. Nifenecker, director of reference, research and statistics for the Board of Education, made public on September 23 by Dr. Harold G. Campbell, superintendent of schools.

According to a memorandum accompanying the statistical table, 91.25 per cent. of the children in the city now are privileged to attend classes on a full-time basis. There were 91,854 pupils on short time a year ago, and now there are 98,817.

The report indicates that the decline in elementary school registration and the increase in the number of high school pupils noticed so markedly in recent years, because of restricted immigration and the declining birthrate, on the one hand, and the scarcity of jobs, on the other, is continuing, although the trends are not so pronounced.

A loss of 6,737 students is noted in the elementary and junior high schools, while the senior high schools have assumed an additional burden of 11,297 pupils.

"Considered apart from the junior high schools, the elementary schools show a loss of 15,408, but nearly half of this is a mere bookkeeping loss because of the transfer of children in the upper grades of elementary school to the junior high school."

In analyzing the figures in this department, the memorandum states:

"The Borough of Brooklyn, for instance, shows a loss of 7,313 elementary pupils against a gain of only 3,439 in the junior high schools. Similarly, Manhattan's loss in elementary school pupils is larger than its gain in junior high-school pupils. In the Bronx, however, the gain in junior high-school pupils more than offsets the loss of elementary school pupils. Even Queens shows a drop of 1,548 in its total elementary registration and a gain of only 371 in the junior high schools."

The total register includes the elementary, junior high, senior high and industrial high schools. Following is a table of the borough totals for this year as contrasted with last:

| | 1934 | 1933 |
|---|---|---|
| Manhattan | 243,191 | 239,790 |
| Bronx | 215,958 | 215,552 |
| Brooklyn | 449,868 | 449,670 |
| Queens | 189,288 | 188,106 |
| Richmond | 31,083 | 31,362 |

These figures do not include the continuation schools which accommodate both children and adults.

The increase of 6,963 in the number of part-time pupils in the day schools over the corresponding period for last year is the result of inability of the city to finance new school construction to keep pace with the increased enrolment, particularly in the high schools.

## THE ROSENWALD COUNTY LIBRARY EXPERIMENT

The first Rosenwald county library experiment to be placed on a permanent basis with public support is that in Richland County, South Carolina, with Columbia as the county seat. A one mill tax has been voted by the state legislature and a county library board has been appointed.

Five years ago the Julius Rosenwald Fund initiated a program of aid to libraries in the south, having for its purpose the development of county libraries which would serve all elements of the population—rural and urban, Negro and white.

To receive a grant a county had to pledge enough local support to bring the total annual library budget to at least fifty cents per capita, including Rosenwald aid. Money from the fund and that raised by the county, which the Rosenwald Fund matched, had to be used entirely for service, that is, books, salaries, etc., but not for buildings. The county provided suitable library quarters and coordinated public library facilities of the county under one head, a trained librarian.

The usual scale of matching was $1 from the fund for $1 from local sources for each of the first two years; $1 from the fund for $2 from local sources for the third and fourth years; $1 from the fund for $4 from local sources for the fifth year. Local money to match aid from the fund must be "new money," that is, funds over and above the library's budget at the time negotiations with the fund began. After the fifth year the local community was to assume responsibility for the entire support with the moral obligation to maintain the service on as high a plane as existed during the period of the demonstration. Because of economic conditions the five-year experiments have been in most cases adjusted to a seven-year period.

Counties which have received grants under these terms include: Walker County, Ala.; Webster Parish, La.; Coahoma County, Miss.; Davidson County, N. C.; Mecklenburg County, N. C.; Charleston County, S. C.; Richland County, S. C.; Hamilton County, Tenn.; Knox County, Tenn.; Shelby County, Tenn.; Jefferson County, Tex.

Reading among rural people in the "Rosenwald counties" increased nearly 200 per cent. in the first two years following the establishment of the experimental service. Among Negroes the increase in reading was well over 300 per cent. More than 250,000 people were offered reasonably adequate public library service for the first time. At the request of the Rosenwald Fund the Graduate Library School of the University of Chicago is now engaged in evaluating the results of the experiments and expects to report on them within the next year.

Significant of the Richland County library's place in public opinion is the fact that in 1932 the library achieved the distinction of being the one agency whose budget the Farmers and Taxpayers League did not recommend cutting.

The first act of the Richland County Library Board just appointed has been to restore some of the cuts which have been in force in library staff salaries.

## THE DOCTORATE OF EDUCATION AT NEW YORK UNIVERSITY

DR. JOHN W. WITHERS, dean of the New York University School of Education, has announced that the degree of doctor of education will be offered by the school for the first time this fall. The general plan for the establishment of the new degree was approved by the council of the university last May, and the program was recently completed by the faculty of the School of Education.

It is the purpose of the doctorate of education to place major emphasis upon demonstrated ability to achieve in the actual work of education. The requirements for matriculation, the program of studies, and the field project or other equivalent requirement in applied education have been established with a view to the fulfilment of this purpose.

General requirements for the degree are: broad general and professional scholarship; evidence of originality and continuous growth in the advancement of education, and demonstrated superior competence in the candidate's major field of educational service.

Candidates admitted to matriculation for the new degree will follow a program of at least three years of graduate study beyond the baccalaureate degree, and the program of studies will be determined by the professional needs of the candidate and by his professional capabilities. Candidates will be required to take a comprehensive written preliminary examination not later than the sixth week in the term or the fourth week of the summer session in which the candidate begins the first course of the last eight required in residence. Courses of study involved in the minimum of three years of graduate study and training for the new degree upon the basis of a recognized baccalaureate degree, or its equivalent, are:

Fifteen full courses, or their equivalents, determined and approved by the sponsoring committee, in consultation with the candidate, according to his interests and needs, and providing:

(a) In general, approximately one third of the courses are to be in the field of the candidate's specialization, another third broadly related to this specialization, and the remaining courses generally cultural in nature.

(b) In general, at least three seminars will be included in the candidate's program: (1) a seminar on problems of contemporary life, (2) a general education seminar on problems of education related to and growing out of the problems of contemporary life, and (3) a general seminar in the candidate's field of specialization conducted in a comprehensive manner so that a well-integrated grasp of these problems may be achieved.

(c) For most candidates two tool courses with reference to the candidate's project based on an actual ''job experience'' in the field of education, such courses to be selected from any one or more of the following groups: (1) languages, (2) educational research, (3) statistics.

In addition to the required comprehensive written preliminary examination and a final oral examination there is required the passing of a final written comprehensive examination in the field of interest towards which the candidate's courses have been directed. The purpose of this examination is to test the candidate's command of integrated knowledge in his field.

## CONFERENCE OF THE NATIONAL COUNCIL OF TEACHERS OF ENGLISH

TRADITION and innovation in the teaching of English in time of accelerated social change is the general topic of the twenty-fourth annual meeting of the National Council of Teachers of English to be held in the Mayflower Hotel, Washington, D. C., from November 29 to December 1, under the presidency of Professor Oscar James Campbell, of the University of Michigan.

Dr. Charles Swain Thomas, of the Graduate School of Education of Harvard University, will preside at the opening session on Thanksgiving Day evening, and Dr. Frank W. Ballou, superintendent of the Washington schools, will give the address of welcome. A representative of the national administration will explain the policies of the New Deal of importance to teachers, and the president's address on "English: Its Domestic and Foreign Policies" will close the program.

At the annual banquet on Friday evening, Stephen E. Kramer, first assistant superintendent of schools, Washington, will be the toastmaster. The speakers will be Reverend Francis P. Donnelly, S.J., of Fordham University; Dr. Allan Abbott, Teachers College, Columbia University; Thomas W. Gosling, director, Junior Red Cross, and Dean Marjorie Nicolson, of Smith College.

Robert Frost and Dr. Esther C. Brunauer, secretary of international relations of the American Association of University Women, will be the principal speakers at the luncheon on Saturday with which the convention will close. Mr. Frost will answer the question, "Can Poetry be Taught?" and Dr. Brunauer will discuss "National Socialist Youth in Germany."

Among those who will take part in the general session on Friday morning and in the sectional conferences are Willard W. Beatty, president of the Progressive Education Association; Bess Goodykoontz, assistant Commissioner of Education; William Hard, political writer and radio news commentator; Thomas L. Stix; Professor Robert E. Rogers, of the Massachusetts Institute of Technology, and Professor Alain Locke, of Harvard University.

Several well-known authors will be the guests of honor at a tea which the faculty of Wilson College will give for the delegates to the convention. A special visit to the Folger Shakespearean Library has also been arranged. Sightseeing trips to the principal points of interest in and around Washington have been planned for the visitors by the local committee.

All who are interested in educational progress and especially in the teaching of English are invited to attend the convention whether or not they are members of the National Council.

The program for the conference on school journalism follows:

''Good Writing, the Basis of All Newspaper Work,'' William Hard.

''School Publications as a Means of Strengthening Public Relations,'' Belmont M. Farley, assistant director of Division of Publications, National Education Association, Washington, D. C.

"Teaching Intelligent Reading of the Newspapers in a Course of Journalism," Arthur S. Flemming, Executive Director, U. S. Society, Washington, D. C.

"What States and Cities Are Doing on Courses of Study in Journalism," Lambert Greenawalt, Adviser, *York High Weekly*, York, Pa.

Chairman, Joseph M. Murphy, Columbia Scholastic Press Association, Columbia University.

## THE CONVOCATION OF THE UNIVERSITY OF THE STATE OF NEW YORK

ONE hundred years of state support of teacher training in New York State will be commemorated at the seventieth convocation of the University of the State of New York, which will be held on October 18 and 19 in the State Education Building at Albany. This annual meeting, arranged by the regents of the university, brings to Albany school people from all over the state. An especially interesting program of addresses by leaders in education and in the arts has been planned for this one hundredth anniversary of the first legislative enactment in America recognizing teacher education as a state function.

The general theme of the convocation will be "The Epic of Teacher Training in America." Among the speakers will be Dr. Walter J. Damrosch, musical counsel for the National Broadcasting Company; Dr. Lorado Taft, lecturer on art at the University of Chicago; Dr. Walter A. Jessup, president of the Carnegie Foundation; Dr. Payson Smith, commissioner of education of the State of Massachusetts; Dr. Henry W. Holmes, dean of the Graduate School of Education of Harvard University; Dr. William C. Bagley, professor of education at Teachers College, Columbia University, and Barrett H. Clark, editor of the Samuel French Publications.

The convocation will be opened on Thursday evening, October 18, by Chancellor James Byrne. The invocation will be pronounced by Dr. George B. Cutten, president of Colgate University. The speakers at this session will be Dr. Harry W. Rockwell, president of the State Teachers College at Buffalo, who will give the prologue "From Time Immemorial"; Dr. Walter A. Jessup, who will speak on "Teacher Education—A State Function?" and Dr. Walter J. Damrosch, whose subject will be "Democracy Turns to Music."

The ceremony of conferring an honorary degree will take place at this session. Dr. Frank Pierrepont Graves, president of the University of the State of New York and State Commissioner of Education, will present the diploma in behalf of the regents.

Following the first session, the Board of Regents and the commissioner of education will tender a reception to the delegates and invited guests in the rotunda of the State Education Building.

The session on Friday morning, October 19, will be opened by Regent John Lord O'Brian, chairman of the Regents Committee for Teacher Education and Certification. The speakers at this session will be Dr. Payson Smith, whose subject is "The Men of Destiny"; Dr. Henry W. Holmes, who will speak on "The Age of Experimentation," and Dr. William C. Bagley, whose subject is "Education Outruns Training."

At the afternoon session on Friday Dr. Lorado Taft will speak on "America Seeks Beauty"; Barrett H. Clark will discuss "New Frontiers for the Drama," and Dr. Charles W. Hunt, principal of the State Normal School at Oneonta, will give the epilogue, "The Century Ahead." This session will be opened and closed by Vice-chancellor Thomas J. Mangan and the benediction will be pronounced by the Rev. Joseph M. Noonan, president of Niagara University.

Music will be given a prominent part on the convocation program. The Fredonia State Normal School Symphony Orchestra and the Potsdam State Normal School A Capella Choir will come to Albany to entertain the convocation audiences. There will also be solos by Harry King, associate head of the Music Department of the Fredonia State Normal School.

The annual meeting of the State Association of Colleges and Universities will be held in Chancellors Hall on the morning of October 18. The Association of State Teachers College and Normal School Faculties will hold its meeting at the same time in the New York State College for Teachers at Albany.

### THE RESIGNATION OF PRESIDENT WALTER WILLIAMS OF THE UNIVERSITY OF MISSOURI

DR. WALTER WILLIAMS, after four years of service as president of the University of Missouri, has resigned the office, effective December 31, or on such date thereafter as the Board of Curators may determine.

The board reluctantly accepted Dr. Williams's resignation, and adopted a resolution expressing its appreciation of his distinguished service to the institution, after the president had expressed his belief that a younger man should be selected to carry on the duties of the office in view of problems and opportunities now confronting the university. He had previously informed the Board that when he accepted the presidency in 1930, it was his desire and intention at that time that he would be relieved of his duties when he reached the retiring age of seventy years.

President Williams was 70 on July 2 of this year, and at that time, in accordance with previous plans, he had prepared his resignation, which was accepted on September 14. Following his retirement from the president's office at the end of the year he will resume his duties as dean of the School of Journalism, a position he still holds, being the founder of the school and its dean since its establishment in 1908.

Upon his return from a trip around the world last year, President Williams learned it would be necessary for him to undergo a major operation. In order that he might complete the work at the university he postponed the operation until after the June commencement when he went to a St. Louis hospital. Following his return, after two weeks there, while convalescing he has spent the entire summer in Columbia at his desk at his home carrying on his duties as president. In tendering his resignation, Dr. Williams told the board that the relinquishing of the large amount of detailed work for the next few months would enable him to regain full health by the time he again assumed his duties as dean of the School of Journalism. He will continue in the meantime to devote his entire time to the major educational and financial problems of the university.

The formal resignation of President Williams follows:

I hereby tender my resignation as president of the University of Missouri, effective December 31, 1934, or as soon thereafter as my successor assumes the duties of the office. I resign in order that a younger man may be chosen for the responsibilities of the presidency.

I can not resign without expressing my thanks to the Board of Curators for honoring me during these most difficult days with the presidency. The days would have been more difficult except for the support given to the administration by the press of Missouri which, with unexampled unanimity, has aided the university as an institution of public service; by the university faculty maintaining university traditions of sound education and constructive research, and by the administrative staff and employees through their loyal and self-sacrificing cooperation; by loyal students and devoted alumni and by the intelligent citizenship of Columbia and Missouri, who have rallied to the university as its welfare was in danger—To all I am deeply grateful.

The university is about to enter on a larger service and I pledge my support to my successor as he leads this great university into this larger service.

I hope that my personal relations with the members of the board which have given me so much pleasure and comfort in troublous times will continue in the more peaceful and progressive days opening before us. For your friendship, forbearance and aid I am indebted now and always.

# EDUCATIONAL NOTES AND NEWS

DR. GEORGE F. ZOOK, who spent the summer in Europe, has now taken up his work as director of the American Council on Education, in succession to Dr. Charles R. Mann. Dr. Zook retired as U. S. Commissioner of Education on July 1. He was succeeded by Dr. John Ward Studebaker, superintendent of schools at Des Moines, Iowa.

DR. JOHN GUNDERSEN ROCKWELL, associate professor of educational psychology in the College of Education of the University of Minnesota, has been appointed State Commissioner of Education. He will fill the balance of the term of E. M. Phillips, who resigned on August 1 after serving one year of the six-year term. Dr. Rockwell was for two years superintendent of the schools of Butte, Nebraska, and has taught for eleven years at the University of Minnesota. Superintendent P. S. Amidon, of Litchfield, has been appointed his deputy to succeed P. C. Tonning, resigned.

THE degree of doctor of laws, conferred upon him by the University of Berlin, was on September 17 presented to Dean Roscoe Pound, of the Harvard Law School, by Dr. Hans Luther, Ambassador to the United States of the German Government.

DR. STEPHEN P. DUGGAN, director of the Institute of International Education, returned to New York on August 28, after nine months absence in Europe.

DR. JOSEPH S. AMES, president of the Johns Hopkins University, who has been traveling in England and Germany for five weeks, arrived in New York on September 19.

DR. R. B. VON KLEINSMID, president of the University of Southern California, is announced as the 1934 recipient of the Northwestern Award of Merit, presented annually by the alumni of Northwestern University to one of its members for "conspicuous achievement in the field of education." Dr. von KleinSmid took his undergraduate work at Northwestern University, receiving the A.B. degree in 1905. He earned the master's degree in 1906 and in 1925 the degree of LL.D. was conferred on him.

THE University Award granted by Rutgers University for distinguished services was presented on September 8 to Albert E. Meder, associate professor of mathematics at the New Jersey College for Women. Professor Meder served as acting dean of the New Jersey College for Women from September, 1932, when Dean Mabel Smith Douglass was granted a leave of absence, to February, 1934, when Dean Margaret T. Corwin was appointed to succeed Dr. Douglass.

OFFICERS of the National Council on Religion in Higher Education for 1934–35 have been elected as follows: *President,* Professor J. Seelye Bixler, Harvard University; *vice-presidents,* Dean Herbert E. Hawkes, Columbia University, and Dean Willard L. Sperry, Harvard University; *treasurer,* Cleveland E. Dodge, New York City.

ELMER J. MCCAUSTLAND, professor of sanitary engineering at the University of Missouri, will retire at the close of the first semester in February, 1935. Professor McCaustland reached the retirement age of seventy years last winter. He went to the University of Missouri in 1914 and since that time has been dean of the School of Engineering and director of the Engineering Experiment Station.

PROFESSOR ROY DICKINSON WELCH, chairman of the department of music at Smith College, will be a visiting professor of music at Princeton University this year. Professor Erwin Panofsky, formerly dean of the faculty of the University of Hamburg, will be visiting lecturer in art.

JAN J. L. DUYVENDAK, of the University of Leyden, has been appointed visiting professor in the Department of Chinese at Columbia University; Professor Frederick S. Boas, of Wimbledon, England, president of the Elizabethan Literary Society, will direct research studies in Elizabethan literature in the Graduate School and will lecture on Elizabethan drama, and Dr. Julius Lips, formerly professor of sociology and ethnology at the University of Cologne, has been appointed visiting associate in anthropology.

JAMES WELDON JOHNSON, professor of creative literature at Fisk University, has been appointed visiting professor of education at New York University and will give ten lectures covering the Negroes' part in racial contributions to American literature. Professor Johnson is a native of Florida, attended Atlanta University and Columbia University, ran a newspaper, studied law and wrote poetry. He has been secretary of the National Association for the Advancement of Colored People.

DR. EVERETT DEAN MARTIN has been appointed director of the new department of social philosophy at Cooper Union, New York City.

SUPERINTENDENT HAROLD E. HEGSTROM has been appointed by the Minnesota State Board of Control the successor of Superintendent J. T. Fulton of the boys training school at Red Wing. Mr. Hegstrom has been superintendent of schools at Stewart, Arlington and North St. Paul.

JOHN J. SKINNER, for sixteen years superintendent of schools at Owatonna, Minnesota, has accepted the superintendency at Fairmont. Mr. Skinner succeeds Claude W. Sankey, who has purchased a newspaper at Belmond, Iowa.

MISS TRESSA C. YEAGER has been appointed chief of kindergarten and elementary education in the Pennsylvania Department of Public Instruction. Miss Yeager is a graduate of Slippery Rock Normal School and the University of Pittsburgh, and obtained her M.A. degree from Teachers College, Columbia University, where she is completing the work for her Ph.D.

DR. ANNETTE T. RUBINSTEIN, formerly of New York University, has become head of the Robert Louis Stevenson School, New York.

DR. DONALD D. DURRELL, associate professor of psychology and director of the education clinic at the School of Education of Boston University, will have charge of the courses in psychology and child psychology at the Garland School, Boston.

DR. HARLAN UPDEGRAFF has been appointed by Dr. James N. Rule, superintendent of public instruction for Pennsylvania, to undertake a six months' assignment for the Committee on Higher Education of the Commission for the Study of Educational Problems in Pennsylvania, of which Dr. Ralph D. Hetzel, president of the Pennsylvania State College, is chairman. He will make a comprehensive study of demands being made upon institutions of higher learning in the state. Dr. Updegraff was formerly professor of educational administration at the University of Pennsylvania, and was later president of Cornell College. In recent years he has conducted two state surveys in New York, two in New Jersey, one in Mississippi and has participated in two national school surveys for the United States Office of Education.

DR. HUGH P. BAKER, president of the Massachusetts State College, has been appointed a member of the advisory committee of the New England Regional Planning Commission. The commission, of which Victor M. Cutter is chairman, is a division of the National Resources Board. Dr. Baker, who was dean of the New York State College of Forestry at Syracuse from 1930 to 1932, has previously served in an advisory capacity to the Westchester Park Commission and other planning activities. He will make accessible to the committee the material available in various college departments.

THE REV. WENDELL PHILLIPS will resign as assistant chaplain of Columbia University on October 1 to become rector of Trinity Church, New Rochelle, N. Y. For the last two years Mr. Phillips has been chairman of the New York Diocesan Committee for work among college students.

EDWARD MCCARTAN, who was awarded the 1933 gold medal of honor given by the Allied Artists of America for a work of distinction in sculpture, has been appointed acting head of the Free Art Schools of the National Academy of Design, New York City.

MISS IDA RICHARDSON HOOD, assistant librarian at the American Museum of Natural History from 1903 to 1926, and since then curator of books and publications, has retired. Miss Hazel Gay has been appointed acting curator of books and publications.

PRESIDENT TYLER DENNETT, of Williams College, was the guest of Wesleyan University on September 26, when he was the principal speaker at a convocation in recognition of scholarship.

SIR RICHARD WINN LIVINGSTONE, president of Corpus Christi College, Oxford, gave the address at the opening of Union College on September 17.

ARNOLD D. MARGOLIN, formerly Justice of the Supreme Court of Appeals of Ukraine, began a special course on "Contemporary Russia" on September 24 at the Washington Square Center of New York University. The course is part of the new program of adult education of the Division of General Education.

"SPECIMENS of Higher Mathematics" is the title of a course of six lectures to be given at the New School for Social Research by Professor Edward Kasner, of Columbia University, on Wednesday evenings, beginning on October 3. Following Dr. Kasner's course and beginning on November 14, Dr. Frederick Barry, of Columbia University, will give a series of lectures on "The Early Development of Modern Science." Dr. Henry J. Fry, visiting investigator at the Cornell University Medical College, who has been associated with the New School for a number of years, will lecture on "The Making of Modern Biology" on Thursday evenings beginning on October 4.

THE fourth annual Conference on Current Problems, sponsored by the *New York Herald-Tribune,* was held at the Waldorf-Astoria, New York City, on September 26 and 27. Mrs. Franklin D. Roosevelt greeted the delegates. The keynote address, entitled "America's Hour of Decision," was made by Dr. Glenn Frank, president of the University of Wisconsin. Dr. Harry Woodburn Chase, chancellor of New York University, spoke on "The Crisis in Education." Dr. Stanley King, president of Amherst College, and Dr. Edward C. Elliott, president of Purdue University, also addressed the conference. Among other speakers was Dr. Harold G. Campbell, New York City Superintendent of Schools, who opened the section of the conference dealing with youth with an address on "Education for Pioneering."

THE annual convention of the National Association of Teachers of Speech will be held at the Roosevelt Hotel, New Orleans, on December 27, 28 and 29. The three-day program will be divided into four main divisions for the study of: (1) Dramatics and Interpretation, (2) Original Speaking, (3) Speech Science and (4) Psychology and Pedagogy of Speech. Teachers of any of these forms of speech at the various educational levels are invited. Officers of the association are: H. L. Ewbank, *President,* University of Wisconsin; Frances K. Gooch, *First Vice-president,* Agnes Scott College; Lionel Crocker, *Second Vice-president,* Denison University; G. E. Densmore, *Executive Secretary,* University of Michigan; H. H. Hudson, *editor of Quarterly Journal,* Princeton University; C. T. Simon, *editor of Research Studies,* Northwestern University.

A CITIZENS' Conference on School Recovery in Pennsylvania will be held at Harrisburg on October 10 and 11. On Wednesday evening, October 10, the Hon. Gifford Pinchot, Governor of the Commonwealth, will preside and the theme will be "The State's Responsibility for Public Education." Addresses will be made on "Education and the State" by Governor Pinchot; on "School Recovery to Meet the Needs of Pennsylvania's Children" by James N. Rule, Superintendent of Public Instruction, and on "Education and the Nation" by Charles H. Judd, University of Chicago. On the morning and afternoon of Thursday, October 11, the topics for discussion will be "Organization of Governmental Units in the Interest of Economy and Efficiency"; "Organization of School Districts in Terms of Needs and Interests of Pupils and Taxpayers"; "The Effective Control of School Expenditures"; "Sources of Adequate School Support," and "The Equitable Distribution of State Subsidies." The speakers will include widely known business and educational executives and economists. Each address will be discussed from the platform by representative citizens. The purpose is to present existing school problems in order that delegates may be thoroughly informed on the immediate and future needs of public school recovery. The conference is intended to pave the way for local citizens' conferences in various communities of the state in which the cooperation of delegates to the state conference will be most helpful.

FRANK G. PICKELL, president of the New Jersey State Teachers' Association, has announced the establishment by the association of an annual award for "distinguished service to education in New Jersey." Mr. Pickell, who is superintendent of schools in Montclair, said that the award, available to any citizen of the state, would be made first at the annual banquet of the association in Atlantic City on November 10.

A GIFT of $10,000, to build a library at the Georgia Normal and Agricultural College for Negroes at Albany, Georgia, has been made by Miss Caroline Hazard, of Peacedale, R. I., well known as an educator and philanthropist. The gift was made to the city commission upon agreement of an annual appropriation of $300 for maintenance of the library.

*The Library Journal* reports that a PWA grant and loan of $650,000 has been made to the Carnegie Public Library, Fort Worth, Texas, for a new site, library building and equipment, of which $172,500 is a gift to the people. Bonds of $472,500, covering the loan, will be submitted to a vote of the people.

THE prospectus of courses, lectures and other educational advantages offered to members of the Brooklyn Botanic Garden and to the general public for the educational year 1934–35 has just appeared as the October issue of the Brooklyn Botanic Garden *Record.* Twenty-one courses are offered for adults. Of these courses nine are especially for teachers and have been accepted by the Brooklyn Teachers Association and the New York Board of Education for credit toward higher teaching licenses. In addition, the course for student nurses which has been given for a number of years in cooperation with the training schools for nurses of a number of Brooklyn hospitals is offered again this year. Nine different courses are offered primarily for boys and girls between the ages of eight and eighteen. The "Prospectus" also includes announcement of opportunities for research under direction and for independent investigation. In this connection the Botanic Garden is in official cooperation with New York University and Long Island University. General statements are given concerning the other educational activities and features of the Botanic Garden, including press releases, broadcasting, popular and technical publications and guide books.

# DISCUSSION

## EXTENDING FRESHMAN WEEK

AT this time of the year colleges all over the United States are opening their doors to the freshmen. Provision for the induction of the freshman into the life of the college ranges from placing a pamphlet into his hands at the time of registration to a full week of freshman activities. While there is some agreement as to the purposes of Freshman Week, it would appear that there is no commonly accepted limits of time for Freshman Week nor of the activities to be included. If there is any one tendency, it is to crowd into the Freshman Week program a multitude of activities, many of which are touched upon but briefly and from which there is probably little satisfactory return either to the freshman or to the college. Too frequently the college assumes that Freshman Week in itself provides adequately for the adjustment of the incoming student to college life and its attendant problems.

Freshman Week began as a method of acquainting the incoming student with the college. Recent trends indicate that the college is becoming increasingly interested in acquainting itself with the student, his limitations, capacities and abilities for achieving satisfactory scholastic work in the college. Many colleges which do not give entrance examinations are making extended use of placement tests in order that the college administration may have an understanding of the background of the incoming student. For the colleges which do not have a restricted enrolment and which do not use the entrance examinations, the placement tests likewise serve as a protective measure for the college administration in the instance of students who do not have the ability or academic preparation that would assure success in college. Placement test results give the college definite record of student achievement apart from the high-school record, which is often an unreliable indication of student achievement. Should a student fail at the end of a semester and the secondary school authorities and parents descend on the college authorities in assumed righteous wrath and indignation, charging the failure of the college rather than of the student, the college is able to point to the record of the student on the Freshman Week placement tests as indicative of the poor preparation of the student and substantiating the claim of the college that the student should be dropped. However valuable the placement tests may be for sectioning purposes or as a college protective measure, the test results should be more valuable for purposes of guidance in assisting student academic adjustment throughout the freshman year.

From an examination of Freshman Week programs, it is evident that Freshman Week activities divide themselves into three phases: First, placement tests; second, a series of very general activities including the usual round of receptions, addresses of welcome, assembly talks, historical lectures, talks on aims and ideals, tours of the campus and learning college songs and cheers; and third, a group of rather specific activities, including talks and discussions on choosing curricula, college organizations, including fraternities, budgeting of time, participation in extra-curricular activities, how to study, use of the library, student conduct, college regulations, vocational guidance and student finance. While the above placement tests, general activities and specific activities may be deserving of a place on a Freshman Week program, it would seem that colleges are shirking responsibilities if they by any chance assume that these activities can be lightly dismissed with the scant attention that is given to them on a program of a few days' duration.

A scanning of the specific activities group will reveal talks, lectures and discussions which merit more than a single hour, and in many cases at least a single semester's consideration. For example, to give full and complete attention to "Use of the Library" in a single hour period of Freshman Week to a group of freshmen, apart from any immediate need for knowing how to use the library, is questionable. To all intents and purposes the students appear interested enough while the discussion is in progress and are likely to say that they understand fully all that has been said, yet the same students later demonstrate only too well that what was explained in the library conference did not register. The same applies equally well to "How to Study" discussions and many of the other specific activities cited above.

This discussion is not aimed as destructive criticism of Freshman Week activities but rather at the naïve assumption that a heavily loaded program of Freshman Week activities will accomplish in itself a full and complete adjustment of the freshman. The college has a responsibility for continuous student guidance for many of the activities which commonly occur on Freshman Week programs. However, there must be a distinction between activities which merit merely discussion, those which can be carried on in conjunction with extra-curricular activities and those which should have a place in the curriculum. Some activities may be carried on in connection with well-organized student-personnel work, other activities may find a place in a specifically organized one-semester college orientation course for freshmen, paralleled by frequent conferences of freshman and student-adviser.

We probably must face the fact that Freshman Week, while laudable in itself, can be no more than an introduction to the entire problem of student orientation and adjustment. Many of the activities begun in Freshman Week must for the most part be continued during the freshman year and possibly to a lesser degree during the sophomore year. For some students this guidance must be continued even longer, but these students should be a very small minority.

FRED G. LIVINGOOD
WASHINGTON COLLEGE

## SOME PHI BETA KAPPA PURPOSES

PROFESSOR JANES'S communication concerning Phi Beta Kappa, published in SCHOOL AND SOCIETY for September 1, makes a reply imperative. At the recent meeting of the eighteenth triennial council an attitude quite the opposite of his was manifest.

In calling the plan to increase the Phi Beta Kappa endowment by $1,500,000 a "grandiose scheme" Professor Janes neglects an italicized statement in the foundation's announcement: "No campaign but steady growth by small and large gifts and bequests." This year two bequests have been made, one of $100 from a non-member and another of a maximum value of about $26,000 from the estate of Miss Isabelle Stone, Wellesley, '05.

This latter bequest, which is for a fellowship in memory of the donor's mother to be awarded alternately in the fields of (1) Greek archeology, history, language, or literature and (2) French language or literature, gives occasion for a statement concerning administration. It is probable that the Senate will request the chapters in 122 of our best colleges and universities to submit nominations for the fellowship and will appoint committees of scholars in the respective fields to make the selections.

Mr. Owen D. Young is chairman of the foundation and Dr. John H. Finley is vice-chairman. The treasurer is Dr. W. Randolph Burgess, deputy governor of the Federal Reserve Bank of New York. The trustees include President Frank Aydelotte, Commissioner Frank P. Graves, Dean Roscoe Pound, Dr.

Albert Shaw, and President Mary E. Woolley. This personnel not only obviates "grandiose schemes" but insures wise administration of trust funds.

There is not the slightest desire or likelihood that Phi Beta Kappa will become an "educational bureaucracy" or use its funds for "publicity and propaganda." Nothing could be more foreign to the spirit of the society or to the tastes of its chapters and officers. It would be difficult to find another society where there is less "standardization" and "laying down the law." The secret of Phi Beta Kappa's vitality and longevity is the freedom of the chapters to adapt themselves to the needs of their own institutions. The ritual referred to by Professor Janes is not required and is not used by many chapters.

Professor Janes's statements concerning *The American Scholar* are far from the truth, except that the subscribers represent about 7 per cent. of the membership. Here it should be noted that over 600 subscribers are not members of Phi Beta Kappa. Since, however, the membership is approximately 70,000, and since the magazine has been built on quality rather than appeals to duty or loyalty, that is rather a figure to be proud of, particularly in view of the fact that the initial number appeared in January, 1932. The subscription list and the quantity and quality of material available have steadily grown more nearly adequate during these difficult years.

It is not true that "most of the articles are of a popular and journalistic character written by professional writers whose names are familiar to readers of current magazines and newspapers." While some of the authors may be essentially journalists, they have for the most part written for *The American Scholar* on subjects on which they are especially informed and therefore almost in the capacity of specialists. Often such writers are needed to interpret for the layman the work of more technical scholars.

Moreover, consider such authors and subjects as the following:

Frederick J. E. Woodbridge, "The Nature of Man."

John Livingston Lowes, "Teaching and the Spirit of Research."

William Rose Benét, "The Ballad of Resurrection Bar" (poem).

Cassius J. Keyser, "The Humanity of Mathematics."

Alvin Johnson, "Intellectual Liberty Imperilled."

Paul Shorey, "American Loyalties."

Hermann Hagedorn, "The Three Pharaohs" (poem).

Gilbert Chinard, "Thomas Jefferson as a Classical Scholar."

James Truslow Adams, "John Marshall."

Bliss Perry, "The Road to Weimar."

Ralph Barton Perry, "William James."

Edgar A. Singer, "On the Contented Life."

Emil Lederer, "Has Capitalism Failed?"

Reinhold Niebuhr, "The Churches in Germany."

Edgar Sheffield Brightman, "Personalism and Economic Security."

Ralph George Hawtrey, "Speculation in American and English Stock Markets."

While it is true that, in addition to the publication of articles by recognized authorities, one of the objectives of *The American Scholar* is the encouragement of young and unknown scholars who have something to say and are able to say it, nevertheless it would be silly to refuse to publish a thoughtful analysis or a creative piece of work simply because the author is well known as a journalist.

Professor Janes's criticism shows that *The American Scholar* is somewhat unique, is steering a course between the technical or specialized type of periodical and the more popular magazine. The purpose is to interpret the realms of thought, values and action in an authoritative, scholarly manner and yet in a literary and interesting style understandable by educated readers who are not specialists in the particular fields entered. What we want to prove is that a substantial discussion and an enjoyable article can be one and the same—that scholarliness can abide with the zest and the clear beauty of a good style.

*The American Scholar* is under no obligation to be "peculiar and original" in all respects. But the society as a whole is seeking a reevaluation of true scholarship and of the criteria of such scholarship. Just as the accumulation of class grades is no longer sufficient to win the key for a student, so the piling up of dry and unrelated items of information can not gain access to the pages of *The American Scholar*. Scholarship with a background of culture, leavened by an authentic sense of values, and an appreciation of its relationship to the realities of living, welcomes *The American Scholar* as a medium for its expression in the interests of our American civilization. What greater and more appropriate service could Phi Beta Kappa render than to serve this type of scholarliness through its magazine?

WILLIAM A. SHIMER,
*Editor*

"THE AMERICAN SCHOLAR"
NEW YORK, N. Y.

# SPECIAL CORRESPONDENCE

## EDUCATIONAL RESEARCH AND EXPERIMENTATION IN CANTON, CHINA[1]

RESEARCH and experimentation, in the sense of systematic and scientific studies in education in any or all of its departments and in the sense of trying out new methods and ideas through objective or controlled methods of procedure are new in China. . . . In the first place, education was only recently conceived of as a separate branch of learning where departmentalization of knowledge and specialization of learning have reached their zenith under the influence of the generally accepted principle of division of labor. And in the second place, like the old civil service examination system and its corollaries, the objectives, methods and contents of instruction called for no innovations and imposed no new demands. In fact, the success of the educative process was often measured according to the degree to which it conformed to the standards set up in the past.

But this situation was disturbed after China's early contacts with the Western world with its challenge to all phases of social, political, economic and cultural life. Since the introduction of Western learning about 1862, more especially since the promulgation of the modern school system in 1903 and the abolition of the civil service examination in 1905, education has increasingly been regarded as a separate branch of learning. Hence all new educational theories and practises are now objects of interest, careful study and experimentation.

The publication of the *New Education Magazine* in 1919, the testing and measurement campaign under Dr. Wm. A. McCall in 1922, the founding of the Chinese National Association for the Advancement of Education in 1921, the establishment of the Dewey School by the Higher Normal School of Nanking in 1920, the organization of the Chinese National Association of Mass Education in 1923 and the undertaking of educational research in the Peking and the Nanking Higher Normal Schools, since 1920, etc., represent initial steps in the progressive education movement.

The foregoing dates go back to the post-war period, the Chinese Renaissance and the lecture tour of John Dewey in China. These factors, as well as the return at that time of many trained students of education from the United States account for these rapid developments.

The world war gave rise to the testing and measurement movement and to an interest in the problem of national illiteracy. The Y.M.C.A. camps for the Chinese laborers in France, during the war, gave added impetus, while the post-war sentiment for democracy and international peace stimulated educators to train along these lines. The Renaissance, led by Hu Shih, Chen Tu-Hsin and others, created an impetus in science and inquiry into all institutions and their functions.

Professor Dewey's lecture tour brought about a stronger conviction of the need for democratic citizenship, education through real life and for new schools, at first experimental, departing from hampering traditions.

For two years this movement was very active. Of the many types of tests made, the intelligence, language and arithmetic tests were the most numerous. The movement has left behind a considerable influence, but has never again been as active as in the first two years. In many progressive centers, especially in Nanking and Shanghai, intelligence and achievement tests have been quite popular in the last few years.

### EXPERIMENTAL SCHOOLS AND EDUCATIONAL EXPERIMENTS

In recent years, it has been common for bureaus of education with progressive tendencies and for universities or teacher-training institu-

[1] Digest of an article by Chiu-Sam Tsang and Chai-Hsuan Chuang, in the *Int. Ztech. f. Erzich. Wiss.*, 3: 1933–1934, Heft 3: 351–61.

tions with affiliated sub-collegiate schools to designate one or more of their schools, especially those of the lower levels, for experimental purposes. Experiments on the Dalton Plan, socialized curriculum, project method, socially-useful labor plan, etc., have been tried out and copied in various places. An examination of their experiments reveals the fact, however, that most of them deal with the details of methods for the improvement of teaching, *e.g.*, the comparison between writing Chinese horizontally and vertically, between deductive and inductive methods in teaching arithmetic, more particularly the improvement of teaching the Chinese language in reading, composition and chirography. For example, of the 44 more significant experiments reported by a writer on the subject, 34 were in Chinese, six in arithmetic and four in miscellaneous subjects.

But far more significant are the educational experiments with a strong social purpose. We refer particularly to the Mass Education Movement, to the Hsiao Chuang (Dawning Village) Normal School experiment, to the Village Reconstruction Institute at Show-Ping, Shantung, and to the rural educational program. The socialization and vitalization of educational experiments in this practical solution of the problems of life and society is truly significant in the movement of educational experimentation in the present-day world.

One of the most important of such activities is the movement for literacy begun by James Y. C. Yen, during the world war, when through the medium of the Y.M.C.A. in France he and his associates selected a working vocabulary and conducted classes in reading and writing for the thousands of illiterate Chinese laborers there. On his return to China after the war, Mr. Yen organized the Movement for Literacy among the Masses, or, as it was later called, National Association for Mass Education. The leaders of this movement, however, did not stop with teaching merely reading and writing, with their by-products of much useful information in civics, history, geography, personal and public hygiene, social and economic conditions, etc., but sought to improve the whole life and especially to solve the problems of rural reconstruction. In 1930 Ting Hsien, a rural district with an area of 480 square miles and a population of 297,000 in the Province of Hopei, was selected to carry on an experiment on a large scale, employing some 200 persons, many of them with university training. It has been largely subsidized (some 60 per cent.) by the China Foundation for the Promotion of Education and Culture, with assistance from the committee in charge of the distribution of the returned portion of the Boxer indemnity by the U. S. Government. Its work includes improvement in illiteracy, agriculture, citizenship, health, social service, as well as promotion of cooperative societies. The experiment has not only aroused great interest but has attained some valuable findings helpful to other similar undertakings.

The work of the Institute for Rural Reconstruction in Shantung was established in 1931. It selects graduates from secondary and technical schools to be trained first in the institute and later sent to various districts to conduct rural schools, training classes for rural school teachers, to carry on the work of the agricultural experiment stations, to take the census, promote cooperatives, etc. It aims, through the ideals of rural life in China, to check the possible incoming evils of over-industrialization and over-urbanization.

Another important experiment is that of Hsiao Chuang (Dawning Village) Normal School in Kiangsu, begun in 1928. It had no definite schedule of work or recitation. Its work centered around the following activities: (1) actual management-teaching in elementary schools and kindergartens; (2) rural improvement; (3) field work and nature study; (4) normal school administration and clerical work. Teachers are called "guides," working and playing with the pupils and observing the same regulations. One of the important purposes is to cultivate friendship with the farmer. At first the villagers were suspicious of the school, but gradually became friendly and often visited the school. The size and renown of the school increased gratifyingly and has left valuable influence, but unfortunately some students abused their freedom and the school has been suspended since 1930.

In February of this year, an experiment combining the rural reconstruction and the research programs of the two experiments described above was authorized by the Ministry of the Interior at Nanking, in conformity with their recent decision to establish one or more political experimental districts in each province for social, political and economic reconstruction. Under the leadership of Mr. T. Mon-Ru, a Columbia University graduate, the experiment in Pin-Yang is making good progress. It is planned to recruit experts in the various fields and by educative and other measures to improve all phases of living—government, reform, farm relief, animal husbandry, water supply, forestry, scientific farming, rural manufactories and industries, etc. It also includes development of self-government by the people and cooperation in road-building and public works. Parallel with this is the training of leaders and workers for further extension of this movement. Such a courageous and comprehensive attempt by the government for a solution of China's rural problem is bound to bear fruit.

A discussion on educational experimentation in China would be incomplete without presenting also the government's experiment on the University Region Plan, part of the University Council Plan, as a possible unit for a proposed national system of educational administration, in the hands of professional educators, withdrawing education from the traditional political influence and incorporating it with research. In October, 1927, a University Council was created in place of the usual Ministry of Education to take charge of all educational affairs of learning, science and art throughout the country. Under this council the University Regions were to take the place of the provincial departments of education on an experimental basis. The president of the university was not only the head of the local university, but also chief executor of all educational affairs in the region. The organization of the university included: a legislative committee, a research institute, a department on higher education (both for the university and the province), a department on general education, an extension department controlling social education, etc. But this plan was soon abandoned.

### Educational Studies and Research

There are many educational institutions engaged in research, such as schools of higher learning, the governmental educational organs, organizations making social experiments, etc.

Among the more noted educational associations in China are: Chinese National Education Association, National Association for Mass Education, National Vocational Education Association, all of them having conducted valuable researches. The National Association for Mass Education, doing notable work in the literacy and social reconstruction movements, has a very large annual budget, hence can assemble many specialists on methods and the most effective procedure for adult education. The National Association for Vocational Education has done some excellent research work ever since 1917, *e.g.*, a survey of more than 50 kinds of vocations, vocational tests in clerical service and aptitudes and interests.

The Institute of Educational Research, at National Sun Yat Sen University, Canton, has conducted research along the lines of improved teaching of Chinese, better methods and contents of adult education, the relationship between education and the economic life of the Chinese people. It publishes the *Chinese Journal of Educational Research*, as well as a series of research monographs and educational data. It has established an extensive library, which has already attracted foreign students of Chinese education.

### An Appraisal

In China, where the old system of education is inadequate and the new system is in the making, experimentation and research are most important. Fortunately, this need is accompanied by the new spirit of science and of inquiry for better ways and means of work and for greater certainties. To look at this movement merely as a conscious or unconscious imitation of current educational trends in the Western world is to miss the very essence of the problem. In looking over the work as presented one may well be satisfied with its past and hopeful for its future.[2]

S. W. Downs

## EDUCATIONAL REFORMS IN PERSIA

"The Parliament gives to the Ministry of Education permission to found in Teheran an

[2] The article concludes with 6 addenda, brief summaries pp. 36–61.

institution called *Daneshgah* (University) for the teaching of advanced courses in the sciences, arts, literature and philosophy," reads the first article of a Persian law approved on May 29, 1934. Persia has no institution of higher education other than the American College of Teheran, and the law quoted apparently marks the beginning of a national Persian university. Already some two hundred thousand square meters of land on the outskirts of Teheran have been purchased as a site for the new institution and two million rials ($125,000) were earmarked in the 1933–34 budget for it.

Six faculties are provided for: Moslem law and theology; natural sciences and mathematics; literature, philosophy and educational sciences; medicine; law, political science and economics; and the practical arts. Each faculty shall have a council made up of its principal and the faculty professors. The university council, which is to be the main administrative body, is to consist of the president, vice-president, principals of the faculties and one professor from each faculty. Professors must be at least 30 years of age; assistant professors, 25, and both in the special subjects they teach are required to have received an academic degree which the council of the university shall consider at least a doctor's degree or its equivalent.

Setting up a national university is only part of a larger plan. A ten-year program of establishing and extending higher and lower normal schools was enacted into law and approved last March 17. It calls for an annual budget in the decennium of 500,000 rials ($31,250) and the founding of twenty-five normal schools in addition to the two now existing. Two of the total will be higher normal schools, one each for boys and girls, which will admit graduates of the secondary schools and give them a three-year course to train them as secondary school teachers. The twenty-three lower normal schools will accept students that have completed the first three years of the secondary school curriculum and offer them two years of training for positions as teachers in the six-year elementary schools. The intention is that all these normals shall be boarding schools and free of tuition charges; temporarily they may be day schools with students given money for expenses of study, under special regulations. Each normal must have attached to it an elementary or secondary school for practise teaching purposes. On admission students give a written promise that after graduation they will teach with pay for five years or accept as a personal charge the amount expended by the government in training them.

The official courses of study for the elementary and secondary (middle) schools are being rewritten with a view to making the former more attractive and practical and much less burdened with memory work. The middle school curriculum of six years' duration was formerly divided into two cycles of three years each. The studies of the first cycle were common for all students; in the second cycle they could choose between a literary and a scientific course. By the new plan there will be a five-year common curriculum and differentiation into special lines in the sixth year depending on the university studies the student wishes to pursue.

Persian educational nomenclature is fixed in a note attached to the law for establishing normal schools:

> Hereafter the elementary school shall be called *Dabistan* and the elementary teacher *Amoozigar;* the middle school shall be called *Dabiristan* and its teacher *Dabir;* the industrial school shall be called *Honeristan* and its teacher *Honeramooz;* each division (faculty) of a higher school shall be called *Daneshkadeh* and the whole institution (university) *Daneshghah* and the teacher in a higher school shall be called *Ostad.*

JAMES F. ABEL

# QUOTATIONS

## THE SEARCH FOR EXCELLENCE

MEN are naturally very imitative. Whether it be personal habit or dress or mode of speech or manners, it is quite usual for the individual human being to fall easily into the habit of imitating his fellows. He who is accompanied with and surrounded by vulgarity, whether of speech, of dress or of conduct, and he who in literature, in the fine arts or in social contacts chooses his companions and guides from the second-rate, will turn his back upon excellence without even realizing that he has done so. It is imperative that education shall hold high standards of true excellence in each one of these fields of endeavor and of interest, as well as lean heavily upon the habit of imitation in making them the guide and the inspiration of youth. Appreciation of what is best in painting, in sculpture and in architecture can be far better gained through association with reproductions and models of excellence assembled in museums, whether large or small, than by any amount of mere reading or talking about them. If any twentieth-century people is to be trained to understand and to appreciate the fine arts, that people must be surrounded by examples of what is excellent, brought together in public collections in their several cities, towns and villages. In literature what is first-rate must always contend with what is for the moment popular. Few things are more distressing than the lists published from time to time of those books which for the time being enjoy chief popularity among readers in various parts of the land. The number of books among these which are really first-rate is so small as to be quite negligible. It is only a generation ago that a well-known professor in old Columbia College used to tell the undergraduates who sat in his classroom that they should not waste time on any book which was less than one hundred years old, since they could not be sure that it was worth while. If this counsel was extreme it was, nevertheless, a hint not to be wholly neglected.

There was a time, not so very long ago, when any one who should address an American audience in any part of this land might safely make reference, by quotation or otherwise, to the Bible or to the works of Shakespeare with a feeling of certainty that the reference would be understood and appreciated by the vast majority of his hearers. That time has passed. The Bible and Shakespeare are now usually read by title only and the superb literature which is their content is, unhappily, no longer part of the ordinary and everyday knowledge of American youth.

In respect to manners and personal conduct, present-day habits, as manifested in every sort of public place and personal relationship, are time and again quite shocking. One wonders why it is that youth can come to full adolescent years with no apparent appreciation of the difference between good manners and their opposite. Manners are manifested through speech, through dress, through personal bearing and through respect for the personality and the opinions of others, particularly those who are older in years or who have justly gained distinction in any walk of life. The family should, of course, be the original source of training and discipline in good manners. The school, also, has its function to fulfil, but too often the school regards its duty as done after very little and merely formal effort to discipline those committed to its care in what good manners really mean and involve.

There is, unfortunately, a very broad distinction between going to school and getting an education. This distinction has become even greater during the past generation than it used to be. It is sixty-five years since James Russell Lowell described the American people as "the most common-schooled and the least cultivated people in the world."[1] That such a judgment could be passed on his fellow countrymen by an outstanding man of letters is sad indeed, but it would be very difficult to confute or to refute him.

Surely these things should not be. If in the family, in the school and in the college we will only fix our minds on excellence and be determined to leave no stone unturned to achieve it, we shall quickly be on the way to remedy such a condition as Lowell described. In order to achieve excellence and to understand it, we must first of all set ourselves standards of judgment. We must realize and recognize the tests which mark the difference between the first-rate and that which is second-rate and yet lower. Some of this knowledge we shall get from imitation of those of our seniors with whom we are associated. The rest can only come from observation and reflection. To this task let every one turn in the year that now opens before us.—*President Nicholas Murray Butler at the opening exercises at Columbia University.*

[1] Lowell, James Russell, "Literary Essays," Boston and New York, 1895, p. 250.

## THE COLLEGE YEARS

I SHOULD like to take just a few minutes to point out what seem to me to be some of the fundamental principles which might guide you in your first year in college and perhaps through the remaining years. A large number of your studies in the first year will be determined by certain requirements, but wherever choice is involved my advice to you is to concentrate your efforts on a subject which you thoroughly enjoy. If you have not yet really become interested in any intellectual activity, your first task in Harvard College is to try to see if you can not find some subject which does interest you. We have in the college an enormous and fascinating variety of intellectual diet. Sample it freely and see if there is not some one aspect of it which particularly appeals to your palate. You will have a great opportunity to find out about such matters quite apart from your courses. There is a tendency to make the fatal mistake in college of feeling that one can learn about a subject only by taking a course in it. This may be true in a few special cases, and often a course is the most convenient and rapid method, but it is by no means the only one. You will have an opportunity of coming to know a great many interesting people: members of the faculty, students in the upper classes, your own classmates. You can acquire much of value by conversation with these people. You can learn of their interests, ambitions and ideals. An incalculably large portion of the value of a college education comes from the fact that the student is living with other men in the stimulating atmosphere of free discussion. You will hear a multitude of divergent opinions and, I trust, learn to be tolerant of many with which you do not agree. In the course of discussions and debates a college student gradually comes to judge the intellectual caliber of his fellow-men and to estimate the soundness of their character. Such judgment of men is of the utmost importance in the world of affairs. It is not to be acquired by any rapid methods, but a serious attitude towards your friends and acquaintances and their problems will do much to develop it.

Aside from your courses and what you learn about your fellow-students around the dinner table, I hope that most of you will have an opportunity to acquire the habit of reading. As I said before, it is not necessary to take a course in order to find out something about a subject. If you learn to read thoughtfully and consistently, you will have laid the basis for continuing your education throughout your life. The world has become so complicated that if a man stops his education when he leaves college or a professional school he is doomed to intellectual mediocrity. There is so much that is interesting that needs to be understood, and things are changing so rapidly! If your talents lead you to such a field as law, medicine or scientific research you will find there is no end to your professional education; it must be kept going by continuous self-directed study. We hope you will have acquired the ability to learn without an instructor. If your intellectual interest is to be used largely as the basis of an avocation, such as literature, music, art, or the study of current history, it is still more important that you acquire in college the habit of thinking for yourself and of being able to keep up an interest without the necessity of having some older man as a teacher.

Finally, I should like to emphasize that Harvard College does not pretend to train its students for any vocation. That is the work of the professional schools. What we hope here is that each one of you will find something which you may study with enthusiasm. Following this track of your own choosing, your four years of college life, rich in a variety of experience, will prepare you either to take up a vocation which requires an academic training or to enter the world of affairs with your vision broadened and your understanding deepened.

Reckoning a generation as between twenty and twenty-five years, you are just a generation younger than I am. You and your contemporaries will have many serious and terrible problems with which to deal, and you may have to deal with them while you are still very young; but you have great advantages. My generation was handicapped by living its youth in an era of security—then came the war, then the "boom," and then the depression. As one of my classmates said, "we have never had a break." In Europe the ranks of my contemporaries were decimated by the war; many who, if they had lived, would have been great leaders of to-day, were shot down in their youth. The generation older than mine lived too long in a period of apparent tranquillity and stability. You, on the other hand, will have known that the world is difficult and uncertain for many years before you enter the struggle. I believe that you, together with your immediate predecessors who are now leaving college, can face many of our problems with more courage and more realism than most of the older men of to-day. At the moment the problem which confronts the country appears to be that of reconciling an awakened social conscience with our older ideal of the liberty of the individual. I do not imagine that a solution can be arrived at in any short time. I feel sure that the way the problem is solved and the value of the ultimate solution will depend largely on the ideals of you young men and your ability to think clearly and without too much emotion. Even in time of war nothing is gained by calling your enemy names, although it may relieve the tension of your nerves. There is a great danger that at times of crisis like the present we shall disappear under a welter of words used in a perfectly meaningless manner—psychology, integration, relativity, complexes, vitamins, service—you have all heard them. Certainly they appeal to the ignorant, but the really educated should be proof against them. The acid test is whether you yourself indulge in them. If you call every one who stands to the right of you a Bourbon and every one who stands to the left a Communist, you are contributing your bit to the confusion and deserve no better fate than to be yourself played upon by those who parade all manner of slogans and catchwords. It is our hope that your experience at Harvard College may help you to escape this fate. If you take full advantage of your four years of college education, we may expect that when your turn comes you will be able to deal courageously and intelligently with great problems.—*President James Bryant Conant in an address to freshmen in Harvard College.*

# EDUCATIONAL RESEARCH AND STATISTICS

## PLACEMENT BUREAUS IN STATE EDUCATION ASSOCIATIONS

IN order to render personal service to its members by placing them in suitable teaching positions, the state education associations in California, Kansas, Michigan, Montana, Nebraska, North Carolina and Utah have organized placement bureaus. The first bureaus were those in the California and Kansas state associations, which were organized in 1920, as shown in Table I.

TABLE I
PLACEMENT BUREAUS IN STATE ASSOCIATIONS, YEAR ESTABLISHED, AMOUNT OF FEES AND COMMISSIONS CHARGED

| Placement bureau | Year established | Enrolment fees | Commissions |
|---|---|---|---|
| California | 1920 | none | 3 per cent. |
| Kansas | 1920 | $1.00 | 3.5 " " |
| Michigan | 1925 | $1.00 | 1 " " |
| Montana | 1931 | $2.00 | 2 " " |
| Nebraska | 1922 | none | 3 " " |
| North Carolina | 1923 | $1.00 | none |
| Utah | 1927 | none | $10.00 |

The enrolment fees to members of the associations are relatively small, while the commissions charged range from nothing in North Carolina to 3.5 per cent. in Kansas, as shown in Table I. Kansas and Utah discontinued their bureaus in 1933 and 1932, respectively. The reasons given were the oversupply of teachers and the increased expense to the associations. It was also felt that the service reached only a very small percentage of the total membership of the associations.

### MEMBERSHIP IN STATE ASSOCIATIONS

The five state associations which at present have well-organized placement bureaus show the same trend in membership growth, as shown in Table II.

The peak in association membership was at its highest in 1931. During the two years previous there was a gradual increase. Since then there has been a gradual decline. The lowest membership total was the last year, 1933.

### BUREAU PLACEMENTS

In regard to the number of registrations in the placement bureaus we note from Table III

TABLE II

State Association Memberships

| State associations | 1929 | 1930 | 1931 | 1932 | 1933 |
|---|---|---|---|---|---|
| California | 34,595 | 36,508 | 37,680 | 37,145 | 33,449 |
| Michigan | 30,731 | 31,996 | 32,238 | 31,253 | 29,637 |
| Montana | 4,438 | 4,838 | 5,207 | 4,543 | 4,004 |
| Nebraska | 12,692 | 12,474 | 12,947 | 12,625 | 11,849 |
| North Carolina | 12,500 | 13,000 | 14,500 | 14,000 | 14,300 |
| Total | 94,956 | 98,816 | 102,572 | 99,566 | 93,239 |

that the peak was in 1932, although this was somewhat clouded, owing to the fact that the Montana bureau had just started the year before with a relatively low registration. It is significant to note the decided drop in 1933 from the registration of 1932, a drop from 7,495 to 5,796.

TABLE III

Placement Bureau Registrants

| Placement bureau | 1929 | 1930 | 1931 | 1932 | 1933 |
|---|---|---|---|---|---|
| California (N. D.)* | 2,775 | 2,053 | 2,685 | 3,113 | 2,300 |
| California (S. D.)† | 2,113 | 2,110 | 2,861 | 2,601 | 1,493 |
| Michigan | 281 | 238 | 254 | 156 | 153 |
| Montana | | | 615 | 1,065 | 1,350 |
| Nebraska | | 461 | 550 | 560 | 500 |
| Total | 5,169 | 4,842 | 6,965 | 7,495 | 5,796 |

* N. D. = Northern Division.
† S. D. = Southern Division.

The number of placements is shown in Table IV. The greatest number was 1,145 in 1930. In 1932 the placements were about one half of those of the year before, dropping from 1,042 to 552. A still lower number of placements occurred in 1933 when only 451 were placed in the six departments.

This decline is strikingly shown in the percentage of placements registered. In 1930, 24 per cent. of those registered were placed, whereas the percentage fell to 7 per cent. in 1932 and 8 per cent. in 1933. In individual states the range is still greater. In 1933 Nebraska placed 7 teachers, or 1 per cent., and the southern district of California placed 171,

TABLE IV

Number of Placements with Corresponding Per Cent. of Registrants

| Placement bureau | 1929 | | 1930 | | 1931 | | 1932 | | 1933 | |
|---|---|---|---|---|---|---|---|---|---|---|
| | Number | Per cent. | Number | Per cent. | Number | Per cent. | Number | Per cent. | Number | Per cent. |
| California (N. D.) | 562 | 20.3 | 601 | 29.6 | 502 | 18.7 | 300 | 9.6 | 202 | 8.8 |
| California (S. D.) | 433 | 20.5 | 470 | 22.5 | 436 | 15.2 | 173 | 6.7 | 171 | 11.5 |
| Michigan | 44 | 15.7 | 27 | 11.3 | 26 | 10.5 | 6 | 3.8 | 11 | 7.0 |
| Montana | | | | | 35 | 5.7 | 63 | 5.9 | 60 | 4.4 |
| Nebraska | | | 47 | 10.2 | 43 | 7.8 | 10 | 1.8 | 7 | 1.4 |
| Total | 1,039 | 20.1 | 1,145 | 23.6 | 1,042 | 15.0 | 552 | 7.4 | 451 | 7.8 |

or 11 per cent. During the peak year, 1930, the northern district of California placed 30 per cent. and Nebraska placed 10 per cent.

According to Table V, there is a wide spread between states in the number of placements. Even in states where the association membership is about the same as in California and Michigan the total number of placements over a five-year period ranges from 3,850 for California and 114 for Michigan. Two other states with comparable association membership are Nebraska and North Carolina, with placements 107 and 500, respectively. Montana, with an association membership of one third that of Michigan, placed more in three years than Michigan did in five.

The type of placements is also revealed in the same table. Few rural teachers are placed by the bureaus. Eight per cent. of Montana's placements were in rural schools. A large percentage of placements were in high-school positions. Thirty-nine per cent. of the placements of the southern division of California were elementary teachers, whereas Michigan placed only 15.8 per cent. in grade schools. Twelve per cent. of Montana's placements were administrators, and only 4 per cent. of the southern division of California's placements were of this type. From the totals we see that 60 per cent. of all the placements were high-school teachers, 31 per cent. elementary teachers and 7 per cent. administrators.

The types of placements for each year can be seen in Table VI. The percentage of high-school teachers remained fairly constant at 60 per cent. for each year. Elementary placements dropped from 35 per cent. in 1930 to 18 per cent. in 1933. Administrative placements increased from 5 per cent. in 1930 to 11 per cent. in 1933. This may be due to a number of fac-

TABLE V

PLACEMENT IN POSITIONS OF DIFFERENT TYPES, 1928–1933

| Placement bureau | Total placement | Teachers: Rural Number | Rural Per cent. | Elementary Number | Elementary Per cent. | High-school Number | High-school Per cent. | Administrator Number | Administrator Per cent. | Others Number | Others Per cent. |
|---|---|---|---|---|---|---|---|---|---|---|---|
| Calif. (N. D.)* | 2,167 | — | — | 540 | 24.9 | 1,426 | 65.8 | 184 | 8.5 | 17 | .8 |
| Calif. (S. D.) | 1,683 | — | — | 664 | 39.4 | 905 | 53.8 | 70 | 4.2 | 44 | 2.6 |
| Michigan | 114 | 3 | 2.6 | 18 | 15.8 | 80 | 70.2 | 12 | 10.5 | 1 | .9 |
| Montana | 158 | 12 | 7.6 | 45 | 28.5 | 82 | 51.9 | 19 | 12.0 | — | — |
| Total | 4,122 | 15 | .4 | 1,267 | 30.7 | 2,493 | 60.5 | 285 | 6.9 | 62 | 1.5 |

(Type of Official: Teachers, Administrator, Others)

* California does not keep a record of rural placements.

TABLE VI

NUMBER OF PLACEMENTS IN DIFFERENT DIVISIONS EACH YEAR 1929–1933 INCLUSIVE

| Year | Total | Teachers: Rural Number | Rural Per cent. | Elementary Number | Elementary Per cent. | High-school Number | High-school Per cent. | Administrators Number | Administrators Per cent. | Others Number | Others Per cent. |
|---|---|---|---|---|---|---|---|---|---|---|---|
| 1929 | 1,039 | 2 | .2 | 329 | 31.7 | 628 | 60.4 | 72 | 6.9 | 8 | .8 |
| 1930 | 1,098 | 0 | .0 | 382 | 34.8 | 654 | 59.6 | 57 | 5.2 | 5 | .4 |
| 1931 | 999 | 4 | .4 | 314 | 31.4 | 590 | 59.1 | 72 | 7.2 | 19 | 1.9 |
| 1932 | 542 | 4 | .7 | 161 | 29.7 | 338 | 62.4 | 37 | 6.8 | 2 | .4 |
| 1933 | 444 | 5 | 1.1 | 81 | 18.3 | 283 | 63.7 | 47 | 10.6 | 28 | 6.3 |
| Total | 4,122 | 15 | .4 | 1,267 | 30.7 | 2,493 | 60.5 | 285 | 6.9 | 62 | 1.5 |

(Type of Official: Teachers, Administrators, Others)

tors. The bureaus may concentrate on specialized positions or the relative number of available elementary teachers is greater than that of administrators. The economic depression may have caused more hiring of local applicants for elementary positions and at the same time it may have caused more shifting in the administrative positions.

### BUREAU'S FINANCIAL STATUS

At the present time all the placement bureaus are either completely independent financially or else they receive a relatively small subsidy from their association. In some, this subsidy takes the form of a cash transfer. In others the associations pay part or all of the overhead, such as salary, rent, heat and light.

### SUMMARY

The following summary and conclusions are drawn from a study of the data compiled from questionnaires sent to managers of bureaus of state associations, of school administrators in Montana, of representatives of units of the University of Montana and of commercial agencies.

(1) Those state associations which conduct well-organized self-supporting placement bureaus are performing a service to a limited number of teachers and administrators. Indications are not clear as to the success or failure of the project. Some bureaus are placing a relatively large number of candidates at a low cost to the person placed. Others place very few at a high cost to the association.

(2) Success or failure of the bureau probably depends upon several factors. The teachers and administrators must take a personal interest in the association and they must have confidence in its officers. A hint of political favoritism will do irreparable harm to the bureau. If the manager takes an active interest in the management of the bureau rather than turn such duties over to an inexperienced office clerk the bureau is more likely to succeed.

(3) Harmony and cooperation must exist between all placement agencies. A closer plan of coordination should, in most cases, be worked out between the placement agencies of the institutions of higher learning and the bureaus of state associations. State institutions should, probably, confine themselves to their own graduates, leaving the experienced teacher members to the state associations.

(4) Both a fee and a commission seem to be the best practise, the fee to be small in order to allow all to join who deserve help and a commission high enough to pay the bureau's costs. The tendency is to make this commission higher within the past few years.

(5) The association in fairness to its membership should not place undue emphasis or grant too large a subsidy to the bureau. After all, a very low percentage of the members of the association are benefited by the bureau.

(6) There is a logical basis for the contention that all placing service should be rendered by the state department of education. This department has charge of the certification of teachers and since placement is simply refined certification they should also be responsible for this service at no cost to the teacher, the public supporting the bureau. In many cases this is not possible. Legal provision is lacking, the state department lacks funds and help and, in some states, politics is apt to color the work. Until such time when society shall have provided a satisfactory economics for its teachers the placement bureaus of state associations will probably have an adequate service to perform for its members.

WILBUR E. MOSER
STANFORD UNIVERSITY

## NEW BOOKS IN EDUCATION

COLE, LUELLA. *Psychology of the Elementary School Subjects.* Pp. xvi + 330. Farrar and Rinehart. $2.00.

COLEMAN, ALGERNON. *Experiments and Studies in Modern Language Teaching.* Pp. xi + 367. University of Chicago Press.

*Course of Study in Science for Grades Seven, Eight and Nine.* Pp. 100. Illustrated. Department of Public Instruction, Commonwealth of Pennsylvania, Harrisburg.

JUDD, CHARLES H. *Education and Social Progress.* Pp. xii + 285. Harcourt, Brace. $2.00.

LAPP, C. J. and others. *Review of Pre-College Mathematics.* Pp. 124. Scott, Foresman.

MORGAN, JOHN J. B. *Child Psychology.* Revised edition. Pp. xii + 502. Farrar and Rinehart. $3.00.

MULLER, HELEN M., Compiler. *The Reference Shelf.* Vol. IX, No. 8: *Federal Aid for the Equalization of Educational Opportunity.* Pp. 121. Wilson.

YOWELL, STELLA. *Robert's School.* Pp. 124. Illustrated. Wheeler. $0.60.

# SCHOOL AND SOCIETY

**WITH WHICH ARE COMBINED THE EDUCATIONAL REVIEW, ESTABLISHED IN 1891, THE TEACHERS MAGAZINE, ESTABLISHED IN 1878, AND THE SCHOOL JOURNAL, ESTABLISHED IN 1874.**

Volume 40 — SATURDAY, OCTOBER 6, 1934 — Number 1032

## FEDERAL SUPPORT FOR PUBLIC SCHOOLS

By Professor JESSE B. SEARS

STANFORD UNIVERSITY

FOR the first time the people of this country are in despair over their schools and are calling to the Federal Government for help. Is this a passing storm or does such a call presage the beginning of a new policy affecting school support? If we accept national support, does that mean the disappearance of the little community school, in favor of a vast bureaucratic system, spreading out from Washington? In view of recent events these considerations can not be passed lightly. I shall try to answer three questions: (1) Are we now facing a serious emergency that requires national aid? (2) Aside from this emergency, can the situation be met, or is national aid a permanent necessity? (3) If we accept national support, must we also accept national control?

### I. ARE THE SCHOOLS NOW IN SERIOUS NEED?

Here are some facts recently assembled by the U. S. Office of Education and the research department of the National Education Association. This year we have a million more high-school students than we had in 1930; but we have 52,000 less teachers. A study of 393 cities shows a 33 per cent. reduction in school budgets since 1930, and school-building expenditures have been reduced by 80 per cent. This year one fourth of our teachers receive less pay than the minimum received by a factory hand under the NRA codes. Two hundred thousand teachers are now receiving yearly salaries of less than $750, and 85,000 are receiving less than $450. On January 1, 1934, some 2,600 schools, affecting 140,000 children, closed their doors for want of funds, and by April 1 estimates indicated that 120,000 rural schools, caring for 1,000,000 children, were closed. Careful estimates indicated that for this school year 2,280,000 of our children received not one day of schooling and that another 800,000 were in school not to exceed four or five months.

These facts show that the financial structure of our schools is not able to withstand the strain of a serious depression. In former depressions Mr. Royce Pitkin has shown that in almost every instance the schools not only withstood the shock, but meantime actually increased their expenditures and their enrolments. We must admit that America's front line of defense for free schools is now broken.

Obviously, this situation must be met. Shall we meet it by alteration of present plans and by applying principles of efficiency; or shall we accept the principle of national support or both? Surely there is something new and strange and dangerous in the situation as it stands.

### II. Does This Call for More than Emergency Treatment by the Federal Government?

Let us consider whether this situation is temporary or whether something basic has given way in our plan of support. Again, I resort to figures. In 1870, 57 per cent. of our 5- to 17-year-old children were enrolled in school; by 1900 this had reached 72 per cent.; and by 1930, 81.3 per cent. Our high-school enrolments accounted for but 1.2 per cent. of these children in 1870; but by 1900 this had grown to 3.3 per cent. and by 1930 to 17.1 per cent. Colleges show even greater growth. Again note: In 1870 the school year was 132.2 days in length; by 1900 it had grown to 144.3 days, and by 1930 to 172.7 days.

Meantime, what of the school program? Figures can not serve us here, but I remind you that in the past fifty years the school has changed its entire philosophy. It was looking mainly backward when this century opened; now it looks forward. It was a mere conservator of culture; now it is an instrument of social progress. School laboratories, libraries, studios, shops, assembly halls, gymnasia and play fields reflect these changes.

All these expansions have been expensive. In 1870 our school properties were valued at $130,000,000, while to-day they are worth above $6,000,000,000. In the last decade alone these values almost trebled. In 1920 our schools were in debt for these buildings to the extent of less than one fourth their value; by 1930 the debt had grown to one third, a shift from $54 to $114 per pupil. Now we are informed that 259 districts have already defaulted on their school bonds. Current costs have likewise mounted. In 1920 operating costs were $864,000,000 and in 1930, $1,843,000,000—an increase of over 100 per cent. Our states spent $1.74 per capita on education in 1919 and $4.55 in 1930; and our cities spent $6.88 per capita in 1919 and $16.28 in 1930.

It is not to the size, however, but to the rate of growth, in these figures that I invite your attention. I have found no evidence that, as totals, they are too large for this country to bear; but, with the virtual establishment of national child labor laws, this expansion is not yet ended. Further, with assurance that we must continuously maintain a large population of unemployed, we must expect further expansion of work in adult education. It will be some years, therefore, before we reach the point where the ratio of school to total population is constant. Till then, school costs must rise.

But how do these rising costs look when set beside our figures on wealth and income? The total value of agricultural property in the country decreased between 1920 and 1930 by 26.5 per cent. Please remember this in connection with the fact of local support for schools. The value of manufactured products in the United States increased less than 12 per cent. in the decade from 1919 to 1929, and the value of products from our mines and quarries by less than 3 per cent. The examples suggest no such rapid growth as we have seen in school expenditures. But what of net incomes? The National Bureau of Economic Research has established the total national income as 29.5 billions in 1909 and 89.5 billions in 1928. That is over 200 per cent. increase in 19 years; and when corrected for change in dollar value it still represents 72 per cent. increase.

I shall make no pretense at great precision by placing figures on rate of growth in school costs over against rate of increase in national income. A 100 per cent. increase in school expense in 10 years against a 48 per cent. increase in national income does not indicate that the schools are going to lead us to bankruptcy. After all, we are spending only from 2 to 2.5 per cent. of our national income on schools.

The difficulty lies, not in these cost totals; it lies rather in the fact that school costs are not pooled on a national scale; they are paid for mainly by the local community. This would be well enough if wealth and income were evenly spread over the country on a parallel with the spread of school children, and if the tax burden for schools were spread evenly upon our wealth and earnings; but neither of these is so. In some states more than 95 per cent. of school costs are borne by the local district. Thus, while the poor district is burdened with taxes the wealthy district scarcely feels it; further, with the outworn general properties tax, rural properties can not escape taxation, while vast amounts of city wealth, being hidden, do escape.

The solution of this question lies, first, in discarding the general properties tax; nor should it be replaced by a tax that is equally noxious, as we have done in California. A second move for solution lies in replacing our antiquated system of small district organization. We must have a larger pooling of effort. We have talked for years about equal burden and equal opportunity in education; about taxing wealth where it is, to support schools where they are; but we cling to the machinery and methods of pre-industrial revolution days. Aside from the present crisis, we should not seek national support for schools until we have applied these two remedies. Let us first reconstruct the tax system, so that the burden will be in alignment with ability to bear it; and, second, let us do away with inefficient and expensive small school districts, placing the burden of school support mainly upon the state, where it obviously belongs. After this we may well consider federal aid.

Let us see how the states actually vary. In 1930 Illinois ran schools for 188.4 days, while Mississippi had but 133.4 days. That year the people of Georgia spent but $31.89 per pupil for schools, while in Nevada they spent $136.18. The increase in cost per pupil in the decade 1920 to 1930 ranged from 3.3 per cent. in one state to 149.6 per cent. in another. The value of school property in 1930 ranged from $72 per child in Georgia to $400 per child in California. These figures show that *we do not have equal educational opportunities throughout the country.*

Is this from choice or from necessity? One has only to look at the various states—their natural resources, the occupations of their people, the density and distribution of their populations—to know that there are vast differences in wealth and in ability to produce wealth, from state to state. The studies of the National Bureau of Economic Research confirm these impressions when they show a per capita net income in one state of $147 and in another of $954. The wealth per child in the states in 1930 ranged from $4,000 to $31,000. Accordingly, we must face the fact that *some states can not have good schools, because the cost is too great.*

If we accept the principle of equal educational opportunity from state to state, as well as within a state; acknowledge that in normal times we do not have this by far; and further admit that we can not have it without imposing a very inequitable burden upon the people of the poorer states; then the only sound conclusion is that there is a proper place for federal aid as a means of equalizing the burden between states.

### III. Does Federal Help Imply a Questionable Change in Policy?

First, this present crisis. The Federal Government has recognized that the schools are helpless, and it has answered the command of the people to help them. Through the Public Works Administration schools are obtaining funds for meeting their school-building needs. Through the Civil Works Administration sums are being granted for building and for repairs.

Also, through the Federal Emergency Relief Administration funds are being made available for the reemployment of teachers and for sending men to college. That is, we have declared and are treating the present school situation as a national emergency. This must continue, at least through this year and next.

And now, has the Federal Government ever helped the schools before? Yes, in 1785 we set aside the 16th section grants of land for the support of schools. In 1862, through the Morrill Act, grants were made for founding our state universities. In 1887, through the Hatch Act the government provided money for establishing agricultural experiment stations. Among important recent items is the Smith-Hughes Act of 1917.

What have these experiences involved in the matter of control of the schools? For the township grants, practically nothing; in the land grants for colleges the government specified training in agriculture and the mechanical arts, and they required military training. This does represent a type of control. The Smith-Hughes Act involved matching a state fund for a specific kind of school service. Here is even more control.

Do these cases represent a progression toward more and more federal control? The answer is yes; and this is a bad tendency. In their effect, however, these grants have all been recognized as highly useful and as in no serious way interfering with the freedom of the state. Personally, however, I do not look with favor upon conditional gifts by the Federal Government to the states. I think our entire history warns against this.

How, then, can we use federal support for schools? In two ways: First, by the highest possible leadership in research, publicity and advice; and second, by direct grants to states, of funds devoted to the task of equalizing the burden of cost for schools. How can these things be done? The first, by greatly increasing the budget of the Office of Education. Let us place more creative scholarship in that office. The second, by establishing a minimum program of instruction to be applied in all states. After each state shall have made a specified sacrifice to raise the money for such program, then apply federal funds to bring it up to this minimum. This can be done between states, as it must be done within each state, in accordance with a statistical formula that is wholly impersonal and which would work automatically.

To sum up what I have said:

(1) America's schools are in desperate need of emergency help. Federal help is now available, and we must continue this help through this year and next.

(2) The cost of schools is growing, and must grow, if we face problems of unemployment, child labor, public health and the American standard of living as we should.

(3) School costs are inequitably borne to-day, and represent a desperate burden upon thousands of districts, and upon many states; first, because of an antiquated tax system; and second, because of an antiquated system of school organization and finance. To revise both of these evils is emphatically step one toward a permanent solution of this problem.

(4) Recent trends in ratio of school costs to wealth and earnings clearly imply that if we are to have equality of educational opportunity for America's future citizens, we must utilize federal support.

(5) America should never give up the principle of state control of education nor the idea that a school is essentially a local enterprise in character. In accepting federal aid, therefore, support and control must part company.

(6) Federal aid should come, first, by enlargement of present service; and second, by financial help; this latter to be

granted as an outright gift to the state for schools, and with no other condition. Amounts made available should be determined by a formula, designed to equalize cost as between states, in terms of a minimum standard program of education.

# EDUCATIONAL EVENTS

## THE EDUCATION IN LONDON OF CHILDREN WITH DEFECTIVE EYESIGHT

THE board of education of London, according to a correspondent of the *Journal* of the American Medical Association, has issued a report on the education of partially sighted children. Schools for them are of much more recent origin than schools for the blind. They began in 1908 with the formation of a "myope class" in London, and the policy of schools for the partially sighted has since rapidly spread all over the world. Myopia is by far the most important condition for admission to these schools. It is generally held that faulty posture in reading and writing, poor illumination and excessive convergence of the eyes, such as may occur in reading small print or doing fine needlework, increase myopia and are only too common in ordinary schools. Evidence was given by ophthalmic surgeons that rapid progress of myopia may be arrested if close work is stopped and attention given to the general health. By reducing the factors causing undue stress on the eyes, some decrease or arrest of the progress of the myopia can be produced, but the result is not always permanent. Some evidence was given that the educational restrictions due to attendance at a special school were not always justified by the results. The committee arrived at the following conclusions: 1. If the eyes show fundus changes indicative of serious myopia, the child should always be admitted to a special school. 2. In the absence of such changes the child should usually be admitted if (*a*) after repeated examinations the myopia is found to be increasing at the rate of more than 1 diopter per annum; (*b*) after a period of slow rate of increase or apparent arrest there is a sudden rise in the rate of progress to more than 2 diopters per annum. 3. The actual amount of myopia should not be the sole factor in determining whether or not a child should be sent to a special school. 4. The age of the child must be taken into account. The younger, the more serious are factors such as the degree of myopia and its rate of progress. In doubtful cases the history of myopia in the family may be a deciding factor. 5. Myopic children with a visual acuity after correction of 6/24 or less should be admitted to a special school. Children suffering from damaged eyes due to the disease should not be admitted to these schools so long as there is any inflammation.

Great difference of opinion was manifested with regard to this. One view was that the danger to the sight of myopic children from reading was so great that they should be discouraged from it as much as possible. Another school would allow books under carefully guarded conditions, holding that the risk was not so great as to justify the loss of educational advantages. The committee took a middle course. It recommended that under the age of 8 books should be sparingly used and the main work done on blackboards, which should be supplemented with books printed in 24 point type as far as is advisable. For older children 18 point type need not be prohibited entirely.

The partially sighted are more likely to become unemployed than are those without this disability. But with good personal qualities they can sometimes work their way into permanent posts of value. The committee is averse to specific vocational training, such as is given to the blind. The object should be to educate these children, as far as possible, to compete on equal terms with others.

## THE TEACHING OF SCIENCE IN THE SCHOOLS

A COMMITTEE of the American Chemical Society has been appointed to study the technical restrictions which tend to exclude scientific men from teaching science in the schools.

Professor Ross A. Gortner, of the University of Minnesota, has been named chairman of the committee, other members of which are: Professor R. E. Swain, Stanford University, *vice-chairman;* F. W. Sullivan, Jr., of the Standard Oil Company of Indiana; Professor Harold C. Urey, Columbia University, and Professor W. L. Evans, the Ohio State University.

It is pointed out that the requirement in many states that teachers in high schools regardless of their training in a particular subject, can not be appointed unless they have had a prescribed number of courses in schools of education is developing a dangerous situation not only for chemistry but for the various sciences, the languages and other subjects. The result, it is said, is becoming more and more intolerable, for it brings into the colleges and universities boys and girls both improperly and insufficiently trained.

The committee has been instructed "to consider the question of the requirements of professional educational courses for chemists entered for the degree of A.B., B.S., A.M., M.S. or Ph.D. before such individuals can teach in high schools." It was also authorized "to enlist the cooperation of other interested societies in studying this situation and formulating a program."

Failure of many universities and colleges to maintain adequate departments for training in chemistry is condemned editorially in the October number of *Industrial and Engineering Chemistry,* a publication of the American Chemical Society, of which Dr. Harrison E. Howe is editor. The editorial reads in part:

Obviously the American Chemical Society can not go to the authorities, the president, or the dean of a school, and make direct recommendations. It would be dangerous to compile an official list of individuals regarded as those from whom department heads and full professors should be chosen. That is not what we have in mind.

We do believe, however, that now and then the time and the occasion present themselves when, in the friendliest spirit of cooperation, some one officially representing the society could approach the responsible official of an institution and express the grave concern of the profession over the noticeable trends in the department of chemistry.

Such an emissary could tactfully disclose the yardstick by which the performance of the department in question can be assured, could indicate the weak spots developing, and could in fact encourage the official by this very display of unprejudiced, impersonal, yet deep concern lest an important center deteriorate. Advice can be forced on no group, any more than a people can be made righteous by legislation, but that does not excuse us from calling attention to defects.

The American Chemical Society, representing our fundamental science in these United States, can not afford to stand idly by and see any weakness develop, whether in our centers of education, in the industry that depends upon our science, or in the activities of its members in pertinent social, political and economic problems.

## HARVARD UNIVERSITY FILM SERVICE AND THE FINE ARTS THEATER OF BOSTON

THE Adult Education Council of Greater Boston has announced that with the cooperation of George Kraska, manager of the Fine Arts Theater, it will provide, as reported in the *Boston Evening Transcript,* programs at that theater which will do what heretofore has been merely talked of.

Beginning on October 4, the Fine Arts Theater will amplify its programs from the resources of the University Film Service (the old Harvard Film Foundation), the film library of the University of Chicago, and that of Erpi, by which name Electric Research Products, Inc., is known.

Professor Kirtley F. Mather, of Harvard University, president of the council, said in making the announcement:

The Adult Education Council of Greater Boston has embarked on a project with reference to the movies and has secured the cooperation of the University Film Service and the Fine Arts Theater. People are apt to forget in the furore over evil films that there are many good ones. Most movements such as the League of Decency are destructive because they merely say keep away from the movies. The council is interested in constructive action that will give a chance to show the good in pictures. I am in sympathy with the opposition of the league to bad pictures, but there are many pictures that give enjoyment and enlightenment at the same time and that besides giving an hour and a half of pleasure afford also a deeper understanding of the world we live in.

The council through its motion picture committee will sponsor the programs at the Fine Arts beginning on October 4. The programs will be arranged by Mr. Kraska in cooperation with the committee. The committee will have the right to veto any suggestion made by Mr. Kraska although there is no reason to suppose that such action will be necessary. Every program will be sponsored by the committee.

The motion picture industry has wonderful resources that have never reached the public because the first run theaters want Mae West. At the Fine Arts there will be a full length feature film as in the past, either a foreign film or one made in Hollywood, selected for entertainment, excellence of acting and subject-matter. We are not interested in selecting pictures merely because they will not offend; we are interested in pictures that will be enlightening as well as entertaining.

The Adult Education Council of Greater Boston was formed early this year and is a branch of a national organization. At its first meeting it was addressed by Dr. John H. Finley, of *The New York Times,* president of the New York Adult Education Council. It represents all interests in the field of adult education in Boston and looks at education from the community point of view rather than from that of an institution. Its purpose is to study, stimulate and coordinate such present and contemplated educational leisure-time programs for adults within the Boston metropolitan area as may tend to promote individual development and effectiveness in the social order.

Last spring the council formed a radio division with Dr. Harlow Shapley chairman and put on programs dealing with vocational guidance and travel, six or eight talks in each, particularly directed toward students graduating and uncertain as to their next step and to people preparing for summer travel abroad.

The most active division has been that on cooperation with the CCC camps which have been visited in an attempt to discover needs on vocational guidance and to outline courses of reading preparatory to return of men from the camps to the average world.

The movement for a motion picture division started this summer. The special committee to study motion pictures is composed of Edward Dewey, *chairman,* Kirtley F. Mather, William Stearns, Father Michael Ahern, S.J., Elizabeth Pigeon, James Rollins Brewster, George Kraska, Dr. Abraham Krasker. Dr. Krasker, director of visual education in the Quincy public schools and instructor in visual education at Boston University, suggested a year ago the establishment of a college of motion pictures. Behind the committee there will be a large group of sponsors, about a hundred prominent citizens representing the whole field of community interests.

## PROVISION AT YALE UNIVERSITY FOR STUDENTS OF SPECIAL ABILITY

At Yale University special attention is now being given to the aptitudes of individual students. As a result, the faculty has made it possible for a freshman of special ability to move from school directly into work more advanced than the regular freshman year curriculum. The boy of exceptional training in English, for example, may start in sophomore courses and go forward as rapidly as he can, thus escaping the boredom which exceptional students sometimes feel in repeating in their first year in college material with which they are already familiar. According to President James Rowland Angell, "the development of this idea of placement in college, for which the stage at Yale has been carefully set, seems to offer great possibilities in breaking what has sometimes been called 'the academic lock step.' Certainly this move has been received with enthusiasm in the better schools, where in the past teaching has sometimes suffered from the looming up of the stone wall of freshman year."

This program is being put into full effect with the present freshman class of 775 students, which includes the highest ranking scholars from thirty-four of the leading secondary schools of the country and which has 163 students who ranked in the highest tenth of their respective classes. More than one third of its members, because of unusual ability, has been permitted to undertake work in subjects more advanced than the regular freshman courses. Last year about twelve per cent. of the entering class took one or more advanced courses. In addition, there were enrolled in the "freshman honors courses," twenty-one in English, forty-eight in history, fifty-two in mathematics, eighteen in chemistry and seventeen in Latin.

These "honors courses" for first-year men have attracted much interest. The special class in freshman English, for instance, covered the essentials of both freshman and sophomore English, and students who completed this course were qualified to take the work of junior English at the end of the freshman year. The classes in history took the form of two special courses which dealt with "Renaissance and Reformation" and "Economic Development of Modern Europe." One or two instructors did seminar work with some of their better students, who were excused from regular classroom appointments in order to pursue individual study.

Recent developments in the curricula of the undergraduate schools provide closer association between student and teacher. About half the students in Yale College may be released, if they desire, from a portion of their classroom work in their junior and senior years, in order to pursue more independently and intensively studies in their favorite subject. Members of the undergraduate faculties assist in this work. The teacher may have general friendly oversight of the student's work, sometimes for three years, with an opportunity to shape his education into a coherent intellectual experience.

## CHILD LABOR DAY

FOLLOWING a custom of nearly thirty years, the National Child Labor Committee has designated the last week-end of January for the observance of Child Labor Day. The key-note this year will be ratification of the Federal Child Labor Amendment. The statement given below has been issued by the committee.

The abolition of child labor in the major industries of the country through the NRA codes has won universal approval. But the codes are temporary—for the period of the emergency only. It is unthinkable that a single inch of the ground gained during these years of depression should be lost. Yet if the Amendment is not ratified and Congress thus empowered to pass a Federal Child Labor Law, a return of child employment must be expected when the codes expire. As soon as employers are once more free to hire children and pay them as little as they please, ''cheap'' child labor will flourish again.

For well over a century, effort has been made to control child labor through state legislation. But while some states have forged ahead, others have lagged far behind in measures to prevent child exploitation. Even to-day there are *nine* states which, through harmful exemptions in their statutes, permit children *under the age of 14* to work in industries, in some cases manufacturing industries, even during school hours. *Eight* states permit children under 16 to work from *nine to eleven hours per day*, and *eleven* states permit children under 16 to work *until 8 p. m. or later*.

Not even the spectacle of millions of unemployed adults clamoring in vain for jobs which mean bread and butter for their families has induced the states to take children out of the labor market. They fear to take the step alone and thus subject their industries to competition with those of states which still permit ''cheap'' children to be employed. As recently as 1933 when unemployment was at its peak, bills to raise to 16 years the age for full-time employment were introduced in 11 states and rejected in all but 2. But only a few months later when 16 years was established as the minimum age for employment *on a national basis* through the emergency industrial codes, it received the unanimous acclaim of industry everywhere.

Federal legislation applying equally to all parts of the country is the only effective method of securing the permanent elimination of child labor from this country once and for all. Twice Federal Child Labor laws have been passed, but the United States Supreme Court has held them unconstitutional. The Federal Child Labor Amendment, now before the states for ratification, is merely an enabling act specifically empowering Congress to legislate on the subject.

Child Labor Day is a fitting time to arouse public interest in this measure, which has been ratified by 20 states. Its progress has aroused those who see their right to employ children placed in jeopardy, and a tremendous campaign of misrepresentation has been launched which must be overcome by making known the correct facts.

The National Child Labor Committee whose headquarters are at 419 Fourth Avenue, New York City, will send a poster, leaflets and other material on the Amendment on receipt of 25 cents for postage.

## THE NATIONAL COUNCIL OF BUSINESS EDUCATION

BUSINESS teachers represent the last major group of teachers to organize a national council. This was accomplished last December at Cincinnati, Ohio.

This council is a federation of national, regional, state and local associations of business teachers. Each affiliated association is entitled to two representatives on the council.

The distinctive function of the council is to

formulate national policies of business education, and then to submit such policies to the member associations for vote. All policies of the council are thus subject to the acceptance or veto of any member association. This procedure is similar to that of the Federal Government in submitting a proposed constitutional amendment to the several states for express action of their legislatures. When such a proposed amendment has been ratified by three fourths of the several states, it becomes a part of the constitution or fundamental law of the nation. Similarly, when proposed council policies are ratified by the several affiliated associations, such policies become the national policies of business education formulated by organized groups of business educators and designed to govern the relations of this important field of education with the other fields of education, with business, and the other major interests of our modern complex social-economic life.

The need of such a council in business education is generally recognized by those in business and in education. The perfecting of a council organization which will best serve to meet this need is still in process of organization. Six standing committees have been appointed by the president of the council for the purpose of collecting points of view from all sections of the country as to the kind of organization which will most fairly and representatively serve every member association.

A printed folder available on October 1, and can be had by writing to the secretary, Miss Helen Reynolds, Ohio University, Athens, Ohio. This folder will explain the purpose, nature and program of the council, and will give the names of the eleven associations which have already become affiliated members in the brief time since last March when the present administration began its organizational work. Each national, regional and state association of business teachers, not already a member, will be addressed by the secretary soon after October 1, urging it to become fully informed about the purpose and work of the council and ultimately to affiliate with it in bringing about unity of effort in business education in matters of national policy.

The officers of the council are: *President,* Paul S. Lomax, New York University, New York, N. Y.; *Vice-president,* Ray Abrams, Samuel J. Peters High School of Commerce, New Orleans, Louisiana; *Secretary,* Helen Reynolds, Ohio University, Athens, Ohio; *Treasurer,* A. E. Bullock, supervisor of commercial education, Los Angeles, California.

## THE ASSOCIATION OF COLLEGES AND UNIVERSITIES OF THE STATE OF NEW YORK

The annual meeting of the Association of Colleges and Universities of the State of New York will be held on Thursday, October 18, in the State Education Building at Albany. The theme of the meeting will be "Who Should Go to College and Why." Dr. Henry T. Moore, president of Skidmore College and president of the association, will preside. Papers will be presented by Dr. William Mather Lewis, president of Lafayette College, and Dr. Herbert S. Weet, formerly superintendent of schools at Rochester, N. Y. The opening session will be concluded with a brief business meeting and the election of officers.

At a luncheon session to be held at the Hotel Ten Eyck the principal address will be given by Dr. Walter A. Jessup, president of the Carnegie Foundation for the Advancement of Teaching. College presidents appointed within the year will be introduced.

The association extends a cordial invitation to all delegates to the University Convocation which meets simultaneously at Albany, and especially to superintendents and to principals of elementary and secondary schools to attend the opening session and the luncheon. Reservations for the luncheon may be made in advance with Dr. Harlan H. Horner, Assistant Commissioner for Higher Education.

The program committee consists of Dr. Herbert E. Hawkes, dean of Columbia College, *chairman;* Dr. C. Mildred Thompson, dean of Vassar College, and Dr. George B. Cutten, president of Colgate University.

## INSTALLATION OF THE PRESIDENT OF UNION COLLEGE

Dr. Dixon Ryan Fox will be installed as twelfth president of Union College at exercises to be held on October 11 and 12. He succeeds Dr. Frank Parker Day, who became president in 1929, but retired last year on account of ill health.

The proceedings will open with a "Conference on College Training for Government" on the evening of October 11. Governor Wilbur L. Cross, of Connecticut, formerly professor at Yale University; Joseph D. McGoldrick, controller of New York City, formerly professor and colleague of Dr. Fox at Columbia University, and Dr. Earl E. Cummins, professor of economics at Union College, will participate.

The induction ceremonies will be held on the morning of October 12 in Memorial Chapel. The proceedings will be broadcast. Dr. Nicholas Murray Butler, president of Columbia University, and Dr. Fox will deliver the principal addresses. Dr. Charles Alexander Richmond, president emeritus of Union College, will give the invocation and benediction, and Dr. Hiram C. Todd, of New York, president of the board of trustees, will officially induct Dr. Fox into the presidency.

A luncheon for 1,000 or more delegates from colleges and universities and learned societies will be held in the Alumni gymnasium. Dr. Livingston Farrand, president of Cornell University, and John H. Finley, of *The New York Times,* are among the speakers whose addresses will be broadcast.

An exhibition, featuring the history of Union College, is being prepared. Numerous valuable documents, which will be on display, have been discovered in attics, library storerooms and among possessions of friends of the college. Some of the history of the college will be reinterpreted in the light of the new material which has been catalogued by Codman Hislop during the summer. The exhibition will portray a student's room as it appeared about 1825. It will include the figure of a student dressed in the period; rooms containing the memorabilia of the six fraternities, founded at Union—Kappa Alpha, Delta Phi, Sigma Phi, Psi Upsilon, Chi Psi and Theta Delta Chi; photographs and biographical sketches of famous alumni and diaries, letters and documents of significant interest.

# EDUCATIONAL NOTES AND NEWS

THE New York City Board of Education has elected Jacob Greenberg, director of foreign languages in the junior high schools, as associate superintendent of schools to fill the vacancy created last February by the elevation of Dr. Harold G. Campbell to the office of Superintendent of Schools.

DR. TYLER DENNETT, who became the tenth president of Williams College this year, was formally inducted into office during exercises that were held on October 5. Dr. Dennett succeeds Dr. Harry A. Garfield, son of President Garfield, who relinquished the office last July. The exercises were attended by Governor Herbert H. Lehman of New York and Governor Joseph B. Ely of Massachusetts, who are trustees of the college.

DR. THURSTON J. DAVIES, formerly secretary of the Graduate Council and supervisor of sports at Princeton University, was installed as president of Colorado College on September 18.

THE REV. DR. FRED P. CORSON, who graduated from Dickinson College seventeen years ago, became president of the college on September 29. The installation ceremony will probably be held next June. Dr. Corson succeeds Dr. Karl T. Waugh, who resigned a year ago.

THE REV. DR. FRANK KINGDON has been elected president of Dana College and the affiliated New Jersey Law School and Seth Boyden School of Business. Richard D. Currier, founder and president of the three schools, who resigned recently, expressed the wish that Dr. Kingdon be elected in his place.

DR. CLAUDE HORACK has been appointed dean of the Duke University Law School. He has been a member of the faculty of the school since 1930 and had previously been professor of law at the State University of Iowa.

BAY EDWARD ESTES, JR., and Edwin Lee Morris have been appointed assistant deans at the Harvard Business School.

SIR MICHAEL SADLER will retire from the mastership of University College, Oxford, on December 31, after having held that office for eleven years. The resignation is not due to ill health, but to a desire for more leisure for writing, and in particular for completing the report of the International Institute Examinations Inquiry, of the English Committee of which he is chairman.

CHARLES RICKETSON ALLEN, educational consultant for vocational education, has retired after sixteen years' service with the Federal Board for Vocational Education.

JOHN PIERSOL MCCASKEY, who for fifty-five years was editor of *The Pennsylvania School Journal,* will celebrate his ninety-seventh birthday on October 9.

THE honorary degree of doctor of humane letters will be conferred on Professor Albert Einstein, of the Institute for Advanced Studies at Princeton, N. J., at the opening of Yeshiva College on October 8.

DR. PAUL RUSSELL ANDERSON, formerly associate professor of philosophy and religion at MacMurray College, has been appointed professor of philosophy at Lake Erie College.

EDWARD J. G. ALFORD has been appointed to the new professorship of fine arts at the University of Toronto. Mr. Alford is now a lecturer to post-graduate students of London University at the Courtauld Institute.

DR. CECIL F. MARSHALL, research associate in history at the University of Iowa, has been appointed assistant professor of European history at the University of Idaho to take the place of Professor Jesse E. Retherford, who died on September 6. Other appointments include Edgar W. Voelker, of the University of Michigan, to be assistant professor of sociology. New instructors are: Dr. Michael Peach, agricultural chemistry, from the Ohio State University; Dr. J. Harold Wayland, instructor in mathematics, from the California Institute of Technology, and Dr. Lowell A. Mullen, instructor in botany, from the State College of Washington.

MLLE. MARGUERITE MESPOULET, formerly professor of French at Wellesley College, has joined the faculty of Barnard College as associate professor in French. Mlle. Mespoulet also will be in charge of graduate work in French. She formerly was a visiting lecturer at the college.

ADDITIONS to the faculty of the Miami University School of Business Administration include Katharine M. Betz, associate professor of secretarial studies; Harold A. Baker, instructor in business, and William J. Vatter, instructor in business.

DR. ROBERT H. SEASHORE has been given a year's leave of absence from the University of Oregon to become visiting professor at the University of Southern California. Dr. Lester Beck, of Brown University, will take Dr. Seashore's work during his absence.

THE Harvard Corporation has granted a year's leave of absence to Professor Calvert Magruder, professor of torts and vice-dean of the Law School, that he may accept an appointment by President Roosevelt as counsel to the National Labor Relations Board. Professor Magruder has already taken up his new work.

DR. HOMER H. DUBS, professor of philosophy at Marshall College, is taking a year's leave of absence to engage in research work at the Library of Congress for the Committee on Chinese Studies of the American Council of Learned Societies. He will make a partial translation of one of the Chinese dynastic histories.

JAMES S. OWENS, director of the New York State Probation Division of the Department of Public Welfare, has been appointed Superintendent of the State School of Industry.

DR. DANA Z. ECKERT, formerly director of curriculum study and research, has been appointed principal of the Henry Clay Frick Training School for Teachers, Pittsburgh. He succeeds Herbert L. Spencer, who has been named dean of the college of the University of Pittsburgh.

SIR JOHN ADAMS, professor of education at the University of California at Los Angeles, died on September 29. He was seventy-seven years old and had been at the University of California for three years. Sir John had been president of the Aberdeen Training School and the Glasgow Training School. From 1902 to 1922 he was principal of the London Day Training College and professor of education at the University of London, from which he retired under the age limit with the title of emeritus. He was knighted in 1925.

WINIFRED LOUISE MERCIER, principal of Whitelands Training College since 1918, died on September 2, at the age of fifty-six years. Miss Mercier had been principal of the City of

Leeds Training College and was later lecturer in education at the University of Manchester.

THE ninth annual Bucknell Conference on Education will be held at Lewisburg, Pa., on November 2 and 3. The program is being built around the one-hundredth anniversary of the passing of the Pennsylvania free school law, with emphasis on the development of the curriculum. Prominent in education at the general sessions will be Ben D. Wood, James N. Rule and Homer P. Rainey. The list of general session speakers is incomplete at the time of going to press. The conferences for school directors and parent-teacher association workers are being given special emphasis this year. Both will be held at four o'clock on Friday, November 2. Chairmen of the meetings include James N. Rule, J. Andrew Morrow, Fred W. Diehl, Carl L. Millward, Florence Rollins, Sylvester B. Dunlap, Robert D. Smink, Frederick L. Padgett, Amelia Clark, Stanley S. Galiley, S. H. Ziegler, Charles S. Sanders, Richard B. Vastine, Gordon Highrighter, Paul H. Humphreys, F. W. Walp and Katherine Reed.

"SOCIAL Goals for Secondary Education" is the topic which will be discussed at the tenth Conference on Secondary Education to be held at Teachers College, Temple University, Philadelphia, on October 19 and 20. Conference speakers will include: Boyd H. Bode, the Ohio State University; John L. Childs and I. L. Kandel, Teachers College, Columbia University, and Eduard C. Lindeman, New York School of Social Work. The general topic for six panel discussions is to be "What Are the Earmarks of a Democratic School?" The chairmen who will lead these discussions are: Burton Fowler, head master, Tower Hill School, Wilmington, Del.; Francis M. Garver, University of Pennsylvania; Jesse H. Holmes, Swarthmore College; Ira R. Kraybill, Cheltenham Township High School; John Lester, secretary, Friends Council on Education, Philadelphia, and Sydney V. Rowland, superintendent, Radnor Township schools.

DR. J. B. EDMONSON, dean of the School of Education of the University of Michigan, has announced that a new type of advanced field course in education will be offered this coming year by the staff of the School of Education in cooperation with the University Extension Division. The course is designed to provide an opportunity for critical appraisal of significant studies of selected educational problems and to assist field workers in the application of findings to the improvement of practice in the schools. It will be administered through the Extension Division of the university with sections of the course offered in seven cities of the state. There will be eight meetings of the course with afternoon and evening sessions. The course will consist of four units, each of which will be presented by a committee of two members of the staff of the School of Education. The four units are as follows: The Improvement of Reading in Elementary and Secondary Schools; The Diagnosis of Behavior Problems of Pupils; The Technique of Instruction for Slow Normal Pupils; The Appraisal and Redirection of Extra-Curricular Activities. The course is intended primarily for those who are engaged in administrative or supervisory work. It is anticipated that more than 50 per cent. of the professional leadership in the schools of Michigan will be reached through this course. A similar course will be offered in 1935–1936 comprising new units of instruction.

WITH the opening of the fall semester of the University of Southern California on September 24 the School of Social Welfare offers a graduate program leading to the degree of master of science in social work, the only such graduate study available in the Southwest, according to Dr. Emory S. Bogardus, director. In addition to the advanced college degree the course of study will qualify the student to receive the provisional certificate in social work authorized by the American Association of Schools of Social Work. The American Association of Schools of Social Work and the American Association of Social Workers have cooperated in jointly determining a program which demands that training in social work be brought rapidly to the same level as for such professions as law, medicine and teaching. The latter organization now requires its members to possess a specific college training, eligibility to membership being impossible through experience alone. Admission to the new graduate program requires the applicant to possess a bachelor's degree with a prescribed amount of undergraduate courses in sociology.

An enrolment of 7,301 students in Harvard University for the current academic year was announced at the close of registration. The total number last year was 7,467. This year's figure is expected to be slightly increased by late registrations. The enrolment in Harvard College is 3,552, as compared to 3,429 last year, freshmen numbering 1,031. Other university figures are:

| | *1934–35* | *1933–34* |
|---|---|---|
| Graduate School of Arts and Sciences | 650 | 757 |
| Medical School | 504 | 507 |
| Dental School | 130 | 121 |
| Law School | 1,422 | 1,413 |
| Business School | 689 | 788 |
| School of Education | 94 | 116 |
| School of Architecture | 45 | 47 |
| Engineering School | 110 | 163 |
| Divinity School | 46 | 54 |
| Landscape Architecture | 15 | 27 |
| School of Public Health | 18 | 17 |
| School of City Planning | 10 | 9 |
| Special Students | 16 | 23 |

The decline in registration in the Engineering School is in line with the recommendation of the faculty of engineering that undergraduates interested in engineering register in Harvard College to obtain a broad general education before beginning their graduate engineering study.

The education committee of the English-Speaking Union of the United States for the current school year has announced through Miss Elizabeth Patch, secretary of the committee, five exchanges for one year between British and American teachers. These include Miss Margaret Coats, of Glasgow, Scotland, who will teach at the Central High School, Tulsa, Okla. She is the third British teacher to visit Tulsa under an exchange teacher arrangement, and Miss Else M. Andrews, of Farnham, Surrey, England, who is changing places with Miss Frances Failing, of the George Washington High School, Indianapolis, Ind. Additional exchanges have been made between Miss B. M. Punter, of Enfield, Middlesex, and Miss Alice M. Connor, of the Commercial High School, New Haven; between Miss M. L. H. Gilchrist, of Glasgow, and Miss Florence Williams, of the Central High School, Flint, Mich., and between Miss Ellen Cumber, of London, and Miss Harriet Howard, of Northfield Seminary, Massachusetts. The exchange sthis year bring to twenty-seven the number of such arrangements made with a similar committee in England since 1925.

The Federal Emergency Relief Administration has made another grant of $13,000, to continue the pre-school centers and the afternoon opportunity schools of Boston. This will furnish employment for teachers who can show actual need. All unemployed teachers who are residents of Boston, whether or not their names appear on the list of candidates eligible for appointment to the Boston service, may apply for assignment to these classes. There will be a change in the manner of selecting teachers, final approval resting with the Federal authorities on the basis of need for welfare relief. Teachers chosen will receive $15 a week.

Backed by the Emergency Relief Administration, the Department of Public Instruction of Wyoming will provide dormitories for rural children of destitute parents who might otherwise be unable to attend high school. It is estimated that between 500 and 600 children, living in districts remote from high schools, will be benefited under the plan, the cost of which is to be repaid by their parents through work on relief projects.

To permit experimental teaching of mathematics in some of the high schools of New York City, five former students of the Institute for Advanced Study at Princeton University have been licensed as substitute teachers of mathematics as a result of a special test given by the New York City Board of Examiners. The five teachers hold Ph.D. degrees and have completed courses in advanced mathematics under Dr. Einstein.

A training course for leaders in Boys' Club work opened its seventeenth consecutive year at the School of Education, New York University, on September 24. This course, sponsored by the Boys' Clubs of America, will be under the direction of R. K. Atkinson, educational director, and Harvey W. Zorbaugh, director of special education in the School of Education. It will provide a study and evaluation of plans and programs that are in operation for dealing with boys in their leisure time under a great variety of auspices. Among those who will appear as lecturers are Roy Smith Wallace, of the National Recreation Association; Mark McCloskey, of the Ethical Culture School; Leonard Mayo, of the New York School of Social Work; Harry Shulman, of the Welfare Council of New York City; Miss Harriett Wright, of the New York Public Library; Palmer Bevis, of the Boys' Club of New York; A. B. Hines, of the Madison Square Boys' Club, and Dr. Anna Y. Reed, Dr. J. B. Nash and Dr. F. M. Thrasher, of the School of Education of New York University.

THE Joint Committee of Teachers Organizations, New York City, announced on September 23 that it had voted to submit to the state conventions of both political parties identical educational planks, as part of a campaign to make sure that the planks adopted pledge adequate safeguards for the schools and the teachers. The plank, prepared by three members of the executive board of the organization, Mrs. May A. Healy, Miss Lillian A. Hatch and Dr. Frederick Houk Law, follows: "The ——— party believes that all the children of the State are entitled to equal educational advantages; and, therefore, (1) That education must be maintained as a State function; (2) That the statutory allotment of State aid must be continued as provided by the Friedsam Commission Act; (3) That the State must continue its control of public education including teachers' salaries; (4) That permanent tenure of positions for teachers is essential to the best interests of the children in the schools; and (5) That, because of the present greatly increased cost of living, steps should be taken immediately to bring about a restoration of the 1932 salaries for teachers and other employees of the Board of Education."

# DISCUSSION

## CONCERNING PROFESSOR BOBBITT'S CRITICISM

THE questioning charges made against the recommendations of the Commission of the Social Studies[1] has prompted me to reread that document. A pronouncement of no less an authority than Professor Franklin Bobbitt can not be dismissed summarily without a most searching consideration. After my first and previous reading I was not aware of the "revolutionary hysteria" imputed to the report by Professor Bobbitt. Even a second reading still leaves me deeply concerned about my own obtuseness in failing to uncover the perfidious meanings detected by Professor Bobbitt. My distress increases as I contemplate Professor Bobbitt's high standing in the field of education and the worthy contributions which he has made to scholarship. My personal chagrin diminishes, however, as his authority is matched with the array of scholarly members of the commission—Beard, Counts, Hayes and others of that level. It is reduced, then, to a matter of choosing between the respected opinions of scholars of equally high rank. If, as Wilson once said, "truth always matches truth," some one must be mistaken.

A second reading of Professor Bobbitt's deprecating rejection of the tenets of the commission forces me to suspect the educator of unwarranted imputations. Charity would prompt me to say that hasty reading may have been responsible. More probably, however, did he yield to a human frailty conducing to reject ideas which do not conform to cherished opinions. We remember that the schoolmen who watched Galileo drop the weights from the Tower of Pisa still believed Aristotle when he said they would fall at different rates. The fathers of the Constitution were considered visionaries by the respectable opinion of the times. Chronological age is sometimes a determinant in an individual's susceptibility to those ideas contradicting stereotyped notions which have been nurtured by social acceptance. "Predominant opinions," said Disraeli, "are the opinions of a class that is vanishing." Men who have been successful under the established rules are reluctant to change those rules. Professor Bobbitt's merited success during an era of economic individualism and acquisitive egoism makes him personally partial to that era. Arnold said, "Men are all tories by nature, when tolerably well off." The history of human progress makes one point unmistakably clear, and that is that change is impeded by the reluctance of the contemporary generations to

[1] SCHOOL AND SOCIETY, August 18.

make the necessary adaptations. The fathers stone the prophets and the children garnish their sepulchers. Lieber said in 1870, "Bismarck proclaims to-day in the Diet the very principles for which we were hunted and exiled fifty years ago." In the light of the foregoing we can understand Professor Bobbitt's tentative rejection of a "frame of reference" which does not conform to his own intuitive credo, acceptable during the era of frontier economy when he evolved his own philosophy of education based on enlightened self-interest. It must be disheartening to see one's published works of a lifetime become obsolescent in a dynamically emerging society. We can justly sympathize without permitting that sympathy to blind our reason in evaluating Professor Bobbitt's resentful indictment.

Let us now examine his disappointment and displeasure with the conclusions of the commission. His first annoyance comes at the commission's use of the term, Collectivism. He is grieved because they avoided the terms, Communism and Fascism, and because they did not name Italy, Germany and Russia as precedents. He does not hesitate to impute bad motive in the use of "favorable euphemisms to avoid popular antagonisms." Therefore, before the professor undertakes to answer the commission, he takes the liberty to reduce all terms to his own mental stereotype, presumably so that his carefully annotated files of ready-made rebuttals might be used without too much adaptation to the real points. Resting heavily upon the special lexicon of the professional patrioteer he employs his whole repertoire of negative sanctions in pummeling his man of straw. "Integration and interdependence" can mean only fascism and communism to Professor Bobbitt, despite the fact that all the dictionaries have apparently overlooked these flexed meanings. However, since there are no syndicated objections to "integration and interdependence," we partly understand the professor's predicament, and sympathize with him in his reiteration of the regimented ideas on regimentation, state paternalism, proletarianism, standardization, wholesale submissiveness, indoctrination, revolutionary trends, etc. "Men are to be nurslings of the state" is the picturesque figure which he uses in restating the recommendations of the commission. "If that is not what the commission means . . . will they explain in a few clear-cut and unambiguous terms exactly what they do mean," demands the confused professor. That is exactly what the commission has done. They have avoided phraseology which means one thing to one sect and something entirely different to another. They rejected the highly charged stereotypes which ignite emotions rather than the mind. Communism has become a label for demagogic opportunists to pin on anything which conflicts with their own interests. It is true that collectivism embraces some of the cooperative techniques of communism without necessarily including the objectionable revolutionary plans and proletarian dictatorship.

To make collectivism mean communism is equivalent to making democracy embrace the outrages of the French Revolution or making governmental systems like that of Chicago include racketeering. In short, Professor Bobbitt objects because the commission chose to be specific and scientific rather than general and unscientific. To me, uninitiated perhaps, words like integration, collective, acquisitive, realistic, individual freedom, functional efficiency, cultural potentialities, many-sided personalities, individuality, creative capacities, etc., are more unequivocal than the words used by the professor to discredit the document.

The most flagrant imputation is that the commission curtly dismisses time-honored democracy without a hearing, thus violating the principles of scientific accuracy. If the commission is clear in one thing, to my thinking, it is that the tradition of popular democracy shall be—not rejected—but *fulfilled.* In addition to the extracts which Professor Bobbitt quoted to support the charge of insincere lip-service, the following excerpt shows the explicit position of the commission on the matter of democracy: "Especially significant, as a conditioning factor in American life, is the well-established national tradition of government and society based on the ideals of popular democracy and of personal liberty and dignity —the tradition that government is organized solely for the purpose of promoting the highest welfare of the governed, collectively and individually, that in all great divisions of economy, administration, and culture the interests of the masses [Professor Bobbitt is alarmed at the implication of "civic degeneracy" in that word] of the people are to be considered paramount, and that, since every person is of moral worth and dignity in himself, no man, woman, or child can be exploited by another without doing violence to the essential spirit of American democracy and liberty" (page 12). Again the commission expressly insists on the retention of democracy "as an accompaniment of the establishment and maintenance of an economically integrated society and as a means of necessary adjustment to new conditions" (page 23). The desirability of the "preservation and the development of individuality in its non-acquisitive expression . . . and the extension to every individual, regardless of birth, class, race, religion, or economic status, of the opportunity for the fullest development of his creative capacities" is aggressively adduced. This in part at least evinces the commission's eager espousal rather than the curt dismissal of democratic principles. Not one word could I find which would warrant a charge of renunciation of democracy, so explicitly alleged by Professor Bobbitt, who then rationalizes by declaring democracy and collectivism irreconcilable. Apparently he can not conceive how a cooperative enterprise can be carried on with the consent of those cooperating. He insists on pointing to Italy and Russia, where dictatorship obtains from above and below, respectively. Dictatorship is the point of variance between the commission's recommendation and the plans of other countries which have become anathema to the conditioned lovers of liberty in America. Both communism and fascism involve autocratic collectivism; the commission projects a democratic collectivism. Collectivism of the process with democratization of purpose might characterize the essential difference between the European precedent and the realistic plan of the commission. Democracy, then, is not to be repudiated by the commission but actually extended to the integrated economy of the emerging society. Democratic control, as now prevalent, has come to affect only the discarded eggshell of the American eagle, which has tended to become a bird of prey as far as a great many wage-slaves are concerned. Extension of the consent of the governed to corporate enterprise would mean a greater fulfilment of the ideals of popular democracy than now obtains under autocratic corporate control, in the opinion of the commission.

Contrary to what Professor Bobbitt would have us believe, the commission does not recommend regimented indoctrination in the education of those who are to enter the new emerging collectivism, but an "enlightened knowledge of realities" and a capacity to cooperate in shaping "the form of that society in accordance with American ideals of popular democracy and personal liberty and dignity." Individualism in its non-acquisitive expression is to be substituted for self-interest. Professor Bobbitt's "frame of reference," from which he educed his philosophy of education, is revealed in his advocacy of "a full self-regimentation, actuated by enlightened self-interest. The function of the school is to attach the needed enlightenment to the self-interest." This needed enlightenment, added to their porcine natures, may account for the activities of our munitions manufacturers and their high-powered salesmen. The commission would put the welfare of the group above the self-interest of any one individual. Is this not democracy? Democratic control must be used to curb, if necessary, the unsocial acquisitive egoism of the individual. Will this produce "nurslings"? It may preclude fatlings. In other words, in a military sense the regiments will determine their own marching orders and will not be subjected to the arbitrary orders of the autocratic industrial colonels. Regimentation for the welfare of the regiments and not for the colonels only will be the new mode. A new social motive is to be substituted for the competitive one in the economic realm. All will cooperate with the aid of technology to gain for every individual freedom from economic stringencies so that all will have time and energy to become culturally what they aspire to be. The commission is expressly "concerned with the development of rich and many-sided personalities capable of cooperating in a social order designed to facilitate the creation of the largest possible number of rich and many-sided personalities." Whether or not this means that men shall become manikins, submissive and meekly compliant to the will of a hostile state, depends upon the perdurance of the democratic techniques in determining our destiny.

In concluding his polemic, Professor Bobbitt attempts to undermine the public confidence in the commission's report by implying that the attitude of the commission was unscientific. He points to the tone of the commission and charges that it is "that of the revolutionary hysteria that grips all the collectivizing nations." He asserts that "the report of the commission is an ominous symptom of unpreparedness on the part of the custodians of the social science to lead the thought required for guiding aright the onward progress of the nation."

A parallel study of the report and its calumniation seems to convict the calumniator of the offenses which are imputed to the members of the commission. At any rate the impassioned rejection of the report by Professor Bobbitt should provoke all to read for themselves the conclusions and recommendations of a commission so significant in the field of interpretative scholarship.

New occasions teach new duties;
Time makes ancient good uncouth.

N. J. Weiss

Albion College

## TEACHING HISTORY OF EDUCATION BY THE LABORATORY-UNIT PLAN

A few months ago there appeared in School and Society an article which challenged the value and purpose of a course in history of education. While there may be no direct carry-over from such a course to the actual teaching of reading, geometry or physics, yet certain lessons in any one of these or other subjects can be better motivated with the background furnished by a comprehensive study of history of education.

When this subject is presented by the laboratory-unit plan the student becomes acquainted with a vast amount of material, some of which can be used in his daily teaching program and all of which develops a "historical consciousness" of the progress of that social institution known as education.

The specific objectives followed in the course taught by the laboratory-unit plan are: (1) To acquaint the student with the most important facts in the development of our school system as it exists to-day. (2) To show the dependence of educational progress upon religious, political, industrial, scientific and economic development. (3) To point out, if possible, ways by which the school may become a dynamic force in bringing about social stability.

The course was organized around six major problems or units, which are: (1) How did the educational program reflect the progressive nature of the Greek Nation? (2) What evidences of the practicability of the Roman People can be found in their educational system? (3) How was learning established and preserved during the Middle Ages? (4) What effect did the Renaissance and Reformation have upon contemporary and modern education? (5) What factors and influences lead to the establishment of state control of education? (6) What is education doing to help meet the present economic and social crisis?

As the name implies, the course was conducted on the laboratory basis. Three semester-hours credit was given for three two-hour periods per week. One of these hours was usually given over to explanation or discussion and the other to supervise study.

A special room was equipped with tables, chairs and book shelves. Two regular texts were used—Cubberley's "A Brief Course in the History of Education" and Monroe's "A Brief History of Education." In addition to these texts all other available material from the college and city libraries were put on the shelves. This included books, bound and current magazines and government bulletins. A count for one semester showed 594 references read by 28 students, or an average of 21 books and magazine articles read by each student in addition to the required text-books.

Approximately three weeks were spent on each unit, during which the students took notes on the readings, the lectures and discussions. At the end of this time the material was organized and in one of the two-hour periods was written in the form of a paper.

The writer has observed the following advantages of the plan: (1) The students take a greater interest in the work. (2) There is more opportunity for correlation with other subjects. (3) An opportunity is provided for knowing the approaches made by different authors. (4) The students learn to collect and organize data pertaining to one central idea or problem. (5) Individual differences are provided for. (6) Present-day trends in education become real issues to the students.

MARY OLA MCCLUSKEY
MORNINGSIDE COLLEGE

# SPECIAL CORRESPONDENCE

## THE PENNINGTON, A FORD SCHOOL

IT is only a one-room school in the very small village of Macon, which is situated in Lenawee County in southern Michigan. There are about ten thousand acres lying about it belonging to Mr. Ford, which he uses for raising soy-beans. The school has about forty pupils and the whole twelve grades. It is organized somewhat on the principle of the Bell Lancaster schools of England with pupil helpers, but it is distinctive and original in nearly every detail.

The building itself represents one of Mr. Ford's hobbies. It was built of cobblestones back in 1851 at a cost of $450.00. It was abandoned in 1866 for the new Macon school, which was twice as large and considered more modern. At this time the old building was sold for $31.50 for storage purposes, and two stores were built in front of it. It remained thus, forgotten by the community, in a general state of dilapidation, until Mr. Ford discovered it in 1931.

Mr. Ford's enthusiasm for antiques is well known. He tore down the two buildings in front and restored the old school to its original condition with the addition of a new slate roof. He heard of Mr. Travis, one of the former pupils and later teacher in the town school, and sent for him to help in the restoration of the interior. He was so much pleased with his local knowledge and educational outlook that he promptly installed him as teacher.

The school has one of the handsomest interiors I have ever seen in any school, but everything is in harmony with the architecture of the period it represents. In the center of the room is a flawless old-time wood stove with a large drum. The desks face the stove from the back and sides. The seats, teacher's desk and window casings are of highly polished black walnut, which was cut from the site and put together with wooden pegs. There is also a black walnut seat running around the room next to the wall, such as was formerly used for recitations. The old-time organ is also of black walnut. The walls are of a dark cream color that harmonizes with the woodwork. The desks and floor are immaculate, as though both had just been washed and rubbed down.

The school is at one end of a square mile of farm land that Mr. Ford has held out of his farm cooperative for special experimenting and whims of his own. There are about eight acres attached to the school, with perhaps five acres under lawn mower for a playground, something like what one would see at Eton or Rugby. At one side is the playground for the little children, with swings, seesaws and other equipment. At the back is a woodlot of ten acres or so that is used at times for school and community picnics. In front of the school is a graveled parking place for about twenty cars. A sidewalk of flat stones leads up to the school building and around on each side to the sanitary toilets in back.

At one side and about two hundred yards back from the road is the old Pennington home with a fine avenue of trees leading up to it, that gives it an almost colonial setting. Mr. Ford has restored it and refurnished it as a pioneer house and uses it to entertain Ford officials and other guests who come to this community.

The curriculum of the school is as interesting and unique as its setting. Mr. Jerome Travis, the teacher, was for many years supervising principal of one of the Toledo high schools. His wife, who assists him, at times, was principal of one of the elementary schools in the same city. There is little teaching in the school. It is essentially a tutorial system, such as has always prevailed in the better English schools and has recently been introduced into the University of Chicago and Yale University. There was about the school a spirit of friendliness and helpfulness such as one seldom sees in a public school. Each child goes ahead in his studies as fast as he is able without waiting for any one else. The big children help the little children if they need it.

The English work has two practical sides. The children conduct the chapel exercises in the morning, and the fifteen Ford schools together publish a magazine, about the size of *Liberty*. Each school has a staff of reporters and sends in news and comment for the bimonthly issues. I have read a number of them and find them interesting and the English exceptionally good.

The children have supervision from Dearborn in music, dancing, nature study and telegraphy. The music supervisor was there at the time we were. We heard the children sing many songs, which were excellent.

Each child is given a garden 60 by 90 feet in dimensions. This is plowed, harrowed, planted and marked for him. He is provided with a hoe and a rake to care for it. All that he raises is his to do with as he chooses.

Mr. Ford is an enthusiast for dancing, and dancing is on the program for all at Pennington. Mr. Ford secured the use of one half of the Macon town school, which had long been unused, and fitted it up as a social hall. Here they have school and community dances and here the morning chapel is held.

The town school is situated about a quarter of a mile from the Pennington, so it makes a short journey to the morning chapel, but not more than academy and college students are accustomed to. The program for the chapel exercises is made out by the children of the Pennington school, and the exercises, including singing recitations and talks, are conducted by them. The town school meets with them and also the children from a rural school about two miles in the country, who are brought in by bus.

The health service is probably as good as is offered to any school in the United States. A doctor comes out from the Ford hospital and gives them all a physical examination in the fall. A dentist cares for all teeth. A nurse weighs and measures them. All children needing any special attention for eyes, ears, adenoids, tonsils or appendixes are taken into the hospital. Fourteen, three of them former pupils, had been taken in by bus the morning we were there. Operations and after care as long as needed are provided at the hospital without expense to the student.

The Pennington school, twelve grades in one room, with one teacher, is a type that the average educator will tell you can not possibly be efficient. But Mr. Travis, who has had many years of educational experience, believes it is a good school. Evidently the community believes it is a good school, as it sends its children in some cases as much as fifteen miles and past several other schools on the way. The children must think it is a good school, as some of them walk in more than six miles every day. I am sure it is a good school in its friendliness, helpfulness and in the work we were able to observe.

I suppose, however, the public would be more interested in the sidelight it gives on Mr. Ford than it would in the school itself. It is about thirty-five miles from Dearborn, but he has already visited it six times in March. His whims and hobbies and also his insight and originality are well illustrated in it. It has the half-time services of a janitor.

Mr. Ford has started no foundation. He makes no large gifts to philanthropic causes. This school and community show a side of him of which the public has seen little. His fifteen schools and the communities around them are his playground. It is hard to see how a man with so many world-wide enterprises (though he says he has nothing to do) can take the time, but he does not hesitate to put off a group of financiers or officials in order to visit one of these schools. He is very fond of the children and seems to know them all by name. In walking across the ground, he always had an arm around a child on each side.

Henry S. Curtis

Ann Arbor, Michigan

# SOCIETIES AND MEETINGS

## A CONFERENCE OF NATIONAL ORGANIZATIONS INTERESTED IN MOTION PICTURES

Entirely apart from the "Legion of Decency" but with a complimentary reference to the legion's activities, the Motion Picture Research Council, now in its seventh year, called a conference of national organizations interested in the improvement of motion pictures for September 28 and 29. Of some thirty-five such organizations, delegates representing twenty-seven and as many more individual educators and publicists attended the conference, which was held on the morning, afternoon and evening of September 28 and the morning and early afternoon of September 29 in the American Museum of Natural History, New York City.

Following the reading of reports and papers by ten invited speakers and discussion in which many took part, the delegates of the national organizations voted informally upon a series of questions which the Committee on National Program of the Motion Picture Research Council put forward. Out of the views expressed as to objectives the committee members expect to develop further statements of principles and methods for a national program which may possibly culminate in a National Film Institute.

Welcomes were extended to the delegates on the opening morning of the conference by Dr. Henry Fairfield Osborn, vice-president of the Motion Picture Research Council, and by Dr. John H. Finley, a member of the board of directors of the council. Dr. Ben D. Wood, of Columbia University, presided as conference chairman.

The outstanding paper of the entire program was probably that of Mr. Arthur Butler Graham, who gave a preliminary report on "trade practices existing in the motion picture in the United States." Mr. Graham stressed the problems involved in "block-booking" and "blind-selling," which compel the local exhibitor to contract for pictures long in advance of their production. If these practises can be stopped and "an open market restored to America, the local exhibitors will have no excuse for exploiting motion pictures in defiance of the wishes of his community and of his patrons." Mr. Graham added that "even though some theaters in a given community were to cater to the demands of the lower elements therein, at least such theaters would come to be known for showing pictures of a low standard while other theaters would be free to build up reputations deserving the respect of the community and the patronage of its respectable elements." There followed discussions by Mr. Abram Myers, of the Allied States Association of Motion Picture Exhibitors, by Miss H. Dora Stecker, a Cincinnati exhibitor, by Mrs. B. F. Langworthy, by Mr. Arthur N. Colton and others.

Organization for community control of exhibition was advocated by Mrs. Robbins Gilman, motion picture chairman of the National Council of Parents and Teachers; by Mr. George J. Hecht, president of the Parents' Publishing Company, and others.

The greater degree of responsibility which would be thrown upon the local community if block-booking is abolished was stressed by Mr. William H. Short, director of the Motion Picture Research Council. Mr. Short believed that "what is needed is a careful, objective, descriptive service rather than opinions." Synopses could be prepared which would enable local exhibitors and committees to know about the pictures offered before acceptance. Mr. Short pointed out that this was different from censorship. "Our purpose is not simply destructive of present abuses but constructive."

Proposals for a National Film Institute were discussed by Dr. Cline M. Koon, of the United States Office of Education, and Mr. Stephen Perkins Cabot, New England chairman of the research council.

"Education in Motion Picture Appreciation" was the subject of a paper by Dr. Edgar Dale, who took part in the research on the motion picture financed by the Payne Fund. Dr. Paul G. Cressy, of the School of Education, New York University, presented his study of the motion picture as "a national school of manners, morals and conduct."

"The European Movie Situation" was sketched by Miss Katherine V. Lyford, of Boston, who told of her recent investigations in England, Holland and Denmark.

The toastmistress at the dinner session of September 29 was Mrs. Walter McNab Miller, field director of the American Child Health Association.

A recent bulletin declares that "three million persons can now be counted officially in the constituency of the Motion Picture Research Council as a result of pledges of cooperation made by national and local organizations." Among the organizations "which have pledged their cooperation to the council" are the National Congress of Parents and Teachers and the Young Women's Christian Association, and national executives of the National Education Association, American Association of University Women,

American Social Hygiene Association, International Council of Religious Education, National Council of the Young Men's Christian Association, Girl Scouts, Boys Club Federation, Camp Fire Girls, Knights of Columbus, Associated Jewish Philanthropies and others.

Raymond Walters

University of Cincinnati

# QUOTATIONS

## THE PLIGHT OF ILLINOIS TEACHERS

### To Chicago Teachers

It seems when this is written, August 18, that you are about to receive checks for your long overdue salaries. The Chicago school district has obtained money from the United States Government to redeem these checks by issuing bonds to the Government and securing them by giving a mortgage on certain valuable school lands belonging to the school district.

It took much hard work to bring about this payment of your salaries; and among the organizations deserving credit for long and continuous effort and the expenditure of a considerable sum of money in the campaign is the Illinois State Teachers Association and particularly its Chicago Division. Please remember these facts:

1. The Chicago Division sent a special representative, Mr. Robert C. Keenan, to Washington, where he put in seven weeks of hard work to get the Federal Congress to make an appropriation of money to lend to school districts for the purpose of paying overdue salaries to teachers. Mr. Keenan actually wrote the amendment to the bill that was sponsored by Representative Sabath and provided for the appropriation of $75,000,000 for loans to pay teachers.

2. The secretary of the I.S.T.A., acting under directions from your agent at Washington, supported his efforts by writing letters and sending telegrams to senators and congressmen from Illinois, and, at a critical time, by writing the secretaries of certain other state teachers associations urging them to use their utmost influence with the senators on a conference committee to which the bill had been referred.

3. The officers and members of the Chicago Division, also following directions from Washington, sent many letters, telegrams and petitions to the President of the United States, to senators and to congressmen urging their support of the measure.

4. The secretary and other agents of the Illinois State Teachers Association and of the Chicago Division at Springfield gave their support to the bill authorizing the board of education to mortgage the school land to the Federal Government; and we opposed the bill providing for amending that law to provide for mortgaging such lands to any bank or trust company.

We do not claim that our organization did it all. But we do claim that without the efforts made and the work done by the organization you would still have little hope of an early payment of your long overdue salaries.

Therefore, the Chicago Division of the I. S. T. A. ought to have a 100 per cent. enrolment of Chicago teachers this year and hereafter, not only as an expression of gratitude for this helpful service, but also as a matter of preparation for the future. The battle is not over; in fact, it may be only beginning.

We rejoice that you are to receive your overdue salaries. But how about your salaries in the future? This federal loan does not solve the problem of obtaining sufficient money to support the schools; in fact it makes the problem more difficult. For the repayment of this loan with interest will add from two to three million dollars a year for the next twenty years to the liabilities in the annual budget that has already been reduced to an alarming degree. Additional revenues must be found and used for schools. We have won only the first fight in a long campaign. Come in and help us win others.

### To Downstate Teachers

No doubt many of you teachers outside of Chicago are wondering whether you may not be treated as well as the city teachers. Some of you have not been paid for several months, or possibly not for a year or two. Many of you are paid wages so infinitesimal as to make the very moderate wages of Chicago teachers seem liberal; so you are probably hoping that your board of education will apply to Uncle Sam for aid to pay you.

For your information we will say that the

Federal Congress appropriated $75,000,000 to be lent on good security to school districts to pay the salaries of teachers due for any time preceding June 1, 1934. If you have salaries due for such time and your district can furnish good security, your board may be able to borrow money to pay you. The Chicago district, as you probably know, is issuing bonds to the government and is securing those bonds by giving a mortgage on valuable school lands.

But please permit us to remind you also that such loans will add to the indebtedness of your district and to the tax levies necessary to pay such indebtedness. It may pay your overdue salaries; but it will increase the difficulties of paying salaries in the future.

What we need most are new and additional revenues so that school districts can meet their necessary current expenditures and their debt liabilities as they fall due. To obtain these additional revenues we must go to our Illinois General Assembly or to the Federal Congress, or to both. Since Illinois is one of the richest of the states, we ought to use our utmost efforts with our own governor and general assembly before appealing to Congress. We admit this is a difficult task; for some of us who have been on the firing line for years have learned that the departments of government are influenced, if not controlled, by certain firmly entrenched financial interests which seem determined to reduce school revenues to the starvation point. Unless we are willing to accept this type of Fascism, approve the meager financial support it is willing to give the schools, and exist on low salaries or no salaries, we must arouse the people to dethrone the Fascist influence in Illinois, to take charge of their own affairs and to restore a democratic form of government.

All this is not only a patriotic obligation challenging the teachers of Illinois, it is also a problem involving their own self-preservation. It is a task that will require the utmost efforts of *all* the teachers of Illinois working together loyally and harmoniously on a definite program. Therefore, the cause of education and the promotion and defense of teachers' and children's welfare in Illinois needs: (1) a 100 per cent. enrolment of teachers as members of the thirteen divisions that are to hold meetings this fall; (2) live working committees that will propose the best possible program of objectives; (3) an energetic, loyal and united support of that program by the officers, committees and members of the association and by the general public. May we count on *you?*—*The Illinois Teacher.*

# EDUCATIONAL RESEARCH AND STATISTICS

## A STUDY OF METHODS OF TEACHING ENGLISH IN THE ELEMENTARY GRADES

As a part of the nation-wide study in English[1] which is being conducted by the Psychological Institute, a sequence for the introduction of phases of usage has been developed as a basis for curriculum revision. The factors considered in its development include the difficulty and the practical utility of each principle of usage as well as its relation to other principles.

The adoption of such a sequence throughout the country would free teachers and pupils from the wasteful practise of devoting time to principles of little importance. It would also insure the introduction of phases of usage in an order consistent with pupils' needs and abilities.

The study was conducted under a grant from the Carnegie Corporation of New York, through the Carnegie Foundation for the Advancement of Teaching. It was sponsored by the Psychological Corporation. During 1934–1938 a cooperative study of teaching methods in English will be undertaken. The results of the surveys already conducted show definitely the need for revising current practises in language instruction and for developing a teaching program embodying scientific findings and designed to meet the practical needs of the pupil.

The sequence on which this teaching study is based is designed not merely to insure emphasis on essentials, but also to insure maximum progress in the mastery of those phases of usage taught. Knowledge of the relative difficulty, as determined by the study, which each phase of

[1] Findings of the English study to date are reported in "Rebuilding the English-Usage Curriculum to Insure Greater Mastery of Essentials," by L. J. O'Rourke. The Psychological Institute, 1934.

usage presents to pupils of each grade made it possible to plan the sequence in such a way that the child is not confused nor burdened with problems beyond his capacity.

Demonstration editions of a complete series of English lessons for grades three and four have been prepared by the institute on the basis of the sequence. These editions are being made available by the institute, through a grant from the Carnegie Foundation for the Advancement of Teaching, at a nominal charge to help cover printing and distribution costs. Any school wishing to participate in the cooperative teaching program may obtain the third-grade edition for use in September. The materials for the fourth grade will be available for use in February, 1935. Later in 1935, the editions for grades five and six will be released.

The lessons are planned to give the pupil adequate training in organizing his thoughts and in expressing them clearly. The child's own experiences at home and at school, his games, his tasks and his travels are utilized as a basis for oral and written expression. The assignments are related to his own life, in order that he may have a background concerning which he can speak and write naturally. As a result, he learns to express himself with a minimum of artificial stimulation. Stories, pictures, poems, letters and word games are so developed as to give the child experience in conversing, story telling, speaking before a group and reporting what he has seen and done. They also relate to social situations the principles of usage he is learning. In planning both oral and written composition lessons, care has been taken to combine the practical and imaginative so that each member of a class will find, in each assignment, a suggestion that appeals to him, and that is within his mental grasp.

Certain of the exercises on each point of usage are so prepared that the pupil corrects his own work, and is automatically referred to any points on which he needs further study. This method has been developed as a result of research carried on by the writer since 1924. Teachers who have used this self-aid technique report that it appeals to the child as a game, leads him to feel his responsibility for improving himself in points in which he is weak, encourages self-reliance and facilitates mastery.

Supplementary exercises are provided to give additional drill wherever the teacher considers it necessary. Tests have been worked out to form an integral part of the teaching method. A comprehensive survey test precedes the course and an achievement test, parallel in form with the survey test, follows the course. Practise and progress tests which have been developed for administration at five intervals throughout the school year enable the teacher not only to measure progress but to determine the special difficulties of each pupil. The pupil is referred to supplementary drills which help him to overcome his specific problems. The provision for supplementary drill to meet individual needs facilitates mastery and enables the teacher to devote more time to oral and written composition.

To have the child carry over into everyday life the habits of correct usage that he establishes in the English class has long been an objective of English teaching. A game technique designed to effect this carry-over has been developed by the writer for use in the program. Children are made conscious of the errors that they make in daily conversation and are provided with a motive for overcoming them. In the past no boy would have had the inclination or temerity to point out speech errors on the playground. The game technique, however, makes challenging his classmates' errors and avoiding errors himself the thing to do. Making an error in English is no longer merely an individual matter, since it causes the pupil's team to lose a point. Each pupil becomes more careful in order to avoid the disapproval of his group.

The following principles of teaching technique have been observed in the preparation of the usage lessons included in the demonstration editions. These methods have been tried in a preliminary program.

(1) In so far as possible, the pupil should see and hear only correct forms. The pupil is shown only correct sentences and phrases. In no instance, except when he is correcting the errors in his own work, is he required to work with erroneous expressions.

(2) Before a principle of usage is taught, the pupil should be made conscious of a need for mastering that principle. The explanation

of principles of usage is, in many instances, preceded by a story, a conversation or a discussion, in which the constructions in question are used. The constantly recurring use of these constructions is stressed. Two or three actual problems are presented to the pupil before a point of usage is explained. He thus sees what specific problem is involved and knows why he is expected to master it. The explanation that follows the examples is thus more meaningful and appears less like a rule to be memorized.

(3) In so far as possible, the problems in drill exercises should duplicate actual speech situations. For example, the pupil is required to rewrite the sentence "He comes home early," adding the word "yesterday." As he writes this sentence, his choice between "came" and "come" is as natural as it is in his ordinary speech and writing. Other devices, such as the use of questions and answers, are equally practical. The pupil's work is made as free from chance results as possible; items requiring direct choice between two forms have been avoided.

(4) Emphasis should vary with the difficulty of the construction. In the exercises, emphasis is given to the forms which are most frequently misused. In drilling "doesn't" and "don't," for example, far more attention is given to the use of "doesn't" with "he," "she," "it," "the boy," and so forth, than is given to the use of "don't" with "I," "we," "you" and "they." The latter constructions present practically no difficulty, and consequently need little drill.

(5) Vocabulary difficulty should not be permitted to impair the effectiveness of teaching materials. In developing the teaching materials, all phrasing has been carefully checked to avoid vocabulary difficulty. As few technical terms as possible are used. At the same time emphasis has been given to vocabulary building as an essential part of language training.

(6) Drills should teach, rather than test. The exercises in this book are designed to lead the pupil to the use of the correct form. They are not tests. They say, in effect: "This is the right word. Let's practice using it together." The examples which accompany all lessons, including reviews, help to give the pupil a feeling of confidence that is essential to learning.

(7) Adequate directions and examples should precede each exercise. Every exercise, including review and test exercises, is preceded by examples. The first item in the exercise is made almost identical with the example, so that the pupil will know exactly what to do and will feel that the problem is a familiar one that he himself can solve.

(8) Every principle introduced should be reviewed systematically and repeatedly, in order to maintain and to increase mastery. A series of systematic review lessons insures that each principle of usage is adequately and repeatedly drilled, so that throughout the course the pupil not merely retains and applies what he has learned, but actually improves his mastery of the principle.

Reviews occur throughout each chapter; the final chapter in each book consists entirely of reviews. The first chapter of the second book of the series provides a thorough review of all the points covered in Book One, and reviews of these points introduced throughout the book continually reenforce the correct usage.

The demonstration edition for each grade includes approximately two hundred pages of lessons, which comprise a full year's course in English. With each copy are provided the tests already referred to and a separate notebook of about fifty pages, especially planned for use with this material. In it the exercise and lesson headings are indicated, and correctly numbered spaces are provided for the words or the sentences to be written. A teacher's manual is also furnished for each class.

Schools wishing to cooperate in the teaching study should address The Psychological Institute, 3506 Patterson Street, N. W., Washington, D. C.

L. J. O'Rourke

## NEW BOOKS IN EDUCATION

Carr, Wilbert L. and others. *The Living Language.* Pp. xvi + 639. Illustrated. Heath. $1.80.

*Experience in English Composition and Literature.* Vol. II, Grades IX–XII. Pp. 480. Illustrated. Francis W. Parker School, Chicago. $1.00.

Haefner, Ralph. *Ted and Polly: A Home Typing Book for Younger Children.* Pp. ix + 107. Illustrated by Eleanor O. Eadie. Macmillan.

Niles, Blair. *Maria Paluna.* Pp. 334. Longmans, Green. $2.50.

Shaw, T. E. *The Odyssey of Homer.* Pp. 327. Oxford University Press. $1.35.

Worcester, Alfred and Henry K. Oliver. *Hygiene for Freshmen.* Pp. vii + 151. Charles C Thomas. $1.50.

# EDUCATIONAL REVIEW

**Edited by Nicholas Murray Butler, 1891–1919, Frank Pierrepont Graves, 1920–1924, and William McAndrew, 1924–**

# COMMENTS ON THINGS EDUCATIONAL

By WILLIAM McANDREW

## SOCIAL STUDIES WITHOUT CONCEALMENT

YESTERDAY I was talking with Richard Welling, who seems to me of all the laymen I know the most in touch with educational trends. Said he, "The English have some very practical ideas on public education."

"Prove it," said I.

"I'll take Mr. Cole," said he, "G. D. H. Cole, Esq., who writes on new education and citizenship in *The New Statesman and Nation.* Cole sees a danger in the indoctrination idea. Russia, Mussolini and Hitler are immersing children of tender years in a continuous bath of political propaganda. Cole dreads that sort of thing for England. The purpose of education as he sees it is not so much to teach facts and doctrines as to cultivate the habit of thinking. This world now sees capitalism threatened with supersession by some form of socialism. It also sees rule by representative legislatures in danger. The usage of settling differences by argument and voting is challenged. The liberal teacher is seeking to save representative democracy by means of education. If he allows himself to keep on being used to preserve capitalism he will wreck education for citizenship. This is the dilemma of the teachers in England. Mr. Cole is a teacher of many years standing. He insists that higher controversial questions should be discussed in school and he is sure he is managing this in his classes without personal bias. He has both sides of public, social, economic and political problems presented without concealment. The fate of democracy depends on a citizenry that knows both sides and that reaches decisions by thinking. If we can not educate the people to this habit some *duce* or *führer,* some panic-mongering demagogue will drive us down a steep place into the sea."

### THE BRITISH ON SOCIAL STUDIES

"Another Britisher," said Mr. Welling, "is Lord Grey of Fallodon. He says that democracy must be strengthened and improved by education of a kind that will create a sound public opinion."

"We were told that," I said, "by one of our own, a hundred and fifty years ago."

"You mean Washington in the Farewell Address: 'Promote as of primary importance institutions for the general diffusion of knowledge. In proportion as our structure of government gives force to public opinion it is essential that public opinion be enlightened.'"

"That is right."

"Well, why haven't you schoolmasters done it? You have twisted the thought of the Father of his Country into the implication that the diffusion of the knowledge of mathematics, languages, science, shopwork and housekeeping satisfies the Washington doctrine. What knowledge does he say it is of primary importance to be diffused? Knowledge that gives force to our structure of government. What does he mean by our structure of government? A rule by the people. If you know anything of the letters and opinions of Washington you know that he insisted that the form was secondary; the primary thing in his idea of American government was the people's knowledge of human rights, ways to preserve these rights and a citizenry active and intelligent in improving their politics. For this your civics is bunk, like Henry Ford's history."

"Our teachers," I said, "are not encouraged by their school boards to let children in school discuss the grip of corporations, light and power companies and employers of labor on the government of the United States. A New York teacher has an idea that if the waste and stealings of local politicians are discussed in school the teacher's safety is endangered."

"So would it be," said the irrepressible Richard, "if he volunteered or was drafted into war. Do you mean to intimate that teachers are cowards?"

"I know they are much less cowardly than

the average citizen. But they are regimented under principals, supervisors, superintendents and school boards. School boards are mostly steered by city halls. You know who runs those places."

"My son, let the teachers of a town or state, through their organizations, pledge themselves to teach the civics that gives force to public opinion. Let them pledge themselves to defend any member who is threatened for such teaching and they can put American education, with loss of only a few martyr patriots, on the plane that the whole galaxy of pioneer statesmen had in mind when they advocated the American system of public schools."

## LABOR'S CRITICISM OF EDUCATION

IN Professor Cubberley's source book, "Readings in Public Education in the United States," he quotes from the report of the Providence board of education, 1900, their statement that the credit for starting public schools in that city belongs to the Association of Mechanics, because of their petition to the Rhode Island legislature in 1799. All the recent histories of education in the United States give credit to the Working Men's Committee of Philadelphia for a vigorous and effective campaign for free schools. The proposals that charity as the motive for free education must be supplanted by the consciousness of education as perpetuation of the Republic, the claim that reading, writing and arithmetic was not enough in the education of citizens, the demand that all the people must be trained to understand the problems of democracy and how to approve or reject measures of government, were characterized by prominent men as preposterous and dangerous. But there can be no real liberty, insisted the Philadelphia working men, unless all are alike instructed in their equal rights and duties as citizens. Simple acquaintance with words and ciphers, said these protesters, must be accompanied by training for the duty of political self-government. No newspaper, magazine or report, read by the average man, now sees anything extreme, absurd or extravagant in those claims of working men three generations ago.

The New York State Federation of Labor, in its recent convention, drove stakes for the educational road ahead they wish to travel. A significant fact is that the markers were furnished by a social science teacher in a New York City high school, Dr. Abraham Lefkowitz, and were set in line as perfectly proper posts prepared in a workmanlike manner.

### TESTS OF CONSERVATISM

Manly Harper's "Social Beliefs and Attitudes of American Educators," F. H. Bair's "Social Beliefs of Superintendents of Schools," Peterson and Williams's "Social Beliefs of Teachers of Teachers" and Claude Arnett's "Social Beliefs of School-board Members," all took as the basis of their study a list of declarations that had been constructed with the aid of persons whose business it is to think public-mindedly. You have an interesting investigation before you if you make an appraisal of yourself and of your educational family by scoring as "favorable," "indifferent" and "unfavorable" your reactions to these demands of the New York State Federation of Labor.

(1) Constructive education, cooperative ideals, must be substituted for mass education dominated by competition and emulation.

(2) All teachers must be trained in social science.

(3) All teachers must hold social good to be above property.

(4) Preservation of democracy demands a more democratic school system.

(5) This requires pupil self-government and the right of teachers to participate in forming educational policies.

(6) Teachers must be given full academic freedom and secure tenure.

(7) Medical service and mental hygiene for children must be guaranteed.

(8) Equality of educational opportunity must be secured without discrimination against districts too poor to raise adequate school taxes.

(9) Vocational training must be directed by those in sympathy with the organized labor movement.

(10) Adult education must be broadened in scope and made a regular part of the public school system.

(11) Adult education must not be used to undermine labor standards.

(12) Boards of education, instead of being dominated by enemies of organized labor, should be composed of representatives of different interests, including organized labor, in order to safeguard the rights of labor and of children.

## SOCRATIC CALIFORNIANS

Rudolph Lindquist, national president of Phi Beta Kappa, who is the director of the University School, Ohio State University, suggested that a good chapter-program would be self-training in conference management. These are the times when the school man must awaken citizens regarding their schools. Instead of talking at them, their own appreciation, understanding and criticism of the public school ought to be brought out as the best accompaniment to informing them of the things the school man knows they ought to know about education. Get a man to talk to you about the things you want to tell him. It warms and opens the brain cells in which you wish to plant the seed. Lambda Chapter, which blooms on the western shores of San Francisco Bay, took up the Lindquist gauntlet. Hyman Haydis, president of that chapter, has sent me the minutes of its fourteen meetings. Schoolmaster Jackson, the secretary, has mimeographed them, making the liveliest, most practical hand-book for a conference or a forum it has so far been my fortune to see.

The vitality of the advice is due principally to the fact that the group secured an expert to steer them. George Mann has trained industrial and commercial executives in the conduct of conferences. He began the first Lambda meeting by asking a pertinent question and himself refusing to answer on advice of counsel. These school men, with a lifelong habit of waiting for teacher to do the trick, had to take the plunge. Thereafter for fourteen meetings there was no ice to break.

Seat your folks around a table. If there are too many people for that use a U formation, leader at the open end. If too many for this form, select a few for seats at a table in sight of the crowd. The others will catch the contagion. The essential is to put everybody at his ease.

What keeps occurring to me as I read Secretary Jackson's narrative, dialogue and portrayal of the quiet influence of Leader Mann is the wish that he had captured my college teachers, my school principal and myself in the long ago. Of all the wooden, perfunctory, spiritless exercises the human mind has devised, none, I think, could equal in artificiality the college classes I attended, even those of eminent scholars. It carried over into teachers meetings. I employed the device of a chairman elected anew by the teachers at each meeting. Most of the dear staff were afraid of me and of each other, no matter how natural we were out of meeting.

The good leader knows the value of argument between members; the too great weight on the leader's side in a dispute, the way to keep unpleasantness out of debate, the tricks of discouraging speech-making, how to avoid the blind-road detours.

These are the conferences these Californians have learned to direct: Teacher and faculty meetings, parent groups, parents and teachers, Dads' clubs, school interpretation meetings with citizens, and so on.

These are the approved ways of dealing with the contentious trouble-maker:

Call on some one else to express an opinion.

Ask the rambler for a concise statement you can write on the blackboard.

Let the others heckle him.

Announce at the beginning that there can be no speech-making—just short direct expressions of opinion or answers to points raised by the conferees.

Turn the objector against the group instead of letting him think he is attacking the leader.

Put the question quickly to a vote: "Shall we hear more of this present line? All in favor say aye. The noes have it."

Call the police.

Or adjourn.

We must all come to this conference business. Adult education is taking the forum form. Taxpayers' associations are warping the intelligence of citizens. Legislatures are pressed by powerful lobbies. Public opinion must be enlightened. The conference is the good old Socratic mind-opener.

# MONTHLY SURVEY OF EDUCATIONAL BOOKS

*Education and Labor's Unending War.* When so sound a patriot as William Allen White calls Louis Adamic's book[1] the best work of the generation on the struggle of the working man, when Robert Duffus of the *New York Times* calls it as challenging a picture of social unrest as has been produced in our time, when the omnivorous reviewer of the *New York Herald-Tribune,* Lewis Gannett, lauds it for bold honesty and direct vision, you may wonder whether your boys and girls ought not to get a first-hand account of the plight of labor, as told by a laboring man with a genius for telling. This is a revision and extension of the work that first appeared in 1931.

After a rapid sketch of early American labor troubles the more conspicuous movements are described at length. These include the Molly Maguires, the riots of 1877, the Haymarket tragedy, the Homestead strike, Coxey's army, the Debs rebellion, the wobblies, the Macnamaras, the Mooney-Billings case, the great steel strike, Sacco and Vanzetti, racketeering and the present situation.

There is much in this book that possibly some of your friends would prefer teachers should not know, or, knowing, should forget. There is, for instance, the typical performance paralleled in almost every corporation or firm in the United States during the war, and likely of recurrence at any moment everywhere.

This was the trick: Toward the middle of 1917 the demand for lumber in various industries became tremendous. The lumber companies, taking advantage of the situation, began to boost the prices sky high. Employers raised the price in three days from $16 a thousand feet to $116 a thousand. Before the end of the year they were selling spruce for airplanes, charging the government $1,200 per thousand feet.

In the various outbreaks described by Mr. Adamic the situation was usually the same: Rising profits brought no share to the workers. Falling profits brought reduction of wages so that dividends and the salaries of officers could be preserved. The conviction of the working man—he and his fellows are the bulk of the population—is that this financial and industrial usage is wrong, those who profit by it will not change it, it will be righted only by compulsion.

American education causes the violence and warfare of the working man. In Europe the poor and lowly have been taught to accept their plight without complaint. Church and school exhort them to the Christian spirit of patience, humility and love. In America the under dog was taught the Declaration of Independence in his public school. It tells him he has equal rights to life, liberty and happiness. It convinces him that he is as good as the next man. School has taught him he should not remain an under dog; he should climb upward. He has the same philosophy of values as the upper dog. He has become convinced that his main duty in life is to succeed, that is, to make money.

Those who have the wealth, as Mr. Adamic shows in countless instances, use force and piracy to get it. Oil magnates crush competitors by underselling and by rebates. Factory owners hire gunmen to shoot down pickets. Employers use force to break up labor meetings. Capital is for war. What else can the workman do for life, liberty and happiness but fight? Well, schoolmaster, what would you advise him to do, you who have thrilled his young mind with the exploits of American fighters?

Americans have been taught self-respect, says our author. To beg a man whom he considers no better than himself for a job is humiliating to a citizen. He resents the contempt shown to the workman. As a gunman or a bootlegger he has a man-to-man chance with an opponent. He can fight it out. In industry he is at the mercy of a huge organization that holds him as of less value than a piece of machinery. Hence poverty in America drives a man into the underworld where the profits of vice and crime promise to make him looked up to or feared, at any rate not despised, by a considerable body of people. The racketeer has little trouble in thinking himself virtuous as compared with the big corporations, the Wall-street gangs and the Napoleons of finance.

An unfounded hope has persisted in America that big business would repent of its sins and

[1] Louis Adamic, "Dynamite." The Viking Press, New York. 495 pp. $2.00.

devote itself to general welfare. Mr. Adamic, like Dr. Niebuhr, John Chamberlain, Lincoln Steffens and the Teachers College group, considers this a wild dream. He shows that business can not be fair, even though wishing so to be.

The answer is compulsion. If there is any other way, what is it?

The average American school board will hardly ask the superintendent to put this book into the high-school library. If Adamic is a public enemy the public defender should know the enemy's tactics. Lafayette, they are here.

*As it looks to a Princetonian.* "The intelligent reader" to whom the Scribners advertise Dean Gauss's[2] meditations is not likely to leave the book until he has profited by every page. It is an unhurried scrutiny of great and obscure events in the history of man, consideration of the wisdom of the sages, always for light on the problems of this day. It is scholarship in timely use, unobtrusive citations fitting smoothly into the theme of the moment. It moves in a graceful manner of speech, soon persuading the reader that he is in the hands of a master of good taste in words and of reasoned argument free of propaganda. The great theme of contemporary civilization is made a matter of personal concern to the everyday American.

Three greatest forces and possible dangers are science, capitalism and nationality. The stream of history has brought these down from a distant and near past. Are there signs that they will be stranded and left behind? The end of any great civilization is not due to snuffing out. Usually no external catastrophe is responsible. The ends come quietly. The oil that feeds the lamp gives out; the flame stops. So was it with Chaldea, Egypt, the Empire of Alexander, Greece and Rome. Their spirit had died before any invaders took possession. Corruption and decay weakened the people's faith. They would not fight for it. With us the defeat of religious interests has been by a process of long-continued sniping. There are many earnest men who cling to their old faith or who strive to make it strong enough to weather modern storms. They tell us that to cure the discontents of the present age the need is for religion. This is true and the predicament is serious. A religion which has been excluded from politics, business, science and public education, from all the fields which mean most to modern man, has naturally lost power and influence. We must realize that we have reduced Him who was once the Almighty to a state of innocuous desuetude.

In the chapter on the rise of capitalism Dean Gauss, fortified by aptly selected facts of history, startlingly establishes the newness of the profit system. By this means he pretty well shatters the argument that you will have to change human nature. One comes through this chapter with much to substantiate a doctrine that the profit system is profoundly unnatural.

There is a challenging chapter on the threat of science. Socrates, Christ, Aurelius and others, still holding the reverence of mankind and unshaken as masters of life, could scarcely hold their own scientifically with a modern schoolboy in a physics class. Not in science but in the humanities is the source of their power. Jefferson, drawing up the Declaration of Independence, was shaping our culture and our history far more than any scientific exploit has done. The most vital questions will not be answered by man as a measurer of numbers but as a person. When the social scientist passes any judgment upon what is just or unjust, good or bad, he steps out of science and into philosophy. This used to be a creditable profession. The fruitful study of politics used to be called political philosophy. It would help to clear the air if we came back to that.

In the lively exposition of disagreement with Professor Millikan's defense of science this book gives you a model of controversy flavored all through with good breeding.

Especially satisfying is the handling of facts bearing upon the inevitable end of nationalism as civilization presses on. America can not live alone. No nation can. This means no loss of the honest love and service one gives his family, his town and his country.

Somehow we must visualize the state, make the nation mean something. On the threshold of a new age this is one of the first problems. Under only democracy can the modern spirit

[2] Christian Gauss, "A Primer for To-morrow." Charles Scribner's Sons, New York. 308 pp. $2.50.

find a sufficient degree of that freedom which is a fundamental craving of all men. Only by giving our republic an inner principle of vitality, a life of its own, can we prevent its disintegration into an impotent, formalistic machine.

My quotations run the risk of implying that this is a book of generalities. It is the opposite. Its conclusions grow from an examination of every side of a series of significant events. Nowhere are you conscious of being argued or persuaded to believe any doctrine. We have imagined that our forefathers solved the problem of setting up free institutions, giving to all the inalienable rights of life, liberty and happiness. The fact that we are forced to face is that under our present economic and political system the citizen does not possess the most elemental economic right, the right to work.

The only impediment to the living conceived by the founders is the recalcitrant spirit of man himself. This is now the last redoubt which we must storm. Our men of letters have been telling us we are on the wrong trail. Our churches are beginning to recognize it; as individuals we must see it for ourselves. Here is the great adventure for education.

*Why marry and abide?* In all probability the primitive man had no conception of that ideal love which binds men and women together in the strongest of human ties. The female's need of protection was not a lasting bond of union, for the female savage, like the female ape, is nearly as strong and capable of self-defense as the male. The source of marriage must be looked for in the helplessness of the offspring. Marriage had its source in the family, rather than the family in marriage. On this thesis Professor Goodsell,[3] of Teachers College, Columbia University, traces the two institutions from primitive times. There are chapters on the Hebrew type, the Greek, the Roman, the influence of Christianity, the Middle Ages, the Renaissance, marriage in England in the seventeenth and eighteenth centuries, the family in the American colonies, in England and the United States in modern times, problems in family conservation.

The most challenging feature of marriage and the family to-day is instability. The modern household is frequently a group of clashing wills. The individualistic spirit has broken the old bonds. Independence has been bought at a heavy price. Writers are not lacking to tell us that monogamy is doomed, that it was based on economic conditions that are passing. The author examines the causes of the change and discusses remedies.

The most critical years of married life, now, are the first five. Forty-three per cent. of divorces are secured in this period. The infrequency of contested divorces indicates mutual unhappiness. Mothers, where there are children, more frequently ask for separation than fathers do. Only 6 per cent. of divorces are asked on account of stated economic reasons; 37 per cent. for alcoholism or drug addiction; 39 per cent. for sex factors. College women, although in recent years the record is improving, number a smaller per cent. of wives than do others. This, Dr. Goodsell shows, is a real loss. The college-bred owe it to the society which educated them to pay back in the coin of children well born and reared.

This book is a master work of scholarly and scientific research, abounding in quaint and fascinating incident and curious reasonings of our forefathers and our contemporaries.

Here is a solid work that in a high-school or college library is sure to be read and to contribute to a vitally important education.

*Marriage and Schoolboard Asininity.* Error, wounded, hasn't writhed in pain and died among her worshipers in the field of argument as to the exclusion of married women from teaching in the public schools. The same "reasons" that flourished in my normal-school days fifty-four years ago, guesses that have been overturned by actual count over and again control the action of the majority of boards of education in these United States in spite of the fundamental civic doctrines of equal rights, life, liberty, happiness, justice and general welfare. This you may see in Dr. Peters's[4] study sponsored by John K. Norton.

The investigator condenses the experience of approximately four thousand teachers, five hun-

[3] Wyllystine Goodsell, "A History of Marriage and the Family." The Macmillan Company, New York. 590 pp. $3.50.

[4] David Wilbur Peters, "The Status of the Married Woman Teacher." Teachers College Press, Columbia University, New York. 97 pp. $1.50.

dred superintendents, principals and supervisors, and the officers of many large industrial and commercial organizations. He wastes no space by padding. His work is continually pertinent. He studies the records of married women in business houses. Employers are influenced by the depression cry that married women are keeping fathers out of positions. Some firms began dismissing wives and abandoned the practise on the ground that it disrupted business and, anyway, employment's natural guidance has to be fitness, not charity. What prevents this consideration applying in the case of teachers? It is a spoils system absorbed from American politics—the job is for the holder and not for the greatest benefit to the public. You see this idea at work in the common opposition of school boards to dropping teachers proven notoriously unfit. Dr. Peters is disconcerted by the number of superintendents who readily build and modify their ideas from those held by whatever school board happens to be in the saddle. He quotes peppery Walter Terpenning, of Kalamazoo Teachers College: "No one can outdo our school men in resourcefulness and versatility in making fools of themselves. For pure unadulterated asininity their records are unsurpassed. The height of jackassery is their reasoning to back up the boards who are getting rid of married teachers."

Dr. Peters does not divulge his own belief. He is impartial in his quotations from a formidable array of studies made by many investigators and from some whose wisdom springs full-panoplied from their speculative heads. The statistics of advancement of pupils of married and unmarried women, teacher-absence and lateness, opposition to professional study and changes, acceptance of in-service training, time of daily preparation, average teaching load, outside recreation, participation in community betterment, leave only this reason for turning out the wives—the quality of service is not so important as the distribution of jobs.

There are two considerations that seem to me important which I have never known to receive the thorough investigation exemplified in Dr. Peters's book. One is to what extent the prohibition of marriage lowers public respect for the woman teacher and her own regard for the profession. From Ichabod Crane to the diatribes of Buchholz, Mencken and *The Saturday Evening Post,* teaching has been subjected to a contempt that has been a serious handicap to a calling that needs, as much as any, a sincere public respect. Any social prohibition not imposed on workers in other positions is a bar to the high regard teaching ought to have.

The other consideration, not uncommonly treated in works by physicians, biologists and mental hygieists but which, out of consideration to social taboos affecting the lay mind and of tenderness toward the feelings of the multitude of unmarried women teachers, appears rarely in educational literature, is, what is the effect of sexual starvation and the denial of love on the fulfilment of life for the continuing maidens in charge of the rising generation? A blunt writer of the science faculty of Northwestern University intimates that daily contemplation of the face of this type of woman is bad for children.

If you live long enough you may see a common rule of school boards amended by insertion of the words below which are printed in italics—"and should a woman teacher *fail to* marry, her place shall be considered vacant."

*Blessings and Blunders of American Diplomacy.* Disarmament conferences, doings of international courts, peace pacts, foreign debts, upsets in China and Japan, keep the question of foreign relations very much alive. Professor Latané's great work, often referred to as the most efficient manual of the subject, came out in 1927. Doubleday, Doran and Company have issued a revise and extension of that treatise done by David Wainhouse,[5] Carnegie fellow of international law. The epochs are thus designated: Republican ideals and principles, defiance, rounding out the borders and looking over seas, safeguarding the Union, expansion in Caribbean and Pacific, intervention in Europe, the post-war period. In this last section are chapters on Pan-Americanism, the Washington Conference, disarmament, the Court of International Justice, Pact of Paris, Sino-Japanese

[5] John H. Latané, David W. Wainhouse, "A History of American Foreign Policy." Doubleday Doran and Company, Garden City, New York. 862 pp. $4.00.

conflict, war debts and reparations, the breakdown of isolation, index.

It is a basal text for college courses in American history or diplomacy. Its subject and style, however, make it valuable for the high-school library as a reference book. It is especially fitted for a source of pupil reports on important measures in various periods of American history.

It treats economic nationalism as a fallacy. It is a plain delusion to think that we can sell and not buy. Our late policy of a prohibitive tariff and a parallel insistence that Europe pay us its war debts is the extreme of nationalism unworkable. It has set in motion a world-wide commercial war paralyzing trade. In this universal dislocation the United States has been the major sufferer, a victim of her own folly of isolation. Seeking to assert our rights as a world power, we avoid the responsibilities of a world power.

Does the victory of the Democratic party mean a revolt against isolation from world affairs? We live in a world which has been transformed by time, technology, international commerce of learning and art. Our eighteenth-century tradition of isolation must yield to a policy of economic and political cooperation in keeping with the realities of present civilization.

*Strengths and flaws in the NRA.* A course of lectures on the National Recovery Administration delivered by Chicago Attorney Gallagher[6] to groups of advanced law students and lawyers has been amplified in popular form and issued as a book. Mr. Gallagher's specialty is constitutional law and the legal powers and limitations of business. His conjectures, therefore, as to what may happen to the recovery program when the Supreme Court has to pass upon any part of it are especially worthy of note. His analysis of the objectives and provisions of the National Industrial Recovery Act, its administration, results of code-making, labor provisions, enforcement, the bearing of the Constitution, are set out with the clarity and exactness of a logical mind.

The NRA has never been considered by the Supreme Court. The act goes on drawing trade and business into its power with a basic constitutional validity undetermined and, in the opinion of respectable authority, gravely in doubt. But what the Constitution is with respect to the NRA is what the Supreme Court will say the Constitution is. The doctrine of precedent does not bind this court. Any rule tested by experience and found inconsistent with the sense of justice or with the social welfare can be abandoned.

Lawyer Gallagher's presentation of the whole matter is singularly clear. His conclusions are positive. Economic research and planning, in his judgment, should continue in the future to be a duty of government. Any scheme will be an experiment subject to change through trial.

*Dr. Dooley's Diorama.* The name of the New York City Textile High School would hardly suggest to a visitor that here he would find notable attention to civics, economics and the newer education to which high schools are being exhorted by the apostles of the social studies. But this institution is a leader in the field. It is largely on account of the dynamic Dooley. This New England schoolmaster organized the Day Industrial School in Lawrence. Fall River called him, where he managed its Technical High School. Next he ran an apprentice school in the Brooklyn Navy Yard in wartime. Fifteen years ago, at the request of Manhattan merchants, he was commissioned by the board of education to organize the New York Textile High School. He is principal of it. He has over five thousand young men and women enrolled. Dr. Dooley has written a book for students, workers and leaders of a great industry.[7] It is an exposition of the science and art of making and selling cloth and clothing. To make the subject of textile teaching appear as a rich carpet in which are woven psychology, sociology, banking, politics, manners, ethics, law, finance, chemistry, mechanics and fine arts is the feat this versatile philosopher-teacher has done with artistry. Teachers of economics will want the text because from 10 to 25 per cent.

[6] Michael F. Gallagher, "Government Rules Industry." Oxford University Press, New York. 241 pp. $2.00.

[7] William H. Dooley, "Economics of Clothing and Textiles." D. C. Heath and Company, Boston. 683 pp. $5.00.

of personal income is spent for cloth. Teachers of home-making will need it for obvious reasons.

*Depression and Recovery.* I have seen no clearer nor better reasoned treatment of present economic upsets than that expounded by two economists on the faculty of the State University of Iowa.[8] They summarize the nature of business cycles, analyze the present depression, treat credit, prices, consumption, production, emergency relief, recovery programs, reflation and reorganization. Because the recovery provisions must be in the nature of experiments these authors give major consideration to the general characteristics and theories leading to these devices. The book is intentionally descriptive rather than critical. It avoids pushing opinions and judgments into the reader's mind. Where there are several possible explanations of an occurrence you are given them all. The book gives you the services of a brain trust gathering facts, quoting authorities and pointing possible outcomes while expecting you to form your own opinions.

*Social Tasks Confronting the Generation.* Cyclopean John Greenan—by this I mean that he has a single eye to the preponderating school duty of training for public welfare and that his industry in turning out texts in the social studies is immense—offers a high-school book on public problems of to-day.[9]

He has taken the voluminous report of the commission on recent social trends and made of it a high-school text with questions and exercises calculated to make the student realize where we are socially, economically and politically. There are eleven units of instruction. They are an exposition of sociology within the comprehension of young people.

The dangers from spoilsmen, political crooks and piratical corporations, the encouragement derivable from gains the better element has given us, the tax problem, the present dangers to democracy, the need for a more enlightened public opinion are earnestly set forth.

8 Dale Yoder, George R. Davies, "Depression and Recovery." The McGraw-Hill Book Company, New York. 298 pp. $2.00.

9 John T. Greenan, "American Civilization To-day." The McGraw-Hill Book Company, New York. 152 pp. 80 cents.

*When We Were a Canal Country.* Mr. Harlow in his absorbing history[10] has saved from oblivion a glamorous and romantic period of American life. He has tramped thousands of miles of canal towpaths, gathered hundreds of rare old pictures which are reproduced in his book, interviewed a multitude of old men and women who treasure memories of departed days of inland navigation, searched state archives, examined records of ancient canal companies and composed a history in which accuracy of fact and date is ample without clogging a moving narrative.

The number of artificial waterways constructed and operated in the United States will amaze the average reader. We dug 4,400 miles of canals before the Civil War. Opposition to canal construction was enormous. "God gave to man the rivers he wished him to use. It is flying in the face of Providence to make others." New York City, to a man, voted against the Erie Canal project. Its completion raised Manhattan from a smaller town than Philadelphia and Boston to the metropolis of the country.

De Witt Clinton's fight for the Erie waterway would have killed an ordinary man. In 1824 by an overwhelming vote of both houses of the New York legislature he was pushed out of his position as a canal commissioner. But he was swept into the governor's chair by a majority of 16,000, the largest that had up to then been given a candidate in that commonwealth. On October 26, 1825, with militia, flags, bands of music and carriages, the notables of the nation assembled in Buffalo and there orated. They marched to the fleet of gaily decorated packets. Governor Clinton took possession of the *Seneca Chief* and began the momentous voyage eastward, followed by the *Superior, Commodore Perry, Buffalo* and *Lion of the West.* Two "elegant kegs" contained water from Lake Erie. As the procession of boats cast loose, a cannon on the towpath fired a salute; another eight miles east responded, and then another and another, all the way to Albany and down the river to New York and

10 Alvin F. Harlow, "Old Towpaths." D. Appleton-Century Company, New York. 409 pp. $5.00.

then back again, eighty minutes each way. Arriving at New York the flotilla proceeded to the Atlantic, into which was poured the water from Lake Erie and some from the Mississippi, Columbia, Thames, Seine, Rhine, Danube, Amazon, Orinoco, Ganges and Nile rivers.

Historian Harlow's narrative is lively with stories of old boating days, ingenuity of American projectors who had no training as engineers, and is indignant at the graft and waste of political contractors. Eighteen grand canals and numerous lesser ones are described and pictured.

The Schuylkill Canal boasted of the first tunnel ever cut in the United States. The newspapers had to explain what a tunnel is. In the days of their glory the boats attempted every color of the spectrum. My father and mother rode from Baltimore to Harrisburg on a crimson packet behind mules with red plumes, nickel-plated harness and silver bells. From Harrisburg to Portage they threaded the mountains in a bright blue bark which a cradle-car carried over the summit ridge and launched into the Conemaugh for Pittsburgh. From Portsmouth on the Ohio to Cleveland they went like the owl and the pussy cat in a beautiful pea-green boat.

An insane appetite for speed, much clever manipulation of rates by the railroads drove the inland waterways out of business. They had brought prosperity to Virginia, Maryland, Pennsylvania, New Jersey, New York, Ohio, Michigan, Indiana and Illinois. If they had been preserved their economic benefit, now, would have been immense. Water transportation has always been, is yet and probably always will be the cheapest mode of carriage. France, Italy, Germany and the Netherlands have maintained their canals and still make others. Lack of foresight in our country lost these costly and useful public carriers. So careful an observer as railroad builder James J. Hill became, in his last years, a believer that the country will have to restore some of its abandoned waterways.

Whether this be so or not, the history Mr. Harlow has written will give the present-day reader much enjoyment.

*A Disappointing Neighbor.* Diplomat Guggenheim was American ambassador to Cuba from 1929 to 1933 when unusual pressure was brought to force the United States into the island disputes. His account of this unsettled domain is peculiarly informative and interesting.[11] It is a study of international relations.

This island has long been a cause of anxiety. The expedition of Lopez, eighty-five years ago, led England to fear that annexation of Cuba would give the American slaveholders such added power that northern hotheads would attempt to seize Canada as an offset. Mr. Guggenheim paints the attempts of American filibusters, Soule and others, the *Black Warrior* episode, the Cespedes revolt, the persistence of slavery till 1886, McKinley's attempt to purchase the island, the probable peaceful transfer without our Spanish war, Spain's preference to loss of the territory by annexation rather than by independence, and various events. His story is animated and made especially valuable by the political implications discussed.

Contrary to general belief, Americans do not own most of Cuba. About 30 per cent. of its area, excluding urban property, the littoral, swamps and rivers, is owned by United States citizens.

The Cuban idea of politics does not recognize service to the people as the prime purpose of statecraft. This view has been responsible for the malfeasance and the revolutions frequent in the life of that republic. Chicago illustrates the same idea. Cubans resent our criticism and point to our similar sins. More than a fifth of Cuban candidates have penal antecedents. These men not only accept graft; they solicit it. The voter has been taught that he has an inalienable right to sell his vote. The president is expected to take illegal profits from all the lotteries. These amount to $3,000,000 a year.

This is a startling book, no less so from the unimpassioned style in which it is written.

*Mind the Facts.* Beginning with a defense of history study, Wisconsin Professor Fish and

[11] Harry F. Guggenheim, "The United States and Cuba." The Macmillan Company, New York. 268 pp. $2.50.

Harvard Professor Wilson[12] have prepared a high-school history of the United States in accordance with their view that the factual aspect of history is of prime importance and so is a presentation vivid, moving and stimulative of imagination.

These authors put much stress upon the formative period of American modes of political thought. The Constitution is praised for its success and not worshipped for perfection. There is an important treatment of the American decline of interest in politics and the diversion of national interest to the great game of making money. The political changes beginning in the Jackson period are unusually well portrayed for a school history. Two hundred sixty pages are devoted to the problems of to-day.

An especially valuable feature is a chronological arrangement of historical events, twenty-seven pages of it. Exercises, studies, projects, readings, previews and index are of high merit.

*Rise of the Middle Classes.* To-day the bourgeoisie rule the world, its governmental, economic, social and religious activities. The middle classes definitely got control in the latter half of the nineteenth century. Since 1870 the new order has effected the greatest changes. Therefore, the Palm-Graham history,[13] beginning with the close of the Napoleonic wars, devotes the larger part of its pages to the period of the greater triumphs of the middle classes.

These are the movements given most attention: The crises of 1848, Cavour's battles, Bismarck's struggles, liberalism in Russia, rise of American bourgeois, Austrian disturbances, mid-Victorian advances, imperialism, international anarchy, the new revolution.

The world war had no victors. Fought by us to make the world safe for democracy, it made it unsafe. Disaster, not democracy, has been the rewards of the smallest as of the greatest national participants. The bubbles of patriotism and idealism burst in the trenches of No Man's Land. Instead of stimulating national trade after the war, governments throttled it with tariffs, the United States leading in this destruction. Instead of trickling down to the worker, the tariff profits have favored a privileged few at the expense of the rest. The war to end war has resulted in spending over $4,000,000,000 in a single year on armaments. Europe is more of an armed camp than in 1914. In this definite manner the authors carry through.

Especially valuable are their summary of war guilt and their cool analysis of the methods of creating war hysteria.

The use of cartoons in the book is striking. The maps are notably good. The narrative strikes me as remarkably clear and vivid. The temper is mostly impartial and judicial.

*High Schools are Looking at Biography.* Forty-four years ago I heard Horace Scudder assert that no type of good literature appealed to high-school students as strongly as well-written biography. Nobody contradicted him; nobody did anything about it. But Miss Hyde[14] has been studying the growth of biographical literature and finds that the general reading public is devouring it, while many progressive high schools are introducing biography as a study. Carleton College, Northfield, Minnesota, established a chair of biography in 1920; Dartmouth, in 1924. Thirty-seven other colleges and universities have introduced courses in the subject. Miss Hyde's text begins with an essay on background. Why read biography? What makes a good one? What have been the famous ones through the ages? What are the characteristics of the "new biography"? There follow two dozen extracts from Mark Twain, Virginia Woolf, André Maurois, Burton Hendrick and others, biographical extracts bearing on Washington, Jackson, Victoria, Lincoln, Sherman, Edison, Pasteur, Barnum, and well-known, admired personalities. Miss Hyde's introductions to the several extracts are stimulating combinations of information and incitement to get the best out of what is coming.

*A Star of Revolution.* A freshening of the national memory for the life and services of

[12] Carl Russell Fish, Howard E. Wilson, "History of the United States." American Book Company, New York. 881 pp. $2.12.

[13] Franklin Charles Palm, Frederick E. Graham, "Europe Since Napoleon." Ginn and Company, Boston. 890 pp. $4.00.

[14] Marietta A. Hyde, "Modern Biography." Harcourt, Brace and Company, New York. 277 pp. $1.12.

one of the stalwart characters of the early days of the United States will result from the publication of Dr. Goodman's life of Benjamin Rush.[15] The author's discovery that no biography of this distinguished patriot and physician exists led to the present intimate and animated history of a stirring and adventurous life. The pictures of boyhood, of student days in Edinburgh, of rebel agitations, of medical service in the Revolution, tireless activity in progressive movements, lively quarrels with everybody worth a quarrel, establishment of Dickinson College, difference and reconciliation with Washington, heroic services in yellow fever scourges, proposals for an educational system suitable for a republic, are graphically revived.

Rush took pains to cultivate every one worth knowing. The painters, Benjamin West and Sir Joshua Reynolds, were his friends. He dined with Sam Johnson and Noll Goldsmith. Franklin, Washington, Adams, Henry and other Revolutionary leaders knew him.

His intimate acquaintance with Generals Conway, Gates and Charles Lee caused him deep regret, much trouble and a lasting cloud, probably undeserved, due to the suspicion by many that he desired Washington's dismissal from the headship of the army.

Dr. Goodman is not blinded by the real glory of the old patriot's career. It is an unvarnished tale as this writer tells it, full of interest withal.

*Correction.* Netta W. Wilson, to whom these thanks, sets right an error in my account of Oscar W. Firkins's language study. The Mrs. Firkins who read to him foreign works of which she understood never a word was not his wife but his devoted mother. Professor Firkins never married.

*Positive Mental Hygiene.* Dr. Symonds was chairman of the committee on mental hygiene in schools when the White-House Conference on Child Health and Protection was making its reports. His recent book[16] is designed for teachers. Its contents should be familiar to parents as well. It emphasizes the positive, preventive side of mind hygiene. We have reached a high level of mental stimulation and excitement. Families are less secure in their economics and contentment than ever before. The future is more terrifying than ever. Added strains are on the business of living. Authorities estimate that one out of every twenty-two persons becomes a patient afflicted with mental disease. The chances of a person of fifteen years contracting a severe neurosis in a lifetime are as one in ten. Symptoms show during school attendance. The school should not dodge responsibility of discovering the unfortunates and of doing what it can to educate them to adjustment.

With an introduction in this tone, Dr. Symonds proceeds to a presentation of drives, behavior patterns, positive habits, sex adjustments, discipline, organization, mental-hygiene tests, case studies and remedies.

Guilt, sin or shame may act as a deterrent, but it carries along with it such mental complications as to be more harmful than serviceable. Habits of right conduct should be encouraged without recourse to the negative. Fretting over failures and disappointments should be avoided, as should a craving for excitement. Comparison with others is usually bad. Enjoyment of misery must be avoided. Let the boy and girl have honest, unexaggerated praise for worth-while things. Let them be encouraged to try things alone without fear, to be glad to try the new and difficult, to see the reason for most that they do, to abandon habitual standards in favor of more intelligent ones, to accept criticism without undue emotion. Teachers are notoriously deficient in this last. A sense of humor, ability to work with others, getting at a task without delay, cheerfulness, patience, enthusiasm, can be taught by example and encouragement. This and much besides, Dr. Symonds expounds with reason and sympathy, illustrating his points with interesting incidents. He fortifies the chapters with well-formed exercises, discussions and problems. The book is a happy departure from stressing particularly a multitude of abnormal cases. It is especially helpful for deans and counselors.

[15] Nathan G. Goodman, "Benjamin Rush, Physician and Citizen." University of Pennsylvania Press, Philadelphia. 421 pp. $4.00.

[16] Percival M. Symonds, "Mental Hygiene of the School Child." The Macmillan Company, New York. 321 pp. $1.50.

*Ups and Downs of Motives for Establishing Schools.* Dr. Cubberley's latest,[17] a source book illustrating the history of education in the United States, would, as I see it, have been a necessity for the schoolman's library under any circumstances. But the hard road education must travel during the coming years gives this chronicle of the struggle of the schools intense importance. A new generation of the unregenerate is marshalling the old arguments against education at public expense. The Cubberley readings revive the attacks and the answers which worsted them. Noah Porter, Henry Barnard, Horace Mann, Daniel Webster, Thomas Cooley, Thaddeus Stevens and a galaxy of lesser stars pierce with brilliancy the objections of the numerous protesters, who, in magazines, pamphlets and newspapers and in appeals to legislatures, blocked and delayed the establishment of free schools.

As you read these impassioned utterances you note a curious fluctuation in the motives behind school advance from period to period. Colonial New England is taxing its citizens for the education of all children on the ground that the old deluder, Satan, will find ignorance the surest aid to win the souls of men away from their duty to the commonwealth. The revolution incites a multitude of statesmen to proclaim the impossibility of maintaining a self-governing nation unless its governors, all the people, are politically enlightened. The Congress, in 1787, the year of the framing of the Constitution, declares that schools and the means of education must forever be encouraged for good government. Messages from state executives to their legislatures repeat the political argument for the taxation of the commonwealth for its own preservation. Mann's contention that the state's laws against infanticide and abortion logically require that forbidding child life to be destroyed must be paralleled by legal provision for developing life —that is, for education. Scores of the extracts argue that education will reduce crime and save the enormous cost of police, courts and jails. Other old appeals are for the diffusion of knowledge in order that wide-spread prosperity and equitable distribution of wealth may ensue. On turning to the last chapter of the book, and reading Pritchett, Coffman and William Russell, you wonder why education has not reduced crime nor equitably distributed prosperity nor created a citizenry intelligent in self-government. This mystery is solved by the conclusion that the motives urged and the promises made by the advocates of tax-supported schools stopped at precept and never got into practise. The numerous extracts showing what the schools were claiming at different periods of our history show acceptance of a political theory, a revolutionary concept of the purpose of education, but no provision for building a curriculum designed to carry it out. It looks as though the brightest days of the American ideal of schools for the maintenance and improvement of representative democracy faded with the passing of Franklin, Washington, Adams, Jefferson, Madison, Monroe, Clinton and Mann. The most rapid expansion of public schools was accompanied by the least discussion of the fundamental justification of making them a tax on all the people. A rush to keep up with the Joneses explains a good deal of education's phenomenal growth in these United States.

Three of Dr. Cubberley's collections of quotations are school-battle chapters. All his extracts are masterfully integrated, developing a particular movement, be it teacher training, obstacles to progress, modifying forces, imported ideas, professional advances, administrative reform, etc. Steps in the history of high schools are especially pertinent. From nursery school through the university, short, vital archives tell the story. Dr. Cubberley issued a work of this sort fifteen years ago, it, like this, being a companion volume to his text, "Public Education in the United States." Now, both that text and the supplementary readings are issued as fresh volumes, rewritten. Cubberley's "retirement" is a delicious joke.

Each volume, the history and the readings, can stand on its own feet. The table of contents of this source book is skilfully prepared for quick location of any extract wanted, but an index of people, places, movements and common educational catch-words will make subsequent editions, if I may say so, a perfect handbook.

[17] Ellwood P. Cubberley, "Readings in Public Education in the United States." Houghton Mifflin Company, Boston. 534 pp. $2.50.

*Education and Missionaries.* Dr. Kandel's annual world survey[18] came late to this reviewery, but it is of lasting importance. It covers educational activities conducted by American missions in Africa, China, India, Japan, Latin America and the Near East. There is a chapter on Roman Catholic agencies. In addition, there are surveys of medical education, agricultural and religious, by the missionaries. There are essays on the place and scope of missionary education, on the history of the movement and its problems and on rural life in the areas of foreign missions.

Dr. Kandel's summary calls attention to the failure of missionary educators to keep abreast of the progress of education in their own country. It is obvious that with this neglect there will be a failure to make any real contribution to the advancement of the people who are served. American education in China, for instance, is not abreast of the times. It suffers from lack of criticism. Educational missions have failed in adapting the teaching to the locality and in developing native leaders.

Pearl Buck's call is applicable to missionary education: "Come to us no more in arrogance of spirit. Come to us as brothers and fellow men. Let us see in you how your education works. No longer stress mere instruction but share with us that better and more abundant life which your educational ideals demand. Give us your best or nothing."

*Dewey's Daughter and Miss Glover.* Children have been living in a world of double standards. The rootless physical science they learn in their schools contradicts the traditional religion which they are taught elsewhere. The system of ethics and morals they absorb in the home, the church and school is repudiated by what they see accepted and approved in the world of business and politics. Their parents train them in one line of conduct and live in another. They have dwelt in a world of chaos, contradiction, and bewilderment. They have no unifying principle of intelligence, no key to understanding their world.

What to do in the upbringing of Uncle Sam's child to lessen the frustrated life that is too often awaiting is the problem two women,[19] experienced in child-welfare work, discuss. They consider the changes in society for which the education of the preceding generation offers little of value. They marshall facts showing an educational failure. Transfer of parental duties to school is futile. Body, mind and character training receive extended treatment in these pages. There is a strong chapter on habit guidance and much on the new type of home, followed by a summary of modern educational experiments of promise.

This is a manual of child-training which takes into account the changes in economic and social life.

*The School Man Must be Up to Tax Reform.* Because of its implications for any state the Blakeys'[20] study of Minnesota is pertinent reading for school superintendents. These economists discuss the taxation of motor vehicles and gasoline, of income, chain stores, liquor and so on. They point out the defects of provisions which have gone uncorrected in spite of the revolutionary changes in economic organization and methods of living. Aggressive improvement in state tax systems everywhere are imperative. The school man must get his community to realize how weak the educational foundation is.

*Chaotic High Schools.* The last Inglis lecture[21] warns that more serious than the economic depression is the spread of skepticism and a common criticism of democracy and its institutions. The fundamental ideals of representative government have been misinterpreted and abused. The reason is to be found not in their obsolescence but in the absence of strong social purpose to give them coherence and meaning. There has been too much reiteration in these states as to the rights of the individual,

[18] I. N. Kandel, Editor, "Tenth Annual Yearbook, International Institute." Teachers College Press, Columbia University. 642 pp. $3.50.

[19] Katherine Glover, Evelyn Dewey, "Children of the New Day." D. Appleton-Century Company, New York. 331 pp. $2.25.

[20] Gladys C. and Roy G. Blakey, "A History of Taxation in Minnesota." University of Minnesota Press, Minneapolis. 88 pp. 75 cents.

[21] Isaac L. Kandel, "The Dilemma of Democracy." Harvard University Press, Cambridge. 79 pp. $1.00.

too little reference to duty and responsibility other than making the most of oneself. So speaks Dr. Kandel from his long experience in appraising the educational systems of the world.

After an illuminating survey of American high-school theories, the substance of a good part of the address, the lecturer offers the view that their chief weakness is the absence of any clear notion of purpose except in terms of individual needs and desires.

Dr. Kandel's address was given earlier than the appearance of the dynamitic report of the American Historical Association's Commission on the Social Studies. Kandel and the commission speak the same language: Objectives are vague; teachers are for subjects; advancement is painfully slow.

Among the commentators on high-school service Dr. Kandel is of the least sensational. His diagnosis is that of the experienced observer without obsessions. What he summarizes is a condition unjustifiable on any logical plan or theory. High-school practise is a chaos of fragments derived from here and there with no guiding principle or principal. Harvard's first professor of education said this forty years ago. Dr. Kandel is sorry it is still true. He sees that the straits we are in must lead to a recast of the high school so as to shift the purpose to civic ends.

*High Class Domestic Teaching.* Dedicating it to their mothers, two professors are responsible for one of the most valuable books for teachers I can name.[22] If you know any of those ancient vintage board members who are willing to be persuaded that homemaking is a fad and a frill, a recital of the battery of requirements these authors demand of the teacher will leave the objector without power of speech.

Here are philosophy, aims, methods, examples, cautions, tests, equipment, community service and a program engaging the highest form of human talent. It is an orderly organized book, clear and definite, soundly professional, a credit to American teaching, for the surveys that have recently searched American high schools show that the high requirements set by Professors Williamson and Stewart are commonly satisfied by women teachers in public high schools.

*Who Goes to High School?* A very present help in planning high-school service for the immediate future is the office of education's bulletin on high school membership.[23] The number of intellectually less competent youths in these grades will continue to increase. In many communities, already, high-school membership is not a selected group but represents the average youth of secondary school age. This means immediate duty of providing courses of study to benefit the new type of membership.

The authors' use of the new facts in such a manner as to show what needs to be done by the high schools makes this monograph something that will have to be carefully studied by those responsible for high-school education.

*Principles of a University President.* Sixteen addresses by President Coffman come from the University of Minnesota Press[24] in a volume handsome for paper, type, presswork and binding. The temper of these speeches, even of the earlier ones a dozen years old, is notably attuned to the present perplexities of national education. A great American tradition that universal education is essential to public welfare has inspired Dr. Coffman's work and utterances during the many years we older men have known and loved him. In his inaugural address he sketched the peculiar American invention of a public school system supported by people who compulsorily taxed themselves to preserve civic liberty by spreading civic education. That a state university is obligated to contribute expert intelligence to the solution of the problems of the commonwealth has been Coffman's guiding principle. University investigations and researches should be offered for public consumption and rewritten in popular language. Com-

22 Maude Williamson, Mary Stewart Lyle, "Homemaking Education in the High School." D. Appleton-Century Company, New York. 500 pp. $2.60.

23 Grayson N. Kefauver, Victor H. Noll, C. Elwood Drake, "The Secondary School Population." Superintendent of Documents, Washington, D. C. 58 pp. 10 cents.

24 Lotus D. Coffman, "The State University, Its Work and Problems." University of Minnesota Press, Minneapolis. 277 pp. $2.50.

posed and delivered in the days of national prosperity the Coffman inaugural declares the main objective of a university to be economic betterment, social and individual justice, intelligence in citizenship. In '21 as in '34 this president, aware of the clamor of university deans for a more closely meshed sieve for keeping out undesired freshmen, held that a university's non-professional courses, a department of liberal arts, could not fortify itself with wall and moat without endangering the fundamental spirit of democracy. In his 1931 discussion, "Flexner and State Universities," this same doctrine brilliantly recurs.

"Ability is distributed without reference to social or economic status. If life is to be made safe, happiness to be promoted and citizenship be made more secure through the professions every possible means must be used to attract the ablest minds irrespective of station."

Dr. Coffman exiles himself from the realm of thought in which Harvard-President Lowell and numerous university professors dwell when he says nothing would pay larger dividends than for faculties to become students of the art of teaching. Professors, he says, are more interested in other things than in becoming better classroom workers.

The Coffman philippic against school wreckers is here, as is the one against the proposed Minnesota law to prevent the teaching of evolution.

There are many crisp pronouncements against persistent fallacies, as, for instance, the assertion that larger classes make poorer learning or that the best scholars keep out of extra-curricular affairs.

You have here the mind of the American educator of the sane progressive type reared and maturing in public school service, keeping his Americanism fresh in spite of alluring examples of some climbers into college presidencies for whom the charm of medieval tradition and cloistered calm have proved irresistible.

*Portrait of a College.* Williams College is the institution chosen by Mr. Jenkins as the background for his relation of the aspirations, experiences and gains of student Ferguson.[25] The spirit of the college, its historic beginnings and the success of its influence are made prominent. Interviews with students to get their estimates of the college effect are given. Faculty and alumni views are reported. Girls, drinking, fraternities, manners, morals, clothes, vernacular, athletics, democracy, professors and all are brought out in the Williams manner.

*Beloved College Teacher.* After "Letters from a Chinese Official" was printed in America and the identity of its author was revealed, books by Lowes Dickinson, "Symposium," "From King to King," "The Greek View of Life," "The European Anarchy," reprinted here, aroused interest in him, leading to his lecturing in many United States cities. Now his admirers may know him intimately through Mr. Forster's memorial volume.[26] How beloved a college teacher may be, how diligent in public affairs, how effective a lecturer while eschewing all recommended details of oratory, how diffident and shy while doing things requiring the highest courage, Dickinson's most intimate friend shows with subtle appreciation. It is a beautiful tribute to an affectionate, unselfish, intelligent, witty, charming, beloved, inspiring teacher. External adventure filled no part of Dickinson's life. He was never shipwrecked or in peril; he was seldom in great bodily pain, was never penniless or starving, never confronted an angry mob or went to prison for his opinions. Fate gave him an easy time, which he very much appreciated. But he suffered bitter pangs of shame and regret at the insanity of a war-seeking world. He was the first to suggest to England a League of Nations. He crusaded for it valorously. He wept over its later decline. His contribution to the thought of the world on contemporary politics, morals and art was prodigious. Mr. Forster's printed list shows 345 titles. Yet Dickinson's letters from America regret that we, over here, are all too rushed, too busy, too concerned with production.

[25] MacGregor Jenkins, "Sons of Ephraim." Houghton Mifflin Company, Boston. 236 pp. $2.50.

[26] E. M. Forster, "Goldsworthy Lowes Dickinson." Harcourt, Brace and Company, New York. 277 pp. $3.00.

# SCHOOL AND SOCIETY

WITH WHICH ARE COMBINED THE EDUCATIONAL REVIEW, ESTABLISHED IN 1891, THE TEACHERS MAGAZINE, ESTABLISHED IN 1878, AND THE SCHOOL JOURNAL, ESTABLISHED IN 1874.

Volume 40 | Saturday, October 13, 1934 | Number 1033

## PREREQUISITES OF INTELLIGENCE[1]

By President ERNEST MARTIN HOPKINS

DARTMOUTH COLLEGE

Dartmouth College is a foundation established for the education of American youth. Its effort throughout its history has been to fulfil this purpose. Its aim to-day remains what it has been. In the variety of its curriculum and in its prescriptions as to how this shall be utilized it seeks a threefold objective. It offers the opportunity of increasing one's store of knowledge; it strives to develop one's intelligence by creating a habit of reflective thought as to how knowledge should be utilized; and it prescribes that study shall be made in some one field of knowledge beyond its elementary stages so that some acquaintanceship shall be had with the method and results of scholarly accomplishment.

If distinction were to be made concerning the relative importance to-day of these three specifications, I should say unhesitatingly that the developing of intelligence must be given first place. But intelligence is dependent upon a wide range of knowledge and upon the discipline of mind which leads one to interpret this knowledge with respect and with discrimination. Hence, neither factual data nor disciplined thinking can be disregarded as prerequisites of intelligence.

There may be perfectly justifiable differences of opinion as to whether the world is most benefited over a long period of time by the contributions of amateur scholars or by those of professional scholars. But as society is constituted at the present day, the general intelligence made pervasive by amateur scholarship is indispensable if the recognition and appreciation of professional scholarship are to be made available for the continued sustenance and development of such scholarship.

Likewise, special circumstances may make it desirable for some individual colleges to make the development of professionalized scholarship their primary concern. But upon higher education in general the responsibility rests first of all for increasing and refining intelligence. Otherwise democracy will destroy civilization by elevating to power the unfit and destroying the influence and the potentiality for accomplishment of the fit. It is no small part of the responsibility of education to develop the confidence in its processes and its effects which shall increasingly give the unfit respect and craving for the cultivated intelligence by which to become fit.

If in such times as those in which we live, higher education should accept a passive rôle or should adopt an attitude of unconcern, arguing that education was not primarily concerned with how society should be organized or declaring that how we

[1] Address at the opening of Dartmouth College, September 20, 1934.

should be governed was outside its ken—if these things were to be, then new dark ages might impend, and civilization would be forced to await the forces of evolution to create some future generation of the fit and to restore such to the legitimate place of influence which should be theirs in conduct of the world's affairs.

On this occasion at the opening of our academic year, I wish to brand as despicable a defeatist attitude. In behalf of Dartmouth and for all colleges I crave the privilege of bespeaking a militant spirit of faith and of courage. And I wish briefly to discuss the details of a few matters with which we have particular concern.

Characterization has been made of our time as a period of frustration. The description is a graphic one, but hardly fair. Man's environment has completely changed within the lifetime of a single generation. It is possible, of course, that man's efforts to adjust himself to this will prove so badly advised as to become entirely futile, but it is not inevitable or even probable. When the history of the world in our time is written, the record will more likely show the present to have been an age of adaptation. Mankind has always been meeting difficulties and eventually lessening these when not entirely dissipating them. In general, the newer and greater difficulties which confront man to-day have been created by man. It is a philosophy of cowardice to assume that the mind of man can not correct them. Obviously, however, despite the vehemence of argument for special devices of government or particular organizations of society, there is no clear knowledge of the exact corrective methods most advisable to apply. The solution must be found by the experimental method. This method presupposes proving certain assumptions false as a concomitant of acquiring proof that others are true. In other words, under necessary acceptance of a method of trial and error, failure may be definitely a step towards success. A noted preacher once said that it was not to be assumed that God didn't answer prayer because he didn't always say "yes." By analogous reasoning, it is not to be assumed that an age is futile or that a generation is wasted because some of its major enterprises do not carry through to success.

On the other hand, under the experimental method it is imperative that projects be intelligently conceived, their development be painstakingly studied, the evidence adduced be critically scrutinized and the eventual conclusions derived be accepted, regardless of doctrinaire opinion or preconceived ideas. Herein I believe lies the greatest basis of doubt in regard to the immediate future in the affairs of government at home or abroad and in regard to desirable social adjustments throughout the world. The query constantly arises in the solicitous mind not so much as to whether the experiments being tried are likely or not likely to succeed, but whether they are being scrupulously examined and studied to learn what factors of promise or fallacy are contained within them. And it is only fair to add that valid judgments upon these seem more likely to be secured from the unbiased minds of men intelligently honest without brilliance than from the minds of men intellectually brilliant, but doctrinaire. Acceptance of this conviction in the conception of desirable educational programs might conceivably modify radically the theory and practise of institutions responsible for higher education.

There is an essay by Dr. F. C. S. Schiller on "Scientific Discovery and Logical Proof" which I wish every undergraduate might read. It is published in "Studies in the History and Method of Science," by Charles Singer. In this there is one particular point that bears upon the matters we are considering; namely, the distinction between the prover and the explorer who may become the discoverer. Dr. Schiller argues that the mental attitude of the one must be quite different from that of the other, that the explorer seldom can be absolutely certain when he has become the discoverer and that verification lies with the prover. To be sure, Dr. Schiller assigns definitely lower rank of the two to the prover in the realm of research in the pure sciences, but from his comments on the inevitably great proportion of failures to successes among explorers, as compared with the provers, it is doubtful if he would make identical contentions in regard to the social sciences. Here inevitably the claims of discovery on the part of the explorers need to be checked by the provers at frequent stages. Unfortunately, the inhibitions of science, as demonstrated in medicine, against hazardous experimentation upon human beings have not become the ethical code of such wielders of vast political powers as a Stalin or a Hitler, for instance. Nor if the aspirations for human welfare of political leadership in America should fail, would we be free in the future from the probability of like experimentation upon ourselves. It is for such reasons that I believe it to be the duty of every real friend of governmental reform and of social advance to insist that provers be given equal place with the explorers in the great social and political experiments of the present day. Even if we accept as necessary a practise of experimentation under a theory of trial and error, provers might recognize error in its early stages and save much that would be lost, if mistake were carried to its final conclusion. As Seneca wrote, "An age builds up cities; an hour destroys them. In a moment the ashes are made, but a forest is a long time growing."

Theoretically, in a democracy the citizens possessed of the vote should be provers, weighing comparative merits and defects of governmental policies and rendering periodical intelligent decision as to the confidence to which these policies had proved themselves entitled. Practically, our political discussions in the past, as they will probably be in the immediate future, have been largely based upon our antagonisms and upon our dislike of specific details of policy, regardless of whether these were at all offset by other policies which in whole or in major part were defining progress or were conserving the national welfare. That this should be so is certainly an indictment of the influence of the educational establishment of a country wherein a quarter of our population, year by year, is enrolled within our schools and colleges, and wherein institutions of higher learning are given the opportunity of working their influence upon more than two million prospective citizens a decade. The responsibility, I believe, rests jointly upon certain attributes of the American college student body and certain defects in our official college conception of what are the real objectives of higher education.

I wish for a moment to leave general discussion and to be quite specific in regard to some aspects of our life together in this college.

In brief review of the history of higher education in the United States through recent decades, certain conclusions seem justified that bear upon the possibilities of common advantage in the relations that begin to-day between the institutional college and the undergraduates.

Important among these I should place the haziness of perception of the average undergraduate about the advantages available to him in a college course and his frequent lack of comprehension of the relative importance of these advantages, one to another. There is no truer saying than that the eagerly sought privileges of one generation tend to become assumed as rights in the next. Consciousness of values then begins to disappear. It is so of higher education in America to-day. Too large a percentage of the undergraduate bodies in colleges to-day are there because going to college is being done. Too small a proportion are there with any consciousness of the values obtainable or with any definite purpose to avail themselves of the particular benefits which will enrich their lives or make these of consequence to the greater welfare of mankind. The man who embarks upon his college course without either knowledge of where he is starting from or where he is going is subject to all the hazards of a mariner at sea without compass or chart.

It is in no censorious mood that I make these assertions, but rather in the hope that in recognition of the facts we may in some measure offset them. They result in some degree from the American aptitude for organization of worthy projects into systems of stereotyped forms, and in some degree from easy assumptions that blessings acquired by self-discipline and effort can be extended without impairment to those who have never labored or imposed any discipline upon themselves. Within the memory of a host of men now living there was no single institution of college grade in the United States that had an enrolment of a thousand students. Without question, even then in individual cases there was no full appreciation of what education was or why its influence was being sought. It would appear, however, from much of the data available in regard to the circumstances of college life of those times that the infrequency of opportunity to attend college, the literal fact that a college man was one in a thousand rather than one in a hundred, gave to individual students a sense of values in college opportunities which led to utilization of those opportunities which could be had to somewhat greater extent than is frequent in our own time. This statement holds in spite of the doubts of an occasional Henry Adams and in spite of the limited facilities of the institutions of higher learning of those days. It seems to be true that the more we have of a thing, the less consciousness we have of its worth, whether this be liberty or health or economic resources. So it is of educational opportunity. Even if, however, these things be necessarily true of students when entering college, there is no need that they continue true among those of a thoughtful group such as an undergraduate body may become.

I have read the editorial comment of undergraduate periodicals in recent years with considerable care. I have listened to extended criticism of college procedures and of college accomplishments in undergraduate groups at Dartmouth and at other colleges. In consideration of these with great interest and with some profit, I have nevertheless had much concern, as forecasting the temper of the great society which college men would later make up, that emphasis has been so largely placed upon what the colleges should do for their men and so little emphasis has been placed upon what these men should do for themselves. Much has been said about making the absorption of learning less difficult, the conditions of college life more comfortable, the procedures and programs more convenient, and the adverse judgments in regard to indolence and indifference less exacting. Little has been said about how learning should be made accurate or about how mental fiber should be toughened or about how intellectual fortitude should be developed.

It is a short step from such attitudes in regard to the relationship of a man to his college to the attitudes of the same man in his relation to government. And though the analogy is not complete, in the large it is true that as a government is what its citizens make it, so a college is what its undergraduates make it. A college may be made a pleasant refuge from ennui between week-ends, or it may be developed into a charming social center, or it may be utilized as an agency for sharpening the predatory instincts of its members and making these effective in relations in later life with their fellow men. On the other hand, a college may be made a sacred temple wherein one finds inspiration to seek truth, wherein are safeguarded treasures of the past whose values have been proved, and wherein one finds courage to abandon the easy assumption of things which are not so.

Quite incidentally also, I should like to refer to the frequent criticism, so vehemently made in the undergraduate press and recently repeated in popular magazines, in regard to the requirements in college curricula of disciplinary subjects requiring exact factual data, of some acquaintanceship with foreign languages and of the ranking system. The hypothesis is usually accepted that except for conservatism and addiction to established forms on the part of the colleges, such requirements would speedily be abandoned. Well, they were abandoned in the most radically experimental project ever undertaken educationally upon a large scale when the Soviet Union set up its system of universal education and founded this on adoption of the project method. What was the result? In a resolution adopted by the Central Committee of the Communist Party on August 25, 1932, the whole plan was declared ineffective and undesirable in that it did not give sufficient general knowledge and failed to teach the essential basic principles of specific subjects. The resolution prescribed a more thorough study of individual subjects, more time to be spent on mathematics, physics and foreign languages, and the reintroduction of examinations and the marking system. The recommendations of this resolution are now being put into effect.

Passing to broader discussion and to other than undergraduate obligations, we must admit the need that the college should accept greater responsibility for articulating itself to the rapidly changing conditions of modern life. We are so much involved in these and so much a part of them that except by definite effort we become insensitive to them. Factual knowledge and philosophical imagination are more indispensable than ever before, but these alone are not enough. The house of truth within which only the college has had justified residence must be expanded into a more ample abode of understanding. A man, for instance, may know all the obvious facts of an industrial dispute and yet have no understanding of it. To possess the latter he must have acquaintanceship with the history of the machine age, the principles of mass production, the theory of capitalism, the influences of the profit motive, the dislocations of labor resulting from wars and tariffs, the effects of monetary manipulation, the physiology as well as the psychology of fear, the incentives of ambition, the contagion of discontent and the cravings for power—to name but a few of the factors involved.

Moreover, and of the greatest importance, any enduring plan for developing industrial peace must reckon with the growing recognition on the part of the working classes that for reasons which they little understand there are rapidly developing conditions in the United States which make it increasingly difficult for a man to change his station in life. The employing class inevitably grows numerically less as technological advance requires more elaborate and more expensive apparatus for the manufacture of products. Then, too, the high degree of specialization required for modern employment tends to separate the working classes into technically trained groups between which there are too few common denominators of experience to make transfer from one to the other at all practicable. Thus the position of the wage-earner tends constantly to become more fixed and access to the employing positions tends to become far less possible than in times not long past. These conditions are all imposed upon a population which has been reared in the conception of America as a land of unbounded and unrestricted opportunity, where any man might become president and where possibility for advancement was unrestricted by any factors except individual ability and individual merit. America still remains a land of opportunity and a land of promise for self-expression of the individual man to greater degree than is true of any other land upon the earth's surface, but it is decreasingly so. The separate facts are known to a multitude of our citizens, but there is little understanding of their implications except among a few.

From a great number of possible examples I have taken labor unrest as a single illustration of the American tendency to classify ills by superficial symptoms rather than by thoroughgoing diagnosis. Wherever we turn to study normalities or maladjustments of mankind in such problems as war and peace, obedience to law or crime, mental hygiene or insanity, democracy or despotism, individualism or collectivism, nationalism or internationalism, we find understanding correspondingly needful and correspondingly difficult. Thus it comes about that few have time or energy to seek understanding and fewer have the background of knowledge and the mental acumen to acquire it. This is the significance of the statement in the report of President Hoover's Research Committee on Social Trends, which declares:

> . . . Modern life is everywhere complicated, but especially so in the United States, where immigration from many lands, rapid mobility within the country itself, the lack of established classes or castes to act as a brake on social changes, the tendency to seize upon new types of machines, rich natural resources and vast driving power, have hurried us dizzily away from the days of the frontier into a whirl of modernisms which almost passes belief.
>
> Along with this amazing mobility and complexity there has run a marked indifference to the interrelation among the parts of our huge social system. Powerful individuals and groups have gone their own way without realizing the meaning of the old phrase, "No man liveth unto himself."

In connection with such an indictment, which must apply particularly to our American system of higher education, the question arises immediately whether it is deserved. In response, the colleges must plead guilty, especially to the charge of "marked indifference to the interrelation among the parts of our huge social system." The criticism can not so fairly be made that our colleges have not done well the things they tried to do as that they have been trying to do other than the most consequential things. Only recently have we begun to pay as much attention to the basic culture necessary for a new civilization as we were giving to the luxury culture designed as an ornament for generations past. As always in change from one practise to another, there is maladjustment from which the colleges are definitely, if slowly, emerging.

There is real basis still, however, for criticism. The reign of science in its development of the scientific method has rendered incalculable service to the cause of education in defining how truth should be sought and in revealing how fallacy may be exposed. Unfortunately, nevertheless, up to the present time this method has dealt so exclusively with static things that its principles are inadequate when applied to changeable human nature. There has been occasional recognition of this among some of our outstanding scientists. Dr. Herbert E. Ives pointed out a few years ago, in an address upon research in applied science, that many of the characteristics necessary for success in human relationships are a positive detriment in scientific research, adding that "the electrons, protons and photons with which modern physics works cannot be stampeded by any emotional appeal.'' On the other hand, it might be added that accomplishment in the field of human relations can not be successful except as the persuasiveness of emotional appeal is utilized to supplement the arguments of logical deduction.

Herein lies the greatest present-day dilemma of the college, that it has become responsible for two entirely different and sometimes contradictory functions. It can not legitimately restrict its efforts to a training for an extension of the boundaries of knowledge. Knowledge once acquired is dependent upon understanding and discriminating interpretation and use if it is to be made of advantage to mankind. The colleges which have been established, endowed and supported by society can not reasonably disregard these obligations to society. They are responsible indeed to a degree never yet formally recognized for much more than training the discoverers and provers of knowledge. They can not justifiably ignore qualities of character, sensitiveness to values we call spiritual or attributes of personality among those of scholastic accomplishment who apply for admission. They can not, in their official awards of merit, logically remain oblivious to those most likely to influence others by attributes supplementary to pure intellectualism such as variety of interest, breadth of comprehension and human sympathy. Through men of these qualities are the fruits of knowledge given their widest distribution. Through men of this type does the college most directly serve democracy. Through men of this type may the claims of education be given appeal to public interest and to public support.

As societies at different times and places differ widely, so educational procedures have differed widely at different times, and so they differ at the present day in different areas of the earth's surface. Consequently, the word ''education'' has many interpretations, and a multitude of definitions have been given to it. The processes of the liberal arts college are devised in the theory that education fundamentally is for the purpose of safeguarding the values which the community has acquired in the past by toil and struggle, adding its due meed to these. Communities, however, are made up of individuals; so education in the liberal college concerns itself primarily with developing and directing the minds of individuals to the end not only that they shall have knowledge but that they shall likewise have intelligence. An intelligent man must have knowledge, but a man may have vast stores of knowledge and yet not be intelligent. Intelligence will demonstrate to any man that he does not and can not live to himself alone. Consequently the college becomes responsible for developing a social consciousness in the minds of men upon whom its influence is operative.

Probably throughout history the distinctions among educational systems among different peoples have been in the conception of what constitutes truth. At any rate, this is so in contemporary times. If final truth is conceived to have been revealed in regard to the preeminence of a hypothetical racial strain, as among one great people in Europe, or in regard to the exclusive right to existence of a single social stratum, as among another great people, or in regard to the ideal form of government, as elsewhere, then in any one of these cases we must grant that all agencies of education should be marshaled in propaganda, training and discipline to compel the acceptance respectively of one or another of these doctrines. If, on the other hand, as in limited portions of western Europe and in the Anglo-Saxon countries, truth is held to be the ultimate of all ideals, approachable but never fully attainable, in search for which an individual or a race possesses itself of intellectual strength, moral stamina and spiritual refinement, the theory and practise of education must be quite different.

Again, the theory and practise of education must be interpreted very differently according to whether we conceive of life in its long continuity and in its changing aspects or whether we yield simply to its contemporary exigencies. In the one case we will adopt the theory of the so-called "liberal" education, while in the other we will tend toward the vocational type and make effort to prepare a man for a given profession or for a given trade. Great, however, as are the problems of adopting the former practise, the problems of doing the latter effectively are almost insuperable and must become more so. In the self-contained community of a century ago, there were combined classifications of professional, agricultural and industrial workers to the number of hardly more than a score. As contrasted with this, the last national census shows a classified index of occupations numbering above twenty-five thousand. In single concerns under the NRA, managements not infrequently find themselves subject to half a hundred involved and intricate codes. Analogous circumstances could be enumerated in considerable numbers. Under a multitude of such conditions applicable to every field of activity in human life, the liberal college argues that that form of education is most desirable which develops its men as a contingent force and gives them such training as will make them available as shock troops to meet any emergency which may arise, rather than trains them simply for one single branch of service. In other words, an education in regard to the general principles by which life has been lived and ought to be lived is likely to be more profitable to society at large than any other, if this education can be combined with enough mental discipline to give fortitude, and enough inspiration to give that form of idealism which constitutes spiritual vision.

It is to be remembered, meanwhile, that truth is a gem of many facets, the brilliancy of any one of which is dependent upon the skill with which the others are cut. Thus the scientist and the artist and the philosopher and the poet and the mathematician and the musician, among others, all have their respective parts to play and their especial surfaces to cut, if the diamond of reality is to have symmetry and beauty. It is with such considerations that we must deal in interpreting the functions of the liberal college—functions inclusive of but far greater than the production of pure scholarship or intellectual brilliancy; functions designed for cultivating wisdom and for developing men of understanding.

# LIBRARIES FOR CIVILIZED LIVING[1]

By CARL H. MILAM

SECRETARY, AMERICAN LIBRARY ASSOCIATION

My thesis is that a system of public and school libraries—which will make books and competent guidance in the use of books easily accessible to every person in the United States—is a necessary part of the public equipment for civilized living under the New Deal.

When I speak of libraries, I do not mean the kind of institution which some of you, unfortunately, have in your towns. A little mausoleum-like building, closed most of the time, presided over by a former mayor's maiden aunt, who selects nice

[1] Address given at the convention of the National Education Association, Washington, July 5, 1934.

clean moral novels for other dear old ladies who just love to read—this is not the kind of library I'm thinking of. Nor am I thinking of the school library which consists of a few locked cases of text-books and supplementary readers dating back to 1880, whose latest purchase was a worthless subscription set bought on the recommendation of a prominent citizen to whom the not-too-honest book agent gave a free copy. Nor of the college library, which begs just any kind of books to bring the total number of volumes up to a quantitative standard set by an accrediting association, and which is manned by some weak brother who couldn't quite get by at teaching or preaching.

There are hundreds, perhaps thousands, of libraries of this sort. They are not simply useless, they are a positive menace to educational and cultural progress, for they give to young men and young women, as they have no doubt given to some of you, a wholly false impression of what a library really is.

When I say "library," I am thinking of an agency maintained by society to make available to all kinds of people of all ages the facts and ideas which the wise men of this and previous generations have recorded in print.

I am thinking, too, of the men and women and boys and girls out of school who want more education and are willing to work for it; of the man who wants to equip himself for a job and keep himself equipped; of the increasing number of men and women who take seriously their responsibilities as citizens; of the student in school or college who is willing to do more than he has to to pass an examination; of the men and women who are not afraid of facts, or of new ideas, no matter how radical; of the scholar who must have access to great collections of books if he is to make his contribution to knowledge without waste of time. I am also thinking of the people who read because they enjoy reading.

The library at its best—whether public, school or college library—is a dynamic, even aggressive institution, which assumes its full share of responsibility for stimulating as well as satisfying intellectual curiosity and reading interest.

The New Deal is expected to bring economic security and more leisure. For what? For "a more abundant life"? If that is our goal, then we must provide for every person, from childhood to old age, opportunity and continuous encouragement for the fullest possible development of personal abilities and social understanding.

Professor William Aylott Orton, in "America in Search of Culture," says: "The state must stand for something in the spiritual life of the community; otherwise it can not stand at all. . . . I contend," he writes, "that even when (such) a state succeeds in the attainment of its purely economic ends—a chicken in every pot, a car to every family, a refrigerator in every kitchen, a radio in every living room—it none the less nurtures the doom of an explosive dissolution. . . . The purposes of the political and economic state have ultimate meaning only in so far as they satisfy the emotional and spiritual needs of the mass of the people."

The goal of a democracy is not efficiency in public administration, nor even universal participation in public affairs—important as these things are. Democracy's objective is the greatest possible advancement of all its individual citizens. To facilitate such advancement, society must provide institutions and agencies: (1) for universal education at the lower levels; (2) for wide-spread education at the higher levels; and also—what is now largely lacking in many areas and only meagerly provided in most—agencies (3) for continuing self-education at all levels; (4) for rapid diffusion of uncensored facts and ideas to all citizens; (5) for wise use of leisure; and (6) for cultivation of appreciation of social and cultural values which will tend to prevent the domination of life by material motives.

Many public agencies exist to serve these needs: schools, libraries, colleges, universities, museums, parks and playgrounds. Many others maintained as private businesses also contribute, such as theaters, moving pictures, orchestras and publications.

Of the public institutions, only the schools are even nominally accessible to all the population. They serve the average person for only a few years. Comparatively few people go to college. Few now have access to museums or organized recreation. Only about 60 out of 100 can borrow books free of charge.

For a very large part of the population, society has failed to provide those public institutions for education, recreation and culture which are looked upon in our more enlightened communities as necessary equipment for civilized living.

Next to the school, the public library is the most basic of all such institutions. It serves art as well as science, hobbies as well as vocations, and education as effectively as recreation. It is the continuation school for every boy or girl or man or woman who cares to use it. It typifies democracy by welcoming and helping the educated and the uneducated, the highest and lowest. It is also intellectually democratic, for it insists upon its right and obligation to furnish material on all sides of controversial public questions.

There are nearly 6,000 public libraries in the United States. They are living monuments to America's faith in education. They have millions of books. They are used by 24 million people. They provide annually hundreds of millions of books for American readers. The public libraries of New York City alone circulated nearly 27 million books in 1932. Some well-operated public libraries serve more than half of the population, regularly, year in and year out. A distinguished educator has said that the public library is one of America's great contributions to civilization.

Yes, we have many public libraries, the best, and perhaps some of the poorest, in the world. The best are providing magnificent service in all fields, and leadership in informal education, though even these have not approached the maximum possibilities of public usefulness. The poorest are so inadequately equipped with books and staff that they can not possibly meet the needs of those who wish to use them. And about 40 million people—most of them in rural areas—have no local public libraries of any kind.

For these 40 million, society has failed to provide one of the essential tools for civilized living; and for the many millions now nominally served by very small libraries, society has done little better.

Good library service, according to present standards, can be had for from one to two dollars per capita per year—only a fraction of what it costs to maintain schools. Most libraries actually operate on much less. Yet, after years of acceptance of the idea of library service, after years of advocacy by school teachers, school administrators, women's clubs and librarians, about four fifths of our rural population and one third of all our total population have no local public library service.

The reason, or at least one reason, is that our units of government are too small to maintain public library service efficiently and economically in areas not thickly populated.

The schools and other governmental agencies have taught us the lesson of consolidation. With us, it must be both consolidation and extension.

Instead of 6,000 public libraries serving 60 per cent. of the population—much of it very badly—we ought to have about 500 libraries serving everybody, or, in the typical state, about 10 libraries instead of 100. Each such library, or library system, would serve a whole metropolitan area, a very large county or several counties. It would consist of a large central library, branches in every town, village and neighborhood, daily exchange of books, thoroughly trained library personnel and service to all equal to that now provided by our best city library systems.

If any such goal is to be achieved in any state within a reasonable length of time, it will be, I think, because the state itself, out of state funds, undertakes to set up and maintain a minimum or foundation program of local public library service. I therefore hope for the assumption by each state of responsibility for establishing and maintaining a system of large unit public libraries which will make library service easily accessible to every inhabitant. For those who believe in local self-determination, let me add that it should be possible under such a system for any unit of government to increase the funds and service of its branch library in accordance with the needs and wishes of the local population.

Each school must also have its library, for the daily use of library materials and service is indispensable to a modern school which endeavors to prepare each individual for a lifetime of self-education.

When I say "library" here, I mean, as always, not simply books, but also professional library service. The larger school, both elementary and secondary, must be provided with organized collections of books and adequately trained personnel; the smaller school should get equivalent service through participation in some plan of large unit administration. I care not at all whether school library service be provided by school authorities or public library authorities. It is essential, however, that the pupil, every pupil if possible, acquire not only the habit of reading, but also, in the interest of his future self-education, the habit of using public libraries.

If, as I believe, it is the business of democracy to provide opportunity for individual development to the highest possible levels, then our national government also has some responsibililty for the institutions of education, recreation and culture. It has for years demonstrated its interest in formal education. Should it not now show a corresponding interest in libraries and other informal agencies for human enlightenment, possibly through national planning for the development of such agencies, possibly through the appointment of a new officer associated with the commissioner of education?

And, if schools and libraries really are necessary, perhaps the Federal Government will also find a way to aid financially.

Let me summarize in conclusion. I believe it is the duty of government to maintain, not only schools, but agencies for informal education, culture and recreation; that next to the school the public library is the most basic feature of all our cultural equipment; that public libraries should be federated and reorganized as large systems; that they should be supported on a minimum basis from state funds; that the Federal Government should participate with the states in planning for their development; and that every school should have such library service as will enable it to train its pupils for a lifetime of self-education and enjoyment with books.

# EDUCATIONAL EVENTS

## SCHOOL GARDENS IN HOLLAND

A MOVEMENT in Holland which began some fifteen years ago with the founding of the Amsterdam Society for School Work Gardens by a small group of men wishing to awaken an interest in nature and in the cultivation of the soil, has spread to other places in the Netherlands. *The Christian Science Monitor* reports that the school gardens have now become a national movement organized in a National Union of School Work Gardens.

Under expert guidance, children from about ten to twelve years of age are enabled to cultivate garden plots of 15 by 20 square yards. The school gardens are quite apart from the elementary schools. The only connection is that in the spring the superintendents of schools are requested to make known to the children that they can obtain a garden of their own upon payment of a fee of 25 cents and the further obligation to pay 15 cents per week toward the running costs of the undertaking. The idea of having a garden of their own is said to appeal strongly to many children. There are now 1,800 children who on Wednesday and Saturday afternoons, from April to the end of October, work in the gardens after school hours.

Each of the four Amsterdam school garden units of five acres each, situated in different sections in the outskirts of the town, has its own plain wooden clubhouse. Here, on rainy days, the weekly lesson on natural science and history is given and a museum containing specimens and pictures of a great variety of plants and flowers is housed. In the clubhouse the garden tools of the children, seeds and other materials are stored as well as aquariums and terrariums, collections of insects and so on.

The work of the children is supervised and guidance is given by trained horticulturists. In each garden the same flowers and vegetables are grown. The soil is dug up and fertilized when the children receive their allotments. For the rest, the sowing, watering, weeding, trimming, binding up and cutting is all done by the children themselves.

The municipal authorities early recognized the importance of this educative work, and the ground for the school gardens is leased at a low rental by the municipality to the society. About 30 per cent. of the running costs are defrayed out of the children's contributions, the rest is paid from subsidies granted by the municipality and the province.

## QUALIFICATIONS FOR TEACHERS IN THE NEW YORK CITY SCHOOLS

GEORGE J. RYAN, president of the Board of Education, City of New York, in a letter to Chairman George J. Smith, of the Board of Examiners, on October 2 called upon the examiners to close the door against all would-be teachers of doubtful loyalty. The full text of Mr. Ryan's letter reads:

It was with great satisfaction that I found in the Board of Examiners' Annual Report to the Superintendent of Schools for the school year 1933–1934 the following sentence: "It is unquestionable that desirable traits of personality and character outrank all others in importance in the equipment of a teacher."

I quite agree with you in this respect and, in view of the fact that you are planning to hold numerous examinations for teachers in the near future, may I urge upon you that even greater attention be given to the personality and character of candidates, and in addition that the Board of Examiners make certain as to their loyalty to their country before admitting them to the school system. The state, as you know, requires an oath of loyalty, but I do not believe that any one should be, or should become a teacher who takes this oath, simply because it is required. Let us have, rather, teachers who deem it an honor and a privilege to pledge allegiance to the state they serve. This is a clear matter of character for, in my judgment, no one is a person of good character who enlists in the service of the state and then withholds his loyalty from the state.

Let us have men and women who know and understand and believe in the principles upon which the American form of government is based; not people who simply know the history of their country, but rather those who take pride in it as well, whether this be the country of their birth or the country of their adoption.

Let us close the door now against any who may seek a teaching position for the purpose of teaching American children un-American or subversive doctrines. It matters not how much book knowledge they may have or how clever they may be at passing examinations, we do not want them in the public schools and I call upon the Board of Examiners to keep them out. You might very well serve notice now upon all who would be candidates in the forthcoming examinations that loyalty to the country whose children they would teach is a fundamental eligibility requirement.

Let us have no one whose professed zeal for "academic freedom" is merely a high-sounding excuse to make an attack upon American ideals. Let us have no more ill-mannered people such as those the Board of Education was forced to dismiss for conduct unbecoming a teacher. Rather, let us have teachers who are ladies and gentlemen in the truest sense of the word.

In so far as possible, I believe the Board of Examiners should interview personally every candidate and not delegate this all-important function.

In brief, let me urge that, in considering candidates in your forthcoming examinations, you make personality and character your first consideration, and that under the head of character you consider loyalty and love of country.

## THE CITIZENS CONSERVATION CORPS AND THE PENNSYLVANIA STATE COLLEGE

THE Citizens Conservation Corps camps in Pennsylvania have turned to Pennsylvania State College for assistance in completing their educational program. Commanders and educational directors from thirty-five localities with Dr. T. Gordon Bennett, educational adviser for the Third Corps Area, recently visited the college, to confer with representatives of President Ralph D. Hetzel, the deans of the college and the head of the college extension service.

According to *The New York Times,* the college was able to make several specific offers and to assure the commanders of support for the program from the entire college as rapidly as details can be arranged.

The fields covered by the forty-two undergraduate curricula were outlined and the camp directors were invited to make selections of courses to fit their programs. The college offered lectures and musical groups for accessible camps, and to set up special classes in shop and manual training for such CCC boys as could be brought to the college campus. It was, however, stated that organization and adaptation of technical subjects for semi-technical instruction would require more specific information.

Dr. Bennett summed up the problem of the camps as "the obligation to fit 15,000 Pennsylvania boys for active and useful participation in American civilization." He pointed out that removing these young men from the street corners and habituating them to regularity of industry is only the first part of this task and that they must be provided with the preliminary training which will enable them to adapt their abilities to a variety of jobs, and give them the mental assurance and moral stamina to go after these jobs. The full implication of the CCC camps, he said, is not only to provide temporary employment but also to supplement the dwindling number of openings in industry for untrained youths and, necessarily, to provide enough of the primary training to enable them to take an active place in the work-day world upon discharge.

## THE HARVARD-YENCHING INSTITUTE FOR CHINESE STUDIES

THE Harvard-Yenching Institute for Chinese Studies, at Harvard University, in the course of the past year has obtained from the Tsukiji Type Foundry Company of Tokyo a font of Chinese and Japanese type containing 10,500 individual characters. The choice of the font is such that any ordinary expression is contained therein and they will be used in the publications of the institute dealing with the history, literature, art and languages of China and Japan. It is the intention of the institute to supplement this font with a rarer and aberrant form of characters as time goes on and the need arises.

The total number of characters met with in the literature of the two countries amounts to some 25,000, but most of these are only rarely met with. About 6,000 characters are really in common use. The quantity of individual characters in the font varies from 500 to 5, the average being about 10.

No other university in the country possesses a font of this type. By arrangement with the American Council of Learned Societies, which combined with the institute to purchase this font, the characters from it may be employed in the publications of that body.

The Harvard-Yenching Institute was founded in 1928 by a large grant from the estate of Mr. Charles M. Hall, of Niagara Falls, N. Y. Its purpose is twofold: to give instruction in the language, literature and history of China, Japan and contiguous countries, and to carry on research work in China through grants in financial aid to six of the universities which have been established by Americans in that country: Yenching University, Shantung Christian University, Fukien Christian University, West China Union University, Lingnan University and the University of Nanking.

Its affairs are conducted by a board of nine trustees, nominated, in the first instance, by the president of Harvard College, the Board of Trustees of Yenching University, and the trustees under the will of Mr. Hall.

The institute carries on, for properly prepared Chinese and Occidental scholars, research and educational work of the type appropriate to a graduate school of arts and sciences, and in so far as it may appear expedient in order to prepare scholars for admission to the work of the institute, to develop through other institutions undergraduate work in China; to explore, discover, collect and preserve objects of culture and antiquities, or to aid museums or others to do so.

In accordance with these purposes, the institute contributes annually to the support of several institutions in China and allots to Harvard University such sums as the trustees deem advisable for the development of teaching and research in the language, literature, history and art of China and Japan. The institute also provides some fellowships for Chinese and Occidental students for study in the Orient or at Harvard.

## THE EDUCATIONAL PROGRAM OF GOUCHER COLLEGE

WITH the opening of the college year 1934–35, Goucher College, the Woman's College of Baltimore, which will soon celebrate the fiftieth anniversary of its founding, enters upon a new educational program.

The general education appropriate for every educated American woman should include, according to the program (1) the establishment and maintenance of physical and mental health; (2) the comprehension and communication of ideas, both in English and in foreign languages; (3) the understanding of the scientific method in theory and application; (4) the understanding of the heritage of the past in its relation to the present; (5) the establishment of satisfying relations with individuals and with groups; (6) the utilization of resources with economic and esthetic satisfaction; (7) the enjoyment of literature and the other arts; (8) the appreciation of religious and philosophical values.

These purposes of general education will be emphasized during the first two years of college and satisfactory progress toward their attainment will be measured in every possible way instead of completion of a certain number of semester hours or even a certain number of required courses. There will be no required credits; there will be no required courses.

Evidences of progress toward the attainment of these realistic objectives in terms of living will be accumulated especially in the first two years of college. All instructors who have an opportunity to observe the student will report concerning her progress, especially the student's guidance officer, who will function like a tutor in an English college. At the end of the sophomore year there will be a general examination on the facts and principles underlying such of the foregoing eight objectives as can be tested; an examination in essay form on one topic chosen by the student from several, for the completion of which three hours will be allowed, and a written project in one field testing the student's ability to use tools in the library or laboratory or both, for the completion of which several days will be allowed. There will also be a reading examination in one foreign language. A board of examiners will consider not only the results of these examinations but all estimates of the student's progress, including reports on the work done in such courses as have been taken and will admit students to the upper division.

The upper division of the college, comprising the third and fourth years, is the period of special education for each student. Every student will devote a quarter of the total of time of her four years in college to work in one of the usual academic fields such as biology, chemistry, English, history, etc., or will devote one third of the total time to a subject which may cross departmental boundaries.

The degree of Bachelor of Arts will be awarded to those who satisfactorily complete a comprehensive examination in the field of concentration, who have a record of satisfactory work not included in the major field, and who show a satisfactory record of progress toward the attainment of the eight objectives.

## LECTURES AT THE AMERICAN MUSEUM OF NATURAL HISTORY

Five free courses for teachers, given by the American Museum in cooperation with the College of the City of New York, are open without cost to its members. A fee will be charged to others. The courses when taken by teachers or matriculated students in the School of Education at the College of the City of New York are credited in the School of Education. Each course is allowed thirty hours' "Alertness Credit" by the Board of Education or credit for one increment. A list of the lectures follows: "Nature Study for City Teachers," "Applied Physiology and Health," "The Museum in Elementary Social Studies," and two courses in "The Mechanics of Visual Instruction." Students in "Applied Physiology and Health" will have the advantage of the results of original research carried on by Dr. G. K. Noble and Dr. H. J. Clausen, of the department of experimental biology, and by Dr. W. K. Gregory, of the department of comparative anatomy.

Four courses, given primarily for teachers, in cooperation with New York University are open to members and friends of the museum upon payment of the regular fees. These are "Astronomy for Teachers," "Survey of Natural History for Teachers," "The Museum in Elementary Education" and "Primitive Culture."

The regular Saturday afternoon showings of motion pictures will be continued, starting on October 6 with the talking picture, "The Silent Enemy."

A series of four Saturday afternoon talks on the Gem Collections of the American Museum will be given at the museum by Herbert P. Whitlock, curator of gems and minerals, on October 20, 27, and November 3 and 10.

The lectures for school children of the city, supplementing their work in science, history and geography, will be continued on Mondays, Wednesdays and Fridays at 10:30 A. M.

The sight conservation classes for children with defective sight will be carried on as they have been for the past twenty-two years.

A new special activity program, consisting of Finger Painting, Nature Crafts and Miniature Group Making, is included in the Exhibition Hall Talks offered to children of the public schools. This is an unusual opportunity for the child to complete, under expert supervision, a definite piece of creative work of his own choosing.

Ten free lectures on biologic science will be offered to students in elementary, general and advanced biology by members of the museum staff.

The Know Your Museum Series for members will begin on October 30. There will be four evening programs, following a plan entirely different from that of previous years.

## THE FOURTH ANNUAL MEETING OF THE NATIONAL ADVISORY COUNCIL ON RADIO IN EDUCATION

The National Advisory Council on Radio in Education held its fourth annual meeting in Chicago on October 8 and 9. Five of the six sessions were held in a hotel and the other at the World's Fair.

At the opening session Dr. Robert A. Millikan, of the California Institute of Technology, chairman of the council, addressed the delegates by radio from London. The other speakers were Dr. Robert M. Hutchins, president of the University of Chicago, who discussed "Radio and Public Policy"; Professor William F. Ogburn, of the University of Chicago, who spoke on "The Changing Social Scene in 1934" and Dr. Frederick P. Keppel, of the Carnegie Corporation, the title of whose address was "Implications of the Changing Social Order in American Cultural Activities."

In the afternoon the speakers and their subjects were: President Robert G. Sproul, of the University of California, "What Radio Broadcasting Has Accomplished as a Cultural Instrument"; Alfred N. Goldsmith, consulting engineer, "Educational Capabilities of Technical Audi-Visual Methods." Grace Abbott, professor of public welfare administration at the University of Chicago, also spoke.

The evening session on Monday was held in the auditorium of the Hall of Science at the fair, with President Rufus C. Dawes presiding. The speakers were Dr. John H. Finley, associate editor of *The New York Times,* and Secretary of the Interior Ickes.

A discussion on "Shall the Government Own, Operate and Control Radio Broadcasting in the United States?" was held on Tuesday morning in the Drake Hotel, when Bruce Bliven, editor of *The New Republic*, advocated government control, and E. H. Brown, chairman of the radio committee of the American Newspaper Publishers Association, advocated private control.

"What should be done to improve American broadcasting" was discussed on Tuesday afternoon. In the evening a dinner was held in the Drake Hotel, presided over by President Walter Dill Scott, of Northwestern University. Speakers at the dinner were Walter Damrosch, musical counsel for the National Broadcasting Company, and Dr. John Erskine, president of the Juilliaid School of Music, New York City.

# EDUCATIONAL NOTES AND NEWS

General Jan Christiaan Smuts, formerly prime minister of the Union of South Africa and in 1931 president of the British Association for the Advancement of Science, will be installed as rector of the University of St. Andrews on October 17. The degrees conferred at the installation ceremonies included the doctorate of laws on Sir Thomas Henry Holland, principal and vice-chancellor of the University of Edinburgh, and on General Smuts.

The degree of doctor of laws was conferred on Dr. Harold Willis Dodds, president of Princeton University, on the occasion of the installation on October 5 of Dr. Tyler Dennett as tenth president of Williams College. President Dodds responded with a brief address.

On the occasion of Founders Day ceremonies at Lehigh University the doctorate of laws was conferred on Dr. Josiah H. Penniman, provost of the University of Pennsylvania, and on Dr. Charles McLean Andrews, emeritus professor of history at Yale University. The degree of doctor of science was conferred on Dr. Irving Langmuir, associate director of the Research Laboratory of the General Electric Company. Dr. Penniman delivered the Founders Day address.

A dinner in honor of Dr. Henry Noble MacCracken was given on October 8 by the trustees of Vassar College to mark his twentieth year as president of the college. Dr. Stephen P. Duggan, director of the Institute of International Education, expressed for the trustees their appreciation of Dr. MacCracken's service. Dean C. Mildred Thompson spoke for the faculty.

Dr. M. Lyle Spencer, dean of the Syracuse University School of Journalism and formerly president of the University of Washington, was elected an honorary member of the New York Press Association at its recent meeting in Syracuse. Dr. Spencer is one of three honorary members the association has had in its history of eighty-one years.

Dr. William R. Price, supervisor of modern foreign languages in the New York State Education Department, has been honored by the French government by the award of the Cross of the Chevalier of the Legion of Honor in recognition of his many years of promoting the understanding of the French language and of the French people. Dr. Price has supervised the instruction of French and other modern languages in the schools of the state since 1911.

The consul general of France, M. René Weiller, acting for his government, conferred the medal of the Legion of Honor on Frank G. Logan, of Chicago, on August 27, in recognition of his and Mrs. Logan's "many years of service to the cause of art, education and scientific research." Mr. Logan is honorary president of the Chicago Art Institute and a trustee of Beloit College. Mrs. Logan has published poems and collaborated with her late brother, Dr. J. L. Hancock, in scientific work.

Dr. Gordon Keith Chalmers, formerly professor of English at Mount Holyoke College, Massachusetts, was installed as president of Rockford College, Illinois, on October 10.

Dr. William Orville Mendenhall, formerly president of Friends University, Wichita, Kansas, was installed as president of Whittier College, California, on September 21.

S. C. Hollister, professor of structural engineering at Purdue University, has been appointed director of the School of Civil Engineering at Cornell University.

Ralph A. Burns has been promoted from an assistant professorship to a professorship of education at Dartmouth College.

DR. EARL CRANSTON, formerly assistant professor of history at Colgate University, has taken up the chairmanship of the department of history and political science at the University of Redlands. Dr. Fred J. Sales, assistant professor of education, has been appointed acting director of personnel. His chief work for the present will be giving educational guidance to students.

AMONG the additions to the faculty of Colby College are the following: associate professor of health and physical education, Gilbert F. Loebs; instructor in health and physical education, Norman C. Perkins; instructor in classical languages, Sharon Lea Finch; instructor in English, John R. Walden. The college opened its one hundred and seventeenth year with 607 students. The entering class of 185 showed a ten per cent. increase over last year.

CHARLES E. CARTER retired on July 1 as superintendent of the Franklin, Pennsylvania, public schools after eighteen years of service. He is succeeded by Karl M. Russell, who was elected supervising principal.

BENJAMIN W. JOHNSON, supervisor of classes for training trade and industrial teachers at the University of California at Los Angeles, will become principal of the Frank Wiggins Trade School, in Los Angeles. Mr. Johnson has been in charge of vocational teacher training at the university for the past eleven years and previously held the same position at Berkeley. He will be succeeded at Los Angeles by Dr. David F. Jackey.

LEAVE of absence until Christmas has been granted to Dean C. K. Burdick, of Cornell University, to enable him to accept Governor Lehman's appointment as chairman of the State's Law Revision Commission. Professor R. S. Stevens will be acting dean in his absence.

PROFESSOR A. F. HINRICHS, of Brown University, has been appointed chief economist of the Bureau of Labor Statistics. Professor Hinrichs has been director of Brown's Bureau of Business Research, and for two years was in charge of research for the New York State Commission on Housing and Regional Planning.

ARNO B. CAMMERER, director of the National Park Service, has been appointed by the Secretary of State a representative of the United States on the International Commission on Historical Monuments.

DR. GEORGE J. RYAN, president of the New York City Board of Education, and Jacob Greenberg, who was recently elected associate superintendent of schools of New York City, have sailed for Europe to observe the school systems in France and Italy.

DR. FRANK D. KERN, head of the department of botany at the Pennsylvania State College and dean of the Graduate School, has returned after a year's leave of absence, during which he served as acting dean of the College of Agriculture of the University of Puerto Rico. He is succeeded by Professor Harry G. Parkinson, head of the department of agricultural education at the State College.

DR. GEORGE B. PARKS, of the Department of English at Washington University (St. Louis), is on leave this year, having received a fellowship for study at the Huntington Library, San Marino, California. Two years ago he was given a year in Europe by the Guggenheim Foundation to prosecute his research on the early English voyages.

DR. CHARLES D. MATTHEWS, professor of Bible at Birmingham-Southern College, returns this fall from a year's study in Palestine, where he was the holder of the Newman Fellowship.

AT Wayne University, city of Detroit, Dr. H. H. Pixley has returned after a leave of absence, during which he served as mathematical economist in the NRA. His promotion to an assistant professorship is announced. In the same department Dr. C. H. Fischer has been appointed instructor.

THE Germanistic Society of America Fellowship of $1,500, which is administered by the Institute of International Education, has been awarded to Vern W. Robinson, instructor in German at the University of Illinois, for graduate study in Germany during the academic year 1934–1935. Mr. Robinson will study at the University of Munich, specializing in the history of the German one-act play. Upon his return from Germany he expects to resume his position at the University of Illinois.

DR. STEPHEN P. DUGGAN, director of the Institute of International Education, who recently returned to New York after an absence of more than eight months in Europe, has been holding conferences with people influential in political, social and economic affairs. Dr. Duggan has been engaged by the Columbia Broadcasting Corporation to deliver over a national hook-up a weekly broadcast upon foreign affairs every Friday at 2:30 P. M., New York time, beginning on October 26 and ending on May 3, 1935. It is hoped that the broadcasts may be of especial interest to college students.

DR. HARLAN H. HORNER, assistant commissioner for higher education of the University of the State of New York, spoke at a recent meeting of the New York State Nursing Association, at which more than 1,000 nurses were in attendance. He discussed his report on a survey completed last spring of the nursing situation in the state. An address was also made by Dr. John Wyckoff, dean of the School of Medicine of New York University.

COLBY COLLEGE has announced its program of evening extension courses for teachers wishing credit from the State Department of Education as follows: "The Public Schools and the New Social Order," by President Franklin W. Johnson; "The Nature of Learning and Teaching," by Professor Edward J. Colgan; "United States History Since 1932," by Professor William J. Wilkinson; "The Language Arts in All the Grades," by Dean Ernest C. Marriner.

DR. EDWIN KNOX MITCHELL, formerly dean of Hartford Theological Seminary, died on October 5. He was eighty years of age.

WASHINGTON UNIVERSITY held a Memorial Meeting to Gabriel Ferrand, late professor of design and head of the School of Architecture, on October 10. Addresses were made by Mr. Ernest Russell, president of the American Institute of Architects; Professor Holmes Smith, for the faculties; Professor Maurice Faure, for the Société Française de Saint Louis; Mr. Clemens Nicholas, for the Alumni. Chancellor Throop presided.

THE American Council on Education held a conference last week at Briarcliff Lodge, Briarcliff Manor, N. Y., with Dr. George F. Zook, director of the council, presiding. Among other officers of the council present were: Dean William F. Russell, of Teachers College, Columbia University, *chairman;* Dr. Sidney B. Hall, of Virginia, of the National Education Association, *first vice-chairman;* the Reverend George Johnson, of the National Catholic Education Association, *secretary,* and President Edward C. Elliott, of Purdue University, and President Cloyd H. Marvin, of the George Washington University, *members of the executive committee.* The meeting was also attended by Dr. Samuel P. Capen, chancellor of the University of Buffalo and first director of the council; Professor Charles H. Judd, dean of the School of Education of the University of Chicago; Dr. R. M. Hughes, president of Iowa State College; Dr. Guy E. Snavely, president of Birmingham-Southern College; Dr. Trevor Arnett, of the Rockefeller Foundation and the General Education Board; Edwin R. Embree, president of the Julius Rosenwald Fund; Dr. W. A. Jessup, president of the Carnegie Foundation for the Advancement of Teaching, and Dr. Frederick P. Keppel, president of the Carnegie Corporation.

THE annual conference of the National Society for the Prevention of Blindness will be held in New York City from December 6 to 8, it is announced by Lewis H. Carris, managing director. Dr. Edward Jackson, of Denver, Colo., will deliver the principal address on "A Wide Basis for Blindness Prevention." Dr. Jackson was the first recipient, in 1925, of the Leslie Dana Gold Medal, which is awarded annually for outstanding achievements in the prevention of blindness and conservation of vision. Among the topics that will come up for discussion at the conference will be: the causes of blindness; sight-saving classes for children with seriously defective vision; prevention of eye accidents, and prevention of pre-natal infections which may cause blindness.

THE Association of Deans and Directors of Summer Sessions will hold its seventeenth annual meeting at Iowa State College on October 12 and 13. The organization was formed to further graduate work in the summer and its members include the deans of colleges and universities which emphasize work for advanced degrees during the summer term. Discussions will be informal. The 1934 officers of the association are: E. H. Hahne, Northwestern University, *president;* P. C. Weaver, Pennsylvania State College, *vice-president;* Dean Foster, *secretary,* and P. C. Packer, University of Iowa, *recorder.*

Harvard University has refused to accept the $1,000 offered for a scholarship by Dr. Ernst F. S. Hanfstaengl, Chancellor Hitler's lieutenant and a member of the Harvard class of 1907. The Harvard Corporation did not meet during the summer, but considered the gift at its first fall meeting on September 24, after which President Conant wrote to Dr. Hanfstaengl as follows: "At a meeting of the president and Fellows of Harvard College, held today, your offer of a traveling scholarship, to be known as the Dr. Hanfstaengl scholarship, was considered. I am authorized to say that, although the corporation appreciates your generosity as a Harvard alumnus, they have voted to decline your gift. We are unwilling to accept a gift from one who has been so closely associated with the leadership of a political party which has inflicted damage on the universities throughout the world. Since your offer was made public and has been the subject of discussion, we deem it proper to make this letter public."

The James Nelson and Anna Louise Raymond Foundation presented a free program of motion pictures for children at Field Museum of Natural History on the morning of Saturday, October 13. The films shown were "Snake Myths" and, in recognition of Columbus Day, the historical feature, "Columbus Sails West."

The initial series of pictures on Child Development produced by Dr. Arnold Gesell, of the Yale Psycho-Clinic, in cooperation with Erpi Picture Consultants, has been completed. The series includes four one-reel pictures, "The Development of Infant Behavior: Early Stages"; "The Development of Infant Behavior: Later Stages"; "Posture and Locomotion," and "From Creeping to Walking."

An International Exhibition of Children's Painting, under the auspices of the Little Red School House, will be inaugurated by Mrs. Franklin D. Roosevelt, on Monday evening, November 12, in the Mezzanine Gallery of Rockefeller Center and will be opened to the general public from November 13 through December 1, every day, except Sunday, from 10 a. m. to 6 p. m. at an admission charge of twenty-five cents. The proceeds will be for the benefit of the scholarship fund of the Little Red School House. This is the first attempt to bring to American parents, teachers and pupils the spontaneous art work of native children from the ages of six to twelve years in forty foreign countries, including China, Bali, Russia and Japan.

Fourteen fellowships and a residential scholarship make up the list of annual awards offered by the American Association of University Women for the year 1935–36. The fellowships are open only to women who are American citizens, except in special instances, and applications or recommendations for them must be received by Mary H. Smith, the secretary of the Committee on Scholarship Awards, 1634 "I" Street, N.W., Washington, D. C., not later than December 1, 1934. Candidates must have completed at least two years of work toward the degree of doctor of philosophy.

The recently incorporated American Students' Foundation has issued a year book listing the scholarships offered by 125 colleges and universities in the United States. These amount to more than $30,000,000. The foundation, a non-profit organization, was founded to fulfil the following needs, according to the introduction of the year book: (1) To create a widespread desire for vocational and college training for the boys and girls of America. (2) To furnish, through the year book, complete tabulated information about colleges, universities, preparatory schools and vocational, technical, trade and professional schools and to assist in determining a child's adaptability to different forms of training. (3) To aid students through scholarships and by providing ways and means for the students and parents to earn educational funds.

Mrs. Annie S. Thomas, the widow of Dr. W. Scott Thomas, who was for many years assistant professor of education at the University of California and examiner of schools, has given to the university a fund of $1,500 to be known as the W. Scott Thomas Loan Fund. The fund, which supplements the Dohrmann and Denicke faculty loan funds, will be available for members of the faculty on the Berkeley campus of the university, and for their widows and children immediately subsequent to the death of the husband or father. It is designed particularly to aid faculty members when they are no longer able to obtain sabbatical leaves of absence, or when they are under heavy expense as the result of illness. For the first year of their existence, the loans will not bear interest, and the interest for succeeding years will be at the rate of 6 per cent. per annum.

Two gifts, one of $50,000 and another of $3,500, have been made to Bennett College for Negroes, at Greensboro, N. C. The first came from Mr. and Mrs. Henry Pfieffer, of New York, and the latter from the Methodist Woman's Home Missionary Society, also of New York.

# DISCUSSION

## LEISURE—A CURSE OR A BLESSING?

How astonished our grandfathers would be if they could hear us solemnly discussing "the problem of leisure time"! A few decades ago the working day of even the white collar class was twelve hours. Factory hands and farm laborers worked fourteen to sixteen hours. There was little leisure time to use wisely or unwisely in grandfather's time. Technological advances of the past half century have shortened working hours first to ten, then to eight and now to seven or fewer hours per day. Our industrial and social experts assure us that, if all able-bodied men would do their share of the world's work, no one would need to work more than twenty-five hours a week. To-day we work less time than our grandfathers had for leisure! This great amount of leisure presents a challenge, a danger and an opportunity to American society and to the American school.

It challenges us because of the undeniable fact that so far we have not learned to use or control it. It is a loose cannon upon the deck of our social ship of state. We have stood helplessly watching this new-found leisure of the masses go madly upon its career of destruction. It is still true, in spite of our boasted civilization, that idle hands are usually employed by the devil. Children forced out of industry gather in street corner gangs and in their early "teens" embark upon careers of petty thievery, car looting and purse snatching. It is no wonder that crime under these conditions continues to grow. Vicious commercial interests have exploited the leisure time of the great mass of our people. The saloon, the cheap dance hall and the lewd or suggestive motion picture are the chief beneficiaries of America's leisure. In the average American city to-day Sally Rand could probably get a larger and more appreciative audience than Schumann-Heink. The age-long struggle of mankind has been for time free from the constant economic struggle, for leisure time. Yet to-day this leisure, now attained, appears to be a Frankenstein monster. Growing crime rates, increasing drunkenness, immorality among our youth, petty crime which is ignored by public officials, graft in high places and filth in low places are the results of this leisure time which we have obtained. Cutten has said, "A civilization which creates a leisure which it does not use in a rational manner is in greater danger than one that has never obtained leisure."

However, in this monster which threatens to overwhelm us there is a possibility for great good. Twice before in history have high civilizations arisen and offered leisure to their people. In the fourth century before Christ, Athens developed the greatest culture of all time out of the leisure of her citizens. It is true that this leisure rested upon the shaking and groaning foundations of human slavery; true it is that barbarian hordes swept over it and destroyed much of it; but we still stand in awe before the broken marble of that age of leisure. With a leisure based upon the enslavement of power and machinery instead of human beings; with a leisure open to not the few of the upper class alone but to all, we should stand to-day upon the threshold of a period which will far surpass in glory the age of Pericles.

We must remember, though, that in the first and second centuries of the Christian era the Romans too acquired considerable leisure. To what did this Roman leisure lead? To-day we see no Parthenon, but instead a blood-stained arena; we hear no music, but instead the cries of martyrs and the howls of savage beasts and a no less savage mob; we see no Socrates, but a Nero as the result of Roman leisure. Cruel bloodthirsty sports, immorality in the home, corruption in the government, crime in the cities, poverty, despair, decay and ruin were the results of the misuse of leisure time by the Romans. The challenge comes to us, "Here is leisure, how will you use it?" The danger is that our civilization will go the way of Rome; we have the opportunity to develop a new culture which will rival that of Athens. The millions of Americans, once engaged in the sole pursuit of earning a living, now may participate in wholesome social enterprises to their own and the community's good.

Nor can we, the schoolmen of America, escape our share of the responsibility for the widespread abuse of leisure time. We have trained students whose literature is "confessions," we have graduated with honors students whose idea of good music is on a level with that of an African savage. Especially have we erred in our failure to make school training an effective force in life. We have taken the student to the door of the school and said to him: "There is the world, Good-bye. If you sink or swim it is nothing to us." We must make the ideals and the culture attitudes which we teach in the formative years of life a constantly growing force throughout all life. We must realize that adult education for cultural improvement is necessary to the solution of the leisure time problem.

We must during the years an individual is in school and in the post-school years definitely train for worthwhile uses of leisure time. We must emphasize hobbies as well as history, libraries for recreational reading rather than literature of a bygone day, games for the sake of games instead of competitive athletics. The public has demanded a "good show" in athletics, and we have given it to them. We have trained girls to hurdle, throw the discus and run the 440. Will some one please find a matron in her thirties who runs the high hurdles during her leisure time?

The school must realize that upon it rests the responsibility to give to each student the urge to do something creative, something for self-betterment, something for the good of the group during his leisure time. Imagine the possibilities of our present society—one half of man's waking hours spent in labor, the other half in producing something for self-improvement or for the cultural advance of the race. During the 1920's a high pressure advertising by creating new markets for consumer goods absorbed the over-production due to technological improvements. For the next century education must absorb the surplus time of the world through raising the cultural, physical and mental standards of living of the masses. Music must bring to mankind a new and more calm emotional outlook. Art must flourish, because many great masters should appear among those freed from the slavery of the economic struggle. Great books can be written and read during the hours of leisure. Great plays, free from the lewd, the immoral and the cheap, must be written, produced and viewed. The general health and physical efficiency of the race must be raised through clean outdoor sport. Great discoveries in medicine, science and philosophy must be made by leaders and intelligently accepted by the people. With all this to do we gaily waste our leisure on the brutal, the animal and the lowest things in life. No present-day institution, except the school, has a physical plant, an outlook or a staff which can be easily adapted to lead this new development in the use of leisure time.

Especially must we develop a new social conscience. We must make all see that parasites upon society must be destroyed. To-day the scum at the top and the dregs at the bottom of society consume the leisure time of the great middle group. The idle, rich and poor both, the criminals, the paupers, the loafers of all ranks and grades consume the leisure time of the great working class. We must teach that abrogation of self for the good of society results in the greatest self-satisfaction. Nor is this task hopeless. Russia's schools and Italy's schools have so trained the youth of their countries that they are fanatically willing to do all within their power to attain the goals set for the country by the school. Let us set for our goal a use of leisure time which will answer the challenge and fulfil the great opportunity which is before us. Then let us train American youths and adults to our standard of clean living, high culture and social good.

W. B. McPherson

Williams Consolidated Schools,
Williams, Minn.

## WHY FEDERAL AID?

A short time ago the newspapers informed us that the Reconstruction Finance Corporation lent the sum of $26,365,000 to Chicago, in order that the back salaries of 14,000 teachers and 3,000 other school employees might be paid. Certainly this was federal aid to education, but not the same sort advised by numerous persons.

The most common proposals have called for an outright grant to states in need of funds to operate schools within their own borders, by the national government. The most generally discussed amounts are $50,000,000 or, more often, $100,000,000, while the radical National Student League has asked $25,000,000 for the state of Minnesota alone. Such funds might be contributed without any provision for use, but in all probability, some form of federal supervision or control would be necessary. Upon the premise that school systems are sorely in need of such help, the question has been almost constantly before us, with numerous arguments advanced, both pro and con. But is this large gift of money an absolute necessity for the schools?

The important contention of the proponents of such legislation is that, since education can not be properly delayed, support of the schools must be always of primary importance. They are, of course, essential. But increased crime makes necessary the maintenance of police departments; increased poverty must be alleviated by poor relief; and our fire, health and public library departments of government must not be too greatly curtailed. If federal aid is given to the schools, why not also to these? Obviously, the ultimate result would be nationalization of every important function, now under control and supervision of state or local governing agents. It is undoubtedly true that the present economic emergency has wrought great hardships upon various school systems, and has necessitated large cuts in salaries, length of term and other expenditures. Nevertheless, aside from the fact that the present state of affairs is considerably brighter than a year or two ago, there are other salient items which must be mentioned in this regard.

The important point is this: Federal loans serve the purpose of grants, and yet entail none of the restrictions which must almost inevitably accompany the latter. These will be discussed in greater length in a moment. If there were no promise of relief from the present depression, loans would, of course, be impossible in certain localities. But all indications point to clearer financial skies; in many places, tax moneys are more plentiful, and nearly two score of cities and towns have increased their budgets for the present school year. This does not mean that federal relief is totally unnecessary, but it does signify that this relief can easily take the form of loans.

Let us suppose that federal aid, in the nature of outright grants, were to be given. Is it not true that, unless definite restriction and control are applied to the application of such funds, the past history of similar grants, a record of tremendous loss through numerous causes including faulty management, will be repeated? Yet this is highly undesirable, because such federal control will inevitably tend toward much greater restriction and regimentation of school policy, a very unsatisfactory phenomenon, which even the most ardent supporters of federal aid must seriously consider.

Therefore we find that it is far more rational to apply federal loans than federal grants to our educational systems. Since they must be repaid, utmost care would be taken in managing and allocating them. Furthermore, since they are loans, federal control, which would produce centralization of school supervision, is both impossible and superfluous. The practicability of these loans is demonstrated by the example, Chicago, pointed out at the beginning of this article. Such a proposal may, quite conceivably, be the salvation of certain sections of our system of public education.

William Kelty

## FOR THE LOVE OF BOOKS

One of the great disasters of the last two decades has been the growth of an unhappy indifference to beauty and an equally unhappy tolerance of ugliness. For a sun-tan and fan-dance generation that may not seem a serious matter, but education as a public process fails in no small degree when it produces such a generation. In some directions forces are unquestionably at work toward the remedying of that evil. We are providing more beautiful and commodious school buildings. We are stimulating interest in music and in pictorial art. We are making the high school somewhat the community center for the presentation of drama.

With all this, however, we have been neglecting one thing of very great moment for the cultural development of our young people. We have failed to make the children who go through our schools lovers of books as books. We permit them to think of the texts that we put into their hands simply as tools for the making of grades. We let them draw their intellectual, social and esthetic nourishment from shabby books, dirty books, germ-laden books, outmoded books; and the inevitable consequence is that they do not love them. For the most part, when they need them no longer for the preparation of their lessons, they part with them as easily as the diner at a restaurant parts with his emptied coffee cup.

The business of public education is largely that of developing in children a finer intelligence, finer tastes and finer human character and quality. For this a love of books as books, not simply as repositories of information, is fundamental. The boy should be taught to accumulate books, to build a library. He should grow to love the sight of a book well made and well bound. He should come to enjoy a clear open page set in good readable type as a thing of good in itself. He should find it an enduring pleasure to linger over beautiful illustrations that are something more than clarifications of the text, illustrations that are enjoyable for themselves and that make the reader reluctant to turn the page. The gathering and preserving and cherishing of such books should be as much a passion for the young man or the young woman going out from school or college into the fuller life of the world as is the collecting of fine china and silver for the woman who delights in having guests about her table.

This passion it is of course impossible to nourish on a fare of badly printed, much pencil-annotated, sadly worn or otherwise shabby books in school and college. The cost of good books is but a negligible fraction of the cost of education in the total. They should constitute a large part of the resources that the student carries on into those hours of leisure in which something fine or something gross, something reposeful or something unsettled and unsettling is to be enjoyed.

It is not simply for the boy himself or the girl that we should cultivate the love of beauty and the hatred of ugliness. It is also for his functioning in society as he becomes an adult that we should train him for the restful tranquilities. To a frenzied world the cultivated man should contribute poise, calmness, assurance, repose. For the fostering of a love of reflective quiet rather than a love of turmoil, a love kept alive by the companionship of good books more than by anything else, the cost of books not dog-eared for the scrap heap is a small price for society to pay. It is ultimate economy to let the children who are to be the future have under their hands day by day things lovingly written, beautifully designed and well made.

Lewis Worthington Smith
Drake University

# SPECIAL CORRESPONDENCE

## THE REORGANIZED SCHOOL SYSTEM OF BULGARIA

After the Agrarian Party under Stambulski came to power in 1920 in Bulgaria, it used its influence to introduce thorough reform in the schools in July, 1921. Some of the new reforms were considered as backward and unprogressive. On the other hand, some of them were useful: The compulsory school attendance was extended up to the fourteenth year of age, and it was provided that in every place where the fourth grade of the elementary schools had more than 20 pupils, there should be founded a pro-gymnasium. The universities were reorganized, and new faculties were added. The Bulgarian priests had been formerly educated in the seminaries, which corresponded to secondary schools. Now a new theological school was established.

With the downfall of the Agrarian Government on June 9, 1923, the way was opened for another reorganization of the Bulgarian schools.

The whole system was reformed by the law of 1924.

The aim of the first three classes of the national schools is the "harmonic evolution of the personality of the child," in order that it would become a useful member of society and that it would gain information needed for higher and professional education.

At the bottom of the educational system is the kindergarten for the children from the ages of five to seven. Here the children learn by plays, singing and manual work. These schools are compulsory in the cities of more than 20,000 inhabitants and in other national communities where elementary schools exist. Such schools can be either private or supported by the state.

The elementary school classes are composed of about 40 children. Its attendance is of four years' duration. Each community which has more than twenty children of school age must create such a school, which is free and compulsory. The school year lasts ten months, and this may be shortened in villages. In the first two years the class hours are limited to four hours a day, and in other classes to not more than five hours. Four hours a week are devoted to visiting factories, walking, etc. Religion, taught one hour a week by the teacher, is a part of the curricula, just as the Bulgarian language, mathematics, Bulgarian geography, civics, drawing, nature study, athletics and sewing are. At the end of the year examinations in biblical history, mathematics, geography and nature study are given.

The "pro-gymnasium" comes next in the scale. It is free and compulsory for all youth up to the fourteenth year. The instruction hours are limited to 28 hours a week, four of which are devoted to the walks into the country, or visiting industrial establishments. The subjects are the same as in the elementary schools, with the addition of the following: Religious Slav language, one modern language (French, English or German), Bulgarian history, general geography, drawing, physics, hygiene and social solidarity, chemistry, economics, agriculture and manual training. Before graduation, the pupil must pass an examination in the Bulgarian language, mathematics, Bulgarian history, Bulgarian geography and nature description.

The elementary and pro-gymnasium schools use a different system of marking than do American schools—the best mark is 6, and the worst 1. The student must have at least a grade of 3 in order to graduate. Those with lower grades than 3 can pass a supplementary examination in three subjects only.

It is interesting to notice that there are numerous places where the pro-gymnasia have less than three-year classes. In 1,299 pro-gymnasia in 1929–1930, there were 116 pro-gymnasia with two classes and 150 with but one class.

The communities with no pro-gymnasium have special courses which are compulsory for the children up to 14 years of age. These last three years, the school year being from September 1 to June 15. The teaching is done in the daytime, evenings or on Sundays. Furthermore, even in the places where a pro-gymnasium is located, there also can be given practical one-year to two-year courses in agriculture, commerce or industry—according to the needs of the region.

The aim of the schools of the third grade is to finish the mental and physical evolution of pupils; to give them necessary information and practical knowledge, and general and civic education. These schools are all named gymnasia. They are divided into those giving general education and those giving special (pedagogical) education. The commercial, agricultural and other special schools are not under the jurisdiction of the Ministry of Education, but under the respective ministries. These gymnasia are either for both sexes or for either sex only. The gymnasia concerned with general education are divided into three classes—classic gymnasia (which teach Greek and Latin), half-classical (which teach Latin) and scientific (which teach a modern language). The number of students in a class is limited to 40. The pupils are taught the Bulgarian language and literature, philosophy, education, one foreign language (French, German, English, Russian, Greek, Latin), mathematics, descriptive geometry and drawing. They are also taught Bulgarian history, general history, Bulgarian geography, general geography, civics and economics, physics, chemistry, nature study and singing. Music, physical education, manual training and shorthand are not compulsory. It is interesting to note that religion is also not compulsory and that physical education was made compulsory only in 1931.

The school administration is composed of a director and the faculty, who have a comparatively large autonomy. The authority of the director is rather extensive. Some schools are visited periodically by physicians and dentists. On the proposal of the faculties, some of the teachers are sent to study abroad for a year or two. Most of these go to Germany.

The University of Sofia is divided into seven faculties—historico-philological, mathematico-natural sciences, legal, medicine, agriculture, theology and veterinary. The term in medical school is 12 semesters; in the veterinary, 9 months; and 8 semesters in the other schools. The technical schools are rated only as secondary schools in Bulgaria, because industry is not well developed.

Sofia also has a "Free University," built on the model of the Paris "École Libre des Sciences Politiques." It is divided into the diplomatic-consular, the administrative-financial and commercial-economic divisions. The courses last three years. Since 1921, the Academy of Art and the Academy of Music have university standing.

It is interesting to notice the proportion of the students failing in their studies in Bulgaria. According to the estimates of Dr. D. Gavrijsky, in 1928–29, only 78.5 per cent. of the children in the elementary schools passed, 0.9 per cent. had to take another examination and 20.6 per cent. of the children failed to pass. Most of the children, 27 per cent., fail to pass the first year of school.

By analyzing the situation in the pro-gymnasia (upper elementary schools), we see that about 60 per cent. of the students pass, 20 per cent. had to take another examination after the summer vacations and 20 per cent. failed. The mortality of the students is the greatest in the first year, that is, 22 per cent. The rate decreases when we come to the gymnasia. During the same year, out of 30,973 pupils 18,624 passed, 3,072 failed, and the rest were allowed to take new examinations. In general, about 10 per cent. of the students failed. The Bulgarian gymnasia students are required to pass the "maturity examination" at the end of their gymnasium studies. Out of 3,405 students, only 2,780 passed, 611 failed and 914 had to repeat it. The same difficulties seem to be confronted by the students from the normal schools; 1,946 applied for the maturity examination, 248 failed and 393 had to repeat the process, so that only 1,305 passed.

In spite of the fact that Bulgaria is said to have made the greatest educational progress in the shortest length of time,[1] the fact remains that Bulgaria has not evolved a systematic plan to improve her conditions in the high rate of illiteracy. Although the country is overcrowded with unemployed intelligentsia, there exists, on the other hand, a number of people who even do not know how to read and write. In 1925–26 41,796 did not even attend the school, and only some 60,000 children completed the attendance to their classes. Hence, during that year 101,512 children, that is, one sixth of the total number of 641,734 children, who were to be in schools according to the law, were out of schools, in spite of the compulsory attendance law. In the next year, the number of the children not attending the school dropped to 95,866. Thus it can be taken for granted that about 5 per cent. of illiterates are being constantly produced. The reasons for the high rate of illiteracy are the indifferent attitude of the parents, the long distance of the homes from the school, physical weaknesses and the work required from the children in families.

The most important factors determining the regular school attendance is the grave economic and social situation in the country. Of the inhabitants, 82.5 per cent. are employed in agriculture, and most of them use primitive methods. Consequently, the people do not understand properly the importance of education.

Another factor determining the unequal spread of education is the considerable racial, cultural and religious differentiation of the country. There are numerous Turks, Armenians, Gypsies and Greeks, who are either educated in state schools or in their own tongue in the backward minorities schools. For example, out of one hundred Bulgarian Turks only eight can read and write.

[1] See: F. W. Russell, "Schools of Bulgaria," New York, Columbia University Press, 1924.

It is worth while to study the Bulgarian educational structure. The whole system provides a complete line of unity, achieved by very few European states. The fundamental characteristic of it is the real aim to achieve democratic features. For example, the secondary education has been co-educational for a long time. Although religion has played a very important rôle in Bulgarian history, religious traditions play very little part in the Bulgarian schools. A very important element is the attention paid to physical education. The typical Bulgarian teacher is very practical and sensible, and is really interested in his career, which is very surprising if we remember his small and irregular income.

JOSEPH S. ROUCEK
PENNSYLVANIA STATE COLLEGE

# QUOTATIONS

## LIBRARIANS IN CONFERENCE

THE schools and the public libraries have cooperated more and more in recent years, and their association seems likely to become closer as the new senior schools develop their curricula and gain a greater knowledge of the needs of boys and girls. Many public librarians seek, with success, to maintain close touch with all grades of schools, with technical institutes and with classes for adult education, and provide many books for advanced students both in the reference department and in the circulating sections. The librarian shares with the teacher the task of awakening a love of literature and a desire to seek for knowledge for its own sake, and in some measure the responsibility of the librarian is greater than that of the teacher. Not only does he need to provide books and advise upon study and research, but he has to select the right books for leisure hours, a task which is not easy at the present time, when so much is published, and when, it appears, almost anything can be published. The Library Association realize that there is here a question which needs threshing out. At their fifty-seventh conference, which opens at University College next Monday, this matter will be exhaustively discussed. The problem is undoubtedly difficult. Almost every public library is now run on the "open access" system. People can go to the shelves, choose the book they want, and take it away with the smallest possible formality. But there are some books, clearly, that should not be available in this way. Many works which it is thought may be harmful to young people are in fact not stocked by the public libraries, or kept apart in a separate place. Any one wanting these books must make a special request to the librarian. A correspondent writing on "Books the Public Wants" in *The Times* recently stated that there was no desire by librarians to set up anything in the way of a censorship. At the same time they rightly consider that they must exercise their own judgment and meet their responsibilities after careful thought. If there is some plain speaking in regard to the type of book which could be eliminated without loss either to literature or to art of writing the Library Association will have performed a useful service.

A great deal of attention is to be devoted during the conference to children and their needs, and it is to be hoped that at the public meeting on "Children's Books" (when the president of the conference, Mr. S. A. Pitt, City Librarian of Glasgow, will be in the chair) the point of view of those who are in daily contact with boys and girls will be put forward and examined. In London the Education Committee's circulating scheme provides opportunity for both class and quiet reading in school, and the holding of library classes is encouraged. The admirable teaching given in infants' schools and preparatory schools enables children to acquire very early the reading habit, and it is not surprising that "children are reading to-day more than they ever did." But they do not read, as often as they might, the books that their parents or their grandparents read. Probably few children at the present day recapture the pleasure with which boys and girls of a former generation steeped themselves in Scott and Dickens, Thackeray and Stevenson. The library has to provide for the needs of a wide public. The children's librarian, it has to be remembered, has to advise the reading of boys and girls with a limited vocabulary and poor mentality, as well as encouraging the normal demands of bright children, who deserve and can appreciate the very best that good books can give them.

For the adult student the public libraries are becoming an increasingly important means for further education. It is illuminating to compare the number of books on general literature available for borrowing in London twenty years ago with the last figures available. The total rose from 657,631 in 1910–11 to 1,173,667 in 1931–32. In the country also the opportunities for obtaining books have greatly increased in recent years, through the generous aid given by the Carnegie United Kingdom Trust. But the existence of a number of small independent urban library areas hampers progress. The Public Library Act of 1892, which extended the powers already conferred on town councils to provide and maintain libraries, gave similar powers to boroughs, urban districts and parishes. This act remains to-day the principal measure relating to public libraries. The Public Libraries Act of 1919 enables county councils to adopt the Public Libraries Acts and abolishes the rate limit of a penny, but it maintains the independence of the existing areas. As was shown in the last Report of the Board of Education, few small authorities have taken advantage of the powers conferred by section 2 of the Act of 1919 to relinquish their autonomy in favor of the county. To-day the number of independent areas with a population of under 20,000 is as high as 216 out of a total of 428. This is unfortunate, as there is reason to believe that the smaller areas find it difficult to maintain an efficient service on the money available from their resources. They can receive help, however, from regional systems which have been set up in certain parts of the country and can arrange for the interchange of non-fiction books and the compilation of a union catalogue. Further aid is obtained from the National Central Library, which with the Scottish and Irish Central Libraries for Students and the National Library for Wales supplements from its own stock and from certain other libraries the supply of expensive or scarce books which local libraries would not feel justified in buying. This problem of the small library needs further consideration, for library activities, it should be remembered, are undertaken without connection with any Government Department. The Ministry of Health sanctions loans for libraries, as for other services, and the Board of Education confirms, allows or disallows by-laws made by public libraries under section 3 of the Public Libraries Act, 1901; but neither department has power to inspect or to regulate the conduct of public libraries. The work of the Library Association is therefore a factor of very great importance in contemporary social life.—*Educational Supplement of the London Times.*

# REPORTS

## THE EDUCATIONAL OUTLOOK IN THE DROUGHT-STRICKEN STATES[1]

THE following statements have been collected from state school officials and from the officers of state education associations during the past few weeks. While a number of officials remark that it is as yet too early to have detailed statistical information, they have supplied these statements in order to give a general review of educational conditions in some of the states included in the emergency and secondary drought areas.[2] This memorandum will be revised from time to time as reports are received from other states and as more detailed statistical information is received.

The scope of the reports submitted to date is indicated in Table 1. The sampling is fairly even for all degrees of severity in the drought states.

*The reports indicate that some schools will be unable to open unless federal assistance is received.* This appears probable in at least 4 states. Texas expects that 75 schools will not open; Arkansas reports 127 districts without funds of any kind; and in South Dakota there will be a few schools unable to open, the exact number depending on the extent to which teachers undertake to conduct the schools without any definite promise of salaries. Michigan reports that "practically all" schools will open. Eight states (Illinois, Iowa, Montana, North Dakota, Oklahoma, Oregon, Utah and Wiscon-

[1] From the Research Division of the National Education Association.

[2] As classified by the U. S. Department of Agriculture, Bureau of Agricultural Economics.

TABLE 1

| | Entirely within emergency drought area | Partly in emergency drought area | Secondary drought area only | Total drought-stricken states |
|---|---|---|---|---|
| Total number of states | 7 | 16 | 2 | 25 |
| States replying to date | 5 | 9 | 1 | 15 |
| Per cent. replying | 71% | 56% | 50% | 60% |

sin) report specifically that they expect every school to open.

*Shortened school terms* are definitely mentioned in the reports received from Louisiana, Nebraska, North Dakota, South Dakota, Texas, Oklahoma, Utah, Arkansas, Michigan, Montana, Oregon and Wisconsin. Terms may be shortened in other states than these twelve. Without federal aid for the extension of school terms it is expected that terms will be shortened in several parishes in Louisiana, in certain school districts in Nebraska and South Dakota. More specifically, Texas anticipates shortened terms in from 1,200 to 1,500 school districts. At least half the districts in Utah will be unable to provide a normal term. Wisconsin reports that 161 rural districts are receiving aid now in order to keep their schools open. Oklahoma can provide from six to six and one half months of schooling, but reports that in some 2,000 school districts the school term will be from two to four weeks shorter than last year unless federal assistance is provided. In Michigan approximately 25 per cent. of the schools will have abbreviated terms. In Arkansas a survey of 3,086 needy districts indicates that there are funds on hand to supply only an average of fifty-one days in each district. From Montana comes the report that funds are available to finance school terms of only four months or less in twenty-three drought-stricken counties.

*With respect to the salaries of teachers,* several states anticipate rather serious delays and irregularities in payments. Illinois, Nebraska, North Dakota and Iowa report that there will be some delays in the payment of teachers' salaries, or in the cashing of salary warrants. Michigan anticipates delays in payment after the first month. From South Dakota comes the report that teachers are finding it necessary to accept "exorbitant discounts" on their salary warrants. Texas reports that fifty per cent. of its schools will expect delays in the payment of teachers' salaries. In Oklahoma, although teachers will receive warrants as usual, the third and succeeding warrants will be non-payable, and although they draw interest at six per cent., these warrants will probably be discounted by the teachers. In Arkansas there is a deficiency of at least two million dollars in the sums needed for the payment of teachers, a condition which according to the State Department of Education means that teachers will have to wait on an average approximately ten months before their warrants can be cashed. As far as the amounts of the salaries fixed for teachers are concerned, the states generally report little or no further downward tendency. The statement from Nebraska is probably typical: "There has been little change in teachers' salaries. They were so low already that there was little chance of any further reductions."

*Heavy tax delinquencies* due to the failure of farmers' incomes resulting from the droughts are reported by most states. Illinois looks forward to some improvement in the school revenue situation. The reports from Nebraska, Oklahoma and Arkansas speak briefly of extensive tax delinquencies. Utah, with an average of 70 per cent. of the taxes paid last year, expects a greater decline in this year's school revenues. From South Dakota comes the report that not more than half of the anticipated revenue for schools from the income tax will be collected.

That *widespread reductions and eliminations of school services* have occurred in past years is now a well-known fact. With the exception of Illinois, none of the states report confidence in the early restoration of these services. Some states expect further curtailment.

*Increases in enrolment of greater or less significance* are reported from Nebraska, Texas, Michigan, Wisconsin, North Dakota, and South Dakota. These increases aggravate the shortage of buildings and place heavy loads on the teachers. In Texas a number of teachers are handling as many as sixty or seventy students in the lower grades.

*Federal aid*—As far as can be judged from

these preliminary reports all the states feel that they need federal assistance in order to operate their schools even on a relief basis. At this early date it is very difficult for school officials to anticipate the extent of this need. A number of states, however, expect that it will be necessary for them to have larger amounts than last year.

# EDUCATIONAL RESEARCH AND STATISTICS

## THE EDUCATION OF TRANSIENT BOYS

The figures to be quoted in this study were taken from the cases of 5,000 transient boys between the ages of 15 and 20 years, inclusive, registered at the Central Intake Bureau of the Transient Service of the Federal Emergency Relief Administration, in Los Angeles. The period covered during this registration was from December 12, 1933, to July 28, 1934.

One further word of explanation should be added. It will be noticed that the state of California is included in the list of those in the study. While state minors are not now cared for by the Transient Service, there was a period during the fall and winter of 1933–34 when such care was extended, and the 111 cases so registered are included here.

The statement has frequently been made that all transients, boys included, are "bums" and "hobos," and the Federal Government has been often condemned for attempting to care for them. Those closest to the field of transient work realize that such a statement is grossly exaggerated; that whereas there are a few transients who might properly fall into one of the above listed undesirable categories, a great majority of them are individuals who have lost their jobs on account of economic difficulties over which they had no control, and who are extremely anxious to rehabilitate themselves. Especially is this true of the army of minor transients, boys under 21 years of age, who have left an undesirable situation at home in order to set out for themselves and make a start in life.

It has been interesting at the Central Intake Bureau of the Department of Transient Service of the Federal Emergency Relief Administration to observe these boys, and to note how eager they are to find work and to help the folks back home. Frequent comment has been made about the degree of education which most of them seemed to possess, and in order to ascertain definitely what the extent of formal education was, this study was made by the supervisor of boys' welfare for Southern California.

Of the 5,000 cases studied, Table 1 indicates the degree of education in each case, the grade cited being that actually completed. In case another grade was started but not finished, the previous one was cited.

TABLE 1

| | |
|---|---|
| Number with no schooling | 41 |
| Number finishing 1st grade only | 11 |
| " " 2nd " " | 23 |
| " " 3rd " " | 28 |
| " " 4th " " | 98 |
| " " 5th " " | 118 |
| " " 6th " " | 222 |
| " " 7th " " | 404 |
| " " 8th " " | 1,097 |
| Number finishing 9th grade | 664 |
| " " 10th " | 882 |
| " " 11th " | 494 |
| " " 12th " | 778 |
| Number having some degree (one year or more) of college education | 110 |
| Number whose degree of education was not accurately ascertained | 30 |

Summarizing these figures, 2,042 had an 8th grade education or less; while 2,928 had some degree of high-school education. The percentage having at least a ninth grade education was 58.9. These statistics have been further broken down and classified by the states where the transient boys have their residence, or in cases where legal residence is doubtful, from where they started their migrations. These figures are contained in Chart I and give an accurate picture of the education of young transients from each state in the Union. (The column "miscellaneous" includes such places as Canada, Mexico, Alaska, Hawaii, the Philippines, England, Ireland, China and Brazil). It is realized that some states have contributed so few boys to the number which reach Los Angeles that it is hardly fair to compare their figures with those of states sending several hundred. Such states are Delaware, Nevada, New

CHART I

FORMAL EDUCATION BY STATES

| | Grades finished | | | | | | | | | | | | | | | |
|---|---|---|---|---|---|---|---|---|---|---|---|---|---|---|---|---|
| State | 0 | 1 | 2 | 3 | 4 | 5 | 6 | 7 | 8 | 9 | 10 | 11 | 12 | C* | ?† | Total |
| Alabama | 2 | | | 2 | 3 | 2 | 15 | 12 | 9 | 8 | 11 | 4 | 5 | 1 | 3 | 77 |
| Arizona | 4 | 1 | 1 | 1 | 6 | 4 | 7 | 10 | 28 | 23 | 11 | 13 | 8 | 1 | 1 | 119 |
| Arkansas | 1 | | | | 7 | 5 | 10 | 9 | 22 | 17 | 7 | 8 | 19 | | | 105 |
| California | 1 | | 1 | 2 | 1 | 2 | 4 | 7 | 22 | 15 | 24 | 12 | 17 | 3 | | 111 |
| Colorado | | 1 | 2 | | | 3 | | 8 | 18 | 14 | 16 | 14 | 18 | 2 | | 96 |
| Connecticut | | | | | | | 2 | 1 | 18 | 2 | 6 | 4 | 6 | | 1 | 40 |
| District of Columbia | | | | | | | | | 3 | 1 | 5 | 1 | 3 | | | 13 |
| Delaware | | | | | | | | | 1 | 2 | 1 | | | | | 4 |
| Florida | | 1 | | 1 | 2 | 3 | 2 | 7 | 10 | 6 | 9 | 3 | 2 | | | 46 |
| Georgia | 1 | | | 1 | 1 | 5 | 5 | 10 | 14 | 10 | 6 | 6 | 6 | 2 | 1 | 68 |
| Idaho | | | | | | | | 1 | 4 | 6 | 5 | 1 | 3 | | 1 | 21 |
| Illinois | 1 | | | | 2 | 4 | 7 | 14 | 77 | 49 | 89 | 62 | 66 | 14 | | 385 |
| Indiana | 1 | | | | | | 3 | 1 | 16 | 10 | 20 | 13 | 26 | 3 | | 93 |
| Iowa | | 1 | | | | | 1 | 1 | 16 | 10 | 11 | 5 | 22 | 5 | 2 | 74 |
| Kansas | | | | | 2 | 2 | 1 | 5 | 23 | 17 | 22 | 14 | 31 | 2 | 1 | 120 |
| Kentucky | | | 1 | 1 | 2 | | 5 | 7 | 14 | 8 | 17 | 3 | 6 | 2 | | 66 |
| Louisiana | | 1 | 1 | 1 | 4 | 5 | 3 | 21 | 25 | 9 | 9 | 7 | 7 | 1 | | 94 |
| Maine | | | | | | | 1 | 3 | 4 | 2 | 2 | | 6 | | | 18 |
| Maryland | | | | | 1 | 1 | 2 | 4 | 5 | 4 | 3 | 1 | 3 | 1 | | 25 |
| Massachusetts | 1 | | | | | | 2 | 8 | 28 | 15 | 25 | 11 | 15 | 4 | | 109 |
| Michigan | 2 | | 2 | 2 | 2 | 2 | 6 | 13 | 45 | 24 | 58 | 45 | 67 | 9 | | 277 |
| Minnesota | | | | | | | 1 | 5 | 29 | 8 | 22 | 7 | 27 | 6 | | 105 |
| Mississippi | 1 | | 1 | 1 | 2 | 6 | 5 | 4 | 7 | 11 | 8 | 4 | 6 | 2 | 1 | 59 |
| Missouri | 1 | | 1 | | 2 | 7 | 8 | 18 | 51 | 22 | 22 | 16 | 30 | 8 | | 186 |
| Montana | | 1 | | 1 | 1 | | 2 | 2 | 10 | 4 | 6 | 2 | 7 | | | 36 |
| Nebraska | | | 1 | | | | 2 | 1 | 17 | 5 | 7 | 6 | 8 | | | 47 |
| Nevada | | | | | | | | | 4 | 2 | | | 4 | | | 10 |
| New Hampshire | | | | | | | 1 | | 3 | | | | 3 | | | 7 |
| New Jersey | 1 | 1 | | | 1 | | 4 | 15 | 29 | 17 | 22 | 9 | 14 | 1 | | 114 |
| New Mexico | | 1 | | | 6 | 2 | 3 | 10 | 22 | 10 | 8 | 4 | 4 | | | 70 |
| New York | 2 | | 1 | 1 | 2 | 6 | 13 | 20 | 98 | 46 | 68 | 47 | 72 | 11 | 7 | 394 |
| North Carolina | | | 1 | | 2 | 3 | 4 | 13 | 12 | 6 | 8 | 1 | 6 | 3 | | 59 |
| North Dakota | | | | | | | | 3 | 4 | 1 | 5 | 1 | 4 | | | 18 |
| Ohio | 1 | | | | 2 | 3 | 6 | 9 | 48 | 43 | 54 | 31 | 58 | 1 | | 256 |
| Oklahoma | 3 | | 1 | 1 | 8 | 7 | 4 | 23 | 37 | 22 | 38 | 21 | 33 | 4 | 1 | 203 |
| Oregon | | 1 | | | 2 | 1 | 3 | 1 | 17 | 11 | 17 | 14 | 9 | | 1 | 77 |
| Pennsylvania | 2 | | 3 | | 3 | 7 | 14 | 20 | 94 | 45 | 53 | 21 | 33 | 5 | | 300 |
| Rhode Island | | | | | | | 1 | 3 | 4 | 4 | 2 | | 1 | 1 | | 16 |
| South Carolina | | | | | | | 2 | 2 | 5 | 2 | 5 | | 4 | 1 | 1 | 22 |
| South Dakota | | | | | | | | | 5 | 1 | 3 | 6 | 1 | 3 | | 19 |
| Tennessee | 1 | | | | 8 | 6 | 5 | 15 | 16 | 9 | 21 | 2 | 11 | 2 | | 96 |
| Texas | 11 | 1 | 6 | 11 | 24 | 27 | 61 | 85 | 91 | 77 | 91 | 30 | 35 | 3 | 1 | 554 |
| Utah | 1 | | | | | | 1 | | 9 | 13 | 12 | 15 | 14 | 1 | 2 | 68 |
| Vermont | | | | | | | | | 1 | 1 | 1 | | 1 | | | 4 |
| Virginia | 1 | | | | | 2 | 1 | 3 | 9 | 3 | 5 | 2 | 2 | 1 | | 29 |
| Washington | 1 | | | | 1 | | | 2 | 25 | 20 | 22 | 8 | 20 | 3 | 1 | 103 |
| West Virginia | | | | | 1 | 1 | 2 | 2 | 15 | 10 | 5 | 8 | 8 | 1 | 1 | 54 |
| Wisconsin | | | | 1 | | 1 | 3 | 1 | 26 | 10 | 17 | 9 | 21 | 2 | 2 | 93 |
| Wyoming | | | | | | | | | 2 | 3 | 2 | 1 | 3 | | | 11 |
| Miscellaneous | 1 | 1 | | 1 | | 1 | | 5 | 5 | 6 | 1 | 2 | 3 | 1 | 2 | 29 |
| Total | 41 | 11 | 23 | 28 | 98 | 118 | 222 | 404 | 1,097 | 664 | 882 | 494 | 778 | 110 | 30 | 5,000 |

* One or more years of college education.

† The exact amount of formal education was not determined.

CHART II

PERCENTAGE OF BOYS HAVING SOME DEGREE OF HIGH-SCHOOL EDUCATION, BY STATES

| | | | |
|---|---|---|---|
| Utah | 83.3 | Oklahoma | 58.4 |
| Wyoming | 81.8 | Arkansas | 58.0 |
| | | South Carolina | 57.1 |
| Indiana | 77.4 | Maine | 55.5 |
| Dist. Columbia | 76.9 | Nebraska | 55.3 |
| Vermont | 75.0 | New Jersey | 55.2 |
| Idaho | 75.0 | Kentucky | 54.5 |
| Delaware | 75.0 | Mississippi | 53.4 |
| Iowa | 73.6 | Missouri | 52.6 |
| South Dakota | 73.6 | Montana | 52.5 |
| Michigan | 73.2 | Pennsylvania | 52.3 |
| Ohio | 73.0 | Rhode Island | 50.0 |
| Illinois | 72.7 | | |
| Kansas | 72.2 | Miscellaneous | 49.6 |
| Washington | 71.5 | Maryland | 48.0 |
| | | Arizona | 47.4 |
| Oregon | 67.1 | Tennessee | 46.8 |
| Minnesota | 66.6 | Connecticut | 46.1 |
| Colorado | 66.6 | Virginia | 44.8 |
| Wisconsin | 64.8 | Georgia | 44.7 |
| Massachusetts | 64.2 | Florida | 43.4 |
| California | 63.9 | New Hampshire | 42.8 |
| New York | 63.0 | Texas | 42.6 |
| North Dakota | 61.1 | North Carolina | 40.6 |
| West Virginia | 60.3 | | |
| Nevada | 60.0 | Alabama | 39.1 |
| | | New Mexico | 37.1 |
| *General Ave.* | 58.9 | Louisiana | 35.1 |

Hampshire, Rhode Island, Vermont, Wyoming and several others. These states could not be merely omitted from the list either, however, so it must be realized that their standings in Charts II and III have been determined by a very few boys only. For that reason too much importance should not be attached to such standings as regards these states.

Chart II portrays by states the percentages of transient boys having some degree of high-school education. As stated before, the general average of the 5,000 cases studied, or rather, the 4,970 cases where the degree of education was really ascertained, was 58.9. More than half, nearly three fifths of the group, had had some high-school training, at least one year of it. As this is broken down by states, the percentage is found to range from 83.3 per cent. in cases of boys coming from Utah (68 cases) down to Louisiana, where the per cent. was only 35.1. It is interesting to note that such high contributing states as Indiana, Michigan, Illinois, Ohio and Kansas rank among the leaders in this chart. One might conclude either that boys as a rule are better educated in these Mid-Western states, or else that these states have sent us some of their superior products. Both statements are probably true to some extent. While it is usual to find the Southern states ranking at the bottom in the matter of high-school education, it is distinctly surprising to observe such ones as Pennsylvania, Connecticut and New Jersey so far below the general average. One would be almost disposed to the opinion that the transient youths from these states did not represent such a high type of boyhood as those from New York or Minnesota or Washington. Oklahoma, with its 203 boys, many more than might be expected, comes the closest to the general average with her 58.4 per cent.

It might be pointed out, before leaving this part of the study, that California does not show up particularly well in the percentage of boys having a 9th grade education or better. While her average is 63.9, it is surpassed by eighteen states and the District of Columbia. Realizing that any deductions from such a superficial study must necessarily be mostly guesswork, one

CHART III

GRADE POINT AVERAGE OF TRANSIENT BOYS, BY STATES

| | | | |
|---|---|---|---|
| South Dakota | 10.47 | Missouri | 9.10 |
| Iowa | 10.15 | | |
| Indiana | 10.10 | *General Ave.* | 9.09 |
| Utah | 10.00 | | |
| Wyoming | 10.00 | Delaware | 9.00 |
| Dist. Columbia | 10.00 | | |
| Minnesota | 10.00 | Oklahoma | 8.98 |
| | | New Jersey | 8.94 |
| Illinois | 9.83 | Pennsylvania | 8.87 |
| Kansas | 9.83 | North Dakota | 8.83 |
| Michigan | 9.81 | Rhode Island | 8.81 |
| Nevada | 9.80 | Kentucky | 8.77 |
| Vermont | 9.75 | Montana | 8.77 |
| Ohio | 9.70 | Maryland | 8.64 |
| Washington | 9.59 | Arkansas | 8.49 |
| Wisconsin | 9.56 | Virginia | 8.48 |
| Idaho | 9.50 | North Carolina | 8.38 |
| New York | 9.49 | Georgia | 8.35 |
| New Hampshire | 9.43 | Tennessee | 8.31 |
| Colorado | 9.41 | Mississippi | 8.27 |
| Maine | 9.38 | Miscellaneous | 8.14 |
| Massachusetts | 9.35 | Arizona | 8.10 |
| West Virginia | 9.30 | Louisiana | 8.06 |
| South Carolina | 9.33 | Florida | 8.02 |
| Oregon | 9.28 | New Mexico | 8.01 |
| Nebraska | 9.23 | | |
| California | 9.21 | Texas | 7.88 |
| Connecticut | 9.15 | Alabama | 7.75 |

might conclude, however, knowing the excellent system of secondary education existing in California, that the higher types of boys there are being cared for through industry or the recreational program, and that the less trained ones only find it necessary to "take to the road."

Chart III points out the average grade attained by the boys. To determine the figures in this chart, each grade was allowed its number, multiplied by the number having completed that grade, the total added, and the sum divided by the number of boys coming from the state. Since the actual year of college work was not ascertained in most instances, fourteen points was allowed in figuring in college or university work. The general average of 4,970 boys was found to be 9.09, or slightly better than a 9th grade education for each boy. This figure might be quoted to those individuals who insist on calling our transient youths "young bums" and "wild boys of the road." It might prove to be that the average education of these "bums" would be better than that of the persons making such statements!

This chart in general tallies with that of the preceding one, with South Dakota, Utah, Iowa, Wyoming, Indiana, District of Columbia and Michigan again among the leaders. Likewise, at the other end are found Louisiana, Texas, Alabama and New Mexico. One word of explanation might be made for Texas. During the period of the study there was an unusually large number of Mexican boys registered at the Intake Bureau. These Mexican boys, most of whom were from El Paso, had had a very little education, and consequently brought down the average of the entire state to a considerable degree. Somewhat the same explanation, to a lesser degree, also holds true for New Mexico, and it must be remembered that the small amount of formal education of the colored boys from the South served to bring down the averages of the states south of the Mason-Dixon Line.

While the educational survey was being made, another was being conducted at the same time as to the cities of origin of the same 5,000 young transients. In this study cities of 25,000 or more population were taken, and those smaller all grouped under the general classification of "Rural." For purposes of contrast the educational figures were also separated into these two groups. In the matter of those having some degree of high-school education, it was found that the average in cities of more than 25,000 population was 64.2 per cent., while that in smaller towns and country districts was 53.8 per cent. These figures are interesting, especially when compared to the general average of 58.9 per cent. The same general comparison holds true in the matter of grade points. While the average of the transient boys as a whole is 9.09, it falls to 8.81 in localities with less than 25,000 population, and jumps to 9.27 in the larger centers. Here again one might conclude that either boys were better educated in the larger cities or else the type of young transients coming from the larger centers was definitely above the average. And here, again, there is probably some truth in both statements.

For one who wishes to study the three charts a great many interesting facts may be gleaned, and comparisons made between various states. The purpose of this study was served, however, when the general averages were compiled, and the fact definitely established that, at least so far as amount of formal education was concerned, boys on the road are not "bums." When a group of 5,000 show a general educational average of 9.09 grades one can not classify them under the usual meaning of the term, to say the least.

It would be interesting to contrast these figures with any available at other centers of boy transiency throughout the country. It is to be hoped that such centers will soon have information available on the education of their minor transients which will either corroborate or change the percentages and state figures as presented here.

George E. Outland,
*Supervisor of Boys' Welfare for Southern California*

## NEW BOOKS IN EDUCATION

*Aids to Teaching in the Elementary School.* Pp. 528. Thirteenth Yearbook, June, 1934. National Elementary Principal, National Education Association.

Strang, Ruth. *Personal Development and Guidance in College and Secondary School.* Pp. vii + 341. Harper. $4.00.

Webster, Hutton and Edgar B. Wesley. *World Civilization.* Pp. xxiv + 844. Illustrated. Heath.

# SCHOOL AND SOCIETY

WITH WHICH ARE COMBINED THE EDUCATIONAL REVIEW, ESTABLISHED IN 1891, THE TEACHERS MAGAZINE, ESTABLISHED IN 1878, AND THE SCHOOL JOURNAL, ESTABLISHED IN 1874.

Volume 40 SATURDAY, OCTOBER 20, 1934 Number 1034

## THE SMALL COLLEGE AND LIBERAL LEARNING[1]

By Dr. DIXON RYAN FOX

PRESIDENT OF UNION COLLEGE

THERE is probably no form of self-expression more treacherous than the inaugural address. The inherent premise, the one article which requires no proof, is that nothing which the speaker says has yet been measured in his practise. His testimonies rest on vague impressions gained from distant view, and he speculates upon the future without that rectifying glass whose lenses time and trial alone can grind for him. Valedictories are far more seemly and certainly more instructive; he who has marched with events and at times determined them is much better fit to guess whither they are leading. Sound sense might dictate silence till, as Milton has admonished us,

> . . . old experience do attain
> To something like prophetic strain.

But custom oftentimes departs from sound sense, and custom has prescribed that, out of his innocence, a new incumbent should set forth what he sees and what he hopes and fears. It is not a little disconcerting, I assure you, when the novice sees before him "old experience" in such numerous and such distinguished instances.

[1] Inaugural address at the installation of the twelfth president of Union College, Schenectady, N. Y., October 12, 1934.

### THE SMALL COLLEGE CHALLENGED

The American college is well represented here to-day; the institutions whose delegates surround us defined the purpose and set the pattern which others by the scores and hundreds have gladly and wisely taken as their own. Sprung from generous and heroic aspiration, designed in affectionate memory of English precedent, founded and sustained by the resolute sacrifice of our own people, molded by our needs and circumstances into something that the world had never seen before, the American college has been cherished more steadily, more widely and more deeply, perhaps, than any other secular institution outside the state itself. In the light of its record, a deliberate attack upon the small, independent college—the historic type—would be met with public scorn.

There has been no deliberate attack that could disturb the most sensitive apprehension, but there have lately come ominous reports and disquieting prophecies. Moreover, they are not the tedious jeremiads of that tribe of critics who love to think that nothing historically American can be right. Rather, in many instances, they proceed from able and far-visioned minds, from men of careful judgment who speak with high authority. Granting the incomparable contribution that the old liberal college has made to the culture of the country, they believe that it has lost adjustment with our modern needs and foresee its slow disintegration.

That which is unique must justify its own unicity. The fact that outside North America other countries, certainly as civilized as ours, have never desired to organize their higher education on our principle may throw some doubt upon its natural perfection. It may suggest that our small four-year college was an admirable issue of expediency under primitive conditions, but is not innately reasonable when circumstances give free choice. It may argue that the attempt to bracket older lads and younger men in one administrative unit gives liberties to youth for which it has not been prepared and prolongs guardianship for those who should be free of it.

### The Junior College

It is nearly forty years since the late President Harper preached the doctrine of the junior and the senior colleges as a solution to the problem, and junior colleges now dot the national map. But the results have not been sufficiently impressive to lead any well-established institution which could afford to carry on effectively its four-year program to relinquish it for this new status, and the correlative senior college has scarcely appeared at all. Brave devotion has gone into the upbuilding of the junior colleges, and one thinks of many instances of solid competence in their faculties, but the institution has not caught the imagination of the country or attracted large endowments. Superimposed upon the secondary school it tends too much to share its spirit; it tends to encourage the prolongation of infancy, which thoughtful observers have long since recognized as a national foible, if not a national disgrace. When standing by itself it marks one more break in the stream of education and finds its best justification, so far, as a convenient stopping place for mediocrity. The reorganization of our education upon the lycée or gymnasium plan has not succeeded far enough at present to menace the existence of the historic college.

### College Interprets Noble Living

But, as in the chemistry of nature, human institutions may undergo fundamental changes in their properties without altering their form. Perhaps the old liberal college is slowly disappearing without our sensing it. The liberal college has existed, I take it, to interpret the possibilities of large and noble living. Taking office in the eighteen forties, a president observed, "Here in college is to be fashioned, in the highest attainable perfection, the scholar, the citizen, the good man, the Christian gentleman." Ghostly predecessors who had wrought the achievements of two centuries could have nodded an emphatic assent, and those who have come after him, to this very day, would scarcely wish to change a word. Eliphalet Nott and Charles W. Eliot and others long ago discerned that life could be interpreted through many approaches, one better for one student, and another for another, but the primary purpose of the college, as professed, remained unchanged. Nevertheless new forces have been working upon it.

### The College and the Professions

Only in theology, whose handmaid the college once had been, was general culture thought to be an essential base for professional training. The so-called university of sixty years ago was a congeries of schools where, so far as entrance standards were concerned, a young man of seventeen might choose at the start whether he would be a cultivated gentleman or a doctor or a lawyer, the latter two being manufactured in a shorter time. The enormous increase in special knowledge necessary to professional practise eventually lengthened the professional courses, but at the same time it came to be realized that a professional man should live as well as earn a living, and that he must understand mankind if he were to keep his bearings in its service. In consequence came professional requirement of a broader and broader basis of general college preparation. But so burdensome became the task of the professional schools in coping with new special knowledge that they found little time for those more general courses which had been a part of their curricula. It was a convenient shift to reshape the college preparation into a fair substitute. The minute prescription of the college work gave the prospective architect little time for chemistry and the prospective physician no time for the fine arts. The college found itself increasingly a service station for the various professions, and what had seemed a victory threatened to be a surrender. In certain university colleges the student taking four years of liberal education became the exception, and even the independent college found its structure badly warped.

### College Faculties and Scholarship

But the small, independent college has much more than this to face. The possibilities of learning in this modern day can not be realized by a master and a pupil and a log to sit on, even if all three are the best of their kinds. The history of higher education in this country is to a considerable degree a history of the log. It has been amplified into academic cities housing marvelous laboratories, libraries, galleries of art—and gymnasiums, perhaps most marvelous of all. The library of one university to-day, with its millions of well-selected volumes, contains a greater number of scholarly books, by far, than were to be found in all America when Mark Hopkins took up his presidency nearly a hundred years ago. It is obvious that the small, independent college can not compete in these facilities with the undergraduate department of any one of our major universities. Moreover, it is argued that the student in the isolated college lacks the stimulus of the scholarly human contacts of the university. The higher learning, it is said, is too expensive to be strewn over the countryside in little centers; in the competition for funds the great universities, with their vast prestige, must always win.

Our student's plight is worse, runs this analysis, because of the teacher's plight, and it is manifest that this strikes at the heart of the matter. A university professor recently published a paper on the independent colleges in which, half humorously, he dubbed them "intellectual graveyards." In it he alleged that the best opportunities for vital thought and the best compensation, and, therefore, the best brains, were to be found in universities, where the college teacher had more time, stimulus and facilities for scholarship, and where some part of the week he met the keen excitement of able graduate student minds. To sum it all, this writer declares in substance that no young man of parts and power would take appointment to an independent college if he had the slightest chance for a place in a university college. Such an appointment is the mark of temporary failure, though final discouragement comes only when all attempts to escape have failed. Then personality rots and withers, and the intellectual graveyard claims another corpse. Many distinguished presidents before me, then, will discover themselves as sextons.

### Alumni of Small Colleges Rank High

This challenge can not be smiled away. It is seriously made and must be seriously answered. Though we live in a swiftly changing world, it might seem that we must, like Patrick Henry, judge the future by the past; and we must judge the past of an institution by its product. When the biographies of "Who's Who" are explored, the witness of the past is strongly reassuring to the smaller colleges. Judged in proportion to their total number of graduates, the independent colleges show a high rating of distinction, at least as it is recognized in that familiar work. In the first fifteen, out of seventy considered, are Amherst, Wesleyan, Trinity, Hobart, Williams, Haverford, Hamilton, Bowdoin and Union—and Lafayette, Dartmouth, Rutgers and Colgate are not far behind. These figures may be crude, but gloss them as you will the small college, so far, has no cause for shame in the assay of American alumni. The graduates of the good small college have for generations sent their sons back to its care, knowing its value in their own lives. After all, the primary purpose of a college is to produce not learned books but able men.

### New Problems

But complacency might well presage degeneration. Perhaps we can not judge the future by the past. It is readily granted that the university as a whole is far less like the small independent college than it was in our fathers' day, and perhaps this makes past comparisons uninstructive. If the university college is now a place of larger and higher life for the undergraduate, the best young men will pass the small college by, for they no longer have the strong appeal of neighborhood convenience. They were scattered through the country just for that. An Oxford or Cambridge family of colleges, serving a nation, would have been impossible in early America, when difficult distances had to be encountered and sectionalism flourished. "It is one of the glories of American colleges," said Theron Baldwin in 1854, "that they are not concentrated in one vast university, but are scattered far and wide among the people, each one filling its sphere, availing itself of local associations and local sympathies. . . ." No one can overestimate what the geographical availability of higher learning has meant to Americans of times past. But now that miles are merely minutes everywhere, geographical availability appeals only to those who must lodge at home. No small college can exist on that alone, or chiefly. The student with a reasonably free choice goes now where he wills, and if the university college is better on all counts it will get him.

### The Teacher's Continuing Education

The future of the small college depends very largely on how it meets the prophecy of an enfeebled teaching faculty. No discouraged man can communicate courage. No man can teach youth to love learning who does not himself continually love learning—not love his own knowledge merely, but the exciting joy of learning. The college which loads a teaching scholar with sixteen or eighteen hours of classroom work soon has nothing but a tired drillmaster. The professor in a small college needs as much so-called leisure for learning as the undergraduate teacher in a university, and a small college which can not afford to give him time for spiritual refreshment will find that young America can not afford to come to him. There is no body of knowledge which, once accumulated in early life, is complete and can be displayed and re-displayed under the name of teaching. As unrevised text-books are soon obsolete and eliminated from the market, so, too, unrevised men become obsolete and ought to be eliminated as humanely as is possible. Academic freedom has never meant the freedom to loaf on students' tuition money.

Able men feel the creative impulse; for the college teacher this is gratified, but only partly gratified, in the classroom. He knows that he can not, generally speaking, meet the judgment of his peers without publication. Though his classes may be more competently critical than he realizes, he is right in doubting the sufficiency of their approval as a test of his new ideas and interpretations. He desires to meet, and should desire to meet, a higher test before the world of scholarship that reads the printed page. Moreover, he desires, and should desire, to contribute to constructive judgment by his own reviews of books from other men in the general field in which he works. He desires, and should desire, to foregather with other scholars in that field at the annual meetings of his learned society and take part in them, at the very least in private discussion of the scholarly papers read.

### The Teaching Scholar

Those who say that the environment of a small college makes real scholarship impracticable do not much impress us. It would be invidious to single out men and women who are to-day the scholarly ornaments of small colleges. To speak of yesterday will be more seemly—and it was a glorious yesterday. To think of Brooks at Hobart, of Emerson at Amherst, of Atwater and Rice and Winchester at Wesleyan, of Tayler Lewis and Laurens P. Hickok, of this institution, and a long list of others, is to illuminate the error in the judgment that small colleges are necessarily graveyards of the intellect. These men had few if any graduate students to whet their minds, and yet their minds did not grow dull and rusty. Their example is still potent. The scholarly world does not demand five-volume works from college teachers—few indeed of these proceed from university college staffs—but in the light of this example it may expect an article or two at intervals.

### "Vacations" for Increasing Knowledge

We may admit again that the facilities of library and laboratory are not as fortunate in country colleges as in university colleges during the so-called academic year. But may I be permitted to suggest from twenty-five years of rather close observation that the data for scholarly writing are not chiefly harvested by college teachers during the "academic year." It is no wonder that the toiling business man is apt to feel that the college teacher's life is soft and easy, when he enjoys nearly a third of the calendar year in what is apparently one long vacation. He does not know that college teachers functioning at par use most of those sixteen weeks in increasing their knowledge and preparing for contribution. Commencement past, the teacher is the whole scholar once again, justifying the academic hood that he has lately worn. He is to be traced in well-planned travel, enriching his observation of the world he is expected to interpret, or, more generally, he may be found among the collections of a notable museum, or ranging with his delicate apprehension the mines of some great library where he suspects the materials of his personal truth may be discovered—truth which he will fit together and define, his contribution to the wisdom of the ages. Or, panoplied with the special implements of his quest, he may be searching the eternal hills themselves to learn their secrets; or with his microscope and test-tube carrying forward no less thrilling venture as a welcome fellow-worker in some famous laboratory. Teachers need a brief holiday of rest and at times prolonged recuperation like other people, but neither more nor less. The teacher who after sixteen weeks returns without his lesson or unable to recite it well is to be marked "unprepared" in any college large or small.

### Teaching Scholar Dramatizes Truth

One hears occasionally of a queer dichotomy which would sharply separate the academic host into two departments, the teachers and the scholars, as if one who seemed to be both must be an optical illusion,

> A faultless monster which the world
> ne'er saw.

Actually, he is the common type. It is a trichotomy that we have before us, in which the central column holding this type is immensely broad, with narrow margins at each side. In one of these margins are listed those with a genius for discovery and literary exposition, but without the power to dramatize accepted truth in classroom colloquy; in the other are their opposites. The former, looking toward the research institute or private study, have little place in the college. The latter, though looking in some cases toward the secondary school, are very welcome, exceptional but welcome, in any college large or small—but let it be remembered that absence of productive scholarship is not in itself a presumption of teaching power. Scattered through the last-named and the great middle column are those who have, too, a genius for friendship with the young and who by constant influence, in the field or by the fireside, an influence as powerful as it is unconscious, build themselves into the enrichment of humanity.

### Friendship in the Small College

In this friendly, fruitful intimacy of old experience and young enthusiasm, the small college, with its close-knit community, has claimed a special advantage; and many a youth turned man traces the guiding vision of his life to the dinner table of a courteous and cultivated professor and his wife, giving their lives to the gracious service of such an institution. Gratitude to them and their kind appears in many a great man's memoirs. But even this generous ministry must be supported by endowments. The college with narrow funds, the college whose necessarily mean stipend confines its teaching scholar to a bare and shabby home, can scarcely hope that his student guest will be subtly reassured with the prospect of a scholarly life. No one pleads that learning should be associated in a student's mind with luxury, but neither can it well be associated with distress. Large-hearted men and women desiring to advance the dignity and charm of learning in this country may well bear in mind that the small college is carrying on its enterprise of education in the homes of its staff as well as elsewhere, and that a modicum of apparatus is as essential there as in the college laboratory. When recently the president of one of our largest universities remarked that his university college assumed no interest in the life of its students outside their academic exercises, President Comfort, of Haverford, welcoming a distinction here implied, took occasion to reply that the small college continued to stand *in loco parentis*. That it does, not in an inquisitorial interference in the sphere of private liberty, not in the imposition of arbitrary rules, but in a humane concern for the growth of fine and rounded personality in every member of its family.

### Small Colleges in Universities

There could be no more impressive recognition of, and no more sincere compliment to, the power of beneficent personal contacts, which has long distinguished the small college, than the recent undertaking of certain large university colleges, with fortune at their beck, arbitrarily to disintegrate themselves, each into a family of small colleges. But it is not unnatural for the historic small college to believe and, perhaps, not indecorous for it to express its belief, that it will not be imitated out of existence.

The high objective of the independent college is liberal education, primarily of its students; but as a means to that end it desires, too, the continuing liberal development of its teaching faculty. The physicist and the classicist, the philosopher and the historian, the economist and the mathematician, are not only in the same institution but in daily neighborly contact and companionship, and constantly aware of the interrelations of the arts and sciences, constantly aware of the oneness of knowledge. It is this which makes for the breadth of college teaching and the richness of the college experience. A liberal college faculty of some fifty men, talking together of an evening, may discover heights of total vision not often achieved in a department meeting of fifty men in a great university.

### The Small College and the Free Life

For long ages it has been necessary for most men and women to work through every day from dawn to dark in order to stay alive. With almost catastrophic force comes the perception in our day that this is no longer true. In some quarters the new leisure in life, by a strange inversion of cause and effect, is resented as the creation of a New Deal in politics. Sudden as is our realization, the fact itself has been emerging for two hundred years, since humble artisans discovered clever ways to lighten the drudgery of spinning yarn, by harnessing the power of falling water. Thousands of generations have struggled with the problem of winning a little time for the free life. The free life now upon us, we are bewildered with the problem of what to do with it. The liberal education was designed for the free life, but it was designed for the fortunate few who had it. Now it is the bounty of the multitude, and it can swiftly ruin the race if put to bad use. How the leisure of commonplace minds should be directed by wise, persuasive leadership need not detain us here, though it is a major problem of our educational statesmanship. The point here is that the free life is available for more able minds than ever before. At the same time that the complication of social effort requires vocational training increasingly intensive and severe, the need of preparation for the free life is, perhaps, even more insistent. For the first time a man may be three days a smith and three days a gentleman; and for the first time, therefore, a liberal education can find fruitage in any able mind.

### State Subsidy of Selected Brains

As a means of discovering, and supporting for the necessary time, minds able to acquire and to use for social benefit the education for the free life, the American governments may well go further along the line of the British government in providing competitive college scholarships. If the state is to dry up the old wells of philanthropy by confiscatory taxation—and at the present moment this might seem to some no mere hysterical fear—it might support the training of its leaders in just this way, through the subsidy of selected brains. Thus would be realized the fine democratic, but anti-equalitarian, ideal of Thomas Jefferson, who desired that leaders be "raked up from the rubbish" by this device. But prudence will watch well to see that it is not selected institutions, far less all collegiate institutions, which are subsidized, but selected brains, with free individual choice among the existing institutions of the country. In the light of history it requires no second sight to see that indispensable state subsidy of institutions means state control, and that universal state control presents grave perils in a society of free men. With the opportunity for free choice among American youth the small college, that is to say the good small college, need not fear extinction.

### Good Small College Need Not Fear

Happily, the wells of philanthropy have not yet been drained, and, somehow, those of us who know the American spirit can not believe that they will be. The long procession of noble men and women who have fed the living streams of learning in this country with their benefactions is not ended, nor will it end. Patrons of humanity in its finest purposes, they have merged themselves into the immortality of American colleges. Moved by affectionate confidence they have seen in each a personality, whose worth had little relation to size or outward grandeur. As it scans the long roll of its benefactors the small college, in its sentiment of gratitude and its conviction of responsibility, finds impulse there, if there were no other, to maintain and to increase its high service to mankind.

# THE CHALLENGE TO EDUCATION[1]

By Dr. NICHOLAS MURRAY BUTLER
PRESIDENT OF COLUMBIA UNIVERSITY

It is my first privilege to offer to President Fox, in this presence, words of affectionate greeting and good will from all those on Morningside Heights with whom he has been so long in intimate association as student, as teacher and as administrative officer. That great company of friends and well-wishers will follow with eager and confident interest the happenings of the new and distinguished career which now opens before him.

The name which this useful institution of higher learning has honorably borne for well-nigh a century and a half is to-day of particularly happy omen. What this disturbed and distracted world most needs at this very hour is just that union which the name of this college betokens. Our slowly building civilization has been broken into a hundred fragments. At the very moment when union of all for all, in the common interest and to promote the general welfare, is the crying and most obvious need, it is disunion—disunion political, disunion industrial, disunion social, disunion moral, disunion intellectual—that forces its disheartening way forward on every side. It is represented by every form and kind of abhorrent voice and influence, from those of simple folly and ignorance to those of dangerous and selfish effrontery, malice and madness. No principle of morals or of organized life is too well established and too clearly based upon unbroken experience to escape ribald and contemptuous attack. No form of folly and no tempestuous phrase-making are too ridiculous to be extolled and to receive a popular acclaim which is by no means always inconsiderable. Culture is laughed at, while scholarship and good manners are looked upon as the marks of a hopeless reactionary. One must no longer save from the fruit of his labor lest he be denounced as preying upon his fellow men. Even the Ten Commandments, the moral law and the multiplication table may be threatened by some new-fangled law of economic relativity. Ideas, policies, slogans which belong to the darkest of dark ages are hailed as progressive, while the finest and best-tested liberalism is hotly denounced as inimical to the interests of the mass of the people.

If any part of the once civilized world has been wholly free from all this disunion and disaster, that fact escapes the attention of even the most patient observer. At the moment, it is the people of Great Britain who are standing most firm upon honored and well-established foundations of ethical and institutional life and of public morals, thereby once more strengthening the honor

[1] An address at the installation of Dr. Dixon Ryan Fox as president of Union College, Schenectady, New York, October 12, 1934.

and esteem in which the thoughtful world has held them for a thousand years. The people of France, while restless and fearful, have not yet broken from their moorings. The Dutch people, with whose spirit of eager adventure and solid progress this Mohawk Valley is intimately associated, are in the front rank of the happy and fortunate few who still hold fast to sound principle. Likewise the Scandinavian peoples who have contributed so much to the population of the United States, particularly in the nearer Northwest, are in these respects companions of the Dutch. Almost everywhere else in the world troublesome and dangerous ferment—moral, political, economic and social—is well under way. Unhappiest of all, the great German people whose literally colossal accomplishments in philosophy and in science, in literature and in the fine arts, in industry and in commerce have played so commanding a part in the world's history for two full centuries, have gone stark raving mad under the pressure and temptation of those rigid and disheartening conditions which attended the writing of the Treaty of Versailles and which have marked the subsequent administration of its drastic and indefensible provisions. No light and no leadership can be looked for from Germany for some time to come. Those people must regain their senses, turn their backs upon the silly and reactionary slogans which are now hurled at them to be received with such highly emotional enthusiasm, before they can resume the intellectual leadership which they had so well won and which some day will again undoubtedly become their right. The world can not do without Germany, no matter how preposterous and reactionary may be its ruling policies and doctrines at the moment.

Here in the United States we are on the border line. In our public policies and public expressions we are falling much below the level upon which the British people stand and we have gone farther toward chaos than the French because of our present restless unhappiness and discontent. At the moment, no political or economic program is too absurd or too unreasonable to receive a certain, often a very considerable, measure of public acclaim among us. Men whose names should never be mentioned save with a smile in any serious society, are extolled by their immediate neighbors, and sometimes over wider areas, as hopeful and promising leaders and guides of public opinion and public action. Promising, yes; but hopeful, no.

One would have thought it quite impossible that after the long record of human experience in the fields of reflection, of action and of experiment such a condition as now everywhere confronts us could exist. Yet it does so. It is marked by disunion of every sort and kind—the breaking up of families and family life; the constant insistence upon selfish and carefully planned industrial war, waged with particular vehemence by those whose every expression as to international war is of opposition and abhorrence; the eager attempt to divide society into fixed and permanent economic and social classes; the subordination everywhere of the moral and the ideal to that greed for gain and for power which is the wickedest manifestation of the unchecked profit motive when unguided by the spirit of service; the vain exaltation of local, sectional and national temporary interests and vanities under the guise of a wholly false patriotism at a time when the satisfaction, the happiness and the progress of every man and of every group of men are dependent upon the quick constitution of an organized world of citizen-nations, to the end that true union may displace forever that disintegrating spirit of disunion which is now so widespread.

The one instrument which humankind

has in its hands to accomplish this revolution forward is that of a liberal education. Narrow preparation for vocations and technical preparation for professions will not do; a liberal education, at least in its elements, must be the foundation of both these. It is the power of liberal education that is challenged by the influences which control the world to-day. A liberal education is not only one which is based upon a true concept and understanding of freedom but it is one which prepares for freedom—freedom from narrow and self-seeking selfishness, freedom from meanness and hypocrisy, freedom from malice and antagonism, whether personal, group or national, freedom from willingness to exploit or impose upon one's fellow men. The man who is truly free will see the world as it is. He will be a stern realist and for that very reason a sincere idealist, since it is ideals, whether true or false, which rule the world.

If these disunions are to be overcome, it can only be through the power of an educated and enlightened public opinion which grasps and is guided by the ideals and convictions of a liberal education.

The American college was in some degree unfortunate in that it began its career as a school whose ideals and methods were, in large part at least, those of vocational preparation. Those who brought the college into existence on this continent had in mind, first and chiefly, the preparation of men for the ministry of the Christian church. It was some little time before those conditions were changed and the college entered upon its long and useful career as a school for the general and liberal education of American youth, no matter what his future calling was to be. As the college multiplied in numbers, its task was steadily increased in difficulty by the progress of knowledge throughout the world. New regions were discovered and new peoples made known. Nature was attacked on every side by observation and experiment and rapidly yielded her secrets with the lessons and consequences that are even now only partially understood. Literature and the fine arts, always untrammeled by either race or language or national boundary, steadily conquered the intelligence and the emotional life of increasing millions of men. Despite these enriching and unifying influences, economic conditions increasingly tended to become such as to lead to the demand that the school and the college offer that instruction which would point the way to earning a livelihood in some specific calling. This is well enough in its way, indeed essential, but it is something which is quite fatal if mistaken for education or allowed to displace it. So in time it came to pass that economic forces which were making for disunion steadily increased their power and influence in the face of the spiritual and intellectual forces which were making for union. The result is sad, indeed disastrous. Until these economic forces are controlled by those which are intellectual and spiritual, the whole fabric of civilization will not be safe. The economic interpretation of history must always be subordinate to its moral and its spiritual interpretation.

To-day the challenge is distinctly to that liberal education which makes for union, that it may give to each of these many separate, often combative, numerators of disunion a common denominator to overcome their disintegrating influences and to bind together parts which should never have been separated. This means steady and persistent emphasis upon the intellectual and the spiritual nature of man, upon his understanding, upon his appreciations and upon his insights—upon all those characteristics and customs which can neither be weighed nor measured nor counted, but which through their presence or absence determine the direction which civilization shall take and the fate toward which it moves.

It is some 200 years since Montesquieu said that society is the union of men and not the men themselves. This union of men involves and depends upon a common foundation for intellectual and moral insight and understanding. It is precisely this which it is the highest business of the twentieth-century American college to furnish. This insight and understanding will be found, as they have always been found, in the interpretation of human insight and human experience. Those masterpieces of the mind which serve as milestones in the history of literature and the arts and those masterful accomplishments in the field of human organization and public service which are the outstanding landmarks of humanity's history, are the material of which this foundation is to be built. The immortality of human effort and human accomplishment surrounds us on every side and if we would understand life and its sternly practical problems, we must grasp the significance of this immortality at any cost.

Happy indeed is the American youth who is led up to the high places from which he can see and appreciate those permanent intellectual, moral and spiritual forces whose working gives to civilization both its meaning and its ideals. What this signifies is that after the technique of apprehension has been gained through a knowledge of arithmetic, algebra and geometry, of grammar and rhetoric, of the elements of scientific method and of at least one other language than that which is native to the student, he shall be offered guidance toward comprehension of fundamental scientific principles, toward appreciation of excellence and beauty in the fine arts, toward a knowledge and love of all that is best and finest in the literature of the world, toward a comprehension of the economic and social influences at work in the world, toward an understanding of that general movement of human forces which is recorded in history, and toward those moral and religious insights and ideals which have always played so controlling a part in shaping human conduct and in providing it with motives. When this shall have been done, the youth will have been offered the training worthy of a free man. He will have gained the basis of a liberal education. It will then be his personal responsibility so worthily to use his knowledge and his training that he himself will steadily grow in mind and in character. His fellow human beings will be better and the richer for his presence in the world and no single one of them will be harmed, much less exploited, by him. It is in this way that the trained youth of the nation can lead and guide our country's public opinion toward that true union of thought and feeling and action, which is not only the basis of strength but the necessity for safety. Longfellow wrote in "Hiawatha":

> All your strength is in your union,
> All your danger is in discord;
> Therefore be at peace henceforward,
> And as brothers live together.

There should ring in our ears across the intervening years the noble words spoken in the Senate of the United States as Senator Lamar of Mississippi, afterwards a justice of the Supreme Court, closed his eulogy of Charles Sumner: My Countrymen, know one another and you will love one another. Only so can we hope to make possible that union which this twentieth-century world so sorely needs.

How fortunate that here in the United States is an honorable institution, ancient as our American institutions go, which is devoted to the accomplishment of these ideals and which, by its very name, emphasizes their essential character and their commanding importance. That the company of scholars, the body of rich alumni sentiment and the fine traditions, all of which unite to make the Union College of to-day, may carry it forward under this new leadership in the very front rank of the forces which would combat and conquer those of disunion, and so lift our people, our country and the world, up to that higher and finer plane of union which is our hearts' desire, is our confident expectation and our most earnest wish.

# EDUCATIONAL EVENTS

## PSYCHOLOGY AND VOCATIONAL GUIDANCE

PSYCHOLOGY as an aid to vocational guidance is discussed among other subjects in a report which has been made to Mr. Oliver Stanley, British Minister of Labor, by a committee selected jointly by the National Advisory Council for Juvenile Employment in England and Wales and the similar council in Scotland. The committee was appointed as a result of a request made by Sir Henry Betterton when Minister of Labor that the councils should review the scheme of vocational guidance which has been in operation for more than twenty-one years. The London *Times* gives the following summary of the report:

Psychological tests alone, the committee state, can not, in their view, afford a sufficient basis for giving advice to the individual on choice of a career. There might, however, be scope for the trained psychologist and the vocational guidance officer to combine their skill and experience in the interests of good advice and placing of boys and girls in employment.

If the further experiments contemplated proved the desirability of extending psychological methods, the committee were of opinion that the psychologist should be responsible for the testing, according to accredited methods, of pupils over a period of years or at the time of leaving school, and, in consultation with the school authorities, for the proper completion of the pupil's record card, which would subsequently form the basis of the school-leaving report. On that report, preferably after personal consultation with the psychologist and the head teacher, the vocational guidance officer should advise finally on the choice of employment.

The committee thought it most important that the final advice should be given by the person in touch with industrial conditions; no system under which the psychologist would be responsible for giving advice and the employment exchange or bureau would be charged solely with obtaining employment in accordance with the advice so given could ever, in their view, produce satisfactory results.

On the whole, the committee was inclined to the view that the application of psychological methods to vocational guidance should still be regarded as being at the experimental stage, although they considered that the results already obtained were sufficiently encouraging to justify the continuance of experiments on a limited scale. They recommended that at least one further experiment should be carried out by the Industrial Health Research Board in cooperation with the Ministry of Labor, and that the ministry should be empowered to lend any necessary support to the work.

The committee attached great importance to the availability of appropriate medical records at the time vocational advice was given or submissions for vacancies were being effected. In their view the full value of medical reports to vocational guidance would not be realized until all education authorities were able to institute a final inspection shortly before the child left school. They also recommended that legislation should be passed to authorize and facilitate consultation between the vocational guidance officer and the school medical authorities in respect of boys and girls who had already left school, concerning whom an independent medical opinion was desirable before advice on choice of employment was given.

Pending this, cooperation on a voluntary basis between the vocational guidance officer and the school medical authorities was suggested. The committee also recommended that the Ministry of Labor should continue its consultations with the Home Office, with a view to the better interchange of information between the vocational guidance officers, the factory inspectors and certifying factory surgeons as to the fitness, or unfitness, of juveniles, within the scope of the examinational provisions of the Factory Acts, for various forms of employment.

## EDUCATIONAL TOURS TO THE WORLD'S FAIR

ARRANGEMENTS for making the utmost use of the educational material at the World's Fair were timed to begin this fall when the schools opened. Student tours, in groups, over planned itineraries for systematic study, was the method adopted. The management has done everything possible to facilitate them and to urge that advantage be taken of this opportunity during the few days that remain before the closing date, October 31.

It is the purpose of the tours that they be a practical part of the educational program of those making them, coordinating with their class work. Accordingly a group composed of university professors, heads of technical schools, supervisors of public schools departments, principals, members of staffs of educational museums and a force of experienced teachers joined with heads of departments and area chiefs of the exposition in a systematic collating of the exhibits for the purpose of arranging itineraries for systematic study that could be carried out in practicable tours. They are so arranged that two tours of two hours each may be taken in a day, with ample interval for lunch and rest.

To further this educational project the fair has made the tours virtually free, with a merely nominal charge of five cents gate admission for students in groups and no admission fee at all for the teacher in charge. Nearly all the purely educational exhibits are free in any case and the concessionaires whose exhibits are collateral with the educational plan are cooperating.

The tours are for elementary, high-school and emergency education students. The age limit is eighteen years. Groups must be of ten or more, in charge of a teacher.

Planned itineraries, syllabi of the subjects and a complete summary of all the educational exhibits are ready in printed and mimeographed form and may be had free by any teacher by writing to the Student Tours Section, A Century of Progress, Chicago. This material includes all necessary information for the handling of student groups at the fair.

It is the first time in the history of education that any exposition has done this work for students. At no previous exposition has the educational material been organized into syllabi offered free to teaching staffs and students. The material and the opportunity for its study in this manner are in accord with the newest ideas in educational progress. There is no other place where there is such a quantity of visual material to make such a project possible. The prepared itineraries have been mapped so thoroughly as to avoid loss of time and exposition guides have been specially trained to assist and direct the groups.

## MUSIC ON THE RADIO

The seventh consecutive season of the organized course in the understanding of good music, the NBC Music Appreciation Hour, was inaugurated by Dr. Walter Damrosch, on Friday, October 5, over the combined coast-to-coast NBC-WEAF-WJZ networks.

More than 6,000,000 school children throughout the country will develop their knowledge of the world's greatest compositions in the 12 weekly concerts by the NBC Symphony Orchestra, in which Dr. Damrosch will demonstrate the various forms of music.

Students' notebooks, giving the themes of the numbers played in each broadcast, and instructor's manuals to assist in interpreting the course are now being distributed from the NBC studios in Radio City. In 1933, more than 17,000 copies of these manuals and approximately 105,000 notebooks were sold.

The 1934–35 course, as in previous seasons, will consist of four series of graded programs for children from eight to eighteen years old. Each Friday morning broadcast from 11:00 A. M. to 12:00 noon, EST, will include programs for two of the series, the remaining two being covered in the broadcast of the following week.

More than seventy stations in the NBC networks, affording local outlets for listeners in every part of the country, will carry the Music Appreciation Hour programs. Previous experience has shown that the concerts with Dr. Damrosch's explanations of the forms and expressions of music are listened to regularly not only by millions of children but by adults as well, for the programs combine both entertainment and instruction.

The enjoyment and benefits of the NBC Music Appreciation Hour are not confined to listeners in America. Last year the programs were heard in Canada, Mexico, Santo Domingo and the West Indies. In addition, requests for the manuals and notebooks were received from cities in Brazil, China, Hawaii, the Philippines, Chile, France and Arabia. The course also has been duplicated during the past summer in South Africa, where several thousands of the notebooks were distributed to school children in Natal.

A steadily increasing number of schools and school children are tuning in on the Friday programs and a growing number of letters are being received from school teachers and principals and from parents, in which the course has been given the highest praise.

## RADIO BROADCASTS ON THE PROBLEMS OF GOVERNMENT

Eighteen weekly programs on "Trends in Government," in the "You and Your Government" series, broadcast by the National Broadcasting Company over an NBC–WEAF network from coast-to-coast at 7:30 p. m., Eastern Standard Time, opened on October 2 with a lecture on "The Crisis in Local Government" by Dr. Charles A. Beard, the economist and historian. Dr. Charles E. Merriam, professor of political science in the University of Chicago, and a member of the Advisory Committee of the Federal Public Works Administration and of the National Planning Board, was heard on the following Tuesday. Dr. Merriam, who has just returned from Europe, discussed "European Local Government."

Thomas H. Reed, professor of political science at the University of Michigan, is chairman of the Committee on Civic Education by Radio which is responsible for these productions. He introduces the speakers each week and keeps the listener informed of the development of the series. Dr. Reed is the director of the Municipal Consultant Service of the National Municipal League, and is in intimate contact with the problems of local and state government which are covered in these broadcasts.

The Committee on Civic Education by Radio includes George S. Counts, of Columbia University; Norman H. Davis; John A. Lapp; Katharine Ludington; Joseph D. McGoldrick, comptroller of New York City; Albert B. Meredith, of New York University; Harold G. Moulton, of the Brookings Institution; Bessie L. Pierce, of the University of Chicago; Frederic A. Ogg, of the University of Wisconsin, editor of the *American Political Science Review,* and Chester H. Rewell, editor of the *San Francisco Chronicle.* This committee was formed by the National Advisory Council on Radio in Education, of which Robert A. Millikan is president and Levering Tyson, director, in cooperation with the American Political Science Association, for the purpose of presenting impartial non-partisan discussions of important governmental subjects. The National Municipal League, a leading organization in the field of local government reform, is cooperating in the presentation of the series.

## THE WORK OF COOPER UNION

Cooper Union begins its seventy-fifth year with an enrolment of approximately 3,000 men and women, according to an announcement made by R. Fulton Cutting, president of the Board of Trustees.

The number of new students is about 500, selected from 4,535 applicants. One out of eight applicants was admitted to the Institute of Technology. There were 842 applicants for admission to the day engineering school, and only 99 were accepted, and more than 1,500 applied to enter the night engineering school, 202 being enrolled. Applications were most numerous for the Night Art School, where 1,693 sought admission to the courses in freehand drawing, the decorative arts, architectural drawing and modeling. Only 120 of the candidates were successful. Eighty students will enter the Day Art School, the applicants numbering more than 500.

Philip Nudd, formerly Coffin Fellow at Massachusetts Institute of Technology, has joined the department of electrical engineering, and Stanley Schauss, of Cornell University, joins the department of physics. Esmond Shaw, the architect, has been named superintendent of the Night Art School. Mr. Shaw, who is chief designer of the New York City Park Department, was formerly a teacher of design at Cooper Union.

Plans for the reorganization of the arts curriculum to include a year's preparatory course on the elements of drawing, painting, picture making, modeling and architecture were also made public. All applicants for architecture, drawing, sculpture, furniture design and other related subjects must now take the same entrance examination and all students will be required to take the preparatory course.

An innovation has been made in the department of painting where a painting laboratory has been established. The best students in the advanced painting class will be permitted to work away from their fellow students in a large room resembling a professional studio.

This year a selected group of advertising students who graduated in June have been asked to return to work under an instructor.

Dr. Everett Dean Martin, director of the newly organized Department of Social Philosophy, announces that the free annual lectures formerly given under the auspices of the People's Institute would begin on November 9.

## VISITING PROFESSORS AT HARVARD UNIVERSITY

As reported in the *Harvard Alumni Bulletin,* an imposing group of distinguished scholars will lecture at Harvard this year.

Dr. Jules Blache, professor of physical geography at the University of Grenoble, is the Harvard exchange professor from France. He belongs to the younger group of distinguished French professors and is a recognized authority in his field. Professor Blache will be in residence during the second half-year. He will conduct a half-course on the "Human Geography of Mountains."

Dr. Eugen Rosenstock-Hüssy, professor of the history of law and of German law at the University of Breslau, who was a visiting lecturer on government last year, returns to the university for the first half-year as Kuno Francke professor of German art and culture. Professor Rosenstock-Hüssy received his doctorate from Heidelberg and began his teaching career at Leipzig. Later he established the Academy of Labor at the University of Frankfurt, and in 1923 he became professor at Breslau. In 1926 he was a lecturer at Oxford.

Dr. Paul Kluckhohn, professor of the German language and literature at Tübingen, has been appointed Kuno Francke professor for the second half-year. After receiving his Ph.D. from Göttingen, Professor Kluckhohn joined the teaching staff of the University of Münster and became associate professor there. Later he held professorships at the Universities of Danzig and of Vienna before his appointment to Tübingen.

Dr. Wolfgang Köhler, professor of philosophy and director of the Psychological Institute at the University of Berlin, is the William James Lecturer in philosophy and psychology for the first half-year. Professor Köhler is prominent in his field. He is a brother of Dr. W. R. W. Köhler, who has been Kuno Francke professor of German art and culture during the past two years and now has the permanent appointment of professor of fine arts.

Dr. Leopold von Wiese, director of the Research Institute in Social Sciences at Cologne, will lecture at Harvard on sociology during the second half-year; Professor Gaetano Salvemini, who was Lauro de Bosis Lecturer on the history of Italian civilization last year, has been reappointed to that lectureship, and Professor Robert Ulich returns for his second year as lecturer on comparative education at the Graduate School of Education. Professor Salvemini has been, successively, professor of history at the Universities of Messina, Pisa and Florence and visiting professor at universities in England and the United States. Professor Ulich was, until recently, professor of philosophy at the Higher Technical School, Dresden.

Professor Samuel Flagg Bemis, A.M. '15, Ph.D. '16, of George Washington University, will lecture, during the first half-year, on history and, as resident tutor in Adams House, will carry on the tutorial work of Professor Baxter while the latter is on leave. Professor Bemis is a former Pulitzer Prize winner in history.

Walter Rice Sharp, of the University of Wisconsin, will lecture during the first half-year on government and also act as a tutor in the division of history, government and economics; Niles Carpenter, Ph.D. '20, of the University of Buffalo, will lecture on sociology, and Professor William R. Dennes, of the University of California, will lecture on philosophy and conduct Philosophy 1, a half-course in logic.

Dr. Hans Zinsser, professor of bacteriology and immunology in the Medical School, is the Harvard exchange professor to France this year. He will be abroad during the second half-year.

## EDUCATION WEEK

The fourteenth annual American Education Week will be observed from November 5 to 11. The program will be built around the theme "Educating for To-morrow." The observance will be a step in the adaptation of education to the needs of a changing social order. The coming American Education Week programs will be sponsored as usual by the National Education Association, the United States Office of Education and the American Legion. Other national organizations whose memberships total millions will cooperate. Each community will adapt the observance to its own needs. Topics suggested for the day-by-day programs follow:

MONDAY, NOVEMBER 5.—"Planning for Tomorrow." Let every community, every school and every organization ask itself the question: "What kind of life do we desire?"

TUESDAY, NOVEMBER 6.—"Developing New Types of Schooling." Discuss the adaptation of the regular school curriculum to the needs of changing social conditions. On this day give special attention to the Tercentenary Celebration in American High Schools.

WEDNESDAY, NOVEMBER 7.—"Improving the Rural School." Achievement of economic security and social well-being of the American farmer is an important step toward national recovery. It is the privilege of the rural school to inspire improvement of country life.

THURSDAY, NOVEMBER 8.—"Financing Our Schools." Show how increasing unity of national life requires that support for education be derived from larger areas. This is the day set aside for mass meetings.

FRIDAY, NOVEMBER 9.—"Quickening the Sense of Civic Responsibility." School observance of Armistice Day. Emphasize good citizenship and Americanism as a part of the Armistice Day Program in cooperation with the American Legion.

SATURDAY, NOVEMBER 10.—"Preparing for New Kinds of Service." Show how the performance of such services as reforestation, beautification of parks and cities, eradication of insect pests, prevention of disease through sanitation, programs of recreation, and the creation of publicly owned art will give employment to many thousands who can not be absorbed in industry and business.

SUNDAY, NOVEMBER 11.—"Enriching Character through Education." Point out the increased importance of strengthening character in times of rapid change in the social structure, in order that the good things achieved in the past may not be swept away merely because they are old, nor new ideals refused trial merely because they have no precedent.

The following complete sets of materials, adapted to the purpose indicated, may be obtained in packet form. Order now. Many of the American Education Week supplies were exhausted early last year.

# EDUCATIONAL NOTES AND NEWS

DR. DIXON RYAN FOX, professor of history at Columbia University, was installed as president of Union College on October 12. The arrangements of the installation exercises were described in the issue of this journal on October 6, and the addresses of Dr. Fox and President Nicholas Murray Butler are printed in the present issue.

DR. ROBERT MAYNARD HUTCHINS, president of the University of Chicago, has been offered a position in the National Recovery Administration, the exact character of which has not been announced at the present writing. It is said that Dr. Hutchins may arrange for leave of absence for a year, or resign to take a permanent executive post at Washington.

DR. EDWIN HATFIELD ANDERSON has resigned after serving for twenty-one years as director of the New York Public Library, and has been made director emeritus by the Board of Trustees. He will be succeeded by Harry Miller Lydenberg, assistant director. From 1906 to 1908 Dr. Anderson was director of the New York State Library and its Library School, resigning to become assistant director of the New York Public Library. After the death in March, 1913, of Dr. John S. Billings, first director of the library formed by the consolidation of the Lenox and Astor libraries and the Tilden Foundation, Dr. Anderson was appointed.

DR. ELMER BURRITT BRYAN, president of Ohio University at Athens, died on October 15. He was sixty-nine years old. Dr. Bryan, after a long career in educational work, was called from the presidency of Franklin College, Indiana, to head Colgate University in 1909. He succeeded the late Rev. Dr. George Edmands Merrill. Before this he had been principal of the Insular Normal Schools, in the Philippine Islands, in 1901–1902, and in the next year he was general superintendent of education for the islands. He had been called to the islands by the late William Howard Taft, then Governor General of the Philippines. Because of illness he resigned in August, 1903, and returned to the United States to take the chair of educational and social psychology at Indiana University. In 1905 he became president of Franklin College.

The formal installation of Dr. Quincy A. W. Rohrbach as the sixth president of the State Teachers College at Kutztown, Pennsylvania, took place on October 19. Dr. Rohrbach was formerly professor of educational administration at the University of Pittsburgh. His inaugural address was preceded by a speech by Dr. James N. Rule, Superintendent of Public Instruction. The ceremonies closed with a luncheon at which Henry Klonower, chief of the teacher division of the Department of Public Instruction, was toastmaster.

Dr. Louis Clinton Wright was installed on October 18 as president of Baldwin-Wallace College, Berea, Ohio.

The Rev. Dr. James H. Franklin, for twenty-two years executive secretary of the American Baptist Foreign Missionary Society, was installed on October 9 as president of Crozer Theological Seminary, Chester, Pa. Dr. Franklin is the third president of the institution. Dr. Homer P. Rainey, president of Bucknell University; Dr. Milton G. Evans, retiring president of the seminary, and Dr. Franklin spoke after the academic procession.

Syama Prasad Mukherjee, son of the late Sir Ashutosh Mukherjee, has been appointed vice-chancellor of the University of Calcutta, in place of Sir Hassan Suhrawardy, whose term of office expires this year.

At the primary election in California there were three candidates for the office of superintendent of public instruction—Vierling Kersey, incumbent, John R. Swan and G. Vernon Bennett. According to the *Western Journal of Education*, "Dr. Kersey made no campaign for the office, but devoted his time exclusively to genuine leadership in educational affairs. He has always been courteous and helpful to school administrators and has an efficient staff of coworkers in the State Department of Education. The final returns gave Dr. Kersey a majority of 83,000 votes over his opponents."

Dr. Arthur H. Wilde, for sixteen years dean of the Boston University School of Education, was the guest of honor on October 13 at a reception attended by graduates of the school, the faculty and students. Following the reception, Dr. Payson Smith, State Commissioner of Education, spoke. A portrait of Dean Wilde by a Boston painter, Miss Margaret Fitzhugh Browne, was unveiled and presented to the university. Underwritten financially by the alumni, faculty, students and administrative staff, "it symbolized the deep affection and high regard in which the dean is held." President Daniel L. Marsh accepted the portrait on behalf of the university. Later, at an informal supper, the principal speaker was Dr. Erik A. Andersen, deputy superintendent of schools at Providence, R. I., who is president of the School of Education Alumni Association.

Dr. William J. O'Shea, who retired in February as superintendent of the schools of New York City, was the guest of honor at an informal luncheon on October 10 held in celebration of his seventy-first birthday. The luncheon was attended by Dr. O'Shea's successor, Dr. Harold G. Campbell, by virtually every member of the Board of Superintendents and by other school officials.

A portrait of Miss Fanny E. Davies, founder and present principal of the Wykeham Rise School, at Washington, Connecticut, was unveiled and formally presented to the school by the alumnae on October 14. Governor Cross, the principal speaker, was introduced by S. McLean Buckingham, State Secretary of Agriculture.

The degree of doctor of humane letters was conferred on Professor Albert Einstein at the opening on October 8 of Yeshiva College, New York City. Dr. David Eugene Smith, emeritus professor of mathematics at Columbia University, presented Dr. Einstein for the degree, and Governor Herbert H. Lehman delivered the address, to which Dr. Einstein replied.

The University of Cambridge will confer, on October 22, the honorary degree of doctor of science on Dr. Lawrence J. Henderson, professor of biochemistry at Harvard University, and on Dr. Karl Landsteiner, of the Rockefeller Institute for Medical Research, at the ceremonies in connection with the opening of the new Cambridge University Library.

Miss Edith G. Wilson, who last year served as acting dean of women at the University of Maine, has been promoted to be dean, serving also as instructor of education.

Nellie Hawkinson, formerly professor of nursing education and dean of the Western Reserve School of Nursing, has been appointed professor of nursing education at the University of Chicago.

Dr. William Clyde DeVane, of Yale University, has been appointed professor of English at Cornell University.

Dr. Glen Haydon, of California, has become head of the department of music at the University of North Carolina.

Dr. Joseph A. Chucka, associate biologist at the Maine Agricultural Experiment Station, has been appointed professor and head of the department of agronomy and agricultural engineering to succeed Professor George E. Simmons, who retired last spring.

Dr. Fritz Morstein Marx, formerly of the University of Hamburg, now a member of the faculty of the department of politics at Princeton University, has been appointed visiting lecturer in government in the Graduate School of New York University for the present academic year. Dr. Marx will give the graduate course in municipal government and administration in substitution for Professor Russell Forbes, New York City Commissioner of Purchase, who is on leave of absence.

Dr. Livingston Farrand, president of Cornell University, has become active chairman of a committee established, in response to an appeal from Governor Lehman, of New York State, by the State Charities Aid Association, to conduct a state-wide campaign for approval at the polls of the $40,000,000 bond issue for unemployment relief.

President Glenn Frank, of the University of Wisconsin, has become a member of the national citizens' committee announced recently by Newton D. Baker, chairman of the 1934 Mobilization for Human Needs. The committee will bring before the public reports on present-day social conditions in American communities preliminary to fall community chest campaigns.

Dr. Robert D. W. Connor, professor of American history at the University of North Carolina, has been appointed the first occupant of the office of archivist of the United States, a post created during the last Congress by President Roosevelt. He will plan and estimate costs of collecting and publishing historical material of importance.

Dr. Roy V. Peel, acting director of the Division of Research in Public Administration at the Washington Square College of New York University, has been granted leave of absence from the university for the current academic year to conduct a survey of public administration in the Scandinavian countries. The expense of the survey will be defrayed by a grant from the Spelman Fund.

Dr. Howard F. Lowry, head of the department of English at the College of Wooster, has been granted leave of absence during the first semester for the purpose of study and research in Europe in connection with the Guggenheim award. In his absence, Professor Frederick W. Moore will serve as acting head of the English department.

Dr. A. E. Joyal, professor of education in the University of Denver, has been chosen to serve as district representative of Phi Delta Kappa in Colorado, Iowa, Nebraska, Minnesota, North and South Dakota and Wyoming. Dr. Joyal will take charge of arrangements of the District Conference to be held on November 9 and 10 in Omaha.

Dr. Richard C. Cabot, professor emeritus of social ethics and of clinical medicine at Harvard University, will lecture on social economy at Simmons College, Boston, during the current academic year.

The Reverend Dr. G. Bromley Oxnam, president of DePauw University, addressed the Methodist sesquicentennial convention at Baltimore on October 12.

Dr. T. A. Harmon, president of Southern State Normal School at Yankton, South Dakota, died on October 10, at the age of sixty-three years.

Charles H. Cooper, for thirty years, until his retirement four years ago, as president emeritus, president of the State Normal School at Mankato, Minnesota, died on October 12. He was seventy-nine years old.

William Dick, for more than fifty years connected with the management of the Philadelphia school system, and secretary of the Board of Public Education for twenty-two years until his retirement in 1928, died on October 11. He was seventy-six years old.

The twenty-first annual meeting of the Association of Urban Universities will be held at the University of Louisville, Kentucky, on November 1 and 2. The speakers and their subjects will be as follows: On November 1, Dr. Fred J. Kelly, of the Office of Education, Washington, D. C., "Federal Plans in Aid of Education"; Dean C. S. Marsh, of the University of Buffalo, educational director of the CCC, "The Educational Program in CCC Camps"; John Lang, president of the National Student Federation, "Some Problems of Youth," and Howard O. Hunter, of the Federal Emergency Relief Administration, "Federal Relief Work." On November 2, papers will be read as follows: "The Integration of High School and College Work," Dr. Henry C. Mills, assistant professor of education at the University of Buffalo; "Experimental College at the University of Minnesota," Dean Malcolm McLean; "The Urban University in Cooperation with Other Institutions," President Philip Nash, of the University of Toledo, and "Evening Session Enrolment During the Depression," Dean Frank M. Debatin, of Washington University, St. Louis.

The tenth annual congress of the National Student Federation of America will be held in Boston from December 28 to January 1. Headquarters for the visiting delegates, college students from all sections of the country, will be at the Parker House. Wesley D. Osborne, a senior student at Boston University, is chairman of the congress committee. There will be discussions on the honor system, athletics, campus government and publications.

By the will of the late J. W. Sparks, of Philadelphia, the Pennington School for Boys, New Jersey, has received a bequest of a million dollars. No decision has been made regarding the disposition of the gift, pending the settlement of Mr. Sparks's estate. Mrs. Sparks, who died in 1932, gave the school $500,000, which was used for general improvements and renovations of the school buildings and equipment.

A bequest of more than $540,000 to Vassar College for an endowment fund is made under the will of Mr. Frank L. Babbott, of Brooklyn. It will establish the Lydia Richardson Babbott Endowment Fund in memory of Mr. Babbott's wife. Previously the college received an endowment fund of $50,000 for scholarships given in 1925 by Mr. Babbott's four children in memory of their mother.

The executors of the estate of John MacLean, president of Princeton University from 1854 to 1868, have presented to the Princeton University Library a collection of Dr. MacLean's letters.

According to *The Christian Science Monitor*, budgets submitted to the State Department of Education by city and county school boards show that with funds expected from all sources during the current school year, two thirds of the schools in Alabama will be closed by February 1. The estimates were compiled in response to a request from the Education Office of the U. S. Department of the Interior. There was, it is reported, no indication in the request as to whether or not the Federal Government intends to aid the schools again this year. Such an interpretation was placed on the request in some quarters as the information was sent to Washington, but Dr. Edgar L. Morphet, director of the research division of the Education Department, said: "We are not optimistic over the prospects of federal aid." If the public schools of the state are to operate for a normal term this year, funds approximating $3,598,294, in addition to present revenues, must be made available from some source. Otherwise, schools in twelve counties and cities will have to close before Christmas. It is said that in only four counties and nine cities will the school authorities be able to operate for a normal term during 1934–35. Dr. Morphet, in explaining estimates, observed that about forty per cent. of state educational appropriations would be paid, while decline in assessed values of property would result in a further decrease in funds available.

An Associated Press dispatch states that Secretary of the Interior Harold L. Ickes has been instructed by President Roosevelt to work out with Harry L. Hopkins, relief administrator, a minimum program to assist in keeping financially distressed schools open for the three months until the Congress and state legislatures meet. Mr. Ickes is said to have stated that $2,000,000 to $2,500,000 would be needed to prevent closing of schools in Texas, Arkansas, Oklahoma, Georgia, Nebraska, Kansas, South Dakota and other states.

*California Schools* reports on the large reductions in expenditures for public schools of that state which have been made during the past four years due to the economic conditions which prevailed. Expenditures for public schools decreased by more than $33,000,000, or approximately 20 per cent. from 1930–31 to 1932–33. A comparison of the expenditures of all other units of government for corresponding years points to the fact that the public schools have borne a larger proportion of the reduction and curtailment in public expenditures than other public agencies. During a like period of time, all other units of government reduced expenditures only $12,063,407, or 3.54 per cent.

IMPROVED financial conditions are apparent as public schools of Pennsylvania start their one hundred and first year. Reports to the Department of Public Instruction, according to the *Pennsylvania School Journal,* indicate that every school in the state will open on the scheduled time. In only four districts has permission been granted for temporary reduction of teachers salaries for 1934–35 below the ninety per cent. level for 1932–33. In no district under 30,000 population has permission been granted to reduce salaries below the ninety per cent. level. In no district to date is the salary schedule below 80 per cent. of the 1932–33 figure. Last year approximately 200 districts applied to Superintendent Rule for permission to reduce salaries below ninety per cent. for the one year. Such permission was granted to less than 100 districts. Most of these were for only 5 per cent. additional reduction. This year only about fifty districts thought it necessary to apply for the permission, but only four have obtained the special grant. In all other cases it has been possible for the Department of Public Instruction to adjust the district finances through more nearly balanced budgets and assistance from the special aid fund of $5,000,000 made available by the 1933 special session of the Legislature. Approximately three fifths of the special aid fund has been used to date. Practically all the $3,000,000 distributed to more than 600 financially distressed school districts has been designated by Superintendent Rule for payment of teachers' salaries and for payment of high-school tuition. The remainder of the fund will be used for the same general purposes during the coming school year.

THE 1933 Indiana state legislature has established three new state taxes other than the property tax to aid public schools. These new revenues are expected to amount to $14,564,654. This sum has been pro-rated among 20,032 teaching units in ninety-two counties of the state on a basis of daily attendance and assessed valuation to supplement the local school levies. The money will be used to pay teachers and bear the expenses of public schools that will serve an estimated daily attendance in the grades of 1 to 12 of 657,682 pupils this year. The three new state tax levies and the sums they produced from August 1, 1933, to July 31, 1934, were as follows: Gross income tax, $8,085,217; excise tax, $1,762,587; intangible tax, $750,533.

TWELVE students of the British Empire, the last of a contingent of twenty-eight who will form the tenth annual group of Commonwealth Fund Fellows, reached New York City recently on their way to seventeen American universities where they will study two years. The new fellows make 260 men and women who have received grants under the fund, which was initiated in 1925 by Mr. Edward S. Harkness, its president, "to promote understanding between the United States and the British Empire."

# DISCUSSION

## REMEDIAL METHODS FOR NON-READERS

MEASUREMENTS have demonstrated that reading ability is distributed along a normal curve with the retarded readers extending from the center to one end. After those with intellectual retardation and visual and auditory defects have been eliminated, the extreme cases of reading deficiency found near the end of the distribution consist of those children who have been able to profit very little or not at all from ordinary classroom teaching. Various terms have been employed to designate these non-readers—developmental alexia, dyslexia, strephosymbolia, inability to read, congenital aphasia, congenital alexia, developmental alexia and congenital word-blindness. Although "word-blindness" has an unfortunate implication concerning the etiology of reading disability, it describes the non-reader rather well. Practically all workers in the field have stressed the inability of these cases to read words as wholes. Perception and memory for words is very inferior. Nearly all the non-readers use inappropriate techniques in their attack on word perception.

The other diagnostic signs of the non-reader are well established. The progress of the eyes over the reading material is extremely irregular both in sequence of movements and duration of pauses. Obviously this indicates a confusion of perceptual processes. Included as important diagnostic signs are: reversing the sequence of letters within words, as *saw* for *was*, and *bread* for *beard;* an inability to distinguish the orientation of certain letters, as *b* and *d,* which results in errors like *dig* for *big;* a lack of ocular-manual dominance; and poor phonetic and spelling ability. Analysis of these diagnostic signs reveals a prominent factor common to all. The signs indicate in one way or another that the non-readers are unable to achieve normal progress in developing orderly perceptual sequences from left to right in their reading or attempts at reading. This tendency, however, is not confined to non-readers. Prior to any training in reading it is quite natural for the normal child to have perception reversals. With maturation and experience the frequency of the reversals declines in normal children but remains prominent in practically all non-readers. The perseveration of this tendency appears to be the important determinant of the reading deficiency.

Successful methods of treatment for the severe reading disability of non-readers have been developed and used by several investigators. Hinshelwood's[1] method is probably the first used. He taught all 12 of his cases to read effectively by the old-fashioned *a-b-c* method. After learning the single letters, the words were mastered by spelling them out loud letter by letter. This spelling was sometimes accompanied by a tracing of the letters on the table with the fingers. Finally the words were recognized by their total form alone.

Fernald and Keller's[2] remedial method for non-readers emphasized kinesthesis. The word to be learned was written in large script on cardboard or on the blackboard. The child then traced over the word with the first two fingers while he pronounced it to himself. When the child was confident he knew the word, it was erased and he tried to write it from memory, pronouncing the syllables as he wrote them. Succeeding stages in the learning process brought the child into contact with simple sentences, new words in a story, apprehension of phrases as a whole, and silent reading for content. New words that were not readily learned continued to be taught by the tracing and writing method.

The remedial program developed by Gates[3] for instructing non-readers is largely intrinsic. In it most of the instruction in phonetics, phrasing and the like is usually part of an actual reading situation. It is really a visual study-and-writing (spelling) method of instruction. Originally this method involved careful observation of a printed word while it was pronounced, attempts to visualize the word during silent articulation, and then writing the word with silent articulation of syllables. The more recent form of Gates' method is much like that of Fernald and Keller. However, print-like characters are substituted for script, and greater stress is placed on similarities and differences in words.

The program of remedial instruction recently employed by Monroe[4] is based mainly on an

[1] J. Hinshelwood, "Congenital Word-blindness." London, England: H. K. Lewis, Ltd., 1917. Pp. x + 112.

[2] G. M. Fernald and H. Keller, "The Effect of Kinaesthetic Factors in the Development of Word Recognition in the Case of Non-readers," *Jour. Educ. Res.*, 1921, 4, 355–377.

[3] A. I. Gates, "The Improvement of Reading," New York: Macmillan Company, 1927. Pp. xii + 440.

[4] M. Monroe, "Children Who Cannot Read," Chicago: University of Chicago Press, 1932. Pp. xvi + 206.

effective drill in phonetics and a kinesthetic technique similar to those cited above.

All these techniques have been employed with marked success in instructing non-readers. Analysis of the methods shows that, in general, one principle overshadows all others. The teaching, when effective, leads to habits of consecutive perception from left to right along the word and along the sentence, with strong emphasis upon developing adequate apprehension of words as wholes. The *a-b-c* method, spelling out the words, tracing and sounding the word simultaneously and phonetics intrinsic to the reading situation all tend to develop more adequate sequences of perception from left to right. As we have seen above, it is the lack of this ability which has been emphasized in diagnosing reading disability. There are, of course, various other factors involved in reading deficiencies and these must receive varying emphasis according to the individual case. Nevertheless, the training to achieve adequate orientation from left to right in perceptual sequences in reading seems to be fundamental. Adequate orientation is practically always absent in severe reading disability, and no satisfactory advance can be made without its correction.

Non-readers usually show an emotional reaction to the reading situation. In one type of case a neurotic constitution is the direct cause of the reading disability. It seems that many neurotics exhibiting impulsive responses, negativistic attitudes and illusions are unable to give the cooperation and sustained effort required in learning to read. For such cases prognosis is poor. Until their emotional adjustments are improved little progress in reading may be expected, even with individual teaching. It has been shown, however, that emotional maladjustment, especially emotional reaction to the reading situation, may be caused by reading disability. Lack of success during early attempts to read produces unfortunate emotional conditioning. Feelings of inferiority arise, and personality and behavior deviations may occur. In most of these cases the substitution of the success for failure in reading causes the unfortunate behavior traits to disappear. This permits normal attitudes of cooperation to develop.

*Motivation is very important in remedial instruction.* The writer believes that it is probably more important than any other factor. Without motivation no progress in reading will occur; with sufficient motivation, any one of the several remedial methods will usually achieve satisfactory results. Practically all non-readers can be taught to read if their cooperation is obtained.

In summary we may say that all non-readers exhibit more or less difficulty in maintaining the proper direction of perceptual sequences from left to right in the reading situation. In the more successful remedial methods, instruction to rectify this tendency is emphasized. *Motivation* is apparently more important than the particular remedial method employed.

Miles A. Tinker
University of Minnesota

## POTENTIAL ECONOMIES IN THE REORGANIZATION OF LOCAL SCHOOL ATTENDANCE UNITS

A study[1] of the school surveys of 223 counties to determine what effect reorganization of schools has on the cost of the school program reveals that this reorganization program would result in a decrease in expenditures for the same type of school program in 213 of the 223 counties. This study is concerned with the cost factor alone, not evaluating the increased educational advantages which will accrue as a result of the consolidation of schools. It reveals that, measured in weighted elementary classroom units or their equivalent, the reorganization of local school attendance units through the consolidation of schools will result in a decrease in cost in 213 counties and in an increase in cost in 10 counties. The mean variation in cost is a decrease of 7.83 per cent. of the original cost. If only the rural schools were included in the basal percentage, the mean decrease would be 9.2 per cent.

It is quite evident from the above facts that it would be to the advantage of all counties to reorganize their local school programs. The small chance which a county would face of increasing its educational cost as a result of reorganization would be more than offset by the improvement in the educational offerings. At the same time it must be remembered that

[1] Harry A. Little, "Potential Economies in the Reorganization of Local School Attendance Units," Bureau of Publications, Teachers College, Columbia University, New York, N. Y. (In press).

the contention that problems of educational finance would be solved by reorganization is not true. The total bill for rural education in the United States is approximately $600,000,000. If the entire rural school area were reorganized, the decrease in cost would be approximately $55,000,000—a very small amount scattered all over the United States. The increase in the efficiency of the schools when coupled with the decrease in cost would more than justify any effort to reorganize the schools according to modern needs and utilizing modern highway facilities.

The schools of the 223 counties studied as they are now organized cost in teaching units 1.36 times as much as they would cost if the same pupils were enrolled in school systems in which no elementary school had less than 290 pupils in average daily attendance and in which no high school had less than 726 pupils in average daily attendance, and where no transportation was required. If these schools were reorganized according to the plans outlined in the surveys studied, the cost would be 1.25 times the proportional cost of larger schools.

It is not to be denied that the consolidation of schools makes possible opportunities for better educational advantages which, if utilized, may increase the cost of the educational program. The better buildings required to put into effect the reorganization proposed in the surveys of these counties would result in additional cost, on the average, of 3.8 per cent. of the original cost of all schools of the county for a period of thirty years. This would mean that until the buildings are paid for, the average decrease in cost would be approximately 4 per cent.

There are three factors which seem to affect the variation in cost resulting from consolidation:

*First,* the amount of consolidation which previous reorganization, natural barriers, community prejudice or other limiting factors will permit. If the schools of a county have already been consolidated, it is natural to suppose that further consolidation will result in a smaller proportional decrease in cost than in counties where no consolidation has been made.

*Second,* the density of population also determines the amount of economy to be gained from the consolidation of schools. Counties which are densely populated have a greater possibility of large consolidation than sparsely populated counties.

*Third,* the number of children per school. This is, in a sense, a measure of the consolidation which has already been effected in the county. Small schools require a larger number of teachers for the same number of pupils than do larger schools. If the schools are already large in number of pupils per school, a smaller decrease in cost is to be expected from reorganization than if the schools were small in number of pupils.

It seems quite evident that county school authorities all over the United States should take steps to reorganize their schools so that modern educational programs could be offered for the least possible amount of money. The county surveys which were used as a basis for this study are excellent examples of educational programs which have included the entire county and which were made with the above purpose in mind.

Some authorities have contended that the reorganization of schools, although offering better school advantages, would be prohibitive in cost. The results of the study mentioned above indicate that this is not the case.

Harry A. Little

Georgia State College
for Women
Milledgeville, Georgia

# SPECIAL CORRESPONDENCE

## RESPONSIBILITY FOR SCHOOL FUNDS

L. A. Whipple, when superintendent of the schools of Bleckley County, Georgia, deposited $3,316.07 with the Cochran Banking Company, as he was told to do by a resolution of the Bleckley County Board of Education designating this bank as the official depository. The bank failed, and the members of the Bleckley County board sued the surety on Mr. Whipple's bond for the loss of funds in the closed bank. The Georgia court held the surety liable.[1]

[1] *American Surety Co. of N. Y. v. N. E. Smith et al.*, 174 S. E. 262 (Ga.), 1934.

Apparently, a public officer is liable for monies in his custody, no matter how careful and prudent he may have been, according to the weight of authority.[2] A public officer is considered an insurer of public funds lawfully in his possession, and any loss, whether due to any fault of his or not, he is responsible for, unless excused by an act of God or public enemy.[3] The courts fear that large sums of public monies in the custody of public officers might be dispensed with by fraudulent means which would be impossible to detect, thus placing public money in jeopardy.[4] Legally, a public officer is considered a debtor, bound to account for exact sums received, on the theory that any other rule would violate public policy.[5] He is liable at all events, regardless of how careful he is in selecting a depository for public funds. He is not considered as a bailee for hire or as a custodian of money in his custody. In most jurisdictions, his liability is absolute.[6]

In a few jurisdictions, a public officer is relieved from responsibility where he deposits public funds in designated depositories apportioned according to the capital and surplus of the depository, unless the said officer contributes to the loss. If he does not deposit the funds according to the capital and surplus of the depository, that officer is said to contribute to the loss, and is personally liable.[7]

In a few jurisdictions, a public officer is not liable for any loss of public funds occasioned by the failure of the depository bank, if he used ordinary care and diligence. In these jurisdictions, he is considered as an ordinary bailee, not as an insurer or as a debtor.[8] This view-point appears to be more in accordance with the old common law rule.[9]

The liability of a surety is coextensive with that of a public officer for whom they have gone bond, whether there was any negligence on his part or not or whether reasonable care was used or not.[10] In the case under discussion, the court held that the surety went Mr. Whipple's bond for the care of school funds which the statute gave into his custody, and for which the statute makes him responsible. In eighteen states the surety has been held responsible.[11] It is the duty of the county superintendent to select the depository, and if he is not satisfied with any resolution of the County Board of Education, he must pick his own depository, since it is he who is responsible for the funds and not any member of the county board.[12]

Where a public officer is liable only as a bailee for hire, the surety is not required to pay for monies taken from the principal by irresistible force.[13] Likewise, where the surety bond states that the surety is liable only for monies which the principal is bound by law to receive, the surety is liable to that extent only.[14]

Because of the strict liability placed on a public officer, many legislatures have relieved him from liability where the loss occurs without any fault of the officer. In most states, legislation of this character has been held constitutional, whether the law relieves the principal and surety, or whether it requires the reimbursement to them of the amounts already paid in by them because of the loss.[15] The majority rule is upheld on the theory that the public can more easily bear the burden where the circumstances make it unjust for the officer to stand the loss.[16] No one but creditors have a vested interest in the funds in the custody of a county officer, and

[2] 46 C. J. (*Corpus Juris*) 1040 gives citations for the rule in the following states: Cal., Colo., Ill., Ind., Kan., Minn., Miss., Mo., Neb., N. J., N. Y., N. C., Ohio, Pa., Tex., Wash., Wis.; *American Surety Co.* v. *Ind. Sch. Dist. No. 18*, 53 Fed. (2d) 178; 81 A. L. R. (American Law Reports) 1.

[3] *Smythe* v. *U. S.*, 188 U. S. 156; Note 18, A. L. R. 982; 32 A. L. R. 1512; 22 R. C. L. (Ruling Case Law) Section 5, page 225.

[4] *Tillinghast* v. *Merrill*, 151 N. Y. 135, 45 N. E. 375; 34 L. R. A. (Lawyers Reports Annotated) 678.

[5] 22 R. C. L. 468, sec. 136; 38 A. L. R. 1512; Supra 3.

[6] Supra 2.

[7] Supra 1.

[8] *U. S.* v. *Thomas*, 15 Wallace 337; Supra 4; 7 L. R. A. (N. S.) 1084, note.

[9] *Perley* v. *Muskegon County*, 32 Mich. 132, 22 R. C. L. 225, Sec. 5.

[10] *People* v. *McGrath*, 279 Ill. 550, 117 N. E. 74; 46 C. J. 1069, Sec. 401; *Luverne* v. *Skyberg*, 169 Minn. 234, 211 N. W. 5.

[11] Supra 1, Supra 2.

[12] Supra 1.

[13] *Newton County* v. *Green*, 104 Ark. 270, 149 S. W. 73; *Bauer* v. *North Ark. Highway Improvement Dist.*, 270 S. W. 533 (1925).

[14] *Mount* v. *State*, 90 Ind. 29, 38 A. L. R. 1512; 41 L. R. A. (N. S.) 97, note.

[15] *Miller* v. *Henry*, 62 Or. 4, 124 P. 197; 46 C. J. 1040, sec. 315.

[16] *Bauer* v. *N. Ark. Highway Imp. Dist.* (Supra 12).

the legislature may relieve him from liability on his bond.[17]

There are some states that hold any laws which attempt to relieve a public officer unconstitutional, on the theory that the vested rights impairing the obligation of a contract are destroyed.[18] The majority of the jurisdictions, however, hold that the vested rights of citizens are not destroyed; that there is no interference with the rights of the political subdivisions for which an officer acts; and that there is no impairment of the "obligation of contract."[19]

PAUL JARVIS

HUMBOLDT HIGH SCHOOL,
ST. PAUL, MINN.

[17] Supra 8.

[18] *Smith* v. *Fuller*, 135 Ga. 271, 69 S. E. 177 (1910); *McClellend* v. *State*, 138 Ind. 321, 37 N. E. 1089; *Bristol* v. *Johnson*, 34 Mich. 123; *Mercer* v. *Floyd*, 53 N. Y. S. 433; *Com.* v. *Tilton*, 111 Ky. 341, 63 S. W. 602. (Most of these cases depend on their own state constitutional provisions.)

[19] 38 A. L. R. 1514; *Miller* v. *Henry*, 62 Or. 4, 124 Pac. 197; *McSurely* v. *McGrew*, 140 Ia. 163, 118 N. W. 415; *Pearson* v. *State*, 56 Ark. 148, 19 S. W. 499.

# QUOTATIONS

## THE AMERICAN COLLEGE

THE installation of Dr. Dixon Ryan Fox as president of Union College at Schenectady—the varied colors of academic hoods matching those of the autumnal foliage—gave occasion for glowing praise of the American college which has been "cherished more steadily, more widely and more deeply, perhaps, than any other secular institution outside of the state itself." The addresses by President Butler and President Fox, his sometime pupil, together make a tractate which deserves to have place with Milton's brief treatise on education. The very name with which this college was endowed gave challenge to that liberal education which makes for union in a distracted world, into which the forces of disunion have thrust their way forward. No part of the civilized world has escaped, and from one (Germany), as President Butler said, not forgetting its "colossal contribution" in the past, "no light and no leadership can be looked for for some time to come." The one instrument which humankind has in its hands to displace forever the disintegrating spirit of disunion "is that of a liberal education," and his definition of it should be emblazoned on the walls of every institution of learning. If it is lived up to, it will indeed be "training worthy of a free man."

President Fox spoke more particularly of the American college as our incomparable contribution to the culture of America and his presentation of the case of the small independent college supports the confident hope that it will not be superseded by the divided college (separated into junior and senior colleges) or imitated out of existence by the disintegration of university colleges into a family of small colleges. It has prospect of immortality as the continuing American type of a liberal education designed as it was for the free life which has now become "the bounty of the multitude."—*The New York Times.*

## THE DIRECTOR OF THE NEW YORK PUBLIC LIBRARY

THE able, quiet, scholarly gentleman who for the last twenty-one years has presided over the Public Library has been so self-effacing that few of the many hundreds of thousands whom he has served, either directly or indirectly, since he became director have ever even heard his name. But to those few the news that Dr. Edwin H. Anderson is retiring as director of the New York Public Library on November 1 comes as a disappointment and brings a sense of personal loss. No longer will they be able to turn to him for advice and guidance. No longer will they see the familiar figure going to and from his office.

To his friends Dr. Anderson's retirement from active duty marks merely the close of one chapter in a long and busy life of usefulness to his community and to the country. Dr. Anderson may seek a change and a rest. But he is not the sort whose career ends with his formal retirement. Behind a modest exterior lies a vigorous and keen mind, ever planning and working to improve library facilities in the country, ever eager to help the libraries to play a more important part in the life of the community. For twenty-one years he struggled to make the always inadequate municipal appropriations which supplement the Public Library's own funds stretch as far as possible. He developed the system of branch libraries. He devised new ways of inducing young people to use the library facilities. Always he was thinking in terms of service—of the library as the tool of the citizen.

His place will be taken by his friend and associate, Mr. H. M. Lydenberg, who has done so much to help Dr. Anderson since he joined the library staff. He will carry on the Anderson policies. To his retirement Dr. Anderson carries not only the satisfaction of a job well done but of a job appreciated by those who know the heavy burden under which he has labored.—*The New York Herald-Tribune.*

### A TEACHER OF TEACHERS

SIR JOHN ADAMS, LL.D., emeritus professor of education in the Universities of London and Los Angeles, died suddenly on September 29, at Los Angeles, at the age of seventy-seven years.

Education in the widest sense of the term owes much to Adams. He was full of vitality and good humor, and the didactic appetite which made him so valuable a force in the educational world was tempered by a genial shrewdness, sound common sense, and well-digested knowledge. When he gave up the post of principal of the London Day Training College he could look back on it as a place where independence of outlook and free intellectual activity, both of the staff and of the students, had been carefully fostered. His methods of training never sacrificed the individual to the machine. He moulded conditions to meet his ideals, while safeguarding the most important interests of the students. He was, in fact, a great teacher who knew how to delegate responsibility to each member of his staff, and his influence was abiding through the organization and atmosphere which he created, and through the books in which he propounded his ideas with characteristic vigor.—*The London Times.*

## SOCIETIES AND MEETINGS

### A NATIONAL ASSEMBLY ON RADIO IN EDUCATION

A VOICE from London opened a conference in Chicago last week—"a demonstration of the rapidity of change in the world to-day." The speaker was Dr. Robert A. Millikan, now abroad, addressing in his capacity as president of the National Advisory Council on Radio in Education the fourth annual assembly of the council.

Audiences of from two hundred to four hundred invited persons from many sections of the country heard the words of Dr. Millikan and those of a score of noted speakers appearing at five sessions on October 8 and 9, including the Honorable Harold L. Ickes, Secretary of the Interior; President Frederick P. Keppel, of the Carnegie Corporation of New York; President Robert M. Hutchins, Professor William F. Ogburn, Professor Paul H. Douglas and Professor Grace Abbott, of the University of Chicago; President Lotus D. Coffman, of the University of Minnesota; President Robert G. Sproul, of the University of California; President Walter Dill Scott, of Northwestern University; Dr. John H. Finley, of the *New York Times;* Director George F. Zook, of the American Council on Education; Mr. Bruce Bliven, editor of the *New Republic;* Mr. E. H. Harris, of the American Newspaper Publishers' Association; Professor John Erskine and Professor Lyman Bryson, of Columbia University; Dr. Walter Damrosch; Mr. H. V. Kaltenborn; Mrs. William Brown Meloney, of the *New York Herald-Tribune;* Mr. Carl H. Milam, of the American Library Association, and Professor W. I. Griffith, of Iowa State College.

The general subject of the assembly was announced as "The Importance of Radio Broadcasting in a Changing Social Order." There was little that was ponderous or dull in the presentation of the subject.

For the spirited debate of the second day the sessions of the first day supplied a factual and historical basis, with lively touches not lacking.

Dr. Millikan, in his broadcast from England, referred to the importance of the radio as "a new and varied social instrument by which the ideas of one man can be projected instantly around the world so that millions of people can come into contact with his personality."

However, the value of instantaneous transmission of the radio will not supplant the printed word.

The ideas of Plato have influenced the ideals of the world enormously and for thousands of years. Words from the mouth of Plato are just as potent to-day as when they were spoken. This is why radio has not as yet played as important a rôle as the printed word and, in my judgment, never can play any major rôle in the more serious side of formal education.

### The Opening Session

President Henry M. Wriston, of Lawrence College, presided at the opening session in the Drake Hotel.

In his address on "Radio and Public Policy," President Hutchins spoke "not as a critic of business but as a member of the educational profession and the consuming public anxious to make a radio more effective in education and more satisfactory to the public." He hazarded the guess that unless broadcasting can be made more successful in these respects, "it will find itself in immediate danger of more drastic regulation, of taxation, of competition with publicly owned stations and even of government ownership." After setting forth specific shortcomings, such as "the delusion that a mass audience is the only audience," President Hutchins concluded:

> If the industry will recognize unequivocally its responsibility to education, if educators will work out a national plan that meets the needs of our people, I believe that the industry will prosper still, that education will be able to use at last the new tool that technology has given it, and that together we may take a significant step toward the civilization of the United States.

Sketching "The Changing Social Scene in 1934," Professor Ogburn declared that "recovery, with occasional retardations, is going forward in all except the durable goods industries." He referred to the extensive use of radio by the administration at Washington as a factor in the present attitude of voters. He stressed the need "to save as much liberty as possible, not only for business but for everybody, while at the same time getting the advantage that comes from effective organization."

Dr. Keppel, in the closing paper of the first session, pointed out the breach between the man in the street and the expert in the natural sciences. The similar gap in the social sciences is even more dangerous. It is "not only the question of old knowledge and new knowledge, it is also the question of old ignorance and new ignorance, the new ignorance being achieved by the process of forgetting old knowledge, tried and proved in man's experience. And, alas, in troubled times like these, men are particularly prone to acquiring stocks of new ignorance in this way."

The process of closing up the gap between knowledge and ignorance—the age-old problem of education—has a new scientific addition in radio. Said Dr. Keppel:

> It really wasn't quite fair of science to crowd us in this way, but the radio is here, whether we like it or not. And again, whether we like it or not, the man in the street, the man on the other side of the gap we have been talking about, will listen to the radio when he won't go to church or to a lecture, or when he declines to pick up the book we think it would be good for him to read. Of course he'll turn the dial if we don't hold his interest, and perhaps he'll make the shift despite our best endeavor, but have we any right to assume this? Don't let us forget the steady rise in the quality of the music demanded by the radio audience, and furnished because demanded. Already the people in a hurry, the people with an axe to grind, the pressure groups and the propagandists have found the radio very well adapted to their needs. Shall we leave the field to them?

### Cultural and Educational Elements

President Coffman presided at the afternoon session of October 8, at which the speakers were President Sproul, Dr. Alfred N. Goldsmith, chairman of the council's engineering committee, and Miss Abbott.

"The real problem that America faces," said President Sproul, "is to keep alive the intellectual and spiritual sparks after our people have finished their formal schooling. To date we have not even approached a solution of this problem. Radio provides a way."

> In this era of change, with its steadily increasing proportion of leisure time, it is imperative that radio broadcasting shall be an instrument of culture and not an agency of confusion. The future of America depends upon our ability to disprove by means of education Lord Macaulay's dictum that democracy is government by count of the polls of the ignorant. Of this process, if it takes place, radio must be an integral part.

Dr. Goldsmith, consulting engineer, outlined possibilities of the future in the development of new tools in educational broadcasting, such as television, facsimile broadcasting and electrical transcriptions. To succeed in full measure in utilizing the new technical audio-visual agencies will, he said, require close cooperation between educators, engineers and technical experts. Dr. Goldsmith urged that the council develop a plan for such cooperation.

"The Radio and the American Home" was the topic treated by Professor Abbott, of the Public Welfare Administration, University of Chicago.

### A Public Meeting

The third session of the assembly, held on the evening of October 8 in the Hall of Science, Century of Progress grounds, was open to the public. There was a large attendance. Presiden Rufus C. Dawes, of the Century of Progress, was chairman. A paper, "The Spoken Word," was read by Dr. Finley, associate editor of the *New York Times*.

The chief address by Secretary Ickes was broadcasted nationally. His presentation of "The Importance of Broadcasting in the Field of Public Affairs" began with a historical sketch of the means of reaching the electorate in earlier eras.

The development of the radio is having a profound effect upon the education and the mobilization of public opinion. As a means of supplementing, in fuller fashion, the news brought to us by the printed page, it seems destined to have an increasingly important place in our lives. By means of the radio the man who wishes to do so can get in full the speeches of those in public life. He has the opportunity of hearing speeches actually delivered. He can judge of the sincerity of the speaker and he can weigh his arguments as his theme unfolds. Not only he and his neighbors, but his fellow citizens in the furthermost corner of the country, can hear the same speech at the same time. Nor do they have to confine their attention to a discussion of one side of a public question. They can hear both sides of it and thus be in a favored position to weigh the merits of the points at issue.

### A Report and a Debate

At the morning session of October 9, Mr. Levering Tyson read his annual report as director and secretary of the council. Of general interest was his reference to the hearings now in progress before the new Broadcasting Division of the Communications Commission. These hearings will either be a mere gesture or a step toward general improvement of American broadcasting, said Mr. Tyson. "Particularly interesting will be the attitude of the broadcasting industry itself." If it defends the *status quo* against all comers, present conditions may persist indefinitely and "broadcasting will be relegated to the minor rôle of a mere entertainment enterprise." The industry, "if it has the sense of its peculiar responsibility and opportunity," may take the lead in proposing changes.

Mr. Tyson, querying as to the attitude of the educators at the commission hearings, declared that "their shortcomings have been as conspicuous as those of the industry, although naturally of a different type." There has been on their part an absence on constructive suggestions. "The net result of a large part of so-called educational programs is parody."

One of the chief handicaps faced, both by the industry and by the educational world, in considering educational broadcasting is failure to realize that, broadly speaking, all broadcasting is educational. The industry and the advertiser have not yet sensed that program practises, whether good or bad, influence for good or ill the cultural development of the nation as a whole. The educator has realized this. For his part, however, he has been unwilling generally to recognize that classroom and lecture hall techniques applied to the radio are the least effective of all broadcasts. The broadcaster has found this out. When both realize their shortcomings and opportunities, American broadcasting will be more popular, and will be subjected to less criticism.

Mr. Bliven, in a lively presentation, supported government ownership of radio in a debate with Mr. Harris. He referred to a magazine article he wrote fifteen years ago about the social possibilities of radio.

So far as America is concerned, these promises have not been fulfilled. I do not want to blame individuals, but we have permitted a system to grow up under which radio is almost useless to-day. What it does in the realm of serious music is a disgrace. What it does in the field of education is pitiful. What it does in the field of news is, broadly speaking, nothing, our friends, the newspaper publishers, having effectively stopped all this work.

To be sure, an opponent of my views can bring forward a few good programs, most of them lasting the conventional fifteen minutes. The answer to that is that it is not the slightest use to have a good minority of programs when the majority consist of unendurable drivel. It is like saying of a beautiful woman that she appeared in a white dress only part of which was dirty.

In advocating government ownership, Mr. Bliven declared that censorship of radio by governments of Europe does not constitute a valid argument against his proposal for the United States. "In countries with a democratic tradition, such as England, government-owned radio is under no more censorship than is the press, and the press is no more censored than is the American newspaper." Mr. Bliven charged that there is censorship of radio in this country now; that programs favor the public-utility "point of view and conservatism in general." In closing, Mr. Bliven made a compromise suggestion of having one nationally owned and operated network. "Let the government summon such a man as President Hutchins, of the University of Chicago, or President Conant, of Harvard University, to be its head. . . . Then let the listeners of America choose between government programs and private ones. I should be happy to abide by the results of such an experiment."

The negative side of the debate was taken by Mr. Harris, who is chairman of the radio committee of the American Newspaper Publishers Association. Mr. Harris gave a detailed analysis of the Communications Act of 1934, by which the Federal Government "may commandeer or seize all radio broadcasting equipment and turn it over to any department of the government." That may "seem to be fantastic in the light of what we still hold to be American liberal ideals; nevertheless, that is a possibility."

Back of all discussions on the subject of the advantages and disadvantages of various systems of broadcasting lies one of two fundamental philosophies. Either we believe in the American ideals of individualism, initiative, trial by error and real democracy, or else we believe in bureaucratic control and social planning under dictatorship. Our belief in one or the other of these systems of broadcasting is nearly always determined by our philosophy of government.

Saying frankly that he believed in "the American ideals" as defined, Mr. Harris opposed government ownership. He cited examples of British censorship. Mr. Stimson, during the 1930 naval conference in London, was required to submit his speech in advance before he could be heard over the English air. The English governmental broadcasting system refused to broadcast the international debate between Harvard and Oxford undergraduates on the subject, "Resolved, That the War Debts Should Be Cancelled." Mr. Harris cited also censorship regulations in ten European countries as instances of what governmental ownership has produced. "The reasons we have poor programs is that we listen and then keep our objections to ourselves." Mr. Harris maintained that "the remedy now lies with us as individual citizens if we care to exercise our prerogatives. The responsibility for securing better programs can not be delegated to the Federal Government without surrendering some of our liberties."

Among those who joined in the discussion after the formal debate were Mrs. William Brown Meloney, editor of the Sunday magazine section of the *New York Herald-Tribune;* Mr. Robert B. Brown, representing the Lawyers' Legislative League; Dr. Morris Fishbein, editor of the *Journal* of the American Medical Association; Mr. Harris K. Randall, and others.

The chairman at this session was Dr. George F. Zook, director of the American Council on Education.

### A Panel on Broadcasting

What should be done to improve broadcasting in the United States was the subject of a panel discussion at the afternoon session of October 9. Professor Lyman Bryson, of Teachers College, Columbia University, was chairman. The members of the panel were Professor Paul H. Douglas, Dr. Zook, Mrs. Meloney, Mr. H. V. Kaltenborn, Mr. Morse A. Cartwright, director of the American Association for Adult Education, Professor W. I. Griffith, Dr. Carl H. Milam, Mother Antonio, of the College of St. Catherine, Minneapolis, and Professor W. W. Charters, of Ohio State University.

The discussion brought out the points that improvements will come by (1) providing special facilities for good educational programs; (2) by fighting to keep on the commercial programs all the best that is there now, and (3) by teaching children discrimination so that the coming generation of listeners will demand and appreciate the best offerings.

### Music on the Radio

Two musicians were the speakers after the dinner which closed the assembly on the evening of October 9. They were Dr. Walter Damrosch and Dr. John Erskine. President Walter Dill Scott introduced them.

Dr. Damrosch recounted his experiences "as a pioneer for music over the radio during the last nine years." He paid his respects to jazz and to crooners. He waxed humorous about the advertisers who engage a great artist and then demand a lowering of the artist's standard "on the plea that the public do not want the particular kind of music which has made that artist famous."

We nevertheless have to-day, said Dr. Damrosch, "quite a formidable demonstration not only of the higher forms of music including symphony concerts by all the great orchestras of the country, but also broadcasts from the Metropolitan Opera House and the Chicago Opera, choral performances and chamber music, beside the charming lighter operas of Strauss and Sullivan.

Now as regards the future of education in radio. My own experiences have taught me that he who seeks to interest our young hearers by such means must himself first learn that the radio is such a different means of approach that he must first learn the technique of proper broadcasting. His pupils can not be eye-minded. They must be ear-minded. That means that first of all he must couch his lecture, his information, his inspiration, in short simple phrases. He himself must learn diction so that he can be easily understood. . . .

At the same time I do not believe that education over the radio can ever take the place successfully of the teacher in the classroom. The two can work wonderfully hand in hand. In music the radio can bring orchestral concerts to the young people and can teach them the tone qualities of the different instruments. They can hear demonstrations of how the great masters of music have used and combined these instruments. They can be taught the whole history of musical forms from its simplest emanations to the most complicated structures of the present day, and these young people can have instilled in them such a love and enthusiasm for music as to make the task of the local teacher comparatively easy. I need but point to the tens of thousands of high-school orchestras that have been formed all over the country, to a great extent as a result of our Friday morning concerts. But it is the local teachers who must teach the notations in music and how to sing correctly and with an unforced, pure quality of tone. It is the local teachers who must give the students a knowledge of playing on the musical instruments, of proper practising to develop their technique and eventually to combine the students of these instruments into orchestras and bands. No radio instruction can act as a substitute for this important part of the child's education.

"Cheap entertainment soon wears thin," said Dr. Erskine. "To survive indefinitely broadcasting must give us programs not only interesting but of permanent merit." After a discussion of advertising and other aspects of radio presentation, Dr. Erskine declared that "if we offer a radio program we must first of all be entertaining, in the sense that we must hold the audience. Why education should not always be entertaining, I never could understand."

Several constructive proposals were made, in addition to the prediction that in the future "music will take up even more time on the air than at present.

Poets and story-tellers must, said the speaker, "recapture the technique of those who wrote for the ear and not for the eye." So doing they may benefit not only radio presentation but "all printed literature."

Dr. Erskine suggested annual reports to go on the air toward the end of each year.

President Roosevelt has won our gratitude by his occasional reports of progress. These reports, of course, refer only to the problems of national government. It would be profitable to have annual reports of progress in science, in exploration, in invention, in each of the arts. We should be glad to know what the year had contributed to American architecture or sculpture or painting or the theater or dancing or music or literature. This kind of progress is a true and permanent addition to the national wealth, and it is precisely the kind about which it is hardest to get information.

If the whole country were told of it, our loyalty would be increased and our ambition stimulated.

Dr. Erskine's closing words were these:

I have tried to suggest that education on the radio must, for various reasons, be quite different from education off it; that the moment the educator talks on the radio, he must be not only learned but interesting; that the radio should not try to rival the schools in work which the schools can do better; and that there is a large mass of information to which as yet we do not have general access and which the radio is well fitted to impart.

RAYMOND WALTERS

UNIVERSITY OF CINCINNATI

# EDUCATIONAL RESEARCH AND STATISTICS

## TRENDS IN THE IMPROVEMENT OF STATISTICAL TECHNIQUES

IN the compilation of an annotated bibliography of statistical articles which have appeared in the last twenty years, certain trends were noted which are of interest. In the making of this bibliography, it was necessary to analyze articles dealing with techniques and devices in educational statistics which have been published in a number of the leading educational and psychological periodicals. The assumption is made that at the time of publication the material presented was unknown to the educational world in general.

In this analysis, only such articles were considered as seemed to represent improvements in existing techniques. This distinction was sometimes hard to make, but in general, the type of article included deals with the development of new formulas and techniques; the refinement of existing techniques; application of statistical devices to new situations; experimental verification of the accuracy of formulas; and constructive criticism of techniques now in use or suggested. On the other hand, the following types of articles were definitely eliminated: formulas and methods developed for the sole purpose of adaptability for machine computation; tables, graphs, charts or printed forms which involve no new principles, but are merely to facilitate computation; discussion of statistical concepts such as the AQ or IQ; formulas for corrections due to chance or guessing in new-type tests.

This principle of inclusion or exclusion was somewhat arbitrary, but was adopted with the intent of restricting the study to what might be termed improvements in pure statistical technique. In case of doubt, the article was included, rather than excluded.

The periodicals used in the study, with the volumes considered, were as follows: *Educational Research Bulletin*—Volume 1 to date; *Journal of Applied Psychology*—Volume 4 to date; *Journal of Educational Psychology*—Volume 1 to date; *Journal of Educational Research*—Volume 1 to date; *Journal of Experimental Psychology*—Volume 1 to date; *Review of Educational Research*—Volume 1 to date.

The words "to date" cover issues to and including June, 1934. Of course it is not claimed that this study covered all articles published which deal with educational statistics, but it is believed that the major portion of such articles has been covered; certainly enough material is included to give a definite indication of any existing trends.

The classification used divided all articles into six general headings, as indicated below. In cases where an article deals with several topics, the attempt was made to classify it under the topic of major importance treated in the article. This classification into broad general

TABLE 1

NUMBER OF ITEMS IN EACH CLASSIFICATION

| | | |
|---|---|---|
| 1. Correlation | | 81 |
| A. Correlation in general | 25 | |
| B. The Pearson product moment formula | 18 | |
| C. Test reliability, particularly the use of the Spearman-Brown formula | 19 | |
| D. Partial and multiple correlation | 19 | |
| 2. Errors in measurement | | 61 |
| A. Significance of differences | 19 | |
| B. Errors in estimated measures | 11 | |
| C. Miscellaneous | 31 | |
| 3. Measures of central tendency and variability | | 14 |
| 4. Comparable scores and equivalent groups | | 14 |
| 5. Scaling and construction of tests | | 13 |
| 6. Miscellaneous | | 13 |
| Total | | 196 |

categories is by no means perfect, but again it serves to indicate trends. The number of items in each classification is indicated in Table 1.

Reference to the table will show that over 40 per cent. of the articles deal with the subject of correlation, over 30 per cent. with errors of measurement. It would be foolish to deny the importance of either of these subjects, but one might well question whether either is of more importance than all remaining classifications in the table. For example, in any study of a standardized test, reliability is of course desirable, but one might question whether at least an equal amount of attention paid to the question of determining test validity might not be worth while. Likewise the question of discrimination might merit some time spent upon it.

Table 2 shows the distribution of the articles under the various classifications, when grouped into three periods of time.

TABLE 2

NUMBER OF ARTICLES IN EACH CLASSIFICATION, BY PERIODS OF TIME

| | Before 1922 | 1922–1927 | 1928–1934 |
|---|---|---|---|
| 1. Correlation | 9 | 29 | 43 |
| A. Correlation in general | 0 | 9 | 16 |
| B. The Pearson product moment formula | 8 | 4 | 6 |
| C. Test reliability, particularly the use of the Spearman-Brown formula | 0 | 11 | 8 |
| D. Partial and multiple correlation | 1 | 5 | 13 |
| 2. Errors in measurement | 4 | 17 | 40 |
| A. Significance of differences | 0 | 6 | 13 |
| B. Errors in estimated measures | 2 | 2 | 7 |
| C. Miscellaneous | 2 | 9 | 20 |
| 3. Measures of central tendency and variability | 0 | 9 | 5 |
| 4. Comparable scores and equivalent groups | 2 | 7 | 5 |
| 5. Scaling and construction of tests | 0 | 4 | 9 |
| 6. Miscellaneous | 2 | 2 | 9 |
| Totals | 17 | 68 | 111 |

Although the numbers are small, consideration of Table 2 seems to indicate certain trends, for example, the growing attention being paid to partial and multiple correlation. The increasing number of articles relating to significance of differences perhaps indicates a realization of the need for care in drawing conclusions from experimental data. Likewise the marked increase in the number of articles dealing with miscellaneous errors of measurement may be indicative of a growing need felt for accuracy of measurement. On the other hand, the decrease in the proportion of articles devoted to the Pearson product moment formula is interesting. A possible explanation is that this technique has been so widely used that the procedure is fairly well stabilized.

In making up the bibliography, it was particularly evident that the large majority of articles was contributed by prominent workers in the field of education. There seemed to be little evidence of any attempt to encourage these along the line of improvement of existing statistical techniques. Several of the articles encountered raised questions which the author frankly admits are unsolved, yet there appears to be no effort by other workers to find a solution.

Perhaps there has been too much emphasis on content, to the exclusion of refinement of tools of research. Since in many cases the soundness of research depends upon the accuracy and applicability of the statistical techniques and devices used, the improvement of such tools of research would seem to offer a fruitful field for research workers in education.

CECIL B. READ

MUNICIPAL UNIVERSITY
OF WICHITA, KANSAS

## NEW BOOKS IN EDUCATION

COLEMAN, ALGERNON. *Experiments and Studies in Modern Language Teaching.* Pp. xi + 367. University of Chicago Press.

FRANK, GLENN. *America's Hour of Decision.* Pp. 263. Whittlesey House, McGraw-Hill. $2.50.

LEGOUIS, EMILE. *A Short History of English Literature.* Translated by V. F. Boyson and J. Coulson. Pp. xvi + 404. Illustrated. Oxford. $2.00.

MELVIN, A. GORDON. *Building Personality.* Pp. 303. John Day. $3.00.

# SCHOOL AND SOCIETY

WITH WHICH ARE COMBINED THE EDUCATIONAL REVIEW, ESTABLISHED IN 1891, THE TEACHERS MAGAZINE, ESTABLISHED IN 1878, AND THE SCHOOL JOURNAL, ESTABLISHED IN 1874.

Volume 40 | Saturday, October 27, 1934 | Number 1035

## EDUCATIONAL GUIDANCE: PROGRESS TOWARDS SCIENTIFIC PROCEDURES[1]

By Dean MAX McCONN

LEHIGH UNIVERSITY

The subject of guidance, as a subject to be taught in teachers colleges and as the center of an educational movement, is comparatively new. But the thing itself—guidance itself—is far from being an entirely new thing in education. Those of us who have been playing the game of educational administration for a number of years can assure the younger members of this audience that we always did quite a little of what would now be called guidance and counseling. That is to say, we always had problem cases, and we talked at length with the boys and girls concerned and found out as much as we could about their situations and problems, and in the end delivered ourselves of advice to them and their parents.

It must be admitted, however, that our earlier guidance procedures were very deficient. They were deficient both quantitatively and qualitatively.

Quantitatively they were deficient in that they were unsystematic and sporadic. We did not regard them as part of our regular job, but rather as works of supererogation and special philanthropy. When we had gone out of our way to handle a problem case humanely, we felt like the boy scout who has done his good deed for the day.

And qualitatively they were deficient in that they lacked scientific basis. We had substantially no scientific instruments to help us in guidance procedures. We were in the position of the physicians of a still earlier day before medical science had acquired the clinical thermometer and the stethoscope and the blood count and the bacteriological examination. Like those earlier practitioners of medicine, we were compelled to base our diagnoses on superficial symptoms only, and naturally we made a terrific number of mistakes—most of which, protectively, we managed to forget, while we remembered our lucky successes.

Of course, in the early period to which I personally refer—the first decade of this century—scientific developments which were soon to come to our aid were already under way. It was early in that decade that Messrs. Binet and Simon in Paris devised their first crude mental test, by means of which they were able to differentiate children whom we should now call morons from children whom we call normal. Their results soon attracted widespread interest among psychologists, especially in the United States, and during the dozen years prior to 1917 a large amount of test-making and study of test techniques was carried on. But this work did not impinge upon the practical activities of

[1] Delivered at the Conference on Individual Development and Guidance, at Teachers College, Columbia University, July 31, 1934.

schools and colleges, except in a very few places, until after the war.

As a matter of fact, the development in the direction of scientific procedures—which it is my business to discuss this evening—may be said to have set in on a large scale in 1917, when certain able and astute psychologists and educators "sold" the mental test to the general staff of the United States Army, which at the moment was bewildered and overwhelmed by the gigantic task of sorting out and assigning literal millions of newly drafted men from every walk of life. The Army Alpha Test, with all its deficiencies, astonished the Army and astonished the nation by the contribution it made to the organization of the A. E. F. and the supporting military and civil activities in this country. Almost immediately after the war revisions of the Army Alpha Test came into use in a few places in connection with admission to college—first, I believe, at Brown University under the leadership of the late Professor S. S. Colvin, and very shortly thereafter at Columbia and elsewhere. About the same time high schools and elementary schools all over the country began to make use of other general intelligence tests adapted to lower age levels. And soon the American Council on Education or Thurstone Test for use with college freshmen came along and was adopted by a number of colleges.

Thus we had acquired, in use, *one* scientific instrument, the general psychological test, and the first step in the direction of scientific procedures may be said to have been taken.

But it soon began to seem as if we were worse off than we had been before. We continued to make terrific mistakes, and we made more of them than ever (I am speaking here of the rank and file of advisory officers who tried to use the tests without knowing too much about them); the reason being, in part, that principals and deans and other counseling officers, armed with this new scientific instrument, acquired a new and injudicious cocksureness. Before we had even the general intelligence test, we knew that we knew practically nothing about our boys and girls, and even the brashest of us were constrained to a certain humility and cautiousness in ladling out advice. But with the new tests in our hands we thought we knew. It was another case where a little knowledge was a dangerous thing. Johnny had been given the Otis Test and had come out with an IQ of 95. That just about settled Johnny. And, at the college level, Jim had taken the Thurstone Test and scored in the lowest decile. So right then we knew what to do with Jim—and we did it!

Now, of course, in a fair number of cases what we did with Johnny and Jim was about right. But in a number of other cases it was far from adequate. And we began to find that out. And other people found it out too—and told us about it. In short, there soon came a swelling tide of protest against the new tests.

As directed against the new tests themselves that protest was in the main invalid and unfair. But as against the use many of us were making of the tests it was thoroughly justified.

I said that the misuse of the tests was due in part to a loss of humility and cautiousness on the part of advisory officers, and I am sure that is true. But in larger part that misuse was simply the carrying over to the new tests of a very ancient educational error. For centuries we educators have been perpetrating exactly the same error in our use of the results of the old essay-type of examination; the error, namely, of assuming that the results of any single examination or any single set of examinations can be regarded as definitive and conclusive and as valid bases for crucial administrative action or crucial advisement. In February and June of each year there are given in your high school and in my college semester and year examinations the results of which determine, wholly or in large measure, promotion or demotion, and in colleges often continuance or exclusion. In June of this year there were held, in scores of centers throughout the country, College Board examinations—on the basis of which spasmodic deliverances, on a few hot June days, under circumstances of special strain, boys and girls are, throughout this present summer, being admitted to higher education or debarred therefrom.

Please note that I have no criticism to make of the College Board examinations as examinations. On the contrary, I am disposed to believe that they probably constitute the finest set of essay-type examinations that have yet been devised—the most carefully and skilfully prepared, the most effectively administered, and the most scrupulously marked. Nor have I anything against the subjective essay-type examination, which, when skilfully handled, I believe to constitute one valuable type of achievement test—inferior in some ways, but superior in others, to the objective achievement test. But I do object to the use we still commonly make of the results of College Board examinations and course examinations, in which we commit exactly the same error we began to make with the new mental tests. With the old examinations we have perpetrated that mistake so universally and so long that it escapes notice. Happily, the minute we began to do the same thing with the new mental tests our malfeasance was spotted and protested. I hope that protest will continue and grow until it overthrows that old error in connection with all kinds of examinations and tests.

But let me continue my historical résumé. Many of you will remember deTocqueville's *mot,* that the cure for the evils of democracy is more democracy. Similarly, a partial cure for the evils of tests has been found in more tests. Despite the protests the test-makers continued their labors. They improved the tests and made more tests, and presently new kinds of tests, so that now we have—in addition to the general intelligence test—special aptitude tests and interest tests and objective achievement tests—yielding an EQ in addition to the old IQ—and personality rating scales. This new series of instruments—a whole doctor's kitful—may be said to constitute the second step.

Again, however, the outcome was sometimes disconcerting to those of us who were on the firing line of actual advisement and counseling. The results of the various new tests did not always seem to gee. A boy might come out with a low IQ and a high EQ. Of course that does not happen often, but it happens sometimes. And what shall the poor adviser do then? More often, of course, we may find a high IQ and a low EQ. The answer to that may be plainer, but it is often not entirely plain. Or a student may show both a low IQ and a low EQ and then make a notably high score on some special aptitude or interest test or in a personality rating. In short, we began to suffer from an embarrassment of riches in the way of scientific procedures. We had attained to the situation of the physician whose stethoscope fails to confirm the heart condition which the blood count says should be present.

But a third step has in large part rescued us from this difficulty. I mean the development of the cumulative record, analogous to the combined medical history and hospital chart of the medical profession. You are all familiar, I am sure, with the two principal forms of cumulative record card now widely used—the American Council on Education form, and the smaller form employed by the Educational Records Bureau. You all understand that the cumulative record brings together, on a time projection scale, all the student's course grades, all his test results in every kind of objective test, and all available factual data in regard to his educational or intellectual biography, thus exhibiting the long-time trends of his aptitudes, interests, and achievements, and the interweaving relationships of his abilities and accomplishments. With this last instrument in our hands, embodying and correlating and almost automatically interpreting the results obtained from all our other instruments, we are at last, I think, in a position to undertake, not without humility and caution still, but nevertheless with some warranted confidence, the dangerous business of advisement and counseling.

But there is at the present time, along with some continuing distrust of the tests, a new protest against the cumulative records as well, arising in large measure from the labor and expense they do admittedly entail, and questioning the large utility which I have just ascribed to them. I beg leave, therefore, to cite, from an earlier paper[2] of mine, three concrete examples of the value, in crucial cases of advisement, of an adequate testing program, summarized, with other data, in a cumulative record.

*Example No. 1:* A principal has in his high school a boy who is planning to prepare for the ministry or for teaching. The principal has doubts. The boy does not do well in his studies. He is probably docile and likable, but when it comes to book-learning he certainly seems to be "slow." But without some evidence from objective tests, what can the principal do about it? Even if he ventures to express his doubts to the boy's mother, who dreams of seeing her son in the pulpit, will he get anywhere? He will not! But suppose the principal has some cumulative record of objective tests. Suppose that in two or three psychological tests it appeared that the boy ranked in the lowest decile of high-school students in bookish intelligence—not according to the principal's personal impressions, or in the opinion of local teachers, but on nation-wide or state-wide percentiles; and suppose that in several annual series of objective achievement tests his scores in such subjects as English, languages and history fell regularly in the lowest quartile—not in the grading of that high school but on experimentally established norms. If those results, from the cumulative record, were carefully and tactfully explained to the boy's father—perhaps to his mother too—there would be some fair chance that that boy, on finishing the high school, would go to work in his father's store or enter the local business school to study bookkeeping, instead of seeking to go on to college and thereafter to theological school or school of education. He would probably make an excellent clerk or bookkeeper, and six or ten years later there would be one less incompetent teacher to constitute a problem for his principal or superintendent, or one less feeble minister to bring religion into disrepute in some community.

*Again:* The principal has another boy who is trying to prepare for a college of engineering. He is something of a mechanical genius. He can always repair the family car and the radio, no matter what has happened to them. And so his father sees him as a future consulting engineer, with $50,000 a year in retaining fees. But the boy finds mathematics a stumbling block. He has to repeat algebra and to be tutored on the side in solid geometry. It is of little use, however, for the principal to cite these facts alone against a college course in engineering. Father will not listen: the high-school mathematics teachers are no good, or they are "down" on his boy. But what if the principal has also, in his cumulative record, achievement

[2] "Educational Guidance is Now Possible," *The Educational Record,* October, 1933.

scores in algebra and geometry and physics and chemistry falling consistently in the lowest fifteen percentiles—not according to the local mathematics teachers but in objective standardized tests? That boy might then be allowed to take a job in a neighboring garage or in a radio supply store down town—which is very likely just what the boy himself is eager to do—and in due course he might have a good garage or radio business of his own. And there would be one less freshman to be brutally "flunked out" from some college of engineering.

*But on the other hand:* The principal has a third boy who stands near the head of his class, whose intellectual curiosity and pleasure in learning and knack for coming out with ideas of his own make him a delight to his teachers. The principal thinks he ought to go to college, talks to him about college. But the boy's father doesn't think much of college, doesn't want to spend the money, and holds the opinion (not without some warrant) that high grades in the Blankville High School don't necessarily mean a whole lot. If, however, the principal's cumulative record shows a series of psychological test scores which say that the boy ranks in the top 3 per cent. of human intelligence and a series of achievement test scores which practically never dip below the top decile, he need only show those records to the boy's mother and tell her what they mean. That boy will go to college. Dad won't have a chance, and the money will be found in the family or in the town. And there will be good reason to hope that a youngster whose superior abilities were on the way to being thwarted and wasted may turn out twenty years later to be a leader or creator in some valuable form of service to society.

Such examples, I hope, may show pretty plainly the value of both tests and cumulative records in making our educational and vocational guidance of individual boys and girls assured (in many cases, at least) and convincing; whereas without such basis it must remain uncertain and unconvincing, as it has too often been in the past.

In my summary of the developments to date in the direction of scientific procedures, I have, of course, touched only the high spots and not all of them. For example, I have said nothing about the large amount of work done in the collection of valuable material in regard to various vocations and the publication of such material in leaflets and monographs to provide a sounder basis for vocational guidance. But I prefer to pass over that and some other points and to devote my last two or three minutes to querying the future. What still further developments may we expect in the direction of scientific procedures?

Well, first of all, we may feel sure that the tests will be still further refined and still further diversified. We may expect many more new kinds of tests. I heard the other night of a new test to measure sense of humor. The mention of such a test almost inevitably provokes a wisecrack to the effect that the propounder thereof must himself lack a sense of humor. But such a test might be extremely valuable, and it may serve as an example of the new things the future may hold in this field.

I think we expect improvements, also, in the current cumulative record forms. In my opinion those forms need both some further elaboration and considerable simplification. Those conflicting desiderata are mechanically difficult to provide. But I think both of them can and will be attained.

Thirdly, we may anticipate the development of entirely new scientific devices to assist us in remedial treatment as well as in diagnosis—devices like the new specialized camera for the photographing of eye movements and the mechanical pacer for eye movements for use in remedial reading, both recently reported from Stanford University.

Fourth, we may hope that in due course the factual data derived from guidance procedures and the attitudes and point of view developed through such procedures will profoundly modify our present courses of study, in the direction of better provision for individual needs and individual development.

But I have held for my final paragraph the new development in the direction of scientific procedures which seems to me most important for the immediate future, namely, the training, and the appointment in schools and colleges everywhere, of skilled advisers, competent to make wise use of the new tests and the new cumulative records, and freed from other duties sufficiently to enable them actually to do this work with living boys and girls. That item is the largest of all. It will be by far the most expensive, by far the most difficult to attain, but it is also a *sine qua non*. If that development does not come, all the rest of our progress, past and future, in the direction of scientific procedures, will be of little avail so far as the boys and girls are concerned. Accordingly, it seems to me that step is the one upon which most of us who are interested in guidance and individual development should chiefly concentrate for the next few years.

# THE SCHOOL FOR THE NEW SOCIAL ORDER

By T. E. WILLIAMS

SUPERINTENDENT, LAWRENCE TOWNSHIP PUBLIC SCHOOLS, LAWRENCEVILLE, NEW JERSEY

A FEW years ago we assumed it was the right of every boy and girl to go through the elementary school and the high school. The tendency in the country, in the towns, in the cities was for education to expand, to cover a wider field and at the same time to become more thorough. We expected teachers to be better and better prepared. It was the feeling among nations that the future of a country depended upon the preparation and development of its youth. Every nation, during a critical time in its history, always emphasized the development of its future citizens. This was the proper and only attitude that could be taken to insure the future preservation of the country. Of over fifty leading nations of the world to-day we are the only one in which there seems to be an organized effort to break down the efficiency of public education.

The opportunities and responsibilities of the future citizens of our country are greater than they have ever been in the past. The inventions in industry or the "machine age" have created a situation in social, economic life from which our nation can never return. Life has changed materially in the last ten years, and there is every indication that the change will be more rapid in the years to come. There is no phase of human existence that has not been affected by this evolutionary process. Life in the home and in the shop has been completely revolutionized. The forms of employment that were open to boys and girls in former years no longer exist. The same preparation for life that obtained a few years ago will no longer satisfy. While this development has been in progress no provisions have been made for the solution of the problems that have come because of the necessary change in the social order. Just how these problems may be solved will be determined largely by the future citizens of our country. How well these solutions may be performed will be determined by the type and efficiency of the preparation that will be provided. It is not less preparation—but more and a different preparation—that our boys and girls need for life in this new social structure. The adult of our country must appreciate and take more seriously its obligation in the training of youth.

The old academic life of our forefathers served its purpose and served it well. It was the proper and natural development of its time. Life has so completely changed that there is scarcely a semblance of the past. Living, as many people of the present generation knew it, is fast becoming a memory. The situations that were common in former days will have no place within the experiences of the future citizens of our country. They will inherit many opportunities and responsibilities that were not known to the older generation and for which they must be efficiently prepared. The young people of our country, in whose hands rests the future destiny of our nation, must not be less equipped to "carry on" in the new social order than were their predecessors in the order in which the requirements and responsibilities were far less exacting.

There never was a time in the history of our country when the need for efficiency in school organization and school administration is more apparent than at the present. The school system, in any community, offers a splendid opportunity for a vast saving to the taxpayers or an undue expenditure of funds. This depends entirely upon the type of school administration and the ability of the administrator to organize and cope with the different administrative problems that are sure to develop in any progressive school system. It should be the duty of every school administrator to develop the most efficient school system at the least possible cost.

There is a general feeling in different sections of our country that our schools are costing too much. This feeling, no doubt, is felt more keenly as a result of the "depression" and the inability of many to pay their taxes. The school is the most important and often the largest business in the community. Much of its support comes from local taxation which usually represents the largest item in the taxpayer's bill. In many instances, in order that the local tax rate might be reduced, schools have been made to suffer regardless of the effect upon the lives of the boys and girls. Much of the local support for public education should be assumed by the state and federal governments. This would tend to preserve its efficiency and prevent its destruction by selfish interests.

In many places in our country school people have been slow in making the proper adjustments to suit the rapidly changing needs in education. Many people do not realize that the degree to which a boy and girl is prepared for life is determined by his or her ability to live, enjoy and participate in the life situations of his fellow beings. It is not the cramming of academic knowledge that makes for the most successful life. One may have all the academic degrees obtainable and still be a failure in the social group. The things that boys and girls learn to do in school only help them to do better the things they learn to do out of school.

Many of the subjects that were termed "fads and frills" by the old traditional school people are being recognized as most essential in the training of youth for citizenship in the new social order. Probably the most outstanding "fad" in many sections to-day is what is commonly known as "home work." Most boys and girls do not know how to study. In many instances little attempt has been made to remedy this situation. As long as most of the studying must be done in the homes this handicap will continue. If schools are organized in such a way that "supervised study" is made a part of the regular curriculum there will be but very little need for "home work." There will be no necessity for home study in the elementary grades, and much of the time that is now being spent by high-school pupils for such work might be employed in a more profitable manner. By "supervised study" is not meant that the teacher is to take on the attitude of a monitor and that the pupil is to be free to study what and how he or she pleases. To be equipped to do this type of work effectively the teacher must have a thorough and special preparation in this particular field. Such a program has a very wholesome effect upon the boys and girls. They are more self-confident, they know how to study and they approach the problems with a more assuring attitude. In fact, they are becoming more able to help themselves and much of the time that is now required to repeat subjects will be eliminated altogether.

All true American citizens want efficient public schools. They desire that the boys and girls be prepared to meet life situations as they may be found in the new social group. Many people feel that the "easiest way out" is to force the bulk of the retrenchment upon the public schools. They fail to realize that the manner and effectiveness with which our country comes out of this "depression" will be determined by the efficiency of the preparation that is provided for the coming generation. The breaking down of public education tends to lower the standard of civilization, creates a feeling of unrest and disorder and delays the return to normal conditions.

Many public schools have been costing more than the people have been able to pay. While our country was prosperous and unemployment was unknown, the support of public schools did not seem to be a burden. The school system that has been economically administered during this period is indeed very fortunate. The local taxing unit can not support the public schools efficiently under the conditions through which we are now passing. Until such time as federal and state support comes to the rescue of the local unit some way must be provided to relieve the local taxpayer of a portion of this obligation. If relief is to be had without destroying the efficiency of the schools much of it must be brought about by organization. This is a subject in which the school administrator should not only have an excellent preparation, but a lot of first-hand experience. Some schools do not have serious organization problems. In many schools these problems either are not recognized or are allowed to go unsolved.

The type of school organization known as the Gary School Plan or the Platoon Plan that was developed several years ago by Superintendent Wirt of Gary, Indiana, came into being to satisfy the need of a rapidly changing society. People came from all over the world to visit and study this type of school organization. A school in which the old academic program had been replaced by one where the boys and girls were allowed to participate in actual life situations was readily accepted by leading school people throughout the country. The growth of the platoon type of school organization has been so rapid in our country that nearly all the large cities and many of the smaller ones have platoon schools. There are now approximately 245 cities in 44 states operating under this type of school organization. The plan is also being operated in the Dominion of Canada and Japan.

The writer was principal for Superintendent Wirt for several years and had some part in the early development of this type of organization. He also adopted and developed the platoon type of organization in the entire system of the East Chicago public schools.

The fact that the platoon organization offered a program to suit the rapidly changing needs of the social order was the dominant factor that caused it to be so widely accepted. This fact alone was a very worthy contribution and one which our schools have sadly needed. There was still another factor that had to do with the adoption of the plan in the East Chicago public schools. This had to do with a more extended use of the school plant. This idea had been emphasized in Mr. Wirt's organization and the writer made use of it in his organization of the East Chicago system, which increased the building capacity 50 per cent.

The Gary and the East Chicago schools were the only platoon schools that maintained the original platoon organization. The original platoon school was organized on the theory that a platoon school would care for two separate complete schools in one building. The only way by which this could be accomplished was to provide for a more extensive use of the school plant. Few people have the ability to reorganize an entire city school system and adopt an entirely new type of school organization. An enriched curriculum, adapted to the different abilities of the boys and girls, was the thing that appealed most to some school people regardless of the saving that might be made in organization. Too much money has been invested in many of our school plants for the little time that they are being used. No business enterprise will continue to pay dividends if the plant is to be used only one fourth of the time. The original platoon school provided that the school plant would be in constant use eight hours each day for regular school work. This was accomplished without lengthening the school day for the pupils and teachers.

There is no doubt that many school systems in our country, with proper leadership, could effect an organization that would materially extend the use of the school plant and provide an enriched curriculum for the boys and girls. A type of school organization that has given excellent satisfaction for years, provided the type of preparation that is demanded for the new social order, and saved millions to the taxpayers, should be worthy of serious consideration by all who are interested in the welfare of our boys and girls and the future prosperity of our country.

# EDUCATIONAL EVENTS

## THE PROPOSED SPANISH–AMERICAN UNIVERSITY

George Howland Cox, writing in *The Christian Science Monitor,* states that the establishment of a Spanish-American University at San Diego, California, is expected within the next few months. General Pascual Ortiz Rubio, formerly chief executive of Mexico, will, it is understood, be elected president.

The purpose of the institution is to promote inter-American cordiality and to encourage commercial relationships among the twenty-one American republics of the western hemisphere.

Discussing plans for the new university, General Rubio emphasizes the opportunity of building up harmony between the United States and the Latin-American nations. Courses for business men and women, and for the public in general, will be arranged dealing with current matters of special interest. Courses in cultural themes, arts, literature and natural science will also be given.

In conjunction with the university idea, it is the plan of General Rubio, and of others interested in cementing international relationships, to institute a Spanish-American University Association arranging courses, throughout the United States, in established educational institutions. It is planned to organize discussion groups and to form societies and associations to study the history, language and civilization of the Spanish-speaking countries.

Included in the curriculum of the university proper are listed five subjects having a direct bearing upon Mexico. From such information as the former Mexican president has given, it would seem fair to assume, according to Mr. Cox, that he is more particularly concerned with the affairs of his own republic than with those of Latin America in general. He makes especial note of the geographical neighborhood of the United States and affirms that a more intimate knowledge of the two countries is desirable. He mentions Mexican legislation, sociology, philology, Mexican and United States journalism and history.

The study of sociology is suggested for persons seeking a general Hispanic American background. It is planned that the Spanish language shall be taught in American universities and that the English language shall be taught in the southern institutions.

Courses in history will include the study of Mexico, Spain, Honduras, Cuba and the United States. The present representatives upon the university's board of patrons claim citizenship in one or the other of these nations. The course will be given without racial, religious and political prejudices.

## YALE-IN-CHINA

ALL branches of Yale-in-China's work have opened for the fall term. The Yali Union Middle School at Changsha started its year with 329 students. Central China College in Wuchang, in which the Yale-in-China Association supports the Yale-in-China School of Science, has opened for its sixth academic year. The Hunan-Yale Nursing School at Changsha reported an enrolment of 101 nurses, a slight increase over last year. The Medical College had 100 students, including a well-prepared entering class.

A number of grants have been announced to the different institutions in which Yale-in-China participates. The Yale-in-China School of Science has received two grants for the year 1934–1935, one of $11,000 Chinese currency, from the National Government and one of $9,000 Chinese currency from the China Foundation, both for science equipment. The National Government has granted to the Medical School $35,000 Chinese currency. The Medical School has also received $20,000 Chinese currency from the China Foundation for equipment and books, and $4,000 Chinese currency from the Rockefeller Foundation for hospital laboratory equipment. It was reported that nearly $10,000 Chinese currency had been raised by the Yale Club of Shanghai in their $50,000 campaign among Yale men and friends in China to endow a chair in the Yale-in-China School of Science.

A recent report from Changsha states that last year's graduating class in the Middle School made a remarkable showing. Twenty-six of the twenty-eight members passed the government examinations creditably. Most of the graduates have entered college or medical school. Three are teaching in Christian schools and one is assisting in the proctor's office at Yali. The demand from business firms, banks and schools for Yali graduates has been greater than the school's supply. Three of the graduating class have entered the Hunan-Yale Medical College.

Of the 329 students in the Middle School, 115 are enrolled in the Senior School and 214 in the Junior School. The senior class has 27 students, one less than last year. The Yali "College Plan" starts its third year of operation. Robert Brank Fulton, Yale '32, of Rockford, Illinois, is house master of the Joy House, while Stephen Walke is in charge of the Thurston House. Students from the three upper classes are chosen to live in the houses so there is a continuity of residence carrying on from year to year. House athletic tournaments, social evenings and club activities are being planned.

## THE THREE HUNDREDTH ANNIVERSARY OF SECONDARY SCHOOL EDUCATION

MOBILIZATION is under way throughout the United States for a parade of secondary schools in recognition of their three hundredth anniversary in 1934–35. Schools and civic organizations are collaborating on ceremonies, orations, pageants, exhibitions, parades and other enterprises. Meanwhile the committee for the national celebration, representing the Department of Secondary School Principals of the National Education Association, is planning radio programs, ceremonies for national conventions, organization of a national high-school band and orchestra, a national high-school fair, a memorial motion picture and the three hundredth anniversary issue of *Scholastic,* the national high-school weekly, to be issued next February, depicting the finest achievements of secondary schools.

The celebration committee has formulated the following objectives for the celebration: to present to the public the aims and works of secondary education; to emphasize the necessity of public secondary education to a free democracy; to acquaint the public with advanced developments in secondary instruction; to improve the chances for every boy and girl to benefit from the full potentialities of the secondary schools.

The celebration of the three hundredth anniversary of secondary education in the United States is to find its most enthusiastic expression in the high-school classrooms during the school year 1934–35. The committee has prepared a number of plans for local celebrations. Among the suggestions are the following: Art classes may make posters and medallions celebrating the anniversary, hanging them in prominent places in the school and in the community. The best of the posters should be sent to the National High School Art Exhibition at Carnegie Institute, Pittsburgh, Pa., in March. English classes may write letters of congratulation to J. L. Powers, head master of the Boston Latin School, the school whose birthday is being celebrated. Prizes will be awarded for the best of these letters. History classes may prepare a history of the local high school, with the cooperation of English classes. Plans are under way to award prizes to schools preparing the best local high-school history. Pupils may participate in the *Scholastic* awards for short stories, poetry, essays and one-act plays. Music classes may rehearse songs popular in the early schools and cooperate with dramatic clubs in presenting pageants and plays.

## SCHOOL COSTS IN NEW YORK CITY

The economy program which the New York City Board of Education has been following in recent years has resulted in a decrease in the *per capita* cost of instruction in the various school activities, according to the annual financial and statistical report of the board.

In all branches of the school system, with one exception, there has been a decided drop in school costs during the last two years. The exception is the industrial high-school division, which shows an increase of more than $8 in *per capita* costs for 1933 over 1932. The figures given in the report based on average daily attendance are summarized as follows in the *New York Sun:*

| | 1933 | 1932 |
|---|---|---|
| Day elementary schools | $ 97.21 | $103.75 |
| Junior high schools | 116.36 | 128.98 |
| Day high schools | 143.63 | 159.67 |
| Industrial high schools | 162.42 | 154.26 |
| Manhattan Industrial High School | 164.83 | 188.88 |
| Parental school | 528.70 | 654.68 |
| Voluntary continuation schools | 5.59 | 6.66 |
| Playground activities | 1.24 | 1.62 |

The table does not show the annual *per capita* cost of compulsory continuation schools and evening schools. These schools are maintained on different schedules of hours and sessions, thus placing them on a different basis from other activities. The *per capita* cost per hour for the continuation schools has been placed at sixteen and a fraction cents for 1933, as compared with twenty and a fraction cents for 1932.

The report shows that the *per capita* cost per hour for the evening elementary schools was slightly over eleven cents in 1933, as compared with twelve and a fraction cents in 1932. In the evening high schools, the 1933 hourly cost was a little over ten cents, while the 1932 cost was twelve and a fraction cents. In the evening trade schools, the hourly cost in 1933 was twenty-four plus cents, as compared with twenty-six plus cents in 1932.

Another table deals with the average daily attendance in day elementary, junior high and senior high schools. It shows that the attendance in day elementary and junior high schools, which had increased steadily up to 1931, is showing a decided and steady decrease. The attendance figure reached its peak in 1931, at 820,675. In 1932, the attendance had dropped to 813,867, and in 1933 it was down to 806,013.

The high schools, however, continue to show a steady increase in attendance with each succeeding year. In 1933, the average daily attendance was 198,322, compared with the 1932 record of 183,535. There are now more than 250,000 pupils in the high schools.

## STUDENT REGISTRATION IN OREGON INSTITUTIONS

AN increase in enrolment of 1,153 students or 21 per cent. in the state institutions of higher education of Oregon is reported to us from the division of information for the state system.

The total number of students enrolled in the six institutions comprising the state system at noon on October 6 was 6,523. A year ago on a comparable date the total enrolment was 5,371. The following table shows the enrolments by institutions and the percentage of increase at each:

| | October 6, 1934 | October 7, 1933 | Percentage Increase |
|---|---|---|---|
| University of Oregon | 2,449 | 2,051 | 19 |
| Oregon State College | 2,508 | 1,885 | 33 |
| Medical School: | | | |
| School of Medicine | 243 | 242 | 0.4 |
| Nursing Education | 293 | 307 | –5 |
| Oregon Normal School | 469 | 396 | 18 |
| Southern Oregon Normal School | 311 | 250 | 24 |
| Eastern Oregon Normal School | 250 | 240 | 4 |
| Totals | 6,523 | 5,371 | 21 |

The increase in enrolment came chiefly in the freshman classes, although substantial increases were recorded at all levels. The following table shows the enrolments in the first-year class at the five institutions which enroll freshmen:

| | October 6, 1934 | October 7, 1933 | Percentage Increase |
|---|---|---|---|
| University of Oregon | 840 | 590 | 42 |
| Oregon State College | 1,019 | 613 | 66 |
| Oregon Normal School | 263 | 227 | 16 |
| Southern Oregon Normal School | 201 | 129 | 56 |
| Eastern Oregon Normal School | 187 | 130 | 44 |
| Totals | 2,576 | 1,752 | 47 |

This unprecedented increase, following as it did larger freshman classes last year, creates a real problem for the teaching faculties at the institutions which had already been cut down to the bare minimum to meet the greatly reduced income. The problem is particularly acute at the state college and the University of Oregon. In some divisions, the increased student load is being met by larger classes and heavier teaching schedules for the present staff. In a few instances, particularly in such basic courses as English and the sciences and in the professional schools of forestry and business administration, it has been necessary to employ added staff members. This has been accomplished with a minimum of cost by restoring some instructors who are on part-time to full-time, or by employing graduate assistants to aid the regular instructors.

## EXTRA-CURRICULAR LECTURES AT HARVARD UNIVERSITY

AN experiment in the history of the instruction systems of American universities will be conducted by the department of government at Harvard University during the present academic year when a series of extra-curricular lectures will be presented by younger members of the department, dealing with their particular fields of research. The lectures, which will begin in the latter part of November, are open only to members of the university and are in no way a required part of the regular government department courses.

The experiment is viewed as consistent with the policy laid down last spring by President James B. Conant's administration of taking away the emphasis from formal, stiff-course requirements and of giving the student greater responsibility in the matters of attendance and records. At that time, it was voted to abolish the return of course grades to the office in November and April, except in courses regularly open to freshmen, and to do away with the return of attendance records in courses taken primarily by juniors and seniors.

The lectures are voluntarily contributed by the instructors, who have expressed the opinion that from the point of view of the material involved they will have a double value. First, they will make available to students research that would ordinarily not fit into any course structure and would therefore not ordinarily be at their disposal until the work had been put into book form. Secondly, the lectures will be valuable as a testing ground for the opinions and theories developed under the isolated conditions of private research.

The formality and location of the lectures has been left entirely to the individual speaker. It is understood that some of the men intend to lecture in regular university halls, while others wish to hold less formal groups, possibly accompanied by discussion, in various units of the house plan. Particular interest centers about this development in the technique of instructing college groups; for it is an interesting outgrowth of the tutorial system.

The lecturers all bear the title of instructor in government and tutor in the Division of History, Government and Economics. The list of speakers and their subjects in the scheduled order of appearance, at dates in the winter yet to be determined, is as follows:

Dr. E. Pendleton Herring, ''Special Interests and the Federal Bureaucracy.''

Dr. Wolfgang H. Kraus, ''The New German State.''

Dr. Mario L. Einaudi, ''Fascism and the Corporative State.''

Dr. Merle Fainsod, ''The Communist Internationale.''

Dr. Payson S. Wild, Jr., ''Topics in the History of International Law.''

Dr. Albert E. Hindmarsh, assistant dean of Harvard College, ''Japanese Foreign Policy.''

Although the subjects are concerned primarily with modern governmental problems, it is emphasized that it is not the main purpose of the lectures to present a survey of contemporary movements. It is the fundamental theory of the series that projects of research carried on by younger members of the government department be outlined, informally, to other members of the university.

## LIBEL SUIT AGAINST DR. WIRT

Dr. William Albert Wirt, superintendent of schools at Gary, Indiana, whose statements concerning the radical intentions of some of President Roosevelt's advisers last spring brought him much publicity and a Congressional investigation, now faces a suit for libel. The plaintiff in the case is Miss Rose Schneiderman, president of the Women's Trade Union League, and the only woman member of the NRA Labor Advisory Board. Miss Schneiderman, through her attorney, Dorothy Kenyon, of Straus & Kenyon, New York City, is asking damages of $100,000 on each of four charges: the publication of a brochure "containing false and defamatory matter concerning the plaintiff," and three subsequent oral statements publicly made by the defendant.

According to the complaint, Dr. Wirt in his brochure stated that the "brain trusters" were assuming that "the America of Washington, Jefferson and Lincoln must be destroyed" as a preliminary to further industrial development, and that they planned to prolong destitution until they had demonstrated to the American people the necessity for government control of industry and commerce. After the term "brain trusters" the complaint inserts the words "meaning thereby the plaintiff and certain others."

In one of the three oral statements alleged to have been made by Dr. Wirt, Miss Schneiderman charges that in an address before a Chicago post of the American Legion on April 30, he referred to her as "the Rose of Anarchy" and stated that she was "in the Virgin Islands in the interest of a socialistic experiment of the brain trust." Later, it is charged, he repeated these statements. Miss Schneiderman's attorney asserts that her client had never visited the Virgin Islands.

The complaint claims that the representations of Dr. Wirt imputed to Miss Schneiderman a belief in "the principles of anarchy, absence of government and the overthrow of government by violence," thereby greatly injuring her in "credit, reputation and business."

Dr. Wirt is represented by Hugo Wintner, who immediately appealed to Federal Judge John C. Knox, into whose court the suit was brought, for a "rationalization of the complaint," stating that "if left in its present state of redundancy and unscientific commingling of causes of action, not alone will there be confusion upon trial of the case, but the defendant's position will be gravely prejudiced."

Dr. Wirt is widely known as the originator of the Gary school system, or Platoon Plan of school organization, which permits the use of one school building for two sets of grades. It is claimed that this system not only effects large economies in the cost of school buildings, but is of educational advantage to the child, making it necessary for him to spend part of the time in the auditorium, gymnasium, laboratories, shops and playgrounds.

### A TRIBUTE TO CLOYD HECK MARVIN, PRESIDENT OF GEORGE WASHINGTON UNIVERSITY

The following resolution was unanimously adopted by the general faculties of the George Washington University, Washington, D. C., on September 14, 1934:

During the past seven years the George Washington University has had the benefit of the educational and financial leadership of Dr. Cloyd Heck Marvin. The last five years of this period have been years of general economic stress, not only in our own country but throughout the world. In the field of higher education the period has been marked in colleges and universities by reductions in salaries, often of major proportions, by curtailments of staff and by elimination of services. In some instances economic pressure has undoubtedly resulted in lowered educational standards.

The faculties of the George Washington University find reason to rejoice that during this period the university's program, under the leadership of President Marvin, has been satisfactorily maintained without sacrifice of educational standards. The administration of admissions has been conducted on a high plane. Student records have been systematized and proper safeguards placed about them.

The educational administration of the university has been simplified and coordinated, particularly as regards graduate studies, the fundamental program of the Junior College, and the work of the professional schools. Academic standards have been steadfastly upheld. The physical plant and equipment have been expanded and improved. The salary scale, materially increased in the early years of President Marvin's administration, has been maintained intact throughout the depression—a record which is unusual among American educational institutions. A generous system of sabbatical leaves was established in 1931–1932 and has been operated until its temporary suspension during the current year.

Faculty prerogatives have been respected and faculty tenure scrupulously regarded. Freedom of thought has been protected. A spirit of cooperation has been fostered throughout the university.

The faculties of the George Washington University face the future with the confidence born of experience. They have faith in President Marvin's leadership and ability, which have been tested throughout this period of association with him in the service of the university. They pledge him their whole-hearted cooperation and support for the coming year and for the years to come.

## EDUCATIONAL NOTES AND NEWS

At ceremonies held on the occasion of the installation of Dr. John Stewart Bryan as president of William and Mary College, the degree of LL.D. was conferred on President Franklin D. Roosevelt, after which he made an address. Dr. Bryan succeeds the late J. A. C. Chandler. Until his election he was vice-rector of the college and is now a member of the International Education Board. He is the president and publisher of the Richmond, Va., *News Leader,* and has been president of the Newspaper Publishers Association.

Colonel Amos W. W. Woodcock, formerly Federal prohibition administrator, was formally installed as president of St. John's College on October 20. Among those on whom the degree of doctor of laws was conferred on the occasion of the installation were Rear-Admiral David Foote Sellers, superintendent of the Naval Academy; Dr. William Mather Lewis, president of Lafayette College, and Dr. Warfield T. Longcope, professor of medicine in the Johns Hopkins Medical School.

Following the resignation of President Williams of the University of Missouri, the Board of Curators authorized appointment of a committee, to consist of three board members, one from the alumni and one from the faculty, for the purpose of making recommendations concerning a new president. This committee as now appointed consists of: Frank M. McDavid, president of the board and chairman of the committee; H. J. Blanton and Mercer Arnold from the board; Robert Caldwell from the alumni and Dr. Winterton C. Curtis from the faculty.

Dr. Flaud Conaroe Wooton has been appointed president of Chevy Chase Junior College, Washington, D. C. Dr. Wooton was called from the Rhode Island State College, where he has been head of the department of education and director of the summer school.

John P. Inglis, formerly principal of the Fremont High School of Los Angeles, has been appointed dean of the Los Angeles Junior College to succeed Dr. W. H. Snyder, who has been at the head of the college since its organization five years ago. Dr. Snyder resigned in June on account of age.

Dr. William Franklin Sands, professor of international relations at Georgetown University, has been named head master of the Newman School, Lakewood, N. J., to succeed William Griffin Kelley.

Dr. William Henry Scott, formerly president of the Ohio State University, observed his ninety-fourth birthday anniversary on September 14. During an interview at that time he stated, "I thought it was time in 1910 to retire as professor of philosophy. I'm not so sure now."

Dr. Thomas F. Holgate, professor of mathematics in Northwestern University since 1893, has retired from teaching and becomes professor emeritus. For seventeen years (1902–1919) he was dean of the College of Liberal Arts, and for two periods (1904–1906 and 1916–1919) was acting president of the university. In 1921–1922 he was visiting professor of mathematics in the University of Nanking, China.

Dr. Collier Cobb, since 1893 professor of geology at the University of North Carolina; Dr. M. C. S. Noble, professor of pedagogy, and Professor A. C. McIntosh have been awarded Kenan emeritus professorships. *The Alumni Review* writes: "The appointments express in a small way the university's appreciation for years of long service of these splendid teachers. Each of the three has contributed much to the sound position of the university in the field of learning, and each is a part of the traditions of Chapel Hill. Each of them has earned the recognition which has come to them. Again there is called to public attention the value to the university of the Kenan Fund which enables the trustees to supplement the state-paid salaries of great teachers. The fund has been a source of life to the university administration during these years of budget cuts, and now the fund steps again into the breach by affording a means of honoring and recognizing the long service of three master teachers, whose total teaching service at Chapel Hill is more than a hundred years."

The resignation of George W. Wickersham as a trustee of Barnard College because of ill health has been accepted by the Board of Trustees. Mr. Wickersham had served on the board since 1918 and was a member of the executive committee and of the committee on education.

Dr. Rose M. Cox, of the English department of the Indiana State Teachers College, resigned from the college faculty at the close of the first summer term to spend some time in travel. Dr. Cox had been a member of the college faculty for thirty-four years. She is now on an extended world tour which will last approximately two years.

Dr. Tempe E. Allison, dean of women at San Bernardino Valley Junior College, California, is on leave of absence this year to accept a temporary appointment as visiting lecturer on drama and the theater at Smith College. During the absence of Dr. Allison, Mrs. Nora McCoy will be acting dean.

Richard Donham has been promoted from instructor in business policy to assistant professor at the Harvard Graduate School of Business Administration for three years, beginning on September 1, 1934.

Dr. Clayton C. Bayard and Dr. Robert S. Holmes have been appointed assistant professors in the department of economics at Oberlin College.

At Stanford University Miss Helen Ederle, who has been a member of the department of education of the Indiana State Teachers College since 1922, has resigned to accept the position of director of Madrone Hall, a dormitory for women graduate students. Dr. Dorothy M. Henderson has been appointed medical adviser to women and director of women's physical education, succeeding Dr. Bertha Sabin Stuart Dyment.

Dr. Martha Tracy, dean of the Woman's

Medical College of Pennsylvania, was recently elected a fellow of the College of Physicians of Philadelphia.

AN honorary degree of doctor of laws was conferred upon Professor Earl W. Crecraft, head of the political science department of the University of Akron, by Franklin College, Indiana, on October 17, at the centennial celebration of the college.

ERNEST CARSON HUNT, who has been a member of the staff of Hunter College for forty-seven years, was the guest of honor at a tea given on October 17, by the Faculty Club of the college. Among those who attended were President Emeritus James M. Kieran, Dr. Eugene A. Colligan, president of the college; Dean Emeritus Annie Hickinbottom Mills, Dean Hannah M. Egan and Miss Alice Hunt.

DR. A. LAWRENCE LOWELL, president emeritus of Harvard University, has been elected chairman of the board of directors of the Boston Municipal Research Bureau.

DAME JANET CAMPBELL has been invited by the Canadian Council on Child and Family Welfare, with the approval of the Dominion Government, to visit Canada during October and November in the interest of maternity and child welfare.

A. W. HICKS, assistant under-secretary of education for New South Wales, Australia, is in the United States to study general administration problems, the articulation of primary and post-primary courses, and the relation of education to industry, under the auspices of the Carnegie Corporation of New York.

DR. H. G. WEISKOTTEN, dean of the College of Medicine of the University of Syracuse, has been chosen to make a nation-wide survey of medical education in the United States and Canada. This survey is sponsored by the American Medical Association, the Association of American Medical Colleges and the Federation of State Boards of Licensure.

A SPECIAL committee of six has been appointed by the Twentieth Century Fund to aid its research staff, which is now making an investigation of government in labor relations. Members of the committee include Dr. Frank Aydelotte, president of Swarthmore College; Dr. William M. Leiserson, professor of economics at Antioch College and chairman of the Petroleum Labor Board; Robert S. Lynd, professor of sociology, Columbia University, and Sumner H. Slichter, professor of business economics, Harvard University. Dr. Roscoe Pound, dean of the Harvard Law School, is a member of the board of trustees.

DR. F. K. KRUGER, professor of political science at Wittenberg College, has been invited as American guest lecturer at the Deutsche Hochschule für Politik in Berlin for the winter semester.

DR. FRANCIS CHO-MIN WEI, president of Hua Chung College (Central China College), Wuchang, China, will give three public lectures on Confucianism at Harvard University, on October 29, 30 and 31, at 8 P. M., in the Fogg Art Museum, Cambridge. The subjects will be "How Has China Come to be Confucian?" "Confucianism as the Chinese Understand It" and "Confucianism and the New China."

INCLUDED among those who will give public lectures at the University of Leeds, England, during 1934–35 will be Lord Rutherford, Professors C. Burt, A. Harden, W. J. Tulloch, B. Melvill Jones, F. A. E. Crew, Hans Driesch, R. W. Whytlaw-Gray, R. Whiddington and Sir G. Elliot Smith.

THE REVEREND JOSEPH REINER, S.J., formerly dean of Loyola University and at the time of his death regional director of sodality work in the Middle West, died on October 14 at the age of fifty-three years.

DR. GEORGE EMERSON QUAILE, founder and head master of the Salisbury School for Boys, died on October 15 at the age of sixty-seven years.

A CONFERENCE of college presidents from the states of Illinois, Iowa, Indiana, Minnesota, Missouri, Nebraska, North and South Dakota and Wisconsin will be held on October 30 and 31 at Galesburg, Illinois, under the auspices of the Association of American Colleges and Knox College. President William Mather Lewis, of Lafayette College, and Dr. R. L. Kelly, of the Association of American Colleges, are speakers representing the association, and almost all the members of the executive committee of the association are participating in the discussions.

The leading subjects under consideration are relationships between the colleges and the federal and state governments, the current practises among the colleges of recruiting and admissions, and the establishment of organic relationships between the colleges and trust and insurance companies and the legal profession, with the view to increasing college endowments.

PRESIDENTS and deans from fourteen colleges met at Middlebury, Vt., on October 19 for the annual two-day conference of the Association of Colleges in New England. The conference opened with a luncheon. The program included a series of round-table discussions at the College Library and Chateau, a tea at the home of President Paul D. Moody, and a formal dinner. Those present included: From Harvard, President James B. Conant, Kenneth B. Murdock and Alfred C. Hanford; from Yale, President James R. Angell, Clarence W. Mendell and Alan C. Valentine; from Brown, President Clarence A. Barbour and Samuel T. Arnold; from Dartmouth, E. Gordon Bill and Lloyd K. Neidlinger; from Williams, President Tyler Dennett, Harry L. Agard and Theodore Clarke Smith; from the University of Vermont, President Guy W. Bailey and Elijah Swift; from Bowdoin, President Kenneth C. M. Sills, Wilmot B. Mitchell and Roscoe J. Ham; from Amherst, President Stanley King and Charles S. Porter; from Trinity, President Remsen B. Ogilby, Morse S. Allen and Roger R. Eastman; from Wesleyan, President James L. McConaughy and J. W. Hewitt; from Tufts, President John A. Cousens and Titus E. Mergendahl; from Boston University, President Daniel L. Marsh and William M. Warren; from Clark, President Wallace W. Atwood and Homer P. Little; from Middlebury, President Paul D. Moody, Burt W. Hazeltine, Charles B. Wright and Edgar J. Wiley.

THE Extension Division of the University of Michigan, in cooperation with the Michigan Congress of Parents and Teachers and the school of education of the university, has announced its fifth annual Parent Education Institute to be held in Ann Arbor on November 1, 2 and 3. The program opens on Thursday morning at 10 o'clock in the auditorium of the University High School and continues through Thursday, Friday and Saturday. Speakers from out of the state will be Dr. LeRoy E. Bowman, of the Child Study Association of America, New York City, and Dr. Caroline Hedger, of the Elizabeth McCormick Memorial Fund, Chicago.

THE annual Rocky Mountain International Clubs Conference will be held at the University of Denver on October 19 and 20, when delegates from four states will meet. The conference is sponsored by the Carnegie Endowment for International Peace. Miss Amy Hemingway Jones, director of the International Clubs, will be the visiting speaker. The principal business of the conference will be round-table discussions of current international problems. More than thirteen colleges will be represented at the conference with over three hundred students in attendance.

A SERIES of thirty weekly lectures, to be given by members of the faculty of Drexel Institute, for the special benefit of the alumni of Drexel and their friends, was begun on October 22. There are six groups of lectures, all to be given on Monday evenings in the Drexel Art Gallery. Each lecture will last one hour, to be followed by an hour of discussion. The groupings are psychology, sociology, history and education; economics, government, law and business; home economics; literature and the fine arts; chemistry, physics, biology and engineering, and library science.

THE University of Denver was awarded the educational medal for distinguished service in promoting international good will and understanding, by the FIDAC, the inter-allied veterans' association, at their annual convention in London. The university was given the award as a result of its being recognized as an outstanding institution in the field of international relations. Dr. Ben M. Cherrington, who has been the executive director for the Foundation for the Advancement of the Social Sciences since its establishment ten years ago, has been chiefly responsible for the development of the university and community programs of the Foundation for the Advancement of Social Sciences. Through a series of programs presented at fortnightly luncheons and at seminars, speakers, distinguished in world affairs, discuss important national and international problems in the fields of politics, law, diplomacy and science.

ANNOUNCEMENT has been made of financial aid for the improvement and extension of Mercer University Library, Macon, Ga., from one of the principal educational foundations of America, including installing of steel stacks and other equipment (from $10,000 to $15,000), the acquisition of additional volumes and collection of research materials in some special field. Mr. J. Kenneth Cameron, general service assistant at the University of Michigan for the past six years, has been appointed librarian to supervise the program.

JUSTICES Van Devanter and Butler have handed down an opinion in the Supreme Court that compulsory military training is not required in land grant colleges and universities under Federal law. Their view was expressed during the oral argument of a case brought to compel the University of California to exempt students from compulsory military training. The two justices held that land-grant colleges and universities were required by Federal law to provide a course in military tactics—but that it was entirely within the control of the college authorities to determine whether such training should be compulsory. John Beardsley, counsel for Albert W. Hamilton and W. Alonzo Reynolds, Jr., conscientious objectors, who were suspended because of their refusal to take military training, insisted that students had the right to attend land grant colleges without surrendering rights they have under the Federal Constitution and the laws of the United States.

# DISCUSSION

## ARE THE CONCLUSIONS AND RECOMMENDATIONS OF THE COMMISSION ON THE SOCIAL STUDIES "STARTLING" OR "ALARMING"?

### I

THE little book entitled "Conclusions and Recommendations" is the final number of sixteen volumes published, or soon to be published, by Charles Scribner's Sons in connection with the American Historical Association Investigation of the Social Studies in the schools. To evaluate the contents of this volume without reference to those on which it is in part based is justified only by the assumption that the commission, or a majority of its members, is convinced that the empirical basis for the statements of fact are contained in the other volumes of the series. The character of the members of the commission is such that this assumption may safely be made.

The eight brief chapters of "Conclusions and Recommendations" deal with "The Obligations and Procedures of the Commission"; "The Frame of Reference"; "Philosophy and Purpose in Education"; "Selection and Organization of Materials of Instruction"; "Method of Teaching"; "Tests and Testing"; "The Teacher"; and "Public Relations and Administration." There follow three appendices: "Next Steps"; "The Work of the Commission"; and a statement of reservations in signing the report by one of its members. Four other members declined to sign; eleven members sponsored the conclusions without reservation.

Whether or not one is pleased with their findings, it is certainly unjustifiable to accuse this commission of a neglect to explain clearly and adequately its assumptions and procedures, and to follow them consistently. In all fairness, such a forthright statement is both the least and the most that students of the report and of education can ask. Whoever believes that the assumptions or procedures are unsound may then dismiss the conclusions and properly assert that in his belief the commission lacks ability or has been careless. Such a belief is, however, no basis for accusing it of obscurity or of malicious intent or of treachery to democracy.

In Chapter I, the commission explains that it felt impelled to consider American civilization as a part of a world order which is now passing through a critical period. While full use was made of scientific procedure to the degree that it could be applied, the commission frankly made judgments and interpretation based on ethical and esthetic considerations—a "frame of reference."

This frame of reference is based on five other volumes of the series and presumably finds justification in the empirical data and cogent reasoning contained therein. It consists of unelaborated generalizations, judgments, interpretations and affirmations concerning (a) the nature and functions of the social sciences; (b) necessarily conditioning factors in American life; and (c) choices deemed possible and desirable in the present and proximate future. Concerning the statements made in the first of these three sections, little question is to be raised. In dealing with conditioning factors and with possible and desirable choices, questions and disagreements are to be expected.

In the second section the commission reaffirms its belief in the perduring vigor and strength of the distinctive aspects, traditions and usages of the American nation, its recognition of the interrelation of the life of America with that of the rest of the world and its faith that the ideals of popular democracy, of personal liberty and dignity and of the paramountcy of the interests of the masses of the people are so strong, so authentic and valid that they will give direction to the further evolution of life and institutions in the United States. There are noted several significant trends that are affecting and will condition social science instruction; the most important of which includes the closer physical unification and ever-closer integration and interdependence of all branches of economy and of social activity within the nation, compelling the individual to depend on corporate organization for employment and income, thereby decreasing the possibilities of individual freedom and equality and developing new problems for American democracy. Faith in economic individualism wanes as the recognition of the growing integration and interdependence of society leads social scientists, philosophers and statesmen to concern themselves with improving its functional efficiency. The collectivistic mode of dealing with common problems of an integrated society will probably be found by a process of experimentation and will probably represent a composite of historic doctrines and of social conceptions yet to appear. Hence the emerging age is one of transition marked by tensions due to the divergence of the trend toward an integrated economy from traditional practises, ideas and institutions of individualism; these tensions will lead either to adjustments or to retrogression into a primitive order of economy and life.

This section of the "frame of reference" includes only the commission's judgments regarding conditioning factors and their meanings and implications. *It has nothing to do with the commission's wishes or its choices.* These are reserved for the third section which follows.

In the third section, after explaining its duty to indicate its judgment concerning the desirable and possible lines of progress, the commission approves a higher standard of living and cultural advance, the employment of every practicable means to avoid the dangers of goose-step regimentation, the retention and fulfilment of the historic principles and ideals of American democracy, the reservation to the individual of the largest possible measure of freedom in the realms of personal and cultural growth and the preservation and development of individuality in its non-acquisitive expressions as the finest flower of civilized society. It favors the steady enlargement of sympathetic understanding and mutual toleration among diverse races and religious and cultural groups, the attainment and spread of accurate knowledge and informed opinion among the masses of the American people, an enlightened attitude toward international relations and a nationalism infused with enlightenment, reason and tolerance. Continued emphasis on the spirit of science and scholarship, liberty of thought and expression, freedom of press and platform and a tolerant study and consideration of diverse ideas are advocated.

The frame of reference, quite inadequately summarized in the preceding paragraphs, conditions the selection and organization of materials of instruction of the social sciences. The commission foresees disagreement with its statements but urges that alternative programs and purposes be prepared as bases of discussion. It asserts that choices must be made, since the very refusal to choose has specific consequences and is therefore a moral act.

In Chapter III, "Philosophy and Purpose in Education," the commission asserts that education is a form of action on the part of some particular social groups; it always expresses some social philosophy, it may be one of the highest forms of statesmanship; it is then concerned with the development of rich and many-sided personalities capable of cooperating in a social order designed for the same ends. Education differs with its geographical and cultural location; hence, in the United States it will be conditioned by the emerging economy which will involve the placing of restraints on individual acquisitive enterprise and on the conceptions, ownership and use of property, and, by the reduction of hours of labor and other measures, will free the individual from exhausting labor and economic insecurity. Therefore, education must promote a recognition among the American people, especially the rising generation, that the old order is passing, that a knowledge of realities and capacity to cooperate are indispensable to American society, and that the rational use of the new leisure requires cultural equipment. Then follow several paragraphs of application of the philosophy to school practises.

II

The judgments and sentiments and the language of Chapters II and III have been challenged several times since the publication of the book. The writer of these pages was, however, quite unprepared for the polemic tone and method used by Professor Bobbitt in his recent article,[1] in which he calls the report "rather startling" and alarming.

Prefacing his attack by a recognition that the American people have been seriously mismanaging their economic-political affairs during the past two or three decades he asserts that "the custodians of social understanding either have been lacking in their supply of it or there has been inefficiency in distributing it to the population."

While both of these alternatives are probably true to a degree, neither of them is necessarily so. The chief difficulty is to be found in the fact that the school, the press, the radio, the stage and even the pulpit—as well as the street corner, the club and the political platform—by which social understandings are transmitted are among the economic-political affairs that are mismanaged. Whatever the efficiency of the "custodians of social understanding," they have had little chance of giving such enlightenment as they have had to a people busy with baseball, jazz, money-making and "social" climbing.

If the nation has lacked guidance, if it even now does lack it, as Dr. Bobbitt implies, the fault lies not so much in the group of earnest and competent men and women who have striven so assiduously for five years to furnish it, as it does in the complexity of the problem and in the almost insuperable difficulties involved in the guidance process. For guidance assumes that a goal is agreed upon, that the persons to be guided desire to reach it, and that the guides know how it may be reached. No one of these assumptions has been clearly and certainly true of the American people "of the last two or three decades," nor is it surely true of them to-day.

Experimentation which Bobbitt ridicules and protests so vehemently is the very heart of democratic and of scientific method. It is based on the best tentative hypotheses that can be formulated and so it differs from mere "trial and error" with which Bobbitt sees fit to identify it.

One of these hypotheses of the commission is that "in the United States, as in other countries, the age of individualism and *laissez-faire* in economy and government is closing and that a new age of collectivism is emerging." Certainly this statement seems humdrum enough. The days of rugged individualism have already been numbered for over a century, as Beard has clearly shown in his article, "The Myth of Rugged Individualism." Not only have intellectual rebels and vigorous reformers—Marx, Bellamy, Henry George, William Demarest Lloyd, Bryan and the rest—foretold its demise, but even so economically conservative a leader as Charles W. Eliot recognized that collectivism was inevitable in a world so complex and impersonal as the one in which he lived at the turn of the century. In the areas of parks and highways, of schools and hospitals, of health protection and social welfare, of insurance and charity, of politics and wage bargaining, and even of industry, transportation and communication, collective ownership and sponsorship and use and social responsibility in response to this collectivism have been recognized for years.

It is supererogatory for Dr. Bobbitt to explain that the commission means by "collectivism" either the form used in Germany and Italy or the form used in Russia (at one point he seems to limit the commission's meaning to communism). The commission elsewhere (pp. 22–23) clearly asserts its opposition to regimentation; it declares its belief that such a process

[1] "Questionable Recommendations of the Commission on the Social Studies," SCHOOL AND SOCIETY, 40: 1025, 201–208.

is contrary to American ideals and traditions and asserts that America can find its own way to collectivism without such regimentation.

It surely was an oversight of Dr. Bobbitt that he seems to indicate it to be the commission's judgment that "all kinds of collectivism are really much alike in spite of their terminology and their pretenses." Probably he would have used parentheses to indicate that this belief is his own had he reread his manuscript more meticulously. Dr. Bobbitt must know, however, that collectivism has progressed in France, Great Britain and the Scandinavian countries almost as far as it has in the fascist countries, and distinctly in the same direction if not so completely as in the Union of Socialist Soviet Republics.

The processes by which collectivism has progressed in the democratic countries of Europe and in America have been very different from those now typical of the fascist and communist states. These processes have not involved "the submission of all to the plans of a few," as Bobbitt accuses the commission of knowing; rather have they been aggressively and resourcefully sponsored and carried through by organized groups—trade unions, cooperative societies, agricultural groups, temperance societies, social welfare organizations, and the like. Indeed, the collectivization movement now in process in Denmark and Sweden and to a less extent in England and Norway, far from involving coercion (which Bobbitt insists "every nation that is now collectivizing its population is forced to use") is clearly related to the educational programs of the adult educational institutions and their sponsoring societies.

The belief that the commission has set forth is that Western Civilization can survive economically only on a collectivistic basis, and it has stated clearly its choice: It "deems possible and desirable the retention and fulfilment of the historic principles and ideals of American democracy" (p. 23). Its statements regarding educational purposes bear no resemblance to Bobbitt's imputation that the problem (as the commission sees it) is "how to educate the people in general for a willing and child-like submissiveness to the wise and benevolent few who are to think and plan their affairs for them."

It is to be regretted that the commission used the word "masses" to signify the hundred and fifteen million American adults and children who have no vested interests in continuance of an economy of scarcity with its production and banking and merchandising for private profit, since the word "masses" is for some reason an emotional word disagreeable not only to Dr. Bobbitt but to many others who perhaps confuse it with proletariat. It may be, too, that the commission should not have dismissed without mention the possibility and desirability of an education that would not concern itself with cooperation or with problems of social evolution or social accomplishment, if such a proposal is one of the alternative possibilities which Dr. Bobbitt implies should have been given a proper hearing, its factors carefully weighed and the reasons why it is not approved cautiously pointed out.

III

It is very difficult for the writer to recognize in the protests referred to in the preceding paragraphs the Franklin Bobbitt whose books and articles have so consistently taken positive position in regard to collectivistic protection of health,[2] large group cooperation and consciousness as a goal of social studies,[3] and the school's paternalistic prescriptions for all pupils of a "general curriculum."[4] Whatever Dr. Bobbitt may suspect or fear that individual members of the commission may believe or desire for American society and for social education, the expressed beliefs and choices contained in "Conclusions and Recommendations" seem to the writer to be in spirit not unlike the conclusions and recommendations for which Dr. Bobbitt himself has been justly praised and once at least wittily criticized by Bode.

Many aggressive educators may regret that the commission's final report contains so much that is obvious. Like the Prince of Wales, the commission is in favor of civilization; it too adds: Why not try it! It is difficult to find in the text any reason for calling it startling or alarming.

Philip W. L. Cox
New York University

[2] *Cf.* "The Curriculum," Part IV, Houghton Mifflin Company, 1918.

[3] *Cf.* "How to Make a Curriculum," Chapter VII, Houghton Mifflin Company, 1924.

[4] *Cf. Los Angeles Research Bulletin,* April 19, 1923.

# SPECIAL CORRESPONDENCE

## THE MEXICAN SCHOOL SYSTEM TO-DAY

### I. FROM MADERO TO CALLES

THE period of 1910–20 was one of great upheaval, due to the revolutionary movements. While in Mexico, as well as in other countries, political questions affected the educational system, educational needs continued to be of definite import.[1] In 1912 Francisco de Madero indicated the serious educational exigency of the republic when he recommended the establishment of elementary schools, an increase in the number of rural schools and an appropriation of eight million pesos to carry on the work.[2] Throughout this period, industrial, agricultural and normal schools continued to be opened throughout the republic. From time to time educational congresses were held and much school work was carried on.[3] However, the destruction wrought by the revolution as far as the educational system was concerned was probably more than the states could overcome.[4]

The weakest link in the educational chain was the preparatory school patterned after the French lycée. It left the great masses of Mexico without an opportunity for education. The result was the rural school, which had made a modest beginning as early as 1913. Mexico's educators realized the need for the reorganization of Mexican education. The general idea was that it should be somewhat empirical. All felt that the races of Mexico were not inferior to those of other countries, but that the Mexican was uneducated. For this reason, Mexico needed instruction in practical things, well-qualified teachers and sufficient budgetary allowance to carry on a good school system.[5]

By 1917 the movement for free schools for all was well on its way. In this year the Constitutional Convention met and wrote the following article into the fundamental law of the republic:

> Instruction is free; that given in public institutions of learning shall be secular. Primary instruction, whether higher or lower, given in private institutions, shall likewise be secular. Private primary schools may be established only subject to official supervision. Primary instruction in public institutions shall be gratuitous.[6]

The program of education in the new government was completely different from that of Diáz. Mexican society under him had failed to reach the millions of Indians and mestizos who are to-day, as at that time, Mexico.[7] By 1921 educational work was begun in earnest. José Vasconcelos, rector of the university, became the Secretary of Education. A budget of 15,000,000 pesos was advanced in 1921, 30,000,000 in 1922 and 35,000,000 in 1923. About 1921, also, the University Extension Service started a campaign against illiteracy. Volunteers were pressed into service to teach adults to read and to write. In Mexico City thousands of such schools were established. The response of the people was immediate. These schools gradually faded out of the picture as the federal schools increased.[8]

An amendment to the Constitution now gave the Federal Government the power to create all sorts of schools in any part of the republic collaborating with the state governments.[9] This step, of course, marked the beginning of the end of state and municipal schools.

What was the aim of Mexican education at this period? The Minister of Public Instruction tells us that it was to make good citizens. ". . . men and women free in spirit, and in fact, able to think for themselves . . . able to earn their own living and to shape the community in such a manner that any earnest worker can attain a comfortable living . . . such has been the purpose of our educational reform."[10]

1 Elizabeth Buckingham, "The Mexican Schools: Past and Present," 167.

2 *Bulletin, Pan-American Union,* xxxvi, 149–51.

3 *Bulletin, Pan-American Union,* xxxvi, 149–51; xxxvii, 44.

4 E. A. Ross, "The Social Revolution in Mexico," 151–55.

5 P. Macharo y Narvaez, "La Enseñanza en Mexico," 9–15.

6 H. N. Branch, "The Constitution of 1857 Compared with the Constitution of 1917."

7 Salvador Alvarado, "La Reconstruccíon de Mexico," 20–100.

8 *El Monumento Educative en Mexico,* 200; 331–34.

9 Buckingham, *op. cit.,* 170.

10 José Vasconceles, "Education in Mexico: Present Day Tendencies," *Bulletin, Pan-American Union,* LVI, 203–44.

## II. From Calles to the Present

The present Mexican school system usually begins with the kindergarten. The next step is the six-year primary school. This school is divided into a four-year elementary, followed by a two-year superior primary. The secondary school takes five years. This period is divided into a three-year secondary school and a two-year preparatory school. The preparatory period is followed by a six- to nine-year course in the university.

The technical, agricultural, industrial and commercial training is given in separate institutions. Frequently these schools are placed under the various departments of government rather than under the Department of Education.

A great many of the schools are still controlled by the states and municipalities. For example, in twelve states, Aguascalientes, Colima, Chiapas, Durango, Guanajuato, Nuevo Leon, Oaxaca, Queretaro, San Luis Potosi and Tamaulipas, the municipalities participate in the support and control of the primary schools.

The Federal Government controls education in the Federal District and in the territories not fortunate enough to have schools. Probably most important of all is the federal program of rural education for over three fourths of the people. According to a document presented to me by the chief of the Division of Rural Education the present (May, 1934) number of rural schools in the thirty states is as follows: 7,945 primary schools, 8,024 special schools (cultural missions, Indian schools, etc.). The number of teachers employed at the present time in the rural system is 11,002.[11]

When the Calles government took over the power, almost every obstacle confronted it that could hinder the educational system. There was briefly a lack of money, lack of adequate teaching facilities, lack of teachers and a lack of enthusiasm on the part of the masses.[12]

The government was strongly behind a wide educational program. Calles, in an interview, said:

> The bed rock of the new system is the rural school and there are now four thousand in operation. They teach the three R's and some manual training, which teaches the child how to use the products of the place in which he lives. Lectures on hygiene and nationalism are given here. My plan is to endow each school with a radio, so as to bring in the news of the world, and so it may become a civic center.[13]

Obviously, the philosophy of John Dewey was to dominate. Dewey later said after a visit to the republic:

> Probably one-half of the children were in school before the Catholic schools were closed. . . . Owing to the destruction of the revolution there are not as many schools as in 1910 in some of the large towns. Four high schools opened recently are crowded. This is a new thing as only preparatory schools were in operation before. A Federal Normal school is housed and equipped to equal any in the world. Open air schools will make compulsory education possible in the Federal District in a short time also.[14]

By far the most interesting development in the Mexican educational system is the rural school. This means a school for the native Indian and in reality a revolution for Mexico. By means of such schools, Mexico is wiping out illiteracy and is incorporating the Indian politically.

The educational program of Mexico to-day was born of the revolutionary movement. The armed country-side, by armed convulsions, was able to communicate its desire for education and it created a system which, without breaking the federal form of government, extends to all corners of the republic. Legally the state governments are not excluded from the work of rural education. The development of action on the part of the Federal Government has become so much greater that it is marching toward open centralization.[15]

The rural school, the chief agent to accomplish the incorporation of the Indian, was initiated under José Vasconceles. The "cultural

[11] Departmento de Enseñanza, Sección de Escuelas Rurales. Forma No. 5.

[12] George Washington A. Luckey, "Outline of the Educational Systems and School Conditions in Latin America," 68–72.

[13] Isaac F. Marcosson, "Calles," *Saturday Evening Post*, February 26, 1927.

[14] John Dewey, "Mexico's Educational Renaissance," *New Republic*, 116–120, September, 1926.

[15] Licenciado Narciso Bassols, "The General Program of Education in Mexico," 6. July 19, 1932.

mission" was evolved to meet the need and to train the rural teacher on the job. In 1928 there were six of these missions. Now there are thirteen (1934).[16] The mission, consisting for the most part of a nurse who gives elementary courses in hygiene, teachers of agriculture, carpentry, sewing, home economics, local crafts, physical education and an educational expert, is either centered or moved to a district. Teachers gather, attend school and go back to their community better fitted to carry on their work.[17]

A teacher in a rural school may have in her charge forty children from seven to fourteen years of age as well as a group of adult students. Often the building is furnished by the community, while the government furnishes the teachers and materials. The teachers must be natives of the particular district in which they teach. There seems to be a preference for married teachers, especially couples who are both able to teach. The response to this program was immediate.[18] Professor Ramirez told me that the Indians would often build houses for schools and then come all the way to Mexico City to beg for teachers. Peones have placed their faith in the school. The creation of thousands of rural schools would not have been possible without the cooperation of the peones.[19] They have laid the foundation for the rural education.

The Federal Government intends to educate entire villages, thousands of Indian and *mestizo* villages. Rural education of this type is directed at the adults. It is the most important department of Mexican education. Other schools have also been organized by the Federal Government. An open-air art school was founded at Santa Anita and by 1926 four other schools of the same type were in operation.[20]

In 1926 an experimental Indian school was established at Mexico City. One hundred ninety-eight pupils were selected from twenty-six different tribes. The term extends for three years and the pupils may do either primary, secondary or industrial work. It is interesting to note that those Indians in the primary course were 95 per cent. successful, those in secondary work 85 per cent. successful, and those in industrial work 63 per cent. successful.[21]

The industrial schools established by the Federal Government have unique features. For example, in Mexico City, the pupils maintain stores where they sell articles. There are many of these stores in operation in the states as well.[22]

There are many agricultural schools, the main ones being located at Hidalgo, Guanajuato, Micheocan and Chíhuahua. These are open to the children of communal ejidos. The course is usually three years long. The school at Hidalgo is especially worthy of notice. It is conducted by a retired graduate of the Agricultural College at Ames, Iowa.[23]

The triple system of federal, state and municipal schools allows the central government to supplement the program where it sees fit. As a rule, one model elementary school is placed in each state, the government maintaining it as a demonstration school. The Federal Government cooperates with the states and seeks to establish schools where no schools have been before.

The Mexican school training is several years shorter than the training in the United States. It consists of a kindergarten, four years elementary primary, two years superior primary, three years secondary, two years preparatory and six years of professional training. Usually the student is ready for his life's work at twenty-three.

The reorganization of secondary education has carried into the university also. Since 1910 it has been the aim of the university to integrate the different professional schools of the university academically as well as administratively. There is no theological school, now that the church and the state are separated and the law school no longer dominates. The modern rector is appointed by the President for three years. He is assisted in his work by the University Council. This body is composed of four professors at large, two professors from the faculty of each department and a student representative from each department. The largest college

16 Secretaria de Educacíon Publica, ''Las Misiónes Culturales,'' 1932–1933, 7.

17 *Ibid.*, 7–15.

18 Robert N. McLean, ''That Mexican,'' 105–10.

19 Bassols, *op. cit.*, 8.

20 Secretaria de Educación Publica, ''Las Escuelas de Pintura al Aire Libre,'' 11.

21 Secretaria de Educación Publica, ''La Casa del Estudianto Indigeña,'' 161.

22 Memoria del Secretario de Educación Publica, 258, 1927.

23 E. Gruening, ''Mexico and Its Heritage,'' 527.

at the university is that of fine arts. There are twice the number of students here than there are in any of the other colleges. A new feature of the university is the graduate school, which does not require residence and has a quantity of extension work in other countries.[24]

### III. PERSONAL IMPRESSIONS

It is impossible to know or to understand the institutions and problems of a people until one knows and understands the people themselves. While in Mexico I made a definite effort to study the Mexicans as individuals. Entering the country at Nogales, Sonora, and following the West Coast Route to Mexico City, I left the Republic at Juarez after traveling throughout the heart of the country. Throughout my travels, the average Mexican citizen I found to be kind, intelligent, considerate and proud of his country.

Within the above specified limits, I had the opportunity of seeing schools of various types. My general impression is that while the Mexican system is not as advanced as ours, it is well on its way. The entire system of education in the republic seems to be dominated by the socialistic as well as the communal ideas. The rural school, for example, is essentially a communal project. The great educational problem of the republic is rural education. With this knowledge firmly in mind I made my way to the office of Professor Rafael Ramirez, chief of the department. We had an interesting conference about educational problems in the republic. I was interested to find out that the rural teachers are selected from the community in which they live. It is the policy of the department never to employ a teacher who is not a native of the locality in which he or she teaches. The main work of a rural teacher is not teaching; it is the work of being an asset to the community. The teacher is the leader of the small centers, gives advice, conducts social affairs, and above all tries to make the people happy.

Very few rural students can hope to attend the university. The university training is more or less reserved for the city people. It isn't generally desirable for rural students to go to Mexico City to attend the university because such a movement would tend to depopulate an already thinly populated area.

[24] E. E. Brandon, "The University of Mexico," *Bulletin, Pan-American Union*, xxxvi, 46.

Adult education is carried on in the rural communities. In many of these the people build the schools and the Federal Government sends out teachers and supplies. Professor Ramirez said that in 1929 the Federal Government had little or no money to carry on this program, but at the present time has the money and is carrying out the program.

The republic is gradually taking over the municipal schools in the provinces. The Federal Government is even bringing private schools under its control. Professor Ramirez predicts that in the very near future the Federal Government will control all the schools in Mexico.

A few days later I visited Junior High School No. 4 of Mexico City. Adalberto Nava, the sub-director, and Miss Lucille Davis acted as my guides and interpreters. The Junior High School No. 4 is housed in an ancient Jesuit school and chapel just adjacent to the University Summer School. I visited classes all day. I was particularly impressed with the courtesy of the students, who rose whenever I entered or left a class. The physical education class was particularly interesting because of the use of the modern methods of the mass drill. Few text-books were in use in the schools. The United States is justly called the text-book nation, but obviously Mexico can not afford that evil as yet. José Calvo, the director of the school, was very agreeable and provided me with much informatory material.

On the whole I came away from Mexico with the feeling that while a definite start has been made toward raising the general level of the Mexican peasant and Indian, who constitute the great rural population, there is still much to be done. The education of these classes is without a doubt Mexico's chief school problem. The upper classes and those of lesser rank who live in Mexico City or any other urban center are provided with adequate educational opportunities, their goal being the university and its specific professional course thereafter. But it is the peasant and the Indian who have had almost no educational facilities at their disposal, until comparatively recently, when the rural school was instituted. The continuous political uncertainty prevalent in Mexico during the greater portion of the twentieth century seems to have left its mark upon the educational development of the country. The principal obstacles standing in the way of progress are the lack of money, the lack of trained teachers and the lack of a more centralized and better organized school system.

ROBERT J. PARKER

TAFT JUNIOR COLLEGE
TAFT, CALIFORNIA

# QUOTATIONS

## CHILDREN'S RIGHTS

NEXT week marks the tenth anniversary of the adoption by the League of Nations of the Declaration of Geneva, the modern charter of children's rights. The twentieth century, early in its course, began to be known in publicists' jargon as "the Century of the Child." In England, at least, the appellation was justified by a spate of legislation having as its prime object the welfare of the rising generation—the Education Acts which saw the new century in, the Midwives Act of 1902, which abolished the untrained midwife, the Notification of Births Act of 1905, and the Children Act of 1908; by the inauguration of a national campaign against infant mortality, the establishment of the first "schools for mothers," and, as the first decade of the century drew to a close, of the first infant welfare centers.

France was a little ahead of us in beginning a national attack on the problem of infant mortality, and, indeed, the earliest British enterprise owed something to French example and inspiration. It was not until 1912, however, that the United States established the Federal Children's Bureau under the aegis of a Department of State, and thus consolidated the national concern for "all matters pertaining to the welfare of children and child life among all classes of our people." Notwithstanding the broad scope of these terms of reference—to be amply justified in later years—it was the excessive infant mortality rates which prompted the American, as the French and, in less degree, the British, efforts towards national child welfare. War losses and the effect of war conditions on the health and general welfare of children aroused in these and in other lands a more acute sense of the importance of safeguarding the youngest citizens, and the child welfare movement began to appear as a definite feature of national life in a well-developed community. National Baby Weeks were inaugurated in England and in America. In Belgium—hitherto a somewhat backward country in this respect—the important and far-reaching *Oeuvre nationale de l'enfance* was established under government auspices.

International cooperation in child welfare may be traced back to 1905, when a conference attended by doctors and social workers from several different countries was held in Paris to discuss the organization of infants' milk centers—the forerunners, both in England and on the continent, of modern child welfare centers. One result of this conference was the formation of the first international child welfare organization, the *Union internationale pour la protection de l'enfance du premier age,* which organized international congresses.

"The protection of children, young persons, and women" is one of the obligations laid upon the League by Part xiii. of the Treaty of Versailles. The work which falls under this head is carried out in part by the International Labor Organization of the League, in part by the Advisory Commission for the Protection of Children and Young People. Its range is comprehensive—a definite advance from that concentration on the prevention of infant mortality and the promotion of infant welfare which was the main characteristic of the earlier efforts of the century, both national and international. The League's activities now include the promotion of measures for the protection of employed women before and after childbirth, for the prevention and control of the employment of children and young persons, for the reclamation of juvenile delinquents, for the suppression of the traffic in women and children and of literature and cinematographic films likely to have a prejudicial effect on juvenile mentality—and the promotion of an international convention on the circulation of educational films—and the study of social conditions, such as unemployment, which are inimical to the welfare of the young.

All these activities tend to conserve the child's rights as defined by the Declaration of Geneva, adopted by the Fifth Assembly of the League just ten years ago (September 26, 1924). The Declaration had been drafted by an English woman, Miss Eglantyne Jebb, whose work as founder of the Save the Children Fund—an international effort for the protection of children—had brought her into close touch with League of Nations activities. In the English version—the original script is in French and is now preserved in the Cantonal archives at Geneva—the Declaration runs as follows:

By the present declaration of the rights of the child, commonly known as the ''Declaration of Geneva,'' men and women of all nations, recognizing that mankind owes to the child the best that it has to give, declare and accept it as their duty that, beyond and above all considerations of race, nationality or creed:

(i) The child must be given the means requisite for its normal development both materially and spiritually.

(ii) The child that is hungry must be fed; the child that is sick must be nursed; the child that is backward must be helped; the delinquent child must be reclaimed, and the orphan and the waif must be sheltered and succored.

(iii) The child must be the first to receive relief in times of distress.

(iv) The child must be put in a position to earn a livelihood and must be protected against every form of exploitation.

(v) The child must be brought up in the consciousness that its talents must be devoted to the service of its fellow-men.

The resolution of the Assembly 10 years ago not only approved the Declaration but invited "the states members of the League of Nations to apply its principles in the work of the protection of childhood," and the President of the Assembly, M. Motta, of Switzerland, said that in so endorsing the Declaration the Assembly had consecrated it as the world charter for the protection of childhood.

Since then the League's approval has been echoed in many individual nations. The Declaration has been signed by the heads of many states and by representative citizens. During the Imperial Conference in London in 1930 the Prime Minister of Great Britain and the leaders of all the delegations, most of them Dominion Prime Ministers, appended their signatures. In Spain, when the new Republican Constitution was formulated in 1932, the Declaration was incorporated *en bloc.* The French Ministry of Education some years ago directed that a copy should be displayed in every state school throughout the country. In Bulgaria—whose king is the only reigning monarch to have set his signature to the document—the Declaration is the focal point of the national "Children's Day," a public festival participated in by the Crown, the Ministry, and the Church, and in Turkey it is the subject of similar emphasis.

On the part of the League itself, a great increase of activity on behalf of the rising generation has marked the past 10 years. When the Declaration of Geneva was adopted in 1924, the League had hardly got into its stride in matters of child welfare. The Advisory Committee on Traffic in Women and Children was the sole committee which took cognizance of the interests of children, and its terms of reference were subject to the limitations indicated in the title. At the meeting of the League Council on December 24, 1924, Sir Austen Chamberlain moved that the Committee be reconstituted under the title "Advisory Committee on Traffic in Women and the Protection of Children" and later the body became, even more emphatically, the "Advisory Commission for the Protection and Welfare of Children and Young People," which is its title to-day. The question of the traffic in women and children was relegated to a sister committee and both, under the leadership of Dame Rachel Crowdy and of her successor, Mlle. Chaptal, have developed a far-reaching program of child welfare. Not the least of the League's contributions to sociology has been the consequent broadening of the definition of "child welfare." Remote, indeed, in some of its phases, from the conception of the pioneers at the beginning of the century, who concerned themselves mainly with the question of establishing milk centers for infants, the modern idea is consonant both with their desire to give children (as the Declaration of Geneva has it) the means requisite for their normal development, and with the new spirit of the times which, expressing itself through the International Boy Scouts and Girl Guides, the Junior Red Cross, the Save the Children Fund, and other organizations, places children above the battle of race, nationality and creed.—*The London Times Literary Supplement.*

# REPORTS

## ACTIVITIES OF THE ROCKEFELLER FOUNDATION

In a detailed report of its activities for 1933 which has just been published, Dr. Max Mason, president of the Rockefeller Foundation, makes the following comments on the work accomplished by the foundation during the year:

The period has been marked by economic, social and political stress in many parts of the world, giving rise to pressing problems of national and international scope. A foundation dedicated to the welfare of mankind, and which has conceived its function in the broad as aid in the process of the rationalization of life, can neither remain indifferent to pressing current problems nor relinquish the support of the fundamentals on which, in the long run, the control of man's destiny depends. In its work for the year The Rockefeller Foundation has been conscious of both types of needs.

While the foundation has continued during the year its activity in furthering the advance of knowledge in the fields of public health, medical science, natural science, social science and the humanities, its work in these fields has been vitally changed in scope through selection, for intensive work, of those subfields which contribute more directly to the general problem of human behavior, with the aim of control through understanding.

In the fields of medical and natural science the major emphasis has been placed on the problem of mental health and on the development of those sciences whose advance is imperatively demanded to form the substantial scientific basis for the rapidly evolving modern science of man. In the social sciences the problems of economic structure and process, international relations and community organization and planning, have been considered of principal importance. The emphasis in the humanities has been on the encouragement of international cultural understanding and the preservation and interpretation of American culture. In the International Health Division, there has been increased attention to studies of disease in its environment, with closely related laboratory investigations.

Early in 1933 a fund was set aside for projects having to do with the present national and world situation. The projects which have been supported fall under two general headings: studies providing for concurrent appraisal and studies furnishing a factual basis for improved planning of important sections of the recovery, relief and reconstruction program; and undertakings involving the collaboration of private agencies in the prosecution of the emergency programs of the federal, state and local governments.

Another emergency requiring special funds was the displacement of eminent scholars in Europe for political reasons and the consequent interruption of important scientific work. Dealing directly with universities in Europe and America which wished to add these men to their staffs, the foundation has contributed toward their salaries. The situation was an emergency; the solution of the problem is as yet on a temporary basis.

During 1933 the Rockefeller Foundation appropriated $9,890,806.31 for various philanthropic projects.

The foundation expended for public health work during the year the sum of $3,286,063.01. It supported laboratories for yellow fever research in Lagos, Nigeria; Bahia, Brazil; and New York City. It completed, in cooperation with various governments of West Africa, an extensive survey which disclosed the areas in Africa where yellow fever occurs; assisted the governments of Brazil and Bolivia in an extensive program of yellow fever control; conducted experiments and studies on the vaccine and virus of yellow fever and on the mosquito vectors of this disease; aided three states in the United States and seventeen foreign governments in antimalaria work; carried out malaria studies and surveys in various parts of the world; engaged in studies of hookworm disease in Palestine, Egypt, Straits Settlements and Puerto Rico; supported studies of *Endamoeba histolytica,* Rocky Mountain spotted fever, tuberculosis, sprue anemia, filariasis, schistosomiasis and the diseases affecting the races of the Pacific; aided the government of India in conducting experiments on the disposal of refuse; sponsored studies of statistical epidemiology; contributed toward the development of state and local health services of fifteen European countries, the League of Nations, five Far Eastern countries, the government of the South Pacific Islands, six countries of the Caribbean region, two countries of South America and the governments of Mexico and Canada; gave assistance to the central health administrations of fourteen states in the United States and to the local health administrations of twenty-three states of the United States, four provinces of Canada and five areas in Mexico, and provided funds for local health units in fourteen other countries; directed the studies of 197 fellows in public health, thirty-two nursing fellows and six nurse visitors; provided financial aid to former fellows in carrying out special studies; and contributed toward the support of schools of hygiene and public health and of centers of public health training in Japan, Puerto Rico, Central America, South America, Europe and the United States.

In the medical sciences the Rockefeller Foundation, during 1933, appropriated $1,173,853. In aid of programs of specific concentration in the fields of psychiatry and public health teaching, appropriations were made to the Johns Hopkins University School of Medicine for research in psychiatry; to University College, London, for work in biophysics and neurophysiology; to Washington University, St. Louis, Missouri, for investigations in nerve physiology; and to the Harvard Medical School and Masschusetts General Hospital for cooperative work in psychiatry. For the development of teaching in public health and preventive medicine an appropriation was made to Dalhousie University, Halifax, Nova Scotia. During 1933 the foundation provided 295 fellowships in the medical sciences. In addition, research aid grants in sums varying from $55 to $3,000 enabled sixty-one scientists or groups of scientists to carry on research work.

Foundation appropriations in the natural sciences amounted to $807,250.

For specific programs of research in the vital processes, particularly in biology and psychology, and in the field of the so-called earth sciences, contributions were made to a number of institutions, among them the California Institute of Technology for research in biology and chemistry; the University of Chicago for biological research; the National Research Council for research in problems of sex and the effects of radiation on living organisms; the Roscoe B. Jackson Memorial Laboratory in Bar Harbor, Maine, for research in mammalian genetics; and the Massachusetts Institute of Technology for aerological research. In addition to the more important grants, awards comparatively small in amount were made for the purpose of exploring new fields of study and increasing opportunities for work which has been retarded because of the present economic situation.

The total number of fellowships in the natural sciences administered by the Rockefeller Foundation during 1933 was eighty-nine. In addition, eighty-eight individuals received new appointments for fellowships administered by the National Research Council with funds supplied by the Rockefeller foundation.

The total amount appropriated for projects in the social sciences during the year was $1,636,000.

In a general program aiding the social sciences as a whole, support was given to twenty institutional centers in the United States, Canada, Europe, the Near East and the Orient.

In support of a program of specific research in economic planning and control, appropriations were made in 1933 to the National Bureau of Economic Research, New York City; to the Financial Section and Economic Intelligence Service of the League of Nations; to the Economic Foundation, New York City, for a study of the history of prices; to the University of Louvain, Belgium, for researches on the business cycle; and to the Industrial Relations Counselors, New York City, for unemployment studies. In the field of international relations, grants were made in 1933 to the Foreign Policy Association, New York City; the Fiscal Committee of the League of Nations, for a study of international taxation problems; the Geneva Research Center, Switzerland; the American Council of the Institute of Pacific Relations; the German School of Politics, Berlin; and the American Geographical Society, for the preparation of a map of Hispanic America on a 1 to 1,000,000 scale. For research in community organization and planning, grants were made to the Social Sciences Research Council's Committee on Government Statistics in Information Service, Washington, D. C.; to the Science Advisory Board, Washington, D. C.; and to the Joint Committee on Research of the Community Council of Philadelphia, Pa.

During 1933, the Rockefeller Foundation provided funds with which 208 active fellowships were maintained in the social sciences. A special fellowship program in agricultural economics and rural sociology which had been supported over a five-year period came to an end on June 30, 1933. In the final year there were 22 men holding fellowships.

The sum of $847,500 was appropriated to projects in the humanities. For planning and development in the field as a whole, funds were appropriated to the American Council of Learned Societies; to the International Committee of Historical Sciences; to the American Library Association; and to Columbia University, Harvard University and the University of Chicago. Within the field of international cultural relations, aid was given in 1933 to the American Council of Learned Societies for studies in the Far East, and to the Orthological Institute of London, in support of various activities directed toward determining the usefulness of Basic English in the Far East. In another field, the preservation and interpretation of American cultural traditions, support was given to the Library of Congress for the accumulation of source materials for American history; to the Virginia Historical Society for the completion of the Virginia Historical Index; to the Bibliographical Society of America for an index of American newspaper files; and to the University of North Carolina toward development of work in American drama.

Grants totaling $589,000 were made by a special trustee committee of the foundation in support of studies of pressing economic problems. Six research agencies and two universities received such aid in conducting special investigations: the Brookings Institution for three concurrent economic studies; the Social Science Research Council for studies of relief cases, unemployment reserves and relief, national policy in international economic relations and the Tennessee Valley development; the American Municipal Association for the work of its Advisory Service on Public Works; the Slum Clearance Committee of New York for its preliminary program; Columbia University for a study of the effects of sales taxes; the University of California for field studies of barter groups; and the New York Adult Education Council and the Committee on the Use of Leisure Time for their general programs. In addition, the foundation arranged for visits to the United States by certain foreign authorities on social and economic subjects, in order that American institutions might profit by their comment and advice.

# EDUCATIONAL RESEARCH AND STATISTICS

## AN EXPERIMENTAL COMPARISON OF TWO METHODS OF CORRECTING THE OUTCOME OF AN EXAMINATION

THE extensive literature devoted to the technique of the examination treats this device almost exclusively as an instrument of rating scholastic achievement. It is easy to list a formidable bibliography dealing with the guessing factor, the reliability, validity and construction of various test forms—problems relating essentially to the refinement of the examination as a technique of measurement. But it is difficult to find any quantitative data relating to the service of the examination as a mode of instruction.[1] As a matter of fact, however, the examination teaches. It arouses serious motivation; it is an occasion for review and orientation; and, if it is a new-type-test, it ingests a wide range of significant subject-matter. If an examination is only busy-work, or even a mild form of pedagogical punishment sadistically inflicted by the instructor, it is rarely ever entirely devoid of instructional value.

In order to secure a quantitative verification for the foregoing view-point, the following experiment was designed. The purpose of the investigation was to determine the relative effectiveness of two methods of correcting the outcome of an examination. The subjects were members of two classes in introductory educational psychology at the University of Michigan. Both classes were taught by the writer according to the same syllabus and by means of the same methodology. At the middle of the semester the two classes took the same new-type examination composed of 47 items covering the first half of the course. One month later the test papers were returned on the same day to

[1] Possible exceptions are: F. D. Curtis and G. G. Woods, "A Study of the Relative Teaching Values of Four Common Practices in Correcting Examination Papers," *School Review*, XXXVII (October, 1929), 615–23. F. D. Curtis and W. C. Darling, "Teaching Values of Common Practices in Correcting Examination Papers—A Second Study," *School Review*, XL (September, 1932), 515–525.

both classes. In the ten o'clock class, each examination question was discussed in detail by the class and the instructor. In the eleven o'clock class, each question was scored in the presence of the group, the students merely indicating on their papers whether the item was right or wrong without any discussion of the evidence for the correct answer. At the end of the period, the test papers were collected from both classes and two days later both groups took the same examination for a second time without having received any warning that it was to be given again. The papers were not returned or further discussed. But the same test of 47 new-type items was given a third time as a part of the final examination at the end of the semester, three weeks after the second and about seven weeks after the first administration of the test.

Forty-eight pairs of students from the two classes were matched on the basis of scores on the Burgess reading scale and the Miller Test of Mental Ability. The results of the intelligence and reading tests and the average scores on the three administrations of the examination are presented in Table I.

TABLE I

The Results of Three Administrations of the Same Examination to the Discussion and Checking Groups

| Group | Intelligence | Reading | First (Examination) | Second (Examination) | Third (Examination) |
|---|---|---|---|---|---|
| Discussion | 92 | 14.2 | 35.8 | 41.4 | 42.0 |
| Checking | 92 | 14.9 | 35.2 | 35.7 | 38.7 |

Table I indicates, first, that the scores for the discussion and checking groups are approximately equal on the reading and intelligence tests and on the first administration of the examination. Second, while the process of checking the rightness or wrongness of the replies did not produce a significant gain on the second examination, it apparently offset the process of forgetting, which, according to the typical curve of oblivescence, should have been considerably advanced by the time of the second examination. Third, the discussion group had a decided advantage over the checking group. This advantage is more striking when a count of the individual subjects indicates, on the one hand, that two members of the checking group made the same score on both the first and second examinations, and that of the remainder only half made a higher score on the second examination, while the other half made a lower score on the second examination. On the other hand, a similar count of the discussion group reveals that with only two exceptions every member of the discussion group made a score on the second higher than on the first examination.

The reduced advantage of the discussion over the checking group in the third administration of the examination may be attributed to the general preparation which both groups made for the final examination. This preparation undoubtedly tended to equalize the background of both groups and partially disturbed the differential influence of the experimental factors.

A further analysis of the data summarized in Table I will elaborate the tendencies revealed there. This analysis consists of an item-by-item comparison of the test papers of the first two examinations for the purpose of classifying each question according to one of the four following categories: (1) the questions that were wrong on the first and second tests, (2) those that were right on both tests, (3) those that were wrong on the first and right on the second test, and (4) those that were right on the first and wrong on the second test. The results of this analysis are presented in Table II.

The data of Table II define in greater detail

TABLE II

Comparative Analysis of the Results of the Discussion and Checking Groups in the First and Second Administrations of the Examination

| Group | Wrong-first Wrong-second (Average number of questions) | Wrong-first Right-second (Average number of questions) | Right-first Right-second (Average number of questions) | Right-first Wrong-second (Average number of questions) |
|---|---|---|---|---|
| Discussion | 3.1 | 8.1 | 33.3 | 2.5 |
| Checking | 7.2 | 4.6 | 31.1 | 4.1 |

the nature of the tendencies revealed in the averages of Table I. For example, in the case of the discussion as compared with the checking group fewer questions persist as wrong responses (3.1 *vs.* 7.2); fewer items, if once stated correctly, are subsequently mistaken (2.5 *vs.* 4.1); more items persist as correct and more items, if once marked as wrong, are corrected on the second examination (8.1 *vs.* 4.6).

As a matter of general interpretation the foregoing data of Tables I and II demonstrate that classroom learning involves the acquisition of correct subject-matter but is also accompanied by a certain residue of tenacious error. This error, however, is more readily corrected by discussion than it is by mere identification (checking). However, even checking the rightness and wrongness of a response serves a useful function of consolidating the preparation made by the subjects up to the time of the first examination. Finally, by correcting false impressions, by filling in sporadic gaps of ignorance and by the confirmation of content already known, the discussion of the specific outcomes of an examination provides a propitious occasion for the achievement of significant objectives of instruction.

In conclusion the writer proposes two specific suggestions: First, the conscience of the teaching profession should be lashed into chagrin at the almost universal, evasive and lazy custom of returning examination papers without comment, not to mention the disgracefully common practise of not returning examination papers at all.

Second, final examinations should be conducted at least one if not two or more periods before the conclusion of a course in order to provide an opportunity to discuss the content of the examination. In other words, examinations should never be final—they should be *next-to-final.* Only carefully planned and stimulating discussions in a final effort to integrate the basic outcomes of the course should be final. The major result, then, of this investigation may be summarized in the following statement: If a unit of curricular material is worth the emphasis of an examination, how much more essential for complete mastery is the examination worth the added emphasis of further instruction. The sequence of instructional activity then becomes not Teach-Teach-Test, but *Teach-Test-Teach!*

### SUMMARY STATEMENT OF THE EXPERIMENT

An experiment was conducted in which two equivalent groups of college students took the same mid-term examination under the same circumstances. One month later the papers were returned to both groups and corrected by two different procedures. The members of one class corrected their papers by checking the rightness or wrongness of each question. The members of the other class participated in a discussion dealing with the evidence for the correct response to each question. Two days later the same examination was given again to both groups without warning; and three weeks later it was administered for a third time as a part of the final examination in the course. The checking group experienced no loss. This result was interpreted to mean that the process of checking the rightness or wrongness of each question overcame the effects of forgetting. The discussion group experienced a marked advantage in the second and third examinations. This result is interpreted as emphasizing the teaching function and value of the examination, and as indicating that the sequence of instructional activity should not be Teach-Teach-Test, but Teach-Test-Teach!

HOWARD YALE MCCLUSKY
UNIVERSITY OF MICHIGAN

## NEW BOOKS IN EDUCATION

*Annual Financial and Statistical Report of the Board of Education of the City of New York, 1933.* Pp. 169. Illustrated. The Board.

BARNUM, MADALENE D. *School Plays for All Occasions.* Pp. x + 188. Grosset and Dunlap. $1.00.

Committee on the Grading of Nursing Schools. *Nursing Schools To-day and Tomorrow.* Pp. 268. Illustrated. $2.00. *An Activity Analysis.* Pp. 214. $2.00. Nursing Information Bureau of the American Nurses' Association.

CORY, DAVID. *Little Indian.* Pp. 128. Illustrated. Grosset and Dunlap. $0.50.

HUGON, PAUL D. *The Modern Word-Finder.* Pp. x + 420. Revised edition. Grosset and Dunlap. $1.00.

KATES, JEROME S. *Minute Stories of Famous Explorers.* Illustrated by HERBERT S. KATES. Pp. 155. Grosset and Dunlap. $1.00.

*Physical Defects: The Pathway to Correction.* Pp. xvii + 171. American Child Health Association, New York.

SMITH, MELVILLE and MAX T. KRONE. *Fundamentals of Musicianship.* Book One. Pp. xiv + 197. 209 figures. Witmark. $2.50.

SCHOOL AND SOCIETY

WITH WHICH ARE COMBINED THE EDUCATIONAL REVIEW, ESTABLISHED IN 1891, THE TEACHERS MAGAZINE, ESTABLISHED IN 1878, AND THE SCHOOL JOURNAL, ESTABLISHED IN 1874.

Volume 40 SATURDAY, NOVEMBER 3, 1934 Number 1036

# ADDRESS AT THE INSTALLATION OF THE NINETEENTH PRESIDENT OF THE COLLEGE OF WILLIAM AND MARY[1]

By President FRANKLIN D. ROOSEVELT

*President Bryan:*

I VALUE far beyond the sentiment conveyed by mere acknowledgment in words the honor that you, in behalf of this historic institution, have conferred upon me to-day.

I well know the great tradition that the College of William and Mary has carried through the centuries. You have taught, you have inspired and you have honored the great and devoted men who were responsible in such large part for the shaping of the cause of American liberty.

Dr. Bryan, on this occasion of your inauguration as president of this institution, I congratulate you on the opportunity of service that lies before you.

The first time I visited Williamsburg was more than twenty years ago. I arrived at Jamestown by boat and started to walk to Williamsburg. I was picked up by an old Negro in a horse and buggy and driven over what was then a nearly impassable road from Jamestown to Williamsburg. Then there was no Capitol building, there was no Palace of the Royal Governors, there was no Raleigh Tavern. Modern buildings had crept into this historic place, almost to the extent of crowding out the fine old Colonial structures which were still standing.

What a thrill it has been to me to return to-day and to have the honor of formally opening the reconstructed Duke of Gloucester Street, which rightly can be called the most historic avenue in America; what a joy to come back and see the transformation which has taken place, to see the Capitol, the Governor's Palace, the Raleigh Tavern, born again, to see sixty-one Colonial buildings restored, ninety-four Colonial buildings rebuilt, the magnificent gardens of Colonial days reconstructed—in short, to see how through the renaissance of these physical landmarks the atmosphere of a whole glorious chapter in our history has been recaptured. Something of this spiritual relationship between the past, the present and the future was expressed by Sir Walter Raleigh:

> It is not the least debt that we owe unto history that it hath made us acquainted with our dead ancestors; and out of the depth and darkness of the earth delivered us their memory and fame.

I am happy to say that the Federal Government, inspired by the fine vision and example of Mr. Rockefeller in recreating Williamsburg, has effectively taken up the preservation of other historic shrines nearby. Six miles to the west of us, we have acquired Jamestown Island, and we are now carrying on the necessary archeological and research work to determine what should be done in the preservation of that

[1] Given at Williamsburg, Va., October 20, 1934.

hallowed spot. Fourteen miles to the east of us at Yorktown the National Park Service has acquired many thousand acres of land, and is actively carrying out the restoration of the symbol of the final victory of the war for American independence. When the work at Jamestown, at Williamsburg and at Yorktown is completed we shall have saved for future generations three historic places—the nation's birthplace at Jamestown, the cradle of liberty of Williamsburg and the sealing of our independence at Yorktown.

It was to William and Mary College that Thomas Jefferson came in 1760. Here he studied for two years, remaining five years longer in Williamsburg to pursue the study of law. It was here in Williamsburg that he was admitted to the bar. It was to Williamsburg that he returned, first as a member of the House of Burgesses, then as Governor of Virginia, following Patrick Henry. He lived in the Governor's Palace during his term and later served on the Board of Visitors of William and Mary. It was largely the result of his recommendations that the curriculum of the college was broadened to provide education in law, medicine, modern languages, mathematics and philosophy. No doubt inspired by his reflections on government, human liberty and the necessity of education, Jefferson throughout his life was interested in designing a system of education for his state and for the nation. I like to think of him, not only as a statesman, but as the enlightened father of American education.

It is entirely fitting that a statesman should have been also an educator. As education grows it becomes the partner of government.

When Jefferson wrote his "Notes on Virginia," he discussed the education then prevailing at William and Mary, pointing out the essentially liberal education that this college was giving to its students. He observed that in order to provide a more advanced type of education, the subjects of the six professorships had been changed after the revolution. It is a matter of very great importance to all of us that one of the six was the professorship of law and of what is now called political science. The teaching of law and of the science of government thus established as an academic discipline in this institution was made significant by the intellectual leadership of George Wythe, who was appraised by Jefferson as "one of the greatest men of his age." The study of this subject, because essentially it touches every human problem, becomes one of the greatest means for the broad education of men who enter every walk of life. It can become the touchstone of universal culture.

Law in itself is not enough. Man must build himself more broadly. The purpose of education, shown by these various subjects of instruction indicated by the builders of William and Mary, was not to train specialists, but to educate men broadly. They were attempting to train not merely doctors, lawyers and business men, but broad-gauged men of the world. They were, in short, training men for citizenship in a great republic.

This was in the spirit of the old America, and it is, I believe, in the spirit of the America of to-day. The necessities of our time demand that men avoid being set in grooves, that they avoid the occupational predestination of the older world and that in the face of the change and development in America, they must have a sufficiently broad and comprehensive conception of the world in which they live to meet its changing problems with resourcefulness and practical vision.

There is in the spirit of a liberal education something of the self-confidence and the adaptability that is characteristic of our country. The pioneer does not call his life a failure if he comes to the end of one path. He knows that there are others, and with a sense of direction and a will to persevere, his life can go on with confidence into the uncertainties of the future.

All of us must honor and encourage those young men and young women whose ambitions lead them to seek specialization in science and in scholarship. Our great universities are properly providing adequate facilities for the development of specialists in science and in scholarship. The nation is using their services in every form of human activity. Private business employs them and so does every type of government. Private enterprise and government enterprise will continue to do so.

But at the same time there is a definite place in American life—an important place—for broad, liberal and non-specialized education. Every form of cooperative human endeavor cries out for men and women who, in their thinking processes, will know something of the broader aspects of any given problem. Government is greatly using men and women of this type—people who have the non-specialized point of view and who at the same time have a general and extraordinarily comprehensive knowledge, not of the details, but of the progress and the purposes which underlie the work of the specialists themselves.

The noble list of those who have gone out into life from the halls of William and Mary is in greater part distinguished because these graduates came to know and to understand the needs of their nation as a whole. They thought and acted—not in terms of specialization, not in terms of a locality, but rather in the broad sense of national needs. In the olden days those needs were confined to a narrow seaboard strip. Later the needs gradually extended to the Blue Ridge and across through the mountains to the fair lands of Tennessee and Kentucky. Later still they spread throughout the great Middle West and across the Plains and the Rockies to the Pacific Ocean.

It is in the realization of these needs in their national scope of to-day that the present and future generations of William and Mary can best carry forward the fine traditions of their centuries.

So I would extend my heartiest good wishes to the College of William and Mary, built early in the morning of American life, dedicated to the education of the makers of a great republic, seeking to enrich and broaden the meaning of an education, and seeking, above all things, to recognize that republican institutions are, in the last analysis, the application to human affairs of those broad humane ideals that a liberal education preserves, enriches and expands in our beloved land.

# INAUGURAL ADDRESS OF THE PRESIDENT OF THE COLLGE OF WILLIAM AND MARY[1]

By Dr. JOHN STEWART BRYAN

I COUNT it a fortunate augury that we are gathered on this day, which has already been blessed by associations with this college. For upon a certain October 20, 1632, Sir Christopher Wren, the architect of this building, was born. Seventy-three years later this building was burned for the first time, on October 29, 1705, but a kind fortune in 1872 sent upon that same date Julian Alvin Carroll Chandler, under whose energetic administration this college attained its present fulness.

So, to-day, we are tied by long associations to this date. But even more significant than the day or month is the year. We engrave 1693 on our college seal. Those figures cut in copper turn with every

[1] Given at Williamsburg, Va., October 20, 1934.

breeze above our heads. Every diploma has embossed on it those sacred numerals. But how many of us recall that 1693 was only five years after the great revolution of 1688, whose scope and magnitude permanently changed for the better life in England, and in the Colonies as well? For the effect of that revolution was to recognize the power of the middle classes in England and to enforce their influence; and by it the dictatorial prerogatives, whether of king or protector, were then definitely, and it seemed, forever curbed.

For these reasons, William and Mary, born as it was when the cheers of the Whigs were still echoing in the halls of Parliament, was almost the child of revolution in America.

Is it not strange how these numerals "93" recur? Look at the next century, 1793. The French revolution was then at its heights of fervor and ferocity, and the little mill of Valmy had become the scene of the defeat of the trained soldiers of Austria by the raw recruits of France. A new force had appeared, and none could stay its course or reckon its sweep from the dust and heat of Spain to the icy steppes of Russia. Once more the sleeping spirit of mankind was awake and active. Once more humanity was on the march to a goal that was not descried, but by a road that was paved with death and suffering.

Or, coming to matters within our own memory, let us look back four decades to 1893. Then, as now, a Democrat and a great leader was in the White House. Then, as now, there was unemployment, hunger, misery, the threat of revolution, and the frequency of riots, men's hearts failing them because of fear. That was a scant forty years ago—a mere tick of the clock of time—and it may well be that future historians will condense the world war into a paragraph while they devote pages to analyzing and describing the forces that gave in 1893 sure evidence of the coming of the storm. At that time Cleveland felt the first angry gusts of the whirlwind of economic change which broke in its fury on President Roosevelt in 1933.

Then as now this nation was fortunate in having a Democratic leader who knew that we are not mere helpless pebbles, tossed hither and thither at random by the purposeless waves of a sea without beginning, without meaning and without end. Both presidents knew that we can control those destinies that are alone of supreme significance—the destinies of faith, of courage, of purpose, of imagination, precisely those spiritual forces that President Roosevelt has summoned to his aid in dealing with the social enemies of doubt, despair, fear and blindness that marked our economic tragedy. The President himself has shown how revivifying the spirit can be when informed imagination grapples courageously with the problems of life, whether those problems be despotism in 1776 or depression in 1933.

Through all these changes and chances the College of William and Mary held to its purpose and pursued its undeflected path, beholding, and ofttimes participating in, but always surviving and surmounting revolution. For this college had sure foundations. Three years before the Mayflower landed its famous band at Plymouth Rock, King James I had issued his letter to the bishops of England for the purpose of collecting funds for a college in Virginia, and on November 18, 1618, the London Company gave orders for the establishment at Henrico of a university of which this Indian college should be a branch, and endowed it with 10,000 acres of land.

At its first session the same House of Burgesses that blazed the way for self-government on this continent petitioned the London Company to send "when they shall think it most convenient, workmen of all sorts, for the erection of this university and college."

It is common knowledge how the Indian massacre of 1622 delayed for nearly two generations the completion of this great idea. Yet, in 1624, the Academia Virginiensis et Oxoniensis was chartered by Edward Palmer, and shortly after, free schools were established in Elizabeth City and in Isle of Wight counties. When finally, in 1693, Their Gracious Majesties, William and Mary, conferred the first Royal Charter in America on this college, education was no untried experiment to the people of the York Peninsula.

There was nothing narrow about the plans that animated the founders of this college, and there was nothing niggardly about its material setting. It was to be "a place of universal study, or a perpetual college of divinity, philosophy, languages and other high arts and sciences."

It was to be established near the Middle Plantation, though by charter it could be moved by reason of its supposed "unwholesomeness." From its inception this college was supported and protected by the Colony of Virginia and by the public at large. In addition to the vast body of land given it by the King and Queen, there were levied for the benefit of the college certain duties on skins and furs, and one penny on all tobacco exported from Virginia and Maryland, except that which went to the British Colonies. This levy doubtless assuaged somewhat the feelings of Commissary Blair, first president of the college, for the rebuff he had received from Mr. Attorney-General Seymour. That gentleman, when pressed to hasten the charter on the ground that the people of the colony had souls to be saved as well as in England, replied: "Souls! damn your souls; raise tobacco!"

Now that tobacco was being raised and taxes were being levied, the government of William and Mary was as much interested in tobacco farmers in 1693 as tobacco farmers are interested in government in 1934.

In 1759 a tax on peddlers—the then protagonists of bootleggers—was levied, and in the very charter of the college itself the office of surveyor-general had been conferred upon the institution, "a union of the College with the principal interests of the Colony," says Herbert B. Adams, "which developed the wisest statesman this country has ever known—George Washington."

Little did William and Mary think, in 1748, that the young surveyor would come back at the end of his unequalled career to be her first chancellor in 1788. Senator Hoar has said: "She gave to Washington her first commission in his youth; he gave to her his last public service in his age."

It is the chief distinction of this college that not only did it commission George Washington as surveyor to set the boundaries of Virginia's dominions, but it also, in 1782, with the honorary degree of doctor of laws, set the stamp of philosophic approval upon Thomas Jefferson, as he began to enlarge the boundaries of Virginia's thought.

In 1776 the income of William and Mary was 4,000 pounds a year, and at that time it was the richest college in America. But wealth was no insurance against the forces of war and revolution, which swept up and down the Peninsula, overthrew the power of the crown in England and created a new form of government in America.

During those battles both Washington and Cornwallis occupied these buildings as headquarters. The president's house was laid in ashes by a fire accidentally started by the French troops who were quartered there, and that building was restored from the privy purse of Louis XVI, who little dreamed how soon thousands of Virginians would forget his generosity in their enthusiasm for his executioners.

Now what account can William and Mary, which has been the recipient of royal, colonial, state and private bounty and benefactions, give of its stewardship?

What returns has mankind received for the outlay of labor, love and wealth that is represented in the founding and support of this college?

We may say that William and Mary has held steadfastly to the idea which the Reverend James Horrocks set forth in 1700, and that this ideal is still controlling it: "The flourishing state of a college," said he, "is not to be estimated by the number of wild and uncultivated minds which may be brought together, but purely by the number of competent scholars and well-behaved gentlemen which are sent by any seminary of learning into the larger society, where they vie to display improved talents for their own benefit and the public emolument."

Who are some of the "competent scholars and well-behaved gentlemen" that William and Mary has sent into the world at large? Amidst so great a concourse of fame, how can the roll be called without omitting some that should be mentioned, unless all the alumni of William and Mary are remembered? Yet who can say how far Thomas Jefferson would have been what he was without his teachers, George Wythe and William Small, at William and Mary?

Even if Jefferson and his Declaration of Independence were all that William and Mary had to offer, this college would stand as one of the great lighthouses of humanity. It took only one St. Francis to immortalize Assisi; it required only one Joan of Arc to make the name of Domremy imperishable. How great, then, must be the glory of a college which can claim Richard Bland, who entered in 1725 and in 1766 announced that Virginia was not a part of the Kingdom of England, except through the nexus of the Crown; Dabney Carr, who entered in 1762 and in 1773 first grasped the idea of colonial federation; Peyton Randolph, who entered in 1735 and in 1774 was first president of the Continental Congress; John Tyler, Sr., who entered in 1765 and carried the proposition for the convention at Annapolis in 1786; Edmund Randolph, who entered in 1766 and in 1787 opened the proceedings at Philadelphia by submitting the "Virginia Plan." In Washington's first cabinet of four men, three had college training and two of those three came from William and Mary. Only a few years after that cabinet had completed its service, another son of William and Mary took oath, as chief justice—John Marshall, the moulder of its plastic form into the vital and self-renewing structure of our constitution.

And yet, after this "long scroll of fame" there are still to be mentioned James Monroe, who established the freedom of the new hemisphere from the interference of the old; President John Tyler, who annexed Texas, and Winfield Scott, the most distinguished commander of the United States Army down to 1861. Of congressmen, senators, governors, speakers of the House of Representatives; of members of the Supreme Court, of diplomatists, judges, chancellors of Virginia, and of the wisest leadership of this state, time is not here to tell.

But it may be urged that it was the fierce heat of the Revolution that evoked the powers of these men, just as an electric current will make the dullest metal throw out a luminous spectrum. To such we would answer: it is true that there are giants on this list. But there are giant potentialities in every man and every age that are as yet unreleased. It was the glory of the sponsors and guides of William and Mary that they have known how to set free those powers.

Look at the evidences of these gifts of liberty.

This college was able to equip her students with the perspective of history and to enlighten them with the experience of mankind. Holding fast to the conquered continents of knowledge, William and Mary was not afraid of the new frontiers.

Adam Smith's "Law of Nations" was a text-book in this college—as the very volumes in our library attest—only eight years after the first edition came from a press to demolish the old mercantilist economy. St. George Tucker's study of the American constitution, probably the first book of its kind, was first studied here.

Can we not read to-day in this recountal of the yesterdays of William and Mary? Is not the analogy between the first and third revolutions apparent? And may we not perhaps, find new purpose for the college and new direction for the nation, if, in some such words as these, we formulate the political creed of those great sons of William and Mary?

They sought something more than learning, and their faces were turned to the past only for examples.

It was in the present they acted, and it was for the future they built.

They were not troubled by any doubts of their own ability to meet and deal with time and chance.

No theory of life which reduced man to a physico-chemical reaction shook their faith or crippled their power.

No doctrine of the control of the conscious choice by the unconscious chooser had been put forward, and to the men who wrought out the salvation of this continent there was no escape from duty by taking flight along the easy path of materialistic determination.

To their mind, the way to destroy evil was by resistance, not by acquiescence.

They knew nothing and cared nothing for the philosophy of surrender; they had the supreme gifts of courage and of vision.

With a certainty that far transcends the conclusions of reason, they both perceived and knew that they were fighting the battles of freedom everywhere.

No specious argument of expediency deflected them from their course; no traitor's thought within, no trampling troops without, could undermine their convictions or shake their fortitude.

With that perfect union of will and faith and action that marks the highest reaches ever attained by self-governed man, all their being flowed in a smooth concurrence to the one great purpose of human liberty.

They believed in themselves; they set up ideals. To these ideals they pressed by conference, by speeches, by writing and by war.

They broke the bands of philosophic doubt and came to grips with reality; they cast off the nightmare of dreadful impotence, and, struggling against all throttling fears, they awoke to find themselves masters of a new world. They made for mankind, not a theory, but a discovery.

Here, if ever, we may say, the will of man wrought out an intended destiny.

That the men who achieved this miracle were the sons of William and Mary is for us inspiring and gratifying. But the future can not be controlled by backward-looking men, not even if their glances rest on these ancient and creative halls. The vital principle of those great sons of William and Mary must be made operative and applicable to-day.

That principle, my friends, is still active and is ready and waiting for our use and service. For the fundamental creed of William and Mary is that of the scholar in politics. The need is self-evident and imperative. The ancient petitions of the Litany against plague, pestilence and famine have been practically granted for our land, but deep disturbances of our social order still remain unsolved. For us, as for the young King Solomon, rises the insistent supplication, "Give thy servant a right judgment in all things, O Lord."

The College of William and Mary had that prayer answered in the revolutionary era of the eighteenth century, and again, as we Southerners believe, in the revolution of 1861. She must make herself worthy now of like direction in the third American revolution.

As the only college in the thirty-six counties of Tidewater Virginia, William and Mary has geographical obligations she will faithfully discharge. Whatever the demands that a proper study will impose upon her in keeping the teaching force of the public school system adequate for most efficient service, she will strive to meet them. The qualified children of her alumni will not knock in vain at her doors for a course in the liberal arts if funds can be had for their instruction. But William and Mary must not consider that her duties end here. She must endeavor, as in the earlier days, so to inspire her students that whatever their chosen sphere of activity, they will restore informed good citizenship to its proper place as the chief avocation of gentlemen.

If, in another two centuries and a half of life, there shall be among her graduates a second Jefferson, another Marshall, or a spiritual successor to Wythe, then those of us who now people her halls shall not have lived in vain.

It does not require such a tragic and heroic setting as the death of Edith Cavell to make us know that mere "patriotism is not enough." True, the great servant of the state must be a patriot. He must be one of whom it can be said: "But that which gave a peculiar grace and glory to all that he did was that he did it for pure love of God and country."

But even so, "patriotism is not enough." And it is to the imperishable glory of William and Mary that her sons to patriotism added scholarship.

I know as well as you that supreme political genius, like the divine gift of prophecy, is not to be brought forth by teaching alone, no matter who the teacher, for the workaday world is not carried along by rare bursts of inspiration; it is by the slow and hard-won experience of mankind in science and government that civilization progresses. It is such knowledge that this college, with its face towards wider wisdom, seeks to give.

Nor is the pursuit of knowledge always a safe and sheltered vocation. Even to-day we have not yet made an end of the danger of discovery or robbed newness of its hazards. As we face the world's future, made dark by the complex forces of narrow nationalism, crushing debt, vast unemployment, imperfect distribution, and, above all, by the universal incertitude that flows from the submergence of old landmarks, we, too, must deal with problems that hold for us as much of menace in their economics as slavery held for our grandfathers in its dramatic emotionalism.

It is the essence of civilization that men learn by experience, and it is the glory and the sustaining purpose of schools of learning that such experience can be vicariously acquired and transmitted.

To evoke these aids, to marshal and equip them, and to prepare the field for their warfare is the essential and incomparable task of the colleges. That task for nearly two and a half centuries William and Mary has sought to discharge.

With all my heart I believe that the blood and background that transfused this nation in 1776 are still present and potent here, and need only the liberating touch of leadership to be set free once more for the nation's welfare.

There is no reward that the nation can give to any man comparable to the inner satisfaction which comes to one who knows the enlarging sense of enduring achievement, and who in contemplating his use of the fleeting moments of this transitory life is able to say:

I sought no reward but the opportunity of service.

I made knowledge the handmaiden of love of my country.

I have fought a good fight and I have kept the faith.

The seed that was sown at Jamestown in 1607—

> Has risen and cleft the soil
> And grown a mass of spanless bulk,
> And lays on every side a thousand arms
> And rushes to the sun.

Animated by that ancestral force, itself transformed by the need of its age and time, William and Mary will press on in sure confidence of the great charter and promise given by Bishop Fuller: "Each of God's children is immortal while their Father hath anything left for them to do on earth."

# EDUCATIONAL EVENTS

## THE PREPARATION OF TEACHERS FOR RURAL SCHOOLS IN HAITI

THE International Bureau of Education has received from the "Service national de la production agricole et de l'enseignement rural de la République d'Haiti" the curriculum of the normal section of the School of Practical Agriculture, published at Port-au-Prince in 1934, from which the following extracts are taken:

The aim of the normal section of the Practical School of Agriculture is to prepare masters capable of teaching in the kind of schools that endeavor to give a thorough education to the rural masses in Haiti. The period of study lasts for two years, but may later be lengthened to three years.

The course in Rural Construction is intended to enable students to undertake or supervise the building of outhouses and plain dwelling-houses made of the materials generally to be found in the rural sections of the country. It also deals with matters relating to reservoirs and wells and with those pertaining to the enclosing of property. The course in topography includes problems of irrigation and drainage and gives some idea of how to level the ground.

In the section of education the students have at their disposal, besides their multigraphed syllabuses, bulletins, reviews, French and English books on various branches and problems of education. A practising school on the farm of Damien, placed under the direction of a competent specialist, gives opportunities to observe teaching methods and to do practical work during the second year.

The section of manual training has the use of a large work shop containing all the tools necessary for teaching carpentry, iron and tin work, weaving and basket work. Spinning wheels and carding tools permit of the use of home-grown cotton for the weaving exercises. A permanent exhibition of work done in the farm-schools is at the disposal of the students.

The following is the detailed curriculum of a few of the courses:

*Rural Education.* The cardinal points of education. The development of agriculture in Haiti. The system of property; the present conditions of agriculture in Haiti. The conditions of life in the rural districts. The rural school.

*Education: Special Methods.* Special methods for the teaching of reading, arithmetic, history, geography and hygiene. Special method for planning the school garden and for the teaching of agriculture. Place of the school garden in our system of education. Arrangement of the playground. Method of teaching to be used in the garden. Agriculture taught by projects.

*Management of the Schoolroom.* The problem of schoolroom management. Standardizing the school routine. Regularity of attendance. Habits of hygiene. Order and discipline. Punishments. The laws of attention. Technique of school teaching. Relations between the teacher and his superiors. The ethics of the teaching career.

*Principles of Education.* Education as a necessity of life. Continuity of life obtained through transmission of values. Education as a social function. The influence of the social environment. The school considered as social environment. The school considered as special environment. Education as guidance. Methods of social guidance. Imitation and social psychology. Education as a development. Conditions of development. Formal discipline and development. Education as formation and reconstruction. Education from the national and the social points of views. The aims of education.

*Special Activities.* Extra-curricular activities. Activities aiming at developing the sense of responsibility in the students, and the habit of doing little daily jobs of importance for the home and the school. Visit to the farm-school of Damien and investigation of the community life of which Damien is the center. Recreational activities in the community. Social work.

## THE SCHOOL FOR ADULT JEWISH EDUCATION

A SCHOOL for Adult Jewish Education is being established this fall by the Menorah Graduate Society of New York, with the cooperation of a group of scholars. The school will be under the direction of Leo W. Schwarz and Rabbi Jacob J. Weinstein. For the present, the headquarters will be at 35 E. 62nd St., New York City. Classes will begin on Tuesday, November 13.

According to Mr. Schwarz, it is the purpose of the school to stimulate and instruct men and women who wish to approach the questions of modern Jewish life on the basis of some critical knowledge of background and precedents, rather than through merely emotional propaganda; it aims to connect the modern Jew with his past, in terms of his present, living day-today interests.

The faculty for 1934–1935 consists of the following:

Elsie Glück, Ph.D., educational director of the New York Women's Trade Union League.

Oscar I. Janowsky, Ph.D., assistant professor of history in the College of the City of New York.

Otto Klineberg, M.D., Ph.D., instructor in psychology at Columbia University.

Joshua Kunitz, Ph.D., formerly instructor in Slavonic languages at the College of the City of New York.

Israel Knox, Ph.D., lecturer in Yiddish literature at the Sholom Aleichem High School.

Koppel S. Pinson, Ph.D., lecturer in the New School for Social Research; an editor of the "Encyclopedia of the Social Sciences."

Shalom Spiegel, Ph.D., professor of Hebrew literature at the Jewish Institute of Religion.

Nathan Reich, M.A., lecturer at Hunter College and Brooklyn College; an editor of the "Encyclopedia of the Social Sciences."

Leo W. Schwarz, director of the New School for Jewish Education of Westchester.

John J. Tepfer, M.A., M.H.L.; Rabbi, fellow in history at the Jewish Institute of Religion.

Jacob J. Weinstein, Rabbi, of the Bureau for Education in Human Relations.

During the first semester, which will begin on November 11, five courses of eight lectures each will be given. The school will be officially opened on Sunday, November 11, when Professor Janowsky will deliver the first lecture of his series on the "Basic Factors in Modern Jewish History." This lecture is to be open to the public.

The other courses to be given are: "Main Currents of Jewish Thought in Modern Times," by Dr. Koppel S. Pinson; "The Jewish Factor in Civilization," by Rabbi John J. Tepfer; "An Introduction to Yiddish Literature," by Dr. Israel Knox, and "A Survey of Current Jewish Events and Problems," by Rabbi Jacob J. Weinstein.

## EXTRA SESSION OF THE HARVARD GRADUATE SCHOOL OF BUSINESS ADMINISTRATION

THE Harvard Graduate School of Business Administration has announced that an extra session designed both for recent college graduates and for men with some business experience will begin on January 28. It will be open to students with degrees from accredited colleges. In addition, well-recommended men who do not hold college degrees, but who have had adequate business experience, will be admitted under the regular provisions governing special students.

Students will have the same instruction under the same faculty as those in the regular first-year class and will be entitled to full academic credit. The session will continue until August 14, thus enabling the students to enter the regular second-year class in September, 1935. By the elimination of vacations, the normal two-year course is consequently compressed into a period of only one year and four months.

The shorter period of time of the session permits a reduction of about 25 per cent. in room and board expense, thus making an approximate cost of $1,000 for room, board, tuition and books for the seven months from January to August. A limited amount of financial assistance will be available to those men who are unable to defray all expenses. This assistance includes various jobs about the school, in the dining halls and on the grounds, as well as grants from the School Loan Fund which is available to properly qualified students.

Decision to hold the extra session in January will make available an opportunity to begin training for business openings without waiting until September. That such openings are available is evidenced by the placement of the 1934 graduating class, over 90 per cent. of whom had been placed by the first of October, and in the two previous years over 85 per cent. of the graduating class had been placed by this date. The jobs which these men secured were distributed throughout the country, and represented affiliations with many different types of business enterprise. In addition, twenty men entered various governmental bureaus and agencies.

## THE JUNIOR SCIENCE WORKSHOP COURSES OF THE AMERICAN INSTITUTE

OVER four hundred advanced science students from the high schools of New York City have been invited to attend two workshop courses in chemistry and biology arranged at the Washington Square College of New York University for the Junior Science Clubs of the American Institute.

L. W. Hutchins, director of the institute, states that the courses will be conducted like college courses, but that they will be perfectly intelligible to secondary school students having a familiarity with chemistry and biology. These courses are in addition to the courses given during the last two years at the museums of the city for the 8,000 members of the Junior Science Clubs. These are held at the New York Museum of Science and Industry, the American Museum of Natural History, the New York Botanical Garden, the New York Zoological Park and the Brooklyn Children's Museum. They have as their basic purpose to give a knowledge of facts and techniques which could not possibly be acquired in the already overcrowded school schedule.

Included in the new courses will be seven lecture demonstrations in biology and nine in chemistry. Each lecture demonstration will be followed by an informal discussion. Special attention will be given to practical applications of the material presented.

The course in biology, under the direction of Associate Professor Harry A. Charipper, chairman of the Department of Biology at the Washington Square College, will be given in the college laboratories on Saturday afternoons, beginning on November 10, as follows:

*Micrurgy.* Associate Professor Ruth B. Howland, assisted by Professor Robert Chambers and Assistant Professor Douglas A. Marsland.
*Cytology.* Professor Alfred F. Huettner.
*Biochemistry and Microbiology.* Associate Professor Kenneth C. Blanchard.
*Endocrinology.* Assistant Professor Hans O. Haterius.
*Physiology.* Assistant Professor George Saslow.
*Genetics.* Assistant Professor Morris H. Harnly.
*Biophysics.* Dr. Alexander Sandow.

Dr. H. M. Partridge, assistant professor of chemistry at the college, will supervise the course in chemistry, in which four hundred students will be enrolled. This course will meet on Tuesday afternoons after school, in the New York University Auditorium, beginning on November 13, according to the following schedule:

*The History of Chemistry.* Professor W. C. MacTavish.
*Microchemical Analysis.* Drs. J. B. Niederl and A. B. Pichler.
*Colloids.* Dr. Henri Mouquin.
*Physical Chemical Measurements.* Dr. R. H. Muller.
*X-Rays.* Dr. William F. Ehret.
*Electrochemistry.* Dr. H. M. Partridge.
*Spectroscopy.* Dr. William West.
*Organic Chemistry.* Dr. J. J. Ritter.
*Toxicology.* Dr. Alexander O. Gettler.

## HEALTH SERVICE IN THE NEW YORK CITY SCHOOLS

As an outgrowth of an experimental project started in 1926 in the West Side Continuation School, a cooperative program of health service, one of three objects of the study, is materializing into a city-wide program for all junior high and elementary school pupils.

Richard Tomkins, correspondent of *The New York Times,* reports that plans for the health program, which will be carried on jointly by the Board of Education and the Department of Health, are nearing completion and will be announced within a few weeks. It is understood that corrective measures rather than mere detection of defects will be emphasized.

A new division has been created in the Department of Health, under Dr. Elwood S. Morton, to deal with the whole problem of personal health among school children, and Charles Degen has been designated as health officer to represent the schools.

Dr. Morton and Mr. Degen were associated in the West Side Continuation School experiment, and it is understood that the technique developed there will form the basis of the program now to be extended throughout the city schools. The program will be carried on under the guidance of a group of specialists announced last spring.

The program will be guided also by the report of a survey of health conditions in the public schools, which was financed by the Metropolitan Life Insurance Company, working in cooperation with the American Child Health Association, the Board of Education and the Department of Health.

Modifications will be made in the technique followed in the earlier demonstration, to apply the health measures to lower age groups. The value of the methods applied in the continuation school, however, is proved by the fact that within six months after the first examination the proportion of defects was reduced 47.7 per cent. in the case of boys and 43 per cent. in the case of girls.

The 1926 experiment was started by the Public Education Association looking toward an improvement in vocational guidance and training, better life and work adjustments of school children, the supervision of personal health, home and occupational environment and toward the practical teaching of rational habits.

The social adjustment phase of the work was reported along with the health work in 1929, but little has been done toward extending the social adjustment plan because of school economies.

The third phase of the experiment was to be an effort to discover through tests the mental capacities, aptitudes and skills of the pupils and to give education not only fitted to them but also to give advice and guidance in regard to the work they could undertake.

Funds for this part of the experiment were not available when the depression set in. Printing tests, tabulating results and other work in connection with the experiment in psychological testing would have cost from $10,000 to $15,000 to get started.

## REVISION OF THE CURRICULUM OF VASSAR COLLEGE

A PROPOSAL to complete the revision of the curriculum of Vassar College has been placed before a faculty committee by Dr. Henry Noble MacCracken, president of the college. The freshman curriculum was changed this year and the extension of a more liberal study plan will be effected to coincide with these initial modifications.

Three purposes are involved: Greater independence of work, more time for the faculty to devote to research and study, and to the obtaining of a broad general foundation for further specialization. The new curriculum will probably be adopted in the spring.

In a preface to his proposal for revision, Dr. MacCracken writes:

In view of the rapid changes now taking place in American society as a whole, and in view of the numerous and serious efforts in educational circles to reconstruct both elementary and college education throughout the United States, it seems to the faculty especially important at this time to undertake a revision of the Vassar curriculum with the threefold object of gaining thoroughness and independence in the work of students, of securing to the faculty more continuous time for study and research, and of securing a broad, general foundation for further specialization.

Essential features of modification include:

As a minimum requirement for the A.B. degree, sixteen one-year courses, or their equivalent, four in each year.

One course in the senior year shall consist of guided preparation for an examination in the major subject, to be taken after the Spring vacation.

Credit for work in the applied art courses.

Guidance in the major field during sophomore and junior years by the appointment of designated officers. Their function shall be to promote successful coordination as the work progresses, to advise on courses and on the work to be taken in vacations.

Honors would be given as at present for work of high quality sustained through the general course. Special honors are suggested for excellence in the major field examination and in work in advanced courses in the major field, as may be recommended by the department concerned.

Courses designated as introductory and other courses with laboratory or field work may have three or more scheduled periods a week. Courses will be regarded as full courses when there are two class periods a week, and a third class period at the option of the instructor.

## THE SOCIAL FRONTIER

The first issue of *The Social Frontier,* "a journal of educational criticism and reconstruction," was published in October. Dr. George S. Counts is the editor, and Mordecai Grossman and Norman Woelfel are associate editors. The leading articles in this issue are:

''Can Education Share in Social Reconstruction,'' John Dewey; ''Property and Democracy,'' Charles A. Beard; ''A Sociologist Views the New Deal,'' Henry P. Fairchild; ''The Importance of a Point of View,'' Sidney Hook, and ''Education *Is* the Social Frontier,'' Goodwin Watson.

Dr. William H. Kilpatrick, chairman of the board of directors, in an introduction entitled "Launching the New Frontier," says:

With this October issue, *The Social Frontier,* ''a journal of educational criticism and reconstruction,'' becomes a reality. Its founding is definitely related to the new spirit of creative social inquiry which has been apparent among American educators and teachers during the past three or four years. If the hopes of its founders are to be realized, this new journal must become the expressive medium of those members of the teaching profession who believe that education has an important, even strategic, rôle to play in the reconstruction of American society. Those who constitute the present Board of Directors of *The Social Frontier* have made the initial effort of sponsorship. Themselves emanating from all parts of the United States but with professional activities centered now in New York City, they know only too well the dangers of provinciality and lack of truly national professional representation on the board as now constituted. It is accordingly their intention to serve merely as a nucleus in the enterprise. As early as practicable during the academic year now dawning, earnest efforts will be made to bring into the membership of the board men and women representative of education and the related professional and cultural fields from other sections of the country. It is the further purpose of the present organization to build up a nationally representative board of contributing editors with the aim of making *The Social Frontier* a prime medium for the development of a constructive social consciousness among educational workers.

Members of the Board of Directors are:

William H. Kilpatrick, *chairman,* Edmund de S. Brunner, John L. Childs, Harold F. Clark, Donald P. Cottrell, George S. Counts, John Dewey, Harrison S. Elliott, Mordecai Grossman, Paul R. Hanna, Heber Harper, Sidney Hook, H. Gordon Hullfish, Alvin Johnson, F. Ernest Johnson, *secretary-treasurer,* E. C. Lindeman, Lois H. Meek, Clyde R. Miller, Jesse H. Newlon, *chairman of the executive committee,* Harry A. Overstreet, Robert B. Raup, Rollo Reynolds, Harold Rugg, Robert K. Speer, V. T. Thayer, Goodwin Watson, Norman Woelfel.

## THE RESIGNATION OF DR. MOTON AS PRESIDENT OF THE TUSKEGEE INSTITUTE

Dr. Robert R. Moton, president of the Tuskegee Institute, Alabama, has resigned after nineteen years as head of the college founded by Booker T. Washington, whom Dr. Moton succeeded.

The announcement of Dr. Moton's resignation, which was submitted at the annual meeting of the board of trustees of the institute, was made public on October 28 by William Jay Schieffelin, chairman of the board. Dr. Moton, who is sixty-eight years old, will retire next May at the close of the current academic year. His retirement will mark the completion of forty-five years of service in educational work, twenty-five of which were spent at Hampton Institute and nearly twenty at Tuskegee. He is expected to serve on the board of trustees of Tuskegee Institute.

In an interview, Dr. Moton said:

I have already passed more than two years beyond the official limit for retirement set by the board for all workers at the institute. I am no longer a young man and am convinced that the best interests of Tuskegee will be served by my retirement. I do not mean to divorce myself entirely from the interests to which I have given practically my whole life, but I believe that I can better serve Tuskegee and the cause for which it stands by spending my remaining years in an atmosphere removed from the pressure of official responsibility and giving myself to the accomplishment of a few cherished objectives which I hope to make my final contribution to the cause which is dear to us all.

In a statement issued by Mr. Schieffelin, referring to the resignation, he said:

The board took no action on the matter at this meeting beyond the unanimous expression of reluctance to concur in his decision, but the insistence of Dr. Moton and a just appreciation of his long years of effective and devoted public service, not only in the cause of education, but in many other fields affecting the progress and welfare of our country, impel us to give his announcement the most earnest consideration.

Whatever its final action, the board will count upon Dr. Moton's continued identification with the interests of Tuskegee Institute and the advancement of the Negro race in general in whatever ways shall be congenial to him and prolong his usefulness to his people and our country.

# EDUCATIONAL NOTES AND NEWS

THE installation of Porter Hartwell Adams as sixteenth president of Norwich University, Northfield, Vt., took place on October 22. Mr. Adams, who has for many years been engaged in the promotion of aviation, assumed the presidency in December, 1933. The exercises were opened by President Paul D. Moody, of Middlebury College. Dr. Vannevar Bush, vice-president and dean of the Massachusetts Institute of Technology, delivered greetings from sister colleges. Greetings were also extended from the faculty, alumni, undergraduates, from the War Department and the Navy Bureau of Aeronautics, after which President Adams delivered his inaugural address. Governor Stanley C. Wilson, vice-president of the university, presided.

DR. HENRY SMITH PRITCHETT, president emeritus of the Carnegie Foundation for the Advancement of Teaching, has been awarded the honorary degree of doctor of laws by the University of Missouri. At the special convocation ceremony before the conferring of the honorary degree, Dr. Pritchett spoke to the student body on "The Relation of Equality to Freedom." The citation by Dean Frederick A. Middlebush, acting president of the university, was as follows: "Dr. Henry Smith Pritchett, native Missourian; distinguished astronomer and professor of astronomy; director of the astronomical observatory of Washington University for fourteen years; superintendent of the U. S. Coast and Geodetic Survey; for six years president of the Massachusetts Institute of Technology; long president of the Carnegie Foundation for the Advancement of Teaching; chevalier of the Legion of Honor of France; honored by degrees from many American institutions of learning; now welcomed into the notable assemblage of our own university's adopted sons. By virtue of the authority invested in me by the Board of Curators, I hereby confer upon you the honorary degree of doctor of laws with all the honors and privileges thereunto appertaining. In token thereof, I now present you with this diploma and invest you with this insignia of the degree."

THE annual Nobel prize in physiology and medicine, of the value of approximately $40,000, has been awarded in recognition of research work which led to the prevention of pernicious anemia. The prize is shared by Dr. George Richards Minot, director of the Thorndike Memorial Laboratory of the Boston City Hospital and professor of medicine at the Harvard Medical School; Dr. William P. Murphy, of the Peter Bent Brigham Hospital and the Harvard Medical School, and Dr. George H. Whipple, professor of pathology and dean of the School of Medicine and Dentistry of the University of Rochester.

DR. ALLAN NEVINS, professor of American history at Columbia University, who won the Pulitzer prize in 1933 for his "Letters of Grover Cleveland," has been appointed to the Watson Chair of American history, literature and institutions at the University of London. He will deliver six lectures at the university during November and December on "The United States in the World Crisis, 1929–1934."

DR. HARRY WOODBURN CHASE, chancellor of New York University, was the guest on October 26 at a dinner of the New York University Doctors of Philosophy Club. Dr. Chase was the guest speaker. Dr. Frederick B. Robinson, president of the College of the City of New York, an alumnus of New York University and president of the club, presented an outline of the plans of the group for the coming year.

Lafayette College conferred the honorary degree of doctor of laws upon Louis Wiley, business manager of *The New York Times,* at the Founders' Day exercises on October 26. Mr. Wiley, in the principal address, made a plea for intelligent newspaper reading and intelligent appraisal of the news.

We note with regret the announcement that Dr. Elmer Ellsworth Brown, chancellor-emeritus of New York University, is seriously ill.

Dr. Lauder William Jones, who for the past five years has been associate director of the Natural Science Division for Europe of the Rockefeller Foundation, is resuming his research and teaching as professor of chemistry at Princeton University.

Professor A. Mendelssohn-Bartholdy has been elected to a senior research fellowship at the University of Oxford. Dr. Mendelssohn-Bartholdy was until lately professor of international law and director of the Institut für Auswartige Politik in the University of Hamburg.

Professor J. C. Jensen has been appointed dean of men at Nebraska Wesleyan University, to succeed Mr. C. Horton Talley. Mr. Jensen, who is professor of physics, has been on the university staff for twenty-six years.

Dr. W. J. Trjitzinsky, of Northwestern University, has become an assistant professor of mathematics at the University of Illinois.

Leonid Kreutzer, formerly professor of piano at the State Academy of Music in Berlin, has been appointed visiting lecturer in music at the New Jersey College for Women.

Dr. Robert W. Karpinski, of the Flint Junior College, Mich., has become a member of the faculty of Science of the Indiana State Teachers College at Terre Haute.

Dr. James Brock has been made chairman of the department of physical science at the Nebraska State Teachers College, Wayne. He succeeds the late Professor I. H. Britell.

Promotions at Wayne University, a unit recently organized by the Detroit Board of Education to include the several colleges under its control, of which Dr. Charles Spain is executive vice-president, include the following: Dr. Charles W. Creaser has been made full professor of zoology; Dr. Floyd A. Stilgenbauer, associate professor of geography; Dr. Harold B. Cutter, associate professor of chemistry; Arthur J. Campbell, Dr. William V. Sessions and Dr. G. Ray Sherwood, assistant professors of chemistry, and Dr. W. C. F. Krueger, assistant professor of psychology.

Members of the faculty of the Indiana State Teachers College, Terre Haute, who were retired at the close of the school year 1933–34 because of the recent action of the college board setting the retirement age at sixty-six years were Professor W. T. Turman, of the art department; Professor J. B. Wisely, of the English department, and Professor Edwin M. Bruce, of the science department. Professor Turman and Professor Wisely had been members of the college faculty for forty years. Professor A. C. Payne, of the department of education, was also retired from active teaching, but is now director of the FERA work being done at the college.

Charles W. Miller has been appointed director of Wrangell Institute, Alaska, a secondary school for natives, under the Office of Indian Affairs of the U. S. Department of the Interior.

Dr. Ruth M. Hubbard, for five years psychologist in the Child Guidance Clinic of the Strong Memorial Hospital, was appointed recently psychologist in the Kalamazoo State Hospital in Michigan.

Professor Robert Murchie, of the University of Minnesota, has been appointed by Governor Olson as director of rural rehabilitation for the State of Minnesota. Mr. Murchie will have charge of all phases of this program, especially in relation to the rehabilitation of the drought areas and to relief and movement of population.

Dr. John W. Studebaker discussed his policies as United States Commissioner of Education at a luncheon of the League for Political Education in the Hotel Astor, New York City, on October 25. The luncheon marked the opening of the League's fortieth season in adult education in New York.

DR. E. E. OBERHOLTZER, superintendent of schools in Houston, Texas, and president of the Department of Superintendence of the National Education Association, will be among the speakers at the convention of the New Jersey State Teachers Association to be held in Atlantic City from November 9 to 12.

FRANCES PERKINS, Secretary of Labor, and an alumnus of Mount Holyoke College, will speak at the Founder's Day exercises to be held on November 8, celebrating the ninety-seventh anniversary of the founding of the college in 1837. The subject of her address will be "Social Security in the Twentieth Century."

DR. WILLIS A. SUTTON, superintendent of the Atlanta, Ga., city schools, and Dr. Frank Porter Graham, president of the Greater University of North Carolina, were the guest-speakers at the recent annual convention of the western branch of the North Carolina Education Association at Asheville, N. C.

DR. ROBERT M. HUTCHINS, president of the University of Chicago, was the principal speaker at the annual meeting of the New York State Teachers Association.

DR. BERNARD FAY, professor of American civilization at the Collège de France, will deliver the second annual Alexander Van Rensselaer Lecture at the Drexel Institute on the evening of November 13. His subject will be "Literature and the Modern World."

DR. ARCH TURNER ALLEN, state superintendent of public instruction in North Carolina since 1923, died on October 20 at the age of fifty-nine years.

S. HOWARD CHACE, superintendent of the Beverly, Mass., schools for twenty-one years, died on October 24 at the age of sixty-three years. He had been previously superintendent of the schools of Ayer and Wilmington.

DR. SILAS EBER PRICE, president of Ottawa University from 1906 to 1924, died on October 27 at the age of seventy-four years.

DR. C. WILSON SMITH, professor of education at Dalhousie University, died suddenly on October 28 at the age of forty-seven years.

PROFESSOR ARTHUR DE PIERPONT, for thirty-two years instructor and professor of modern languages and literature at the Rensselaer Polytechnic Institute, died on October 20 in Aye, Belgium. Professor de Pierpont was decorated twice by Belgium in recognition of his contributions to education. Born at Liége in 1858, he came to this country in 1893. During five summer sessions, from 1916 to 1920, he was visiting professor at Columbia University.

WESTERN RESERVE UNIVERSITY is planning a program in honor of the formal opening of the Leonard Case Library, the Graduate School and the School of Library Science, and will dedicate the new building, Thayer Hall, in which these schools will be housed. The program will be held in the building on November 9, that being the eighty-first birthday of Dr. Charles F. Thwing, president of the university from 1890 to 1921, when he became president emeritus. The afternoon reception and tea will be for the Graduate School and the School of Library Science. Dean Elbert J. Benton, of the Graduate School, and Mrs. Benton, Dean Herbert S. Hirshberg, of the School of Library Science, and Mrs. Hirshberg, will receive students and members of the alumni bodies of the two institutions. The evening program will formally honor Dr. Thwing. Guests will include trustees of the institutions, faculties and friends. They will be received by Mr. William G. Mather, president of Case Library, and Mrs. Mather; President Winfred G. Leutner, of Western Reserve University, and Mrs. Leutner; Dr. Charles F. Thwing and his sister, Miss Harriet Thwing. There will be a musical program arranged by Professor Arthur Shepherd, while in the afternoon there will be displays of valuable items included in the library. Case Library was founded in 1846. It was endowed by Leonard Case, who also founded Case School of Applied Science. It became a part of Western Reserve University ten years ago. Two years later it was moved to temporary quarters on the campus. In Thwing Hall its valuable collections will be available in the most modernly efficient manner.

EXERCISES for the laying of the cornerstones of Goodell Library and Thatcher Hall Dormitory, new buildings now under construction at the Massachusetts State College, as emergency public works projects, will be held on November 3. Governor Joseph B. Ely, president of the Board of Trustees, will lay the cornerstone for the library and Nathaniel I. Bowditch, of Framingham, vice-president of the Board of Trustees, will lay the cornerstone for Thatcher Hall. The exercises will be held in connection with the celebration of Fall Alumni Day. They will begin at 10 o'clock at Thatcher Hall with President Baker presiding. Addresses will be given by the Honorable Charles P. Howard, chairman of the State Commission on Administration and Finance, and by Dr. Henry Lefavour, chairman of the Massachusetts Emergency Public Works Commission, formerly president of Simmons College. Exercises at Goodell Library will begin at 11 o'clock, with President Baker presiding. Addresses will be presented by Kenyon L. Butterfield, who was president of Massachusetts State College from 1906 to 1924; by Charles H. Gould, alumnus of the college and member of the Board of Directors of the Associate Alumni.

THREE days of study will be provided for alumnae of the New Jersey College for Women next month. The project, a week-end seminar on "Social Change," will be a first trial in the extension of educational services to graduates of the college. A nursery school on the campus will care for children of alumnae, while their mothers attend the sessions, which will be held on Friday, Saturday and Sunday, November 23, 24 and 25. They will open on Friday night with a round table on "Social Change in the United States," at which speakers will be Dr. George P. Schmidt, associate professor of history; Dr. Miriam West, assistant professor of economics, and Dr. Mildred Moulton, assistant professor of political science. The Saturday morning session will be on "The NRA in Operation" and two members of the faculty of Rutgers University will speak—Dr. John J. George, associate professor of political science, and Thomas W. Holland, assistant professor of economics. On Saturday afternoon the topic will be "Aspects of Social Change Abroad"; the speakers will be Dr. Harold A. Van Dorn, associate professor of political science; Dr. Emily G. Hickman, professor of history, and Dr. Francis W. Hopkins, assistant professor of economics. Commissioner William J. Ellis, of the Department of Institutions and Agencies, will discuss "Social Relief in New Jersey" at a dinner session on Saturday, and Miss Eleanor J. Flynn, assistant professor of sociology, will speak on "Current Policies of Social Service." The closing seminar session will be on Sunday morning, when "Present Issues Seen in Perspective" will be discussed by Dr. Harry R. Rudin, assistant professor of history at Yale University.

DR. JAMES N. RULE, head of the State Department of Public Instruction, will speak on "Education That Matters" at the annual Thiel College Convocation, Greenville, Pa., to be held on November 9, which seeks to honor students who have attained a high scholastic average in their last year's work. The institution has organized two new educational projects. An Institute on Parenthood and Home Relations to be held at the college will be inaugurated on November 15, 16 and 17. Among the speakers will be: Dr. Garry C. Myers, professor of parent education at Western Reserve University; Mrs. Alice Liveright, Pennsylvania state secretary of welfare; Dean H. L. Spencer, the University of Pittsburgh; Miss Jean Brigham, director of the Child Guidance Nursery School, Pittsburgh; Dr. Frank Reiter, chief of special education, Pennsylvania Department of Public Instruction; Miss Myra Woodruff, state supervisor of emergency nursery schools for parent education; Miss Zoe Hirt, high-school counsellor, Erie; as well as members of the Thiel College faculty. In order to provide an adult education program for the winter months, the college will initiate a series of popular lectures. The first lecture will be given on Tuesday, November 20, by President Rudisill, entitled "Education and the Present Uncertainty." There will follow lectures on politics, economics, literature, science, art, speech, athletics, ancient civilization, psychology and religion.

DR. ELIOT G. MEARS, professor of geography and international trade and dean of the summer session at Stanford University, has been named director of the twelfth session of the Institute of World Affairs to be held at the Riverside Mission on December 9 to 14. Current international problems will command the attention of the one-week gathering to be attended by official faculty delegates from universities and colleges of the western portion of the United States. Reservations have been made for representatives of the University of Montana, the University of Nevada, the University of Arizona, Brigham Young University, Scripps College, the California Institute of Technology, Occidental College, Pomona College and the University of Redlands. In addition to Dr. Mears Dr. William B. Munro, of the California Institute of Technology; Dean Henry F. Grady, of the University of California; Dr. Charles E. Martin, of the University of Washington; Miss Lillian B. Getty, of the Los Angeles University of International Relations of the University of Southern California, and Dr. R. B. von KleinSmid are members of the executive committee.

PRESENTATION of the eight murals hung in the Iowa State College Library was made on October 22 in connection with the annual dinner of Iowa artists given by the Memorial Union. Grant Wood, associate professor of graphic arts at the University of Iowa, under whose direction the murals were painted by twenty-one public works artists at Iowa City last winter, will present them to the college. Judge E. C. Carlson, of Des Moines, a member of the State Board of Education, will accept the murals. Three of the murals portray agriculture, three engineering and two home economics.

To provide a study and recreation center for its large group of students from abroad, the George Washington University will open an International House this fall. A building has been acquired by the university especially for this purpose. International House will contain lounge and study rooms for the use of members of the foreign student group, and also will be the meeting place for the International Student Society and will provide offices of the adviser to students from foreign countries, Professor Alan T. Deibert. International House also will house the quarters of the Center of Inter-American Studies, of which Dr. A. Curtis Wilgus is director. Students from forty foreign countries are enrolled in the university, forming one of the largest foreign student groups in universities of the United States.

# DISCUSSION

## VISIT OF ITALIAN STUDENTS TO THE COLLEGE OF THE CITY OF NEW YORK

THE faculty of the College of the City of New York desires to state its position in regard to the disturbance at the City College on October 9. The facts in the matter are the following:

(1) The president of the college invited a group of Italian university students to visit the college on October 9. The invitation was extended at the request of a committee of distinguished American citizens, including the Honorable Breckenridge Long, United States Ambassador to Italy, Gustavus T. Kirby, head of the Amateur Athletic Union, and Dr. John H. Finley, formerly president of the college. The president of the college was assured that the visit was entirely non-political in purpose and was intended to strengthen the bonds of friendship that should exist among universities and colleges the world over.

(2) A group of students of the college who were aggrieved at the proposed visit because they erroneously fancied it to be an indication of approval of the principles of Fascism was authorized by the dean of the college to hold an anti-Fascist demonstration in the stadium of the college at the same time that the reception was being held in the Great Hall. These students, acting in concert and under the aegis of the student council, did not avail themselves of the dean's authorization, but instead came into the Great Hall, interrupted the proceedings with hissing and shouting and finally engaged in a disorderly brawl.

(3) A representative of the student council had requested permission to speak at the reception to the Italian students. He had agreed to make no derogatory remarks and to confine himself solely to a friendly welcome. He was permitted to speak, but immediately proceeded to make a derogatory and insulting remark. His failure to stop when requested by the chairman of the meeting precipitated the disorderly scene referred to above, which brought the exercises to an abrupt close.

(4) Shortly thereafter a group of students,

after leaving the Great Hall, held an unauthorized meeting at the flagpole on the campus, in direct defiance of the orders of the dean. The dean had forbidden the use of the flagpole for this purpose, but, as previously stated, had authorized the use of the stadium. Only after this meeting, at which several students spoke, did the group finally move to the stadium. This stadium meeting was in turn interfered with by a very small group of students, apparently attempting to retaliate because of the preceding disorders.

Without enumerating further particulars, we have here instances of direct disobedience of college authority, of deliberate defiance of college regulations, of failure to observe the most elementary rules of hospitality, of grossly discourteous conduct and of acts subversive of all discipline and order.

The faculty of the college is charged with the responsibility for the conduct of the institution and is clothed with the necessary authority towards that end. When its authority is challenged by deliberate disobedience and gross discourtesy, the faculty has no choice but to take prompt and vigorous disciplinary action against the offending students and student groups.

In an institution so large as the City College, a very considerable number of the student body proceed about their regular duties in entire ignorance of such occurrences and of their significance. Many members of the student body as well as of the outside public who are not so familiar as the faculty with the precise details of this and previous difficulties may readily be misled as to the issues involved. Superficially it may be said: "Here are boys protesting against military training; they are expelled. Here are boys determined to prevent war; they are censured. Here are boys denouncing Fascism; they are disciplined. It doesn't seem right." As a matter of fact, many of the faculty are opposed to military training, all are united in detestation of war; the great majority disagree emphatically with the principles of Fascism. The faculty and the great majority of the student body are as one in their devotion to the principles of democracy and to the cause of peace.

But the faculty and a small minority of the student body must part company when a philosophy of conduct is introduced which justifies anything done in furtherance of noble aims, whether by fair means or by foul. The faculty does not believe that the use of foul, dishonorable, unworthy means is justified under any circumstances. The faculty feels that it is intellectually dishonest for any student or group of students to attempt to excuse unlawful and disgraceful conduct by wrapping around themselves the cloak of the ultimate objectives hoped for.

The faculty of the City College still adheres to the democratic methods of tolerance, of liberalism and of peaceful persuasion in advocating political and economic changes. When college students refuse to listen to opposing views, they are themselves intolerant and it ill behooves them to declaim against the intolerance of others. When they attempt to interfere with the conduct of others with whom they are not in sympathy, they are acting in an illiberal fashion and are denying to others the right of free speech to which they claim themselves to be passionately devoted. When they resort to shouting, hissing and booing to express their sentiments, they have descended far indeed from the level of gentlemanly conduct which is the duty as well as the prerogative of the scholar. Such conduct appears to the faculty to be disgraceful, and it does not propose to condone it. It is not merely a lack of manners that might be overlooked as a superficial deficiency but an indication of a narrow, illiberal and intolerant mind.

In this era of rapid economic and social change, it is natural that college students should express their opinions strenuously and energetically; at the same time it is expected that they will express themselves decently and with dignity. Tolerance implies the widest possible freedom to express opposing views; it does not imply permission to ignore established regulations, to violate the elementary rules of hospitality or to act in a disorderly and discourteous manner. The faculty has indeed failed in its mission if it can not succeed in making the student body understand the distinction between freedom of expression, which is permitted and encouraged, and disrespectful and insubordinate conduct, which would be subversive of all orderly progress.

## BETTER ENGLISH FOR STUDENT-TEACHERS

Every teacher should have a ready command of good English. Many prospective teachers, while in their college training, do not take this matter very seriously, and the result has been that many such students have been graduated and have been permitted to go out into teaching positions with very poor language habits.

Believing that the teacher-training departments are responsible for such situations, and desiring to produce teachers with the best command of the English language possible for each one, the College of Emporia, through its department of education, introduced a new plan last year. The plan is this: No student will be permitted to do practise-teaching at the city high schools until he has proved his ability to use the English language skilfully.

In order to determine the student's ability to write and speak good English, each one is required to take a standardized test. These tests are offered twice a year, and the students are required to pass this test with a satisfactory ranking during the semester preceding the semester of their practise-teaching. Those who fail to show satisfactory results are placed under special guidance of the department of English of the college, and are given intensive tutoring in English composition and rhetoric for that semester. At the end, the students who previously failed are given a final opportunity to satisfy the department of their ability to use English acceptably.

The plan has been in operation just one year, and it has been highly successful. It has stimulated interest in good English, and the students are making remarkable progress in their development along this line. Only two students have been unable to satisfy the requirement. They were, of course, not permitted to enroll for practise-teaching. Unfortunately, they found it possible to go to another college which did not have this requirement. Of course, they could not get a teaching certificate in the state without having had practise-teaching.

The results of this plan thus far have been so satisfactory that the plan has been adopted for permanent use by the department of education. One of the values which have accrued is the increased professional attitude on the part of the students. They are taking the teaching profession more seriously than before, and they are rapidly losing the accursed idea that teaching is a temporary stepping-stone on which any college graduate may stop for a short time while he is casting about for something better.

The students themselves have had a very kindly attitude towards the plan, and they seem to realize that it is for their good. Personally, I believe that their appreciation of the teaching profession has also been increased by it.

The local high-school authorities have welcomed the plan as a progressive step both for the college and for the high schools. They have been embarrassed a few times in the past by student-teachers who could not speak correctly before a class of high-school pupils.

John Harvey Furbay
College of Emporia

# QUOTATIONS

## EUROPEAN ACTIVITIES OF THE INSTITUTE OF INTERNATIONAL EDUCATION

It would be a fortunate thing for our country and for civilization in general were either our military or naval attaché in foreign countries to be replaced by an educational attaché. While it is difficult to understand just what service the military or naval attaché renders to the country, there can be no doubt of the possibilities of service that a well-selected scholar might render as an educational attaché. If the term "educational" be understood in its broad sense, not only might he be an authoritative source of information about education *per se* but about every aspect of the spiritual life of the country to which he is sent—and surely the things of the spirit are as important as those that have to do with war.

I am prompted to write thus by the careful study I made of the splendid results of the establishment during the war of the two branches of the American University Union in Europe, the one in Paris and the other in London, which we administer. They are veritable educational embassies. There are more than a thousand American students in France and between seven and eight hundred in Great Britain. The number of American professors and scholars who engage in research in those countries is large. The number of native students and others of those countries intending to visit the United States or wanting information about it is also large. For all these people the Union offices are real mines of information. In both cases their directors are in close touch with the officials and cultural agencies of France and England, respectively. Moreover, the American embassies, almost as a matter of course, turn over to the Union offices practically all inquiries and activities of a cultural nature.

It is unfortunate that the funds at our disposal do not permit us to assist financially the Amerika Institut in Berlin, for that also is performing an admirable service with inadequate finances. In 1926, the Director of the American Council on Education and the undersigned, as the result of a careful study of the problem, recommended to the Carnegie Endowment for International Peace the allotment of a subsidy for the maintenance of some four offices in foreign cities where our cultural interests are extensive. As yet this has not been done. But if the United States is to make its civilization properly appreciated in those countries as well as to make their civilizations appreciated at home, it is upon such agencies as the Endowment that we must rely. The French, Germans, Italians and some other nationals in those foreign centers look for cultural support to their governments at home—and get it.

The Institute is the representative in the United States of nearly all the important summer sessions of universities in foreign countries. Most Americans attend those summer sessions to study the language of the countries involved. The American Institute of the First Moscow University has just been established with a different point of view, *viz.*, to offer courses on many aspects of Soviet civilization. Moreover, the courses are given in English, there being few Americans who could understand Russian. The interest in the new régime in Russia that prevails in the United States is made evident by the fact that some two hundred persons attended this summer session, more than is true of any other foreign institution. Moreover, they included college professors, research students, teachers and undergraduates. The Institute was asked to sponsor this enterprise and I was invited to Russia primarily to help in its organization. This was necessary because of the great difference between Russian and American standards of living and methods of instruction. It was a difficult task on account of the ignorance that prevails in Russia of our conception of scholastic work. The Institute agreed to sponsor the enterprise for a year as an experiment and then to determine what its permanent relation to it would be.

The activity which we organized last year, namely, the Emergency Committee in Aid of Displaced German Scholars has been maintained throughout the year with a great deal of success. There is almost no great university in which a German scholar, displaced because of race, religion, or political opinions, has not been received in some department of scholarship, and this is also true of several of the most important colleges. At this date, October 1, some fifty professors eminent in the various fields of learning, are giving instruction or engaging in research to the great profit of our students. And I should like to emphasize again that these professors have been received into our universities without any addition to the university budget, the money having been provided for this specific purpose from outside sources. In this way all competition with our own unemployed teachers has been avoided.—*Dr. Stephen P. Duggan, director of the Institute of International Education, in his annual report to the trustees.*

# SOCIETIES AND MEETINGS

## THE ASSOCIATION OF AMERICAN UNIVERSITIES

The effect of the depression upon college and university teachers and the placement of graduate students were topics of broad interest discussed at the thirty-sixth annual conference of the Association of American Universities, held on October 25, 26 and 27 at the University of Chicago. There were four sessions and a formal dinner which fifty-five delegates and guests attended, representing thirty member institutions and several additional universities and foundations.

That college and university teachers fared better during the depression than most other groups in the community was the conclusion reached by Professor S. H. Slichter, of Harvard University, in his "Survey of the Economic Condition of the Academic Profession," a paper read, in the absence of Professor Slichter, by Dean F. K. Richtmyer, of Cornell University, at the evening session of October 25. "The drop in academic employment has probably been less than 10 per cent.," according to Professor Slichter's findings, as "contrasted with a drop of 28 per cent. in the salaried employees of factories between 1929 and 1932 and of 50 per cent. in the salaried employees of steam railroads during the same period. Among wage-earners the drop was somewhat greater. . . . The annual income of lawyers diminished 39 per cent. between 1929 and 1932 and the annual income of consulting engineers 58 per cent."

In his study of 246 colleges and universities, Professor Slichter ascertained that private institutions made a reduction of 7.3 per cent. in the size of staff, and public institutions made a reduction of 6.5 per cent. An analysis as to grades showed that 248 full professors were dropped, 465 assistant and associate professors and 1,196 instructors and assistants. "The shrinkage in the number of professors was much greater in private institutions than in public."

Since 1931, salary cuts "have been made by virtually all institutions." During the depression the cost of living dropped 24 per cent., so that this factor at least offset the drop in professional salaries.

Preliminary figures for the present year "indicate a distinct change for the better," both as to additions to the reduced collegiate staffs and as to partial restoration of former salary levels. Professor Slichter was not optimistic, however, about the effect upon teachers of the revival of business. Such revival will enable many institutions to balance their budgets at the present salary scales, but "it will substantially reduce the purchasing power of salaries and accentuate the financial problems of teachers."

As to the future, Professor Slichter's estimate was that "the demand for college and university teachers will increase at a decreasing rate."

The population of the country is expected to cease growing about 1950. High-school enrolment has not yet reached the saturation point but seems, nevertheless, to be in sight of it. In 1930, 85 per cent. of the population 15 years of age was attending school, 66 per cent. of the population 16 years of age, and 48 per cent. of the population 17 years of age. It is impossible to estimate the saturation point for colleges and universities, because this must be determined largely by the educational standards which these institutions choose to maintain. . . .

Ever since 1890, enrolment in institutions of higher learning has been diminishing relative to high-school enrolment. In 1890 it was two thirds as large as secondary school enrolments; in 1930 it was little more than one fourth as large.

The great drop in college and university enrolment relative to high-school enrolment might seem to indicate that there is much room for growth in college and university enrolment. At present it is about 1,250,000. He would be optimistic, however, who would predict that in the next twenty or thirty years it would rise to 2,000,000. Such an enrolment would require an increase in teaching staff from about 90,000 as at present to approximately 150,000. At that point or probably below it, the demand for college teachers will shift from an expansion to purely a replacement basis.

How the output of graduate schools of the United States compares with employment opportunities was revealed in papers also read at the evening session of October 25 by Professor E. J. Moulton, of Northwestern University, and by Professor George E. Carrothers, of the University of Michigan. Professor Moulton considered a restricted phase, the placement of graduate students in mathematics, with some few estimates as to the sciences. The study of Professor Carrothers included a summary of the National Research Council's statistics for doctorates in the sciences and a check on doctorates in other subjects at Michigan.

For the ten-year period, 1924 to 1933, the total number of doctorates in science granted by American universities was 9,458. During the same period the University of Michigan awarded 663 doctorates, of which 288 were in fields other than the sciences. Applying the Michigan ratio, Professor Carrothers estimated that the total in non-science fields in American universities was 7,263 graduates. "This would mean a grand total of approximately 16,721 doctorates of philosophy awarded in the ten-year period."

To the question "What to do with the product?" Professor Carrothers considered answers in terms of college teaching and of teaching in secondary schools. He cited findings of Dr. J. G. Umstattd, showing that in colleges "the average number of appointments per institution decreased from 10.7 in 1920–21 to 6.9 in 1931–32, a decrease of 35 per cent. . . . The problem will become more acute as the surplus of unemployed college teachers increases, and should receive immediate, nation-wide consideration."

A further consideration, Professor Carrothers thought, was the new policy of the North Central Association by which "a wider base" is indicated for judging the competence of college faculties "than merely that of holding advanced degrees." Professor Carrothers' conclusion was that in the smaller colleges "in the future considerably less emphasis will be placed on the holding of the doctor of philosophy degree than has been true in the past."

A career in the secondary school as an outlet for the young doctor of philosophy was then considered by Professor Carrothers. "There appears to be very little question as to the need for better trained teachers in secondary schools." Whether the present type of doctors of philosophy would meet the need was largely doubted by a group of leading high-school principals in the Middle West to whom Professor Carrothers addressed inquiries. They agreed that teachers in secondary schools would gain "by a broader and deeper acquaintance with the subject being taught." Some of the principals expressed disappointment in their experience with teachers in the secondary schools who have the doctor's degree.

Professor Carrothers concluded that "if holders of doctors' degrees are to become teachers in secondary schools, either the point of view of employing officials will have to be changed or doctors with different personal qualifications and a different sort of training must needs be produced."

There was much discussion from the floor. Dean L. P. Eisenhart, of Princeton University, thought it desirable to approximate in the United States what has gone on for years in Europe, where holders of the doctorate and producers of research and literary work are teachers in the lycée and gymnasium. Dean Charles B. Lipman, of the University of California, wondered whether the objections of secondary school officials to holders of the doctorate were based on a sufficient number of cases for valid judgment. It was the opinion of Dean Carl E. Seashore, of the State University of Iowa, that present opinion may be due to the fact that thus far those who have gone into secondary schools have been the less able doctors who did not obtain positions in colleges. "The day is hastening when able holders of the doctorate will go into secondary schools, especially into superintendencies. To help this we must live down the imputation that the university graduate schools are over-emphasizing research." Dean Henry G. Gale, of the University of Chicago, considered it essential that "we should not try to put into the secondary schools those graduate students who have gone straight through to the doctorate without experience as secondary school teachers." Dean Fernandus Payne, of Indiana University, reminded the conference of studies disclosing that "a large proportion of recipients of the American doctorate have had considerable teaching experience before or during graduate courses." Referring to the possibility mentioned in Professor Carrothers' paper of decreasing emphasis upon the doctorate for college faculty positions, Dean Edgar S. Furniss, of Yale University, said that his experience is that, at present, the small colleges decline to consider any applicants except those holding the doctorate. He felt, along with Dean Eisenhart, that the secondary schools would gain by taking on doctors of philosophy who have the requisite personal qualifications for teaching younger students. Dean Furniss expressed, in closing, his conviction that the executives of graduate schools might well consider other fields than teaching and research as outlets for their product, fields such as public service; and that the graduate school should re-examine all it is doing as to objectives and methods.

Another angle upon the subject of the overcrowding of the graduate schools and of the educational and scientific professions was brought forward at the morning session of October 26.

Professor Anton J. Carlson, of the University of Chicago, took definite exception to the doctrine of restricting enrolment because these fields are crowded. "Is it such a waste if a Ph.D., unable to find a place in education or science, goes into industry or business?" Professor Carlson opposed limitation in the professions, following the old guild system. "Who are we to say nay to those who want to go ahead regardless of the risks?" Dean Lipman seconded this view, saying he objected to such limitation, just as he objected to telling a farmer how much he may plant. "We don't know enough about the future to determine now the number of Ph.D.'s it will need." President Ray Lyman Wilbur, of Stanford University, added his approval of this point of view. He has advocated it, he said, as applied to the profession of medicine.

At the afternoon session of October 26, Director W. T. Couch, of the University of North Carolina Press, summed up "ways in which a university press may aid scholarship":

It can encourage the writing of manuscripts on important subjects not already adequately treated. It can organize experimental publishing projects. It can help to raise the quality of scholarly publishing by adopting a more critical attitude toward works submitted. It can offer an economical and efficient mode of publishing manuscripts of limited interest. It can solve special regional publishing problems. And finally, since it is forced to give careful attention to the more general problems of scholarship, it may succeed in helping to bring order into what appears to be chaos, and it may succeed in securing the wider adoption of the methods and spirit of scholarship.

Other papers were read before the conference as follows: "Admission Policy of Graduate Schools with Reference to the Accepted List," Dean Payne and Dean Furniss. "Research Fellowships: Their Purpose and Effectiveness," Dr. Donald Young, of the Social Science Research Council, and Dean George H. Chase, of Harvard University. "The Language Requirements of the Graduate Schools," Dr. J. M. Stalnaker, of the University of Chicago, and Dean Roy J. Deferrari, of the Catholic University of America. "University Training in the Social Sciences under a Divisional Organization," Dean Robert Redfield, University of Chicago. "A Survey of Existing Equipment of Graduate Schools," President R. M. Hughes, Iowa State College. "Post-Doctorate Education," Professor C. A. Kraus, Brown University.

Reports of standing committees were presented at the business session on the morning of October 27. Upon recommendation of the Committe on Classification of Universities and Colleges, the following were added to the accepted list of the association: Antioch College, Hollins College, Seton Hill College and, under technological institutions, the Texas Agricultural and Mechanical College. The Massachusetts Institute of Technology and the California Institute of Technology were elected to membership in the association.

RAYMOND WALTERS

UNIVERSITY OF CINCINNATI

## NEW BOOKS IN EDUCATION

*Applied Social Science: Journal of the National Institute of Social Sciences.* Vol. XVI–XIX. May, 1931—December, 1934. Pp. 196. F. W. Faxon.

BEATY, JOHN Y. *Story Pictures of Farm Animals.* Pp. 155. Beckley-Cardy. $0.70.

BERRY, LILLIAN G. *Proficiency Tests and Workbook for Second-Year Latin.* Pp. 142. Silver, Burdett. $0.56.

*Cardinal Objectives in Elementary Education: Trends in Unit Teaching.* Bulletin 1043. Pp. 153. Illustrated. University of the State of New York Press.

COWLEY, ELIZABETH B. *Solid Geometry.* Pp. ix + 230. Illustrated. Silver, Burdett. $1.28.

EBY, FREDERICK and CHARLES F. ARROWOOD. *The Development of Modern Education.* Pp. xxiv + 922. Illustrated. Prentice-Hall. $3.50.

*Fraternidad Hispana.* Pp. 80. Illustrated. Fordham University.

HEGLAND, EDWINA K. and SHERIDAN HEGLAND. *The Open Door: A Library Reference Work Book.* Pp. 36. Stanford University Press. $0.35.

HULL, OSMAND R. and WILLARD S. FORD. *Survey of the Los Angeles City Schools.* Pp. xxviii + 395. Los Angeles City School District.

*Le Rayon: Annuaire du Cercle Francais de L'Universite Fordham, 1934.* Pp. 79. Illustrated. Fordham University.

MORRIS, ALBERT. *Criminology.* Pp. xii + 590. Longmans, Green. $3.50.

MYERS, GARRY C. *I Am Growing Up.* Book I: *Conduct.* Pp. 48. Book II: *Manners.* Pp. 48. School and College Service, Delaware, Ohio.

SHARMAN, JACKSON R. and others. *Current Problems in Camp Leadership.* Pp. 120. Ann Arbor Press. $1.25.

*Supervised Correspondence Study: August Conference at Teachers College,* Columbia University. Pp. 66. International Textbook Company. $0.25.

# EDUCATIONAL REVIEW

**Edited by Nicholas Murray Butler, 1891–1919, Frank Pierrepont Graves, 1920–1924, and William McAndrew, 1924–**

# COMMENTS ON THINGS EDUCATIONAL

By WILLIAM McANDREW

## DEADLY COMMUNITY CIVICS

SOME of the handsomest books used in high schools are the beautifully illustrated texts describing the waterworks, the parks, the fire and police departments and the set-up of government. A friend recently described to me a high-school course in which the principal, once a week, gives a lecture illuminated by lantern slides and moving pictures. Food and sanitary inspection, street maintenance and repair, public utilities, libraries, educational facilities, sewage disposal and industries are presented with vividness and artistry. It is twenty weeks of glorious "my city 'tis of thee," the sort of thing that brings the principal the plaudits of the Chamber of Commerce and of the Associated Realtors of the town.

I asked my informant how much attention in these lessons is given to the way citizens could reduce profits going to favored contractors, pipe layers, excavators, school builders and friends of the political boss. He could think of no teaching with that in view, direct or indirect. On the contrary, he sniffed contemptuously at me that it isn't the school's duty to train fault-finders.

There's a hint of the infantilism of much of this community-civics performance.

There is, for instance, the fourth annual handbook of the National Council for the Social Studies, National Education Association. The high-school teachers who gave their time and labor to the preparation of its papers are highly respectable educators. Harvard Professor Wilson, introducing the report, notes that social-science teaching is bewildered by the people's current ills. But the writers of the book show little disturbance of this kind. They are as calm and sure as teachers of geometry. In one of the volume's preliminary papers Chicago Professor Judd notes that pupils studying government get no concrete ideas about the needs of the community closest to them. They do not get the sense that they are obligated to do anything. Little if anything in the teachers' plans making the bulk of this book would leave any impression that local government needs critical examination. The social studies we have are not likely to divert from his career any future Boss Tweed, Boss Platt, Boss Quay or Boss Anybody who is now in high school. Cincinnati Charles Taft insists that what you civic teachers need to organize is classes in wrath. Not a spark of indignation is visible in any of these lovely outlines. It is as if a committee called upon to advise regarding a very leaky ship should find the original plans of it and offer them as a report of its present condition.

### COMPLACENT COMMUNITY CIVICS

Meantime the number of men worth listening to who say that "the nation's current ills" are in no small part due to an unenlightened public opinion, untaught, are increasing.

In this line is a cold, factual essay from the University of Chicago Press[1] which is a short outline of local government as it is, a survey on the line of Richard Welling's "Civics as it Should Be." Government is not of, for or by the people; it is not based on an intent to render public service; it interferes with education; it prevents individual development. So says Fairweather.

This surveyor, whose facts are universally known, sees signs of a wide-spread inclination of citizens to organize, as in Cincinnati, to break away from party subserviency and to govern their communities on a non-partisan basis. The necessary steps for popular control he outlines, with full acquaintance of the obstacles to be encountered.

The failure of education he treats with profound regret, putting no blame on any but the whole population. Public education, he says, is the finest plan in the output of democracy.

[1] George O. Fairweather, "Wanted: Intelligent Self Government." University of Chicago Press. 52 pp. 25 cents.

It was designed to train in cooperative government. The great justification in taxing all the people for educating the children of some is the equipment of citizens to operate government for the general welfare. The civics these young people are taught can not be found outside of school.

Would it not be better to discontinue the present community civics? They are anesthetic to civic responsibilities. They foster a do-nothing pride in a dream city. They give no spur to achieve it. They are head-burying exercises in an educational sand pile. Few things in after life damage more a man's opinion of his teachers than to discover they taught him things that aren't so.

## HOW ONE MAN TEACHES SOCIAL SCIENCE

DR. BALLOU, who directs the public schools in probably the most perplexing area in the United States—the District of Columbia, where more than 57 varieties of educational policies are yearly brought to the capital by officials with children, found the report of the Commission on Social Studies too sweeping for him to sign. He wouldn't indict a whole people such as are the teachers of these subjects. If some beneficent foundation would pay the expenses of Dr. Ballou and me for visiting classes in these critical topics we might prepare an eye-opening report on how teachers' fear of dynamite is possibly exaggerated.

I could start with Milo Whittaker, for example.

Here is no wild-eyed Communist but an observant American quietly teaching teachers in the State College at DeKalb, Illinois. As I listened to him tell what is being passed to the students in the social studies there, it struck me that in DeKalb, at least, the worship of the divinity, Status Quo, is no more. Mr. Whittaker's youngsters say "there is in America a death-grapple with entrenched forces of capitalism," "we are in a revolution," "government is giving the people a new system of social justice."

"Tut, tut," says Professor Whittaker, "you know better than that. No social reform can be *given* to a people. Stop expecting any magic-working revolution. No revolution ever brings reforms. It only clears the deck. Use your history. Examine your French, your American, your Russian revolutions. Whatever general welfare is gained will have to come from your informed, enlightened selves."

As I gather from my short visit the DeKalb social-science students realize, as all of that Insull realm understands, that no profit-making corporation can be expected to conduct its affairs for the common good. Industry will not, these young people think, submit to control. The task of education is to awaken the citizenry to the fact that complacency brought the country to this pass; complacencies will bring us to a worse.

"What," asks Teacher Whittaker, "has been the trouble with education before this crisis?"

Up stand those who want to answer. One sober-looking young chap ventures, "I think the schools have not taken notice of the situation. My school filled my mind with interesting things that had no connection with making this a government by the people for the general welfare."

"What," asks the professor, "is the reason the law makes all the people pay school tax?"

"To save and improve representative democracy."

"Right, of course," assents the instructor. "But who of you ever heard of a school issuing a report of the work for good government done by its graduates?"

Nobody answered.

"What do they boast of?"

"Athletic games won." "Victory in debates." "High scores in studies." "Prizes."

Some startling convictions come to the participants as the result of discussions in the Whittaker classes. "Unless a better citizenry results from the public schools, they'll have to stop taking tax money."

"Education must give itself a new deal."

"Education has devoted itself to praising our economic system."

"Education has not shattered the American idol—the man of wealth. It has helped in the worship of it."

Professor Whittaker's beliefs as to the teaching needed are that political problems must be substituted in the place of information upon the forms of government. The teaching must be alive with challenge. Youth must be taught to think rather than to believe. The passage of boys and girls through high school who come out with the belief that the statesmen have solved or will solve all the problems should be prevented. The prohibition of controversial matters must be repealed. The absurd prominence given to "the background" in the social studies must yield to the foreground—the present situations in the local and state area. There must be ample practise in real government in the school. The extreme form of autocracy typified in many high schools and colleges should be replaced by self-government sympathetically guided, but a real and not a fake democracy. Teachers should share in it and give it educational potence.

To my mind this quiet Illinoisan, continuously directing the view of his students beyond the campus fence, is rendering a great and timely service to his commonwealth.

## GEESE FOR PROPAGANDA

MORE than a friendly curiosity and well-wishing is due the British Association for Education in Citizenship. You might send it a dollar for a year's subscription and get some of its enlivening announcements. The minimum annual fee is two shillings, sixpence. The office is at Morley College, 61 Westminster Road, S.E. 1, London. Sir Henry Hadow is president. Among the directing council are Rt. Hon. H. A. L. Fisher, Professor Gilbert Murray, Lord Lytton, Sir Norman Angell, Delisle Burns, Miss Jebb, Cyril Norwood, Professor Sir Percy Nunn, Mrs. Sidney Webb. The objects of the association are to collect information on what training in citizenship is being done in the schools of the world, to work out new courses to urge bodies having control of education to improve political teaching in schools. There is need, says the prospectus, for more direct training for the public duties of citizens in a democratic state. British economic and political problems are so complex that a more specific education is required. The growth of authoritarian governments demanding unreflecting obedience and docile devotion is a menace. Their principles are being inculcated in children by mass propaganda. If democracy is to survive, our educational system, say these Britons, must develop men and women loving freedom and trained to independent political thinking. It is in the school, the college, the university and the adult class that the working of democratic institutions will be determined. There are various methods by which the duties of a democratic citizenship can be encouraged in school. The association expects to make these methods more widely known and to stimulate and help those who so far have done little.

In listening to Mr. Kingsley Martin, a member of the association's council, speak of education for citizenship I easily imagine him among the most plain-speaking of our American Committee on the Social Studies.

Experience, said Mr. Martin, has exposed the absurdity of the idea held by the more sentimental of the early democrats that almost any one, by the mere light of nature, is capable of forming an intelligent opinion about public affairs and even of administering them.

### DETERIORATION OF EDUCATIONAL IDEALS

WE Americans are pretty well saturated with that fallacy, too, I confessed. We began with a higher standard. Only the more intelligent were allowed to vote. Our statesmen were distinguished men. But with Andrew Jackson the notion swept the country that any one can be mayor or governor, an Andrew Johnson can be President. Our civil service requirements are flouted by our political bosses. Our educational requirements in granting the franchise make little demand for a knowledge of public problems.

It is the lack of such knowledge, said Mr. Martin, that may seem to the man in despair of reform to justify him in calling democracy a failure. He is asserting that the common man is incapable of forming reasonable decisions even on the broader issues and does not care for an individual life within the community but wants a disciplined and militarized existence in which all he has to do is to obey the orders of those who do his thinking for him.

We do not know, said Mr. Martin, how far the ordinary man is capable of understanding democratic principles and problems because he never has had the chance. Democracy is not an exploded ideal but a goal to win. We are watching the nemesis of plutocracy, not the failure of democracy. No democratic thinker from Aristotle to Mill ever believed that democracy would work unless deliberately based on an educational system designed to make intelligent citizenship possible.

That, ventured I, was the idea of the men who set up our republic. Our first educational law was in 1787. It said schools and the means of education shall forever be encouraged for the preservation of good government. Washington, Adams, Jefferson, Madison and Monroe, in turn, proposed public schools devoted to political education rather than to scholarship.

What happened to the scheme? asked Mr. Martin.

We were too busy making money to bother with it. We let the schoolmasters prattle along with the educational ideas we had brought over from the reign of your James the First.

None of us, said Mr. Martin, can put on many medals for victories in education for democracy, but we can, within the existing order, carry on genuine experiments to prepare children of ordinary men and women for the decisions they will have to make as citizens. We can definitely try to develop critical readers of the newspapers and listeners to speeches, informed and intelligent voters. We can agree that "civics" does not satisfy the need. We can abandon the aim of making scholars and experts and substitute a purpose of giving to the country a citizenry that will have an understanding of the social and political world so as to be saved from being flocks of geese to be driven by the propaganda of millionaire press-lords or of aspiring dictators.

# MONTHLY SURVEY OF EDUCATIONAL BOOKS

*Asleep at the Microphone.* Time is tempering some of the claims of the extreme advocates of radio in education. No teachers have been displaced by it. No one now claims that everything can be taught by it. Not all subjects are as much at home on the air as music. The printed page is superior for many children, though not for the particularly ear-minded. The broadcast enthusiasts have become more serious in their thinking. So muses Professor Charters in Directors Tyson's[2] and Waller's forecast. Their study examines the directions of present trends. The government might regulate the programs, or, as in England, it might take them over, delegating them to licensees, or, as in Russia, Germany and Italy, it might boss the whole business. Mr. Tyson reviews government activities of the past five years. It is a disappointing history. Radio needs a strong organization of educators. The profit system is preventing the use of the great invention as it should be used—for public welfare. If educators can offer what the public will want there will be little trouble in getting governments' backing. You can't force intellectuality down democracy's throat unless it opens its mouth. So far its teeth have been tightly clenched.

Director Waller summarizes the achievements of educational radio during the last five years. A serious defect is the lack of appraisal of the programs after their broadcasting. Insufficient attempt has been made to improve the educational output. If the work of the past five years had been left entirely to educators the programs to-day would be nil and the audiences zero. The National Education Association is asleep at the microphone. But information is wanted by thousands of listeners. It is the educators' task to learn how to give it simply and effectively. New techniques are being successfully employed in the movies, in entertainment, in the schools. Why should education's methods stand still on the radio? As a practical substitute Miss Waller outlines objectives and organization of a university of the air.

*Wit, Wisdom and Age.* When, forty-eight years ago, my high-school boys referred to me as "the old man" I remember I took it as a compliment. It is no especial credit to be young. One is born so. But to be old means conservation, staying-power and other com-

[2] Levering Tyson, Judith C. Waller, "Future of Educational Broadcasting." University of Chicago Press. 32 pp. 25 cents.

mendable qualities. One always puts affection into "old" when he speaks of old Wesleyan. The youngest colleges in their songs call themselves dear old whatsitsname. Dear old Brigham is, at 90, the state librarian of old Iowa, where the corn grows tall. He has issued a book full of charm.[3] It is a collection of what the witty and the wise have said of the usefulness, the works, the happiness of old men and women. Here are the sayings of several hundred thinkers from Confucius to Clarence Darrow: Sophocles and Cicero, Shakespeare and Shelley, Walt Whitman and Rabbi Wise, Charlie Mayo and Michelangelo, with many timely tips by Johnson Brigham, himself. DeWitt Talmadge used to tell of an insane chap who stood on the street corner wagging his finger at every male passer and crying in a warning voice, "Maybe you'll be an old man." The Brigham message is, "If you're lucky you'll be one."

This is a good book for the tables in the waiting rooms of leisurely dentists and Long Island physicians. Teachers attending conferences with recovery administrators should take a copy along.

*Mens Felix in Corpore Pulchro.* A physical education practitioner must know a normal body when he sees one. He must know how it functions to maintain proper posture and to perform efficient movements. Accordingly, Professor Rathbone[4] puts the reader of her book through a thorough set of lessons on the foot, the lower leg, the knee and hip, the spine, the arm and the properties of muscular tissue.

In the reconstructive program Professor Rathbone fortifies the prescriptions with the authority of abundant clinical experience. Appeal to psychology is especially notable. No system of gymnastics that fails to emphasize joyous activity can have any claim for improving the body. The dance systems now in vogue are as valuable as body builders as they are developers of art appreciation if they are expressive of joyous emotion.

[3] Johnson Brigham, "The Youth of Old Age." Marshall Jones and Company, Boston. 209 pp. $2.50.

[4] Josephine Langworthy Rathbone, "Corrective Physical Education." W. B. Saunders Company, Philadelphia. 292 pp. $2.50.

I know a high school with six women teachers of girls' classes in physical education. Four of them are sad-eyed sisters of sorrow in whom the joy of life flickers like a candle in the rain. The other two are married women who haven't discovered the depression. I noticed in visiting the class of one of these two that every few minutes the faces of the girl pupils burst into smiles like the flash of ripples on breeze-swept water in the sunlight. The mystery was cleared up when I was taken by the principal to the back of the gymnasium. From there we could see that the teacher laughed now and then when her class did the stunts to suit her. In the classes of these two teachers there were no requests backed by physicians' certificates for excuse from exercises. In the classes of the four crepe-hanging ladies the principal said often half the pupils, duly certificated, were sitting on the benches because of the menstrual period. No joy means no jumping.

Another point Miss Rathbone makes is that gymnasium costumes should be abbreviated. How, asks the author, can you expect a person to get the concept of the beautiful body if he never sees one? Prudishness kills physique.

Here is where, again, I use the barrage of a book review to slip a bit of autobiography into print. Gordon Grant illustrated a students' handbook for the Washington Irving High School when I was principal of it. One of his dainty drawings represented a girl of fourteen in a white blouse, dark skirt to the knees, black stockings and gymnasium shoes. The great Maxwell put me on the carpet for it.

"But what's wrong with it, Doctor?"

"The legs."

"What's the matter with them?"

"They show."

Ten years later when the physical education women of America held a convention in Brooklyn, the Maxwell Training School gave a program for the visitors at the Academy of Music which was packed with *intelligentsia mascula atque femina.* The hundred young women performers, striplings you would say, were costumed according to the motto, not how much but how good. And in a box, applauding, was my corrector, as delighted a spectator as ever you saw.

A third principle of a good gymnastic system is the constant warming of hope and belief that it is making you healthier and handsomer. Mankind has for thousands of years suspected this, remarks the Rochester surgeon, Charles Mayo, but now he knows it. The experiments and demonstrations of Cushing, Cannon and Crile, to name but three, have made of it a scientific fact. Mind does make body.

Dr. Rathbone's corrective exercises for every fault are illustrated by hundreds of snappy pictures. There is a knowing chapter on mental hygiene, the effect of good and bad states of mind on the frame. The school problem as treated extensively here is full of powerful incentives to educational reform. It is inescapable that the abundant evidence that the child leaves school with more defects than he has on entering demands attention all along the line.

This book is clear, interesting, full of dignity, beauty and cheer.

*The Change in Physical Education.* Teachers soon became averse to being called physical "culturists." With exploration of educational values and changes of practise the teaching and training for health and bodily development expanded beyond what satisfied the school a generation ago. A book expanding and applying the new principles comes from the Saunders press.[5] The authors make clear the educational aims and objectives and put this teaching on a high professional plane. They make much of mental and moral outcomes, show the implications of increasing leisure time, decry the evils of competition, oppose concentration or teams, insist on work by all the pupils and stress attention to individual differences. The great purpose of public education, they insist, is better community life. How this line of teaching must contribute to the general welfare is cogently argued.

*Here we Rest.* Here is a curious fact that may have some highly important implications. Intense mental action is accompanied by muscular rigidity or stretching. Thinking hard how you shall answer a disconcerting question you probably have a straining of the muscles around the chin, cheeks and throat, possibly in the arms and legs. Nerve impulses, maybe, are overflowing from the seat of thought into the muscles. A detailed and interesting discussion of this opens Dr. Jacobson's exhortation to keep yourself calm.[6] On the other hand, tense muscles may keep the mind in action and prevent rest. For those who need to relax and can't this explicit manual gives directions and exercises.

*Why Do You Do This?* Do you remember the old story of the man who had rapped the wheels of the passenger cars for thirty years? When the president of the road in casual conversation asked what he expected to find, he replied, "I don't expect nothin'; I just taps 'em." I wish I had a dollar for every time I have heard that story told at teachers institutes to shame us into motivating what we do. Forty years ago our school superintendent had us make plan-books of the term's lessons we taught. The opening pages had to be devoted to the "objectives"—the changes to be effected in the pupils by our teaching of the subjects. When he visited a class he asked first for the plan-book. Later he said he never found that any teacher ever thought of objectives after the first day they were written down. I knew a principal who asked each teacher what purpose the lesson the principal was about to observe had in the teacher's mind. Two of his girls were transferred to the school I was in charge of. They left their objectives behind them. The School of Education in the University of Minnesota made a canvass of its students to find what they wanted most. Methods outranked principles by a long shot. I remember hearing Hugo Munsterberg when at the height of his popularity ask a gathering of school men "Why do you fuss with aims? The German schoolmasters are the best in the world. They have no aims other than teaching their subjects."

I have just finished reading a bright book by Professor Downing[7] of the University of

[5] Eugene W. Nixon, Frederick W. Cozens, "An Introduction to Physical Education." W. B. Saunders Company, Philadelphia. 262 pp. $2.50.

[6] Edmund Jacobson, "You Must Relax." McGraw-Hill Book Company, New York. 201 pp. $1.50.

[7] Elliot Rowland Downing, "An Introduction to the Teaching of Science." University of Chicago Press. 287 pp. $2.00.

Chicago. He opens with a conversation between an inspector and a teacher.

*Inspector:* "They have mastered this material very well. What is your objective? Why are you having them do this work?"

"Why, it is a part of the course of study."

Cautious and considerate, the inspector tried by this question and that to find out what human product milady was aiming to develop. The most he could get was that the lesson was in the book. In the course of a term the book would be injected into the children. At the end, if the pieces of it that were indicated by the examination could be found to the extent of 60 per cent. of them, the pupil achieving this record was "passed."

It is happening all the time, protests Dr. Downing. General science, biology, chemistry, physics, are crammed into the heads of pupils with no definite notions of the habits to be achieved.

It seems like an age-long struggle to get the teaching mind to think of other than covering the subject. Montaigne ridiculed the instruction of his day for this lack. As a young man, Edward Thorndike was urging that education is the process by which a boy is changed from what he is to what he ought to be. A Siglar School up the Hudson dropped "teacher" and "instructor" from its vocabulary and substituted "influencer." Private schools, like Miss Aiken's, here and there were organized on the psychology basis, attempting to avoid organization around subjects but to center on observation, perception, concept-forming, induction and deduction.

Dr. Downing enumerates goals. Science, he says, has helped to change man from a careless to a helpful thinker. It has taught him what are the elements and safeguards of scientific thinking. So the teacher must direct the pupil's change from a careless thinker to a scientific thinker.

I recall a positive introduction to a physics syllabus in Pittsburgh many years ago: "Physics teaches us to observe all the pertinent facts in a situation and to reason carefully to a conclusion." But I remember, too, the head of a science department in a large high school who put all his savings into a wild investment scheme, the physics teachers following his lead. The "facts" observed were only those in the mining company's prospectus. No science teacher consulted any one whose business it was to go examine investments.

The upsetting suspicion hovering over the whole educational system is that observation and thinking in any school exercise will be confined to it and go no further. The everlasting picture of the absent-minded professor as type of the result of study gives us the shivers.

We have the Judd doctrine to fall back upon: that after a mode of thought has been mastered in a particular problem the teacher should get, from pupils' suggestions and his own knowledge, situations in real life for using the same or similar kinds of thinking. Dr. Downing in this treatise often reverts to this need of generalization. One would think the cultivation of "scientific thinking" so important that every chapter of a school text in science would conclude with life problems quite different from the specific points of the chapter. The model tests in Dr. Downing's book have nothing of this sort. But the experiments he quotes that were made in teaching pupils to think indicate the success of motivated study. Then, we have the records of Otis Caldwell's reduction of gullibility by instruction in science.

The Downing book is a stimulating survey of principles and practises, the present curriculum and how it should be improved, science methods, supervised study and testing pupils. It surely will help its teacher readers to realize that giving science as information is not giving mental skill. Many school systems have a psychologist for the sake of subnormal children. If I were a principal I should want one for the normal boys and girls. His job would be to search through the classrooms looking for teaching that was developing the habit of thought.

*Physiology de luxe.* Why may a dyspeptic digest a large Christmas dinner although often an ordinary meal gives him distress?

Why do adults have more trouble learning drawing or languages than history or mathematics? How can you develop the qualities of loyalty, generosity and honesty?

When you fret over washing the dishes do you come into more or less fatigue than usual?

What are the dangers of acting as though you believed in superstitious notions?

Questions like these abound in many parts of Dr. Jesse Williams's new book. No, it is not a psychology nor an ethics, although it has much of each. It is an applied physiology.[8]

The questions and exercises are in the modern mode. They should please Dr. Julius Boraas, who says he has been looking all his life for high-school examination questions that will use the pupil's known power of thinking rather than let him by on a mere memory countersign.

Dr. Williams, or his printer, or both, have reached the prize row in text-book making. The type is notably handsome, the paragraph headings are skilfully composed; the abundant drawings, diagrams and photographs are easy to understand. The terseness, clarity and simplicity of the author's language make the multitudinous complexities of modern physiology and hygiene intelligible to the high-school pupil. The scope and treatment are also admirable for a college course.

*Beautiful Bird Book.* If Professor Roberts ever has a dull moment let him get his latest book[9] and gloat over it. It is a sumptuous family album of exceptional beauty, showing birds found throughout northern United States and southern Canada east of the Rocky Mountains. The author of the text, Professor Roberts, fills the chair of ornithology in the University of Minnesota and is director of the Minnesota Museum of Natural History. He supplements the pictures by descriptions and bird anecdotes. Plumage, nest, eggs, songs and habits are detailed. There are 561 bird portraits in color. The treatment of the subject is such that you have here a work appealing to the trained ornithologist and to the beginner in the kindergarten of bird-lore.

*The Newness of Biology.* Biology is the oldest of all branches of learning, say the authors of a new Ginn book,[10] and proceed to make it distinctly modern, stressing its continuous usefulness. Here are the food necessities of the world, the struggle for existence, the domestication of animals, the fight against disease, the factors of inheritance, the enjoyment of science, served in a tempting manner with an abundance of teaching aids and allurements to life-long interest in the wonders of nature. Dr. Caldwell, of the Lincoln School, New York, has here effective matter on cultivating the scientific habit of mind and curing gullibility. The other two authors are science teachers in the high school of the University of Michigan. Dr. Curtis is also professor of the teaching of science in the university.

*General Science for College.* The traditional science offerings of the higher institutions were specialized. Their relation to the whole cosmos failed to integrate. The same causes which led to a general science study in high schools apply to college. For him who seeks a broad education and does not intend to specialize in any one branch of science a general view of the world is indicated. After trying the new idea for a number of years with classes of college students the three experimenters[11] consult Professor Samuel Powers, Teachers College, Columbia University, and with his editorial collaboration bring out a survey of the physical universe. Astronomy, physics, geology, geography, meteorology, physiography, evolve from this general concept. The application of natural laws, their measurement, their use in machines and life situations are presented. Of course there are questions, readings, references, pictures and an index.

In book II, this treatment continues through the presentation of plants, animals, growth, evolution, reproduction, heredity, hygiene, culture, social problems and new discoveries affecting physiology.

8 Jesse Feiring Williams, M.D., ''Healthful Living.'' The Macmillan Company, New York. 622 pp. $1.56.

9 Thomas Sadler Roberts, ''Bird Portraits in Color.'' Plates by Allan Brooks, W. A. Weber, Francis Lee Jaques, George M. Sutton, W. J. Breckenridge, Louis Agassiz Fuertes. University of Minnesota Press, Minneapolis. 906 pp. $3.50; limp cloth, $2.50; Pictures in portfolio with index but no text, $1.50.

10 Francis D. Curtis, Otis W. Caldwell, Nina Henry Sherman, ''Biology for To-day.'' Ginn and Company, Boston. 727 pp. $1.76.

11 Frank Covert Jean, Ezra Clarence Harrah, Fred Lewis Herman, ''An Introductory Course in Science for Colleges.'' Book I. The Physical Universe. 524 pp. $2.20. Book II. The Biological World. 589 pp. $2.40. Ginn and Company, Boston.

*Mathematics Adults Should Know.* Professor Walker's short treatise on statistics[12] is a self-teaching manual. It defines, illustrates and furnishes exercises and tests for mathematical operations required in the preparation of statistics. In order to understand the modern world, to read the rapidly expanding literature of business, science, education and government one needs the fundamentals of applied mathematics. Dr. Walker's text, used by her in curing much mathematical inferiority complex found among her graduate students, is designed to lead the adult through necessary algebraic operations and know no pain.

*A Bright Star Book.* Give a hand to Professor Baker, chair of astronomy, University of Illinois. He can describe the heavens without lugging in mathematics. In a beautifully pictured book, in the sort of language you would want if a knowing friend were walking with you under the stars this scientist presents the heavens as "the grandest spectacle ever seen."[13] Sun, moon, planets and stars, constellations, galaxies, meteors, comets, nebulae, starclouds, all that is in the heavens above, have the stories of their birth and the courses which they run told in more than an easy manner—it enthralls.

*Putting Hate Out of Text-books.* The library of The League of Nations is making an international collection of school books. What for? Gilbert Murray, at a League assembly in 1927, said that in most countries, in the ordinary education given, there is inculcated an excessive sense of the military glories of the particular country, an overdone emphasis of difference from neighboring nations. "We find instilled into the minds of the young the germs of contempt for other peoples. This is pure poison. It is not patriotism."

At the same assembly our Professor Millikan suggested the proper influence should be put on all publishers presenting all subjects, especially history.

[12] Helen M. Walker, "Mathematics Essential for Elementary Statistics." Henry Holt and Company, New York. 246 pp. $1.50.

[13] Robert H. Baker, "When the Stars Come Out." The Viking Press. New York. 188 pp. $2.50.

An extensive memorandum[14] for eliminating from school texts passages compromising to world peace is available in English. Resolutions have been passed with acclaim and have remained platonic, says the report. Programs of action have been set up and there they stand, unused. The League of Nations adopted the positive Casares resolutions stimulating the National Committees of Intellectual Cooperation to action on text-books, but the resolution is rarely applied.

The teachers of France, at their Strasbourg congress in 1926, blacklisted twenty French schoolbooks among those most widely used in classrooms. These books have passed out. Their publishers, unable to sell them on account of the boycott, have published revised, unobjectionable editions. In France, in contrast to the usage in other European states, teachers can choose their own texts.

Many organizations have endorsed a proposal to create an international body whose task would be to deal with schoolbooks. The International Committee of Historical Societies urges a procedure of international cooperation in requesting authors of history text-books to submit proof-sheets to examination by their colleagues in other countries, advice being solicited at the same time.

The present volume reports work done up to the time of publication, the League operations, the activities of the Committee for Disarmament, what twenty-one governments have done, the work of seventy-six international and national associations, regulations of forty-four governments regarding the adoption of school text-books and cognate matters. A study of the volume leaves me with a sense of the absurd delay in doing what ought to be done. I feel like shouting what Papa Bernstein did from the family box after seeing his actor son, through five acts of a play, still standing with his gun before the palace gate: "Jakey, for Gott's sake, start someting." You get, too, a shock from realizing what an insignificant part this nation is playing in the whole business.

[14] International Institute of Intellectual Cooperation, "School Text-book Revision and International Understanding." League of Nations Agency, Palais Royal, 2 Rue de Montpensier, Paris (Ier). 191 pp. $2.00.

*National Issues for the School Student.* Massachusetts, California and North Carolina supply the authorship[15] of a new sociology for high schools. It abounds with ventures into what have long been forbidden fields in public-school topics. Particularly take up controversial issues, it says. Include such publications as *The New Republic*, *The Nation* and *The Forum.*

The young student is warned against school propaganda for going to college so as to make more money. There is a surplus of college-trained men and women. The country has a right to expect of its college graduates much volunteer unpaid service to the community.

These authors tell the young student the cold truth about much that has been glorified too much in the past.

Newspapers to increase sales search for and stress the sensational. Crime, divorce, accidents, suicides and misunderstandings that may lead to war are constantly dwelt upon. The wholesome is not supposed to have news value. You can't expect newspapers to mend their ways until more readers demand information instead of sensation.

Free speech is encouraged in the Constitution but has been resisted from the foundation of the Republic and often by those responsible for education. In 1828 an Ohio school board refused the use of the schoolhouse for a discussion as to whether the town should join in promoting a railroad. Railroads, said the board, are not to be discussed in a schoolhouse. They represent rank infidelity. There is nothing in the word of God about them. If he had designed that we should have them he would have foretold them through his holy prophets.

This book, organized into nine units, opens with a history of social advance and takes up economics, marriage, public health, recreation, housing, planning, population, immigration, the Negro problem, crime, labor conflicts, government regulation of business, politics, war, education and the enlightenment of public opinion. It is handsomely illustrated. It is well supplied with notebook problems, subjects for special reports and questions for class discussion. It presents recovery measures as well as current political issues with clear summaries of the common arguments for and against.

*Common Fallacies Regarding Negroes.* Seventeen professors of education, psychology, anatomy and anthropology contribute to a notable volume on the education of the Negro.[16] Their studies cover race psychology, physical constitution, the mulatto hypothesis, Negro-white differences in non-intellectual traits, in special aptitudes, in general intelligence in scholastic achievement, in the incidence of mental disease.

Professor Thompson's chapter recounts the views of scientists experienced in race problems. Exactly the same number believe the Negro inferior in mentality, as report themselves of the opinion that there is no difference in native ability between the Negro and the white.

An excellent summary of each essay is contributed by Walter Dearborn, of Harvard, and Howard Long, of the Washington public schools. A common assertion crops out in most of the essays: that the tests, samplings and other investigations employed to compare the two races are too crude to establish much scientific conclusion.

*One Town's Community Civics.* Radburn is a town in New Jersey, ten miles from the center of Manhattan Island. It is being built for families of moderate means, who want a separate home and a car. It is, in the opinion of the officers of the American Association for Adult Education, being built with such intelligent consideration for reasonable civilized living that the association publishes a book[17] describing the objectives in the planners' minds, the physical layout, the administration, the people, the community activities, discussion courses, recreations, religions, citizenship and child care.

The inhabitants have a Radburn Citizenship

15 Ruth Wood Gavian, A. A. Gray, Ernest Rutherford Groves, "Our Changing Social Order." D. C. Heath and Company, Boston. 577 pp. $1.80.

16 Charles H. Thompson, Editor, "The Physical and Mental Abilities of the American Negro." Department of Education, Howard University, Washington, D. C. 564 pp. $1.50.

17 Robert B. Hudson, John O. Walker, "Radburn, A Plan of Living." Association for Adult Education, 60 E. 42nd Street, New York. 118 pp. $1.25.

Association with committees. There are Democratic, Republican and Socialist clubs, a live Parent-Teachers Association that makes house-to-house canvasses, a volunteer fire department, a borough council, a zoning commission, a shade-tree board and a health officer. What the Radburners read, what radios, movies and theaters they enjoy, and what they think of their town makes an interesting and edifying case study of a real community.

*Going to Have a Forum?* Mr. Fansler[18] and Mr. Ozane, whom the American Association for Adult Education use as eyes and ears for the Macedonian cries of eager communities; Mr. Bryson, who directs a California Association for Educational Service to grown-ups, are authors of three timely books fitting into the present demand. Mr. Fansler does the service of reporting the actual happenings, questions, answers and comments of men, women and leaders of forum events in which the problems are typical of most such occasions. There are studies of symposiums preceded by a lecture, of informal group discussions as at meetings of clubs; there is similar treatment of the new-fangled panel discussion; and there is a wise discourse by the author touching on objectives and measures of success.

Mr. Ozane treats of a dozen actual surveys of communities and develops the educational implications.

Mr. Bryson's essay is an account of adult education experiments in California, of forums, of library clubs, of arts and crafts, of the training of teachers for this special service, of broadcasting and of a plan for an entire state. His account has the advantage of reality, being chiefly a description of movements actually at work.

*High School Economics.* The head of the department of Social Science of the High School of Commerce, Springfield, Massachusetts, offers an introduction to fundamental problems of economics written for students of secondary grades.[19] It concentrates on such matters as the author believes essential to the understanding of the business world. It uses discussion, projects, special pupil research and collateral readings freely. It begins each chapter with a statement of aims. Especially new are the presentations of international trade, tariffs, distribution, wages, profits, labor problems and economic reform.

*Tension, East and West.* Bringing into our picture the less-known nations of Asia, the John Day Company puts out an account of changing civilizations spreading over the globe. The spread of western influence brings crisis in its wake. The Japanese workers march, fifty thousand of them, with paper lanterns and national flags and numerous brass bands, to the imperial palace. They sing:

Hear ye the voice of the people  
In shadow and sorrow lamenting.  
Money, now, is too powerful;  
Justice and mercy have vanished;  
There is no freedom for workers;  
Weeping they stand in the twilight.  
Therefore our song rings for justice.  
Let peace in her turn be prevailing.  
As wealth in the land is triumphant.  
Freedom is banished by money.  
Shall riches prevail over justice?  
Is money more precious than people?

This book, for world unity, describes the unrest which Europe and America have spread over the world. It lays down rules of conflict and understanding, outlines the political problem, the culture clashes, the social complexities, the factor of Bolshevism, the economic difficulties, the new prospects in world politics. It contains a bibliography of the questions of Orient and Occident in general.[20]

*Sprightly World History.* Mr. Coulomb, who is an assistant superintendent of Philadelphia public schools, enjoyed himself writing a history of the world for children of the seventh grade or thereabouts.[21] You may establish this

18 Thomas Fansler, ''Discussion Methods for Adult Groups.'' American Association for Adult Education, 60 E. 42nd Street, New York. 149 pp. $1.50. Jacques Ozane, ''Regional Surveys.'' 48 pp. 90 cents. Lyman Bryson, ''A State Plan for Adult Education.'' 69 pp. 50 cents.

19 Augustus H. Smith, ''Economics.'' McGraw-Hill Book Company, New York. 542 pp. $1.60.

20 Hans Kohn, ''Orient and Occident.'' The John Day Company, New York. 140 pp. $1.75.

21 Charles A. Coulomb, ''World Backgrounds.'' The Macmillan Company, New York. 552 pp. $1.48.

surmise from the pleasure you derive from reading the book. This story of man from prehistoric ages to the present day is a moving tale, as this author tells it. The freshness and interest of the illustrations are superb. He wants the boys and girl to enjoy history. Dear teacher, he says, don't worry if many facts fade out. The more pleasureful the study the longer the results will last. As a questioner and exercise-maker Master Coulomb loses none of the sprightliness he exhibits as a writer. He has the knack of provoking thought in the study helps at the end of the units.

Assisted by two supervisors experienced in the newer methods, he issues also a fourth school grade text covering history to the circumnavigation of the globe.[22] Both books are composed with an eye on approved word lists for the grades covered. Both are triumphs of the bookmaker's art in print, paper, design and binding.

*History Units in Social Science.* In their world history,[23] Teachers Greenan and Gathany have followed the course advocated by leaders in the social studies. The authors minimize detail and throw institutions and movements into bold relief. Their treatment of history by units takes, for instance, the orderliness brought into the world by feudalism and makes this theme decide what events shall be given prominence. The next unit is the overthrow of feudalism by the kings, the rise of strong, central government. The unit on the growth of liberty, the one on commercial rivalries and consequent wars, are particularly impressive. The last four units carry into the problems of civilization versus war, individualism and the economic revolution, democracy or dictator, and a summary of recent social progress.

The authors have been experimenting with these lessons for three years and use their experience in providing a copious amount of study helps and teacher assistance: vocabulary drills, review facts, thought questions, reference readings, report topics, map studies, debates, floor talks, dramatization, composition and encouragement for illustrations by pupils. The publishers have put the text into alluring form with numerous maps, portraits, photographs and colored plates. Chronology is simplified by "stairways of time."

*Plain Words from Australia.* A disconcerting criticism is issued by the Melbourne University Press.[24] It is a study of the taste and training of a modern community in regard to English literature. Mr. Braggini set out to find where the ordinary Australian stands in the matter of literary appreciation. Dr. Leavis, of Cambridge University, who writes an introduction to this work, believes the findings are applicable to England as well. The testimony of English-Professor Leigh Hunt, of the College of the City of New York, brings us into the same degenerating class.

Mr. Braggini reprints an extensive collection of tests in which good literature is set alongside of tawdry writing for the student to say which extract he prefers and why. The patients in this clinic were 528 college and university students, juniors, sophomores, commerce first and second grade classes and public school teachers in training. The readiness with which the majority of these good people preferred the poorer extracts, the infantile reasons they gave for their choice, are set forth with interesting comments. Mr. Braggini hesitates to expose this distressing situation as a grave reflection on local culture. Before any American can sniff at Australia, or, considering Dr. Leavis's judgment, at England, fairness would require giving these same tests to teachers, business college students and undergraduates in a department of liberal arts.

The constructive essay on the teaching of English, in which the surveyor modestly suggests what might be done, is extensively pencil-marked for approval by Dr. Frederick Keppel, of the Carnegie Corporation, who had my copy for a while. The author refers often to the unnatural mental atmosphere commonly found in school and college classrooms. The student or the professor, or both, have created a tradi-

[22] Charles A. Coulomb, Emma Dowling, Anna A. Rapp, "Beginnings in the Old World." The Macmillan Company, New York. 278 pp. 96 cents.

[23] John T. Greenan, J. Madison Gathany, "Units in World History." McGraw-Hill Book Company, New York. 710 pp. $1.96.

[24] Ernest Gordon Braggini, "English in Australia." Melbourne University Press. (New York Office, Oxford University Press). 134 pp. $1.00.

tion that lectures and recitations are "a desirable nuisance." The university professor who does not notice the elation of his class when the session is shortened or postponed is an unobservant man. There seems to be a professorial agreement to let this stifling influence continue.

I was never in Australia, but like most of my classmates in a university in this land of freedom, I knew that we ought to have been made to take our rations seriously. Winchell, the geologist; Frieze, the Latinist; Thomas, the Germanic scholar, knew we were using our minds in low gear—they told me so after I had been teaching for a few years. They, like the Australians of Mr. Braggini's acquaintance, seemed content to prescribe the food without making us chew and digest it. When I asked Professor of Education William H. Payne whether it would be a good thing to adopt James Rice's scheme of grading professors' pay by the number of their students who passed tests showing growth he was of the opinion that the most eminent of the faculty would apply for positions in other schools.

In Australia, according to this treatise, the student resents being pressed to use his own mind. He resorts to subterfuges; he goes to more trouble to avoid thought than he would be put to if he undertook it. He prefers note-taking, formulas, authoritative opinion and doing everything but harnessing his understanding. If we would cultivate his taste for good literature we must throw him on his own resources and discourage him from all others.

In many localities where I have undertaken to steer high-school teachers in round-table discussions—teachers of the school grade where real thinking is urged by every author whose secondary-education books are sent here for review—the first meetings disclose what seems like a conspiracy to perform the mental acts of only listening, absorbing and giving back everything in the form received. I am for the good old Chinese custom of his solitary confinement in a cell until the student pierces the artificial shell of his own understanding and starts the ratiocinative wheels in his head working. A mild substitute for such compulsion I have seen successful. A professor says to a student, "My son, you are stalling. The materials for an intelligent answer are in your possession. You will not need to consult any book or person. Write the question, now, and the next time we meet answer it and defend your answer." Howison, of the University of California, used this method, as did Lattimer of New Platz. But, alas, they have both gone where the spirits of just men have been made perfect.

The Braggini comments and proposals are so universal that their application in high school and college will, in the judgment of Dr. Leavis, produce desirable results in a very few hours of determined employment.

*Laugh, My Lady, Laugh.* It may seem that in an hour of nation-wide depression, laughter is a poor offering, suggest Mesdames Bruere and Beard[25] in their jolly big book on women's humor in America. Wit and humor, insist these cheery authors, evolve strength out of failure and temper too much success. Their nutriment is absurdity, incongruity and conflict, no less than satisfaction, security and peace. The sharp edge of laughter can cut the mistakes of man from Moses to Mussolini. Dean Swift was not fooling when he poked fun at incompetence, selfishness and bigotry. Lincoln used laughter to strengthen the force of action. Under stress it is especially important to remember laughter, for it is more than a defense mechanism, a means of adjustment, a safety valve against despair—it is an agency of constructive enterprise. So here is a book about America, its humors, cheerfulness, buoyancy, playfulness, stolidity or bile. Who says the female type must be somber? How relieved the tension among nations would be and how much brighter international discourse if the nations would no longer picture their militancy in the form of woman—armored ladies symbolizing war, preparedness and patriotism.

As Americans have advanced from coast to coast they have guffawed, wise-cracked, joked and giggled. Fondness for laughter has been styled our national complex.

Up to 1885 collections of humorous poetry of

[25] Martha Bentley Bruere, Mary Ritter Beard, "Laughing Their Way." The Macmillan Company, New York. 295 pp. $4.00.

the United States represented not any women. In that year Kate Sanborn published an antidote in her review of women's witty observations on the American scene. Now come into this volume three score of laughing gentlewomen with hundreds of jolly pieces from the widow Bedott to Gertrude Stein. Here are Mary Mapes Dodge, Grace King, Ruth McEnery Stuart, Samantha Allen, Emily Dickinson, Edna Millay, Carolyn Wells, Myra Kelly, Anita Loos, Dorothy Parker, Cornelia Skinner and Josephine Daskam Baker, along with others whom you will be happy to meet. Each type of writing is given an appraisal; cartoons are reproduced, and a sketch of the end of the century abounds in pleasant reminiscence. In your school library order, Schoolmaster, don't forget that more than half of your readers are girls and that these are sad days.

*Discovery of a Defeated Genius.* One afternoon in 1925 Mr. A. J. A. Symons learned of a rare book, "Hadrian the Seventh," a few copies of which had been sold since its publication twenty years earlier. On reading it he felt an interior stir of a transforming experience. He thought, and still thinks, the book one of the most extraordinary achievements in English literature. To learn more of the obscure author became in Symons a quest beside which all other occupations seemed colorless. This adventure of rediscovery constitutes one of the most discussed books[26] of the season in England. The maker terms it "an experiment in biography." You follow the author pursuing clews, as a detective, from England to Scotland, to Wales, to Rome, to Venice. Piece by piece the life of an arrogant, brilliant, untiring, malignant, quarrelsome dead-beat is pieced together. You put the book down resolved, as you would decide in the case of a personal contact with such a pervert, to have nothing more to do with him. You are drawn back again to see what further excess of labor or penury or ingratitude the errant genius will disclose. One after another men attempt to help him. They are dazzled by his genius; they are appalled at his egotism; they are stung by his invective. The adventure includes literary people, clergymen, priests, Americans, well-known publishers and benevolent possessors of wealth. The proud youth is drawn to the Catholic faith and hopes for ordination as a priest. He is rejected. A high-born woman befriends him in Italy. He returns to England as Baron Corvo. He lives on the edge of starvation, a haggard, shabby, shy, priestly-visaged master of a superior technique of insulting those who help him. He repays succor with scorn; kindness, with curses. It is impossible to withhold from him admiration and pity. Something had early given him the complexes of inferiority and persecution—overdeveloped his defense mechanism. He gets himself to Venice, fleeces hotel keepers and benefactors. He announces a plan of producing a pornographic work in Italian, French and English, to be published at Paris for fifty francs, with the initials of one of his benefactors and the family coat of arms of another on the cover so as to shame them in the eyes of the world.

Invaded by swarms of rats, threatening suicide, he falls dead of a heart attack in Venice in 1913. He had made for himself two epitaphs: "Pray for the repose of his soul; he was so tired." "Selfish, yes, selfish. The selfishness of a square peg in a round hole."

*Rally for the Library.* The careful and comprehensive Mr. Duffus, whose mission it is to get to the bottom of topics of current importance, has gathered the distressing facts of the status of public libraries and set them down in a book.[27] It is a first-hand investigation of ten typical cities—Detroit, Chicago, Indianapolis, Louisville, Knoxville, Richmond, Baltimore, Brooklyn, New York and Springfield, Massachusetts. In each of these chapters the story is of constant interest; the conduct of the library people, heroic. In his argumentative paragraph Mr. Duffus speaks from a long acquaintance with a library stringency dating years before the depression. Demands upon the libraries are everywhere increasing; funds are cut down. Intellectual starvation is no

[26] A. J. A. Symons, "The Quest for Corvo." The Macmillan Company, New York. 293 pp. $2.50.

[27] R. L. Duffus, "Our Starving Libraries." Houghton, Mifflin Company, Boston. 148 pp. $1.25.

pleasant thing to contemplate. There ought to be a revolt led by the library patrons, the best citizens, against fiscal policies that cripple libraries. There is no more profitable investment than in the intellectual fertilization of the community.

*Encyclopedia of Library Information.* If anything printed on libraries since 1920 escaped the scrutiny of the forty searchers whose work has been published by the American Library Association[28] you may guess it is not of much account. These assiduous collectors set out to bring Cannon's bibliography of library economy, a librarian's bible, up to date. They listed library articles in periodical literature indexes; they listed leading essays in the numbers of eighty-two journals and periodical bulletins issued by libraries of the country; they included all books upon the subject; they sorted and alphabetized the thirty-four thousand cards. The monument to this cooperative task shows "art departments in city libraries," "zoning," and 430 solid pages of information in between. "School Libraries" has over 800 references, covering administration, training of school librarians, guidance, supervised study, book selection, budgets, circulation, equipment, discipline, inventories, picture collections, relations with teachers, standards, student assistants, platoon schools and much beside.

*Country Library.* Miss Lathrop, of the United States Office of Education, specializes in school libraries. The Carnegie Corporation has done the country schools the service of printing and distributing, free, the progressive rural-library manual which this gentlewoman has prepared.[29] It covers the United States, suggests what books are most in demand, outlines various kinds of service, describes different projects worked out by children in the rural school libraries, discusses reading clubs, recommends cooperation of the Parent-Teacher Association and contains significant pictures.

*An Interesting Grammar.* Why the old grammar is too shaky for satisfying use Dr. Aiken[30] discusses in a readable preface. The body of her book is a presentation of grammar in its functional aspects, six of them, rather than building the treatise on the eight parts of speech. Twenty-four chapters with examples and questions cover all the current concepts used in the common schools. The book presupposes a knowledge of grammar in the reader and serves as a clarifier of grammatical knowledge. It is full of interest and will be a gratifying aid to teachers.

*Columbia's Classics.* The faculty of Columbia University believes that any book famous among general readers can be read with profit by any fairly intelligent person. A Columbia course in which a group meets once a week to discuss such a book after reading has been found more profitable than a lecture. An expanded list of books of this kind has been prepared by members of the faculty.[31]

The plan of the book is that of recommending the edition to be read and of furnishing lists of supplementary books bearing on the classic. Thus are treated the main books of the Bible, the Greek and Roman masters, the Christian Fathers, the sagas, the classics of the Renaissance and the enlightenment, Grotius, Hobbes, Descartes, Spinoza, the dramatists, the philosophers, the novelists, the economists, the historians, the poets, the popular scientists, Karl Marx, Dostoevsky, Nietzsche, concluding with Sigmund Freud.

*Not Enough Libraries.* So late as 1925 over half the population of the United States lived in territory that had no library service. Director Fair, of the Library School of the New Jersey College for Women, addresses herself to the problem of getting this area civilized.[32] Like a general planning a campaign, the author uses sixty-eight reports and articles written by researchers of library extension. The result is a variety and interest you would never expect from the book's title. Many of the chapters are

[28] Lucile M. Morsch, Editor, "Library Literature 1921–1932." American Library Association, Chicago. 430 pp. $10.00.

[29] Edith A. Lathrop, "A Study of Rural School Library Practises and Services." American Library Association, Chicago. 103 pp. Free.

[30] Janet Rankin Aiken, "A New Plan of English Grammar." Henry Holt and Company, New York. 216 pp. $1.40.

[31] J. Bartlet Brebner, John Erskine, Everett Dean Martin, "Classics of the Western World." American Library Association, Chicago. 128 pp. $1.00.

[32] Ethel M. Fair, "Countrywide Library Service." American Library Association, Chicago. 208 pp. $2.50.

as adventurous as tales of other kinds of pioneers.

*Essays Again.* What essays have proved most satisfactory in high-school classes? On the answers of hundreds of teachers and students the selection of a text issued in 1926 was based. A recent similar canvass has brought out a new and enlarged edition.[33]

Fifty-two essays, including the works of Bacon, Emerson, Swift, Lippmann, Broun, Chesterton, Galsworthy, Leacock, Morley and Woodrow Wilson, are supplemented by hints to teachers and students, bright essays on the essay as a literary form, aids to appreciation, composition suggestion and a guide to reading.

*Delight in English-Teaching.* To begin a school text with a few lines of exhortation to the pupil is common enough, but to carry the whole course of lessons through on the idea of self-study, self-knowledge and self-improvement and to do this with a maintenance of lively interest is the sign of rare talent. Three New York high-school teachers[34] have done this successfully. Up to the last chapter they are asking the pupil whether he does this or that and why or why not. If he is doing the wrong thing, why doesn't he try this exercise, such as good speakers and writers have used to improve themselves? The essentials of good speech are covered by lessons from which boredom has been driven out by incident, by example and by stimulating encouragement. The old complaint of dullness in English teaching has no leg to stand on with a book like this at hand.

*Literature in the High School.* Scott, Foresman and Company offer a new series providing an organized course in literature for secondary schools.[35] Its range is from Homer to Carl Sandburg, stories of adventure, legend, history, poetry, industry, outdoor life, beauty, art and a dozen pieces on the spirit of good citizenship. There are hints on study and reading, explanatory comments, pictures of action, biographies of all the authors, sixty-eight of them, two indexes and a pronunciation list.

*Books in Demand.* For a list of simply written, informative and readable books suitable for use in connection with current adult educational activities being conducted by government and other agencies, American librarians studied the subjects most frequently mentioned by readers. For these subjects a list of books is now ready.[36] This list covers history, biography, economics, political problems, labor, war, literature and the arts, self-development, child care, and much besides.

*Ruminative Reading.* The University of Minnesota publishes seventeen critical, epigrammatic, witty essays of its brilliant Professor Firkins.[37] Art, taste, humanity, life, death, patriotism, literature, drama, undepicted America, novelists, Babbitts, diseased writing, realism, morale, liberty, evolution, Christianity, self, decency and events near and far are mined for treasure by a master prospector.

It is what you call a delicious book, quotable from every page, a provocative, persuasive, satisfying exposition of things that matter much.

*Short Stories for School.* With a historical sketch of the short story and a discussion of essentials, with biography and criticism of each, author Schweikert's collection appears with additions, bringing the number of complete tales up to thirty-eight.[38] Most of them are by living writers, American and European.

*Ideals and Adolescents.* In the form of conversation and dialogue between a wise physician and high-school boys, two experienced boys' club workers[39] present most of the problems that bother youth, to whom religion is ceasing to be an unexamined package. Science, religion, personality and other large themes are discussed in simple language.

33 Essie Chamberlain, "Essays Old and New." Harcourt, Brace and Company, New York. 460 pp. $1.00.

34 Charles Robert Gaston, Abby Forbes Chapin, Munjon Moses Nagelberg, "English in Daily Life." Ginn and Company, Boston. 547 pp. $1.40.

35 Edwin Greenlaw, William H. Elson, Christine M. Keck, Dudley Miles, "Literature and Life, Book One." Scott Foresman and Company, Chicago. 640 pp. $1.80.

36 Doris Hoit, "Books of General Interest for To-day's Readers." American Library Association, Chicago. 59 pp. 25 cents, ten or more 15 cents each.

37 Oscar W. Firkins, "Selected Essays." University of Minnesota Press, Minneapolis. 298 pp. $2.50.

38 H. C. Schweikert, "Short Stories." Harcourt, Brace and Company, New York. 612 pp. $1.08.

39 W. Ryland Boorman, James Johnston, "Independent Young Thinkers." The Christopher Publishing House, Boston. 171 pp. $1.50.

# SCHOOL AND SOCIETY

WITH WHICH ARE COMBINED THE EDUCATIONAL REVIEW, ESTABLISHED IN 1891, THE TEACHERS MAGAZINE, ESTABLISHED IN 1878, AND THE SCHOOL JOURNAL, ESTABLISHED IN 1874.

Volume 40 | Saturday, November 10, 1934 | Number 1037

## AMERICAN EDUCATION AND THE NEGRO

By JAMES A. SCOTT

CHARLES HENRY TURNER SCHOOL, ST. LOUIS

According to the Biennial Survey of Education—1926–1928—there were, in sixteen states reporting, 7,432,066 white and 3,104,992 colored children of school age. These figures—partial as they are—lend definiteness to the assertion that in America two large groups of future citizens are being educated in almost completely segregated institutions by groups of teachers between which professional conference is rare. Of added significance is the point that the individuals of both races must, as adults, participate in a common national life in such activities as will involve numerous contacts with one another. What can be done in the public schools of to-day to make these future associations of the most socially desirable nature possible is, therefore, a highly pertinent question for American education to ask itself.

If one investigates the sources from which the majorities of white and colored children at present derive their concepts of each other, the problem becomes recognizably serious. In all too many localities our daily press still headlines the Negro as a criminal or buffoon. Furthermore, traditional animosities, fears and biases of parents constitute a large measure of the formative social heritage of both groups. And most disturbing of all is the subtle and frequently unintentional indoctrination of the very texts used in the public schools. If one were to cull the allusions to the Negro from the social studies books of the average classroom and classify them according to their socializing, indifferent or anti-socializing effects on white or colored children, he would find the third column lamentably long. Foundational apperceptive backgrounds basic to future racial attitudes are, on the whole, being so built as to perpetuate rather than eliminate the maladjustments of the present social organization—maladjustments of sufficient scope to evoke numerous books, articles and discussions of a so-called "Negro Question."

Towards the solution of this American problem educators of both races can make determinative contributions. Assuming that the modern school purposes to develop in its pupils social attitudes based on undistorted truth and to send forth a generation enthusiastic with the resolve to speed to consummation a society based on the principles of justice, one clearly sees the necessity for a definite cooperative race relations program in the two sets of schools. The two bodies of teachers should know each other's objectives and procedures in handling this particular content so that their efforts may be complementary. Wisely planned functional instruction in social studies by elementary and high-school teachers of to-day would mean that the white adult of to-morrow would be freer from prejudice born of misconceptions and nurtured by passions and that his colored contemporary would possess to a smaller degree attitudes conditioned by the consciousness of that prejudice in those about him.

Details of such a bilateral program must obviously be the result of painstaking research and cumulative experience. Its essential objectives, however, might perhaps be stated under three main headings:

(1) Development in the Negro of rationally founded attitudes towards himself ethnically and development in the whites of corresponding attitudes towards him based upon acquaintance with the same scientifically ascertained facts.

(2) Development in the Negro of desirable racial characteristics which are the natural outgrowth of his background and nature, and development in whites of appreciations for the social and cultural values of these characteristics.

(3) Familiarizing the Negro child with the social channels through which the contributions of his race have flowed or may now flow into the larger American life and demonstrating to the white child the enrichment of national culture which would result from the multiplication of these channels.

That there is real necessity for developing in Negro boys and girls healthier attitudes towards themselves and their problems no one familiar with present-day conditions can deny. Pathological results of past neglect of this objective are evident about us. In a highly revelatory study of the racial attitudes of Negro students at the University of Iowa, the author, Mr. H. C. Jenkins, cites a number of examples of the aloofness, bitterness, reticence, uncertainty and hyper-sensitivity consequent upon the previous racial experiences of many colored students there. And even now among some rather well-trained Negroes exists a decided aversion for the spirituals because of the painful circumstances associated with their creation. "That's something we're trying to get away from," is an expression not uncommonly heard. This desire to escape the circumscriptions of race reaches, perhaps, its climax in certain groups of college graduates who prefer menial work in northern cities, where unsegregated enjoyment of cultural and recreational facilities is accessible, to possible leadership in centers of large Negro populations, where they must generally suffer the chafing inconveniences of a ghetto. In the face of these facts, educators of Negroes throughout the country are adopting as one of their paramount aims the buttressing of racial self-respect and loyalty.

How to accomplish this end is a practical problem of Negro education. It involves, first of all, the displacement of the Negro's present unscientifically acquired conception of his orientation in American civilization with an interpretation based on the findings of conscientious research in the fields of modern psychology, anthropology and history. Perhaps the one agency devoting all its energies to assembling material of this sort is the Association for the Study of Negro Life and History, with national headquarters located at Washington, D. C. By its well-trained staff is gathered information which possesses the authenticity of sound scholarship and the functional value of inspiring in Negro boys and girls a more accurate appreciation of their place in the American environment. At every stage of this country's development and in every crisis of its national life the Negro has played a constructive part. Understanding of what his group's contribution has been—in agriculture, road-building, exploration, science, art, education, literature and music—is the birthright of every Negro boy and girl. And the dissemination of such knowledge—if not its compilation—devolves primarily upon his teachers. Only through their unflagging persistence in the task may be attained a racial morale which will be basic to further racial achievement. Of so fundamental importance is this objective felt to be that colleges and high schools for colored youth are rapidly introducing courses in Negro history. One of their first concerns is that the students shall not disprize themselves.

In such a program sonorous hortation and chauvinistic braggadocio have no place. By the cold, clear light of depersonalized research, the Negro must face truth. Thus only may be attained an objectivity requisite to intelligent social perspective. For the fact of racial handicap may have any of a number of effects on the individual in his efforts at life adjustment. Confronted by it many a student has given up in despair, while others have gone through college on a motive power of angry defiance which drove them to achievement. The problem of educators of Negroes is to present the added hindrances to successful accomplishment imposed by race as challenges to the individual's stamina but not insuperable obstacles. Properly interpreted, the handicap can become a means for strengthening rather than undermining the personality fiber of the race.

Particularly effective for this purpose is the practise of keeping the boys and girls in touch with the present progress of the group in its ascent in American civilization. It is significant that the race has generally glorified the "first Negroes" to achieve distinction in specific fields with almost Lindberghian acclaim. The first college graduate, the first Phi Beta Kappa, the first doctor of philosophy have all been greeted with loud hosannas by press and pulpit. Some Negro leaders have deplored these enthusiastic outbursts on the ground that the people so heralded have accomplished no more than innumerable whites about them. The point, however, is that for the minority to which they belong, these "firsts" do symbolize not only an upward step in an uncertain struggle but also the demonstrated possibility of worthwhile achievement in spite of race. The attendant publicity fortifies the racial self-respect and racial self-confidence of many others. It inspires the youth with new social courage.

But *pari passu* with the program for the inspiration of an invigorating race pride in Negro youth must go an equally intensive one for the spread among white boys and girls of truthful information concerning Negro life and achievement, since otherwise still further maladjustment would obviously result. For such an undertaking by educators of white youth, the present is ripe. There is abroad in the land to-day a healthy irreverence for the opinionated oracles of this expiring social order. Modern teachers are in the ideally strategic position of facing a generation which questions the doctrinaire assumptions of its elders and prefers truth to propaganda. The opportunity is theirs to present available social data from such a view-point as to make more satisfactory the human relationships of to-morrow. The accepted thesis of planned economy is an implicit recognition of the existing need for intelligently directed social evolution, and the responsibility of charting the course of American civilization lies to no small extent in the hands of teachers. It is peculiarly their province to determine how men shall think and feel.

Simply stated, the problem of teachers in white schools is to see that their pupils derive impressions of Negro character from unbiased sources and that they get a picture of the whole. Before the bar of crystallizing public opinion the Negro has had no fair hearing. His crimes have been broadcast in sensational detail; his virtues have not been "news." That there is criminality among Negroes no one denies or doubts. The injustice of the situation is that this aspect of his racial life has been altogether disproportionately emphasized.

It is, of course, proper to discuss the Negro as a criminal when criminals are being discussed; but it is false to the ideals of this nation to dilate upon such characters to the exclusion of those which have made him an asset to American civilization. Equally with other races, the Negro has a right to be appraised at his best—or at least at his average—rather than at his lowest. He does not deserve the opprobrium which comes from the limitation of the horizon of his fellows to a knowledge of his undesirables.

Material for more comprehensive understanding of the Negro is increasingly available. The romantic facts of his career on this continent are being systematically unearthed and appreciatively told. There is no more fascinating content than the humanized results of research in this field. It possesses inspirational values for all. Incorporation of such historical and biographical data in our text-books and unbigoted presentation of it in the classroom will reveal to the children of America the facts that the Negro has achieved distinction in every type of endeavor followed by his fellow citizens and that he has made an original contribution to American culture. It will lead them to image him not as a beast or a clown but as a man. The theory of racial inferiority is in scientific disrepute. Public education must make it popularly so.

If, then, the current misconception of the Negro which vitiates the public mind is supplanted by rational evaluation, the program of racial advancement can more easily be made one of self-realization rather than self-renunciatory imitation. The teleology of the Negro educator should be the harmonious development in terms of the American environment of the natural capacities and traits of his pupils. Such an objective is, of course, axiomatic in any sound philosophy of education. With one eye on the child and the other on the changing social scheme in which he is to function, the teacher should so stimulate each pupil that he becomes a self-adapting unit of an evolving order. This means that those in charge of our schools must possess an intimate understanding of the children they teach and a broad comprehension of the civilization that environs them. For the Negro teacher, it implies unusually clear social and psychological insight.

It might be objected here that the conclusion of modern psychology is that there are no distinctly innate racial characteristics. We will not quarrel. But it is a fact established that among the masses of Negroes in America is to be found a certain *modus vivendi*—a way of thinking, feeling and acting—which constitutes their life pattern. Like other social patterns, it is composite of biological and environmental elements. Obviously discernible in it are the gifts of song and laughter, kindliness and understanding of human nature, social adaptability and boundless capacity for the enjoyment of leisure. These are traits now virtuous in any group. They are the psychological bases upon which modern civilizations must be rebuilt. In the Negro they have been the products of hard racial experiences under constantly threatening circumstances. Whether they be specifically racial attributes or general human qualities acquired in response to specific situations is not germane.

The significant consideration is that the survival values which gave them birth may, by educational processes, be transmuted into adaptive ones. What modern social need is more immediate than the patience to endure an undesirable situation combined with alertness to seize an opportunity to change it—not the patience of resignation but that of temporary toleration? When was the gift of humor more sorely requisite—not for the purpose of laughing out of consciousness the baffling problems of our economic day but of laughing them into perspective? What race can make a more healing spiritual contribution to modern life than one which, amid the demoralizing experiences of human slavery, could sublimate its miseries in melodies of dauntless faith? When was the capacity for sheer *joie de vivre* a more vital asset than in this era of increased leisure? Above all, what social habit could be more timely than that of sharing food and shelter with neighbors in distress—a folkway which has caused social workers to observe that among the lowest classes of Negroes in urban centers there seems to exist a loose form of communism? When was the cultivation of human sympathy and understanding more necessary than now? These traits are the essence of the Negro's racial heritage. They are virtues in contemporary life.

We can not, therefore, too variously emphasize the principle that the job of the Negro educator is not to create in his pupils a new set of virtues but to guide them to fulfilment of themselves on the level of their richest potentialities. It is his to see that the boys and girls under his tutelage are exposed to the best American culture has to offer and that they assimilate it in such expressions of their own nature as to give them the fullest possible personal satisfactions and at the same time enable them to contribute most worthily to American life. And never should he allow himself or them to lose sight of the inspiring fact that individuals of the race have already accomplished in every field of human activity and that to do so they had but to be themselves—their truest, wisest selves. That is the highest education of the Negro. It is the highest education of any race—and the only kind by which a group is lifted from one plane of living to a better. Ignorance of this psychological truism has been the failure of many a well-intentioned missionary enterprise.

And as the Negro educator stimulates to maturation in his pupils abilities and traits which are at once continuous with the line of their racial evolution and functional in modern life, it is the part of the white educator to develop appreciation of these characteristics in the environing majority. Abundant opportunity for so doing surrounds him if he but realizes that nothing more conduces to better understanding than wisely chosen interracial exposures—the establishment of contacts with Negroes in the study of their finer achievements. It is encouraging to note that teachers of social problems at many colleges—both north and south—are including in their course requirements direct contact with institutions and individuals representative of the best in Negro life. The action of the University of North Carolina, for example, in entertaining James Weldon Johnson as guest lecturer for a period of a week was a triumph of courageous liberalism. It has been widely and profitably emulated elsewhere. One danger of this procedure unsupplemented by further experiences, however, is that some students tend to regard such an individual as exceptional and retain their original idea of the race. A line must be determined by more than one point.

What is already being attempted at many colleges and universities is also possible in high and elementary schools. The life of most communities affords ample opportunities for enlightening interracial contacts on all grade levels. The coming to the local theater of such plays as "Green Pastures" or "Porgy" might appropriately be made an occasion for calling attention to the achievement of the Negro on the legitimate stage. A program in town by Roland Hayes, the Hampton Choir, or the Fisk Singers makes timely emphasis upon the Negro's contribution to music. Publication of such epicly American books as "Along This Way" and their advertisement at the local bookstore might be used to arouse interest in the Negro's present efforts to express himself literarily. The teacher need only be conscious of the happenings about him and quick to relate them to the work of the social studies hour.

These efforts to give white children first-hand knowledge and appreciation of Negro achievement at its highest should be accompanied by the attempt to give them a more intimate understanding of the Negro life in their own community. How this may most effectively be done will vary with local conditions. Certainly, however, they should know sympathetically and vividly the worthwhile aspirations and attainments of the darker minority in their midst. They should be made conscious of the fact that across the social *impasse* of race lies a world very similar to their own in which individuals with motives and abilities like theirs pursue kindred life purposes. Fair interpretation of this almost foreign land to the children of the country is as fundamentally the duty of the public school as the interpretation of English, French or any other life to which they have little access but understanding of which is essential to modern good citizenship. Possession of authentic information in this regard will create in them a receptivity for the contribution the Negro educator is preparing his pupils to make. It will also increase their cultural capacities.

It is important, then, that modern education inculcate in the present school generation more rationally founded attitudes on the part of the Negro towards himself and of others towards him; that it guide to fruition in useful patterns the traits and abilities indigenous to his social and biological heritage; and that it awaken in those about him an appreciation for his actual and potential contributions to American progress by providing opportunity for more intimate acquaintance with them. Its remaining task is to familiarize Negro boys and girls with the ways in which those of his group who have succeeded in spite of racial odds have done so, and to lead white boys and girls to a realization of the increased richness of American life which would result from the making possible of a greater number and variety of such contributions.

In the educational systems of all rapidly changing periods and of all rapidly progressing groups, the philosophy of opportunism must have prominent place. For the Negro the slogan of *carpe diem* has already proved the soundest of pragmatic wisdom. Because the children of this race are given fewer opportunities than the offspring of other elements of the American population they should be led to specific study of those they have with the aim of fully exploiting and increasing them. Considerable racial energy is expended—and rightfully so—in protest against the limitations placed upon the Negro's possibilities for advancement in various areas of the nation's life. Not enough is given, however, to analytical scrutiny of the ones he has. In the course of seventy years of struggle towards freedom there has been accumulated by numerous individuals a wealth of racial experience in specific ways of circumventing prejudice and succeeding in spite of it. Much of this material is in printed form. It should be made easily accessible to Negro pupils of the public schools. Any education worth the name will encourage boys and girls to study in detail the careers of people who faced problems similar to their own and solved them. Biographies like that of James Weldon Johnson—in which is depicted practically every type of situation a Negro in America may face, and the reaction to it of a great and generous mind—are at once inspirations and texts.

A whole science of living is here involved and awaits organization by the only one who can organize it—the teacher of Negro youth. His failure to do so will mean that one of the most vital needs of the young people he serves will go unmet. Negro boys and girls coming out of school should not be forced to learn—or not learn—entirely by the wasteful process of trial and error the avenues by which the abilities they have acquired may find useful expression in the larger community life. Techniques gleaned from the successes and failures of Negroes who have tried before should be part of the equipment with which they leave. They should also go forth cognizant of the current forces for and against them in their efforts to succeed, and motivated to alertness to take advantage of every fortuitous combination of circumstances which may speed them to a higher goal. This is differential education only in the sense that every intelligent educator studies the life needs of his pupil and seeks to meet them through the instrumentality of an elastic curriculum.

And as the Negro educator focusses the attention of those he instructs on specific strategies in utilizing the opportunities they have, it is the rôle of the white educator to demonstrate to his pupils the benefits to modern civilization which would inevitably accrue from the multiplication of such channels. In the age of machine-made plenty, at the threshold of which we have arrived, the old factor of cut-throat competition for the means of bare subsistence is scheduled to pass from our life into our history. One of the most pregnant causes for the denial of opportunities to Negroes in many fields has been the conviction—at least subconscious in the mind of the dominant group—that the more desirable opportunities were given to Negroes, the fewer there would be for themselves—that the progress of the race must be inversely proportional to theirs. "Holding the Negro down," therefore, was to a large degree an expression of the survival instinct and characteristically the attitude of those most closely in competition with him. But in this period of transition from an individualistic to a social economy, it can be emphasized that in the reorganized industrial régime which is before us there will be material sufficiency for all—that none need be denied to provide enough for another. The pointing out by educators that the economic motive for circumscribing the opportunities of Negroes has been out-evolved will tremendously weaken opposition to his advancement.

They can do more. Upon the shoulders of American education rests the responsibility of giving to every class of our citizenry a comprehension of the truth already accepted by the more thoughtful that the self-realization of one individual or group increases the possibilities for self-realization of all others. Humanity's highest achievements are quickly communized. On the plane of the civilization to which we must advance unless we retrogress into barbarism, the contributions of each will be the property of all. The presence in our culture of such living examples of the developed genius of a race as Johnson, Hays, Braithwaite and others like them makes accessible to the entire nation a greater variety of finer satisfactions than it otherwise would have. If America can be made to see this fact and to see, further, the social waste which results from the denial of avenues for fullest development to millions of these men's compatriots there will arise thousands of white people working as hard on their side of the barrier to remove the impediments to the race's advancement as Negroes are working on theirs; until the structure of American society has been so channeled and its spirit so enlightened that all who come bearing gifts may be graciously received at the altar of a common culture.

The sum of our hopes, therefore, is that modern education shall see this problem clearly and whole, to the end that teachers in every section of the country and at every level of instruction will work upon these aspects of it immediate to them, conscious of the relation of the parts they play to the synchronized efforts of others. The result will be the production, on one side, of a generation of racially self-respecting Negroes seeking the fullest possible self-development and continuously alert for occasions to serve American life, and, on the other side, of a generation of whites unprejudicedly evaluating their darker fellow-citizens, acquainted with their accomplishments, and actively sympathetic with their aspirations for more adequate outlets. Such is the specific educational attack on a problem which has hitherto been tacitly evaded as a dangerously "delicate" matter. It concerns itself with the treatment of deep-lying causes rather than superficial effects.

And let it be remembered, too, that we are here considering a question which is more than a matter of securing justice for an overwhelmed minority. It is *in micro* the problem of the modern world. The survival of civilization ultimately hinges on the ability of peoples widely differing to live side by side, equal yet not identical, integrated yet not amalgamated, each more nurturing to each because of their varied individualities. Unless, then, America can equitably solve its Negro question, it must confess the failure of the principle upon which its government rests and leave to others demonstration of the ways in which diverse races may live side by side to their common elevation. There lies the challenge to the modern educator. On the very frontier of social change, in a nation which was established as the testing ground of democracy, he has the privilege to stand—uncompromising and unapologetic—upon a platform of equality of opportunity which will be significant for times to come. Only through him can American idealism preserve its soul.

# THE AMERICAN FEDERATION OF TEACHERS

By Dr. HENRY R. LINVILLE
PRESIDENT, LOCAL 5, NEW YORK CITY

PROBABLY there is no disagreement among teachers on the need for them to take an active part in their own defense and in the defense of public education. But the American Federation of Teachers holds that the old methods of trying to improve the professional status of teachers by exhortation or by administrative measures have failed. We still have before us the problems of developing better teachers and better teaching conditions, and we have now the additional problem of contending with the social forces that threaten to impede the progress of education by cutting down expenditures and by eliminating services. So far as we of the American Federation of Teachers can see, there is no way to work through these problems to a solution, except by developing a deeper interest in the problems on the part of teachers and on the part of other social groups. Following the development of interest and understanding there must be organization. Teachers themselves must organize for definite objectives, and they must secure support from the socially minded groups in the community.

It seems to us in the teachers' unions that organization is more likely to be effective if it is fundamentally social in character, extending down into the realm of the groups that belong to the producing class of our people. The basic concern of this class is economic; we believe that economic interest is the basic concern of all workers, including teachers. The trade union movement itself is without question the most definitely economic type of social organization that has yet been developed. Its spread throughout the world is evidence of its basic appeal and of its validity as a social movement.

Valid tests of the fundamentally social character of the trade union movement may be cited in the nature and the extent of its contributions to the general welfare. The American Federation of Labor and its predecessors in the field of labor in this country have made many such contributions. No other power would have cut down the hours of labor for all workers or would have raised the wage scale and the standards of living for the great majority—even for those who were never members of the organization. No other power would have brought about the installation of safety devices in industrial plants or would have gone so far in securing protection for the health of workers. No other agency has striven so effectively for the protection of women and children in industry. Indeed, no other agency has given so much support to the public schools for the entire period of one hundred years in which public schools have existed in this country. By all these tests, and by still others, the American labor movement is fundamentally social in character.

In the period of the depression the drive for retrenchment in the legitimate costs of public education has been engineered and directed by real estate, industrial and banking interests, motivated chiefly by the desire to maintain the old levels of dividends and profits. There were two reasons why organized labor came to the rescue of the schools in this period. The first reason was that the deflation of the salaries of public-service employees threatened the income and the standards of living of all wage-earners. The second reason was the historical interest of the American labor movement in the public school as an institution through which the children of the workers would have the same opportunities as the children of the well-to-do. Prior to one hundred years ago the free school in this country was either a charitable institution or a religious school. In the period from 1828 to 1834 the trade unions and the Workingmen's Party, acting chiefly in the industrial states of the Atlantic Coast region, kept up an incessant demand for what they called "free and equal, tax-supported public education." Although Horace Mann in Massachusetts, Henry Barnard in Rhode Island and Connecticut and Thaddeus Stevens in Pennsylvania were the chief public leaders of this movement, the labor movement provided the social force that completed the drive. The labor movement is still true to its historic rôle of defending the public schools against the profit-seekers and in behalf of all the children.

The American Federation of Teachers, which since 1916 has been affiliated with the American Federation of Labor, is frankly an economic organization. But it is much more than that. It has a program which includes the improvement of the status of the profession of teaching, the improvement of education and the defense of education against those who would curtail educational services in the interest of dividends. We would improve the status of teachers by striving for the establishment of salary schedules on the basis of the value of the work to society. We would work for the establishment of adequate pensions and would try to secure legal tenure for all teachers after a short probationary period. We would seek to abolish all systems of the compulsory rating of the service of teachers, and would substitute intelligent, cooperative supervision for the petty, fault-finding supervision which is now in vogue. We would improve the status of teachers by discrediting all attempts at supervising their out-of-school activities, their wearing apparel or their points of view. We would improve the effectiveness of teachers by showing them that freedom in the classroom and social interest, both in the classroom and out of it, are among the best stimuli to good teaching, and for satisfactory personal and group living. In short, we would destroy all barriers that tend to place teachers under disciplinary restraint as if they were wards of the state and would establish the conditions that tend to create a self-respecting and socially efficient profession.

We would improve public education by endeavoring to set up in every school system an experimental school into which new materials and ideas for education could be brought, and where new methods of presenting subject-matter could be tried out, and also where the learning process itself could be studied. Such an experimental school could serve further as a laboratory for the education of teachers.

Certain locals of the American Federation of Teachers have already done a great deal in the preparation of studies that show the source of the attacks on public education by the "vested interests." The Teachers Union of New York City has recently pointed out to the members of a group of five distinguished educators the impropriety of their serving as an advisory committee to the New York State Economic Council, which has fought all propositions for maintaining the statutory appropriations for public education and has claimed as one of its successes the defeat of the Child Labor Amendment in the 1934 session of the New York State Legislature. This council has also recently proposed that all persons who receive public relief shall be disfranchised. The Teachers Union holds that it is unprofessional for educators to ally themselves, even in an imaginary advisory capacity, with the obvious enemies of the general welfare.

The American Federation of Teachers first pointed out the economic necessity of a federal system of taxation for public education that would tap all sources of wealth, inasmuch as neither local land taxation nor state taxation of incomes will provide the funds which the schools must have. Some well-known authorities in school finance have accepted our idea of federal taxation, which would not involve federal control of educational policy. And the National Education Association has supported in part our demand for $600,000,000 yearly from the Federal Government by demanding an annual appropriation of $500,000,000.

The question of the relation of teachers to the social order has often been raised. Our answer to that question is that whatever the future holds in store for this country, the American Federation of Teachers is committed to the principles of political, social and educational democracy. It will endeavor to promote the welfare of teachers and the progress of education through these principles. By direct implication the organization is opposed to all forms of dictatorship in political government, in social and industrial relations, as well as in education. The organization regards as futile any talk of the teachers as a class fighting for a form of government different from that in which the school may function normally as a part of the general social set-up. The public school never has been, and never can be, a revolutionary element in civilization. The consensus of opinion among us is that our objectives are most likely to be attained, and the perpetuation of the public school as a sound social institution assured, under some form of political collectivism.

As an outcome of the organization's stand on democracy in education, we can not logically support the announced plan of the National Survey of the Education of Teachers by which the work and the qualifications of teachers are to be improved by a method that is chiefly administrative and compulsory in character. In a preliminary announcement made by the survey in 1931 all tenure laws are to be scrapped and the certification of teachers made for periods of five years with renewable certification on proof of professional improvement. Under such a system teachers could never be sure of their tenure beyond the five-year period, and all the benefits of the civil service features of tenure would be lost to us. We oppose propositions of this kind, not because we want to protect incompetence, but because we believe that school officials can not protect competence, ruled as most school officials are by the exigencies of partisan politics or by the dictation of the special interests. We believe that in the long run the profession, organized on the basis of a program to develop its own standards, can be trusted to maintain those standards, as other professions are trusted. The present system of officially controlled advancement which the National Survey Commission would continue has produced unsatisfactory results, granting to the full the desire of the commission to improve the profession. In the face of lack of interest on the part of a largely indifferent profession, compulsion simply will not work. There must be developed the necessary cooperation through participation and interest.

Another phase of our program for the improvement of the professional status of teachers is our position on the interference of partisan politics with the promotion to the higher positions in the educational service. In New York City and in many other places all high positions in educational administration are political prizes. We condemn this system unqualifiedly, and also decline to take part in political trading for the support of any of our measures in state legislatures or in Congress. Our answer to solicitous politicians is that we presume that whatever support they give to our measures is given in the public interest.

We hold that the welfare of education is bound up with other phases of a society that promote the well-being of all the people. Therefore, we are opposed to war and to its cause, the exploitation of the many by the privileged classes. We are opposed to military training in the schools and colleges and to the development of the war spirit everywhere.

We are not unaware of objections to affiliation with teachers' unions that are held by a considerable number of teachers in all grades of the education service from kindergarten to the university. For example:

(1) It is held to be improper for teachers to join a union because teaching is a profession, and teachers should never lower the standards of their own profession by affiliating with groups that are not professional, such as miners, iron-workers, masons and the like.

(2) It is held to be disloyal to the public for teachers to affiliate with the labor section of the community against the community as a whole.

(3) Teachers in a union are believed to be liable to be called out on strike, either a sympathetic strike or a strike for a direct objective of their own.

(4) Some assume the attitude of direct attack by saying that the labor movement in this country is too conservative and, indeed, is reactionary. Furthermore, it is maintained that labor leaders are not educated enough to head a movement for social and educational reconstruction.

The following interpretations are offered as answers to these objections:

(1) If the members of any occupational group find themselves exploited or discriminated against by another social group, as by employers or government officials, or find it impossible to protect the standards by which living and working are carried

on, the distinction between a profession and a trade tends to disappear. For example, when the professional actors found that the theater managers meant to increase their profits by refusing fair pay or by dismissing at will, the actors took the advice of the organized stage carpenters and formed the Actors Equity Association, which has been affiliated with the American Federation of Labor for several years. Actors are now guaranteed pay for all performances and freedom from other discriminations. Similarly, another self-respecting profession has been protecting itself through the American Federation of Musicians. Teachers are not yet in the position to maintain an attitude of professionalism superior to that of the actors or of the musicians. But they could develop an attitude of professionalism through effective and general organization into unions, backed by the social power of the trade union movement.

(2) On the second point of being disloyal to the community, we are in an especially favorable position now to raise the question of who constitute the community. Is it all the people or is it the controlling elements in the community, such, for example, as chambers of commerce or the owners of the industrial institutions or the merchants' associations? As a matter of fact, the community is not the majority of the people. It is rather the minority groups who own and control, together with their representatives in the local governments. We maintain that what organized teachers have done in this country has been in the interest of the community as well as in the interest of society as a whole. We are willing to have our work estimated on that basis.

(3) On the point of the strike, we question the understanding of those who raise the issue. First of all, the American Federation of Labor is what its name implies—a federation of independent national bodies. No part of the federation has the right, or may assume the power, to compel any other part to participate in a strike. Moreover, whenever strikes in industry have been successful, they have been won because there has been cohesive power in the union and in the national body of which the union was a part. Furthermore, there had to be a certain amount of economic control of the output in the industry in the hands of the union. In the third place, there had to be definite public support of the striking union to set off against the public inconvenience which might be caused. Do any of our critics seriously believe that American teachers have cohesive power, or are likely soon to develop it, or that they have control of educational output, or that the public would support a strike of teachers as a policy? It is well known that the Board of Education of the city of Chicago, throughout the long period of the grievous exploitation of teachers, faced with equanimity the possibility of a strike among Chicago teachers, many of whom belonged to the unions. The board would have welcomed a strike, because a strike could have been charged as default of contract and as an excuse for employing substitute teachers or other persons at lower pay—or at promised pay. The constitution of the American Federation of Teachers contains no strike provision—a fact which together with a non-strike policy adopted in 1920 would appear to settle the question. It is true that unorganized, desperate teachers in this country have gone on strike. It is also true that the organized teachers of France have engaged in successful strikes on several occasions.

(4) In answer to objection Number 4, it will be granted that organized labor in this country is a conservative force. But first of all, its conservatism has had the effect of preserving the rights and the standards which by its own efforts the movement

built up out of an environment and social situation which were inimical to its entire program. As a matter of fact, every success of the labor movement in this country has been attained in the face of charges of radicalism made by opponents, and even in the face of unfair court decisions and legislation. Every demonstration of the economic power of labor, from strikes through picketing, from opposition to so-called "yellow-dog" contracts to success in collective bargaining, has been denounced, not as proof of conservatism and reaction, but as proof of radicalism and even of "revolutionary designs."

It will be granted, also, that the tendency of organized labor in this country has been to hold zealously to its gains and, in some quarters, to oppose with attitudes of violence such political movements as appeared to be directed toward the capture or the destruction of the American Federation of Labor. Among those who complain of the reactionary tendency of the American labor movement and denounce its leaders as "labor fakers" or as "betrayers of the workers" are those who would set up in this country a left-wing political dictatorship. It is a credit to the labor movement that it opposes not only political dictatorship, but industrial and economic dictatorship as well.

It may be granted, further, that in the fifty-three years of the existence of the American Federation of Labor some unprogressive leadership has developed. But the leadership has one great advantage over leadership in the field of education as thus far developed. The social experience of labor leaders has had fundamental educational effect in giving them social understanding of the problems of human existence. In the long run labor leadership becomes as progressive and as aggressive as the exigencies of the economic existence of the class it serves require it to be. If those who sit in academic chairs and charge labor with being reactionary were fortunate enough to be subjected to similar social discipline, our academic education might be more effective socially than it is.

Among those labor leaders who have attained eminence as citizens and have demonstrated in their social outlook and in their character the educative possibilities of participation in the labor movement is the able president of the American Federation of Labor, Mr. William Green. Mr. Green has recently spoken to the teachers of this country, in part as follows:

> Let the teachers organize and organize effectively for mutual help and mutual protection. The opportunity is here and the organization which the teachers of the nation ought to join is functioning. The hosts of labor, those who make up the great organized labor movement, appeal to the teachers to join with them, to come with them and to work with them in the establishment of higher living standards and in the fight which the wage earners and the salary earners of the nation are making to bring about the realization of American ideals.

# EDUCATIONAL EVENTS

## TEACHER-TRAINING IN PALESTINE

A Department of Education, whose primary purpose is to improve the quality of teacher-training in Palestine, is the latest development announced by the Hebrew University, Jerusalem, whose head is Dr. Judah L. Magnes, an American, formerly connected with Temple Emanu-el, New York, and a leader in educational and liberal movements in this country.

An American has been chosen to head the new department, which will be organized along the lines of the latest developments in educational work in the United States, including the establishment of a practice school. Dr. Alexander Dushkin, at present head of the Chicago Board of Jewish Education, has been appointed to the post of associate professor in educational method and administration, and will leave for

Palestine in December of this year, to take up his new work.

The new department is sponsored by a group of American teachers, educators and social workers, under the chairmanship of A. P. Schoolman, director of the Central Jewish Institute of New York. The committee plans to raise the sum of $10,000 annually, to provide for the appointment of several assistants to Dr. Dushkin, and a psychologist to be attached to it. The practise school is expected to be self-supporting. The American committee will endeavor to supply funds for scholarships for talented, but needy students.

The department will be established as part of the Faculty of Humanities (equivalent to our School of Arts and Sciences), and will provide opportunities for graduate studies in pedagogy by teachers employed in the public and private schools of Palestine. It is planned that the department will also carry on research and experimentation with the idea of improving the standards of the Palestinian school system.

Mr. Schoolman points out that "An outstanding need of the educational system of Palestine is the better training of teachers. The Palestinian teachers' seminaries are in reality secondary schools, on the model of the European gymnasium, which make provision only during the last year for imparting pedagogic principles and practise. Educators and parents in Palestine are pleading for more adequately trained teachers, as well as opportunities for post-graduate training for teachers already in the school service. It is only natural that the Hebrew University, which is the crown of the Palestinian school system, should supply this need."

Mr. Schoolman states that the Hebrew University has the staff and also the equipment for training teachers adequately to instruct students beyond the elementary school system. The practice school which the American committee hopes to see established and opened by Dr. Dushkin by the fall of 1935 will provide students in the new department of education with opportunities for practical training, and will enable experimentation to be conducted along the lines of modern progressive educational principles.

Dr. Dushkin has been connected with the Jewish schools of Chicago for the past eleven years, and has also been a member of the lecturing staff of the University of Chicago during that time. Previous to his removal to Chicago, he was associated with the Bureau of Jewish Education in New York as teacher and principal in its schools. He is the author of a treatise on "Jewish Education in New York City," published in 1918, which is said to be a classic reference book in the field. He has been the editor of *The Jewish Education Magazine,* and is the author of numerous articles on that subject.

Dr. Dushkin was the first Jewish inspector of schools appointed by the Government of Palestine under Sir Herbert Samuel, during his residence in that country from 1919 to 1921. During that period he was associated with the Zionist Board of Education, and taught in the Hebrew Teachers' Seminary in Jerusalem.

In addition to Mr. Schoolman, other members of the American Committee for Support of the Department of Education include Dr. Samson Benderly, director of the Bureau of Jewish Education, New York; Dr. Adele Bildersee, dean of the Women's Division, Brooklyn College; Israel S. Chipkin, director of the Jewish Education Association; Professor Morris R. Cohen, of the Department of Philosophy, College of the City of New York; Professor A. J. Goldforb, of the College of the City of New York; Professor Isaac Husik, of the Department of Philosophy, University of Pennsylvania.

## LOANS TO STUDENTS OF COLUMBIA UNIVERSITY

MORE than $1,500,000 has been loaned to students of Columbia University during the past twenty-five years, according to a report of the Loan Fund made public by Nicholas McD. McKnight, associate dean of the college and chairman of the Loan Fund Committee. Loans amounting to $183,000 were made to 974 students during 1933–34.

A decrease in the number of applicants for loans, which is evident this fall, it is pointed out is "an evidence that the depression is on the wane." Loans this year will total about $150,000. The report says:

About 97 per cent. of the loans are used to pay

tuition fees. The smallest loan is for $22.50, usually given to a student who has failed to include the student activities fee as part of his expenses. The largest is $265.00, tuition at the Medical School.

Last year students from practically every department of the university received loans, with 289 students in the college leading. Loans made to students in the Graduate Faculties numbered 176; the Law School, 124; the Summer Session, 26; the Medical School, 58; Engineering, 50; Business, 71; Dentistry, 38; Extension, 54; University Undergraduates, 26; Optometry, 11; Seth Low Junior College, 12; Library Service, 12; Journalism, 12; Architecture, 15. Barnard College and Teachers College have their own loan funds.

The Columbia Loan Fund was organized on a small scale about thirty years ago, but as the university expanded and the number of self, or partly-supporting students increased, the officials looked for ways and means of giving the students financial aid. The loans are just what they imply. They are not scholarships, for the students pay an interest rate of 5 per cent. and eventually return the principal, either during their college career or shortly after they are graduated and obtain employment.

In 1926 the Loan Fund was reorganized to meet the ever increasing needs of the students and also to encourage worthy students to remain in college.

There is an element of competition in the awarding of loans; each applicant must be acceptable to three officials in three different departments of the university. The first official that the student comes in contact with when applying for a loan is the dean of the school in which he is studying. The dean passes upon his academic ability, personal fitness and decides whether the student will be worth the investment.

The latter problem touches upon the possibility of the student completing his courses, obtaining a degree, and otherwise being worthy of aid. Naturally, if a student is careless, shows little interest in his studies, and may drop out of college after a semester or two, there is no need of aiding him because the money can be applied toward the expenses of a more worthy student.

Once an applicant receives the approval of his dean, the secretary of appointments looks over the record of the student to see what he is doing in regard to obtaining part-time employment as a means of earning his way through college. The bursar considers the applicant from the viewpoint of his financial record, whether he has been given previous loans and paid them back, and whether he is earning money on part-time employment.

Most of the loans are repaid in installments, usually of $5 or $10, so that there will always be money available for other needy students. No loans are made for over a period of one year, but the notes are renewable upon payment of interest.

The principal of the Loan Fund is about $700,000, this money having come from gifts, appropriations by the university, and, in many cases, the returning to Columbia of money equal to the scholarships former students once held. Former students who have received loans from Columbia paid back $183,000 to the university during the last twelve months, some of the money having been loaned as far back as 1911. As notes are being repaid nearly every day, the money can be used over and over again.

With $183,000 loaned last year, the sum being about equally divided between the first and second semesters, the Loan Fund reached a new high. The previous academic year, $173,000 was loaned. In 1931–32 the figure was $145,000; 1930–31, $116,000; 1929–30, $109,000; 1928–29, $78,000; 1926–27, $77,000.

Members of the Loan Fund Committee, in addition to Chairman McKnight, are Dean Joseph W. Barker, School of Engineering; Professor James P. Gifford, School of Law; Professor Edgar G. Miller, Jr., Medical School, and W. Emerson Gentzler, secretary of appointments.

## STUDY OF THE FEDERAL GOVERNMENT BY STUDENTS OF YALE UNIVERSITY

A PLAN for a week's visit in Washington next spring by a selected group of juniors and seniors, for the purpose of studying the Federal Government in action at short range, was announced to-day by Professor Nicholas J. Spykman, Sterling professor of international relations at Yale University. About a dozen young men will be chosen on the basis of interest and proficiency in the field including the honors students in the department, and others whose major subject is government. The trip will be made during the spring reading period, and the bulk of the expenses of those selected will be paid by the university from the funds of the Block Foundation, established at Yale by Paul Block, of New York City. The work done in Washington will count as an important part of the students' honors or course work for the year.

The program will be arranged in cooperation

with the recently established National Institution of Public Affairs in Washington. The group will be under the guidance of Professors Spykman and Harvey C. Mansfield, who will also make the trip and will direct conferences and discussions each day, based on the day's activities. It is planned to include visits to each branch of Congress and their committees, the Supreme Court, the Executive Offices at the White House, and the principal administrative agencies, together with the press bureaus and the headquarters of important lobbying organizations. Preliminary reading will be assigned and done in advance, so as to insure the maximum benefit from the short time available for the field work. After the trip is over each student will write a paper dealing with some phase of the week's activities. In this way it is hoped that by a short and intensive period of study those who make the trip will obtain a more real and concrete appreciation of the functions and working of the federal government than is possible in the classrooms and library alone.

This trip will therefore carry out the general purpose of the Block Foundation to promote a better understanding of the press and public opinion in their relation to government, and will, it is also hoped, encourage a more active participation by college men in the affairs of the national government. If the experiment proves successful, it may be possible to make the arrangement a permanent feature of the offerings of the Department of Government.

## AN EMERGENCY COLLEGE AT YONKERS

In response to the request of the Commissioner of Education and of Dr. L. A. Wilson, in charge of extension work for the University of the State of New York, President Frederick B. Robinson, president of the College of the City of New York, consented to canvass the feasibility of establishing an emergency college at Yonkers. The problem was to determine how many superior graduates of high schools residing in Yonkers there were who were fully eligible for college but who could not go to college because of financial disability.

Superintendent Lamont F. Hodge, of the Yonkers schools, has been cooperating in this survey. He and Deputy Superintendent William R. Williams supplied the various high-school principals with the regular application blanks of the College of the City of New York so that application could be made on the same forms as those used by the college in dealing with its own students.

The Commissioner of Education requested President Robinson to preserve the same standards in the emergency colleges as those maintained at the College of the City of New York itself so that students admitted to the college and completing its courses could have credit which would be acceptable should the students later find themselves able to be transferred to other institutions of higher learning.

The officers of administration and instruction at the College of the City of New York have generously given their help in this undertaking and have been evaluating the application blanks. It appears, on the whole, that most of the superior students of Yonkers who wished to go to college have been sent to college and have been cared for, and that relatively few are now left who require the assistance of the emergency college, but there is a large group of what might be called border-line cases, namely, those who have their diplomas and have very respectable grades in the various subjects but who have not reached the level ordinarily required by the College of the City of New York for admission. In conference with Deputy Superintendent Williams, President Robinson agreed to take in this group of students on what will be known as a C probation. They will be assigned a program of studies less than that given to the students fully meeting college entrance requirements and they will be allowed to continue in residence only so long as they maintain an average grade of C in their college work. It is understood that probationary attendance of this sort is in lieu of entrance examinations, which it is not possible to conduct on short notice at the emergency college. After a staff has been organized for the college, and for future terms, the exact standards of the College of the City of New York can be imposed because those who have not maintained the superior average required for admission on certification can then be given opportunity to demonstrate their capacity for college work by entrance examinations.

President Robinson states that very successful work has been achieved in the emergency college at Garden City, Nassau County, and at the emergency college in White Plains, Westchester County, under his general supervision, and he has every reason to hope that a superior center can be established in Yonkers. The only question that is uncertain at this time is whether or not the number of persons in Yonkers who are qualified for college admission and who have not already been taken care of in excellent colleges is sufficiently great to enable the administration of a fairly extensive program of college subjects.

## EDWARD W. BROWNING'S BEQUESTS FOR PUBLIC WELFARE

BY the will of the late Edward W. Browning, of New York City, the income from his residuary estate, said to be over $5,000, will be divided into six equal portions and such portion be devoted each year as a prize for the results achieved during such year in the six classes or purposes outlined in the will which are to be known as the Browning Prizes. The classes are as follows: "The prevention of cruelty to children or animals, or the promotion of peace and international harmony.

"The spreading of the Gospel under Protestant auspices, either by distinguished example, effective teaching or exceptional service.

"The uplifting of the moral condition of the world, either by some direct and positive service or example to that end, or by the introduction or furtherance of methods most successful in decreasing vice, gambling, intemperance; or dishonesty and corruption in government and politics.

"The production of the most serviceable invention or useful discovery; or architectural improvement in fireproofing and sanitation or otherwise; or the most important work of art in painting, sculpture or literature.

"The most widely beneficial discovery or new method in medicine, surgery or in the prevention of disease.

"The increased production or improvement of fish, birds or animals; the conservation of forests; the irrigation of arid lands; the increase or improvement of crops, flowers or plants." The value of Mr. Browning's estate is said to be $7,000,000. The testament, dated in December, 1912, named as trustees of the prize funds the late Dr. Elmer Ellsworth Brown, formerly chancellor of New York University; Dr. Nicholas Murray Butler, president of Columbia University; Dr. John H. Finley, Robert T. Morris, M.D.; Dr. Henry S. Pritchett; The Rev. Henry A. Stimson, and the late Clarence H. Kelsey.

## LECTURES AT COOPER UNION

SIXTY-SEVEN lectures by professors of Columbia, Cornell, New York University, College of the City of New York, the New School for Social Research, and other schools and universities constitute the free educational program of the new Department of Social Philosophy at Cooper Union for 1934–35, as announced by Professor Everett Dean Martin. Numerous study and discussion classes will also be held.

Carrying on the work of the People's Institute, which was discontinued recently after an existence of thirty-seven years, the department will maintain at Cooper Union a free platform for the discussion of philosophical and social problems.

The lectures, which it is planned to conduct "in a spirit of scientific inquiry and academic freedom," will be given in the Great Hall of the Union and are expected to attract an attendance for the year of 75,000. There will be no charge for admission, no requirements for registration and no academic credit. "Can the Economic Problem Be Solved without Resort to Dictatorship?" was the subject of the opening lecture by Professor Martin Friday evening, November 9. Professor Martin will deliver twenty other Friday evening lectures in a course entitled "What Will the American People Do in the Present World Crisis?" Discussing "In Defense of the Individualist" on November 11, John Erskine, president of the Juilliard School of Music, will open a series of Sunday evening lectures on the general theme "What Can People Believe in the Modern World?"

Other Sunday evening lecturers include: Dr. Horace M. Kallen, New School for Social Research; Professor Robert M. MacIver, Columbia University; Professor Morris Cohen, College of the City of New York; Professor Richard McKeon, Columbia University; Dr. C. R. Stockard, Cornell Medical School; Professor Harry A. Overstreet, College of the City of New York;

Dr. Henry P. Van Dusen, Union Theological Seminary; Professor Scott Buchanan, University of Virginia; Professor Edward G. Spaulding, Princeton University; Professor Irwin Edman, Columbia University; Professor George S. Counts, Teachers College, Columbia University; Professor Mortimer J. Adler, University of Chicago; Houston Peterson, lecturer at Columbia and Rutgers Universities.

Professor Allan Nevins of Columbia is among twenty-three lecturers who will speak in a symposium styled "Can People Be Happy in a Planned Economy?" beginning on November 13 and ending on April 30. "Self-Regulation in Industry: Its Possibilities and Its Limits" will be the subject of Professor Nevins, who was recently appointed to the Sir George Watson chair of American history, literature and institutions, to lecture at the University of London this winter. Other lecturers in this series are: Professor Robert S. Lynd, Columbia University; Clifton Fadiman, writer; Professor Buchanan; Professor McKeon; Dr. Henry J. Fry, Cornell Medical School; Professor Lyman Bryson, Teachers College, Columbia University; Professor Frederick Barry, Columbia University; Professor Adler, Dean Howard Lee McBain, Graduate Faculties, Columbia University; William B. Curry, Dartington School, England.

## RADIO TALKS ON PUBLIC HEALTH

SIR ARTHUR NEWSHOLME, formerly head of the public health service in England, will speak from London on November 18, at 12:45 P. M., Eastern Standard Time, over a WABC–Columbia network, on "Medical Care for All."

This is a special broadcast in the Public Health series—entitled "Doctors, Dollars and Disease"—sponsored by the National Advisory Council on Radio in Education.

The regular series will be resumed on Monday, November 19, when Thomas Parran, Jr., State Health Commissioner of New York, speaks on "Public Health Needs." The time is advanced a quarter of an hour, to 10:30 P. M., Eastern Standard Time.

Other speakers who will be heard on Monday evenings include Ray Lyman Wilbur, president of Stanford University, formerly Secretary of the Interior in the Hoover Cabinet; Edward A. Filene, of Boston; Dr. George H. Bigelow, of the Massachusetts General Hospital; Professor Paul H. Douglas, of the University of Chicago; Dr. William T. Foster, director of the Pollak Foundation; Dr. Michael M. Davis and C. Rufus Rorem, of the Julius Rosenwald Fund; I. S. Falk and Edgar Sydenstricker, of the Milbank Memorial Fund; William Hard, publicist; Frank Van Dyk, executive-secretary of the Hospital Council of Essex County, New Jersey; Homer Wickenden, director of the United Hospital Fund of New York; Miss Katharine Tucker, director of the National Organization for Public Health Nursing; Nathan Sinai, director of research of the Michigan State Medical Society; Dr. Haven Emerson, formerly president of the American Public Health Association; Harry H. Moore, director of study of the Committee on the Costs of Medical Care, and Dr. Livingston Farrand, president of Cornell University.

These programs aim to stimulate discussion of public health problems, the costs of medical care, the relation between the medical profession and the public, and ways of reconciling the interests of the two groups. They do not advocate any one solution, but simply furnish reliable information as a basis for the solution of the problem, mainly economic, of the under-employed and poorly paid doctor and nurse, and the uncared-for patient.

Three addresses were presented in October, by Dr. Robert Jolly, president of the American Hospital Association; Dr. C.-E. A. Winslow, of the School of Medicine of Yale University, and Dr. Walter P. Bowers, editor of the *New England Journal of Medicine*. The Public Health Committee of the National Advisory Council on Radio in Education is composed of Surgeon-General H. S. Cumming, Senator Robert F. Wagner, Dr. Haven Emerson, Dr. George E. Vincent, Dr. Alice Hamilton, Dr. Thomas Parran, Jr., Dr. Ray Lyman Wilbur and Dr. William Trufant Foster, *chairman*. "The problem," according to the committees, " is to bring doctors and dollars and diseases into such helpful and continuous contact with each other that the practice of medicine can keep pace with the science of medicine."

# EDUCATIONAL NOTES AND NEWS

Dr. Arthur A. Hauck, formerly dean of Lafayette College, was installed on November 3 as the eighth president of the University of Maine. He succeeds Dr. Harold S. Boardman, whose resignation became effective in June. In his address Dr. Hauck outlined a program for the development of the university. Other speakers were Edward E. Chase, of Portland, a member of the board of trustees, and Bertram E. Packard, Commissioner of Education for the state of Maine. Speakers at the alumni-faculty luncheon included Governor Louis J. Brann, Dr. Morland King, head of the department of electrical engineering at Lafayette College, who brought greetings to the university from Dr. Hauck's former associates, and George S. Williams, of Augusta, president of the General Alumni Association.

Donald William MacKay was installed as first president of the New Mexico Junior College at Portales on October 6, in the presence of citizens and representatives from institutions of higher learning in New Mexico and neighboring states.

Dr. W. H. Cramblet, for many years treasurer of Bethany College, has been elected president of the institution, a position his father, Thomas E. Cramblet, held from 1901 to 1919. He succeeds Dr. Joseph A. Serena, who resigned last June.

Allan Vanderhoef Heely, a member of the department of English and assistant dean at Phillips Andover Academy, has been appointed head master of the Lawrenceville School, N. J. He will be installed on November 29, Thanksgiving Day. Mr. Heely succeeds Dr. Mather A. Abbott, who died on May 7.

The *Journal* of the National Education Association writes: "Agnes Samuelson, a member of the executive committee of the National Education Association, and state superintendent of public instruction for Iowa, recently received unique recognition when the Democratic state committee voted not to nominate a candidate in opposition to Miss Samuelson, who is a Republican. This, in effect, takes the state superintendency for this year out of politics and leaves Miss Samuelson unopposed for the election."

An informal tea for Professor Gilbert D. Harris, who this fall retires from active teaching, was given on October 21 by members of the faculty of geology at Cornell University and of the two geological fraternities Chi Upsilon and Sigma Gamma Epsilon. The out-of-town guests included several former students. Numerous telegrams were received and letters of greeting from friends and students now engaged in geological work throughout the United States, Canada, South America and South Africa.

Dr. John H. Wyckoff, dean of New York University College of Medicine, has been made president-elect of the American Association of Medical Colleges. He succeeds Dr. Ross V. Patterson, dean of Jefferson Medical College, Philadelphia, who will preside at the Toronto meeting next year.

J. W. Potter, since 1927 superintendent of the Carlisle schools, has been elected president of the Southern Convention District of Pennsylvania.

Dr. T. Gilbert Pearson, executive head of the National Association of Audubon Societies for the last twenty-four years, has retired and has been elected president emeritus. Kermit Roosevelt has been elected president and John H. Baker, who until now has been chairman of the board of directors, has been named executive director.

McCready Huston, associate editor of the *Scranton Republican,* has been appointed professor of journalism at the University of Pittsburgh.

At the University of Maine, Dr. Edward F. Dow, who, since the retirement of Dr. Caroline Colvin, has been acting head of the department of history, has been appointed head of the department with the rank of associate professor. Professor Weston S. Evans has been promoted to be the head of the department of civil engineering.

Through a reorganization of the administrative policy of the Colorado Agricultural College last spring, heads of divisions have been made deans of divisions. The following are the present deans: agriculture, Dr. E. P. Sandsten;

engineering, E. B. House; home economics, Inga M. K. Allison; science, Dr. G. H. Whiteford; veterinary medicine, Dr. I. E. Newsom; men, S. Arthur Johnson, and dean of women, Mrs. Amy O. Parmelee. Charles A. Lory continues as president.

DR. EUGENE HILTON, principal of the Edison Elementary School, Oakland, California, has been appointed supervisor of social studies through the elementary, junior and senior high schools of Oakland.

ALVIN W. SHEPARD, director of intermediate school grades in the public schools of Buffalo, N. Y., has submitted his resignation. Mr. Shepard has been connected with the Buffalo schools for thirty-nine years.

DR. WILLIAM A. HOWE retired on October 1 as chief of the Medical Inspection Bureau of the New York State Department of Education after a service to the department and to the schools of the state of nearly twenty years.

ROGER PIERCE, formerly secretary to the Harvard Corporation and bursar and business manager of the Harvard Medical School, at one time secretary of the Harvard Alumni Association, has been elected president of the board of trustees of Milton Academy. He succeeds N. Penrose Hallowell, who has filled the office of president since 1921. Mr. Hallowell has been a trustee of the academy for twenty-seven years and will remain a member of the board.

WILLIAM B. ASPINWALL, president of the State Teachers College at Worcester, Mass., has been elected vice-president of the board of trustees of Leicester, Mass., Academy.

T. JEFFERSON COOLIDGE has resigned as president of the board of trustees of the Boston Museum of Fine Arts, on the ground that his work as Under Secretary of the U. S. Treasury makes it impossible for him to give adequate time to the interests of the museum.

DR. GEORGE CANBY ROBINSON, professor of medicine at Cornell Medical College and director of the New York Hospital-Cornell Medical College Association, sailed for Europe on November 3. Beginning on January 1 he will lecture at the Peiping Union Medical College as visiting professor of medicine.

DR. HAROLD BENJAMIN, assistant dean of the College of Education, of the University of Minnesota, returned on October 10, after having spent a month in Chile, attending the International Conference on Education held at Santiago.

DR. EDWARD L. THORNDIKE, professor of educational psychology at Teachers College, Columbia University, lectured on "Learning in Adult Years" at the Twentieth Century Club in Boston on October 17, under the auspices of the Massachusetts Society for Mental Hygiene.

DR. L. A. PECHSTEIN, dean of Teachers College, University of Cincinnati, addressed the West Virginia State Education Association at Parkersburg on Friday, October 26. The topic of his address was "Children for To-morrow."

DR. ELMER ELLSWORTH BROWN, chancellor of New York University from 1911 until his retirement as chancellor emeritus in 1933 died on November 3, at the age of seventy-three years. Dr. Brown had been previously U. S. Commissioner of Education and professor of education at the University of California and the University of Michigan.

DR. HERBERT RONELLE PURINTON, professor of Biblical literature and religion at Bates College from 1908 to 1932 and before that instructor and professor in Hebrew and church history at Cobb Divinity School, died on November 5, at the age of sixty-seven years. Dr. Purinton was director of the Northern Baptist Education Association, a trustee of the Maine Council of the Religious Education Association, and a trustee of the New England Baptist Conference.

DR. GEORGE MATHER FORBES, professor emeritus of the University of Rochester and president of the Rochester Board of Education from 1906 to 1912, died on October 30. He was in his eighty-second year.

HERBERT CLAY FISH, for fourteen years professor of American history in the Washington State Normal School at Ellensburg, died at the age of fifty-six years on October 22. Professor Fish was an authority on Pacific Northwest history and Indian lore. During the years from 1907 to 1915 he was curator of the State Historical Society at Bismarck, North Dakota, and for four years subsequently served as professor of history in the State Teachers College at Minot, North Dakota.

CLINTON B. PRICE, who retired in 1920 as business manager and treasurer of Union Theological Seminary in New York, died on November 4 at the age of eighty-four years.

HONORING the memory of the late Dr. Mather A. Abbott, head master of Lawrenceville School, a special service was held on November 4 in the Edith Memorial Chapel. Dr. William Lyon Phelps, professor emeritus of English literature at Yale University, conducted the service and unveiled a tablet in memory of Dr. Abbott, who was head master from 1914 until his death last May.

A BRONZE plaque has been unveiled at the New York School for the Deaf (Fanwood) to Edwin Allan Hodgson, who died on August 13, 1933, and who for more than fifty-seven years was connected with the school as instructor and editor of the *Deaf Mutes Journal*. The memorial, the work of E. E. Hanan, a deaf sculptor who was present at the unveiling, was made possible by the contributions of Mr. Hodgson's former pupils and other friends.

IN honor of William Holmes McGuffey, the author of a series of eclectic readers, a monument was dedicated recently at Washington, Pennsylvania. The memorial was established through the efforts of Henry Ford who with Mrs. Ford was in attendance at the ceremonies. The principal address of the occasion was delivered by W. J. Cameron, of Detroit, whose subject was "What William Holmes McGuffey Means to the Present Generation." The dedication ceremonies took place on the one hundred and thirty-fourth anniversary of his birth. The shrine was erected on the site of the log homestead of Henry Holmes, grandfather of Dr. McGuffey, where he was born.

THE Fidac International Congress in London has announced through the National Headquarters of the American Legion the awarding of the medals of honor to colleges and schools in the allied countries for their achievements in the field of international relations as part of the peace program of the Fidac, which groups some eight million world war veterans in eleven allied nations. The American Legion is the member society of Fidac in the United States. The Fidac medals offered to educational institutions in the United States are awarded as follows: one medal to a university, one to a college, and one to the university or college doing the most to promote an interest in the Far East. The following three American institutions won the medals this year: in the class of universities, the University of Denver; in the class of colleges, Earlham College; for work relating to the Far East, the University of Washington. The American Jury of Award consisted of Gen. L. R. Gignilliat, superintendent of Culver Military Academy, Culver, Ind., chairman; Dr. John J. Tigert, president of the University of Florida and former United States Commissioner of Education, Gainesville, Fla.; Dr. Lindsey Blayney, dean of Carleton College, Northfield, Minn.; Dr. Thomas H. Healy, assistant dean of Georgetown University School of Foreign Service, Washington, D. C., and Louis Johnson, American vice-president of Fidac, Clarksburg, W. Va.

A SCHOLARSHIP has been established in the State College of Agriculture, Cornell University, in memory of Charles R. White, president of the New York State Federation Farm Bureaus.

THE estimated total resources of Columbia University as of June 30, 1934, aggregate $152,594,964, according to a summary of university statistics just made public. Capital endowment excluding value of plant was $84,497,019.94. The estimated total value of lands, buildings, and equipment was $57,864,276.11. The annual budget for 1934–35 aggregates $14,224,348.46. The teaching staff last year numbered 2,833. These figures include Barnard College, Teachers College, the College of Pharmacy, Bard College at Annandale-on-Hudson, and New York Post-Graduate Medical School. The number of employees in the university, exclusive of affiliated institutions, was 2,532. Tuition, computed at $10 per point, ranges from $365 to $545 per year. The annual expenses of the average student are $622, the low figure being $476. There are more than 85,000 living graduates.

PROPOSALS for the revision of the administration of the teachers retirement funds of the State of Washington have been drawn up by a committee of the State Educational Association. The actuary has been working on the cost of a plan to include tentatively the following features: Consolidation of city and state funds.

Execution of annuity contracts already matured. Credit on new plan of all payments of present membership. Pension of $20 a month after age 60 to all members who retire, paid by the state from current funds. Annuity of $20 from individual endowments contributed by members, and an additional $10 unit if desired. Refund on withdrawal. Accrued liabilities of present members to be paid in part by the state. Disability provision optional on self-supporting basis. Conditions of retirement similar to those of present funds. These are to be considered not as final but as indicative of the present opinion of the committee.

IN order to increase its educational services to the people of New Jersey, Rutgers University will establish a new college to be known as University College, which will administer the evening credit and certificate programs formerly conducted by the Extension Division. President Robert C. Clothier, in announcing completed plans for the new unit, stated that courses will be offered in business administration and general subjects leading to the degree of bachelor of business administration. Professor N. C. Miller, director of the Extension Division, will be acting director of University College. The purpose of the college will be to offer academic training to high-school graduates who must seek employment for maintenance, and to adults who desire further training, but whose present employment prevents attendance at classes during the day. No time limit is prescribed for degree, but it is believed that a student will be able to earn sufficient credit in from five to nine years, depending upon the amount of time available for study. There are at present approximately 1,500 students taking evening courses under the Extension Division, and these students will constitute the undergraduate body of the new unit. Actual operation of the college will begin not later than September, 1935.

A NEW field, that of social and political science, has been opened up to intellectual cooperation as a result of the initiative taken in 1933 and 1934 by Professor James T. Shotwell and M. Edouard Herriot, chairman of the governing body of the International Institute of Intellectual Cooperation. According to *The Christian Science Monitor,* it is proposed: 1. To draw up a list of the institutions and organizations which engage, in the different countries and internationally, either in research or teaching in the field of social and political science; 2. To initiate research into the principles and methods of the various subjects into which they may be divided, and 3. To undertake a series of studies of certain specific problems. The first of these studies will concern the effects of mechanization on modern civilization. Another proposal, in the educational sphere, is that which concerns the revision of school text-books. The committee on intellectual cooperation contemplates supplementing the improvement schemes now in existence by the preparation of a standard draft bilateral agreement for the abolition of differences in the interpretation of certain historical events in the text-books now in use.

THE distribution of 1,000,000 copies of a new health newspaper issued by the New York City Board of Education started on October 1 in the public schools of the city. It is a monthly publication known as *The Health Broadcaster.* It is published by the division of health education of the Board of Education, and is edited by Dr. I. H. Goldberger, assistant director of health education, in collaboration with members of the division. The paper will be distributed in every elementary and junior high school to all teachers and pupils. Principals have been advised to instruct pupils to take their copies home for the information of parents. It is pointed out that the paper will contain accurate and timely information for parents as well as for teachers and pupils.

ACCORDING to a wireless despatch to *The New York Times* from Rome, a program providing for a considerable increase in elementary educational facilities in Italy was announced at the conclusion of a cabinet meeting on September 20. The program calls for the opening of 1,250 elementary schools before the beginning of the next academic year. Of these, 250 will be in sparsely populated rural districts where, in many instances, children have received no elementary education, because they have lived far from schools and transportation has not been available. Eleven new institutions of higher learning will be opened at the same time. Hundreds of new courses will be added to the curricula in the various grades. This program has been necessitated by the increase in the school population from 3,800,000 in 1926 to more than

5,250,000 last year. In the same period the proportion of the population attending schools has risen from 97 to 126 a thousand. This increase in school attendance has been accompanied by a marked decrease in illiteracy. The last three censuses showed the proportion of illiterates in the population, 38 per cent. in 1911, 27 per cent. in 1921 and 21 per cent. in 1931.

# OBITUARY

## SIR JOHN ADAMS

(1857–1934)

Sir John Adams, who died at Los Angeles on September 29, was not only a pioneer in the professional study of education; he remained to the end one of the most scholarly and productive members of his guild. When he became professor of education in the University of London in 1902, the persons holding this title in all universities the world over could have been assembled in a small classroom. He lived to see this group grow until it numbered two thousand and more. Indeed, the growth of this group in size and in influence has been one of the outstanding phenomena in the history of modern education, and in this movement John Adams played a very significant part.

Throughout his active life Adams was a teacher. After graduating from the University of Glasgow with first honors in mental and moral science he became a teacher in and head master of the Jean Street School in Port-Glasgow. Later he served as rector of the Grammar School at Campbeltown. With this background of experience he became a teacher of teachers, first at the Aberdeen Training College and then at the Glasgow Training College. He served as principal of both of these institutions, and in 1902 he was called to London as principal of the London Day Training College and professor of education in the University of London. These two posts he held until 1922, when he became professor *emeritus*. The remainder of his life was spent chiefly in Los Angeles, where he wrote some of his best books and also lectured at the University of California. He was knighted in 1925, a recognition of which his successor at the University of London, Sir Percy Nunn, was also a recipient a few years later upon the nomination of the Labor Government.

Adams's first book, "Herbartian Psychology Applied to Education," was published in 1897. Both in England and in America the Herbartian movement was at its height, and this book, far more interestingly written than most of the works on pedagogy, was warmly welcomed and exerted a wide influence.

Another piece of pioneering came in 1902, when Adams was invited to study the Protestant schools of Quebec. His report was one of the earliest of the publications that now constitute so important a part of our professional literature—the "survey" documents.

Adams was forty years old when his first book was published. Twelve others appeared between 1901 and 1932. They include a "Primer on Teaching" (1902), "Exposition and Illustration in Teaching" (1909), "The Evolution of Educational Theory" (1912), "The Student's Guide" (1917), "Modern Developments in Educational Practice" (1922), "Errors in School" (1927), "Educational Theories" (1927), "Everyman's Psychology" (1929), and "The Teacher's Many Parts" (English edition, 1930, American edition, 1932).

Adams's writings are characterized by both erudition and a charming style. More than once he protested against the dullness of our professional literature, and his own books are evidence that he could set a new and better standard. He was particularly apt in coining effective words and phrases. His term, "educand," as designating the pupil or student or learner, might have become current, but the ways of words pass human understanding, and it remains unique to Sir John. In discussing some of the difficulties in selecting effective illustrations in teaching, he warned against illustrations that pass the "threshold of stun." When in 1929 he was completing his excellent exposition and criticism of the prevailing "schools" of psychology, he wrote that he was somewhat worried about the title. He desired to call the book, "Psychology with the Chill Off." He apparently had to compromise, but "Everyman's Psychology" is not a bad substitute.

Personally, Sir John Adams was a most delightful friend and companion. A modest, unassuming, cultured gentleman, a democrat by conviction and practise, devoted to his students and his colleagues, proud of his profession as a teacher and a student of education, he was desirous above all, perhaps, of contributing to the advancement of that profession. And this he did in a rich and enduring measure, not only through his teaching and his writing but also through personal charm, gentle manners and genuine culture, which gave to all who knew him an enhanced respect for the profession which he served so well and represented so worthily.

WILLIAM C. BAGLEY

# DISCUSSION

## THE LIBRARIAN AS AN ASSOCIATE IN COLLEGE INSTRUCTION

THE ever-increasing recognition being given to the importance of books and of libraries in effective college education is well illustrated by two recent articles in SCHOOL AND SOCIETY.[1] Both Mr. Allen and Mr. Shores plead for a vital relationship between the library and college instruction. Mr. Allen proposes departmental reference librarians who are acquainted with the literature in their special fields and who are likewise conversant with the instruction given in their respective departments. He proposes definite conferences between the reference librarian and students who are working on term papers in his own special department (or departments). The results of such conferences are to be available to professors, who in turn keep the reference librarian informed of significant contacts which they may have with students.

In his "Modest Proposal," Mr. Shores goes a step further, for he suggests a "library arts college" in which there are no professors—only librarians who completely take over the functions of the instructional staff.

As far as the writer can learn, no college has yet had an opportunity to demonstrate the practicability of the above proposals. A library program now being conducted at Stephens College is, however, making it possible for us to try out a number of these and related procedures.

For the past two school years we have been engaged in a library program at Stephens College, one of the major objectives of which is to make the library the center of our instructional activity.[2] To further this objective, the librarian has the dual position of librarian and dean of instruction. As librarian, he must know what is in the library; as dean of instruction, he must be familiar with classroom teaching. This organization makes it possible for the librarian to offer teachers a type of assistance which might otherwise be quite difficult.

In a college with six hundred students and a teaching staff of more than sixty, it is, however, impossible for one person to be thoroughly conversant with the instruction offered by every instructor. It seems quite clear, therefore, that library-instructional relations of the type in which we are interested may be facilitated by giving additional members of the library staff certain responsibilities which will lead to a better acquaintance with instruction in various instructional divisions.[3]

During the first two years of our library program, a number of procedures have been used for encouraging more effective instructional use of books. As a part of our plans it has been our purpose to bring about situations which make it possible for students and teachers to work together in the presence of books. Classroom libraries have been used extensively by classes in English, science and foreign language. Classes in English, art, natural science, psychology, sociology and French have used our general library for reading periods during

[1] Paul Allen, "In the Liberal Arts College—the Reference Librarian, a Professor?" SCHOOL AND SOCIETY, 39:231–236, February 24, 1934; Louis Shores, "A Modest Proposal," SCHOOL AND SOCIETY, 39: 570–571, May 5, 1934.

[2] A second major objective of the total program relates to the stimulation and guidance of pleasure reading. As an aid to furthering this objective, libraries for recreational reading have been set up in each of the college's six residence halls. This article is concerned solely with the instructional aspect of our library developments, and will not, therefore, deal with dormitory libraries, their administration or their use.

[3] In 1930 Stephens College discarded the usual departmental organization in favor of a divisional organization under which courses are grouped in the following four divisions: Humanities, social science, natural science and skills and techniques.

regular class hours. Teachers of English and humanities (an orientation course) have held office hours[4] in the library in order that they might have an opportunity to confer with students in the presence of books.

These procedures have resulted not only in *increased* use of our libraries,[5] but also, we are convinced, in more *effective* use of our book collections. An additional development pointing toward still greater coordination of classroom and library service is the "division library."

In the fall of 1933, we opened a social science division library immediately adjacent to the offices and classrooms of the division. This library has a seating capacity of twenty-five and contains more than twelve hundred books, twelve magazines and four newspapers selected by the social science faculty. In charge of the library is an assistant who has her master's degree in sociology and who has had a rich background of experience in social service work.

The location of the library increases the opportunities which teachers and students have to work together in the presence of books. During their study hours in the social science library students frequently encounter problems and items of interest which they take across the hall and discuss with their professor. From time to time during class hours professors send to the division library for books which will throw light upon a problem that has arisen during class discussion. Upon a number of occasions professors have requested individual students or groups of students to leave the classroom and go to the division library to consult books regarding queries which have been raised during the class hour.

The specialized training and interests of the social science librarian and her location immediately adjacent to the offices and classrooms of the division make it logical for her to become acquainted with the instruction in the division. During the second semester of the 1933–34 school year the librarian and the director of the social science division have cooperated with the division librarian to the end that she might become acquainted with the instruction given in the division and become a more vital part of it. The schedule of the division librarian was so arranged that each week she visited at least one section of each course offered in the division. This experience, plus conferences with professors, provided her with a background which aided her in her efforts to stimulate and guide students as they came to the library with questions and problems.

The director of the social science division has, in cooperation with the division librarian, taken several additional steps toward vitalizing the library-instructional relationship. Early in the second semester, the professor told all his students that in the future he wished them to have their individual conferences with him, as in the past, but that in addition he wanted them to have regular individual conferences with the social science librarian regarding the problems and projects upon which they were working. He then gave the division librarian the names of all his students, together with the problems upon which they were working. The librarian then prepared bibliographies on the various problems on which students were working. She also made a $4 \times 6$ card for each student, recording on the card the student's name and the problems or projects upon which she was working. Following each student conference the librarian recorded on the card impressions of the student and her work. Every ten days the professor who was trying this plan held a conference with the division librarian. Together they noted each student's card and discussed the student, her strong points, her weak points and methods of guiding and stimulating her to more effective work. Frequently, as the professor passed the division library, he stopped to discuss with the librarian situations which he had encountered with specific students. Such contacts have, in the opinion of both the librarian and the director of the division, resulted in a more thorough understanding of the individual student and have been instrumental in guiding and stimulating many students to do more effective work.

We have, to be sure, tried this plan for a

4 One member of our English staff spends more than thirty hours a week in the stacks of our general library conferring with individual students regarding their reading.

5 During the first two years of our library program, the circulation of books and library attendance have increased 82 per cent. and 73 per cent., respectively.

short time only. We are convinced, however, that it is worth continued trial and are, therefore, making plans for extending our instructional-library relationships.

During the past semester several professors in the social science division have become interested in the work that the director of the division has been carrying on in cooperation with the division librarian, and have indicated that they wish to establish a similar cooperative relationship with the library staff. During the present year, the division librarian is therefore extending her instructional contacts to include other classes than those which she served last year. She is continuing her weekly visits to at least one section of each course offered in the division. In addition to this she teaches one section of our introductory social problems course—a course which is taught by every faculty member in the division. This means that as a faculty member in the division, the division librarian participates in the weekly meetings which the division holds to discuss the social problems course.

Our plans, in summary, give the social science librarian the following contacts with instruction in the division: (1) She visits weekly at least one section of each course offered in the division. (2) She holds regular conferences with the students of several professors and keeps a record of the results of such conferences. (3) In regular conferences with professors she discusses with them the work of individual students. (4) She teaches one section of the social problems course. (5) As a teacher of social problems she meets weekly with faculty members of the division to discuss the social problems course and such other situations as may arise.[6]

It is our belief that the close relation which the division librarian has with instruction will enable her to work with increasing effectiveness with students and teachers.

We are not committed to the policy of division libraries at Stephens College. We are, however, committed to the policy of placing the library at the hub of our instructional wheel. We are eager, therefore, to experiment with any plan which gives promise of aiding us in pressing toward our objective. We are convinced that such promise is embodied in the division library with a librarian who knows the instructional program and is in reality a part of it.

B. Lamar Johnson

Stephens College

[6] A library with a similar purpose and organization has been set up for our natural science division. This library began functioning at the opening of the fall semester.

## PROFESSIONAL COORDINATION IN TEACHER PLACEMENT

In School and Society for September 29, 1934, Wilbur E. Moser gave a very illuminating report of the accomplishments of placement bureaus operated by state teachers' associations. The impressive thing is the meagerness of the accomplishment. Only six state associations seem to have any definite organization for placement. The placement bureaus enroll only 6 per cent. of the membership of the associations in these six states, the highest in any state being about 12 per cent. Less than 8 per cent. of those registered were placed in 1933, the highest in any state being less than 12 per cent., and the lowest between 1 and 2 per cent.

When a state teachers' association organizes a placement agency that merely adds another to the existing agencies competing with one another for the placement of teachers, it is scarcely to be expected that any more favorable results will be secured. It costs money to be successful in this competitive game. The placement bureau of the California association, one of the oldest in operation, has discovered that successful work can not be done without a substantial fee from those benefitting by its services, and now charges 3 per cent. of the first year's salary. This is three fifths of the standard fee of the commercial agency, and the commercial agencies are not getting rich on the 5 per cent. fees. If college and university placement bureaus had to be fully self-supporting, including a fair proportion of the salaries of the directors, they would be unable to do successful work with any smaller fee.

There is a service in teacher placement that may be performed by a state teachers' association that is more needed than the establishment of an additional competing agency. Some professional group needs to coordinate the activities of the existing agencies, especially those connected with the normal schools, teachers' colleges and universities.

In some of our states these agencies are rather numerous. If each one carries on its own advertising campaign well enough to get attention from the employing officials, it becomes very expensive in proportion to the number of teachers who secure positions through the aid of the bureau. The number of these advertising appeals becomes so great that an increasing number are consigned immediately to the waste basket. If an employing official who desires to be courteous and fair to everybody gives information of a vacancy to every bureau operating in the state, and each of these bureaus recommends only a moderate number of candidates, there will be an unwieldy number of applicants for the position vacant. The individual candidate must spend a large amount of time and money for a small chance of success.

The existing type of unregulated competition among the bureaus makes it to the advantage of each bureau to recommend several, rather than one, candidate, for the more candidates the bureau has applying for the place, the greater the probability of one of them being successful. Thus when each bureau seeks its own advantage single-handed, even if its methods are intentionally honorable, the result is an unreasonable number of candidates for each position. It becomes impossible for the employing officials to examine the credentials well enough to select the best.

In many ways the state teachers' associations are in the best position to bring about cooperation among these bureaus. They have a professional prestige. They have a freedom from political fears, such as often deter state departments of education from taking the initiative in such movements. Nearly twenty years ago Dr. Charles H. Judd predicted that the state departments of education would become the centers of teacher-placement, but not much progress has been made in that direction.[1]

In working out the details, a state association would have to find its way as it proceeded; but to make the proposal more concrete, a suggestive plan of procedure is added in conclusion. Let the association appoint a commission on teacher placement. Let this commission call a meeting of representatives of all placement agencies operating in the state. The state teachers' association could thus arrange to take over the work of collecting information of vacancies, and each bureau would obligate itself to recommend only its one best candidate.

The confidence of three groups must be won before the plan will be completely carried out: the school officers charged with the selection of teachers, the institutions that prepare teachers and the candidates for positions. All three groups would ultimately find the plan to their advantage.

L. O. McAfee

Albany College
Albany, Oregon

# QUOTATIONS

## CHANCELLOR BROWN

To Chancellor Brown the lines of a great modern poem which he knew in its entirety, "The Testament of Beauty," are peculiarly applicable; for his "mortal sensibility" had

> A wide jurisdiction of range in all degrees
> From mountainous gravity to faintest tenuities.

As a philosopher he knew the mountainous heights of human thinking, and as a man of deep poetic feeling he had a wide human sympathy, an appreciation of beauty as eternal essences and a skill in the written word—for he "knew himself to sing and build the lofty rhyme." He was a best exemplar of that liberal education in which, as he once said, "the golden threads of one's own essential being are picked up."

There are many ways in which the miracle of discovery and development are wrought. He suggested some of them in an address which he made a few months ago when proudly welcomed back to his alma mater, the University of Michigan:

> Some will find themselves most of all in the majestic lines of the Hebrew Scriptures. Some will meet themselves face to face in the "glory that was Greece and the grandeur that was Rome,"

[1] *Elementary School Journal,* April, 1916, pp. 442–448.

or in the wide-pervasive history of the Christian Church; or in the singularly stirring legend, art and letters of the Middle Ages; or, further afield, in the myth and beauty of the Orient—Chinese, Persian, Indian; or in the compelling sweep of these past three centuries and more of modern music; or in the briefer and more marvelous development of modern science.

Familiar with all these sources of self-discovery and self-advancement, he was eminently fitted in his own person to give guidance and leadership to a university which seeks to serve most helpfully the nation by serving most effectively and intimately the highest cultural and civic interests of this vast community.

The period of his "emeritus" tenure was regrettably brief—too brief, it is feared, to have allowed him to complete the history of education in America which he was equipped above all others to write, too brief and too much intruded upon by illness to permit him to receive expressions of the gratitude of the Republic and, above all, of this city. But he had a notable part as United States Commissioner of Education in making that history. He did an even greater work in giving vital succession to ideas that founded and maintained New York University through a century; and has endowed it with his philosophy of life and of education for the centuries that lie ahead. Those who knew him well would be ready to say of him what Phaedo said of the ancient great philosopher: "He was the wisest and justest and best man I have ever known."—*The New York Times.*

NEW YORK UNIVERSITY mourns the loss of a man who has been her leader for a quarter of a century of rapid growth in power. By temperament he was the scholar and the man of culture. The freshness and the richness of his mind, his fine and gentle spirit, his friends alone knew.

Destiny had made of him an administrator and to the task of administration he gave himself without reserve; always kindly, just and thoughtful—always regardless of self. He brought the university through a difficult and trying period with a steady advance in its standards and distinctions.

But steadily he looked forward to the day when release from administrative duties would bring him leisure for research and writing. Despite ill health, he had already begun work with enthusiasm on a history of American education, a field which he had already enriched by his contributions.

To him the university owes a profound debt of gratitude and it deeply grieves at his passing. —*Dr. Harry Woodburn Chase, Chancellor of New York University.*

# SOCIETIES AND MEETINGS

## THE ASSOCIATION OF URBAN UNIVERSITIES

WAYS in which current federal aid to education is operative in colleges and universities, with particular reference to city institutions, formed the chief topic of the twenty-first annual meeting of the Association of Urban Universities, held on November 2 and 3, at Louisville, Kentucky, with the University of Kentucky as host. There were in attendance about 40 delegates, representing 21 of the 32 institutions holding membership in the association.

Nine formal papers and addresses were given at the four sessions, including a dinner at the Pendennis Club, at which many Louisville citizens were present.

The Federal Emergency Relief Administration honored the association by sending as its representative Mr. Howard O. Hunter, who is in charge of the administration's office at Chicago. Mr. Hunter's address on "Federal Relief Work" was informal and was indicated as not for quotation.

A general statement on "Federal Plans in Aid of Education" was given at the morning session of November 1 by Dr. Fred J. Kelly, of the U. S. Office of Education. Dr. Kelly's chief point was that, quite apart from our individual feelings as to what it should be, the actual policy of the Federal Government, historically and at present, is not to give money directly for education. He sketched the historical background, going back to the ordinances of 1785 and 1787 providing for federal aid through grants of land. The definite policy of the founding fathers not to appropriate directly for schools was reaffirmed recently by the Congress, said Dr. Kelly, when it declined to pass recommendations that one hundred million dollars be appropriated directly to keep schools open in the present economic emergency. Instead, provision was made for this same purpose by having the Federal Emergency Relief Administration make amounts available to the states as a part of general relief, with the states distributing the aid to education. The present administration appears to consider any departure from the traditional policy so large a question as to prefer to postpone definite action until a calmer period.

Dr. Kelly indicated that the Federal Government has in the past fostered types of education which it regarded as vital for national development. Examples of this were the Morrill Act, providing for agricultural training in land-grant colleges not afforded in the academic colleges of the 1850's, and the 1917 act, providing for vocational training not afforded in the high schools of the period.

Stress was laid by Dr. Kelly upon the President's order of June 27, 1934, by which earlier rules of apprenticeship in the trades are replaced by regulations approached from the view-point of labor and not the view-point of education. A nation-wide system of apprentice education is being established in which full and final authority rests with the Secretary of Labor, who has an advisory committee.

"Economic Aspects of Federal Aid" was the subject of a paper following that of Dr. Kelly, presented by Professor Ernest H. Hahne, of the department of economics, Northwestern University. Dr. Hahne said, at the outset, that the problem of federal aid was one of concern to urban universities because they "have the especial responsibility of safeguarding and directing the social well-being of the communities in which they are located."

That the economic view-point leads to approval of increasing federal aid to schools was the conviction of Dr. Hahne. He thought the general property tax unjust, and federal aid an advantage in relieving the public school system from this injustice. "Taxpayers who rebel against the general property tax may ultimately and unintentionally cause the public schools to suffer." Dr. Hahne cited nine reasons to show that the depression has accentuated the injustice of reliance upon property tax. He said that in England the "movement towards central aid during the past century has led toward increasing reliance upon the funds of the Exchequer for the support of schools and has afforded greater and greater relief for the owners of land. To some extent the same movement is now under way in the United States in the shifting of the burdens of school finance whereby greater reliance is being placed on federal aid, since the Federal Government raises substantially no money from land taxes."

Dr. Hahne discussed some of the new economic problems created by the federal aid program, "if it is to become a permanent policy for school finance." One of the most difficult of these problems is "to determine the proportion of financial responsibility for schools that attaches to state, local and federal governments."

Dr. Hahne believed that a reasonable increase of federal control over the school system would be establishing a national minimum rather than an equalization of educational opportunities. "What this national minimum should be is distinctly a problem for the educational leaders and not for the economists, except in so far as they inquire whether they get their money's worth from the expenditure of federal funds."

How one municipal university has cooperated with local agencies in adult education under the Federal Emergency Relief Administration was reported by President Philip C. Nash, of the University of Toledo, on the morning of November 2. At Toledo, an opportunity school is operated by the university as one of the several emergency schools of the city, with FERA funds. Classes are organized for citizens "not able to pay for regular evening college instruction but who wish seriously to study some intellectual interest. . . . Last year about 1,400 people registered with us in the emergency school in over 150 classes of college grade taught by 77 well-qualified instructors." The instructors of the opportunity school are not the members of the university faculty, but local citizens, "experts in their field, willing and able to make this contribution to the community."

In the discussion of President Nash's paper, it was suggested that a wide expansion of free instruction might endanger the evening extension work of universities, for which there is rarely endowment support and which must accordingly pay its own way.

Another type of educational work made possible by federal aid was reported by Dean C. S. Marsh, of the University of Buffalo, who is at present serving as educational director of the Civilian Conservation Corps. That the educational program now being conducted in the camps of the Civilian Conservation Corps "is a great American folk-school movement" was the theme of Dean Marsh's paper, read at the afternoon session of November 1. "It is an educational enterprise for adults and for older youths growing out of the native culture of a people who want to learn the things that are of most interest or importance to them. It is not imposed from above, it does not prescribe an individual's curriculum, it meets the immediate needs and interests of the people. In the folk school one group may be studying their social and economic problems, another their vocational problems, another may be satisfying their yearning for self-expression."

Dean Marsh traced the development of the educational program since the CCC Camps were set up in the spring of 1933. The camps are operated by the War Department, "the United States Army assuming this burden in addition to its ordinary duties." The educational program is operating in 1,468 of the 1,728 camps, with a total enrolment of about 300,000 men out of approximately 370,000. Details of the program were given in Dean Marsh's paper, which will be published later in SCHOOL AND SOCIETY.

A proposal for federal aid in a new direction was made before the association by Mr. John Lang, president of the National Student Federation. Mr. Lang, who is a recent graduate of a Southern college, made an impassioned plea for consideration of the plight of youth. "A whole generation faces dry-rot," he declared, unless economic opportunities are soon offered to the six millions of the nation's youth now idle. "Their cries ring out for a salvaging hand and for a chance to do something before it is too late."

Mr. Lang proposed a Federal Youth Service in the Office of Education, Department of the Interior, which would coordinate the work of present federal agencies, state and city agencies. He said:

> The detailed duties of the Youth Service would be many. In addition to conducting extensive studies, disseminating information and consolidating scattered efforts, the agency would experiment along new lines. There would be an enlistment of the initiative and enterprising efforts of communities, towns, cites and states in tackling the current difficulties, devising new, useful occupations in undeveloped fields. Private organizations would be asked to cooperate. Schools and colleges would be encouraged to revise their curricula and practises to train youth more satisfactorily for the realities of life. Every possible means for the guidance and counseling of youth would be stimulated. Nation-wide testing would be fostered so that those fitted for college could be directed there; those prepared for high school sent there; and those of other bents guided to vocation schools or projects for refurbishing the community. Improved leisure time programs would be drawn up and made public. Adjustments would be attempted with organized economic and industrial groups to permit youth the training facilities and share of work which rightfully belong to him. Opportunities for apprenticing young persons to public officials and professional leaders would be encouraged. . . . Throughout its many activities the Washington agency would operate in an advisory and leadership capacity.

### OTHER TOPICS AND BUSINESS

Two significant activities in urban universities were set forth on the morning of November 2 in papers by Dr. Henry C. Mills, of the University of Buffalo, and by Dean Malcolm McLean, of the University of Minnesota.

Dr. Mills reported findings of an intensive study during the past three years at the University of Buffalo on "The Integration of High School and College Work." Dean McLean read a paper on "The General College of the University of Minnesota."

Registrations of 27 of the 32 members of the association as of October 1 showed an increase in total enrolment of 5.6 per cent. over those of October 1, 1933, as reported by Dean Frank M. Debatin, of Washington University. The current totals were 192,946, as compared with 182,664 a year ago. The liberal arts enrolment totals for these 27 universities show 58,311 undergraduates, compared with 56,837 in 1933. The number of graduate students is 8,041, a decrease of 97. As to extension enrolment the total is 80,484, or 13,484 more than last year.

At the business session, Dean Everett W. Lord, of Boston University, was elected president of the association for 1934–35, with the choice of the meeting place for 1935 as Boston.

In resolutions passed upon recommendation of a committee headed by President Parke R. Kolbe, the association approved the CCC educational program with suggestions for more adequate funds; approved "the policy of including general education in the relief program"; recommended that, in view of "the distressing plight of American youth in these years," the U. S. commissioner of education should "carefully consider the possibilities of effective coordination of the various agencies and activities designed to solve the problem"; and heartily thanked President R. A. Kent and the University of Louisville for "the fine hospitality which they have extended to us."

RAYMOND WALTERS
UNIVERSITY OF CINCINNATI

# EDUCATIONAL RESEARCH AND STATISTICS

## A SHORT ORAL GROUP INTELLIGENCE TEST

RESULTS of investigations on auditory *vs.* visual method in teaching, learning and testing indicate much evidence in specific advantages for the auditory method. Investigation of the auditory methods are assuming increasing importance with the wide-spread introduction of radio in education for school children and for adults.[1]

The feasibility and possible practical applications of an oral group intelligence test were demonstrated over a national radio network by Frank N. Freeman in 1933. A number of investigators have reported significant correlations ranging from + 0.55 to + 0.90 between general intelligence tests ratings when administered visually to groups (the visual procedure wherein the subject reads the questions and writes the answer) and orally (wherein the examiner reads the question aloud and the subject writes only the answers).[2]

The present investigation is based on the Chapman Oral Intelligence Test for grades 6 to 12. In administering this form of 100 questions to groups of children approximately forty minutes are necessary.

A shorter oral group intelligence test which may serve as a "dragnet" device in general testing and broad classification programs in schools seems especially desirable. By distributing the odd and even items on the original Chapman test, two forms of 52 items each were made. Each form hereafter is referred to as Form A and Form B. Either form requires approximately 21 minutes total administration time when presented to a group of school children.

Both forms were given at different times in the seventh and eighth grades of the New York City Public Schools to 88 boys and girls. Their IQ's, based on the National Intelligence Test, ranged from 76 to 126. The coefficients of correlation in Table I show that either form A or B

TABLE I

CORRELATION OF THE NATIONAL INTELLIGENCE TEST WITH SCORES ON THE SHORT ORAL GROUP INTELLIGENCE TEST. (N = 88)

| | r | $PE_r$ |
|---|---|---|
| Form A and IQ | 0.70 | ± 0.03 |
| Form B and IQ | 0.69 | ± 0.03 |
| Form (A and B) with IQ | 0.69 | ± 0.03 |

1 Research Problems in Radio Education, National Research Council on Radio in Education, Information Series, No. 4, April, 1934; Group Listening, Information Series, No. 8, October, 1933.

2 R. C. Chapman, *Jour. Educ. Research*, December, 1920, 777–786, and April, 1925, 269–279; H. C. Lehman, SCHOOL AND SOCIETY, October 5, 1929, 470–472; M. B. Jensen, SCHOOL AND SOCIETY, November 19, 1930, 675–677; V. M. Sims and L. B. Knox, *Jour. Educ. Research*, 23: 656–62, 1932; T. H. Briggs and G. H. Armacast, *Jour. Educ. Research*, 36: 595–96, 1933; C. C. Ross and P. D. Gard, *Bulletin Bureau of School Service*, College of Education, University of Kentucky, Vol. 11, No. 4; H. N. De Wick, Pub., University of North Carolina, May 20, 1933; M. E. Carver, Unpublished Harvard Ph.D. thesis, 1934; H. L. Ewbank, *Quart. Jour. Speech*, November, 1932, 4, Vol. 18, 561ff.

is equally satisfactory in revealing a measure of general intelligence. The consistency with which either form measures the relative capacity of an individual—or the reliability of the test—was obtained by correlating form A and B. This gave a coefficient of $0.86 \pm 0.01$.

The differentiation between IQ levels by the abbreviated form of oral intelligence test is shown in Table II. Form A scores are consistently lower than Form B. This seems to indicate that Form A is more difficult, since this form was administered after Form B.

TABLE II

RAW SCORE ORAL GROUP INTELLIGENCE TEST

| N.I.T.I.Q. | N | Average | Median | Range |
|---|---|---|---|---|
| *Form A* | | | | |
| 110 and above | 17 | 29.6 | 30.0 | 24–34 |
| 90–109 | 49 | 25.0 | 25.0 | 17–35 |
| 89 and below | 22 | 19.4 | 19.4 | 13–27 |
| *Form B* | | | | |
| 110 and above | 17 | 35.9 | 36.7 | 28–42 |
| 90–109 | 49 | 31.3 | 32.0 | 15–40 |
| 89 and below | 22 | 24.9 | 24.8 | 15–35 |
| *Form A and B* | | | | |
| 110 and above | 17 | 65.4 | 67.6 | 52–72 |
| 90–109 | 49 | 55.5 | 55.7 | 32–73 |
| 89 and below | 22 | 43.1 | 43.0 | 31–61 |

Results of this preliminary study suggest that further investigation may reveal a special value for the oral group intelligence test. In large scale testing programs in the schools, it is considered good procedure to give two "verbal" group intelligence tests. Frequently one verbal group intelligence test is supplemented by a non-language group intelligence test. The advantage in utilizing two tests is obviously to allow for errors in measurement due either to disturbing or unusual conditions, to handicaps in speed and comprehension of reading and to visual perception and language difficulties.[3] Further consideration should be given to the relative advantages and disadvantages of the visual as contrasted with the oral presentation of group intelligence tests. A careful standardization of an oral group intelligence test would be especially desirable in view of the fact that among school children there are wide differences in reading ability and visual perception. There is also consistent evidence that individual differences must be taken into account in determining the relative effectiveness in teaching, learning and testing by the visual as compared with the oral method of presentation. An oral group intelligence test combined with a verbal group intelligence test (visual presentation) and a non-language group intelligence test should yield more accurate classification and provision for individual differences by means of the group-testing programs.

The value of the oral individual intelligence test for school children is evidenced in the results obtained by the Binet-Simon test and its various revisions. Commonly known verbal group intelligence tests are more or less judged by comparing them with the degree of accuracy in classification obtainable in the Binet-Simon test. Similarly, further experimentation should aim to reveal evidence on the relative merit of the oral group intelligence test as compared with the ordinary verbal group intelligence test in predicting levels of general intelligence as measured by the various revisions of the Binet-Simon Test.

RICHARD S. SCHULTZ
THE PSYCHOLOGICAL CORPORATION
GILBERT S. MACVAUGH
THE NATIONAL HOSPITAL FOR SPEECH DISORDERS
NEW YORK, N. Y.

[3] D. D. Durrell, *Jour. Educ. Psychol.*, 24: 412–416, 1933; O. F. Litterer, *Jour. Applied Psychol.*, 17: 266–276, 1933.

## NEW BOOKS IN EDUCATION

JORDAN, A. M. *Objective Tests on Educational Psychology.* Pp. 67. Holt. $0.50.

KUNITZ, STANLEY J. and HOWARD HAYCRAFT, Editors. *The Junior Book of Authors.* Pp. ix + 400. 260 illustrations. Wilson. $4.00.

*Our Year's Work: Annual Report of the Board of Education of Evansville, Indiana, for the School Year Ending July, 1934.* Pp. 78. The Board.

STEESE, RUTH Z. *Choral Music in the American Colleges.* Pp. v + 31. Eastman School of Music, University of Rochester.

SWIFT, FLETCHER H. *European Policies of Financing Public Educational Institutions: II, Czechoslovakia.* Pp. x + 181–250. *III, Austria.* Pp. x + 251–344. University of California Press.

# SCHOOL AND SOCIETY

WITH WHICH ARE COMBINED THE EDUCATIONAL REVIEW, ESTABLISHED IN 1891, THE TEACHERS MAGAZINE, ESTABLISHED IN 1878, AND THE SCHOOL JOURNAL, ESTABLISHED IN 1874.

Volume 40 | SATURDAY, NOVEMBER 17, 1934 | Number 1038

## THE AMERICAN SCHOLAR TO-DAY

By Professor GUY STANTON FORD

DEAN OF THE GRADUATE SCHOOL, UNIVERSITY OF MINNESOTA

ON August 31, 1837, the old meeting house of the First Parish in Cambridge, Massachusetts, was filled with a distinguished audience come at the opening of a new college year to hear the annual oration of the Phi Beta Kappa society. In the audience were names great and to be great—Norton, Palfrey, Ware, Holmes and Lowell. The speaker was a Harvard graduate of the class of 1821 whose wide-ranging mind had not distinguished him in college as an outstanding student. Ralph Waldo Emerson had left to others the bondage of books and had sought in study new freedoms for a spirit part Yankee, part German, part mystic and part rational, and yet wholly of the New Englander's Puritan rigor. Slender, grave, benign and untroubled by an audience in which half were apprehensive of a new heresy and half were expectant of a new declaration of independence, Emerson advanced to the platform to read an historic address on "The American Scholar."

Almost a century has passed and yet Emerson's address remains the most profound and significant of the thousands of addresses given under the auspices of the Society of the Phi Beta Kappa. Lowell, an auditor, characterized it justly as an "event without any former parallel in our literary annals, a scene to be always treasured in the memory for its picturesqueness and its inspiration. What crowded and breathless aisles, what windows clustering with eager heads, what enthusiasm of approval, what grim silence of foregone dissent!" Carlyle in far-away Chelsea read it and exclaimed, "God be thanked for it! I could have *wept* to read that speech."

Perhaps it may not be without profit for us to review that address a century later on a campus that in 1837 was part of the wilderness of the West. On the day when men wearing the key of this society, tense with eager expectation, crowded even the window niches in the old church in Cambridge, Indians trailed their paths across the campus of the University of Minnesota to set up their tepees by the Falls of St. Anthony. Within sound of those falls, now muffled by great mills and the thunder of transcontinental trains, lived and died Oscar W. Firkins, the most distinguished of Emerson's biographers. The Indians are gone, the West has sunk beyond its last horizon, tens of thousands of students make paths like the Indians but amid a new wilderness of colleges and courses. Some seek freedom on the terms the Indians sought it, in absence of restraint; a few find it, and I hope they are among those who wear the emblem of this venerable society, in the freedom and grave self-trust that Emerson proclaimed.

The subject of his address, "The American Scholar," was already hackneyed when

Emerson accepted it as the one which custom dictated for the occasion. Great orators like Everett and Channing had used it for a theme, but not as Emerson did nor to the same purpose. So different was his purpose and doctrine from the usual and traditional that some might say that he did not really consider the American scholar in any sense usually attributed to these words singly or in combination. They would be essentially correct from our standpoint, for Emerson saw in the occasion an opportunity to proclaim a new philosophy, held as his own till the moment came to share it. Few things he wrote are so distinctly Emersonian as this address, and none is a better or more pregnant introduction to the Transcendental movement that we associate with the Concord philosopher.

What was it that Emerson said that the young men in his audience felt should be treasured in memory? What made it for them an event without parallel till then in American literary annals and why among some of their elders that "grim silence of foregone dissent"? What could any one say about the American scholar that would divide an audience? What were Emerson's criteria for the American scholar? How have they stood the test of time? Are they the characteristics that have marked American scholarship in the intervening century? If not, what are the characteristics of American scholarship as we know it to-day?

It is to these questions, and perhaps one other, which I shall propose later, that I want to direct your thoughts for a moment this evening.

Emerson proclaimed the day was at hand when "this continent will . . . fill the postponed expectation of the world with something better than the exertions of mechanical skill. Our day of dependence, our long apprenticeship to the learning of other lands, draws to a close." He believed that the time had come when great things were ready to say or sing themselves, if man would be their voice. But man had become so divided into men that planter and tradesman, priest and lawyer and laborer, did not lift their eyes from their task; each was "ridden by the routine of his craft and the soul is subject to dollars." In such a society the scholar must be the delegated intellect, he must be not a thinker but "Man Thinking." This Man (and Emerson capitalized the word), this scholar, was to be the true master. He was to catch up in his soul the soul of all men; his voice from the depths of his self-knowledge, from the heights of his self-trust, would go forth to be recognized by all men as their voice proclaiming the universally true.

How was he to be trained? First by Nature, the web of God, till he learned by joining fact with fact into one great law that he was one with Nature. Second by the Past in books, but books not as masters or compelling authority but as instruments in his rôle of "Man Thinking." "I had better never see a book," said Emerson, "than be warped by its attraction clean out of my own orbit and made a satellite and not a system." Books for Emerson's scholar were but the raw material for inspiration and immortal thoughts. Only the mind of the multitude could accept books, harden them into dogmas, build colleges upon them and send forth a book-learned class that held fast to Locke or Bacon, forgetting that Locke and Bacon when they wrote were only young men in libraries. How often to-day we need to remind ourselves and our students, as the Soviets did the Russian peasants, that a book is not something to be feared, for a book is after all only a man talking. "Books are the best of things, well used, abused among the worst." Emerson would not underrate them, but he would not be pushed down by them. By creative reading the American scholar could go on to creative thinking. Colleges likewise had their place. In them there must be laborious reading in history and exact sciences, but their purpose was "not to drill but to create"; the light concentrated in their halls from every prophet in every age should set the hearts of youth aflame. If colleges forgot this and turned to ceremonies and endowments they "will recede in their public importance whilst they grow richer every year."

To Nature and books Emerson adds action and free contact with men, humble and revered alike, as the school of the scholar. His scholar is to be no recluse, sneered at by "practical men." Action for the scholar is essential, even though it be subordinate. No sloth or timidity should rob him of any opportunity for action, and every lost opportunity to act is a loss of power. Let the scholar plunge into the world, this shadow of his soul, this other self that lies wide around him. "Life is our dictionary." Colleges and books only copy the language which the field and the workyard make. "The scholar loses no hour which the man lives." "Only be this limitation observed, that a man shall not for the sake of wider activity sacrifice any opinion to the popular judgments and modes of action."

To you, listening to this paraphrase of Emerson's section on the scholar in the school of life and action, it may seem as though the mild and retiring Concord philosopher were uttering a challenge to the scholar to enter the forums of public life and service. It sounds perhaps like a section inserted from another unfinished oration on "The Scholar in Politics." It might well be or have been to the youth who heard it as a challenge to public service and activity in a day when slavery was a rising issue and democracy had taken unto itself a new meaning after eight years of Jacksonian rule.

But those who followed such a practical interpretation were not the full embodiment of Emerson's American scholar, of the "Man Thinking." To Emerson such living and acting would be only another demonstration to the scholar of the oneness of all men, whether speaking in books or laboring in farm and factory. When the scholar spoke his inmost thought, and to do that in full self-trust was the all-comprising duty, he would find that he was the "world's eye" and "the world's heart." ". . . In going down into the secrets of his own mind he has descended into the secrets of all minds" . . . and "is the master of all men whose language he speaks. . . ."

"Free should the scholar be,—free and brave." His greatness lies not in his power to alter matter but to alter states of mind. He must have an abiding faith in his own instincts, in the truth in his own bosom and in the unsearched might of man. If to this high faith the scholar be true, walking on his own feet and speaking his own mind, then here in America, grown timid by listening too often and too long to the muses of Europe, "a nation of men will for the first time exist, because each believes himself inspired by the Divine Soul which also inspires all men."

As one reads Emerson's address a century later or hears even such a summary as I have just concluded, he must agree with the judgment of the listeners that something had that day been said that time would not dim nor let die. It is itself a demonstration of its own philosophy that he who speaks the faith that in him lies will find that other men respond to it in glad surprise. Not in the thinker's own age alone but in all ages inarticulate men will say of it, as they do of the utterances of any emancipating spirit, "Those are the things I believe and would fain have said for myself."

When one turns from Emerson's vision

of the American scholar as he was to be to the theme that I have chosen, the American scholar as he evolved in the nineteenth century and as he is to-day, it must be admitted that the historian who traces the development of American scholarship in the last century will pass by Emerson and all his works. His address was without directive force or influence on the course or contributions made by the American scholar within or without college walls. Indeed, I have just read the manuscript of a young New England scholar who has with great acumen surveyed the social philosophy of great American educators, and Emerson is not only not given space but I doubt if his name appears even in the index as one who contributed to the basic philosophies of those who shaped the nation's thinking in the last century about education at any level.

In the practical field where educational institutions have been built and the conditions for the nurture of scholarship set up, one reads to-day not the utterances of Emerson but of Horace Mann, Henry Barnard, Charles W. Eliot, Daniel Coit Gilman, Andrew D. White, William Watts Folwell, John Dewey and a score of others. These men, many of whom did their greatest work within Emerson's lifetime, some of whom were beginning it even as the echoes of his great address were heard beyond the walls of First Church, proclaimed no new independence of Europe but rather the opposite as they applied lessons learned abroad, chiefly in nineteenth century Germany, to American education from the public schools to the founding or refounding of great universities. These men had much to do with creating institutions that were, in Emerson's words, in large part their own lengthened shadows.

It is not with institutions or institution makers primarily that one concerns himself when he seeks to appraise American scholarship and the American scholar since 1837. Emerson's chief concern was with the scholar as prophet and philosopher. He was freshly returned from his European travels. He had seen a Europe still in the age of Metternich, still struggling to throw off fetters that his own land had never known. What a vision of a new independence in culture and thought such a contrast engendered in the New England iconoclast! The new American scholar was to lead in founding a new American nation with its own culture derived not from books and the past but from within the scholar's own mind, inspired by the events of his own day and his own land.

If in any sense the American scholar has played a formative rôle in the past century it is in quite another way than Emerson foresaw and under influences more European than American. In so far as American scholarship has made a distinct contribution in method or results it may be said to have turned its back upon the independence and individualism and self-sufficiency that were the guides Emerson set before it. It has produced few philosophers, none who were exponents of the Oversoul, and if there have been prophets among American scholars, they have been without honor in their own land.

What the American scholar is and what he has done are worthy achievements, but they conform in no visible sense to the Emersonian pattern, granted that Emerson was really defining the American scholar and not expounding transcendentalism. They are respectable enough to deserve the brief survey I propose to give them to-night, set against the background I have given in Emersonian terms.

At the outset of any survey of the American scholar since 1837 one must note that Emerson set up two qualifications that had become impossible at almost the very moment when he uttered them. The retirement of John Quincy Adams in 1829 from what he called "the perpetual motion and crazing cares" of the President's office ended the line of public men associated with the making of the nation and with service because of special fitness. He was the last scholar in the White House for many a day. Andrew Jackson of Tennessee and his followers came in with new concepts of public life and service. From their day almost to our own public evidence of scholarship and special preparation have been a bar to elective office in a democracy where any man was qualified by the counting of votes. A few months before Emerson spoke the presidency had been assumed by a manipulator of men trained in the factional strife of New York politics. To Jacksonian indifference to anything but personal loyalty Van Buren added the arts of a machine politician. The scholar in politics might be eulogized later by Phi Beta Kappa orators, but they talked of something which had scarcely existed and had become impossible in the democracy that was taking color and characteristic attitudes as Emerson spoke.

Equally futile was the call to independence from Europe. In the audience to which it was addressed were undoubtedly men, the first of a long procession ever increasing in numbers, who had made the pilgrimage to German universities. Ticknor, Motley, Bancroft and Longfellow had already made Göttingen their goal. They had come back imbued with the methods of painstaking German erudition. Others interested, like them, in literature, philology and history gave way in time to a still broader stream of those interested in mathematics and the sciences. The American scholar became in the decades between Emerson's oration and his own death in 1882 the product not of a new American culture but of German university training. Only one of Emerson's auditors, James Russell Lowell, remained primarily American in his training, and even he made the rounds of European universities on the eve of a Harvard professorship. And it was Lowell alone who sought the ear of the American electorate on public questions, and that only by the indirect route of the Biglow Papers and essays in the *North American Review*.

So far as independence in scholarship was concerned, Emerson in 1837 was truly a voice crying in a wilderness. American scholarship had before it a long apprenticeship to Europe in the ways of meticulous research and the effort to follow observed facts dispassionately. That the success and effect of this would in the long run be most patent and nationally significant in the physical sciences and biological sciences rather than in the social sciences was determined by three things. The European universities, despite their boasted academic freedom, were kept safe and sane under European monarchs and petty princes in all the fields that touched public affairs, and the revolution of 1848 only emphasized for the ruling class in Europe the wisdom of keeping the attention of professors and their students confined to the distant origins of human institutions and the study and exposition of the *status quo*. In the fields of politics, government and even history, continental European professors under Louis Philippe and Napoleon III or the German rulers, small and great, and then under Bismarck, knew before their appointment in what directions it was safe to explore freely.

Even if this view of their nineteenth century *Lehrfreiheit* is too unfavorable, the continental universities, imbedded in a political and social system alien to that of America, had little but method to impart to students of the social sciences from the western democracy. As those methods could be and were best exemplified in history, it is not surprising that in the group of studies that had to do with man in society the first German-trained American scholars were historians such as Motley and Bancroft, and in the universities the first trained leaders of seminars were Andrew D. White, Charles Kendall Adams and Herbert Baxter Adams in the field of history. Even such a sport in American academic life as Henry Adams at Harvard in the seventies used themes and methods in historical research that were Teutonic rather than American. In all other fields the dynastic nationalism of Europe and the self-satisfaction of an America given over to acquisitive exploitation of apparently inexhaustible resources and the political appeal of short views and expedient policies combined to leave no place to learn or to apply scholarship in public affairs.

Moreover, scholarship in America, whether native or foreign in training in the fields of politics or economics, was not sure of its position in the nineteenth century if it disagreed with the existing American political and economic order in any degree. Professor Perry at Williams and William Graham Sumner at Yale, who were opponents of protection in the eighties, were under constant fire as unsafe men to instruct American youth. In my sophomore year at Wisconsin, where La Follette was beginning his career, Richard T. Ely, professor of economics, was subjected to a heresy trial before the regents because he explained socialism to his classes and wrote a harmless and still useful little book on social thinkers of the nineteenth century from Saint-Simon to Marx and Lassalle. Three years later President Andrews of Brown University created a tremendous furor in the East by favoring Bryan and free silver and shortly afterwards transferred to the chancellorship of the University of Nebraska. Clearly there was no place yet for the independent, self-sustained Emersonian scholar in the social sciences in the America of the last century and it is yet to be proved that he has a secure place in the twentieth century. If he ever existed in many European countries he has disappeared from their universities during the years when you have been earning a Phi Beta Kappa key. His ultimate fate in America may be one of the major national issues before many more annual orators have appeared before you.

Other factors, however, determined that American scholars should seek and Europe, again with German universities in the lead, should give training to large numbers in the natural sciences and medicine. Here was a free field for scholarship where both continents needed and quickly recognized and applied the results of the scholar's work in the laboratory. It is true that the theologians tried to save their cherished creeds by crying out that science was undermining religion. But industry and commerce were more concerned with chemistry than they were with creeds. The bourgeoisie and not the bishops ruled the economic life of the new nations in Europe.

Science helped make cities through its contributions to industry, it helped feed them by its contributions to crop production and it made life in them possible by its contributions to sanitation and its success in combatting epidemics. It enabled nations to make war more efficiently and it perfected surgery and aseptic treatment of the wounded through the opportunities given it by these wars. Even a nation as reckless in wasting its natural resources of men and materials as the United States gave public lands to found state universities that would serve agriculture and the growing industries. American educators learned from Europe that these objects could be accomplished only through advance in the basic sciences and put the funds to better uses than Congress had ever intended or state legislatures dreamed. But it was the European universities that led the way. The German universities, serving the economic and industrial interests of the new empire after 1870, enabled it to overhaul England and outstrip all other countries. America was Germany's most apt pupil. Emerson and his prescription for the American scholar became "alms for oblivion" as tasks for schoolboys studying English. The brooding Oversoul, one with all nature, had fled from American hills denuded of their forests, from streams harnessed to mill wheels and prairies turned into food factories. "Man Thinking" had concentrated upon a test-tube or a ticker tape.

Emerson lived to see American scholarship as we understand it well on the way to great things in a Harvard where Eliot had taken charge and in Johns Hopkins under Gilman, and the beginnings of things a few like Folwell of Minnesota dreamed in the state universities of the Middle West. He did not live to see its most characteristic expression. That was reserved for the twentieth century.

Perhaps that peculiar and typical and non-Emersonian characteristic of American scholarship in our own day may best be exemplified by incidental experiences of my own. I recall that in a seminar on American history its leader, Frederick Jackson Turner, was commenting on Schouler's "History of the United States." He remarked that a few years before he had reviewed it rather adversely and added, "At the next meeting of the American Historical Association I met the old gentleman and found him so charming that I am not sure my review would have been so pointed had I known him first." The effect on book reviews of personal acquaintance with the author is the apparent point. The real one became clearer in the following seminar on English constitutional history under Professor Haskins, when we were all advised at the outset of our careers to join this same national organization of professional scholars in history. Organization and emphasis upon professional group interests and cooperation were thus brought definitely into the consciousness of the American neophyte in scholarship.

Many years later, in 1924, I was asked by one of the foundations to make a survey of the universities of central Europe. The purpose was to see what was necessary to save them from the debacle due to the collapse of their economic life and the fantastic inflation of their currency. In the execution of some of my own recommendations, I was associated with Professor Coss of Columbia in an attempt to select a representative in each of the countries who would be a resident representative of the foundation to select fellows. I knew from my student days in Germany and France how much more difficult that task was in Europe than it would be in America. The reason was that professionally European scholars were still wholly individualistic. They had no effective national organizations whose officers you could consult. Within any single university there was no idea of a department as we understand it, no cooperation and little common interest among men who with us would be in close association as departmental colleagues. I recall that in my Berlin student days two of my professors in the same department were engaged in a vigorous *Federkrieg* over a moot historical point, the dating of an interview in Bismarck's memoirs. In a seminar one professor referred to his colleague as a very industrious person but very mediocre in penetration and intellectual ability and therefore quite incompetent to judge the evidence. Then he gathered up his papers and bustled out, while I went into an adjoining room to hear a lecture by this dull and mediocre fellow-professor in the history department. How was organization and cooperation, apparently so easy and characteristic of American scholarship, possible among scholars in whom such an attitude as I have illustrated was equally characteristic?

This contrast between the atmosphere of continental university halls and that of our own campus can be illustrated by two other incidents. A few years ago the newly elected president of a great university came to Minnesota to spend a few days in observation. At the end of the first day he came into my office and said, "I want to ask you three questions. The first is how do you get cooperation at the University of Minnesota?" I broke down and confessed that our staff was just that kind and that you could pick up cooperation on the run almost anywhere on the Minnesota campus. The other incident was the pleasure of entertaining as a guest three weeks ago a seaboard scholar who had assumed executive responsibiity in an important piece of cooperative research. On the advice of all those he had asked he had come to Minnesota to get first-hand information on the major problem confronting him in his new responsibility—that of securing collaboration. My experiences are not unique nor is the situation on the Minnesota campus one that could not be duplicated in other universities. Their interest lies in the fact that they are typical. They epitomize what any objective observer would perceive was a truly characteristic feature of American scholarship and its approach to its task to-day.

The chief feature that such an observer of present-day American scholarship would note is organization on a grand scale and in every discipline and in the many subordinate divisions into which specialization has divided all the major fields of research. These organizations on a national basis by subjects are crossed and recrossed by regional and state and local organizations in the same fields. A national organization of physicists or chemists or historians is only the most manifest form of scholars' organization. Each in turn is broken up into many more. Biology in its two great divisions, animal and plant, has nearly forty national organizations of the specialties in this field. Above even the most inclusive national organizations stand super organizations like the Triple A. S. or the National Education Association with many sections and a membership so numerous that their annual meetings tax the hotel capacity of the largest cities. Their significance is as organizations of scholars rather than as organizations of scholarship. They are sometimes even cited as evidences of the extent to which America tends to divert or dilute scholarship by organization.

They are not so significant of what is really happening in research and investigation as are three great and more recent organizations which might be compared to holding companies, yet with independent operating functions of their own carried on over long periods and uniting in cooperative study many scholars of diverse disciplines upon great and many-sided problems. They are not only attempts to organize scholars but to organize scholarship. They have assumed the high responsibility of planning major movements along a wide front and of mobilizing all specialties and many specialists within their domain into a unified attack upon unsolved problems. They seek to cross-fertilize specialism by cooperation between allied disciplines. They command considerable funds when any major attack is planned and they support and direct the training of younger scholars by extensive systems of resident and traveling fellowships. They have headquarters and permanent secretariats that formulate plans for general staff approval and then keep the lines of attack and the supporting funds in motion.

These three organizations for national planning in scholarship are the National Research Council in the field of the physical and biological sciences, the Social Science Research Council, an incorporation of three representatives from each of the national societies in history, economics, political science, sociology, anthropology, psychology and statistics, and the American Council of Learned Societies, which includes a number of fields in the social sciences and adds the humanities in the widest sense, including philosophy, languages and literature and archeology. To these might be added the recently reorganized American Council on Education. Among them these four divide and include the whole range of American scholarship. They have some joint membership, some common activities and an occasional unofficial observer from one group attending the sessions of another. They are clearly not rivals, except that some unkind interpreter of what I said to Sigma Xi a year ago might point out that the constituencies of the National Research Council are bent on upsetting the world faster through discovery and invention than the social scientists can adjust mankind to the necessary changes; and all that may be left, if the resulting strain blows up civilization, is that the archeologists from the Council of Learned Societies will have the melancholy pleasure of gathering up and labeling the fragments.

Coincident with these organizations of scholarship and even preceding them is the establishment of an even more distinctly American manifestation, that of wealth combined with faith in education and scholarship—I mean the great foundations set up in many cities but centering chiefly in New York. The total list of more than one hundred and ten have an aggregate endowment approximating a billion, and I do not believe we are yet at the end. In no other age or land have such tremendous funds been mobilized for the support of research and the training and application of scholarship. They are organized like great universities without faculties. They do not, in the main, operate directly in research and teaching but rather make possible the programs and efforts of scholars in other university organizations or in national groups such as the major ones mentioned above. Their place in the picture of American scholarship is well in the foreground and their responsibilities for its future development equal or exceed their great resources. To be a trustee or responsible staff member of such a foundation is a place of power in determining the future of American education that finds no parallel in the cultural or social life of any other nation. The policies and decisions of the great foundations are determining in our day almost as much as the universities to what extent the mobilized scholars of America, not the individual prophet of Emerson's vision, will make an impress upon American civilization and institutions in the twentieth century. As the operations of many of the greatest of these foundations are not limited to our own country and their funds are being allotted to mature scientists and to scholars in training in all lands, their ultimate influence is limited to no century and to no one nation.

The contrast between the American scholar of Emerson's vision and the one we know to-day as a contributor to cooperative researches would be complete only if we described some of the many far-flung investigations now in progress. One might choose any field within the compass of the three major organizations. I think first of the study of sex directed by the National Research Council. Its origin lies in the experience of a man of wealth on a grand jury that had to investigate prostitution. Appalled by what he had learned, he set aside a sum to investigate the biological rather than the social aspects of a basic phenomenon of life. That study to my knowledge has been under way for ten years. Its centers and cooperating scholars are as far separated as New York, Chicago and California. This study, like the equally significant one on drug addiction, is planned and coordinated by a competent advisory committee. The contributors are not mere subordinates or cogs in a machine. They are outstanding scholars in many fields whose independence is jealously guarded but whose labors fit into the joint enterprise. In the seventeenth century a French scholar like Du Cange might undertake single handed a dictionary of medieval Latin. In our day, its revision is the cooperative task of hundreds of scholars in many lands. Sixty years ago von Ranke, single-handed and half-blind, began a "History of the World" in his eighty-first year. At his death ten years later he had reached 1500 in nine stout volumes. A similar task undertaken seriously to-day involves scores of scholars in many lands combining to produce the serried volumes in the Cambridge history series. The Social Science Research Council, now ten years old, has expended in that decade three million dollars, most of it in support of cooperative studies of the social and economic problems confronting American society.

The annual reports of these organizations, significant as they are, present but a partial picture of organized research in America. One finds it on every great campus where endowments or gifts are at the disposal of the university staff organized in councils, committees and institutes. Certainly no one at the University of Minnesota should want for examples when so many of the staff are in service on nationally planned researches and where our Employment Stabilization Institute has given in the past three years a brilliant example of the coordinated effort of many men and disciplines in studying such a disturbing phenomenon of the capitalistic system as the insecurity of labor and the equal insecurity of heedless industries.

No one would accept what has been said to-night as a complete picture of American scholarship. The effort has been primarily to describe its most characteristic national feature in our day. Nor is exposition of this feature meant in any sense to be exaltation. I do not believe that scholarship begins at forty, that nothing can be done or is being done until forty scholars have enlisted in cooperative research on one problem. What we have seen is a typical and in general a commendable effort in America, more distinctly than in any other land, to overcome the disadvantages of extreme specialization when faced with social and scientific problems so complex that they yield to the efforts of no one man or one discipline. We may recognize the advantages, the sheer necessity of such mobilization without worshipping at the bottom of a statistical column, without feeding our scholarly spirit solely on raw data, without minimizing the flash of a single scholar's intuition or the devotion or achievements of the lone seeker after truth. But when we have done that we do not escape the conviction that we have been reviewing in all these evidences of organized scholars and organized scholarship a challenging and significant manifestation of our national life. To my mind its significance does not lie in the field of scholarship alone. The attention of any student of social evolution who is scanning the horizon for signs of planning and indications of the rôle of individualism in the future might well consider the tendency that is revealed by scholars, who by tradition and training are the most individualistic group in all ages and all nations.

For two sufficient reasons I have drawn no comparison between what Emerson said of the scholar in his relations to his fellow men and their problems and the place of the present-day scholar in public life. In the first place, Emerson is here more Emersonian than at almost any other point in his address and chiefly concerned with the effect of such contact on the scholar's inner life. In the second place, the theme as it would be interpreted to-day is far too vast for a paragraph and too important from the standpoint of the scholar and the public to be touched and dropped. I commend it to some future Phi Beta Kappa speaker who is free to start with some other address than Emerson's.

At the opening of this address I asked and have sought to answer certain questions about the historic address of 1837. Its main philosophy explained how it affronted many in the smug Unitarian Harvard audience. The criteria Emerson set up for the scholar, the training he outlined, were those of his own philosophy, not of scholarship as men understood it then or have understood and exemplified it since. The characteristics he felt essential have in no visible sense been the characteristics of American scholarship in the last century.

There remains the question I did not ask. It has, however, its proper place at the conclusion of any such address as this to young scholars. What significance have the words of Emerson to you, to any reader a century later. Certainly it is something to rise even for a moment to new intellectual levels with a great poet and essayist. That elevation of the spirit Emerson's address shares with all great literature. It is sheer gain to stand, as you do in reading his words, in the presence of a "Man Thinking." Such men are so few, so precious, so in danger of being overwhelmed by the turbid floods of speech and print that we must seek them out and turn aside with them into quiet bypaths where we can hear their voices. When we do, it is to listen to one who interprets to us our own noblest impulses, our abiding heart's desire. It is this that Emerson can still do for each of us according to the measure of our spiritual apperception.

We turn from all the triumphs of a century of scholarship in ways unknown to Emerson to reaffirm with him that the American scholar to-day, to-morrow, must be free. What he claimed for the scholar's sake alone we claim for the sake of civilization itself in a world where nation after nation has condemned the "Man Thinking" to silence or exile. And this because his greatest power is not to change the material world but to change states of mind. If stupidity and dumb acquiescence are the price of physical survival they are equally a sentence to spiritual torpor and death. The complexities of science are being solved by the cooperation of free scholars. The complexities of our political and social life can be solved only by the cooperation of free men, of free men thinking. If the American scholar to-day can be assured the freedom that Emerson demanded as his birthright, a freedom that all ages have shown is even more essential to the orderly evolution of society, then, and then only, will "this continent . . . fill the postponed expectation of the world with something better than the exertions of mechanical skill."

# EDUCATIONAL EVENTS

## THE ENGLISH LABOR PARTY AND EDUCATION

AT the Labor Party Conference recently held at Southport, England, Sir Charles P. Trevelyan, presenting the labor and education section of the executive report, urged that the short and non-controversial discussion of the topic should not be mistaken by anybody as indicating any lack of its importance in the eyes of the labor party. He stated that the report was definite and strong, but that a longer restatement of the party's whole educational policy would be issued by the executive committee under the title of "Education in Power." A summary of Sir Charles' remarks, as reported in *The London Times Educational Supplement*, follows:

The public ought to know that the labor party stood for big changes in the national education system—for the raising of the school age to 16 in two rapidly succeeding stages; for the freeing of secondary education in all state-aided schools at once, thereby abolishing the mainstay of class distinction in educational opportunity; for the improvement of primary schools at once by drastic alteration of the size of classes and of the standards required in the teaching profession; for drastic dealing with the bad buildings among the schools, and for other changes dealing with books and curriculum. There would be a wide extension throughout the country of nursery schools, and school feeding would take a far more important part in our educational system. Almost all these things could be attained at once without legislation, though there would have to be legislation for raising the school age.

When a Labor Government came into office with power its whole energies would be absorbed at once by the task of nationalizing the banks, the land, the mines and other industries. There should be no doubt about the intention of the party to lay the foundations of an equal system of education for all. The whole system had to be reshaped and the teaching profession reorganized, but to do all these things at once would require Parliamentary time, and that might divert attention from the great things educationally which might be done at once through administration. In the Labor Government of the future the minister of education ought to be more important than the minister of war. He ought to have under his control all the universities and public schools and the whole of the educational systems. As a party they had made up their minds that the economic revolution which they were planning and plotting at that conference had to be accompanied by a mental growth in the population such as demanded a higher and more universal system of education. The program to achieve that end was not speculative, it was a mandate to the next Labor Government for immediate action.

Three composite amendments to which the Cambridge University Labor Party was a party either as mover or seconder were accepted in principle by Sir Charles Trevelyan for inclusion in the extended report. They provide for the elimination of all teaching calculated to encourage militarism or imperialist ideas; for passing all children of all classes through the public primary schools, and for securing equal access of all persons to the universities, the sole condition being intellectual capacity.

The education report was then approved, but before the vote was put there was an echo of possible trouble in store over the religious issue in education. Sir Charles Trevelyan, speaking in reply to an amendment, which was later withdrawn, considered it important, but a detail.

## COURSES IN PUBLIC ADMINISTRATION IN THE HARVARD BUSINESS SCHOOL

The Harvard Business School announced recently the inauguration of a program in public administration, designed primarily to prepare students for the business aspects of public service. In addition the new program, which has been under consideration for some years, will supply necessary background for men entering private business by training them to deal with questions arising out of the relationships of government and business.

A two-year curriculum is being set up diverging from the established courses in business administration at the middle of the first year's work for those desiring to specialize, but offering all men, whether or not specializing in public administration, an opportunity to elect courses giving a foundation in the business aspects of government and in the relationship between the two.

A substantial beginning in this work will be offered to a limited number of men entering for the extra session beginning January 28, 1935, for graduation in June, 1936. In addition, men who entered this fall will be able in their second year to lay a foundation in government subjects from courses in the new field.

In connection with the regular work in private business, new courses will be organized in public administration, the agricultural industries and the relations of government to business. Close cooperation will be maintained between the school and the departments of economics and government in the university in providing a background in the general problems and in the theory of government.

Wallace B. Donham, dean of the school, in commenting upon the proposed plan said in part:

> The creation of this program in public administration is the result of several years of such preparation on the part of the faculty. It grows directly out of the belief that further opportunity to study the interrelations of business and government and the business problems of government

must be provided if men entering business are to be of maximum value to business and of greatest possible service to the community.

The organization of this program in public administration is made possible by a recent modification made by William Ziegler, Jr., donor of the William Ziegler Memorial Fund established by him in the school in 1927, which makes income from this foundation available for the new objectives. A professor of public administration will be appointed under this fund.

The school intends to conduct this new program in such a manner that men electing the new work will in every case take a large proportion of their instruction in courses primarily emphasizing private business in order that they will be prepared to enter business, if they desire, either at once or after a period in government service. Such men will be more and more useful to private business.

When the Harvard Business School was founded in 1908, it was originally conceived as a School of Public and Private Business, but the idea of direct preparation for government services was abandoned as offering at the time too restricted possibilities for graduates. In offering a program in public business to-day, in addition to its training for private business, the school is carrying out one of the objectives for which it was originally planned.

## TEACHER TRAINING AT THE UNIVERSITY OF VERMONT

THE University of Vermont has made an important announcement with reference to its future plans for teacher training. For many years it has maintained under its College of Arts and Sciences a four-year course for teachers leading to the degree of bachelor of science in education. The graduates of this course have been able to qualify either for secondary or for elementary school teaching. The university has also offered a two-year course for elementary school teachers, under the direction of its department of education.

In the past the articulation of this course with the requirements for the B.S., in the case of those who wished to continue their studies and obtain a degree, has presented a difficult problem. The official statement, given out by the university, is as follows:

The University of Vermont and State Agricultural College announces that commencing with the college year 1934–1935 the present two-year teacher training curriculum will be extended so as to provide for two more years of teacher training, thereby resulting in a complete four-year elementary education curriculum. Through this arrangement, a student who satisfactorily completes the prescribed four-year course will be awarded the degree of Bachelor of Education. The candidate for this degree will be recommended to the Committee on Degrees by the head of the Department of Education and the committee in turn will make their recommendations to the Board of Trustees.

The two-year curriculum was established in 1921 at the request of the State Board of Education and has been continued since that date. Only such modifications have been made as have been agreed to by the university and the State Board of Education. The inauguration by the university of the extension of the present two-year course, thereby providing a complete four-year elementary education curriculum leading to the degree of Bachelor of Education, will enable those who so desire to complete their teacher training at the university rather than to be obliged to go outside the state for that purpose. Graduates of other two-year teacher training schools, either in Vermont or in other states, will be admitted to the third year of this curriculum provided they present recommendations and credits that are satisfactory to the university. The development of this curriculum will not in any way affect the four-year teacher training curriculum leading to the degree of Bachelor of Science in Education. Students who are candidates for the new degree will be eligible for aid from university funds on the same basis as any duly enrolled candidate for any other degree.

In formulating its building program, consideration is to be given to the development of the Department of Education into what may eventually prove to be a School of Education.

## THE SCHOOL FOR WORKERS IN INDUSTRY AT THE UNIVERSITY OF WISCONSIN

MORE than 13,000 citizens of Wisconsin have taken part in the five events which made up the program for 1933–34 of the School for Workers in Industry at the University of Wisconsin, according to a report made public recently by Dr. Alice Shoemaker, director of the school.

The total cost to the university for carrying on the school during the year was $4,720. This amount provided for classes in economics in nine Wisconsin cities, with a weekly attendance of 275 citizens; sponsored talks on economic subjects at union meetings, with a total attendance of 10,500 persons; institutes held in four Wisconsin cities with a total attendance of 2,800; a training center for FERA teachers at the university during the summer, attended by 32 men and women, and the regular six-week summer school for workers, which had an attendance of 90 students.

The classes in economics and general education were held in the cities of Green Bay, La Crosse, Beaver Dam, Kenosha, Sheboygan, Waukesha, Racine, Oshkosh and Madison. Attendance in these cities ranged from 20 to 60 citizens a class, and according to the report, there was "universal enthusiasm and appreciation." Besides these classes, talks on economic questions were given in Milwaukee.

A feature of the winter program were the labor institutes held in Milwaukee, Sheboygan, Madison and Kenosha, at the request of and with the cooperation of the central labor bodies. The institutes lasted from three to five days, and many well-known teachers, including members of the faculty of the university, spoke on current economic topics.

The scope of the 1934 summer session was enlarged by the addition of two government projects. The University of Wisconsin was chosen as one of a half-dozen leading educational institutions as a training center for unemployed teachers who are to be used in the FERA workers' education program for the coming winter. The territory covered by the center includes Michigan, Minnesota, North and South Dakota, besides Wisconsin.

The second government project was the addition of a unit of 55 unemployed women workers to the school for workers, increasing the total enrolment to 90 for the six-week courses in economics, English and history.

The Wisconsin School for Workers celebrated its tenth anniversary last summer with a week-end of festivities, which brought back to the campus former students from ten cities and from seven of the nine previous sessions.

## EDUCATIONAL WORK OF THE MUSEUM OF THE UNIVERSITY OF PENNSYLVANIA

WITH the completion of an additional junior studio the University Museum of the University of Pennsylvania will greatly expand its program of educational work for children this year, according to a statement made by Horace H. F. Jayne, director of the museum.

The program, which will include three separate projects designed to encourage an interest in art and archeology among children ranging in age from six to fifteen, will be under the direction of Eleanor M. Moore, a member of the museum staff who has returned from Czechoslovakia, Rumania and Hungary, where she studied for three months in the International School of Art.

The extensive collections of the museum have been drawn upon to transform the two junior studios into temporary homes of the South American Indians, and in these rooms, beginning on October 27 and continuing until April 6, children's classes in pottery, wood carving, modeling and water color painting will be conducted every Saturday morning by experienced teachers.

A second project for children will be the "How-to-Make-It Club at Home," the members of which will receive from the museum at monthly intervals complete materials and directions for making unusual and interesting objects used by past civilizations or primitive peoples in various countries.

The list of eight objects to be made includes an Eskimo hunter's helmet, Babylonian queen's jewelry, Tewa Indian mask, Egyptian pen and ink case, Maya flower pot, South Sea Island brush, Japanese fish kite and South American pan pipes.

Finally, there will be special junior memberships to whose holders there will be mailed each month, from November to April, an entertaining story about people in foreign countries. In addition, these junior members will receive one how-to-make-it gift during the year, and two admission cards for the museum's annual junior entertainment.

## LICENSING MOTION PICTURES IN NEW YORK STATE

THE Motion Picture Division of the State Education Department reviewed and licensed 1,769 films during the year beginning July 1, 1933, and ending June 30, 1934, according to the annual report submitted by Irwin Esmond, director of the division, to Commissioner of Education Frank P. Graves. Of these 1,769 films,

286 were approved with eliminations. Fifteen pictures were rejected entirely, of which two were later revised and approved with eliminations.

The net revenue to the state for the year amounted to $170,670.79. Receipts for the year were $231,497.88 and expenditures were $60,827.09. The net revenue is $8,973.32 greater than last year's revenue. Since the organization of the Motion Picture Commission in 1921 the total net profit to the state over and above all expenditures has been $1,688,764.63.

The Motion Picture Division is charged with the duty of reviewing and licensing of motion pictures, except news releases, previous to exhibition in New York State. It is also charged with the duty of inspecting theaters or any place where motion picture films are exhibited, stored, kept or used, for the purpose of ascertaining whether such films have been licensed, the license leader is displayed on the screen in accordance with the statute and the eliminations have been made pursuant to directions of the division. Mr. Esmond reports:

The fact that 8,362 reels of film were reviewed during the year, that 15 pictures were rejected outright, and that 2,195 eliminations were made on statutory grounds, will give some idea of the amount of work that is done. During the entire time that this division has been in operation, we have succeeded in keeping off the screen pictures exploiting prostitution, venereal disease, white slavery, narcotic drugs, unnatural love, sterilization, nudism, and films destructive of our form of government. We have also eliminated a very great number of scenes of lust, crime, indecency and immorality, as well as scenes that are inhuman and sacrilegious.

In administering the motion picture law, the Motion Picture Division has always kept in mind the rulings and procedure of the courts in construing and applying similar language used in statutes over which the courts have been called upon to exercise jurisdiction. We have consistently maintained a sane, conservative and constructive administration of the motion picture law in this state. In doing this, we have acted carefully under the statute to the end that our actions may be wholly defensible if called in question either before the Commissioner of Education or before the courts.

The 2,195 eliminations are classed as follows: indecent, 838; inhuman, 79; tending to incite to crime, 511; immoral or tending to corrupt morals, 752; sacrilegious, 15.

## THE GENERAL EDUCATION BOARD'S GRANT TO NEW YORK UNIVERSITY

NEW YORK UNIVERSITY has received an emergency grant of $50,000 from the General Education Board to conduct a program of teacher training and research in connection with the emergency adult education activities in New York City. A part of the grant will be used to strengthen the administrative and supervisory staff conducting the work in adult education.

The program will be under the direction of Dr. Ned H. Dearborn, acting director of the Division of General Education, and will be planned and conducted in cooperation with Dr. L. A. Wilson, assistant state commissioner for vocational education, who is in charge of emergency education for New York State; Superintendent Harold G. Campbell, Associate Superintendent William E. Grady and Dr. Morris E. Siegel, director of evening and continuation schools, all of the New York City Board of Education.

According to Chancellor Harry Woodburn Chase, the General Education Board's emergency grant will supplement the $1,500,000 of relief funds which has been appropriated for the State Adult Education project in New York City. It will enable New York University to continue and extend the "in-service" training of more than 1,200 New York adult education emergency teachers and supervisors started at the university last summer. The grant also provides for a study of the character and results of the New York emergency education program which is expected profoundly to affect practises in adult education throughout the country and safeguard the future work of adult education in New York City.

Actual work under the grant will be started when the immediate supervision of emergency education is transferred from the State Department of Education to the City Board of Education, according to Dr. Dearborn.

Dr. Dearborn is at present assisting in the organization of a staff of supervisors for special fields, including art, music, dramatics, payroll and statistics, and leisure time activities, which will be composed of men and women regularly employed by the state and city departments of education, supplemented by special supervisors provided for by the grant from the General Education Board.

Dr. Dearborn pointed out that limitations in the use of relief funds make it impossible to employ the quantity of men and women needed for the administration and supervision of the adult education program or to provide the amount of in-service education of teachers, leaders and supervisors that is imperative if high standards of instruction are to be maintained. Neither can relief funds be used to provide the research work needed to guide in making changes in the programs from time to time in terms of actual adult needs and to evaluate the year's work. All these important factors will now be made possible by the subvention of the General Education Board.

### THE NATIONAL COUNCIL OF GEOGRAPHY TEACHERS

THE National Council of Geography Teachers will meet in Philadelphia on December 26 and 27.

Wednesday morning will be devoted to discussions of geographic field work and its relation to planning toward better utilization of natural resources. The session will open with a paper by Earl Hanson, of the Water Resources Section of the National Resources Board, who will discuss geographic research in national planning. The morning program includes reports of specific field work as it now is being carried on in given college, high-school and elementary classes, and suggestions for making use of further opportunities for such work.

The Wednesday afternoon discussions will center on "Developing Independence in the Use of Geographic Tools." An hour will be given in the afternoon, in which a large group of council members will participate in an attempt to answer briefly specific questions which are being received from teachers in many sections of the country about the teaching of geography. Questions for discussion should be sent to the director, Miss Erna Grassmuck, State Teachers College, Indiana, Pennsylvania.

The Thursday morning session will stress urban studies. Professor Preston James, of the University of Michigan, and Professor Lewis F. Thomas, of Washington University, St. Louis, are representative of those who will present content studies, based on recent research in specific cities. They will be followed by a discussion of "Organizing Urban Material for Classroom Use" by Miss Ruby Harris and other specialists in this field.

Dr. William Scott Gray, of the University of Chicago, who has recently made a study of the education of teachers, will be the guest of honor and the first speaker on Thursday afternoon. This session will be devoted to "Teacher Education." Dr. George F. Howe, of New Britain, Connecticut; Dr. Leonard O. Packard, of Boston, and Miss Pearle Blood, of Towson, Maryland, will also speak. Specialists in promoting the progress of the in-service teachers of geography will speak on this aspect of teacher education.

At the banquet, on Thursday evening, the speaker will be Dr. Isaiah Bowman, director of the American Geographical Society of New York City.

## EDUCATIONAL NOTES AND NEWS

WILLARD E. GIVENS, superintendent of schools at Oakland, Calif., was elected secretary of the National Education Association by the board of trustees at a special meeting in St. Louis on November 10. He succeeds J. W. Crabtree, who has been secretary since 1917, and who has reached the age of retirement, having been born on April 18, 1864. Mr. Givens will take charge of the national headquarters in Washington on January 1. All members of the board of trustees were present at the meeting. These are: Joseph H. Saunders, superintendent of schools at Newport News, Va., *chairman;* Henry Lester Smith, dean of the School of Education of Indiana University, now president of the N. E. A.; Joseph M. Gwinn, technical adviser of the public schools of San Francisco; A. L. Whittenberg, secretary of the State Examining Board for Teachers' Certificates, Springfield, Illinois, and Edgar G. Doudna, secretary of the Board of Normal School Regents of Wisconsin.

DR. CHARLES S. MILLER was formally installed as president of the State Teachers College at

Slippery Rock, Pa., on November 10. Dr. Carmon Ross will be installed as president of the State Teachers College at Edinboro, Pa., on November 24.

DR. SHELTON JOSEPH PHELPS was installed on November 9 as president of Winthrop College at Rock Hill, South Carolina. Dr. Phelps succeeds Dr. James P. Kinard, now president emeritus, who served after the death of the first president of the college, Dr. David Bancroft Johnson.

DR. RUFUS B. VON KLEINSMID, president of the University of Southern California, has been given the degree of doctor of laws by DePauw University. President von KleinSmid was head of the departments of psychology and education at DePauw from 1905 to 1914, prior to his election as head of the University of Arizona. He was made president of the University of Southern California in 1922.

THE degree of doctor of letters was conferred on Dr. Arnold Wolfers, formerly director of the School of Politics in Berlin and visiting professor in the Department of Social Sciences at Yale University, at the Founder's Day exercises at Mount Holyoke College on November 8.

A DINNER in honor of Dr. Arthur E. Bostwick was given on October 1 to celebrate his twenty-fifth anniversary as librarian of the St. Louis Public Library. About 125 members of the library staff and members of the Board of Directors and former board members attended. Charles H. Compton presided. Marion C. Early and John B. Edwards, of the board, spoke of the growth of the library system under Dr. Bostwick's guidance. Miss Marjorie Doud, chief of the Readers' Advisory Service, expressed the high esteem in which Dr. Bostwick is held by members of his staff.

DR. JOSIAH H. PENNIMAN, provost of the University of Pennsylvania and professor of English literature, has been awarded the Cross of the Legion of Honor of France by the President of the French Republic. The award was made on the recommendation of the French Ambassador in recognition of Dr. Penniman's services to French literature and Franco-American intellectual relations. It was formally presented by Marcel deVerneuil, French consul general in Philadelphia, at a brief ceremony conducted in Dr. Penniman's office on November 14.

DR. MICHAEL DEMIASHKEVICH has been awarded by the French Government the title of *Officier d'Académie* and the decoration known as the Academic Palms. This honor is in recognition of Dr. Demiashkevich's scholarly contributions to the literature of comparative education.

THE Academy of Physical Medicine at the recent New York meeting conferred the title of fellow of the academy upon Dr. Robert Tait McKenzie, physician and sculptor, professor of physical education at the University of Pennsylvania.

DR. MARION R. TRABUE, professor of educational administration and director of the Bureau of Research in the Department of Education of the University of North Carolina, has accepted appointment as director of a national research project which will attempt to reclassify occupations and to develop new technique for fitting the unemployed into current work opportunities. The project is being sponsored jointly by the Social Science Research Council in New York City and the United States Employment Service. Dr. Trabue's headquarters will be in Washington and branch bureaus will be established throughout the country.

DR. MAX FÖRSTER has been appointed visiting professor of English at Yale University. Dr. Förster has held university posts at Würzburg, Halle, Leipzig and Munich. He was for a long time one of the editors of the German Shakespeare Year Book, and is now first vice-president of the German Shakespeare Society.

DR. JOSEPH D. MCGOLDRICK, comptroller of the City of New York, will resume his position as professor of economics at Columbia University after he leaves office on January 1.

DR. FRANK P. GRAHAM, president of the University of North Carolina, has been appointed chairman of an advisory committee on economic security named by President Roosevelt to submit for his consideration a broad program covering the whole field of social problems. Dr. Grace Abbott, of the University of Chicago, formerly chief of the United States Children's Bureau, is a member of the committee.

A DINNER in honor of Mrs. Mary K. Simkhovitch, founder and director of Greenwich House, New York City, was given on November 15, at which Gerard Swope, president of the house, presided. Mrs. Franklin D. Roosevelt attended the dinner and presented to the founder of the settlement a check representing contributions for furthering health and recreational activities of the settlement.

DR. HENRY PITNEY VAN DUSEN, dean of students at the Union Theological Seminary, was elected a charter trustee of Princeton University at the annual meeting of the board of trustees held on October 25.

DR. CHARLES TIPPETTS, head of the School of Business Administration of the University of Buffalo, has accepted a similar position at the University of Pittsburgh.

DR. JOSEPH S. ROUCEK, who has been visiting professor of sociology in the Pennsylvania State College, has been appointed lecturer in social studies in extension. In addition to his adult education activities throughout the State of Pennsylvania, Dr. Roucek is also engaged in experimental educational work at the Rock View Penitentiary.

WALTER H. PISTON, assistant professor of music at Harvard University, has been granted leave of absence for the second half of the current academic year.

KENNETH BINNS, librarian of the Commonwealth Parliamentary Library at Canberra, Australia, has returned from a visit to the United States and England where he investigated library methods and policies.

DR. WILLIAM MATHER LEWIS, president of Lafayette College, and Dr. Robert C. Clothier, president of Rutgers University, were the speakers at a dinner given on November 8 on the occasion of the celebration of the one hundred and sixty-eighth anniversary of the founding of Rutgers University.

DR. JAMES MARK BALDWIN, formerly professor of psychology at Lake Forest College, the University of Toronto, Princeton University and the Johns Hopkins University, who has resided in Paris since 1912, died on November 8 at the age of seventy-three years.

DR. BENJAMIN RAND, librarian emeritus of the Emerson philosophical library at Harvard University, died on November 9 at the age of seventy-eight years. Dr. Rand built up the library of philosophy in Emerson Hall, Cambridge, making it the most complete library of its kind in North America. He had been an assistant and instructor in philosophy at Harvard in the days of William James, Josiah Royce, George Herbert Palmer, George Santanya and Hugo Munsterberg and was appointed librarian in 1906, retiring in 1933 because of his health. The library of philosophy was distinct from the Widener Library of the university. It was housed in a separate building and was accessible to all students.

DAVID B. OLIVER died on October 21, just ten days before he was to have observed his one-hundredth birthday. *The Public Education Bulletin* of the Department of Public Instruction of Pennsylvania says: "Mr. Oliver's life paralleled within a few months the first century of free public education in the state of his adoption. At the time of his death and for fifty-four years preceding, he was an active member of the Pittsburgh Board of Education, a record probably unequaled in the United States. One of his greatest contributions to public education in Pennsylvania was direction of the drafting of the School Code of 1911."

DR. ALICE HAMLIN HINMAN, formerly head of the department of philosophy and psychology at Mount Holyoke College, died on October 29 at the age of sixty-six years. Mrs. Hinman was the daughter of the Reverend Cyrus Hamlin, founder of Robert College, Istanbul, Turkey.

L. ALLAN COMPTON, assistant professor of physical education at Rutgers University and a member of its physical education department since 1924, died on November 7 at the age of thirty-two years.

PROFESSOR ABRAHAM OCHOA, director of La Ceiba College, Tegucigalpa, Honduras, was killed in a duel on November 6.

A BRONZE plaque in memory of Charles William Eliot, formerly president of Harvard University, was presented to the university on November 8 by members of the Harvard Memorial Society. The plaque was placed in Room 11 of Holworthy Hall, where Dr. Eliot lived as an undergraduate. Speakers at the dinner given on the occasion were Roger B. Merriman, professor of history and political science; Joseph H. Beale, professor of law, and Herbert M. Irwin, president of the memorial society. Samuel Eliot Morison, professor of history, was toastmaster.

DR. MARY E. WOOLLEY, president of Mount Holyoke College, during the Founder's Day exercises announced a gift of $150,000 for library endowment from the Carnegie Corporation, which in 1921 gave $75,000 for general endowment and in 1930 $25,000 for the purchase of books for the library.

BY the will of the late Fred M. Preble, of Ludlow, Vt., Colby College received the sum of $6,000 to be added to the endowment funds of the college, $3,000 to establish the Fred M. Preble scholarship fund, and the residue of the estate, the extent of which is not yet determined. The sum of $1,900 is left to the Coburn Classical Institute to be added to the endowment funds of the school.

SIX Henry Fund Fellowships, each having a value of £500, will be offered this year to American students for a year's study at Oxford or Cambridge Universities. Candidates must be unmarried American citizens, men or women. Preference will be given to those who are in their last year of undergraduate work or who have just started upon graduate work in a recognized college or university in the United States. The American Committee of Management consists of the following six trustees of the fund: President James B. Conant, Jerome D. Greene and Dean A. Chester Hanford, who represent the Harvard Corporation, and President James Rowland Angell, Mr. Carl A. Lohmann and Mr. George Parmly Day, who represent the Yale Corporation. The choice of subject of study to be undertaken by a Henry Fellow is unrestricted, provided the plan of work meets with the approval of the committee of management and of the university to which the fellow is assigned. Men fellows have a free choice of studying at either Oxford or Cambridge Universities. Women may apply for appointment to any college or school which regularly admits women to departments of study in these universities.

DR. H. W. STOPHER, director of the department of music of Louisiana State University, has completed arrangements with the Mozarteum, Austrian National Conservatory in Salzburg, whereby two students from that school will be exchanged with two students from Louisiana State University for a year's study. The plan will become effective in 1935–1936. The students will be chosen on a competitive basis.

GIFTS to Columbia University aggregating $51,543.01 were announced on November 8. This includes $25,000 from the Carnegie Corporation of New York, for the maintenance of the School of Library Service. For the study of rheumatic fever, directed by Dr. Walter W. Palmer, of the School of Medicine, the W. K. Kellogg Foundation contributed $10,000. A group of donors founded an Italian Societies Endowment Fund with $1,730. The income from this will be used for research and study in the fields of Italian culture. Another group gave $370 for a study of racial and social differences in mental ability, conducted under the Council for Research in the Social Sciences.

IN neither England, France or the Scandinavian countries has the depression been permitted to strike the blow at education that we have permitted in the United States, Dr. Glenn Frank, president of the University of Wisconsin, says in a chapter on "Education Hamstrung" in his recent book entitled "America's Hour of Decision." "A sword hangs over education throughout the United States," Dr. Frank writes. He also says that never before in the United States has a depression been permitted "to scuttle the schools and rape the intellectual resources of the national future." Reviewing the effects of past depressions on education, Dr. Frank points out that the panic of 1837 ended in the renewal, not in the ruin, of the schools. Between 1837 and 1843, he notes, leading American states increased their support of education as much as 34 per cent. "The panic of 1857," Dr. Frank continues, "left the schools unharmed. The panic of 1873, despite its severity, did not result in any backward step in education. In 29 representative states, the financial support of the schools was averagely increased by more than 50 per cent. The depression of 1893 did not reduce the support of the schools. The depression of 1907 did not tamper with the public investment in education. And the depression of 1922 saw no educational retrenchment."

The Carnegie Trust for the Universities of Scotland in its thirty-second annual report, as reported by *Nature,* directs special attention to the operation during the last five years of its schemes for the endowment of post-graduate research. The principal scheme, under which fellowships, scholarships and grants are awarded, has now been operating for thirty years, during which period scientific investigation in the universities by 1,162 persons has been subsidized by this means to the extent of more than a quarter of a million sterling, the expenditure for the six quinquennia beginning 1903–08 having been: £27,754, £35,698, £27,640, £39,465, £51,047 and £69,268. "What this has meant to the enrichment of the intellectual life of the Scottish universities may in part be inferred," says the report, "from the fact that the total publications received have numbered 227 volumes and 2,002 other original contributions." The problem has been, not to find suitable and well-qualified applicants, but to find sufficient means to finance them, and in order that the amount available should meet the requirements of the situation so far as possible, the value of the individual awards for 1932–33 was reduced, fellows' stipends being lowered from £300 to £250, senior scholarships from £200 to £175 and other scholarships from £175 to £150; and it has now been found necessary to place all scholarships on the uniform level of £150. A welcome indication of better times is afforded by the fact that resignations on account of appointment to salaried posts have again become numerous. Other financial aids to research are provided by the trust in the form of grants towards the maintenance of the laboratory of the Royal College of Physicians of Edinburgh, amounting during the last quinquennium to £9,369, and awards to university assistants and lecturers devoting not less than half their time to research, amounting during the same period to £18,329.

# DISCUSSION

## PURPOSE OF THE COMMISSION ON THE SOCIAL STUDIES IN THE SCHOOLS

The article by Dr. Franklin Bobbitt, professor of educational administration in the University of Chicago, entitled "Questionable Recommendations of the Commission on Social Studies" in the issue of School and Society for August 18 raises some questions about the problem and purpose of the commission. May I ask you, therefore, to publish the enclosed statement which in a sense represents the composite view of the commission on these questions. It was prepared originally as the preface to the volume of "Conclusions and Recommendations" of the report. As such it was submitted for approval to all members. It was given its final form at a meeting at which E. E. Day, G. S. Ford, C. E. Merriam, Jesse H. Newlon, G. S. Counts and C. J. H. Hayes, as well as the writer, were present. Whatever their differences on other points, these members of the commission agreed upon this preface as indicating their conception of their task and the spirit in which they had sought to accomplish it. It was omitted, perhaps unfortunately, in the final printing of the volume because it was disproportionately long compared to the main document, because most of what it recited had been published before and because it seemed certain that no one would question the purposes of the commission. Since a question has been raised, I hope that the preface may now be printed in the journal.

A. C. Krey,
*Chairman of the Commission of the Social Studies in the Schools*

### Preface Originally Prepared for the Volume of Conclusions and Recommendations of the Commission on Social Studies in the Schools

This volume presents the conclusions of the Commission on the Social Studies in the Schools sponsored by the American Historical Association. It marks the close of five years of study and deliberations. Perhaps it would be more correct to say eight years, for those who planned the investigation during the preceding three years became members of the commission. The joint efforts of social scientists and educators, representing two great fields of scholarship, are here focused upon the problem of a more adequate preparation of American youth for effective participation in the emerging society in which they live and which they must shortly direct.

The problem, or host of problems, to which the commission addressed itself arose out of the world-wide changes that have bred new problems as a heritage to the new generation. The program of training for participation in society which the schools were largely following had been laid down at the beginning of the present century. Yet the society for which the pupils were being prepared was not static but dynamic. It was and is undergoing many and far-reaching changes. A basic question before the commission, therefore, was how much of this change was of a permanent character requiring a modification of the school program. There were individuals who had predicted as early as 1910 that the school program must be altered to meet the changes which were already apparent to them, but at that time society at large was by no means convinced of that necessity.

The material changes wrought by science and its handmaiden, technology, were obvious. Basically significant were the improvements in methods of communication which integrated the whole world. The constant improvement of the automobile and the rapid extension of its use to include virtually the whole population could not be without important consequences for society. To all this was added the development of the airplane, the cinema, the press and the radio, by means of which not only men and materials but ideas as well were being transmitted more rapidly and more widely. Nearly every field of industry had availed itself of the fruits of technology either to increase production or to produce equally with more mechanical and far less manual labor. The material aspects of these changes were almost immediately appreciated and quite universally adopted. Only a few recognized the fact that such changes were bringing fundamental social changes as well. What these social consequences were, how fundamental and far-reaching and to what extent they called for modifications of government, business and social organization were questions which had to be met, not avoided or too long postponed.

If there were some who as early as 1910 felt the need of modification in the agencies of social control and direction, their vision was apparently lost in the blood-red mists of a world war. The emotional disturbances and social dislocations caused by that catastrophe clouded more years than the duration of the war itself. It was difficult, if not impossible, for even the most perspicacious to distinguish between temporary social disturbances due to the war and those more permanent shifts in value dependent on other factors such as the consequences of technological development. It was not until the third decade of the century was well advanced that thoughtful people became generally aware of the magnitude, pervasiveness and permanence of the changes which had their beginnings about the opening of the century. A few startled and timid souls even suggested that research in natural science be arbitrarily halted until research in social science and its translation into suitable institutions and patterns of thought could be brought abreast of the world remade by the natural sciences and technology.

Fortunately it is not possible, nor is it necessary, to halt research in natural science or advance in technology. But the increasing strain involved when men think in old ways and live in a new world was an unavoidable challenge to educators. The answer was not obvious and the rewards of success in seeking it neither certain nor material, yet the challenge was accepted by a great influx of able youth into fields of social science research. Economics, political science and sociology expanded into many specialized forms. Recognized scholars in these fields were enabled by grants from educational foundations to devote themselves solely to research with the help of the more youthful scholars. The danger of futility resulting from a separated and limited attack upon problems in which all the social sciences were concerned was early recognized. Coordination of this research was attempted by several agencies and at length strongly promoted through the organization of the Social Science Research Council. One of the early achievements of this cooperative research was the study of

"Comparative Civic Education," which proved of great value to the present investigation.

The national government had likewise come to recognize the importance of scholarly research into the conditions and trends of contemporary society. Under its auspices a series of investigations were projected and carried out on a scale unprecedented in the history of this country and perhaps unequalled by any similar society at any time. In addition to the regular investigations, such as the United States Census of 1930 and the investigations of school problems by the United States Office of Education, there were a number of commissions appointed by the National Executive—the National Commission on Law Observance and Enforcement, the President's Conference on Home Building and Home Ownership, the White House Conference on Child Health and Protection, the President's Conference on Unemployment, the Committee on Recent Economic Changes and, finally, the President's Research Committee on Social Trends, which reported early in 1933. In all these studies government and social science scholarship cooperated cordially and effectively.

Whatever shortcomings may have appeared in the work of these commissions, they have given ample evidence of ability and courage. They represent a more comprehensive and scholarly effort to appraise the conditions and trends of contemporary society than had ever been undertaken. The results of these investigations have yielded bodies of data for the guidance of authorities in government, business and social administration unparalleled in national history. They have been sufficiently impressive to encourage the hope that, if so much has been accomplished in so short a time, research in social science can be made to meet more adequately in the near future the challenge which a world transformed by science and invention has laid down. The results of all these investigations have enabled this commission to proceed with greater certainty on its task of recognizing the more permanent changes in our society and trying to prescribe a more effective program of education for our youth in dealing with them. To our present generation, whose patterns of thought were so largely formed by thinkers and educators still one further generation removed from the world, these studies revealed one thing. That, however, was only part of the problem, the easiest part. To arrange this material into the shape and form through which our children could go forth prepared, not for their grandfathers' world, but for their own, was an infinitely greater and more difficult task. This demanded not only the fruits of scholarship treated with humility and patience, but also a practical knowledge of the best in educational method and management. No one could be a builder who did not know materials and have a vision of the thing he builded and one with him in importance and responsibility was the teacher and administrator who prepared each stone for its appointed place and lifted and fixed it there to become a bearing member of a new educational structure.

In the decade from 1920 to 1930 no less than a thousand organizations of citizens whose membership was at least nation-wide recommended more or less extensive modification in the program of social education. Such development betokened not merely the traditional faith in the force of education, but quite definitely marked the widespread recognition of education as one, if not the chief, instrument through which society could most effectively adapt itself to new and changing conditions.

Fortunately, the schools had been undergoing many important modifications during these years, some of which at least helped to meet the additional demands. Most important of these modifications was the extension of the years of universal education. Described as a nation of sixth grade education in 1917, the country at the present time finds nearly all or most capable of academic education enrolled in high school, if not also in junior college. Beside this change in the schools, all the other changes, such as the improvement in methods of instruction, especially in the earlier grades and methods of educational administration, important as these are, pale almost into insignificance. For it is the addition of these years to universal education that offers to the schools the greatest prospect of meeting the additional load which the increased complexity and quickened tempo of modern society have placed upon them.

School authorities shared with other thoughtful citizens increasing awareness of the extent and depth of the social changes which were occurring. Few indeed among them did not try to meet the needs, as these became known, with all the resources at their command. The more seriously and actively they strove, the sooner they realized that the problems with which they were dealing were so complex, so far-reaching, that no school system had within itself the resources sufficient to cope with them. Nor was their problem lightened by the flood of demands from various groups of citizens which called for many and specific changes. Though the purpose of these demands was usually worthy and engaged the sympathy and approval of the school authorities, the specific changes demanded were too often made without knowledge of the technical process of education nor the ultimate import of what was asked. More often than not, adoption of the specific change demanded could only operate to defeat the very end which the group of citizens sought to serve. With their own efforts unavailing and the volunteered aid of the many lay organizations confusing, school authorities found it necessary to seek help elsewhere.

In this dilemma the school administrators turned to their national organizations for aid and direction. National educational associations, centers of educational research, philanthropic organizations interested in education, all answered the appeal. School authorities appealed also to the national associations of scholars concerned with the study of society. Like the educational associations, these also responded, each separately and to the extent of its own resources. From all these sources school authorities received suggestions and recommendations. Since, however, each of these organizations had worked separately upon a problem common to all of them, their recommendations were overlapping, sometimes conflicting and in many respects inadequate. There was clear need for the effective coordination of all important elements concerned in the major problem of social education.

The situation called for another effort which should somehow bring together the resources of social science and educational research in a united attack upon the problem of educating the youth of the land for participation in the society of a new and puzzling age. The American Historical Association, oldest of the national social science organizations and the one most intimately associated with the program of the schools, was asked to sponsor such an undertaking. Its committee recommended in 1925 that a satisfactory treatment of the problem could only be accomplished by a directing body which should include economists, political scientists, sociologists, geographers, scholars in educational research, educational administrators, as well as historians. The trustees of the Commonwealth Fund provided sufficient funds for the formulation of a plan on this basis. This plan was presented to the American Historical Association in December, 1926, and approved by it. The execution of the plan called for a sum of money beyond the resources of any, or all, of the scholarly associations represented. At this juncture the trustees of the Carnegie Corporation lent their support to the undertaking. After a preliminary grant to develop the plan in its practical details, the trustees of the Carnegie Corporation toward the end of 1928 voted sufficient funds to carry on the investigation for the first year of its five-year program. The commission to direct the investigation was appointed by the American Historical Association at the end of December of that year and began its work in January, 1929. The trustees of the Carnegie Corporation have continued their support by annual appropriation to the completion of the program in 1933.

Many members of the commission had been closely associated with antecedent efforts to deal with the problems involved in its work. Other members as well as some of these were serving in the vast national investigations of social conditions and trends conducted concurrently. They were able, therefore, to bring to bear upon the task of this commission immediately much of the findings of these other investigations. Others, as educational administrators, were dealing at every level of the educational scale with the problems facing the commission. The commission was thus fortified in its work by a knowledge of the trends of contemporary society and of exigent problems it laid daily upon the educator.

Under these circumstances, the commission was able from the outset and throughout its investigation to take a broad conception of its work. The purely technical or professional study of the teaching of the social sciences in the schools could only be a part of its inquiry. Nor could it confine its operations to a correspondingly narrow examination of public education. On the contrary, it was forced to direct its attention not only to problems of a pedagogical nature, but also to the most profound considerations of the history and policy of the nation in its world setting, to the relation of school and society, to the conflicts and tensions in economy and social relations, to the meaning, purposes and potentialities of American life. If a function of the social science studies in the schools was to prepare the youth in the schools more adequately to deal with the society of which they were a part and of which they would later become the directing part, the most thorough and extensive knowledge of that society which the commission could bring to the problem would be none too much.

As indicated in the *Charter* with which this report was begun, the commission has reexamined the traditions of our American society. It has recognized the closer interrelationships of local with national, and even international affairs, as these were reported by the several investigations, especially by the Commission on Social Trends. Nevertheless, as both the *Charter* and this volume of conclusions reveal, the commission, after its survey of all pertinent evidence, believes that all necessary adjustments to the conditions which have developed and are developing, can be made without the sacrifice of any of the finest traditions of American life and history. It likewise believes that all necessary adjustments can be made by our society without resort to the extreme measures which other peoples of the world have taken. It is in this spirit that the commission offers its report.

The detailed procedure of the commission, the steps in its progress from January, 1929, to December, 1933, and the acknowledgment of the aid which it has received are told elsewhere. The host of problems with which the commission has dealt involve many technical aspects, each the object of great study and an extensive literature. In order to furnish teachers and school authorities with more detailed assistance in meeting their practical needs, the commission early decided to entrust the study of these technical aspects to individuals expert in each field. As each of these studies has been completed it has been submitted to the criticism of all the members of the commission. The suggestions which the latter have made have been accepted or rejected by each author according to his own best judgment. For the fourteen major, and the several supplementary, studies the commission therefore assumed primarily the responsibility of sponsorship. The relation of each volume to the report as a whole is indicated in the separate preface accompanying the volume. The commission assumes full responsibility, however, for the *Charter,* in which was set forth the host of problems to be attacked, and for this volume of conclusions in which the principles of the commission's findings are applied. This volume of conclusions, therefore, is intended to serve less as a self-contained document than as the commentary of the commission on the several phases of the work which are treated in detail in the other volumes of the report.

## COLLEGE IN THE MOVIES

I AM not a movie addict. Sometimes I do go, usually as a passive companion to my wife, but now and then to see what should be a good picture. Several times recently we have happened upon films which portrayed college life, either as the *raison d'être* of the plot or as the incidental background. To me they have been so ludicrous that I can no longer wait for some more talented individual to cry out against them.

Perhaps college is still a life apart, very different from the everyday environment off the campus and known to the uninitiated only through song, story or movie. It may even be difficult for scenario writers to ascertain just what goes on under the elms. Certainly they show little understanding of undergraduates and their activities, so little in fact that one doubts whether they ever got closer to a university than the stadium. Above everything else, they find college life carefree—it is the state of no responsibilities, no fixed employment, no serious work. Parties, dances, games, girls and semi-riotous living wile away the hours, interrupted only by a professor or dean, who is either a buffoon or an obvious fool. He exists primarily to be outwitted, thus adding a little slap-stick to the comedy.

Nowhere can I recall the portrayal of an instructor, other than a coach, who has had a deep influence for good on his classes, or who has had any part in molding the life of a character. Easily, however, there comes to mind a college president shaving on the platform of the auditorium while the faculty and students assemble, and a dean so stupid as to allow himself to be photographed repeatedly in compromising situations. Indeed, the college teacher of the movies must be recruited from the madhouse rather than the graduate school. Quite in contrast is he to the handsome, well-groomed students, masters of the campus and themselves. What a shame they should have to associate with such a lot of moronic old fossils!

And the singing! Movie collegians are all members of the glee club; they burst forth at the least provocation into their Alma Mater, they sing outside the windows of the faculty room, as they leave chapel, while walking anywhere, before and after conversations and as serenaders. After supper at a movie college must be a veritable paradise of song, for do not even Princetonians of the screen loiter beneath their dormitory windows singing, singing, as the twilight deepens?

Cheering runs a close second. When the college crowd can't think of anything else to do, it cheers, for the professors, for the girl, for the stars, for the team, for the president, in fact, for anything. Not infrequently it even stops singing just for a cheer.

If a person knew nothing of North American college life except through the moving picture, his summary of impressions would be something like this: A college has small, banner-lined rooms to sleep in and a concrete stadium to play in. The professors are very stupid, in fact, the students are largely educated by fooling them. The administrators, especially the deans, are the most stupid of all, but the presidents run them a close second. Sometimes the students go to class, but not very often; they couldn't and still find time for taking part in games, cheering and singing, singing and cheering, dancing, moonlight strolls, locker room conversations and the hundred and one other diversions which take up their time. The best-looking boys and girls in the country go to college; they're always falling in love, particularly freshmen; it's impossible to be sure that they all get married and live happily ever after, though it would seem so. It is most exciting when a college hero wins the affection of the most beautiful co-ed. Then the whole institution turns out and cheers; very often they do a dance, and then sing, my, how they do sing as the girl falls into the hero's arms. Maybe there are courses in unembarrassed public love-making; anyhow, it's a fine life, but it's not surprising that they don't learn much at college.

I suggest that a fair sampling of directors and scenario writers be sent to college for a semester, say on government funds, RFC, AAA, HOLC or NRA. We might then hope for at least as large a number of pictures true to college life as are now true to other subjects—one per cent., isn't it? Furthermore, some of the "forgotten men" might learn that serious work, character training, cultural contacts, stimulating teachers and other worth-while things form the back-bone of our colleges and universities.

E. Newbold Cooper

Girard College

## RACE PREJUDICE

I believe that some readers of School and Society may be interested in a paragraph which I quote verbatim from a letter of one of my former students, a man who was granted the Ph.D. degree from the University of Minnesota and whose record in the Graduate School of Minnesota shows that he is capable of high scholastic achievements. Unfortunately, his skin is black and he is now on the staff of a Negro college in the South. He writes as follows:

> I am stranded, scientifically speaking. Haven't seen a journal since I left Minnesota. Being in the South I am denied the privilege of visiting Public Libraries or libraries connected with white colleges and universities. This is a great handicap, but something over which I have no control. If you have the time I should like to know of any new publications in our field.

Perhaps comment is superfluous. I would simply like to suggest, however, that all persecution of scientists is not confined to—may we say Russia?

R. A. Gortner

University of Minnesota

# SPECIAL CORRESPONDENCE

## EDUCATION IN MEXICO'S SIX-YEAR PLAN

The six-year plan of the National Revolutionary Party in Mexico, covering the period of the 1934–1940 presidential administration, gives ample evidence that the Mexican educational reform movement which has attracted so much attention among foreign observers during the last twelve years is continuing to receive loyal support from the revolutionary chiefs and their followers. General Plutarcho Elias Calles, President Alberto L. Rodriguez and General Lazaro Cardenas, as well as many other well-known revolutionary leaders and government officials, have taken active part in the formulation of the plan and have supported it vigorously.

The program is more than a mere party platform. It was drawn up by technical commissions working under the direction of the national executive committee of the National Revolutionary Party, but it has been concurred in by the Federal Government, and it carries all the weight of an adopted national policy.

The plan is directed toward the attainment of three main goals: (1) final solution of the agrarian problem, (2) complete organization of the United Front of Workers to make effective a marked elevation of the national standard of living, and (3) development of an adequate educational program for all Mexicans, whether children or adults. This ambitious program is based on the frankly declared principle that "in the Mexican revolutionary concept, the State is an active agent of management and direction of the vital phenomena of the country; not a mere custodian of national integrity, peace, and public order."[1]

Those responsible for drawing up this plan have clearly recognized that education is a crucial factor in the solution of the country's agrarian, labor and general economic problems. In proposing a better distribution of land and water for farm purposes, for example, the plan adheres firmly to the concept that new human resources as secured from more and better education are fully as necessary if not even more important than new economic resources in the solution of the problem. In that portion of the plan dealing with labor, moreover, where the government is pledged to support the individual's right to work, to enforce complete unionization of industry, to maintain satisfactory wage-scales and conditions of labor and to provide for obligatory social insurance through cooperation of the state, the employers and the workers, there is a recurrent emphasis laid on the state's duty to educate its members and to keep them educated.[2] In the program for public health a similar tendency is evident. The Federal Government is pledged to increase the percentage of its annual budget allotted to the Department of Public Health, from 1.93 per cent. in 1926 and 3.03 per cent. in 1933 to 3.40 per cent. in 1934, 3.86 per cent. in 1935, 4.20 per cent. in 1936, 4.60 per cent. in 1937, 5.00 per cent. in 1938 and 5.50 per cent. in 1939. These increased expenditures are to be devoted particularly to raising standards of hygiene in living quarters, developing pure water supplies and fighting infant mortality, tropical diseases, leprosy, tuberculosis and venereal diseases. It is obvious that much of this department's increased activity will be largely educational in nature.

The strictly educational portion of the six-year plan is designed to answer four main questions: (1) How much money is going to be spent on education in the next six years? (2) How are educational facilities going to be expanded and improved by these expenditures? (3) What measure of freedom will be given to teachers and local educational authorities in working out their school programs? (4) How will scattered educational efforts of various private, corporate and governmental organizations be correlated?

To these questions of so crucial importance to the people of Mexico, the National Revolutionary Party and the Federal Government

[1] El Comité Ejecutivo Nacional, "Plan Sexenal del Partido Nacional Revolucionario," p. 17, México, D. F., 1934.

[2] *Ibid.*, pp. 23–45.

have furnished rather detailed and clear-cut answers.

With respect to financial support for schools during the period 1934–40, the plan declares that the Federal Government, the local governments and the corporations *for no motive and under no pretence* should reduce from now on the percentages of their budgets destined for education. The Federal Government is pledged to assign not less than 15 per cent. of its total expenditures to education, and local governments are called upon to hold to their 1933 percentages as minimum standards. The National Revolutionary Party also declares that any assignment of funds for educational purposes in excess of these minimum standards will demonstrate that the governing authorities have a high concept of their responsibility and obligation to revolutionary principles. The Federal Government promises, furthermore, that its own budget will have the following percentages devoted to education during the six-year period: 15 per cent. in 1934, 16 per cent. in 1935, 17 per cent. in 1936, 18 per cent. in 1937, 19 per cent. in 1938 and 20 per cent. in 1939.

In answer to the question of how educational facilities are going to be expanded and improved, the party and the government declare frankly that rural education will receive the major share of their attention during the six-year period. Federal rural schools are to be increased by at least 1,000 in 1934, 2,000 in each of the years 1935 to 1938, inclusive, and 3,000 in the year 1939. This scheme of minimum increases, if carried into effect, will more than double the number of federal rural schools during the six-year period.[3]

The Federal Secretary of Public Education, in a detailed plan for 1934, to show how the six-year plan is going to be put under way, promises that in addition to 1,000 new rural teacher positions, making a total of more than 12,000, the secretariat is taking the following forward steps during the current year: (1) Employing a new specialist in rural education and 22 more rural school inspectors. (2) Establishing two new cultural missions, making 16 in all. (3) Organizing six more regional agricultural schools, making eight in all, and building two new buildings for such schools. (4) Carrying on a campaign to force ranches and factories to provide schools for their workers—causing at least 1,500 more new schools to be established.[4]

In the field of technical education the plan pledges the government to increased effort. At least three new regional schools of agriculture will be established each year. A new Technical Council of Agricultural Education, composed of an equal number of representatives from the Secretariat of Agriculture and the Secretariat of Public Education, will be charged with approving organizational plans and programs of studies for the agricultural schools. The system of fellowships in technical education, already established by the Federal Government, will be extended on the theory that the living expenses of workers and workers' children who are securing technical training is a proper part of the state's share in the cost of technical instruction. The establishment of an institute of vocational guidance, designed to explore and define the aptitudes and interests of persons called to receive technical teaching, is also proposed.

The National Revolutionary Party declares that the exercise of particular professions is a social matter and not at all an individual right of professional people. It proposes, therefore, to regulate very strictly the conditions of entrance to all professions and of work within them. No general expansion of facilities for professional training on the university level is contemplated for the period 1934–1940, but an increase of support for research institutes and laboratories is promised.

In defining the measure of freedom to be granted to teachers and school authorities, the party and the government flatly deny the right of any private party or organization to establish and direct educational institutions outside the control of the state. The control of the state will be exercised over the aims of all schools to see that they are scientific, non-religious and socialist in their orientation, over the professional preparation of all supervisors and teachers and over the hygienic conditions under which the instruction is carried on. The nature of the state's control over the orientation of the school may be inferred from the statement that "the primary school, besides excluding all religious teaching, will give a true,

[3] *Ibid.*, p. 84.

[4] *Ibid.*, Appendix.

scientific and rational answer to each and every question which ought to be solved in the minds of those being educated, to form for them an exact and positive concept of the world which surrounds them and of the society in which they live, since by any other outcome the school will not fulfill its social mission."[5]

Aside from general recommendations that more attention be paid to rural, agricultural, technical, scientific, health and physical education, however, the framers of the six-year plan avoid any attempt to tell the teachers and the educational administrators of the country just what they should do. A program of increasing normal school facilities indicates that the Mexican political leaders are adhering to the principle that the best way to make a new social order through education is to educate teachers in the principles of the new social philosophy and then give them a broad enough technical preparation to enable them to find and use methods appropriate for carrying the principles into practise.

With respect to the problem of correlating the scattered educational efforts of governments, corporations and private agencies, the plan provides for conferences between representatives of local authorities and the Federal Government at which agreements of cooperation will be drawn up. These agreements shall be based on the following principles: (1) that the educational obligations of local authorities shall not be reduced, and (2) that the final word in the technical and administrative management of all schools shall rest with the Federal Government.

Harold Benjamin
University of Minnesota

# QUOTATIONS

## "DOCTORS, DOLLARS AND DISEASE"—RADIO EDUCATION OR PROPAGANDA

In 1929 a series of meetings called by the American Association for Adult Education resulted in the formation of a body known as the National Advisory Council on Radio in Education, Inc. Its general purpose is said to be to "further the development of the art of radio broadcasting in American education." Recently, Congress enacted some legislation entitled "The Federal Communications Commission Act," which automatically abolished the Federal Radio Commission. This act also makes it mandatory on the new commission "to study the proposal that Congress by statute allocate fixed percentages of radio broadcasting facilities to particular types or kinds of non-profit radio programs" and to report to Congress by February 1, 1935.

The National Advisory Council on Radio in Education, Inc., is exceedingly interested in this problem, because it has made education of the public over the radio its particular province since the time of its organization. The council wants more time on the air for education. In a recently issued circular, the director says, "The council is an organization independent of faction, non-partisan in its procedure, disinterested as to personnel and non-commercial in operation." Notwithstanding these assertions, the medical profession is now confronted with the promotion by the National Advisory Council on Radio in Education, Inc., of a series of broadcasts under the title, "Doctors, Dollars and Disease," said to be presented by the Public Health Committee of the National Advisory Council on Radio in Education, Inc. These programs are offered every Monday evening over WABC, Columbia network, extending from coast to coast, at 7:45 Pacific time, 8:45 Mountain time, 9:45 Central time and 10:45 Eastern time.

Let us then view the nature of the organization of the Public Health Committee which prepared the program and the nature of the program itself to see to what extent the National Advisory Council on Radio in Education, Inc., has fulfilled its claims of being independent of faction and non-partisan in procedure. The Public Health Committee includes as its chairman William Trufant Foster. This is the same Foster, an economist and not a physician, who attacked organized medicine bitterly at a conference held in Philadelphia last February, fully reported in the *Journal,* March 3, page

[5] *Ibid.*, p. 85.

701. Associated with Mr. Foster on this committee are the following physicians: Ray Lyman Wilbur, chairman of the Committee on the Costs of Medical Care and signer of its majority report; Thomas Parran, Jr., health officer of the state of New York, committed in repeated addresses to compulsory health insurance and measures leading to the socialization of medicine; Haven Emerson, formerly a president of the American Public Health Association and a signer of the majority report. Included with these four are Alice Hamilton, a distinguished investigator in industrial diseases, whose writings indicate nevertheless that her pity for the sad fate of the majority of mankind overbalances her scientific judgment in matters of social control, and, last of all, Dr. Hugh S. Cumming, surgeon-general of the United States Public Health Service. It will be obvious to any one that this Public Health Committee of the National Advisory Council on Radio in Education, Inc., is overwhelmingly controlled by the state medicine and socialization of medicine points of view, and that it contains no definite representative of the 100,000 physicians organized as the American Medical Association.

The radio program developed under the auspices of this committee is, as might have been expected, overwhelmingly for the socialization of medical care. It contains the name of but one person who signed the minority report of the Committee on the Costs of Medical Care, and there are indications that he accepted under a misapprehension as to the nature of the program and will not appear. Those who are to discuss the future of medical care and the subject of medical economics are for the most part non-medical men, unfamiliar with medical practise and for the most part definitely opposed in their writings to the policies of organized medicine. Representing the opposite point of view are Walter P. Bowers, editor of the *New England Journal of Medicine,* who has made that periodical largely the organ of the majority report of the Committee on the Costs of Medical Care, Thomas Parran, George H. Bigelow, Haven Emerson and Ray Lyman Wilbur, who speak as physicians on this program. These are, all of them, proponents who would change seriously the nature of medical practise. Among the laymen listed are such well-known names as Edward A. Filene, Michael M. Davis, C. Rufus Rorem, Nathan Sinai, I. S. Falk, Edgar Sydenstricker and Harry H. Moore. It calls the roll of the agitators from the Committee on the Costs of Medical Care. Other speakers include Foster, Paul H. Douglas, of the University of Chicago, Robert Jolly, of Houston, Texas, and Livingston Farrand, president of Cornell University, the latter as an M.D., who has for long been somewhat out of touch with medical affairs.

It should be clear to any physician that this program indicates an attempt on the part of the interests represented in the majority report of the Committee on the Costs of Medical Care to further its propaganda. In developing a program of this type the National Advisory Council on Radio in Education, Inc., has been untrue to the principles on which it was established. Thereby it fails to merit support from the medical profession. Nevertheless, physicians will do well to be aware of the matter and to use such influence as they may possess with the radio stations that carry such material to bring about a realization of its true nature.

It might have been within the province of the National Advisory Council on Radio in Education, Inc., to develop a series of useful lectures on the prevention of disease and on the maintenance of health. It might have used some of the time, which apparently it is able to get without charge from the broadcasting chains, for the enlightenment of the public on many of the scientific fallacies promoted by commercial interests. It has, however, failed to avail itself of these opportunities, devoting itself and its time instead to what constitutes essentially an undermining of the medical profession of this country. It would be interesting to know the motives that animated the executive officers of the National Advisory Council on Radio in Education, Inc., to lend themselves to this propaganda.—*The Journal of the American Medical Association.*

## TENNESSEE VALLEY AUTHORITY ON A FEDERAL RADIO PROGRAM

In the few specific recommendations that I shall make, I am representing the Tennessee Valley Authority.

As I sat through the program this morning, I was impressed by the sincerity of the speakers but amazed at some of the radio activities which they term "educational." I, also, have had some experience in the field of education. This experience has extended over a period of twenty-seven years and has included teaching, supervision and administration at every level, from the elementary school through the college and the university. For the eight years preceding my appointment as director of personnel of the Tennessee Valley Authority, I was engaged in teaching courses in education at the University of Chicago.

I recognize the great values that radio has brought to American education, but I am also convinced that there are potential values that can never be secured without some modification in the present method of administration and control.

The Tennessee Valley Authority now has more than twelve thousand employees and the number is increasing rapidly. In the personnel division of the Authority, which is under my immediate direction, there is a section which provides a broad adult education program for employees. If the radio were available for use on a non-commercial basis, I am certain that it could be made a much more effective instrument for spreading education and general culture than it now is, not only among our own employees but among others as well.

The present plan for providing radio facilities to the American public is not satisfactory from the standpoint of meeting the needs of the educational and cultural agencies of America. I recognize that the radio can never take the place of the teacher in the schools, but if radio programs were properly coordinated and given adequate time and suitable wave-lengths at satisfactory hours, the radio could become a more valuable supplement than it now is to the classroom teacher.

America is entering a period of great expansion in adult education. It is difficult to overestimate the values that might be derived from the radio in the development of such a program. These benefits can not be secured, however, when radio service is maintained almost entirely for profit and is financed by advertising. Commercial programs have forced many adult education programs off the night air waves, and adult education is impossible without night programs.

There should be an opportunity for people to hear a reasonable amount of educational and cultural broadcasting free from advertising. It should not be forgotten that freedom of speech needs to be safeguarded not only from interference by political forces but also from interference by commercial forces. This can not be accomplished with all or almost all the radio channels operated under commercial ownership. The public should own the air and should rule as to what is sent over it.

If we are to get the benefits of radio in education, some method must be found to secure talent of such a quality that large groups of people will desire to listen to it. To secure this talent, planning on a national scale is necessary.

When radio is maintained on a commercial basis, it must cater to the widest possible audience in order to make the most effective use of the advertiser's time. Its main interest is not that of trying to elevate the public standards, but of getting the maximum return for its advertisers. Most educators who have made a study of radio education agree that the radio should be used more widely for educational purposes. It seems probable that the radio could be employed with powerful effect in every public school in the country, if adequate facilities were provided. This can not be accomplished so long as the system is operated entirely on a commercial basis. Even though a majority of the people may be satisfied with the types of programs given over the radio, there are several million, at least, who are disgusted with them. In all fairness to these dissatisfied people, there should be at least proportional representation in radio programs. Those who desire better entertainment and educational materials should have an opportunity to secure them.

*It is recommended, therefore:*

(1) That the United States Government own and operate a national system of radio stations, giving full-time coverage over the entire country through suitable allocation of frequencies;

(2) That these frequencies be allocated with a

view to as little disruption of present commercial broadcast facilities as possible;

(3) That the mechanical operation be financed by the Federal Government;

(4) That the control of programs be under the direction of a committee representing foremost non-profit national educational and cultural agencies, these agencies to be designated by the President of the United States;

(5) That these facilities be available to non-profit organizations, including governmental departments, for educational and cultural programs.

Those opposed to plans of the type suggested have argued that educational and cultural agencies, such as universities, have not found it possible to produce programs of a type such that large numbers of people enjoy listening to them. In a measure, this has been true, but it in no way condemns the plan proposed. There has never been a real opportunity to develop such programs. An organization, nation-wide in scope, is necessary to develop such programs, in order to have available always the best talent. Furthermore, supervision and administration of the type suggested will make it possible to utilize some of the best talent that has been developed in commercial radio, as well as the best talent from other sources.

A major advantage of the method suggested would be that the listener who wants good programs would always know where to turn the dial to get what he wants.—*Testimony of Floyd W. Reeves, director of personnel, Tennessee Valley Authority, before Federal Communications Commission, October 19, 1934.*

# EDUCATIONAL RESEARCH AND STATISTICS

## THE MENTAL ABILITY OF TWINS

Twenty-six thousand eight hundred and eighty-three seniors and 32,676 sophomores in Wisconsin public and private high schools were given the Henmon-Nelson Test of Mental Ability, Form B, for grades 7 to 12, in December, 1933, as part of the Wisconsin Cooperative Testing program. One hundred and eighty-eight pairs of twins were among the 59,500 high-school students tested. Fifty of the pairs of twins were opposite sex twins, 59 pairs were both boys, and 79 pairs were both girls.

TABLE I

| Percentile | All twins | Boy twins | Girl twins | Unlike sex twins |
|---|---|---|---|---|
| 90–100 | 23 | 7 | 7 | 8 |
| 80–89 | 37 | 14 | 11 | 11 |
| 70–79 | 24 | 6 | 12 | 6 |
| 60–69 | 28 | 11 | 11 | 6 |
| 50–59 | 52 | 18 | 15 | 18 |
| 40–49 | 20 | 8 | 11 | 4 |
| 30–39 | 64 | 18 | 30 | 14 |
| 20–29 | 40 | 8 | 22 | 11 |
| 10–19 | 41 | 11 | 17 | 12 |
| 0–9 | 47 | 17 | 22 | 10 |
| Totals | 376 | 118 | 158 | 100 |
| $Q^3$ | 66.43 | $Q^3$ 67.73 | $Q^3$ 61.36 | $Q^3$ 70. |
| Median | 39.38 | M 46.25 | M 36. | M 47.5 |
| $Q^1$ | 21.5 | $Q^1$ 21.88 | $Q^1$ 30.23 | $Q^1$ 22.73 |
| Q | 22.46 | Q 22.92 | Q 15.56 | Q 23.63 |

The test scores made by the twins were converted into percentiles. The percentile ranks equivalent to the raw scores were computed for the seniors from the distribution of the test scores made by the entire group of high-school seniors tested, and the percentile ranks for sophomores were computed from the distribution of the test scores of the entire sophomore group.

The 376 twins were distributed as shown in Table I. This table shows that the medians of all the twins, of like sex twins and of unlike sex twins are lower than the median (50) of the entire group of high-school students. The opposite or unlike sex twins approach the median most closely, and the girl pairs of twins are lowest. The quartile deviation of the girl twins is nearly ten points lower than the quartile deviation of the normal group; that is, the girl twins are clustered around the median percentile of 36. more closely than a normal sampling of the students would be grouped around the median.

The relation between the test results of each of the 376 students with his or her twin was determined by correlating the Henmon-Nelson test percentiles made within the pairs of the twins. The correlations in Table II were found.

The highest coefficient of correlation is found in the twin pairs of girls. The twin girls also have the lowest median percentile and the small-

TABLE II

| | Number of pairs | Coefficient of correlation | Probable error |
|---|---|---|---|
| All twins | 188 | .609 | .03 |
| Boy twins | 59 | .598 | .056 |
| Girl twins | 79 | .645 | .044 |
| Unlike sex twins | 50 | .423 | .078 |

est quartile deviation. When both like sex and opposite sex twins are grouped together, the next highest coefficient of correlation is found; the next to the lowest median and next to the smallest quartile deviation is also found in this all-twin group. The smallest degree of correlation is found between the twins of unlike sex; these twins have the highest median percentile and tend to deviate most from the median.

Of the 79 pairs of girl twins: In 17 pairs both girls made test scores above the 50th percentile; in 40 pairs both girls made test scores below the 50th percentile; in 22 pairs one girl was below and the other above the 50th percentile.

Among the girl twins there was no pair who made test scores which placed one girl above the 75th percentile and her twin below the 25th percentile.

Of the 50 pairs of unlike sex twins: In 17 pairs both twins made test scores above the 50th percentile; in 18 pairs both twins made test scores below the 50th percentile; In 15 pairs one twin was above and one below the 50th percentile.

In four pairs of the unlike sex twins one of the pair made a test score placing him above the 75th percentile, while his twin made a test score placing him below the 25th percentile.

Of the 59 pairs of boy twins: In 18 pairs both made test scores above the 50th percentile; in 22 pairs both made test scores below the 50th percentile; in 19 pairs one twin was above and one below the 50th percentile.

Among the boy twins there was only one pair who made test scores which placed one boy above the 75th percentile and his twin below the 25th percentile.

When the 188 pairs of twins were considered it was found that: In 52 pairs both made test scores above the 50th percentile; in 80 pairs both made test scores below the 50th percentile; in 56 pairs one twin was above and one below the 50th percentile.

In only five pairs of twins was the difference between test scores so great as to place one twin above the 75th percentile and the other below the 25th percentile.

The conclusions which may be drawn from this study of the scores made by 188 pairs of twins in the Henmon-Nelson test of mental ability are:

(1) That the median test percentile of the 376 twins is more than 10 points lower than the test percentile of all the high-school students tested in this program, and that the first and third quartile points are also lower for the twins than for the entire group of high-school students.

(2) That the 158 "both girl" twins have a median percentile 14 points lower than the entire group of high-school students and that the girl twins deviate less from the median percentile than does a normal group.

(3) That 118 "both boys" twins have a median percentile 10 points above the girl twins and less than 4 points below the median of the whole group of students.

(4) That the unlike sex twins have the highest median percentile and deviate most from their median. It should be noted that it is this group of twins which does not include identical twins that tends to measure up most closely to the entire group of students.

(5) That when an analysis was made of the relation between the mental test score of each twin with his or her twin it was found that the girl twins resemble each other most and the unlike sex twins resemble each other least.

RUTH BYRNS
UNIVERSITY OF WISCONSIN

## NEW BOOKS IN EDUCATION

BLACKHURST, J. HERBERT. *Humanized Geometry.* Pp. 206. Illustrated. Author, Drake University.

GRAY, RUTH A. *Bibliography of Research Studies in Education, 1932–33.* Pp. xiv + 349. Bulletin No. 7, 1934. U. S. Government Printing Office. $0.25.

LEONARD, STERLING A. *The Atlantic Book of Modern Plays.* Revised edition. Pp. xiii + 401. Little, Brown. $1.28.

SLAVSON, S. R. and ROBERT K. SPEER. *Science in the New Education.* Pp. xii + 396. Prentice-Hall. $2.50.

# SCHOOL AND SOCIETY

WITH WHICH ARE COMBINED THE EDUCATIONAL REVIEW, ESTABLISHED IN 1891, THE TEACHERS MAGAZINE, ESTABLISHED IN 1878, AND THE SCHOOL JOURNAL, ESTABLISHED IN 1874.

Volume 40 | Saturday, November 24, 1934 | Number 1039

## WORK OF THE COMMITTEE ON THE PLACE OF SCIENCE IN EDUCATION

By Professor OTIS W. CALDWELL

INSTITUTE OF SCHOOL EXPERIMENTATION, TEACHERS COLLEGE, COLUMBIA UNIVERSITY

In 1924, when addressing the American Association for the Advancement of Science, President Coolidge said, "It is a wonderful thing to live in a time when the search for truth is the foremost interest of the race. It has taken endless ages to create in men the courage that will accept the truth simply because it is the truth." That eminent speaker knew too much about human nature to permit him to argue that *all* people always regard the search for truth as of supreme interest, or that *all* people have the courage to accept the truth simply because it is the truth. Even some of the scientists to whom those words were addressed may sometimes have seemed to their associates as less than "100 per cent." in their exemplification of unbiased interest and courage for the truth, the ideals the President thus stated. On one of the walls of the Hall of Science at the Century of Progress Fair in Chicago, among other interesting quotations, was one from A. D. Little, "More important than particular truths is the love of truth." That, like the preceding quotation, has a pleasing sound to scientific people, but it also causes queries to arise. Did Dr. Little mean that particular truths, facts, knowledge, are not of consequence, but that desire for these is the thing of consequence? He could hardly have meant that. Indeed, such men as Dr. Little are conspicuous for their ever-ready possession of much exact knowledge. It seems safe to assert that no one, whether scientist or not, acquires a real love for truth except through the experience of long and faithful search for the specific facts of science. Most of us are fearful of oratorical advocacy of generalized ideals, unless abundant place is given to the many specific achievements which manifest the generalized qualities that are advocated. Thus, in considering the place of science in education, it has seemed to many able minds that, while slogans, fine phrases and much talk about universal possession of scientific methods may all be excellent, what is most needed is increased effort directed toward specific types of truths. By such efforts the desired generalized results may perhaps be developed. Their development is likely to be slow, however, and seems likely to be accomplished only through the actual performance of many specific and detailed operations.

Because of such considerations as these, the American Association for the Advancement of Science voted in 1923 to establish its Committee on the Place of Science in Education. It appears that no one expected that such a committee would endeavor to do such idealistic things as to have all citizens all the time gaining their chief pleasure through scientific research;

or to have every one always exhibiting the courage to accept and live by the truth simply because it is the truth; or to have folks constantly caring more about their love for truth than they do about specific truths. The approval of these fine ideals was implied in some sort of televisionistic way, though there can not have been much hope of measurable results during the life of any single committee.

The initial commitment did not relate chiefly to science in schools and colleges, though that was included. Rather, the committee was charged with doing any specific tasks it could find to do within the whole range of science in its educational relations. That was a large assignment. In the eleven years that have passed much has been accomplished in this broad field by many agencies, and the committee is glad to have been among them. The committee members have been chiefly occupied with their own professional work, so that their activities in this particular commitment have had to be fitted into otherwise busy lives. Also, it was not clear just what might be attempted or accomplished. A statement of the general purposes of the committee was published in *Science* for December 12, 1924. A few concrete tasks have been undertaken. Some of these will be described below, with a double aim—first, to illustrate and to encourage further work upon these specific ventures, and second to elicit ideas and support for later endeavor by this committee or by some other group or groups that may be working with similar purposes. The ideas justifying such a committee as this should be progressively plastic.

Although people not professionally engaged in scientific research or advanced science teaching have constituted an always increasing part of the association's membership, yet there were many years when interest in the meetings of the American Association for the Advancement of Science was almost restricted to technical scientific reports. As research became increasingly specialized it became more and more apparent that those who were in attendance at the sessions of one association section or one scientific society really had little appreciation of the work presented at sessions of other sections or societies. Meantime, the public, though curious about what scientists were doing, usually received only such knowledge of the meetings as was provided by the press. Until about 1922 the daily papers generally gave but very inadequate reports of association meetings, and the excellent science stories that are now common in newspapers at all seasons, but especially throughout the week of the great annual meeting of the American Association for the Advancement of Science, represent a development of the last ten or twelve years. This remarkable development has stimulated and encouraged public interest in science and it continues to do so, along with other agencies.

Partially in response to this trend of the times and with clear realization that the general dissemination of scientific knowledge of all sorts among the people should constitute one of the principal objectives of such organizations as the American Association, the Committee on the Place of Science in Education arranged a general session for the public at the Kansas City meeting, held in December, 1925. That session was held in a large, well-filled auditorium. The program included addresses by Burton E. Livingston ("The Obligation to Distribute Knowledge"), by the late E. E. Slosson ("Action and Reaction") and by Michael I. Pupin ("Science and Service"). I quote the closing paragraph of Dr. Livingston's address:

With this great task of distributing knowledge we must be constantly engaged, and later generations must continue to carry on. The task is as endless as is the duration of humanity and the growth of knowledge. But it varies in method and means as evolution proceeds and it has unsurpassed capacity for supplying us with well-filled and happy hours over which there is not likely to be serious subsequent regret.

In the following year, at the fifth Philadelphia meeting the committee again presented a program for the public, the lecture topics being as follows: "Biology and Better Beef," by W. A. Cochel, editor of the *Kansas City Weekly Star;* "Newer Knowledge of the Chemistry of Nutrition," by H. C. Sherman, of Columbia University; and "Science Spirit in a Democracy," by L. H. Bailey, then president of the American Association for the Advancement of Science. Since 1926, the enlarged program of public lectures by the association itself has generally provided abundant opportunities of this type, and no more such programs have been organized by the committee. This sort of public educational effort by the association has been extended at some meetings so as to present scientific knowledge in still more popular fashion, to appeal to young people of school age and others whose interest in science is little more than nascent. Further development of this phase of work is surely desirable, by whatever effective means may be feasible, for, as every one knows, the future of our democracy and the future of our science must both depend largely on impressions gained by our people in early youth.

There had long been need for a carefully prepared bibliography related to the use of science in schools. The committee arranged for the preparation of such a bibliography by Earl R. Glenn and provided him with a trained worker and the requisite clerical assistance. The bibliography, which was published in 1925, by the office of the U. S. Commissioner of Education, was distributed widely for use by persons engaged in any kind of investigation of science teaching. The preface set forth the committee's credo about science, which was rendered specially desirable at that time by public interest in the famous Scopes trial. Copies of this book are still to be obtained from the U. S. Superintendent of Documents at a price of twenty-five cents each. Of course it is not now as useful as when first issued, since eight active years have passed since its completion.

A pamphlet attempting to outline current thought regarding certain phases or problems of science education was prepared under the direction of the committee and was published in 1928 under the auspices of the association council. Copies are available for free distribution by the Washington office of the American Association for the Advancement of Science in the Smithsonian Institution Building, Washington, D. C. Among other topics discussed in that pamphlet are: "The Search for Enduring Facts and the Growth of Confidence in the Guidance of Scientific Truth"; "The Obligations of Scientific Knowledge"; "Science Subjects in Educational Programs"; "Summaries of Types of Specific Studies Relating to Educational Uses of Science"; "Those Who Teach" and "Those Who Have Developed Science." The three following recommendations were made:

(a) That some organization of national scope, such as the United States Bureau of Education, or the Research Division of the National Education Association, be asked by this committee to undertake a comprehensive and intensive study of the situations, tendencies and needs of science instruction in educational systems.

(b) That the services of a field secretary be secured, to work with existing agencies, to distribute information on research in science education, to stimulate further research, to operate as a sort of clearing-house agent and to continue the organizing of new groups of science teachers, writers for popularization of science, etc. This field secretary should work under the guidance of the Committee on the Place of Science in Education, or under the guidance of a national council of science teachers if such a council should be formed.

(c) That a national council of science teachers be organized to advance science teaching, to increase public appreciation of science and to secure for science teachers increased facilities and a wider usefulness. The services of a field secretary would be very useful in the organization of such a council.

The larger part of the first of these recommendations was realized in the publication of the important study made by G. W. Hunter, of Claremont College, California, with the title, "Science Sequence in the Junior and Senior High Schools," published in *School Science and Mathematics,* Volume 33, 1933. The second recommendation has not yet been realized. A movement is now on foot that may result in the realization of the third recommendation. This will receive attention below.

Through adherence to the time-honored custom of adding to the personnel of a committee those persons who are bold enough to evince particular interest in its work, the Committee on the Place of Science in Education grew until its roll included twenty-nine names. A final report, recommending the discharge of the committee, was presented to the Association Council in 1929. The report was accepted and approved, and a new committee was appointed, which has continued to function along the general lines of the older one and under the same name. The present membership of the Committee on the Place of Science in Education is as follows: J. McKeen Cattell, chairman of the Executive Committee of the American Association for the Advancement of Science; Karl T. Compton, president of the Massachusetts Institute of Technology; Jerome Isenbarger, of the Wright City Junior College, Chicago; Burton E. Livingston, of the Johns Hopkins University, general secretary of the American Association for the Advancement of Science; Morris Meister, of the Haaren High School, New York City; and Otis W. Caldwell, of Columbia University, chairman.

In 1929 the association council approved a new plan of this committee, which aimed to enlist the special interest of superior high-school students in active science work. Students were invited to write competitive essays on any of over fifty selected topics or upon any other topic that had been previously submitted to and approved by the committee. It was thought that the preparation of such essays would be profitable to the student authors and the results might subsequently be stimulating and helpful to others. It was hoped that the writers might be led to an increased appreciation of the significance of responsible authorship. Experience of this sort, as distinct from that of pastime writing and class-assignment writing, should be engaging and lastingly productive. A prominent scientist remarked, capable students often "need some form of hook on which to hang their endeavors." The approved topics were representative not only of the main fields of natural science but also a number of phases of the social and industrial uses of science. The plan was widely announced throughout the United States and Canada. The committee realized the need of curbing the use of high-school essays as means of objectionable propaganda, and it consequently invited to this essay competition only such superior students as could engage in this activity without harm to their regular school work. Even so, the plan partook of the nature of propaganda, but in a good sense.

Obviously, such a contest required the preparation of a workable plan of operation in the judging of the essays that would be submitted, since they would represent a wide diversity of topics and methods of treatment. The plan adopted was devised by a special committee, consisting of: M. F. Carpenter, of Iowa City, Iowa; Claudia E. Crumpton, of Detroit, Michigan; Newton B. Hammond, of Yonkers, New York; R. L. Lyman, of Chicago, Illinois; Percival M. Symonds, of New York City; Lucy A. Terrell, of Cleveland, Ohio; and G. M. Ruch, of Berkeley, California (chairman). The same special committee acted as judges, and finally reported on 120 essays. The judges had no knowledge of either names or locations of the essay writers. An account of the judging methods employed and a list of the 20 winning essays with the names and schools of the authors may be obtained from the chairman of the Committee on the Place of Science in Education.

"Recognitions of Achievement" awards were made on account of the winning essays. Funds for prizes and for the other expenses of the project were composed mainly of gifts from anonymous friends of science. A small appropriation was made by the American Association. Twenty cash prizes were awarded, the highest being $200 and the lowest $50. An important feature of the award was that no prize was given to any student author; instead, the prizes were given to the schools attended by the successful students. It was specified that prizes should be used only for the purchase of additional science books for the school libraries to which cash awards were made, but the books were selected by those in charge of the libraries. The American Association supplied a bit of suggestive guidance by furnishing to each of these school libraries a set of its Popular Science Book-Lists. These authoritative, useful and attractive little booklets, representing as many fields of knowledge, were prepared by the American Association for the Advancement of Science Committee on Popular Science Book-Lists, of which the chairman is Joseph L. Wheeler, librarian of the Enoch Pratt Free Library, of Baltimore, Maryland.

Each of the books thus purchased was inscribed with a statement showing that it was contributed to the school library as a result of the association prize-essay contest, also showing the name or names of the successful student authors whose winning essays had made this addition to the library possible. In some of the schools that received prizes students of the art departments prepared special bookplates for use in these books.

Each of the student-authors of winning essays received added personal recognition in the form of a copy of the two-volume edition of Wells, Huxley and Wells' "The Science of Life," accompanied by a page of signatures of past presidents of the American Association for the Advancement of Science.

The essay contest just described was in some part an experiment. Whether it is desirable to try to have such contests repeated at intervals may be left as an open question. Some students of popular education appear to think that student competition of this literary sort is fundamentally undesirable, but many others have expressed the wish that this project might be repeated soon. Inquiries are still being received from schools that desire to have the project repeated and some students are reported to be even now at work on essays that they hope to submit in some future competition. From the view-point of superior students there seem to be few, if any, objections to the general plan.

On the other hand, it should not be forgotten that such essay contests must necessarily demand an enormous amount of work on the part of those in charge, and it may not always be easy to enlist the requisite number of capable and willing cooperators in such undertakings. Furthermore, the financial aspect of any essay contest that may be planned must inevitably be given prime consideration; such projects require funds and they can bring no financial income to the sponsoring organization.

Competition among school students with regard to scholarship and literary ability are surely just as desirable as are competitions with regard to athletic ability, which appear to be generally approved at the present time. Muscular prowess and bodily agility guided by quick minds are certainly excellent. Scholarly prowess and engaging literary expression surely are even more commendable, however, though not now so popular. We are apt to express surprise when an outstanding athlete becomes known as an outstanding scholar, though the occasion for such surprise is confessedly rather infrequent.

With regard to another of the recent phases of activity of the Committee on the Place of Science in Education, it has been pointed out from time to time that some sort of national organization of teachers of science is highly desirable. Although several effective organizations of sectional or state groups of such teachers are in existence, it seems that a national organization might accomplish much good. This question received serious attention in a special conference held in connection with the fifth Boston meeting of the American Association, in December, 1933. The papers presented dealt partly with the problems of the educational uses of science and partly with a suggested national organization of science teachers. At this conference W. L. Eikenberry, of the New Jersey State Teachers College, at Trenton, spoke on "Types of Useful Organizations of Science Teachers." His address was published in *Science Education,* 1933. Reprints of that address may be obtained from the New York office of the Committee on the Place of Science in Education. Also a special committee was organized to study the question concerning a national organization. It was voted to request the American Association to arrange for an additional conference to be held at the third Pittsburgh meeting of the association in December, 1934.

Such a conference has been planned and its program will be presented on December 29, 1934, at Pittsburgh. The special committee under the chairmanship of H. A. Carpenter, specialist in science in the schools of Rochester, New York, will present its report. In connection with that conference the Committee on the Place of Science in Education will also present a program dealing with phases of newer knowledge that will be of interest to all science teachers. A Pittsburgh local committee, of which the chairman is John A. Hollinger, is assisting in the arrangements for these sessions. Because of the important question before the science teachers' conference, all teachers of science are invited to attend. Copies of the day's program will be sent to all who request it from the Committee on the Place of Science in Education, 433 West 123rd Street, New York, N. Y.

This account of work by the Committee on the Place of Science in Education may seem to consist of brief descriptions of unrelated ventures. They are not unrelated. As indicated above, the large purposes of science in education are to be attained not directly but through the doing of no end of specific things. Each specific task has its own special purpose which is a consistent part or component of the larger purpose. By taking many separate steps the whole road may be finally traversed. Although the details of each step hold attention for the time being, yet, when many steps have been accomplished they leave results that fall into place as parts of the larger purpose. Every good science teacher knows this. For example, in the study of absorption, diffusion and imbibition in plants, each of these topics calls for specific accomplishment, the discovery or appreciation of specific facts and relations; but it is only through knowledge of such details, and many others, that a student may be expected to envisage the performance of such a thing as a tree and its place in nature—how it gains material and energy from its complex surroundings, transports and uses them in many ways, grows or is dormant according to the changing seasons throughout a century, and finally returns its materials and energy to the surroundings, from which they may subsequently be taken into other organisms, possibly of very different kinds. Such a broad conception can be attained only through many intermediate steps.

It is true in many ways that the "search for truth is the foremost interest of the race," but I doubt if a very large proportion of our people are aware of that. It is true that "the courage that will accept the truth simply because it is the truth" is a highly desirable human trait, but there are many individuals who, before accepting and acting on what seems to be truth, wish to know to what extent acceptance would affect some of their personal wishes. It may even be true that "more important than particular truths is the love of truth," but the repeated and habitual use of many truths is surely the best way to establish a "love of truth."

# PARENT EDUCATION IN THE EMERGENCY[1]

By EDNA NOBLE WHITE
DIRECTOR, THE MERRILL-PALMER SCHOOL

In spite of the tremendous difficulties faced by public schools during the period of the depression, it is interesting to note that during the present fiscal year (1933–1934) the Federal Government spent the largest sum it had ever devoted to educational purposes. Until this time educational enterprise had to a large extent been dependent upon local and state resources. When these resources failed, the Federal Government found it necessary to expand its expenditures enormously in order to keep schools open, employ teachers and maintain educational programs.

One of the most important of the federal programs was that termed emergency education. About $15,000,000 were expended on this program during the past year. The program undoubtedly had its origin in the desire to give employment to the large number of teachers thrown out of work by the economic crisis. It was also believed that educational programs ministering to needy families and unemployed adults would help to raise the morale of those suffering from unemployment and the consequent financial stress and strain. On August 19, 1933, Harry L. Hopkins, federal emergency relief adviser, issued his first statement authorizing the hiring of unemployed teachers to teach in rural schools that would otherwise be closed and to instruct illiterate adults. On September 26 authority was given to employ teachers for general adult education, vocational education and rehabilitation. On October 23 emergency nursery schools were authorized.

The original plans of the Federal Government called for parent education only in connection with the nursery school program. Within a short time, however, it became apparent that a much larger place would be given to this type of education in the actual working out of the educational programs. In such states as Iowa, where parent education programs had been established for a considerable period, it was at once recognized that the plan of conducting parent education programs for parents of preschool children alone was far too restricted. There was an immediate demand for the instruction of parents of children of different ages and educational

[1] Given at the eighth Iowa Conference on Child Development and Parent Education, June 21, 1934.

levels. Furthermore, a number of leaders in the field of adult education conceived of their programs as being especially concerned with family life rather than with individual development, probably because the whole emergency education program had arisen out of a crisis that vitally affected families. Uncertainty about incomes, the vast expansion of commercialized leisure-time activities and rapid changes in standards of all sorts had made the problems of parents acute, and they demanded help. These problems were probably much more urgent in urban than in rural areas.

Vocational leaders had already included parent education as a part of their program in many states. They offered instruction in the care and guidance of children, making and remaking clothing, the selection and preparation of food, family relationships, the adjustments of families to new conditions, and so forth. In a few localities instruction in parent education was included in the literacy program, though there was little material available on this level.

Educators have begun to feel, of course, that parent education is an integral part of the education of children, owing largely to the activities of such organizations as the parent-teacher associations and the American Association of University Women.

Another urgent demand for the inclusion of parent education in programs for adults comes from the recognition of the social work group that such instruction is an important instrument in social reconstruction. In one large city the social worker in charge of family case work stated that, owing to the enormous increase in the number of clients brought about by unemployment, it was no longer possible to do intensive case work of the type essential in rehabilitation problems. Since the major difficulty in any case was unemployment and not disintegration, the social worker had found that bringing small groups together under efficient leadership to discuss the family problems rising out of their situation was an effective method of dealing with the problem.

Under these various circumstances, leaders in parent education believed it was necessary to coordinate and guide these activities as far as possible. Application was made to a foundation for a grant for this purpose under the sponsorship of the National Council of Parent Education, which is made up of fifty leading national agencies in the field.

This grant was made late in 1933, and the duties of the supervisory service thus made possible were accepted by the Office of Education. Bess Goodykoontz, Assistant Commissioner of Education and also a member of the governing board of the National Council of Parent Education, was made directly responsible. The program was developed under Ralph P. Bridgman, director of the council, with the assistance of Agnes Tilson and Muriel Brown.

The service was announced to the state superintendents of education in a letter from George F. Zook, United States Commissioner of Education, dated January 3, 1934. Following the usual policy of the Office of Education, no staff member in parent education went into a state except at the invitation of the state superintendent. Upon invitation, staff members assisted with the organization of the program in the state and advised concerning the choice of a special state assistant in this field. Since there was no provision in the state relief administration funds for supervision, the salaries of these state assistants were paid out of the foundation grant.

In the federal office, which was housed with the educational division of the FERA, the parent education staff wrote a handbook on parent education for the use of the leaders and assembled 1,000 packets of material, including bulletins and other printed material from many sources. News letters, accompanied by material for the special assistant or for parents themselves, were also sent out.

In spite of the brief period during which the program was in operation (January 3 to April 2), the parent education staff worked in twenty-one states. In fourteen they worked with the nursery school program, in ten with adult education, in three with vocational education and in one with the literacy program. In six states the parent education program was a part of two divisions of the federal emergency program. Incomplete reports up to May 1 showed that the work had reached approximately 20,000 parents. Each state worked out its own scheme for training leaders and planned a program fitted to its special needs.[2]

The federal program was directed by a committee from the governing board of the National Council of Parent Education, of which Bess Goodykoontz and George D. Stoddard, director of the Iowa Child Welfare Research Station, were members. This committee was responsible for a program presented to state superintendents meeting with the American Association for Adult Education in Washington, D. C., the week of May 20. At that meeting a resolution was prepared and sent to Harry L. Hopkins, pointing out the use that had been made in the states of trained workers in parent education since they had been made available by the Office of Education and the actual demand for instruction in parent education in many phases of the emergency education programs. The resolution asked that in the future these needs be specifically recognized and provided for in emergency education projects.

Just what the future of the program may be we can not say. In so brief a period only the beginning of a program was possible, and the results were necessarily fragmentary. However, the program did demonstrate the need for trained guidance and a demand for its continuance. In some states the program will probably result in the appointment of a permanent staff member to the state department of education; in others it may mean a specialist in extension.

The fundamental social importance of the movement is difficult to estimate. Economists tell us that our power to develop material resources has greatly exceeded our understanding of how to use and distribute them. Likewise it is certainly true that our knowledge of how to develop creative human relationships has not kept pace with the increasing complexity of these relationships in modern family life. If this program in emergency parent education has contributed to this end, as we hope, our time, energy and money have been well expended.

# EDUCATIONAL EVENTS

## THE TWENTY-EIGHTH ANNIVERSARY OF YALE-IN-CHINA

FOUNDERS' DAY exercises at Changsha on November 16 marked the twenty-eighth anniversary of the establishment of the educational work of Yale-in-China. The Yali Union Middle School enjoyed a holiday with the morning given over to a meeting at which representatives of the government, the board of governors and the city spoke. Dinner was followed by an afternoon of sports and field events. Friends and former staff members of Yale-in-China in New Haven celebrated the occasion with a Chinese dinner.

The Yali Union Middle School occupies a forty-acre campus outside the north gate of Changsha and enrolls some 329 boys in its six years of college preparatory work. Registered

[2] "Parent Education Programs," *School Life*, 1934, 19, 170.

with the Ministry of Education and recognized as one of the leading preparatory schools in China, Yali has realized many of the hopes of its founders, as they set up the first school session on November 16, 1906, in a small Chinese building in the center of the city of Changsha.

The aim of Yale-in-China has been to maintain a school of a distinctly Christian character, holding up the highest possible scholastic standards. The trend has been toward making the school more Chinese and more financially independent. To-day Yali is governed entirely in China by a Board of Governors sitting in Changsha, the majority of whom are Chinese. The faculty is entirely Chinese, with the exception of the Department of English, which is composed of Yale men on short-term teaching appointments. The budget of $60,000 Chinese currency is met from Chinese sources for the most part, only $10,000 coming from the cooperating mission boards in the United States.

A unique feature of the school is the short-term "bachelor" appointment to the teaching faculty. Annually two men are selected from the senior class to teach English at Yali for two-year terms. Five Yale men are now resident in Changsha on such appointments. The work of these men includes teaching, study hall supervision, coaching athletic teams, direction of dramatics and glee club and cooperation of religious activities.

Plans for Yale-in-China were first formulated in New Haven in 1901. At the home of Dr. Anson Phelps Stokes informal discussions crystallized into an actual program which chose China as the field and higher education as the type of work to be engaged in. The Yale Foreign Missionary Society was incorporated in 1903. Lawrence Thurston was the first representative to China, but he died in California in 1904 from illness contracted in service. A preliminary survey was made in 1904 by Harlan P. Beach and Brownell Gage, who traveled to Changsha to investigate the situation at the invitation of missions in the city. The following year Dr. Gage, Warren B. Seabury and Edward H. Hume took up residence in the city and property was purchased in 1906. The two large family houses which were purchased were remodeled and ready for occupancy in November of 1906.

## THE FEDERAL CHILD LABOR AMENDMENT

A LETTER from President Roosevelt approving ratification of the Federal Child Labor Amendment as a method of making permanent the outlawing of child labor under the national recovery act has been made public by Courtenay Dinwiddie, general secretary of the National Child Labor Committee.

Mr. Roosevelt's letter reads:

> One of the accomplishments under the national recovery act which has given me the greatest gratification is the outlawing of child labor. It shows how simply a long desired reform, which no individual or state could accomplish alone, may be brought about when people work together. It is my desire that the advances attained through the NRA be made permanent. In the child labor field the obvious method of maintaining the present gains is through ratification of the Child Labor Amendment. I hope this may be achieved.

Mr. Dinwiddie predicted that the President's statement would strongly influence the twenty-four state legislatures who would vote on the amendment this winter. Twenty states have ratified the amendment and sixteen more are needed to complete the three fourths approval which would write it into the Constitution as the twenty-second amendment.

States which have ratified are Arizona, Arkansas, California, Colorado, Illinois, Iowa, Maine, Michigan, Minnesota, New Hampshire, New Jersey, North Dakota, Ohio, Oklahoma, Oregon, Pennsylvania, Washington, West Virginia and Wisconsin.

Of the twenty-eight states which have not approved the amendment, four—Kentucky, Louisiana, Mississippi and Virginia—do not have regular legislative sessions scheduled for 1935.

The remaining twenty-four, out of which proponents of the amendment must gain sixteen ratifications to make the measure law next year, are: Alabama, Connecticut, Delaware, Florida, Georgia, Idaho, Indiana, Kansas, Maryland, Massachusetts, Missouri, Nebraska, Nevada, New Mexico, New York, North Carolina, Rhode Island, South Carolina, South Dakota, Tennessee, Texas, Utah, Vermont and Wyoming.

The Texas Senate voted down a ratification motion last February, as did the Virginia Senate. No ratifications were obtained from the nine state legislatures which held regular sessions, although one of these previously had ratified the amendment. Opponents of the measure have protested the reintroduction of the ratification question before legislatures which previously had rejected it.

Mr. Dinwiddie reported that the child labor provisions of the NRA appear to be well observed by employers. Complaints rarely involve the use of children under sixteen years of age. Only two out of more than 12,000 employees in the cotton garment industry in 1934 were children under that age. State and city authorities who issue work permits have given excellent cooperation.

If and when the amendment is ratified, the National Child Labor Committee will seek the enactment by the Congress of a federal child labor law embodying provisions similar to those temporarily in force through the industrial codes. These provisions will include a sixteen-year age minimum for employment, with light work in certain industries permitted outside of school hours at fourteen years, and an eighteen-year age minimum for employment in hazardous occupations.

## CHILDREN'S CLASSES AT THE GERMANIC MUSEUM OF HARVARD UNIVERSITY

In collaboration with A. F. Burke, director of art education in the Cambridge public schools, the Germanic Museum of Harvard University is conducting an extensive program of art history and appreciation with public school children. *The Boston Evening Transcript* reports that experiments along these lines were carried out last year with such success that the work this year will be conducted as a regular extra-curriculum course for eighth-grade students.

Twelve weekly meetings are held on Saturday mornings running throughout the winter. At these meetings an illustrated talk is given to about two hundred children on some phase of the history of art. The talk is followed by an appropriate moving picture dealing with a similar subject.

If, for example, the talk is on medieval art, the children are shown a film depicting the making of a stained-glass window; if Egyptian art is to be the subject of the meeting, a film on Egyptian peasant life is run. The program is broad in scope and covers the history of art from ancient times to the present day. The combination of illustrated talk and moving picture makes the art of a particular period vivid and alive to the children. From time to time selected groups of children are conducted through Fogg Museum or the Boston Museum of Fine Arts so that they may be brought into contact with original works of art.

Last year, in spite of the fact that attendance was purely voluntary, more than a thousand children came to the course. It is expected that during the current season this number will be greatly increased.

The course began on November 17 with the first of two programs on the Art of Egypt. A film, The Daily Life of the Egyptians, was shown. The remainder of the course on the following Saturdays are:

The Art of Egypt, II; film, Digging into the Past.
Minoan Art; film, The Gorgon's Head.
Greek Art; film, The Making of a Bronze Statue.
Roman Art; film, Glass Blowing, with specimens of ancient and medieval blown glass.
The Middle Ages—The Cathedral Age; film, The Making of a Stained-Glass Window.
The Middle Ages—The Age of Castles and Chivalry; film, A Visit to the Armor Galleries, Metropolitan Museum.
The Lives of Christ and The Virgin; film, The Nativity and Passion of Christ.
The Renaissance; film, Art Treasures of the Vatican, Historical Episode in the Life of Michelangelo.
Woodcuts, Engravings and Etchings; film, The Etcher's Art.
Colonial Art; film, The Silversmith.
Modern Art; film, Lorado Taft, Sculptor; The Pottery Maker.

## PLANS FOR AN ADVANCED SCHOOL OF EDUCATION

Dr. William F. Russell, dean of Teachers College, Columbia University, in his annual report, recommends the establishment of a new school at Teachers College, to be known as the Advanced School of Education, where exceptionally able students should be trained to provide leadership in American education.

Dean Russell suggests the raising of an endowment fund of $3,000,000, the income of which would be used so that graduate students would receive advanced training without cost. Only the best men and women of the country, selected through a process of rigid examinations, would be admitted. Once the student entered, however, he would be guaranteed economic security and given a position for life.

Pointing out that he is patterning his proposals upon the Ecole Normale Superieure School of Paris which he visited last spring, Dean Russell reports that he feels confident that a similar school can be set up at Teachers College. As at the Ecole Normale, stringent examinations would eliminate the mediocre students, leaving as graduate students the best minds that this country can offer.

Dean Russell states further that, following the French plan, the Advanced School of Education cauld be established on the model of the Ecole Normale, with the rest of Teachers College, Columbia University, Union Theological Seminary, the Juilliard School and other institutions in the same relationship to it as the University of Paris to the Ecole Normale. Thus, while it would be necessary to have a place for the students to gather and to work, a library and adequate laboratories, no exclusive faculty would be needed, as professors in Teachers College could be assigned for full or part time.

In his report, Dean Russell says:

> Young graduates of highest promise could be retained on three-year terms to work with these students. The students could spend their time anywhere in the university, and if deemed wise, at the Sorbonne, University of London, Harvard, Yale, Chicago, the Brookings Institution, or anywhere else.
>
> Sometime this school could have a great building, facing the college on 122nd Street. There should be a great social hall with a wood fire burning and plenty of books. There should be a large auditorium for general lectures. There should be smaller conference rooms, offices, a great study hall, a library and special laboratories like the statistical, curriculum and guidance laboratories.
>
> There should be apartments for married students, a wing of rooms for single men and one for single women, and apartments for the director and a few of the staff. Here would be a modern Solomon's house, accepting only the best, graduating only the most able, attacking on all fronts the problems of education. It would be an honor to be a member—a privilege highly to be appreciated.

The school would be composed of three departments: Educational Research, Practical Science and Professional Education. The offerings of the school would be limited to perfecting the scholarship, research and professional abilities of its students. Courses offered elsewhere would not be duplicated.

In outlining further his belief in the advisability of this new school, Dr. Russell writes:

> If you can assure the ablest students of a permanent post for life, you can attract thousands to turn their hopes in your direction. If, in addition, you can eliminate the economic barrier, by providing all expenses over a period of years, you can be assured that the ablest will take the examination.
>
> Even if your examination system is imperfect, and even if you can not be sure that you judge either fairly or accurately, none the less you will have a first-rate body of students. Then, if you provide a place for study, an adequate library, good laboratories, and if there is a rich offering of lectures and classes in other educational institutions nearby, to which you can send your students and in addition you have an adequate system of supervision and periodic examinations, then you need have no faculty of your own.
>
> I should like to see something like this at Teachers College. Under present conditions we could not offer free maintenance, but at least we should consider whether it might not commend itself to the Trustees of Teachers College to try to raise $3,000,000, the income from which could be used for this purpose.

## MEETING OF SCIENCE TEACHERS WITH THE AMERICAN ASSOCIATION FOR THE ADVANCEMENT OF SCIENCE

THE Council of the American Association for the Advancement of Science has authorized its Committee on the Place of Science in Education to prepare a one-day program to be given in Pittsburgh, at the Athletic Association Building, on Saturday, December 29. This is the result of the request made at the meeting held in Boston last year. Invitation to participate is extended to delegates from science teachers' organizations and to individual teachers of science from elementary and high schools, colleges, universities and state administrations. The Pittsburgh Athletic Association is near the buildings where the other meetings of the American Association for the Advancement of Science will be held.

The program will be opened by Professor Otis W. Caldwell, chairman of the Committee on the Place of Science in Education, who will speak briefly on the purpose of the meeting. The subject of the morning session, over which Dr. Wilhelm Segerblom will preside, will be "Newer Knowledge of Interest to Science Teachers," when papers will be presented on "The Influence of Certain Gases upon Plants," by Dr. P. W. Zimmerman, assistant director of the Boyce Thompson Institute for Plant Research; on "Research in Sound and Communication," by Dr. Harvey Fletcher, of the Bell Telephone Company Research Laboratories, and on "The Present Status of Knowledge of Cosmic Rays," by Professor Robert A. Millikan, Norman Bridge Laboratories, Pasadena, California. Each paper will be followed with a discussion by an invited speaker.

In the afternoon a symposium has been arranged by the special committee appointed at the Boston meeting on "A National Organization of Science Teachers," at which a report on the work of the committee will be presented by the chairman, Harry A. Carpenter, specialist in science, Rochester Public Schools, Rochester, N. Y. Others taking part in the discussion will be John H. Harms, physics teacher, Ames Senior High School, Iowa; Earl R. Glenn, head of the Science Department, State Teachers College, Montclair, N. J.; Florence Billig, assistant professor of natural sciences, Wayne University, Detroit; Harry A. Cunningham, professor of biology, Kent State College, Ohio; Mary Gilliam, teacher and secretary, Science Section, Virginia Education Association, and Philip G. Johnson, science supervisor, Teachers College, University of Nebraska. Those taking part in the discussion that will follow the symposium include: E. J. Cable, State Teachers College, Cedar Falls, Iowa; Ivan G. Hosack, chairman of the General Science Teachers Club, Perry High School, Pittsburgh, Pa., and Elbert C. Weaver, president of the New England Association of Chemistry Teachers and teacher in Bulkeley High School, Hartford, Conn.

At the luncheon Professor Edward L. Thorndike, president of the American Association for the Advancement of Science, will make an address on "The Psychology of Attitudes," after which scientific men who are invited guests will be presented.

Reservations for the luncheon, which will be served at noon at the cost of $1, should be sent to the local chairman, Dr. John A. Hollinger, Administration Building, Bellefield Avenue at Forbes, Pittsburgh, Pa. The final program, giving the names of the speakers, will be sent on application to the Committee on the Place of Science in Education, 433 West 123rd Street, New York, N. Y.

## DINNER OF THE ASSOCIATE ALUMNI OF THE COLLEGE OF THE CITY OF NEW YORK

More than seven hundred alumni, professors and officials of the College of the City of New York attended the fifty-fourth annual dinner of the Associate Alumni in the Hotel Commodore on November 17. For the second year since its organization in 1853 distinguished alumni of the college were honored for their post-graduate achievements in various lines of endeavor and for their service through alumni activities to the college.

The principal speakers were the Honorable Gerald P. Nye, United States Senator from North Dakota, and Professor Felix Frankfurter, of the Harvard Law School. Other speakers were Charles J. Hardy, president of the American Car and Foundry Company, who represented the fifty year class; George L. Cohen, who represented the twenty-five year class, and President Frederick B. Robinson, who spoke of the work of the college during the past year. The toastmaster was Dr. Stephen P. Duggan, president of the alumni and director of the Institute of International Education. The invocation was asked by the Rev. Walter Krumwiede, pastor of the Grace Lutheran Church of Rochester, N. Y.

At the dinner three men prominent in education were presented with the Townsend Harris medals "for postgraduate achievement." The citations were:

Stephen Pierce Duggan

You gave the college inspired teaching and creative administration during the years when you built the departments of education and of government and when you established the evening session and the extension courses for teachers. It was not surprising, therefore, that those who desired a scholar to stimulate and direct intellectual cooperation among the peoples of the earth should lift you to a wider field of endeavor. You have enlarged your classroom so that it now contains the students of the world. In you Alma Mater finds particular reason to rejoice.

FELIX FRANKFURTER

Scholar, teacher of lawyers, valiant champion of due process and of complete justice for all men, you have realized the best traditions inherent in the common law. You have held public trust with high distinction and you have rejected public office with rare courage. Interpreter of the ideals of the United States before the University of Oxford, honored teacher in the oldest of American tradition in uniting the law with social justice. In you Alma Mater finds particular reason to rejoice.

FRANK SCHLESINGER

Worthy successor of Copernicus and of Galileo, leading scholar in the great University of Yale, you have helped men to understand the expanse and the mystery of the universe. What your own eyes have seen and what, through the medium of great telescopes from New Haven to Johannesburg, you have enabled other men to see has vastly enriched the world's knowledge of the most ancient of the sciences. In you Alma Mater finds particular reason to rejoice.

# EDUCATIONAL NOTES AND NEWS

DR. EDWIN W. CHUBB, since 1907 dean of the School of Liberal Arts of the Ohio University, has been named acting president. He succeeds Dr. Elmer Burritt Bryan, who died on October 15 after serving as president for thirteen years.

DR. THEOPHIL H. HILDEBRANDT has been appointed chairman of the department of mathematics at the University of Michigan. He succeeds Professor James W. Glover, who recently resigned in order to devote more time to research problems and investigations dealing with the federal government plans for economic security for the individual. Professor Glover remains as James Olney Professor—a "distinguished professorship" created for him.

AT Princeton University, Associate Professor Elmer G. Butler has been appointed chairman of the department of biology. After the retirement of Professor Edwin G. Conklin last year Professor Butler served as acting chairman of the department. Dr. Edward Sampson, associate professor of geology, will succeed Professor Alexander Hamilton Phillips as head of the department of geology.

DR. MARSTON MORSE, professor of mathematics at Harvard University, has accepted a call to a professorship of mathematics at the Institute for Advanced Study at Princeton, New Jersey. His associates in the School of Mathematics of the institute will be the present permanent group, namely, Drs. Albert Einstein, Oswald Veblen, James Waddell Alexander, John von Neumann and Hermann Weyl.

PROFESSOR EDMUND S. CONKLIN, of the University of Oregon, has been appointed professor and head of the department of psychology at Indiana University, to succeed Professor William F. Book, who has retired with the title of professor emeritus.

PROFESSOR B. P. HEUBNER recently joined the department of education and psychology of the University of Denver. Professor Heubner was formerly head of the departments of education at Ripon, Wisconsin, and at Wichita, Kansas. He succeeds Dr. G. L. Maxwell, who is now serving as director of adult education in Colorado.

AT a reunion of former students of the department of chemistry at the Ohio State University on November 17, presentation was made by the alumni of a portrait of Dr. William McPherson, professor of chemistry and dean of the Graduate School. The portrait, the work of Professor James R. Hopkins, of the faculty of fine arts, was presented by George A. Burrell, '18, consulting chemist of Pittsburgh, Pa.

A PORTRAIT of Professor Emeritus William H. Hobbs, formerly head of the department of geology of the University of Michigan, was recently presented to the university by the department of geology. The portrait is the work of Leon A. Makielski. A large group of colleagues, students and friends of Professor Hobbs attended the presentation ceremonies, which included addresses by Dr. John G. Winter, president of the Research Club, and Dr. Ermine C. Case, chairman of the department of geology. President A. G. Ruthven accepted the gift for the university, after which Professor Hobbs responded.

Dr. Tyler Dennett, president of Williams College, on November 17 received the degree of doctor of laws from Amherst College. In conferring the degree, Dr. Stanley King, president of Amherst College, said that Amherst desired to make Dr. Dennett a foster son "in recognition of a common heritage and like traditions, in token of friendly rivalry in sports, and in anticipation of many happy years of work together in the common enterprise of learning."

Dr. Frank P. Speare, president of Northeastern University, was presented on November 14 with the gold key and honorary membership in Sigma Epsilon Rho, scholastic honor fraternity of the evening school of business, "in recognition of his extraordinary executive ability as typified by the growth and development of Northeastern University."

The Nobel prize in chemistry has been awarded to Dr. Harold C. Urey, professor of chemistry at Columbia University, for his discovery of deuterium.

Dr. Michael I. Rostovtzeff, Sterling professor of ancient history and classical archeology at Yale University, has been elected an honorary member of the Royal Irish Academy. Professor Rostovtzeff was last year elected a corresponding member of the Academy of Athens, and an associate member of the Belgian Academy of Sciences, Letters and Art.

Dr. Robert C. Clothier, president of Rutgers University, has been elected an honorary member of the Kappa Phi Kappa, national honorary education fraternity.

Frederick A. Ashley, superintendent of the Everett, Mass., schools, has been elected president of Boston University's chapter of Beta Gamma Sigma, national honorary fraternity in collegiate schools of business, for 1934–35. He succeeds Aaron R. Davison.

Congressman Clarence E. Hancock, Republican representative from the New York Thirty-Fifth District in Washington since 1927, has taken up his work as visiting professor of government at Wesleyan University.

Professor Walther von Wartburg, director of the seminar in Romance Philology at Leipzig and an authority on linguistic atlases, will substitute for Professor T. Atkinson at the University of Chicago this winter. He was recently awarded the Prix Volney by the French Institute.

Dr. Gabriel Szegö has joined the faculty of Washington University as visiting professor of mathematics. He is on leave of absence from the University of Königsberg, where he has been professor of mathematics since 1926.

Alexander Fichandler has been appointed head of Junior High School 136, Brooklyn, N. Y., and Samuel M. Levenson has become head of the new Junior High School 40 in the Borough of Queens, N. Y. The latter appointment becomes effective when the school opens for the first time in February.

Dorothea A. Pohlman has been appointed educational director of the Dayton Art Institute in Dayton, Ohio. She was formerly a member of the staff of the St. Louis Art Museum.

Dr. Robert Maynard Hutchins, president of the University of Chicago, and Dr. Charles S. Johnson, head of the department of social science at Fisk University, have been elected trustees of the Julius Rosenwald Fund.

Dr. D. B. R. Johnson, dean of the school of pharmacy at the University of Oklahoma, has been named chairman of the committee on relations of boards and colleges of the American Association of Colleges of Pharmacy.

Dr. George J. Ryan, president of the Board of Education, and Jacob Greenberg, associate superintendent of schools of New York City, returned from Europe on November 14 after an absence of six weeks, during which time they visited schools and universities in Italy and France. During their tour abroad they inspected the schools of Naples, Rome, Florence, Cannes and Paris. Dr. Ryan lectured on the American system of education in several of the Italian universities. The University of Bologna conferred on him the degree of doctor of letters.

Bess Goodykoontz, Assistant United States Commissioner of Education, was the guest speaker of the New York University chapter of Pi Lambda Theta, national honorary educational sorority, on November 17. Miss Goodykoontz is the national president of the organization.

Dr. Walter Scott Athearn, president of Oklahoma City University, died on November 15 at the age of sixty-two years. Dr. Athearn was at one time president of Butler University at Indianapolis. He had also been dean of the school of religious education and social service at Boston University and professor of religious education at Drake University.

Dr. Ellsworth G. Lancaster, professor of education at the University of Florida, died on November 11. He retired at the close of the spring session of 1933 at the age of seventy-two years because of failing health. Dr. Lancaster was for eleven years president of Olivet College, Olivet, Mich., and for several years taught psychology at Colorado College before going to the University of Florida.

The Rev. Albert Biever, S.J., died on November 14 at the age of seventy-six years. He was the founder and for nine years president of Loyola University.

Dr. Daniel W. Redmond, from 1926 to 1932 dean of the School of Liberal Arts and Sciences at the College of the City of New York, died on November 14 at the age of fifty-eight years.

Dr. W. W. Long, for twenty-two years head of the extension division of Clemson College, S. C., died on November 13. He was seventy-three years old.

Henri Verbrugghen, formerly conductor of the Minneapolis Symphony Orchestra, died on November 12. For the past two years he was professor of chamber music and appreciation and chairman of the department of music at Carleton College.

A service in memory of LeBaron Russell Briggs, formerly dean of Harvard College, dean of the Faculty of Arts and Sciences, president of Radcliffe College and teacher of English at Harvard University for forty-two years, will be held on December 11, his birthday, in Memorial Church, Harvard University. Dean Briggs died on April 24. President James B. Conant has appointed the following committee to arrange details of the service: Kenneth B. Murdock, dean of the Faculty of Arts and Sciences, *chairman;* Charles F. Adams, member of the Board of Overseers; Willard L. Sperry, dean of the Divinity School; Frank W. Taussig, professor of economics, and George L. Kittredge, professor of English literature, and Robert S. Hillyer, associate professor of English.

At the annual Alumni Week-end on November 17, Wesleyan University laid the cornerstone for a new squash courts building and unveiled six memorial tablets, one commemorative of the career of Woodrow Wilson as professor of history and political economy at Wesleyan University from 1888 to 1890. George W. Davison, of New York City, president of the board of trustees, presided, and Mrs. Charles L. Denison laid the cornerstone. The Wilson tablet was placed in the Memorial Chapel at a point near which the former President held his classes. Tablets were unveiled in the chapel also in memory of Professor Calvin S. Harrington, professor of Greek from 1863 to 1886, of John Gribbel, of Philadelphia, president of the board of trustees from 1920 to 1927, and of Wesleyan men who died in the Civil War. A tablet in Judd Hall memorializes Professor Wilbur C. Atwater, professor of chemistry from 1874 to 1907.

The election of officers, including Dean E. L. Cloyd, of North Carolina State College, Raleigh, as president, marked the closing session of the North Carolina College Conference at Greensboro, N. C. Dean Cloyd succeeds Dr. Frazer Hood, of Davidson College. Dr. Howard Omwake, of Catawba College, was elected vice-president, and Dr. N. W. Walker, of the University of North Carolina, Chapel Hill, was reelected secretary-treasurer. Members of the executive committee include the officers of the conference and Dr. Hood, Dean D. B. Bryan, of Wake Forest College, and Miss Hazel Morrison, of Flora Macdonald College.

The National Council of Teachers of English will meet in Washington, D. C., on November 29 and 30. Included among those who will address the meeting are Henry A. Wallace, Secretary of Agriculture; Robert Frost, poet; Dr. Edwin D. Starbuck, director of the Institute of Character Research, University of Southern California; Dr. Esther C. Brunauer, International Relations Secretary of the American Association of University Women; Bess Goodykoontz, Assistant U. S. Commissioner of Education; Willard W. Beatty, president of the Progressive Education Association and superintendent of the Bronxville Public Schools; Professor Robert E. Rogers, Massachusetts Institute of Technology; Alfred S. Dashiell, managing editor of *Scribner's,* and William L. Chenery, editor of *Collier's.* Tradition and innovation in the teaching of English in a time of accelerated social change has been announced by Dr. Oscar James Campbell, of the University of Michigan, president, as the general topic for the convention.

John W. Studebaker, U. S. Commissioner of Education, has announced that the annual meeting of State Superintendents and Commissioners of Education in the United States will be held in Washington, D. C., on December 10 and 11. Called by State Superintendent Charles A. Lee, of Missouri, president of the council, the meeting this year will take up a number of important educational problems. Commissioner Studebaker has urged not only state directors of education to attend the meeting, but also state directors of research or statistics, inasmuch as a number of problems to be considered involve detailed records in relation to the Federal Emergency Educational Program.

The Educational Research Association of New York State, of which Dr. Harry S. Ganders, of Syracuse University, is president, and Dr. Wayne W. Soper, State Education Department, is secretary-treasurer, will hold its annual luncheon meeting in Syracuse at the Hotel Syracuse, Thursday, December 27, in conjunction with the meetings of the Associated Academic Principals and other allied associations. The general subject of the program will center around the progress that has been made in the selection of candidates for teacher training, the pre-service and the in-service training of teachers. The following program has been arranged: "Selective Admissions in Teacher Training Institutions," Dr. Oscar E. Hertzberg, State Teachers College at Buffalo; "The New Curriculum for the Education of Elementary School Teachers," Dr. Hermann Cooper, assistant commissioner for teacher education, New York State Education Department; "Practical In-service Training of Teachers," W. Howard Pillsbury, superintendent of schools, Schenectady; "A New Venture in Research," Dr. Paul R. Mort, director of the School of Education, Teachers College, Columbia University.

At the ninth annual Conference on Education of Bucknell University, held at Lewisburg, Pa., on November 2 and 3, nearly two thousand were in attendance at the several sessions. Dr. James N. Rule, state superintendent of public instruction; President G. Morris Smith, of Susquehanna University; Dr. Charles F. Sanders, of Gettysburg College; Dr. Ben D. Wood, of Columbia University, and President Homer P. Rainey, of Bucknell University, were the speakers at the general sessions. Following the general session on Saturday, Dr. Wood and President Rainey were made members of the Bucknell Chapter of Kappa Phi Kappa. Wilson MacDonald, the Canadian poet, spoke at the banquet on Friday evening. Those with records of fifty or more years of educational service were honor guests. The sectional meetings were generally well attended, several of them having in the neighborhood of a hundred people in attendance. The general subject of the meeting was "One Hundred Years of Education in Pennsylvania." On the program was a pageant written by three Bucknell students and produced by groups of high-school students from Lewisburg, Sunbury and Milton.

A conference on "More and Better Wills," under the auspices of the Commission on Endowment and Trust Funds of the Association of American Colleges, was held at Davidson College, North Carolina, on November 21. F. L. Jackson, treasurer of Davidson College and chairman of the commission, was responsible for the arrangement of the program. Among the speakers and their subjects were P. C. Whitlock, American Trust Company of Charlotte, who spoke on "Why Have an Attorney Prepare Your Will?"; R. G. Stockton, of the Wachovia Bank and Trust Company of Winston-Salem, on "Why Have a Trust Company Administer Your Will?"; Gilbert T. Stephenson, vice-president of the Equitable Trust Company, Wilmington, Delaware, on "Making the American People Will-Minded"; President Clyde A. Miller, Guilford College, N. C., on "Why Put Colleges in Your Will?" and Dr. R. L. Kelly, executive secretary of the Association of American Colleges, on "The Future of College Finance."

THE University of Wisconsin Graduate School announces the establishment for graduate students of twelve or thirteen research fellowships in the sciences for the academic year 1934–35. These fellowships have been made possible by a grant of $10,000 from the Wisconsin Alumni Research Foundation. The stipends will vary between $750 and $1,000. In selecting the candidates emphasis will be placed on scholarship, personality and originality. The fellowships are open to men from any state in the union as well as from foreign countries. Fellows will be appointed at any time during the current year when a suitable candidate is discovered.

ALL school teachers, men and women, including instructors in the girls' section of the Ballila (Fascist Youth) organization, will wear uniforms from now on in the compulsory military culture courses that will be given in every high school and college in Italy. The innovation is said to be a part of the government's plan to militarize the country.

# DISCUSSION

## MORE COMMENT ON BOBBITT'S CRITICISM

PROFESSOR BOBBITT'S criticism of the conclusions and recommendations of the Commission on the Social Studies[1] may prove to be a distinct service to the teaching profession, although probably not in the way he intended. It will be likely—at least so we hope—to stimulate more careful scrutiny of the report of the commission, as is already evidenced by the reply of Professor Weiss.[2] And since Professor Bobbitt's article misrepresents so flagrantly the point of view expressed by the commission, it seems almost a foregone conclusion that the final outcome will be a greater acceptance of the spirit of the report than if Professor Bobbitt had not spoken.

The surprising feature of the criticism is that so outstanding an educational leader should understand so little of what has been happening during the past few years as to take so reactionary a stand. It is hard to believe that a thoughtful man would fail to grasp the distinction between democracy and laissez-faire individualism, and the distinction between a democratic collectivism and either Russian communism or Italian fascism. But since Professor Weiss has already discussed very adequately this feature of Bobbitt's criticism, it is unnecessary that I follow it further.

An additional point of interest to me is that Professor Bobbitt's article illustrates very beautifully the utter failure of the method for achieving social progress which Bobbitt long has favored. I refer to the theory that "leadership and the enlightenment necessary for a wise management for economic and political affairs" can be "entrusted (completely) to the specialized economists, political scientists, sociologists, historians and geographers."[3] In other words, I refer to the idea that it is the business of general education to train "followers" and that the training of leaders should be left to higher professional schools. In this particular instance, Professor Bobbitt speaks as a layman—thus a "follower"—and says that although the American Historical Association did the right thing in appointing a committee of experts to report upon needed changes in the teaching of the social sciences, nevertheless he does not like the report which the experts have produced. And this, surprisingly enough, from the man who points to that as the only method of social progress! Moreover, the basis for his objection is exactly that which the reactionary layman will always make when expert recommendations

[1] SCHOOL AND SOCIETY, 40: 1025, 201–208, August 18, 1934.

[2] SCHOOL AND SOCIETY, 40: 1032, 446–449, October 6, 1934.

[3] SCHOOL AND SOCIETY, 40: 1025, 201, August 18, 1934.

are not to his liking, namely, that the committee is either not competent or is wilfully attempting to mislead the public. Haven't we heard enough of that in recent months?

In order to put a slightly better face on the matter Professor Bobbitt accuses the committee of being highly emotionalized, and for this reason unscientific. Why should the announcement of a scientific conclusion not be emotionalized, so long as the emotion has previously served as a vitalizing force in driving the investigators to examine most carefully and painstakingly the accuracy and adequacy of the conclusions reached? Great scientific discoveries have probably always been accompanied by highly emotionalized states on the part of the discoverers, both prior to and following the discoveries. The point is that to reject expert recommendations merely because they are emotionalized is very dubious business. Moreover, as Professor Weiss has pointed out, the comments of the critic seem to a disinterested observer to be much more highly emotionalized than the report of the commission.

The difficulty with the leadership-followership notion is, as Suzzallo has pointed out, that no individual is always and forever either a follower or a leader. He is sometimes one and sometimes the other, and always somewhat of both. It is therefore important that every citizen in a democracy be as capable as possible in passing independent judgments, since no one can avoid the necessity for passing, from time to time, upon the capabilities of experts and the dependability of their judgments. Every one must be trained for leadership as well as for followership. That Professor Bobbitt's theory carries with it no basis for training in passing critical judgments is shown by the almost total lack of any logical or rational basis for the criticisms which he levels at the commission.

Speaking practically, the idea of leaving to experts alone the matter of making social changes or of passing judgments regarding the desirability of social changes, and expecting the mass of humanity to follow along in a docile manner, simply will not work. A people brought up in an atmosphere of democratic idealism will never tolerate domination of this kind if they believe it exists. The expert and the layman must cooperate in making the decision. If we take democracy and the scientific method seriously we will have to prepare all members of society, to the limits of their various capacities, to arrive at their own judgments in regard to perplexing matters, and thus in that sense to become leaders. It requires independent thought to pass upon the judgments of others, as well as to make judgments one's self. The schools have no alternative in determining whether or not influential judgments will be cast by the lay public. Whether the experts like it or not, public opinion will crystallize, and must be taken into consideration. The only thing that the schools may possibly do is to train up a citizenry which becomes progressively more able to arrive at intelligent judgments, rather than judgments which are based on emotion and popular tradition only.

We really owe Professor Bobbitt a vote of thanks for his courage and frankness, thus providing this opportunity for bringing into the open problems which need to be discussed thoroughly and with candor. It is only as we air our differences that we will ever be able to harmonize them and reach that professional accord which is needed if progress is to be made.

Ernest E. Bayles
The University of Kansas

## WHAT ONE STUDIES, NOT HOW

If designing autocrats were to suggest a formula for misdirecting education through the years to their own advantage they could not do better than hold for method as against subject-matter; they could do no better than to join hands with those who think it makes little difference what is studied, the manner and act of studying being considered more important.

What one studies is far more important than how one studies; and if one studies something interesting and important the method will largely take care of itself.

The world has been going wrong because of lack of knowledge at the right spot. Technique is always good, but substance is better. And it is amazing how technique straightens itself out if a person would learn.

Curriculum studies are accordingly to be rated rather above the more filmy sections of treatises on the technique of teaching and repetitious portions of texts on educational psychology. And schools and colleges of education have a large and urgent order in the matter of routing their students through fields of subject-matter which in the light of the hour pertain. It would appear from the ills of society that subject-matter had suffered a neglect.

Arland D. Weeks
North Dakota Agricultural College

# SPECIAL CORRESPONDENCE

## THE EDUCATIONAL PROBLEM PRESENTED BY THE SPANISH-SPEAKING CHILD OF THE SOUTHWEST[1]

The Southwest is an extensive territory with a relatively small population. Four of the states of the Union border upon the Republic of Mexico—Texas, New Mexico, Arizona and California. The distance along the border (roughly from Brownsville to San Diego) is more than 1,800 miles, or about the distance from the city of Washington to Denver. The state of Texas alone has an area greater than that of Massachusetts, New York, New Jersey, Pennsylvania, Ohio, Indiana and Illinois together. Yet the state of New York, with one fourteenth of the area of the border states, has a greater population. Ohio has a population density of 163 per square mile, California 36, Texas 22, New Mexico and Arizona a little less than 4.

Within the states the population is unevenly distributed. Texas and California have five cities each of more than 100,000 inhabitants. On the other hand, there is a large rural population. In the four states together more than two fifths of the population live in the country, in non-incorporated places, or in incorporated places of less than 2,500 inhabitants. There is at the one extreme the isolated rural child with no near neighbors and at the other the child of the city tenement district where hundreds of others live almost within a stone's throw.

The first aspect, then, of the problem presented by the Spanish-speaking child, as of all other children of the Southwest, is the vastness of the area, its sparseness of population and its extreme range of conditions from the tenement district to the isolated ranch home.

Turning now from this general geographic background, let us consider the Spanish-speaking population more specifically. The total population of the four border states in round numbers was 12,360,000 in 1930. Of these about a million and a half, nearly one eighth of the total, are Spanish-speaking. In the several states the proportion varies. While exact numbers are unknown, estimates are about one twelfth in California, one eighth in Texas, three tenths in Arizona and one half in New Mexico. But their distribution in different localities does not correspond to the distribution of the total population; in some districts all the inhabitants are Spanish-speaking, in others none, and in still others various proportions. In California, for example, the Spanish-speaking population is confined very largely to the southern part of the state. Los Angeles County alone has nearly half of the total of the state. Taylor reports that in 1927 Mexican children constituted 17.1 per cent. of the total enrolment of elementary school children in Los Angeles. In El Paso, Texas, the Spanish-speaking population is about two thirds of the total, in San Antonio about two fifths, but in Dallas only about one thirty-third. There is frequently a tendency also for the Spanish-speaking people of a given community to concentrate in one or more sections rather than to distribute themselves over the whole.

The problem is further complicated by local conditions, which vary from state to state and community to community. Among these is ability to pay for educational opportunities. To take a single illustration, El Paso County, Texas, has a very large Spanish-speaking population and Dallas County a very small one; but El Paso County has an assessed valuation per scholastic (in 1931) a little less than two thirds that of Dallas County.

Another variable is the number of children belonging to other racial or linguistic groups in a given community or state. Texas has 850,000 Negroes distributed for the most part in Central and East Texas. California has

[1] Grateful acknowledgment is made of the generous financial assistance of the Fund for Research in the Social Sciences of The University of Texas.

165,000 Japanese, Chinese and Filipinos. New Mexico and Arizona have 70,000 Indians. And in all these states there are numbers of foreign-born belonging to still other groups. The first two generations of foreign white stock, except Spanish-speaking, constitute a proportion of the population varying from 6 per cent. in New Mexico to 37 per cent. in California. As in the case of the Spanish-speaking people, these various racial and linguistic groups are unevenly distributed within the several states.

The title of the paper and the discussion to this point assume that the Spanish-speaking child constitutes an educational problem somewhat different from the English-speaking child, for otherwise there would be no point to the discussion. The nature of the problem must now be made more explicit.

Let us look first at the school record of the Spanish-speaking child. As in all large groups, some children do very well indeed and some do very poorly. The individual differences in every respect are very large. On the average, however, the record is discouraging. Studies in various states have revealed serious retardation in the progress of these pupils through the schools. Figures for only two states will be given here. A survey in Texas a few years ago found that nearly half of the Spanish-speaking children who were enrolled at all were in the first grade, nearly three fourths in the first three grades, and only 3 or 4 per cent. in the high school. In the third grade the Spanish-speaking child was about three years older than the English-speaking child. Some schools, of course, had less retardation than this, while others had more. Computations from the report of the Division of Statistics and Information of the State Department of Public Instruction of New Mexico for 1932–33 show that 34 per cent. of Spanish children are enrolled in the first grade as compared with 16 per cent. of other children and that the median age of Spanish children in the third grade is 10.1 years as compared with 8.8 years for other children.

Standard tests give results equally discouraging. To illustrate their achievement, reference will be made to a study of reading and arithmetic in the Lower Rio Grande Valley of Texas. On the basis of results for ages 8 to 12 in grades 2 to 8 these are the findings: In arithmetic the Spanish-speaking children have a score slightly in excess of chronological age at eight years, but at successive age levels the score falls farther and farther behind. Their reading age at the eight-year level is below their chronological age and the gap widens with advance in age. On the average the Spanish-speaking children are about a year and a half below the English-speaking children of the same age in arithmetic, and in reading a little over two years below. On the whole the Spanish-speaking curves rise very slowly. With some variation in details, this illustration is probably more or less typical of conditions in general. One significant feature is definitely supported by Tireman's report, in a New Mexico study, that the reading scores of Spanish-speaking children were progressively lower than those of English-speaking children with advance in grade.

It is evident, then, from the school record that the schools of the Southwest are finding the Spanish-speaking child a serious problem. Indeed, a study of the situation would lead us to expect difficulties.

Consider the language situation, for example. Each year in these border states the Spanish-speaking children who become of school age—35,000 of them—enter the school, if they go at all (and many of them do not), with little or no knowledge of English. They are taught from the beginning in a language which is foreign to them and, in most of the public schools at least, have little or no contact with written forms of their native language until they enter the high school. At the same time, outside of school most of them have little contact with English. As a result many of them never have the opportunity to gain a mastery over either Spanish or English. No one knows the full extent of this handicap both in the work of the school and in later social adjustment.

A second factor of great significance is their generally low socio-economic level. While some are from well-to-do homes and homes of high culture, the average for the area as a whole is far below that of the English-speaking population. Often there is extreme poverty and a correspondingly low cultural level. Many are the children of migratory laborers. Some who are now desperately poor are from homes which have seen better days; many, however, are from families which for generations have known only extreme underprivilege.

There is some tendency to seek an explanation of their school difficulties in their intelligence quotients. As a matter of fact, the average IQ's reported by investigators are usually much below 100. Averages ranging from 78 to 97 may be found in the literature. Here, however, we are dealing with a situation in which it is difficult to distinguish cause and effect and in which our customary inferences from test scores are even more precarious than usual. It is certain that these IQ's must not be taken at their face value as a measure of the possibilities of these children. The depressing effect of extremely unfavorable environment is well established in other connections; and when English is involved in a test, the handicap of a Spanish-speaking child is more or less obvious. It is probable that low IQ and low school achievement are in part at least the result of common causes. There are, of course, many who in spite of their handicaps exhibit superior ability both in the test situation and in their work.

Various differences between the Spanish-speaking population and the English-speaking population and the exaggeration of actual differences through lack of understanding add to the difficulties of education. Many of the parents, for example, are foreigners, and the native people tend to treat them as groups have always treated those who have not "belonged." Even children who by virtue of birth on American soil are citizens of the United States are victims of the suspicion and antagonism commonly shown toward the foreigner. As a matter of fact, many Spanish-speaking families are descendants of colonists who came into the Southwest long before those who spoke English. It is important to remember that this region was colonized from the South as well as from the East. But these facts are apparently overlooked by a certain part of the English-speaking population who seem to think that they have some kind of a divine right to the territory.

Another difference is that of race. While some of the Spanish-speaking people are pure white (if one may properly speak of pure races), others are Indian (that is, Mexican Indian), and still a larger number in this country are a mixture of white and Indian. The darker skin color which commonly goes with Indian blood is undoubtedly the cause of some prejudice on the part of groups whose skin color is lighter. And of course where prejudice appears, the problem of the school is rendered more difficult.

Differences in custom, also, sometimes rather trivial, often serve as a barrier between Spanish-speaking and English-speaking groups; and in some cases lack of home training in the ways of this country place an added duty on the schools.

Perhaps this paper has been disappointing in that it has not set up Americanization as *the* educational problem presented by those Spanish-speaking children who come from immigrant homes. To be sure, it is a problem to make citizens out of the children of immigrants, but it is a problem also to make citizens out of other children—and the process is not far different. Of course, some things have to be taught the immigrant child which other children learn at home. But effective citizenship is not taught by talking about it; it is developed through participation. So far as these children are concerned, it would be better to drop Americanization out of our vocabulary and simply give our attention to providing an educational opportunity for them suited to their individual and social needs just as we do in the case of others.

Prejudice and indifference toward the Spanish-speaking child are in many communities among his greatest enemies. While some districts are sincerely attempting to give him the education he needs, in others he faces indifference or actual antagonism. At least in Texas, where the writer is best acquainted with conditions, there are some communities in which no serious attempt is made to get the Mexican child into the school, and frequently the opportunities provided are quite inferior to those provided for other children.

It is obvious that out of the situation which has been briefly described grow many problems of administration, supervision, curriculum and method. For example, how can an adequate educational program be provided in communities that are now indifferent or antagonistic to the education of these children? What opportunities can be offered to the children of migratory families? How can effective supervision be applied in sparsely settled areas? How may the abilities of these children be adequately appraised? How should they be taught so that their transition to English may be accomplished with the least possible loss? How can their opportunities for mastery of English be increased? What modifications of curriculum are necessary to adjust to their peculiar background of experience and to meet their social needs? How may the school become an active force for the improvement of the home of the underprivileged child? What elements of Spanish and Mexican culture should be saved to enrich our common store? These and many others constitute the educational problem presented by the Spanish-speaking child of the Southwest.

This paper should not give the impression that the educational condition of the Spanish-speaking child of the Southwest is wholly unfavorable or that only feeble efforts are being made to solve such problems as are presented. On the contrary, many educators are fully alive to the situation, many schools are doing excellent work, and in various centers productive research is going forward. These are not mentioned in detail here, for it is the purpose of this paper to set forth the nature and extent of the problem rather than to describe attempts to solve it.

H. T. MANUEL

UNIVERSITY OF TEXAS

# QUOTATIONS

## PRESIDENT BUTLER AND FASCISM

*The Nation* has received the following communication from President Butler, denying the charges contained in the article "Fascism at Columbia University," printed in *The Nation* last week:

A reading of the anonymous article in *The Nation* of November 7, to which my attention is directed by your letter of October 30, makes it plain that *The Nation* has been imposed upon. This article is one more exhibition of the prevailing tendency to persecute, even maliciously, any one whose opinions or supposed opinions differ from those of the writer. The article is a curious hodge-podge of falsehood, misrepresentation and half-truth, with the result that it ends in utter nonsense.

No member of Columbia University is ever questioned as to either his political opinions or his religious beliefs. These are matters for himself alone. The university concerns itself with character, scholarship, teaching power and personality. There is not now and never has been any attempt on the part of the distinguished scholars, so recognized on either side of the Atlantic, who are responsible for the conduct of the university's work in all that relates to Italy to discriminate against any one, either teacher, student or visitor, because of his political opinions, which, indeed, are usually unknown. On the contrary, these scholars have promptly declined every suggestion that action of this sort be taken when made to them from sources outside the university.

The Casa Italiana, which is the generous gift of men and women of Italian origin living in New York, is wholly without political purpose or significance. In this respect it does not differ one iota from Schermerhorn Hall, the scientific laboratory building upon which it looks. The Casa Italiana is admirably equipped for the study and teaching of all that relates to Italy and its civilization—the history and geography of the country, the language and the literature and the art of its people, together with their social, economic and political institutions as these have developed through the centuries. In all that concerns scholarly endeavor it stands to Italy in precisely the same relationship that the Maison Française stands to France, the Deutsches Haus to Germany, the Casa de las Españas to Spain and the coming Japanese House to Japan.

The article to which you direct my attention mentions the names of Count Sforza and Senator Croce, both of whom are my warm personal friends and constant correspondents. Count Sforza, a distinguished European statesman of high rank and large experience, has often visited us on Morningside Heights and will soon do so again. If his engagements permit he will certainly speak at the Casa Italiana within a few weeks. Senator Croce, who is the outstanding philosophical mind of this generation, has frequently been invited to Columbia but has not been able to accept our invitations. Only within the last few days has he finally decided that he can not arrange to come to the United States in the near future, on the invitation of the Carnegie Endowment for International Peace, in order to address the American Historical Association on the occasion of its annual meeting at Washington in December next. Had Senator Croce been able to accept that invitation, he certainly would have spoken at Columbia to our students of philosophy and to those of Italian.

Senator Guglielmo Ferrero, whose name is also mentioned in this article, was invited by the director of the Casa Italiana in person to speak at the Casa, but was compelled to decline to do so. Signor Ferrero, however, accepted an invitation to lunch here as the guest of the Casa Italiana and met a number of members of the university faculties.

The Casa Italiana has entertained in its rooms Jews and Catholics, fascists and non-fascists in large numbers. No inquiry has ever been made as to the political beliefs of any one of these guests. Among the well-known anti-fascists who have recently received prolonged hospitality at Casa Italiana are Signor Max Ascoli and his wife. Signor Ascoli is now a professor at the New School for Social Research.

Professor Arthur Livingston, to whom reference is made, is one of our most valued scholars, and has for some years been classed as a member of the Department of Romance Languages with the group in French rather than with the group in Italian for budgetary reasons only, and without the slightest reference to any political opinions that he may hold. At the moment he is directing the work of candidates for the degree of doctor of philosophy whose major subject of study is Italian, and he is carrying to completion a translation of the monumental work of the outstanding Italian social philosopher, Pareto.

The Department of Italian at Columbia as now constituted has been in the habit of recommending for appointment to professorships of Italian in other institutions outstanding scholars, always because of their fitness and without any regard whatever to the fact that they might have publicly made anti-fascist declarations. One scholar, in particular, who was appointed not long ago to a professorship elsewhere on the recommendation of our department was a signer of Senator Croce's well-known manifesto.

*The Nation's* anonymous contributor is singularly misinformed as to the director of the Casa Italiana. When Professor Prezzolini first came to Columbia more than ten years ago as a member of the staff of the Summer Session, it was Professor Livingston who had suggested and urged his appointment because of his reputation in Europe as an outstanding scholar and man of letters. Those who supported this proposal were assailed at that time for having invited to this country so conspicuous an anti-fascist as Professor Prezzolini. When Professor Prezzolini was named director of the Casa Italiana, he occupied the distinguished post of chief of the literary section and of the information section of the Institute of International Cooperation of the League of Nations at Geneva. It may be of some interest to know that he was elected to that post by the votes of all the members of the League of Nations with the exception of Italy and Paraguay.

I can only repeat that *The Nation* has been imposed upon by a contributor who fails to accept public responsibility for his misstatements. My answer to your question is that Dr. Butler will not act for the convincing reason that there is nothing for him to act upon.

[Signed] NICHOLAS MURRAY BUTLER

*The Nation* received President Butler's letter with mingled feelings of satisfaction and sorrow: satisfaction because the letter itself is a complete refutation of the charge that *The Nation* has been imposed upon; sorrow because it is clear that Dr. Butler has been grossly deceived by subordinates in whom he has apparently trusted. Dr. Butler has been imposed upon, not *The Nation*. Despite its sweeping denials and general assertions, Dr. Butler's letter with its numerous irrelevancies fails to answer or even to mention many of the specific points made in the article on "Fascism at Columbia University" and the editorial which accompanied it in last week's *Nation*. Among these are the following:

1. That the Casa Italiana has refused to permit in its publications any opinion at variance with fascist doctrine.

2. That such noted Italian liberals as Count Sforza and Professor Salvemini have never been invited to speak at the Casa, whatever visits any of them may have made to the university.

3. That Professor Prezzolini, director of the Casa and former liberal journalist, in 1933 announced outspoken support of Mussolini and fascism.

4. That Professor Riccio's dissertation linking Prezzolini and the *Voce* movement to fascism was "fraudulent in conception and execution and could not have borne the imprimatur of a university unless special pressure was at work."

5. That Prezzolini was aware of the purpose and nature of this dissertation and aided in its publication. (Here let us state that we have learned

that the printing of Professor Riccio's scandalous dissertation was subsidized by the Casa Italiana.)

6. That Professor Riccio was secretary of the committee in charge of arrangements for the recent visit of the Italian university students to this country and that on October 23 he received a medal from the Italian Government for his services in its behalf.

7. That an intimate association and regular correspondence exist between the Italian Embassy at Washington, the Italian Consul-General's office in New York, the office of the *Fasci all' Estero* of Rome and the Casa Italiana.

8. That student gatherings for the purpose of discussing fascist rule are forbidden at the Casa.

9. That the real purpose of the Casa educational bureau is to carry on fascist propaganda among the Italian American population of New York.

10. That the Consul-General's office last year gave $3,000 to the Casa, and that the Italian Government originally donated most of the furnishings.

11. That the *Italy-America Monthly*, the official publication of the Casa, is frankly fascist in character, that it has not once carried a controversial article in its nine months of existence, and that its leading article has consistently been written by Beniamino de Riti, a fascist propagandist who is not affiliated with Columbia University.

Let us now deal specifically with the denials and counter-charges contained in Dr. Butler's letter.

1. The reason for the anonymity of the article will be obvious to any one who understands the methods employed by fascist agents and organizations. The identity of the author is known to *The Nation*, his reliability is beyond question, and he is prepared to accept responsibility for his statements if any legal challenge is offered.

2. Dr. Butler calls the fascist professors mentioned in the article "distinguished scholars, so recognized on either side of the Atlantic." Professor Riccio's dissertation would hardly entitle him to this rank. His dissertation has been sharply attacked as a miserable fraud. (See Professor Gaetano Salvemini's article in the Belgian review *Res Publica*, December, 1932, Brussels, and the pamphlet issued last year by Carlo Rossi and Antonio Marchi, "An Academic Scandal at Columbia University.") Has Dr. Butler ever read either the dissertation or the pamphlet which demolishes it?

3. To say, as Dr. Butler does, that the Casa "is wholly without political purpose or significance" is merely to substitute an ideal for a fact. In 1926 the Italian consuls in the United States were designated as lieutenants of Il Duce himself, and all persons of Italian origin living in America were placed under their direct orders and absolute obedience was demanded of them. The Casa Italiana has been and is subject to the orders of the Italian Consul-General in New York through its director, Giuseppe Prezzolini, who is still an Italian subject. All its "splendid physical resources" have been, with the exception of the Paterno Library which is a part of the university library system, exclusively controlled by the fascist group. Thus the Casa Italiana bears no similarity to Schermerhorn Hall or the Maison Française.

4. *The Nation's* contributor did not question the personal relationships existing between Count Sforza, Senator Croce, Guglielmo Ferrero and Dr. Butler, or the fact that Count Sforza has "visited us on Morningside Heights." The article did not imply that either Columbia University as a whole or President Butler as an individual was fascist. The fact remains that, in spite of Dr. Butler's friendship and his undoubted influence at Columbia, not one of these distinguished gentlemen has ever spoken at the Casa Italiana. To say that Count Sforza will speak there in the future and that Senator Croce "certainly would have spoken . . . to students of Italian" had he come to Columbia, raises the question of Dr. Butler's speculative powers. It is our guess that, in the future, the Casa will think it wise to include a few non-fascists among its speakers, if any is willing to accept.

5. Dr. Butler asserts that Guglielmo Ferrero was invited to speak at the Casa Italiana by Prezzolini. If so, *The Nation's* article was in error on this point. However, he did not speak. Nor did the Casa Italiana, as Dr. Butler claims, invite Signor Ferrero to luncheon during his visit to Columbia. Professor Prezzolini, acting as an individual, invited Ferrero to a luncheon at the Faculty Club which was attended by "a number of members of the university faculties." This luncheon was not even under the auspices of the Casa.

6. *The Nation's* contributor did not state that either Jews or Catholics were excluded from the Casa. But what anti-fascists have been "recently" entertained there? Professor and Mrs. Ascoli were housed there for three weeks in 1931, two years before Professor Prezzolini became an avowed fascist. Dr. Ascoli's letter to *The Nation*, although revealing a regrettable error of fact, reveals also his clear understanding of the political nature of the Casa.

7. Count Facchetti-Guiglia, a leader among Italians of fascist sympathies in New York, made a speech at a banquet at the Hotel Commodore in 1927 to raise money for the Casa. He denounced Professor Arthur Livingston as an anti-fascist, and stated that no money for the Casa would be forthcoming from Italian Americans sympathetic to fascism until Professor Livingston's connection with the Casa and the Italian Department should be severed. If Professor Livingston was transferred to the French Department for "budgetary reasons only" shortly after Facchetti-Guiglia's speech, the coincidence seems strange indeed. In any case, we should like an explanation of the "budgetary reasons" for Dr. Livingston's removal from the Italian Department. Might they not be related to the fact that places had to be made for two additional professors: Riccio, author of the dissertation on Prezzolini, and Prezzolini, director of the Casa?

8. Dr. Butler also states that Prezzolini was brought to Columbia by Professor Livingston and not by Professor Bigongiari. If this is so, *The Nation's* investigator was misled by public declarations to the contrary made by Professors Bigongiari and Riccio and others at the Casa on numerous occasions.

9. Dr. Butler's reference to Prezzolini as "so conspicuous an anti-fascist" must seem more humorous to us than to the director of the Casa himself. Prezzolini was indeed considered an anti-fascist—ten years ago when he first visited Columbia—but when he changed his allegiance and came out in support of the dictatorship of Mussolini, he permitted—even aided—the publication of Riccio's dissertation, which had as its purpose the reconstructing of Prezzolini's past to make it appear as a forerunner of fascism. "The Threshold of Fascism" was the title of the work. Prezzolini can not have it both ways; since he has chosen the fascist interpretation of his life's work, we have a right to ask that President Butler do the same.

The charges made in *The Nation's* article last week were sound. The fascist control of the Casa Italiana is beyond dispute. It is a matter of grave public concern when even a single department of a great American university is controlled by representatives or adherents of a foreign dictatorship and its activities turned to partisan political ends. President Butler has refused to act. He asserts that "there is nothing for him to act upon." We have no doubt that the information he received from the "distinguished scholars" in the Italian Department only served to fortify his natural belief in their integrity and academic standing. We ask him again, most earnestly, to go behind these returns and check the facts for himself. There are impartial scholars at Columbia who could tell him the truth. If he does not care to find it out, there are others who do; undoubtedly the Congressional Committee on Un-American Activities would be happy to investigate the relations of the Casa and the Fascist Government. But that should not be necessary. Columbia should be able to clear its own name.—*The Nation.*

## MERITED SEVERITY

The decision of the City College faculty to expel twenty-one students and to impose lesser penalties on sixteen others who took leading parts in the disorderly demonstration of October 9 has been described as the most drastic disciplinary action ever taken at the college. So drastic is it that there may be a tendency to condemn the professors for undue severity in decreeing what, in effect, is an end to the academic careers of the expelled students.

Before the faculty is judged, however, it would be wise to consider the happenings which led it to impose such extreme punishment. For several years City College has appeared in the news as a place where ill-mannered young dissenters insisted on having their own way, regardless of how their actions might affect the rights or the safety of others. True, they constituted a small minority of the 7,000 to 8,000 students of the day session who, for the most part, preferred to go about their studies rather than to take part in the "mass picketing" which the young radicals at City College seem to have developed to a high point of efficiency. But the fact that the demonstrators were in a minority did not lessen the harm which the prestige of the city's free college suffered.

The disorder on October 9 took place while the college was holding official exercises to welcome a group of visiting Italian students. City College men who purported to see in the exercises an official sanction of Fascism had been told they might hold their protest in the college stadium. This did not appease them. When they insisted on disrupting the official greetings in the great hall of the college the faculty properly decided that discipline must be enforced. Even then it did not act hastily. It waited more than a month, until it had made a thorough investigation. Its discipline is severe but just.—*The New York Sun.*

### CREATING "GUTTERSNIPES"

THE continued uproar at City College is but one example of the unrest sweeping American colleges. It is only natural that, in a time of wide-spread economic distress, students should become vitally interested in social problems. It is also natural that, seeing the wreckage made of education and of free thought by Fascist régimes in Europe, our students should become conscious of and frequently overwrought by the menace Fascism holds for free institutions.

Where college executives are wise and well balanced, this new interest has been welcomed as a stimulus to serious study and discussion. Issues have been thrashed out in the classroom from every possible angle, and what had before seemed dull subjects and humdrum courses have been made of immediate interest and concern.

Certainly from the standpoint of the true teacher, interested not in regimenting his students but in opening their minds to the wonders of science and the great problems of society, the new attitude must seem a blessing.

Unfortunately, some college presidents have turned a blessing into a cause of continual wrangling. Teachers have been muzzled and students have been stigmatized as "Communist." Supposed "educators" who saw no harm in the vacuous folk who went to college for football and frat dances drew back in horror at students really interested in the world about them.

Dr. Frederick B. Robinson, president of City College, seems to be that kind of educator. He shows a bad temper and lack of tact in handling young people. The attitude of young people toward them is usually a good index to the real character of their elders.

If Dr. Robinson is unable to keep order at City College, the fault may be his students'. The fault may also be Dr. Robinson's. And the clue to that fault may well lie in the drastic action just taken by the faculty under pressure from Dr. Robinson and over the recommendations of the dean. The expulsion of twenty-one students is extraordinary even at City College.

Dr. Robinson has been trying to keep order by strongarm methods for a long time—ever since he became president. He has sought to control student newspapers, suppress student self-government and crush free speech by the faculty. If the result is a plague of riots, picketings, sidewalk scribblings and a long list of protests unbecoming both to students and to the college, the cause may be found in this repressive attitude, an attitude that hardly breeds respect.

Dean Gottschall, after an investigation, merely recommended suspensions on the grounds that disorder during the reception to the Italian Fascist delegation "was not the result of a carefully arranged plot to disrupt the meeting or gain possession of the platform." He could have added that there might have been less disorder had Dr. Robinson not called his own students "guttersnipes" when they booed references to Fascism.

Though the students may have been unruly, Dr. Robinson himself should have used better judgment. Dr. Robinson's attitude breeds "guttersnipes."—*The New York Evening Post.*

## REPORTS

### SECONDARY SCHOOL POPULATION

DESPITE the fact that the democracy of public education in the United States has brought into the high schools a larger proportion of pupils from varied intellectual, social and economic groups than ever before, "there is still considerable economic selection, a selection which keeps down the proportion of children from the lower economic levels completing the work of the secondary schools." This is the general conclusion of the National Survey of Secondary Education as reported in a monograph Survey report, "The Secondary School Population," available from the Government Printing Office, Washington, D. C.

Within 50 years, 1880 to 1930, enrolment in high school advanced from 3 per cent. of boys and girls between 14 and 17 years of age in the nation to more than 46 per cent. Of the 3,940,000 young people from 14 to 17 years of age throughout the country in 1880, few more than 110,000 were enrolled in public secondary schools. In 1930, by way of contrast, of the 9,340,000 young people within this age group in the United States, 4,399,000 were enrolled in public secondary schools. This increase in high-school enrolment proves a corresponding growth in popularization of secondary education, the National Survey report indicates.

Prepared by Grayson N. Kefauver, Victor H. Noll and C. Elwood Drake, specialists in school organization of the National Survey of Secondary Education, this monograph is one of 28 now in process of publication. The study involves an analysis of changes in secondary-school population and in characteristics of secondary-school pupils. The latter investigation concerned pupils in full-time schools and is based upon visits to 34 schools in 13 cities.

The National Survey of Secondary Education was conducted under the auspices of the Federal Office of Education by authority of Congress, with Dr. William John Cooper, who was then United States Commissioner of Education, as director. Dr. Leonard V. Koos, professor of secondary education, University of Chicago, was associate director. The major burden of directing and handling the survey was entrusted to Dr. Koos, eminent in the field of secondary education. The study, which results from a 3-year investigation by a distinguished group, it is emphasized by Carl A. Jessen, survey coordinator and present Federal Office of Education specialist in secondary education, aimed primarily at discovering and studying not the usual but the unusual practises, not the ordinary but extraordinary ones.

It is noted in the study of the secondary-school population that the increase in its popularity has occurred more rapidly in urban schools than in rural schools. For example, 67 per cent. of pupils 14 to 17 years of age were enrolled in urban high schools in 1930 compared with less than half of this number, 31 per cent., in rural high schools. The proportions of pupils in this level of education, it is pointed out, vary from state to state and from one type of community to another.

The results of a study of Seattle and Bridgeport, dealing with the social composition of the high-school enrolment, disclose striking increases from 1920 to 1930 in the proportionate representation in the high school of all occupational levels. This finding harmonizes with the general conclusion that there is a rapidly increasing popularization of high-school education.

However, when the increases of the different social and economic groups represented in the high school are compared, for Seattle the groups of the upper levels during the period, already larger at the outset, were gaining on the groups at the lower level. The gains were larger, for example, for the proprietary and professional groups than for skilled and common labor. For Bridgeport, on the other hand, the proportions at the different levels appeared to be drawing together.

"The evidence presented seems to indicate progress toward intellectual democratization," the survey report reveals, "that is, toward increased representation in secondary schools of intellectually less competent youth. It is not that intellectual selection is no longer operative, but that it is less operative than formerly. There is evidence that in many communities the secondary-school population as a whole is not far from being a representative cross-section of at least the total literate population. The data at hand are not sufficient to yield a statement of the exact degree of progress toward intellectual democratization of education at the secondary level."

Regarded as an important conclusion is the finding that secondary education is becoming intellectually more democratic through the extension of courses to include vocational and other non-college subjects.

The analysis of secondary school characteristics involved more than 17,000 pupils. The analysis includes pupils as well as schools, intelligence and success of pupils in school work, social and economic status and other characteristics of pupils and parents such as birthplace, education and occupational status.

Pupils whose fathers were engaged in upper economic levels or professional groups were found to take a larger proportion of academic and scientific courses in high school. Pupils from lower economic levels were found more frequently studying household and industrial arts courses. About one fourth of the high-school pupils taking academic and scientific courses were from homes in which fathers were at the semi-professional level. About one sixth of the pupils in household arts and industrial arts groups came from this level. About one tenth of the pupils studying academic and scientific courses came from the professional level.

In the study of other pupil characteristics, the National Survey school population study revealed that nearly all pupils were born in the United States. Forty-three per cent. of the fathers of pupils enrolled in trade schools included in the study were born in this country. The percentage of foreign-born parents varies among the other types of schools included in the survey. From 10 to 20 per cent. of the pupils' mothers were found to be employed outside the home.

Practically all the pupils, in the full-time schools examined, plan to graduate from high school. Pupils from all schools plan to go to college, but the proportions are much larger for the academic groups. As many as one fifth of the pupils in the industrial group and in the comprehensive and general schools are ambitious to enter college. Approximately the same proportion in the commercial group express this desire.

# EDUCATIONAL RESEARCH AND STATISTICS

## AN OBJECTIVE ENGLISH SCHOLARSHIP EXAMINATION

### I. The Competitive Examinations

The University of Chicago offers once a year a series of scholarship examinations to senior high school students. In May, 1934, 894 students from 108 high schools took the examinations in Chicago and seventeen outside centers. On the basis of the results of three hours of testing, twenty-five full scholarships and twenty-two half scholarships were awarded. Past records show that these students are destined to be the most successful group of students at the university—more successful than students selected in any other way.

According to the present program, scholarships are awarded on the basis of the combined scores on three one-hour examinations in three different subjects which the student has previously selected. The only restriction placed on his choice is that he take at least one examination from the following subjects: English, world history, mathematics, Latin, French, German and Spanish, and not more than two from physics, chemistry and biology.

### II. The English Examination Problem

The candidates are informed in advance that the examination in English composition and literature will be based on "College Entrance Requirements" in the field; at the University of Chicago, the entrance requirement is any three units approved by the high school. Obviously, with more than one hundred high schools from many parts of the country involved, no uniformity of curriculum or reading requirements exists. Such a condition makes almost impossible the task of constructing an examination which will not arouse protest.

The conditions under which the examinations are given impose certain restrictions. Sixty minutes is a short time for testing a very general and difficult field. Because the tests must be scored, the necessary statistical computations made, the various test scores combined, lists of student names made and scholarship winners determined within five hours after the examination is given, completely objective tests must be used. Other valid reasons for the use of objective tests in scholarship examinations have been given.[1] A further restriction is that the tests must be sufficiently difficult to differentiate among the top ranking ten or twenty students.[2]

Because of the nature of the curriculum and the usually ineffective teaching in high-school English, the students who take this examination

[1] John M. Stalnaker and M. W. Richardson, "Scholarship Examinations," *Journal of Higher Education*, V (1934), 306.

[2] The distributions of scores should be positively skewed. As the test is designed to select from eight or nine hundred students the top twenty or thirty, it is of no consequence if half of the students get a score of zero, so long as the remaining students, particularly at the top, have scores which are distinguishable from one another.

are frequently not so well prepared as are students who take the examination in, say, mathematics or physics. Furthermore, the group which takes the English examination includes not only those students whose special ability lies in the field of English, but many another who, having selected two other fields because of his aptitude in them, decides that, after all, English is any one's field.

Is it possible to devise a test, completely objective, sixty minutes in length, on which the high ranking students will be highly successful in college composition and literature work? The problem, at first glance an appalling one, seems less hopeless when one bears in mind the purpose of the examination—to select from the group the most potentially successful students—and the fact that the content of the examination need not be restricted to material covered in the average high-school English course. General information about the field, advanced knowledge and skills, reasoning items and intelligence test items are quite permissible.[3] In fact, it is probably true in the field of English literature more than in any other, that the superior student will have knowledge and familiarity with material beyond the limits of the curriculum.

### III. The Examination

The May, 1934, examination consisted of eight sections. The student was free within the sixty minutes allowed to devote as much time as he chose to any one section. The first section was a vocabulary test of the recall type—typical intelligence material—which consisted of twenty-five sentences, in each of which one word was omitted except for the first letter. The student, aided by one or two synonyms, was to determine the missing word.

*Example:* All my life, he has been held
up to me as a p—(pattern,
model of excellence). . . ________

The highest score obtained was eighteen out of a possible twenty-five; the average score (mean) was six (standard deviation, four). Six per cent. of the group received a score of zero. No item was failed or answered correctly by all the students. Although on the average this section constituted only 7 per cent. of the total score, the correlation between the scores on this section and the scores on the total test was .65. (See Table 1 for complete data.)

TABLE 1

The Behavior of the Various Sections of the English Scholarship Test, 1934

| Section | Maximum points possible | Average score | Sigma[1] | Sk.[2] | r with total[3] |
|---|---|---|---|---|---|
| (1) Vocabulary | 25 | 5.7 | 4.0 | +0.47 | .65 |
| (2) Word change | 20 | 7.9 | 4.8 | +0.13 | .58 |
| (3) Categories | 36 | 19.7 | 7.6 | −0.07 | .73 |
| (4) Poetry identification | 24 | 7.5 | 6.4 | +0.18 | .68 |
| (5) Verse forms | 18 | 9.6 | 4.4 | −0.12 | .65 |
| (6) Prose and criticism | 35 | 11.5 | 9.1 | +0.40 | .63 |
| (7) Poetry appreciation | 25 | 8.7 | 6.8 | +0.37 | .49 |
| (8) Topic sentence | 14 | 6.1 | 4.8 | −0.01 | .23 |
| Total | 197 | 77.4 | 28.4 | +0.24 | |

[1] Sigma is the standard deviation of the distribution.

[2] Sk. is the measure of skewness. $Sk = \frac{3(M-Md)}{\sigma}$

[3] r is Pearson coefficient of correlation.

The second section, which was also intended to measure verbal or linguistic intelligence, was patterned after an exercise in the Scholastic Aptitude Test of the College Entrance Examination Board. The student was asked to find, in each of ten paragraphs, the one word which had been changed so as to destroy the meaning of the paragraph.

*Example:* George Moore says that happiness is no more than a faculty for being surprised; and it is the sudden vista, the beauty of a city square seen through falling snow, a street-car drama, the face of a passing woman, the dialogue of friends, which make the commonplaces for the man with the eye for copy.

Although these items had not been subjected to a careful experimental check in advance,

[3] Stalnaker and Richardson, *op. cit.*, 309.

they were, with one exception, satisfactory. In the example given, the correct word, *commonplaces,* was marked by 43 per cent. of the students. The average score on the total examination of this group was 92.[4] *Copy,* an incorrect word, was marked by 20 per cent. of the students, who averaged only 70 on the total examination. A few students marked: *happiness, no, faculty, surprised, sudden, vista, square, passing, dialogue, make* and *man.* The average score of these students was 69. Selections for such a test which are both satisfactory and of the correct degree of difficulty are not easily found. The average score on the exercise was four items; two of the 373 students answered all ten items correctly; twenty-nine students answered none correctly. The correlation between this section and the vocabulary section was .41.

The third section—herein called "Categories" —was designed to measure factual knowledge of literary history. It consisted of twelve lists of authors, each list containing six names, five of which were related in some way. The student was asked to check the one name in each list which had no relation to the others, to indicate the period during which the remaining five lived and to identify the *genre* in which their work falls.

*Example:* ——— Period
——— Category
——— Bennett, Arnold
——— Conrad, Joseph
——— Dickens, Charles
——— Galsworthy, John
——— Maugham, Somerset
——— Wells, Herbert George

In the example given, the correct period is *20th century;* the category, *British novelists;* the incorrect name, *Charles Dickens.* One student obtained a score of thirty-five out of the thirty-six points possible. Six students scored zero. This section proved a little too easy for a scholarship examination: the distribution of scores was approximately normal, rather than positively skewed.

Section four required the identification of the authors of nine short but characteristic passages of American poetry. Nine poets were listed, although not all of them were represented by selections, and some had more than one selection. The task thus narrowed itself down to recognizing which of the nine poets listed might most likely have written a given selection. In the example given, Masters is the author, and 16 per cent. of the students so marked the selection, although 18 per cent. attributed it to Sandburg, 12 per cent. to E. A. Robinson, 7 per cent. to Robert Frost, 7 per cent. to E. E. Cummings, etc.

*Example:* Where are Elmer, Herman, Bert, Tom and Charley,
The weak of will, the strong of arm, the clown, the boozer, the fighter?

Twenty-two per cent. of the students could identify none of the selections. Six students (2 per cent.) received perfect scores. In general, Robinson, Millay, Masters, Whitman, etc., are not read in the high-school classroom, but superior students interested in literature should be familiar with American poetry.

Section five (Verse Forms) called for the classification of each of nine poems according to its form—ballad, blank verse, couplet, etc. This exercise proved to be easier than other sections, although only 4 per cent. of the students received a perfect score and 3 per cent. identified none correctly. The average score was 9.6 (total possible, 18). This section measures factual knowledge, but knowledge slightly off the beaten track. The example given is blank verse.

*Example:* I shall not go back.
We pay for going back; and all we get
Is one more needless ounce of weary wisdom
To bring away with us.

The next part of the examination was an experimental form aiming to measure the students' feeling for language. To be sure, it was made on a reasonably low level, but the linguistic ability of senior high school students is poor. Seven selections of prose, from ninety to two hundred and fifty words in length, and varying in style from that of John Dewey to that of Hemingway, were given, together with a critical descriptive comment on the style of each selection. The student's task was to match the

[4] The average score for all students was 77; standard deviation, 28. See Table 1.

comment with the prose selection to which it referred. The total possible score was thirty-five; the average score was 11.5, or slightly over two correct matchings. About 4 per cent. of the students answered the entire exercise correctly, and 19 per cent. scored zero. Because this exercise has been thoroughly described elsewhere, no illustration is given here.[5]

An ingenious poetry appreciation test devised by Professor Walter Blair, of the University of Chicago, was used in section seven. A poem was rewritten in four different versions, each version introducing some obvious flaw. The student was to select the best version, and to identify the defect in each of the other four from a given key, such as: (1) too sentimental, (2) faulty rhythm, etc. Although 5 per cent. of the students received a perfect score on the exercise, 21 per cent. did not have even one correct response. The original poem was voted, not the best, but third best. The first ranking poem, in the judgment of these students, started:

> Steeped in dust sleeps a pallid lady:
> Thin and tall and blonde was she; . . .

The second ranking poem is in the Guest style:

> Here slumbers a wonderful mother
> Bereft and sad her children three
> They sadly mourn for their wonderful mother
> Who taught them all to pray at her knee. . . .

The average score was 8.6 out of 25, or somewhat more than one of the five marked correctly. Such a brief exercise is of course not very reliable, but it measures an ability of considerable significance.

The final section consisted of two paragraphs, the topic sentences of which were to be underlined. This exercise was not found to be satisfactory.

## IV. An Analysis of the Results

Unquestionably, the teacher who had stressed in his cramming class the typical English course content would be distressed to find an objective examination of the type here described. But is the examination of value? Is it worth while? One measure which is generally made is of the consistency or reliability of the examination. The reliability of this examination (odd *vs.* even items) was .88. Even correlating the scores on the four odd-numbered sections with the four even-numbered sections, and then estimating the reliability in the usual way, gave a coefficient of .76, a high reliability in view of the lack of homogeneity of material and the shortness of the sections. The total examination gave the desired positively skewed distribution of scores, on the basis of which it was possible to differentiate easily among the high ranking students.

The most significant measure of success of the examination would be the subsequent records in college of the highest ranking students. This obviously can not be determined at once. An additional complication is the fact that the scholarships are awarded on the basis of three examinations in three different subjects. The five highest persons in the English examination were also sufficiently high in their other examinations to be awarded full scholarships. Students ranking in sixth, eighth and tenth positions in the English examination did so poorly—below the average of the group—in one of their other examinations that they were not in the scholarship range. The ninth ranking student was awarded a full scholarship and the seventh ranking student a half scholarship. Obviously, the English examination selected students who were found by the other examinations to be superior: seven of the highest ten students were awarded scholarships.

## V

The examination here described was not built of carefully analyzed test items; its items will not be used again; it will not be standardized, published or sold. It was devised and constructed for a specific function—to select the best of a group of highly selected students. Such post-analysis as is given here is for the purpose of improving the next examination. Test forms, rather than specific content, are being analyzed. The content appears to be unorthodox, but the examination is reliable, and as far as present measures of validity are possible, it appears to be valid.

John M. Stalnaker
The University of Chicago

[5] See John M. Stalnaker, "The Cream of the Crop in English," to be published in *The English Journal*.

# SCHOOL AND SOCIETY

WITH WHICH ARE COMBINED THE EDUCATIONAL REVIEW, ESTABLISHED IN 1891, THE TEACHERS MAGAZINE, ESTABLISHED IN 1878, AND THE SCHOOL JOURNAL, ESTABLISHED IN 1874.

Volume 40 SATURDAY, DECEMBER 1, 1934 Number 1040


## THE HISTORY OF STUDENT RESIDENTIAL HOUSING


By Dr. W. H. COWLEY

THE OHIO STATE UNIVERSITY


To achieve an understanding of the present-day residential housing situation for students in the American college and university one must review with some care the pressures from the past which have produced it. One of three major philosophies, developed largely from historical accidents, has consciously or unconsciously dominated the thinking of every dormitory builder and every student residence planner since the erection of Harvard Hall in 1639. These philosophies can neither be comprehended nor evaluated without being traced both to and from their sources. An awareness of the influences of former times may be expected to illuminate and perhaps to give better direction to present and future practises.

### STUDENT HOUSING IN THE MIDDLE AGES

Housing, whether for citizens or for students, always becomes a problem when population takes a sudden turn upward. How and where to house students became a matter of concern in the universities of the Middle Ages chiefly because thousands of vagantes, or wandering students, flocked to the seats of learning at Bologna and Paris and Oxford. In 1262 the Bologna faculties were lecturing to almost 10,000 students. In 1257 Oxford enrolled 3,000; and Paris in the same century numbered 30,000. That the influx of these hordes of students created a housing problem of considerable magnitude is clear when one remembers that medieval cities seldom numbered more than five thousand.

Moreover, these multitudes of students were practically all in their teens, and the majority of them not over 14 or 15. Although they organized into self-governing (and faculty-governing) groups, the need for discipline and control grew the more they fought among themselves, with the townsmen and with the civil and ecclesiastical authorities. Many students, furthermore, were poverty-stricken. Sons of wealthy men could hire suites or houses for themselves and their retinues, but some provision became necessary for the poor beneficiarii whose resources often amounted to no more than the scant clothes upon their backs. In the early days of Bologna and Paris students lived anywhere they could find lodging. Some rented garrets, some boarded with masters, still others with townsmen, and a few took over houses of their own. Slowly from this confusion there grew up a housing plan which, in its general outlines, has continued at Oxford and Cambridge ever since.

Some time during the twelfth century the students at Bologna began to withdraw from the homes of townsmen and masters and to organize into groups called socii. They hired houses and set up establishments known as hospicia or hostels. The plan spread to Paris and to Oxford. At the former they were first called paedagogies and at the latter halls and colleges. Each group elected one of its number to manage its affairs. On the Continent these leaders were known as regents or paedagogues and at Oxford as principals.[1] The university had no control over either the halls or their principals.[2] They were democratic, self-governing groups which set up their own financial and disciplinary regulations and their own methods of enforcement. Each student maintained his personal autonomy, however, and could move freely from one establishment to another if he found the food or his associates or the discipline distasteful.

### The Growth of the Oxford and Cambridge Colleges

In the course of time special hostels were organized and endowed by pious founders to provide residences for the poorer students. According to Rashdall,[3] these establishments were "mere eleemosynary institutions for poor boys. . . . The objective of the . . . founders was simply to secure board and lodging for poor students who could not pay for it themselves." Over these endowed hostels or domus pauperum the universities gradually asserted authority. They began by insisting upon approving the principals or paedagogues elected by the students. Soon thereafter they took over the prerogative of nominating the principals, and with this arrangement well established they appointed older students, and later members of the faculty. By the time Elizabeth came to the throne of England, the complete responsibility of the university authorities for the halls had been permanently fixed.

Meanwhile the ability of the student to move from one hospicium to another had been limited first at Paris and then at Oxford and Cambridge. In 1452 the chancellor of Paris ruled that no paedagogue could receive into his house a student who had left another paedagogium to avoid correction. Five years later he ordered that all students were required to live in paedagogies and that no new halls could be established without his permission. In the course of two centuries the houses which students had established on their own initiative had passed entirely from their control into the hands of the university authorities.

The Oxford and Cambridge colleges of to-day have come down through the centuries step by step, following this chain of developments. After 1284, when John Peckham, Archbishop of Canterbury, spoke of Walter of Merton as the "founder and planter of your college," the endowed halls at Oxford and Cambridge came in time to be known as colleges. At the beginning of the fourteenth century three colleges and 300 halls were flourishing at Oxford, but by the beginning of the sixteenth century 10 colleges had appeared and the number of halls had been reduced to 55. To-day Oxford[4] is made up of 23 colleges, all separate corporations, one public hall and seven private halls. One of the colleges and four of the halls are for women. They are all, as at Cambridge, under the control of the faculties. Student self-government has slowly worn away through the centuries.

### The Disappearance of Colleges on the Continent

The residential colleges at Oxford and Cambridge were duplicated from the fourteenth to the eighteenth centuries in

[1] H. Rashdall, "The Universities of Europe in the Middle Ages," Vol. I, p. 481. Oxford, 1895.

[2] *Ibid.*, Vol. II, p. 607.

[3] H. Rashdall, *Op. cit.*, Vol. I, pp. 482 and 495.

[4] Cambridge comprises 18 colleges for men and two for women.

France and from the fourteenth to the sixteenth centuries in Germany. During the fourteenth century 40 colleges were in operation at the University of Paris. The collegiate system, indeed, originated at Paris and had been taken over to Oxford and Cambridge during the middle of the thirteenth century. In Germany,[5] upon the founding of the great universities during the 150 years preceding the Reformation, halls or Bursen were organized. The Reformation, however, changed the structure of the universities of Central Europe, and the Bursen[6] disappeared to give place, in the course of time, to the boarding house system in vogue to-day. The French retained their colleges more tenaciously, but all educational institutions in France closed their doors during the Revolution. Upon their reorganization in 1808 the residential foundations vanished.

Besides the Reformation and Revolution other factors contributed to the abandonment of the residential system in continental countries. Before the Lutheran revolt all members of German faculties were required to live in Bursenzwanz or celibacy. The great majority of them, therefore, were clerics who favored the monastic mores of their orders. In about 500 St. Benedict had brought to Europe the monastic system which had become so prominent a part of the religious life of the East and the Near East. He substituted, however, group life for the eremitical practises which predominated among oriental Christians. The establishment of the Benedictine and later orders and the setting up of monasteries influenced all the life of the Middle Ages and in turn had its effect upon the universities. With the break from the church which followed Luther's theses, the monastic system waned in Germany. As it waned in religious groups it all but disappeared from the universities. Members of the faculty married, the clerical garb which scholars had universally worn gave way to civilian dress, and the majority of students were no longer clerks reading for holy orders.

The German Bursen, moreover, had been of a different character from the French and English halls. Large sleeping rooms or dormitories were more common than the smaller studies and bedrooms in France and England. Students, sometimes as many as 200, slept in large rooms, and often at the command of their provincial rulers they lived in barracks, better to be hardened for military service. The disappearance of the monastic system brought these large sleeping apartments into disrepute because of their close resemblance to the dormitories of the religious orders. The Bursen, in fact, disappeared entirely.

Still another factor entered into the situation. Both German and French educators, during the latter part of the eighteenth century, under the influence of the Encyclopedists, gave all their enthusiasm to scholarship and the advancement of knowledge. What monies they had available they preferred to devote to instruction and research. When the University of Berlin was established in 1809 no provisions were made for the housing of students, not only because the need of dormitories was no longer apparent but also because the leading spirits in its founding preferred to put all their emphasis upon spreading the frontiers of knowledge. But following the characteristic British method of procedure, Oxford and Cambridge muddled through with the college system which it had inherited from Paris. The insularity of England protected it from the direct impact of both the Reformation and the Revolution, and the

[5] Frederick Paulsen, "Geschichte des Gelehrten Unterrichts," Vol. I, pp. 260–261. Leipzig: Verlag von Veit und Comp., 1919.

[6] Wilhelm Bruchmüller, "Der Leipzigen Student, 1409–1909," p. 142 *ff*. Leipzig: Teubner, 1909.

colleges continued in the original continental design.

### The American Heritage from England

If the Reformation and the French Revolution, with their attendant influences upon continental education, can be thought of as historical accidents, then the colonization of America, chiefly by Englishmen, may be similarly characterized. The present American system of higher education obviously would not and could not have been developed had Frenchmen or Spaniards dominated America. The colonial American college followed the British pattern because its founders knew no other. More than twoscore Cambridge graduates migrated to the Massachusetts Bay Colony during its first three decades, and naturally enough they brought with them a predilection in favor of the educational structures which they knew in England. With the exception of James Blair, founder of William and Mary, who had been graduated at Edinburgh, all the founders of the colonial colleges were Oxford and Cambridge graduates or Americans who had been educated in England or in the early American colleges established by Englishmen.

The British background of the pre-revolutionary college organizers had more to do with the establishment of residential colleges in America than any other factor. There were, however, several others of importance. College students of the seventeenth century usually entered at 13 or 14 years of age, and since communities were small and travel difficult it was to be expected that the college would board and room them. The founders, moreover, were all devoutly religious men who conceived of the college more as a religious institution than as a seat of learning. Students had souls to be saved and the early faculties were bent upon saving them. To have a student entirely under their control from the 5 A.M. rising time until lights out at 9 gave them the opportunity they sought to minister continuously to the souls' welfare of their charges. Professors and tutors were expected to pray regularly, morning and evening, with their students, and if a youngster misbehaved they believed with certainty that they were exorcising the devil when they whipped him.

It should be observed that the heritage from England by no means completely controlled early American institutions. In both Oxford and Cambridge the universities consisted of a growing number of independent foundations or colleges. In America the collegiate system never developed, chiefly because of the sparsity of the population and its relative poverty. One college at Harvard, one at William and Mary and one at Yale were all that the founders could achieve. They may have had plans for universities just as those in England, but the environmental forces of pioneer America directed their energies into the establishment of institutions which were English in general point of view but American in its implementation. Thus English precedences implanted the residential principle, but American contingencies modified it to fit the colonial situation. In time American colleges and universities were to grow as large and even larger than those in England, but meanwhile English ties had been broken and the American college followed its own course of development. Dormitory buildings were erected, but the British system of coordinate colleges came in for no serious thought until Wilson[7] tried unsuccessfully to introduce it at Princeton in 1905, and Harvard and Yale inaugurated their house plans in the late twenties.

[7] Princeton had made an unsuccessful attempt in 1818 to introduce the British tutorial system. See Varnum Lensing Collins, "Princeton," pp. 134–135. New York: Oxford University Press, 1914.

The chief point of difference between the British and American philosophies of student residential housing has amounted to this: at Oxford and Cambridge the residential colleges developed into highly significant educational agencies; in America dormitories during the nineteenth century became little more than body shelters. The British have used their housing units to bring dons and students together, not only for formal individual conferences upon their academic work but also for social and intellectual intercourse. Kept small by design, the colleges have supplied the Empire with men at once splendidly trained intellectually and admirably cultivated socially. Without labeling oneself an Anglophile one can assert with assurance that Oxford and Cambridge have come nearer satisfying the scholar-and-gentleman ideal than the universities of any other nation.

The early American college might have developed in much the same fashion, had not the pioneer situation and more particularly the bogey of student discipline persistently interfered. Oxford and Cambridge tutors were fortunately relieved of practically all disciplinary responsibilities during the eighteenth century.[8] Deans, proctors and bedels were charged with keeping the peace, and the dons were unhampered by the necessity of enforcing administrative regulations. From this student-teacher relationship the Oxford and Cambridge intellectual and social esprit has grown and flowered.

In America, on the other hand, the faculty member living in the dormitory became the student's natural enemy. Circumstances made him a martinet, and conscientiously he lived up to his responsibilities. The results are well known. Student riots and rebellions against the faculty have bespattered the historical records of every American college up until the inception of athletics and extra-curricular activities in the last decades of the nineteenth century. Students lived under the suspicious eyes of clergyman-professors who, as one historian remarks, were "also required to be detectives, sheriffs, and prosecuting attorneys." "It was my privilege," wrote President White,[9] describing his experiences as an undergraduate at Hobart, "to behold a professor, an excellent clergyman, seeking to quell hideous riot in a student's room, buried under a heap of carpets, mattresses, counterpanes, and blankets; to see another clerical professor forced to retire through the panel of a door under a shower of lexicons, boots and brushes, and to see even the president himself, on one occasion, obliged to leave his lecture-room by a ladder from a window, and, on another, kept at bay by a shower of beer-bottles."

At Dartmouth unpopular members of the faculty were visited by groups of students who would stand outside their windows and blow tin horns late into the night. At Princeton in 1802 the students burned down Nassau Hall, the only college building, and in 1814 for no particular reason they set fire to one of its outhouses and again almost wrecked the hall itself by exploding two pounds of gunpowder in a corridor. A few years earlier the undergraduate body at Williams, chafing under the severities of several of the tutors, petitioned their removal, and when President Olds refused to treat with them the entire junior class stayed away from recitations for almost a week. At Yale in 1828 the food at the commons precipitated the famous "Bread and Butter Rebellion." Two years later the sophomore class none too politely declined to recite their mathe-

[8] Ralph Durand, "Oxford, Its Buildings and Gardens," p. 23. London: Grant Richards, 1909. Also V. L. Collins, *Op. cit.*, p. 191.

[9] "Autobiography of Andrew Dickson White," Vol. I, pp. 18–20. New York: The Century Company, 1905.

matics as the rules required, and the riots that ensued have come down in history as the "Conic Section Rebellion." George Bancroft, greatest American historian of his day, lost an eye when as a Harvard tutor he attempted to quell an incipient uprising. Another Harvard tutor went through the remainder of his life with a limp after an encounter with a group of student assailants. And many were the black eyes and bruised skulls nursed by students and faculty alike.

These citations might be multiplied, but they are enough to demonstrate the faculty-student antipathy in nineteenth century American colleges. Fortunately, Oxford and Cambridge, either by accident or design, avoided these catastrophies by separating their proctoring and instructional functions. Students and tutors became intellectual and often close friends, while in America they battled one another. The more cordial the relationships of the English don and student grew, the more liberal became the instructional procedures. The rigid rules of the proctors and bedels[10] have been unchanged for centuries, but the academic abracadabra of compulsory class attendance, point systems and daily quizzes typical of the American college never appeared. The individual student has been put upon his own in a stimulating educational environment.

Meanwhile disciplinary problems in the American college took on such importance that the dormitory never developed into a meeting place of expanding minds. The office of tutor brought from England in the early days disappeared entirely by the middle of the nineteenth century. Residence halls became places for students merely to sleep, to eat and occasionally to study. The opportunity to make them the core of the educational program has been lost in the disciplinary muddle. The attempts being made to-day at Harvard and Yale to reclaim the dormitory for educational purposes will very likely be successful, but the typical American college will perforce follow the American rather than the British pattern.

10 Called bulldogs by undergraduates.

### THE PARTIAL DISINTEGRATION IN THE NINETEENTH CENTURY

Chiefly because of the messiness and magnitude of the disciplinary problem dormitories came in for a series of attacks during the nineteenth century. In 1830 a speaker at a convention held in connection with the founding of New York University inveighed against dormitories because of the importance which discipline had assumed. His reasoning[11] proceeded as follows:

> It is proper to touch here one peculiar feature of the system of education of the United States . . . , namely, the collegiate life. It is, historically as well as by the name itself, well known to be of monkish origin; it is the remnant of the habit of educating youth in convents; it is the constant source of dissension between the faculty and the student. . . . The education of the young man and its corporal feeding must be separated. A place where a college is placed must afford the student the means of decent living; if it does not, it shows that it is too much secluded from the society of men, to be able to educate a man for the society he is destined to enter.

President Henry Philip Tappan, of the University of Michigan, led the onslaught in the fifties, following the point of view early expressed by the New York University speaker and by President Francis Wayland of Brown. He had been a professor at New York University and, soon after becoming the president of Michigan in 1852, he converted the one dormitory that had been built into classrooms. He expressed the philosophy behind his action as follows:[12]

11 F. Hasler, *Journal of the Proceedings of a Convention of Literary and Scientific Gentlemen*, pp. 262–263. Common Council Chamber of the City of New York, October, 1830. New York: Leavitt and Carvill, 1831. (Reprinted by New York University, 1933.)

The dormitory system is objectionable in itself. By withdrawing young men from the influences of domestic circles, and separating them from the community, they are often led to contract evil habits, and are prone to fall into disorderly conduct. It is a mere remnant of the monkish cloisters of the Middle Ages, still retained in England, but banished from the universities of Germany.

One of the historians of the University of Michigan further illuminated the Tappan point of view when he wrote in 1891 that:[13]

. . . To a certain extent the system of espionage is a necessary concomitant of dormitories, and their abolition was the beginning of a broader and more liberal method of discipline. The charm of dormitory life—for such a charm there doubtless is—was exchanged for the ordinary life of an ordinary lodger. The result was twofold at least. In the first place, it prevented to a great extent concerted attempts at practical jokes and more serious follies of college life, which do not add to proficiency in studies or to the dignity of young manhood, and, secondly, it made the students feel to some extent that they were not a distinct and privileged order of beings, but were of the same clay as the rest of the world around them. . . .

The Tappan philosophy rapidly predominated in the Middle West and West, but there were other points of attack besides discipline. In the first place, Tappan had become enamored of German as opposed to British educational ideology. German thought had begun to attract attention in the United States early in the century upon the occasion of the publication of Madame De Staël's book, "Germany." In 1829 John Griscon's book, "A Year in Europe," appeared, followed in 1831 by an English translation from the French of M. Victor Couzens' "Report on the State of Public Instruction in Prussia." These volumes found no American reader more interested than Dr. Tappan, who later traveled in Germany and brought home with him the conviction that the Prussian educational system must be "acknowledged to be the most perfect educational system in the world." He made every attempt, therefore, to transplant the Prussian program to the University of Michigan and to the schools of the state.

Since German universities paid no attention to students outside of the classroom and since they insisted that they find their own social life and boarding and rooming facilities, Tappan introduced the same methods at Ann Arbor. With the rapid growth of state universities immediately after the Civil War, his ideas came in for considerable vogue. The German point of view also gained strength from the return to the United States of hundreds of professors who had taken graduate work at Berlin, Leipzig, Heidelberg and Göttingen. The German point of view, in fact, ruled, and as it grew in popularity dormitories were frowned upon, occasionally abolished, and seldom built at state universities.

The financial situation in these new institutions fanned the flame of disapproval. All available monies were needed for instruction. Dormitories were expensive to build and state university administrators, anxious for their institutions to become the academic equals of those in the East, put all their funds into salaries, classrooms and laboratories. Moreover, state university students were, in general, poor boys and girls who could ill afford to pay for dormitory residence. In order to secure an education, in the terms in which they conceived it, they were willing to live in inexpensive rooms and frequently in garrets and cellars. If they could live at home while attending college, so much the better. The great growth of the junior college[14] since 1900 has come about chiefly because

12 Henry S. Frieze, "A Memorial Discourse on the Life and Services of Henry Philip Tappan," p. 35.

13 Andrew C. McLaughlin, "History of Higher Education in Michigan," p. 52. Bureau of Education Circular of Information No. 4, 1891. Washington: Government Printing Office, 1891.

14 L. V. Koos, "The Junior College," Vol. I, p. 124. Minneapolis: University of Minnesota, 1924.

of the inability of many parents to educate their children away from home.

As American institutions of higher education grew in size, the possibility of erecting dormitories to care for more than a small percentage grew less and less remote. The upward trend in college registrations, so marked in recent decades, began ten years after the Civil War, and few colleges, whether east or west, were unable to keep pace with the multitudes of students who were clamoring at their doors. All resources were needed for strictly academic activities. Fraternities and sororities, which were originally organized as social and intellectual groups, took on residential functions. Since the eighties fraternity and sorority houses have become fixtures on most college campuses chiefly because students needed places to live and eat, and the colleges were unable, if not unwilling, to provide them.

The dormitories built early in the nineteenth century continued in operation, but many of them had been allowed to fall into semi-decay. "When I lived in the college dormitory," observed President Eliot in 1909,[15] "the water often stood two feet deep in the spring in the cellar. I frequently had to put on rubber boots in order to go down cellar to get coal. There was no running water in any of the buildings. We all had to draw our own water by means of two pumps in the college yard, located quite out in the open. There was no gas in any of the buildings when I lived in the college dormitory and no means of lighting, except whale oil, and a very inflammable liquid which was called appropriately 'burning liquid.'" The conditions under which Eliot and his college generation lived continued at Harvard long after the public had become accustomed to better living arrangements.

As at Harvard, so also in most other colleges and universities. Students, irked by the primitive conditions under which they were expected to live, moved out in large numbers to fraternity houses, private residences, and at Cambridge to the dormitories which private individuals had built for profit. During the same period the rise of fraternity houses at Amherst became so pronounced that the administration abandoned its newest dormitory. Its number of students in dormitories had diminished from 53 per cent. in 1870 to 24 per cent. in 1905. By 1900 no dormitories had yet been built at most state universities. The Eastern and the small Middle Western liberal arts colleges continued in general to defend and promote the residential philosophy, but the Zeitgeist prevailed against its extension and even against its claim to academic desirability.

(*To be concluded*)

15 C. W. Eliot, *Religious Education*, Vol. 4, p. 56, 1909–10.

# THE BLENDING OF EDUCATION WITH PSYCHIATRY

By Dr. FREDERICK L. PATRY
UNIVERSITY OF THE STATE OF NEW YORK

IT is a significant observation that certain educators are envisaging mental hygiene or preventive psychiatry to be as broad as education itself with respect to cardinal objectives.

Formal education has delegated a threefold function of the school: (a) To prepare the school-age child for productive, useful and cooperative citizenship; (b) to assist him in gaining an orientation and preparation for his future means of employment in life; and (c) to develop his capacity for profitable and cultural utilization of leisure time.

But the goals and functions of education, fortunately, are of a receding nature. New knowledges and social conditions bring about the need of reshaping and enlarging the schools' usefulness to society. To be sure, the basic or tool subjects—reading, writing and numbers—are insisted upon during the elementary school period. Moreover, certain minimum standards, and fortunately with no attempt to circumscribe maximum attainments, are insisted upon for purposes of grouping of pupils, promotion and certification. But the progressive wing of education is more and more emphasizing the need of capitalizing the school as a place where children may learn to live happily and effectively as social units. The acquisition of knowledge, skills, appreciations and interests are properly regarded as merely means toward the social objective. In its essence, however, it should not be overlooked that the optimal development of a vigorous, noble and loyal character are focal points to be reached after.

Psychiatry, on the other hand, in its preventive or mental hygiene aspect, aims at the promotion, to the optimum, of individual and group health, happiness, efficiency and social adaptation. The need for educating the emotions as well as the intellect is conceived as equal if not of greater importance. We aim to unfold and bring to well-rounded maturity each pupil's constructive potentialities, in the light of his needs and opportunities. Marketability or employability are viewed as essential criteria of the worthwhileness of education, since this must show in concrete performance, in the light of appreciation by others as well as individual satisfaction. Individual differences are respected and cultivated, but not to the neglect of developing and respecting worthwhile individual likenesses. We aim to conserve and prevent not only maladjustments to life but also to enlarge and enrich actual living, day by day.

Education has witnessed tremendous growth in responsibility to the school-age child. From a skeletal elementary schooling of the three R's we have now national free and compulsory education for all children from the age of five to eighteen, at least in New York State. This tremendous responsibility to educate all the children of all the people for some twelve to thirteen years largely determines what and how we shall teach these children. Whereas in a former generation the school could promptly reject pupils as unprofitable material who failed to complete the sixth or eighth grade at the age of fifteen or sixteen, to-day such is not the case. Even the atypical child who is handicapped by varying degrees of mental retardation or deficiency, physical disabilities, visual and auditory defects and special learning disabilities must be provided for in our schools. Interesting enough, the main force behind raising the age of compulsory school education comes not from within the school but from organized labor. The struggles for an economic subsistence is of fundamental importance to adults and must not be jeopardized by juvenile competition in the employment market. Thus there has been thrust upon our schools new responsibilities to differentiate courses of instruction which will profitably utilize the time and growth as well as social, cultural and marketability opportunities of all children.

The motives underlying the reshaping of the school curriculum have also changed in the past two generations. The knowledge motive which emphasized the acquisition of facts has proven inadequate, since most people do not live by what they know but by how they feel and the habit organization thereof. Although leaders in educational thought have emphasized character building as the highest motive, yet we see this coming to the front with a reemphasis upon socialization. It is now realized that it is more important that children learn to get along happily and effectively with each other and in groups than that they acquire any amount of information. Thus the happy child as a primary motive holds greatest significance, since in the vast majority of cases all other desirable part-steps are forerunners to this emotional and social objective.

But we must also ask ourselves the question: For what purposes are we seeking to develop the happy socialized child. Surely we must envisage desirable development in the light of marketability or employability. Thus the work motive as well as profitable and constructive utilization of leisure and citizenship obligations must be kept in mind as cardinal objectives.

In order to develop latent potentialities with

respect to worthwhile individual differences in a differentiated occupational distribution, we must give ample opportunities to discovering creative and inventive contributions, new interests and a keener capacity for discrimination and evaluation of concrete performance. We now realize that too much emphasis upon purposes, goals and objectives may blind us to the ever-evolving new combinations of thought, feeling and action which must be eagerly sought after if we are to reach higher levels of performance which meet the ever-changing needs and new opportunities. Thus freedom of activity must not be too rigidly controlled by adults. Grown-ups must divest themselves of anything which smacks of omniscience or a Jehovah complex. We are all fundamentally doers or actors. This fundamental trait must be respected for what it is and may evolve, such as new interests, new concepts and latent ability for self-criticism, self-direction and self-government.

Keeping in mind the pivotal importance of functioning and behaving rather than behavior as a concept, we should strive for a differential type of unity wherein each teams up to best advantage with his fellow in meeting the moment-by-moment needs, opportunities and obligations. But, you ask, should we not train our youth for leadership? To be sure, human nature craves varying degrees of leadership as well as independence of thought and action. But since leaders are born with these potentialities we should not deceive ourselves in thinking that nature has short-changed any of us because we fail to arrive at a position of leadership. Our obligation is to provide adequate opportunity for fanning the sparks of constructive innate tendencies, whether they be in the nature of leadership, specific talents or creative interests. To be sure this will lead to inevitable inequalities. But such a fact must be accepted, in the light of the facts of human nature, as incontrovertible. Unfair competition and the clouding of individual initiate need not become a significant problem if we become sufficiently imbued with the spirit of democracy which keeps us ever mindful of our fellow's welfare as well as that of our own. Moreover, since capacity for leadership is restricted to a relatively few persons, we must seek to early develop capacity for discrimination or choice and decision with respect to the selection of most promising examples in leadership. For the vast majority of us, capacity for followership is the most essential need. At the same time, no one should be denied the opportunity of developing initiative, leadership or any other constructive qualities which he may possess.

The psychiatrist working with the educator would seem to be an essential aid, not only in the detection and prevention of undesirable deviations from the norm of the individual as well as that of the group, but also from the point of view of conservation and development to the optimum of individual innate potentialities which have social significance. The psychiatrist is essentially an integrator who obligates himself to bring to optimal adjustment and functioning the whole child in view of his past, present and probable future considerations with respect to the total situation and a multiplicity of results which are often unpredictable. Of particular moment is the harmonious development of emotional and volitional qualities, although intellectual knowledge is not minimized. We aim to fructify in actual living the optimal balance of personality traits. These fundamentally depend upon emotional control and direction rather than the recently acquired intellect. Each of us reacts as a total unit with varying degrees of intellectual, emotional, volitional and concrete performance or overt activity components. But the basic and primarily motivating force at the present stage of human evolution is our instinctive-emotional life, which must be respected and more or less satisfied and that in the light of social demands. Thus the need of compromise, substitution, sublimation and renunciation of primitive, anti-social or asocial reaction patterns are essential experiences to be woven into the learning process. As the centuries roll on, *pari passu* with the increasing complexity of the integration of human nature, we have reason to hope that man's behavior will become more and more motivated by rationalism, which upholds the best welfare of the greatest number, and less and less by primitive impulsiveness and rationalization. We must be brought to a full recognition of healthy respect for our emotions and instincts. Our most important obligation in the next thousand years is, and will be, the education of our feelings, emotions and instinctive drives. Until we strike the golden mean of harmoniously balancing emotions, intellect and actions, we may expect recurring wars, economic depressions, political corruption, glorification of crime, increasing mental sickness and dependency, alcoholic and drug intemperance, sexual debauchery and paralysis of democratic principles and practises.

One of the greatest needs of to-day is the espousal of critical experimental education. As public opinion becomes molded to the need of supporting such a type of school program which concerns itself with the education of the total child on a twenty-four hour basis throughout the most plastic period of his life, and follows this up to see that each individual becomes a happy and socialized marketable product, we will witness more and more realization of such forward-looking educational practises.

Our pupils and students need a dynamic, genetic, flexible educational program of activities to achieve personality stability of integration by virtue of adequate and purposeful planning on the part of thoroughly trained and experienced personnel who know how to guide but rarely dictate or coerce pupil activity. Every school should be imbued with the spirit of bringing to realization the following quotation:

> As one star differs from another in glory, so do children of men differ in power and strength. Each child . . . has his place in the great scheme of life in which under proper guidance he can find happiness and usefulness.

# EDUCATIONAL EVENTS

## A NUTRITIONAL INVESTIGATION OF BRITISH SCHOOL CHILDREN

*The British Medical Journal* states that, in view of a statement by the head teacher of one of the schools in Middleton that "lack of nourishing food" was the cause in the children of an inability to concentrate, a deterioration in physique, a lowered standard of work, and an absence of vitality and pluck, an investigation of 217 unselected children in various departments of that school was arranged by Dr. S. T. Beggs, medical officer of health. Weights and heights were correlated, and shown to be average on the whole, although there were several individual exceptions. Most of the children had too little sleep, however, and the foodstuffs they received were sometimes most unsuitable. The school conditions were not altogether satisfactory, there being too much noise from adjoining classes—an important factor in feebleness of concentration. This investigation led to an inquiry being made in other schools, a questionary being sent to head teachers. The number of children found to be under the average height and weight amounted to 34.45 per cent. The percentage of children not receiving properly prepared meals at home was 8.61, having no milk 11.26, and having an excessive amount of tea 12.58. In 62.26 per cent. there was insufficient sleep. Overcrowding was found in 31.79 per cent., unemployment was possibly concerned in 49.67 per cent. and various physical defects were present above the average. Suitable instructions were accordingly issued to parents. The average of thirty-two estimates by clinic mothers of the cost of an economy diet weekly for a family of mother, father and one child aged 5 was 16s. 8½d., as against the British Medical Association's figure of 13s. 8d. Current food prices were shown to be higher than those noted by the British Medical Association. It is concluded that the causation of ill nutrition in growing children is complex in nature, but that sufficiency of sleep is a major factor in determining the growth and development of the school child. The excessive physical defects are to be related to the nutritional state. Home management in a number of cases requires drastic correction, but the school environment also needs improving sometimes. The amount of money expended on food in the homes of necessitous cases is below the minimum for the satisfactory growth and health of the children. The mothers' estimates as regards the food requirements of a family closely approximate the British Medical Association figure, but the local prices of foodstuffs are higher than those estimated by the association in the proportion of 24s. to 20s.

## SUSPENSION OF A BONN PROFESSOR

DR. KARL BARTH, the distinguished Swiss theologian of the University at Bonn, has been suspended from his professorship by Dr. Bernhard Rust, Prussian Minister of Culture, according to *The New York Times,* on the ground that he refuses as a state servant to take the oath of personal loyalty to Chancellor Hitler as provided in a law of last August 20. It was also announced that disciplinary proceedings would be instituted against Dr. Barth before a court to be appointed by the ministry. Dr. Barth's name has been closely associated with the present struggle in the church, and he has written a series of articles and several pamphlets attacking Dr. Mueller. Although he still retains his Swiss citizenship, as a professor in a German university he is legally obliged to take the oath of allegiance to the Reichsführer. The Swiss Government has informed the German authorities, however, that if Swiss professors in German universities are dismissed for political reasons the Swiss Government will reply by dismissing all German professors in Swiss universities.

Dr. Barth is reported to have told a *New York Times* correspondent that he had not refused to take the prescribed oath but that three weeks ago he had requested permission to swear a formula of his own choosing. He was prepared to take the regular oath, he said, with the addition of "so far as I can defend it as an Evangelical Christian." This formula was rejected by Minister of Culture Rust.

Dr. Barth is a naturalized German, but has not renounced his Swiss citizenship. He has held professorships in German universities since 1921 when he went from Safenwil, Switzerland, to Göttingen, transferring later to Münster and to Bonn, where he has been a member of the faculty since 1930.

There are at present two other professors of theology of Swiss nationality lecturing at the University of Berlin.

## CHANGES IN THE CURRICULUM OF BELOIT COLLEGE

THE faculty of Beloit College recently voted changes in the curriculum and in entrance and graduation requirements in order to stimulate students to do better work. The changes, which are regarded as a liberalizing of old requirements, are now gradually taking place.

Under the new plan a foreign language will no longer be required for admission, but students must study one in college if they have not previously, and all students must pass a proficiency test in a foreign language before they are eligible for a degree. With this arrangement advanced students may pass the requirement upon entering Beloit and other students whenever they have reached the degree of "proficiency."

Algebra and geometry are no longer considered essential for admission, and neither must entrants have credits in history, but a deficiency in history must be made up by taking a year course in Beloit.

Students who have maintained high grades during their freshman and sophomore years may voluntarily work for "honors" during their remaining two years. For such a student a thesis will be required and a six-hour comprehensive examination at the end of the college year in addition to fulfilling the general requirements. Special help from members of the faculty will be given to those students who try for honors.

The more than twenty departments in Beloit college have been combined into three broad divisions: sciences and mathematics, social sciences, and languages, literature and arts. Students will no longer choose a "major" but will select a "field of concentration." General graduation requirements have been lessened so that students may study more extensively in their chosen field and also take related subjects.

High-school students standing in the upper one fifth of their class will be admitted without question as to subject-matter; those who stand in the middle section must have English and a certain number of units of "academic" credit, and those standing in the lowest one fifth will not be admitted under any circumstances.

## COURSES IN LARGE SCALE PLANNING AT CORNELL UNIVERSITY

IN response to a growing public interest in the general field of large-scale planning, the Board of Trustees of Cornell University has authorized the establishment in the near future of a special group of courses on this subject, to be offered to all students of the university. A grant from the Carnegie Corporation of New

York will finance the project for a period of three years.

The board also announced the appointment of Gilmore D. Clarke, of New York, as professor of regional planning to supervise the new enterprise. Mr. Clarke is well known throughout the country as a consultant on many large-scale developments.

While specialized courses have been established at other institutions, notably at Harvard University and at the Massachusetts Institute of Technology, primarily for the training of city planners, the offering at Cornell University will be in the nature of an experiment along new lines. The attempt will be made to develop an understanding of the subject among students whose main interest lies outside the technical planning field.

This idea is based on the belief that actual accomplishment in large-scale planning must rest on the cooperation of many diversely trained individuals united through an informed interest. While recognizing the importance of the specially trained city planner as a coordinator, the Cornell plan will attempt to present the idea of collective control of environment to as many students in as many different fields as possible, not as a matter of professional training, but as a supplement to their normal major interests. Such a course, it is felt, will assist rather than compete with the professional courses already in operation elsewhere.

The specific program of work to be offered proposes:

1. An introductory course for juniors and seniors, dealing with the history, theory and development of large-scale planning. This course will be the main feature of the program. It will be entirely non-technical in character so that students from the College of Arts and Sciences, Law, Medicine or Agriculture will be as well able to follow it as those from engineering or architecture.
2. An advanced course to follow the introductory course.
3. Seminars in special fields.

While these courses are not intended primarily for the technical student, the very existence of the new department and the consequent additions to the faculty in a related field will undoubtedly be felt in at least three special subjects.

In the College of Architecture special work in cooperation with the faculty in landscape architecture on their most advanced planning problems, and criticism of thesis problems as they develop will be given. In the College of Engineering work will be carried on in cooperation, particularly with the department of highway engineering, intended to reinforce and extend the offerings of the department. Special emphasis will be placed on the social and esthetic aspects of highway and parkway problems. In the College of Agriculture where already much work has been done on the problems of land use and rural social organization, the courses will be made to reinforce one another.

## PROPOSED CENTER FOR GRADUATE WORK AND RESEARCH AT ATLANTA

THAT the coordination of Emory University, Agnes Scott College and the Georgia School of Technology into a great university center is desirable and feasible is brought out in a preliminary report made by leaders in education who have been studying the project for nearly a year under the auspices of the Lewis H. Beck Foundation.

Written by Dr. George A. Works, of the University of Chicago, who also planned the reorganization of the University System of Georgia, the report recommends the following seven major steps toward the goal of making Atlanta a recognized center of graduate work and research:

Organization of a "Council on the University Center," consisting of the chief executive officers of each cooperating institution, one representative of the board of trustees of each, and an equal number of representative citizens who are not identified with the institutions in any capacity.

Consolidation of smaller classes in certain departments at Agnes Scott College and Emory University, and concentration of all instruction in engineering at the Georgia School of Technology, thus releasing time and energy of many faculty members for graduate work and research.

Development of graduate work on a cooperative basis leading to the Ph.D. degree in the social sciences; in the biological sciences, especially those identified with medicine, and in the physical sciences and mathematics, which are closely related to engineering.

Organization of a school of social work, and expansion of the courses in business administration and in the fine arts.

Enlargement of library and laboratory facilities.

Provision of "an endowment running into millions that will make it possible for the proposed university center to attract and hold outstanding scholars in the several fields that are desirable to develop."

Erection of a new science building and a new library at Agnes Scott College, an auditorium at the Georgia School of Technology, and new buildings amounting to approximately $1,000,000 at Emory University.

It is pointed out by Dr. Edwin Embree, president of the Julius Rosenwald Fund, in a preface to Dr. Works's report, that by eliminating duplication and concentrating its efforts on a limited field each institution could, even on present funds, do much to realize the first five of these aims.

Besides Dr. Works and Dr. Embree, the members of the committee, which began its study last January, included Dr. L. D. Coffman, president of the University of Minnesota; Edmund E. Day, director of the social sciences for the Rockefeller Foundation; Dr. Robert M. Hutchins, president of the University of Chicago, and Dr. William F. Ogburn, professor of sociology at the University of Chicago. The presidents of the three Atlanta institutions, Dr. Harvey W. Cox, of Emory University; Dr. J. R. McCain, of Agnes Scott College, and Dr. M. L. Brittain, of the Georgia School of Technology, who requested the Beck Foundation to finance the investigation, were *ex-officio* members.

Members of the faculty committee on coordination at Emory University are Dr. G. C. White, *chairman;* Dr. F. M. Green, Dr. R. C. Rhodes, Dr. J. M. Steadman, Jr., and Professor J. G. Stipe. The Agnes Scott committee consists of Professor S. G. Stukes, *chairman;* Professor Robert B. Holt, Dr. Mary S. MacDougall, Dr. Philip Davidson and Professor Lucile Alexander.

Success of the university center in Toronto, Canada, where the educational offerings of a provincial university, a Catholic college, a Methodist institution and a Presbyterian school have been coordinated into a unified whole, has been cited as proof that the plan proposed for Atlanta will work.

The Georgia School of Technology is a state-owned institution, Emory University is Methodist and Agnes Scott College is affiliated with the Presbyterian Church. All three are on the approved list of the Association of American Universities.

## A TRAINING SCHOOL FOR GOVERNMENT SERVICE

THE apprenticeship system of training young people for government service will make its appearance on a national scale in the United States early in 1935, according to *The Christian Science Monitor*.

Under the auspices of the National Institution of Public Affairs, between 50 and 125 college students will go to Washington for the months of February and March to study the government at first hand by actually working in various offices. The lecturers will be officials of the government, and the teachers will be social science professors on leave of absence from their colleges.

Candidates for the first class of the school are now being chosen by faculties in accredited colleges in all sections of the country. Final selection will be made on a regional basis by an educational committee, of which Dr. Arnold Bennett Hall, director of the Institute for Government Research of the Brookings Institution, formerly president of the University of Oregon, is chairman.

Students will be selected from juniors, seniors or recent graduates on requirements similar to those for Rhodes scholars. Scholastic standing, interest in political affairs and qualities of leadership will be considered.

Although the plan for this type of training was first expounded publicly by a member of the administration, Chester H. McCall, assistant to the Secretary of Commerce about a year ago, the institution is non-partisan, non-political, privately financed and self-governing. Its board of trustees is composed of Louis Brownlow, director of the Public Administration Clearing House; Eugene Meyer, formerly Republican governor of the Federal Reserve Board, and William E. Sweet, formerly Democratic governor of Colorado. Otis T. Wingo, Jr., is executive secretary.

The program is designed to supplement classroom instruction in political science with practical experience. Students will be divided into small groups for individual contact with government officials. Each will serve an "internship" of actual administrative work and duties in a government agency of particular interest to him. At the close of the term he will be required to write a report or thesis, submitting one copy to the institution and one to his college.

Special attention will be devoted to the Congress, with groups of students spending an entire day in the galleries of the Senate and the House, watching the work and procedure of Congress. In addition, there will be lectures by Senators and Representatives. The various departments and major independent agencies and commissions will be studied in much the same way.

A restricted number of scholarships will furnish transportation to and from Washington, in addition to board and room for two months.

## THE TWENTY-FIFTH ANNIVERSARY OF THE PRESIDENT OF CARLETON COLLEGE

AT a special chapel service held in Skinner Memorial Chapel, Carleton College, on October 27, members of the Carleton faculty presented Dr. Donald J. Cowling with a silver entree dish in recognition of his twenty-five years of service as president. Dr. Cowling was installed as president of Carleton College on October 18, 1909. Presentation of the gift was made by Dr. Curvin H. Gingrich, chairman of the department of mathematics. Dr. Gingrich also joined the faculty in 1909, and has completed a quarter of a century of consecutive service as professor of mathematics.

A correspondent writes: "In the twenty-five years of Dr. Cowling's administration Carleton College has grown from a small institution to the position of one of the most solidly established and most widely known liberal arts colleges in the United States. In 1909 there were less than 300 students, a faculty of twenty teachers, and a graduating class of less than fifty seniors. By 1934 the college had increased about threefold. The student body now numbers between seven and eight hundred, the faculty numbers 66, and the senior class has approximately 150 students. The total assets of the college were $819,330 in 1909. On June 30, 1934, they had increased to $4,315,255.

"The college in 1909 had seven major buildings. It now has seventeen buildings. Five new dormitories have been built with accommodations for the entire student body. These new buildings include Davis, Burton and Severance Halls for men and Nourse and Margaret Evans Halls for women. Music Hall, Skinner Memorial Chapel, Leighton Hall of Chemistry, Laird Stadium and a modern central heating and power plant, have also been erected. Since 1909 the campus has been greatly extended. Lyman Memorial Lakes have been developed and an arboretum containing about 360 acres has been added to the college grounds, which also include a college farm of about 300 acres.

"In spite of the heavy demands which the growth of the college during the last twenty-five years has made upon the time and the energy of President Cowling, he has been able to carry many responsibilities outside of his immediate college relationships. He has been president of the Association of American Colleges and of the American Council on Education; a member of the division of educational relations of the National Research Council, chairman of the Congregational Tercentenary Commission, member of the executive committee of the Pilgrim Memorial Fund Commission; chairman of the Congregational National Council's Commission on Missions; a trustee of the corporation for the National Council of Congregational Churches; trustee of the Congregational Foundation for Education; trustee of the Chicago Theological Seminary, of Pillsbury Academy and of the American University Union; president of the Religious Education Association; member of the state executive committee for the Minnesota Y. M. C. A.; chairman of the Minnesota branch of the League of Nations Association; chairman of the Minnesota State Crime Commission, and president of the recently formed Minnesota Law and Order League."

## MEETING OF THE HOUSE OF DELEGATES OF THE NEW YORK STATE TEACHERS ASSOCIATION

A MEETING of the House of Delegates of the New York State Teachers Association opened at

Niagara Falls on November 22. In his report as president of the association, according to *The New York Times,* George R. Staley, of Rome, stated that the office building for the association, now in process of construction at Albany, would be completed next year; that Governor Lehman had promised to give the full state aid to schools in 1935, and that the plea of the State Economic Council for a budget reduction had been met by a teachers' investigation in Little Falls.

Arvie Eldred, of Albany, executive secretary, recommended in his report that the association stand "four square" behind the Friedsam act. He also urged improvement of the teaching profession by requiring increased qualifications from entrants, tenure and extension of tenure for all teachers, including those now in non-tenure areas, and a united front by teachers.

The proposal for higher certificate requirements for teachers was outlined by Dr. Hermann Cooper, assistant commissioner for teacher education and certification of the State Department of Education. The present schedule calls for the application of the qualifications on and after September 1, 1935, but would not be retroactive and would not apply to those already enrolled and studying for the present certification requirements.

The increased requirements, Dr. Cooper said, are designed to protect parents, children and teachers. They call for an additional year of study by those seeking to become elementary school teachers.

In addition, both elementary and high-school teachers, granted a provisional certificate, will be required to study an additional year "in service" before they are eligible for a "renewal certificate," the final form of certificate.

W. Howard Pillsbury, of Schenectady, treasurer, reported that on August 31 the association had total assets of $271,211, compared with $205,458 on the same date in 1933. Income for the year, however, was $2,950 less than for the previous year, being $104,055. His report showed 45,415 members on August 31, compared with 45,804 at the end of the previous year.

The annual report of the New York State Teachers Retirement System was made at a separate meeting. It showed a membership on July 1, 1933, of 43,715, of whom 36,859 were women, and a gain to June 30, 1934, of 3,864 to 43,790, of whom 36,539 were women. Annuitants receiving benefits on July 30 numbered 3,743, of whom 3,272 were women. Assets were $59,267,044 on July 1.

At the annual banquet, the principal speaker was Allen D. Albert, of Chicago. Other speakers were Dr. H. H. Horner, representing Commissioner of Education Graves; Daisy Lord, of Waterbury, Conn., and Dr. James F. Taylor, of Niagara Falls.

Miss Mabel Simpson, director of elementary grades at Rochester, was nominated for president of the association.

## THE TERCENTENARY OF AMERICAN HIGH SCHOOLS

THE Department of Secondary School Principals of the National Education Association is taking the leadership in sponsoring a nation-wide observance of the tercentenary of American high schools. It is planned to enlist the support of every high school in America, so that the year 1935 may be as significant to secondary education in the years to come as the year 1635 has been to the past 300 years.

On April 13, 1635, the freemen of Boston, Massachusetts, passed the following order: "Likewise, it was then generally agreed upon that our brother Philemon Pormont shall be entreated to become schoolmaster for the teaching and nurturing of the children with us." Thus was founded the Boston Latin School, the first secondary school in America.

It is proposed that state departments of education shall promote the tercentenary through special and regular publications. In many states the governor has already issued a special proclamation for its observance. Where this has not been done it is expected that steps will be taken to secure such a proclamation.

Superintendents are requested to appoint committees representing the various high schools of the city to be responsible for the celebration in the local community, to prepare plans for the future development of the high schools and to present them to the community for approval.

Principals of high schools will appoint committees for observance in individual schools and it is hoped that teachers colleges will encourage the writing of masters' theses on the history of a single high school, or of the high schools of a county or a state.

The letter from President Franklin D. Roosevelt given below has been released through the office of the secretary of the National Education Association:

The year 1935 ushers in an important anniversary in the life of the American people. Three hundred years ago the first American high school—the Boston Latin School—was founded. It was established in 1635 only fifteen short years after the landing of the Pilgrims. From a small beginning with one instructor and a handful of students has grown the splendid service now provided for more than 6,000,000 young Americans by 26,000 public and private high schools. These schools are developing the most precious resource of our nation, the latent intelligence of our young people. It is worth noting that social progress in the United States is following swiftly on the heels of the remarkable expansion of educational opportunity at the high school level.

I hope that the young people of every high school in the United States will celebrate this three hundredth anniversary. I hope they will celebrate it in a manner which will bring vividly before parents and fellow townsmen the significance, the contribution and the goals of their schools.

# EDUCATIONAL NOTES AND NEWS

AT the annual meeting on November 21 of the trustees of the Carnegie Foundation for the Advancement of Teaching, Dr. Walter C. Murray, president of the University of Saskatchewan, Canada, was elected president; Thomas W. Lamont was elected vice-president, and Frederick C. Ferry, president of Hamilton College, secretary. New trustees elected were Chancellor E. H. Lindley, of the University of Kansas; Dr. Edward C. Elliott, president of Purdue University, and Dr. James B. Conant, president of Harvard University.

ROBERT M. LESTER, assistant to the president of the Carnegie Corporation since 1926, was elected secretary of the corporation at a meeting of the trustees held on November 20, to fill the place made vacant by the death of James Bertram. John M. Russell, administrative assistant of the corporation, will succeed Mr. Lester as assistant to the president.

CLYDE A. ERWIN has been appointed superintendent of public instruction in North Carolina. He succeeds Arch T. Allen, who died on October 20.

THE REVEREND PAUL LINDBERG has been elected president of Luther College, Wahoo, Nebraska. He succeeds the late Dr. A. T. Seashore, and will assume his new office next September.

DR. ABRAHAM LEFKOWITZ, legislative representative of the American Teachers Union, was given a testimonial dinner on November 24 on the occasion of his fiftieth birthday. Included among the sponsors were Dr. George J. Ryan, president of the Board of Education of New York City, and Dr. Harold G. Campbell, superintendent of schools. Dr. Harold Rugg, professor of education at Teachers College, Columbia University, was the principal speaker.

PROFESSOR ALBERT H. GILMER, head of the department of drama and public speaking at Lafayette College, and Associate Professor Theodore E. Norton, librarian, have been elected members of the French Academy of Education in recognition of outstanding contributions to the cultural and educational life of France.

DR. ARTHUR H. COMPTON, professor of physics at the University of Chicago, was awarded the honorary degree of master of arts on the occasion of the opening of his lectures as George Eastman visiting professor at the University of Oxford.

MARCHESE MARCONI was elected rector by a majority of a hundred votes over the other candidate, Sir James Jeans, as the result of the St. Andrews University rectorial election.

H. S. COOKE, lecturer in education at the University of Reading, England, has retired on the completion of fifty-one years' service in education, thirty-seven of which have been spent in Reading.

PROFESSOR JAMES E. POLLARD has been named acting head of the School of Journalism of the

Ohio State University. He succeeds Professor Joseph S. Myers, formerly director of the school and now emeritus professor of journalism.

DR. ELMER P. KOHLER, who since 1914 has been Abbott and James Lawrence professor of chemistry at Harvard University, has been elected Sheldon Emery professor of organic chemistry. Dr. Lawrence J. Henderson, who had been professor of biological chemistry, has been elected to succeed Professor Kohler as Abbott and James Lawrence professor of chemistry.

E. V. ELLINGTON, head of the department of dairy husbandry of Washington State College and Agricultural Experiment Station, was recently appointed vice-dean of the College of Agriculture and assistant director of the station.

DR. ALEXANDER GRAY, professor of political economy at the University of Aberdeen, has accepted the professorship of political economy and mercantile law at the University of Edinburgh. He succeeds Professor F. W. Ogilvie.

DR. HAROLD W. DODDS, president of Princeton University, was elected president of the Municipal League, which met at Pittsburgh on November 26. Dr. Dodds succeeds Murray Seasongood, formerly mayor of Cincinnati. The league is composed of public officers, experts in government and league workers.

DR. F. L. MCVEY, president of the University of Kentucky, was elected president of the Association of Land Grant Colleges and Universities at the recent Washington meeting. Dean J. G. Lipman, of the College of Agriculture at Rutgers University, was elected vice-president. Dean Thomas P. Cooper, of the University of Kentucky Agricultural College, was reelected secretary and Dean F. B. Mumford, of the University of Missouri College of Agriculture, was reelected for a five-year term on the executive committee.

DR. L. A. PITTENGER, president of Ball State Teachers College, Muncie, Indiana, has been elected president of the Indiana Schoolman's Club.

L. E. NOLLAU, professor of mechanical drawing in the University of Kentucky College of Engineering, has been elected president of the Kentucky section of the Society for the Promotion of Engineering Education.

DR. C. MACFIE CAMPBELL, professor of psychiatry at the Harvard Medical School, has been elected president of the Massachusetts Psychiatric Society.

DR. LUTHER A. HAAR, professor of finance at the Wharton School, University of Pennsylvania, has been appointed secretary of banking for the State of Pennsylvania.

DR. STEWART SCRIMSHAW, professor of industrial relations at Marquette University and a member of the faculty of the College of Engineering for twelve years, has been granted a leave of absence until June 30, to accept an appointment to the National Labor Relations Board.

DR. FRANK A. PEARSON, professor of prices and statistics at the College of Agriculture, Cornell University, who, with Professor George F. Warren, is credited with originating many of the federal administration's monetary policies, has returned from a month in western Europe where he made a study of commodity prices. From headquarters in London he traveled in England, France, Germany, Holland, Belgium and Italy.

DR. HARLEY L. LUTZ, professor of economics at Princeton University, has been granted leave of absence from the university for the second term of the current academic year.

DR. JAMES B. CONANT, president of Harvard University, was the first speaker at the annual convention of the Middle States Association of Colleges and Secondary Schools on November 30 and December 1. Other speakers were Dean Chauncey S. Boucher, University of Chicago; William John Cooper, formerly U. S. Commissioner of Education; Thomas Alexander, chairman of New College, Columbia University; Wilson Farrand, head master of Newark Academy, and Frederick M. Davenport.

DR. DAVID L. CRAWFORD, president of the University of Hawaii, was a recent guest speaker at the University of Denver. His lecture, "The Paradox of the Pacific," was sponsored by the Foundation for the Advancement of the Social Sciences.

DR. GOODWIN WATSON, professor of education at Teachers College, Columbia University, addressed a general convocation of university students on November 27 at the University of Kentucky. His topic was, "Building a New America."

Gleb V. Anrep, professor of physiology in the Egyptian University of Cairo, will deliver the 1935 series of Lane Lectures at Stanford University School of Medicine in April.

Memorial exercises to the late Francis Preston Venable, member of the faculty of the University of North Carolina for fifty-three years and president for fourteen years, were held on November 17. Dr. Charles H. Herty, head of the department of chemistry from 1905 to 1916, spoke of Dr. Venable as a scientific man and Dr. H. V. Wilson spoke of him as a colleague and as president of the university. The faculty committee in charge of arrangements for the exercises were Dr. H. M. Wagstaff, *chairman,* Dr. H. V. Wilson, Dr. W. C. Coker, Dr. A. S. Wheeler and Dr. J. M. Booker.

Dr. Alexander Graham, who started to teach at the age of sixteen years and who, ever since, has been active in educational affairs in North Carolina, died on November 2 at the age of ninety years. He was superintendent of the Charlotte schools for twenty-five years and at the time of his death was superintendent emeritus. Dr. Graham's son, Dr. Frank Porter Graham, is president of the University of North Carolina.

Dr. George Barlow Penny, emeritus professor of musical history and theory at the Eastman School of Music, died on November 14 at the age of seventy-three years. Dr. Penny had been connected with the Eastman School of Music since 1918. He went to Rochester in 1910 to join the faculty of the Rochester Conservatory of Music and to become conductor of the Rochester Oratorio Society. When the conservatory was bought by George Eastman and made the Eastman School of Music, Dr. Penny joined the faculty.

Dr. Calvin H. French, for fourteen years president of Hastings College, and president emeritus since last spring, died on November 22 at the age of seventy-two years. Dr. French was president of Rollins College from 1917 to 1919.

Professor George L. Richardson, Jr., director of admissions at Phillips Exeter Academy, died on November 21 at the age of thirty-nine years.

J. C. Merrill, principal of Washington Academy, East Machias, Maine, was killed on November 23 when his automobile stalled at a railroad crossing.

The Reverend John J. Biggane, professor of English at Niagara University, died on November 22 at the age of thirty-five years.

Dr. Wendell Christopher Phillips, president of the American Medical Association in 1926–27 and founder of the American Federation of Organizations for the Hard of Hearing, died on November 17 at the age of seventy-one years.

Students and members of the faculty of Harvard University on November 26 attended exercises in commemoration of the three hundred and twenty-seventh anniversary of the birth of John Harvard, founder of Harvard College, who was born November 26, 1607. As reported in *The New York Times,* the ceremonies opened in the Harvard Memorial Chapel, where the Reverend Henry Wilfer Foote, minister of the First Unitarian Church of Belmont, Mass., delivered the commemorative address. The audience then sang a hymn written by Lionel de Jersey Harvard, a lineal descendant of John Harvard, for the Harvard commencement of 1915. A wreath was placed on the statue of John Harvard in the yard by Herbert M. Irwin, Jr., of Port Washington, N. Y., president of the Harvard Memorial Society, and Daniel E. Burbank, of Springfield, Mass. Both are sophomores of Harvard College. The statue on which the wreath was placed is not the likeness of Harvard's founder. Daniel Chester French, the sculptor, could find no portrait of John Harvard and he modeled the figure from Sherman Hoar, a Harvard graduate of the class of '92.

The Joint Commission on the Emergency in Education has issued invitations to a Conference on State School Legislation and Long-Time Educational Planning, to be held on Tuesday, Wednesday and Thursday, December 11, 12 and 13, in the Board of Directors' Room, National Education Association, Washington, D. C. The purposes of the conference are: (1) to get and to give help with relation to state school legislation to be enacted in 1935; (2) to take counsel together on a long-time program of educational planning, recovery and reconstruction. Invitations to the conference are being extended to state superintendents and commissioners of education, presidents and secretaries of state education associations, and chairmen of committees on legislation, or other officers of corresponding rank. The first session is to be held on Tuesday evening, December 11, at 8:00 P. M., following the adjournment of the annual convention of the National Council of State Superintendents and Commissioners of Education.

WITH the second biennial report of the Oregon state board of higher education now on the press, Willard L. Marks, president of the board, has submitted to Governor Meier his official letter of transmittal in which he states that the six institutions under the control of the board have helped to reduce the tax burden during the depression years, have maintained high quality of service and instructional standards despite financial handicaps, and have arrived at a settled policy as to major curricula allocations. Operation of the system on state income 40.5 per cent. under that enjoyed by the institutions before the single board was given complete charge has not been accomplished without curtailment of important services to the state and students, or without imposing emergency conditions on staff members that can not be expected to continue. Nevertheless, standards have been well maintained under the difficulties encountered. President Marks asks only that higher education be allowed enough money to maintain itself on the present restricted level of operation and that its staff members be accorded the same treatment as to restoration of salaries that the legislature may provide for other state employees. He adds that these cumulative salary reductions in all funds handled within the system will amount to approximately $1,020,000 by the end of the present fiscal year.

THE Board of Trustees of Stanford University, on receipt of the reports of the president and comptroller as to the financial operations of the university for the academic year 1933–34, has decided there is a sufficient surplus to warrant a payment to the faculty of half of the ten per cent. cut made in all salaries of $1,000 and over. This will be paid in a lump sum within the next few weeks. At the time of the adoption of the budget for the year 1933–34 it was necessary to make a ten per cent. reduction in all salaries, but it was agreed by the Board of Trustees that, should the income be more than was anticipated or should savings be made, the members of the faculty were to get the benefit of any such surplus. This action has no reference to the current academic year, the financial outcome of which will not be known until next October.

REPRESENTATIVES of 33 foreign nations are enrolled in the student body of the Massachusetts Institute of Technology this year. One hundred and forty-nine students, or nearly six per cent. of the entire student body, are citizens of countries outside the United States and its territories and dependencies. The group does not include those American-born students whose background has been predominantly foreign. Leading all other countries in number of students is China, with 31. Canada stands second with 29, while Great Britain ranks third with 13. There are nine students from Japan, seven from Cuba, six from India, and four each from Spain and Germany. Other nations represented are the Argentine Republic, Australia, Austria, Belgium, Brazil, Colombia, Czechoslovakia, Ecuador, Finland, France, Holland, Hungary, Iraq, Mexico, Newfoundland, Norway, Panama, Poland, Siam, South Africa, Switzerland, Soviet Russia, Syria, Turkey and Venezuela. Of the entire foreign group, 88 are undergraduates and the remaining 61 are carrying on advanced studies in the Graduate School.

A DISPATCH to *The New York Times* reports that the historic insignia of the German University at Prague were transferred on November 26 to the rector of the Czech University, following an agreement reached between the rector of the German University and the Minister of Education. Despite this accord there were renewed disorders. Thousands of students gathered around the Czech University, cheering the rector's announcement that the insignia were now in his custody. The scepter seal and chain of office, adopted by the university when it was founded in 1348, had been retained by the German branch when it separated from the Czech in 1920. Nationalist students organized anti-German demonstrations in several parts of the city. Discontent manifested itself not only against Germans but also against the Jewish population. Disorders among German nationalist students are also reported at Vienna.

*The Times* also reports from Cuba that high-school students disarmed policemen in the down-town section of Havana on November 26, seized a man whose name is believed to be Lozango and took him to a secret place for a student trial. The man had been captured in front of the high-school building facing Central Park, but the police intervened. A few minutes later while the prisoner was being taken to a station some forty students rushed the police and seized the prisoner. It is said that if the prisoner is convicted at the trial he will be shot, as happened in September, 1933, when a student spy named Soler was tried, sentenced and killed by a student firing squad. A police guard has been thrown around the high-school building and an attempt is being made to apprehend the students and their prisoner.

A WIRELESS dispatch to *The New York Times* states that in order to intensify national defense the Estonian Government intends to extend military training to all schools. Hitherto only the students in the higher schools have been instructed in gas warfare, air defense and military strategy, but henceforth the same instruction will be given in the primary schools in towns and later in all the rural schools. The students also will be sent to camps for ten days every year. This system is similar to the one in effect in Latvia.

# DISCUSSION

## FUNCTIONAL AREAS IN THE COLLEGE CURRICULUM

THE doubling of college attendance each decade, during the past thirty years, and the presence now of a million students are facts sufficient to compel a reconstruction of the college. Significant reconstructive movements are already under way, as we well know, in certain pioneering institutions. There is a general conviction that, for the great majority of students, something must be offered that differs materially from the traditional conceptions of scholarship; and there is much agreement that this should consist of non-professional training for high-level and efficient living in a real and social world.

Reforms are various. But of chief importance, it would seem, is the establishment of a curriculum that is functional with respect to civic and personal needs. When this problem is honestly attacked, it becomes evident that certain familiar practises are inadequate—for example, the system of majors and minors, with its canalizing of studies and its implication that the student is to be a specialist in some academic field. Likewise, the offering of various narrowed and split courses, usually in the category of electives, with their inevitable effect of disintegration. Thinking is now leading clearly away from these practises—at least, for the typical student who will become neither a professional man nor a scholar.

Movement is toward a curriculum worked out upon the principle of a functional analysis. The purpose is to survey actual needs that appear upon the level of educated living. Such a survey shows that knowledge is interrelated and not compartmented, and it reveals the necessity for a curriculum that is sanely inclusive in scope. These conclusions lead to an organization of instruction within large, natural areas. These areas could not, in the logic of the case, be regarded as mutually exclusive; but they would serve, nevertheless, as convenient groupings of function.

The purpose here is to present a curricular organization of the kind suggested. The following should prove adequate.

*The social-economic field.* The purpose here is to provide, throughout the college course, a continuous study of problems selected because of their significance in the world of practical events. It is not to be based upon a few disconnected, text-book courses, but upon an inclusive and unified program. This field would consist of social science in a real and useful sense. Each problem would be attacked without regard for the artificial boundaries of economics, political science, geography or history. The purpose would be to secure and analyze all the pertinent facts, not as an exercise in "research," but as an experience in the methods and materials available to the common man. No more would students be able to graduate with little or no social science, save, perhaps, a book-bound course in constitutional government or a history of colonization in the Southwest or similar dehydrated pabulum. The social-economic field would lie across the student's whole curriculum. It would tie in with all the other fields and give a progressive experience in the real business of directing life in an organized world.

*The field of human nature and personality.* Man should understand man, biologically, psychologically and as a social being. Such understanding should be a major outcome of a college education for all. This purpose can not be accomplished in a few technical courses that some students "take" and some omit. The need demands a kind of instruction that is adept in selecting essentials from an ocean of materials, most of which are meticulous and of importance only to the specialist. It is appalling how little the average student learns through college instruction about himself and his fellows as human beings. So meager is his instruction in this field, as a rule, that he goes into the world emotionally juvenile, a prospective dupe for advertisers and propagandists, unfreed from superstitions, uninformed as to the laws of his own nature, lacking the principles for wise self-guidance in wholesome living, and, except for what he has picked up, uninstructed as to marriage. Training in this field would disregard the property rights of old-line subjects; but it would appropriate all useful materials in general psychology, physiology, sociology, mental hygiene, genetics, medicine or any other available branch of knowledge.

*The field of personal and community health and recreation.* While this field is closely related to the preceding one, its purpose is less a matter of knowledge to be acquired and more one of practical experience in the art of healthful living. At the present time, the activities of the college along this line are chiefly and notoriously those of intercollegiate athletics. There is also some "required" physical education; and there is military drill, including bayonet practise, in which young men learn the most effective methods of mangling. In a reasonable system, much of a formal nature would have to be learned concerning the principles of personal and community health; but more important would be the provision for activities from which the students might acquire energetic interests in personal well-being and gain motives for healthful pleasure. This field would contribute greatly to a solution of the leisure time problem. It would include generous opportunities for real play and real participation in college and community recreation. It would never be limited to physical activities, but would embrace all kinds of occasions for play and pleasure in handcrafts, art, music, dramatics, debating and practical science.

*The field of the natural sciences.* The object is an understanding and an appreciation of nature, a knowledge of the significant applications and services of science to life, and a grasp of great unifying principles and illuminative facts. This would take precedence over minute and piecemeal practise in scientific method. Such a statement constitutes heresy as most college professors of science see it; for in their minds no comprehensive over-view of science can equal in value one single course—botany, for example—if it requires the student to spend a hundred hours peering through a microscope and drawing the structures of cells. And there is nothing so healthful for the mind, it is believed, as an intense struggle with the mathematical complications of Mendelian law.

The natural sciences, in truth, hold thrilling possibilities. The microscopic world is an exalting revelation; likewise astronomy. The keys to life and cosmos are in science. But we forego these for our students in favor of a tedious methodology in some little subdivision. A liberal study would not neglect the scientific method, but would exemplify it broadly throughout—in the social sciences as well as the natural. The general student would become imbued with it as a principle, which would be far more valuable, for him, than an isolated practise.

*The field of the social technologies.* This would include the various useful means by which men record and communicate ideas and attack their practical problems. Here we should find written and oral English, general mathematics, drawing, logic of science, familiar statistical procedures, common techniques such as are employed in social economics, insurance and banking; and possibly some materials selected from applied psychology.

This field, we should hope, would be a reply to that just and wide-spread criticism of so many graduates of our liberal arts colleges—that they can not write good English, that they can not express themselves on their feet, that they have learned no practical usages and that their education has been in the clouds. In the teaching of this field, every part of it would be purged of the notion that its intensive study conveys a mystical training of the mind and would be treated as an instrumentality for high-level, intelligent living.

*The field of liberal culture.* Here we find materials from literature, art, music, languages, narrative history, archeology, anthropology, the history of science, philosophy and whatever subjects may contribute to good taste, sensitive appreciation, cultured criticism, knowledge of fine works and possession of motivating interests in the things that ennoble life. To one capable of thinking only in terms of the traditional college courses, which are minute subdivisions of subjects, it must seem that the topics mentioned are far too numerous for any curriculum. But the point is that these would be treated in an entirely different way. They would be amalgamated and humanized. So far as they contribute to this field of liberal culture, there would be no intention of developing experts. The students would be led to read extensively; art and music would be presented; literature and philosophy would be inspiringly interpreted. The field would be entrusted to princes of the faculty whose minds exceed the limits of specialized fields.

*A field of personal choice.* The preceding fields would be organized to meet the needs of an educated person as these are determined by the conditions of modern life. They are the common ground of culture and social efficiency. But we must also recognize the need for differentiation and personal interest. Without question, every student must be given an opportunity to develop a talent or to pursue a study of his own choice. His selection might be vocational or preprofessional, it might be academic, it might lie in one of the arts. In any event, it would comprise a sequence of courses—perhaps one or two each semester—leading to the satisfaction of a personally felt want.

The seventh field would in part answer the protest of those who will declare that, by exposing our students to six common fields, we are cutting them to a pattern. Those who make this protest should also object to the practise of rearing several children in the same family, for fear they will turn out alike. Personalities are not made uniform so easily as that, even with similar inheritance. Nevertheless, within the common fields there would no doubt be provision for a certain amount of election on the part of the student. And furthermore, the fields would not consist of dogmas, indoctrinations or authoritarian pronouncements. They would comprise organizations of studious experience in which initiative and independent thinking would be the challenge all along the line.

When proposals such as those here presented are laid before the academician, he demolishes them with one devastating remark: "All this is nothing but a glorified high school course!" This criticism betrays the amazing inconsistency of the professorial mind. College professors are notorious in their disparagement of the mental capacities of the majority of their students. They believe that most students are inferior to the standards of genuine scholarship. But if they are right, why do they so loudly condemn the "glorified high school course"? This would seem to be the kind of a course that all but a few of their students need. The high school admits that its chief concern is to train young people in a well-balanced way of life. Is it not a primary function of the liberal college to do the same thing—on a higher level, but not on a different kind of a level?

P. F. Valentine

State Teachers College
San Francisco, Calif.

## MATHEMATICS IN WEBSTER'S NEW INTERNATIONAL DICTIONARY, SECOND EDITION, 1934

IN view of the extensive use of Webster's dictionaries in the schools of our country teachers are naturally interested in the recent greatly enlarged edition of the most complete volume of the series. The successive revisions show that we are living in an age of progress and they should tend to increase our readiness to consider points with respect to which further progress seems desirable, especially when they relate to subjects taught in the common schools. The attitude of mind which is looking for further improvement in our material of instruction is fortunately in line with the spirit of the times even as regards the definitions of terms commonly employed in our schools and in common conversation.

In the edition named in the heading of this article there appears under the entry "logarithm" the following statement: "Tables of natural logarithms were published by John Speidell (London, 1619); of common logarithms by Briggs (1624, 1633)." Under the same entry it is noted correctly that Briggs died in 1630; that is, about three years before he is here said to have published a table of common logarithms. This disparity of dates is probably less annoying to the thoughtful reader than the fact that J. Speidell is here, and in many other places, credited with the publication of tables of natural logarithms long before the base of this system was determined.

Under the entry "algebraic operation" there appears the following definition: "A combination of a finite number of the fundamental algebraic operations addition, multiplication, subtraction and division." The term "algebraic operation" is now usually employed with a wider meaning so as to include at least the extraction of roots. On page 140 of Felix Klein's "Elementary Mathematics from an Advanced Standpoint," 1932, it is noted that it is desirable to say that certain equations are algebraically solvable even when they can not be solved in terms of radicals and that it is not at all necessary that they can be reduced to a set of pure equations in order to be thus solvable. The four fundamental operations noted above are commonly called the rational operations.

Although the term "group" is not as elementary as the two terms to which we just referred it is being used more and more widely in common conversation on the part of educated people. H. Weyl recently wrote, "the concept of group is one of those very few primitive and fundamental ideas which play the part of an ordering, suggestive, and guiding principle in all branches of mathematics and wherever mathematics is applied." Those who consult the dictionary under consideration for a definition of this term will find under the entry "group" the direction to see the term "distribution." Here they find the following statement: "Arrangement of objects in classes called *parcels* when the order is indifferent, and *groups* when it is essential." Practically the same statement appears in the preceding edition of this dictionary.

Notwithstanding the fact that I have been interested in group theory for more than forty years and have read this quotation a number of times I confess that I can not yet connect any meaning with it which seems to correspond with the facts. If it is retained in a later edition of this dictionary the question of elucidation might be considered. The part of the definition of the term group which appears under this entry is quite incomplete, but it conveys important elements of the definition of this term as a technical mathematical term. An explicit statement of the fact that it does not aim to be complete would have improved it from the standpoint of the student of mathematics.

The preceding remarks are explicitly made with a view towards progress and not primarily with a view towards exhibiting the nature of the recent revision as regards the mathematical terms contained in this dictionary. The latter would have required a more extensive study in view of the great number of additions and the numerous changes. There seems to be no question about the fact that students of mathematics will find the present edition much more useful than the earlier ones, but it should be used with a feeling that it is not as nearly perfect as one might infer from some of the advertisements relating thereto. An enlightened public is more desirable than one which fails to realize the room for improvements.

G. A. MILLER

UNIVERSITY OF ILLINOIS

## EDUCATIONAL BROADCASTING

As a former president of the National Association of Educational Broadcasters and as a director of an educational station which has been on the air since 1922, I am of the opinion that Miss Florence Hale made several statements which are contradictory to the facts, in her testimony before the Federal Communications Commission on the question of the application of broadcasting facilities for education, religion and other non-profit agencies.

While all of us in educational work desire to give full credit to the part the National Education Association has done in its radio work, such statements as "These broadcasts constitute the first regular, sustained programs of a purely educational nature given over the air, extending over a long period of time" are not correct. Such a statement might be true if she had made it clear that she was talking about broadcasts over the chain. There are hundreds of purely educational programs being given by university-owned stations each year and our only handicap has been lack of proper facilities to reach a sizable audience.

In another instance she says: "I have found that most of our educators who propose carrying on educational broadcasting independently have little realization on the practical problems involved." Apparently she is not thoroughly familiar with the personnel in educational broadcasting over stations owned and operated by colleges and universities.

JOS. F. WRIGHT

DIRECTOR OF STATION WILL

# QUOTATIONS

## DOLLARS AND BOOKS

DEVALUATION of the American dollar has presented the nation's libraries with a difficult problem. When the dollar's exchange value fell, library heads were hard pressed to keep their foreign periodical and book purchases abreast of the times.

Inquiries by scholars for the latest in foreign literary and scientific works now are being met with the reply that budgets will not permit purchases of publications that, as a result of the dollar's fall, in some instances, cost 50 per cent. more now than formerly. Librarians are sympathetic, but can do nothing to help the knowledge-seeker.

Buried in the Library of Congress' forthcoming report for the fiscal year 1934 is a pregnant paragraph by Linn R. Blanchard, chief of the accessions division.

"In common with other American libraries," Mr. Blanchard declares, "the Library of Congress has been confronted with a serious financial problem because of the fall in the exchange value of the dollar, thus greatly increasing the cost of foreign books. This loss in buying power is felt the more keenly by the Library of Congress since foreign books and periodicals make up such a large percentage of its total purchases."

However, Mr. Blanchard explains, the Library of Congress is more fortunate than any other library in the country because of the fact that it benefits by copyright privileges. Through this system, the library receives two copies of every book copyrighted, after the Copyright Act provisions have been complied with.

But even the benefits from the copyright books are not enough to permit the Congressional Library to make the purchases of foreign books and periodicals that it used to make before the fall of the dollar. And this, according to Mr. Blanchard, is a serious condition when it is realized that the Congressional Library is the country's heaviest buyer in foreign book markets, much heavier than any university library.

One of the East's most important university libraries recently has informed its trustees that purchases of foreign books and periodicals have been seriously curtailed by the fall in the exchange value of the dollar. Since a vast amount of this library's books are for research problems and investigations, the scholars have been having a difficult time.

In normal times, about 68 per cent. of this library's expenditures are for purchases of books and periodicals made abroad. At present these same purchases cost the library, in dollars, approximately 50 per cent. more than they formerly cost.

Last year, as a result of a conference between the library heads and booksellers of a foreign country, substantial discounts were received. However, whatever advantage was thus obtained was more than wiped out by the fall in the exchange value of the dollar. The result: Foreign books could be ordered only when special funds were made available.

This state of affairs, according to Herbert Putnam, chief librarian, Library of Congress, is indicative of conditions prevalent among the rest of the nation's libraries, university and privately endowed, that specialize in foreign books and periodicals.

However, Mr. Putnam declares, students at the Library of Congress have less to worry about than any other library group in the country. Latest figures reveal there are approximately five million books and pamphlets on file at the Congressional Library. These are in addition to more than a million maps and views, more than a million music volumes and a half million prints.—*United States News.*

DIFFICULTIES of administration growing out of the depression face Harry Miller Lydenberg, new director of the New York Public Library, who has assumed office this month with the retirement of Edwin H. Anderson.

The major problem confronting Mr. Lydenberg, as was the case with his predecessor, is economic. It is the necessary restriction of library service because of reduced budget, a problem which only recovery is likely to solve.

In discussing the library Mr. Lydenberg explained that much as he deplored its handicapped services, he did not in any way blame the city administration.

"The city has given us as much as it can give us," he said. "There is no arguing that point. The city has always looked at the library with creditable foresight and shown itself ready to meet our needs."

Because of reduced appropriations the library faces, among other things, the gradual disappearance of its stock of circulating books. When books wear out now only an inadequate appropriation is available for replacements, so that the supply available for the public is gradually diminishing.

In 1932 the library appropriation for purchase of new books for circulation was $256,500. In 1933 the amount was reduced to $57,000, which included also the allowance for binding and periodicals. In 1934 the appropriation was reduced still further to $50,000, but for 1935 it has been raised to $60,000. Books are being mended and remended to prolong their service to the limit, but eventually they deteriorate to a point at which they are no longer usable.

"Not to be able to meet public needs is one of the librarian's tragedies," Mr. Lydenberg explained. "The librarian devotes his life to the satisfaction of this human need for books. For the librarian to find himself suddenly unable to meet this need, which he has done much to recognize and stimulate, is pathetic."

Another of the problems engaging the new director is the inadequate number of branches and sub-branches in the Bronx. This, again, is basically an economic problem, Mr. Lydenberg explained, which can not be solved wholly until recovery makes money available for new buildings and extended service.

Mr. Lydenberg has become director of the library after having been in its service thirty-eight years. He began as a cataloguer, and for three years subsequently was in charge of manuscripts. From 1899 to 1908 he was assistant to the director, later chief reference librarian, and until recently assistant director. —*The New York Times.*

# EDUCATIONAL RESEARCH AND STATISTICS

## A FOLLOW-UP STUDY OF EARLY SCHOLASTIC PREDICTIONS IN THE UNIVERSITY OF MINNESOTA

IN connection with the counseling system begun in 1915 in the College of Science, Literature and the Arts of the University of Minnesota, continuous efforts have been made to discover valid information to be given entering freshmen regarding their prospects for success in college. This advice has been given, not to discourage any one or to serve any selfish interest of the college, but to save students from failure and to help them find, if possible, the vocations and types of training most suitable to their abilities. Systematic studies in the prediction of scholarship were begun with the class which entered in 1917 and have been carried on continuously with subsequent freshman classes. For the period 1921 to 1928, these studies involved the use of rank in high-school classes and a psychological test composed of an adaptation of Moore's completion questions, a short opposites test and two recognition vocabulary sections. This test was constructed and standardized by Professor D. G. Paterson. The total percentile rank of the test, based on college freshman norms, was averaged with the percentile rank in high-school scholarship, based on grades for three and one half years, to derive the college aptitude rating. The early studies of these predictive devices have been reported elsewhere.[1]

These early studies showed that college scholarship could be predicted with a high degree of success from high-school percentile rank and the college aptitude test; the best prediction was obtained by averaging the two ranks. Prediction of failure (or less than an average grade of C) was especially efficient for students with a college aptitude rating below 26. For the period 1923–1927 only 1.1 per cent. of students with C.A.R. below 26 received an average grade of C. On the other hand, some students high in C.A.R. failed to maintain a scholastic performance commensurate with their ratings. For the period 1923–1927 96 per cent. of students with C.A.R. above 90 received an average grade of C or higher.

Most of the studies referred to above were based on grades obtained during the freshman year (in some studies, on the first two quarters of residence). One study, however, examined the correlation between the C.A.R. and the scholarship throughout a four-year period for the group which entered in 1921.

The results of this study were summarized by Johnston as follows: "It is to be noted that a high correlation exists between the predictive ratings and the length of residence and that no student graduated or made four years' progress in a professional course whose rating was below the 'threshold of ability.' Those who made four years' progress with scholarship marks of D plus were in schools which do not require the average of C. The combined ratings are evidently a good measure of ability for the four-year course as well as for the first one or two years."[2]

It is important to extend these studies to determine the validity of the prediction based on the C.A.R. with reference to the scholastic records made by students during their entire residence in the university. Accordingly, such a follow-up study has been made for the freshman classes of 1923, 1924 and 1925, involving a total of 1,085 students.[3] This study, made at this time, has the further advantage that it takes into account those students who, after a period absence, returned to the university to complete their course. The study of the 1921 group was made immediately at the end of the four years following entrance.

The results of this follow-up study are reported in Table I in terms of the number of students, at each level of college aptitude rating, receiving C grades but withdrawing from college without a degree (column 3); the number at each level receiving a degree only in this college (column 4); the number receiving a degree from the Arts College and other colleges of the university (column 5); the total number of degrees from the Arts College (column 6); and the corresponding percentage (column 7). Students beginning in this college, but graduating from another college of the University of Minnesota prior to June, 1933, are classified in column 8, with the corresponding percentage (column 9). In view of the fact that the purpose of the early studies was to predict grades and progress in the Arts College, it is necessary

1 J. B. Johnston, "The Liberal College in a Changing Society," Century Company, 1931; J. B. Johnston, "Who Should Go to College?," University of Minnesota Press, 1930.

2 J. B. Johnston, *University of Minnesota Bulletin*, Vol. XXX, No. 75, November 8, 1927.

3 In the Arts College honor points are assigned as follows: 3 to each credit of A, 2 to each B, 1 to each C, none to grade D and minus 1 to F grades. The honor point ratio is computed by dividing the total number of honor points earned by the total number of credits carried.

TABLE I

RELATION BETWEEN COLLEGE APTITUDE RATING AND GRADUATION FROM THE ARTS COLLEGE COMPARED WITH GRADUATION FROM OTHER COLLEGES OF THE UNIVERSITY OF MINNESOTA FOR 1923–1924–1925, MEN AND WOMEN COMBINED

| 1<br>C. A. R. Percentiles | 2<br>Total number students | 3<br>Satisfactory grades in S.L.A. and no degree from U. of M. | 4<br>Degree in arts *only* U. of M. | 5<br>Degree in arts and adv. degree or degree from other colleges U. of M. | 6<br>Total degrees in arts | 7<br>Per cent. of total with degrees in arts* | 8<br>Degrees other colleges U. of M. | 9<br>Per cent. of total with degrees other colleges U. of M. |
|---|---|---|---|---|---|---|---|---|
| 96–100 | 36 | 6 | 11 | 12 | 23 | 63.9 | 7 | 19.4 |
| 91– 95 | 59 | 10 | 17 | 9 | 26 | 44.1 | 18 | 30.5 |
| 86– 90 | 61 | 9 | 19 | 9 | 28 | 45.9 | 18 | 29.5 |
| 81– 85 | 61 | 8 | 13 | 7 | 20 | 32.8 | 19 | 31.1 |
| 76– 80 | 66 | 11 | 13 | 5 | 18 | 27.3 | 22 | 33.3 |
| 71– 75 | 48 | 9 | 8 | 7 | 15 | 31.3 | 15 | 31.3 |
| 66– 70 | 66 | 6 | 13 | 7 | 20 | 30.3 | 19 | 28.8 |
| 61– 65 | 74 | 12 | 12 | 6 | 18 | 24.3 | 18 | 24.3 |
| 56– 60 | 69 | 7 | 11 | 5 | 16 | 23.2 | 18 | 26.1 |
| 51– 55 | 77 | 10 | 12 | 4 | 16 | 20.8 | 18 | 23.4 |
| 46– 50 | 64 | 3 | 11 | 6 | 17 | 26.6 | 14 | 21.9 |
| 41– 45 | 71 | 5 | 14 | 1 | 15 | 21.1 | 10 | 14.1 |
| 36– 40 | 76 | 3 | 5 | 4 | 9 | 11.8 | 13 | 17.1 |
| 31– 35 | 67 | 3 | 10 | 1 | 11 | 16.4 | 10 | 14.9 |
| 26– 30 | 50 | | 3 | 2 | 5 | 10.0 | 11 | 22.0 |
| 21– 25 | 46 | | 2 | 0 | 2 | 4.3 | 2 | 4.3 |
| 16– 20 | 39 | | 2 | 0 | 2 | 5.1 | 5 | 12.8 |
| 11– 15 | 25 | | 1 | 1 | 2 | 8.0 | 3 | 12.0 |
| 6– 10 | 20 | | | 0 | | 0.0 | 3 | 15.0 |
| 1– 5 | 10 | | | 0 | | 0.0 | 0 | 0.0 |
| | 1,085 | 102 | 177 | 86 | 263 | | 243 | |

* *e.g.,* 23 of the 36 students with C. A. R.'s between 96 and 100 received degrees in arts.

to study separately the question of predicting grades in other colleges by means of the early tests. In this study no attempt has been made to determine the number of students failing to obtain degrees in the university but subsequently graduating from colleges other than those in the University of Minnesota.

One hundred and two students maintained average grades of C or higher in the Arts College, but withdrew from the university for reasons other than low scholarship. Since none of these withdrawing freshmen had college aptitude ratings below 31, it is quite evident that the predictive measure was valid in the cases of these students. A total of 263 students eventually received degrees from the Arts College. Eighty-six of the 263 received, in addition, degrees from other colleges in the University of Minnesota. The C. A. R.'s of this latter group appear to be slightly higher than is the case for those students receiving degrees only from the Arts College. Only one of these students receiving two or more degrees had a C. A. R. below 26. This student, whose C. A. R. was 12.5, received the B.S., M.B. and M.D. degrees. The distribution of college aptitude ratings of these students graduating from the Arts College (column 6), resembles to a surprising degree the distribution presented by Johnston in "Who Should Go to College?" Johnston found that only three of all freshmen entering this college for the years 1923 to 1927, inclusive, and with college aptitude ratings below 26 maintained C or higher grades in the first few quarters in college residence. Table I, column 6, shows that only six students with college aptitude ratings below 26 eventually graduated from this college; this is 4.3 per cent. of students at this level with degrees as compared with Johnston's report of 1.1 per cent. of students with C or higher average grades.

Johnston reported 19 students with college aptitude ratings between 26 and 35 inclusive who maintained C or better grades, whereas in Table I, column 6, there are 16 such students. Since Johnston's study was based upon 2,212 students and this present study includes only 1,085, the percentage of successes at this level is greater in this follow-up study. These facts would indicate that a few low aptitude students who do poor work in their first and second quarters in college eventually raise their college marks at least to the minimum C level.

Johnston's early studies showed that the college aptitude rating gave better prediction of grades in college than did percentile rank in high school scholarship or college aptitude test alone. A similar comparison is made in Table II for the present follow-up study. It is apparent that Johnston's early conclusion that C. A. R. yielded the best prediction for these Arts College students has been verified by this follow-up study. Not only do fewer students with low C. A. R.'s get degrees, but a larger percentage of those with high C. A. R.'s are successful, than is true for high-school percentile rank or college aptitude test alone.

TABLE II

COMPARISON OF C. A. R., HIGH-SCHOOL PERCENTILE RANK AND COLLEGE APTITUDE TEST, BY LEVELS WITH REGARD TO PERCENTAGE OF STUDENTS GRADUATING FROM THE ARTS COLLEGE

| | College aptitude rating | High-school scholarship percentile rank | College aptitude test percentile rank |
|---|---|---|---|
| | Per cent. S. L. A. degrees | Per cent. S. L. A. degrees | Per cent. S. L. A. degrees |
| 96–100<br>91– 95 | 51.6* | 41.7 | 42.2 |
| 86– 90<br>81– 85<br>76– 80 | 35.1 | 34.3 | 31.9 |
| 71– 75<br>66– 70<br>61– 65<br>56– 60<br>51– 55 | 25.4 | 25.8 | 23.7 |
| 46– 50<br>41– 45<br>36– 40 | 19.4 | 16.7 | 17.5 |
| 31– 35<br>26– 30 | 13.9 | 12.6 | 25.0 |
| 21– 25<br>16– 20<br>11– 15<br>6– 10<br>1– 5 | 4.3 | 6.6 | 13.3 |

* The other 48.4 per cent. includes those who cancelled with C or higher average grades (Table I, column 3), or graduated from another college (Table I, column 8). Similar interpretations should be made of other percentages presented in Table II above.

To turn to an analysis of the predictive value of C. A. R. for other colleges of the university, column 8 of Table I indicates the number of these freshmen who transferred from the Arts College and eventually graduated from some other college. There were 13 students with college aptitude ratings below 26 included in this group. Table III gives the college aptitude rating, the honor point ratio received in the Arts College and the degree received by these 13 students. One student graduated from Business, two from Dentistry, three from Dental Hygiene or Dental Nursing, four from Education, two from Engineering or Architecture, and one from Law. From this table, it is evident that only one of the thirteen students who eventually graduated from these various colleges had a standing of one honor point per credit carried while he was a student in the Arts College. The college aptitude rating is not supposed to be a measure of the special aptitudes required for success in these various colleges.

This illustrates very clearly what Johnston constantly said in all the years when the method

TABLE III

Students with College Aptitude Ratings Below 26 who Graduated from Other Colleges in the University of Minnesota

| Students number | C.A.R. | Total credits in S.L.A. Carried | Total credits in S.L.A. Earned* | Total number honor points earned in S.L.A. | Degree in other colleges, U. of M. |
|---|---|---|---|---|---|
| 1 | 24.0 | 125 | 117 | 109 | L.L.B. |
| 2 | 7.0 | 99 | 82 | 31 | D.D.S. |
| 3 | 18.5 | 41 | 37 | 21 | D.D.S. |
| 4 | 11.0 | 68 | 29 | − 29 | B. Arch. Eng. |
| 5 | 17.0 | 156 | 150 | 164 | B.B.S. (Business) |
| 6 | 19.5 | 151 | 131 | 90 | B.S. (Educ.) |
| 7 | 14.5 | 15 | 5 | − 10 | B.E.E. |
| 8 | 18.0 | 80 | 77 | 62 | Dent. Hyg. |
| 9 | 9.0 | 15 | 5 | − 10 | Dent. Hyg. |
| 10 | 21.5 | 46 | 43 | 36 | B.S. (Educ.) |
| 11 | 19.5 | 105 | 95 | 95 | B.S. (Educ.) |
| 12 | 11.5 | 72 | 66 | 41 | B.S. (Educ.) |
| 13 | 8.5 | 40 | 25 | − 10 | Dent. Nurse |

* Credits carried refers to the number for which the student registered; credits earned refers to the number for which he received passing grades.

of selecting students by means of a college aptitude rating was being developed and explained. The college aptitude rating and the method of obtaining it were empirically worked out with students in the Arts College on the basis of their scholastic records. The college aptitude rating technique was found empirically to yield the most valid prediction of future scholastic standing in the Arts College when applied to freshmen at the time of entrance. The claim of validity for this particular technique was made only in the case of Arts College students. Other colleges whose faculties or administration wish to secure corresponding services for their students must work out a technique which is applicable to the students, curricula and standards of those colleges. For this purpose an instrument like the Arts College aptitude test may be tried and used if it proves to be valid; but its validity for Arts College students can not be affected by such trial with students in other colleges. This extended statement is necessary because some persons have failed to understand this simple principle of calibrating each predictive device for each college or curriculum.

Only five of the thirteen students in the above table graduated from a professional college which requires an average of C for graduation. All thirteen met the requirements of their respective professional colleges, but in courses taken in the Arts College, only one met the standard of one honor point per credit carried, the criterion used throughout the studies of the validity of predictive devices. Some of those with low ratings took longer than the normal period to complete their professional courses. Table I shows that six or 4.3 per cent. of the 140 students who had a rating of 25 or lower in C. A. R., devised for the Arts College, graduated from the Arts College, while an additional thirteen or 9.3 per cent. (column 8) graduated from other colleges during the same period. This is evidence that the C. A. R. is less valid, although still valuable for these other colleges.

The early studies of prediction for Arts College students, verified by the data presented in Tables I and II, led to the arrangement of special curricula in this college for low-aptitude students. The performance of these students under such special conditions offers another source of evidence as to the validity of the C. A. R. as a predictive device. Under this arrangement, students who had low ratings were enrolled, during the four years 1928–29 to 1931–32, as "non-candidates for a degree." The following account of the results of that experiment is abbreviated from the dean's report to the president for the biennium 1930–32.[4]

The hypothesis on which that experiment was based was that those students whose college aptitude ratings indicated very poor prospects for successful work in the regular curriculum would find it more profitable to omit technical and tool subjects which prepare for scholarship, and spend their time on studies useful for some vocation or in preparation for the duties of citizens. It was known that the large majority of these students would stay in college less than two years, and a

[4] *University of Minnesota*, Bulletin, Vol. XXXV, No. 64, pp. 103–108.

large part of them only one or two quarters. In addition to the plan to give this group of students instruction which might help them to discharge their duties as citizens, the college had the object of putting its space, its equipment, and the time of its staff at the disposal of those students who gave promise of using these facilities in higher education and in the later service to society in the more important and complex social, economic, and political problems. During the past four years, then, the group of students indicated was not allowed to elect at the beginning of their freshman year foreign languages, laboratory courses, mathematics, English constitutional history. Other subjects open to freshmen were open to them: Modern world history, human geography, descriptive economics, drawing, shopwork, etc., lecture courses in zoology, botany, and geology.

To show in the most general way the grounds on which the group in question was segregated, it may be said that whereas 96.6 per cent. of the students with ratings between 96 and 100 did satisfactory work in college, there is a steady decline in the percentage until at 26 to 30 in the scale, only 6.4 per cent. did satisfactory work, and at 1 to 15 in the scale, none did satisfactory work.

At the end of the first year (1928–1929) of this segregation of the low aptitude students it was observed that they had secured on the average higher grades than the students with corresponding ratings had secured in previous years. On examining the scholarship record of the low rating students subject by subject in the year 1926–27, it was evident that these students secured higher grades in economics, history, and lecture courses in science than they did in languages or laboratory courses in science. This, together with later examination of the records of the low aptitude students in various subjects, seems to show that such students secure better grades in discursive subjects such as economics, history, and general survey lectures in sciences than they do in the close, detailed study required in languages or in laboratory courses. Therefore, the limitation of these students to certain subjects enabled them to secure higher scholarship standings.

It should be said that the identity of the low aptitude students was known to only a few administrative officers and advisers. The teachers in whose classes they were enrolled had no means of knowing who they were.

During the four years there were 996 students assigned to the non-degree group. They were distributed over the four years as follows: 274, 296, 208, and 218. In the first two years those students who had college aptitude ratings of 35 or lower, and in the last two years those who had ratings of 25 or lower, were assigned to this group.

The degree of success of these students in the training offered by present colleges and schools is evident from the figures in the above tables (See Report to President). Of the total number 996, 236, or 23.7 per cent., have been dropped from college during or at the close of the first three quarters of residence. The proportion of all freshmen dropped over a period of years has been eight or nine per cent. An additional 386 did not return to college after varying periods of residence. . . . Of the 274 who entered in 1928–29, 80 were dropped and 156 did not return, or 86 per cent. of the group. Of the same year group 2 (0.73 per cent.) were graduated from this college and 4 (1.46 per cent.) from professional schools in June, 1932. In his study of "Student Survival" (1925) Mr. West[5] found that of those entering this college as freshmen 6.7 per cent. graduated in four years from this college and 17 per cent. either graduated from professional schools or made four years' progress in combined courses. Since none of the students in question are enrolled in combined courses, it is correct to say that 2.19 per cent. of the 1928–29 group have graduated in four years as compared with 23.7 per cent. of all freshmen enrolled in September, 1920.

Of the 239 from all four years who have remained in this college until June, 1932, 59 have been in residence for three years and 11 for four years, of whom 5 have been promoted to the Upper Division and 2 of the 5 have graduated. Of the 62 who have been in residence two years, 2 are now eligible for promotion to the Upper Division and 5 to professional schools. This means that out of 778 from the three years, 132 have remained in this college long enough to complete the Lower Division work; of whom 12, or 1.54 per cent. have made normal progress. From the same three-year groups 73 have transferred to professional schools, of whom 2 have been dropped and 4 have taken degrees. There were 69 in residence in professional schools in June, 1932, a large part of whom will presumably reach graduation in those schools.

It is necessary now to call attention to the fact that of the 996 students who have been treated alike administratively, 176 were assigned to this group on the basis of their ranks in college aptitude tests alone. These were persons whose high school ranks were not reported to us. . . . Of the 820 whose classification was based on the complete C. A. R., 9.39 per cent. secured an average of C in all work carried (See Table IV below). . . .

[5] R. M. West, *University of Minnesota Bulletin*, Vol. XXVIII, No. 4, Feb. 10, 1925, pp. 3–50.

This favorable record is fully explained in my opinion by the fact that students of this type secure higher grades in the subjects which were open to these students than in those required subjects which were closed to them.

From this experience of four years some inferences can be drawn with regard to the prospects for students of the type here studied, going on to graduation in the college or the professional schools. Of the first year group, 2 have graduated in this college, from the second year group 3 have been promoted to the Upper Division, and from the third group 2 are ready for promotion to the Upper Division. If the fourth year group should do equally well, there may be 10 students out of the total 996 to enter the Upper Division and probably to graduate. This is 1 per cent. of the entrants.

At the same time 73 students have entered the professional schools and 5 are now ready to enter; 2 have been dropped, 4 have graduated, and 27 show good records at present. If 5 others enter professional schools from the fourth year group there will be 74, of whom 40 or 50 may graduate. It is noticeable that students frequently make distinctly better records in professional schools than they do in this college. If a maximum of 50 may be expected to graduate from professional schools in a normal period, that would be 5 per cent. of the total entrants. This does not take into account possible deferred graduations such as Mr. West studied for the freshman class of 1920.

TABLE IV

Relationship Between C. A. R. and Scholarship in the Arts College of 820 Non-candidates for Degree*

| C.A.R. | F− −1.00 − .51 | F+ −.50 −.01 | D− .00 .49 | D+ .50 .99 | C− 1.00 1.49 | C+ 1.50 1.99 | B− 2.00 2.49 | B+ 2.50 2.99 | A 3.00 |
|---|---|---|---|---|---|---|---|---|---|
| 31–35 | 9 | 12 | 44 | 36 | 12 | 4 | 1 | ...... | ...... |
| 26–30 | 16 | 26 | 44 | 24 | 15 | 1 | ...... | ...... | ...... |
| 21–25 | 37 | 36 | 42 | 44 | 13 | 2 | ...... | ...... | ...... |
| 16–20 | 19 | 34 | 51 | 28 | 8 | 2 | 1 | ...... | ...... |
| 11–15 | 30 | 26 | 36 | 22 | 7 | 2 | ...... | ...... | ...... |
| 6–10 | 17 | 25 | 27 | 13 | 5 | 2 | ...... | ...... | ...... |
| 1– 5 | 21 | 13 | 9 | 2 | ...... | 1 | 1 | ...... | ...... |
| | 149 | 172 | 253 | 169 | 60 | 14 | 3 | ...... | ...... |
| | Total | | | | | | | | 820 |

* Table VI in the Dean's Report to the President, 1932, p. 108.

As a phase of a counseling system, the use made of a college aptitude rating has been twofold. On the one hand, the counselor acquainted the student with the general probability of success or failure in the work which he was about to undertake. On the other hand, the counselor undertook to find out whether the unpromising student had qualifications for a vocation which requires non-college training beyond the high school. In these services, the counselor was often able to rescue the student from danger or disaster and to help him on the road to success in some field suited to his interests and abilities. These efforts have led to further development of instrumentalities, such as the University Testing Bureau, for securing more complete and reliable data.

Table I (columns 3, 6 and 8) shows that 56 per cent. of the students entering the Arts College proved to be fitted for the work of that college or of some professional school in the university. This situation has suggested two other main lines of effort. The first of these is to discover whether the failing students may be given help through the improvement of health, the correction of speech defects, training in methods of study or otherwise by correcting or supplementing the training they have been given at the secondary level. All these counseling methods are being used extensively at the present time; additional experience will show to what extent they should be developed and to what individuals such special services should be furnished.

The second line of effort is the attempt to discover whether any new or modified form of instruction at the college level is more suited to students who can not profit from the curricula of the traditional college or professional schools. In Minnesota this search has led to the establishment of the University General College, which enrolled, among others, the type of students described above as "non-candidates for a degree." In connection with the General College, a third indication of the validity of the C. A. R. is found in the scholastic records of two groups of students: those who protested against assignment to the General College and were accepted in the Arts College, and those who were transferred to the Arts College after a period of successful residence in the General College. This third study of the validity of the C. A. R. supplements the one summarized in Tables I and II and the second study quoted from the dean's report to the president.

The university board of admissions, acting in cooperation with committees of the various colleges, has had to deal with students who protested against assignment to the General College and who insisted on admission to the college of their choice. The Arts College required for admission a C. A. R. higher than 35. In the two years since the opening of the General College, 169 such protestants have been admitted to the Arts College on probation. The performance of these students in Arts College classes is the proper test of the wisdom of the committees concerned in yielding to the students' persistence and insistence.

Sixty-nine of the total of 169 were accepted under these conditions in 1932–33, of whom 28 remained in this college one quarter, 7 remained two quarters, 11 remained three quarters, and 22 went on through the second year (4 quarters in one case, 5 quarters in two cases). Ten students secured an average of C in their whole work, one for two quarters, one for three quarters and eight for six quarters. Of those who did not secure a standing of C, 1 cancelled in the first quarter, 28 were dropped for low scholarship, 7 were advised to transfer to the General College, 8 did not return after one, two or three quarters, 1 was transferred to the School of Nursing and 14 continued in the second year.

An additional 100 were admitted in 1933–34, of whom 1 cancelled during his first quarter without grade, 47 remained through one quarter, 17 through two quarters and 35 through three quarters. Three secured an average of C for one quarter, two for two quarters and 12 for three quarters. Thirty-four fell below the satisfactory standing of C but without disciplinary action, and 48 were dropped for low scholarship. Of those dropped for low scholarship, 39 were allowed to enter the General College.

Some persons have made the observation that the students who have the poorest equipment for college work are the ones who are most persistent and most certain that they can succeed. This is obviously not the whole of the matter, for the very qualities of persistence and self-confidence are themselves important in college work, and with these qualities usually goes serious effort.

Since the 169 students above described were granted a special privilege on their urgent request and were on probation from the start, we must assume that they made conscientious efforts to succeed. Of this group, 27 or 16 per cent. did satisfactory work in this college as compared with 18 or 7 per cent. of the 257 freshmen with C. A. R.'s below 36 (see Table I) who received degrees from the Arts College only.

After a period of residence in the General College, a student whose record has been satisfactory may be recommended by the director of that unit for transfer to the Arts College. The students' work committee of the Arts College requires "honors" standing in the General College and may require special supplementary aptitude tests. During the past two years, 53 students have been transferred to the Arts College on the basis of this policy. The bearing of the success of these students on the validity of the college aptitude rating lies in the fact that some students enter the General College whose college aptitude ratings are satisfactory for entrance to the Arts College, and that those who are transferred include some with C. A. R. below and some with C. A. R. above the minimum set for entrance to the Arts College.

In deciding the problem of transferring these students, the Students' Work Committee exercised great care and made use of all available data. In general, the college aptitude rating did not play a primary part. When the C. A. R. was low, it was superseded by the record from the General College. When the C. A. R. was high, it was accepted as corroborative evidence.

Of the 53 transfers, 30 did satisfactory work in the Arts College and 23 did not. In order to consider what would have been the effect of basing transfer on the college aptitude rating only, 44 students can be taken into account, since the C. A. R. was not available in the cases of nine. For these 44 students the record is as follows:

RECORD MADE IN THE ARTS COLLEGE

| | Average of C or higher | Below C average |
|---|---|---|
| Transferred on General College record | 26 | 18 |
| C. A. R. above 35 | 16 | 6 |
| C. A. R. 35 or lower | 10 | 12 |
| C. A. R. above 25 | 24 | 12 |
| C. A. R. 25 or lower | 2 | 6 |

The results of the first two years can not be regarded as conclusive. It can be said only that they do not furnish positive evidence that a period of study in the General College will serve as a means of overcoming an original handicap of low aptitude for studies in the Arts College. The number of successes among students with low C. A. R. is possibly to be attributed to the known ability of competent advisers to discover individuals who will do better than is indicated by their college aptitude ratings because of inaccurate test ratings, ambition, specialized aptitude for particular courses and other factors which operate to produce inaccuracies in general predictions of marks.

The writers are of the opinion that the examination of all available evidence, which they have attempted to set forth above, clearly shows that the college aptitude rating offers a dependable and just basis for the counseling of students under the conditions prevailing at such institutions as the University of Minnesota. Its use for the assignment of students to different colleges without counseling, however, is not recommended. If so used, it should be limited to those students who fall below the 15 or 20 percentile level.

The essential principle of the C. A. R. is found in the combination of two or more criteria or measures. Our experience points unquestionably to the desirability of adding further tests or other measures to those now being used. Experiments with this in view have been carried on for several years and are being expanded during the year 1934–35 to provide a sampling of students' educational background in the subject-matter fields of science, mathematics, history and contemporary affairs (or current events). These extensive samplings will supplement those used heretofore, namely, the college aptitude test, high-school scholarship percentile rank and a test of English grammar, spelling and usage. In addition, the present research program will include a study of the early form of the college aptitude test used in the years 1921 to 1928; this analysis will provide a further comparison of present prediction with that of the period 1923–1925 inclusive.

J. B. JOHNSTON
E. G. WILLIAMSON
UNIVERSITY OF MINNESOTA

## NEW BOOKS IN EDUCATION

BERMAN, ISABEL R. and others. *Vocational Interest Scales.* Pp. 35. University of Minnesota Press.

*Development of Social Intelligence through Part-Time Education.* Pp. ix + 67. U. S. Government Printing Office. $0.10.

GIDEONSE, HARRY D. *America in a World Economy.* Pp. 56. American Association of University Women, Washington, D. C.

HILL, DAVID S. *Control of Tax-Supported Higher Education in the United States.* Pp. 383. Carnegie Foundation for the Advancement of Teaching.

HOUSE, HOMER C. and SUSAN E. HARMAN. *College Rhetoric.* Pp. ix + 321. Prentice-Hall. $2.25.

MORT, PAUL R. and EUGENE S. LAWLER. *Taxation for Adequate Support of Educational Services.* Pp. 24. American Association of University Women.

PALEY, WILLIAM S. *Radio as a Cultural Force.* Pp. 29. Columbia Broadcasting System.

PETERS, CHARLES C. and GEORGE W. HARTMANN. *Abstracts of Studies in Education at The Pennsylvania State College.* Part IV (1934). Pp. 80. Pennsylvania State College.

*Report of Conference on Supervised Correspondence Study, Held at Teachers College, Columbia University.* Pp. 66. International Textbook Company. $0.25.

TIBBITTS, F. LYMAN. *Platooning the Church School.* Pp. 86. Burkhart Press, Tulsa.

TILDEN, F. F. *You Don't Say! . . . Or Do You?* (A Pronunciation Test). Pp. 51. Author, Boston.

WHITMER, T. CARL. *The Art of Improvisation.* Pp. 73. Witmark. $2.50.

# EDUCATIONAL REVIEW

**Edited by Nicholas Murray Butler, 1891–1919, Frank Pierrepont Graves, 1920–1924, and William McAndrew, 1924–**

# COMMENTS ON THINGS EDUCATIONAL

By WILLIAM McANDREW

## LOST PROVINCES OF EDUCATION

IN the monthly tramp to the parlors of publishers where books are exposed from which there must be selected some to keep this reviewery's shelves well-stocked I came upon Philophilus beaming more than usual.

"Phil," said I, "happiness is radiating from you like the sparks from an electric welder."

"O terque quaterque beatus," he answered, "that's from our edition of Vergil."

"If you publish it you ought to know how to pronounce it. What has happened to you?"

"Vacation, old dear. I'm off for a month, first time in ten years, and I'm driving my new flivver."

"Alone?"

"Unless you come wi' me, me lad."

"You can't bluff me, Phil. I'll go. When do we start?"

"To-morrow, sun-up."

See us, then, next day, gliding along the Boston Post Road like riding on a velvet-footed, softly-purring pussy. New Haven, first stop.

"There's a meeting here," said Phil. "Want to go?"

"I thought this was vacation."

"Comrade, where's your psychology? Don't you know the best vacation is one you spend among people you like the most? Come and see Connecticut teachers; they're real."

We went into the hall of the commercial high school. It was full. Another hall in New Haven and two in Hartford were brimming with the cream of Connecticut.

Egbert Case, Willimantic schoolmaster, was speaking when we came in. After listening to his quiet presentation for a minute we noted, as his audience realized, that he was picturing the present educational crisis with an understanding and a purpose the likes of which neither of us has ever heard surpassed.

"It is folly," said Student Case, "to relapse into the old educational dream that the schools are secure. We didn't fight the battle that established the schools. We accepted them as a divine gift, a manifest destiny.

"But we have neglected preparedness for defense. We have lost provinces. The chief of these is the reverence of the public mind. The family still spends for what it wants: World's Fair, Mae West, more booze than ever, and kicks on the 14 cents a day tax on a $7,000 house.

"Another lost province is professional standing. People do not take us seriously as able to make a diagnosis of civic ills and as promoters of remedial thinking. Yet, on promise that this would be our function, the founders made us public officers.

"We have, in the minds of our political masters, become lucky job-holders. Professional skill is no consideration in the opinion of the dispensers of patronage. Appointment is decided by place of birth, marital condition or financial need. The public has not been taught that teaching-skill is a possession acquired by much labor and expense of time and brains.

"The tax-resisting part of the public is finely organized. Possessors of wealth are opposing the use of their money to educate other people's children. These few could be voted down in the good old days. But now the millions who thought themselves moderately well-to-do are submerged by the wreckage of instalment buying, supersalesmanship and speculation."

What we liked about Case was his definite plan of organizing teachers and citizens to study the tax problem, the school dollar, the need of an educated citizenry, provisions that bonds be dependable investments, the dependence of prosperity on schooling, and insuring that the people prevent the legislature from wrecking the schools.

Especially we admired the persuasive urge to teachers to take a leaf from the physician's note-book and to keep out of our educational meetings the speakers bidding by sensation for mention in the newspapers. These are the wild boys who call the school a failure, useless preparation for life. We must cure our educational diseases not before the none-too-friendly public.

## HURRIED AMERICA

From New Haven to Bear Mountain bridge is, as the Ford flies, a matter of thirty-odd miles, but what a picture book to set right the misguided American who thinks the English country-side the acme of loveliness! Behind their stone fences the descendants of the Davenports, Winthrops, Trumbulls, Websters, Hopkinses, Wolcotts, Ellsworths and Touceys look from their white houses on well-trimmed lawns under the majestic trees. Although their valleys are deep the streams are in no hurry to leave this lovely land. Whisk, we are riding through Newton on its hilltop, a village claiming to be the cleanest in the United States. Danbury is a dear. A modest sign tells us we are crossing to New York. It is the lake country supplying the metropolis with much water. Here, my host informs me, the troops of Connecticut and New York were ready to fight for ownership of the land, but eastern Long Island was turned over by the Nutmeg State to its greedy neighbor and the boundary we now go over was settled. How does Philophilus know the particular history needed at various moments on our long journey to the banks of the Missouri? I solved the secret later, finding in the boot-box behind the car a small library of "Seeing This" and "Seeing That," which this tireless vacationer diligently peruses after his companion has gone to sleep.

Like a spider on wheels we traverse the thin web that spans the Hudson and get a moment of melancholy by the sight of the long stretch of this majestic stream without a boat in sight. In old pictures of Sunnyside the river is dotted with sails. In Clinton's day a signal could be waved from Albany and repeated, seen from steamer to steamer, all the way to Sandy Hook. America finds navigation all too slow. Her river and canal fleets have gone. Continental Europe goes on cutting canals and dredging rivers, keeping down transportation costs and keeping travel picturesque. This steam and gasoline whizz flips the pages of the picture book so fast that the enjoyment of scenery is dying out.

More melancholy is due at Port Jervis, where, no more, hung daringly above the waters of the Delaware, the boats of the famous old canal make the crossing. We old men remember when it was a favorite jaunt to follow the towpath, no dust, no smell, no dodging the traffic, from Honesdale to New Paltz, to Newburgh, through a green paradise.

But there is recompense. Milady of the Port Jervis inn serves slices of cold lamb, mint jelly, hot biscuit, honey and the milk that makes the Jerseys famous.

Huntingdon, Pennsylvania. For two days, like Phaeton of old, Philophilus has gone now high, now low, through green valleys and over bare mountain tops. Often he sings, no words, only ah-ah, but the tune is of "America the Beautiful." He knows the value of silent conversation. For hours we ride without a word. Often he stops on some commanding height and we gaze, like the men of Cortez, silent on a peak in Darien. Some music is not helped by the teacher's effort to tell the children what to hear. Some pictures are best gazed at quietly. Some of the best poems can be read without analysis. Why must the teacher play the part of demonstrator in a dissecting room?

My host's route, zigzagging, has method in it. We are held up in different towns while he gets into deep conversation with different bright men and women, sometimes over a meal in a hotel, sometimes in a schoolhouse, while he jots down notes. What is it about? A text-book is to go into a revised edition. Philophilus is sounding teachers who are using the work. And this is a bookman's vacation! It reminds me of a kinsman of mine who sailed his ship into New York harbor from Japan around Cape Horn. I wished to show him attention and took him to dinner at John Hill's swank Café Mazarin. What did this sailor, home from the sea, ask for? Corned beef, his regular fare on shipboard for half a year!

## TEACHERS' INSTITUTE AS WAR TRAINING

At Huntingdon the teachers of the county were streaming in from Waterfall, Hares Valley, Cedar Rock, Shady Gap, Coles Summit and other villages whose names paint pictures in your imagination. What journeys these bright folk have had this sunny morning! God bless Henry Ford! We follow the caravan and learn what an educational institute is like in these days of crisis. A speaker is telling the faithful that they must look back to the days of 1773 when committees of correspondence organized the defense. This is the public's danger, but the public doesn't know it. No one knows it so well as the teachers. No people are more able to organize for work than they. But the campaign must show itself as a people's movement. The nucleus of it has to be the teachers of each district. Form your committees, now. Don't wait until you see the whites of the enemy's eyes. Meet once a week. Rehearse. Have at your tongue's end the things education has done for the commonwealth. Know the history of the long fight for public schools in Pennsylvania, the work of Franklin, Benjamin Rush, John Dickinson, Thaddeus Stevens, Wickersham, Schaeffer and Finegan. Study Mulhern's book. Know your state educational history. It's full of interest, a long fight for schools. Show how education is the foundation of prosperity and order. Show what an immense saving the public schools effect by their systematic organization. Show what it would cost families if they had to fall back on tutors as they did in the old days. These arguments should be rehearsed and practised in your teacher committees. You must make lists of your leading citizens and see that they are interviewed by two missionaries at a time. Draft citizens from your parent-teacher association. Keep a record of the people you interview. Are they for, against or undecided? Get your storekeepers. You are their customers. Get your labor organizations. They did more in the early days to make education a state concern than any other group. Get your clergymen. Get your board members and former ones. The majority of the people are for the school, but they are not organized. Paid agents of hostile associations are on the job every day. You are as intelligent as they, but you have been civically lazy. Take a lesson from the "drives" of the Red Cross, of the old lightning-rod canvassers, of the automobile sales forces. Education is in serious danger. Old-age pensions are coming. Unemployment insurance will be put through. These will take a lot of money from the taxpayer. Unless you stir yourselves a good part of this will be taken by reducing school funds.

Keep your association representative at Harrisburg active. Get your warning bulletins from him regularly. Have your citizens pledged to send the letters and telegrams to their representatives in the legislature when the word comes. Any man experienced in government will tell you that these messages do have immense influence. Know the representative from your district in both houses at Harrisburg. Have your best committee call on these men and inquire exactly how they stand. Make your own hesitant teachers work. They dread to ask strangers to support the schools. They try to persuade themselves that playing politics is wrong. Their bosses often give them this notion. This is not playing politics. It is making politics work for the salvation of your country.

I thought from the agreement, approval and applause of these teachers that they could be much more effectively led into a patriotic nation-saving campaign than their predecessors could.

### QUICKENING THE TEACHER

SHEETS outlining the program of the State Education Association were handed to each member of the audience. The agenda included maintenance of the Edmunds Act until a better plan can be secured, at least one third of the cost of education to be borne by the state, a revision of the tax and assessment system, a new and simpler state constitution, enforcement of unpaid tax-claims upon corporations, maintenance of the teacher-retirement system, a tenure law, new and better child-labor laws and restoration of the school program now crippled by emergency legislation.

Harrisburg. "If more men saw the sunrise this would be a better world" was the reason the tireless Philophilus gave for our leaving the huge old Leister Hotel before daybreak and without breakfast. The sun met us in "the Big Valley," where full-bearded religious men, opposed to automobiles, drive their horse-drawn wagons from big barns to market. We had the quiet and companionable Mifflin County superintendent Sipe as breakfast guest in the famous old iron town of Lewistown and followed the winding Juniata through its mountain valleys eastward. Look for them, and every now and then you will see the ruins of the old stone locks that functioned when the great Pennsylvania canal was the highway to the west. In 1848 my father and mother, moving from Baltimore to Ypsilanti, rode by water through this lovely land.

Our visit to the state Capitol was to hear the speakers at the Citizens Conference on School Recovery. The State Superintendent, James Rule, outlined the situation plainly. The well-being of the state depends on the schools. It has been said so often that you accept it as true and sufficient. But education is no monument fought for, set up and needing no further thought. It is a living organism unable to subsist without steady public approval and support. The Rule presentment portrays the civic life for which the school must prepare the American youth. The different competences he must have are described. The number of persons to be educated is made clear. Dr. Rule presents a list of vital questions for each community to ask regarding its schools. He shows the impossibility of adequate service in present circumstances. His exposition has been printed in a pamphlet, "The Three R's of Public-School Recovery." They are reorganization, revision, reconstruction. The presentation is plain talk, fortified with facts, persuasive and appealing in tone, strengthened with pictures and charts. We must have better schools, concludes the superintendent, or pay a heavy penalty in decreased economic efficiency, a lowered moral tone and heavier costs for delinquency and crime.

We had a flock of Pennsylvania schoolmen at McNally's, facing the Capitol grounds, for dinner. My guess is that these jolly fellows are not all awake yet. Some don't know where the strength of their friends is. They haven't counted the heads of the enemy. They seem waiting for a leader. Mass meetings, "inspirational" addresses, whoopee, are very well in their way. Pennsylvania needs more house-to-house canvassing and organized defenses. The strength of woman campaigners isn't understood so well as New York senses it.

Philophilus told the diners this. It was startling to hear him, who had been so soothingly silent on his rides, muster tips from his experiences in getting text-book adoptions and apply them with a niagara of ideas, plans and strategy to the work in hand.

Next morning we turned our radiator toward Detroit.

# MONTHLY SURVEY OF EDUCATIONAL BOOKS

*A College Dean's View of Education.* We older University of Michigan Alumni hold John Johnston in high regard. He put life into his instruction in zoology when he was in the family of our alma mater. His contributions to neurology are distinctive. Anatomy, eugenics, sociology, have been enlivened by him. His latest book[1] teems with constructive educational philosophy and "doctrine attainable by living men." From here and there terse statements will make a dent in the reader's cortex.

"Democracy is at the crossroad with a path to fascism to the right, one to communism to the left, and one straight ahead that needs grading and paving." Dean Johnston is an efficient grader and paver.

"The greatest need of education to-day is that its principles should be understood and supported by the whole people. Education should now be an almost constant topic for consideration. One of the best opportunities for informing the public is contacts made by teachers."

As a democracy we have frequently been mistaken in the leaders we have followed, he says. Factory owners have been placed in the position of leaders of national policy. Go-getters have been allowed to mow down the forests and let the soil formed through millions of years wash away to the sea. Great fortunes have been made by corporate manipulation. No regard

[1] John B. Johnston, ''Education for Democracy,'' The University of Minnesota Press, Minneapolis. 280 pp. $2.50.

was shown for the safety of investors. The nation's wealth has been taken by a few through laws framed by lobbyists.

We have had fascism, masked, worked behind the scene.

It is the function of our educational system to introduce, into democracy, self-control and ordered management for general welfare. This management must depend on accepted leaders. What leaders the people will follow depends on the intelligence and ideals of the citizens. Public education should be the chief influence in shaping civic ideals. The burden of selecting proper leaders is laid upon the schools.

But, he continues, in the minds of many, support of education is maintained in the hope of personal advantage to be obtained.

The number of persons seeking higher education is out of proportion to the pecuniary or personal advantage gained.

Legislative appropriations and private endowments are not for the personal advantage of those who are in school and college. As a beneficiary of a trust no student has the right to accept of it and loaf.

The rapid increase of enrolment without increase of funds has made it impossible to maintain standards. Budgets per student are lower than they ever have been.

Thousands are finding that they are immune to the education offered by the colleges. Other thousands are confronted with overcrowding in their professions.

So-called democracy, instead of organization to meet social needs, has attempted to educate every one for the highest or most attractive types of service instead of training each one for what he is fitted.

Dean Johnston's enumeration of the details of present maladjustment of education is extensive and severe. The major part of his book is concerned with needed adjustments and is confidently constructive.

In the reform of education more importance must be given to estimating the native abilities, interests and aptitudes of children and to the resulting educational guidance which will become concrete and positive after the age of twelve to fifteen years.

As experimental techniques mature college faculties must give reliable guidance. As measuring and estimating native abilities is shown to be dependable, admission to any particular phase of higher education will be based on the fitness of the individual to profit by this training and to make adequate returns to society. At present all sorts are accepted as students in college courses without regard to their ability to profit from instruction.

The new education, he says, will realize that the differences between individuals constitute one of society's greatest assets. The cultivation of the individual's most pronounced traits and highest skills will give society the greatest effective purpose.

"Educators should lead the integration of the many diverse elements of American life into a new social order."

The dean discusses at length the formation of an American aristocracy of character. The time is ripe, he says, for the assertion by colleges of the right of trained minds to leadership among men.

Here he goes into a battlefield that has been fought over for many years. The right of an institution for general education and supported by general taxation, or private endowment, to decide whom it shall benefit has been the claimed prerogative of college since John Harvard made his will. The propriety of exclusion of the unfit from medical school, law school, engineering, dental, pharmaceutical, veterinary and other departments whose graduates should be protectors of life and property has no formidable opposition. The right of a college of literature, science and the arts, that is, a nonprofessional school, a general education department, a liberal-arts college, to say whom it will admit is another matter.

Within the memory of living men such exclusion was practised in all grades of education. The naughty child could be "expelled" from the first grade. High schools determined by examinations who should be let in. High-school teachers, by maintaining "standards of scholarship," eliminated the "unfit." A nation-wide insistence on education as a right for all and, later, as a duty of democracy, has pretty well pushed the sieve-idea out of the picture of public education from kindergarten through junior college. No education for democracy can very well defend the proposition that state-supported colleges of liberal education may operate on a policy different from the rest of the public school system of which they are parts. It is true that the canvass made of deans by Professor Gauss of Princeton shows them in agreement that the college should be allowed to pick its clientele. So were the majority of high-school teachers in 1900 practically unanimous that they should determine who should have high-school instruction.

Dean Johnston's hope that college will perfect a technique for discovering what a boy is best fitted for is shared by all the high-school people. The persistence of college entrance requirements utterly remote from testing fitness or even for determining success in the studies arbitrarily required after the boy gets into college throws a fog over expectation that the higher institutions will care so much for what a youth should do as for whether he fits the college course as is. Isn't it true that determination of ability and subsequent guidance is a technology originating and getting its development in the organizations devoted to the professional training of teachers? Also, who are more opposed to the professional study of education than are the professors in colleges of liberal arts?

Accepting Dean Johnston's patriotic concept of the college as an organizer of the whole people to secure the welfare of all, believing with him that public welfare can not be organized by special interests, that the intelligence, the planning must come from an institution representing the whole people, the public-school men in large numbers resist the proposal that college shall sift the country's youth to cast aside those whom the college deems unworthy of initiation into the aristocracy of brains. For some time to come we are likely to be governed in accordance with the votes of a majority. If a tax-supported college, or a private one relieved of taxation, is devoted to improving civic conditions, why, for the land's sake, should we approve of its debasing our citizenry by pushing into it all the youth whom the college considers unfit? If these, failing to meet entrance requirements, were at once put to death the logic of the solution would be evident. The élite theory of education is, if Dr. Kandel's yearly surveys may be relied on, passing away in Europe. Dean Gauss finds it non-existent in the rank and file of the American people.

What will happen and is happening in American colleges is a shift from emphasis on courses, on scholarship, on research and other traditions long worshipped by faculties. In place will come the belief, here and there in his book ably presented by Dean Johnston, that the main business of college is all sorts and conditions of men. A readily adjusted treatment calculated to make of these the most intelligent and efficient citizens possible is demanded. College management needs to worship its tools less and study its raw material more.

Dean Johnston's conception of education's main purpose illumines this entire book. Democracy, he keeps saying, can succeed only by organizing all the people for the common good. This is the business of education.

"The educational system when true is altruistic and spiritual; the industrial system, individualistic and selfish."

Now it is high time for education, says the dean, to bestir itself and to render the service that is rightly to be expected from it by bringing into the consciousness of our people the problems of well-being that are to be solved through public service.

Our people have been tutored into a materialistic patriotism—"trade follows the flag." The flag which flies over every schoolhouse is the flag of the army, ready to fight for trade.

"Special interests desire to dictate what the schools shall teach. They do not want the truth to be taught."

"Contrary to this is the duty of education to prepare a planned society, not exploitation of the country by a few, but a government bringing comfort and satisfaction to all."

Dean Johnston's comprehension of the whole national situation, his emphasis on specific reforms in school practise, his straightforward, lucid speech, make this one of the powerful books of the year.

*Claims of Catholic Education.* Father McGucken, S.J., writes a little book well worth your study.[2] He writes it "for mothers and

[2] William J. McGucken, "The Catholic Way in Education." The Bruce Publishing Company, Milwaukee. 131 pp. $1.50.

fathers, for sensible teachers who are really educating the youth of the country, but most of all for the Catholic laymen and laywomen who are making heroic efforts to support Catholic education." This, Father McGucken insists, is most emphatically not the public-school way. The fundamental theory of all non-Catholic theory is the robot one which makes of man a soulless machine; which sees in his every action the inevitable result of chemical and physical reactions; which rejects freedom of will and morality. The Catholic theory, says our author, is the opposite of this in all things. "It would be nonsense for a Catholic to maintain that he has no quarrel with the public school. As an American citizen he claims a right to criticize any institution paid for by taxes derived from Catholics and failing to satisfy his conscience."

Father McGucken's chapters treat of modern trends in American education, the educand, the supernatural, the Catholic college, a model educational system, whose is the right to educate, modern psychology and the Catholic way in character education.

Rousseau, Eliot, Dewey, says the author, these three and their satellites are responsible for most of the unsound philosophy underlying most of our educational endeavor. It is a philosophy of humanitarian idealism intermingled with pragmatism culminating in a naive doctrine of essential progress. "Of the effect upon the whole fabric of American life it is hardly necessary to speak. Only in America could a bootblack turned cinema star become a nation's idol." "Only here could mountebanks like Aimee McPherson and Billy Sunday be regarded as religious leaders."

"It is high time American schools ceased cheapening education by applying it to processes that can be learned equally well in a factory or shop."

The testing movement is roundly trounced, as is "the nonsense of dressing up in Roman togas or building project books illustrative of classical life and calling it the teaching of Latin." "In the ideal Catholic school little will be said of mathematics and science except, to the scandal of the moderns, they will be given a subordinate place." The Thorndike tests, failing to discover the general mental training claimed for Latin and algebra, are dismissed as proving nothing. The proper teaching of Latin is outlined.

Arguments are presented for a division of the public-school money so as to give the church a part.

That the state is supreme in education Father McGucken says is a new idea, or better, a very old pagan one reborn in modern times. It was abhorrent to all of Christendom during Christian centuries. The American school, he says, was for several decades a religious one more or less under the direct control of the local church. The assertion of the state's duty to educate was not a cherished idea of the fathers of the American Republic. It was the proclamation of the bloody doctrinaires of the French Revolution. On Horace Mann lies the responsibility of implanting the germ of the idea of the supremacy of the state in education. This, says the author, was in 1840. It required only three generations for the average American to hold as a primary article of his creed that the public schools are by the intention of the founders of the republic to be completely free from all religious color.

We who have read our Elwood Cubberley, our Charles Beard, our Edgar Knight and, especially, our Allen Oscar Hansen, can hardly follow Father McGucken's excursion into educational history. Jefferson is an obstacle in this path, as are Noah Webster, Benjamin Rush, Madison, Monroe and the Ordinance of 1787 setting aside government funds to support public schools in order that "good government and the happiness of mankind" might be promoted. It was not in 1840 but in 1791 that the objection to alliance of public education with any religious creed was notably at variance with the idea defended by Father McGucken. Instead of ninety-four years ago it is a hundred and forty-three since the defenders of the Constitution yielded to clamor demanding that the fundamental law keep clear of religious alliances. Even then this could hardly have been a strong American feeling of only that year.

*Appalling Information.* Dr. Caldwell and Mr. Lundeen[3] give a list of two hundred works

[3] Otis W. Caldwell, Gerhard E. Lundeen, "Do You Believe It?" Doubleday, Doran and Company, Garden City. 307 pp. $3.00.

mostly devoted to superstitions. You and I have been reading such books off and on for years, finding much entertainment in them. In their own treatise these two Columbia University experimenters discuss the most common fool ideas that are known to the average American. This is made an amusing and instructive account enlivened by delicious black-and-white sketches by A. J. Iorio. Although the authors maintain the reserve of scientists along with a graceful style such as would please a group of congenial literary people at a club meeting the conclusions the average reader will come to are disconcerting enough. This will be inevitably so with teachers who peruse the book. For, after many pages of entertainment, the authors introduce the results of investigations they and others have been carrying on for some years. They tabulate one hundred questions on dreams, journeys, the number 13, crossed fingers, Friday, knocking wood, red hair, funerals, lucky numbers, black cats, horseshoes, spilling the salt, sneezing, and so on. The average high-school pupil is, according to extensive samplings, obsessed by twenty-two of these utterly absurd superstitions. Girls believe in a larger number of false ideas than boys do. Worse yet, forty-four and nine tenths per cent. of these superstitions, or of similar ones, are believed by the numerous young persons tested who are preparing to be teachers. Returns from 2,379 instructors, in 13 states, showed more than half believing the claims made in advertisements of antiseptics, dentifrices and other health and beauty preparations. Here, too, the returns showed women more gullible than men.

Especially significant are the records of the effect of training in science. In all the researches it has been found that those who have had science courses are freer from superstitions.

It will occur to you that the Caldwell-Lundeen volume is something to get pupils and teachers to read. Once beginning it you will go through. It affords numerous texts for interesting assembly talks. It confirms me in a notion I have had for some time that there ought to be classes in thinking maintained in all high schools. I fail to see why writing, swimming, spelling, reading, singing and other school arts do not have as a companion the art of thinking given a distinct period and regular practise. Here is a country devoted to universal education and notoriously failing to train its citizens to think. Dr. Julius Boraas, long a state inspector of high schools, insists that they deliberately sidestep thought in favor of memoriter recitations. The bulk of books coming to this office for review cry for a thinking public. Sir John Gorst found us weak-minded in civic problems. President Butler says we are political morons. The subject-specialists contend that a thorough grasp of Latin, of geometry, of history, of shopwork, establishes the mental power. "Try to get it by direct methods and all is lost." Caldwell and Lundeen take the opposite view. "In teaching a subject you can form attitudes. Why not teach with this as a conscious aim?" They would have you make a specific attack on common and influential superstitions, on unfounded beliefs.

We ought to be for that. With all the claims that the scholar is in pursuit of truth, why wouldn't it be possible to lead the rising generation to tackle Pilate's question, "What is truth?" With all the practical psychology in print why not put the high-school boy and girl through a course of mental sprouts for knowledge of what is meant by "thinking," what "analysis," "induction," "deduction," "probability," "demonstration," "conjecture," "proof" are? Then turn them loose on these superstitions and on civic, economic and political problems, graded as in a geometry and used not for propaganda but as geometry is used for exercise in thinking?

*The Great N. E. A.* Within the year of its date and in its usual satisfying typography and snug binding comes what has long been conceded to be the big book of American education.[4] Dr. Crabtree, the secretary, in his seventeenth year of service, notes improved working arrangements with the National Congress of Parents and Teachers, the American Association of University Women, the League of Women Voters, the General Federation of Women's Clubs, the American Legion, and many other civic and welfare groups. He does

[4] "Addresses and Proceedings, 1934, Vol. 72." National Education Association. 1201 Sixteenth St., Washington, D. C. 1006 pp. $3.00 to nonmembers.

not say, what is being said more and more, out in the field, that one of the organizations participating in these working agreements needs a gentle hint that the National Education Association does not stand for all the principles of all the organizations which have working agreements with it. From here and there, voiced by respectable school people, come protests against the attitude by one of these groups which assumes too patronizing an attitude toward the schools and too much tendency to tell them what and what not they must teach. Time to quote Rupertus Meldensus: *in necessariis, unitas; in dubiis, libertas; in omnibus, caritas,* which, on being translated, is: in educational essentials, unity; in class politics, separation; in all, affection.

Dr. Crabtree summarizes the wreckage of school service, notes the beginning of recovery, estimates that federal aid saved the schools, outlines association policies including freedom to departments, giving special importance to the welfare of the classroom teacher, and abating any hostility that may exist between schoolboards and schoolmasters.

Principal Jones, the necrologist, pays an unusually well-expressed tribute to the two thousand members dying since the last report and lists their names by states.

You will note with satisfaction the fullness of "Association records and information." The usage here observed of transcribing stenographic reports of the business meetings, etc., not only makes interesting reading but is valuable as establishing the real intent of resolutions and actions if ever, as they sometimes become, they may be subject to different interpretations on later dates.

The addresses and forum discussions appertaining to both conventions—Superintendents in Cleveland, others at Washington, are, as usual, the largest part of the volume. Here is the place to repeat that nowhere in the world is there to be found so valuable an annual educational encyclopedia. The proportion of outside eminences, inside notables and worthwhile workers of merit, is beyond criticism. A sniffy complaint that some people are put on too many programs does not stand actual count. It strikes me, as a long-time spectator from the side lines, that the National Association program is a masterly service by the highest order of unselfish, industrious, patriotic men and women.

*A Strong Professor.* Two of his colleagues[5] have done a masterly biography of the late George Holmes Howison. They are happy in their delineation of his superiorities as scholar, teacher and man. They are honest in presentation of qualities that made him unpopular to some. My recollection of Professor Howison is tinged with resentment at the way he was treated at Ann Arbor. The young cubs there, of whom I was one, had, in the Department of Literature, Science and the Arts, altogether too much of the foolish notion that study wasn't the main business of a college student. One son of a prominent Chicagoan spent several semesters in the university without attending any classes until an easy-going administration found it out. Howison held that the requirements for work maintained in the engineering, medical, dental and pharmacy classes could be enforced in the college of liberal arts. The philosophy courses were considered as "snaps." When Howison came a horde of easy-goers elected his course. His teaching was solid, never dull, but exacting. His attitude toward a bluffer was indignant—that of a foreman who had carefully prepared a project and considered himself insulted by the indifference of those who paid scant attention to it. He made it clear enough that his course required reasonable preparation by us and that lack of it would bring the logical result. We were used to threats which never came true. Dear old geologist Winchell passed everybody. So did Hennequin in French. Vaughn's and Sewell's courses were brilliant lectures with no responsibility on the hearers. My four years were mostly exercises in loafing. But Howison, somehow, pushed me into his honest belief that college meant work. As I remember it, about five of us escaped the "F" at the end. Among these was Novy, a digger, who afterward, in Koch's laboratory, and in Pasteur's, as well as by contributions to the studies of French, Belgian and American scientific societies, won medals and awards galore.

[5] John Wright Buckham, George Malcom Stratton, "Howison, Philosopher and Teacher." University of California Press, Berkeley. 418 pp. $2.50.

At final examination of the Howison course Novy so warmed to his work that a bottle of some chemical in his pocket blew out the stopple and scented the room with fumes.

Howison must have felt lonely in the namby-pamby atmosphere of the Ann Arbor of those days. What he thought of the place the gracious biography before me gives no hint.

It is a prime book for teachers, professors and students. The biography is enlightening and spirited. The professional habits are engrossing. The selected writings on idealism, evolution, modern science, pantheism, immortality, freedom, poetry, the university's obligation to the state, a liberal education, are great themes superbly handled.

*Mind-care.* Mr. Kirkpatrick's latest publication on human nature[6] maintains the happy combination of scientific fact and everyday English which marks his numerous earlier studies of mind and work. This is a classroom text especially valuable to college freshmen and to intending teachers. It is well supplied with case studies, questions and reading references.

It covers mental health, poise, principles of adjustment, individuality, maturing, conscious personality, foundations of healthy living, conventional requirements, mental hygiene as a school duty, diagnosis and correction.

The author is notably liberal in his views, quite free of the New England Puritan influence.

A society, he says, that is over-protective and restrictive may greatly diminish its security; it offers too many temptations for law-breaking. The problem of mental hygiene in the making of rules and laws is to give every person a high degree of security and to restrict few to such an extent that they are likely to disobey.

Laws regulating eating and drinking are usually met with resistance or evasion. Regulations regarding the sex impulse are not based on the nature of the sex act but upon all sorts of ideals, unfounded beliefs and superstitions. Marriage laws have been almost wholly negative. Experience is accumulating that reveals family life as one of the most important sources of mental health. The schools that teach young people the principles of married life, the making of a happy home, the wisdom that is the bearing and rearing of children, are doing a high patriotic service. The question of freedom of speech needs more attention by educators. The constitutional safeguards of liberty are being sadly weakened.

Author Kirkpatrick knows his field. His presentation is singularly interesting, important and persuasive.

*The Anatomy, Physiology and Hygiene of Character.* Michigan's state superintendent of public instruction,[7] a well-known pioneer in character education, offers a work on the theories underlying this service. He develops it through wishes, values, emotions, ideas, structures, ideals, conflicts, discrimination, choice, attitudes, expression, environment and integration.

The objectives of character education, we are reminded, are hardly to be separated from the total aims of education in general. These aims have not been prominent enough nor means of achieving them effectively used. The present economic and political dilemma of our country makes the thinking citizens conscious of the inadequacies of the civic intelligence. The people have shown themselves unable to prevent the disasters that have fallen upon us. Crime, vice, dishonesty in business and in politics, narrow partisan thinking, indifference to injustices, are our common lot. Most of us came through the public schools. We must develop a new type of citizen who is able and inclined to make a maximum contribution to a better economic and political social structure.

So runs the introduction. The need is for a coordination of effort, a revision of the curriculum so as to contribute a maximum to getting the people's ability directed to the country's needs, individual guidance, trained teachers for character, trained parenthood, redirection of community forces.

Education, says the author, must have a wider scope. At present it aims too narrowly at acquisition of knowledge as knowledge, or, in the higher grades, at original search for

6 Edwin A. Kirkpatrick, "Mental Hygiene for Effective Living." D. Appleton-Century Company, New York. 387 pp.

7 Paul F. Voelker, "Character in the Making." E. M. Hale Company, Milwaukee. 163 pp. $1.50.

truth. This is not enough. Education must concern itself more with emotions leading to a better social and civic menage.

As Dr. Voelker sees it, the kind of individualism the school must develop in America is that of defending a principle which the holder believes to be right and which, standing on his own feet, he will push in spite of public sentiment. The man of principle will appeal to the judge within his own breast and regard the verdict as of more value than the applause of the rest of mankind.

*May and Must in Education.* When, says Professor Leacock,[8] I became a schoolmaster I handed out the same flogging treatment I had had in my school days. When I look back at it now I marvel at the barbarity of it; but not then. The boys whom I licked the most seem to cherish the kindest memories; and seem to have succeeded best. Looking back on the list, I find that I have licked no less than eight cabinet ministers, two baronets and four British generals—to say nothing of about one half of the bench and the bar in Toronto. Whether these men would have come to the front without this assistance I do not discuss.

This confession occurs in a delicious little book reproducing a Kappa Delta Pi lecture of the many-sided McGill professor of economics and political science who is, by the way, an often-mentioned choice of the Mark Twain Association, which wants him to be a traveling professor of humor.

In speaking of cap and gown Professor Leacock says a notion of equality and democracy has created a public opinion against them. They have to go. Public opinion killed them. The good old gown, like charity, covered a multitude of shabby clothes. It obliterated distinctions between rich and poor and therefore was a promoter of democracy.

Read and enjoy his comments on the written examination, on the study of literature, on lectures, absurd compulsory studies and the quickening of the spirit.

*A Lure to Science.* Liveright has brought out a new printing of Sir Arthur Thomson's popular little talks on scientific curiosa,[9] a big book for a dollar. Here is an alluring bridge that will carry many of your boys and girls into serious study in the great field. Sir Arthur has the human touch. His style is familiar; his language, simple; his choice of subjects, made with a rare sense of satisfying the curiosity of the average man. He reviews theories, facts or discoveries appertaining to such themes as the beginning of life on the earth, why we fall asleep, why our hair turns white, animals' fear, the cause of laughter and tears, what settles sex, behavior of plants and animals, credulities, evolution, the awesomeness of nature, the emancipation of mind, why we die—threescore and ten puzzles of the universe and what man is doing to solve them. The science teacher who is keen to keep alive the healthy curiosity of youth will find this book a potent helper. Yourself will find it a rare combination of instruction with entertainment.

*The Universe is Ruled by Mind.* "For a wider outlook, a keener realization and a greater enjoyment of nature's wonders and glories" the Macmillan Company enlists a galaxy of teachers of science who in sixteen short essays[10] talk of the stars, the universe, the earth as the home of man, the ascent of mind, the oneness of life, the romance of the plant world, chemical wonders, nature's plan, design and purpose, mysteries, the breakdown of materialism and the wonder of life.

The chapters are distinctly alluring in subject and treatment. High-school students in science classes will find them attractive.

The materialistic fallacy that gripped the world in the last century, proposing that the universe and all its manifestations are the results of chance, finds no echo in these pages. The authors, eminent each in his own branch of science, see ordered harmony, mathematical precision and a great design pointing to a purposing and directing mind back of the great drama of creation.

8 Stephen Leacock, "The Pursuit of Knowledge, a Discussion of Freedom and Compulsion in Education." Liveright Publishing Corporation, New York. 48 pp. $1.40.

9 J. Arthur Thomson, "Riddles of Science." Liveright Publishing Corporation, N. Y. 387 pp. $1.00.

10 Frances Mason, Editor, "The Great Design." The Macmillan Company, New York. 324 pp. $2.50.

The spirit of the essays is in agreement with Sir Oliver Lodge's summary: If we limit ourselves to material considerations we get depressed, downhearted, pessimistic. We do not and can not see the ultimate outcome; we are afflicted with doubts as to whether there is any ultimate outcome. But if we admit the activity of the spiritual world let us be consistent. Let us trace and utilize its activity throughout. It is the effort of religion to utilize this help and knowledge. In spite of many blunders the religious feeling, apart from forms and ceremonies, is as alive and as energetic as ever. Philosophy justifies it and science contributes an element toward justification. The spiritual world is the great reality. All else, however beautiful and interesting, is temporary and evanescent. The universe is ruled by mind. Whether it be the mind of a mathematician or of an artist or of a poet, or all of them, and more, it is the one reality which gives meaning to existence, enriches our daily task, encourages our hope, energizes us with faith, wherever knowledge fails and illuminates the whole universe with immortal love.

*How Much for Junior High School?* This generation has seen the school principal and superintendent develop into an estimator of costs. Change from an 8–4 plan of public schooling to the scheme of three units is not uncommonly opposed on the grounds of increased expense. The study of Dr. Gooch, with supporting data for its conclusions,[11] is based on the 6–3–3 type in cities of not less than 5,000 inhabitants. Costs per pupil in 107 systems in six eastern states show the mean for kindergarten through the sixth year to be $96.23: for years 7–9, $128.80; for grades 10–12, $162.23. In the systems studied which have the 6–3–3 system the total costs are less than in the 8–4 systems. Dr. Gooch has a chapter on cost of a standard junior high school. The ratio of junior-high-school costs to K–6 costs vary to a high degree in different states. No community need be deterred from the 6–3–3 type by fear of increased expense. The investigator shows that junior high-school teachers are, in large numbers, unprepared for the special problems. They need a different rather than more training. A valuable element of the study is demonstration of unharmful economies in the junior high school.

*Guiding the High-School Teacher.* It is sad to observe Dean Collings begin his work on high-school supervision[12] by saying that the theory of passive receptivity of boys and girls in accordance with which the mind is a blank for the record of traditional facts still controls the practises of teaching in the traditional high schools of to-day. The regret that this should be said is deepened by recollection that T. Briggs often says the high schools teach less well than the elementary grades, by the fact that most of the treatises on high-school teaching that come to this office note neglect of exercises in thinking and because works like those of Henry Morrison show teachers how to mend their ways. Professor Collings puts heavy demands on high-school teachers. He asserts that, as the requirements have been met in a number of high schools through a period of years, proper supervision will bring anywhere the results desired.

The book, therefore, is a specific manual for supervising the work of teachers to the end that a high school may be turned from a theory of passive receptivity to one that interprets learning as the improvement of complete functioning in real-life situations. It is a text for high-school principals, for heads of departments and for teachers. It guides teachers in studying how boys and girls grow, what the purposeful activities of boys and girls are. It describes the ways to bring teachers to integrate subject-matter in the purposeful activities of the students, to plan, perform and measure teaching procedures. It treats of supervisory guidance of teachers of social science, of natural science, of communication, of occupation, of fine art and of play. Complete detail of selection of activities, stimulation of motive and direction of the work is offered in connection with each project.

*Debunking Vocational Prophecy.* How trustworthy and useful can educational and voca-

[11] Wilbur I. Gooch, "Junior-High-School Costs." Teachers College Press, Columbia University, New York. 160 pp. $1.75.

[12] Ellsworth Collings, "Supervisory Guidance of Teachers in Secondary Schools." The Macmillan Company, New York. 613 pp. $2.50.

tional guidance be made? If the guidance now given is beneficial but can be made much more so by methods which cost no more, will you change to better methods? A corps of investigators under the direction of Dr. Thorndike[13] studied over two thousand children for eight years.

Among the various conclusions reached is one concerning the truth of the stay-in-school exhortation. "To assume that if all boys stayed in school until 21 they would earn as much as do the specially able boys who now graduate from college at 21 is indefensible and mischievous." School-conduct marks have no predictive value. Neither has attendance record. No combination of facts regarding any boy or girl at the age of fourteen enables a counselor to foretell much better than by a sheer guess how successful the person will be at mechanical work six or eight years later. Of the one or two persons in each hundred who went criminal the investigator found their school records at 14 years of age inferior in all respects. Contrary to common opinion, the wages of white-collar workers are generally greater than those of mechanical workers. The tables, tests, appendices, etc., and the excellent index afford the student of vocational guidance assistance in following this extensive research. It is to be continued until the pupils studied reach the age of 32.

*Stiffening the Grown-ups.* Bigger and better, occasionally exulting, the Handbook of Adult Education for this year[14] contains accounts of work and plans by a score of leaders covering agriculture, alumni education, the arts, correspondence schools, classes for the foreign-born, forums, library service, lyceums, chautauquas, museums, music, dramatics, puppetry, settlements, unemployment, the movies, vocational guidance, the physically handicapped and workers in industry. The book has a national directory of organizations with adult education programs listing the membership, objectives, activities and publications of each. The contrasts in awareness of present needs are striking in the accounts of alumni education by different universities. Little Emory University in Atlanta should have first prize. She has a four-day alumni conference every year. The one listed here is entirely devoted to current politics. New York University's Alumni meet has for its theme "the inside of politics." Connecticut Wesleyan gives its graduates a five-day session for the discussion of current problems in economics. The University of Virginia has an annual two weeks' Institute of Public Affairs, at which political problems of local, state and national bearing are discussed by civic administrators from all parts of the United States. The University of Washington, Seattle, reports a thousand alumni participating in a three-day program of discussion of present-day economic and political problems. My dear Mater-Michigan's report shows her back in the good old far-off things and battles long ago—European politics (are those of the home state in no need of attention?), sidelights on American history (why not turn the front lights squarely on Michigan banking or into the dropping of music, art, domestic science and other subjects from the high schools of the state because the funds are insufficient to carry these along with the algebra and foreign languages required for college certification?). But since this handbook was printed, Michigan University has put on another alumni program, this one bristling with current political problems. This book's list of the Harvard alumni service shows that the number of present civic and economic matters taken up is 0. Yale ties her in this score. It is amazing how many institutions of higher learning in this day of a nation-wide attention to perplexities of the here and now live up to the traditions that the vanes upon their towers are steadied by the breeze that blows out of antiquity. As to the women, Goucher reports concentration on central Europe and our foreign policy; Smith gives Great Britain first place, Downer takes up present economic problems, Mount Holyoke concentrates on art. Pennsylvania Women's College leads off with French conversation; Radcliffe

13 Edward L. Thorndike, Elsie O. Bregman, Irving Lorge, Zaida F. Metcalfe, Eleanor E. Robinson, Ella Woodward, ''Prediction of Vocational Success.'' The Commonwealth Fund, 41 E. 57th St., New York. 284 pp. $2.50.

14 Dorothy Rowden, Editor, ''Handbook of Adult Education in the United States.'' American Association for Adult Education, 60 East 42nd Street, New York. 383 pp. $2.00.

with astronomy, but lists economics as one of five themes. Vassar says nothing of current politics; Wells and Wellesley do; Wheaton lists contemporary dramatists. Taken by and large, this display of university activity in educating its alumni shows a strange preference for "there, there!" instead of for "here, here!" As you recall your childhood you remember that "there, there" was mother's message when you needed to be soothed; but a common wording of father's sharp correction was "here, here." It wouldn't be a bad idea, for a while, to drop "alma mater" as the designation of a college and substitute "urgens pater." Suggestion, said Comenius, worketh wonders.

*Preparing for the Press.* Get shears, paste, clips and pencils with heavy lead, tackle the first piece of copy in the Harrington-Wolseley workbook,[15] master the eighteen lessons: headlines that click, weeding out hackneyed expressions, trimming copy, avoiding libel, rewriting poor copy, editing special departments, making streamers, handling pictures, reading proof, making dummies, etc. By this time you should be able to improve at least your school paper.

The first-named author is director of the School of Journalism in Northwestern University. The second is a teacher of news-writing and editing in the Englewood High School, Chicago. Their book has a chart of proofreading signs and a dictionary of common newspaper terms. There is a chapter on the use of capitals, numbers and punctuation which has many surprises.

"Do not use Mr. when initials or Christian names are used, except when mentioning teachers in a school paper. Use Mrs. or Miss when Christian names are given. Omit Miss when writing of high-school girls."

Custom is breaking school text-book rules more and more, cutting down capitals and punctuation marks. When a comma makes the sense clearer, use it. "Whatever is, is right."

Designed as a work-book, with the materials and spaces for practise bound in it, the text, nevertheless, has an extensive coverage of the essentials of getting out a paper, is designed for classes in journalism, for guiding amateurs editing a school paper, and is full of valuable information for any one who writes for printing.

If you are reporting an event you are not to speak of an *interesting* meeting, a *splendid* attendance, a *convincing* speech or a *masterful* argument. These words are reserved for editors. Reporters are not permitted opinions.

Liability to action for libel is hovering even over the high-school paper. The offending action, in the eyes of the law, lies not in the writing, but in the circulation. You may not accuse an official of being mentally or morally unfit for office. You may not accuse a professional of lack of knowledge or skill. You may not defame or bring ridicule on a person, especially a woman.

*The High-School Paper.* Two high-school teachers who have done work in outside journalism and are the staff advisers of school papers[16] are authors of a book appropriate for upper classes which do or do not publish a paper. Its purpose is to aid the adolescent to observe, to think, to record and to express himself. The abundant illustrations, examples and models in the text are taken from a wide variety of school journals, editorials, news and special articles.

*Grammar for Encouragement.* Mr. Beal, of the Boston Mechanics Arts High School, wishes to help the many youngsters whom the complexity of grammar disheartens. He puts into book form[17] the material which, by trial and alterations for six years with high-school classes, he has found better than the old style grammatical teaching. He makes the sentence the master key to spoken and written speech. He gives to words much dramatic content, motivates technical necessities with natural interests, stresses abundant usage, employs a wealth of practise sentences, and employs novel forms of diagramming. This book has a remarkably full index.

[15] H. F. Harrington, R. E. Wolseley, "The Copyreader's Workshop." D. C. Heath and Company, Boston. 341 pp. $1.32.

[16] William M. Otto, Mary E. Marye, "Journalism for High Schools." Harcourt, Brace and Company, New York. 412 pp. $1.48.

[17] Kenneth Beal, "Grammar for Speaking and Writing." Harcourt, Brace and Company, New York. 489 pp. $1.40.

# SCHOOL AND SOCIETY

WITH WHICH ARE COMBINED THE EDUCATIONAL REVIEW, ESTABLISHED IN 1891, THE TEACHERS MAGAZINE, ESTABLISHED IN 1878, AND THE SCHOOL JOURNAL, ESTABLISHED IN 1874.

Volume 40 SATURDAY, DECEMBER 8, 1934 Number 1041

## THE TEACHER'S PART IN PROMOTING THE SCHOOL CHILD'S HEALTH

By Dr. J. HOWARD BEARD

UNIVERSITY OF ILLINOIS

WHAT progress! In sixty years we have acquired more knowledge concerning disease, its control and prevention than in all that vast period from 1870 to when our ancestors took up their residence in caves. In a few decades infant mortality has been reduced to one half and tuberculosis to one fourth their previous rates. Dipththeria ceases to cause terror, Asiatic cholera visits us no more, and yellow fever has been eradicated on this continent. In a generation, fifteen years have been added to the average life expectancy.

Science has created an industrial era, made great cities possible, urbanized more than half the population, revolutionized communication, altered living conditions, changed social outlook, made thousands go to bed hungry in a land of plenty and, because of or in spite of our knowledge, the enrolment of our institutions for the defective, deficient, delinquent and dependent is increasing more rapidly than our colleges and universities. Speed, strain and stress are destroying lives by automobile accidents saved by the control of communicable disease, filling sanatoria and providing a harvest for the psychiatrist. Phenomenal changes! But where are we? What of the future?

Physical and mental impairment are due largely to the conditions under which men are compelled to live. If an organism is forced to make a marked change in its environment or mode of life, it becomes especially subject to disease. When the Indians were housed, tuberculosis increased among them. The Eskimo brought to our great cities develops pneumonia. Measles introduced to the Fiji Islanders killed half of them. Biological adaptation to new conditions takes time; if external changes are more rapid than the power of adjustment, extinction is inevitable.

The position of civilized man to-day is not unlike that of his primitive brother who suddenly finds himself living under conditions for which his biological inheritance is inadequate. Human evolution, generally speaking, has occurred in a slowly changing natural environment and not in rapidly changing artificial surroundings which make it impossible for the adaptation of the individual to keep pace with the demands of his habitat.

The need of the hour is for men who are physically, mentally and morally able to live successfully in this largely artificial world. How shall they be obtained? We can not wait for the slow natural process of organic evolution to produce them. Therefore, the race is between education and catastrophe with the result in doubt. If education can give the child the habits, knowledge and ideals, to conserve rather than destroy human life and motivate them, our march towards a far distant Utopia continues; if not, we shall become as extinct as the great civilizations of the past.

With the teacher lies victory or defeat. It is his part to give in a large degree to those who are under his charge the health which renders them capable of living most and serving best—the power to rise above their environment in their struggle for the redemption of man and the attainment of the abundant life.

He must write across the sky in the largest letters of flaming crimson so the world may read—the better the education, wider the application of science to human welfare and the greater the building of character, the less need there will be for hospitals, asylums, laws, police power and prisons, evidence of physical, mental and moral deterioration.

### THE TEACHER'S PART

The primary consideration of the teacher in promoting the health of school children is to keep ever before herself the all-important facts clearly expressed in the quatrain,

> Sow a thought, reap an action;
> Sow an action, reap a habit;
> Sow a habit, reap a character;
> Sow a character, reap a destiny.

The most effective means for the promotion of health commensurate with individual and social needs are the formation of sound health habits, the impartation of health information and the development of a health conscience sensitive to the significance of physical, mental and moral values in the production of vigor, character and progress.

No teacher who can not see the mighty oak in the acorn is adequately equipped to protect the health of children. Unless she appreciates that habits determine disposition, shape behavior patterns, create a philosophy of life and render the individual an asset or a liability to society, she is unprepared for her task. Likewise in dealing with children at an age when their plasticity and retentivity are at the maximum, she must know the influence of example far exceeds that of precept, pedagogical technique or the subject-matter she presents.

In promoting the health of the school child, the teacher must have as goals the inculcation of correct hygienic habits of posture, diet, elimination, sleep, work, play, cleanliness, etc. She must cultivate proper attitudes of mind in the children under her charge, and guide them in the conservation of their mental energy. She must help them in the avoidance of worry, the banishment of fear, the facing of the facts of existence and in the development of patience, courage, magnanimity and initiative.

The teacher can do much to promote the development of a social sense of responsibility which will control the instincts of acquisitiveness and reproduction to the best interests of the individual and of society. By such action, antisocial tendencies, criminality and selfishness are nipped in the bud and the great driving forces of natural impulse are sublimated and used for the advancement of civilization.

The teacher must teach her children something of the supreme value of beauty, goodness, truth and the meaningfulness of life. They must be made to understand there is neither abiding health nor happiness in life for those unable to assume a satisfactory relationship to those "forces that lie at the heart of the world and determine its destiny."

The provision of an environment in which physique may develop without handicap, the mind attain knowledge and wholesomeness, the spirit aspire to nobleness and high ideals come to happy fruition will test the ability of the most gifted teacher. But such is the aim of education.

For this end, philanthropists endow colleges, legislatures appropriate funds for instruction, and citizens carry the burdens of taxation.

### WHAT THE CHILD SHOULD CARRY OVER INTO LIFE

The teaching of health must be integrated with every part of school life to produce the most fruitful results in the individual and in the community. It is one thing for a teacher to have in mind the aims she would attain, but it is an altogether different thing to have the child carry over into life the precepts and practises which will make him able to protect himself and his family and to function as an informed citizen in all matters of civic betterment.

Habits tend to become static. They only are dynamic and meet the needs of a changing environment when they have meaning and the basic principles upon which they rest are understood. In no branch of human endeavor is "What one knows" so unproductive until it is applied and "What one does" so important as in the promotion of personal and public health. Neither knowledge without action nor the best intention without motivation corrects a single defect or prevents an epidemic.

Health knowledge must be made a part of the child's conditioned reflexes. This is a task of the first magnitude because what the teacher may do in the few hours her pupil is in school may be undone by unfavorable conditions on the playground, in the home or in the community. If the teacher has committed herself to the policy of doing all she can for the children under her charge, she will have to associate herself with all enterprises in the community to make it a better place in which to live.

A teacher will be a brilliant success if she can fix in the minds of her children that science and not superstition is the foundation of health, that to-morrow's health depends upon to-day's prevention and that health can not be preserved after it is lost. As trite as are these facts, lack of their appreciation deprives health departments of adequate support, fills the hospitals, turns loose epidemics in the community and perpetuates quackery.

In health education, subject-matter, technique and tact must be appropriate for the circumstances, age and the ability of the child. Suitable instruction and routine practise should begin the day the child enters the first grade and continue until it is handed its high-school diploma. This does not mean formal instruction for each of the twelve grades. In the first, the teaching may be as simple as advising that pencils be kept out of the mouth, that hands be washed before eating or that a pint of milk be taken every day. In the senior year of high school after the child has had biology and physiology, the information given him should make it possible for him to protect his own health and that of his family and to function intelligently as a citizen in making his community conducive to vigorous, sane, prosperous and contented living.

Specifically, no child should be permitted to pass out of the public school system who does not know the physiological basis of sound health habits, the various food elements essential for adequate nutrition, and the meaning of normal mental action and the conditions underlying the common deviations from it. He should have a general understanding of the sex instinct in man, the stages of its development, its normal expression, sublimation and the penalities attached to its perversion and anti-social tendencies. He should know that improper habits predispose to degenerative diseases and their relation to premature senility and the breakdowns of middle life.

The high-school graduate should know the factors determining infection and resistance, the principles of artificial immunization, and he should be a living example of sane precaution by being protected against smallpox, typhoid fever and diphtheria. Thus will he be forearmed against the health hazards of his own community or the localities he may visit. He is unprepared to be a responsible citizen if he is not aware of the dangers inherent in unpasteurized milk, polluted water, the unscientific disposal of wastes, overcrowding, improper housing, inadequate playgrounds, noise, dust, gangs, etc.

The counselors an individual selects are indicative of his knowledge and the soundness of his judgment. In no phase of human need is this so true as in the choice of a dentist, a physician or a surgeon. If the child on leaving school understands that training, experience and character are the qualifications of experts, and acts accordingly, his teacher has served him and his community well. Before the child leaves school, he should be taught something of the important public health problems of his community, the general methods of attacking them, and the results to be expected from efforts directed intelligently towards their solution.

Unless teachers in cooperation with parents, dentists, physicians and public health officials will lead in giving children the benefit of the health knowledge now available, neither this nor the next generation will obtain more than a small part of the good to be derived from the practical application of the epochal discoveries of the last sixty years and those which are being made yearly in chemistry, physics, biology, engineering and medicine.

### Promoting and Protecting the Health of Children

How much farther the teacher will have to go in the promotion of the health of the school children under her care than her endeavor to have them form sound health habits, to give them instruction in biology, physiology and hygiene, and to strive to have them develop a health conscience, will depend upon the size of her school, whether or not she is the principal of it, and whether or not there are dentists, nurses or doctors available to examine and supervise the health of her pupils.

Even if the school can arrange for doctors to give the children an annual health examination, dentists to inspect their teeth at least once a year, nurses to follow them up to see that their defects are corrected and a dietitian to provide at nominal cost warm school lunches for those who do not eat at home and special diets for the undernourished, the teacher must give them her support and cooperation. If she is in a school which makes no provision for the general health of its pupils, she will have to assume in some degree the rôles of doctor, dentist, nurse, food expert and sanitary inspector.

She will have to be alert to detect pupils with acute illness and those developing communicable disease. It will be necessary for her to seek the cooperation of local doctors, district nurses, dentists, the parents of the children and her school board to have her pupils examined, their teeth inspected and to follow them up until their defects are corrected. The able teacher will use every available agency at her command. She will seek the assistance of boards of health, of public officials, the association of commerce, the Rotary Club, etc.

She must know a 100 per cent. education can not be acquired through eyes whose errors of refraction leave them only 50 per cent. function. She must appreciate that the neglect of diseased tonsils and the inadequate care of children with communicable disease often lead to heart lesions, permanently damaged kidneys and semi-invalidism. She must understand that physical defects are related to truancy and delinquency and must strive to prevent potentially useful citizens becoming serious social liabilities. She must realize that the plasticity, reserve and vigor of the young give corrective and remedial measures the best chance to convert the defective and the ill into efficient normals—an opportunity which in a few years may be lost forever.

The school should set the standard for the community in sanitation as well as in education, recreation and culture. The beauty and tidiness of its grounds are largely dependent upon the interest, the ideals and the ability of the teacher to cultivate a taste in her children and in their parents for timeless values which make health more than mere physical fitness and life more than "a galling load along a rough and weary road." The attractiveness of its appearance and the correctness of its furniture and equipment are largely determined by her. She should appreciate the importance of making the drinking water arrangements, the heating, ventilation, lighting, school meals, washing facilities and toilet provisions, the means for inculcating health habits and the teaching of sanitation.

Inconsistency comes in full bloom when teachers strive to promote the health of their pupils and lose sight of the hygienic management of their schools. The methods they employ should be wholesome. The program of the school should be permeated with the consideration of health. The length of the school day should not cause excessive fatigue, examinations and tests should be reasonable, and grading and promotion should leave no cause for a feeling of resentment or injustice. Recesses should be arranged and supervised with the view of giving them the greatest possible recreational value. The requirements of home work should be made with regard to the health and best interest of the pupil in the broadest sense.

Special classes for unusual children are an important means for the promotion of health. The teacher should attempt to discover as early as possible exceptional pupils in her school and give them the advantages, the instruction and the guidance indicated by their peculiar abilities and physical defects. In the large school she may have to form classes for gifted children, the mentally deficient, the physically handicapped or the subnormal; in the small institution she will have to care for the exceptional child by special assignments, more individual attention, a seat closer to the front of the room, greater encouragement, or by persuading the parents to arrange for the child's attendance at a school equipped to deal with his particular type of defect.

The teacher should remember that although special classes afford the unusual pupil an opportunity to make the most of himself by giving him the benefit of favorable surroundings, special equipment and especially trained instructors, they have the disadvantage of segregation and a tendency to create a feeling of inferiority. They also cultivate an undemocratic desire for special privileges, and increase the per capita cost of education.

The value of special classes for the mentally deficient is well recognized. Their advantages are great and their segregation is beneficial rather than injurious. They largely prevent the development of the feeling of being peculiar, avoid the accentuation of handicaps by comparison with the greater accomplishments of the mentally normal, and tend to offset the child's retardation by special methods of training.

The teacher can contribute to the health of her pupils by her attitude towards and her participation in an adequate and rational program of physical education. In the large school, her efforts should be given to the procurement of well-equipped playgrounds, an athletic field, a gymnasium and competent supervisors; in the small school, she will have to enter more intimately into the games and activities of those under her charge. She will have to provide opportunities for play and will have to direct her pupils in the utilization of such outdoor facilities as may be available. The teacher is often able to reach children on the playground or athletic field who seem inaccessible in the classroom. Such contacts are mutually beneficial. They may provide an opportunity for her to get some needed exercise out-of-doors, to change improper behavior patterns in the children or to learn the reason for their scholastic difficulties.

Health in its comprehensive sense is the quintessence of life—the foundation of personal welfare, spiritual development and progress. Only the robust individual can make all his potential gifts actualities and all his natural endowments contributions to social betterment. The dependence of physical vigor, mental efficiency and moral stamina on normal physiological processes make health essential to intellectual achievement, the excellence of personality and abiding happiness. In the language of Spencer, "to be a good animal is the first requisite to success in life, and to be a nation of good animals is the first condition to national prosperity."

The teacher's part in the promotion of the health of the children under her charge is a large and responsible rôle—one that is becoming greater and more difficult as the centers of hygienic, social and moral training move steadily away from the home towards the school. But it is a glorious opportunity to save one's life by spending it for others and to help mankind continue its march from the jungle to the high destiny which awaits those who look up, aspire and climb.

# THE HISTORY OF STUDENT RESIDENTIAL HOUSING. II

By Dr. W. H. COWLEY
THE OHIO STATE UNIVERSITY

### THE TWENTIETH CENTURY REVIVAL

The attacks upon dormitories in eastern colleges and the indifference toward them of state university administrators in the Middle West and West continued without abatement until the 1890's. The importation from Germany of the university idea, which brought Johns Hopkins, Clark and Chicago into existence and which changed Harvard, Columbia and other institutions from colleges into universities, accentuated the swing from the British heritage to a distinctly German emphasis. But the old-time American college was not to die easily. It had been essentially an Alma Mater, "knowing her children," as Cardinal Newman expressed it, "one by one." It was not, he pointed out, "a foundry, or a mint, or a treadmill." Yet in the opinion of a large number of educators the university idea had transformed the college into just what Cardinal Newman said it ought not to be. Those who raised the protest agreed with Newman's judgment of the nature of a college, and although they recognized the need of explorations in search of new knowledge, they strongly dissented against the slaughter of Alma Mater as a burnt offering upon the altar of research and scholarship.

Several examples from a large array are perhaps sufficient to illustrate how strongly many college-minded professors felt about the matter. One comes from Yale and one each, interestingly enough, from Harvard and Chicago. Overwhelmed by the shattering of "college life" over the country, Arthur T. Hadley, who was soon to become president of Yale, asked these questions in 1895:[16]

> Can Yale preserve its distinctive features as a *college* in the midst of its widening work as a university? Can it meet the varying intellectual necessities of modern life without sacrificing the democratic traditions which have had so strong an influence upon character? Can it give the special education which the community asks without endangering the broader education which has produced generations of "all round" men, trained morally as well as intellectually?

He went on to point out that "these are questions which every large college has to face. They are not peculiar to Yale. If Yale feels their difficulty most, it is because she is the largest representative of the traditional American college idea, which Harvard has, to all intents and purposes, abandoned."

Even before Hadley's pertinent queries, the residential idea, so strongly entrenched at Yale, had begun to penetrate into the Middle West. William Rainey Harper, a Yale professor of Hebrew, had organized and become president of the University of Chicago in 1893, and he brought with him an enthusiasm for dormitories. He built four (57.3 per cent. of the total building cubature at Chicago in 1893 was in dormitories[17]) in the first group of university buildings and sought money for more. In 1900 he had erected seven "in spite of the prejudice against them at the time in the West on the ground that they were mediaeval, British and autocratic."[18] The Chicago leadership, so potent in all other matters of higher education, had its important influence upon arousing other Middle Western institutions to an interest in housing.

Soon after Hadley's plea for the college as opposed to the German university idea, important developments began to take place at Princeton. In 1901 a graduate department was organized under the deanship of Andrew F. West, and in contrast to the graduate work being done at Hopkins, Harvard, Columbia and Chicago major emphasis was to be put upon the educational environment. The Princeton people insisted that:

> . . . the conditions surrounding the daily lives of graduate students at Princeton should be reenforced and elevated, and the satisfaction of the double purpose pointed directly at a residential college where this body of advanced scholars would mingle freely in common daily association with one another, not leading solitary existences scattered over the town, but securing in their distinctively graduate life the enriching advantages of mutual incentives and community of intellectual interests coupled with an identity in mode of living, advantages obtainable in no other way so well as in residential intimacies like those so peculiarly characteristic of Princeton undergraduate life.[19]

The building of the beautiful graduate school at Princeton several years later implemented this philosophy, but meanwhile Woodrow Wilson, who had been inaugurated as president in 1902, established the preceptorial system in 1905, modeled directly after the systems in vogue at Oxford and Cambridge. Since Princeton dormitories were not adapted to the complete taking over of English methods, Mr. Wilson in 1907 proposed a scheme for social coordination known as the Quadrangle Plan. This contemplated the grouping of the dormitories of the university into a number of quadrangles and the housing of unmarried members of the faculty with students in order "to bring them in close

[16] Arthur T. Hadley, "Four American Universities," pp. 83–84. New York: Harper and Brothers, 1895.

[17] Floyd W. Reeves, Ernest C. Miller and John Dale Russell, "Trends in University Growth," p. 158. The University of Chicago Survey, Volume I. Chicago: University of Chicago Press, 1933.

[18] Edwin E. Slosson, "Great American Universities," p. 422. New York: Macmillan Company, 1910.

[19] V. L. Collins, *Op. cit.*, p. 267.

habitual natural association with undergraduates and so intimately tie the intellectual and social life of the place into one another.''[20]

Because the quadrangle plan involved the abandonment of the strongly entrenched club system at Princeton, alumni, students and some members of the faculty rose in vigorous protest. In much bitterness President Wilson dropped his project; but the stir which his writings and addresses created, not only at Princeton but throughout the United States, focused attention once again to the important values of the English residential system and brought a resurgence of interest and even enthusiasm for reintroducing into American colleges the programs of Oxford and Cambridge. The Princeton program unfortunately met serious snags, but President Lowell, who twenty-five years later introduced the house plan at Harvard, began actively upon his succession to the Harvard presidency in 1909 to work toward the Wilsonian objectives.

Lowell had been influenced not only by Wilson's ideas and experiences at Princeton, but he very likely also read the articles of Edwin E. Slosson on higher education which appeared in fourteen issues of *The Independent* during 1909 and early 1910, and which were later published as a volume entitled ''Great American Universities.'' One dominant motif pervaded Slosson's book—the need of individualization in the colleges! ''Here,'' he wrote,[21] ''is the weak point of all the great colleges, and even of the smaller ones—the lack of personal contact between teacher and student. It is not due to the influx of an overwhelming number of students, because the faculty has generally grown in proportion or more. It is partly due to defective organization and partly to the development of a new school of teachers, who detest teaching, who look upon students as a nuisance, and class work as a waste of time. . . . Almost every educator, if asked what was the main fault of our large colleges, would have said that it was the loss of personal relationship between instructor and student, resulting in ill-adapted and careless teaching on the one side and in diversion of interest on the other. Teacher and pupil were not even on opposite ends of the same log. They were at opposite ends of a telephone working only one way.'' Mr. Slosson even went so far as to point out that at Harvard (Eliot had just resigned and no one knew who would follow him) ''it will be the duty of President Eliot's successor to see that individualized education is applied.''

Whether or not Mr. Lowell read Mr. Slosson's articles, certain it is that he began even in his inaugural address to sponsor the doctrine to which Slosson gave voice and for which Wilson had worked so vigorously at Princeton. He devoted his address entirely to Harvard College and its needs, neglecting even to mention research and scholarship. He talked about the values of ''college life,'' a phrase which Eliot never used. He suggested that graduate education had sabotaged the distinctive functions of the college. He urged that dormitories, especially for freshmen, be built and that everything within reason be done to develop undergraduates as people as well as students. ''Among his other wise sayings,'' he pointed out,[22] ''Aristotle remarked that man is by nature a social animal; and it is in order to develop his powers as a social being that American colleges exist. The object of the undergraduate department is not to produce hermits, each imprisoned in the cell of his own intellectual pursuits, but men fitted to take

[20] Woodrow Wilson, *The Princeton Alumni Weekly*, June 12, 1907.

[21] Edwin E. Slosson, *Op. cit.*, pp. 17–18, 76.

[22] A. Lawrence Lowell, ''Inaugural Address,'' quoted by S. E. Morison, ''Development of Harvard University, 1869–1929,'' p. lxxix. Cambridge, Mass.: Harvard University Press, 1930.

their places in the community and live in contact with their fellow men."

The program which Lowell inaugurated in 1909 moved forward slowly during his twenty-four-year administration, bringing concentration of studies in special fields after the sophomore year, comprehensive examinations, reading periods, tutorial work and finally the much-discussed House Plan. What Wilson had failed to accomplish by direct attack Lowell achieved two decades later by Fabian indirection. But meanwhile other influences in favor of dormitories were accumulating. Three of these deserve discussion: First, the effect upon all institutions of the several women's colleges in the East; second, the emphasis placed upon dormitories, especially in the Middle West, by deans of women, and third, the clamor of students and alumni in defense of "college life" and the dormitory as a means thereto.

Mount Holyoke, Wellesley, Vassar and Smith had all been organized during the second half of the nineteenth century on distinctly residential bases. It might be very well for men's colleges and coeducational institutions to put students upon their own, but few in those days were willing to allow young women undergraduates to shift for themselves. The notion that women were physically unequal to higher education had by no means completely died down, and the Victorian morality left no room for anything but strict housing regimentation.

In time these women's colleges grew to considerable influence, especially in coeducational institutions. Many of their graduates joined the faculties of Middle Western colleges and universities, and they brought with them the housing philosophy. Some of them became deans of women, and charged with the social and physical welfare of their students, they gave devoted and continuous attention to housing.

The first deans of women, although usually called preceptresses, had been appointed in the early days in the Middle West, but in the late nineties their numbers grew, and in 1902 a small group of them met at Northwestern University and laid the foundations for a permanent organization. To-day this organization totals some 1,500 members, and during the past three decades it has been a powerful influence, especially in the direction of bringing the attention of administrators to the housing of women students. The annual meetings of the National Association of Deans of Women always devote considerable time to housing, and in its first years a large fraction of their discussions were on this topic. Considering the primitive conditions of rooming houses as they existed in the Middle West, even in the first decade of this century, it is no wonder that the deans have been persistent in their efforts to create better living arrangements for their charges.

A survey of rooming houses at a Middle Western institution in 1906 brought out these facts:[22a]

> . . . that 18 of the 40 householders admitted both sexes; that approximately 30 householders permitted students to provide and prepare their own food; that cooking, eating, sleeping and studying were done in the same room; that in these houses girls had no parlors in which to entertain friends or callers; that none of the houses provided single beds; that only six had bathrooms and inside toilets; that ten had furnace heat; that three still used kerosene lamps. . . . Those doing light housekeeping might wash and iron in their own rooms, where kitchen duties were usually taken care of on kerosene stoves. . . .

By slow, persistent effort the deans of women have succeeded in improving the rooming houses in which a large percentage of their students are still forced to live. Much remains to be done, but the appear-

22a Caroline Grote, *Housing and Living Conditions of Women Students.* T. C., Columbia University, Contributions to Education, No. 507, 1932, pp. 25–26.

ance on many campuses of new dormitories during the past thirty years has considerably ameliorated the situation. Dormitories have not only put marginal rooming houses out of business, but they have also set standards for those that remain.[23] The deans of women have made a large contribution to improving the living and, therefore, the educational environment of students. Their vigilance, moreover, continues and will very likely always be one of their dominant interests.

In turning to the third of these supplementary influences toward a revival of interest in student housing, it must be remembered that "college life," as we understand the term to-day, has grown up since the 1860's. The first intercollegiate athletic contest of any sort was a boat race between Yale and Harvard in 1852 on Lake Winnipiseogee. Seventeen years later the first intercollegiate football game took place, but in general both sports and social life were undeveloped. During this period a few student publications existed, but they were in general poorer than the journalistic ventures of our preparatory school students of to-day. Because a large percentage of students planned careers in the ministry and in the law, debating had some vocational value, but intercollegiate contests did not begin until the seventies in the Middle West and not until the nineties in the East. Fraternities had been part of the college scene for four or five decades, but the fraternity house had not yet appeared and the societies were comparatively few in number and insignificant in prestige. The guitar and banjo had recently been introduced, but polite people still considered dancing a libidinous device of Satan.

The football played in those days resembled a street brawl more than a game, since twenty-five men made up a team, and the players wore no uniforms. Yale played Columbia in 1872 with twenty men on a side, and Princeton and Harvard played in 1876 with fifteen men on a side. It was not until 1880 that the eleven-man team became standard, and until 1890 paid coaches had not yet appeared. Basketball, hockey, soccer, tennis and swimming were not to become college sports for some years, and track had not begun until the seventies. Athletic letters were not generally awarded until the last decade of the century. Athletic cheers and cheer leaders arrived with their questionable pageantry about the same time. College colors came in with athletics, Yale first adopting green in 1853, and Harvard crimson at the suggestion of Eliot when, as a member of the crew that rowed against the Boston Irish in 1858, he and another oarsman wore crimson handkerchiefs upon their heads. "Fair Harvard" had been written in 1836 on the occasion of the bicentennial anniversary of Harvard's founding, but most of our present-day college songs did not come into vogue until after athletic contests grew in popularity.

By the beginning of the century this new type of college life had become thoroughly entrenched in practically every college and university in the country. It had likewise become an important part of the system of values of the great majority of alumni. To many graduates the contributions to their education from athletics and from extracurricular activities in general appeared to them to be more important and more lasting than their classroom and laboratory work, and they sought to foster every instrument that would keep or expand the active give-and-take of intimate undergraduate life. The alumni were chiefly responsible for scuttling Wilson's Quadrangle Plan at Princeton because it seemed likely to undermine the undergraduate social system; they gave Eliot many uneasy

[23] "Survey of Land-Grant Colleges and Universities." U. S. Office of Education Bulletin, 1930, No. 9. (Directed by A. J. Klein.) Vol. I, p. 426.

days and nights; and even Hadley at Yale, though generally sympathetic with their notions, had difficulty in keeping them from stealing the academic show. At Columbia, where the absence of residence halls had interfered with the development of a college life as colorful as at other comparable institutions, the alumni in the nineties set up a demand for dormitories. In 1896 the Board of Trustees capitulated and adopted a resolution in favor of raising money for student buildings. The action brought immediate alumni enthusiasm and attracted considerable newspaper attention. University officials were interviewed, and among their statements was one from Dean Van Amringe which appeared in the *New York Evening Post* of November 21, 1896, and which summarized the situation:

> . . . Since the acquisition of the new site, there is, perhaps, no single matter connected with the college that has received more general attention and more hearty commendation than the dormitory system. It has been looked to by students and alumni as a means of supplying what the college has always lacked, an opportunity to cultivate what is distinctly known as college life. . . .

The rejuvenation of the belief that where and how students live is of large educational significance has by these several means been achieved; the Hadley protest at Yale, the establishment of dormitories at Chicago, the efforts of Wilson at Princeton, the Lowell program at Harvard, the residential philosophy of the eastern women's colleges, the work of the deans of women and finally the hue and cry for more student life from students and alumni. The opinion built up by these several forces in favor of dormitories accumulated to such potency that it rapidly spread through the country. Cornell, which had been under the Tappan influence in the person of President White, built a small cottage for women in 1898 and its first large dormitory in 1914. Minnesota erected its first building for women in 1897, Illinois in 1916, and even Michigan fell in line with two in 1915. Hundreds of other colleges and universities have followed these Eastern and Middle Western leaders, and the movement has gone steadily forward. It has been considerably hampered by the depression, but it has remained actively alive. That it will continue to become even more important can hardly be doubted.

### THE THREE DOMINANT HOUSING PHILOSOPHIES

Proponents of dormitories have accomplished much of educational importance during the past thirty years. It must be pointed out with emphasis, however, that the great majority of dormitories, even those built in recent years and many now being erected, have not been conceived primarily as educational agencies. They house students in comfort and almost complete safety, and they serve vitally in the social development of undergraduates. Organically, however, they are separate from the curriculum and the active intellectual life of the colleges. Few housing plans, besides those in effect at Harvard and Yale, at once house students and bring them into daily formal and informal relationship with members of the faculty. Expensive plants, such as those at Harvard and Yale, will never be possible for more than a small fraction of American colleges and universities, but the values which accrue from this interlinking of living arrangements and educational effort (especially at Harvard) will more than likely lead to the adaptation at other institutions of buildings, which are now merely dormitories, into residences which more actively contribute to the educational process.

This brief critical discussion upon the foundation of a historical review gives point to contrasting three major housing philosophies, all of which have their adherents in American institutions of higher education. First, the British point of view exemplified best at Harvard and to a degree at Yale; second, the German philosophy still dominant at the Universities of California and Nebraska; and third, the American method which has developed from the impact of British[24] and German principles. The British system makes the residence hall the center of the student's formal as well as his informal education. The German principle rules out the desirability of any concern with the student outside the lecture hall and, therefore, eschews dormitories. The American compromise gives students body shelter (sometimes only a small fraction of the total enrolment) and varying degrees of social education, but as yet it remains considerably apart from the curricular life of the campus.

[24] The English provincial universities have not followed the example of Oxford and Cambridge. Founded in the nineteenth century or later they have encountered the same financial problems as American state universities.

# EDUCATIONAL EVENTS

## THE SCHOOL STRIKE IN MEXICO

Harold B. Hinton in a wireless dispatch to *The New York Times* from Guadalajara, Jalisco, Mexico, reports that on December 3 thirty per cent. of Jalisco's school children failed to attend school, in defiance of the federal law. According to a statement of Acting Governor Ignacio Jacobo, the state is deferring for the present any move to punish the parents while the situation is being studied.

The school strike springs from a misunderstanding, according to Señor Jacobo, the parents believing that the federal "socialistic education" system, opposed by Mexican Catholics, is already in effect. As a matter of fact, he states, Jalisco has given its teachers no instructions.

The State University was closed two months ago by the authorities because of the refusal of the students to admit the right of the government to prescribe the governmental theories to be taught. The fight on "socialistic education" is the front on which the Catholic Church is now concentrating its forces, believing that the proposed primary instruction definitely renounces God and the family.

Señor Jacobo stated that priests in Jalisco were obeying the restrictive laws in general in so far as the authorities were aware, except in exhorting parents from the pulpit and at the confessional to keep their children out of school in the hope that the government will modify its program.

In the neighboring State of Durango it is said that indignant fathers are kidnapping teachers who have indicated their willingness to impart "socialistic education." As a result, Governor Carlos Real has announced that for every teacher kidnapped he would imprison one priest.

Schools in other parts of the country are not in session now. An organization has been formed in Mexico, D. F., however, to exhort mothers to keep their children out of school, and to pay the fines of those punished for doing so.

Mr. Hinton reports that there is no doubt that the Catholics feel that if they can influence the government to modify its school program an end of the whole anti-church campaign is possible.

## MILITARY TRAINING AT THE LAND GRANT COLLEGES

The Supreme Court on December 3 handed down an opinion unanimously sustaining the right of the University of California and other land grant colleges to require military training as a part of their curricula and to deny admission to students refusing to comply, thus upholding the suspension by the regents of Albert W. Hamilton and W. Alonzo Reynolds, Jr., who refused because of religious and conscientious objections to submit to military training.

In an opinion read by Justice Butler, the court said:

> Government, federal and state, each in its own sphere owes a duty to the people within its jurisdiction to preserve itself in adequate strength to maintain peace and order and to assure the just enforcement of law. And every citizen owes the reciprocal duty, according to his capacity, to support and defend government against all enemies.
>
> The privilege of the native-born conscientious objector to avoid bearing arms comes not from the

Constitution but from the Acts of Congress. That body may grant or withhold the exemption as in its wisdom it sees fit; and if it be withheld, the native-born conscientious objector can not successfully assert the privilege.

No other conclusion is compatible with the well-nigh limitless extent of the war powers as above illustrated, which include, by necessary implication, the power, in the last extremity, to compel the armed service of any citizen in the land, without regard to his objection or his views in respect of the justice or morality on the particular war or war in general.

The opinion quoted from the court's decision in upholding the Massachusetts compulsory vaccination law, where it outlined the liberties guaranteed to the individual under the Fourteenth Amendment, but said:

And yet he may be compelled, by force if need be, against his will and without regard to his personal wishes or his pecuniary interests, or even his religious or political convictions, to take his place in the ranks of the army of his country and risk the chances of being shot down in its defense.

Plainly, there is no ground for the contention that the regents' order, requiring able-bodied male students under the age of twenty-four as a condition of their enrolment to take the prescribed instruction in military science and tactics, transgresses any constitutional right asserted by these appellants.

The contention that the regents' order is repugnant to the Briand-Kellogg peace pact requires little consideration. In that instrument the United States and other high contracting parties declare that they condemn recourse to war for the solution of international controversies and renounce it as an instrument of national policy in their regulations with one another, and agree that the settlement or solution of all disputes or conflicts which may arise among them shall never be sought except by pacific means.

Clearly there is no conflict between the regents' order and the provisions of the treaty.

Justice Cardozo, who was joined in his opinion by Associate Justices Brandeis and Stone, expressed agreement, but made the point that the conscientious objector, if his liberties were extended as suggested in the current case,

might refuse to contribute taxes in furtherance of war, whether for attack or defense, or in furtherance of any other end condemned by his conscience as irreligious or immoral.

The right of private judgment has never yet been so exalted above the powers and the compulsion of the agencies of government. One who is a martyr to a principle—which may turn out in the end to be a delusion or an error—does not prove by his martyrdom that he has kept within the law.

While affirming the action of the university regents and concurring in the opinion of the majority, Mr. Cardozo held that:

There is no occasion at this time to mark the limits of governmental power in the exaction of military service when the nation is at peace.

He pointed out that the petitioners had not been required to bear arms for any hostile purpose, offensive or defensive, and said:

If they elect to resort to an institution for higher education maintained with the state's moneys, then and only then they are commanded to follow courses of instruction believed by the state to be vital to its welfare. Instruction in military science, unaccompanied here by any pledge of military service, is not an interference by the state with the free exercise of religion when the liberties of the Constitution are read in the light of a century and a half of history during days of peace and war.

## WILLIAMS COLLEGE AND FEDERAL EMERGENCY RELIEF

Dr. Tyler Dennett, president of Williams College, on November 25 answered the attack made as a result of his refusal of Federal Emergency Relief Administration funds by Harry L. Hopkins, Federal Relief Administrator. Dr. Dennett in a speech on the general subject of "Our Bureaucracy," which inaugurated the season of the Williams College Forum, took as an example the recent incident of Mr. Hopkins's attack on his stand against FERA aid to needy students. He had earlier maintained that under a bureaucracy there was a tendency for the system to become bigger and bigger, the conception being that the larger the more important, and that the bureaucrat finally ended by regarding the taxpayer "as a public enemy."

Mr. Hopkins, in a speech to presidents of land grant colleges and universities, had mentioned Dr. Dennett's earlier refusal of federal financial aid, saying it was "a lot of nonsense," and criticizing Williams and the few other New England educational institutions which have refused government funds as "overly-endowed aristocratic institutions . . . who claim that they have certain privileges that the rest of us shall not have."

Dr. Dennett stated that:

In order to maintain in college this year its worthy students in need of aid, this college has not only expended every nickel of its funds derived from endowed scholarships but has also dipped into the general funds to the extent of about $30,000 for additional student aid. . . . We preferred to help our own rather than call upon the American taxpayer to do it for us.

Only a few weeks ago the president made an appeal for private philanthropy to exert itself to the utmost this winter, and then, when Williams College, along with some others, agreed to carry through the year all its students who are judged to be worthy of and also in need of financial assistance without recourse to the FERA, Mr. Hopkins comes along and, instead of recognizing a public spirit, calls us snobbish. Have we reached such a pass in this country that every one who refuses federal aid is a snob? . . .

Williams College has always welcomed poor boys. I was one of them thirty-three years ago. Every one who knows Williams College, as Mr. Hopkins evidently does not, knows that there is no college in the country where the poor boy is more welcome or gets a better break. There is no campus that is more uncomfortable for the poor little rich boy who comes to college with money and nothing else and thinks money will get him through. . . .

As for the assumption that every boy ought to have a college education merely because he wants to go to college, that is pure sentimentalism. Of course, boys faced with the alternative of college or greasing cars in a gas station will prefer college. But it does not follow that because a boy prefers four years of excitement on a college campus that he ought to have it. Least of all should he have it at the expense of the American taxpayer. . . .

Williams College is still proud of the fact that it is not taking FERA money. If there is any professor here that approves of the New Deal he is perfectly free to say so. But if he does not approve of it he at least does not have the embarrassment of knowing that when he teaches that FERA economics are bad he is arguing against his own salary.

## STRIKE OF STUDENTS OF JOURNALISM AT THE STATE UNIVERSITY OF LOUISIANA

Students of journalism at Louisiana State University stayed away from their classes on November 28 in a protest strike against the suspension of twenty-six students and against censorship of *The Reveille,* the undergraduate newspaper, by university authorities, said to have been undertaken at the command of Senator Huey P. Long. The twenty-six students suspended signed a petition to Dr. James M. Smith, president of the university, demanding freedom of the campus press from the censorship, and reinstatement of the newspaper staff, who resigned on imposition of the censorship.

Dr. Smith on November 28 conferred with student leaders and members of the faculty, but announced at the end of the day that the situation had not changed. He is reported to have said:

About fifteen of the twenty-six students who were suspended have asked for reinstatement. Being a reasonable man, I will consider each application on its merits. Thus far, however, there have been no reinstatements and there is no change in the situation. I'm in this thing as a matter of principle and I'm going to see it through. If the board of supervisors does not see fit to back me up they can get a new president. I'm going to stick with it, and I don't give a hang what any board member thinks.

New petitions demanding reinstatement of the twenty-six suspended students have been started in a series of protest meetings of journalism students.

According to the newspapers, the censorship order was issued by university authorities on the direction of Senator Long, who is said to have recently had himself appointed a member of the board of supervisors after having seen in an advance page proof a letter from a student critical of his efforts to make Abe Mickal, university star halfback, a member of the State Senate "without an election." After several days the censorship was lifted, but it was later reestablished. An Associated Press dispatch, dated December 3, reports that Senator Long states that he has "never censored or undertaken to censor anything published at Louisiana State University."

## THE CCC CAMPS AND THE AMERICAN ASSOCIATION OF UNIVERSITY PROFESSORS

The American Association of University Professors at its recent meeting in Chicago, prompted by the recent action of Robert Fechner, CCC director, in banning from the camps the book "Men and Machines," passed a resolution, proposed by Dr. F. K. Richtmyer, dean of the Graduate School of Cornell University, requesting President Roosevelt to take action in the matter. The treatise, which deals with the effect of increasing mechanization on craftsmen, was written by Professor William F. Ogburn, of the University of Chicago. The resolution follows:

> The association is informed that the director of the Civilian Conservation Camps shows a disposition to interfere with the freedom of teaching and to obstruct the program of the educational director of the camps.
>
> This association respectfully requests President Roosevelt, to whom the director of the CCC is alone responsible, to review the matter.
>
> Furthermore, this association requests President Roosevelt and the Congress to expand greatly the educational program of the camps in order that the young men may have the opportunity of becoming more intelligent with regard to the industrial and social problems which confront the civilized world.

In a recent statement, Dr. Charles H. Judd, dean of the School of Education at the University of Chicago, says:

> Educators will regard the decision to suppress this pamphlet as a very serious matter, because it raises the important question whether information about economic and social problems can be taught in public institutions. The pamphlet contains a perfectly innocent and quite useful discussion of the social implications of the machine. It was written by a leading authority on that subject. It was approved by competent educators. There is no point in herding 300,000 boys together unless we can do something for them intellectually as well as physically. The educational reading materials available at the camps are certainly now inadequate.

Dean Judd reported that several prominent educators in the East are already actively interested in knowing the reasons for the banning of the pamphlet. Dr. Ogburn's pamphlet, he explained, is the first of a series now in preparation for CCC use which have been made possible by a grant of $40,000 for that purpose by the General Education Board of New York. The educational program of the CCC was drawn up by the office of education of the Department of the Interior. Dean C. S. Marsh, on leave of absence from the University of Buffalo, is in immediate charge of the CCC educational work.

## THE NATIONAL INTERFRATERNITY CONFERENCE

THE National Interfraternity Conference, at the closing session on December 1 of its twenty-sixth annual meeting at the Hotel Roosevelt, decided, according to a report in *The New York Times,* to commit itself to a policy of complete cooperation with college administrators as a means of increasing the popularity of national college fraternities. It was the opinion of the delegates from the sixty-six fraternities represented that such a policy was necessary to restore to the undergraduate societies the prominent position which they had once held.

The future course of the association was outlined by LeRoy E. Kimball in an address following his induction as chairman for the ensuing year. Mr. Kimball stated that there has been much talk as to the existence of an unfriendly feeling in the colleges towards the fraternities, adding that he knew "of no college president or dean opposed to the ideal social fraternity. It will be the aim of the new administration to press forward with intelligent optimism and intelligent competence. We shall get nowhere unless we work hand in hand with the colleges."

It was stated at the conference that national college fraternities and their individual chapters are facing the greatest crisis in a generation, and the subject was discussed by representatives of the National Undergraduate Interfraternity Council, which met in conjunction with the National Interfraternity Conference. A more favorable picture of the trend of national fraternities was given by Peter C. Hitt, a senior at Yale and a member of Beta Theta Pi. He said that at Yale University there has been a revival of interest in the campus fraternity, due mainly to the college house experiment instituted there. The effect of the house unit plan will not be to exclude the fraternity but to complement its activities. There will still be a definite need for the undergraduate societies.

Unsafe and unsanitary conditions in fraternity houses were decried by several speakers who dealt with the maintenance question. The discussion on this subject was led by George Starr Lasher, of Athens, Ohio, national president of the Theta Chi fraternity, in whose house at Dartmouth nine men died on February 25 of asphyxiation caused by defective flues. The conference adopted the following resolution submitted by Mr. Lasher:

Resolved, That the National Interfraternity Conference, through its executive committee, make a thoroughgoing and persistent appeal to college and university authorities for expert investigation semi-annually of all dormitories, fraternity and sorority houses and large rooming houses as a protection against fire, gas and sanitation hazards.

Another resolution adopted by the conference asked that colleges where fraternities included in the National Fraternity Conference are represented be sounded out to determine the extent to which they will cooperate with the fraternities in establishing resident adviserships.

The meeting closed with the luncheon of the College Fraternity Editors' Association, at which Arthur S. Draper, editor of *The Literary Digest,* was guest speaker.

## THE NEW LIBRARY OF COLUMBIA UNIVERSITY

Columbia University on November 30 formally opened South Hall, the new library erected at a cost of $4,000,000, the gift of Edward S. Harkness. Addresses were made by Dr. Nicholas Murray Butler, president of the university, and Dr. John Buchan, English author and member of Parliament for the Scottish Universities.

The building is in Italian Renaissance style and was designed by James Gamble Rogers, architect of the Sterling Library at Yale University. It is the twentieth of the twenty-nine buildings in the original design of the Columbia campus on Morningside Heights as planned in 1893. There are accommodations for 3,000,000 volumes and future provision can be made for an additional million.

A frieze around the top of the fifth story bears the names of eighteen men of letters, while panels under the large front windows are inscribed with the names of twenty-four American statesmen and authors.

Reproduced on the three panels over the main entrance is the seal of King's College, used from 1754 to 1784; the seal of Columbia College under the regents of the University of the State of New York, in use from 1784 to 1787, and, in the center, the seal of Columbia College, which has been in use since 1787, and is used by the entire university to-day.

South Hall contains sixteen special reading rooms, in addition to the main reading room and the departmental seminar and work rooms. Fifteen tiers of book stacks occupy the central portion of the building, each air-conditioned to provide the best conditions of book storage. On the ground floor is the Harkness Academic Theater, an assembly room seating about 300 persons.

Dr. Butler referred to the library as a laboratory, where students at Columbia may have facilities for reference to sources and authorities such as they have never before enjoyed. "This building," he said, "is not only a monument to academic progress, but it is a prophecy of academic accomplishment yet to come."

Dr. Buchan, in his address, stressed the importance of the "humanities" as the ideal of education rather than the mere "acquisition of learning."

Mr. and Mrs. Harkness sat in the audience. On the speakers' platform were Roger Howson, librarian of Columbia University; Dr. Herbert Putnam, librarian of Congress; Harry M. Lydenberg, librarian of the New York Public Library; Professor Roswell Magill, of the Columbia Law School, and James Gamble Rogers, trustee of the university.

# EDUCATIONAL NOTES AND NEWS

Katharine F. Lenroot, daughter of former Senator Lenroot of Wisconsin, acting chief of the Children's Bureau of the U. S. Department of Labor, has been appointed chief to succeed Miss Grace Abbott, who resigned on July 1 to become professor of public welfare in the School of Social Service of the University of Chicago. Miss Lenroot has a record of nineteen years of continuous service in the bureau and has held the position of assistant chief since 1922.

DR. ROBERT ALLEN ARMSTRONG was elected acting president of West Virginia University on December 1. He will take office on January 1 and will serve until June 30, 1935, or until a new president is elected.

A DINNER on the occasion of the forty-fifth anniversary of Barnard College, Columbia University, will be given on December 11 in honor of George A. Plimpton, who has served the college as trustee since its establishment and for forty-one years as treasurer. Speakers at the dinner, which will be presided over by Mrs. Henry Wise Miller, a trustee, will include Dean Virginia C. Gildersleeve, Dr. Nicholas Murray Butler, Mrs. George Haven Putnam and Mr. Plimpton.

DR. ROBERT EMORY BLACKWELL, for over thirty-two years president of Randolph-Macon College, who received the degree of master of arts from the college in 1874, celebrated his eightieth birthday on November 14.

DR. FREDERICK B. ROBINSON, president of the College of the City of New York, has taken up his work at the college after an absence of three weeks caused by illness.

DR. ROBERT C. CLOTHIER, president of Rutgers University, was elected president of the Middle States Association of Colleges and Secondary Schools at the recent meeting at Atlantic City. Dr. George William McClelland, vice-president of the University of Pennsylvania, was named secretary, and Stanley R. Yarnell, principal of the Germantown Friends School, treasurer.

MISS MABEL E. SIMPSON was elected president of the New York State Teachers Association at the conclusion of its eighty-ninth annual meeting at Rochester, N. Y., on November 27. Miss Zoraida E. Weeks was chosen vice-president.

COLUMBIA UNIVERSITY conferred the honorary degree of doctor of letters on December 3 on John Buchan, British author and lecturer and member of Parliament from the Scottish universities. Dr. Buchan delivered the principal address at the formal opening of the new library.

PROFESSOR IRA EUGENE CUTLER, chairman of the division of biological sciences and professor of zoology at the University of Denver, has been made professor emeritus. Professor Cutler has been connected with the university for thirty-six years, first as professor of both botany and zoology, and later of zoology. Dr. Humphrey Gray Owen, associate professor of zoology, has been appointed to succeed Dr. Cutler.

DR. CHARLES S. TIPPETTS, professor of economics at the University of Buffalo, has been appointed dean of the School of Business Administration at the University of Pittsburgh. He will take office on February 1.

DR. J. H. SMITH, formerly superintendent of schools at West Aurora, Ill., has been appointed director of the Training School of the State Teachers College at Oshkosh, Wis.

CLARA BRIAN was recently appointed dean of women at the Northern Montana College.

DR. ARTUR SALZ, formerly professor of economics in the University of Heidelberg, is spending the year at the Ohio State University as visiting professor of economics. He is conducting a seminar on "Technical Progress and Capitalism."

THE REV. CLAUDE JENKINS, fellow of King's College, London, dean of the faculty of theology and professor of ecclesiastical history in the University of London, has been appointed to the canonry of Christ Church and regius professorship of ecclesiastical history in the University of Oxford, to succeed the Rev. E. W. Watson.

ACCORDING to the London *Times,* a chair of national health was inaugurated on November 1 at Munich by Dr. Gerhart Wagner, head of the German Medical Association, who stated that the new chair would form a model for others. The first professor of the new faculty is Dr. Schultze, the Bavarian state commissioner of health.

A BRONZE wall plaque of Professor Joseph S. Myers, professor in the School of Journalism of the Ohio State University from 1914 to 1927 and director of the school from 1927 until his retirement with the title of emeritus last July, was presented to the university on November 23 at the annual Hall of Fame dinner. Karl B. Pauly, of the *Ohio State Journal,* made the presentation on behalf of graduates and former students, and Vice-president J. L. Morrill accepted the plaque on behalf of the university. The plaque, in bas-relief, is the work of Professor Erwin F. Frey, of the department of fine arts. A cast of the plaque was unveiled at the time of presentation, and the bronze itself is to be completed in time for Alumni Day next June.

A PORTRAIT of Dr. Hugh D. Reed, since 1906 professor of vertebrate zoology at Cornell University, was presented to the university on November 17 by his graduate students and colleagues in the department. It was formally presented by Dr. Julian D. Corrington, of Rochester, who was one of Dr. Reed's students, and officially accepted for the university by President Farrand. Professor Simon H. Gage described the early history and development of the department of zoology and the methods of teaching that were used before 1900, when Dr. Reed joined it as assistant. Professor Benjamin F. Kingsbury told of their acquaintance and of Dr. Reed's work as a student, graduate and member of the faculty of the university. The presentation was followed by an informal reception.

THE Penrose Medal of the Geological Society of America has been awarded to Dr. Charles Schuchert, emeritus professor of invertebrate paleontology at Yale University. The medal, which was established in 1925 by the late Dr. R. A. F. Penrose, Jr., is given for distinguished service and fundamental contributions to the advancement of geologic science. It will be presented to Dr. Schuchert at Rochester, N. Y., on the occasion of the annual dinner of the society on December 28.

E. E. OBERHOLTZER, superintendent of schools at Houston, Texas, and president of the Department of Superintendence this year, has completed his work for the doctor's degree at Teachers College, Columbia University. His dissertation is entitled "An Integrated Curriculum in Practise."

SPENCER LEESON, head master of Merchant Taylors' School, has been appointed head master of Winchester College. Mr. Leeson succeeds Dr. A. T. P. Williams, who was recently appointed dean of Christ Church, Oxford.

A. E. FOOT, for the past eleven years assistant master of Eton College, has been appointed head master of the Delhi Dun Public School, Delhi, India, which will open next March. The sum of £150,000 has been collected to erect the school, which will be run on English lines adapted to Indian needs and environment.

GARTH H. AKRIDGE, formerly superintendent of schools at Norphlet, Ark., has accepted a newly created position with the Julius Rosenwald Fund. He will act in a fact-finding and advisory capacity to state departments of education and the Federal Emergency Relief Administration on the Emergency Education program, particularly as it affects the Negro.

DR. MARY DABNEY DAVIS, who organized the FERA emergency nursery school program, has been appointed full-time nursery-kindergarten-primary specialist of the Office of Education. Dr. Grace Langdon, formerly with the Institute for Child Development, Teachers College, Columbia University, and Mrs. Jane E. Lubald, formerly critic teacher, will carry on the administrative functions. Dr. Langdon has worked with Dr. Davis in the emergency nursery school development since its inception a year ago.

ASSOCIATE SUPERINTENDENT MARGARET J. MCCOOEY, in charge of education for handicapped children, has been reelected for her third six-year term by the New York City Board of Education.

WALTER H. KLAR, instructor in the summer school of Pennsylvania State College from 1927 to 1934, has been appointed to be supervisor of fine and industrial arts of the Springfield, Massachusetts, public schools.

ARTHUR A. BALLANTINE, LL.D., Harvard University, assistant secretary of the United States Treasury from 1931 to 1933, and member of the law firm of Root, Clark, Buckner, and Ballantine, has been elected by the trustees of Teachers College, Columbia University, a member of the board.

JOSEPH W. BARTLETT, '98, a business man of Newton, Mass., chairman of the Emergency Finance Board of Massachusetts and formerly chairman of the board which administered the

Civil Works Administration in the state, has been elected a member of the board of trustees of Massachusetts State College.

THE REV. DR. WILLIAM GREENOUGH THAYER died on November 24 at the age of seventy-one years. From 1894 until 1930 he was head of St. Mark's preparatory school. On his retirement the alumni established a fund of $250,000 in honor of him and Mrs. Thayer.

DR. DUDLEY WILSON WILLARD, head of the department of sociology at George Washington University, died on November 27 from the results of the explosion of an oil furnace in his home. He was forty-two years old.

DR. FRANK COE BARNES, who has been a member of the modern language department of Union College for thirty years and its chairman since 1906, died on November 30, at the age of sixty-seven years.

MRS. HELEN M. SCOVILLE, principal emeritus of the Scoville School for Girls, New York City, died on November 30, at the age of seventy-six years.

THE VERY REVEREND GEORGE MILLIGAN, professor emeritus of divinity and biblical criticism at the University of Glasgow, died on November 26, at the age of seventy-four years.

NEW YORK UNIVERSITY was presented by the French Government at ceremonies held on December 3 with the university medal of the "Groupe Americain, Société des Architectes Diplômes" recently awarded for excellence of work done in the department of design of the department of architecture of the College of Fine Arts. Frank Cheney Farley, president of the society, made the presentation, and Harold O. Voorhis, secretary of the university, accepted the medal in behalf of Chancellor Harry Woodburn Chase. David Sarnoff, president of the Radio Corporation of America and a member of the council of the university, delivered an address on "Art in the Radio Age."

THE 1935 meeting of the World Federation of Education Associations will be held next August in England, either in Oxford or in Cambridge. The meeting will be held in conjunction with the International Federation of Teachers' Associations and the Bureau International de L'Enseignement Secondaire, looking to a more complete consolidation or coordination of these international societies working to the same end. It is expected that the invitation of Japan for 1935 will be renewed for 1936. The tidal waves and typhoons of the Philippines called for so much relief that finances could not be arranged for the 1935 regional conference, for which the association had been invited. Teachers and others who contemplate attending the 1935 meeting in England should communicate with the headquarters office of the World Federation of Education Associations, 1201 Sixteenth Street, Washington, D. C., at an early date.

SIXTEEN western colleges and universities are to take an active part in the twelfth session of the Institute of World Affairs to be held at Los Angeles from December 9 to 14. On the program of the six-day session as special lecturers and round-table leaders will be fifty-five speakers on international problems, representing Stanford University, the University of California, the California Institute of Technology, the Universities of Washington, Montana, Nevada, Arizona, University of Denver, Brigham Young University, Mills College, Occidental, University of California at Los Angeles, Scripps College, Redlands University, Pomona College and the University of Southern California. Dr. Eliot G. Mears, of Stanford University, is director of the 1934 institute, which is sponsored by the Los Angeles University of International Relations of the University of Southern California. Political and economic problems of international concern will be discussed at morning round-tables, afternoon general sessions and evening lectures.

A CORRESPONDENT writes: "Far back into the mountains of West Virginia near Ripley, where it is reported that a Negro has not been seen in forty years, a group of colored citizens journeyed on November 15 to take part in an educational meeting. The meeting was a part of a government project for adult education. The audience consisted exclusively of over four hundred white people, including farmers, common laborers and small business men. The discussion centered round the contribution of the Negro to American life. The addresses were delivered by I. J. K. Wells, state supervisor of Negro schools of West Virginia; Harry W.

Greene and Thomas E. Posey, professors at the West Virginia State College. Music by others of the colored group was rendered. The program was most enthusiastically received, and the whole affair was regarded as one of the finest steps toward more and better wholesome race relations in West Virginia."

ACCORDING to information from the office of the president, J. Nelson Norwood, Alfred University, in cooperation with the Education Department of the State of New York, has organized two new emergency collegiate centers, one at Salamanca, and one at Medina. Two centers were organized last year at Bath and Jamestown. There are now about 250 students in these four centers under the auspices of Alfred University. James G. Stevens has been appointed supervisor of the centers, with headquarters at Alfred.

THE five-year program, financed by the Rockefeller Foundation, in child guidance at the University of Rochester, terminated on September 1. This clinic was originally established for the intensive study of behavior problems in children of pre-school age and preadolescent period. While the clinic will continue, it will be on a restricted basis, owing to this reduction in the budget.

COLORADO STATE TEACHERS COLLEGE summer school, 1935, will be conducted on a plan that will take into consideration the desire of students to attend the National Education Association meetings in Denver. In the belief that a large number of students will want to combine business, study and recreation, Teachers College is preparing for a large enrolment and at the same time arranging the summer school program so that there will be ample time for mountain trips and a week off for the meetings. Two sessions are to be held, one of nine weeks, with a week's intersession during meetings, and one of six weeks, beginning on the day following their close.

PENNSYLVANIA MILITARY COLLEGE, for 114 years a privately owned institution, has been transferred to public ownership, it has been announced by John G. Pew, a member of the newly created Hyatt Foundation. Mr. Pew stated that the college has been purchased from the Hyatt family, which has owned it for three quarters of a century, and that it is to be operated as a purely non-profit institution in the future by the foundation. In transferring the college to public ownership Mr. Pew said that the Hyatt family, of which Colonel Frank K. Hyatt, president of the college, is a member, had made a generous contribution to establish the Hyatt Foundation. The reason for the change, he said, was to assure the perpetuation of the college beyond the lives of present members of the Hyatt family and to give it an opportunity to enhance its work through the creation of endowment funds.

# DISCUSSION

## THE TRUANT CHILD

TRUANCY, especially in our city schools, presents a persistent and serious problem. Juvenile court statistics list this form of behavior as delinquency, and as such it constitutes a major item in all reports of this nature. The child who absents himself from school may be doing so in order to preserve his sense of adequacy by escaping from a situation in which his inferiority undergoes constant magnification. An inferiority feeling of this type is often traceable to low mentality, a speech defect or some specific disability concerning a particular subject. Upon being questioned with regard to his truancy the child may declare that he does not like school; but the underlying cause for his defection is rarely revealed.

Intensive investigations of child life and behavior have taught us that the individual is frequently unable to supply the correct reason for his conduct. As adults we are aware that our motives in most cases skilfully elude us, leaving only the dregs of rationalization. Most truants fail to point out an acceptable reason for their absences because the real cause may be obscured by a complexity of factors not obvious either to themselves or the teacher.

To the teacher, on the other hand, the problem reduces itself to a question of whether or not the child will conform to the attendance requirements. Rarely does she seek underlying causes. In many schools the psychologist is non-existent, and where he does function his services consist of mental examinations to determine intellectual status. The possibility of emotional conflicts associated with truancy are not considered. When repeated warnings fail, court action and coercion are resorted to as a final alternative. The truant officer (whose insight into psychological mechanisms of human behavior is regrettably deficient) is expected to "adjust" the child.

Our experience with a great many truants has convinced us that excessive absence from the classroom may have its roots in an intrapsychic conflict traceable to the home situation. This factor might be suspected in cases where the child is of average intelligence and where truancy is apparently unmotivated by some gross misalliance between the child and his school. An example will demonstrate a problem of this type.

A boy of average intelligence appeared to develop a strong antipathy toward the school and began to truant excessively. He was invariably found at home. Initial questioning elicited the statement that he "did not like" school. Investigation revealed no difficulty with school subjects. Our findings, after a careful study of the case, showed that the parents were extremely incompatible, that the mother was a hysterical personality who controlled her otherwise stable husband by frequently threatening suicide. The boy remained at home in order to guard against the fulfilment of her threats.

Another case concerns a boy of very superior intelligence who remained away from school until he failed most of his subjects. An analysis proved that he was addicted to auto-erotic practises and feared that his classmates could read the results of these practises in his features.

In both these cases adjustive work resulted in marked improvement and adjustment to the school and home. Force and threats might only have intensified the problem. Persuasion would have been futile.

We have also learned that truancy might be caused by inadequate clothing which engenders a sense of shame in the child. A poor home environment in which home study facilities are absent also contributes to truancy by reason of the fact that the child is loath to attend classes when his work is consistently poor.

Truancy, as these examples will indicate, is by no means a simple problem of whether or not the child is willing to conform. It must be regarded as a *symptom* of some fundamental maladjustment. Psycho-therapeutic measures are indicated when truancy is not caused by patent mental retardation or through the influence of bad companions. The work of the visiting teacher in conjunction with that of the school psychologist is of paramount importance in this connection. Truancy is frequently a personality problem. Recourse to court action by the school should be resorted to only when all other efforts at adjustment have failed.

Fred Brown
Alfred Willson Children's Center
Columbus, Ohio

## THE COURSE AS A UNIT OF TEACHING

We hear a great deal to-day of teaching by larger units. It makes us think of problems, projects, challenges, jobs, activities, etc., all designed as progressive methods by which the student is encouraged "to learn by doing." A series of such activities constitutes a course; a series of courses, which is only the name for larger units, is in turn designed to lead the learner to a goal—graduation.

The life of each individual must be evaluated in terms of its integration, its unity. If this be true, and we believe so, then our schools and our teachers need to adopt a new outlook. As it is, we appraise the product of our schools by the accumulation of units or credits, which are based on so many courses more or less successfully covered. It also indicates a certain amount of time served, each course representing a quarter, a semester or some such time-unit.

Surely, all of us have at times felt some apprehension over this system of judging a pupil's or student's educational achievement. The point in view for our discussion is that the content of a course is so often broken up into fragments and presented to the learner, who is expected through some mysterious process to put the mosaic together and see the course as a beautiful well-ordered whole. Unfortunately such optimism too frequently goes unrewarded. The teacher may or may not know the ultimate aim of his own course, and the best means and methods to get there; the learner certainly has a task on his hands when he sets out in the dark on his course or courses, attempting in self-defense, perhaps, to acquire enough of more or less unrelated facts to satisfy the standards as required by the teachers. If such is the case within a course, what can we expect between courses?

We are all no doubt aware of the situation, but do little about it. Each teacher is an accepted expert in his field, and tends to view those in other fields with an amount of caution, at times culminating in open rivalry, if not hostility. He may even go to the length of belittling the work done by colleagues, keeping his own courses from contact with others for fear of possible contamination. It reminds one of the now so popular Cellophane wrapping. The whole matter appears inexcusable and ridiculous in view of the fact that the only divisions of knowledge which we have were set up by the human mind. And when we find that the lines of demarcation have become so sharp as to threaten the efficiency of our educative process, then we back up, using "larger units" as ways and means to reach the desired end—integration. We have become aware that problems in life are not solved by courses, but by our fused knowledges, our integrated experiences.

The elementary school people have been first to recognize this fact in their activity program, an extension of the project-method, socialized recitation, etc. It is an attempt to correlate the phases of school work so the learner may more or less consciously appreciate the relationship of the facts and phenomena that have bearing on the solution of the problem at hand. Such a procedure will make a better educated person than could possibly result from the mere passing of courses.

Wood to become really useful needs a period of seasoning; otherwise it tends to dry in such a way as to shrink and warp. The same is true of knowledge. The hurried and superficial passing of courses in our schools does not permit the students' mastery of subject-matter necessary to retention and efficient use. They are rushed through, arriving at graduation in a state of confusion and weariness, wondering what it is all about—if they do wonder.

Some of our schools are trying to bring order out of chaos by inaugurating comprehensive examinations. The underlying principle is that it will further correlation, attainment, skill, power to think—not mere memory of unrelated facts. It is probably too early to draw definite conclusions as to the merit of this practise; but it seems promising in ways.

The educational menu which we spread before the learners to-day is largely cafeteria style. Unfortunately, many of our customers lack foresight and experience as well as knowledge to select a balanced meal. The result in many cases is mental indigestion. One dish does not agree with another. Probably what we need as much as anything is to help our students to see the relation of ideas, and thus of subject-matters. If we are to retain the course as one of the large units of instruction, its contents and its method should be evaluated in terms of its contribution to the whole—the growth, or education of the learner. No course can stand on its own merit; it is merely a unit in the learner's total experience, and in that total experience it must be submerged. It must find its proper place in the hierarchy of knowledges, skills and attitudes which are being inculcated in the learner. In that case it will reinforce other courses, and in turn be reinforced by them.

And finally I believe that there should be some central super-integrative principle toward which every course, every activity should drive. I mean to say that the sum total of our educative endeavors should be woven about a dominant, dynamic ideal. It should stand out like a shining beacon, at all times showing the way. If such were the case, correlation and integration would of necessity follow. Some denominational schools recognize such a principle in their religion, and strive for the education of what they call "the whole man." But the rest of us, particularly in state institutions, can not for obvious reasons adopt that principle. We speak rather glibly of education for citizenship, education for progress, social service, democracy. We honestly try to achieve such or similar noble ends, but can we do it by the present system of leading our students through one course after another, the relationship of which even we teachers may not appreciate? That the minds of our students appear rather befuddled should not surprise us.

President Hutchins, of the University of Chicago, says: "The most characteristic feature of the modern world is bewilderment; we do not know where we are going, or why; and we have almost given up the attempt to find out."

It may not be as bad as that, but it seems high time that we get together and fully realize that each of us is merely contributing a share to the total education of our students, that we and our courses are but units of the whole. Strictly speaking, we are not teaching courses but young people. In the words of Matthew Arnold, let us help them to "see life steadily and see it whole."

GUSTAF FREDEN

LOUISIANA POLYTECHNIC INSTITUTE

### DEPRESSION AND THE TEACHER

IN quest of a teaching position in the secondary schools for the year 1933–34, the results set forth herein were secured. These should be of interest to those in the teaching profession and of some significance to the general public. A brief tabulation of the facts should have some value.

A total of two hundred and sixteen individually typed applications were mailed to that number of secondary school districts out of the three hundred and eleven such districts listed in the Directory of California Secondary Schools (December 15, 1933). One hundred and twenty-four of these application letters carried a self-addressed postal, to facilitate reply. This large number of applications yielded ninety-five responses, or 44 per cent. Of these fifty-seven were on the self-addressed cards, thirty-six were in the form of letters and two were on mimeographed cards. A majority of the principals answered immediately, though belated cards continued to arrive till the opening of the school year.

The responses of the principals varied greatly in their nature and length. Some were polite letters, others brief and curt. Two cards contained only the two words, "No vacancies." One principal answered in pencil, with parentheses and double underscore, "No vacancies this year. Wish you success." The spirit is appreciated. None of the replies was encouraging. Only in one instance was a second communication received from a principal, and this in a case where former relationship entered into the candidate's application.

Apart from the letters mailed to the districts, notices of eight vacancies were received from the California Teachers Association, two others arrived from a teachers' agency and one came from a leading university. Six trips were made in following up these notifications but without positive results. These trips varied in length from thirty to six hundred miles. Approximately one hundred and fifty dollars were expended in carrying out this entire program.

This sums a season's efforts to secure a position by a teacher with eight years' experience, four of which were in two of the most prominent school systems of California, a teacher with an M.A. in education from Stanford University, and an administrator's credential. It would therefore appear that there is little left to do in continuing the effort apart from applying to the SERA.

The tabulated results would not be significant were they particular to the individual involved, but they are not. They typically represent the conditions confronting hundreds of teachers of commendable ability and experience. A reasonable and applicable solution is advisable and urgent.

HOWARD RENNICK,
*Stanford, '30*

## SPECIAL CORRESPONDENCE

### EDUCATION IN BULGARIA

THE TRAINING OF TEACHERS

PROFESSIONAL education of Bulgarian teachers is, as everywhere else in Europe, a matter of most serious concern to the state. A Bulgarian authority estimates that about 61 per cent. of the elementary school teachers get their education in normal schools; the rest are graduates of gymnasia, seminaries and other schools, and about 1.1 per cent. even lack secondary education.[1]

In 1928–29 Bulgaria had 13 normal schools for the training of elementary school teachers: the teaching staff comprised 155 male and 162 female teachers and the students numbered 3,439 men and 3,132 women.[2]

The normal schools have a curriculum which is nearly identical with the gymnasia. The subjects taught are the Bulgarian language and literature, pedagogy, psychology, logic and ethics, Bulgarian general and church history, Bulgarian and general geography, a choice of modern languages (French, German, English or Russian), civics, mathematics, natural history, physics and chemistry, popular hygiene, political economy, the science of cooperative movements, drawing, modelling, handicrafts, needlework, music and singing, gymnastics and special lectures on physical culture and shorthand. Special attention is paid to musical education. At the end of the course, students take the matriculation examination and become qualified for appointments as teachers in elementary schools.

Most of the students come from peasant families. The matriculation fees are high, according to the Bulgarian standards, but they cover the expenses for books and other needs, and for uniforms, which must be worn by all Bulgarian students who are in the third category of schools. The training is open to students, not above 20 years of age, who are physically fit and have completed the prescribed course at a lower gymnasium successfully. Each institution is connected with a training school for teachers. Some normal schools also offer courses for kindergarten teachers and for teachers of delinquent children.

Only about 54 per cent. of the pro-gymnasia teachers are specially trained for their subjects; about 34 per cent. had attended some secondary schools, 5 per cent. the universities and 4 per cent. had attended a university or some other higher institution of learning without graduating.

[1] Václav Příhoda, Jednotná Škola Bulharská, p. 23. Prague, Orbis, 1934.

[2] The Near East Year Book, 1931–32, p. 243.

According to the law of 1909 special courses for the pro-gymnasia teachers, known as the "Teachers' Institutes," were established. Its attendants must be graduates of gymnasia or of normal schools. There are only two of these schools in Bulgaria, one in Shemen and one in Plovdiv. Its subjects are divided into general—pedagogy and introduction to philosophy, foreign language, hygiene and popular medicine—and special. The professional courses are divided into humanistic and mathematical and natural science. Under the first group come Bulgarian religion, history, geography and civics; under the second come mathematics, physics, chemistry and natural sciences. Drawing, physical education, music and handicrafts are selective. Each institute has its own training pro-gymnasium. The training is free and continues for two years; it is now decided that it will be extended by another year.

There is a tendency in Bulgaria to raise the standards of the teachers. It is now required that the future teacher must first of all be graduated from a gymnasium, and then must specialize in pedagogical studies. In October, 1930, a one-year "teachers' course" was opened in Lord Gladstone's gymnasium as an experiment. The first year, only 30 students were registered. The experiment must have proved successful, because the pedagogical committee of the Ministry of Education recommended the extension of the course from one to two years.

The education of the gymnasia is primarily technical. The students register also in the universities to study courses in pedagogy. After finishing their university studies, the graduates are usually put on probation for one year as teachers in the Lord Gladstone's gymnasium in Sofia. During the first semester they attend a pedagogical course dealing with the theory of education, didactica, psychology, school hygiene and school organization and school legislation. During the second semester they carry on practical research under the direction of the experienced teachers. Only after the graduation of this probationary year are the candidates allowed to pass state examinations.

The training of women-teachers in home economics in gymnasia and technical schools is well taken care of. They are trained in a two-year course in the professional school of Maria Louise in Sofia, which will be extended to three years, according to the recommendation of the council for the technical education of the Ministry of Education. The students must be graduates from gymnasia or technical schools, so that the school has a character of a semi-higher institution of learning. As is the usual case with the technical and professional schools of Europe, the curriculum is so crowded with courses that the students spend even 44 hours weekly in the classroom.

In general, the education of Bulgarian teachers of all categories conforms to the needs of the country. In contrast to the other European countries, the pedagogical schools of the teachers for elementary schools have the standing of the secondary schools and require an attendance of five years. The requirements for teachers in pro-gymnasia are also rather high. The organization of the training for secondary school teachers is of much higher standard than it is in the neighboring countries. There is no question that the Bulgarian educational system is one of the best in the Balkans.

### The New System of Physical Education

Bulgarian history has been characterized by wars. The geographical situation of the country is readily conducive to frequent armed struggles. It is quite natural that the Bulgarian state is especially interested in the improvement of the physical education of its members. The law of March 10, 1931, provides the new foundation for such an educational aim.

This law concerns all the youth up to the twenty-first year of age. Up to that age, physical education is made compulsory, with the exception of the sick people and married women. The education is taken care of not only in all the grades and varieties of schools of Bulgaria, but also in the organizations not connected directly with the educational system. A special section for physical education was organized in the Ministry of Education.

The elementary schools now must spend one half an hour daily in plays. Furthermore, four hours of one afternoon are devoted to a walk into the countryside, or to a visit of industrial establishments; the same applies to the pro-gymnasia (higher-grade elementary schools). Furthermore, in pro-gymnasia, one hour is devoted weekly to the systematic physical training; during the other five school-days, half an hour is spent daily in plays and group plays in the open air. Larger pro-gymnasia must employ a professionally trained instructor. The gymnasia (corresponding to English public schools or colleges) must devote two hours a week to physical education and from 25 to 30 minutes daily in group plays. During the winter, one day every month is utilized for an excursion into the countryside, and two days during the summer. The students of the higher educational system are obliged to be members of some student organization interested in sports and must schedule two hours weekly in physical education courses.

The law also makes provisions for physical education apart from the school system. Every private and public establishment must be responsible for giving physical education to its employees. The workshops or factories employing more than 100 workers are obliged to build up their own playgrounds, a gymnasium and to make provisions for showers. If they do not conform to such requirements they must send their employees into the local organizations and pay 36 *leva* yearly for each member. The non-observance of the law is punished by a fine of 100 *leva* for each employee.

The young people who had gone through five years of physical training complete the training by an examination and receive special privileges, in the military service and in the execution of the civil obligations. The public authorities keep a check on the regular attendance, because it is provided that the youth must attend the local organizations, which are parts of the schools and directed by a teacher-physician or by a physician.

Special courses have been established for the education of the teachers of physical education. All teachers of the subject must pass the courses, and it is also their duty to give their services to the physical education organizations, which are not parts of the school system. They receive credit from two to four hours weekly for such activities. The graduates of foreign state institutions are certified as regular teachers.

To give the benefits of this training even in the smallest and out-of-way villages, each community must create an athletic association, headed by a committee of six members. The physician, mayor, secretary of the villages and teachers are *ex-officio* members of the committee.

The Bulgarian example is undoubtedly one of the most advanced and progressive that can be found in Europe.

Joseph S. Roucek
The Pennsylvania State College

## TRAINING TEACHERS FOR EMERGENCY NURSERY SCHOOLS IN WASHINGTON

The work on the emergency nursery school program in Washington started on January 6, 1934, in the State Department of Education. A state advisory committee of five members assisted. By January 10 a state supervisor had been assigned by the Federal Government to the State Department of Education to serve as supervisor of emergency nursery schools. A week later fifty-four teachers were in training at the Washington State Normal School, Ellensburg. These teachers were given an intensive training for two weeks before being assigned to their posts. Again in the summer, from July 16 to August 11, the teachers were given a month of more thorough training in anticipation of the work for the ensuing year.

The emergency nursery school for training was established on the ground floor of the campus training school. Following the teacher training period of last winter the unit was maintained in order to continue the service to needy families. The school consists of four rooms—a reception room, equipped with cloakroom space and toilet and washing facilities, a sleeping dormitory, a large playroom and a kitchenette for use in preparing and serving foods and liquids. The toys, supplies and equipment were gathered mostly from other school-rooms, Sunday-school rooms and homes of P. T. A. members. The lockers, cupboards and some of the furniture were constructed by CWA carpenter labor. A fenced playground was also made available.

The teaching staff consists of a trained director with a full-time assistant. The cooperating members of the school staff are: nurse, nutritionist, educational supervisor, speech specialist. An experienced woman is employed to cook, clean and launder.

Only children of needy parents are accepted. The purposes of the program as outlined by the state supervisor are pertinent here. (1) To serve the emergency needs of preschool children and their parents who are suffering from current social and economic difficulties. (2) To carry improved methods of child care and guidance into the home. (3) To employ needy qualified workers. (4) To carry on an educational and health program for children and their parents. (5) To demonstrate to local communities and school authorities methods of caring for the educational and physical needs of preschool children.

The teachers in training were given instruction in child development, nursery school procedures, principles of nursery school education, food planning and menus, parent education and administration of the emergency nursery school. A portion of each day was given over to the observation of each phase of the work and each teacher was given an opportunity to teach. Those experiences were followed by conferences with the state supervisor and other instructors.

Although the period of training has been altogether too short, the fact that the teachers selected were individuals who formerly had at least two years of collegiate training and in most cases either training or experience on the preschool, kindergarten or primary levels facilitated the program. It was necessary that they understand the federal program and the suggestions for local administration. They needed to have a point of view which is peculiar to this emergency relief program.

The organized class work, in an intensive manner, insured a sensitivity to the whole program. It gave a point of departure for continued growth in the study of nursery school literature. It embraced instruction in all phases of child guidance toward health habits, emotional control and stability, bodily skill and coordination, desirable attitudes, appreciations and wide interests. An outline of the courses of instruction would be valuable here, but space does not permit.

The parent education phase of the program has been demonstrated through listening to and participating in conferences with parents.

The instructional staff included specialists in parent education, nursery education, home economics and nutrition.

In evaluating the results of the training we must turn to the testimonies of the teachers and more especially to the reports of the state supervisor. The former are unhesitating in their favorable response. The training was absolutely indispensable to their success. But the reports of the latter offer the best criteria. In her judgment the two-week training period at the beginning was of inestimable value. The whole program may have failed without it. But the longer period during the summer has been even more fruitful.

The value of the whole program to the people of Washington may be told in part by the following facts: (1) Six hundred children and nearly as many homes were provided with an educational and health program. Most of these children were literally hungry and without decent clothing. (2) Employment for 54 unemployed teachers and from 35 to 40 other workers was provided. (3) Many educators, many parents and others have learned much about nursery school education. (4) The letters and oral testimonies from hundreds of parents attest to the fact that they received mental as well as physical relief.

ROBERT E. MCCONNELL
WASHINGTON STATE NORMAL
SCHOOL, ELLENSBURG

# QUOTATIONS

## AN APPRAISAL OF THE "ECONOMY PROGRAM" OF THE CHICAGO SCHOOL BOARD

THE *Elementary School Journal* has, from time to time, called the attention of its readers to the drastic economy program initiated by the Chicago Board of Education in July, 1933. This program, it will be recalled, put into operation the following drastic measures: (1) The only junior college maintained by the city was closed. (2) All junior high schools were abolished. (3) Kindergarten teachers were reduced by 50 per cent. (4) Principals of the elementary schools were reduced in number with no principal having less than two schools under his supervision. (5) Instruction in manual training and household arts was discontinued in the elementary schools. (6) Facilities for guidance were practically abolished. (7) The teaching load for high-school teachers was increased to seven classes a day. (8) The teaching of physical education in the elementary schools was discontinued. The Board of Education attempted to justify this despoiling of the school system of Chicago on the ground that it would result in an annual saving of some ten millions of dollars. Everyone at all familiar with school finance in Chicago knew perfectly well that this claim was absurd, but citizens generally had no way of knowing the truth because the board consistently refused to divulge the facts on which its sweeping estimates of economy were based. It was not until the board reported its expenditures for the school year 1933–34 that it was possible to know exactly the economies effected by the board's policies.

The following statement published in a recent number of *Chicago's Schools,* the official organ of the Citizens Save Our Schools Committee of Chicago, reveals that the net savings resulting from the board's program are, in fact, only a small fraction of the amount which the board claimed it would save.

> Although an annual public audit is required by law, no complete audit of the board has been made for several years. On August 22, however, a report of expenditures was made for the school year 1933–34. By this time the economy program had been in effect a full school year for which the large savings of $10,000,000 had been predicted.
>
> But the report shows no such results. It shows instead a net difference of only $3,446,943 between the expenditures for the education, building, playground and text-book funds for the school year 1933–34 and that of 1932–33. The other funds, bond redemption and interest, and teachers' pension and retirement, which the board handles are fixed in expenditures by law. . . . Of this net difference, $1,194,395 had been caused by closing school one additional week over the curtailment of the previous year and by an additional cut in teachers' salaries. Both of these reductions had been made before July 12, and had never been

claimed as a part of the "economy" program. Therefore, only $2,252,548 of the net difference could have any connection with the board's plan.

A further analysis of this amount shows that $495,033 of it had been saved by closing Crane Junior College on its 4,500 students and $270,000 had been saved by demoting half the elementary principals to teaching positions. The board has since reversed its action on both of these points. Three junior colleges have opened to take the place of Crane, and the principals have all been returned to their schools. Thus the "economy" in closing Crane and providing a half principal to a school is admittedly a mistake. If the amounts thus "saved" and since returned to the budget are deducted from the $2,252,548, it leaves the momentous total of $1,487,515 chargeable to the economy program.

Against this number of dollars is weighed the smashing of the junior high school system, wiping out all guidance activities in the high schools, dismissing 1,400 teachers from the system, eliminating the manual arts from the elementary schools and reducing the efficiency of the kindergartens. In the light of the social and spiritual values of the services which were discontinued, the comparatively small amount of money "saved" dwindles into absolute insignificance. During the year of the economy program, the county government kept illegally an amount much larger than the "savings" which should have been turned over to the Board of Education.

A percentage analysis of the annual "savings" of the economy program also shows that the heavy cuts were made in the schools themselves. Expenditures for instruction dropped 11 per cent., and teacher payrolls dropped 12 per cent., while operation costs (sweeping and dusting of the school buildings) dropped but 9 per cent. The payroll for school clerks increased 3 per cent. during the same period.

The tendency of expenditures for this year of the school crisis is indicative of the trend of the Chicago Board of Education for many years. . . . The tendency since 1924 [has been] to spend large and larger amounts on the departments which supply easy political jobs and contracts, at the expense of instruction and adequate working material for teachers and pupils.

As is indicated in the foregoing quotation, in the autumn of 1934 three new junior colleges were opened in Chicago, and a principal was restored to each elementary school. No doubt the board was, in a measure, impelled to take this action because of the persistent opposition to its policies by the city superintendent of schools, by many powerful groups of organized citizens, and by some of the leading newspapers of the city, notably the *Chicago Daily News* and the *Herald and Examiner*. No doubt, too, the board was influenced by the relatively small savings which resulted from its policies. But perhaps the real reason for restoring the junior colleges and the principals is that those political and financial interests which dictated the board's economy program have come to realize that, after all, the economies accomplished are too slight to be of any serious concern. Whatever may be the explanation of the new attitude of the board, citizens of Chicago should continue to press for the reestablishment of junior high schools, for the restoration of instruction in manual and household arts, for adequate kindergarten facilities and for an effective guidance service in the schools.—*The Elementary School Journal.*

## DISPLACED GERMAN SCHOLARS

At a recent meeting of the Academic Assistance Council and at meetings of representatives of other academic organizations held in London it was possible to report substantial progress.

Of the German scholars and scientists displaced since April, 1933, 200 have found permanent places and 325 have been provided with temporary facilities for continuing their research outside Germany. This means that at least two thirds of the total number who are justified in hoping to continue their scientific work have been assisted to remain in the academic world. The activities of the academic assistance committees have been coordinated on an international basis, and the real size and nature of the problem are now known.

The total task is limited and manageable, but requires steady and energetic work for a long time. So far as the Academic Assistance Council is concerned we are at present giving emergency grants to 71 scholars and scientists in the universities of this country to maintain them while seeking permanent posts. Of the scholars to whom the council made grants before April, 1934, approximately one third have already found positions outside this country, and we are convinced that this absorption will continue, provided that emergency grants-in-aid can still be given. There is serious danger, however, of funds being exhausted before permanent placement is achieved. Some national committees on the Continent are already faced with collapse, and the resources of the Academic Assistance Council will be brought to an end in July, 1935, by its present commitments.

The council decided that its emergency work of grants-in-aid, payment of traveling expenses and loans for reestablishment must continue, but that, in addition, it should make a more permanent contribution to the defense of academic freedom by the creation of a limited number of research fellowships available in the British universities for scholars and scientists of special standing in their subjects.

The council proposes, therefore, to issue in the coming spring an appeal for funds to enable it (1) to continue its desperately urgent emergency work, and (2) to establish a trust for the creation of a limited number of research fellowships. The council has never, in principle, confined its emergency assistance to the persons displaced from Germany alone, and proposes that the fellowships also should be available for scholars and scientists of distinction in any country who are unable to continue their work for reasons of religion, political opinion, or race.

I am glad to be able to say that for a constructive program of assistance on an international basis there is already the prospect of obtaining from an American source funds for the creation of 36 fellowships of three years' duration available in the universities of the British Dominions.—*Lord Rutherford, president, Academic Assistance Council, in the London Times.*

# EDUCATIONAL RESEARCH AND STATISTICS

## TWENTY YEARS AFTER

THERE are 196 members of the American Psychological Association now living who received the doctorate prior to 1915. The intervening twenty or more years have served to establish this group in various positions—positions ranging from university president to research fellow. Classified, they fall into the following categories:

| *Position* | *Number* |
|---|---|
| College teaching | 131 |
| College administration | 18 |
| School systems | 8 |
| Consulting psychologists | 5 |
| Miscellaneous positions | 18 |
| Address only given | 16 |

Obviously the majority of these individuals is engaged in teaching. Psychology claims 93, education 13, philosophy 9, educational psychology 7, pedagogy and physiological psychology 2 each, sociology, parent education, zoology, neuropathology and anthropology 1 each. The percentage in teaching is inordinately high. Only 15 per cent. of the whole group is engaged in work not connected with the university or college. It is unlikely that this percentage will remain so low unless psychology of the academic variety expands more rapidly than we can reasonably expect. In 1903, Cattell wrote of 200 eminent psychologists: "Nearly all the men are engaged in teaching. . . . There is, indeed, not a single person who has not been engaged in teaching. There are at present only eight who do not earn their livings by teaching or administrative educational work. . . . It is fortunate for psychology that there are in the country so many teaching positions to be filled. Still the conditions present certain serious drawbacks. . . . In most sciences there is applied work into which those who prove inept for research work can overflow."[1] In an address to the American Psychological Association 13 years later, the occasion of the twenty-fifth anniversary of the founding of the society, Cattell further observed that "272 of our 307 members are now or were recently engaged in teaching. This is a larger percentage (88 per cent.) than in any other science except mathematics. Most of the remaining 35 have also taught. There are 16 connected with boards of education, hospitals, laboratories of reformatory and charitable institutions and the like. It is not impossible that this group, now so small, may at our fiftieth anniversary surpass in numbers those engaged in teaching.[2] The fiftieth anniversary of the association will

[1] J. McK. Cattell, *Am. Jour. Psychol.*, 14: 310–328, 1903.

[2] J. McK. Cattell, *Science*, 45: 275–284, 1917.

occur in 1941, six years hence, and as yet there is little indication of the fulfilment of that prediction.

The 131 members who have elected to stay in teaching are distributed by rank as follows:

| | |
|---|---|
| Professor | 114 |
| Associate professor | 12 |
| Assistant professor | 1 |
| Instructor | 2 |
| Lecturer | 2 |

Thus we see that 87 per cent. of this group have scaled the academic ladder. Nine per cent. is engaged in college administration, including nine presidents of institutions of higher education, one vice-president and eight deans. The national school systems support only eight of the pre-war Ph.D.'s; two of these are principals of secondary schools, and the remaining six are supervisors, commissioners, school psychologists, etc. This field seems to be one that offers a greater number of opportunities to the young Ph.D. than it has in the past. Especially is this so for women psychologists. A random sample of the entire 1934 yearbook shows that school systems claim the second largest group of our female psychologists—the largest group, of course, being teachers of psychology. Consulting psychologists must be of a more recent vintage. Only five of our early group list themselves as such. Various other positions account for eighteen of the group, and sixteen appear to have retired from active work, as they list only addresses in the directory.

Can to-day's Ph.D. anticipate success equal to that of the old guard? Certainly not, if he prefers an academic position. There are no longer "plenty of teaching positions to be filled." The youngest of the 131 teachers listed above is about 43 years old, so we can expect the whole group to have retired in the next twenty years. But if we continue to turn out Ph.D.'s as we have in the last four years, there will be 2,090 applicants for their vacated positions! The following table shows the number of Ph.D.'s in psychology given each year since 1921.[3]

| | | | |
|---|---|---|---|
| 1921 | 26 | 1927 | 74 |
| 1922 | 32 | 1928 | 66 |
| 1923 | 46 | 1929 | 112 |
| 1924 | 51 | 1930 | 97 |
| 1925 | 51 | 1931 | 105 |
| 1926 | 60 | 1932 | 104 |

[3] Data from C. J. West and C. Hull, *Science*, 72: 357, 1930; 74: 659, 1931; 76: 296, 1932.

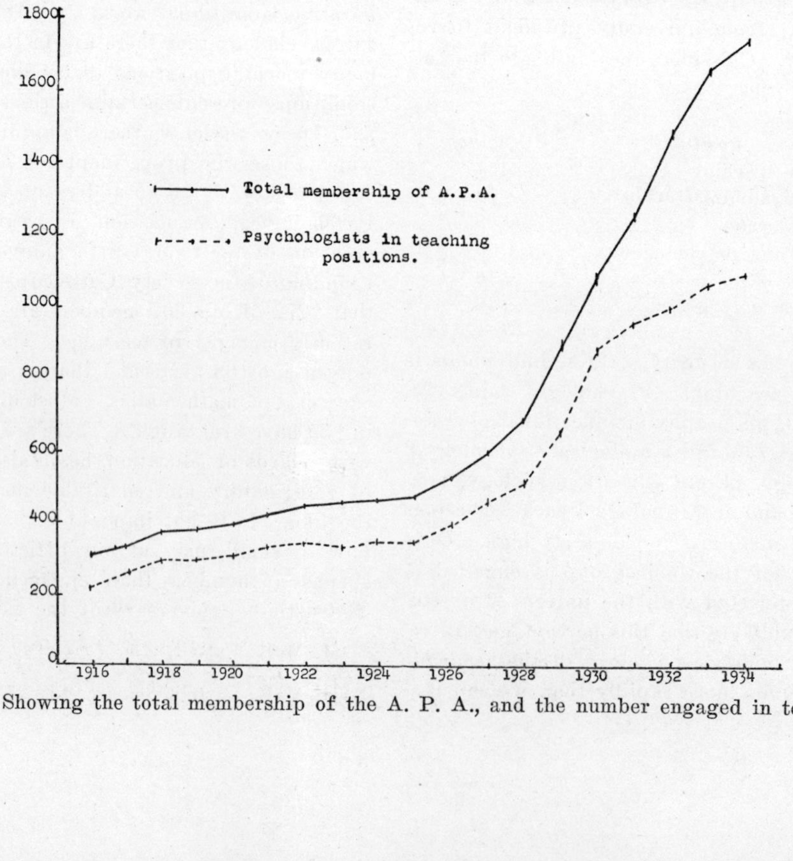


FIG. 1. Showing the total membership of the A. P. A., and the number engaged in teaching.

Up to recent years, educational expansion has absorbed these growing numbers. Fig. 1 shows the total membership of the American Psychological Association from 1916 through 1934, with the number of those in teaching positions for the same years. This latter figure was computed by counting all those who are listed in each of the yearbooks as instructing in some subject. While there are probably many errors in using these data to indicate the number of teaching jobs in psychology, still we find that our figures compare favorably with those obtained by the Committee on the Ph.D. in Psychology and reported to the association in 1933.[4] From this graph we can see that the two curves run fairly close together up until 1931. We can not expect educational expansion to continue as rapidly as it did in the 1920's. Although psychology is a relatively new science, and should be still in its growth period, the supply has already surpassed the demand. Fig. 2 represents what we may call our supply and demand chart. The solid bars indicate the yearly production of teaching jobs, that is, the yearly increase in the number of those individuals listed in the yearbook as instructing. In 1919 and 1923 there were fewer than in the years just preceding. For the most part, however, and especially in the last half of the 1920's there was a marked increase in the number of new teaching positions, the greatest single increase coming in the psychological boom year of 1930. From that time on placements have declined markedly. Yet, as the cross-hatched bars illustrate, there has been a steady rise in the number of Ph.D.'s granted.

Even more discouraging are the figures given by the previously mentioned committee of the American Psychological Association. The table following, taken from their report, shows the number of Ph.D.'s placed in the various positions by the institutions reporting for the year 1932–1933.

| | |
|---|---|
| *Academic* | |
| Teaching psychology | 11 |
| Teaching other than psychology | 2 |
| Research | 9 |
| *Non-Academic* | |
| Clinical and testing | 4 |
| Industrial and personnel | 0 |
| Child guidance | 2 |
| Research | 1 |

[4] *Psych. Bull.*, 30: 648–653, 1933.

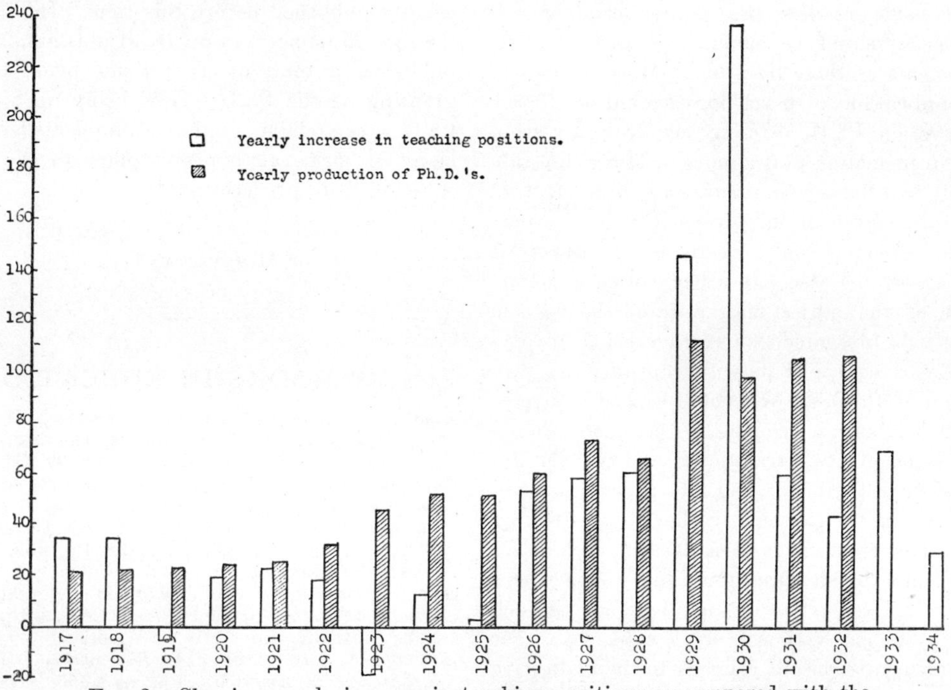


FIG. 2. Showing yearly increase in teaching positions as compared with the yearly production of Ph.D.'s.

Only 29 Ph.D.'s placed in the whole year! The committee concluded their report with these words: "The trend is certainly for the supply of both Ph.D.'s and M.A.'s to exceed the demand. The remedy must be either to decrease the supply or to increase the demand, or both. It is easier to decrease the supply than to increase the demand. But this remedy must be applied with great caution."

Let us canvass the possibilities for increasing the demand. It is no longer "those who prove inept for research work" who will go into applied fields. Business, under the New Deal, should be able to use men of psychological training just as it is recruiting men from all other sciences. Business personnel, student personnel, industrial psychology, vocational guidance and child welfare present opportunities for the psychologist. But for this sort of work he must be specially prepared. A rather perfunctory beginning was made at the business meeting of the association in 1933 when it was voted "to instruct the committee to consider the problem of redirecting graduate training in psychology in such a way that professional psychological service can make increasing contributions to community life." The gravity of the situation demands more drastic steps. Course schedules and sequences should be modified to meet the requirements of these positions. More courses in the applications of psychology should be offered. The average Ph.D. of to-day acquires only scholastic information plus a more or less well-established "readiness" to regurgitate bits of it at intervals. Even in our present courses in vocational, personnel and advertising psychology is this largely the case. In other words, either by virtue of the subject-matter or of the way in which it is presented, the average Ph.D. in psychology is equipped only to continue the production of Ph.D.'s. We would hazard a suggestion that laboratory courses for beginners should drop some of their traditional and usually unsuccessful experiments and add practise in constructing advertisements rather than picking good ones from magazines, testing each other for occupational capacities and achievement rather than for extent of knee jerk, rating each other as to motivation or work capacity rather than rating patches of color as to their affective value, and what not. There can be no harm in presenting, along with the methods of psychology, a little information that will be more immediately useful in the interpretation of human conduct. Profiles, check-charts, cumulative records, rating scales and their uses could be presented along with, or in place of, the usual elementary statistics. For advanced students, there should be courses in which practise in "the procedures in employment psychology" or in "the principles of advertising" would be available. Practise should supplement principles and procedures.

Without revision of the educational set-up, however, the outlook is rather gloomy. Teaching will take care of but few of our new Ph.D.'s. They are prepared neither for the practical application of psychology, which of all sciences should have the most immediate utilization, nor are they particularly well equipped for independent research. The average Ph.D. to-day is urged to receive his degree three years after the baccalaureate—three years in which to take a certain number of prescribed courses, complete one major piece of research and write a thesis. This leaves little time for independent investigation. The average Ph.D. of 20 years ago received his doctorate at the age of 28 and had usually published before this time. In fact, of the first 25 names on our list of oldsters, 20 had published a total of 47 articles prior to the granting of the Ph.D. How many of to-day's Ph.D.'s can claim similar attainments? How many of them can hope to follow in the footsteps of their predecessors?

E. DONALD SISSON

UNIVERSITY OF MINNESOTA

## NEW BOOKS IN EDUCATION

*American Council of Learned Societies, Proceedings Number.* Bulletin No. 22, October, 1934. Pp. 236. The Council, Washington, D. C.

CRAYTON, SHERMAN G. *A Proposed Program for the Care and Education of Kentucky's Handicapped Children.* Bulletin of the Bureau of School Service, Vol. VII, No. 1. Pp. 268. University of Kentucky.

GRUEN, FERDINAND B. *English Grammar in American High Schools Since 1900.* Pp. xi + 292. Catholic University of America.

LOWELL, A. LAWRENCE. *At War with Academic Traditions in America.* Pp. xiv + 356. Harvard University Press. $4.00.

# SCHOOL AND SOCIETY

WITH WHICH ARE COMBINED THE EDUCATIONAL REVIEW ESTABLISHED IN 1891, THE TEACHERS MAGAZINE, ESTABLISHED IN 1878, AND THE SCHOOL JOURNAL, ESTABLISHED IN 1874.

Volume 40 SATURDAY, DECEMBER 15, 1934 Number 1042

## STATISTICS OF REGISTRATION IN AMERICAN UNIVERSITIES AND COLLEGES, 1934

By Dr. RAYMOND WALTERS

PRESIDENT OF THE UNIVERSITY OF CINCINNATI

WITH help from the Federal Emergency Relief Administration, approved colleges and universities of the United States have gained 5 per cent. in the totals of their full-time students over last year, with an increase of 14 per cent. in the numbers of freshmen. Enrolment levels are now not much lower than the prosperity plateau of a half dozen years ago.

There are increases for 1934 over 1933 in all geographical divisions except one, the largest percentage advances being recorded in the Mountain and West South Central divisions. As to types of institutions, the universities, colleges and technical schools under public control show decided enrolment gains as compared with corresponding institutions under private control, probably due to the heavier tuition and other expenses in the latter.

Reports have been received from 567 institutions on the lists approved by the various regional associations as published by the American Council on Education. The figures, compiled as of November 1, 1934, show 655,725 full-time students and a grand total (including part-time and summer-school registration) of 978,632 who are enrolled in 104 universities, 347 colleges of arts and sciences and 116 technical institutions. These totals include all but a very few approved institutions. The report does not in general include normal schools (the American Council list is followed for teachers colleges) nor junior colleges. In regard to junior colleges it may be mentioned that the American Association of Junior Colleges in February, 1934, reported 105,457 students in 519 junior colleges for 1933–34, as compared with 106,016 students in 497 junior colleges for 1932–33.

The classification devised in 1932 is repeated in the summary table herewith and in Table I. Under this scheme there are groupings of universities and large institutions of complex organizations, with 55 under public control and 49 under private control; colleges of arts and sciences, 347; and technical institutions, of which 47 are classified as technological schools and 69 as teachers colleges. Total enrolments for these groups are given in Table I.

The summary table herewith, covering 563 institutions which reported last year and this, discloses that 55 universities under public control have 17,198 more full-time students than in 1933, or 9.1 per cent. increase (as compared with 3.7 per cent. decrease in this group for 1933 under 1932); that 49 universities under private control have 2,166 more students, or 1.3 per cent. increase (as compared with 3.6 per cent. decrease in this group for 1933 under 1932); that 344 colleges of arts and sciences have 5,350 more students, or 3.3 per cent. increase (as compared with 5.3 per cent. decrease in this group for 1933 under 1932); that 47 technological schools have 6,975 more students, or 12.9 per cent. increase (as compared with 6.4 per cent. decrease in this group for 1933 under 1932); that 68 teachers colleges have 3,731 more students, or 7.4 per cent. increase (as compared with 13.8 per cent. decrease for 1933 under 1932).

As to grand-total enrolments in these 563 institutions, the 1934 totals are 975,218, an increase of 7.5 per cent. over the 907,200 totals of 1933. There may be interest in the part-time and summer-session totals of these institutions: 55 universities under public control, in 1934, 96,426; in 1933, 80,560; 49 universities under private control, in 1934, 109,090; in 1933, 98,888. 344 colleges of arts and sciences, in 1934, 54,894; in 1933, 52,709. 47 technical institutions, in 1934, 16,751; in 1933, 13,813. 68 teachers colleges, in 1934, 44,563; in 1933, 43,183. Totals of 563 institutions in 1934, 321,724 part-time and summer-session students; in 1933, 289,153 part-time and summer-session students. These figures do not include non-resident, home-study and correspondence students.

To represent more fully the scope of the current study the order of presenting statistical tables has been changed from that of preceding years and a geographical table and a summary of freshmen have been added.

All universities and senior colleges on the list of "accredited institutions" compiled by the American Council on Education as of October, 1934, were asked to report their enrolment figures; nearly all responded. Table I gives reports on this list which includes institutions approved by the Middle States Association of Colleges and Secondary Schools, the North Central Association of Colleges and Secondary Schools, the Northwestern Association of Secondary and Higher Schools, the Southern Association of Colleges and Secondary Schools and the institutional members of the New England Association of Colleges and Secondary Schools. Of the 567 institutions herewith reported, about 275 are also on the accepted list of the Association of American Universities, which is a national list. In Table I institutions are classified in accordance with the recommendations of a committee of the Association of American Colleges, of which the present writer was chairman. There are obvious advantages in comparing data of institutions which are alike in organization and purpose. Should there be misinterpretations in the listing under the several headings of Table I, the writer will be pleased to hear from the heads of the institutions concerned.

Table II is new in this series. It assembles full-time student totals according to the accepted geographical divisions of the United States. There would appear to be interest and value in this new presentation.

Table III gives figures in detail for thirty universities which have been included for many years in statistical articles in *Science* and later in SCHOOL AND SOCIETY.

Table IV gives a list of the twenty-five largest universities of the United States reporting in this study.

Tables I, III and IV are arranged to bring out clearly the enrolment of full-time and of part-time undergraduates. The full-time student is defined for this series as a student who has completed a high-school course and is devoting substantially his full time to study during the collegiate year. The student whose main time and attention are given to some other employment and who takes college and university courses in late afternoon, evening and Saturday classes is listed as a part-time student. The grand-total figures for 1934 include full-time students, part-time students and summer-school students of 1934, but do not include extension and correspondence students, who are, however, recorded in Table III.

The part-time and extension figures suggest the measure in which the urban and state universities have extended their educational offerings. The part-time reports are in general for collegiate work available in late afternoon, evening and Saturday classes, attended by secondary school teachers and business and industrial employees.

### THE EXTENT OF FERA AID

In accordance with past federal policy, continued by the Roosevelt Administration, the financial aid of the Federal Emergency Relief Administration is not given directly to colleges and universities for routine educational purposes but is allotted, through

TABLE I

I. UNIVERSITIES, AND LARGE INSTITUTIONS OF COMPLEX ORGANIZATION
(For both men and women, unless otherwise indicated)

1. UNDER PUBLIC CONTROL

| Institution | Students Full-time | Students All Residents | Teaching Staff |
|---|---|---|---|
| C. C. of New York **M** | 8,030 | 27,248 | 937 |
| Indiana U. | 4.607 | 5,943 | 324 |
| Louisiana S. U. | 3,907 | 5,693 | 220 |
| Miami U. | 2,427 | 2,937 | 169 |
| Michigan State C. | 3,073 | 3,667 | 288 |
| Mun. U. of Wichita | 1,332 | 1,662 | 95 |
| Ohio State U. | 10.012 | 12.556 | 985 |
| Ohio U. | 2.102 | 3.544 | 221 |
| Penn State | 4,879 | 7.250 | 1,073 |
| State C. of Wash. | 3,205 | 3.727 | 221 |
| State U. of Mont. | 1,692 | 2,266 | 84 |
| U. of Akron | 1,220 | 1,610 | 90 |
| U. of Alabama | 4,484 | 6.528 | 300 |
| U. of Arizona | 2,220 | 2,736 | 170 |
| U. of Arkansas | 1.844 | 2,217 | 214 |
| U. of California | 18.892 | 21,210 | 1,700 |
| U. of Cincinnati | 3,887 | 9.534 | 602 |
| U. of Colorado | 3,022 | 5,654 | 326 |
| U. of Delaware | 736 | 1,133 | 91 |
| U. of Florida | 2,635 | 3.641 | 159 |
| U. of Georgia | 2,404 | 3.598 | 151 |
| U. of Hawaii | 1,247 | 2.566 | 115 |
| U. of Idaho | 2,243 | 2,885 | 154 |
| U. of Illinois | 10,747 | 12.363 | 1,032 |
| U. of Iowa | 4,943 | 7,661 | 575 |
| U. of Kansas | 3,832 | 4.637 | 223 |
| U. of Kentucky | 2,567 | 3,904 | 261 |
| U. of Louisville | 1,452 | 2,445 | 272 |
| U. of Maine | 1,427 | 1,733 | 161 |
| U. of Maryland | 3,072 | 4,213 | 558 |
| U. of Michigan | 9,005 | 11,138 | 708 |
| U. of Minnesota | 12,188 | 16,275 | 655 |
| U. of Mississippi | 1,226 | 1.413 | 75 |
| U. of Missouri | 3.420 | 5.295 | 336 |
| U. of Nebraska | 5,111 | 6,812 | 307 |
| U. of Nevada | 865 | 938 | 72 |
| U. of New Hampshire | 1,529 | 1.784 | 144 |
| U. of New Mexico | 983 | 1,827 | 77 |
| U. of N. Carolina | 2,706 | 3,514 | 201 |
| U. of N. Dakota | 1,518 | 1.906 | 151 |
| U. of Oklahoma | 5,064 | 6.533 | 279 |
| U. of Oregon | 2,496 | 3,599 | 159 |
| U. of S. Carolina | 1,231 | 1,722 | 88 |
| U. of S. Dakota | 719 | 1,003 | 89 |
| U. of Tennessee | 2.719 | 4,1[illegible]0 | 154 |
| U. of Texas | 6,836 | 10,771 | 454 |
| U. of Toledo | 1,342 | 2,212 | 111 |
| U. of Utah | 3,248 | 3,978 | 174 |
| U. of Vermont | 1,261 | 2.044 | 194 |
| U. of Virginia **M** | 2,251 | 3,699 | 274 |
| U. of Washington | 7.541 | 10,991 | 506 |
| U. of Wisconsin | 8,053 | 10,743 | 505 |
| U. of Wyoming | 1,207 | 1,794 | 116 |
| Wayne U. | 2,931 | 8,360 | 253 |
| W. Virginia U. | 2,465 | 3,229 | 190 |
| Totals | **206,055** | **302,481** | **18,043** |

2. UNDER PRIVATE CONTROL

| Institution | Students Full-time | Students All Residents | Teaching Staff |
|---|---|---|---|
| Boston C. **M** | 2,711 | 2,976 | 175 |
| Boston U. | 5,316 | 8,350 | 519 |
| Brigham Young U. | 1,738 | 2,337 | 86 |
| Brown U. | 1,801 | 2,011 | 172 |
| Catholic U. of America **M** | 1,077 | 2,688 | 164 |
| Clark U. | 363 | 516 | 39 |
| Columbia U. | 13,819 | 25,770 | 2,182 |
| Cornell U. | 5,717 | 7.474 | 946 |
| Creighton U. | 1,465 | 2.002 | 220 |
| Dartmouth **M** | 2,480 | 2,480 | 251 |
| De Paul U. | 2,023 | 5.684 | 154 |
| Drake U. | 1.000 | 1.529 | 84 |
| Duke U. | 3,076 | 4.008 | 264 |
| Emory U. | 1,136 | 1.592 | 286 |
| Fordham U. **M** | 3,566 | 6,215 | 382 |
| Georgetown U. **M** | 1,998 | 2.116 | 390 |
| George Washington | 1,695 | 6.026 | 334 |
| Harvard **M** | 7,671 | 9,177 | 1,728 |
| Howard U. | 1,253 | 1,711 | 228 |
| Johns Hopkins | 1.798 | 4,405 | 601 |
| Lehigh **M** | 1,319 | 1.506 | 148 |
| Loyola, Ill. | 2,397 | 4.577 | 568 |
| Loyola, La. | 690 | 1,783 | 110 |
| Marquette | 2.535 | 3.155 | 336 |
| New York U. | 12,347 | 27.682 | 1,599 |
| Northwestern | 5.371 | 13,210 | 700 |
| Princeton **M** | 2,622 | 2,622 | 313 |
| Rice Inst. | 1,282 | 1.282 | 84 |
| Rutgers | 2.562 | 3.276 | 299 |
| St. John's U., N. Y. | 5,883 | 6,094 | 194 |
| St. Louis U. | 3,796 | 5.967 | 600 |
| Southern Methodist U. | 1,423 | 2,591 | 106 |
| Stanford | 3,670 | 4.018 | 636 |
| Syracuse | 4,764 | 6.420 | 562 |
| Temple | 5,483 | 8.603 | 728 |
| Tulane | 2,607 | 3,9[illegible]8 | 414 |
| U. of Buffalo | 1,452 | 3,828 | 479 |
| U. of Chicago | 5,950 | 11,320 | 771 |
| U. of Denver | 1,480 | 3,167 | 169 |
| U. of Notre Dame **M** | 2,637 | 3,390 | 187 |
| U. of Pennsylvania | 6,115 | 10,813 | 1,269 |
| U. of Pittsburgh | 5,723 | 9,767 | 723 |
| U. of Richmond | 969 | 1,427 | 75 |
| U. of Rochester | 1,653 | 2,353 | 139 |
| U. of Southern Calif. | 3,927 | 12.061 | 500 |
| Vanderbilt | 1,393 | 1,393 | 351 |
| Washington | 3,400 | 4,462 | 432 |
| Western Reserve | 3,350 | 7,765 | 646 |
| Yale | 5,036 | 5,082 | 730 |
| Totals | **163,539** | **272,629** | **23,073** |

TABLE I—(*Continued*)
II. COLLEGES OF ARTS AND SCIENCES
(For men and women, and privately controlled unless otherwise indicated
**Pub.** = Publicly controlled. **M** = Men. **W** = Women)

| Institution | Students Full-time | Students All Residents | Teaching Staff |
|---|---|---|---|
| Adelphi **W** | 394 | 413 | 32 |
| Agnes Scott **W** | 485 | 489 | 43 |
| Alabama C. **Pub. W** | 811 | 1,230 | 79 |
| Albany | 206 | 206 | 29 |
| Albertus Magnus **W** | 113 | 141 | 33 |
| Albion | 619 | 622 | 43 |
| Albright | 322 | 365 | 30 |
| Alfred U. | 592 | 665 | 48 |
| Allegheny | 580 | 655 | 45 |
| Alma | 250 | 322 | 25 |
| American Int. | 345 | 352 | 24 |
| American U. | 335 | 531 | 64 |
| Amherst **M** | 778 | 778 | 72 |
| Antioch | 607 | 612 | 56 |
| Arkansas S. C. **Pub.** | 425 | 884 | 25 |
| Atlanta U. | 44 | 649 | 27 |
| Augustana, Ill. | 566 | 736 | 55 |
| Augustana, S. D. | 379 | 522 | 32 |
| Baker U. | 298 | 324 | 27 |
| Baldwin-Wallace | 506 | 583 | 50 |
| Bates | 666 | 868 | 43 |
| Baylor C. **W** | 570 | 902 | 57 |
| Baylor U. | 1,188 | 1,966 | 101 |
| Beloit | 504 | 512 | 42 |
| Berea | 675 | 821 | 54 |
| Bethany, Kans. | 241 | 369 | 33 |
| Bethany, W. Va. | 304 | 320 | 29 |
| Birmingham-South. | 747 | 1,223 | 55 |
| Blue Mountain **W** | 244 | 474 | 25 |
| Bowdoin **M** | 578 | 578 | 56 |
| Bradley Polytech. In. | 653 | 848 | 48 |
| Brenau **W** | 297 | 382 | 36 |
| Bridgewater | 211 | 215 | 19 |
| Brooklyn C. **Pub.** | 5,090 | 12,138 | 397 |
| Brothers | 118 | 118 | 45 |
| Bryn Mawr **W** | 458 | 492 | 85 |
| Bucknell U. | 838 | 1,076 | 79 |
| Butler U. | 1,186 | 1,879 | 81 |
| Calvin | 348 | 357 | 20 |
| Canisius | 570 | 927 | 61 |
| Capital U. | 540 | 649 | 68 |
| Carleton | 685 | 704 | 57 |
| Carroll, Wis. | 482 | 540 | 30 |
| Carson-Newman | 374 | 474 | 22 |
| Carthage | 277 | 310 | 26 |
| Catawba | 332 | 586 | 47 |
| Centenary | 408 | 538 | 38 |
| Central | 463 | 575 | 33 |
| Centre | 350 | 377 | 32 |
| Citadel **Pub. M** | 558 | 558 | 39 |
| Claremont C. | 105 | 105 | 80 |
| Clarke C. **W** | 336 | 502 | 40 |
| Coe | 635 | 732 | 56 |
| Coker **W** | 206 | 206 | 21 |
| Colby | 599 | 608 | 44 |
| Colgate **M** | 990 | 990 | 99 |
| C. of Charleston **Pub.** | 367 | 568 | 28 |
| C. of Emporia | 276 | 276 | 28 |
| C. of Idaho | 355 | 394 | 31 |
| C. of Mt. St. Joseph **W** | 209 | 400 | 38 |
| C. of Mt. St. Vincent **W** | 403 | 703 | 43 |
| C. of New Rochelle **W** | 700 | 706 | 61 |
| C. of Notre Dame **W** | 121 | 192 | 28 |
| C. of the Pacific | 506 | 827 | 60 |
| C. of Puget Sound | 556 | 910 | 39 |
| C. of the Sacred Heart **W** | 247 | 488 | 36 |
| C. of St. Benedict **W** | 183 | 332 | 28 |
| C. of St. Catherine **W** | 544 | 823 | 50 |
| C. of St. Elizabeth **W** | 327 | 591 | 33 |
| C. of St. Rose **W** | 254 | 367 | 29 |
| C. of St. Scholastica **W** | 225 | 305 | 25 |
| C. of St. Teresa **W** | 308 | 522 | 47 |
| C. of St. Thomas **M** | 509 | 521 | 46 |
| C. of Wooster | 859 | 905 | 66 |
| Colorado C. | 526 | 545 | 62 |
| Columbia C., Ia. **M** | 347 | 681 | 23 |
| Columbia U., Port'd, Ore. | 272 | 272 | 21 |
| Concordia | 410 | 410 | 36 |
| Connecticut C. **W** | 627 | 645 | 63 |
| Connecticut S. C. **Pub.** | 767 | 773 | 85 |
| Converse **W** | 283 | 283 | 33 |
| Cornell C. of Ia. | 475 | 619 | 41 |
| Culver-Stockton | 171 | 259 | 19 |
| Dakota-Wesleyan | 352 | 470 | 32 |
| Davidson **M** | 655 | 702 | 40 |
| Denison U. | 761 | 854 | 63 |
| De Pauw | 1,230 | 1,239 | 96 |
| Dickinson | 559 | 566 | 34 |
| Doane | 190 | 253 | 23 |
| Dominican **W** | 161 | 490 | 45 |
| Drury | 378 | 401 | 34 |
| D'Youville **W** | 263 | 263 | 29 |
| Earlham | 359 | 373 | 39 |
| Elmhurst | 232 | 243 | 20 |
| Elmira **W** | 322 | 325 | 47 |
| Emmanuel | 335 | 335 | 35 |
| Emory & Henry | 350 | 521 | 16 |
| Erskine | 341 | 343 | 22 |
| Eureka | 224 | 224 | 21 |
| Evansville C. | 339 | 510 | 28 |
| Fisk U. | 277 | 429 | 41 |
| Florida S. C. for **W. Pub.** | 1,542 | 2,108 | 110 |
| Franklin C. of Ind. | 265 | 273 | 25 |
| Franklin & Marshall **M** | 657 | 657 | 42 |
| Friends U. | 229 | 368 | 29 |
| Furman U. | 501 | 892 | 31 |
| Geneva | 568 | 996 | 36 |
| Georgetown, Ky. | 251 | 399 | 21 |
| Georgian Court | 151 | 249 | 22 |
| Georgia S. C. for **W. Pub.** | 1,160 | 1,623 | 79 |
| Georgia S. W.'s C. **Pub.** | 335 | 337 | 20 |
| Gettysburg **M** | 483 | 533 | 43 |
| Gonzaga U. | 567 | 900 | 79 |
| Goucher **W** | 613 | 621 | 81 |
| Greensboro **W** | 243 | 243 | 27 |
| Grinnell | 658 | 672 | 59 |
| Grove City C. | 655 | 769 | 38 |
| Guilford | 288 | 323 | 20 |
| Gustavus Adolphus | 311 | 316 | 27 |
| Hamilton **M** | 487 | 487 | 46 |
| Hamline U. | 500 | 528 | 41 |
| Hampden-Sydney **M** | 331 | 331 | 16 |
| Hanover | 339 | 343 | 20 |
| Hastings | 626 | 669 | 40 |
| Hardin-Simmons U. | 515 | 664 | 36 |
| Haverford **M** | 333 | 333 | 40 |
| Heidelberg | 312 | 321 | 33 |
| Hendrix | 312 | 339 | 30 |
| Hillsdale | 336 | 349 | 35 |
| Hiram | 330 | 412 | 28 |
| Hobart **M** | 293 | 293 | 38 |
| Hollins | 265 | 276 | 36 |
| Holy Cross **M** | 1,141 | 1,141 | 77 |
| Hood **W** | 398 | 443 | 47 |
| Hope | 458 | 465 | 24 |
| Howard C. | 564 | 1,047 | 40 |
| Hunter C. **Pub. W** | 5,949 | 10,606 | 535 |
| Illinois C. | 402 | 438 | 31 |
| Illinois Wesleyan | 632 | 675 | 50 |
| Immaculata **W** | 206 | 426 | 35 |
| Immaculate Heart **W** | 306 | 618 | 21 |
| Incarnate Word **W** | 343 | 743 | 39 |
| Intermountain Union | 146 | 193 | 15 |
| Iowa Wesleyan | 239 | 334 | 21 |
| James Millikin U. | 349 | 373 | 34 |
| Jamestown | 338 | 377 | 27 |
| John B. Stetson U. | 501 | 579 | 44 |
| John Carroll U. **M** | 508 | 847 | 29 |
| Johnson C. Smith U. | 254 | 497 | 25 |
| Judson **W** | 177 | 184 | 30 |
| Juniata | 452 | 542 | 45 |
| Kalamazoo | 307 | 316 | 25 |
| Kenyon **M** | 237 | 239 | 25 |
| Keuka **W** | 202 | 203 | 24 |
| Knox | 488 | 513 | 38 |
| Lafayette **M** | 798 | 810 | 90 |
| Lake Erie **W** | 112 | 112 | 26 |
| Lake Forest | 295 | 311 | 25 |

TABLE I—(*Continued*)

| Institution | Students Full-time | Students All Residents | Teaching Staff |
|---|---|---|---|
| La Salle C. **M** | 286 | 362 | 22 |
| Lawrence | 686 | 686 | 51 |
| Lebanon Valley | 383 | 470 | 32 |
| Lenoir-Rhyne | 336 | 572 | 25 |
| Lewis Inst. | 969 | 2,999 | 93 |
| Limestone **W** | 308 | 319 | 24 |
| Lincoln U., Mo. | 316 | 443 | 24 |
| Lincoln U. Pa. **M** | 273 | 298 | 25 |
| Lindenwood **W** | 360 | 361 | 40 |
| Linfield | 462 | 479 | 30 |
| Loretto Heights **W** | 116 | 189 | 22 |
| Louisiana C. | 303 | 411 | 21 |
| Loyola C., Md. **M** | 216 | 216 | 19 |
| Loyola U., Cal. **M** | 472 | 472 | 40 |
| Luther **M** | 298 | 321 | 24 |
| Lynchburg | 255 | 278 | 22 |
| Macalester | 632 | 642 | 37 |
| MacMurray C. **W** | 343 | 361 | 32 |
| Manchester | 592 | 968 | 39 |
| Manhattan **M** | 1,202 | 1,209 | 70 |
| Marietta | 387 | 402 | 30 |
| Marshall **Pub.** | 1,628 | 2,631 | 87 |
| Mary Baldwin **W** | 292 | 301 | 25 |
| Marygrove **W** | 355 | 508 | 52 |
| Marylhurst **W** | 87 | 207 | 21 |
| Marymount, Kans. **W** | 105 | 241 | 35 |
| Marymount, N. Y. **W** | 135 | 135 | 34 |
| Maryville, Tenn. | 832 | 835 | 45 |
| Marywood **W** | 500 | 610 | 48 |
| Mercer U. | 477 | 696 | 24 |
| Meredith | 501 | 518 | 40 |
| Mercyhurst | 162 | 237 | 21 |
| Middlebury | 649 | 1,148 | 61 |
| Mills **W** | 446 | 650 | 75 |
| Millsaps | 379 | 521 | 27 |
| Mississippi C. | 351 | 516 | 20 |
| Mississippi S. C. for W. **Pub.** | 866 | 866 | 60 |
| Mississippi Woman's C. | 195 | 195 | 20 |
| Missouri Valley | 202 | 253 | 19 |
| Monmouth | 510 | 561 | 34 |
| Moravian **M** | 127 | 157 | 21 |
| Morehouse **M** | 320 | 893 | 45 |
| Morgan | 420 | 631 | 41 |
| Morningside | 561 | 707 | 39 |
| Mount Angel | 127 | 179 | 36 |
| Mount Holyoke **W** | 965 | 1,019 | 114 |
| Mount Mary **W** | 184 | 481 | 37 |
| Mount St. Joseph **W** | 228 | 517 | 37 |
| Mount St. Mary's, Cal. | 203 | 590 | 29 |
| Mount St. Mary's, Md. **M** | 356 | 396 | 21 |
| Mount St. Scholastica | 182 | 409 | 31 |
| Mount Union | 543 | 622 | 32 |
| Muhlenberg **M** | 425 | 693 | 31 |
| Muskingum | 613 | 979 | 45 |
| Nazareth, N. Y. **W** | 222 | 322 | 24 |
| Nebraska Wesleyan | 400 | 591 | 47 |
| Newcomb **W** | 630 | 645 | 63 |
| New Jersey C. for W. **Pub.** | 919 | 934 | 99 |
| N. Y. S. C. for Teachers | 1,319 | 2,522 | 82 |
| Niagara U. **M** | 701 | 776 | 59 |
| North Central | 449 | 463 | 35 |
| Norwich U. | 223 | 223 | 31 |
| Notre Dame, O. **W** | 150 | 298 | 33 |
| Oberlin | 1,569 | 1,639 | 153 |
| Occidental | 597 | 634 | 56 |
| Ohio Wesleyan U. | 1,336 | 1,342 | 107 |
| Oklahoma C. for W. **Pub.** | 803 | 803 | 49 |
| Ottawa U. | 285 | 357 | 22 |
| Otterbein | 272 | 315 | 37 |
| Pacific Union | 328 | 490 | 30 |
| Pacific U. | 257 | 257 | 20 |
| Park | 495 | 500 | 35 |
| Parsons | 295 | 402 | 26 |
| Pennsylvania C. for W. | 268 | 281 | 32 |
| Phillips U. | 392 | 594 | 30 |
| Pomona | 684 | 716 | 74 |
| Presbyterian **M** | 279 | 280 | 18 |
| Providence | 678 | 838 | 46 |
| Radcliffe **W** | 845 | 986 | 300 |
| Randolph-Macon **M** | 244 | 244 | 16 |
| Randolph-Macon **W** | 572 | 603 | 58 |
| Reed | 362 | 440 | 36 |
| Regis **W** | 293 | 293 | 31 |
| Ripon | 325 | 329 | 26 |
| Roanoke | 349 | 439 | 22 |
| Rockford **W** | 319 | 425 | 39 |
| Rosary **W** | 343 | 868 | 43 |
| Rosemont **W** | 204 | 272 | 35 |
| Russell Sage **W** | 436 | 453 | 45 |
| St. Ambrose **M** | 340 | 600 | 30 |
| St. Benedict's **M** | 288 | 288 | 27 |
| St. Bonaventure **M** | 447 | 758 | 44 |
| St. John's **M** | 265 | 268 | 25 |
| St. Joseph's, Md. **W** | 168 | 168 | 37 |
| St. Joseph's, N. Y. **W** | 360 | 360 | 45 |
| St. Joseph's, Pa. **M** | 400 | 400 | 32 |
| St. Lawrence U. | 656 | 796 | 45 |
| St. Mary of the Woods **W** | 232 | 954 | 36 |
| St. Mary's **M** | 479 | 534 | 36 |
| St. Mary's of Notre Dame **W** | 249 | 471 | 50 |
| St. Mary's of the Springs **W** | 83 | 140 | 30 |
| St. Olaf | 817 | 830 | 53 |
| St. Thomas **M** | 549 | 745 | 32 |
| St. Vincent **M** | 452 | 627 | 63 |
| Salem, N. C. **W** | 263 | 275 | 37 |
| San Francisco C. for W. | 115 | 200 | 21 |
| Scripps **W** | 172 | 172 | 24 |
| Seton Hall **M** | 245 | 245 | 22 |
| Seton Hill **W** | 214 | 552 | 43 |
| Shorter **W** | 224 | 224 | 29 |
| Shurtleff | 116 | 210 | 17 |
| Simmons C. **W** | 1,456 | 1,671 | 144 |
| Simpson | 457 | 564 | 33 |
| Sioux Falls | 264 | 345 | 24 |
| Skidmore **W** | 547 | 583 | 67 |
| Smith **W** | 2,005 | 2,292 | 208 |
| Southwestern, Kans. | 531 | 629 | 30 |
| Southwestern, Tenn. | 350 | 378 | 29 |
| Sth'west. Louisiana I. **Pub.** | 978 | 1,326 | 61 |
| Southwestern U. | 306 | 442 | 29 |
| Spelman **W** | 237 | 252 | 29 |
| Spring Hill **M** | 190 | 395 | 22 |
| Sterling | 142 | 210 | 22 |
| Susquehanna U. | 238 | 383 | 33 |
| Swarthmore | 610 | 613 | 86 |
| Sweet Briar **W** | 406 | 406 | 46 |
| Talladega | 278 | 278 | 25 |
| Tarkio | 198 | 262 | 19 |
| Texas Christian U. | 591 | 917 | 47 |
| The St. Mary C. | 136 | 309 | 29 |
| Thiel | 259 | 266 | 22 |
| Transylvania | 438 | 652 | 29 |
| Trinity, Conn. **M** | 483 | 608 | 44 |
| Trinity, D. C. **W** | 300 | 331 | 49 |
| Trinity U. | 287 | 332 | 24 |
| Tufts | 2,036 | 2,036 | 529 |
| Tusculum | 250 | 251 | 18 |
| Union, Ky. | 273 | 273 | 16 |
| Union, N. Y. **M** | 805 | 805 | 72 |
| U. of Chattanooga | 454 | 630 | 30 |
| U. of Dayton | 495 | 885 | 48 |
| U. of Dubuque | 244 | 319 | 24 |
| U. of Redlands | 543 | 657 | 48 |
| U. of San Francisco **M** | 847 | 1,082 | 78 |
| U. of Santa Clara **M** | 396 | 396 | 45 |
| U. of the South **M** | 257 | 257 | 28 |
| U. of Tulsa | 524 | 1,171 | 60 |
| Ursuline **W** | 209 | 209 | 27 |
| Ursinus | 462 | 462 | 40 |
| Valparaiso U. | 428 | 506 | 40 |
| Vassar **W** | 1,223 | 1,227 | 165 |
| Villa Maria **W** | 149 | 211 | 28 |
| Villanova **M** | 759 | 2,186 | 118 |
| Va. Mil. Inst. **Pub. M** | 552 | 552 | 48 |
| Virginia S. C. **Pub.** | 665 | 1,208 | 62 |
| Wabash **M** | 367 | 373 | 29 |
| Wake Forest **M** | 1,005 | 1,386 | 38 |
| Washburn | 755 | 970 | 75 |
| Washington C. | 278 | 282 | 24 |
| Washington & Jefferson **M** | 455 | 582 | 35 |

TABLE I—(*Continued*)

| Institution | Students Full-time | Students All Residents | Teaching Staff |
|---|---|---|---|
| Washington & Lee **M** | 858 | 858 | 55 |
| Webster **W** | 156 | 244 | 35 |
| Wellesley **W** | 1,537 | 1,537 | 173 |
| Wells **W** | 258 | 258 | 37 |
| Wesleyan C. **W** | 241 | 249 | 33 |
| Wesleyan U. **M** | 649 | 651 | 73 |
| Western C. **W** | 315 | 315 | 38 |
| Western Maryland | 522 | 907 | 45 |
| Westminster, Mo. **M** | 320 | 321 | 16 |
| Westminster, Pa. | 647 | 670 | 44 |
| W. Va. State C. **Pub.** | 608 | 1,217 | 38 |
| Wheaton, Ill. | 762 | 930 | 39 |
| Wheaton, Mass. **W** | 445 | 445 | 55 |
| Whitman | 519 | 533 | 36 |
| Whittier | 435 | 495 | 45 |
| Whitworth | 177 | 177 | 22 |
| Wiley | 459 | 807 | 26 |
| Willamette U. | 514 | 572 | 46 |
| William Jewell | 299 | 355 | 23 |
| William & Mary | 1,141 | 1,309 | 76 |
| William Smith **W** | 131 | 132 | 38 |
| Williams **M** | 790 | 790 | 73 |
| Wilson **W** | 447 | 449 | 43 |
| Winthrop **Pub. W** | 1,228 | 1,366 | 63 |
| Wittenberg | 802 | 1,154 | 71 |
| Wofford **M** | 428 | 539 | 22 |
| Woman's C. of Ala. | 248 | 312 | 31 |
| Woman's C., U. N. C. **Pub.** | 1,283 | 1,657 | 116 |
| Yankton | 316 | 429 | 31 |
| Totals | **170,666** | **226,351** | **16,335** |

## III. INDEPENDENT TECHNICAL INSTITUTIONS

### 1. Technological Institutions

| Institution | Students Full-time | Students All Residents | Teaching Staff |
|---|---|---|---|
| A. & M. C. of Texas **Pub. M** | 2,915 | 3,559 | 202 |
| Alabama Polytech. Inst. **Pub.** | 1,688 | 2,889 | 143 |
| Alaska C. of Ag. & S. of M. **Pub.** | 142 | 170 | 18 |
| Armour I. of T. | 773 | 819 | 62 |
| Battle Creek College | 237 | 400 | 27 |
| California Inst. Tech. **M** | 750 | 781 | 137 |
| Carnegie Tech. | 2,159 | 3,719 | 339 |
| Case S. of Ap. Science **M** | 579 | 822 | 63 |
| Clarkson C. of Tech. **M** | 332 | 334 | 28 |
| Clemson Agr. C. **Pub. M** | 1,215 | 1,437 | 103 |
| Colorado Agr. C. **Pub.** | 1,303 | 1,976 | 122 |
| Colorado S. of Mines **Pub. M** | 521 | 649 | 50 |
| Drexel Inst. | 1,342 | 1,469 | 97 |
| Georgia S. of Tech. **Pub. M** | 1,773 | 1,842 | 132 |
| Hampton Inst | 725 | 1,416 | 96 |
| Int. Y. M. C. A. **M** | 511 | 571 | 41 |
| Iowa S. A. & M. **Pub.** | 3,719 | 4,348 | 377 |
| Kansas S. C. of Ag. **Pub.** | 2,724 | 3,191 | 307 |
| Louisiana Polytech. Inst. **Pub.** | 1,101 | 1,574 | 61 |
| Mass. Inst. of Tech. **M** | 2,507 | 3,433 | 483 |
| Massachusetts S. C. **Pub.** | 1,316 | 1,358 | 109 |
| Mich. C. of M. & Tech. **Pub.** | 491 | 623 | 68 |
| Mississippi S. C. **Pub.** | 1,164 | 1,164 | 86 |
| Montana S. C. **Pub.** | 1,064 | 1,081 | 91 |
| Montana S. of Mines **Pub.** | 205 | 205 | 23 |
| New Mex. C. of A. & M. Arts **Pub.** | 471 | 632 | 51 |
| N. Car. S. C. of Ag. & Eng. **Pub.** | 1,802 | 2,074 | 133 |
| N. Dakota Agr. C. **Pub.** | 1,364 | 1,389 | 107 |
| Oklahoma A. & M. **Pub.** | 3,284 | 4,248 | 233 |
| Oregon S. Ag. C. **Pub.** | 2,534 | 2,924 | 229 |
| Polytech. In. of Brooklyn **M** | 512 | 1,898 | 116 |
| Purdue **Pub.** | 3,773 | 4,264 | 324 |
| Rensselaer Polytech. In. **M** | 1,215 | 1,245 | 118 |
| Rhode Island S. C. **Pub.** | 1,062 | 1,235 | 81 |
| Rose Polytech. In. **M** | 188 | 188 | 26 |
| S. Dak. S. C. of Ag. & M. Arts **Pub.** | 732 | 866 | 86 |
| S. Dak. S. S. of Mines **Pub.** | 261 | 261 | 23 |
| Stevens Inst. of Tech. **M** | 468 | 575 | 38 |
| Texas C. of A. & Ind. **Pub.** | 558 | 1,389 | 41 |
| Tex. S. C. for W. Ind. Arts **Pub.** | 1,665 | 2,626 | 103 |
| Texas Tech. College **Pub.** | 2,181 | 3,950 | 128 |
| Tuskegee N. & Ind. Inst. | 598 | 720 | 101 |
| U. S. Military Acad. **Pub. M** | 1,277 | 1,277 | 170 |
| U. S. Naval Acad. **Pub. M** | 1,704 | 1,704 | 240 |
| Utah Ag. C. **Pub.** | 2,056 | 2,056 | 110 |
| Va. Polytech. Inst. **Pub.** | 1,421 | 1,746 | 150 |
| Worcester Polytech. In. **M** | 549 | 585 | 68 |
| Totals | **60,931** | **77,682** | **5,941** |

### 2. Teachers Colleges

| Institution | Students Full-time | Students All Residents | Teaching Staff |
|---|---|---|---|
| Arizona S. T. C., Tempe **Pub.** | 882 | 1,198 | 51 |
| Arkansas S. T. C. **Pub.** | 565 | 1,236 | 33 |
| Ball State T. C. **Pub.** | 946 | 1,726 | 52 |
| Bowling Green S. C. **Pub.** | 901 | 1,505 | 60 |
| Colorado S. T. C. **Pub.** | 1,353 | 3,167 | 98 |
| Concord S. T. C. **Pub.** | 576 | 1,120 | 30 |
| Delta S. T. C. **Pub.** | 275 | 467 | 29 |
| East Carolina T. C. **Pub.** | 1,005 | 1,369 | 46 |
| Fresno S. T. C. | 1,704 | 2,280 | 94 |
| George Peabody C. for T. | 363 | 2,271 | 66 |
| Harris T. C. **Pub.** | 278 | 278 | 17 |
| Henderson S. T. C. **Pub.** | 396 | 595 | 28 |
| Idaho S. N. S., Albion **Pub.** | 278 | 278 | 23 |
| Idaho S. N. S., Lewiston **Pub.** | 403 | 403 | 25 |
| Ill. S. N. U., Carbondale **Pub.** | 1,404 | 2,134 | 114 |
| Ill. S. N. U., Normal **Pub.** | 1,642 | 2,864 | 157 |
| Illinois S. T. C., Eastern **Pub.** | 887 | 1,376 | 68 |
| Illinois S.T.C., Northern **Pub.** | 732 | 1,106 | 61 |
| Illinois S. T. C., Western **Pub.** | 920 | 1,562 | 68 |
| Indiana S. T. C. **Pub.** | 1,079 | 2,458 | 95 |
| Iowa S. T. C. **Pub.** | 1,475 | 2,851 | 160 |
| Kansas S.T.C., Pittsburg **Pub.** | 1,172 | 1,172 | 129 |
| Kent S. C. **Pub.** | 1,147 | 1,838 | 91 |
| Kentucky S. T. C., Eastern **Pub.** | 801 | 1,777 | 53 |
| Kentucky S. T. C., Western **Pub.** | 1,426 | 2,746 | 104 |
| Louisiana S. N. C. **Pub.** | 1,176 | 1,956 | 87 |
| Michigan S. N. C. **Pub.** | 1,231 | 2,675 | 178 |
| Michigan S. T. C. Central **Pub.** | 613 | 1,387 | 65 |
| Michigan S. T. C., North. **Pub.** | 506 | 795 | 49 |
| Michigan S. T. C., West **Pub.** | 1,375 | 2,383 | 177 |
| Mississippi S. T. C., Hattiesburg **Pub.** | 434 | 1,246 | 35 |
| Missouri S. T. C., Central **Pub.** | 767 | 767 | 54 |
| Missouri S. T. C., Northeast **Pub.** | 465 | 1,148 | 49 |
| Missouri S. T. C., Northwest **Pub.** | 610 | 1,098 | 51 |

TABLE I—(*Concluded*)

| Institution | Students Full-time | Students All Residents | Teaching Staff |
|---|---|---|---|
| Missouri S. T. C., Southeast Pub. | 692 | 1,176 | 41 |
| Missouri S. T. C., Southwest Pub. | 880 | 1,903 | 59 |
| Montana S. N. C., Dillon Pub. | 330 | 555 | 28 |
| Montana S. N. S., Billings | 313 | 313 | 14 |
| Morehead S. T. C. Pub. | 624 | 1,195 | 34 |
| Murray S. T. C. Pub. | 748 | 1,120 | 47 |
| Nebraska S. N. C., Chadron Pub. | 409 | 812 | 40 |
| Nebraska S. T. C., Kearney | 648 | 1,714 | 60 |
| Nebraska S. T. C., Wayne Pub. | 725 | 1,409 | 50 |
| Oregon N. S., Monmouth Pub. | 470 | 777 | 52 |
| Oregon N. S., Eastern Pub. | 256 | 256 | 18 |
| Peru S. T. C., Pub. | 493 | 606 | 45 |
| Radford S. T. C., Pub. | 463 | 1,015 | 46 |
| Sam Houston S. T. C. Pub. | 686 | 1,925 | 43 |
| San Diego S. T. C. Pub. | 1,303 | 1,628 | 59 |
| Stephen F. Austin S. T. C. Pub. | 602 | 1,886 | 51 |
| Stout Institute | 400 | 683 | 44 |
| Sul Ross S. T. C. Pub. | 288 | 1,149 | 26 |
| Tenn. S. T. C., Johnson City Pub. | 495 | 603 | 40 |
| Tenn. S. T. C., Memphis Pub. | 920 | 920 | 34 |
| Tenn. S. T. C., Murfreesboro Pub. | 612 | 1,080 | 30 |
| Texas S. T. C., East Pub. | 999 | 3,509 | 66 |
| Texas S. T. C., North Pub. | 1,525 | 4,407 | 100 |
| Texas S. T. C., Southwest Pub. | 945 | 953 | 49 |
| Texas S. T. C., West Pub. | 833 | 1,839 | 52 |
| Va. S. T. C., Farmville Pub. | 609 | 873 | 51 |
| Va. S. T. C., Fredericksburg Pub. | 627 | 935 | 36 |
| Va. S. T. C., Harrisonburg Pub. | 711 | 1,230 | 62 |
| Washington S. N. S., Bellingham Pub. | 653 | 1,232 | 50 |
| Washington S. N. S., Ellensburg Pub. | 332 | 666 | 39 |
| Western S. C. of Colo. Pub. | 320 | 577 | 29 |
| Wisc. S. T. C., La Crosse Pub. | 645 | 660 | 50 |
| Wisc. S. T. C., Milwaukee | 1,247 | 2,553 | 85 |
| Wisc. S. T. C., Oshkosh | 664 | 1,040 | 50 |
| Wisc. S. T. C., Superior Pub. | 687 | 1,188 | 52 |
| Totals | **54,534** | **99,489** | **4,129** |

the state relief administrations and the colleges and universities, to individual students for their financial needs. As Administrator Harry L. Hopkins expressed it in a letter on July 3, 1934, "the principal objective of using relief funds for student aid is to increase the number of young men and women going to college." The corollary was, of course, to decrease the numbers of young persons looking for jobs.

That this objective is being attained appears clear from the present statistics of attendance. The FERA funds are obviously a considerable help. They are enabling 94,331 students in 1,466 institutions to earn an average of $15 a month from September, 1934, to the close of the academic year next May or June, a governmental expenditure of $1,414,940 a month. Each college and university accepting the arrangement (Harvard, Yale and Williams were among the few which declined) has agreed to put the students at "socially desirable work, including the sort customarily done in the institution by students who are working their way through college, such as clerical, library and research work." The general opinion among college and university administrators is that the students are serious, faithful and useful in these jobs.

Of the 94,331 students so engaged in all 1,466 institutions of the country, approximately 76,000 young men and women are in approximately 560 of the institutions reported in the present approved list. According to the initial stipulation, now waived, "at least half of the funds allotted must be paid to new students"; the number of freshmen who from September to November were receiving aid through jobs paying from $10 to $20 a month was therefore approximately 32,500 in these approved institutions. The accompanying freshman table reveals that in 487 of these institutions there are 155,212 freshmen in the fields of liberal arts, engineering, commerce and agriculture, or 19,148 more than in 1933.

Although FERA aid is a factor, it does not account for the whole trend. This may be deduced from the figures already cited for two groups: part-time students now in colleges and universities and students attending the 1934 summer schools. Neither group was announced as eligible for FERA jobs (although later justifiable exceptions were made in part-time cases). Nevertheless, the 1934 total of these two groups for 563 institutions is 321,724, as compared with the 1933 total of 289,153. The increase is 11.3 per cent., which is distinctly

TABLE II

Geographical Division Summary

| Division and state | Institutions | Full-time students 1933 | Full-time students 1934 | Per cent. change, 1933 to 1934 |
|---|---|---|---|---|
| (1) *New England* | *39* | *53,733* | *54,546* | + *1.51* |
| Maine | 4 | 3,249 | 3,270 | + .64 |
| New Hampshire | 2 | 4,034 | 4,009 | − .62 |
| Vermont | 3 | 2,120 | 2,133 | + .61 |
| Massachusetts | 21 | 33,404 | 33,918 | + 1.54 |
| Rhode Island | 3 | 3,530 | 3,541 | + .31 |
| Connecticut | 6 | 7,396 | 7,675 | + 3.77 |
| (2) *Middle Atlantic* | *93* | *135,602* | *135,086* | − *.38* |
| New York | 42 | 85,726 | 85,236 | − .57 |
| New Jersey | 8 | 7,359 | 7,412 | + .72 |
| Pennsylvania | 43 | 42,517 | 42,438 | − .19 |
| (3) *East North Central* | *106* | *130,801* | *136,777* | + *4.57* |
| Ohio | 32 | 36,779 | 38,639 | + 5.06 |
| Indiana | 17 | 18,173 | 18,816 | + 3.54 |
| Illinois | 29 | 39,204 | 40,775 | + 4.01 |
| Michigan | 16 | 20,709 | 22,135 | + 6.89 |
| Wisconsin | 12 | 15,936 | 16,412 | + 2.99 |
| (4) *West North Central* | *83* | *74,339* | *79,612* | + *7.09* |
| Minnesota | 12 | 16,222 | 17,312 | + 6.72 |
| Iowa | 16 | 14,263 | 16,022 | +12.33 |
| Missouri | 20 | 17,463 | 17,666 | + 1.16 |
| North Dakota | 3 | 2,862 | 3,220 | +12.51 |
| South Dakota | 7 | 2,692 | 3,023 | +12.30 |
| Nebraska | 9 | 9,426 | 10,067 | + 6.80 |
| Kansas | 16 | 11,411 | 12,302 | + 7.81 |
| (5) *South Atlantic* | *88* | *67,481* | *71,102* | + *5.37* |
| Delaware | 1 | 744 | 736 | − 1.08 |
| Maryland | 13 | 9,932 | 9,931 | − .01 |
| District of Columbia | 6 | 6,937 | 6,658 | − 4.02 |
| Virginia | 22 | 14,004 | 14,267 | + 1.88 |
| West Virginia | 4 | 4,470 | 5,005 | +11.97 |
| North Carolina | 14 | 12,365 | 13,749 | +11.19 |
| South Carolina | 12 | 6,812 | 6,945 | + 1.95 |
| Georgia | 13 | 8,145 | 9,133 | +12.13 |
| Florida | 3 | 4,072 | 4,678 | +14.88 |
| (6) *East South Central* | *41* | *29,917* | *32,833* | + *9.75* |
| Kentucky | 10 | 8,055 | 8,857 | + 9.96 |
| Tennessee | 13 | 8,356 | 9,252 | +10.72 |
| Alabama | 10 | 9,153 | 9,785 | + 6.90 |
| Mississippi | 8 | 4,353 | 4,939 | +13.46 |
| (7) *West South Central* | *40* | *45,795* | *51,947* | *+13.43* |
| Arkansas | 5 | 3,194 | 3,542 | +10.90 |
| Louisiana | 9 | 11,103 | 11,800 | + 6.28 |
| Oklahoma | 5 | 9,034 | 10,067 | +11.43 |
| Texas | 21 | 22,464 | 26,538 | +18.14 |
| (8) *Mountain* | *27* | *25,317* | *29,340* | *+15.89* |
| Montana | 6 | 3,454 | 3,750 | + 8.57 |
| Idaho | 4 | 2,661 | 3,279 | +23.22 |
| Wyoming | 1 | 968 | 1,207 | +24.69 |
| Colorado | 8 | 7,696 | 8,641 | +12.28 |
| New Mexico | 2 | 1,254 | 1,454 | +15.95 |
| Arizona | 2 | 2,596 | 3,102 | +19.49 |
| Utah | 3 | 5,842 | 7,042 | +20.54 |
| Nevada | 1 | 846 | 865 | + 2.25 |
| (9) *Pacific* | *41* | *53,334* | *58,251* | + *9.22* |
| Washington | 8 | 11,527 | 13,550 | +17.55 |
| Oregon | 10 | 6,463 | 7,660 | +18.52 |
| California | 23 | 35,344 | 37,041 | + 4.80 |
| (10) *Hawaii* | *1* | *1,210* | *1,247* | + *3.06* |
| (11) *Alaska* | *1* | *140* | *142* | + *1.43* |

TABLE III

| | California | Chicago | Cincinnati | Columbia | Cornell | Harvard | Illinois | Indiana | Iowa | Johns Hopkins | Kansas | Michigan | Minnesota |
|---|---|---|---|---|---|---|---|---|---|---|---|---|---|
| College men | 5544 | 1537 | 573 | 2157 | 1242 | 3595 | 2103 | 1409 | 1932 | 489 | 1373 | 2772 | 2347 |
| College women | 5727 | 1155 | 561 | 991 | 538 | .... | 1491 | 787 | 1090 | .... | 852 | 1602 | 1908 |
| Engineering | 1828 | .... | 1189 | 233 | 954 | 123 | 1555 | .... | 330 | 318 | 493 | 1360 | 1617 |
| Law | 562 | 413 | 201 | 628 | 179 | 1445 | 289 | 201 | 220 | .... | 133 | 539 | 323 |
| Medicine | 292 | 566 | 291 | 424 | 287 | 523 | 614 | 445 | 360 | 274 | 299 | 468 | 645 |
| Graduate school | 2081 | 1347 | 171 | 2643 | 607 | 741 | 911 | 215 | 319 | 279 | 152 | 1204 | 942 |
| Agriculture | 685 | .... | .... | .... | 1149 | .... | 888 | .... | .... | .... | .... | .... | 913 |
| Architecture | 133 | .... | .... | 76 | 172 | 67 | 225 | .... | .... | .... | .... | 187 | .... |
| Art | 171 | .... | 237 | .... | 19 | .... | 127 | 14 | .... | .... | 215 | * | .... |
| Commerce | 1208 | 243 | 244 | 363 | .... | 721 | 1582 | 647 | 287 | 90 | 189 | 110 | 418 |
| Dentistry | 144 | .... | .... | 256 | .... | 135 | 125 | 167 | 142 | .... | .... | 177 | 277 |
| Divinity | .... | 195 | .... | .... | .... | 56 | .... | .... | .... | .... | .... | .... | .... |
| Education | 1791 | .... | 222 | 5333 | 657 | 208 | 400 | 530 | .... | 11 | 71 | 235 | 1269 |
| Forestry | 192 | .... | .... | .... | 41 | .... | .... | .... | .... | .... | .... | 71 | * |
| Journalism | .... | .... | .... | 74 | .... | .... | 126 | 96 | .... | .... | .... | * | .... |
| Music | 74 | .... | .... | .... | .... | .... | 149 | 65 | .... | .... | * | 175 | .... |
| Pharmacy | 264 | .... | .... | 337 | .... | .... | 257 | .... | 82 | .... | 65 | 65 | 157 |
| Other courses | 49 | 791 | 297 | 385 | 782 | 57 | 375 | 141 | 211 | 337 | 84 | 162 | 1475 |
| Deduct duplicates | 1853 | 297 | 99 | 81 | 910 | .... | 470 | 110 | 30 | .... | 94 | 122 | 103 |
| Total | **18892** | **5950** | **3887** | **13819** | **5717** | **7671** | **10747** | **4607** | **4943** | **1798** | **3832** | **9005** | **12188** |
| Part-time | .... | 2200 | 5084 | 3970 | .... | .... | .... | 205 | 923 | 2048 | 138 | .... | .... |
| Summer session | 3738 | 4580 | 886 | 10281 | 1757 | 1506 | 2605 | 1601 | 2650 | 959 | 1142 | 3272 | 4087 |
| Deduct duplicates | 1420 | 1410 | 323 | 2300 | .... | .... | 989 | 470 | 855 | 400 | 475 | 1139 | .... |
| Gd. tot., Nov. 1, '34 | **21210** | **11320** | **9534** | **25770** | **7474** | **9177** | **12363** | **5943** | **7661** | **4405** | **4637** | **11138** | **16275*** |
| Gd. tot., Nov. 1, '29 | **25274** | **12747** | **10891** | **33367** | **7915** | **10866** | **13883** | **5517** | **7988** | **5992** | **5472** | **11800** | **21027** |
| Gd. tot., Nov. 1, '24 | **24112** | **12015** | **6442** | **30021** | **7302** | **9490** | **11513** | **5448** | **6995** | **4622** | **4916** | **10656** | **13313** |
| Exten. courses | 10182 | .... | .... | 450 | .... | .... | 86 | 4244 | .... | .... | 68 | 1568 | 1686 |
| Teaching staff | 1700 | 771 | 602 | 2182 | 946 | 1728 | 1032 | 324 | 575 | 601 | 223 | 708 | 655 |
| Administrative staff | 60 | 55 | 14 | 73 | 14 | 163 | 86 | 31 | 102 | 7 | 18 | 72 | 25 |

* Included elsewhere.

higher than the increase for full-time students who are the chief recipients of FERA aid.

Moreover, as to full-time students generally there are reports of somewhat improved financial capacity, as represented in fewer applications for instalment payments of tuition and notes payable after graduation. Better financial conditions in parts of the West are indicated in the striking percentage gains in student enrolment presented in the accompanying geographical table.

### GEOGRAPHICAL DISTRIBUTION OF ENROLMENT INCREASES

Inasmuch as collegiate attendance is a significant index of economic conditions, it seemed advantageous to assemble attendance data on a geographical basis which would suggest how different sections of the country are faring. Table II presents a mass of interesting details regarding full-time attendance, which has additional importance when compared with a similar compilation for 1931 and 1933 made by Mr. C. L. Constance, of the University of Oregon, utilizing the present writer's SCHOOL AND SOCIETY statistics for those years.

The largest percentage gain for 1934 as compared with 1933 is that of the Mountain division, in which an increase of 15.9 per cent. is registered in the totals of 29,340 full-time students attending 27 approved institutions in the states (given in the order of percentage increase) of Wyoming, Idaho, Utah, Arizona, New Mexico, Colorado, Montana and Nevada. In 1933 the full-time attendance of 22,413 in 20 institutions in the Mountain division was a decrease of 6.2 per cent., as compared with 1931.

The second largest percentage gain for 1934 as compared with 1933 is that in the West South Central division, in which there is an increase of 13.4 per cent. in the totals of 51,947 full-time students attend-

TABLE III—(*Concluded*)

| Missouri | Nebraska | Northwestern | Ohio State | Pennsylvania | Pittsburgh | Princeton | Stanford | Syracuse | Texas | Tulane | University of Washington | Virginia | Washington University | Western Reserve | Wisconsin | Yale |
|---|---|---|---|---|---|---|---|---|---|---|---|---|---|---|---|---|
| 849 | 1013 | 1225 | 1415 | 1034 | 1263 | 2118 | 2628 | 937 | 2462 | 592 | 1975 | 1307 | 737 | 975 | 2511 | 2802 |
| 387 | 662 | 1078 | 567 | 320 | 826 | .... | 1042 | 698 | 1745 | 509 | 2664 | 9 | 616 | 666 | 1393 | .... |
| 611 | 497 | 238 | 1344 | 387 | 578 | 217 | 214 | 323 | 806 | 260 | 975 | 143 | 295 | .... | 1090 | 181 |
| 175 | 189 | 259 | 274 | 416 | 232 | .... | 159 | 100 | 489 | 128 | 267 | 298 | 146 | 204 | 374 | 350 |
| 80 | 337 | 588 | 371 | 681 | 265 | .... | 218 | 190 | 355 | 472 | .... | 246 | 348 | 275 | 316 | 212 |
| 148 | 158 | 341 | 828 | 374 | 1044 | 287 | 270 | 254 | 207 | 119 | 781 | 187 | 359 | 82 | 894 | 653 |
| 423 | 470 | .... | 913 | .... | .... | .... | .... | 9 | .... | .... | .... | * | .... | .... | 653 | .... |
| * | 47 | .... | * | 137 | .... | .... | .... | 51 | * | 37 | * | 39 | 68 | 49 | .... | 98 |
| 83 | 91 | .... | * | 34 | .... | .... | 18 | 387 | .... | 134 | * | .... | 279 | .... | .... | 274 |
| 159 | 758 | 410 | 1883 | 1725 | 600 | .... | 85 | 761 | 310 | 177 | 1135 | 169 | 191 | .... | 169 | .... |
| .... | 59 | 382 | 198 | 327 | 183 | .... | .... | .... | .... | .... | .... | .... | 148 | 116 | .... | .... |
| .... | .... | .... | .... | .... | .... | .... | .... | .... | .... | .... | .... | .... | .... | .... | .... | 218 |
| 203 | 848 | 289 | 1602 | 315 | 545 | .... | 107 | 289 | 223 | * | 118 | 61 | 43 | 237 | 577 | .... |
| .... | .... | .... | * | .... | .... | .... | .... | 469 | .... | .... | 224 | .... | .... | .... | .... | 33 |
| 333 | 186 | 121 | * | .... | .... | .... | 39 | 13 | * | * | * | .... | 16 | .... | 100 | .... |
| * | 137 | 198 | * | 21 | .... | .... | .... | .... | .... | 34 | * | .... | .... | .... | 115 | 87 |
| .... | 71 | .... | 181 | .... | 185 | .... | .... | .... | 104 | .... | 156 | .... | .... | 99 | 82 | .... |
| 11 | 118 | 242 | 489 | 358 | 9 | .... | 2560 | 471 | 135 | 212 | 27 | .... | 154 | 690 | 100 | 128 |
| 42 | 530 | .... | 53 | 14 | 7 | .... | 3670 | 188 | .... | 67 | 781 | 208 | .... | 43 | 321 | .... |
| **3420** | **5111** | **5371** | **10012** | **6115** | **5723** | **2622** | **3670** | **4764** | **6836** | **2607** | **7541** | **2251** | **3400** | **3350** | **8053** | **5036** |
| 446 | 616 | 6197 | 147 | 4055 | 2634 | .... | .... | 290 | 662 | 554 | 1207 | 120 | .... | 3781 | .... | .... |
| 1778 | 1777 | 2300 | 3088 | 1368 | 2611 | 121 | 605 | 1484 | 4673 | 787 | 2739 | 1702 | 1062 | 1205 | 3457 | 109 |
| 349 | 692 | 658 | 1291 | 725 | 1201 | 121 | 257 | 118 | 1400 | .... | 496 | 374 | .... | 571 | 767 | 63 |
| **5295** | **6812** | **13210** | **12556** | **10813** | **9767** | **2622** | **4018** | **6420** | **10771** | **3948** | **10991** | **3699** | **4462*** | **7765** | **10743** | **5082** |
| **6020** | **9394** | **13558** | **13179** | **13828** | **13932** | **2459** | **4468** | **7236** | **8523** | **4373** | **9908** | **4410** | **4343** | **12454** | **13486** | **6184** |
| **5156** | **8237** | **8864** | **10547** | **15285** | **9408** | **2392** | **2949** | **6299** | **7241** | **3849** | **7225** | **4167** | **3559** | **4691** | **10972** | **4731** |
| 834 | 324 | .... | 338 | 1613 | 768 | .... | .... | .... | 332 | .... | 2447 | 944 | 2545 | .... | 20800 | 259 |
| 336 | 307 | 700 | 985 | 1269 | 723 | 313 | 636 | 562 | 454 | 414 | 506 | 274 | 432 | 646 | 505 | 730 |
| 39 | 17 | 42 | 13 | 119 | 56 | 38 | 83 | 25 | 33 | 25 | 41 | 21 | 21 | 3 | 38 | 96 |

*** Included elsewhere.**

ing 40 approved institutions in the states (in order of increase) of Texas, Oklahoma, Arkansas and Louisiana. In 1933 the full-time attendance of 34,746 in 23 institutions in the West South Central division was a decrease of 1.4 per cent., as compared with 1931.

Third in point of percentage increases for 1934 over 1933 is the East South Central division, in which there is an increase of 9.8 per cent. in the totals of 32,833 full-time students attending 41 approved institutions in Mississippi, Tennessee, Kentucky and Alabama. In 1933 the attendance of 15,348 in 21 institutions was a decrease of 15.5 per cent., as compared with 1931.

The Pacific division is fourth in percentage increases, with a gain of 9.2 per cent. in the 1934 totals of 58,251 attending 41 institutions in Oregon, Washington and California. In 1933 the attendance of 45,454 in 23 institutions was a decrease of 9.3 per cent., as compared with 1931.

Fifth in percentage gains is the West North Central division, with an increase of 7.1 per cent. in the 1934 totals of 79,612 attending 83 institutions in North Dakota, Iowa, South Dakota, Kansas, Nebraska, Minnesota and Missouri. In 1933 the attendance of 64,880 in 58 institutions was a decrease of 11.7 per cent., as compared with 1931.

The South Atlantic division shows an increase of 5.4 per cent. in the 1934 totals of 71,102 in 88 institutions of Florida, Georgia, West Virginia, North Carolina, South Carolina, Virginia, Maryland, Delaware and District of Columbia, the last three reporting slight decreases. In 1933 the attendance of 57,684 in 71 institutions was a decrease of 9.3 per cent., as compared with 1931.

The East North Central division has a percentage increase of 4.6 in its 1934 enrolment of 136,777 in 106 institutions of Michigan, Ohio, Illinois, Indiana and Wisconsin. In 1933 the attendance of 114,793 in 91 institutions was a decrease of 14 per cent., as compared with 1931.

The New England division has an increase of 1.5 per cent. in its 1934 enrolment of 54,546 in 39 institutions of Connecticut, Massachusetts, Maine, Vermont, Rhode Island and New Hampshire, the last named having a decrease of less than one per cent. In 1933 the attendance of 51,729 in 33 institutions was 4 per cent. below that of 1931.

The Middle Atlantic division, with 1934 full-time enrolment totals of 135,086 in 93 approved institutions, records a decrease of .4 per cent., as compared with 1933. New Jersey's approved eight institutions show a gain of .7 per cent. New York's 42 approved institutions have enrolments .6 per cent. less and Pennsylvania's 43 approved institutions have enrolments .2 per cent. less than last year. In 1933 the attendance of 126,015 in 82 approved institutions was 2.2 per cent. lower than in 1931.

TABLE IV

| University | Full-time students | Rank | All resident students | Rank |
|---|---|---|---|---|
| California | 18,892 | 1 | 21,210 | 4 |
| Columbia | 13,819 | 2 | 25,770 | 3 |
| New York U. | 12,347 | 3 | 27,682 | 1 |
| Minnesota | 12,188 | 4 | 16,275 | 5 |
| Illinois | 10,747 | 5 | 12,363 | 8 |
| Ohio State | 10,012 | 6 | 12,556 | 7 |
| Michigan | 9,005 | 7 | 11,138 | 12 |
| Wisconsin | 8,053 | 8 | 10,743 | 16 |
| C. C. of N. Y. | 8,030 | 9 | 27,248 | 2 |
| Harvard | 7,671 | 10 | 9,177 | 20 |
| U. of Wash. | 7,541 | 11 | 10,991 | 13 |
| Texas | 6,836 | 12 | 10,771 | 15 |
| Pennsylvania | 6,115 | 13 | 10,813 | 14 |
| Chicago | 5,950 | 14 | 11,320 | 11 |
| Hunter C. | 5,949 | 15 | 10,606 | 17 |
| St. John's | 5,883 | 16 | 6,094 | ...... |
| Pittsburgh | 5,723 | 17 | 9,767 | 18 |
| Cornell | 5,717 | 18 | 7,474 | 25 |
| Temple | 5,483 | 19 | 8,603 | 20 |
| Northwestern | 5,371 | 20 | 13,210 | 6 |
| Boston U. | 5,316 | 21 | 8,350 | 22 |
| U. of Nebraska | 5,111 | 22 | 6,812 | ...... |
| Brooklyn C. | 5,090 | 23 | 12,138 | 9 |
| Oklahoma | 5,064 | 24 | 6,533 | ...... |
| Yale | 5,036 | 25 | 5,082 | ...... |
| Iowa | 4,943 | ...... | 7,661 | 24 |
| Southern Calif. | 3,927 | ...... | 12,061 | 10 |
| Cincinnati | 3,887 | ...... | 9,534 | 19 |
| Western Reserve | 3,350 | ...... | 7,765 | 23 |
| Wayne U. | 2,931 | ...... | 8,360 | 21 |

1934 AND 1933 CLASSIFICATION COMPARISONS
INSTITUTIONS
Totals of Full-time Enrolment

| Classification | 1934 | 1933 |
|---|---|---|
| 55 Universities, public | 206,055 | 188,857 |
| 49 Universities, private | 163,539 | 161,373 |
| 344 Colleges | 169,997 | 164,647 |
| 47 Technological Institutions | 60,931 | 53,956 |
| 68 Teachers Colleges | 53,786 | 50,055 |
| 563 Total | 654,308 | 618,888 |

### HOW MANY FRESHMEN ARE THERE?

A new feature of the present study is an analysis of the number of freshmen this year and a comparison with the number a year ago. This is valuable, because it reveals the upward turn in enrolment more specifically than do the figures of total enrolment. The senior classes which went out last June were large; the freshman classes which came in in September, 1933, were small and, as sophomores, they continue small. The totals of 1934 enrolment are therefore kept low as compared with 1933. In the number of new students entering this fall a more definite measure is afforded of the immediate trend.

Of the 567 approved institutions in the present list, 487 were able to supply comparative figures for freshmen for 1933 and for 1934 in the four large fields concerning which inquiry was made: liberal arts, engineering, commerce and agriculture. The findings are given in some detail in the accompanying table of freshmen.

In the 487 institutions reporting there are 155,212 freshmen in these four fields, or 14 per cent. more than the 1933 totals of 136,064.

FRESHMAN ENROLMENT

| | Liberal Arts | | Engineering | | Commerce | | Agriculture | |
|---|---|---|---|---|---|---|---|---|
| | 1933 | 1934 | 1933 | 1934 | 1933 | 1934 | 1933 | 1934 |
| 53 Universities, public | 26,776 | 31,213 | 5,810 | 7,621 | 5,247 | 6,792 | 2,135 | 3,041 |
| 47 Universities, private | 19,832 | 20,340 | 2,689 | 2,801 | 5,076 | 6,182 | 373 | 399 |
| 336 Colleges | 52,331 | 56,818 | 994 | 974 | 1,154 | 1,494 | 108 | 100 |
| 44 Technological Institutions | 2,390 | 2,965 | 7,311 | 8,849 | 1,363 | 1,921 | 1,597 | 2,707 |
| 7 Teachers Colleges | 690 | 770 | 29 | 38 | 143 | 164 | 16 | 23 |
| 487 Totals | 102,019 | 112,106 | 16,833 | 20,283 | 12,983 | 16,553 | 4,229 | 6,270 |

As to liberal arts, the total of 112,106 freshmen is 9.8 per cent. greater than a year ago. The increase is 16.5 per cent. in liberal arts freshmen in the 53 universities under public control; the increase is 2.5 per cent. in the 47 universities under private control; and 8.6 per cent. in the 336 colleges of arts and sciences.

As to engineering the total of 20,283 freshmen is 20.5 per cent. larger than in 1933. The increase is 31.1 per cent. in the universities under public control; the increase is 4.1 per cent. in the universities under private control; the increase is 21 per cent. in the technological institutions (38 per cent. for 35 under public control and .6 per cent. for 12 under private control).

As to commerce or business administration, the total of 16,553 freshmen is 27.5 per cent. larger than in 1933. The increase is 29.4 per cent. in the universities under public control; the increase is 21.8 per cent. in the universities under private control. There are 1,494 freshmen recorded for commerce in the colleges of arts and sciences, a gain of 29.4 per cent. over 1933. The increase is 40.9 per cent. in the technological institutions, which this year have 1,921 freshmen in this field.

As to agriculture, the total of 6,270 freshmen is 48.3 per cent. larger than in 1933. The increase is 42.4 per cent. in the universities under public control, and 69.5 per cent. in the technological institutions.

## INTERPRETATIVE SUMMARY

In accordance with the thought that facts without interpretation are of little use, the present writer hazards this interpretative summary of the statistics of this report:

1. The enrolment increases in approved colleges and universities of the United States this year—5 per cent. for full-time students and 14 per cent. for freshmen—may be explained as being due somewhat to student aid by the Federal Emergency Relief Administration; somewhat to the difficulty high-school graduates have in finding jobs these days; somewhat to improved economic conditions in certain sections of the country; somewhat to the persistent faith of American fathers and mothers that higher education will benefit their children so that they make sacrifices to send them to college.

2. These statistics reveal a trend toward greater attendance in universities, colleges and technical schools which are under public control, doubtless due to the heavier tuition and other expenses in institutions under private control.

3. Liberal arts continues to be the chief training sought by those entering American colleges and universities. The proportion, however, is somewhat lower this year than last. In 1933, 75 per cent. of the freshmen entering 487 approved institutions chose a liberal arts curriculum; this year it is 72 per cent.

4. As compared with 1933, there is a re-

turn this year to practical courses. There is an increase of 20.5 per cent. in engineering freshmen; an increase of 27.5 per cent. in freshmen taking courses in commerce or business administration; and an increase of 48.3 per cent. in the freshmen taking courses in agriculture. In comparing these percentages with the 9.8 per cent. increase in liberal arts freshmen, account must be taken of the actual numbers. These are: 112,106 freshmen in liberal arts courses in 487 institutions; 20,283 freshmen in engineering; 16,553 freshmen in commerce, and 6,270 freshmen in agriculture.

5. The present rate of freshman increase would indicate a speedy return to the prosperity plateau of collegiate enrolment. This will depend, however, on factors such as the continuance of FERA aid to students, business and industrial revival, which sometimes leads away from college instead of to it, and other elements which the future may introduce.

### EXPLANATORY PARAGRAPHS

The thirty universities having statistics in detail in Table III are those to which this annual study was restricted for many years. The following paragraphs explain statistics given in the table and give additional information, including, for comparison, the full-time enrolment at each university five years ago.

The statistics in the first column of Table III are officially reported for the "University of California, Berkeley, Los Angeles, San Francisco and elsewhere." Of 1,828 students listed under engineering, 455 are in chemistry. The 49 students indicated under the term other courses are taking nursing. Of 1,791 students listed under education, 1,170 are in the Teachers College, University of California at Los Angeles, 587 are in the non-professional Graduate School, and 34 are included also under liberal arts. The 1934 summer session attendance (including duplicates) was made up as follows: intersession (Berkeley), 974; summer session (Berkeley), 1,795; summer session (Los Angeles), 1,167. The notation for the teaching staff reads that the 1,700 include "minor members of the teaching staff." Separate figures for the University of California at Los Angeles are of interest: The full-time students there number 6,107. There are 2,525 men and 1,971 women in liberal arts courses. The enrolment in education is 1,170 and in non-professional graduate study, 231. For the entire University of California the special report on freshman enrolment shows that there are 2,589 freshmen in liberal arts, 319 in engineering, 224 in commerce and 116 in agriculture, as compared with a November, 1933, enrolment of 2,541 freshmen in liberal arts, 260 in engineering, 191 in commerce and 92 in agriculture. Full-time students, 18,892; in 1929, 17,242.

In scanning the column of the University of Chicago, it should be considered that education is now a department and not a separate school and that students in education, in art and in music are included in the totals for college men and college women. The 791 listed under other courses embrace 734 in the school of social service administration, 36 "students-at-large" and 21 in the graduate library school. In determining the grand total, the compiler of this study has deducted the same number of duplicates as were reported for deduction last year, no deduction being included in the present report. There are 752 liberal arts freshmen this year as compared with 732 last year. Full-time students, 5,950; in 1929, 5,867.

The liberal arts enrolment at the University of Cincinnati, 1,134, is slightly larger than last year, although the freshman class was somewhat smaller. As to the engineering enrolment it should be explained that the 1933 figures of 1,231 covered all in the College of Engineering and Commerce, whereas the 1934 report gives, under the column heading commerce, the 244 students now taking the new course in business administration in the College of Engineering and Commerce. Of these 244 students, 158 are freshmen. There are 333 freshmen in the cooperative engineering courses, as compared with 257 last year. As to the figures for education, it should be pointed out that the 222 listed for Teachers College include those in the three upper years of the five-year program, the freshman and sophomore years being included in the liberal arts college. The term other courses here means 179 students in the school of household administration and 118 in the school of nursing and health. Full-time students, 3,887; in 1929, 3,964.

In the Columbia University statistics in Table III, the liberal arts figures of 3,148 are made up as follows: Columbia College, 1,701 men; Barnard College, 991 women; Seth Low Junior College, Brooklyn, 200 men; Bard College at Annandale (formerly St. Stephen's), 113 men; "university undergraduates," 143. The 256 students listed under dentistry include 59 in oral hygiene. For Teachers College the report shows 3,219 graduate students, 1,814 undergraduates and 300 in New College. The term other courses here takes in 300 students in library service and 85 in optometry. There are 892 liberal arts freshmen who are new at Columbia this year, as compared with 775 last year. The number of engineering freshmen is exactly the same, 68. There are 64 business administration freshmen, or nine less than last year. The figures for teaching and administrative staffs are those for 1933–34. Full-time students, 13,819; in 1929, 14,952.

The engineering total of 954 in the Cornell University column includes 144 in chemistry. Under other courses are included 446 in home economics, 179 in hotel administration and 157 in veterinary medicine. The Cornell special report on freshmen shows 427 in liberal arts, 212 in engineering and 315 in agriculture, as compared with 421 in liberal arts, 209 in engineering and 299 in agriculture in November, 1933. Full-time students, 5,717; in 1929, 5,500.

In the consideration of Harvard's statistics it should be noted that the 721 listed under commerce are in the graduate school of business administration; that the 67 students in architecture include 19 in landscape architecture; that students taking forestry and music are included under nonprofessional graduate enrolment; and that the total of 57 for other courses takes in 28 special students, 19 students in public health and 10 students in city planning. As to freshmen, there are 1,111 in liberal arts and 374 in commerce, as compared with 1,052 in liberal arts and 401 in commerce a year ago. Full-time students, 7,671; in 1929, 8,377.

In the University of Illinois figures the 1,555 reported under engineering include 437 in chemistry, who are also reported under liberal arts and sciences; a proper deduction is of course made in the table for duplicates. The term other courses here embraces 284 in the school of physical education, 47 library and 44 landscape architecture students. As to freshmen the comparisons are: 1934 liberal arts, 1,501; engineering, 424; commerce, 693; agriculture, 377; 1933 liberal arts, 1,298; engineering, 358; commerce, 550; agriculture, 313. The report states that the number of 1,032 in the teaching staff "does not include 267 non-paid part-time clinical staff." Full-time students, 10,747; in 1929, 12,413.

As to the returns for Indiana University it may be said that other courses means 141 students in nurses training, and that there are 847 freshmen in liberal arts and 231 freshmen in commerce, as compared with respective figures of 632 and 193 in November, 1933. Full-time students, 4,607; in 1929, 4,177.

The figures of 1,932 men and 1,090 women listed as taking liberal arts college courses in the University of Iowa column include students in art, education, journalism and music. The term other courses here means 211 students in nursing. There are 1,194 freshmen in liberal arts and 100 in engineering, as compared with 948 and 82 in the same fields a year ago. Full-time students, 4,943; in 1929, 5,106.

The engineering total of 318 given for Johns Hopkins University includes 24 in graduate courses in engineering and 21 taking chemistry. The enrolments reported as full-time and totalled in the table under other courses include 245 in "afternoon and evening courses" as distinct from part-time and 92 students in the school of hygiene and public health. The 1934 freshmen at Johns Hopkins are 178 in liberal arts, 80 in engineering and 17 in commerce, as compared with 150 in liberal arts, 112 in engineering and 27 in commerce a year ago. Full-time students, 1,798; in 1929, 1,468.

Students in architecture are included in the 493 reported for engineering in the University of Kansas column. Other courses here means 94 students in nursing. There are 857 freshmen in liberal arts and 139 in engineering, as compared with 751 and 114 in these fields a year ago. The 223 reported for the teaching staff are "full-time only." Full-time students, 3,832; in 1929, 4,227.

In the University of Michigan statistics students listed under architecture include some in the fine arts, and the liberal arts total includes certain students in journalism. Other courses here takes in 139 students in nursing, 21 in dental hygiene and two in anesthesia. There are 1,089 freshmen in liberal arts and 285 in engineering, as compared with similar enrolments of 978 and 226 in November, 1933. Full-time students, 9,005; in 1929, 9,688.

The engineering totals in the University of Minnesota report include 1,034 in engineering and architecture, 376 in chemistry and 207 in "mines." There are students in forestry and in home economics included in the agriculture enrolment of 913. Under other courses the specific registrations are 932 in the general college, 429 in nursing, 63 in dental hygiene and 51 in university college. The 1933 freshman numbers are 1,751 in liberal arts, 237 in engineering and 329 in agriculture, as compared with 1,552 in liberal arts, 196 in engineering and 226 in agriculture of November, 1933. The registrarly notation is that the grand total of 16,275 "includes duplicates between the summer session of 1934 and the full enrolment of 1934." Full-time students, 12,188; in 1929, 10,657.

The report of the University of Missouri as usual includes, in the engineering total of 611, the 350 students in the School of Mines and Metallurgy at Rolla. It is of interest that the Rolla enrolment numbers eleven women who are studying in various engineering and scientific fields. Students taking courses in architecture and music on the Columbia campus are included in the total of 83 for fine arts. The summer session enrolment includes students at Columbia and at Rolla. As to freshmen, the report shows 556 in liberal arts this year, as compared with 455 last year; 177 in engineering, as compared with 121 last; 162 in agriculture, as against 97 last year. Full-time students, 3,420; in 1929, 3,710.

In the engineering totals of the University of Nebraska, 497, there are 51 in chemical engineering. Under other courses there are 118 students in nursing. The 1934 freshman enrolments are: liberal arts, 626; engineering, 183; commerce, 346; agriculture, 119; in 1933: liberal arts, 579; engineering, 132; commerce, 210; agriculture, 60. Full-time students, 5,111; in 1929, 6,038.

The one necessary explanation about the Northwestern University tabulation is that other courses here means students in speech. There are 785 freshmen in liberal arts and 76 in engineering, as compared with 784 and 69, respectively, a year ago. In the school of commerce, which requires two years of college work for entrance, there are 210 entering students as against 193 a year ago. Full-time enrolment, 5,371; in 1929, 5,804.

It may be mentioned, in regard to the enrolment figures of Ohio State University, that students in architecture are included under engineering; students in art and in music are included under education; students in forestry are included under agriculture, and students in journalism are included under commerce. The other course details are: veterinary medicine, 273; applied optics, 109; arts-education, 86; nursing, 21. The 1934 freshmen include 871 in liberal arts, 446 in engineering, 810 in commerce and 397 in agriculture. In 1933 the freshman enrolments were 805 liberal arts, 251 engineering, 607 commerce and 291 agriculture. Full-time students, 10,012; in 1929, 10,557.

These points may be observed in the University of Pennsylvania statistics: The engineering count of 387 includes 123 students in chemical engineering and 46 in chemistry. The medical figures are made up of 529 in the school of medicine and 152 in the graduate school of medicine. The 125 students in architecture include seven doing graduate work and 12 in landscape architecture. There are 1,669 students in the Wharton School and 56 in the graduate course in business administration. Other courses in the table mean veterinary medicine 171, nurses training 162 and oral hygiene 25. There are 320 in the newly established liberal arts college for women. As to freshman comparisons the figures are: 1934 registrations, 486 liberal arts, 47 engineering, 427 commerce. 1933 registrations, 507 liberal arts, 68 engineering, 429 commerce. Full-time students, 6,115; in 1929, 7,119.

The engineering enrolment of the University of Pittsburgh as given in Table III is made up of 476 in engineering and 102 in "mines." As to the 545 students in education it should be explained that they are upper classmen, the freshman and sophomore years being included in the liberal arts college. The term other courses here covers seven students in retail training. There are 809 freshmen in liberal arts, 207 in engineering and mines and 232 in commerce, as compared with corresponding freshman enrolments a year ago of 805, 126 and 164. Full-time students, 5,723; in 1929, 5,646.

As to the Princeton statistics it need only be explained that the summer session is attended solely by Princeton undergraduates; and that the freshman registration this year is 570 in liberal arts and 74 in engineering, as compared with 542 in liberal arts and 75 in engineering in November, 1933. Full-time students, 2,622; in 1929, 2,459.

As usual Stanford University statistics are reported so as to cover all the university registration under college men and college women, with deduction for duplicates below. It is of interest that the number of women students at Stanford, restricted for many years to 500, is now 1,042. There are 635 freshmen this year in the lower division, as against 549 last year. Full-time students, 3,670; in 1929, 3,535.

The figure of 387 under art in the Syracuse University statistics takes in students in music as well as in fine arts. The other-courses total is made up as follows: Home economics 215, nursing 116, school of speech 79, Wanakena Forest Rangers 50 and library school 11. There are 507 freshmen in liberal arts, 86 in applied science and 250 in business administration, as compared with corresponding numbers of a year ago, 508, 80 and 215. Full-time figures, 4,764; in 1929, 4,989.

The report of the University of Texas includes 355 students in the medical branch at Galveston. Students in architecture are counted under engineering and those in journalism under liberal arts in Table III. There are 135 students in nursing recorded under other courses. The grand total of students is reduced by the compiler of this article by 1,400, the number of duplicates reported last year. There are 1,070 freshmen in liberal arts and 201 in engineering, as compared with corresponding freshman registrations a year ago of 909 and 152. Full-time students, 6,836; in 1929, 5,822.

Tulane University of Louisiana includes 61 students in chemistry in its report of 260 engineering students. The liberal arts college figures include students in education and in journalism. There are students in social work, a professional course, and in the graduate school of medicine in the 76 total reported under other courses. Freshmen this fall are 443 in liberal arts, 114 in engineering and 54 in commerce. The similar distribution of freshmen a year ago is not available. Full-time students, 2,607; in 1929, 2,405.

The University of Washington (Seattle) comment is that the figures of 1,975 men and 2,664 women are for University College, which comprises the departments formerly in the colleges of liberal arts and sciences. These include students in architecture, art, journalism and music. Other courses in this case means librarianship, with 27 students. The freshman comparisons are as follows: 1934, University College 1,921, engineering 391 and commerce 584; 1933, same, 1,566, 328, 453. Full-time students, 7,541; in 1929, 7,258.

In the University of Virginia total of 143 for engineering, 30 students in chemistry are included. Courses in agriculture are given in the college of arts and sciences. First-year students are made up of 459 in liberal arts, 49 in engineering and 63 in commerce, as compared with corresponding fields in 1933 of 385, 39 and 84 first-year students. Full-time students, 2,251; in 1929, 2,269.

Of the column for Washington University (St. Louis) it need be noted only that certain students in social work are included in the 191 total for commerce, and that the 154 listed under other courses are students in nursing. The grand total of 4,462 does not allow for duplicates. There are 572 freshmen in liberal arts and 96 in engineering, as compared with 411 and 106, respectively, a year ago. Full-time students, 3,400; in 1929, 3,398.

The liberal arts enrolment at Western Reserve University, given under college men and college women, includes students in art, commerce and music; but some of these are included under education. Other courses here means applied social sciences, 337 students; nursing, 287 students, and library science, 66 students. There are 453 freshmen in liberal arts as compared with 473 a year ago. Full-time students, 3,350; in 1929, 3,496.

In the engineering enrolment of 1,090 reported for the University of Wisconsin, 175 are students in chemistry and chemical engineering. Home economics is included under agriculture. Other courses here means graduate nurse course, 62 students, and library school, 38 students. The freshman figures are: liberal arts, 1,604, engineering 285, agriculture and home economics 225, as compared with 1933 corresponding registrations of 1,312, 211 and 159. Full-time students, 8,053; in 1929, 9,468.

The report of Yale covering art in Table III includes students in painting, sculpture and the drama. There are 128 students in nursing listed under other courses. Yale has 781 liberal arts freshmen as compared with 838 in November, 1933. Full-time students, 5,036; in 1929, 5,084.

# EDUCATIONAL EVENTS

## MILITARY TRAINING IN THE SCHOOLS OF ITALY

*The Educational Supplement* of the London *Times* states that the Italian Minister of Education, Signor Ercole, has addressed an official circular to the rectors of universities, to the directors of higher educational institutions, and to local authorities for education, announcing the formation of a general inspectorate for "pre-military and post-military" training in schools. General Grazioli has been appointed as head of the new inspectorate, with Commendatore Angelo Senesi as chief inspector on behalf of the ministry.

The circular states that "in conformity with the new Mussolinian conception of a military nation, based on the principle that the functions of citizen and soldier are inseparable in the Fascist State," the Fascist formula "Book and Rifle" now finds application in the Italian educational system, from elementary school to university. This has been achieved by the regulations for pre-military instruction, now compulsory for all citizens from the age of eight to the age of 21. Every division between the conceptions of civil and military life is, it is stated, being eliminated; the barriers between civil and military institutions are being demolished; a fusion is being effected of the youth organizations, the armed forces, and the schools; and military education, recognized as of high moral value, is becoming a substantial element of general education.

"It is my firm intention (the Minister adds) that the aim of the government shall be realized in full, without hesitation or delay." The educational system is the "great forge of the Fascist régime," and will not fail to look upon the task set it in the light of the Duce's words: "If it is to be true peace, that fruitful peace which must be accomplished by justice, we can adorn the barrels of our rifles with branches of olive. But if it should not happen thus, be sure that we, men tempered in the climate of the Littorio, will adorn the points of our bayonets with the laurel and oak of victory.

"I am certain that the whole educational system, from the elementary school to the university, will in a single unanimous and passionate cry answer 'Present' to the Duce's call. I will impart to you further instructions as soon as the relevant measures have been translated into laws. In the meantime the Inspectorate-General for pre-military and post-military training has this day (October 29) been solemnly constituted by the head of the government, and the preliminary work is being set in hand. I direct that in all schools under your authority, of whatever order, type, or grade, the measures be given the widest possible circulation and their meaning and importance duly explained. The aim is progressively to excite in the school population the sentiments of love and admiration for the glorious Italian Army, to dispose the pupils to accept willingly and joyfully the new military teaching, and to draw from it the utmost profit, for the advantage of the motherland."

Those to whom the circular is addressed are asked to "collaborate assiduously and intelligently" with the representatives of the administration and of the armed forces so as to enable them to carry out in the best possible way the task that lies before them in the schools, giving them for the purpose all necessary information and anything else they may require.

## THE HARVARD UNIVERSITY LIBRARY

The total number of books in the Harvard University Library at the end of the academic year 1933–34 was, according to the *Harvard Alumni Bulletin,* 3,602,040. Of that number, 126,935 volumes and pamphlets were added during the year.

The Harvard University Library, which includes the College Library, the various departmental libraries and the collections in the seven residential houses, is the largest university library in the world, and only six libraries of any kind have a larger number of volumes, namely, the British Museum, the French National, the Library of Congress, the New York City Public Library, the Leningrad Public Library and the Moscow Public Library.

The Harvard College Library contains 1,960,762 volumes and pamphlets, the departmental libraries 1,576,859, and the house libraries 64,419. These totals do not include thousands of broadsides, posters, programs, play-bills, leaflets, clippings, autographs, photographs and engravings.

Of the 126,935 volumes and pamphlets added last year to the University Library, 66,885 went to the College Library, 52,676 to the departmental libraries and 7,374 to the house libraries. The Baker Library of the Graduate School of Business Administration had 17,207 accessions last year—the largest number received by any departmental library; then came the Law School with 13,490 additions, and the Medical School with 8,544.

The College Library received last year gifts amounting to $111,306 in cash as well as 20,718 books and 31,899 pamphlets.

Dr. Robert P. Blake, director of the University Library, says in his annual report that the circulation of books last year was 235,258. This was 2,259 smaller than the circulation in 1932–33, but larger than the circulation in 1931–32 (232,338), 1930–31 (210,981) and 1929–30 (182,429).

Dr. Blake's report continues:

The reference and circulation departments report for the first time in many years a decrease both in the registration of the users of the library and in the actual circulation of books within and without the building. This decrease is probably not attributable to any one cause, but appears to be proportionate to the slight decline in registration throughout all the departments of the university.

The number of visiting scholars also shows a slight decrease over the peak figure of last year. Though the number of such scholars is large, 637, the majority of them stay with us for only brief intervals and the bulk of their visits falls during the summer, when it is easy to accommodate callers from outside.

Inter-library loans likewise manifest a slight decline from the total of last year. The borrowing institutions are widely distributed over America. While the work involved in this service is very considerable, it is something we do gladly, as it is a point where we can be of the greatest service to our sister institutions and to scholars throughout the United States.

## THE FINANCES OF YALE UNIVERSITY

IN its review of the financial operations of Yale University for the fiscal year ending June 30, 1934, the treasurer's report, issued on December 7, states that 7,148 alumni cooperated with the university through the Alumni Fund during 1933–34—a larger number than in any year since 1930–31. Total expenses for last year were $6,810,164 (as compared with $7,720,829 in 1930–31), the largest single item, aside from salaries for instruction in 1933–34 being $642,752 for assistance to students in need of financial aid; the total number helped being 1,571. In addition to the amount thus expended to assist them, the university made loans aggregating $194,428 to self-supporting students during the fiscal year, at the same time obtaining employment for many of them through its Bureau of Appointments, which states that the grand total of all reported earnings and scholarship aid during the year was $1,053,149.

Gifts to the university through the Yale Alumni Fund Association aggregated $273,831 for the year, $127,324 of this amount representing interest on the principal of the Alumni Fund, and $146,506 annual contributions and bequests received from 7,148 contributors.

Other gifts and bequests for endowment, exclusive of contributions to building funds, aggregated $417,666 for 1933–34; gifts to income for special purposes $892,821, and gifts to income for general purposes, including the contribution of the Alumni Fund, $266,482. In order to provide for expenditures made for scholarship aid in excess of the income available from endowment of scholarship funds, the corporation authorized an appropriation of $135,879 from funds available for such use in its discretion; at the same time appropriating a total of $147,751 from Contingency Reserve Fund to meet other heavy demands upon the current resources of the university, such as the payments for the group insurance plan covering the staff and for faculty retiring allowances and pension reserves, for which there is no special endowment.

In commenting on the loans of $194,428 made to students in all schools and departments of the university during the year just closed, the report points out that for these loans notes are taken payable, as a rule, in from two to five years after graduation. No interest is charged where notes are paid promptly when due, but after the date of maturity interest at the rate of six per cent. a year is added. Notes outstanding at the end of the fiscal year amounted to $1,028,800, as compared with $951,775 one year ago.

Loans made from the Teachers Emergency Loan Fund during the past year amounted to $47,238, as compared with $32,740 in 1932–33, the total of notes outstanding on June 30, 1934, being $18,305. These loans, which are made to members of the faculties of the various schools, are repayable in monthly instalments from salary payments, in accordance with the conditions governing the foundation, which was established by a gift of $15,000 from "A Graduate of Yale College" on November 30, 1910. Since that time loans aggregating $474,641 have been made from this revolving loan fund to 847 borrowers.

Total payments made by the university from its own general income for premiums under the Group Insurance Plan covering all Yale's staff, for faculty retiring allowances and for reserves to provide for the assumption of pensions previously assured to members of Yale's staff under the former Carnegie Plan, aggregated $153,884 in 1933–34, as compared with $151,847 for the previous year.

## THE SOCIAL SCIENCES IN THE CURRICULUM OF NEW YORK UNIVERSITY

Greater emphasis on the social sciences in college curricula, and in general a training more useful for the problem of living to-day, was urged by a majority of 714 alumni of Washington Square College, New York University, as the result of a questionnaire made by the committee on curriculum, of which Professor Clyde Eagleton is chairman.

English composition, English and American literature, psychology, American government, American history and economics were the courses most favored by the alumni, according to Professor Eagleton. Over half the alumni favored the requirement of at least one natural science, one modern language, philosophy and public speaking.

The survey of the day alumni was made by the Washington Square College Alumni Association and a committee of evening alumni submitted a report to Dean Milton E. Loomis, of the college. More than 200 courses not now offered by Washington Square College, many of them with technical and vocational emphasis, were suggested. Among those most favored were courses in mental and sex hygiene, philosophy of etiquette, vocational guidance, how to study, stenography and typewriting, contemporary civilization, contemporary literature, oriental languages and history, and comparative religion. Special interest was indicated in courses which would help an individual to get along with others in the world in which he must live. The questionnaire included questions on vocations, examinations, course organization and instruction as well as on curriculum.

The committee pointed out the desirability of introducing into the curriculum, as alternative choices to present courses, a course in economic and political problems with special reference to the United States; a course in the history of civilization; a mathematics survey course for students neither majoring nor minoring in mathematics or the sciences, nor preparing to study medicine; a course in the biological sciences that would include chemistry and some laboratory work; a course in music and the fine arts; and a survey of physics for students not majoring or minoring in science that would touch on astronomy and geology and that would include some laboratory work. Other alternative courses proposed for the two-year curriculum would be in hygiene, philosophy, psychology, a modern language, English composition and English and American literature.

Of the 714 alumni who participated in the questionnaire survey 626 indicated that they had come to Washington Square College with vocational preparation as a major objective. One hundred fifty-four of this number changed their choice of vocation after entering the college. Those at present unemployed number eighty-six and 158 are studying further. Among the 470 now working, the eleven leading occupations represented are as follows: teachers, 103; lawyers, 88; doctors, 47; clerical workers, 40; secretaries, 27; business men and women, 20; social workers, 18; salesmen, 16; accountants, 10; dentists, 8, and advertising workers, 7. Eighty-six graduates are now employed in 40 other miscellaneous occupations. Among them are a clergyman, an anthropologist, a policeman, a librarian, a radio announcer and a statistician.

## ONE-TEACHER RURAL SCHOOL DISTRICTS IN NEW YORK STATE

*The New York Sun* reports that Governor Lehman's planning board in a recent statement recommended purchase and reforestation by New York state of all the land in the small, one-teacher rural school districts. These regions have rugged, poor soil and are gradually being abandoned.

"Though unfit for farming, they are well suited for timber production and recreation uses," the board experts said. "Under state ownership the taxpayers would be saved the expense of schools and roads, the state would in time benefit greatly from timber production and the present owners would have opportunity to move to areas where better livelihood might be obtained."

Under the board's plan the people of these districts could be absorbed in the populations of more fertile and prosperous sections, and hundreds of rural schools that have an average of five pupils or fewer could be abandoned. These schools cost the state thousands of dollars, and it is contended that if their pupils could be sent to schools in more populous districts they would enjoy much better educational advantages. As an argument for its plan the board points out that in eight of these schools there is only one pupil each.

"These eight youngsters," says the statement, "each has a heated and lighted schoolhouse to himself and the exclusive attention of a whole-time teacher."

The cost to the state of maintaining one of these pupils is $1,166 annually, and the cost to the state where there is an average daily attendance of one or two pupils is $866 a pupil. Contrasted to this is the $55 cost a pupil in the one-teacher schools with an average attendance of twenty-eight or more.

Of the 6,000 one-teacher school districts in the state there are 245 with five or fewer students. Eight of them have one pupil each, fifteen have two, fifty-three have three, seventy-two have four and ninety-seven have five.

"These are the sort of facts," said the report, "that are being correlated and brought to light by the technical staff of the New York State Planning Board. They reveal the enormous waste of public funds inevitably associated with an antiquated system of public administration and the saving to taxpayers that could be effected through intelligent and continued state planning."

## THE UNIVERSITY OF THE AIR

THE third year of the WEVD University of the Air was inaugurated during a two-hour program before an audience of sixteen hundred at the Town Hall, New York City, on the evening of December 8. Among those participating were Professor John Dewey, Chancellor Harry W. Chase, of New York University, Fannie Hurst, Dr. Harry W. Laidler, Heywood Broun, Michael Strange, B. Charney Vladeck, Dr. Sandor Lorand, Alla Nazimova, Dr. Sigmund Spaeth and Mrs. Franklin D. Roosevelt.

Dr. Dewey's address, of which the following is a summary, was entitled "Radio's Influence on the Mind":

> The radio is the most powerful instrument of social education the world has ever seen. The eye is superior to the ear with respect to the understanding of physical and technical matters. But in all social matters the mass of people are guided through hearing rather than by sight. The progress of democracy has been greatly hindered by the fact that modern means of exchange of physical things has advanced far beyond the means for exchange of knowledge and ideas. The radio brings us the possibility of redressing the balance.
>
> It is only a possibility, not as yet an accomplished fact. The radio lends itself to propaganda in behalf of special interests. It can be used to distort facts and mislead the public mind. In my opinion, the question as to whether it is to be employed for this end or for the social public interest is one of the most crucial problems of the present. Upon the way in which it is practically answered depends to a larger extent than we yet realize the formation of that enlightened and fair-minded public opinion and sentiment that are necessary for the success of democracy. The radio even when in private hands is affected with a profound public interest. For this reason every attempt at genuine education of the millions who daily listen in is of greatest concern. That is one reason, and a great one, why I welcome the endeavors of Station WEVD to conduct the University of the Air. May it succeed and may its influence spread till every broadcasting organization follows its example.

Due to the intervening Christmas and New Year holidays, the other courses will begin the week of January 7. They are:

*Wednesdays,* 10:15 P. M., "Education for a New Social Order," Professor John Dewey, Professor William H. Kilpatrick; *Thursdays,* 8:15 P. M., "Economic Planning—Society in the Making," Professor Henry Pratt Fairchild, John T. Flynn, Dr. Harry W. Laidler; *Fridays,* 10:15 P. M., "Psychoanalysis To-day," Dr. Sandor Lorand, Dr. A. A. Brill; *Sundays,* 10:00 P. M., "University of the Air Forum."

Later in the season the following will be offered:

"Labor Faces the Future," William Green, Sidney Hillman, Elmer F. Andrews; "Literature and Drama," Fannie Hurst, Heywood Broun; "Studies in a Museum," Professor Henry Fairfield Osborn.

## THE SIXTY-FIFTH ANNUAL MEETING OF THE DEPARTMENT OF SUPERINTENDENCE

THE *Journal* of the National Education Association reports that the sixty-fifth annual meeting of the Department of Superintendence will be held from February 23 to 28 at Atlantic City, New Jersey. President E. E. Oberholtzer is organizing the programs around specific problems in educational recovery and improvement. Members of the department will take part not only in the deliberations of smaller groups but may join in the panel-discussion on the controversial issues represented in the 1935 Yearbook which will be specially featured at one of the general sessions. The subject of the Yearbook is "Education for New Social and Economic Relationships." Its preparation is undertaken by a commission headed by U. S. Commissioner of Education J. W. Studebaker, who will present it to the convention and act as moderator of the panel discussion. Topics to be emphasized in the give-and-take of this new informal platform method include "Changing Ethical Standards," "Individualistic Versus Collective Social Planning," "What Lies Ahead in Government" and "The Relationship of the Teaching Profession to Social Policy."

Two afternoons of the convention will be devoted to forum-discussion groups. The topics to which these groups will devote themselves and their respective leaders follow:

"The Support and Control of Public Education in a Democracy," David E. Weglein, Baltimore.

"Personnel Problems in Educational Administration," Carroll R. Reed, Minneapolis.

"Educational Interpretation Dealing with Recent Trends, Practises and Developments Toward a New Educational Program," Ben G. Graham, Pittsburgh.

"Administrative Problems," George C. Bush, South Pasadena.

"The Outlook for New Educational Programs with Special Emphasis on Social-Economic Phases," A. J. Stoddard, Providence.

"Curriculum Trends and Controversies," H. B. Bruner, Columbia University, N. Y.

Members of the department will be asked to make special studies in advance of the convention. Reports of these studies will be made in a series of meetings known as study-discussion groups. Twenty-five or thirty sections will be organized for this purpose.

President Oberholtzer is arranging a general program which includes the participation of prominent government officials, and nationally known leaders in various professional and industrial fields. These speakers will be presented at the morning and evening sessions.

Elementary school principals are planning special programs, which include a panel discussion similar to those in which the general department will engage. This feature of the convention will be directed by J. Cayce Morrison, assistant commissioner for elementary education, State Education Department, Albany, N. Y., and President M. Emma Brookes, of the Department of Elementary School Principals, principal of the Miles-Cranwood Schools, Cleveland, Ohio.

# EDUCATIONAL NOTES AND NEWS

DR. EDWARD L. THORNDIKE, head of the work in psychology at Teachers College, Columbia University, will preside at the ninety-fifth meeting of the American Association for the Advancement of Science, which will be held at Pittsburgh from December 26 to January 2. Dr. Henry N. Russell, research professor of astronomy at Princeton University, will give the address of the retiring president, which is entitled "The Atmospheres of the Planets." At a dinner on the evening of the twenty-eighth the addresses will be given of the retiring vice-presidents of the section of psychology and the section of education. Professor Walter R. Miles, of Yale University, will speak on "Training, Practise and Longevity," and Professor Walter F. Dearborn, of Harvard University, on "The Mental and Physical Growth of Public School Children." Dr. J. McKeen Cattell will preside.

THE Board of Curators of the University of Missouri have voted to postpone acceptance of the resignation of Dr. Walter Williams as president of the university until April 1. A previous order appointing Dr. Frederick A. Middlebush as acting-president was reaffirmed by the action of the board.

DR. HENRY HARBAUGH APPLE, for twenty-five years president of Franklin and Marshall College, Lancaster, Pa., submitted his resignation to the trustees on December 7. He said that he "could not hope to continue to serve long enough to complete any extended plans" and that such plans should properly be the function of his successor. A committee was appointed by the trustees to select a successor.

DR. DAVID LINN EDSALL, dean of the Medical School and of the School of Public Health of Harvard University, will retire with the title of dean emeritus at the close of the academic year.

DR. FRANKLYN B. SNYDER, professor of English at Northwestern University, has become dean of the Graduate School.

THE New York City Board of Superintendents has promoted Elizabeth A. Walsh, acting head of the bureau of children with retarded mental development, and Margaret C. Holmes, acting director of kindergartens, to the directorships of their divisions.

DR. LOREN C. PETRY, professor of botany since 1925, has been appointed director of the forty-fourth summer session at Cornell University. Beginning next summer the separate schools formerly held by the endowed colleges and the state colleges will be combined as a single enterprise.

HOWARD W. HOPKIRK, of Montclair, N. J., will become superintendent of the Albany, N. Y., Home for Children on January 1. Mr. Hopkirk has been connected with the Child Welfare League of America in New York City.

DR. MARTHA M. ELIOT, of the Yale Medical School, has been appointed assistant chief of the Children's Bureau. She succeeds Miss Katharine Lenroot, who was recently named chief of the bureau. Dr. Eliot will have special responsibility for the bureau's child and maternal health program.

DR. GEORGE H. WHIPPLE, of the School of Medicine and Dentistry of the University of Rochester, and Dr. George R. Minot and Dr. William P. Murphy, of the Harvard Medical School, joint recipients of the Nobel prize in physiology and medicine, were present on December 10 at the ceremonies held in Stockholm on the occasion of the presentation to them by King Gustaf of the diplomas, gold medals and money award. Professor Harold C. Urey, of Columbia University, who was awarded the prize in chemistry, was unable to be present. The value of each prize is about $40,000.

DR. OTIS W. CALDWELL has been elected the first honorary member of the Central Association of Science and Mathematics Teachers. This announcement was made at the recent annual dinner of the association at which he was toastmaster. Dr. Caldwell was one of its founders and is the oldest living past-president.

DR. LLOYD NICOLI YEPSEN, director of the psychological clinic of New York University in the Washington Square College, received the Medal of Merit of the Republic of Chile at a dinner of the Kappa Delta Pi and Phi Delta Kappa fraternities in New York City on December 8. The presentation was made by Roberto Gatica. The medal was bestowed upon Dr. Yepsen in recognition of his work in the development of schools for feeble-minded and retarded children in Chile in 1929 and 1930.

IN recognition of his contributions to humor and biography, the Mark Twain medal has been awarded by the International Mark Twain Society to Dr. Stephen Leacock, professor of political economy at McGill University. Next year Professor Leacock will be the speaker of honor at the University of Missouri at the Mark Twain Centenary celebration.

PROFESSOR C. P. BABER, head librarian at the

Kansas State Teachers College of Emporia, was elected president of the Kansas Library Association at the recent meeting in Manhattan. Miss Nora Daniels, librarian at the Emporia Public Library, was elected vice-president.

The *Kansas Teacher* writes: "The victory of State Superintendent W. T. Markham in the recent election is without doubt one of the outstanding surprises of Kansas political history since Kansas was a state. According to press reports based upon unofficial returns, it appears that while Governor Landon, the Republican nominee for governor, carried the state by more than 60,000 votes, Mr. Markham, the Democratic nominee for state superintendent of public instruction, rolled up a majority of approximately 40,000 votes over the Republican nominee, Mr. Seaman."

Former students in the department of student personnel administration of Teachers College, Columbia University, have recently been appointed to positions as follows: Miss Alice Brown (M.A., 1934) has been appointed head of residence at the New Jersey College for Women, New Brunswick; Miss Marion Galton, who completed her work for the master's degree during the 1934 Summer Session, has been made dean of women, State Teachers College, Slippery Rock, Pa.; Miss Emily Post (Teachers College, 1933–34) has been appointed dean at Fairfax Hall, Waynesboro, Va.; Mrs. Mary F. Swaney (M.A., 1934) has been appointed academic dean at The Dearborn-Morgan School, Orange, N. J.; Miss Alida P. Banks (M.A., 1934), formerly assistant to Dean Slowe, of Howard University, has been appointed dean of women at West Virginia State College, Institute, W. Va.; Miss Harriet Harrison (M.A., 1934), formerly head of the department of physical education at the State Teachers College, Duluth, Minn., has been appointed dean of women in that institution.

John H. Manning Butler has been appointed professor of elementary education at the National Teachers College of Manila. After thirty-two years of service in the Bureau of Education of the Philippine Islands and as superintendent of schools. Dr. Butler retired on reaching the age limit last March. He was the first superintendent to be retired at the highest rate of pension.

F. A. Meier, at present head of the science department at Rugby School, England, will become head master of Bedales—the co-educational school at Petersfield, Hampshire. He succeeds Mr. J. H. Badley, head master and founder, who retires next July.

C. E. Douglass, formerly assistant superintendent of schools at Baltimore, Md., has been elected superintendent of schools at Newark, Del.

I. E. Stutsman, formerly superintendent of schools at Greeley, Colo., has been appointed superintendent at St. Joseph, Mo.

Dr. James Kieran, president emeritus of Hunter College, sailed for Europe on December 8.

Miss Lulu Holmes, dean of women at Drury College, Springfield, Mo., has been granted a year's leave of absence and is teaching history in Kobe College, Japan.

Arthur Pope, professor of fine arts at Harvard University, has leave of absence for the academic year 1934–35, during which he has undertaken advisory work in connection with projects in art education for the Carnegie Foundation.

A memorial assembly was held on November 14 in honor of the late W. A. Lewis, president of the Kansas State Teachers College at Fort Hays.

Dr. Palmer C. Ricketts, president since 1901 of the Rensselaer Polytechnic Institute, a member of the faculty since his graduation in 1875, died on December 10 at the age of seventy-eight years.

Dr. Theobald Smith, from 1896 to 1915 professor of comparative pathology at Harvard University, and from 1915 to 1929 director of the department of animal pathology of the Rockefeller Institute for Medical Research, and at the time of his death president of the board of scientific directors of the institute, died at the age of seventy-five years on December 10.

Dr. George Herbert Betts, professor of education and director of research at the School of Education of Northwestern University, died on December 8, at the age of sixty-six years.

Professor W. H. Hulme, who retired as

head of the English Department of the Flora Stone Mather College of the Western Reserve University in June, 1933, died in Freiburg on December 6, at the age of seventy-two years. Professor Hulme was a member of the Modern Language Association of America, and of the Delta Kappa Epsilon and Phi Beta Kappa fraternities.

EDWIN PUTNAM BROWN, principal of Wayland Academy Preparatory School since 1901, died on November 26 at the age of sixty-five years.

OSBERT CROOME ROACH, head of the personnel department of the United States Rubber Company and formerly owner and head master for fifteen years of the Repton School for Boys at Tarrytown, N. Y., died on December 4. He was fifty-four years old.

HENRY WALROND SIMPKINSON, sometime assistant secretary of the British Board of Education, died on November 24 at the age of eighty-one years.

A GIFT of $95,000 to the Students' Aid Association of the College of the City of New York has been announced by Professor Alfred D. Compton, secretary. The donor wishes to remain anonymous, and for some time only the income on the investment of the money will be used. On November 1, according to the financial report, the Students' Aid Association had a balance of $1,769, after having paid out in loans, gifts and scholarships the sum of $11,478. The total receipts during the year were $13,248. On November 1, 1933, a year ago, the balance on hand was $4,379. This year loans were granted to 240 students, ten times as many as in 1928, before the depression. Scholarships this year were given to 83 students, as compared with only 29 that year. In 1933, 56 students received the scholarships.

ACCORDING to reports in the daily press, Professor Johannes Leisegang, of the University of Jena, was sentenced on November 30 by the Emergency Court at Weimar to six months' imprisonment, because he called Chancellor Adolf Hitler's oration at the funeral of von Hindenburg an "election speech." The state's attorney asked for eighteen months' imprisonment on the ground that Dr. Leisegang is one of those who are responsible for training German youth. He was convicted for "wilful circulation of untrue assertions of a factual nature" and not for disrespect to the chancellor. He was taken into custody and began to serve his sentence immediately.

ON November 22 *The New York Times* received the following wireless dispatch from Berlin: "Foreign study for German students has been made virtually impossible, except in Switzerland or under one of the rare exchange student arrangements through a ruling by the currency exchange control office. The ruling declares that applications for exchange to make possible study abroad, except as they apply to Switzerland, are not to be granted. Switzerland has been made an exception because of the special character of the Reichsbank's exchange arrangement with the Berne government, which is calculated to present as little interference with the free flow of goods and services as possible. The Third Reich's academic relations with foreign countries are becoming steadily less intimate as German universities take on an increasingly Nazi character. The number of foreigners registered for degrees in German universities decreased in two years from 4,403 to 2,962 last winter."

A SPECIAL cable to *The New York Times* from Rio de Janeiro reports that a strike committee named on December 2 by students of Sao Paulo University distributed among students of secondary schools in the city a manifesto calling on all to walk out. Police barriers erected around the Polytechnical School were torn down during the night. Molten lead was poured over the locks on doors so that policemen with axes had to smash the doors to admit faculty members. The dispute between students and educational authorities is over a bill, now under consideration in Congress, that would abolish final examinations and base promotion on grades attained in the regular term's work. Prominent teachers declare the measure encourages "national mediocrity."

A CAMPAIGN against illiteracy in Portugal has been undertaken by the Government. About seventy-five per cent. of the people are reported by the *Christian Science Monitor* to be still unable to read or write. Immediate steps are to be taken to build 20,000 schools for primary instruction all over the country. They are to be in working order within two years' time. This decision has resulted from a tour of the provinces by the Ministers of Instruction and Public Works. At all the higher schools a special chair is to be established for colonial instruction, and propaganda films exhibited, thus continuing the work done by the Portuguese Colonial Exhibition at Oporto, which has just closed. Excellent results are said to have been obtained by the Government's action in ordering enforced instruction to recruits and soldiers. Now in every barracks in Portugal two hours are scheduled in the daily routine for instructing the soldiers and the recruits for obligatory service how to read and write. A stimulating reward to learn quickly is given by shortening the term of military service and by the promotion of soldiers to the rank of corporal.

ENGLISH is to be the principal foreign language in Latvian schools—replacing German and Russian—according to a decree recently published by the Latvian Minister of Education, and reported by *The Christian Science Monitor*. Henceforth, in all Latvian towns children will begin to learn English at the age of nine years, while children in the country will start at twelve years. Only the minority schools will keep their own language. The government's measure is described as a gesture to meet England's friendly attitude toward the Baltic States. It is also ascribed to a desire to build a language barrier against any undue German or Russian cultural influence. Until now English has been little used in Latvia, where, besides Lettish, mostly Russian and German is spoken.

ACCORDING to the *Journal* of the American Medical Association, the department of physical education of Tokyo has reported a recent investigation of the weak boys and girls in 541 primary schools containing 694,147 children in which methods differing from any previous investigation were used. The department asked the teachers to report the number of boys and girls whom they thought to be too weak, physically or mentally, to be among the normal boys or girls. Formerly this was usually done by means of physical or mental examination by specialists. The following seven items were reported on by the teachers: (1) inferior mental power; (2) feeblemindedness; (3) reduced hearing; (4) weak sight; (5) stammering; (6) sickliness; (7) deformity. A comparatively small number was so reported. The criteria were whether weak boys or girls should be specially educated. The numbers were as follows: (1) 7,783, (2) 7,206, (3) 1,023, (4) 2,020, (5) 2,880, (6) 3,841, (7) 1,865. Special classes for such children are as yet insufficient but the authorities are making a great effort to establish special schools.

A WIRELESS dispatch to *The New York Times* on November 14 reads: "The independence of the historic student corps in German universities and of individual students is threatened again by a reorganization order issued for the benefit of the much organized students by Minister of Culture Bernhard Rust. Andreas Feickert, chief of the German Student League, has been directed by the Minister to turn over Nazi "point of view" instruction to the much more radical Nazi Student League, which is controlled by student leaders made famous by the book-burnings last year. The solution of the problem of the comradeship houses, which threatened to destroy the old German fraternity system, has also been turned over to the small and revolutionary Nazi Student League, enemy of fraternity tradition and the pre-war German conception of the university as essentially an institution affording an opportunity for individual research work. The original Nazi program for universities, before it was softened by Herr Feickert, would have forced every student to spend his first two years in a comradeship house in which he would be under semi-military discipline and would have a thorough Brown Shirt training. It is believed recent decrees may be the first step toward reinstating the original program."

LEADERS in education from many parts of Pennsylvania and other states attended at Hershey on November 15 the dedication of the new buildings of the Hershey Industrial High School, an institution for educating and training orphan boys for positions in business, commerce or trade for which they are best suited. The group of buildings includes a junior-senior high school and trade shops having a capacity for 1,500 students. A large auditorium, gymnasium and swimming pool have been provided. The institution was founded by M. S. Hershey in 1909 and the new buildings are a gift from the founder. The trade school opened on September 5, with an enrolment of 86 boys. Present plans call for a three and one half year trade course making eligible boys of fourteen years or older who have completed successfully the first half of the ninth grade.

# DISCUSSION

## THE BIRTH OF A HOBBY

I HAVE had many hobbies in my lifetime; as a boy I collected butterflies, stamps, old coins, fossils and innumerable other things valuable and of lesser value. In my twenties I followed musical hobbies, piano, violin, clarinette, even the accordion. Not of those short-lived enthusiasms, however, do I wish to speak to-night. With your permission I shall take you into my holiest of holies and make known to you the hobby which during the past five years has become one of the dominating influences in my life, the inspiration of which will, I believe, keep me active and enthusiastic for many years to come.

The seed of this hobby was planted nearly thirty-five years ago as I stood gazing at the gray, ivy-covered walls of the ancient University of St. Andrews in Scotland, wishing, as intensely as only an eighteen-year-old boy can wish, that I might devote my life to study. I knew this desire could never be fulfilled. Even the optimism of youth could not reconcile the long, expensive preparation necessary for an educational career with the knowledge of a mother and several young sisters dependent upon me for support. Mine must be a better paying business.

I cherished the dream, however, as a fetish, throughout my business career, which has covered two continents. In the early part of my life I clung to it desperately as to a forlorn hope. As the years went on and the struggle for success in business became more intense, making ever-increasing demands upon my time and energy, my ardor gradually gave place to a settled and somewhat sad conviction that my seed would never germinate. It was a holy thing, however, that dormant, inert, undeveloped seed, that carried in it apparently only the lost hopes and ideals of an enthusiastic boy.

About five years ago I felt a strange stirring within me. Was there a possibility? Could I dare to hope that after all these years my dream might become a reality? Back of this diffident, yet hopeful agitation was a chance remark of the dean of a great university college which devotes itself to the enrichment of living among men in my situation. "Why don't you go on," he asked, "and work for your bachelor's degree?" I scorned the idea. A middle-aged business man, nearly thirty-five years out of school, to become a student in a university! The very thought was preposterous. In his calm, kindly way the dean replied: "There's nothing so very ridiculous about that I assure you. Only last year we graduated a business man of seventy-five."

Immediately I became interested, and listened eagerly as he mapped out a program which seemed both reasonable and possible. In spite of my willingness to be convinced my common-sense would not allow me to overlook the nearly insurmountable obstacles. Besides business responsibilities, I had duties to my wife and daughter, and social obligations in my community. I played golf, and I was a member of a debating club. Repeatedly I told myself it could not be done, yet the dream of my youth stood steadily before me pleading for fulfilment. My business friends told me I was crazy. My wife, sympathetic as she is, looked doubtful at the thought of thirty-six courses for one of my limited leisure.

Yet the idea fascinated me, and unconsciously I began to rationalize concerning it. I could not, of course, at this late date, expect a scholarly career, nor did I indeed wish it. Was there a chance, however, that my dream might come to fruition as a hobby? Other men had hobbies, expensive hobbies some of them. Many of my friends spent more time and money at golf than I would need to devote to study. So I reasoned.

Arnold Bennett's "How to Live on 24 Hours a Day" helped me to realize the possibilities of conserving time. In true business fashion I made a list of the activities of my leisure time, hoping by elimination to gain time for study. Forty-five minutes twice a day in the suburban train, in the past devoted to the morning and evening newspapers, could be salvaged for more serious reading. Twenty-five minutes three times a week devoted to systematic exercises at the Y. M. C. A. would keep me in better condition than my evenings at golf. My debating club failed to yield profitable dividends and could be given up. I could without inconveniencing any one study at least one hour most evenings and perhaps several hours on Sunday. Yes, I decided, it could be done.

I laid my plans before my wife. Like most modern women she has many interests outside of the home, and she knows the fascination of hobbies. While rather fearing the effect of such an indoor activity upon my health, in addition to the confinement of business, she encouragingly told me to go ahead. The days immediately succeeding this momentous decision were busy and exciting. I wrote to Scotland for my high-school record of long ago, and proceeded to adjust my life to the new conditions.

I was as enthusiastic as a boy—the dream of long ago was at last to be realized. With a thrill I registered for my first course at a University-College, for on that day my seed burst its covering, my hobby was born.

JOHN A. LOW

GLEN ELLYN, ILLINOIS

## SCIENTIFIC BOOKS IN THE EARLY WEST

MOST people are inclined to think of the Mississippi Valley in the second half of the eighteenth century as completely backwoods and the few people there as dwelling in a cultural dark age. Saint Louis was then a village of fewer than a thousand people, and lay a thousand miles or more away from any place of greater size or importance, but it was no more isolated intellectually than it was commercially. A number of private libraries contained, among other things, the soundest works of the time on commerce, finance, history, law, agriculture. One finds that these libraries had even a certain amount of scientific literature.

Of the scientific works, the most important class is, reasonably enough, the medical. Auguste Condé, an inventory of whose estate was made the twenty-eighth of June, 1778, left seventy-two volumes of "chirurgie et autres." Claude Mercier, another physician of the village (his estate was inventoried 23 May, 1787), left twenty-eight books concerning surgery and medicine. Unfortunately, I have not been able to find detailed lists of these libraries. Pierre Joseph Didier, curé of the parish at the end of the century, left behind him a Dictionary of Medicine in six volumes, a treatise of surgery by the famous Ambrose Paré and a two-volume work on medicinal chemistry. In an inventory made in 1778 of the estate of Pierre LaClède we discover that the founder of the town possessed one volume entitled "Maitre de Chirurgie," one "Recoeuil de Recettes de Chirurgie," a third which was an "abridgment of anatomy," and two volumes by Simon André Tissot, who, if not the most famous doctor of his day, was certainly the most popular medical writer. One of the Tissot volumes was his most popular and best-known work: "Avis au peuple sur la santé." Auguste Chouteau apparently began to collect his library in the 1770's. Among his books we find Barthesi's "Maladie Gouteuse" (two volumes), Buchan's "Médecines domestiques" (five volumes), Leroy's "Médecine curative" (five volumes), a one-volume work on yellow fever and one or two other medical works.

Of scientific works other than those concerned with medicine we find some not insignificant. LaClède had a five-volume work on experimental physics, a two-volume essay on electricity, Belidor's "Architecture hydraulique," an eight-volume work on natural history and the two-volume Dictionary of the Arts and Sciences of the French Academy. Père Didier had a seven-volume work on chemistry. Auguste Chouteau had a two-volume study of electricity, Guyot's "Amusements Magnetique" (one volume), "Leçons de phisique experimentale" (five volumes), "Physical and Chimical Essays" (one volume), and thirty-three volumes on natural history, including Saint-Pierre's "Études de la nature," Deville's "Histoire des plantes" and Buffon's "Histoire naturelle." He had also the "Dictionnaire des Sciences" in thirty-five volumes.

This sketch gives an idea of the works of scientific nature which were to be found in Saint Louis in its first forty years. The list is by no means complete, for we do not have inventories of all estates in Saint Louis in this period. Furthermore, when we do have such inventories they are not always made in detail. I have mentioned that the Condé and Mercier libraries are not detailed. In addition to these I may say that Laurent Trudeau in 1772 left twenty-three books, Captain Fernando de Leyba, Commandant, left seventy-four in 1780, Louis Perrault left (in 1783) among others twelve books of "different treatises," Louis Dubreuil (1796) left ninety-seven volumes, Père Didier (1799) left seventy-six "other books." It is quite possible—and even probable—that among these unknown volumes were other works of a scientific nature. It is clear, then, that Saint Louis at that time was in possession of some scientific literature.

In Ste. Genevieve, some sixty miles below Saint Louis, a village of much the same size and existing under like conditions, we find more private libraries containing books of much the same order. The most interesting is that of Pierre Peyroux, Commandant of Ste. Genevieve, inventoried in January, 1795. Nearly one third of his 160 volumes are concerned in some sense with science. He had, for instance, a "Dictionnaire de Phisique" (four volumes), the "Dictionnaire des arts et metiers" (five volumes), "L'art veterinaire" (one volume), "Secrets des arts et metiers" (two volumes), and a variety of others. But the largest portion of these works are the books of an engineer. These vary from such assorted reading as "L'art de la verrerie" ("glass-making"; one volume), "L'art de foudre (?) de fer" (iron-working; one volume), "Instruction de Pilotes" (one volume) and "Voyages metallurgiques" (three volumes), to a treatise on carpentry and another on surveying (the first in two volumes, the second in one). He had also Belidor's "Science des Ingenieurs" (two volumes), two or three works on shipbuilding, and no less than five titles on architecture (eight volumes).

The French of the Illinois country were by no means—even before the Americans swarmed over the Mississippi Valley—without sound reading matter, far as they were from the cultural centers of the world.

JOHN FRANCIS MCDERMOTT
WASHINGTON UNIVERSITY,
SAINT LOUIS

## OUR PRESIDENTS

THE fourth best of the ten most recent presidents of the United States—that is where students of political science at Stanford University rate Franklin D. Roosevelt.

The students' ratings list the presidents in order of effectiveness as follows: Woodrow Wilson, Theodore Roosevelt, Grover Cleveland, Franklin D. Roosevelt, Herbert Hoover, William McKinley, Calvin Coolidge, Benjamin Harrison, William Howard Taft and Warren G. Harding.

The students' verdict, given at the end of a quarter term of United States history study covering the period 1890–1934, shows a slight change from their opinions of the same presidents before study of their administrations. At the beginning they rated the presidents in this order: Theodore Roosevelt, Wilson, Cleveland, F. D. Roosevelt, Hoover, Coolidge, McKinley, Taft, Harrison and Harding.

As the names of the presidents were presented to the students in paired comparison form it was possible to determine just how much more efficient any president was considered over any other. On the first test Theodore Roosevelt, rated the best, was considered 2.3 times more efficient than Harding, judged the least efficient. On the retest, Harding was judged still less efficient, while Wilson, judged the most efficient, was considered 3 times more effective than Harding. T. Roosevelt was now considered only 1.3 times more efficient than Harding.

Presidents rated as possessing only average presidential ability were McKinley and Coolidge. Hoover, F. D. Roosevelt, Cleveland, T. Roosevelt and Wilson were all considered to possess more than average presidential ability, and Harrison, Taft and Harding were judged to possess less than average presidential ability.

At the end of the quarter of study Franklin D. Roosevelt was rated more than twice as efficient as Harding, while at the beginning of the quarter he was only rated 1.7 times more efficient.

One pronounced effect of the study of the administrations of these presidents was to lengthen the concept of the range of abilities of the presidents as judged by the students.

In conjunction with this study the students' ratings were also secured on the first ten presidents. They were listed in order of effectiveness after a quarter of study as follows: Washington, Jefferson, Jackson, Monroe, John Adams, Madison, J. Q. Adams, W. H. Harrison, Van Buren and John Tyler. In this list Washington was rated just twice as efficient as Tyler. Jackson, Monroe, John Adams, Madison and J. Q. Adams were considered to possess average presidential ability, Washington and Jefferson were considered to possess more than average presidential ability, and W. H. Harrison, Van Buren and Tyler were judged to possess considerably less than average ability as presidents.

LEONARD W. FERGUSON

STANFORD UNIVERSITY

# SPECIAL CORRESPONDENCE

## TURKISH SCHOOLS, SEEN THROUGH THE EYES OF AN ENGLISH VISITOR

THE following is a brief account of a visit which I was enabled, by the great kindness of the Turkish Ministry of Education, to pay to Turkish schools last Christmas. It is based on a stay of three days in Ankara, a week in Constantinople, two days in Scutari and one in the country. This was all the time that my vacation allowed me to spend in Turkey. If I had not met with kindness and help at every turn, I might have learned nothing at all in so short a stay; but the converse does not follow—if my observations make any contribution towards a coherent picture of an educational system, they are yet no measure of the vast kindness of the Turkish officials and teachers.

Turkey has a great opportunity educationally, and a visitor can not fail to be impressed by the extent to which she is aware of the opportunity and by the enthusiasm and devotion of the teachers who are trying to seize it. They are able, through circumstances which I hope to mention, to make almost a fresh start, to tend as it were an educational system as a gardener tends a plant which he has grown himself from seed. What is remarkable is the selfless eagerness with which they are giving themselves to the work.

Two instances must suffice to demonstrate this. The first is their acceptance of the surprisingly rapid change of leaders. I met more than one man who said, "When I was on the staff of the Gazi Institute. . . ." Now the Gazi Institute is the "école normale supérieure" of Turkey; these men had given their best to it and had been removed to more routine positions. This is made more acceptable because there are no large salaries in Turkey, where important officials often live in a few rooms of a school building and head teachers receive only a small bonus in addition to their salaries as teachers; this softens the feeling of disgrace when a man is removed from an influential position. People in responsible places are often removed as soon as they have made their distinctive contribution. Detractors from the system would say that they are displaced merely because they or others more important than them who have patronized them have fallen from favor; but even this can be explained on the ground that throughout Turkish political life men with ideas are encouraged and given scope to put their ideas into practise. This means that others are displaced in favor of the new man and those who have his confidence; and he must expect to be removed himself when he has had his chance. But the vitality of the system is so great that these changes are not as disturbing as they would be in our more settled organizations. A living organism can stand shocks—it does not need bolstering up. Nor are the changes as much resented by the people affected as we should expect; perhaps the fact that there is always a post for him to go to helps to distinguish the displaced Turk from a worker in almost any other civilized country who loses his job!

The other instance is the teachers' interest in the theory of teaching, in which they attend courses of lectures. An inspector of primary schools told me that he is now in the second year of a "three-year plan" of lectures to the teachers in his area. He has discussed the teaching of writing and is now beginning on arithmetic; but he has given most of the time to "project-work," of which I saw examples in every primary school I visited and in the work of the Constantinople Normal School for Girls. (It is even said that teachers fresh from training know more about project-teaching than they know about subject-teaching.) He has gone into details of the method, advocating, for example, the use of "folders" for written work instead of exercise books. Attendance at these lectures has been compulsory, but the inspector has also given courses which have been voluntarily attended; for instance, on contact with parents, how to conduct parents' meetings, and so on; I also met members of another small class of teachers whom he is taking in elementary German, so that they may be able to read works on advanced educational thought; they were delighted to be able to get into touch with me through a few German sentences.

Many things which we consider very modern are being generally practised in Turkey primary schools. Free discipline is the rule. There are no rewards and no punishments, except reprimands and exclusion. "Committees of honor"—pupils' disciplinary committees—though not common are not unknown in secondary schools, and some primary schools have pupils' conferences of the whole school, which must be very like shareholders' meetings or the town moots of some American schools. Children scramble in and out of classrooms at the beginning and end of lessons and rush noisily about the corridors during the intervals. My entry, with the head master, into a classroom was regarded with frank interest, but it rarely for long repressed the exuberance with which the children were responding to the lesson—I had almost written "were 'conducting' it"!

I think the reason for the universal acceptance of advanced ideas is that the modern teacher in Turkey has had no established system to contend against. Practically speaking, any education there was under the Sultans was bad, and young teachers are encouraged by the government to think that it was. It was the acquisition of largely useless knowledge under compulsion; and the present generation of teachers, younger on the average than English teachers, and working under inspectors, trained for the most part in America or Vienna, have a boundless belief in the educational possibilities of subject-matter which is suitable and agreeable to the children. Thus I was assured that fear of punishment never makes a child work harder; and even when I pretended jokingly to support corporal punishment, I never got any one to agree with me!

It is not only in matters like discipline and the school-store (*co-operatif*) that there is "student-government" but in the class-work of the children. In one school I saw a geography lesson with the oldest class, at the end of which the children noisily decided, with the teacher's help, how they should spend the next lesson—that is, the period immediately following, *not* the "next geography lesson." Work in another subject, on a topic related to the geography lesson, was chosen. This kind of teaching is made more possible because there is no formal division of the work into subjects for the first two school-years—*Gesamtunterricht*—and because the body of matter to be learned is much more amorphous than, say, the English curriculum, which is still influenced by the nineteenth-century practise of "payment by results" in sharply defined subjects.

From the primary schools of Constantinople and Scutari I have brought back an impression of "child-centered schools," directed by keen and open-minded teachers. The tangible results they are getting are good, the intangible are very good. In the contest with nation-wide illiteracy the less-gifted children are perhaps likely to be too much overlooked; sterner methods would perhaps produce better results from such children; but one hopes that by the time the educators become conscious of them, there will be time and money for intelligence-testing and the provision of special schools for defective children and special classes for very backward children. At present the idea of grading by ability was thought mistaken by those to whom I mentioned it, even where there are two parallel classes in the same age-group in a school. I think the teachers I met are likely to combat the problem of backward children not with harsher discipline but with *Gesamtunterricht,* "projects" and friendly personal contact with the child. Under rules introduced two or three years ago, a child has the same teacher throughout his life in the primary school; and he is known personally to the head teacher, for primary schools are small—200 to 500 pupils.

I visited also a number of country schools, where the same general characteristics were to be found as in the city schools. Here, as in the town, the teachers felt that about a quarter of the time of the upper classes could profitably be given to project-work, but of course projects would be connected with gardening, carpentry and so forth, sides which were weak in town schools, through lack of equipment, though treated thoroughly in the training colleges.

One village, inhabited by Turks "exchanged" from Macedonia under the Peace Treaty, deserves more detailed description. I visited it in the company of as many inspectors as could conveniently be packed into one small taxi-cab. Part of the way lay along the magnificent Constantinople-Adrianople road, along whose 200 miles there is a 'bus service joining the two cities; but the rest was along roads which could better be said to separate than to connect the villages. The peasants whom we passed in the fields were working with every sort of plough, from the latest iron contrivance imported from the West, to the wooden ploughs used probably in these fields when the Turks were still Central-Asiatic nomads. Turkey has a long way to go!

We were received by the policeman, the priest came down from the mosque to shake hands with us, the inhabitants raised their hats and the children, who were at play, sang the national anthem for us.

There were three teachers and ninety children in the school. The children seemed, after the teachers, by far the most civilized thing in the village; the girls were dressed in neat smocks with white collars, and one of the boys signed his name very well in an autograph book which I keep for children's names. They were eager that I should stop and see them at their afternoon lessons; my ignorance of the language prevented me from knowing whether they were going so far as to suggest that afternoon school should be begun earlier for my benefit!

The village was built up the side of a low hill. The mosque, a former Christian church with a minaret added, was at the top; below it a brand-new school building with three classrooms, below that again a modern dispensary, with three beds for serious cases, and an old building converted into a minute village-hall. Beneath these again were the houses.

There are still many villages without schools. The money for buildings has to be raised locally; in some places, I was told, the peasants have been unable to produce money but have instead given their labor and knocked up a school building themselves. Central schools, at which the children can live, bringing their food for a week, are projected, but in sparsely populated areas like parts of Thrace, villages are too remote from one another even for this. There is everywhere a great shortage of teachers, and so, although there is some local bias in training colleges in small towns (*e.g.*, in the Adana district, where cotton-growing is studied), a teacher who wants to teach in a city school is sure to be able to get a position in such a school. Buried in the country, he would probably meet no one with any pretensions to intellectuality, and he would be unable to get to a town except at rare intervals; some one on whom he could try the remains of his French might not visit the place once in five years.

On the other hand, the country teacher can be a great power in the village if he can persuade the people to accept him. The priest, the other educated person in the village, is unfitted by training and often by age for any sort of leadership under modern conditions. Teachers are *ex-officio* members of the "village councils" which the government is trying to set up in every village and hamlet. They are often local librarians, getting books through the post from the nearest central town.

The country teacher will perhaps find the people suspicious at first. One village teacher told me he had overcome this suspicion by making beehives, and demonstrating that hives which he made, and could teach others to make, cost only one seventh of the commercial price. Better still, his hives had an (unnecessary) glass panel through which the gratified owners could watch the bees crawling about at work!

The country schools are one of Turkey's greatest educational problems. With the present generous expenditure on education—one hundred new schools have been built in Constantinople in the last ten years, and many old buildings, like the Ottoman Debt building, have been converted into schools—the towns will within a measurable time be adequately equipped with buildings; and there will in time be a satisfactory supply of teachers. But the rural districts offer a much less simple challenge—a challenge all the more stirring because it is in the countryside that the purest-bred Turks are found; and it is the pure Turk, rather than the cosmopolitan citizen of Constantinople, who is to be the backbone of the new state.

On the secondary level, Turkish schools are like secondary schools everywhere—the interests of the subject-matter tend to preponderate over the interests of the pupils. Higher education is free and open to all, but the schools are not numerous enough to make small classes usual. Teaching methods are naturally different from the methods of the primary school, but the differences seem exaggerated. A child who has been taught on collaborative lines with forty or fifty others in the primary school may find himself in a secondary school in company with seventy or even eighty others in a small room learning a foreign language by taking his turn at working on the blackboard under the teacher's eye. If there are even fifty children in a class, and each child works for five minutes at the blackboard, it will be seen that a child is lucky if he is noticed once a week by the subject-teacher. I was present at a number of lessons in secondary schools and rarely saw any child in the back half of the classroom take more than a passive part in the teaching.

Much of this passivity is unavoidable. The opportunity for movement is very restricted with large classes, and written work must be infrequent, because there is a limit to the amount of marking which any teacher can do. But one can not depict the average Turkish secondary school teacher as a man or woman with the primary school teacher's attitude towards teaching, struggling against adverse circumstances. The cleavage between the two schools is not of this order. The child who goes from the primary school to the secondary passes from a system inspired largely by American and German ideas to one inspired by French. Teaching-method is at a discount in secondary schools. An evening course in secondary school-teaching method, which it is possible for undergraduates to take, is now accepting no more entrants; instead, a department of pedagogy has been started at the university within the faculty of psychology; one of the professors told me, "We study children, not teaching ('pedalogy, not pedagogy'): 'method' is for primary schools—in the lycée, teaching is naturally didactic."

It seems a mistake deliberately to make this distinction, while admitting children indiscriminately into the higher schools. Returning through Belgrade, I found that Yugoslavia is moving in exactly the opposite direction, by starting a college for secondary school teachers.

Turkey has some fine new secondary school buildings, but here the trade schools and higher technical institutes excel the secondary schools. Some of the higher technical and professional schools and institutes of Ankara are among the finest and best-equipped buildings in Turkey, and the instruction given in them is worthy of the buildings.

Both in the higher technical schools and in the university at Constantinople one finds many foreign teachers. In the summer of 1933, in one of the complete upheavals which I have said are not uncommon, every member of the university staff was dismissed. This made an opening for a number of German professors, who had been removed by the new régime in Germany or had left because of it. German professors, and a few French, were engaged for periods of five years. The instruction of their students, one of them told me, is only a secondary consideration in their engagement—and it will indeed be a difficult task, for they have to lecture through interpreters to students who have very few text-books. Their primary task is to build a body of knowledge, in books, in their subject, and to train their Turkish assistant professors to succeed them. The foreign professors are as a body incomparably more distinguished than their predecessors; it remains to be seen what they can make of their material. Two of them told me that they were satisfied with their students; and many, perhaps most, of the assistant professors will be men who have already studied in the West.

A word should be said of the numerous foreign schools, both primary and secondary. They were founded, mostly in or near Constantinople, by national or racial minorities for their own children. A number of Turkish children attended them, for they often gave as good an education as was available in pre-war Turkey.

They will eventually be an anomaly in the complete national organization, but their suppression now would leave a gap which the Turks are still far from being able to fill. Where the government does not suspect that the private school is doing religious propaganda among its pupils, the official attitude is not unfriendly, but the schools are handicapped by a recent regulation compelling them to give up five hours a week for the study of Turkish and five hours for history and geography, to be taught in Turkish. Ten weekly periods are thus in the hands of a visiting Turkish teacher, who is not responsible to the head of the school. This arrangement handicaps, for example, the English high schools if they want to prepare children for examinations for English certificates, and discourages students whom the American Robert College would attract, but who have no interest in Turkey.[1]

The whole question is a legacy from a very different past and it would be hard to make any prophecy of its eventual disposal.

If I have given the impression already that Turkish educators start, as it were, with a clean sheet, with few old traditions and standards to encumber them, I have yet no more than begun the tale. Turkish statesmen and Turkish educators begin, as it were, with a new people. For six hundred years the simple Turks have been under the rule of the Ottoman Turks. According to Mme. Halidé Edib's account, the true Turk was almost everything that the Ottoman Turk was not—homely, unaggressive, honest and half-pagan. His rulers were warlike and ostentatious and despised him, calling themselves "Ottomans" and using the word "Turk" as a term of contempt. The enlightened movements of the last century came from the Ottomans; it was only when the Sultan and his government were discredited after the war that Mustapha Kemal found in the Anatolian Turk the true national. By imposing a democratic form of government on the country, and by relegating Constantinople to the status of a provincial seaport, Mustapha Kemal has dissipated the Ottoman dominance and is making a state of which the true Turk is the typical citizen. He is clay ready to be moulded by the educator.

It is sometimes argued that it is absurd to educate a people that has once been great in any other way than so as to lead it to express itself again in the fashion in which it once lived so fully. That is almost the same as to say that the son of a general will never be a full man unless there is a war. But even if it were true, it would not apply to Turkey, for the spirit we think of as Turkish, the spirit which animated the Turkish army before Vienna, was not Turkish but, according to Mme. Halidé Edib, Ottoman and Macedonian. The real Turk is unknown to the West, except as the private soldier of the war.

This new people is illiterate, and there is therefore in the hands of the educators the power to teach it almost anything through the medium of the new accomplishment—reading. More than that, as the people are learning to read only the Latin alphabet, the government need not proscribe books published before the revolution, for the masses can not read them, and even if they could read the characters, they could not understand the inflected Persian and Arabic words with which the former written language abounded, and which are being purged out of the new written language—the uninflected language of ordinary speech.

From what little I could see, the government was not abusing in the schools the power which these circumstances give it. The clearest proof of this is the fact that so much stress is laid on the development of individuality. How far the present Turkish government is democratic is a matter for students of politics; but one can not shut one's eyes to the evidence on every side that children are being prepared for democracy as surely as they are in America or were in Social-Democratic Germany. The Gazi Mustapha Kemal is revered, but there is no mention of the "leader-principle." The nation is perhaps being treated as a child, but it is being prepared for self-reliant manhood.

A last experience may illustrate this. I went one evening to an adult class in reading, writ-

[1] The history book had not been translated when I was in Turkey, but I understand that it begins with an introduction on the lines of Mr. Wells's "Outline of History," skims rapidly over general history and then treats in detail the war of liberation and the history of the republic.

ing and arithmetic. In the early days these classes were very numerous, and every one under forty-five who could not read was supposed to attend them. As a result of these classes, and of the work of the schools, 22 per cent. of the population can now read and write, where only 5 per cent. could do so ten years ago.

The course takes three hours a week for four months, and a test is given at the end; a higher certificate is awarded to those who take a further four months' course in citizenship, the history of the revolution and hygiene. At the school I visited, these courses were taken concurrently—the elementary one from seven to eight o'clock, the advanced from eight to nine.

The students were all men but one—a servant-girl sent by her employers; they were mostly between thirty and forty years old, and only one had been to school as a child. They were workers on the roads or in a neighboring factory. They did not seem to mind sitting at desks made for children, and all were remarkably keen on the work. The top division were being helped by a discussion of the meaning of difficult words, and one man, who had been attending for four months, was a very passable reader. In the bottom division was a youth who had only begun that night, and who seemed more interested in the servant-girl than in the blackboard!

In the more advanced course, the teacher gave in this particular lesson a brief outline of the history of Turkey in the years immediately before the revolution, touching on the ineffectiveness of the old régime and the immoral life of the Sultan. He then spoke of the war of liberation, illustrating his lesson with a map made by the children in the day-school, which showed Turkey as divided by the Treaty of Sèvres, and as united and unified by the Treaty of Lausanne.

At the end of the lesson, Hifzirrahman Rasit Bey, the assistant director of education for Constantinople, who had accompanied me, pointed out to the class how different was the new dynamic spirit of freedom and hope from the old one of suppression and fatalism: as illustrated particularly by these classes in reading and writing, which the old government would never have started, preferring that ordinary people be kept in uncritical subjection. The new government had given them something to live for and to look forward to.

I almost wished that some of the English were illiterate, so that we might have the excuse to bring them together for such stirring talks on public affairs and the meaning of citizenship!

I went to Turkey principally in order to see whether it was possible to reconcile nationalism and the mass-education of a backward people with the cult of individualism, of which one read in accounts of Turkish schools. It appears that a very fair balance is being held between individualism and indoctrination, and that the guiding principle is education of a hitherto submerged people on sound modern lines. The Turkish leaders are not, on this interpretation, westernizing orientals. It may be that they are moving too fast, paying too little regard to such roots as are really Turkish. On the other hand, I would point out that both adults and children seem eager for the new things, and that, if a visitor can trust the evidence of his eyes, the children are at least as much at home in the new schools as our own western children would be.

BRIAN STANLEY
THE UNIVERSITY OF MANCHESTER

# QUOTATIONS

## CHILD GUIDANCE IN LONDON

IN the four and a half years of its existence the London Child Guidance Clinic has now dealt with nearly 1,900 cases. In the beginning its organization was largely experimental, but it has now evolved the lines upon which it intends to progress. It was designed from the outset to serve two functions—the treatment of children and the training of students—and early in 1933 it was divided into two separate departments for treatment and training. Each child is treated by a team consisting of a psychiatrist, a psychologist, and two social workers; the same psychiatrist handles each case throughout to ensure continuity of treatment, and the unit members deal directly with the doctor, teacher or parent referring the case. The course of training includes lectures, discussion groups and seminars held at the London School of Economics, and supervision of the practical work of the clinic. The report of the clinic for the years 1932 and 1933 states that students who complete this course are being widely accepted for responsible posts where a trained social worker is required, for it is being realized that some such training is necessary to equip workers in psychiatric and child guidance clinics and out-patient departments of hospitals. The clinic also gives candidates for the academic diploma in psychology of the University of London their practical work in child guidance, and supervises and instructs students attending the course in child development at the Institute of Education, who come to the clinic for observation of play groups and for instruction in remedial teaching. The division into two sections has increased the efficiency of both aspects of the work. Members of the clinic have travelled all over England delivering lectures on child guidance, with the result that knowledge and acceptance of the subject have widely increased. The number of children seen at the clinic has steadily grown, and in 1932 an extra psychiatrist and a social worker were appointed. The children have come from all over the British Isles, but the practical difficulties in the way of lodgings near the clinic for regular attendance are great, and satisfactory treatment will be possible for all only when clinics are available throughout the country. During the two years under review the clinic dealt with 973 cases. Children tend to be referred at an increasingly early age—a satisfactory development. Many are sent from the schools and school care committees of the London County Council, and by magistrates and probation officers. A considerable number of cases attended only for examination, and a large number were given some special type of service, including individual psychotherapy, remedial teaching or education in play groups. The clinic claims to have secured adjustment in the mentality of about half the children it has treated. About a quarter are discharged partially adjusted, and about one fifth can not be improved. These results seem fully to justify the expenditure of time, energy and ingenuity. The progress of child guidance work in this country has been slower than in some others. This is not altogether a bad thing in an enterprise which is so novel and which is capable of such extremes of theory and experimentation. There is a refreshing absence in the report of the effervescence which is apt abroad to discourage sympathizers with the movement. The clinic shows great promise of success in this important necessity of modern civilization. This particular method of tackling the problems of modern childhood came to us from the other side of the Atlantic, under the auspices of the Commonwealth Fund. The time has now come when that fund may legitimately say, and does in fact say, that the clinic has either proved its worth or its worthlessness, and that the people of this country must either support it or close it down.—*The British Medical Journal.*

## EDUCATIONAL LEADERS AMONG THE NEGROES

The past school year has witnessed the passing of a number of conspicuous leaders among Negro educators whose names must endure as shining lights in the progress of the race. Among them Nathan B. Young, of Florida A. and M. College, and other institutions including Tuskegee, for years the dean of Florida's teachers, Lucy Laney, of Haynes Institute, Augusta, the pioneer in secondary education in Georgia, J. W. E. Bowen, of Gammon Theological Seminary, for years the foremost real scholar among his people, and more recently S. G. Atkins, of Winston-Salem Teachers College, the Christian sage of North Carolina, and J. W. Rowan, of Alcorn College, the patient persistent pioneer of Mississippi, are representatives of the first fruits of education in the Negro race, which were at once its justification and the means of its expansion and perpetuation.

They stand for the same thing in the second generation of Negro progress after Emancipation as the names of Armstrong, Cravath, Ware, Rendall, and Silsby did in the first. They were the black children of the education movement begun by white leaders immediately after the Civil War, and as inheritors of its best traditions passed them on faithfully to the next generation of their people with the stamp of their own personalities upon them.

Each was a character to adorn any race, made conspicuous by the substantial service they rendered over a long period of years and by the ripened fruit of their characters which grew richer with the passing of time. They were school men (and this includes Lucy Laney) all of them. Education was their native element and in it they achieved a distinction comparable to that of earlier names in the field of politics and their contemporaries in the church. They touched other fields, some of them, but education was their first love and their last and toward it they manifested a devotion as honorable to themselves as it was to the profession they served.

Where will we find their like again? Their only peers are their contemporaries who survive them. In them character came to its full flower. They were not the products of schools so much as they were of life, the combined result of their own struggles and the impress of their teachers. Their successors are distinguished more for their degrees than for their constructive abilities, for their attainments in formal scholarship than their achievements in public service, for erudition rather than original thinking. Both have their value to the race, but the latter are more difficult to find and more essential to progress, and their names longer remembered.—*The Tuskegee Messenger.*

# REPORTS

## WESTERN REGIONAL CONFERENCES OF THE JOINT COMMISSION ON THE EMERGENCY IN EDUCATION

A SERIES of regional conferences west of the Mississippi River has just been completed (October 27 to November 17) under the auspices of the Joint Commission on the Emergency in Education. These conferences were called by Chairman John K. Norton and were held under the immediate direction of Herbert S. Weet, a member of the commission. Conferences were held at Chicago, Minneapolis, Cheyenne, Ogden, Portland, Oakland, Los Angeles and Austin.

The conferences are part of the program being developed by the Joint Commission in response to its instructions from the National Education Association and the Department of Superintendence. Two general phases of this program are recognized: (a) To study and to attempt to meet the emergency problems, especially those of a financial nature, now confronting the public schools; (b) to develop and encourage long-term educational planning in order that the schools may meet more effectively the demands of the present day. The commission therefore attempted to secure a first-hand knowledge of the emergency problems confronting the various states and to discover what is already being done in the nature of educational planning. Since several states were represented at all but one of these conferences, those present could exchange experience concerning educational developments in various parts of the country. Certain publications summarizing educational trends in the nation as a whole were also distributed and discussed at each conference.

The conferences were attended by consultants of the Joint Commsision and other educational leaders invited by the local committees on arrangements. The consultants include the state superintendents of public instruction and the officers of state and national education associations, state and national parent-teacher associations and other representative groups. All states west of the Mississippi, with only two exceptions, were represented at one or more of the conferences. The eastern states were covered by a previous series of conferences.

The principal conclusions which emerge from this series of conferences concern: (a) the nature of the emergency in certain states, (b) federal participation in school finance, and (c) the development of educational planning.

*Emergency conditions.*—An educational emergency, due primarily to a lack of sufficient current income to finance education, even at a low level, exists in large areas of the tier of states ranging from Arkansas to North Dakota. Other areas, such as the Texas and Oklahoma panhandles and certain counties of Colorado and elsewhere, are also in this type of most serious emergency. The drought of last summer, culminating a series of years of subnormal rainfall, has left agriculture in these states at a low economic ebb. This condition, of course, indirectly affects all other occupations. Representatives from the most severely affected areas stated emphatically at the conferences that legislation within the states could not meet the emergency existing in the current school year. About 150 schools were already closed in Arkansas and no provision made for the education of some 50,000 children who would normally be enrolled. Some public high schools are charging tuition fees. Many teachers are working without pay or accepting warrants which have little or no cash value. At the time of the conference, no federal assistance had been extended this year to open schools where state and local funds were exhausted.

*Federal financing of education.*—Discussion of federal aid for education at these conferences involved several issues. The first has already been suggested: securing federal funds to keep certain schools open on a relief basis during the current year. It was stated that the Federal Emergency Relief Administration plans to allot funds to keep schools open in Arkansas and the Dakotas until January, 1935. It was the general opinion that this promised action was a step in the right direction but that the program was too limited in area, too short in duration and too late in going into effect.

A related issue arises from the federal emergency education program which allots work-relief funds for unemployed teachers in nursery schools and various types of adult education. Opinions regarding this federal program varied. Perhaps about seven out of every ten of the educational leaders expressing themselves on this point were inclined to criticize the emergency education program as at present administered. This attitude did not indicate disapproval of nursery schools or of adult education; many voiced enthusiastic support for these types of educational service. The fundamental objection seemed to arise from the fact that, under present conditions, such education is necessarily an incident to the relief program. Among the criticisms made occurred the following: That it is difficult to secure qualified teachers from relief rolls; that relief is not an appropriate channel for financing schools; that unqualified teachers have sometimes been employed to the detriment of the educational service; that relief wages undermine professional salary schedules; that the earmarking of federal assistance to the schools is wrong in principle; that federal money for education should be allotted to the states without designating a particular service to be supported; that state and local school officers can determine the services needed by their own communities better than a national relief bureau; and that the present program acts as a barrier against securing a type of federal assistance for education which is sound in principle.

On the other hand, some vigorously defended the existing program. They asserted that it has fostered desirable new types of educational service; that earmarking of funds and a reasonable amount of federal supervision are not objectionable; that the federal program of aid for college students has been especially successful; and that, as a practical matter, no other federal assistance can be secured, and therefore, what is available should be accepted and used as intelligently as possible.

However, even those who made no serious criticism of the present emergency programs, agreed, almost without exception, that these programs are temporary expedients and that every effort should be made to develop a federal policy of permanent and substantial support for the schools. Such a policy was adopted by resolution at practically all the conferences.

*Planning.*—Finally, almost every state has under way some form of long-range educational planning. Such planning varies from state to state in its scope, machinery and definiteness. In Michigan, for example, there is the State Educational Planning Commission, a lay group appointed by the State Superintendent of Public Instruction. In Iowa, certain educational planning is administered and financed as a subdivision of the State Planning Board, a subsidiary of the National Resources Board. In Wyoming, educational planning is developed by representatives of various educational interests at a seminar held by the state university each summer. The problems recognized by the different states are, on the whole, rather uniform. Practically all the states are concerned with the development of state equalization funds, the improvement of state revenue systems, the provision of larger school units. An urgent educational problem in many states is the unemployed high-school graduate who lacks opportunity for further education or other purposeful activity. Another problem mentioned at several of the conferences is the coordination of the various levels of education both with respect to curriculum and finance. State educational planning is also frequently concerned with devising a curriculum more definitely related to the needs of modern life.

*In summary,* and omitting many problems peculiar to a single state or to a few states, these regional conferences reveal:

1. That in certain areas serious educational emergencies now exist.
2. That the consultants, almost unanimously, favor permanent federal assistance in the support of education without federal control.
3. That most of the states have under way definite planning programs, not only for better school financing but also for the improvement of the school system itself.

# EDUCATIONAL RESEARCH AND STATISTICS

## THE YOUNG COLLEGE STUDENT[1]

WHILE numerous studies have shown the superiority of the young college student as contrasted with the typical or average student, this investigation represents a new approach to the problem in that it compares the young and superior student to college entrants who possess equal ability and differ only in the single variable, age. The young group included all students, 57 in number (32 men and 25 women) who entered the University of Buffalo at the age of sixteen or under during the years 1925 through 1928. Each member of the control group, selected from students whose average age was two years greater, was matched with one of the accelerated group on place in graduating class based on average school grade, size of high school, centile ranking in the American Council on Education Psychological Examination, average New York State Regents grade earned during high school and sex. The mean age at entrance for the accelerated group was 15.97 years, for the control 17.90. Both groups achieved a centile rating of 59 in the American Council on Education Psychological Examination and a Regents average of slightly over 81. Very similar amounts of high-school training could be claimed by both the young and older students, the former having earned an average of 16.6 units, the latter 16.9.

The college records of these 114 students were investigated to discover any difference in mortality, class performance and participation in extra-curricular activities. Particular attention was given to the freshman records, since the work at that level was deemed more amenable to comparison than that done later when more differentiation occurs and students leave to enter the several professional schools. When freshman grade averages for the two groups were computed, the difference in performance was found to be negligible, an average of 4.25 (C+) resulting for the accelerated and 4.23 for the control group. When specific courses were considered, no significant differences were evident, but there was some indication of a dissimilarity in consistency between the older and younger students, with a tendency toward greater variability within the more mature group.

While the later work of the students is conceded to be interesting, it was much more difficult to analyze and evaluate due to transference to other divisions of the institution or other institutions. A few more young students completed the arts course, but this was balanced by a greater tendency on the part of older students to transfer earlier to the professional schools. There was a marked degree of agreement between the proportions of the two groups receiving distinction at graduation. Contrary to earlier studies, practically equal percentages of the accelerated and control groups completed their college courses (earned a college degree). This may be at least partially explained by the similarity of ability characterizing both groups of students acting as subjects of this investigation.

The degree of social adjustment achieved was

[1] This study was made possible through a grant from the General Education Board. The author is indebted to Dr. Mazie Earle Wagner for suggesting the problem, which is treated at greater length in "Studies in Articulation of High School and College," *The University of Buffalo Studies*, Vol. IX, Chapter V.

measured by answers to questionnaires which included the question, "What extra-curricular activities interested you most? List high school and college activities separately." The questionnaire was submitted to the total number (114) students, and the resulting data were later checked with the activities listed for the respective students in the yearbook. Although the average number of activities found interesting by both groups was almost identical, it did appear that the young students tended to be extremists; that is, more were to be found at the lower end of the distribution (reporting either no or a single extra-curricular interest), or at the top (reporting at least five such diversions), while the older students more closely approximated the normal curve of distribution. Contrary to previous findings, the types of activity found interesting by the two groups were very similar, another indication of the previously mentioned similarity of ability. An analysis of the data relating to the high-school situation showed that college interests of a social nature seem to follow along the paths laid out during the secondary school period.

The questionnaire also contained material relating to the early educational history of the two groups. While it was found that the accelerated student entered school at an age approximately six months younger than the members of the control group, he increased this advantage through the device of "skipping" grades. About one third of the questionnaires returned by the young group showed that these students had completed high school in three years or less. Finally, the young student was asked to express his opinion concerning acceleration on the three educational levels, during the grades, high school and college; whether or not he was handicapped, and in what way, physically, intellectually or socially. The chief disadvantage noted was the social one, which appeared to be most frequent in high school and became slightly less important on the college level. Only an insignificant number of students reported any evidence of either physical or intellectual handicap at any time during their academic careers. The findings reported above concerning extra-curricular activities showed a marked degree of diversity of social interests and social participation on the part of many of the young students. The question is therefore raised: May not the feeling of handicap be either the result of an exaggeration of the importance of the social aspect of life or merely a reflection of popular opinion concerning the inadequate social adjustment of the young high-school student?

Because of the amount of discussion that has revolved about the relative values of the enriched versus the accelerated curriculum, the subjects of the study, accelerated and control, were questioned concerning their experience in this connection. It would seem that the enriched program, so far as the students returning questionnaires were concerned, is little more than a myth, as all but three young students denied any acquaintance with enriched curricula. When the subjects of the study were asked what age they deemed most desirable for college entrance, each group tended to favor its own experience; that is, the young student would, given another opportunity, enter college younger and advise other students to enter at an earlier age than the older students felt desirable.

To summarize, this investigation shows: (1) The young student is capable of keeping abreast of the superior student of normal age in the college population; (2) he participates to a considerable extent in extra-curricular activities; (3) he continues his education fully as far as the student who is two years older; (4) a large proportion of the young group found the experience of acceleration of such a nature that they were not only willing to repeat it but would also advise other students to follow their example; (5) the enriched curriculum, so far as this investigation is concerned, seldom functions as an educational device; (6) at present acceleration constitutes the most practical and most commonly accepted solution to the problem of what to do with the superior student.

MARY E. SARBAUGH

UNIVERSITY OF BUFFALO

## NEW BOOKS IN EDUCATION

HATHAWAY, ESSE. *Romance of the American Map.* Pp. ix + 316. Illustrated. Whittlesey House, McGraw-Hill. $2.00.

LAPP, C. J. and others. *Review of Pre-College Mathematics.* Pp. 124. Scott, Foresman.

SCHUBERT, MARIE. *Famous Paintings.* Pp. 48. Illustrated. Grosset and Dunlap. $1.00.

SHEDD, CLARENCE P. *Two Centuries of Student Christian Movements.* Pp. xxii + 466. Association Press, New York. $3.00.

# SCHOOL AND SOCIETY

WITH WHICH ARE COMBINED THE EDUCATIONAL REVIEW, ESTABLISHED IN 1891, THE TEACHERS MAGAZINE, ESTABLISHED IN 1878, AND THE SCHOOL JOURNAL, ESTABLISHED IN 1874.

Volume 40 | Saturday, December 22, 1934 | Number 1043

## THE BASIC FUNCTION OF SECONDARY EDUCATION[1]

By Dr. GUSTAVE A. FEINGOLD

PRINCIPAL, BULKELEY HIGH SCHOOL, HARTFORD, CONNECTICUT

Recognizing that there are pronounced mental and physical differences among human beings, and still other differences due to economic and social conditions, it becomes the imperative duty of education in a democracy to provide the necessary flow and distribution of those educational opportunities and instrumentalities which will best maintain a constant contact between the various levels of society, ranging all the way from those who are in the van of human endeavor to those who are in the most receding ranks of the national life. Since the national life can not stand still, and since it would be suicidal to return to primitive forms, the opportunities and instrumentalities of education must be such as will best foster the spirit of leadership and growth in every conceivable department of that national life. All public education must be spun and woven on this fundamental pattern.

Now, it is obvious that leaders in any field of endeavor can advance only as far as the rank and file are able to follow them. Statesmen and scientists, ministers and artists, physicians and lawmakers—all those who have the inborn urge to carry onward the flame of human development—more often than not see their efforts frustrated, their hopes shattered, their plans vilified and their works destroyed in the void which exists between themselves and the masses of mankind who, through ignorance and inability to understand, are ages removed from their leaders.

We have had a striking example of this in Russia under the Czars. The trouble with Russia prior to 1917 was not that it lacked great artists and scientists, great writers and composers, but that the masses were kept in such a deplorable state of ignorance that the works of the national leaders were wholly lost to their own people. The result was scintillating flashes of Russian genius which arrested the attention of the rest of the world, but which did not exist for the mentally moribund millions of Russian peasants. If we accept this fundamental principle of public education, and I do not see how any other theory can even find a place for serious discussion in a democracy, all our misunderstandings and petty differences as to objectives and the mode of procedure vanish into thin air.

To illustrate, if a constant and unbroken contact is to be maintained between those who are in the foremost ranks of the science of health and sanitation, let us say, and the millions of people who quite naturally are in the receding ranks of that branch of

[1] Address delivered before the National Council of Education, Washington, D. C., June 30, 1934.

learning, then there is nothing left for education to do but to provide opportunities and instrumentalities for the passing on of the great discoveries and the vast body of knowledge which exist in those fields to each successive receding rank in terms and language understandable by it. This means, for example, that the knowledge contained in the fields of botany, biology, zoology, chemistry, bacteriology and kindred subjects must be imparted to our children in both elementary and secondary schools and, of course, to the public in general through adult education.

To make the currents of civilization accessible to all the people means, in the first place, that they have to be reduced to a few main streams in order to bring the individual to the point where he is ready to depart on his life's career; and in the second place, it means that the currents have to be tempered to the general capacities of the large groups into which the growing individual naturally falls.

Education, no less than business and politics, has its catchwords and popular phrases, and the objectives of education have been greatly confused, I fear, by these catchwords. On the one hand, we hear it said that the purpose of education is to train for "citizenship"; on the other hand, it is to train for "service." At one time the slogan is "Educate for leadership"; at another time it is "Educate for character." This is the latest shibboleth. I sometimes suspect that the "citizenship" slogan emanates from the patrioteers, while the "service" cry is raised by the profiteers. The "leadership" notion is strongly tinged with the sentiment of self-regard, while the "character" shibboleth is the smokescreen of those whose philosophy of education is rather vague.

How much saner, it seems to me, is the principle we are enunciating to-day—education for national growth or broad human development; that is, the object of education should be to maintain a constant contact within the ranks of humanity from highest to lowest.

In the light of this principle, the folly and the crime of trying to segregate children in their early teens into water-tight compartments on the basis of selective tests or try-out courses, and to deny them forever the privilege of making the mental contacts we refer to, become quite obvious. A youngster may be very poor in technical grammar and wretched in spelling, and yet have a fine appreciation of the beauties of literature. Should he be denied the opportunity to study the English classics; and should he be shunted into the manual training or the commercial course on that basis? Why maintain, for instance, that only those children who show unusual aptitude in numerical manipulations be allowed to go on with the study of mathematics and guide the others into something else? Is this procedure in accordance with the pattern of life? Is life made up wholly of "either, or," with no middle ground? Who can build a road between two blades of grass without destroying both?

I believe that the greatest enemies of education are in our own midst; and it is they who bring the public schools and the teaching profession into ill repute through their groundless utterances. Here, for instance, is a progressive educator making the astounding statement that "95 per cent. of the schools in the United States are entirely out of step with contemporary life."[2] If 95 per cent. of the schools of to-day are out of step with contemporary life, then certainly that proportion must have been out of step ten, fifteen and twenty years ago—that is to say, 95 per cent. of our citizens are out of step with modern trends. Who, then, creates the contemporary life? Surely, it is not the

[2] Professor J. Ralph McGaughy, address before Progressive Education Association, Hartford, Connecticut, May 12, 1934.

remaining 5 per cent. If anything, this statement proves just the opposite of what it intends—namely, that the emphasis placed in the public schools upon the basic principles of knowledge is most conducive to preparing the individual for contemporary life.

Education to the progressive educator means not the acquisition of knowledge about the things that constitute the framework of our civilization, but rather the slow development of something vague and uncertain called inherent interests. All standards and norms must be discarded. To set them up as goals of attainment is considered a cruel practise. Teachers must cease to think that they are leaders; rather are they to follow the blind, groping child. Their function is merely to act as feather dusters, so to speak. They are to remove from the child's path all obstacles that may hinder him in his career of self-evolution, and these obstacles are usually the fundamentals of school learning.

The interests of the young person are to become the prime movers in the educational process. How these interests are to be determined, how we are to discover whether they are permanent or transitory, whether they are native or merely imitative—these are matters about which the progressive educators leave us very much in the dark. They pattern the philosophy of education on the model of adult life and maintain that inasmuch "as in real life our interests are the determining factors of our professional pursuits," therefore, the interests of young children and adolescents should be the guiding factors in their educational pursuits.

There is a peculiar fallacy in this argument, it seems to me. It assumes either that the education of thirty and forty years ago was of a progressive nature, developing the interests which determine the life of the present adult generation, or that it was as bad as it is to-day, but that somehow we, adults, were able to break away from its baneful influence and pattern our life in accordance with our interests after all. We know that the former assumption is not true to fact; if the latter assumption is correct, then there is nothing detrimental to adult life in the substantial program of education offered to-day.

The other argument of the progressive educator, namely, that "we learn by doing," is equally weak in that it denies the power to the human mind to make deductions whereby the individual is able to leap over obstacles by an act of thought rather than by breaking his mind and body against them before achieving a deed of significance. It is true that the race as a whole learns by doing in the course of centuries, but to assume that the individual has to recapitulate the experience of the race in his own development is denied by the very fact that the people who use books, that is, we who enjoy western civilization, are where we are; whereas those who learn by doing—primitive people—are still where their ancestors were ages ago. I wonder how many of us have ever thought of the numerous times that we have escaped serious bodily injury or even death by doing, or refraining from doing, certain things which our very existence proves that we did not learn to do or to shun through personal experience. In these matters we guide ourselves by deductions formulated from the experiences of others, and this is true in most of our life. Of course, actions which are purely mechanical or physical have to be learned by the individual through "doing," but not the whole of one's life consists of merely physical actions.

Another dangerous and unfounded doctrine which has been gaining ground with increasing impetus in recent years is that the bulk of our high-school population is moronic and unfit for the profitable pursuit of high-school studies, as we know them.

We have been hearing of late, for instance, that 50 per cent. of the high-school enrolment is made up of the sons and daughters of conductors, factory workers and scrubwomen, and since they themselves will become motormen, truck-drivers and charwomen, the education of the high school ought to be of a type which will prepare them for that sort of life.

I believe that never was a more dangerous policy advocated by people of professional responsibility. It is for this reason that increasing pressure is being brought to bear on administrators to convert the junior and senior high schools of the country into trade, handicraft and commercial schools. More and more pupils are flocking into the commercial courses until now 50 per cent. of those enrolled in urban high schools are devoting from one quarter to one half of their time to the study of typewriting, bookkeeping and stenography; and this in spite of the fact that fully 80 per cent. of those who graduate with the commercial course fail to secure positions which involve the use of the skills they acquire in school.

It is for this reason, too, that foreign language study, the English classics and the sciences are being crowded out of the high-school curriculum, and cooking and sewing, woodworking and auto mechanics are being introduced in their place. The object, you see, according to this type of education, is to turn out a completely physically rounded individual—one who will know how to make his own bed, to cook his own meal, to mend his own shirt, to drive his own car and to fix his own carburetor. And then he will be happy! And then too he will fit perfectly into Shakespeare's description of the Neapolitan prince of whom Portia says, "He makes it a great appropriation to his own good parts that he can shoe his horse himself."

The spreading of the idea that 50 per cent. of the high-school enrolment is unqualified for the traditional high-school studies is nothing less than a libel against the youth of the nation. What are the facts? The prosperous era starting in 1926 caused a tremendous influx into the high school because parents were able to get along without the financial assistance of their children. The subsequent depression, starting in 1930, increased the high-school population still more, owing to the fact that the children could not secure employment. This, of course, threw a certain type of pupil into the high school who, in normal times, would have avoided the thankless task of trying to secure information out of books and would have gone to work.

But what is the actual proportion of this type of pupil? A recent survey made by the writer shows that not more than 10 per cent. of the present high-school enrolment falls into the group of IQ 89 and below. Perhaps another 10 per cent., which may be called borderline cases, should be added. This, then, is the element which constitutes the serious problem. But it is not so large as to justify the destruction of the educational opportunities for the other 80 per cent. To say that the only way to remedy the scholastic difficulties encountered by two out of every ten high-school pupils is by decrying education measured in terms of "intellectual activity,"[3] and by attempting to smash the high-school curriculum is like throwing the baby out with the bath.

In brief, 33 per cent. of the high-school population have IQ's below 100; 34 per cent. have IQ's between 100 and 109; and 33 per cent. have IQ's of 110 and above. This is not bad at all, and is far from the imaginary 50 per cent. who are said to be doomed to become truckmen and scrubwomen and on whose account we are asked

[3] U. S. Senator Royal S. Copeland, address before the National Education Association, Cleveland, February 28, 1934. Also SCHOOL AND SOCIETY, May 12, 1934.

to sell the very basis of our civilization for a pot of porridge. I am not at all convinced that individuals with IQ's of 105 or even 100, provided they have the necessary motivation, will-power and persistency, may not become successful in some of the professions. Indeed, some of them may succeed in becoming mayors, or state and national representatives, or school principals, or school board members, in which case a high-school education along the traditional lines would not be to their disadvantage in the least.

The need of preserving the educational standards of our high schools is greater now than ever before, because now the high schools are really the people's university, not only by virtue of the large variety of educational offerings, but more especially because of the large numbers attending and remaining for the full four years. With an enrolment of five million youths and graduating classes which constitute from 60 to 80 per cent. of the original numbers entering, the potential power of the American secondary school for public good is prodigious. Not only do these millions of young people have their appetites for further education sharpened, not only are new vistas of life and learning opened to them, but by coming under the influence of their teachers who, on the whole, are well-educated, idealistically inclined, cultured men and women, the character training our boys and girls receive from these contacts must be enormous. Furthermore, the mere living together of so many young people in large groups, subject to relatively uniform rules and social controls, prepares them in a most marvelous manner for that type of civic cooperation and responsibility which the welfare of modern society demands. In brief, what the rustic life of the early history of our country did for the development of the rugged individual, the American high school is now doing for the development of the cooperating, socialized individual.

It is obvious, however, that the time has long since arrived for a radical change in the policy which prevails in the secondary school. We are no longer preparing the vast number attending high school for college only. Not more than 15 per cent. are now headed for college. The other 85 per cent. are receiving all the formal education they ever will receive and are preparing for life. It is the duty of us educators, therefore, to concentrate our efforts upon this vast majority in order to help it fit into the American scene, so to speak; to judge things, to do things and to evaluate things from the American point of view and in the American spirit.

What is this American spirit? More than a quarter of a century ago, Dr. James Muirhead described it more completely and more explicitly than any writer has done before or since his time. The American spirit includes:

(1) A sense of an illimitable expansion and possibility.
(2) An almost child-like confidence in human ability and fearlessness of both the present and the future.
(3) A wider realization of human brotherhood than has yet existed.
(4) A greater theoretical willingness to judge by the individual rather than the race.
(5) A breezy indifference to the "weight" of authority and a positive predilection for innovation.
(6) A marked alertness of mind and a manifold interest.
(7) And above all: an inextinguishable feeling of hope and courage.

These seven traits of Americanism are on the whole quite desirable. At least there is nothing in any of them which, in the process of realization, would require the suppression or extinction of other peoples, races or individuals. It is a formula, a world outlook, which may be adopted by all mankind and in all lands with grace and dignity.

Is there a place in the high school where these American traits can be developed and integrated in the life of the American youth? I believe there is, and it is the duty of the high-school teacher and administrator so to adjust the educational situations that these ideals or characteristics of the American spirit may find their greatest fulfilment.

The strongest power in the educational process for character development is the influence which the teacher exercises over his pupils through his personality. Unfortunately, on the secondary school level there are many factors which impede the pupil-teacher contact or make it altogether impersonal. There are, in the first place, the totally unrelated subjects that the pupils pursue. In the second place, there is the lack of integration or departmental cooperation in the teaching of the various subjects. Thirdly, the pupil has as many different teachers a day as he has subjects on his program. Fourthly, the large classes and short recitation periods prevent the teacher from doing more than merely to call on the pupil to answer a question or two during the day. In the fifth place, and particularly in the case of large schools or schools conducted on the double session plan, there is a lack of both time and place for the teacher to meet the pupil outside of school hours for personal conference, acquaintance and influence. And finally, the semi-annual promotion system which prevails in so many city schools destroys the last opportunity for pupils and teachers to become acquainted with one another. But these are mechanical hindrances which should and can be overcome. School executives and school boards who fail to recognize their interference with the educational process are simply mentally obtuse and misplaced in their responsibilities.

The first step in the process of remedying the weaknesses of the high school, as I see them, is to develop an educational institution which shall furnish a two-year training course for grammar school graduates who have been found by long and careful observation to be unqualified for a high-school education, as we understand that term. This school should offer light training in modern arts, crafts and skills. The establishment of such a school was recommended by the writer eleven years ago, and it is interesting to note that New York City, the largest school system in the world, is only just now planning to establish this type of school in the fall of 1934.[4]

Such a school is the place where pupils might well be offered the opportunity to read newspapers and popular magazines and to spend part of the day in receiving visual instruction. On the completion of the course, the graduates of such a school, having passed the compulsory attendance age, would be in a position to choose what they should do. Those with pronounced mechanical leanings may then go on with specialized training in a trade or technical school. Those who show leanings for book learning would undoubtedly be encouraged to enter a regular high school. The others would try to find their place in industry and commerce. They would be old enough to do this without risk to their health and morals, yet not too old to begin at the bottom where individuals of this type have to begin anyway—whether it be at the age of sixteen or nineteen; and it is better that they start at sixteen than at nineteen.

In these depression times, however, I do not see much hope for the erection of such schools to take care of the 20 per cent. of our adolescents now misplaced in the regular high school. The solution of the prob-

[4] G. A. Feingold, "Intelligence and Persistency in High School Attendance," School and Society, October 13, 1923. Also the *New York Times*, June 27 and July 16, 1934.

lem of poor scholarship and the presence of the non-bookish pupil in the regular high school must be brought about, therefore, by the establishment of parallel curricula. This process has been going on gradually for the past ten years, and I believe that it is one of the most notable achievements in secondary education in the United States.

This procedure, however, requires careful accumulation of records, both mental and achievement, starting early in the grades. It requires wise counseling and guidance. But it enables us to place the slow type of pupil in groups of his own kind and to offer him English, general mathematics, sciences, social studies and other subjects which are less exacting in their content than those taken by the pupils of better ability. I am not worried about the danger that boys and girls of pronounced ability would drift into these minimal courses. Neither am I concerned about the danger of debasing the high-school diploma because it would be awarded to youths of such limited attainment. I am much more cheered by the prospect that the 80 per cent. who have average and more than average ability, being freed of this encumbrance in the classroom, would be able to benefit by the offering of the high school in the greatest measure.

Another step in the improvement of the high school is to simplify the curriculum by reducing the subjects of instruction to five or six main fields such as English, mathematics, science, foreign language and social studies. These subjects should constitute the backbone of the youth's education. In addition to these, but occupying a less important place and offered as extras —not as substitutes—should be manual training, commercial training, art, vocal and instrumental music and household science. There is no objection to specialization in these fields, but that specialization should be deferred to the last two years of the school course, when the pupil is old enough to manipulate the special tools required and can make progress twice as fast as when he begins fumblingly in his freshman year.

Finally, to bring about the educational and character improvement so sorely needed these days it is necessary to effect a greater consolidation of the small rural schools and to break up the abnormally large city high schools. No high school can adequately educate the individual for modern society if it is as badly crippled in equipment and personnel as most country schools are; nor can it provide the necessary character education if the opportunities for personal contact among pupils, teachers and principal are so scattered and desultory as in the city high school of three thousand pupils or more. Character building—that is to say, the development of socially desirable attitudes and sentiments —can not be brought about by a study of text-books dealing with that subject. The study of ethics does not make a person more moral. On the contrary, it may make him more shrewd and more circumspect in his immorality. Character, good or bad, is developed through the subtle influences that one individual has on another, or that the group has on the individual. It is mere lip service, therefore, to clamor for character development rather than for intellectual activity without providing the necessary conditions for such development.

With proper emphasis on the essentials of sound learning and proper opportunities provided for the concomitants thereof, such qualities as character, citizenship, service and leadership will be realized in their own time and in their own way. We must not diminish the opportunities of our children, especially during the adolescent period of life, to develop those powers of mind and understanding and those educational and cultural tools which will furnish a channel through which all the fruits of our civilization may be passed on from individual to individual and from group to group for the benefit and enjoyment of all our people in accordance with their capacities. This is what H. G. Wells means when he declares that in order to establish a satisfactory social order, "it is first necessary to provide an educational and cultural substratum." And how can such a substratum be developed in our country unless it be through emphasis on a liberal rather than a technical education in the American high school? In education, as in law, we must find a common denominator which will assure a happy society through the development of an intelligent, well-read, broad-minded individual. Teach your children things, and they will become robots. Teach them ideas, and they will become intelligent human beings.

It is only when we develop among the millions of prospective American citizens a common sense of power that they will acquire a common sense of worth. And when the people of a nation have a unified sense of worth, they are not likely to allow themselves to be cajoled or bulldozed into the worship of the golden calf, nor to bow before the priests thereof. Not in the lap of the gods, but in the halls of the American high school, rests the fate of the American nation.

# NONSENSE IN HIGHER EDUCATION

By Dr. GUY E. SNAVELY
PRESIDENT, BIRMINGHAM-SOUTHERN COLLEGE

NONSENSE in higher education is a term that would include the frills, fads and fancies that creep into education on the college and university level. The term, however, is a relative one. What would seem like frills in a liberal arts curriculum would be quite in order for a curriculum with a definite vocational label. A course in dress design would certainly be in order for a bachelor of science degree in home economics but of certain dubiety in a bachelor of arts course of liberal culture.

That phase of college organization which has been attacked most vigorously in recent years is the program which permits a student to obtain a bachelor's degree simply by the accumulation of a certain number of units in courses which may or may not show a definite correlation. This state of affairs came about by the adoption of the free elective system which came into general usage a generation or two ago. There can be no real defense of a curriculum which permits choice of subjects without reference to some sensible plan of grouping.

In more recent years, the tendency has been quite in the other direction. Practically all colleges have adopted "major" and "minor" requirements with certain allowances in the choice of electives. No college has been really as guilty as the critics would have us believe. It is quite the vogue at present for the curriculum to be divided into upper and lower divisions. In the lower division, which covers the first two years in college, the courses are specified with almost the same rigor as was done in the college curricula of the days before President Eliot, of Harvard, made his pronouncement concerning free election. In the upper division, covering the last two years of the curriculum, the student is required to choose studies that complete "major" and "minor" requirements and is allowed quite a latitude in the election of other studies.

In some colleges much more freedom is

being given the individual student. He is being exempted even from class attendance. The comprehensive examination is being substituted practically for all other requirements. This plan obviously has merits. It seems too expensive in its operation for most institutions. After listening to a full exposition of its operation given by Dean Boucher, of the University of Chicago, I have been convinced of its meritorious claims.

Though frankly admitting the claim that a student has obtained a college education if he meets the acid tests of comprehensive examinations, I am so old-fashioned that I still believe in the value of the association of young students with mature and trained faculty minds in the "give and take" of the classroom.

My Utopian college will certainly have as its main attraction a conspicuous faculty group. Each one should be an intellectual luminosity and a radiant personality with character beyond reproach.

Nonsensical is the undue emphasis given by some colleges to intercollegiate athletics. Football is the chief offender. What explanation can justify a higher salary for the coach than for the other regular members of the faculty? It is reputed even in some few institutions the football coach receives more pay than the president.

A few years ago one of the regional standardizing associations dropped a college from its membership primarily because of its over-emphasis in intercollegiate football. The college in question had become hopelessly involved in debt because of the money spent in the construction of an enormous athletic stadium. Quite a number of other institutions have succumbed to the craze of building large stadia. The financial outlay in this particular has been decidedly lop-sided compared with expenditures made in other departments of college and university administration.

Frequently a good football player is pushed through high school because of the strength exhibited in his back and legs rather than in his mind. The gravest sort of injustice is done such a young man. He wakes up too late to find that he is utterly unprepared for college. However, it has been rumored that he is even carried some time in college by the aid of good tutors and his assignment to the so-called "snap" courses.

The past year the Southern Association of Colleges and Secondary Schools has appointed a committee to survey the athletic situation among its college members. The committee is making a study at present of the scholastic records of the members of the football squads. Scrutiny is being made not only of the high-school records but of the standing of the men in their college work. Doubtless, the committee will later look into the other questions, such as unfair recruiting and partiality in the award of scholarship and other grants.

If college faculties and administrators would only decide to agree positively to intercollegiate football of definite amateur standing and submerge the ambition to have a winning football team at any cost, the situation would be straightened out promptly. Intercollegiate football does give a glamor to college life, and it does have a far-reaching appeal.

In the realm of social life there is frequently a tendency to over-emphasis. It is readily conceded that a college training includes social development as well as physical, spiritual and mental. However, frills can easily develop in this feature of college training.

A dean of women in a reputable college once told me that she was worn out chaperoning college dances. She was obliged to attend two or three a week on the average. These dances were given under the auspices of college classes, the social sororities and fraternities, the professional and honorary organizations and other groups. A student could easily spend most of his time attending these functions, thus wearing himself out physically as well as finding little or no time for his studies, the main reason for his enrolment in college. A moderate amount of social life, whether stimulated by fraternities or other groups, is certainly in order. Social fraternities can be and very frequently are valuable aids to the development of good habits of study on the part of their members.

Under the head of frills would come certain vocational subjects, especially when offered by certain types of institutions. Secretarial courses are legitimately the province of business colleges. Though a limited amount of work in this field might be permitted in courses leading to vocational degrees in certain colleges, that certainly would be out of place in a liberal arts curriculum.

Similarly, a limited number of courses in fields of home economics and physical education could be approved as parts of a regular curriculum for certain bachelor of science degrees. They should surely come under the head of extra-curricular offerings in a liberal arts program.

Our college committee on advanced standing had a case a few years ago that illustrated the point in question. After spending a year or two carrying regular courses in a standard college, the candidate for admission to advanced standing drifted around several summers to conspicuous summer schools. She offered from one nationally known institution a course in poultry husbandry and from another of international recognition a course in a certain phase of fancy swimming. Our faculty committee declined to accept either course. They could not help but feel that too much time was wasted on the characteristics of the rooster.

General acceptance is being accorded the result of the findings of committees of college and university associations with regard to the importance of a limited amount of training in methods of teaching. I feel personally that the college curriculum can easily include too many such methods courses. Why can not a course in the principles of education be comprehensive enough to include principles of high-school education as well as principles of elementary education?

A year or two ago I had an interesting experience as a member of an advisory committee of twelve which was completing an investigation of teacher-training institutions under the leadership of the United States Office of Education with a grant from the United States Congress. Statistics showed that the liberal arts colleges turned out a far larger portion of high-school teachers throughout the United States than any other type of college.

A good teacher certainly can not know too much of the content of his chosen subject. He may be thoroughly drilled on how to present it, but he will be a decided failure if he has not sufficient material to present.

Most foolish of all and most difficult of solution is the continuance in office of the poor teacher and the ineffective administrator. The college administrator has not the heart to drop an instructor after he has lost his efficiency. Frequently the trustees hesitate for many years to make emeritus a president who has lived beyond his most effective period.

Courage is required to ban the nonsense that creeps into the college curriculum. The inescapable obligation is to the eager youth enrolling in our colleges and universities in order to find the truth that will make them free.

# EDUCATIONAL EVENTS

## PROPOSED INCREASE IN THE SCHOOL LEAVING AGE IN WALES

ACCORDING to *The Educational Supplement of the London Times,* about twenty of the Welsh local education authorities have passed resolutions in favor of raising the school age from 14 to 15. The case for raising the age is aided by the fact that in Swansea about half the pupils who may leave school at 14 prefer to remain at school rather than to wait outside until they obtain work. At the same time that the Cardiganshire Education Committee passed a resolution in favor of raising the school age to 15 it was decided as a necessary condition to consider a plan for the reorganization of the schools. Most of the Cardiganshire schools are either two-teacher or three-teacher schools, the majority with a head master aided by an uncertificated or supplementary teacher. If the school age were raised the present head teachers of these small schools would be given an almost impossible task, for they already have to provide instruction for pupils of ages ranging from seven or eight up to 14, in schools not too well equipped and certainly not fitted for modern methods. The director of education, in a comprehensive report, states that the raising of the school age would increase the present numbers by about 600. It is estimated, however, that the total number of children in the schools will fall in the next 10 years from the present number of 6,600 to about 5,300, and among these the pupils from between the ages of 11 and 15 will number from 2,200 to about 2,000.

Three alternative schemes for training these older boys and girls have been put forward. The first, and probably the best if the schools be properly organized, is to transfer them to the secondary schools, enlarging the present and building two new schools in southern and north Cardiganshire. The cost of the conveyance of pupils to the schools is estimated to amount to about £7,000 a year, and the provision of additional premises to about £55,000, an expenditure which the Board of Education is not likely now to sanction. A second plan would be to transfer pupils living within a distance of 10 miles to the secondary schools and to form "higher tops" for the less fortunate who live outside that district. But the cost of this is also prohibitive. The third is to organize six central schools similar to that already established at Lampeter, forming senior classes at selected centers for those pupils living too remote from any of the proposed new schools. The cost of the conveyance of pupils would amount to £3,400, and of additional premises £27,000 and the expenditure on staffing would not be so much as in the other two schemes.

## PROFESSIONAL PRACTISE AT THE UNIVERSITY OF CALIFORNIA

A STATEMENT of the general policy to be followed by the University of California in making its facilities available for the use of the public or of private business, and the extent to which faculty members will be permitted to engage in private employment has been issued by President Robert G. Sproul.

In order to aid in directing the new service policy, an advisory committee of faculty members and university alumni has been named to cooperate with the administration. It includes: Dean Charles Derleth, of the College of Engineering; Dean C. B. Hutchison, of the College of Agriculture; Professor B. M. Woods, chairman of the department of mechanical engineering; Dr. R. E. Davis, professor of civil engineering; Dean F. H. Probert, of the College of Mining; Alex J. Dickie, '98; Donald L. Kieffer, '19; E. L. Oliver and Max Thornburg, '21.

The service policy outlined provides that:

> Members of the university may render professional service for compensation as long as such service does not interfere with their prescribed duties and unless their university employment forbids them to accept additional employment, or their appointment requires them to render a consulting or advisory service without charge.
>
> Within these limits, teachers of professional subjects are encouraged to engage in the practise of their professions so far as may be necessary to maintain professional competency. Such activities are to be engaged in under private arrangement, and fees charged are to be on a scale prevailing within the professions practised. The university will not approve the employment of its members, however, in routine tasks of a commonplace type,

undertaken primarily to supplement personal income.

The participation of the university itself in tests and investigations shall be limited to activities leading to the extension of knowledge or increased effectiveness in teaching. No tests or investigations shall be undertaken by the university which might interfere with the teaching responsibilities of a faculty member.

The results of all tests and investigations made by the university shall be available for common use by the public and shall not be for the exclusive use of parties sponsoring or conducting the work.

The laboratories of the university shall not be made available for tests of a purely commercial nature unless satisfactory facilities for such tests do not exist elsewhere.

Commercial tests involving controversial elements are not to be undertaken except at the direct and unanimous request of representatives of all parties to the controversy.

The university is to make a charge ample to cover all direct and indirect costs of all tests or investigations which it undertakes.

The use of the name of the university for purposes of advertising will not be tolerated.

## PROSPECTS FOR JEWISH PRE-MEDICAL STUDENTS

A MEMORANDUM signed jointly by President James Lukens McConaughy, of Wesleyan University, at Middletown, and Dr. Edward Christian Schneider, professor of biology, on the prospects for Jewish pre-medical students at Wesleyan University has been made public. The text of the memorandum follows:

We are sending you this memorandum in order that there may be no misunderstanding regarding the rather difficult situation which you may face if you are planning to seek admission to a medical school.

It is important to recognize that the opportunity to study medicine is definitely limited by the medical schools in this and other lands. In our country each year between 6,200 and 6,300 medical freshmen are chosen from a field of approximately 14,000 applicants. Furthermore, foreign study is restricted in that almost impassable barriers have been established in many countries abroad, and by legislation in most of our states. Any young man wishing to study abroad must first get permission from the state in which he wishes to practise. Most states are refusing to accept the foreign diploma.

While the racial question does enter somewhat into the selection of students, it does not enter as much as some claim. The Association of Medical Colleges reports that 17 per cent. of the freshman students in medical school are Jews. It is pointed out that in this country, out of a population of more than 120,000,000, there are probably between 5,000,000 and 6,000,000 Jews. They, in round numbers, make up not more than 5 per cent. of the entire population. It has further been reported that over 50 per cent. of the applicants for entrance to the medical schools in 1933 were of Jewish ancestry.

The above facts explain why it is difficult for Wesleyan to place her graduates of the Jewish race in medical schools. It should be apparent that in selecting its freshmen each medical school will feel some degree of responsibility for the graduates of the institution with which it is associated, and it therefore is impelled to accept the promising applicants within its own borders. It is now quite generally admitted that, after that selection has been made, very little room is left for Jewish candidates from other institutions.

We have no desire to discourage you in your hope for a medical career, but feel that it is only fair that you should know the circumstances. We have been disturbed at the difficulties which some of our students, even after a very good Wesleyan record, have encountered in the last few years in securing admission to medical school.

Dr. McConaughy later amplified the memorandum with the following statement:

This is a part of the vocational guidance program of the college, whereby we try to show each boy who tells us that he is interested in a certain profession the difficulties and opportunities of it. In view of the number of applicants for medical schools and the difficulty of admission thereto, we felt that the Jewish boys who are interested in medicine ought to know the facts early in their college course. Those who want to continue preparing for medicine, which probably will be most of them, we will assist in every way we can and help them to secure admission to medical schools they will want to enter. There is no anti-Jewish feeling here.

## THE NEW COUNCIL AT THE OHIO STATE UNIVERSITY

PRESIDENT GEORGE W. RIGHTMIRE, of the Ohio State University, early in November announced the establishment of a new university council to coordinate the student personnel activities of the university.

The new organization is to be known as the personnel council. Thirteen members of the faculty and administrative staff have been appointed to membership. These include the president, the vice-president, the examiner, the dean of men, the dean of women, the director of the Student Medical Service, one representative of the council on student affairs, two junior deans, two college secretaries and two members of the general faculty.

The council will meet fortnightly to discuss the many extra-instructional relationships of students with the university. President Rightmire's statement follows:

In 1895 the university enrolled 695 students. To-day more than ten thousand students are registered. This tremendous growth has brought many problems of administration, and of necessity many new agencies have been established to prevent the size of the university from interfering with the personal growth of the individual student.

In 1912 we appointed our first Dean of Women. In 1920 we created the office of the University Examiner to administer the work of admitting students. In 1921 we set up the Student Medical Service to guard the health of students. Seven years later we established the office of Junior Dean in our five large undergraduate colleges so that students, especially freshmen and sophomores, might readily find counsel upon their many and ramified problems. And then in 1929 we appointed a Dean of Men.

These several student personnel agencies have all been working effectively in their various sectors, but now we feel the need of coordinating their activities. All are working toward a common end, *i.e.*, the adjustment of the student to the university and, equally as important, the adjustment of the university to the student. In order to bring all student personnel officers into closer relationship to one another the Personnel Council is being organized.

The new council has no legislative or administrative responsibilities. It is an informal coordinating medium with these functions:

To serve in an advisory capacity to the president in all student personnel matters.

To serve as an advisory and coordinating agency of all student personnel activities of the university.

To keep informed of all student personnel activities of the university.

To promote improved techniques of administration in student personnel offices.

To conduct research on student personnel problems.

To develop, in cooperation with the director of publicity, methods of publicizing the student personnel activities of the university.

To submit an annual report to the president on the status of student personnel administration of the university, summarizing the work of all functional divisions of student personnel administration.

Professor W. H. Cowley, of the Bureau of Educational Research, has been named as chairman of the new council.

## SUMMER SEMINARS IN THE HUMANITIES

PRELIMINARY notice is given of opportunities to be offered during the summer of 1935 to mature scholars for expanding their interests and competence in fields generally underworked by Americans. A series of seminars will be held similar to the Summer Seminars on Far Eastern Studies at Harvard University and the University of California in 1932 and 1934, designed not as ordinary summer-school courses, but specifically for providing mature teachers in universities and colleges with information and techniques not readily obtainable at any other time.

The section on Chinese and Japanese studies will be part of the summer session at Columbia University from July 5 to August 16, 1935. L. C. Goodrich will direct the section and will teach the Chinese language. Arthur W. Hummel, of the Library of Congress, will teach Chinese history; Benjamin March, of the University of Michigan, Chinese art; Carl W. Bishop, of the Freer Gallery, the pre-history of Asia; Ryusaku Tsunoda, of the Society for Japanese Studies, the Japanese language; Shunzo Sakamaki, of Columbia University, the history of Japan, and H. G. Henderson, of Columbia University, Japanese art. Other eminent specialists will lecture on specific topics.

The second Russian Language Institute will also be held at Columbia University from June 25 to August 31. Instruction will be in charge of George Z. Patrick, of the University of California, assisted by lectors. An elementary course will be planned to give a useful control of Russian materials to students of history, political economy and other subjects to whom these materials are necessary. The advanced course will be intended for those already having some command of the Russian language. The experience of the first institute at Harvard University in 1934 indicates that extraordinary success can be expected from this kind of intensive study of a language, properly directed, on the part of mature scholars who realize the necessity of acquiring such a tool.

A seminar on Arabic and Islamic studies is being planned at Princeton University, to run approximately from June 20 to July 31. It will be offered, if funds can be secured, under the direction of Professor Philip K. Hitti, of Princeton University, and will be designed for medievalists, historians of science, the fine arts and Eastern Europe, linguists, scholars of Romance languages and others to whose interests the Arabic-Islamic field is peripheral and who find some competence in it desirable. Special work in the Arabic and Turkish languages will be available.

It is hoped that some financial assistance can be offered to a few qualified scholars who might otherwise be prevented from attending any of these seminars. Further information can be obtained from Mortimer Graves, American Council of Learned Societies, 907 Fifteenth Street, N.W., Washington, D. C.

## RADIO RESOLUTION OF WISCONSIN TEACHERS

The Wisconsin Teachers Association in annual convention adopted unanimously the follow resolution concerning radio education:

Be it Resolved, That, recognizing the great present and potential future influence and value of radio in education, we, the representatives of twenty thousand teachers, in behalf of their constituencies in maturity and youth throughout the state of Wisconsin, in annual convention assembled, reaffirm our support of the general idea of education in radio, and support the demand which the organized agencies of education, culture, and morality throughout the nation are making for the right of clear and unlimited broadcasting channels by government, education, religion, through nonprofit broadcasting stations.

*We urge* the establishment of a national policy which shall assure the development of radio in true public interest;

*We take pride* in the fact that WHA, the state station at Madison, was the first radio station in the United States, or anywhere, to institute broadcasting programs; and,

*We commend* the outstanding work being done by the Wisconsin state-owned and operated stations at Madison and Stevens Point in providing a broadcasting service of high informational, educational and cultural programs adapted to children and youths of the home and the school, and to adult citizens, generally;

*We urge* adequate financial support by the state of Wisconsin for the continuing growth and development of this meritorious, and now nationally recognized, pioneering adventure;

*We take genuine satisfaction* out of the prompt action of the new Federal Communications Commission in its present investigation and hearings on the educational and cultural uses of radio in the public interest.—Unanimously adopted by the Wisconsin Teachers Association, Milwaukee, Wisconsin, November 1–3, 1934.

## EDUCATIONAL RESOLUTIONS BY THE AMERICAN LEGION

The following resolutions were passed by the American Legion at the National Convention, 1934:

*Resolved,* That the American Legion does hereby in convention assembled, and in the interest of public education, endorse the following five points:

1. That education, because of its vital relationship to American ideals and institutions, be given special consideration by the legislative bodies and not be made to bear a disproportionate share of the sacrifice for economy.

2. Because of a growing inequality of wealth among the states, certain communities and even whole states are no longer able to offer their children adequate educational opportunities, that Federal aid without Federal control of educational policy within the states be endorsed as a necessary step to insure adequate funds for public school purposes.

3. Since the reorganization of industry has made it impossible for a large number of our youth below the age of eighteen to be employed in gainful occupation, that both the extension and broadening of school opportunities for such youth be encouraged.

4. Since shorter hours of employment have given the great mass of people more abundant leisure, it is imperative that greater opportunities for wholesome recreation be provided since

we have in America great facilities for recreation under the control of the public school system, that local boards of education be encouraged and empowered to make a wider use of these facilities for the non-school population of their communities.

5. That only competent, professionally trained and carefully selected teachers be employed, that they be citizens of unquestioned patriotism and advocates of American ideals.

*Be it further resolved,* That each Post of the American Legion be urged to appoint an Education Committee, this committee to be constantly watchful of the problems of education, and especially cooperate with school officials in the annual observance in November of American Education Week, with the giving of school awards and other education activities.

## A HEALTH SURVEY OF NEW YORK CITY SCHOOLS

Dr. George T. Palmer, secretary of the Department of Health of New York City, gave as the reason why less than half of the New York public school children with severe defects of sight, hearing and teeth are being properly taken care of is the lack of efficiency and adequate facilities in the schools themselves, rather than the poverty of the parents.

He spoke at the "Know Your City" forum of the Women's City Club, on the recently published report, "Physical Defects: The Pathway to Correction," which is the result of a two-year study of the health service for New York City public school children, made under the auspices of the American Child Health Association, with the cooperation of the Department of Health and the Department of Education.

The American Child Health Association began a study in January, 1932, with the support of the Metropolitan Life Insurance Company, to find the reasons for the lack of correction in the cases of a great many school children with serious physical handicaps. They examined 25,000 children in the fifth and sixth grades, and grave conditions, especially with regard to eyesight, were brought to light.

Of 5,000 children whose eyes were tested, 14 per cent. were found to have severe defects, a visual acuity of 20/50ths or worse, as compared with 11 per cent. elsewhere in the country. Although half of these children in New York City wear glasses, outside New York only a third of the children with serious deficiencies wear glasses. Of those now wearing glasses, two thirds received the impetus from the schools.

Out of a typical one hundred children with uncorrected vision defects, it was learned that only two were in the process of obtaining glasses. In the other ninety-eight cases the children either were recorded as being normal, there was a conflict of opinion, the case had been arbitrarily dropped from the records or the parents were still unconvinced. In only eight instances was the matter dropped for financial reasons.

The charts in the report which deal with teeth defects reveal that seven per cent. of the children have severe defects, compared with fourteen per cent. outside of New York. About two thirds of those who had been receiving continuous dental attention received the original impetus from the school health departments.

The methods of testing hearing are still in an early stage of development. Comparatively few records of hearing defects were found at all. About one third of the severe cases were on record. Dr. Palmer recommended a more thorough use of the audiometer in schools.

## GRANTS FOR RESEARCH AT WESLEYAN UNIVERSITY

Wesleyan University's interest in research, which has already brought endowments of more than $100,000 for this work, has resulted in a special grant of $9,500 by the trustees to supplement the endowment funds. The previously established endowments for research work include the Charles Himrod Denison Foundation for biological research of $75,000 and the Atwater fund of $30,000 to support research in chemistry. The position of a research associate in astronomy is also regularly maintained.

The grant for the current year is to be used for needs not supplied from these funds. A portion is allotted to secretarial service in various departments of the college, while $1,000 is set aside as a travel fund to defray expenses incurred by members of the faculty in attending meetings of learned societies. The balance is given to aid special projects.

In the department of astronomy a grant is given to Professor Slocum for employment of student computers in connection with the observatory program of study of stellar parallaxes. Professor Williamson, of the department of economics and social science, is given a grant for assistance in collecting material for a treatise on public finance and taxation.

Professor Banks, of the English department, is given funds to employ a professional copyist to search records in England in connection with the identification of a Spenserian character. In the department of geology a grant is given to Professor Foye for chemical analyses of minerals in connection with his study of the differentiation of the Tariffville lavas. Professor Curts, of the German department, is given a grant to provide for a typist familiar with German in connection with his preparation of a text in scientific German.

In the department of history and government a grant is given to Professor Bell for research assistance in connection with his biography of Lord Palmerston and to Professor Dutcher for extra secretarial aid in connection with work on the Historical Publications of the Connecticut Tercentenary Commission; to Assistant Professor Thomson for photostatic or copying work of manuscripts in connection with a biography of Denzel Holles, an English Parliamentarian (1599–1680), and to Assistant Professor Schattschneider to help defray the expenses of publication of his study of the Hawley-Smoot tariff bill. Professor Camp, of the department of mathematics, is given funds for special assistance in connection with mathematical problems which have been submitted by the research committee of the American Statistical Association. These are chiefly economic problems of which a statistical analysis is desired. A grant is given to Professors Cady and Van Dyke, of the physics department, for a research program on piezo-electricity and related problems. These investigations are of importance in the science of radio transmission. Assistant Professor Langlie, of the department of psychology, is given a grant for secretarial help in connection with his personnel work with Wesleyan students and his special studies on relation of learning and temperament.

In the department of Romance languages a grant is given to Professor Bussom to provide a typist who can use French in connection with a study on Alphonse Daudet.

## ANNIVERSARY CELEBRATION OF THE SCHOOL OF EDUCATION OF THE UNIVERSITY OF PITTSBURGH

ARRANGEMENTS for a celebration on February 2, 1935, of the twenty-fifth anniversary of the establishment of the School of Education at the University of Pittsburgh are now being made by a committee composed of interested groups.

Plans include a dinner meeting with several guest speakers and an illustrated brochure depicting the history and development of the school. The groups cooperating in formulating plans for the celebration include Xi Chapter of Phi Delta Kappa, Tau Chapter of Kappa Phi Kappa, Delta Chapter of Pi Lambda Theta, School of Education Alumni Association, the first graduating class of the School of Education, Pittsburgh public schools, School of Education faculty, the University of Pittsburgh administration, the General Alumni Association of the University, Pittsburgh Principals' Club, Pittsburgh Teachers Association, Allegheny County public schools, Allegheny County Principals Round Table, Western Convention District of the Pennsylvania State Education Association, Western Pennsylvania County Superintendents Association and the superintendents of the independent districts of Allegheny County. Dr. C. A. Buckner, head of the professional division of education, is correlating the work of these groups.

Five committees as follows are in charge of preparations: Program—Dr. C. A. Buckner, professor of education, University of Pittsburgh; Charlotte Truby, principal of Humboldt and Wickersham schools, Pittsburgh; Dr. J. Freeman Guy, associate superintendent of schools, Pittsburgh; tickets—Dr. J. C. Werner, superintendent of schools, Coraopolis; Dr. C. R. Foster, president, State Teachers College, Indiana; Dr. J. B. Ritchie, superintendent of schools, McKeesport; J. C. Syling, superintendent of schools, Lawrence County; Paul C. Trimble, J. C. Winston Company; publications—Dr. P. W. Hutson, associate professor of education, University of Pittsburgh; Dr. R. V. Morrissey, instructor in botany, University of Pittsburgh; S. H. Replogle, assistant superintendent of schools, Allegheny County; Dr. F. D. Zuerner, superintendent of schools, North Braddock; luncheon and guests—Myrle

Eakin, teacher, Gladstone Junior High School, Pittsburgh; Ora Leona Eimer, teacher, Schenley High School, Pittsburgh; Helen Heazlett, high-school teacher, Wilkinsburg; William A. Dannels, principal of the Allen School, Pittsburgh; J. P. Runk, supervising principal of schools, East McKeesport; publicity—Theodore A. Siedle, assistant to the dean of the School of Education, University of Pittsburgh, and Dr. Frank M. Gatto, assistant director of curriculum study and research division, Board of Education, Pittsburgh.

# EDUCATIONAL NOTES AND NEWS

DR. E. W. JACOBSON, assistant superintendent of schools, in charge of instruction, at Oakland, Calif., has been appointed superintendent. He succeeds Willard E. Givens, who resigned to become secretary of the National Education Association.

THE board of trustees of Rensselaer Polytechnic Institute have elected Edwin S. Jarrett, consulting engineer of New York City, vice-president of the institute with the duties and powers of the president until the appointment of a successor to Dr. Palmer Chamberlaine Ricketts, who died on December 10.

DR. GEORGE W. COLEMAN, president of the Babson Institute, will retire at the end of the next academic year to become president emeritus. He will continue as president of Webber College, a business school for women. Dr. Carl D. Smith, dean of Northeastern University, Boston, will succeed Dr. Coleman as president of the institute.

DR. DIXON RYAN FOX, president of Union College, was the guest of honor and principal speaker at the annual reunion dinner of the Alumni Association of Union College in New York City on December 13. James E. Finnegan, president of the Alumni Association, presided.

DR. MARION E. PARK, president of Bryn Mawr College, was given a dinner by the alumnae of the institution on December 11. During the dinner plans were outlined for the celebration, early next year, of the fiftieth anniversary of the founding of the college.

A DINNER was recently given in honor of Dr. W. B. Bizzell, president of the University of Oklahoma, by the staff of the university to commemorate his twenty-fifth year as a college president and his tenth year as president of the University of Oklahoma. Dr. Bizzell was president of the College of Industrial Arts, Denton, Texas, from 1910 to 1914, president of the Texas Agricultural and Mechanical College from 1914 to 1925 and since then has been president of the University of Oklahoma.

DR. HARVEY N. DAVIS, president of Stevens Institute of Technology, was the guest of honor and principal speaker on December 14 at the annual dinner of the Alumni Association. Other speakers were Professor Richard Francis Deimel and Albert C. Wall, a trustee of the institute. Dr. Davis spoke of Dr. Palmer C. Ricketts, president of Rensselaer Polytechnic Institute, who it had been hoped would attend the dinner, as "the undisputed dean of engineering college executives."

DR. ROBERT CLARKSON BROOKS, professor of economics at Swarthmore College, received on December 14 at a dinner in New York City the honorary degree conferred upon him *honoris causa* by the University of Berne in Switzerland on the occasion of its centenary last June. Dr. Brooks was unable to attend the ceremony in Berne. The speakers included Marc Peter, minister of Switzerland to the United States; Dr. Adolf Meyer, of the Johns Hopkins University; Dr. Eric C. Kunz, president of the Swiss Society of New York, and Dr. Frank Aydelotte, president of Swarthmore College. Dr. Victor Nef, Swiss Consul General at New York, was toastmaster.

THE New York State Vocational Association, at its meeting held in Syracuse, will award on December 27 to Dr. Lewis A. Wilson, assistant commissioner of education of the State of New York, a medal for distinguished service to vocational education. The presentation will be made by Dr. Harold G. Campbell, superintendent of schools of New York City. This is the first award of its kind to be made by the association.

Dr. Stephen Pierce Duggan, director of the Institute of International Education, was reelected on December 18 as president of the Associate Alumni of the College of the City of New York.

Dr. Herbert E. Hawkes, dean of Columbia College, Columbia University, was elected president of the Association of Colleges and Universities of the State of New York at the recent annual meeting. He succeeds Dr. Henry T. Moore, president of Skidmore College.

Dr. Vierling Kersey, superintendent of schools for California, has been elected by the National Council of State Superintendents and Commissioners of Education its president for 1935. Francis L. Bailey, of Vermont, was named secretary in place of Dr. Ernest W. Butterfield, of Connecticut.

Dr. Charles Swain Thomas, of Harvard University, has been elected president of the National Council of Teachers of English. Other officers for the next year are: Dr. Dora V. Smith, University of Minnesota, *first vice-president;* Holland D. Roberts, Stanford University, *second vice-president;* W. Wilbur Hatfield, Chicago Normal College, *secretary and treasurer.* Other members of the executive committee are Dr. Stella S. Center, Theodore Roosevelt High School, New York City; Dr. Walter Barnes, New York University, and Dr. Oscar James Campbell, University of Michigan.

The Chandler Medal for 1934 for "conspicuous work in the field of chemistry" was conferred by Columbia University on December 14 on Dr. Jacob Goodale Lipman, dean of agriculture at Rutgers University and director of the New Jersey Agricultural Experiment Station, for "his outstanding achievements in the field of agricultural chemistry." Dean Howard Lee McBain, of the graduate faculties of Columbia University, made the presentation before nearly four hundred scientific men. Mrs. Charles F. Chandler was present.

Dr. Walter P. Steinhaeuser, president of Le Master Institute, New Jersey, until it closed this year due to lack of funds, has been appointed professor of business administration and education at Shenandoah College in Virginia.

Dr. Stanley F. Howard, associate professor of economics at Princeton University, has been appointed chairman of the department, and Dr. Edward Sampson has been appointed chairman of the department of geology.

At the University of Nebraska, Professor W. C. Brenke has been made chairman of the department of mathematics. The retiring chairman, Professor A. L. Candy, will continue to teach in the department.

The Rev. Dr. William Adams Brown, senior fellow of the Yale University Corporation, has resigned, and the trustees have elected to succeed him the Right Rev. Henry Knox Sherrill, Bishop of Massachusetts. Dr. Brown, who is Roosevelt professor of systematic theology at Union Theological Seminary, has been a member of the corporation since 1917.

The Rev. Dr. Wilbur T. Clemens has resigned as associate general secretary of the Greater New York Federation of Churches to become general secretary of the New York State Council of Churches and Religious Education.

Dr. W. Taylor Thom, Jr., associate professor of geology at Princeton University, has become special assistant to the Subsistence Homestead Division of the Department of the Interior, contributing his services as director of a survey of the coal-mining industry.

Dr. Otis C. Trimble, associate professor of psychology at Purdue University, has been allowed a grant-in-aid by the National Research Council for a special research project in audition.

Dr. John H. Finley, formerly commissioner of education of New York State, will be the principal speaker at the New York State Association of Academic Principals meeting in Syracuse on December 27.

Dr. Richard Henry Tawney, professor of economic history at the University of London, has been appointed Ford lecturer at the University of Oxford for the year 1935–36.

Professor W. L. Bragg, Langworthy professor of physics at the University of Manchester, will deliver the Children's Christmas Lectures at the Royal Institution in December and January. The subject of the lectures will be "Electricity."

THE biennial award of the Oberly Memorial Prize (in memory of the late Eunice Rockwood Oberly, formerly librarian of the Bureau of Plant Industry, Washington, D. C.), for the best bibliography in the field of agriculture or the natural sciences has been postponed until March, 1935. This prize consists of the income from $5,000 for a biennium and is awarded every two years.

PROFESSOR FEDERICO AGENO, director of the National Library at Rome, died on December 1 at the age of forty-nine years.

DR. HORATIO STEVENS WHITE, professor emeritus at Harvard University, died on December 13 at the age of eighty-two years. From 1876 to 1878, Dr. White was assistant professor of Greek and Latin at Cornell University; and from 1891 to 1902 he was head of the German department. In 1902 he was called to Harvard University, where he was for seventeen years professor of German.

DR. BEN M. CHERRINGTON, director of the Foundation for the Advancement of the Social Sciences of the University of Denver, and Henry W. Toll, of the American Legislative Association, sponsored a three-day "planning session" for some fifty Colorado legislators on November 26, 27 and 28. The six meetings were held at the State House and considered the issues which will face the legislature in the coming session. It was hoped that such a conference would enable the legislature to put through a wiser program with less delay than it could otherwise.

BUILDINGS erected at a cost of $400,000 for the Westminster Choir School were dedicated on December 13. Given by an anonymous donor, the campus group consists of an administration building, two dormitories and a chapel, all constructed of red brick in the colonial style. A joint concert of the Westminster Choir and the Philadelphia Orchestra, with Leopold Stokowski conducting, featured the dedication ceremonies in the Princeton University Chapel. The Reverend Dr. John Finley Williamson, president of the Westminister School, delivered the address, and the Reverend Dr. J. Ross Stevenson, president of Princeton Theological Seminary, presided. Others who participated were the Reverend Dr. Robert R. Wicks, dean of the Princeton University Chapel, and the Reverend Dr. Charles H. Erdman, a former moderator of the Presbyterian General Assembly.

ELMER E. WHITTED, who until his death recently was a well-known lawyer in Denver, Colo., willed to the University of Denver his library, consisting of about fifteen hundred volumes of well-selected biographies, histories and literature, especially essays, both English and American.

DR. BENJAMIN RAND, who died on November 9, provided in his will that the proceeds from the future sale of his books shall go to the president and fellows of Harvard College to establish the Benjamin Rand Philosophical Fund for the general advancement of philosophy. The residue of his estate goes to relatives in trust. At their death, three quarters of the residue goes to Harvard and the other quarter to Acadia University in Nova Scotia. Dr. Rand was connected with the department of philosophy at Harvard from 1897 until his death; since 1933 he had been librarian emeritus of the Philosophical Library.

DEAN VIRGINIA C. GILDERSLEEVE, of Barnard College, has announced the plan decided upon by the faculty committee for awarding the fellowship established by the $30,000 gift from the Women's Organization for National Prohibition Reform. The gift represents the surplus funds for the repeal organization headed by Mrs. Charles H. Sabin. Under the terms of the gift an annual fellowship of $1,300 will be awarded to the successful candidate for a year's graduate work at an approved college or university in one or more of the related fields of history, economics, government and social science. The fellowship will be awarded each year by the college not later than May 1, beginning in 1935. Candidates must be citizens of the United States and have received a bachelor's degree not earlier than June, 1929, from a college or university on the accepted list approved by the Association of American Universities. They must have shown special ability in the field of political science and show promise of future usefulness in public service. The faculty committee on the fellowship award includes Professor Emilie J. Hutchinson, *chairman;* Professor Eugene H. Byrne, Professor Raymond Moley and Dean Gildersleeve.

THE Paris correspondent of the London *Times Educational Supplement* writes that on the completion of his inquiry into the recent school teachers' congress at Nice, at which strong attacks were made on the government, M. Berthod, Minister of Education, has ordered one of the speakers at the congress to be severely reprimanded and another to be brought before the departmental council. In a circular addressed to the education inspectors in each department the minister calls on them to show the reports of their speeches at the congress to certain teachers, to ask them whether they were faithfully reported, and to demand an explanation. M. Berthod adds that where a teacher refuses to answer he is to be told (*a*) that even outside school hours a teacher must think of the effect of his words and deeds on the good name of the school and on his own authority in the eyes of pupils and their families; (*b*) that a congress exclusively composed of teachers, with an agenda containing, with other things, the definition of their rôle in the state and their attitude towards the authorities, can not be regarded as divorced from their professional activities; and (*c*) that in no case can union discipline absolve them of the duty to obey the orders of their superiors. M. Berthod concludes by ordering that if, by his refusal to reply, a teacher shows that he does not share these views, he is to be immediately reprimanded, without prejudice to any later punishment which may be inflicted.

A UNITED PRESS dispatch from Istanbul reports that more than twenty-seven thousand pupils are attending foreign or minority schools there. This situation is considered by the Turks a remnant of the former system of capitulations, and the policy of the Kemalist government clearly is directed toward gradually replacing the schools operated by foreigners with national Turkish establishments. Americans maintain, besides Robert College in the suburb of Bebek, four primary schools at Istanbul, attended last year by 1,453 pupils, while the college numbered 489 students. Virtually all were Turkish subjects. Since the American College at Ismir, Smyrna, closed in June, no more educational establishments are maintained by Americans outside of Istanbul. The English have only two schools, with a total of 371 pupils. The French, who were the first to open schools under concessions dating as far back as the seventeenth century, maintain fifteen primary and eight secondary schools, as well as six colleges directed by Roman Catholic priests or nuns. The pupils in these schools numbered last year about 5,036. The Germans possess one college with 878 pupils, and the Austrians have two schools with 596 pupils.

THE academic requirements and other preliminary plans for the establishment of a school for social work in New Jersey have been outlined by a committee representing the New Jersey Chapter of the American Association of Social Workers, and the New Jersey Conference of Social Work. The committee announced that the establishment of a graduate school of social work can be adequate only if set up by the standards of the American Association of Schools of Social Work. The school will be an individual unit and will have a full-time director. It will be designed to train new entrants to the field of social work. The students must have a bachelor's degree in social science as an entrance requirement.

# DISCUSSION

## A PLAN OF EDUCATION

EDUCATION at public expense is designed to train youth in citizenship. Too much time and money have been spent on one phase of this task, the imparting of information in the attempt to fix habits of thought and action deemed most desirable for an ideal citizen to possess. This type of education has failed to develop personality and the ability to meet new situations as they arise. Efforts to remedy these defects have usually taken the form of courses in character education, vocational guidance and other related activities. These attempts to train for situations through elaboration of education more or less formal may become highly artificial through neglect of that unity of experience and unity of personality which determine attitudes and actions in actual life.

Instead of a more specialized curriculum there must be comprehensive programs for the development of personality. Herein public education should seek to know and coordinate all community resources within which a given group of pupils is growing from childhood to manhood. School life is only one of the many experiences that influence children. Too long it has been overworked by attempting to crowd into a few daily hours and terms of school attendance a heterogeneous series of facts and exercises labeled "curriculum."

In an attempt to carry out the dictum, "School is not preparation for life, but life itself," ambitious educators have bit by bit brought life experiences into the school, but valuable as these may be in their natural setting, they lose when torn out and reproduced in school their relationship to total situations. Hence, deprived of educational values, these activities may become mere items of casual information or forms of amusement.

Instead of attempting to build an education with parts selected from wholes it should be possible to utilize actual life situations. Too long the school has sought to educate with facts selected arbitrarily from miscellaneous fields of knowledge. Often this information has been further alienated from the child by classifying it into the logical categories of adults. Efforts to integrate this material are the result of a worthy desire to overcome its inadequacy.

It should be possible to go further and give children experience, information and attitudes through guided realistic living. To do this, public education must recognize the opportunities that already exist in community life. Instead of trying to make the school a cross-section of life, artificial at the best, it should aim to coordinate life itself as lived at home, in play, at club and church, so that to live it will be to learn and become adjusted.

Besides a "school curriculum" there should be for each community a "Plan of Education" in which schoolroom experiences will be an element, but not the only one, for child development. This "Plan of Education" will use the resources of the community, social and material, each to the best advantage, for all the twelve months of every year. It would develop common policies and aims toward which each agency might contribute its share in social training, religious training, health and recreational activities, vocational insight and civic loyalties. All these advantages could be attained through the wise coordination of agencies already existing in every community.

Such a working together of agencies would not only prevent overlapping but would serve the more important purpose of clearing up the confusion from which children suffer when exposed to many unrelated influences, worthy as each may be.

The school itself, freed from the necessity of imitating life, may devote more of its time to the study of life in its natural functioning—through excursions, discussions and evaluation of things done and observed. More time then could be given to the creative work of recording impressions and developing appreciations.

W. S. DAKIN
STATE DEPARTMENT OF EDUCATION
HARTFORD, CONN.

## THE AMERICAN FEDERATION OF TEACHERS

HAVING spent some time during a decade or longer in studying the unionization of teachers, we read Dr. Henry R. Linville's recent statement with considerable interest.[1] Sixteen years of teaching in Chicago afforded opportunity to observe results at first hand.

Investigation of the publications of the American Federation of Teachers, now readily accessible, indicates that teacher unionization in New York differs greatly from that in Chicago. The earliest affiliation of teachers in Chicago with organized labor occurred in 1902.[2] Classes were then so large that there was much illness among teachers.[3]

We have Dr. Linville's own statement that there has been a period of grievous exploitation of teachers in Chicago. He is entirely correct about this matter, since classes increased further in size in 1933. Physical education teachers in high schools must teach 35 periods per week. A charming woman, little more than fifty years of age, died a month ago. She was a physical training teacher in a large Chicago high school. She had studied thoroughly the laws of health

[1] SCHOOL AND SOCIETY, 40: 1037, November 10, 1934.

[2] *Chicago Teachers' Federation Bulletin*, November 14, 1902, p. 4.

[3] *Ibid.*, April 11, 1902, p. 1.

and she practised what she preached. After nearly a third of a century of teacher unionization Chicago teachers are still exploited; hence it does not appear that Dr. Linville's remedy is effective.

Dr. Linville says: "We maintain that what organized teachers have done has been in the interest of the community as well as in the interest of society as a whole." If he means all types of teachers' organizations, we agree with him, but if he means unionized teachers only, we feel that his statement is open to question.

The American Federation of Labor publishes reports of proceedings of annual conventions. In 1933 it was evident that the Actors' Equity as a union had suffered great decline in membership, due to the depression.[4] It should be remembered that the actors carried on a successful strike in 1919.

It is true that the American Federation of Labor is a conservative force. However, a week spent at the headquarters of the organization in Washington, late in September, 1934, was sufficient to impress me with two facts: (1) The American Federation of Labor expects unionized teachers to pay national dues. (2) Other labor unions have carried on strikes to enforce just demands, but the unionized teachers have failed to do so.

CAROLINE BENGTSON

HASTINGS, NEBRASKA

# SPECIAL CORRESPONDENCE

## PUBLIC HEALTH ON THE RADIO

"DOCTORS, Dollars and Disease" is the title of a series of radio programs on the subject of medical economics, broadcast under the auspices of the National Advisory Council on Radio in Education. This is the council's first venture in the field of public health, and seems to be arousing much interest and some controversy.

As our original announcement states: "The purpose of this series of radio talks is not to advocate any one solution of the problem, but to furnish reliable information and stimulate discussion. The recent progress of the science of medicine has been little short of miraculous. Physicians as a rule have shown fine professional spirit and have given freely of their time without pay. Yet more than fifty million persons in the United States either do not receive the care which they need, or are heavily burdened by its costs, while many practitioners and agencies for health are under-employed and poorly paid. The barrier is mainly economic. It stands between the doctors and the dentists and the nurses who are able and eager to serve and the patients who are sorely in need of the service. The problem is to bring doctors and dollars and diseases into such helpful and continuous contact with each other that the practise of medicine can keep pace with the science of medicine. That is the central theme of this series."

Many solutions are proposed. Some of them —including certain plans for group payment of medical services on an insurance basis—are widely approved, because it is believed that under such plans most families would be able to budget the otherwise unpredictable and possibly unbearable costs of medical care. Other plans —including some forms of state medicine—are widely opposed because of the fear that they will lower the quality of medical services.

In the first program in the series, Dr. Foster sketched all the questions that would be raised in these programs and summarized: "Do all these questions lead to 'state medicine'? (Should medical care be provided for everybody at public expense?) Some of the speakers in this series may think so. Others, I am sure, believe that the government already has gone too far toward paternalism. Many doctors are gravely concerned, as you shall hear in these talks, lest 'state medicine' or even group practise lower the quality of medical service. In particular many doctors fear that the proposed reforms may destroy the precious confidential relations between physicians and patients. Indeed, many of us outside the profession believe that we should make haste slowly; in particular, that we should guard against the real danger of in-

[4] Report of the Proceedings of the Fifty-third Annual Convention of The American Federation of Labor, 1933, p. 36.

terference with the scientific phases of medical service by those who lack scientific equipment. The chief safeguard against all these dangers is informed public opinion, and that is the sole object of these Monday evening talks."

The list of speakers includes many prominent men in public life, in the field of education, in health and welfare activities and in the medical world. In at least half of the programs, the speakers are doctors of medicine. Because School and Society of November 17 reprints an editorial from the *Journal* of the American Medical Association, attacking the program as "propaganda for the socialization of medical care," I want to add that five very prominent members of what might be termed the conservative wing of the American Medical Association were invited to participate in this series, in addition to the doctors who are actually on the program. More than one fourth of the total time available was offered to the following representatives of the organized profession who declined to speak: the president of the American Medical Association; the president of the American College of Surgeons; Nathan Van Etten, M.D., member of the House of Delegates of the American Medical Association and a leader of the minority who declined to sign the report of the Committee on the Costs of Medical Care; Roger Lee, M.D., a member of the House of Delegates of the American Medical Association, and Richard Smith, M.D., of Boston.

There are nineteen programs in the series, every Monday from 10:30 to 10:45 P. M. Eastern Standard Time, through February 25, when President Livingston Farrand, M.D., of Cornell University, will speak. All the talks are being published by the University of Chicago Press, 5750 Ellis Avenue, Chicago, Illinois, and they are available for fifteen cents each, or two dollars for the series of nineteen.

The Public Health Committee, under whose direction these programs are presented, includes Dr. William T. Foster, as chairman, and Drs. H. S. Cumming, Haven Emerson, Alice Hamilton, George E. Vincent, Ray Lyman Wilbur and Senator Robert F. Wagner.

To date the speakers in the series have been Dr. William T. Foster, director of the Pollak Foundation for Economic Research; Dr. Walter P. Bowers, editor of the *New England Journal of Medicine;* Dr. C.-E. A. Winslow, of the School of Medicine at Yale University; Robert Jolly, director of the American Hospital Association; Sir Arthur Newsholme, of England; Dr. George H. Bigelow, director of the Massachusetts General Hospital; Edward A. Filene, of Boston, and Dr. Ray Lyman Wilbur, president of Stanford University, formerly president of the American Medical Association, and Paul H. Douglas, of the University of Chicago.

The remainder of the program is as follows:

Dec. 24. "Tiny Tims of To-day," William Trufant Foster, Ph.D., director, Pollak Foundation.

Dec. 31. "Progress in 1934," Michael M. Davis, Ph.D., and C. Rufus Rorem, Ph.D., C.P.A., Julius Rosenwald Fund, Chicago.

Jan. 7. "Budgeting Hospital Bills," Frank Van Dyk, executive secretary, Hospital Council of Essex County, New Jersey, and Homer Wickenden, A.M., general director, United Hospital Fund, New York City.

Jan. 14. "The Nurse's Part in Public Health," Miss Katherine Tucker, R.N., general director, National Organization for Public Health Nursing, Inc.

Jan. 21. "Mutual Health Service," Nathan Sinai, D.P.H., director of research, Michigan State Medical Society.

Jan. 28. "The Government's Part in Medical Care," William Hard, L.D.H., journalist, Washington, D. C.

Feb. 4. "Where Doctors are Lacking and Why," Haven Emerson, M.D., College of Physicians and Surgeons, New York; formerly president, American Public Health Association.

Feb. 11. "Present Trends in Health Insurance," I. S. Falk, Ph.D., and Edgar Sydenstricker, Milbank Memorial Fund, New York City.

Feb. 18. "The Man from Mars asks Questions," Harry H. Moore, Ph.D., director of study, Committee on the Costs of Medical Care.

Feb. 25. "Next Steps," Livingston Farrand, M.D., president, Cornell University.

Levering Tyson

Director of the National
Advisory Council on Radio
in Education

# QUOTATIONS

## THE SUPPORT OF ENDOWED UNIVERSITIES

No thoughtful observer of the struggles through which our social and economic life has been passing but must have wondered more than once whether our American confidence in education as the great safeguard and support of democracy were ill-founded, and at all events whether the nature of that education must not be fundamentally reconstructed. This thought has certainly occurred repeatedly to the thousands of embittered graduates of our colleges who, after years of hard grinding sacrifice to win an education, have recently found themselves walking the streets in search of a job—any job that would give them food and shelter. And their sense of the futility of it all has often been most acutely directed toward our higher education. But sober second thought can only reinforce the conviction that, whatever their shortcomings and whatever transformations it may be expedient that they should undergo, in their essence the colleges and universities represent indispensable intellectual and spiritual values which our social order, if it is to endure at all, simply can not afford to forego. The distressing fate which has overtaken many of the continental universities, ravaged of their independence and prostituted to the dictates of political expediency, may well serve us as a grim object lesson of the evils which may flow from violent social upheaval.

. . . . . . . .

As is well understood, institutions of the type represented by Yale have recently suffered bewildering shrinkage of capital funds and staggering losses of income, but there are other more remote consequences of the depression which I believe to be potentially far more sinister. Current social and political trends, accentuated, if not directly provoked, by the economic depression, contain a menace for the great endowed institutions which should not be overlooked. Counting among their number the most venerable and many of the most important of our universities, they have owed their power to assemble great bodies of scholars to create great libraries and laboratories and museums, very largely to the gifts of generous benefactors, often in the form of legacies. If the present tendency to excessive taxation of personal income persists, or increases, as it may, and if this be coupled with further assault by inheritance taxes upon testamentary estates, the two largest sources of income for these institutions will almost inevitably dry up or, in any case, be gravely impaired. If on top of these procedures exemption from taxation of gifts to philanthropic and religious organizations should be repealed, as has already been energetically proposed, the consequences would again be extremely destructive to endowed educational foundations. If, finally, the widespread effort to tax their physical properties were successful, their plight would be most critical.

Tuition charges, apart from endowment the only source of income, could not possibly alone support these institutions of learning, unless, on the one hand, educational standards were ruthlessly sacrificed and the methods of teaching were radically and disastrously modified (*e.g.*, by discharging many of the teachers and employing a few lecturers to address huge classes) or, on the other hand, the fees were greatly increased, which at present would, as a financial device, defeat itself by greatly reducing attendance. Adequate scholarships would help solve the problem, but these rest almost invariably upon endowments or private gifts and would be subject to the same malign influences already pointed out. Whether the social order in America can afford seriously to cripple these endowed institutions, and possibly to destroy some of them, should be conscientiously considered by the advocates of taxation methods the results of which are reasonably certain ultimately to undermine the vitality of the universities.

A complete reorganization of education in the United States, with a shift in its objectives and a complete change of its center of gravity, may, as some persons believe, be highly desirable; but to bring this about by indirection and more or less unintentionally as a result of a panic-stricken effort to mitigate through injudicious taxation the effects of a transient economic crisis, or as the result of a merely emotional assault upon the results of thrift and industry, would be a sorry product of our democratic society, and one ruinous to some of the highest values which have been built up in our century and a half of national life. In any case, thoughtful people should not be oblivious to the obvious implications for higher education of certain of these current trends.

As a consequence of these circumstances, Yale finds itself in grave need of additions to its capital resources adequate to make good the losses of income which in common with all other endowed institutions it has of late suffered.

Funds for scholarships are urgently needed, especially in the undergraduate divisions, where fifty could be used to the greatest advantage. The report reveals that the university has had to curtail its budget by nearly one million dollars as compared with 1931.—*President James Rowland Angell in his report to the trustees of Yale University.*

# REPORTS

## THE WORK OF THE CARNEGIE CORPORATION

DR. FREDERICK P. KEPPEL, president of the Carnegie Corporation of New York, states in his annual report that of the $5,000,000 voted from the income of the corporation during 1933–34 only $40,000 was appropriated for emergency and other grants falling outside the normal program, as against nearly a million dollars voted for the same purpose in 1932–33. Sixty-four per cent. of the year's grants were devoted to fields in which the corporation has long been active—library interests, adult education, the arts, research studies; eighteen per cent. of the grants were made for the initiation of new activities; and ten per cent. were made on the basis of long-continued relations with the institution or individual in question or because of matters involving inter-foundation comity.

The number of proposals and suggestions presented to the corporation during 1933–34 was nearly twice that of the previous years. Of the proposals 255 resulted in grants, 847 received unfavorable consideration, and 556 were carried over for consideration in 1934–35, or thereafter.

A word may be said as to the device, which seems to be growing, of bombarding a foundation with letters and telegrams of endorsement when some particular proposal is up for consideration. *Bona fide* support from those who have first-hand knowledge is always welcome and frequently very helpful in reaching a decision, but it is no compliment to the intelligence of foundation trustees to assume that they can not distinguish between such communications and the wholesale product of pressure group methods.

Appropriations to "general education" constitute the most frequent type of grant made by the corporation. Mr. Keppel defines this type of education as "concerning itself not with the fortunes of any particular institution, but rather with the fuller understanding of the laws of learning and their application at different levels and for different purposes and with the broader provision which society is making for the adjustment of the individual to his environment." The purpose of these grants is to bridge the gap, brought about by changing conditions, between the layman and the professional in the educational field.

The corporation is contemplating two general studies, one on support for scholarly publication and one on grants to operating organizations for general expenses as contrasted with grants for specific programs. Regarding the study of scholarly publications, Mr. Keppel says, "It will be interesting to see whether careful inquiry will confirm the opinion frequently expressed that careless preparation for publication results in the printing of material far too bulky for effectiveness to say nothing of being unnecessarily expensive. Furthermore, it is said that the material is not only poorly organized, but when published it suffers by comparison with corresponding material appearing in other countries."

Of the independent college with a limited endowment Mr. Keppel says: "There must be a fundamental change in the attitude of the institution towards the individual student and also, a different conception on the part of the student as to what he is there for, a different use of his energies and capacities. Advance will be made by an effective study as to the application of what we now know regarding individual difference, interests and motives, mental hygiene, the technique of continuous record, the uses of comprehensive and other examinations."

For some years to come the total income of

the corporation that is available for grants will be considerably reduced because of the policy of the Finance Committee to place security above yield in making new investments.

The largest grants voted during 1933–34 were $500,000 for permanent funds of the American Library Association; $538,000 to the American Law Institute for the Re-statement of the Common Law; $300,000 for support of the Institute of International Education; $250,000 for the continuation of the Australian Council for Educational Research and for the establishment of a similar institution in New Zealand; $238,000 for support of the American Association for Adult Education and the National Occupational Conference. New undertakings include an endowment grant of $100,000 to the Museum of Modern Art, $200,000 divided among the universities of Western Canada, and grants, from the British Dominions and Colonies Fund, aggregating $205,000 to finance a general survey of Southern and Equatorial Africa, to contribute toward social research in the Union of South Africa, and to support a three-year program in the interest of over-seas students at the Institute of Education, University of London.

# EDUCATIONAL RESEARCH AND STATISTICS

## WHAT THE PUBLIC SCHOOL ADMINISTRATOR THINKS OF PROFESSIONAL TRAINING IN EDUCATION[1]

IN the course of its study of the value of "Required Courses in Education" Committee Q of the American Association of University Professors sent a questionnaire to the principals or head masters of 136 private secondary schools and to 1,800 high-school teachers for the purpose of ascertaining the attitude of these two groups toward required courses in education.[2] Replies were received and used by Committee Q from 83 head masters and from 391 high-school teachers, or 61 per cent. of the head masters of private schools and nearly 22 per cent. of the high-school teachers to whom questionnaires were sent. On the basis of replies to its questionnaire the committee presents certain generalizations and recommendations which seem to be wholly unwarranted.[3]

Just why the committee selected the 136 head masters of private schools as a group from whom it might secure valid judgments concerning any aspect of the preparation of teachers for the public schools is difficult to understand, unless one assumes that the committee had previously decided what conclusions it wished to reach from its investigations and then submitted the questionnaire to a group of school men who would be quite certain to support the preconceived generalizations. Certainly no well-informed educator would regard the judgments of head masters of private schools as having any considerable degree of validity in the matter of professional training of teachers for the public schools. The reasons for this are so obvious that it seems scarcely necessary to present them. Many of the head masters of private schools have had little or no professional training and naturally they feel no need of it. Their pupils are a select group, coming largely from our better homes. The school is usually far removed from the community from which its pupils come and consequently feels no need of adapting its educational procedures to the varying demands of the local situation. Preparing pupils for college entrance is the sole objective of many of these private schools; thus their educational function in society is very simple as compared with the public school.

In order to ascertain the attitude of the public-school administrator in Indiana toward professional courses in the training of teachers the writers submitted the same questions which Committee Q used in its study to all public-school administrators in the state. The writers are perfectly clear in their own minds as to the value of the questionnaire method as a basis for

[1] This study was done in cooperation with the Alpha Chapter of Phi Delta Kappa of Indiana University. Alpha Chapter kindly distributed the copies of the questionnaire. The writers tabulated and analyzed the results.

[2] A condensed form of the committee's report is found in the *Bulletin* of the American Association of University Professors, Volume XIX, Number 3, March, 1933. Committee Q was appointed by the American Association of University Professors to investigate the professional requirements for teachers in the secondary schools.

[3] For a critical evaluation of the report of Committee Q the reader is referred to University of Kansas Bulletin, "The Value of Professional Training in Education," by Smith, O'Brien and Bayles, December, 1933.

conclusions concerning the value of professional training. The problem under consideration can never be answered by the collection of opinions of any group of individuals. However, if we must rely upon opinions of any group, then certainly there is no group whose opinions should be more seriously considered than the school men who employ, observe and supervise the teachers who have had varying amounts of professional training.

### THE EXTENT TO WHICH INDIANA SCHOOL MEN BELIEVE IN AND USE PROFESSIONAL EDUCATION

Our questionnaire was adapted from the two questionnaires used by Committee Q. It was made up by adding two questions to their "Questionnaire to Private Schools." One of the added questions (No. 2) was set up to duplicate the first question in the original list, but with a different point of reference. The other question (No. 5) was taken directly from their "Questionnaire to High School Teachers." Certain minor changes were made in the statement of some of the questions so that the questionnaire would be applicable to the public-school situation. Also, in order to be somewhat more systematic, the check lists of possible answers were rearranged and extended somewhat. While the questionnaire was not well adapted to the Indiana situation with regard to teacher-training requirements, it was felt that in order to make valid comparison with the results obtained by Committee Q it should not be modified in any of its essential aspects.

The questionnaire, as thus formulated, is as follows:

1. In selecting and recommending teachers (for appointment to positions in your school system) who have not already had considerable experience, are you influenced by the amount of professional training (courses in education and psychology) the prospective teacher has had?—Answer by checking the appropriate response.

——No, emphatically
——No
——Almost none
——No, with reservation
——Yes, emphatically
——Yes
——Yes, with reservation
——Yes, a moderate amount
——Yes, very little
——Yes, due to requirement
——Yes, adversely
——No inexperienced teachers considered

2. In selecting and recommending teachers (for appointment to positions in your school system) who have had even considerable experience, are you influenced by the amount of professional training (courses in education and psychology) the prospective teacher has had?—Answer by checking the appropriate response.

——No, emphatically
——No
——Almost none
——No, with reservation
——Yes, emphatically
——Yes
——Yes, with reservation
——Yes, a moderate amount
——Yes, very little
——Yes, due to requirement
——Yes, adversely

3. If attention is paid to professional training, what is the type of such preparation (nature of courses) that is desired?—Answer by checking the specific course or courses.

——Philosophy
——Philosophy of Education
——Educational Sociology
——History of Education
——Principles of Education
——General Psychology
——Educational Psychology
——General Methods
——Special Methods
——Practice Teaching
——School Administration
——(Write in) ————

4. Have those of your teachers who have had extensive specific "pedagogical" training proved, in your judgment, more skillful in imparting knowledge, and more successful in stimulating interest and study than those who have had no, or little, such training?—Answer by checking the appropriate response.

——No, emphatically
——No, a hindrance or handicap
——No
——Not to a great extent
——Not necessarily
——Yes, emphatically
——Yes
——Yes, as to imparting knowledge
——Yes, as to stimulating interest and study

5. What, in your judgment, is the relative value of the different types of professional training (professional courses)?—Answer by ranking the following courses according to importance, the most important first, the next most important second, etc. In the blank spaces provided for the purpose, simply write the respective ranks, 1, 2, 3, etc., to 12.

——Philosophy
——Philosophy of Education
——Educational Sociology
——History of Education
——Principles of Education
——General Psychology
——Educational Psychology
——General Methods
——Special Methods
——Practice Teaching
——School Administration
——(Write in) ———

6. Remarks

This questionnaire was mailed to 1,004 school men, including all school men who are concerned with the supervision of high-school teachers in the public schools of Indiana. The sampling included 662 principals of township high schools, 160 town and city superintendents, 92 county superintendents, 50 members of college faculties in departments of education and 40 Phi Delta Kappans not definitely classified.

Replies were received from 623, or 62 per cent. of the men to whom the questionnaire was sent. This number included 368, or 55 per cent. of the principals of township high schools; 82, or 90 per cent. of the county superintendents; 118, or 74 per cent. of the town and city superintendents; 48, or 96 per cent. of the members of college faculties, and 7, or 18 per cent. of the unclassified Phi Delta Kappans.

Table I shows the extent to which the school men in the present sampling are influenced by professional training as a basis for selecting and recommending relatively inexperienced teachers for positions in their school systems. Here it will be observed that 586, or 94.06 per cent. of the school men make use of professional training for the purpose indicated, while only 27, or 4.33 per cent. do not so use professional train-

TABLE I
DISTRIBUTION OF REPLIES TO QUESTION NO. 1

| General classification | | Yes, emphatically | Yes | Yes, a moderate amount | Yes, with reservation | Yes, very little | Yes, due to requirement | Yes, adversely | No, emphatically | No | Almost none | No, with reservation | No inexperienced teachers considered | No answer recorded | Total |
|---|---|---|---|---|---|---|---|---|---|---|---|---|---|---|---|
| 1. Principals of township high schools | N | 67 | 110 | 76 | 57 | 14 | 18 | ...... | 4 | 8 | 2 | ...... | 2 | 10 | 368 |
| | % | 18.20 | 29.89 | 20.65 | 15.49 | 3.81 | 4.89 | ...... | 1.09 | 2.18 | 0.54 | ...... | 0.54 | 2.72 | 100 |
| 2. County superintendents | N | 11 | 33 | 18 | 16 | 1 | ...... | ...... | ...... | 3 | ...... | ...... | ...... | ...... | 82 |
| | % | 13.41 | 40.24 | 21.96 | 19.51 | 1.22 | ...... | ...... | ...... | 3.66 | ...... | ...... | ...... | ...... | 100 |
| 3. City superintendents | N | 25 | 46 | 20 | 12 | 1 | 6 | 1 | 1 | ...... | 1 | 3 | 2 | ...... | 118 |
| | % | 21.19 | 38.98 | 16.95 | 10.17 | 0.85 | 5.08 | 0.85 | 0.85 | ...... | 0.85 | 2.54 | 1.69 | ...... | 100 |
| 4. Members of college faculties | N | 27 | 14 | 3 | 3 | ...... | ...... | ...... | 1 | ...... | ...... | ...... | ...... | ...... | 48 |
| | % | 56.25 | 29.17 | 6.25 | 6.25 | ...... | ...... | ...... | 2.08 | ...... | ...... | ...... | ...... | ...... | 100 |
| 5. Unclassified | N | 7 | ...... | ...... | ...... | ...... | ...... | ...... | ...... | ...... | ...... | ...... | ...... | ...... | 7 |
| | % | 100 | ...... | ...... | ...... | ...... | ...... | ...... | ...... | ...... | ...... | ...... | ...... | ...... | 100 |
| 6. Entire sampling | N | 137 | 203 | 117 | 8 | 16 | 24 | 1 | 6 | 11 | 3 | 3 | 4 | 10 | 623 |
| | % | 21.99 | 32.58 | 18.78 | 14.13 | 2.57 | 3.85 | 0.16 | 0.96 | 1.77 | 0.48 | 0.48 | 0.64 | 1.61 | 100 |

*Summary:* Number making use of professional training ............ 586 (94.06%)
Number not making use of professional training ............ 27 (4.33%)
Number not replying to the question ............ 10 (1.61%)

TABLE II

DISTRIBUTION OF REPLIES TO QUESTION NO. 2

| General classification | | Yes, emphatically | Yes | Yes, a moderate amount | Yes, with reservation | Yes, very little | Yes, due to requirement | Yes, adversely | No, emphatically | No | Almost none | No, with reservation | No answer recorded | Total |
|---|---|---|---|---|---|---|---|---|---|---|---|---|---|---|
| 1. Principals of township high schools | N | 42 | 107 | 82 | 57 | 27 | 10 | ...... | 4 | 16 | 6 | 7 | 10 | 368 |
| | % | 11.41 | 29.07 | 22.28 | 15.49 | 7.34 | 2.72 | ...... | 1.09 | 4.35 | 1.63 | 1.90 | 2.72 | 100 |
| 2. County superintendents | N | 9 | 27 | 14 | 12 | 4 | ...... | ...... | ...... | 4 | 1 | ...... | 11 | 82 |
| | % | 10.98 | 32.93 | 17.07 | 14.63 | 4.88 | ...... | ...... | ...... | 4.88 | 1.22 | ...... | 13.41 | 100 |
| 3. City superintendents | N | 16 | 45 | 23 | 14 | 3 | 2 | ...... | 1 | 4 | 5 | 2 | 3 | 118 |
| | % | 13.56 | 38.14 | 19.49 | 11.87 | 2.54 | 1.69 | ...... | 0.85 | 3.39 | 4.24 | 1.69 | 2.54 | 100 |
| 4. Members of college faculties | N | 19 | 21 | 1 | 3 | 1 | 2 | ...... | 1 | ...... | ...... | ...... | ...... | 48 |
| | % | 39.59 | 43.75 | 2.08 | 6.25 | 2.08 | 4.17 | ...... | 2.08 | ...... | ...... | ...... | ...... | 100 |
| 5. Unclassified | N | 6 | 1 | ...... | ...... | ...... | ...... | ...... | ...... | ...... | ...... | ...... | ...... | 7 |
| | % | 85.71 | 14.29 | ...... | ...... | ...... | ...... | ...... | ...... | ...... | ...... | ...... | ...... | 100 |
| 6. Entire sampling | N | 92 | 201 | 120 | 86 | 35 | 14 | ...... | 6 | 24 | 12 | 9 | 24 | 623 |
| | % | 14.77 | 32.26 | 19.26 | 13.80 | 5.62 | 2.25 | ...... | 0.96 | 3.85 | 1.93 | 1.45 | 3.85 | 100 |

*Summary:* Number making use of professional training .......... 548 (87.96%)
Number not making use of professional training .......... 51 (8.19%)
Number not replying to the question .......... 24 (3.85%)

TABLE III

DISTRIBUTION OF REPLIES (CHECKS OF ENDORSEMENT) TO QUESTION NO. 3

| General classification | | Philosophy | Philosophy of education | Educational sociology | History of education | Principles of education | General psychology | Educational psychology | General methods | Practise teaching | Special methods | School administration | Miscellaneous (written in) |
|---|---|---|---|---|---|---|---|---|---|---|---|---|---|
| 1. Principals of township high schools (368) | N | 34 | 123 | 94 | 63 | 160 | 171 | 221 | 215 | 258 | 184 | 90 | 12 |
| | % | 9.24 | 33.42 | 25.54 | 17.12 | 43.47 | 46.46 | 60.05 | 58.42 | 70.10 | 49.99 | 24.45 | 3.26 |
| 2. County superintendents (82) | N | 8 | 21 | 28 | 18 | 33 | 39 | 44 | 54 | 58 | 35 | 38 | 15 |
| | % | 9.76 | 25.61 | 34.15 | 21.95 | 40.24 | 47.56 | 53.66 | 65.85 | 70.73 | 42.68 | 46.34 | 18.29 |
| 3. City superintendents (118) | N | 16 | 49 | 43 | 33 | 67 | 58 | 94 | 76 | 91 | 84 | 26 | 5 |
| | % | 13.56 | 41.52 | 36.44 | 27.96 | 56.78 | 49.15 | 79.66 | 64.40 | 77.11 | 71.18 | 22.03 | 4.24 |
| 4. Members of college faculties (48) | N | 4 | 33 | 15 | 11 | 34 | 26 | 45 | 27 | 46 | 38 | 16 | 8 |
| | % | 8.33 | 68.75 | 31.25 | 22.92 | 70.83 | 54.17 | 93.75 | 56.25 | 95.83 | 79.17 | 33.33 | 16.67 |
| 5. Unclassified (7) | N | 3 | 5 | 6 | 2 | 4 | 6 | 7 | 6 | 6 | 6 | 3 | 2 |
| | % | 42.86 | 71.43 | 85.71 | 28.57 | 57.14 | 85.71 | 100.00 | 85.71 | 85.71 | 85.71 | 42.86 | 28.57 |
| 6. Entire sampling (623) | N | 65 | 231 | 186 | 127 | 298 | 300 | 411 | 378 | 459 | 347 | 173 | 42 |
| | % | 10.43 | 37.08 | 29.85 | 20.38 | 47.83 | 48.15 | 65.97 | 60.67 | 73.67 | 55.69 | 27.77 | 6.74 |

TABLE IV

DISTRIBUTION OF REPLIES TO QUESTION NO. 4

| General classification | | Yes, emphatically | Yes | Yes, as to imparting knowledge | Yes, as to stimulating interest and study | No, emphatically | No, a hindrance or handicap | No | Not to a great extent | Not necessarily | No answer recorded | Total |
|---|---|---|---|---|---|---|---|---|---|---|---|---|
| 1. Principals of township high schools | N | 89 | 117 | 27 | 35 | 2 | ......... | 17 | 31 | 39 | 11 | 368 |
| | % | 24.18 | 31.79 | 7.34 | 9.51 | 0.54 | ......... | 4.62 | 8.43 | 10.60 | 2.99 | 100 |
| 2. County superintendents | N | 15 | 36 | 4 | ......... | ......... | ......... | ......... | 6 | 8 | 13 | 82 |
| | % | 18.29 | 43.90 | 4.88 | ......... | ......... | ......... | ......... | 7.32 | 9.76 | 15.85 | 100 |
| 3. City superintendents | N | 28 | 43 | 12 | 8 | 2 | ......... | 4 | 7 | 9 | 5 | 118 |
| | % | 23.73 | 36.44 | 10.17 | 6.78 | 1.69 | ......... | 3.39 | 5.93 | 7.63 | 4.24 | 100 |
| 4. Members of college faculties | N | 22 | 15 | 3 | ......... | 2 | ......... | ......... | 2 | 1 | 3 | 48 |
| | % | 45.83 | 31.25 | 6.25 | ......... | 4.17 | ......... | ......... | 4.17 | 2.08 | 6.25 | 100 |
| 5. Unclassified | N | 5 | 1 | ......... | ......... | ......... | ......... | ......... | ......... | ......... | 1 | 7 |
| | % | 71.42 | 14.29 | ......... | ......... | ......... | ......... | ......... | ......... | ......... | 14.29 | 100 |
| 6. Entire sampling | N | 159 | 212 | 46 | 43 | 6 | ......... | 21 | 46 | 57 | 33 | 623 |
| | % | 25.52 | 34.03 | 7.39 | 6.90 | 0.96 | ......... | 3.37 | 7.38 | 9.15 | 5.30 | 100 |

*Summary:* Number believing that professional training contributes materially to teaching success ........ 460 (73.84%)
Number believing that professional training contributes somewhat but not necessarily to teaching success ........ 103 (16.53%)
Number believing that professional training does not contribute to teaching success ........ 27 (4.33%)
Number not committing themselves on the question ........ 33 (5.30%)

ing, and 10, or 1.61 per cent. do not express themselves either way. It will be observed also that the different groups of school men use and believe in professional training to about the same extent. The members of college faculties seem to favor strongly professional training, while the principals of township schools tend to respect professional training somewhat less than the other groups.

Table II shows the extent to which Indiana school men are influenced by professional training as a criterion in selecting experienced teachers. The picture in this case is much the same as in the previous case. Extensive use is made of professional training in selecting and recommending experienced teachers. Approximately 88 per cent. of the school men so use professional training; 8 per cent. do not, and 4 per cent. do not commit themselves on the issue.

The types of professional training that the school men desire for the prospective teacher are indicated in Table III. This table shows the frequency with which the different professional courses were checked as desirable in teacher-training. According to these data, practice teaching stands first; educational psychology, second; general methods, third; special methods, fourth, and so on down to philosophy, eleventh, as desired types of professional training.

The extent to which the different groups of school men and the entire sampling believe that professional training functions is indicated by the data presented in Table IV. These data show that the different groups believe strongly in the influence of professional training on the success of the teacher. In all, 460, or 73.84 per cent. of the school men believe that professional training contributes materially to the success of the teacher; 103, or 16.53 per cent. believe that professional training contributes somewhat, but not necessarily, to the success of the teacher; only 27, or 4.33 per cent. believe that professional training does not contribute anything toward successful teaching, and 33, or 5.30 per cent. do not commit themselves.

The relative importance of the different types of professional training, according to the opinion of the school men involved in the sampling, is shown in Table V. The values presented in this table are the *number* of times the particular subject was rated; *average rank,* average of the ranks assigned as directed in question No. 5, and *rank order,* order of preference based on the *average ranks.*

Table V is largely self-explanatory. But, for the sake of emphasis, it should perhaps be pointed out (1) that in order of preference the different subjects stand as follows: First, practise teaching; second, educational psychology; third, general methods; fourth, special methods; fifth, general psychology; sixth, principles of education; seventh, philosophy of education; eighth, school administration; ninth, educational sociology; tenth, miscellaneous subjects (written in the space provided in the questionnaire); eleventh, history of education, and twelfth, phi-

TABLE V

THE RELATIVE IMPORTANCE OF THE DIFFERENT PROFESSIONAL COURSES (IN TERMS OF THE RATINGS ASSIGNED IN ANSWER TO QUESTION NO. 5)

| General classification | | Philosophy | Philosophy of education | Educational sociology | History of education | Principles of education | General psychology | Educational psychology | General methods | Practise teaching | Special methods | School administration | Miscellaneous (written in) |
|---|---|---|---|---|---|---|---|---|---|---|---|---|---|
| 1. Principals of township high schools (368) | Number | 335 | 328 | 285 | 284 | 332 | 335 | 326 | 364 | 343 | 339 | 315 | 53 |
| | Average rank | 8.54 | 6.59 | 7.57 | 8.14 | 5.08 | 4.72 | 3.95 | 4.03 | 3.75 | 4.26 | 7.55 | 8.39 |
| | Rank order | 12 | 7 | 9 | 10 | 6 | 5 | 2 | 3 | 1 | 4 | 8 | 11 |
| 2. County superintendents (82) | Number | 57 | 60 | 61 | 59 | 62 | 63 | 67 | 69 | 70 | 62 | 61 | 10 |
| | Average rank | 9.27 | 7.51 | 6.88 | 8.37 | 5.37 | 5.09 | 4.31 | 3.98 | 3.08 | 4.41 | 6.24 | 6.88 |
| | Rank order | 12 | 10 | 8.5 | 11 | 6 | 5 | 3 | 2 | 1 | 4 | 7 | 8.5 |
| 3. City superintendents (118) | Number | 88 | 98 | 97 | 95 | 104 | 99 | 108 | 104 | 107 | 106 | 87 | 14 |
| | Average rank | 8.74 | 6.53 | 6.90 | 8.10 | 4.64 | 4.75 | 3.43 | 3.95 | 3.30 | 3.93 | 7.11 | 8.50 |
| | Rank order | 12 | 7 | 8 | 10 | 5 | 6 | 2 | 4 | 1 | 3 | 9 | 11 |
| 4. Members of college faculties (48) | Number | 40 | 45 | 42 | 43 | 46 | 44 | 48 | 42 | 46 | 44 | 43 | 13 |
| | Average rank | 9.19 | 5.00 | 7.53 | 8.38 | 4.78 | 5.95 | 3.72 | 5.27 | 2.72 | 4.44 | 7.99 | 7.25 |
| | Rank order | 12 | 6 | 9 | 11 | 5 | 7 | 2 | 4 | 1 | 3 | 10 | 8 |
| 5. Unclassified (7) | Number | 5 | 6 | 6 | 6 | 5 | 6 | 6 | 5 | 6 | 5 | 5 | 5 |
| | Average rank | 9.20 | 7.17 | 7.00 | 8.83 | 4.60 | 4.83 | 2.33 | 3.00 | 4.83 | 5.20 | 8.40 | 6.20 |
| | Rank order | 12 | 9 | 8 | 11 | 3 | 4.5 | 1 | 2 | 4.5 | 6 | 10 | 7 |
| 6. Entire sampling (623) | Number | 525 | 537 | 491 | 487 | 549 | 549 | 555 | 584 | 572 | 556 | 511 | 95 |
| | Average rank | 8.66 | 6.51 | 7.41 | 8.19 | 5.03 | 4.90 | 3.90 | 4.15 | 3.51 | 4.26 | 7.40 | 8.11 |
| | Rank order | 12 | 7 | 9 | 11 | 6 | 5 | 2 | 3 | 1 | 4 | 8 | 10 |

losophy, and (2) that the different groups of school men are closely agreed as to this rank order of the different subjects.

### Conclusion

This survey of opinions indicates very clearly that Indiana school administrators and teacher-trainers in general are strongly in favor of professional training for prospective teachers. A large majority of the administrators make extensive use of professional training in selecting teachers for positions in their school systems. This is the case whether the candidate for a position be an inexperienced or an experienced teacher.

The types of training most generally used in this connection are: (1) Practise teaching, (2) educational psychology, (3) general methods, (4) special methods, (5) general psychology and (6) principles of education. Other types of training are used as criteria, of course; but these six types are the most frequently used, and they are used in the order listed. Indeed, the state certification requirements include the six types of training listed here and a number of other types; and it might be thought that the different types are used just because of this requirement. But it is obvious from the questionnaire reports that this condition is not the case: only approximately 4 per cent. of the school men involved in the sampling said they considered professional training as a criterion, just because it was required.

As a matter of fact, school administrators are at least apparently convinced that professional training contributes materially to teaching success. At any rate, three fourths of those who replied stated as much; and a large percentage of the remainder stated that they considered professional training as of value.

It is very apparent from the comments of prominent school men in Indiana that there is an insistent demand for a more intelligent and a more rigid selection of students in our teacher-training institutions for admission to teacher-training courses. It is also evident that in the consideration of prospective teachers school administrators believe teacher-training institutions should place more emphasis on the matter of personality than has been done in the past. (A survey of the material under "Remarks" was made, but on account of its length could not be included in this article.)

The results of this study present an almost complete refutation of the generalizations reached by Committee Q, especially in so far as these generalizations pertain to the attitude of school men toward professional courses in education. Since the present sampling of school men is much larger and since it includes all types of public-school administrators, it is legitimate to conclude that the results obtained by Committee Q, together with the sweeping generalizations based thereon, have practically no validity so far as training teachers for our public schools is concerned.

Many of the public-school administrators state that the requirements for professional training of teachers should be revised. There is no consensus of opinion, however, as to just what changes should be made. The authors of this report are in perfect agreement with these school men and also with Committee Q's report on this point. But it must be pointed out again that revision does not necessarily mean either decreasing or increasing professional requirements. Improvement in teacher-training, whether this means decreasing or increasing professional requirements or any other requirements, is the one desirable objective upon which all educators are agreed. Revision to secure such improvement should obviously represent the combined efforts of public-school administrators and officials of teacher-training institutions who are intimately associated with the work of the public schools.

The late G. C. Brandenburg
O. C. Trimble
Purdue University

## NEW BOOKS IN EDUCATION

Adler, Herman and others. *The Incidence of Delinquency in Berkeley, 1928–32.* Pp. x + 102. University of California Press. $2.00.

*Annuaire International de l'Education et de l'Enseignement, 1934.* Pp. 482. Bureau International d'Education, Geneva. Frs. suisses 12.

Brown, Lynn E. *Housing of Women Students at the Normal Schools and Teachers' Colleges in New York State.* Pp. xi + 241 + x. H. L. Hedrick, Columbus, Ohio.

*l'Admission Aux Ecoles Secondaires.* Pp. 222. Bureau International d'Education, Geneva. Frs. suisses 5.

McLean, Beth B. *Good Manners.* Pp. 128. Manual Arts Press. $0.72.

# SCHOOL AND SOCIETY

WITH WHICH ARE COMBINED THE EDUCATIONAL REVIEW ESTABLISHED IN 1891, THE TEACHERS MAGAZINE, ESTABLISHED IN 1878, AND THE SCHOOL JOURNAL, ESTABLISHED IN 1874.

Volume 40 | Saturday, December 29, 1934 | Number 1044

## THE CHALLENGE OF THE FRONTIER[1]

By Dr. ROBERT LINCOLN KELLY

PERMANENT EXECUTIVE OFFICER, ASSOCIATION OF AMERICAN COLLEGES, NEW YORK CITY

More than forty years ago the Census Bureau of the United States announced the fact that the frontier was ended. The frontier, terminated by this edict, was the frontier of free government lands, of expanding railroad construction, of staked claims and golden dreams. It was, however, but the last of a series of challenges to sturdy yeomen. It, as its predecessors, had drawn into its westward current many men and women, restless, discontented, ambitious, vaguely optimistic and youthfully buoyant. The same government at Washington to-day (and be it noted the government of the United States is one of the few really ancient governments now in existence) is urging some of the disillusioned westerners, and some who refuse to be disillusioned, to vacate their arid lands and move back—or forth—to more propitious habitats.

But it was not "a fact" that the frontier was ended in 1890. Within the intervening forty years frontiers have sprung up, in numbers, like the armed men from the dragon's teeth of Cadmus. Increasingly, men and women have exhibited pioneer states of mind, as they have fared forth to accept challenges to heroic adventure. And they have not ceased to dream the American dream. In a rapidly contracting world, college administrators in a peculiar sense still have the feeling of vast open spaces. Like nature, they have abhorred these vacuums and in the midst of their Herculean labors have had in some measure the experience of pushing ahead the van, if not of civilization, toward which hopeful ones aspire, at least of such culture as we possess.

Along with other forward-looking citizens of the republic, they have transcended national frontiers—all, in mind and spirit; some, in fact—and have ventured into oceanic, climatic, aerial, stratospheric, bathyspheric, interelectronic, internebular areas of truth seeking and finding. Neither heights nor depths nor any other creature can baffle the true pioneer. Every new college administrator consciously stands in awe, like Immanuel Kant, at the starry heavens above him and the moral law within him.

*The Intellectual Frontier,* within the four decades, has challenged in cumulative fashion the energies of many college men. Such watchwords of this movement as independent study, study for honors, comprehensive examinations, are but signs marking a certain degree of progress. Phi Beta Kappa, harking back to Emerson, has launched its magazine, *The American Scholar,* and is taking steps to designate its

[1] Delivered at the installation of William Orville Mendenhall as president of Whittier College, California, on September 21, 1934.

future members by means of those more refined and trustworthy processes of selection which are in general use among progressive educators.

Within the undergraduate colleges this movement is at one and the same time away from high intellectual specialization and in the direction of achieving a synthesis of fundamental values. At the hands of some college pioneers it has become a doctrine of aristocratic intellectualism. In less extreme manifestation, there is increasing respect both among teachers and students for intellectual achievement. The "bad lands" of the conservation and increase of knowledge, at times rather lightly abandoned because of their supposed aridity, have been fertilized and vivified through the discovery within the student consciousness of deeply hidden springs. We have scarcely arrived at the status of the French intellectual, but there is a marked seriousness of purpose within the area of this ever-expanding frontier.

*The Frontier of Appreciation* is a relatively new discovery by the colleges. At last we are beginning to study the arts in colleges of liberal arts. To be sure, faculties are rightly conservative as the arts including music claim a place in the college programs of study. The conservatism is justified in the light of the horrible examples of art and music that have too frequently been cited for academic recognition.

In this area of pioneering the secondary schools often surpass the colleges in the quality of their achievement. Many students lose in college the ground they have gained in high school. College art and music have been their own worst enemies. They have made their academic conquests doubly difficult.

But some kind of appreciation and performance is as inevitable as human development itself. They are appetites inherent in the human constitution. The occupancy of this frontier has made rather striking progress in recent years in architecture, landscape gardening, dramatics, household art, folk art and music. The most successful college programs in music are those that offer to the public the highest grade of performance. The mediocre and bad are losing their popularity. In some sections it is claimed college music has gone highbrow. As a passing word, it may be recorded that the greatest and most enduring achievement on the Broadway boards during the last season was written by a former faculty member of Whittier College. Indeed, at the summer session of the University of Cambridge just closed, that great English critic Wilkinson asserted "America is leading in the writing and producing of plays. The hope of the modern drama is in America."

Great foundations are contributing factors in these pioneer efforts to encourage the various types of artistic appreciation. The Association of American Colleges in its studies and books has set forth the best aspirations of our greatest architects. The forthcoming report on music in the colleges will reach a high-water mark in measures of quality in musical appreciation and performance.

The arts have a remarkable history and a vast literature. There is adequate subject-matter here for scholarship and research. We find in them a universal language. We move toward civilization as we learn to adore beauty. There are those high among the counselors in art who find in it a consummation of the highest synthesis. They superimpose the musical scale upon the elevation of the Acropolis and demonstrate a most striking identity. They assure us that Plato and Pythagoras discovered the unity of architecture and music through the medium of mathematics. Shall mathematics assume over-lordship here, also, as she has with the help of her hand-maid, physics, among the sciences? In any event, architecture is more than frozen music; it is music alive and vibrant to those who have eyes to see and ears to hear. The same harmonies appeal to the eye of man and to the ear of man and to the soul of man, because God made man that way. The colleges may help to make explicit and understandable this ultimate synthesis.

*The Frontier of the One and the Many.* Perhaps we do not call it that now. Our language is less euphonious. We are disturbed about the conflict between rugged individualism and integrated and regimented masses. But it is the same old problem of human relationships. Shall the frontier be occupied happily through the prohibition of plenty, through the cheapening of money, through the abandonment of the profit motive, through the substitution of coercion for freedom, through a return to paternalism, through the increase of armaments as we seek national isolation? Will the debt to end debts which now hovers as a black cloud above us and about us have more success than did the war to end wars? Does peace and security, domestic and foreign, come this way?

But all the armed men in this frontier can not be summoned to the present scene. Manifestly the function of the colleges is to maintain among their sons and daughters a sense of perspective and balance, to develop an appreciation of values and to conserve those values as a precious heritage of the race. Through discrimination and critical and fearless interpretation, through an enlarged vision of the wholeness of life, we may pass beyond our period of chaos, and move on to a more rewarding adjustment of the one and the many. Without the abandonment of liberty new methods of cooperation may lead us to social control.

At this moment, when history is becoming "the descriptive study of how human behavior patterns change from one generation to another," and therefore is becoming "the central nervous system, the mechanism by which man coordinates his thinking and doing," helpful lessons may be gained from science, which, far in the lead, is emancipating itself from mechanism and, impressed with its own social implications, is recognizing the help of common sense, intuition, revelation, mysticism, religion, if the depths of truth are to be penetrated in a rewarding fashion. A distinguished portrait artist, highly gifted with insight and sanity, remarked the other day, "chaos always precedes the greatest constructive work."

That this frontier has an amazing appeal to high-spirited collegians is reflected in the decisive trend, through current systems of elections, to the offerings of the classroom in the social sciences, an enrolment that promises this year to be larger than at any time in history. But it transcends the opportunities of the curricula and leads students into manifold clubs and societies dedicated to economic, sociological and political discussion and performance.

That section of the field which may be called the frontier of social work, because it seeks the prevention of social calamities, the rehabilitation of individual victims and the care of those who are in distress, is of especial interest to the students of the group of which Whittier is a conspicuous example. What hordes of student volunteers are enrolling for vacation service within the coal fields of West Virginia and the general area of the Tennessee Valley Authority, under the guidance of such organizations as the American Friends Service Committee! From a number of the leading colleges for women throughout the country the largest proportion of the students, upon graduation, enter this challenging field of social work. In like fashion, this new vocational pattern is attracting the interest of many college men. It is a vivid and practical manifestation of their yearning for social justice.

*A Series of Expanding Frontiers.* This

pioneering industry is quite in line with the theory and practise of the members of the Society of Friends. George Fox was a pioneer into the realm of the spirit of man and so have been all his conspicuous disciples. If we confine our view to the United States and to that section of Quakerism devoted to education, we shall discover a series of expanding frontiers.

Shortly before the proclamation of the Census Bureau, to which reference has been made, Johns Hopkins, a Baltimore Friend, established a hospital and a park in his home city and conceived the idea of establishing a college which he endowed so generously with money and with freedom to develop that Gilman created the pioneer graduate university of our country. With an entirely different conception of the function of a university, another Friend, Ezra Cornell, had promoted and secured the establishment of the institution at Ithaca, which bears his name, welcoming to the offerings any subject with which the human mind might seriously be concerned. It was a striking case of the democratization of higher education. State universities in practise now approximate this type. In the same spirit, a group of Philadelphia Quakers established Bryn Mawr College and opened up to the women of America opportunities not only for a thorough but for an advanced education. These institutions and others under Friendly influence not now named, while representing educational pioneering, do not so perfectly illustrate the Quaker college pattern.

Something like a quarter of a century ago, Earlham officially recognized the college as a social institution and among the first of a large and constantly enlarging group of colleges constructed a program of studies upon the foundation of student interests and capacities, with such flexibility as to guarantee a partial realization of these interests and capacities without destroying the sound development which comes through continuity and unity of study; somewhat later Swarthmore discriminated sharply between the pass student and the honor student and developed a unique honors system which has been a source of inspiration everywhere; Haverford demonstrated her leadership among all American colleges which have submitted themselves to modern testing methods for the determination of student growth during the four years of the college course. We find Guilford blazing new paths in the South in phases of curriculum construction, and Friends University developing a remarkably rich intramural life which has penetrated helpfully into the heart of the social and civic activities of the city and the larger community.

Whittier's elaboration of a series of coordinations of subject-matter with fundamental life situations has attracted the commendation of educational specialists across the continent. There is nothing more needed in our time than a successful plan for such psychological, economic, social and religious organization of the individual and of the family in terms of experience and knowledge.

I suppose when one is in California he should do as Californians do. Speaking of epics, therefore, Quaker educators have also written an epic during the years.

*The Frontier of Moral Control.* As a constant note running through this Quaker educational epic, there has been a deep moral concern. Whatever the type of pioneering effort, this concern has played a continuous accompaniment to the event. Quaker educators are always desperately in earnest.

Perhaps the frontier of moral control is the most difficult of all. Sir James Jeans in his vigorous reply to those critics who have blamed science for war and unemployment argues that the greatest danger to civilization lies in man's lack of moral control. "Scientific knowledge," he asserts, "is transmitted from one generation to another, while acquired characteristics are not. Thus, in respect to knowledge, each generation stands on the shoulders of its predecessor, but in respect to human nature both stand on the same ground. These are hard facts, which we can not help or alter and which—we may as well admit it—may wreck civilization."

Admitting the significance of heredity and environment and the influence of the moral earnestness of the teacher, it still remains that character is built up from scratch. There is always a new beginning with each individual and each group. Perhaps moral control will, in the nature of the case, always be behind scientific knowledge.

But this college has one advantage. She hath inherited a more excellent name. It is a smart saying that we outlive our poets, seers and prophets. Of course we do not outlive them; we only forget them. The poetic talent of Whittier, the Patron Saint, was obscured at times by the intensity of his convictions and the tumultuousness of the struggle in which he was engaged. He did not have time to dot each "i" and cross each "t," while urging his fellow citizens to strike off the shackles of slavery. Not only was he a saint; he was a mystic and a politician. He served two terms in the legislature of Massachusetts, he missed Congress only because of the frailty of his health and because he refused to be muzzled. He was a trusted counselor to what we to-day would call the political bosses and he was a presidential elector in each of the Lincoln campaigns. A college that stands for freedom from modern forms of slavery—for freedom of speech and press and ballot—for freedom to think, to work, to worship, to serve, may well seek guidance from the Quaker poet and reformer—the fighter not only for the man in shackles, but for the common laborer—the forgotten man—and for him who would lift up society, the state, the church.

Would our earnest college student have a goal of personal attainment?

The Word, which the reason of Plato discerned;
The truth, as whose symbol the Mithra-fire burned;
The soul of the world which the Stoic but guessed,
In the Light Universal the Quaker confessed.

Do we seek to worship according to the dictates of our conscience? Whether Methodist or Mormon or Episcopal or Reformed we cry:

Dear Lord and Father of Mankind
Forgive our feverish ways.

Is interracial tolerance a vital need of the times?

For a sense of the Goodness revealed everywhere,
As sunshine impartial, and free as the air;
For a trust in humanity, Heathen or Jew,
And a hope for all darkness the Light shineth through.

Does the modern student rebel against sectarianism?

One holy name bearing, no longer they need
Credentials of party, and pass-words of creed:
The new song they sing hath a threefold accord,
And they own one baptism, one faith and one Lord!

Is it the problem of war and peace that disturbs the minds of this generation?

No honors of war to our worthies belong.

And in "Yorktown,"

Let Freedom, in whatever clime
She waits with sleepless eye her time,
Shouting from cave and mountain wood
Make glad her desert solitude,
While they who hunt her quail with fear;
The New World's chain lies broken here!

On this great day in the history of Whittier College, I do not sing with Vergil of arms and the man—I sing of the college and the man.

If the college has been dedicated to truth and freedom, the man—William Orville Mendenhall—has been brought forth for service. He is a mathematical wizard and therefore an integrator and coordinator; he is welcomed to the high councils of the denominational and interdenominational societies, local, national and international; he is a seasoned college administrator and executive; he is an inspirer and leader of youth with rare penetration and insight; he is a loyal and trusted friend, sincere and unselfish; he is a Christian gentleman.

May not this man, as Tennyson's Ulysses, issue the call?

Come, my friends,
'Tis not too late to seek a newer world.
Push off, and sitting well in order smite
The sounding furrows; for my purpose holds.
To sail beyond the sunset and the baths
Of all the western stars, until I die.

. . . . . . . . . . .

Tho' much is taken, much abides; and tho'
We are not now that strength which in old days
Moved earth and heaven: that which we are, we are:
One equal temper of heroic hearts
Made weak by time and fate, but strong in will
To strive, to seek, to find and not to yield.

# NO MORE LARGE GIFTS?

**By ARNAUD C. MARTS**
NEW YORK CITY

"There will be no more large gifts to education and philanthropy in the years ahead of us." This prophecy has wide currency at the moment and its constant reiteration by many educational and religious and philanthropic leaders is having a noticeable effect upon the hopes and plans of our colleges, hospitals, churches and humanitarian institutions.

A prophecy which affects the further development of these institutions merits careful analysis, for such institutions comprise a very important section of American life, more important, I believe, than is generally recognized. Our philanthropic enterprise, that is, our agencies and institutions which are supported by voluntary gifts, is a vast undertaking. It includes, for instance, 210,000 churches. In many Christian nations the churches are supported in whole or in part by taxation, but in America they are supported entirely by the voluntary gifts of people who wish to support them. If these churches were set side by side, they would occupy a continuous strip from New York to Los Angeles, a "Bible Belt" which would be worthy of even Mr. Mencken's attention.

Of our 907 colleges and universities, 526 are supported by voluntary gifts and private foundations. Students and teachers at these colleges supported by private philanthropy are equal in number to the entire population of the city of Washington, D. C. Among our 7,000 hospitals, 2,738 are supported by private philanthropy and the 300,000 beds in these hospitals would hold all the people of the city of Louisville, Ky. The Boy Scout Movement is another type of agency supported entirely by voluntary gifts. There are over 700,000 boys enrolled in this great movement at the present time, and over 5,000,000 have been enrolled since its inception. There are over 300,000 girls enrolled in the Girl Scouts, also carried forward by voluntary gifts.

There are 535 of our libraries that are supported by philanthropy. We have 1,000 Y. W. C. A.'s and 1,100 Y. M. C. A.'s, all supported by voluntary gifts. We have a thousand or more settlement houses, tens of thousands of local welfare, charity and humanitarian agencies. We have the Red Cross Society, anti-tuberculosis, anti-cancer, anti-leprosy societies and scores of other health organizations, with many local branches, all supported by private giving. We have local, state, national and international societies devoted to widely divergent humanitarian and cultural purposes from the prevention of vivisection of a stray puppy to the advocacy of the League of Nations, all of which depend upon voluntary gifts for their maintenance.

During the 1920's we gave away over two billion dollars per year to these philanthropic agencies, and even in the depressed 1930's we are still giving to them, voluntarily, at least a billion dollars per year. Millions of our best citizens experience their greatest satisfaction of patriotic and social expression as trustees, directors, committeemen and volunteer workers in these philanthropic undertakings. The degree of one's interest in these institutions may well be regarded as the measure of the cultural caliber of the average American. Gloomy or unwarranted prophecies about the financial future of philanthropy are, therefore, treading on premises which are sacred to the very best instincts and expressions of American life, and should be appraised with great care. I, for one, believe the prophecy referred to should not be accepted on its face value without strict questioning and I propose to question it, briefly but pointedly, on six counts.

First, we are in no proper state of mind to prophesy about the future. After five years of depression-shock, the only future in which we can believe is a gloomy one. The only prophets whom we consent to honor to-day are the prophets of pessimism. This particular prophecy seems to me to reflect our general pessimism of the moment rather than any prescient understanding of the future.

Second, the prophecy seems too sweeping. We have been misled recently by other sweeping prophecies uttered in a national mood of pessimism or exaltation. "We are in a new era, wealth is unlimited"—1928. "Prices of stocks will never go down"—1929. "Prosperity is just around the corner"—1930. "Our industrial machine is hopelessly smashed—technocracy is our only way out"—1931. "Prices can never go up again"—1932. One who trusted these prophecies is cautious in accepting another prophecy that is as sweeping and radical in its terms.

Third, we have no certain knowledge yet of how far the New Deal will go in changing traditional American life. The prophecy we are considering is based, of course, on the expectation that the New Deal will make great fortunes impossible in the future through the withdrawal of special privileges and through heavy taxation. While this is undoubtedly the trend of Mr. Roosevelt's policies, it is too early to know how far the program is intended to go or how far it will be permitted to go in that direction. It may be fairly doubted that the New Deal will bring about such a sharp curtailment of individual wealth as this prediction takes for granted. We read of a resident of Chicago who has filed a tax return on an income of $4,000,000 in 1933; we read of a young man conferring million dollar gifts on his bride in 1934; we know of corporations still willing to pay enormous salaries to men competent to manage their complicated affairs; and we observe many other evidences that great wealth has not been legislated summarily out of existence. Unless the New Deal should be replaced by a system of government far more radical it is quite probable that Americans of unusual business and inventive genius will continue to be permitted to accumulate and hold great fortunes.

Fourth, we have not given so lavishly to our cultural and philanthropic institutions in the past that the curtailment of riches need force the curtailment of giving. The implication in the prophecy is that we have been giving such a large proportion of our income that decreased incomes will necessarily cut into our giving ability. The facts are to the contrary. Mr. Robert R. Doane, author of the valuable book published recently by Harper Brothers, "The Measure of American Wealth," sets forth the amounts which we did actually give to our philanthropic enterprises in 1929, a year of great incomes. Approximately a million people paid income taxes to the Bureau of Internal Revenue that year on incomes of $5,000 or more. They reported an aggregate income of $20,050,000,000. They were permitted to make certain deductions on their tax returns for their gifts to philanthropy up to 15 per cent. of their income. According to Mr. Doane, they listed such deductible gifts at only $380,000,000, or 1.9 per cent. of their income. After spending all they could, or were obliged to spend, for clothes, food, rent, recreation, travel, taxation, etc., they were able to put back 36 per cent. of their income in savings and new investments. This means, of course, that though many people were giving most generously to the philanthropic institutions of the nation, still more persons who were amply able to give were giving little or nothing.

Fifth, I question the validity of this prophecy on the grounds of the development of a new social consciousness which may more than counterbalance the decreased incomes. The reason so many of the million persons referred to in the preceding paragraph gave nothing to the nation's cultural causes in 1929 was because they had no interest in such causes. The formula for large giving is not simply a large bank account. It is a large bank account plus a sense of social responsibility. For my part, I would rather take my chances of obtaining a gift of $1,000,000 for a humanitarian purpose from a man worth $2,000,000 who has a social sensitiveness than from a man worth $50,000,000 who is a social illiterate.

There are evidences all about us of a decided growth in this sense of social responsibility. Men are asking themselves: "What is wealth for? Why do I have it? Will I be permitted to keep it? Could I get greater happiness by using it for humanity than in holding it for myself? Do I not owe some of it to society?" The whole nation is going these days to a school of social consciousness, the attendance at which is compulsory. New social ideas are penetrating unaccustomed hearts. Is it not quite possible that this new social sensitiveness may more than compensate in the matter of giving for any actual decrease in wealth?

Finally, I question the prediction because everyday events refuse to conform to it. The very distinguished president of one of our greatest universities laid down this prophecy a year ago:

> In the history of the University we have arrived at the end of an era during which most generous and great gifts were received from many different individuals for the endowment and enrichment of the work of the University. . . . The great fortunes and the large accumulations which made these benefactions possible are either dissipated or destroyed. . . . Should these great fortunes be renewed, either in whole or in part, an extravagant government stands ready to take a great proportion of their annual income in taxation. . . . A steady flow of gifts from the alumni, moderate in amount but large in number, must be one of the University's chief sources of dependence for its continued usefulness in the years that lie just ahead of us.

Six months later the gifts to the university in the interim were made public. They totalled $655,499, rather a neat little sum for six months of a year as depressed as 1933. Had this come in the "steady flow from the alumni, moderate in amount but large in number"? On the contrary. $400,000 had come from one generous man and $245,000 of it had come in lesser individual amounts from wealthy persons and foundations created by wealthy persons. Only $9,550.67 had come from the "steady flow."

Early in 1934 a conference of many of the nation's religious leaders was called to exchange views on the financial status of the church. The following quotation sums up their belief on the matter under discussion. "It would seem that the day of large gifts may be over. If income and inheritance taxes absorb the wealth which has been available in the past, then the loss must be made up by the larger number of small givers." Within ninety days of that meeting a modest gentleman of quiet religious faith died and named two denominational boards which had been represented actively at the conference as the legatees of his residuary estate of $10,000,000, without doubt the largest single gift those boards had ever received. Certain of the decedent's disappointed relatives wish he had not died before learning that large-scale philanthropy was no longer expected.

In April, 1934, several hundred presidents and officers of colleges met to confer over the financial outlook. The following excerpts are quoted from the public utterances on that occasion: "There will be fewer men giving millions of dollars to this or that institution; this seems to be clearly proven by the evidence of the last three or four years, so the college which is going to grow and develop in answering the social needs of the future must look about for new means of support. . . . Certainly one solution will be found in the building up of a number of small contributors." Again, "There will be increasingly fewer great fortunes from which universities may hope to draw support. . . . Universities will do well to turn their energies to the solicitation of small gifts in large numbers." Others spoke in the same vein, but the sequence to which I wish to call attention is that within ninety days colleges announced publicly gifts and bequests during the academic year as follows: One for $1,300,000; one for $1,000,000; one for $516,154; one for $500,000; one for $402,213; one for $350,000; one for $250,000; three for $100,000; one for $93,424, and so on and on to a total of many millions.

I have not endeavored to prove, or even to claim, that great gifts to philanthropy will be resumed on the grand scale of the 1920s. On the contrary, I have endeavored simply to neutralize the extreme pessimism of the current prediction and to suggest that perhaps the event will not be as discouraging as the prophecy.

May I suggest further that it is poor strategy

for our philanthropic leaders to continue to reiterate this prediction, even if they could prove its warrant. Its effect on prospective large donors is bad, for they need stimulus and inspiration to give rather than ready-made excuses for not doing so. Its effect on the rank and file donors is equally bad, for they can not be inspired to give more generously by the plea that persons better able to give will or can do so no longer. Most of us give to philanthropy because others do rather than because others do not.

It would seem to me that a far more effective theme for the pronouncements on this subject by our cultural and religious leaders would be a strong emphasis upon the urgent need for the further development of character and culture. Recent world events provide abundant material for such emphasis. The one lesson which looms with ever-increasing clarity against the background of world tragedy is that brute strength and selfish greed in modern civilization succeed ultimately only in destroying themselves. Vast material wealth has turned to ashes in the very hands of its possessors; only cultural and spiritual values remain intact.

These latter are the values, of course, which our philanthropic institutions, our colleges, churches, libraries, hospitals and other agencies have been created to produce. In a world of material overproduction, these abiding values, alone, have been underproduced. Can not the challenge to strengthen the agencies which produce character, intelligence and good will be invoked by our cultural leaders in a manner so impressive that a continued outpouring of great gifts shall be inspired?

# EDUCATIONAL EVENTS

## THE HEALTH OF THE BRITISH SCHOOL CHILD

THE annual report for 1933 of the Chief Medical Officer of the British Board of Education was published on December 3, under the title of "The Health of the School Child."

According to a summary in the *Times,* after a preliminary sketch, in which the objects and achievements of the school service are dealt with, Sir George Newman states that during 1933 upwards of 3,000,000 children passed under definite medical review and that subsequently nearly 2,000,000 reinspections were carried out. Of the 1,855,499 children submitted to routine examination, 20,579, or 11.1 per 1,000, were found to be "mal-nourished" and requiring treatment, and 23,760, or 12.8 per 1,000, were found to be undernourished and requiring observation. The figure for 1932 of "malnourished" children requiring treatment was 10.7 per 1,000, and that for 1931 11.2 per 1,000.

This massed return for 1933, compiled from figures submitted by 316 local education authorities, indicated that the condition of nutrition of school children throughout England and Wales in 1933 was similar to that of 1931 and 1932, and showed no general deterioration.

The total number of meals provided in the year 1933–34 was 68,800,000, an increase of 6,500,000 on 1932–33. The number of children who received meals was 414,800, as compared with 399,400 in 1932–33.

Sir George Newman considers that the evidence indicated definitely that the general health and nutrition of the population of England and Wales, taken as a whole, was well maintained in 1933, in spite of economic and social difficulties, distressing as these had been. "There can be no question," he adds, "that the nutrition of the English people is better to-day than at any past period of which we have record. But that does not say or mean that present standards of health and nutrition can not be or should not be improved."

Discussing physical training in junior technical schools, he states that the picture disclosed by the survey is not bright. "Thus, only about half of the existing schools have the use of suitable gymnasiums or halls, and a number of them are under the necessity of omitting physical exercises altogether from the curriculum because there is nowhere, either indoors or outdoors, where they can be carried on."

In regard to unemployment Sir George writes:

> A state which allows its young people to degenerate, physically or mentally, because of unemployment is incurring a very grave responsibility. Perhaps of all the disadvantages of

prolonged unemployment in youth the worst are the disappointment and demoralization which ensue on this enforced idleness and the more or less complete wreck of psychological aspirations and hopes. Such young people are liable to become embittered and mentally depressed, and they lose the ground of hope. Have authorities failed hitherto to recognize this?

## ADMINISTRATION OF HIGHER EDUCATION IN CALIFORNIA

THE functions of the junior colleges, the teachers colleges, and the University of California, is the subject of a report of the State Council on Educational Planning and Coordination made public on December 14 by Dr. Will C. Wood, chairman of the council. The council, under provisions of the last legislature, investigated the situation and needs of California as regards higher education and the report has been sent to the State Board of Education and the Regents of the University of California.

The council, created by the legislature of 1933, was appointed jointly by Vierling Kersey, state superintendent of public instruction, and Robert G. Sproul, president of the university. Allen T. Archer, of Los Angeles, represented the State Board of Education and Chester Rowell was *ex-officio* member for the regents. The other five, lay members, are: Will C. Wood, Oakland; Mrs. William J. Hayes, Burlingame; Miss Annie Florence Brown, Oakland; Charles Albert Adams, San Francisco, and Gurney Newlin, Los Angeles.

The following recommendations are made:

*Junior College Functions:* strong semi-professional and vocational curricula designed to give the student in two years sufficient skill to meet the demands of employers; curricula for life needs, covering in an explanatory way entire fields of thought; one or more lower division curricula modeled after those of the higher institutions to which the particular junior college sends most of its students to complete a four-year course; and adult education such as that now provided in several junior colleges. It recommends strongly against adding two years at the top to the junior college as at present constituted.

*Teachers College Functions:* The function of the teachers colleges should be to prepare teachers for the elementary schools, for the intermediate or junior high schools and for such phases of supervision of instruction and administration in the elementary schools as do not involve courses on the graduate level; teachers college should perform in its region those functions of the junior college for which a part of its program is well adapted.

As a distinctly minor function, the teachers colleges should prepare students for special high school credentials as long as there is no other adequate provision, and should serve as centers for adult education in their regions.

Neither educational theory nor public policy would seem to justify the conversion of teachers colleges into liberal arts colleges in name or, to any great degree, in purpose.

*Functions of the University:* The functions of the university are three and they are coordinate: professional training, development of the individual and research in all matters that are of significance to the human race.

To meet such a comprehensive obligation a university must offer both college and professional curricula. The college curricula should be of two kinds: those designed as backgrounds for the professions and those designed to produce clearer thinking and nobler living.

The university should, through its extension division and in cooperation with other educational agencies, extend its opportunities as widely as possible among persons of all ages, regardless of their geographical distribution.

## ENTRANCE REQUIREMENTS AT THE UNIVERSITY OF MICHIGAN

AT the December meeting of the regents of the University of Michigan the present system of entrance requirements was modified in favor of a program of flexible "sequence requirements" replacing prescribed standards.

Under the new admission plan high-school credits are divided into five general groups—English, foreign languages, mathematics-physics, the sciences and social studies. Entrants must be high-school graduates and have earned fifteen units in these fields, but units are classified into "sequences," permitting a choice of subjects, instead of being rigidly prescribed.

Required under the new set-up are two major and two minor sequences. A major sequence consists of three or more units in one of the five groups, while a minor is two or two and one half units. This allows the main requirements to be met from four of the five groups, while the balance of the fifteen units may be made up of any studies giving credit toward high-school graduation.

The sequence system, which has been worked out by the faculties of the various schools and colleges in the university after a year of study, applies to all divisions admitting students direct from the high school, including the colleges and schools of literature, science and the arts; engineering, dentistry, education, architecture, pharmacy, music and nursing; the requirements of the professional schools, however, are varied to fit the particular needs of such programs of study.

Dean Edward H. Kraus, of the College of Literature, points out that

> The modernization of entrance requirements, permitting greater flexibility to fit individual cases, recognizes the variety of subjects now well taught in our high schools. From another aspect this increase in flexibility is an expression of the conviction that a student's ability to do college work has but little causal relationship with the subjects pursued in high school. On account of the increased complexity of work at the college level, the ability of the student and a record of cumulative study have greater significance in so far as his college achievement is concerned than the specific subjects taken in the secondary school.
>
> This increase in flexibility will permit the high school to carry the able pupil farther in the subjects in which he shows the greatest interest and ability. It is the expectation that, in consequence, these students will receive a more thorough preparation for college and university work. It will also be possible for the able students to enter the university from the small secondary schools where the curricula may be more limited than those of large city schools. The proposed plan further provides a means whereby the decision to attend college can be made relatively late in the high-school course without the imposition of a prohibitive amount of extra work.

## SCHOLASTIC HONORS AT HARVARD UNIVERSITY

AN increase in the number of Harvard undergraduates applying for scholastic honors is shown in statistics on candidates for distinction at Harvard College made public by the Committee on the Choice of Electives.

Achievement of scholastic honors is registered on the student's degree as *cum laude,* "with distinction"; *magna cum laude,* "with high distinction"; *summa cum laude,* "with highest distinction." The award of honors in special subjects is made on the basis of high course records, individual research, usually in the form of an honors thesis, and a high showing in the general examinations given at the end of the senior year to determine the student's mastery of his field of concentration. Award of general honors is made on the basis of a specified number of high course grades.

This fall, 1,066 sophomores, juniors and seniors, representing 42 per cent. of the upperclassmen, are listed as candidates for honors in special fields. This is the largest percentage so registered since 1930. The figures for 1930 to 1933 indicate a general rise, as follows: 1930, 38 per cent.; 1931, 39.3 per cent.; 1932, 41.5 per cent.; 1933, 40.8 per cent.

The figures show that the departments of astronomy, biochemical sciences, classics, history and literature, literature, mathematics, philosophy and physics have the largest percentage of their concentrators registered as candidates for honors. In each of these fields, more than 50 per cent. of the students are competing for distinction.

Leading the fields of concentration in numbers of men applying for honors are history with 126 candidates; English with 122; the biochemical sciences, with 112, and economics, with 106.

Last spring, for the first time in the history of Harvard College, more than half the whole undergraduate body, including all four classes, were approved candidates for honors. Of 3,325 undergraduates, 1,665, or 50.2 per cent., were so listed. Previous to last spring, the highest percentage was in the spring of 1933, when out of 3,271 undergraduates, 1,601, or 48.9 per cent., were candidates for honors.

Since 1927, the percentage of all Harvard undergraduates, including the freshmen who had announced their choice of a field, registered in June as approved candidates for honors has increased steadily as follows: 1927, 30.2 per cent.; 1928, 30.4 per cent.; 1929, 32 per cent.; 1930, 32.4 per cent.; 1931, 34.4 per cent.; 1932, 38.1 per cent.; 1933, 48.9 per cent.; 1934, 50.2 per cent.

Last spring, 280, or 37.2 per cent., of the seniors received degrees with distinction. The number of degrees with honors has been increasing steadily since 1931, as follows: 1931, 220, or 28.5 per cent. of the graduating class; 1932, 256, or 32.6 per cent.; 1933, 272, or 35.8 per cent.

The rise in the number of degrees with honors is due to an increase in the number of successful candidates for special distinction. Since 1931 there has been a slight tendency for the number of degrees with general honors to decrease, as follows: 1931, 50 men, or 6.5 per cent. of the graduating class received general honors; 1932, 38, or 4.8 per cent.; 1933, 39, or 5.1 per cent.; 1934, 35, or 4.7 per cent.

## THE CORNELL UNIVERSITY THEATER

Five three-act plays and a production of the Gilbert and Sullivan "Pinafore," in which ninety-two students will take part, are on the list of productions for the first term of the academic year, according to an announcement by Professor A. M. Drummond, director of the theater and head of the Department of Public Speaking and Dramatics at Cornell University. The plays for the first term, according to *The New York Times,* include "Private Lives," "The Far-Off Hills," "The Queen's Husband," "The Late Christopher Bean" and "Clear All Wires."

The production of "Pinafore" will be presented on December 15 and 16 as a joint performance of the Cornell Dramatic Club and the Cornell Musical Clubs.

New impetus was given to work in dramatics at Cornell this year by a grant from the Rockefeller Foundation. Under Professor Drummond's direction, the university theater has expanded from a small group giving one-act plays in the main lecture room of Goldwin Smith Hall to an organization in which more than 400 students work in the various departments of production in the completely equipped theater in Willard Straight Hall.

Weekly performances are given of three-act plays, ranging in scope from Shakespeare to O'Neill and including the first American débuts of many noted European playwrights, such as Pirandello. In the course of its twenty-five years of existence the Cornell Dramatic Club has produced 136 three-act plays and 636 one-act plays, fifty-one of which were original Cornell plays.

The dramatic program at Cornell University is fourfold in its aim. Its purpose is to give as many students as possible the opportunity to hold responsible positions in the activities of the theater; to provide experience and training so that students after graduation may contribute something to the theater as professionals, as community leaders of amateur groups, as members of dramatic departments in schools and colleges, or as informed play-goers; to produce plays that will not only entertain the audience but that will enrich its experience; to experiment in methods of presentation and to encourage the writing of original plays by offering an opportunity for their production.

## THE NEW WOMAN'S DORMITORY AT THE GEORGE WASHINGTON UNIVERSITY

A gift to the George Washington University, to be used in the erection of a hall which will house 200 women students, has been made by Mrs. Henry Alvah Strong, a member of the board of trustees.

President Cloyd H. Marvin, at a meeting of the Board of Trustees on December 12, stated that he regarded the announcement as of utmost importance and significance in connection with the development of the university. He said: "Through Mrs. Strong's generosity we will be enabled to give appropriate housing to the many women students who come to the George Washington University from all parts of the country, and to provide a center for all women's activities on the campus. This is a need that long has been keenly felt. Mrs. Strong's gift makes it possible for the university to develop in a direction in which hitherto it has been hampered by limited facilities. It is an action which exemplifies her creative attitude toward life, and is representative of her interest in education and in young people. Mrs. Strong has the heartfelt gratitude of all associated with the George Washington University, and who will be associated with it in the years to come."

Work will begin at once on plans for the building, and construction will be pushed to completion before the opening of the academic year next fall.

Mrs. Strong has been a trustee of the George Washington University since 1931. For many years she has interested herself in the education of young people and in 1928 founded the Hattie

M. Strong Foundation for the purpose of continuing in a more permanent form the policy of lending money to students which had been carried on by her for a number of years on an informal basis.

A resident of Washington since 1926, Mrs. Strong is internationally known for her philanthropies. The Cross of the Legion of Honor was bestowed upon her by the French Republic in grateful recognition of her gift of a chateau where crippled war veterans find a home. She has likewise been decorated by the government of Jugoslavia with the Cross of the Order of St. Sava, in recognition of her generosity to Jugoslav students.

The George Washington University, largest in the South Atlantic section, was founded in 1821. It enrolls some 7,000 students from every state in the United States and from 40 foreign countries, approximately one third of whom are women. In addition to undergraduate and graduate work in letters and sciences, the university offers training in eight professional fields, including government, law, education, engineering, library science, fine arts, medicine and pharmacy.

## THE NEW SERIES OF LECTURES AND GALLERY TALKS AT THE METROPOLITAN MUSEUM

DURING January, February and March the Museum will continue the program of educational work which has aroused so much interest since its beginning last October. The success of the new plan of giving free talks on the collections every day in the week except the two pay days (Monday and Friday) is indicated by the number of people who have attended them—more than six thousand during the first seven weeks.

These free gallery talks, which will be continued through the winter, will include as before general tours and historical surveys of the collections, short courses on various subjects, and single talks, often of timely interest. In addition there will be more formal lectures by invited speakers. Special lectures for the deaf and deafened and story hours for children are also included among the free educational activities. For members of the museum and for teachers in the city public schools special courses have been planned.

Offered for the first time this year will be the Matthews Lectures on Gothic Architecture to be given by Professor Joseph Hudnut of Columbia University. This series of ten illustrated lectures is endowed by the bequest to the university of the late Charles T. Matthews. Admission to these is free.

A new pamphlet of free gallery talks and other lectures, which will be sent upon request to any one desiring it, lists by day and hour all the three hundred appointments for the period with subjects and names of speakers.

*The New York Times* writes editorially as follows:

The interest in the educational program of the Metropolitan Museum of Art is gratifying. It was thought by the authorities when the free gallery talks were announced that there would be an attendance of not more than twenty-five or thirty at any one time, but the numbers have frequently exceeded 200 for single talks, with a total attendance of more than 10,000 for the ninety-three given during October and November. One by-product is a greatly increased demand upon the museum library for books relating to arts and crafts.

At a talk in the painting galleries, for example, there were considerably more than 200 present—nearly all of whom were adults—who stood for an hour, save a few who had provided themselves with camp stools. They listened with closest attention, and many of them took notes. This is a distinct forward step in making the museum one of our great popular educational institutions.

## THE WASHINGTON MEETING OF THE AMERICAN HISTORICAL ASSOCIATION

THE American Historical Association will hold its fiftieth anniversary meeting in Washington on December 27, 28 and 29. The Mayflower Hotel will be the headquarters, and with but few exceptions, will house the general sessions and the sectional meetings. The Honorable William E. Dodd, of the University of Chicago, American Ambassador to Germany and president of the association, will deliver his presidential address.

The program, as prepared by a committee under the chairmanship of Dr. Samuel Flagg Bemis, includes seven sessions devoted to papers and discussions of specific phases of historical interest, five joint sessions where allied organizations join together in consideration of problems of mutual interest, four general sessions, seven luncheons and luncheon-conferences and four dinners of which the outstanding one will be that of Saturday, December 29, in honor of the five surviving founders of the association. About a thousand members are expected to be in attendance. Local arrangements are in the hands of a committee of fourteen with Dr. Leo F. Stock as chairman.

Each year since the founding of the association in 1884, with the exception of the year 1918, annual meetings have been held, many of them in Washington. This meeting marking the close of the first half century is, therefore, the forty-ninth. Five members of the original group survive and in their honor a Founders' Dinner is being arranged as the climax of the fiftieth anniversary meeting. The surviving founders are: Clarence W. Bowen, Davis R. Dewey, Ephraim Emerton, J. Franklin Jameson and Henry E. Scott.

In accordance with custom, several organizations having kindred interests are meeting concurrently with the American Historical Association. Among these are the Mississippi Valley Historical Association, the Conference of State and Local Historical Societies, the Agricultural History Society, the American Society of Church History, the American Catholic Historical Association, the History of Science Society, the Bibliographical Society of America, the Medieval Academy of America, the Association of Research Libraries and the National Council for the Social Studies.

## THE ATLANTA MEETING OF THE ASSOCIATION OF AMERICAN COLLEGES

THE twenty-first annual meeting of the Association of American Colleges is to be held at the Atlanta Biltmore Hotel, Atlanta, Georgia, on the 17th and 18th of January, 1935. It is to take somewhat the form of a celebration by the association of its coming to age. The outlook is for a very large attendance not only from the Southern states but from other sections of the country, New England, the Middle Atlantic states, the Mississippi Valley states and the Far West.

Among the speakers who are announced for this meeting are four who are to present the progress of the American college during the last two decades: President Frank Aydelotte, of Swarthmore College, from the standpoint of intellectual achievement; President Frederick C. Ferry, of Hamilton College, from the standpoint of artistic appreciation; Dr. Edwin Mims, of Vanderbilt University, from the standpoint of social insight, and Rector James H. Ryan, of the Catholic University of America, from the standpoint of moral control.

There is to be a series of sectional meetings. One is to be devoted to Modern Measurements of Achievement, led by Dean C. S. Boucher, of the University of Chicago, and Dr. F. S. Beers, of the University of Minnesota, secretary of the Committee on Educational Testing of the American Council on Education. Another section will undertake to answer the question, "If Guidance is Inherent in Higher Education, Who Shall Guide?" This section will be led by Dean Eugenie A. Leonard, of Syracuse University, and will be participated in by many personnel workers of national prominence, among whom may be mentioned Professors Sarah M. Sturtevant and Esther Lloyd-Jones, of Teachers College; Dean Agnes Ellen Harris, of the University of Alabama; Mr. J. H. Miller, dean of students of Bucknell University; Dean Mary Louise Brown, of American University; Dean Sarah G. Blanding, of the University of Kentucky; Mrs. Ruth Schiffman, of the Institute of Women's Professional Relations; Dean H. L. Spencer, of the University of Pittsburgh, and Dr. Anna Y. Reed, of New York University.

A third section, under the leadership of President W. M. Lewis, of Lafayette College, will consider the present-day financial relationships of the colleges, and a fourth will concern itself with an investigation which is now being made by the Association of American Colleges of methods of recruiting for admissions, to which field a number of abuses have recently come. The leader of this section is President C. J. Turck, of Centre College.

The presidential address for this year will be given by President W. M. Lewis and the annual report of the executive committee and executive secretary by Dr. R. L. Kelly, of New York City, the permanent executive officer for the past seventeen years.

Among others whose names appear on the program are President John J. Tigert, of the

University of Florida; President James L. McConaughy, of Wesleyan University; Treasurer F. L. Jackson, of Davidson College; President Daniel L. Marsh, of Boston University; President Henry M. Wriston, of Lawrence College; Mr. Henry James, president of the Teachers Insurance and Annuity Association of America, New York; Dr. W. W. Cook, of the American Association of University Professors, Washington, D. C., and John A. Lang, of the National Student Federation of America, New York.

The railroads of every association in the United States and Canada are offering special rates and certificates may be secured by applying to the office of the association at 111 Fifth Avenue, New York.

# EDUCATIONAL NOTES AND NEWS

THE present issue of SCHOOL AND SOCIETY completes the twentieth year and the fortieth volume of the journal, the first number having appeared on January 2, 1915. The weekly journal *Science,* under the same editorship, on which to a certain extent SCHOOL AND SOCIETY has been modeled, completes at the same time its fortieth year and eightieth volume.

A BUST of Abbott Lawrence Lowell, formerly president of Harvard University, has been presented to the university by a group of his friends. It was executed by John Wilson, instructor in modeling in the Harvard School of Architecture, and has been placed in the faculty room of University Hall. It is slightly more than six feet in height and represents Dr. Lowell in academic robes. The head and shoulders are modeled out of Carrara marble. The square pedestal is of verde Soria marble.

DR. WILLIAM H. S. DEMAREST, president of the New Brunswick Theological Seminary, has announced that he will resign on December 31, after holding the office for ten years. The board of directors, in accepting the resignation, elected him president emeritus. Dr. Demarest, who served as president of Rutgers University from 1906 to 1924, and in 1909 as president of the General Synod of the Reformed Church in America, stated that his resignation was prompted by his wish to be relieved of administrative routine and responsibility.

DR. LEVI L. SPRAGUE, president of Wyoming Seminary of Pennsylvania for fifty-two years and a member of the faculty for sixty-eight years, celebrated his ninetieth birthday on December 23. Dr. Sprague is active in the affairs of the institution. He spends at least four hours of each day in his office; conducts daily chapel exercises and faculty meetings and attends all campus activities.

DR. NICHOLAS MURRAY BUTLER, president of Columbia University, sailed on December 22 for the West Indies.

DR. ERNEST HOPKINS, president of Dartmouth College, sailed for Europe on December 14. He plans to be abroad for two months, which he will spend in France and Italy.

DR. FREDERICK P. KEPPEL, president of the Carnegie Corporation, will sail from Los Angeles on January 9, to visit various British dominions and colonies in connection with the British Dominions and Colonies Fund program of the corporation. He will stop in Honolulu, will spend February in New Zealand, March and April in Australia, and May in Africa. Dr. Keppel expects to attend a conference of Jeanes school teachers at Salisbury, Southern Rhodesia, from May 26 to 29, and will be in London during June. In England he is planning to attend a conference on examinations and a meeting of the Carnegie Corporation advisers for the British Empire. He will return to the United States in July.

DR. HEBER HARPER, professor of international relations and social reconstruction at Teachers College, Columbia University, has been granted a year's leave of absence. He plans to sail on January 3 for Russia, where he will make a survey of the universities, higher technical schools and scientific research laboratories of the Soviet Union to ascertain the possibilities now available for American graduate and special research students. He will act as one of the directors of the summer session of the University of Moscow.

A DINNER in honor of Professor Wesley C. Mitchell, of Columbia University, was given by his associates and some of his former students at the Columbia Faculty Club on December 17. More than 100 guests, including many members of the faculty of the university, attended the dinner. Professor Frederick C. Mills was toastmaster. The speakers included Professor Edwin R. A. Seligman, of Columbia; Professor Edwin F. Gay, of Harvard; Professor Joseph H. Willits, of the University of Pennsylvania, and Willard Thorpe, chief of the Consumers' Division of the National Emergency Council. A volume of economic essays, written and compiled by his former students, was presented to Dr. Mitchell.

THE insignia of a chevalier of the French Legion of Honor was recently presented in Paris to Dorothy F. Leet, for the past twelve years head of Reid Hall, Paris center for American university women. Dr. S. Charléty, rector of the University of Paris, made the presentation. Among the other speakers were André Siegfried, French economist; Mme. Veiller Duray, president of the French Association of University Women, and Dr. Horatio Krans, director of the University Union at Paris.

THE degree of doctor of science was conferred on November 22 by the University of London on Dr. Karl Pearson, professor emeritus, formerly Galton professor of eugenics and director of the Francis Galton Laboratory for National Eugenics.

DR. DAVID SAVILLE MUZZEY, formerly professor of economics at Columbia University, will give courses on American history and civilization at the coming summer session of the University of California at Los Angeles.

ERIC REGINALD PEARCE VINCENT, Christ Church, Oxford, has been elected professor of Italian at the University of Cambridge to succeed Professor Edward Bullough, who died last September.

WILLIAM A. JENNER, of Potsdam, N. Y., has been appointed director of the Bureau of New York State Institution Farms by Charles H. Baldwin, State Commissioner of Agriculture and Markets. He succeeds E. C. Pooler. Mr. Jenner has for two years been assistant director. The bureau supervises the activities of forty-five state-owned and twenty-four state-rented farms.

EARL W. BARNHART has been reappointed chief of the Commercial Education Service in the Division of Vocational Education, Office of Education, from which position he resigned in October, 1934, to accept a place on the staff of the College of the City of New York.

MISS LAURA STILLEY has been appointed state supervisor of Emergency Nursery Schools in Louisiana. She will spend four weeks at the training institute at the National Child Research Center preparatory to taking up this work.

DR. ARTHUR N. HOLCOMBE, professor of government at Harvard University, has been granted sabbatical leave for the second half of the academic year to assist in the formation of a new Chinese constitution. He leaves on January 3 for Nanking.

DR. LEON WHIPPLE, professor of journalism at New York University, has been granted a leave of absence from January 7 to February 17 to deliver a series of thirty lectures before the adult education forums of the Des Moines, Iowa, schools. The forums are supported by the Carnegie Foundation through the Adult Education Association of America.

DR. JOHN G. BOWMAN, chancellor of the University of Pittsburgh, and Dr. William Mather Lewis, president of Lafayette College, were speakers at the annual dinner in New York City of the Pennsylvania Society held on December 15.

DR. MILO SMITH KETCHUM, dean emeritus of the College of Engineering at the University of Illinois and director of the Engineering Experiment Station, died on December 19, in his sixty-third year.

DR. ROLAND BURRAGE DIXON, professor of anthropology at Harvard University since 1916, died on December 20. He was fifty-nine years old.

DR. HENRY G. BAYER, associate professor of French at New York University, where he had been a member of the faculty since 1916, died on December 23, at the age of sixty-seven years.

DR. JEAN CHARLEMAGNE BRACQ, professor emeritus of Vassar College, historian of France and of French colonization, died on December 18, at the age of eighty-one years. Dr. Bracq served as professor of Romance languages at Vassar College from 1891 to 1918.

DR. ARTHUR WINSLOW PEIRCE, head master of Dean Academy, Franklin, Mass., died on December 20 at the age of seventy-four years. From 1882 to 1891 Dr. Peirce was a teacher and in 1891 was chosen head master of Goddard Academy at Barre, Vt., where he remained until 1897, when he received the appointment at Dean Academy.

HOWARD DYKMAN, assistant dean of the College of Business Administration at the University of Florida, died as the result of an automobile accident on December 23. He was thirty-eight years old.

THERE was held on December 13 and 14, at Central Normal College, Danville, Indiana, the tenth annual Indiana State Conference on Supervised Student Teaching. This meeting was sponsored by C. L. Murray, state director of teacher training and by Waldo E. Wood, president of the Central Normal College. The subject of the conference was given as "More Emphasis on Character Development in Supervised Student Teaching." In addition to numerous local speakers, Dr. Edwin D. Starbuck, of the University of Southern California, spoke on "Educating the Whole Personality."

STEPS looking toward the consolidation of library systems, new legislation designed to secure adequate library support and certification of librarians were the topics considered by several hundred librarians and library trustees at the midwinter Conference of the American Library Association in Chicago on December 27, 28 and 29. National and state planning for libraries was the main subject of discussion. Forty states and the District of Columbia have planning boards actively at work evaluating existing library machinery and working toward universal service with adequate support, and reports on their activities were presented. There were two sessions of the Council of the American Library Association, the policy-forming body of the association, numbering about 125 members, at which reports were considered on federal relations, minimum requirements for teacher-librarian training agencies, unemployment of librarians, library revenues, recruiting for library service, and a summary of the three-year investigation of association activities by a special committee. Groups holding separate meetings included the League of Library Commissions, College Librarians of the Middle West, Normal School and Teachers' College Librarians, Librarians of Large Public Libraries, University and Reference Librarians, the Trustees Section, the Board of Education for Librarianship and the Library Extension Board.

THE inaugural dinner of the newly established American Institute of Cinematography was held on December 14. The institute seeks to act as an objective non-partisan clearing house for the helpful exchange of national and international opinion on the many problems presented by the motion picture. The membership, and the Advisory Board, will include representatives selected from the film industry (executives, directors, writers and actors), from the faculties of colleges and universities, and from various professions and groups representing the public at large. Such an organization, neither existing for propaganda nor representing any specific point of view or minority, has long been needed in the United States. It is believed that the dignified and successful film institutes of England, Italy, Japan and many other countries demonstrate the practicality of this venture. The meeting was addressed by the director, Dr. Rufus B. von KleinSmid, and by representatives of the various departments of the film industry.

ANNOUNCEMENT is made by Dr. Samuel J. Crumbine, general executive of the American Child Health Association, of the eighth Health Education Conference, to be held in Iowa City, from June 19 to June 22, 1935, at the invitation of the University of Iowa. The conference will be held in conjunction with the ninth annual Iowa Conference on Child Development and Parent Education, which will meet from June 17 to 19 inclusive. The American Child Health Association held its first Health Education Conference in 1922. Since then, three conferences have been held in New York State and others in California, Massachusetts, Illinois and Michigan. These conferences are for the exchange of experiences and for free discussion of current problems in the field of health education. The Iowa Conference on Child Development and Parent Education is sponsored by the Iowa State Council for Child Study and Parent Education. The program is under the direction of the Iowa Child Welfare Research Station and the Extension Division of the State University of Iowa, cooperating with the council, Iowa State College of Agriculture and Mechanic Arts, and Iowa State Teachers College. On June 19, with both conferences in session, the two programs will be arranged jointly. The Child Development and Parent Education Conference will be open to all who care to attend. Dr. George D. Stoddard, director of the Iowa State Child Welfare Research Station, is arranging its program. The Health Education Conference will be primarily a working conference, and for the working sessions attendance will be limited to about two hundred.

*Nature* reports that the twenty-third annual Conference of Educational Associations will be held at University College, London, from December 31 to January 7, under the presidency of the Marquess of Lothian. The presidential address, entitled "Liberty and Collectivism," will be delivered on December 31. On January 2, a joint conference on "Education for Leisure" will be delivered, when the principal speakers will be the Hon. Mrs. Franklin, Mr. Gerald Heard and Mr. A. C. Richmond. On January 5, a conference on educational and vocational guidance methods will be held at the National Institute of Industrial Psychology, to which members of the Conference of Educational Associations who are actually working in this field are invited. Among the subjects of discussions to be held at the conference at Gower Street are the following, together with the principal speakers: "Biology and General Science in the First School Examination," J. K. King, J. Line and W. Sumner; "Zoos in their Educational Aspect," Professor Julian Huxley; "Psychology and Religion of the Future," The Very Reverend the Dean of St. Paul's. Among the lectures to be delivered are: "The Objects, Value and Methods of International Teaching in the Schools in Terms of the New World Situation," Dr. Delisle Burns; "The All-Importance of the Study of Habits for the Knowledge of Evolution," Professor E. W. MacBride; "Some Reflections on the Scottish Mental Survey," Professor James Drever.

Dr. Elmer Ellsworth Brown, chancellor emeritus of New York University, who died on November 3, provided for division of his estate into twenty-four parts. New York University, of which he was president for more than twenty years, and the University of Michigan, his alma mater, were named among the beneficiaries. The value of the estate has not been disclosed.

The Julius Rosenwald Fund has set aside $2,500 to be devoted to one fourth of the cost of constructing a public school building for Negroes at Warm Springs.

South Carolina institutions of higher learning have the authority to grant competitive scholarships in spite of a legislative act abolishing free tuition, according to a recent ruling of John M. Daniel, state attorney-general. The state scholarships, awarded by Clemson College, the University of South Carolina, the Citadel and Winthrop Colleges, also exempt the recipients from payment of tuition fees. Approximately 2,000 students in the four state institutions were recipients of free tuition during the school year just past. Charges have been raised from $40 to $60 for next year.

By decision of the board of trustees of Rutgers University, it has been decided to offer to students at New Jersey College for Women for the coming year 200 scholarships, in the amount of $175 each, to students who plan to live on the campus. This sum is the equivalent of the college charge for dormitory accommodations. Each award will be made for one year by the scholarship committee, on the basis of scholarly ability, and general character as determined by the high-school record, a psychological examination and financial need. These scholarships will be available for members of all four undergraduate classes.

Yale University School of Medicine announces the establishment of five fellowships by the Rockefeller Foundation for the study of adolescence, which will be approached through studies of anatomy, physical anthropology and anthropometry; physiology, biochemistry and nutrition; psychology and psychiatry; medicine, particularly pediatrics and immunology, and education and social adjustments. It is hoped to discover the methods by which data can be obtained on the growth and development of individuals during the second decade of life. The medical school has also effected a working relationship with the university department of physics. Appointments are to be for two years and they are to expire in alternate years so that one of the two men will always have had one year's experience on the project.

A "DEGREE with distinction," a new honor established at the Stevens Institute of Technology, will be awarded for the first time in 1936. Members of the present junior class will be the first to be eligible for the new degree. Candidates for the degree, chosen by the committee on graduate instruction, must be on the dean's list of honor students at the beginning of the second term of the junior year, carry special work and prepare a thesis on a subject approved by a special committee of two faculty members.

# DISCUSSION

## 1935 AS A CENTENNIAL YEAR IN THE HISTORY OF EDUCATION

IN continuation of previously published lists[1] of centennial dates in the history of education, the following group of significant 1935 dates is presented. Additional details regarding events and persons mentioned may be found in the encyclopedias and histories of education.

A. D. 35

Birth of Quintilian, foremost Roman writer on educational practise, whose "Institutes of Oratory," a manual on the training of a public speaker, constituted an outline of a liberal education.

A. D. 735

Birth of Alcuin who, under Charlemagne, laid the foundation of the Frankish schools.

Death of the Venerable Bede, whose "Ecclesiastical History" of England gives the chief picture of English education of his period.

A. D. 1535

Death of Sir Thomas More, author of "Utopia," English humanist.

A. D. 1635

Establishment of the French Academy by Richelieu.

Founding of Jesuit Mission school at Quebec.

Founding of the first American Latin grammar school at Boston.

Death of Ratke (Ratichius), German educator, who was the first to apply Francis Bacon's ideas to education, and whose "Methodus Nova" was the pioneer work on school method.

Founding of Kiralyi Magyar "Pazmany Peter" Tudomany Egyetem, state university of Hungary.

A. D. 1735

Founding of the University of Rennes, France.

[1] See SCHOOL AND SOCIETY, January 6, 1934, for list for 1934 and for references to similar lists from 1926 to 1933.

A. D. 1835

Founding of Albion College, Michigan.

Founding of Marietta College, Ohio.

Resignation of the president of Delaware College as a protest against the acceptance of "tainted money" from lottery licenses.

Birth of William T. Harris, United States Commissioner of Education from 1889 to 1906.

Death of Wilhelm von Humboldt, philosopher and scholar, one of the leaders in the regeneration of Prussia.

Organization of the first "Training College" for teachers in England.

Reprinting, in New York City, of the famous "Report on the Condition of Public Instruction in Germany, and Particularly Prussia," by Victor Cousin, with resultant important influence on educational conditions in the United States.

Adoption of state constitution by Michigan, upon entrance into the Union, providing for the first permanent state superintendent of public instruction in any state.

Requirements for admission to the University of North Carolina raised so as to include all arithmetic and "Young's Algebra to simple equations."

WALTER CROSBY EELLS
STANFORD UNIVERSITY

## BETTER SPEECH FOR TEACHERS

A PROFESSOR of education remarked recently that students trained in speaking seem to be conspicuously effective in practise teaching. To me, this observation is not startling, inasmuch as teaching is a speaking situation, one of social adaptation and control. The class is the audience which responds in some definite way to the teacher's purpose, albeit at times by indifference and boredom. To know how to stimulate and fashion that response is the open sesame for teachers or for any one who would influence the behavior of others. This capacity to influence human behavior is central in both teaching and speaking. That which makes for effectiveness in the one contributes to proficiency in the other. Professors of education and school administrators would probably agree that nothing is more basically needful in the teacher's equipment than this ability to capture the interest and enthusiasms of those who come under his charge. Modern speech teachers would say the same for the speaker. It is not surprising, then, that students who speak effectively should be noticeably capable in the classroom.

In the current number of SCHOOL AND SOCIETY (November 3) John Harvey Furbay points to a serious lack in the average student-teacher, namely, the inability to use the English language acceptably. When the surfeit of traditional English courses in both secondary schools and colleges is considered, one is constrained to ask why this deficiency should obtain. Figures from "Recent Social Trends" (p. 331) strikingly reveal that, in 1928, of all the pupils in public secondary school 93.1 per cent. were enrolled in English; while only 13.6 per cent. were enrolled in biology, 17.9 per cent. in American history, and 5.1 per cent. in economics. The average student takes twice as much course work in English as he does in all the sciences combined, and American history comes in for only one fifth as much time. This shows that our average student is not neglected in the academic routinism of English teaching. English is the white-headed boy of the curriculum not only in secondary schools but also in our colleges.

Again figures from "Recent Social Trends" (p. 339) show that English courses lead the field by a large margin in the records of one hundred typical members of the June classes of the colleges of the University of Chicago. Thus we see that opportunities for English instruction are not lacking in high school or colleges. Yet students come to their last year of college woefully deficient in their ability to express themselves in good English. The Carnegie Report of the comprehensive tests given in Pennsylvania colleges would tend to strengthen that indictment. Mr. Furbay shows how this lack is readily repaired when the student is confronted with the teaching exigency. The import of his conclusion is tantamount to saying that students will not improve their English until they are faced with necessity. Is not Mr. Furbay unconsciously indicting the non-functional red-ink technique in the teaching of English?

His happy experience with the quick results under social pressure and the education professor's observation merge to key a clue to the whole problem. Good English is motivated by need and is incidental to the whole matter of socialized expression. The urge to be effective in a social situation will provide impetus for the individual to discipline whatever powers that effectiveness may require. If careless grammar or enunciation is a barrier to proficient debating, the aspiring debater will remove that barrier through concentrated application. Mr. Furbay's student-teachers readily compensate for wasted opportunity when they are made conscious of the imperative of good English. Recognition of immediate use is a spur to better usage. Participles which have persisted in dangling, despite the unremitting badgering of grammar-centric celibates, submit to treatment when the social occasion demands. Faith in rule-book pedantry, without the works of social confrontation, is dead.

Is not our problem one of providing the social situation for that student who would facilitate his expression in the English language? And do we need to wait until he assumes control of a class in practise-teaching? In order to make the teaching of English functional, we need to change the whole approach. The emphasis should be placed on social adaptation, coordination and control; all of which is included under what is now known as speech. In this field the student is given opportunity to interest, stimulate and control his fellows in a face-to-face group situation. Use of language is a part of the whole picture.

The student desirous of "getting across" in the classroom will discipline himself in that which most aids him in this desire. To get and hold the attention of an audience and to elicit favorable response is the highest achievement in social control. The speech teacher in his classroom makes such achievement his central objective. For that reason it is my contention that much of the time-serving in English classes should give way to speech activities. Continue to call it English, if you will, just so long as the speech situation is maintained and the English usage is made a contributing factor in the whole matter of social acceptance. Increasingly the integrated and interdependent society into which we are emerging will require members who have the capacity to cooperate with and to influence the behavior of others. The teacher must not only possess that quality but also must be able to stimulate it in the unfolding lives of those who are to carry on.

Professor Roswell H. Johnson, writing on "A Technique for College Teachers,"[1] maintains that "all aspirants for college teaching would do well to take a course in public speaking and to participate in debating." Could that hold for any kind of teaching? It is not the lack of correctness that handicaps the prospective teacher; but rather the lack of freedom, differentiation, directness, animation, flexibility and personality effectiveness.

Not *more* English for teachers but *better* speech!

N. J. WEISS

ALBION COLLEGE

## THE CHILD'S NEED IN SCHOOL ADMINISTRATION

EVERY child's greatest need in education is recognition of his individuality; but in order to provide this recognition, hard-and-fast standards of promotion and classification must be abandoned; fixed curricula must be made elastic; stereotyped programs of the past must be made over to accord with each child's individual need; grade norms for speed and accuracy of performance must be ignored as educational aims; and all administrative devices which presuppose mass teaching must be forgotten. Uniformities that now hamper teaching rest upon the long-established methods of mass teaching. In spite of progressive educational theory, many teachers still instruct groups instead of individuals and expect each separate child to learn successfully and to pass the hurdle of a fixed grade standard. Before teachers can adapt their teaching to the needs of each child, they and their supervisors must cease to expect standard performance from a non-standard pupil. The paraphernalia of mass instruction must be superseded in every detail by a system which recognizes individuality.

### NOT GRADE STANDARDS BUT INDIVIDUAL

The pursuit of grade standards is a very fallacious procedure. Schools in their anxiety to attain a statistical median or grade norm often forget the needs of the bright child who attains the norm with little effort and spends the rest of his time in idleness. They concentrate a high-powered remedial attack on children whose native capacity prevents them from reaching the grade norms; and the total result is disappointment, discouragement, excessive retardation, bad social attitude on the part of the pupil and unnecessary strain upon the teacher. The school might as well attempt to make a child seventy inches in stature when nature has designed him to be only sixty.

The concentration of attention upon the lower half of a class to bring each individual up to an established norm is fallacious even from a statistical standpoint. If all schools should succeed in the attempt, the norm would be reestablished necessarily upon a higher basis, leaving the school to chase the pot of gold at the end of a receding rainbow. It should be the purpose of the school to help each child reach his own maximum achievement without necessary reference or comparison to grade norms. When an individual standard supersedes the grade norm as a goal for the effort of both teacher and pupil, the undue stress will be removed from the dull child and the brighter children will extend their knowledge and enrich their training in response to a new challenge.

Standardized tests are valuable in helping to ascertain the individual needs of each child; they are valuable also in measuring levels of achievement. They should never be used, however, as impossible hurdles for the backward child or as educational goals that are too easy for the bright.

### FALLACY OF MINIMUM ESSENTIALS

The doctrine of minimum essentials in education is based upon a recognition of the fact that all persons must accept a common number system, a common language and a common citizenship; but it disregards the further fact that

[1] SCHOOL AND SOCIETY, June 16, 1934.

these common elements in society are social characteristics, that they develop independently of the school, that they will develop even in spite of the school. The doctrine merely misapplies a fundamental idea by seeking to require all children to master facts arbitrarily selected at certain stages of their development. The minimum essentials of knowledge and skill should be acquired by each child, but not in a specified grade. The acquisition should come when individual need, capacity and opportunity are coincident.

### Error of Homogeneous Classification

A uniformity in classification known as homogeneous grouping is an effort to recognize individual differences by mass methods. But even if mass instruction were needful, the usual bases of homogeneous grouping are unsound. To treat children educationally in the same way because their intelligence quotients are equal is ludicrous. Physicians might as well prescribe the same treatment to all patients of like stature. Two pupils having an identical intelligence quotient may be very dissimilar in their educational needs, even when enrolled in the same grade. Health, life interests, special aptitudes, emotional characteristics and many other personal qualities enter into a proper determination of need.

Some educators, discerning the inadequacy of the intelligence quotient as a basis for grouping, have modified their formula by adding achievement standards, mental ages, social ages and various other data. Again referring to the analogy drawn from medical practise, physicians might as well classify patients for treatment on the combined basis of stature, weight, temperature and blood pressure. Neither in the practise of medicine nor in the field of teaching does such a conglomerate grouping of individuals for professional attention serve any valuable purpose. The individuals so grouped are not necessarily alike in anything. Similarity of pedagogical need would be the most logical basis for homogenous grouping; but even then such grouping has doubtful value because it tempts the teacher to forget the individual and to think only of the mass.

Children who are to become dependents or institutional cases because of mental deficiency should be kept out of the regular classes. Their education will differ from that which is due normal children in preparation to occupy independent stations in life. Special classes for children who are merely dull or backward, however, to be known in the community by humiliating names, should go into the discard. These classes have served a good purpose in the past by obtaining recognition of the need for individualization of teaching; but they have not served to educate the children enrolled in them to any higher degree than was possible in a regular class. On the contrary, measurable results indicate that children who remain in regular classes accomplish more than those of equal ability who are placed in the special classes. Long ago by force of enlightened opinion the dunce cap disappeared from the school; but the dunce category, in the form of a special class or a "Z" group, is still with us.

Every child, dull or bright, should be given the right to pursue school work with reasonable joy and with the possibility of success. Teachers can do this only when their superior officers throw the modern dunce cap in the waste basket, cast aside the idols of uniformity and grant both teachers and children a better recognition of individuality.

Geo. R. Johnson

Board of Education
St. Louis, Mo.

## "WE AIN'T GWINE NOWHERE"[1]

On a country road, near Atlanta, a friend of mine met three colored men. "Where are you all going?" he asked.

"We ain't gwine nowhere," was the answer. "We's *been* where we's gwine."

If the teachers of the United States were asked to-day, "Where are you all going?" and they answered, "We ain't gwine nowhere," the answer would be grammatically wrong and therefore shocking. But if such an answer is factually right, that ought to be still more shocking.

During the past five years, have the schools of the country, considered as a whole, been going anywhere? Have they progressed in teachers' salaries, in security of tenure of office, in freedom of speech, in blocking political

[1] Notes from the address at the annual meeting of the Missouri State Teachers' Association, at Kansas City, Thursday, November 8, 1934.

interference or in gaining effective recognition of the crucial importance of public education? Have there been gains, meanwhile, in the quality and morale of the profession? During that period, in my visits to each of the forty-eight states, I have observed notable achievements in schools, here and there. I have found many individual teachers who have triumphed over all the depressing influences of these years. But for the country taken as a whole, my impression is that the schools have been going nowhere.

Collectively, the members of the profession have failed to command the respect which is due their cause. They have not used their potential influence. Was it for this reason that the Federal Government this year, despite all entreaties, ignored the largest organization of teachers, even though this body was meeting in annual convention within the shadow of the White House? The President did not even send a word of greeting. This same President, however, did speak at the annual convention of the American Legion, and so did his predecessor. He did speak at the annual convention of the American Bankers Association, and so did his predecessor. Why were the teachers ignored?

The American Legion, asking huge appropriations for themselves, demanded attention and received it. The American teachers, asking comparatively small appropriations for the nation's children, meekly asked a little consideration and received none. Why this discrimination?

And why did the bankers command attention? Was it because they had so successfully managed our banks? As a matter of fact, if the banks had been conducted for the common good as efficiently as the schools, there would have been no major depression. If the banks had been as sound in their financial operations as the teachers' associations, there would have been no need of closing the banks. No, it is not that legionnaires or bankers themselves deserve more respect or that their cause is of greater moment. It is partly—not wholly, of course, but partly—because they are so organized as to command a hearing. The teachers are not.

Chicago has dramatized the story. So feeble is the voice of the disorganized profession that the Chicago teachers were unable to get pay for seven months. The people of Chicago could not find eighteen million dollars with which to pay the teachers, at the very time when the people of Chicago found eighteen million dollars with which to start a world's fair.

Did you ever hear of bricklayers working seven months for nothing—or mill hands or railroad men or bankers or members of Congress—or, for that matter, any other large group except teachers?

What the teachers of the nation did collectively in this emergency is a short, short story. They did nothing. Even the National Education Association did not use the most obvious means of protest: it did not decline to hold its annual convention in the city which had spent its eighteen millions on a world's fair instead of on seven months' back pay for teachers.

Meantime the Chicago teachers themselves showed the incapacity for concerted action which characterizes the profession. Instead of uniting under one leader they split up in conflicting groups. The Women's High School Teachers Federation had its own ideas about what to do. So did the Men Teachers Union and the Chicago Principals' Club. These ideas did not exactly suit the Chicago Teachers Federation or the Chicago High School Teachers Association; nor did anybody's ideas suit the Subscribers, a Fascist organization which was open only to men teachers. Dissatisfied with all other groups, some of the teachers formed the Volunteer Emergency Committee. There was, in addition, the Chicago Division of the Illinois State Teachers Association. Here were at least eight organizations of Chicago teachers, incapable of effective mass action and in some cases actually working at cross purposes.

What was true of Chicago is true of the country as a whole: "We ain't gwine nowhere." The teaching profession is a house divided against itself. Large numbers of teachers are members of no national body whatever. The largest organization comprises less than one fifth of all those engaged in education. Most of the college and university teachers have nothing to do with any of the large teachers' associations. Most of the private school teachers keep aloof from public school teachers. Most of the men teachers do not attend the meetings of the National Education Association. There are more than 100 teachers' associations and more than 250 national deliberative committees which have no means of concerted action for a common cause.

Yet we live in an era of protest against extreme individualism. Group solidarity and group action are marching on. Unless teachers work *collectively* for the advancement of the profession, they are out of step with the times.

There should be an all-inclusive legion of the nation's teachers. It should be dominated not by superintendents but by the rank and file. At its head should be a permanent executive of highest caliber. The baseball industry took a federal judge for its full-time, permanent executive and paid him a substantial salary. The motion picture industry took a member of the President's Cabinet. Bringing up the next generation is an industry almost as important—speaking moderately—as baseball or the movies. Potentially the leadership of the educational forces of the nation is a job worth all that any man has of brains and energy and devotion.

For the first three years of the depression the Federal Government gave emergency relief to every large cause except education, to every large group except teachers. Even the unskilled ditch-diggers had their champions. The original NRA blanket code prescribed a minimum annual wage of $750 for common labor, while 85,000 teachers were receiving less than $450.

One reason for this neglect was the neglect of the teachers collectively to express their convictions and to authorize somebody to speak for them.

Even so, the scuttling of the schools might have been worse. How much more thorough it would have been if the National Education Association had not succeeded, against great obstacles, in making its membership twenty-two times as large as it was at the close of the war! How much worse off certain states would have been this year if the threat of further scuttling had not precipitated the most effective group action of the teachers in all their history. What we have done here and there, in this emergency, shows what we should do everywhere, as a long-range policy. Then we would be going somewhere.

WILLIAM TRUFANT FOSTER

# SPECIAL CORRESPONDENCE

## THE NEW SCHOOLS OF MEXICO

DESPITE eighteen years of political sobriety in Mexico we are so conditioned to the idea of revolution in relation to our Latin-American neighbors that no particular attention is drawn to one's conversation by remarking "I was in on a revolution in Mexico this summer."

But the current revolution puts education on the front page and into conversation, a subject for tremendous enthusiasm or deep resistance. Education has become news, spread to the feature section, over to the editorial column, and one holds suspect even the advertisements.

Education is the concern of the political as well as the educational leaders, and the public schools of Mexico have become socialist. In the state of Sonora the new program went into effect with the opening of the fall term; administrators and teachers have been working under a pressure not usually associated with mañana and three hours for lunch. But traditional courtesy remains unhurried, and educators have been generous in sharing their plans with visiting teachers.

To the repeated query, "Precisely what is socialized education and the socialist school?," the reply of the state director of public education, Fernando Dvórak, summarizes the challenging conceptions of all to whom the question was put. It is, he said, that the *obreros* (workers) of education stretch out their hands to the *obreros* of muscle. The teachers become the social factors in the state, instructing the workers in their rights and how to organize to obtain them. Socialized education must lift the workers so that they can live better, can fight for and maintain their rights. Socialist schools aim definitely at improving economic conditions so that all are well fed and none go naked, so that all have the benefits of hygiene and bodily health, and enjoy the pleasures and diversions of a richer living.

Whether because I was a teacher or a Californian I do not know, but no one ever presumed that I could entertain any developed concept of socialism. A discussion therefore of political theory and the philosophy of socialism was the essential introduction to that of current pedagogical practise. One so instructed would never waver from the position that Mexican socialism is Mexican to fit Mexico and beds not with any other variety, Marxian or Russian. It is not to be confused with communism. Nor with capitalism. The specifically Mexican product embraces the productivity of capital, yes; the slavery of capitalism, no. The industrial trinity is the triune worker dividing returns with capital and the manager or "owner."

The duty of the new schools is to provide practical education for solving actual problems of the day—its point of departure being the welfare of the masses, and its enthusiasm the power of all individual efforts united to better immediately present economic conditions. Uneconomic distribution of work, class differences, the iniquities of capitalism, become the textual material of education. The socialist school instructs the proletariat that in the decadent capitalism of to-day there are only two classes, the exploiter and the exploited. The *Educación Socialista* is to lift the culture of the workers sufficiently for them to fulfil their mission in contributing to the evolutionary march of humanity—that they may build a new society in which each man is a worker, well paid and well nourished and well dressed; where not one child goes to school with his stomach empty, or once there is mystified by the mental soporifics which have made of school life a touching picture enclosed in a box, while life throbbed outside in its own cruel realities of economic inequality. The leaders assert that the socialist school will cement the foundation of socialist society.

Why does such a program result in student strikes that can at one time close three of Mexico's great universities (including the oldest one in America) and can cause the National Secretary of Public Education, Eduardo Vasconcelos, to warn students that the government will close preparatory schools in the capital and devote its resources entirely to rural education if they insist in their protest against the education imposed by the government? Because pedagogically all seven cardinal principles of socialist education are aimed at combating *alcoholismo* and *fanatismo,* in which the leaders see the poisons that over the centuries have repressed the Mexican worker—one by cooking his intestines with mescal and the other by stupefying his mentality with the hopes and fears of ecclesiastical teaching. To be instructed in the evils of *alcoholismo* is familiar enough. But to be instructed that *fanatismo* is similarly destructive is not so familiar to the Mexican parent. And just here, in the use of the schools to combat the influence of clerical concepts, does the new education find its practical expression and meet the resistance of many parent and student groups.

Only an understanding of the influence of the historic church in Mexico, of its political activities since the conquest and of its educational system, can help one appreciate how vigorously an educational movement that is socialist in concept makes its major attack one against clerical ideology. As preparation, the priests were expelled, services prohibited and the churches given to the workers as cultural centers on the request of their organizations. This summer the leaders of the new education in Sonora, following the plan instituted by the national government, provided "cultural Sundays" in the theaters (gatherings well and noisily attended) with the purpose of educating parents in the problems of the present as against any clerical instruction. *Anti-fanatismo* is the characteristic philosophy of the *educación socialista.*

The methods by which the schools are to realize this new order? Since the course of study is in the making, few detailed plans were available, but in form these presented a not unfamiliar aspect of aims and bases of the new education, the manner in which these were to be approached and realized, the texts for basic instruction, the material to be covered by units and the margins of change by teachers relative to peculiarly local problems.

The difference in organization exists in the courses which one by one unroll as being obligatory if the student is to complete the secondary school. English, French, Spanish, history (Mexican and world), geography (Mexican and universal), mathematics (algebra, geometry, trigonometry), physical education (hygiene, sports, dancing), physics, logic, astronomy—one can stumble no further down the list of required courses without confusion at the prospect of "high school students one has known" contributing to the socialist state by virtue of studying logic and astronomy.

How deeply intentioned is the structure behind the educational revolution in Mexico appeared in the energetic explanation of Sr. Dvórak by which he integrated logic and astronomy as rich sources of the new education. The aims and objectives of these courses focus on the destruction of current religious concepts traceable to the biblical account of creation, and with these concepts, an order of thinking which the present leaders condemn as being at the root of all resistance to change.

Our own preoccupation with providing for individual differences makes no schism in the revolutionary program. The secondary school course is planned for the student in his group for each year with the intent of raising the level of the entire group. There is no differentiation to meet special interests until the secondary school is completed, but the individual is not quite so brutally disregarded as one at first supposes. The primary school is a school of learning by observing and doing (John Dewey is loved and very practically interpreted), and regimentation is not extreme. Compulsory education does not extend beyond the completion of the primary school course. Following the three-year course of the secondary school, the student proceeds to normal schools, professional schools or the university. The greatest revolutionary changes concern the normal schools, whose purpose is the training of teachers, and here, obviously, the entire program is one of specialization.

It is still possible for a person to enter upon a teaching career in Sonora after twelve years of public school preparation—three years of normal school topping the three of secondary and the six of primary training. Certification to teach is provided by the state office on evidence of one's ability in the material one undertakes to teach. Many engineers and lawyers are on the teaching staffs. Language teachers must receive their linguistic training in the country whose language they teach and their pedagogical training in Mexico. French and English are both required for two years in the secondary school. (In the case of English, even in the usual classes ranging from thirty-six to forty-six students, the two-year period is probably something of a refinement, since so many pupils are familiar with English as spoken in Los Angeles, Watts and Eagle Rock, Texas.)

In respect to academic freedom, although one infers that material which might lead a California teacher afoul of the criminal syndalism act is quite in order in Sonora, one also infers that teachers who simulate a support of the educational program, while in reality they differ in aim and ideal, have little place in the school system. Cases of resignation or discharge, however, resulting from this conflict are first-page news.

The rural school is the special province of the Federal Government, to the end that rural education in Mexico receives an emphasis common to few educational programs. The *plan sexenal* calls for establishing 30,000 rural schools in the country at a minimum of 1,000 a year. Fifteen per cent. of the national income goes directly to rural education. Federal support for rural schools and state support for village and city schools separates the unity of instruction not at all. The purpose of education, state or federal, has been succinctly phrased by General Calles: "Debemos entrar y tomar posesión de la conciencia de los niños, de la conciencia de los jóvenes"—"We must enter in and take possession of the consciousness of the children, of the consciousness of youth."

Not, reply the critics of the revolutionary plan, when the leaders have taken the educational bases of other countries and are experimenting in applying them to Mexico without any sensible consideration of the character of Mexican civilization. This opinion considers the National Revolutionary Party and the educators who support it to be tyrants who will never succeed in changing the soul of a people violently.

Perhaps not. But the educational activity of our neighbor is worthy of our attention. For among all those connected with the schools there is a tremendous enthusiasm. Possibly enthusiasm resounds in the mind too explosively, is too tied with what we like to term the Latin temperament or too much characteristic of the untried hopes of youth. But the temperament may be discounted, and even the youth. Many young people are indeed involved in this movement to use the schools to better the economic conditions of a state. The man who is responsible for unifying the program, however, the state director of public education, has been an educator for forty-four years. His enthusiasm is as energetic and vital as that of youth. One encounters this enthusiasm among administrators and teachers; in public schools; in private schools; in plan and in practise. And this enthusiasm one catches everywhere is enthusiasm for education. It is enthusiasm for education that is close to the life of the people and their present problems.

ANITA RISDON

ELK GROVE, CALIF.

# QUOTATIONS

## CONSTRUCTIVE ACTIVITIES OF THE FOUNDATION

THE reader of a report of this character may very possibly wonder whether the writer has not taken unfair advantage of the opportunity which the occasion offers to air his personal views about foundation matters in general, instead of confining his efforts to a brief record of the year's operations in his own organization. If the practice can be justified, it will not be on the basis of the profundity of the opinions expressed, but for other reasons. Whether one considers the foundations merely as repositories of nearly a billion dollars of our national wealth, or thinks of them in terms of what they have actually accomplished or of their potentialities for the future, one can not fail to be impressed by the lack of public interest and understanding of this particular type of social instrument. Any serious and reasonably well-informed expression of opinion may, therefore, find justification should it serve to provoke discussion, to offer suggestions to those contemplating the creation of new trusts, or warning to those in control of existing trusts that their responsibilities are not of a private but of a public nature.

The freedom of foundations to carry out the purpose of their founders and, from another point of view, the evidence of public confidence in their social usefulness, lie in the exemption from taxation which they have shared with religious, educational and charitable institutions. While the great majority of foundations recognize their responsibility to the public and make public record of their grants and their investments, this is not uniformly the case. Furthermore, in these days of eager search for possible sources of public revenue, signs are not lacking that the complete exemption from taxation which has hitherto been enjoyed by all the institutions mentioned may no longer be taken for granted. Under all these circumstances, a foundation executive may be forgiven if the expression of his interests and concerns are not confined to the affairs of his own particular bailiwick.

In his report as acting president of the corporation in 1923, Dr. Henry S. Pritchett stated that one of the basic conditions for the creation of foundations in any country is the social tradition which favors private as against government initiative in philanthropy. Those responsible for the administration of existing trusts in the United States to-day are faced with a situation very different from that which existed when Dr. Pritchett made this statement. The recent entry of our Federal Government into many fields in which the foundations have been, and are to-day, devoting a large share of their resources is a phenomenon of great significance. That the immediate cause of this change in federal policy can clearly be traced to the economic crisis through which we have been passing is obvious, but there can be little doubt that not a few of the changes will prove to be permanent. There has always been some common ground, as for example in geological and agricultural research, but generally speaking, experiment and trail-breaking in the natural and social sciences alike, have in the United States been left to individual universities or similar institutions, often with financial aid from foundations, or to the initiative of the foundation itself. The most striking feature in the recent change is that it is precisely into these fields that government has entered.

Not only is there a shift in the sources of support for social and educational experimentation, but the underlying purposes of such experimentation are themselves shifting in these days of rapidly changing values. For a foundation to take sides as to which changes are socially desirable and which modifications in our planning are wise would lead it into the dangerous terrain of indoctrination, if not of active propaganda; but the opportunity to contribute toward the cost of providing factual information upon which the personnel which conducts our many-sided educational and social programs, and the lay public, which ultimately pays the bills, may base their conclusions, has thus far constituted one of the great privileges of the foundation. In view of the rôle now played by government and of the present confusion in men's thinking as to what the next step should be and why, the foundations may well ask themselves what the future has in store for them. In the past foundation aid has been far from a negligible factor in social progress. It is true that no foundation has been or will ever be ideally organized or ideally directed, and there will always be definite limits as to the uses to which a trust fund may wisely be put. But the foundation has corresponding advantages. It can engage in long-range activities; it can move quickly to meet emergencies; it can turn from creative tasks to relieve distress, as practically all foundations have done in the past three years; and it can turn back, though this has proven to be a much more difficult job. Must the foundations now look forward to an inevitable reduction in the social usefulness of their activities, or can government with its practically unlimited resources and the foundations with their strictly limited funds work profitably together? Or, may the foundations, by turning their activities into fields in which government is not as yet a friendly competitor thus maintain their usefulness to society?

Whatever happens, the foundations can find useful things to do with their funds. They could, if they so decided, return to their earlier practise of contributing to the general purposes of worthy individual institutions; they could expand their existing contributions to the advancement of "pure" scholarship, to fundamental research conducted without reference to practical application. The question which these recent activities have raised has to do with the range of fruitful foundation activity, and it is one which can not be answered in a day or a year.

That the best opportunity for a foundation lies in creative and constructive activities, rather than in palliative or remedial, is becoming generally realized. It is also becoming realized that the best results can be obtained by a reasonable limitation of its field of activity. What is not so generally understood is that in creative and constructive work, money can of necessity play only a secondary part; the fundamental contribution must be made by some individual, more rarely by a group. But money, though secondary, has its place, and there is never enough of it to go around, less than ever in these days. It should be axiomatic that foundation money must be reserved to fill the gaps—the occasions in which the funds needed can be provided from no other source. To discern with complete accuracy just which these occasions are would, however, require a seventh sense which has not been vouchsafed to erring mortals. That mistakes of judgment are often made either as to the importance of the work undertaken, or the necessity of a foundation contribution, no one realizes better than those in responsible charge of foundations. They hope they may be credited with making every effort to avoid them, and they hope also that in the intelligent public opinion to which all foundations are in the last analysis accountable, such errors of judgment as will inevitably occur may be forgiven in the light of the instances in which the foundation has been the means of providing the funds necessary for some work of permanent usefulness to mankind.—*President Frederick P. Keppel, of the Carnegie Corporation, in his annual report.*

## THE GAME AND THE CANDLE

President Keppel of the Carnegie Corporation refuses any credit for courage in saying what he has set down in his report about the immediate past and the future of the American college. As to the past up to the moment of the present, he says, it is a question (all the colleges and all the students being taken into consideration) "whether the game has proved to be worth the candle." There are approximately a million college and university students of whom "every year thousands . . . profit and profit richly from the opportunities which the colleges now offer." Still his conclusion stands, as to the mass, taking into the reckoning not only the price in money but in "the years of youth."

Generally speaking, colleges have sought to improve conditions by "tinkering with the curriculum" rather than by concentrating upon the student himself. Particularly is the question raised touching the independent colleges of limited endowment in which are one-third of all American undergraduates. This will come with a shock to many who have found from experience that in such institutions attention has been especially concentrated upon the student himself rather than upon the program of study. The exceptions to his generalization which Mr. Keppel cites tend rather to prove the rule. The enrichment of undergraduate life at Harvard and Yale, the specially mentioned exceptions, accentuates the concentration upon the student made possible not only by the division into smaller units but by the generous support of Mr. E. S. Harkness. The gifts that have been made within the last few weeks to Amherst, Wesleyan and Trinity indicate that commensurate endowments may continue to come to the independent colleges as well as to the multiple colleges in a university environment.

The American college single or multiple, as Mr. Keppel suggests, must be built "on the personality of the existing faculty," with an effective study as to the application of what we now know regarding "individual differences interests and motives, mental hygiene, the technique of continuous record, the uses of comprehensive and other examinations." These essentials may still be developed and provided without large expenditure even in the independent college. The Carnegie organizations, which have done so much in the past for improving the teaching in the American college, are still giving effective assistance of a nature to help the student in his self-education—as a major part of all education must be.

The inference that one wishes to be warranted in drawing from Mr. Keppel's observations is not that too many young men and women go to college, but that the college has not made the game worth the candle for all of them.—*The New York Times.*

# REPORTS

## THE PHI BETA KAPPA ANNALS

The Phi Beta Kappa Society has issued the first number of its *Annals,* an interesting book designed to keep the 70,000 members of the society in touch with its ideals and activities, and to secure their participation in its work, either directly or through advice, so making the society's contributions to the world of scholarship more vital.

The book starts with an introduction by President Clark S. Northup, followed by a brief historical sketch of the society. The three types of members elected and their proportion of the whole; the organization of the First National Council and the creation of the United Chapters; the admittance of women to membership; abandonment of secrecy in the affairs of the chapters; and the conversion of the society from a social to a purely honor society are some of the outstanding developments of the first century of existence. Starting with the chapter as the unit of organization, the extension of the society through alumni associations is noted.

The list of talks given to both chapter and association groups is an index of their wide interests. And a suggested lecture or study course as an amplification of this feature shows how the members, either through their alumni groups or individually, might stimulate and have a real effect upon a community's thinking, were a series of lectures or discussions along such lines sponsored by the members of Phi Beta Kappa, and reported in the local press. Such subjects are suggested for discussion as: "Crime-Breeding and Mental Hygiene," "The Fate of Rural America," "Unemployment," "Taxation," "War," "The Fate of Religion." Various suggested approaches to the different subject are given in the form of questions. Under the subject of "Whither is Education Headed?," for example, are the following questions:

Do political and economic crises condemn our educational systems?

How should education prepare for increased leisure?

What is the relation of specialized to liberal learning?

How can we, in school and college, learn to grasp and do, not merely to know facts?

Should not lectures, recitations and examinations be abolished?

A group of reading courses, prepared by the president of the society, Dr. Clark S. Northup, is given in detail.

The work of the Phi Beta Kappa Foundation for scholarship is treated of and its developing needs pointed out. The undertakings of the United Chapters are stressed, particularly the work done by *The American Scholar,* the society's quarterly, in providing an audience for scholarly appraisal of values in current thought along all lines, and the encouragement incidentally given to the production of publications of this caliber in America.

The discussions at the recent eighteenth triennial council are summarized and attention given to the new plan of granting charters to institutions. Hitherto institutions have been nominated by votes by chapters, but this triennium the choice was made by a committee on qualifications after intensive study. Three charters were granted under this new plan: Delta of Connecticut, Connecticut College, New London; Alpha of Florida, Florida State College for Women, Tallahassee; Alpha of Utah, The University of Utah, Salt Lake City. A description of each of these institutions of learning is given.

Two new sections were authorized to existing chapters: The chapter at the University of Pennsylvania was empowered to establish a section in its new College of Liberal Arts for Women, and the University of North Carolina chapter received similar authorization for a section in The Woman's College at Greensboro.

A new vitality is stirring in Phi Beta Kappa, chiefly as a result of proposed basic revisions of principles and methods to which the senate has directed the attention of the chapters and the triennial council. These propose to increase Phi Beta Kappa's influence (a) by concentrating the attention of the collegiate chapters upon undergraduate scholarship in the liberal arts and sciences; (b) by chartering graduate chapters for the nearly 70,000 Phi Beta Kappa members no longer on the campus; (c) by encouraging institutions to strengthen their work in the liberal arts and sciences; and (d) by keeping the members and others aware of Phi Beta Kappa's work and ideals through *The American Scholar* and the *Annals.*

The word "liberal" in defining a liberal arts course was taken to mean that only students 75 per cent. of whose work was "designed primarily for a knowledge or understanding or appreciation of the natural and social world," as contrasted with "training intended primarily to develop skill or professional techniques," should be eligible for membership in course. The membership committee is besides to take into consideration "the results of such methods as honors work, comprehensive examinations and aptitude tests, as well as the opinions of deans and teachers who have recently had the candidates in class, concerning the character, capacity, scholarly achievement, breadth of interest, and general promise of each candidate."

The limiting of the election of alumni and honorary members to an average of one a year of each class, by any chapter, was recommended.

The plan to give greater importance in the society to alumni associations, the changing of their name to graduate chapters and granting them a limited rôle in the council, was favorably referred to a committee *ad interim* for consideration and presentation of the next council.

A suggestion for a council chapter, or membership at large, was defeated, largely owing to difficulties of administration.

District organization, for the purpose of nominating institutions for membership, was discussed fully pro and con, and referred to the *ad interim* committee.

In considering the relationship between the general society and the council, the committee on which two of the oldest chapters, Harvard and Bowdoin, were represented affirmed its conviction (1) that some increase in the authority of The United Chapters over individual chapters is desirable in matters affecting the national reputation of the society, especially in the matter of elections to honorary membership; (2) that, since chapters may deteriorate and in time bring discredit to the society, constitutional provision should be made for the revocation as well as for the granting of charters; and (3) that individual chapters should continue to be allowed, in the determination of their policies and the conduct of their affairs, the maximum of freedom compatible with the purposes and well-being of the Phi Beta Kappa Society at large.

The committee recommended that the *ad interim* committee give careful consideration to the fundamental and complex issues concerning the relation between the general society and the constituent chapters.

Those who have been puzzled to know which form of pronunciation is correct for the society's name "Phi Bate" or "Phi Beet," failed to gain relief. The senate's recommendation in favor of the uniform anglicized pronunciation was not adopted. A majority of the delegates seemed to believe that usage would still overrule logical consistency.

Dr. Voorhees was appointed by the council as life historian of the society. He tells of his work in preparing the official history of the society, with its many compensations in the discovery of important old documents bearing on the history.

An appreciation of Dr. Voorhees' long and devoted service to the society was adopted; as was a resolution prepared by Dr. Voorhees regarding the faithful and efficient service given the society for twenty-one years by David Layton.

Names and addresses of chapter and association secretaries and presidents are given.

R. W.

# EDUCATIONAL RESEARCH AND STATISTICS

## HOMOGENEOUS GROUPING AS A TECHNIQUE FOR IMPROVING PREDICTION COEFFICIENTS[1]

THIS study is the result of trial-and-error efforts to improve the prediction of college performance. It is the outgrowth of a very intensive study of prediction coefficients[2] in which the best measure of average freshman-sophomore college success was the New York State Regents Examination average of all "academic" subjects passed in high school. Herein is reported the correspondence between the criterion and this best measure of success for the following more homogeneous subgroups: sex, age at high school graduation, high school which graduated the student, amount of secondary school content repeated,[3] amount of foreign language spoken in the home, position among siblings in the family, and degree sought.

Secondly, group differences in school success were investigated for the two academic levels. Thirdly, differences in college performance as related to high-school attainments were studied to see, for example, whether a boy completing high school at sixteen years or less with a Regents average of 90 had as good a chance, a better or a poorer one of making A grades in college than one completing at eighteen. Fourthly, some attempt is made to understand the reasons for the higher relationships obtained within certain groups and the relative lack of consistency of performance within others.

The following groups show a correspondence between our two variables of r. 80 or over:[4] all bilingual, or "youngest," or preprofessional girls, girls from Buffalo schools No. 1 and 4,

[1] This study was made possible through a grant from the General Education Board. For a detailed report of results see *Jour. of Appl. Psychol.*, 19: 5, 1935.

[2] M. E. Wagner, *The University of Buffalo Studies,* 9: 125–173 and 184–209, 1934. Also SCHOOL AND SOCIETY 40: 367–368, 1934. An r .65 was obtained between the total "academic" New York State Regents average and a freshman-sophomore college average for the total 750 college students investigated.

[3] M. E. Sarbaugh, *The University of Buffalo Studies,* 9: 174–183, 1934. For this portion of our investigation, the number of subjects was considerably less—about one half the number used for the other comparisons.

[4] In the earlier study, with the same group of subjects used herein, the best multiple correlation coefficient obtained between our variables was R .67 (between two-year college average and a combination of Regents average and Iowa High School Content Examination). The inclusion of other variables in this combination did not increase the size of this *R*. In a review of the literature, two authors were found who reported multiple *R's* of .80 or over and two more between .70 and .80. The remaining studies showed *R's* of less than .70.

and girls who completed high school at nineteen years or over, together with "only" children of both sexes. In addition, the following classifications show an *r* of .70 or over:[5] girls as a total group or from all Buffalo schools as a group, together with those completing high school at seventeen years of age; boys from No. 6, from Buffalo suburban high schools and those graduating from high school at sixteen years of age or less; and the combined girls and boys who repeated examinations to raise passing grades (in competition for scholarships). Groups showing especially low relationships are: total non-Buffalo schools, especially rural village and non-Buffalo city secondary institutions, those who repeat examinations because of previous failure, all those who complete high school at eighteen years of age, all "middle" children and predental boys.

Given a definite Regents average, a girl will achieve slightly more in college than a boy; a Buffalo student, slightly more than a non-Buffalo high-school product; students from certain Buffalo schools, more than those from others; bilinguals slightly more than monoglots. Those who repeat Regents examinations in scholarship competition are more successful at every level of Regents performance than those who do not repeat; boys sixteen years or less and twenty years and over at high-school completion and girls sixteen or less or eighteen years of age or over are more successful than those of the same Regents average and of another age at secondary school completion. Predental boys achieve less than those of the same high-school success who seek other degrees. "Only" children (those with no siblings) with superior Regents averages are more sucessful in college than non-only boys and girls of the same secondary school achievement. However, with inferior Regents grades, the "only" child is less successful in college than children with siblings of the same high-school performance.

The following factors seem to make for ease of prediction within groups studied—(1) a high average Regents average, (2) high motivation and (3) relative homogeneity within subgroups. Examples of the first are (a) girls as contrasted with boys, (b) Buffalo schools as contrasted with non-Buffalo schools, (c) sixteen-year-old boy high-school graduates and seventeen-year-old girl graduates, and (d) degree sought. As examples of relative homogeneity within the subgroups investigated, we may consider sixteen-year-old boys who, as a group, must needs be bright and more motivated than average as contrasted with those boys completing high school at eighteen, many of whom may be bright but lacking in motivation, or highly motivated and dull, or again atypical in neither ability nor motivation. Or again, the "only" child has a more constant sibling relation than a group of "middlers," some of whom may be the middle of three, the second of ten or the ninth of ten. The bilingual or the preprofessional girl is probably more motivated than the average. The sixteen-year-old boy graduate is probably more motivated than those older, as too may well be those nineteen or twenty and over at secondary completion. Undoubtedly those competing for scholarship or for other reasons repeating a previously passed examination to raise grades are highly motivated.

In concluding, the authors wish to make the point that this investigation is in no wise conclusive. It may well be that similar results would not be forthcoming at another institution. Except for homogeneity grouping by graduating school and sex, findings here reported are but suggestive. It is hoped that investigators at other institutions may report similarly planned researches.

Mazie Earle Wagner
Eunice Strabel
The University of Buffalo

[5] It might be of interest to note here that an *r* of .70 increases the accuracy of individual case prediction by about 30 per cent. over chance. An r .86 increases this accuracy 50 per cent. over chance. See Holzinger, K. J., "Statistical Method for Students in Education," pp. 166–167. Boston: Ginn and Co., 1928.

## NEW BOOKS IN EDUCATION

*Carnegie Corporation of New York: Report of the President and of the Treasurer; For the Year Ended September 30, 1934.* Pp. 167. The Corporation.

Compton, Charles H. *Who Reads What?* Pp. 117. H. W. Wilson.

Krofta, Kamil. *A Short History of Czechoslovakia.* Pp. v + 198. McBride. $2.00.

Nichols, Frederick G. *The Personal Secretary.* Pp. xii + 105. Harvard University Press. $2.00.

Robertson, Stuart. *The Development of Modern English.* Pp. ix + 559. Prentice-Hall. $2.25.